CRICKLADE COLLEGE

A66636

KU-510-532

WITHDRAWN

THE SHORT OXFORD HISTORY OF THE
MODERN WORLD

General Editor: J. M. ROBERTS

THE SHORT OXFORD HISTORY OF THE MODERN WORLD

General Editor: J. M. ROBERTS

THE CRISIS OF PARLIAMENTS: ENGLISH HISTORY 1509–1660
Conrad Russell

EMPIRE, WELFARE STATE, EUROPE: ENGLISH HISTORY 1906–1992
Fourth Edition
T. O. Lloyd

THE OLD EUROPEAN ORDER 1660–1800
Second Edition
William Doyle

ENDURANCE AND ENDEAVOUR: RUSSIAN HISTORY 1812–1992
Fourth Edition
J. N. Westwood

THE BRITISH EMPIRE 1558–1983
T. O. Lloyd

MODERN INDIA: THE ORIGINS OF AN ASIAN DEMOCRACY
Second Edition
Judith M. Brown

BARRICADES AND BORDERS: EUROPE 1800–1914
Robert Gildea

REBELLIONS AND REVOLUTIONS: CHINA FROM THE 1800S TO THE 1980S
Jack Gray

BRITISH HISTORY 1815–1906
Norman McCord

THE EUROPEAN DYNASTIC STATES 1494–1660
Richard Bonney

THE LIMITS OF LIBERTY

AMERICAN HISTORY

1607–1992

MALDWYN
A. JONES

Cricklade College LRS

CRICKLADE COLLEGE

WITHDRAWN

ANDOVER

LRC

Oxford New York

OXFORD UNIVERSITY PRESS

Oxford University Press, Great Clarendon Street, Oxford OX2 6DP
Oxford New York
Athens Auckland Bangkok Bogotá Buenos Aires Calcutta
Cape Town Chennai Dar es Salaam Delhi Florence Hong Kong Istanbul
Karachi Kuala Lumpur Madrid Melbourne Mexico City Mumbai
Nairobi Paris São Paulo Singapore Taipei Tokyo Toronto Warsaw
and associated companies in
Berlin Ibadan

Oxford is a registered trade mark of Oxford University Press

Published in the United States by
Oxford University Press Inc., New York

© Maldwyn A. Jones 1983, 1995
Second Edition 1995

All rights reserved. No part of this publication may be reproduced,
stored in a retrieval system, or transmitted, in any form or by any means,
without the prior permission in writing of Oxford University Press.
Within the UK, exceptions are allowed in respect of any fair dealing for the
purpose of research or private study, or criticism or review, as permitted
under the Copyright, Designs and Patents Act, 1988, or in the case of
reprographic reproduction in accordance with the terms of the licences
issued by the Copyright Licensing Agency. Enquiries concerning
reproduction outside these terms and in other countries should be
sent to the Rights Department, Oxford University Press,
at the address above

This book is sold subject to the condition that it shall not, by way
of trade or otherwise, be lent, re-sold, hired out or otherwise circulated
without the publisher's prior consent in any form of binding or cover
other than that in which it is published and without a similar condition
including this condition being imposed on the subsequent purchaser

British Library Cataloguing in Publication Data
Jones, Maldwyn A.
The limits of liberty.—(Short Oxford history of
the modern world)
1. United States—History
I. Title
973 E178
ISBN 0-19-820572-4 Pbk

5 7 9 10 8 6

Printed by
TJ International Ltd,
Padstow, Cornwall

AUTHOR'S PREFACE

THE preparation of this book has extended over a number of years and many people have helped me bring it to completion. My great indebtedness to the work of other scholars is, I trust, sufficiently acknowledged in the Bibliographical Essay. But I should also like to thank a number of friends and colleagues for specific assistance, so generously given. To John Roberts, the general editor of the series, who honored me with his invitation to write the book and who patiently endured what turned out to be its unduly long period of gestation, I am under a particularly heavy obligation. He read my entire manuscript, gave me the benefit of his learning and experience, and made invaluable suggestions about content and style. Esmond Wright, Melvyn Stokes, and H. G. Nicholas read and commented on parts of the book in draft, to my very great benefit. For ideas and information I am indebted to Marcus Cunliffe and the late Wallace E. Davies, as well as to many historians at those American universities at which I have been fortunate enough to hold visiting appointments: Chicago, Pennsylvania, Harvard, Princeton, Cornell, and Stanford. I am grateful also to Nazneen Razwi for her tireless labors in typing and retyping successive drafts of the book and to Kathleen Edwards and Irene Leonessi for their part in typing the final version. My thanks are due also to Ivon Asquith of Oxford University Press for his many courtesies and his long-continued encouragement and to Gill Wigglesworth, whose skilled copy-editing greatly improved the manuscript. Finally, I should like to thank my wife for her shrewd—though not always welcome—criticisms, for her willingness to share in the drudgery inseparable from the preparation of a book, and for much else besides.

University College London April 1982   M.A.J.

CONTENTS

LIST OF MAPS   xv

LIST OF TABLES   xvii

1. *Colonial Foundations, 1607–1760*   1
The Physical Setting   1
The American Indian   2
England and Colonization   3
The Structure of Government   13
Mercantilism and the Imperial System   15
The Colonial Economy   17

2. *Provincial Expansion, 1700–1763*   19
Population and Immigration   19
White Servitude and Black Slavery   21
Colonial Society and Culture   23
Colonial Religion   26
The American Enlightenment   29
Education   30
Law and Legal Institutions   31
Indian Wars and the Contest for Empire   32

3. *Revolution and Independence, 1763–1783*   37
Imperial Reorganization and Colonial Protest   37
The Stamp Act Controversy   40
The Townshend Duties   40
The Boston Tea Party   43
The Continental Congress   44
The Declaration of Independence   46
The Revolutionary War   49
Military Operations: Long Island to Saratoga   50
The French Alliance   51
Problems of War-making   54
Military Operations: The Southern Phase   55
Peacemaking, 1781–1783   56

4. *The Revolutionary Transformation, 1776–1789*   58
The American Revolution   58
The State Constitutions   62
The Articles of Confederation   63
The Federal Convention   70
The Ratification Debate   73

5. *The Federalist Age, 1789–1801*   76
   Organizing the Federal Government   76
   Hamilton's Financial Program   79
   Foreign Affairs   82
   The Rise of Political Parties   84
   The Adams Administration   85
   The Election of 1800   88

6. *Jeffersonian Republicanism, 1801–1824*   90
   Jefferson in Power   90
   The Louisiana Purchase   93
   The Neutral Rights Controversy   97
   Indians and Frontiersmen   100
   The War of 1812   101
   Political Transition and Postwar Nationalism   106
   Sectional Strains   111

7. *The Expanding Union, 1815–1860*   113
   The Transport Revolution   113
   Foreign Trade and Shipping   116
   The Westward Movement   117
   Urban Growth   121
   Slavery and the Cotton Kingdom   122
   The Growth of Industry   126
   The Rise of Mass Immigration   129

8. *The Politics of Egalitarianism, 1824–1844*   134
   A Society of Equals?   134
   Political Democracy   135
   John Quincy Adams and National Republicanism   137
   The Jacksonians   138
   Jackson's Presidency   140
   The Nullification Crisis   142
   The Bank War   145
   The 'Second Party System'   149
   Van Buren's Presidency   151
   The 1840 Election and the Whig Eclipse   152

9. *Social and Cultural Ferment, 1820–1860*
   Struggle for Cultural Independence   156
   Americans at Worship   160
   The Reform Impulse   161
   Utopian Experiments   162
   Prison and Asylum Reform   163
   Americans at School   164
   The Temperance Movement   167
   The Peace Crusade and Women's Rights   168
   Antislavery and Proslavery   170

10. *Westward Expansion and Sectional Conflict, 1844–1850*   177
    Manifest Destiny   177
    The Election of 1844   180
    Polk and Expansionism   181
    The Mexican War   183
    Slavery in the Territories   187
    The Election of 1848   190
    The Sectional Crisis   191
    The Compromise of 1850   192

11. *The Road to Secession, 1850–1861*   196
    Sectionalism and the South   196
    Pierce and the Revival of Conflict   199
    The Kansas–Nebraska Act   201
    Antislavery, Antiforeignism, and Political Realignment   203
    Bleeding Kansas   205
    James Buchanan, the Dred Scott Decision, and the Lecompton Constitution   206
    The Lincoln–Douglas Debates   209
    John Brown's Raid   210
    The Election of 1860   211
    The Lower South Secedes   213
    The Failure of Compromise and the Sumter Crisis   215

12. *The Civil War, 1861–1865*   218
    The First Modern War?   218
    The Confederacy and the Union   219
    Slavery and the Border States   220
    Wartime Politics and Policies   220
    Behind the Lines   222
    The Confederate States of America   223
    The War: Bull Run to Antietam   224
    The Emancipation Proclamation   227
    The War: Gettysburg, Vicksburg, and Chattanooga   229
    Europe and the Civil War   231
    Grant versus Lee   233
    The Election of 1864   233
    The Final Campaigns, 1864–1865   234

13. *Reconstruction, 1865–1877*   237
    The Legacy of War   237
    Presidential Reconstruction   238
    Congress versus President   241
    Radical Reconstruction   244
    The Impeachment of Andrew Johnson   245
    The Election of 1868   247
    The Grant Administration   248
    Liberal Republicanism   249

Political Scandals   250
Reconstruction in the South   251
Black Aspirations and Achievements   254
Instruments of Radical Rule   255
Undermining Radical Rule   256
The Disputed Election of 1876 and the Compromise of 1877   258

14. *The New South and White Supremacy, 1877–1914*   260
Southern Agriculture   260
Southern Industry   262
Bourbon Rule   265
The Erosion of Black Freedom   267
Black Responses: Accommodation and Protest   270

15. *Taming the West, 1865–1900*   275
The Wild West   275
The Mining Frontier   276
The Cattle Kingdom   278
The Destruction of the Plains Indians   281
Spanning the Continent   285
The Farmers' Frontier   288
Conservation   291

16. *The Growth of an Industrial Economy, 1865–1914*   295
The American Industrial Revolution   295
Inventions and Improvements   297
Railroads and their Critics   300
Steel, Oil, and Finance   304
Big Business: Apologia and Attack   307
Curbing the Trusts   309
Trade Unionism: Progress and Problems   310
The Growth of Industrial Conflict   313
Industrialization and the Condition of Labor   317

17. *Society and Culture in the Industrial Era, 1860–1910*   319
Population Trends   319
Urban Growth   320
The New Immigration   321
Transport, Safety, and Public Health Problems   324
Retailing and Advertising   325
Urban Architecture and Planning   326
The Slum Problem   327
Class Division and Social Mobility   329
Women, Marriage, and Divorce   330
The Impact of Technology on Everyday Life   331
Entertainment, Sport, and Leisure   332
Challenge to Religion   335

Educational Advance 339
Libraries and the Press 341
Literature and the Arts 343

18. *Politics from Conservatism to Revolt, 1877–1896* 347
    The Political System 347
    The Political Parties 350
    The Money Question 352
    Factionalism and Spoils 352
    Civil-Service Reform 353
    Presidential Negativism 354
    The Agrarian Revolt 358
    The People's Party 360
    The Battle of the Standards 363

19. *The Progressive Era, 1900–1917* 368
    Progressivism: Sources and Characteristics 368
    Municipal Reform 372
    Progressivism in the States 372
    Women's Suffrage, Prohibition, Child Welfare 374
    Theodore Roosevelt and Progressivism 377
    Taft and Republican Insurgency 382
    The Election of 1912 386
    The Climax of Progressivism 388

20. *The United States and World Affairs, 1865–1914* 393
    Isolationism and Indifference 393
    Post-Civil War Diplomacy 393
    From Introspection to Imperialism 396
    The Spanish–American War 400
    The Development of Far Eastern Policy 404
    The Acquisition of the Panama Canal Zone 407
    Policing the Western Hemisphere 408

21. *The United States and the First World War, 1914–1920* 412
    The Problems of Neutrality 412
    The German Submarine Campaign 415
    Propaganda and Preparedness 417
    The Election of 1916 419
    Wilsonian Peace Efforts 420
    America Goes to War 420
    The American Contribution to Victory 424
    The Home Front 426
    Wilson and Peacemaking 428
    The Senate and the Versailles Treaty 430

22. *After the War, 1919–1929*   432
    The Age of Disillusion and Reaction   432
    Normalcy in Action   435
    Nationalism, Conformity, and Social Disunity   438
    Coolidge, the Business Boom, and the Cult of Prosperity   444
    American Society in the Jazz Age   448
    Literature and Rebellion   450
    The Election of 1928   451

23. *The Great Depression, 1929–1939*   453
    Origins of the Depression   453
    Hoover and the Depression   455
    Franklin D. Roosevelt and the Early New Deal   457
    Critics of the New Deal   461
    The New Deal: Second Phase   462
    American Society during the Depression   465
    The Supreme Court Controversy   471
    The Ebbing of the New Deal   473
    The New Deal in Retrospect   475

24. *Foreign Policy between the Wars, 1921–1941*   477
    The Aftermath of Versailles   477
    The Washington Conference   478
    The Kellogg Pact   480
    War Debts and Reparations   480
    Origins of the 'Good Neighbor' Policy   481
    The Far East   483
    New Deal Diplomacy   484
    Isolationism Triumphant   487
    Challenges to Isolationism   491
    Lend-Lease and its Consequences   494
    The Road to Pearl Harbor   496

25. *Global War, 1941–1945*   499
    Civil Liberties in Wartime   499
    The American War Effort   500
    American Society in Wartime   503
    The Grand Alliance   504
    The Defensive War, 1941–1942   506
    The Mediterranean Campaigns, 1942–1943   508
    The Assault on Nazi-Occupied Europe   509
    The Pacific War, 1943–1944   511
    Wartime Politics   511
    The Yalta Conference   512
    The European War: Final Phase   513
    Truman Takes Hold   514
    The Reduction of Japan   515

26. *Cold War Tensions, 1945–1960*   517
    The Cold War   517
    The Containment Policy   519
    China Goes Communist   520
    The Korean War   522
    Truman and Domestic Affairs   524
    The Election of 1948   527
    Communist Subversion and McCarthyism   529
    The Eisenhower Landslide   531
    The Eisenhower Presidency   533
    Eisenhower's Second Term   535
    Dulles and the Cold War   537

27. *The Troubled Years, 1960–1980*   543
    The Election of 1960   543
    John F. Kennedy and the New Frontier   544
    Lyndon B. Johnson and the Great Society   550
    The Warren Court and Judicial Activism   552
    The Black Revolt   553
    Resistance to Communism: the Caribbean and Vietnam   554
    The Election of 1968   556
    Nixon's Foreign Policy: Vietnamization and *Détente*   558
    Nixonian Conservatism, the Imperial Presidency, and Watergate   559
    The Ford Interlude   564
    The Carter Presidency   567
    The Election of 1980   570

28. *American Society and Culture, 1940–1980*   573
    Population, Immigration, and Mobility   573
    The Urban Crisis   576
    Economic Growth and Technological Change   578
    Minority Problems: Blacks, Chicanos, and American Indians   581
    The Women's Movement   584
    Religion in American Life   586
    Problems of Mass Education   588
    American Culture: Science, Literature, and the Arts   590

29. *The Conservative Counter-Revolution, 1980–1992*   596
    Conservatism Resurgent   596
    Reaganomics   597
    Reagan and the 'Evil Empire'   596
    Reagan's Second Term   602
    The Reshaping of the Supreme Court   604
    Corruption and Scandal   606
    The Iran–Contra Affair   607
    Reaganism in Retrospect   609
    The Presidential Election of 1988   610
    Bush and the End of the Cold War   612

The Gulf War   615
Bush at Bay: Recession, Taxation, Racial Tension   618
The Election of 1992   621
Population and Immigration Trends   624
Social Issues: Abortion, AIDS, Drugs, Gun Control   628

BIBLIOGRAPHY   633

MAPS   673

TABLES   690

INDEX   699

MAPS

1. Physical Map of the United States   673
2. Political Map of the United States   674
3. Colonial Grants   675
4. The Struggle for America   676
5. English Mainland Colonies, 1763   677
6. The Northern Campaigns of 1775–1777   678
7. The Seat of the War in the South, 1779–1781   679
8. The New Nation   680
9. Growth of the United States, 1776–1853   681
10. Railroads and Canals, 1840–1850   682
11. The Mexican War   683
12. Eve of the Civil War   684
13. The Civil War, 1861–1865   685
14. The New West   686
15. Final Stages of the War in the Pacific   687
16. The Vietnam War   688

TABLES

1. Population of the United States, 1790–1990   690
2. Immigration to the United States, 1820–1992   694
3. Admission of States to the Union   694
4. Presidential Elections   695
5. Justices of the United States Supreme Court   698

1. *Colonial Foundations, 1607–1760*

The United States began as an extension of Europe. In some important respects it has remained one. American religion, law, education, literature, philosophy, art, and science—and of course language—all bear the mark of European origins. Long after they became politically independent, Americans remained in a state of cultural (and to a lesser extent, economic) dependence upon Europe, reading European books, aping European fashions, drawing on European technological 'know-how' and recruiting European labor to till their fields and develop their mines and factories. Yet even the first colonial settlements were never an exact replica of Europe. Right from the start American society and culture diverged from European models. The American environment had dissolving effects: it demanded and encouraged new ways of thinking and behaving and forced European settlers to modify the institutions they brought with them. The sheer size of America, its remoteness from Europe, its climatic and topographical peculiarities, its seemingly endless economic opportunities, the extraordinary energies required to subdue the wilderness—these factors helped to form a fluid, mobile society and bred a temper that was at once restless, optimistic, enterprising, reckless, and impatient of external restraint. A further source of divergence was that Americans drew not on one European tradition but several. Although during the crucial early decades of settlement English influences were paramount, by 1760 there was a sufficient non-English leavening to give the population a distinctive spice. In the nineteenth century America attracted vast numbers of immigrants from every country in Europe—and from other parts of the world. A unique blend of peoples and cultures was to result. Americans, then, remained in Europe's debt but evolved a distinct society with an ethos and an idiom of its own.

The Physical Setting

White settlement of the continental United States, an area three-quarters that of Europe, required continuous adaptation over a period of nearly three centuries to a succession of strange and widely different physiographic regions: forests, grassy prairies, treeless plains, swamps, deserts, mountains, saline sinks, and high, semiarid plateaux. Westward advance was made more difficult by the fact that the natural grain of the North American continent is longitudinal. Two great north– south mountain systems serve to wall in the continental heartland. On the east the Appalachians, consisting of a series of parallel mountain ranges bordering a fringe of coastal plain, extend a thousand miles from Newfoundland to Alabama. On the west the towering peaks and rugged masses of the Cordilleras, the giant mountain chain comprising the Rockies, the Cascades, and the Sierra Nevada, straddle the backbone of the continent all the way from Alaska to central New Mexico. Between these two mountain barriers lies a vast sprawling plain drained by one of the world's great river systems—the Mississippi and its tributaries—which flows southward and empties into the Gulf of Mexico.

The first settlers were however fortunate in that the side of the North American continent facing Europe was more penetrable than that facing Asia. Along the Atlantic coastline they found an abundance of good harbors, a relatively deep coastal plain suitable for agriculture, and numerous navigable rivers affording access to the interior. But if these physiographic features—none of them duplicated on the Pacific coast—invited settlement, European newcomers had to endure greater extremes of climate than they had been used to: summers were hotter and more humid, winters (north of the Chesapeake at least) longer and more severe. They were also confronted with dense forest on a scale unknown in Europe for centuries. But while this was an obstacle to travel and agriculture it was vital to the settlers' survival. It furnished timber for shelter and fuel and its abundant wildlife—notably deer, bears, beavers, badgers, wild turkeys, and pigeons—constituted a rich source of food and clothing. It also yielded lumber, naval stores, and furs for which there was a demand in Europe. Hardly less valuable were the fish which teemed in American rivers and lakes and in even greater variety and profusion on the continental shelf, the underwater ledge jutting out from the coast into the Atlantic. Except in New England, the Atlantic coastal plain (once cleared of trees) consisted of fertile farmland particularly favorable to the cultivation of Indian corn and tobacco, the two most important plants North America has given to the world. However, the early settlers introduced a variety of European edible plants and vegetables and, since the dog was the only domestic animal then existing in America, they also imported horses, cattle, sheep, and pigs.

The American Indian

When the first settlers arrived in America early in the seventeenth century, they found a land unexplored but by no means uninhabited. Most scholars are agreed that the misnamed 'Indians' descend from Mongoloid immigrants arriving from Siberia by way of the Bering Strait at least 30,000 years ago. From Alaska they slowly fanned out across the length and breadth of the Americas. In 1600 there were perhaps one and a half million Indians in what is now the United States. While they shared common physical features—black hair, high cheekbones, and some shade of coppery skin—the Indians were culturally very varied. Some tribes were nomadic, others sedentary; some were pacific, others warlike; some lived in bark wigwams, others in skin tepees, others again in adobe or stone cliff-dwellings. There were more than six hundred different Indian languages.

In parts of central and south America some Indian peoples had become highly advanced: the civilizations of the Mayas and the Aztecs of Mexico and of the Incas of Peru were their achievements. But the tribes of North America were relatively primitive. They knew nothing of the wheel, the horse, metal cooking utensils, or firearms. They thus had much to learn from the white man. However they had much to teach him in return: how to grow maize or Indian corn, for example, and how to cultivate, cure, and use tobacco. Despite this mutual dependence relations between the races were soon to fall into a pattern of hostility. White men long had little understanding of, or sympathy with, a polytheistic (and thus in their eyes 'pagan') culture which found the concept of the private ownership of land not only alien but repugnant. Cultural differences bred friction, skirmishing, and finally open warfare. In the end, the Indians were no match for a technology vastly superior to their own, while the intruders, for all their avowed intention of converting the Indians to Christianity, saw the tribes essentially as an obstacle to be overcome or removed, along with other perils of the wilderness. Most of the story of the white man's treatment of the Indian is a dreary record of dishonored treaties, encroachments on Indian hunting-grounds, and the crushing of those not cajoled, bribed, or intimidated into relinquishing their patrimony. Over a period of three centuries relentless white pressure, the white man's diseases, and the white man's alcohol would demoralize the Indians, destroy their culture, and all but rob them of a sense of identity. By 1900, when the whites had spread over the whole continent, there were fewer than 250,000 Indians in the United States, most of them herded into reservations, chronically poor, diseased, and disoriented. Place-names were almost the only legacy of their presence: of the present fifty states over half bear names of Indian origin.

England and Colonization

Among the white newcomers to the New World, the English were late starters. Adventurous Norse seafarers from Iceland and Greenland had reached Newfoundland and Labrador at the beginning of the eleventh century and may even have attempted to settle. But nothing had come of their discoveries. Columbus's first voyage of discovery in 1492, undertaken in the belief that Asia could be reached by sailing west across the Atlantic, opened the age of American colonization. It produced prompt results. Spain, eager for the riches America was believed to hold, at first laid claim to the whole of the New World but in 1494 concluded with Portugal the Treaty of Tordesillas which established a north–south demarcation line 370 leagues west of the Cape Verde Islands: everything west of the line belonged to Spain, everything east of it to Portugal. Accordingly, in the early decades of the sixteenth century, Portugal established a colony in Brazil while Spain explored much of the rest of South America and the Caribbean. Soon, some Spaniards ventured northward from Mexico in their search for precious metals. In the 1530s and 1540s expeditions led by Hernando de Soto and Francisco Vasquez Coronado traversed wide stretches of the Mississippi Valley and the Great Plains but, finding no gold, concluded that the region had little to offer. Apart from leaving a fort at St. Augustine, Florida and a number of missions in the Southwest, Spain turned her back on America north of the Rio Grande in the later sixteenth century, though without relinquishing her claims there. But Spain's apparent success led England, France, the Netherlands, and Sweden to defy those claims and plant colonies on the North American mainland.

English interest in the New World dated back to 1497 when Henry VII sent John Cabot—like Columbus a Genoese—in search of a westward passage to the Orient. For most of the sixteenth century England did not challenge Spain's imperial dominance, but by 1580 the Tudor monarchy had consolidated its authority and the Elizabethan settlement had achieved a religious equilibrium. The defeat of the Spanish Armada in 1588 then ended the threat of invasion. At about the same time, the growth of joint-stock trading companies like the Muscovy Company (1555), the Levant Company (1581), and the Barbary Company (1585) was kindling wider interest in America as a route to the East and provided means of raising the capital needed for colonization. Meanwhile, a sharp rise in England's population and new problems of rural employment as grain-growing gave way to wool-growing fed impressions that the country was overpopulated. In 1584 an Oxford geographer, Richard Hakluyt, brought out a promotional tract, *A Particular Discourse concerning Western Discoveries*, setting forth the case for colonization. Colonies would, he said, buy English manufactures, make England self-sufficient in colonial products, offer homes and land to her surplus population, furnish bases for attacking the Spanish empire, and enable the gospel to be carried to the Indians. Hakluyt's arguments, elaborated in later works, were well received. Already, in 1583, one of his friends, Sir Humphrey Gilbert, with the Queen's approval, had led a colonizing expedition to Newfoundland (he had been lost at sea on the voyage home). A few years later Gilbert's half-brother, Sir Walter

Raleigh, made a series of attempts to found a colony on Roanoke Island, off what later became North Carolina. But in 1591 a relief expedition found Roanoke utterly deserted and what happened to the 'lost colony' was never discovered. Yet in spite of failure, these efforts demonstrated two things: the inadequacy of one man's resources to finance such enterprises and the necessity of keeping colonists supplied from England. England came to dominate the colonial scene because these lessons were learned.

The thirteen mainland colonies which were ultimately to band together to form the United States of America were haphazard creations. The unity born of their common English heritage was small, and was subtly replaced as time passed by a different kind of unity, one shaped by New World experiences and the New World environment. They were founded by unconnected private ventures with aims ranging from the utopian to the mundane. Appearing over a period of a century and a quarter and strung out along 1,500 miles of Atlantic coastline, they were to develop at widely different rates, evolving dissimilar economies, forms of government, and religious codes, and attracting populations of diverse ethnic and racial makeup. The first of them was founded because of a desire for profit.

In 1606 James I granted a charter to two groups of merchants, the London Company and the Plymouth Company, giving them the right to colonize North America between the 34th and 45th parallels. Neither group envisaged agricultural settlement, but aimed at establishing trading posts to collect furs, fish, and timber, manufacture tar, pitch, and potash, and mine precious metals. The Plymouth Company's first colony (on the coast of Maine) lasted only a few months. The London Company's enterprise further south was successful after repeated disasters and disappointments. In December 1606 the Company sent out three small ships, the *Susan Constant*, the *Goodspeed*, and the *Discovery* with 104 men and boys. They entered Chesapeake Bay in May 1607 and founded Jamestown on the James River. Several hundred additional settlers joined them in the next two years. Though hardly any were of noble birth, the early colonists represented a rough cross-section of English society. Most of them came from the squirearchy or from yeoman stock or were the sons of substantial merchants. What they sought was quick wealth.

The colony ran into trouble from the start and for more than a decade hovered on the brink of extinction. The site was swampy. Few of the settlers possessed either an inclination to work hard or farming skills. They quarreled among themselves and wasted their energies looking for gold instead of growing food. The mortality was appalling; during the 'starving time' of 1609–10 famine and disease reduced the population from 500 to 60. The colony survived only because of the resourceful leadership, first of a colorful soldier of fortune, Captain John Smith, and then of Sir

Thomas Dale, a stern disciplinarian who assumed control in 1611. Their efforts would have been in vain, however, without continued support by the London promoters. Reorganized in 1609 as the Virginia Company, they continued to send out supplies and reinforcements. In order to recruit settlers the Company offered new incentives, giving the settlers a share of the Company stock and allowing them to cultivate their own land instead of working communally. In 1618, a 'headright' system gave every person who imported a settler or servant into the colony fifty acres of land. Meanwhile, it had been discovered that tobacco would grow successfully in the colony. Tobacco altered the venture's original purpose and quickly became the basis of Virginia's economy; in 1618 fifty thousand lbs. were exported, in 1626 more than six times as much. The stabilizing of the colony was clearly reflected in the Company's decision in 1619 to send out shiploads of women, "Whereby the Planters' minds may be faster tyed to Virginia by the bonds of Wyves and children." At the same time, self-government, which would serve to distinguish all the English colonies from the colonies of other European powers, was introduced. In 1618 the Virginia Company had ordered the calling of an elective assembly and it met for the first time in the church at Jamestown on July 30, 1619. Yet the future was still uncertain. In 1620 Virginia had less than a thousand settlers and two years later was almost wiped out by Indian attack. But by 1624 the crisis was over. It then became a royal colony because the Company had gone bankrupt, the Crown reluctantly continuing the right of representation.

Maryland differed from Virginia in being the creation of a single proprietor rather than a company. George Calvert, Lord Baltimore, was a Roman Catholic convert. Long interested in colonization, he induced Charles I in 1632 to make him a vast land grant north of the Potomac river. The new colony (named 'Maryland' after the queen, Henrietta Maria) was to be at the same time a feudal lordship, a source of income to the proprietor, and a refuge for Calvert's co-religionists. Since Calvert died before the charter was sealed it was actually issued to his son, Cecilius, the second Lord Baltimore, who in late 1633 sent two ships and between 200 and 300 passengers to settle the family province. The expedition included two Jesuits and most of its leaders were Roman Catholics, but most of its members were Protestants. Profiting from Virginia's experience and mistakes Maryland escaped the hardships and misfortunes of its neighbor and, like Virginia, based its economic life on tobacco. The land was parceled out into large manors, but the relics of feudalism soon disappeared, and although the charter had made the proprietor the sole source of political authority, subject only to the advice and consent of the freemen, things worked out differently in practice. An assembly first met in 1635 and quickly won the right to initiate legislation. The most celebrated enactment was the Maryland Toleration Act of 1649, passed at Lord Baltimore's insistence to protect the colony's dwindling minority of Catholics. It did not, as is often claimed, mark a general acceptance of the principle of religious toleration and was repealed in 1654.

Meanwhile other Englishmen had settled six hundred miles to the north in 'New England', a region explored by Captain John Smith and named by him. This movement involved many more people than the Chesapeake enterprises and had religion as its mainspring. The pioneers were a little band of Separatists from Scrooby, Nottinghamshire; in 1608 they had gone to Holland to escape ecclesiastical and popular hostility and after a decade in exile had decided to seek a fresh refuge across the Atlantic. With financial help from a group of London merchants, they set sail from England in the *Mayflower* in September 1620. Though they were only about a third of the *Mayflower's* 102 passengers, the Separatists—or 'Pilgrims' as they styled themselves—effectively controlled the enterprise. Whether by accident or design, they made a landfall at Cape Cod and on December 16, 1620 landed at what is now Plymouth. Being outside the jurisdiction given to Virginia by James I the Pilgrims were dubious about their legal status. Before disembarking, therefore, they drew up the celebrated 'Mayflower Compact', which bound the signatories to form a 'civil body politic'. It was to remain the basis of government throughout the colony's history.

Like the Jamestown settlers, the Pilgrims faced appalling hardships. During the first winter half of them died, including nearly all the women. Several lean years followed before the development of farming and fishing secured the colony's future. Even then Plymouth grew only slowly and remained isolated until absorbed by Massachusetts Bay colony in 1691. This had been a far more significant foundation. The Puritans who settled Massachusetts Bay not only placed a distinctive stamp on New England but were long to influence American life and thought. Strictly speaking they were not religious refugees; nor did they go to America to establish the principle of freedom of conscience. Far from being driven out of their native land, they left it voluntarily and with royal blessing, though for religious reasons. They (unlike the Separatists) had wanted to reform the Church of England from within, but that aim seemed unattainable once Charles I had successively made their chief opponent, William Laud, Bishop of London (1628) and Archbishop of Canterbury (1633).

In 1629 Charles I granted a charter to the Massachusetts Bay Company, a body which had fallen under the control of a group of prominent Puritans. At a meeting at Cambridge the stockholders decided to remove both the charter and the Company to America. As governor of the proposed colony they elected John Winthrop, a Suffolk lawyer and landowner and a fervent Puritan. He was to become the dominant figure in early Massachusetts. It is also true that although the Puritan leaders were generally well-to-do, some of them had suffered from inflationary price rises, a depression in the cloth trade, and a succession of bad harvests. Yet there can be no doubting that religion was the main force moving them. They wanted to move to New England to establish a Bible Commonwealth based on Puritan beliefs under a form of government in church and state that would both satisfy their own aspirations and serve as a model for those left behind. Toleration they bitterly repudiated. They went into the wilderness to practice what they deemed to be the one true form of worship, and believed it would be sinful to allow any other.

The Puritan 'Great Migration' was the largest exodus in the history of seventeenth-century English colonization. In 1630 seventeen vessels carried Winthrop and nearly a thousand settlers to Massachusetts Bay. In the next ten years twenty thousand more followed them. At first, chiefly from East Anglia and the West Country, two of the staunchest Puritan strongholds, emigrants came later from all over England. Most were of above average wealth and education and, unlike the first settlers of the Chesapeake area, generally brought their families with them. They were also frequently accompanied by their pastors, whole congregations often emigrating in a body.

The founders of Massachusetts insisted on orderly and well-regulated settlement. In 1630 they established Boston and half a dozen other towns along the shores of Massachusetts Bay. Soon afterwards they planted a circle of secondary settlements twenty or thirty miles inland. By 1640 there were more than twenty towns; though little more than villages, they contrasted sharply with Virginia's scattered farms and plantations. They served as political and administrative units, controlled their own internal affairs, and regulated land distribution so that persons of wealth and social position received larger grants than others. After the usual early hardships the settlers took to growing food on land cleared and abandoned by the Indians and were soon self-sufficient. Massachusetts had a harsh climate and stony soil and no staple commodity to export, but it had other resources, notably timber and fish. Shipbuilding began as early as 1631 and before long lumber, fish, and grain were being exported to the West Indies and southern Europe.

The leaders of Massachusetts Bay believed that the mass of the people were unfit to rule. Authority, they thought, should be exercised by those whom God, in Winthrop's words, had made "high and eminent in power and dignity", in other words, themselves. But except at the very beginning oligarchical control was never absolute. In part this was because of the way the Company's charter was adapted to serve as the constitution of the colony. The charter had vested control of the Company in the freemen or stockholders but in 1631, in order to perpetuate the Puritan character of the enterprise, political participation was made dependent on church membership rather than on ownership of stock. That membership was restricted to 'visible saints', certified by the clergy after rigorous examination, but at least during the early years this meant a large proportion of the adult males. Moreover, further concessions had soon to be made to meet complaints against authoritarian rule. In 1632 the freemen gained the power to elect the governor directly; two years later they were empowered to select deputies to represent them in the General Court, which acted as a legislature and possessed the right to levy taxes. Finally, in 1644, the General Court became bicameral, the upper house consisting of the governor and his 'assistants', the lower house of the deputies. The consent of both houses was to be needed to enact legislation.

Representative government weakened neither Puritan control nor the religious character of the Bible Commonwealth. Massachusetts was not strictly a theocracy since the clergy did not hold secular office, yet Church and State were closely intertwined. Puritan preachers, as the sole authorized interpreters of the Scriptures, were highly influential: leading divines like John Cotton, "the foremost scholar and official apologist for the New England Way", were regularly consulted by the political leaders. As in Europe, it was taken for granted that the state had the duty to maintain and protect religion. Every town was required to build a meeting-house, taxes were levied to pay ministers' salaries, and laws prescribed church attendance and restricted Sabbath-day activities. Moreover, the civil authorities dealt harshly with the heterodox. Blasphemers had their ears cropped, Baptists and Quakers were whipped, fined, and expelled. Once, four Quakers who returned to the colony after having been banished, were hanged on Boston Common.

Intolerance in Massachusetts Bay encouraged settlement elsewhere in New England. The founders of Rhode Island had been expelled from Massachusetts for their opinions. The most celebrated of them were Roger Williams and Anne Hutchinson. Williams was a minister, a Separatist, and a leveler, who denied the validity of the Massachusetts charter on the ground that the land belonged to the Indians and questioned the rights of civil magistrates to control consciences and beliefs. When the alarmed authorities ordered him to leave Massachusetts he went to Narragansett Bay and established the town of Providence on land bought from the Indians (1636). Soon afterward Mrs Anne Hutchinson, the wife of a Boston merchant, stirred up religious dissension there. She challenged clerical authority and insisted that faith alone was necessary for salvation. Tried for sedition and heresy, she was sentenced to banishment (1638), and (with her family) followed Williams to Narragansett Bay. Before long the exiles came together to form the colony of Rhode Island, which in 1644 obtained from the Long Parliament a charter providing for the separation of Church and State and for absolute freedom of conscience.

New Hampshire, too, was founded as a religious refuge—in 1638 by followers of Anne Hutchinson. But the other colonies spawned by Massachusetts Bay resulted largely from a desire for wider economic opportunity. The Reverend Thomas Hooker, who led an overland exodus to the Connecticut Valley in 1636 and founded the town of Hartford, may have had differences with the Massachusetts authorities but had religious and political opinions much the same as theirs. The constitution he drew up for Connecticut, the Fundamental Orders, took Massachusetts as its model. In any case, his followers, like other Puritans later in the 1630s, were prompted by the need for more fertile land. The colony of New Haven, founded in 1638 by yet another group from Massachusetts, was perhaps an even stricter Bible Commonwealth than the Bay colony itself. It was unique among the Puritan colonies in denying jury trial because it was not mentioned in the Scriptures. (Too small to exist independently, New Haven was absorbed into Connecticut when the latter colony obtained a royal charter in 1662.)

The English Civil War brought emigration temporarily to an end in 1642. By then, a group of virtually autonomous Puritan communities had taken firm root in New England. Their *de facto* independence grew during the period of the Commonwealth and Protectorate when Englishmen were preoccupied with domestic affairs. The need for united defense against the Indians, the Dutch, and the French prompted Massachusetts, Connecticut, New Haven, and Plymouth to form the New England Confederation in 1643. Rhode Island, thought by her neighbors to be disreputably liberal, was excluded. The Confederation was no more than a loose league but was the first experiment in federation in American history. Though weakened by intercolonial jealousies, it held together long enough to wage King Philip's War (1675–6), the most devastating Indian War of the century, and was not dissolved until 1684.

The restoration of Charles II in 1660 opened a new phase of colonization. The next twenty-five years brought English settlement to the South Atlantic seaboard and the Middle Atlantic region between New England and the Chesapeake. Unlike Virginia and Massachusetts Bay, all the Restoration colonies resembled Maryland in being based on royal grants to individual proprietors or groups of proprietors. In charters of 1663 and 1665 Charles awarded Carolina, a vast tract of land immediately south of Virginia, to a group of eight proprietors, all prominent politicians. One of them, Sir Anthony Ashley Cooper, later Earl of Shaftesbury, together with his physician and adviser, the eminent philosopher, John Locke, drew up the Fundamental Constitutions, an elaborate frame of government for the new colony. It envisaged a highly stratified society ruled by a hereditary aristocracy; it also provided for religious toleration and Negro slavery. Both the latter provisions were in fact implemented but otherwise the Fundamental Constitutions proved unworkable. Government in the new colony came to resemble that of other proprietary colonies in having an appointed governor and council and an elected assembly. The northern and southern halves of the Carolina grant were geographically distinct and the northern region around Albemarle Sound was soon colonized by a group of settlers from Virginia. Within a few years they were profitably engaged in growing tobacco and raising naval stores. Further south the bulk of the early settlers were small planters from Barbados, displaced by the extensive cultivation of sugar by slave-labor. In 1669, together with some settlers direct from England, they established themselves inland on the south bank of the Ashley river, and a decade later moved to the present site of Charleston. Hopes of producing silk came to nothing, but rice and indigo proved valuable staples and a lucrative trade developed with the Indians in deerskins and furs. In 1712 the proprietors appointed separate governors for North and South Carolina.

New York, the first proprietary colony in the Middle Atlantic region, was created in 1664 when Charles II granted the territory between the Connecticut and Delaware rivers to his brother James, Duke of York (afterward James II). The area, though long claimed by England, was first under Dutch occupation and was known as New Netherland. Yet the Dutch were primarily interested in the fur trade not colonization, and by 1650 there were still only 3,000 people in New Netherland. Already, land-hungry Puritans from Connecticut had crossed to Long Island and were pressing toward the scattered Dutch settlements. In the Second Anglo-Dutch War the Duke of York's forces had little difficulty in forcing the surrender of the weakly held colony. Apart from renaming the towns— New Amsterdam became New York—the proprietary government changed little, leaving the Dutch undisturbed in their religion, commercial privileges, and estates. James in fact continued the Dutch practice of bestowing vast tracts on a few favorites, and since the great landowners, Dutch and English alike, refused to sell land and exploited their tenants New York attracted relatively few settlers. James also granted freedom of conscience, a code of laws which included jury trial and even a limited form of self-government, but did not accede until 1683 to the demand for an elected assembly. Its first act was to adopt a Charter of Liberties, which James repudiated. On his accession to the throne in 1685 New York was transformed into a royal colony.

James, almost as soon as he received his proprietary, had given away the lands between the Hudson and the Delaware, the southernmost part of what had been New Netherland, to two of his friends, both Carolina proprietors, Lord Berkeley and Sir George Carteret. The new colony was named New Jersey (after the Channel Island where Carteret had been born). In 1674 the proprietors divided their grant in two. Berkeley took the western half, Carteret the eastern, and Berkeley at once sold West

Jersey to members of the Society of Friends. In late 1675 it began to be settled by English Quakers. Meanwhile East Jersey had been filling up with transplanted New England Congregationalists and Baptists, attracted by the promise of religious freedom and an elected legislature. They were soon at odds with the proprietors over land titles and rents. Since their animus towards Quakers was unabated, they became still more discontented when in 1682 a wealthy Quaker syndicate headed by William Penn bought East Jersey from Carteret's heirs. Finally in 1702 East and West Jersey were reunited as a royal colony, though disputes over land were to persist well into the eighteenth century.

Although New Jersey thus became a refuge for Quakers, William Penn wanted a colony of his own for his co-religionists. Quakerism, at once the simplest and the most mystical of the unorthodox sects that sprang from seventeenth-century Puritanism, denied the necessity for a special priesthood and for outward rites, its central idea being the doctrine of the "inner light"—that inspiration comes from within each individual. They attracted almost universal hatred in England not only by rejecting prevailing ideas of ritual and church government, but also by their democratic scorn for all forms of authority and a tendency to disorderliness that contrasted strangely with their peaceful professions. Penn, the son of an admiral who was one of Charles II's staunchest supporters, had become a Quaker in 1667 but had retained his connection with the Court. In 1681, in payment of a debt owed to the deceased admiral, Charles II granted Penn an extensive tract of land beyond the Delaware. This was to be Pennsylvania. The following year Penn bought the former Swedish settlements along the Delaware from the Duke of York; these "three lower counties" were granted their own representative assembly in 1703 and became the separate colony of Delaware.

Though Penn's 'Holy Experiment' was idealistic and generous, he intended that Pennsylvania should at the same time yield a profit in the form of land sales and quitrents. He sold large tracts to rich English, Welsh, and Irish Quakers and promoted emigration from Continental Europe with pamphlets in several languages. By 1685 religious toleration and easy terms for land purchase had attracted eight thousand colonists from the British Isles, Holland, and the German Palatinate. Penn himself sailed to his colony in 1682 to lay down careful plans for a capital city named, appropriately, Philadelphia (Greek for 'brotherly love'). The following year a group of German settlers founded Germantown, near Philadelphia. Needing the financial backing of well-to-do Quaker associates Penn had to water down his commitment to popular rule; the Pennsylvania 'Frame of Government' provided for an elected assembly, but left power mainly with an appointed governor and council. And although Pennsylvania's Quaker elite was soon to become a minority, it dominated the colony's politics down to the American Revolution. Penn himself derived little profit from his proprietary; indeed it nearly bankrupted him. But Pennsylvania itself prospered.

Pennsylvania was the last seventeenth-century foundation. It gave England a continuous string of seaboard colonies from French Canada almost to Spanish Florida. The settlement of Georgia in 1732 completed the pattern. The group of wealthy philanthropists headed by General James Oglethorpe, to whom George II granted a twenty-one year charter in 1732, intended it to serve as an asylum for debtors and hoped to develop the Southern fur trade. The British government, for its part, saw Georgia as a buffer against Spanish and Indian attack. There was even a utopian dimension to the enterprise: it sought to promote virtue by forbidding slavery and rum and by limiting land holdings to 500 acres. Oglethorpe became the colony's first governor. By 1740 the trustees had sent out 1,500 colonists, only a few of them debtors. Besides Englishmen, Scots, and Swiss, they included German Protestant pietists called Salzburgers. The first two decades were difficult. Vineyards and mulberry trees proved unsuccessful and settlers complained continually about the restrictions imposed on them. The trustees eventually gave way, first over rum, then over slavery and land policy. This opened the way to large-scale cultivation of rice and indigo, but Georgia grew only slowly, even after 1751 when it became a royal colony. As late as 1760 its population was barely six thousand.

The Structure of Government

All the colonies, whether royal, proprietary, or corporate, eventually came to have a more or less identical governmental structure. This consisted of a governor, a council (which acted as the upper house of the legislature), and a legislative assembly. Except in Rhode Island and Connecticut, where he was elected by the legislature, the governor was appointed by the Crown or the proprietor and in theory he possessed sweeping powers. As the king's official representative he was head of government, chief magistrate, and commander of the armed forces; he could summon and dissolve assemblies, veto their laws, and appoint lesser officials. But in practice the governor's authority was limited. Generally resented as an outsider, he had also to contend with the colonial assemblies upon which he was dependent for appropriations and, because of Parliament's refusal to vote money for the purpose, even for his own salary. In every colony the assembly was elected (and, it might be added, much more representative than the British Parliament). The ownership of property was so widespread that it has been estimated that between 50 and 80 percent of adult white males were entitled to vote, though the proportion which actually did so was much lower. Moreover, prevailing notions of deference ensured that those elected were generally men of position and substantial property.

This did not make the assemblies any less insistent on the self-government provided for in the colonial charters and which they claimed was their birthright as Englishmen. Following the example of the House of Commons in its struggle with the Stuarts, the assemblies used their control of the purse to encroach on the governors' prerogatives and by the beginning of the eighteenth century they had already won a large measure of autonomy in local affairs. In particular they enjoyed the right to initiate legislation, levy taxes, and supervise expenditure. Colonial laws needed the approval of the Privy Council, but when they were disallowed—a fate suffered by only 5 percent of the 8,500 measures submitted to London between 1691 and 1775—colonial legislatures would generally reenact them in slightly amended form.

In local government institutional structures reflected the differing social and economic conditions of the colonies. In New England, where settlements were relatively compact and tightly organized, authority over local affairs was vested in town meetings in which all freeholders had voting rights; these assemblages fixed town tax-rates and chose selectmen to administer the town's business. When New Englanders moved to other colonies they carried their township system of government with them and even today it provides a forum for deciding local matters in many parts of the United States. In the more sparsely scattered Southern colonies, the basic unit of local government was the county. No provision was made for direct democracy on the New England township model. The county court, an administrative as well as a judicial body, consisted of justices of the peace appointed by the governor—usually in practice for life. The sheriff, too, was appointed by the governor. As the chief executive officer of the county, he was charged (like his counterpart in contemporary England) with keeping the peace and supervising elections and also with collecting taxes.

Though political parties were unknown in the colonies political factionalism was endemic and political controversy intense. The most persistent disputes were those between creditors and debtors over paper money and between frontiersmen and seaboard oligarchies over land, political representation, and frontier defense. On several occasions sectional and class conflict led to violence, an early and dramatic example being Bacon's Rebellion in Virginia in 1676. Though sparked off by a clash between frontiersmen and Indians, it exposed divisions within white society. When the royal governor, William Berkeley, refused early in 1676 to take appropriate action against marauding Indians he incensed frontiersmen already exasperated by his refusal to open more western land for settlement. They suspected that the sympathy Berkeley and his associates in the planter ruling class displayed toward Indians stemmed from a selfish desire to protect their fur-trading interests. Nathaniel Bacon, a wealthy young planter recently arrived from England, threw in his lot with the frontiersmen and, having raised a volunteer army to fight the Indians, marched on Jamestown and seized the government. But after Bacon had died of swamp fever, Berkeley regained control and executed thirty-seven of the rebels.

Mercantilism and the Imperial System

Unlike France and Spain, England was slow to develop either a comprehensive policy for supervising the colonies or effective machinery for implementing it. Struggles between King and Parliament pushed colonial questions into the background and the colonies were allowed to go their own way. But by the end of the Civil Wars their place in a general scheme of empire required consideration. Attempts began to be made to establish closer control over them. The imperial system that resulted was based, like that of other European powers, on an economic philosophy, later to be called mercantilism, which held that economic self-sufficiency was the key to national wealth and power. Mercantilists assumed that colonies existed solely to serve the interests of the mother country, to supply her with raw materials, absorb her manufactures, and provide employment for her shipping. Between 1651 and 1673 Parliament put these ideas into a series of Trade and Navigation Acts designed to establish an English monopoly of the colonial carrying trade, the colonial market, and certain valuable colonial products. All cargoes to or from the colonies were to be carried in ships built and owned in England or the colonies and manned by predominantly English crews. In addition, certain 'enumerated' commodities—sugar, cotton, indigo, dyewoods, ginger, and tobacco—could only be exported direct from the colonies to England even if their ultimate destination lay elsewhere. Finally, European goods bound for America had, with few exceptions, to be landed first in England and then reshipped.

During Charles II's last years the tendency towards control from London became more pronounced. In 1675 a special committee of the Privy Council—the Lords of Trade and Plantations—was established to oversee colonial affairs. In 1684 Massachusetts, which had persistently violated the laws of trade, was deprived of its charter and placed under a royal governor. Then in 1686 the process of centralization reached its climax when James II combined all the New England colonies into a single unit, the Dominion of New England. The existing assemblies were abolished and a governor appointed with autocratic powers. Later on New Jersey and New York were added to the Dominion. The Glorious Revolution of 1688 soon ended this experiment. When news reached Boston of James II's fall a popular uprising overthrew the new regime and there were similar events in other colonies. In Maryland Protestant insurgents drove out the representatives of the Catholic proprietor and elected a convention to choose a new governor. In New York a German merchant led a rebellion and took over the government; his reluctance to surrender power resulted ultimately in his being hanged for treason.

Under William and Mary the abolished colonial legislatures were revived, but attempts to tighten royal control went on. By a new charter of 1691, Massachusetts became a royal colony with a governor appointed by the Crown; so for a time did Maryland. By the middle of the eighteenth century only three proprietary colonies (Pennsylvania, Maryland, and Delaware) and two corporate colonies (Connecticut and Rhode Island) remained outside the direct control of the Crown. Even they had their quota of royal officials. In 1696 a new body, the Board of Trade, was given wide powers over the colonies and new machinery to ensure compliance with the laws of trade. English colonial policy remained strictly mercantilist. The list of enumerated commodities was steadily extended until by 1763 it included practically everything the colonies produced except fish, grain, and lumber. Laws were also passed to check colonial manufacturing; the Woolens Act of 1699 forbade the export of woolen yarn and cloth outside the colony in which it was produced and the Hat Act of 1732, passed in response to complaints of colonial competition from London feltmakers, prohibited the export of colonial beaver hats and instituted a lengthy apprenticeship for colonial hatters. Additional slitting mills and plating forges and the export of colonial iron outside the empire were forbidden by the Iron Act of 1750. Finally, restraints were placed on colonial-currency issues, British merchants having become alarmed at the instability and rapid depreciation of the colonial currency.

Nevertheless, elaborate though the legal and administrative framework became, the colonies were never effectively brought under imperial control. Distance was partly to blame. Administrative confusion compounded the problem. The colonies were administered not by a single government department but by several. The Board of Trade shared responsibility with a number of other departments and agencies, notably the Treasury, the Admiralty, and the Secretary of State for the Southern Department. Nor was the character of the officials sent to America always calculated to promote imperial interests. The chief posts in the colonial customs service came to be sinecures, filled by placemen who remained in England and sent deputies to perform their duties. Rarely men of ability and integrity, the wretchedly ill-paid deputies found it hard to resist bribes to wink at infractions of the laws of trade. Another reason for laxity of control was the 'salutary neglect' that came to prevail during Robert Walpole's long ascendancy (1721–42). Calculating that strict enforcement of the laws of trade would simpy limit colonial purchases from England, Walpole deliberately relaxed them. And although Halifax, as president of the Board of Trade between 1748 and 1761, tentatively attempted to tighten imperial control, the colonies remained for the most part loosely governed until after 1763.

The Colonial Economy

British mercantilist policies affected colonial economic development less than was once thought. There was no serious American complaint about mercantilist regulations before the imperial system was reformed in the 1760s and even then they were not a crucial grievance. Some aspects of the system were undoubtedly damaging to the colonies. Not all the provisions of the Acts of Trade and Navigation could be easily evaded. Burdens have to be weighed, however, against the substantial benefits the colonists received as members of the British empire. Colonial products enjoyed a protected market in England. Parliament granted generous subsidies (amounting to $300,000 a year by the 1760s) to producers of such colonial commodities as naval stores, indigo, and lumber products. The colonial shipbuilding industry profited by the exclusion of foreign ships from colonial trade. By the time of the Revolution one-third of the British merchant marine had been built in the colonies, especially New England. Nor on the whole did the laws regulating manufacturing have much impact. Only the Hat Act appears to have been effective. The Woolens Act affected Ireland more than the American colonies, as indeed it was meant to. The prohibitions of the Iron Act were openly disregarded: some colonial assemblies even carried defiance to the point of subsidizing new slitting mills. Not that the Iron Act was wholly restrictive. Though designed to check the expansion of the iron-finishing industry it sought to encourage crude-iron production and allowed colonial bar and pig iron to enter England free of duty. Partly because of this the colonies had outstripped England as producers of crude iron by the time of the Revolution. But whatever the effect of particular measures, the British mercantilist system as a whole was not so restrictive as to inhibit the development of a flourishing colonial economy. On balance it may even have been economically advantageous to the colonies.

The growth of a flourishing iron industry should not be taken as evidence of economic sophistication. Most of the slitting mills, furnaces, and forges were small, employing only handfuls of workers. So did shipbuilding yards. Most colonial manufactures—textiles, boots, and shoes and the like—were products of domestic industry. Farming remained the dominant economic activity, employing perhaps 90 percent of the working population. Agricultural techniques were primitive and improvident, at least by comparison with the best contemporary European practice. Only the most rudimentary farm implements were used. The abundance of land and the scarcity of labor discouraged manuring and crop rotation. Even so, virgin soil produced high yields. The maturity of colonial agriculture was reflected in its

degree of specialization. In the South tobacco remained the most important export staple and the mainstay of the economy. Although tobacco
cultivation tended to exhaust the soil and some planters, especially those
who moved inland to the Piedmont, turned to wheat-growing, tobacco
exports rose from about 14 million pounds in the 1670s to 100 million
pounds a century later. The eighteenth century also saw spectacular
increases in the export of Southern rice and indigo. The Middle Colonies
became a granary, exporting wheat to other mainland colonies, the West
Indies, and southern Europe. New England remained a land of small subsistence farms, but 'farming the sea' provided it with a profitable alternative. From the Newfoundland Banks and the shores of Nova Scotia
Yankee fishermen brought back great quantities of cod and mackerel, to
be dried and exported, along with livestock and lumber. More than half
of New England's thriving export trade was with the West Indies, which
supplied her in return with sugar, molasses, and other tropical products.
New England distillers turned molasses into rum, most of it for domestic
consumption, rum being almost a dietary staple of the colonists. But considerable quantities were used as an outward cargo in the notorious tri-
angular trade between New England, West Africa, and the West Indies.
New England slavers would carry rum and other commodities from Boston
or Newport to the Guinea coast, then slaves from Africa to the West
Indies, and finally sugar and molasses from the West Indies to their home
ports. New England's West Indian trade seemed likely to be crippled,
along with her rum industry, by the Molasses Act of 1733. Passed in
response to complaints of foreign competition from the sugar planters of
the British West Indies, it placed prohibitory duties on sugar and molasses
imported into the mainland colonies from French, Spanish, and Dutch
possessions in the Caribbean. But the measure proved largely a dead letter
and the illicit trade with the foreign West Indies persisted.

Thus for all its apparatus of regulation and control the British imperial
system was in practice easygoing. No other colonizing nation conceded to
its colonial subjects the degree of autonomy the inhabitants of British
America enjoyed. Right from the beginning the English colonists had been
allowed a great deal of latitude in running their own affairs. The imperial
system was intended to enrich the mother country, and it certainly did
that, but it could hardly be called tyrannical when the colonists were more
lightly taxed than Englishmen or when they were as prosperous and as
lightly governed as any people in the world.

2. Provincial Expansion, 1700–1763

Population and Immigration

Between 1700 and 1763 an unprecedented surge of expansion transformed the English colonies. The settled area doubled, the population increased eightfold to reach two million—about a third of the population of England and Wales. Meantime the character of immigration changed and with it the ethnic composition of the population. Expansion brought new problems and challenges but by the end of the Seven Years' War a self-assured and distinctive colonial society had emerged and the colonial economy had developed into one of the richest and most productive in the world.

The astonishing growth of population, much greater than that of contemporary Europe, was due mainly to a significantly lower death-rate. That in turn was attributable to the relative youthfulness of the population, the absence of famine, epidemics, and similar demographic crises, and the better diet made possible by the high productivity of American agriculture. Once the early 'starving times' were over the mortality-rate, especially of infants, fell dramatically—though more slowly in the hot, humid, and malaria-ridden environment of the Chesapeake colonies than in New England—and life expectancy soared. At Andover, Massachusetts, for example, the average age at death of the first male settlers was 71.8 years—higher, that is to say, than that of men in the United States today.

A steady influx of immigrants helped further to swell the population. Up to about 1700 the great majority were English. By then, though, the mercantilist view that people were a species of wealth, an indispensable resource to be husbanded at home rather than dispersed abroad, had won official favor. Thus emigration was discouraged, though it was never prohibited, except in the case of skilled artisans. The authorities only remained anxious to speed the departure of undesirables, shipping out vagrants, paupers, and political and military prisoners like those captured after the Jacobite rebellions of 1715 and 1745, as well as convicted malefactors. The practice began early in the seventeenth century but reached its height only after 1717, when Parliament created the new legal punishment of transportation. Despite colonial protests at least thirty thousand felons were transported to America during the eighteenth century, most of them to Virginia and Maryland.

Toward the end of the seventeenth century the colonies began to receive significant numbers of non-English immigrants. Thus began what was to become a persistent and indeed distinguishing theme in American development: the contacts and conflicts of people of different ethnic groups and races. Among the first were the French Huguenots, forced to flee when Louis XIV deprived them of freedom of worship by revoking the Edict of Nantes in 1685. Mostly craftsmen, merchants, and professional people, they tended to settle in seaport towns like Charleston, Philadelphia, New York, and Boston. Much larger numbers came from Germany and from the German cantons of Switzerland. A few belonged to pietist sects—Mennonites, Moravians, Dunkers, Schwenckfelders, and Amish—seeking refuge from religious persecution, but most to Lutheran or German Reformed (Calvinist) communities, driven out by economic pressure, more particularly the devastation of the Palatinate during the wars of Louis XIV. Germans settled variously in North Carolina, Georgia, and upstate New York, but their favorite colony was Pennsylvania. By 1766 economic opportunity, a generous land policy, and religious freedom had attracted so many of them that, according to Benjamin Franklin, they constituted one-third of Pennsylvania's population. They had a well-deserved reputation as stolid, pacific, and deeply pious folk, and were widely admired for their neatly kept farms and careful farming methods. The 'Pennsylvania Dutch', as they were generally known, clung to their own language and customs while the sectarians among them, especially the Amish, led an austere, isolated existence which their descendants preserve even today.

The largest group of eighteenth-century immigrants were the Scotch-Irish, descendants of Scottish Presbyterians who had settled in Ulster at the beginning of the seventeenth century. By 1776, a total of 250,000 Scotch-Irishmen had emigrated to the colonies. Their main reasons for leaving Ulster were economic—discontent with the land system, recurrent bad harvests, and the decline of the linen trade—though religious and political disabilities provided an additional impetus. The Scotch-Irish first made for New England but, meeting with an unfriendly reception, turned instead to Pennsylvania. There they were encouraged by the provincial authorities to settle on the frontier as a barrier against Indian attack. They poured into the Cumberland Valley and the trans-Allegheny region beyond the German settlements and then moved southward into western Maryland, the Valley of Virginia, and the Carolina back country. By the 1750s there was a continuous chain of Scotch-Irish frontier settlements all the way from Pennsylvania to Georgia. Intensely religious and fiercely intolerant, the Scotch-Irish deserve the major credit for establishing Presbyterianism in America. They were, however, notoriously undisciplined, turbulent, and restless. Unlike their German neighbors, with whom they were frequently at odds, they were careless farmers, partly; it would seem, from a psychological repugnance to commit themselves permanently to a particular locality.

While foreign immigration drastically altered the ethnic composition of most of the colonies, New England was an exception. Discouraging strangers lest they jeopardize the success of the Puritan experiment, it remained as ethnically homogeneous as its name implied. But elsewhere the population was in varying degrees cosmopolitan. In addition to the Scotch-Irish, the Germans, and the French Huguenots, there were scatterings of Scots, Welshmen, Irish Catholics, Dutchmen, and Sephardic Jews. But except in the towns there was little intermingling. Each ethnic group tended to cluster in separate areas and its members did not marry outside it. Not without reason has the population map of colonial America been likened to a mosaic.

Indentured Servitude and Negro Slavery

Few immigrants to the colonies crossed the Atlantic under their own resources. They tended to travel in groups, either as part of colonization schemes or, more frequently, under a system of temporary servitude designed to meet the chronic labor shortage. The system enabled the less well off to obtain free passage by entering into a contract or indenture pledging their labor for a specified term of years, usually four. During the colonial period between half and two-thirds of all white immigrants— except to New England—are believed to have done so in this fashion. By the early eighteenth century the traffic in indentured servants had become systematized and largely concentrated in the north of Ireland and in Holland. Merchants and ship captains would make regular recruiting tours of the hinterland, employing a variety of unscrupulous methods. On arrival in the colonies servants were publicly offered for sale in much the same way as Negro slaves. Closely related to the servant trade was the redemptioner system under which poor people were given free passage on the understanding that friends or relatives would 'redeem' them on arrival in America. If not redeemed, they were sold off into servitude. So, too, were the motley group—kidnaped vagrants and children, transported convicts— who left England involuntarily. Convicts were, however, in a special category: their period of servitude generally lasted fourteen years.

Most indentured servants went to work either in the Middle Colonies, especially Pennsylvania, or, until about 1700, when they began to be replaced by Negro slaves, in the Southern colonies. Their lot was generally harsh. The work was often difficult and exhausting, the penalties for carelessness or wrongdoing severe. Servants could not marry without their masters' consent, nor even stay out late at night. Yet they retained all their political and legal rights save those explicitly denied by the terms of their indentures. They had, for example, the right of recourse to the courts.

And when their terms expired they were free to choose their own occupations and were entitled by custom or statute to certain 'freedom dues'—clothing, and, in most cases, tools, seeds, and provisions. But since land was not normally included, only a small proportion became independent farmers. A few of them rose to fame and fortune. But the majority either became wage-laborers on farms and plantations, or drifted to the towns or the frontier. Some even returned to Europe.

None of these options was open, however, to black slaves. The first Negroes to reach the mainland colonies arrived in Virginia as early as 1619. Their numbers at first grew very slowly: even in the 1670s Virginia's Negro population did not exceed 2,000. Nor at first were blacks geographically concentrated: New York City in the 1690s had proportionately as many as Virginia. Initially the legal status of Negroes was indeterminate, though from an early date custom probably assigned them a special and inferior position. After about 1660 legislation began to define their status more precisely, in particular differentiating them from white servants. Virginia and Maryland passed laws declaring Negroes to be slaves for life and that the children of Negroes and mulattos were likewise slaves. Later laws expanded and added to these distinctions. Thus blacks were forbidden to possess weapons, sexual relations between them and whites were discouraged or prohibited, and slave manumission was made more difficult.

About 1700 the importation of slaves rose rapidly and slavery took firmer root, especially in the Chesapeake colonies. Soil exhaustion, increasing competition, and dwindling profit margins were compelling tobacco planters to search for a more stable, more disciplined, and more economical labor force. Masters had never found indentured servitude wholly satisfactory. It was expensive since the term of service was relatively short; servants frequently absconded and were not easy to trace. Negroes possessed neither of these disadvantages, being permanently enslaved and easily identifiable by color. And although the initial investment in slaves was high, they were self-producing and when employed in gangs constituted an efficient and economical work-force. A further attraction was a fall in slave prices after 1697, when the Royal African Company lost its monopoly of the African slave-trade and English and colonial merchants joined in. The slave-trade now entered its heyday. The Negro population of the colonies soared from under 20,000 in 1700 to about 350,000 in 1763. Negro slaves were to be found in every colony, though over four-fifths of them were in the Southern plantation colonies. In Virginia in 1756 blacks made up 40 percent of the population (120,000 out of 293,000), while in South Carolina in 1751 they outnumbered whites by almost two to one (40,000 blacks to 25,000 whites). Despite their servile status they were a potent influence in the South, their presence reflected in many ways from the Africanisms in Southern speech to the uniquely restrictive features of Southern legal codes.

Population growth was accompanied by—indeed, largely explained— the spread of settlement. In 1713, when the Treaty of Utrecht ended a long period of colonial warfare with France, the British settlements were still confined to a narrow coastal strip. Nowhere had the frontier advanced beyond the fall line of the rivers. In the next half-century, however, it was carried steadily westward, in places by as much as a hundred miles. With previously unsettled lands in older regions filling up as well, the occupied area more than doubled. In New England settlers advanced up the Connecticut River into New Hampshire and along the coast to Maine. In the interior of New York fingers of settlement reached out into the valleys of the Hudson, the Mohawk, and the Schoharie before being checked by Indian attack. Further south the frontier advanced more rapidly. In the Tidewater region of Virginia and Maryland enterprising planters abandoned worn-out tobacco lands and worked their way inland into the Piedmont, the region between the fall line and the Blue Ridge. Meanwhile the stream of migrants moving westward in Pennsylvania, mostly Germans and Scotch-Irish, had run up against the Appalachian barrier and then swung southward into the great interior valleys between the Appalachians and the Blue Ridge. Entering the Valley of Virginia in the 1730s, the Carolinas in the 1740s and 1750s, and Georgia in the 1760s, this southward thrust created an exposed, relatively primitive, back-country region different from and frequently at odds with the older settled east.

During the colonial period there were only five towns of any size, all of them seaports: Boston, Newport, New York, Philadelphia, and Charleston. Their population increased, but more slowly than the population as a whole. Their combined population in 1720 of about 36,000 was about 7 percent of the total; in 1760 it was 73,000, only 3.5 percent of the total. Up to 1700 Boston was easily the largest American town but thereafter it was overtaken by Philadelphia and New York. By the time of the Revolution Philadelphia had 40,000 inhabitants and was the second largest city in the British Empire—although it hardly rivaled London with its population of 750,000.

Colonial Society and Culture

By the middle of the eighteenth century the colonies had attained a measure of maturity and a culture at once derivative and distinctive. English institutions, English ideas, the English tongue, people of English stock were everywhere in the ascendant. English forms still provided the model in law and education. No distinguishing American idiom had yet appeared in literature, art, or architecture. Yet not everything transplanted from

England had survived the ocean-crossing unchanged. The wilderness environment had created a society that was un-English in its ethnic and racial variety, its pluralistic religious structure, its fluidity and mobility. Americans were more self-reliant, adaptable, and enterprising than Englishmen, more severely practical, more conscious of their rights, less inclined to accept traditional moral and social values.

As to language, the process of Americanization was already under way. A few nouns like *toboggan, moccasin, canoe*, and *wigwam* had been borrowed from the Indians; the French had contributed *portage, prairie, chowder*, and so on; Dutch settlement had supplied other borrowings: *boss, cookie, waffle, Yankee*. A sprinkling of Americanisms had arisen through new combinations of familiar English words (*bullfrog, catbird, groundhog, snowplow*). A number of other English words had acquired new meanings: *bluff*, meaning cliff, *branch* and *creek* meaning stream, *neck* meaning isthmus. But although in 1756 the great lexicographer, Dr Samuel Johnson, felt justified in referring to an 'American dialect', most eighteenth-century visitors to the colonies noted not only the absence of regional dialects but the proper and grammatical English spoken by Americans of all classes.

In fact the inhabitants of the separate colonies had not yet begun to think of themselves as one people. The word 'American' was mainly a geographical expression. Most colonists considered themselves English. There was a good deal of intercolonial jealousy and constant intercolonial squabbles over boundaries and land claims. Within colonies, seaboard communities disputed with those in the back country. Yet a sense both of unity and of difference from England was all the while being fostered by a century and a half of isolation and change.

Although the structure and functions of the family were the same as in Europe, American conditions tended to loosen family ties and undermine parental authority. The easy availability of land encouraged young people to leave the parental roof in order to set up on their own and at the same time weakened the ability of fathers to influence marriage choices by withholding their sons' inheritance. These tendencies were reinforced in the South by a relatively high mortality-rate which made anyone over fifty a rarity. Another destabilizing influence was the distorted sex ratio resulting from the heavy preponderance of men among the first settlers. In 1700 there were still three men for every two women in Virginia: even in New England (where family migration had long been common) women were still in a minority at that date. The imbalance between the sexes explains why the average age of marriage for women was substantially lower than in Europe. According to some historians it also helped to raise the status of women. Whether in fact they enjoyed a higher status than in Europe seems doubtful. Irrespective of wealth or condition they were assigned a subordinate role within the family and were denied the political and civil rights enjoyed by men.

At first glance colonial society resembled that of England. Distinctions of rank and status were universal and jealously preserved. Men of property and standing were addressed as "gentlemen" or "esquires", church pews were assigned according to social class, students listed according to their "dignities". In every colony by about 1700 a wealthy elite had emerged whose preeminence was evident in its homes, possessions, and lifestyles, and in its oligarchical control of politics. The great Virginia planters—Fitzhughs, Byrds, Carters, Lees, Randolphs—who made up the colony's upper class, had their counterparts in the Dutch and English landed families of the Hudson Valley—Van Rensselaers, Schuylers, Morrises, Van Cortlandts, Phillipses. In the seaport towns the growth of trade had brought into being a mercantile aristocracy: Browns, Cabots, Hutchinsons, and Belchers in Boston, Quakers like Edward Shippen and Isaac Norris in Philadelphia. In New York City in 1703 the richest 10 percent of the population owned just under half the taxable property. Meanwhile indigence was becoming a chronic problem in the seaports, necessitating the building of almshouses, the founding of charitable societies, the adoption of a warning-out system. In the southern back country, too, especially at the rim of settlement, there were families living in degradation and squalor. The bottom of the social structure, of course, was permanently constituted by Negro slaves, nearly a quarter (23 percent) of the population by 1760.

Even so English America was, in Richard Hofstadter's phrase, 'a middle-class world'. The groups which formed, respectively, the apex and the base of the English social pyramid—the nobility and the destitute—were almost entirely unrepresented in America. The absence of such props of a privileged order as a Court, rotten boroughs, an officer caste, an entrenched Church, and exclusive universities helped further to undermine the attempt to transplant the English class structure. It was difficult, too, to maintain traditional social distinctions when the daily struggle to eke out an existence from agriculture compelled masters and servants to live and work cheek by jowl. The availability of land meant also that, unlike those in England, where farm tenancy was the rule, the great majority of colonial farmers—and hence of the male population—tilled their own acres. In the cities again, artisans capitalized on their scarcity value not only by demanding (and getting) high wages but by declining to accept a subordinate status. Pauperism, even in the towns, was never the dreadful evil it became in England. Beggars were rare and the numbers needing poor relief a tiny fraction of the population.

As for the colonial upper class, it was not really an aristocracy in the English sense: its origins were too recent, its status too insecure, its membership too wavering, its resources too limited, its connections with moneymaking too close, its opportunities for leisure too restricted for it to have been taken for—or acknowledged by—the genuine article. Nor could the colonial elite be distinguished by speech. In the colonies accent was not a badge of class, as it was—or became—in England. Spurred on by the illusion of Cavalier origins, though in fact most were descended from merchants and yeomen, the great Virginia planters consciously modeled themselves on the English landed gentry. They sat prominently in church, served as vestrymen and as justices of the peace, rode to hounds, and even sported family coats of arms. Yet they were hard-working capitalists, intensely and of necessity absorbed in land speculation and in the details of raising and marketing a commercial crop. Since their capital was largely tied up in land and slaves, their liquid assets were not all that impressive by European standards. Indeed, they were constantly and embarrassingly in debt. Largely for that reason no Virginia plantation home could compare with Chatsworth or Woburn Abbey, or even with an English country gentleman's manor-house. Such leading examples of Georgian architecture as Westover, the residence of the Byrds on the James River, were elegant and dignified but nonetheless modest edifices, notwithstanding their rich imported furnishings, while George Washington's Mount Vernon, on the Potomac, suggests nothing grander than a plain, solid, commodious farmhouse.

Claims that class lines were fluid, opportunities for social mobility unequaled, should nonetheless be kept in perspective. A handful of individuals did indeed rise from humble beginnings to wealth and power. Two of the wealthiest landowners in Maryland, Daniel Dulany and Charles Carroll, started from little or nothing; Benjamin Franklin's father was a tallow-chandler and soap-boiler; Sir William Phips, the first royal governor of Massachusetts, was born in poverty. Governor Phips owed his great fortune to luck: he married a wealthy widow and discovered a sunken treasure. Even so most of the colonial elite came from families of substance. In Maryland before 1660 indentured servants rose rapidly after being freed, but opportunities subsequently dwindled almost to vanishing point. Recent studies have demonstrated also that as communities emerged from the frontier stage, rates of upward mobility declined. Nonetheless,—and despite evidence that inequalities increased during the eighteenth century—colonial society was extraordinarily mobile by European standards.

Colonial Religion

In contrast to England and other countries of western Europe there was no dominant religious denomination in the colonies. The tendency towards schism, particularly marked in New England, together with the immigration of sectarians from several different countries produced a multiplicity of denominations, none sufficiently numerous to dominate the rest. This made toleration a practical necessity, even where the law enjoined religious conformity. Except in Rhode Island, Pennsylvania, Delaware, and New Jersey, where there was no connection between Church and State and where a large measure of religious freedom existed from the start, Established Churches were the rule—the Church of England in all the southern colonies and in four New York counties, the Congregational Church in New England outside Rhode Island. In New England, however, Puritan control began to break down by the end of the seventeenth century. Witchcraft hysteria in Salem, Massachusetts in 1692 led to hundreds of arrests and nineteen executions, but this proved to be the last spasm of persecution. The revised Massachusetts charter of 1691 had undermined religious exclusiveness by making property qualifications rather than church membership the test for voting. By 1700 or so both Massachusetts and Connecticut had granted Anglicans, Baptists, and Quakers the right of open public worship and in the 1720s allowed them to earmark for the support of their own churches what they paid in church-rates. As for the colonies where the Church of England was legally established, Anglicans were nearly everywhere too few to make establishment a reality. Only in Virginia was establishment effective enough to impose serious obstacles to dissent, and even there freedom of worship could not be denied once Scotch-Irish and German sectarians had taken possession of the Virginia back country. However, formal religious liberty would not be achieved in Virginia, or, indeed, in the rest of the colonies, until the Revolution.

The history of Virginian Anglicanism illustrates how traditional institutions either did not work or were subtly and unintentionally transformed in the New World. The failure of the Church of England to appoint a bishop for the colonies meant not only that churches could not be consecrated or parishioners confirmed but also that clerical discipline could not be enforced. Moreover the absence of central ecclesiastical authority opened the way for a kind of Anglican congregationalism. Parish affairs came to be controlled by lay vestrymen who, among other things, appointed and dismissed the clergy in a manner reminiscent of New England Puritanism. Low salaries made it difficult to attract parsons of the right caliber: many clergymen were ill-prepared and neglectful. But the sheer extent of Virginia's parishes, a reflection of its plantation economy, militated against proper pastoral care. The isolation of churches also meant that marriages and funerals were generally performed at home, while the dead were interred in gardens or orchards rather than in churchyards.

By the late seventeenth century the religious ardor of the early settlements was on the wane. That, indeed, was partly why toleration gained ground. With the advance of settlement, the growth of material prosperity, the spread of Enlightenment ideas, a more secular and rationalistic outlook came to prevail. In New England especially the harsh rigidities of Puritanism were progressively softened. The process began with the Half-Way Covenant of 1662, when a Massachusetts ministers' synod decided to grant partial church membership to members' children who had not themselves experienced conversion. The Salem Witchcraft Trials were followed by a revulsion against ecclesiastical authority and in 1699 came the first definite departure from orthodoxy, the founding in Boston of the Brattle Street church which dispensed with the requirement that only God's elect could qualify for membership. By the middle of the eighteenth century some of the New England clergy had even abandoned the Calvinist doctrine of predestination and were preaching salvation to all who accepted Christ's teaching. In the Middle Colonies a more humanistic view of religion likewise gained ground in denominations as varied as the Presbyterian, Lutheran, and Dutch Reformed churches, as well as among the Quakers. In the Southern Colonies, too, religion had lost much of its inner spirit, the prevailing temper being latitudinarian and worldly.

Suddenly, however, Calvinism was revitalized by a wave of religious revivals, emotional and evangelical in tone, known as the Great Awakening. It began in the Middle Colonies in the 1720s with the preaching of Theodore J. Frelinghuysen, a German-born minister of the Dutch Reformed Church, and of William Tennent, a Scotch-Irish Presbyterian clergyman who in 1736 was to found a celebrated 'Log College' in frontier Pennsylvania to train ministers. Their message, emphasizing the individual's personal relation with God and the necessity of salvation through conversion, was taken up with great success in the South by the Presbyterian Samuel Davies and by an army of Methodist and Baptist preachers. Religious ferment was further stimulated by the arrival in 1739 of one of the greatest of English evangelists, George Whitefield, whose preaching tours drew enormous crowds from Georgia to Maine. The outstanding intellect of the Great Awakening, however, and the foremost religious controversialist produced by colonial America, was Jonathan Edwards, a Congregational minister in Northampton, Massachusetts. Defending traditional Calvinism against the inroads of rationalism, Edwards terrified congregations with graphic descriptions of sin designed to bring home the need to rely on God's mercy.

The Great Awakening certainly awoke controversy and division. Conflicts arose between laymen and clergy, between different denominations, and within existing religious organizations. 'Old light' conservatives, along with exponents of rationalist religion, were outraged by the extravagances of revivalism, its weeping, shrieking, and emotional paroxysms. 'New light' revivalist preachers, for their part, condemned 'unregenerate' ministers for their lack of piety and encouraged congregations to challenge ministerial authority. Not infrequently the result was schism, the Presbyterians splitting into 'Old Side' and 'New Side' factions, Congregationalism losing adherents to newly formed separate or New Light Baptist churches—and to Anglicanism as well. The principal beneficiaries of the religious excitement were the smaller dissenting sects, notably the New Side Presbyterians and the different free-will Baptist persuasions. These new sects appealed particularly to the poor and uneducated, to whom they offered a religion that was meaningful and personal.

Some historians believe that the Great Awakening aroused a democratic spirit that contributed to the Revolution. This seems overstated. The Great Awakening had leveling implications, but its appeal was not limited to any one class, and if it tended to undermine the position of the clergy it did not develop into a general challenge to traditional forms of authority. The philosophical basis of the American Revolution is more readily discerned in the thought of those New England rationalists like the Reverend Jonathan Mayhew who stood at the opposite extreme to revivalism and who constituted its fiercest critics. Mayhew's widely circulated sermon, *A Discourse Concerning Unlimited Submission* (1750), rejected the notion of absolute obedience to authority and affirmed the right of resistance to the illegal encroachments of arbitrary power. His political ideas were derived from the writings of a group of early eighteenth-century radicals and Whig politicians (see Chapter 4) as well as from the celebrated Lockean concepts of natural rights.

The American Enlightenment

The speed with which Locke's natural-rights philosophy was accepted in the colonies was one indication among many of the influence of the Enlightenment. The Enlightenment belief in Natural Law, its insistence upon man's innate goodness, its supreme faith in human reason and perfectibility, all gained a large following among the colonial intellectual elite and permeated every branch of thought from religion to science, from economics to literature. Even an eminent Puritan divine and pillar of orthodoxy, Cotton Mather (1662–1727) proved surprisingly receptive to Newtonian science, though it should be added that Mather, like Jonathan Edwards later on, and Newton himself, saw in the findings of reason only a confirmation of revelation. A more genuine scientific spirit was displayed by such men as the Harvard astronomer and physicist John Winthrop IV (1714–79), a descendant of the first governor of Massachusetts Bay, who popularized rational scientific explantions of such natural phenomena as eclipses and earthquakes, and the botanist John Bartram (1699–1777), who collected and classified American plants, shrubs, and trees.

Benjamin Franklin (1706–90). the most representative and at the same time the most cosmopolitan product of colonial civilization, best exemplified the American Enlightenment. Franklin was a many-sided genius who succeeded in everything he attempted—journalism, business, science, invention, politics, diplomacy, and love (or "venery" as he candidly called it). Born in Boston and largely self-educated, he moved as a youth to Philadelphia where he prospered as the owner of a printing business and as editor of the *Pennsylvania Gazette*. A prolific pamphleteer on politics, economics, religion, and other topics, he became even more widely known through his *Poor Richard's Almanac* (1732–57), a compilation of homely maxims extolling prudence, common sense, and honesty. Franklin's passion for learning and civic improvement led him to play a leading role in founding among other things a circulating library, a city hospital, the American Philosophical Society (1744), and the College of Philadelphia. He was elected to the Pennsylvania Assembly, served as deputy postmaster general of the colonies (1753–74), and represented Pennsylvania and other colonies as agent in London (1757–62 and 1766–74). Meanwhile he had become famous both in America and Europe as a result of his inventions (which included the lightning-rod, the Franklin stove, and bifocal spectacles) and still more for his scientific researches into the nature of electricity. In all his endeavors Franklin displayed a skepticism, a faith in reason and in progress, a passion for freedom, and a humanitarianism that were characteristic of the Enlightenment. But his utilitarian, pragmatic cast of mind and his relative lack of interest in pure science or abstract philosophical speculation mark him out as typically American.

Education

Educational provision in the colonies varied widely, with the Middle and Southern colonies lagging far behind New England. To the Puritan founders of New England education was vital primarily for religious reasons: to qualify for a state of grace a man had to be able to read the Bible. The Massachusetts Bay Acts of 1642 and 1647, which became models for the rest of New England, placed an obligation on parents to ensure that their children were taught to read and required the establishment of elementary schools in towns of more than fifty families and of Latin grammar schools in towns exceeding one hundred families. These laws did not, however, compel parents to send their children to school as would be the case with the nineteenth-century public-school system; they simply laid down minimum standards of literacy while seeking to make formal education at community expense universally available. By about 1700 the spread of settlement and the waning of Puritan spiritual intensity had brought a degree of laxity in the observance of these laws but New Englanders nonetheless remained a highly literate and well-educated people. Elsewhere in the colonies the picture was bleak. Pennsylvania and New York had only a handful of schools, mostly maintained by the churches. In the Southern colonies, where the dispersal of the population increased the difficulty of establishing schools, education was regarded as a family matter rather than a community responsibility. Wealthy planters commonly employed private tutors or sent their sons to England for their education.

The first institution of higher learning in the colonies dates from 1636 when Massachusetts Puritans, dreading "to leave an illiterate ministry to the churches when our present ministers shall lie in the dust", founded Harvard College. That Harvard fulfilled the hopes of its founders was shown by the fact that over half its seventeenth-century products entered the ministry. The second colonial college, William and Mary, was established in 1693 as a bulwark of the Anglican Church in Virginia, while the founding of Yale (1701) represented an attempt to counteract the unorthodoxy taking root at Harvard. The four new colleges established under sectarian auspices in the mid-eighteenth century—Princeton (Presbyterian, 1746), Brown (Baptist, 1764), Rutgers (Dutch Reformed, 1766), and Dartmouth (Congregational, 1769)—resembled their predecessors in being set up to raise learned ministers. But the argument that they were the product of the Great Awakening is overstated. None was narrowly sectarian in curriculum or outlook and only Princeton, founded in the immediate aftermath of the revivals, could claim to be directly and unequivocally the product of religious zeal. The impetus for the rest came from growing population and prosperity, an impetus that led also to the establishment in New York of the interdenominational King's College (1754), afterwards Columbia, and the completely secular College of Philadelphia (1755), which grew into the University of Pennsylvania. Initially the curricula of the colonial colleges resembled those of Oxford and Cambridge in consisting largely of the classics and theology, but in the course of the eighteenth century, under the influence of the Enlightenment, such subjects as logic, mathematics, and the natural sciences were added. American colleges also diverged from their English models in developing a system of external ownership and control. Instead of being autonomous corporate bodies of scholars and masters, they were governed by outside groups of nonresident laymen or trustees.

Law and Legal Institutions

The development of colonial law and legal institutions afforded a further demonstration of how American conditions defied efforts to reproduce English forms and practice. Divergence was inevitable when few were learned in the law, even judges commonly lacked legal training and law books were scarce. Often the best the early lawmakers could do was to apply to American problems a half-forgotten layman's understanding of the peculiar technical language of the English legal system—itself far from uniform. For a long time cases were not printed, judges gave no reasons for their decisions, and legal proceedings were conducted orally rather than by the exchange of written pleadings. Not until the mid-eighteenth century did the practice of law become a profession. Even then it was not the specialized, elaborately organized, and stratified profession it remained in England. In the absence of licensing guilds like the London Inns of Court distinctions between barristers, attorneys, solicitors, and scriveners were unknown and legal knowledge, instead of being an esoteric, upper-class monopoly, became simplified and widely (if thinly) diffused. Crimes were everywhere less harshly punished than in England, death and imprisonment being less commonly prescribed than whipping, branding, or the stocks, and in New England, where Puritan "admonition" was as important as punishment, practice was often more lenient than mere statute would suggest.

Indian Wars and the Contest for Empire

Except briefly at the beginning of settlement warfare was a constant fact of colonial life. To secure their foothold on the continent the colonists had to overcome the resistance of the Indians, often supported and organized by England's colonial rivals. The earliest settlers were fortunate: the tribes they faced on the Atlantic coast were less powerful and warlike than those further inland and relations with them were at first friendly. At Plymouth the Wampanoags instructed the Pilgrims in wilderness ways and enabled them to survive. At Jamestown the marriage of Chief Powhatan's daughter, Pocahontas, to a leading settler seemed an augury for peace. But as the whites encroached more and more upon traditional Indian hunting-grounds the alarmed tribesmen attempted to halt the advancing tide. In Virginia in 1622 Powhatan's successor, Opechancanough, fell suddenly upon outlying English settlements, killing some 350 people. The whites exacted bloody retribution. Thereafter hostilities went on intermittently until 1644, by which time the Indians had been dispossessed and all but wiped out. In New England the clash of two incompatible economic systems led to the Pequot War of 1637, in the course of which the Pequot nation was annihilated and the Connecticut Valley opened for settlement. Disregard for Indian rights and susceptibilities gradually soured relations even with the Wampanoags and resulted finally in King Philip's War of 1675–6. A score of New England settlements was destroyed and over 1,000 whites killed before the war ended—as all Indian-white wars would ultimately end—in Indian subjugation. This happened on the New York frontier in the 1640s and in the Carolinas during the Tuscarora War of 1711–12 and the Yamassee War of 1715–18. The whites vied with the Indians in savagery, burning villages and cornfields, butchering whole populations, cutting off scalps as trophies. Virtually the only settlers to show much concern for Indian rights were the Pennsylvania Quakers. A celebrated peace treaty between William Penn and the Delaware Indians in 1682 marked the beginning of half a century of harmony. Penn and his successors kept their promises. But the Scotch-Irish influx into Pennsylvania undermined their tolerant policy. Sharing the almost universal frontiersman's conviction that 'heathenish' tribesmen had no moral right to occupy land 'when Christians needed it on which to raise their bread', the Scotch-Irish promptly harried the Delawares out of their patrimony.

Towards the end of the seventeenth century warfare between colonists and Indians merged with a larger international struggle for the mastery of eastern North America. The English colonies, strung out along the Atlantic seaboard, were beginning to expand into the interior and encroach upon the claims of England's Continental and colonial rivals. Spain, confined to the Florida penisula and only weakly established there, was a minor obstacle. The main threat came from France, which had established settlements at Port Royal in Acadia (Nova Scotia) in 1605 and at Quebec in 1608, that is at virtually the same time that the first English settlers landed at Jamestown. Gradually French explorers, missionaries, and fur traders penetrated into the region of the Great Lakes and the Mississippi Valley. In 1682 the explorer La Salle reached the Mississippi delta, took possession of the surrounding country for Louis XIV and named it Louisiana. Early in the eighteenth century French colonists settled there in strength, introduced Negro slaves, and established a plantation economy. By 1720 or so a huge arc of French forts, trading posts, and settlements stretched all the way from Louisbourg on Cape Breton Island to New Orleans.

Between 1689 and 1763 England and France fought four successive wars: the War of the League of Augsburg (1689–97), the War of the Spanish Succession (1702–13),the War of the Austrian Succession (1744–8), and the Seven Years' War (1756–63). The first three started in Europe and only later spread across the Atlantic. That the colonists viewed them essentially as foreign wars in which they became embroiled only as subjects of the English Crown was evident from the labels they attached to them: King William's War, Queen Anne's War, and King George's War. Nonetheless they were eager for the defeat of neighbors they regarded with fear and suspicion. The Catholicism of the French—and of the Spanish, for that matter—was anathema to them. They resented the competition of French fur traders and fishermen. Above all they felt threatened by the French alliance with the warlike tribes of the Ohio Valley.

During King William's War and Queen Anne's War the French and their Indian allies carried out savage attacks on the frontiers of New York and New England. Settlements like Schenectady, New York, and Deerfield, Massachusetts, were put to the torch, their inhabitants scalped, tortured, or carried into captivity. The colonists made retaliatory raids on the Indians and struck at French strongholds on the St. Lawrence. Great Britain was too long absorbed in European theaters of war and apparently too indifferent to the fate of the colonists to send them much help; most of the fighting was left to the colonial militia and such Indian auxiliaries as they could muster. The English colonists outnumbered the French fifteen to one, but intercolonial disputes and jealousies largely offset their advantage. All the same they won some notable victories. In 1710 provincial forces captured Port Royal and were instrumental in turning French Acadia into British Nova Scotia. Then in 1745 came a major military achievement: the storming of the massive French fortress of Louisbourg. This rare cooperative effort by several colonies also had an improvised quality that was coming to be recognized as characteristically American. It was planned and executed by amateurs and, according to one contemporary, "had a lawyer for contriver, a merchant for general, and farmers, fishermen and mechanics for soldiers . . .". Proud of their victory the colonists were understandably mortified when the Treaty of Aix-la-Chapelle (1748) handed Louisbourg back to France.

The peace was no more than a truce. No sooner had it been signed than English and French colonists redoubled their efforts to control the Ohio Valley. Matters came to a head when a group of prominent Virginia planters, bent on land speculation, organized the Ohio Company and secured from the British government a grant of some 200,000 acres in the trans-Allegheny region. When the French began to build a chain of forts between Lake Erie and the Allegheny River a Virginian force commanded by a youthful militia colonel, George Washington, was sent to forestall them. But Washington found that the French were already in possession of the key to the Ohio Valley, the forks of the Ohio (the site of present-day Pittsburgh), where they were busy constructing Fort Duquesne. In the fighting that followed Washington was forced to surrender (July 4, 1754). Thus for the first time in the long drawn-out Anglo-French duel for empire hostilities had begun in America rather than in Europe. The war was as yet undeclared but in 1755, in response to Virginian appeals for help, the British government dispatched General Edward Braddock to America with two regiments of regulars. But on his way to Fort Duquesne Braddock blundered into a French and Indian ambush, was killed, and his army routed (July 9, 1755). This disaster exposed four hundred miles of the Pennsylvania and Virginia frontier and in the next two years Indian war parties devastated scores of settlements.

Braddock's defeat was due in part to unfamiliarity with forest warfare, but even more to his lack of Indian auxiliaries. Already in 1753 the Board of Trade had recognized that Indian support would be vital in the coming struggle. It called upon the colonies from Virginia northward to send delegates to a meeting at Albany to concert Indian policy. The Albany Congress, meeting in June 1754, failed to secure an alliance with the Iroquois, the best disposed of the tribes towards the British, but it adopted a scheme drawn up by Benjamin Franklin for a permanent intercolonial confederation. Franklin's Plan of Union envisaged an elected colonial Parliament, or Grand Council, with authority (subject to royal approval) over Indian affairs and defense and with power to levy taxes to support an army. The British government might well have vetoed the proposal since it went much further than it had intended. But local particularism saved it the trouble. The colonial assemblies either rejected or ignored the Plan.

In 1756, two years after the initial skirmishing at the forks of the Ohio, England declared war on France and the climactic struggle for empire began. The Seven Years' War—or the French and Indian War, as it was known in America—developed into a worldwide conflict; there was fighting in Europe, the Mediterranean, the West Indies, and India as well as in North America. At first things went badly for the British. The French general Montcalm captured Fort Oswego on Lake Ontario in 1756 and Fort William Henry at the southern end of Lake George the following year. These reverses reflected the inability of the new British Commander-in-Chief, Lord Loudoun, to induce the colonists to unite in their own defense. Parsimonious colonial assemblies, dominated by representatives of the secure and prosperous seaboard, were unperturbed by the threat to remote frontiers. Most colonies were indifferent to what went on beyond their borders: those from Pennsylvania southward in particular were unwilling either to help each other or to relieve New York and New England by joining in a general assault on the French.

Only in 1757 when William Pitt was recalled to power by George II did the tide begin to turn for Great Britain. Pitt dispatched an expeditionary force of 25,000 regulars, the largest army yet seen in North America, and paid for raising a further 25,000 American provincials. In 1758 British forces again captured the fortress of Louisbourg and then cut the link between Canada and the Mississippi Valley by taking Fort Frontenac on Lake Ontario. This led to the fall of Fort Duquesne, renamed Fort Pitt. The climax of Pitt's grand strategy came in 1759 with a converging three-pronged assault on French Canada from the mouth of the St. Lawrence, Lake Ontario, and Lake Champlain. Wolfe's defeat of Montcalm on the Plains of Abraham (September 12, 1759) gave the British Quebec and effectively destroyed French military power in Canada. In 1760 Amherst took Montreal and the conquest of Canada was complete. Fighting continued in other parts of the world but by the terms of the Treaty of Paris (1763) which brought the war to a close Great Britain received Canada and all the French possessions east of the Mississippi; she also acquired Florida from Spain in exchange for the return of Cuba and the Philippines, conquered in 1761; to compensate Spain for the loss of Florida, France ceded 'Louisiana' to her, that is, roughly the whole of the Mississippi Valley to the west of the river as well as New Orleans on its eastern bank.

Great Britain emerged from the war as the world's leading colonial and maritime power. France's North American empire had been entirely lost. Yet the very completeness of the British triumph prepared the ground for the American Revolution.

3. *Revolution and Independence,*
1763–1783

Imperial Reorganization and Colonial Protest

At the close of the Seven Years' War in 1763 hardly any of the American colonists are likely to have harbored thoughts of independence. For all their varied origins they were closely bound to Great Britain by ties of interest and affection. They were proud to be members of the British Empire and rejoiced in its great triumph over France. They cherished the British tradition of political liberty and, though chafing at certain aspects of the imperial economic system, were reasonably content with it. Yet when George III's ministers attempted to tighten control over colonial economic and political life, there was prompt and vigorous resistance. Interpreting the new British moves as a deliberate attempt to subvert their freedom, the colonists began to reexamine their position in the imperial structure. Ten years of controversy culminated in armed revolt. Finally, in 1776, the colonists decided, as the Declaration of Independence put it, "to assume, among the Powers of the earth, the separate and equal station to which the Laws of Nature and of Nature's God entitle them".

However it may have seemed in America, the British purpose in reforming the old colonial system was not to establish a tyranny but to deal with the results of the war. The extensive additions to Great Britain's already large American empire created difficult new problems. Government had to be provided for 80,000 French Canadians, alien in language and religion, and unfamiliar with British law and political forms. A coherent Western policy was needed to reconcile the conflicting needs of land settlement, the fur trade, and the Indians. Above all, the sudden transformation of what had been a commercial into a territorial empire necessitated new provisions for defense.

It should not have been difficult to foresee what the colonists' reaction would be to greater metropolitan involvement in their affairs. When during the war the British had tentatively tried to strengthen control there had been vehement protest and questions of constitutional principle had been raised. In 1761 the use of writs of assistance—search warrants—to stamp out smuggling and trading with the enemy was denounced by a young Boston lawyer, James Otis. Parliament, he contended, possessed only a limited power of legislating for the colonies; any act like that authorizing the writs, which violated natural rights, was null and void. In the 'parson's cause' in Virginia two years later Patrick Henry advanced a still more radical constitutional doctrine. Attacking the Privy Council for having disallowed a Virginia law providing that the salaries of the Anglican clergy, customarily paid in tobacco, should instead be payable in money at the depreciated rate of twopence a pound he declared that the king had "degenerated into a tyrant, and forfeited all rights to his subjects' obedience".

These warnings of future trouble were, however, ignored by George Grenville, the king's chief minister on whom the task of imperial reorganization fell. The first requirement was a new frontier policy, a need shown almost at once in Pontiac's rebellion of May 1763. Angered by the frauds of British traders and fearing further encroachments on their lands, the Ohio valley tribes, led by the Ottawa chief, Pontiac, rose in revolt and destroyed every British post west of Niagara, except Detroit. In an effort to prevent further trouble a royal proclamation of October 7, 1763 prohibited settlement beyond the Alleghenies as a temporary measure to allow time for a comprehensive policy to be worked out. But frontiersmen were not to be restrained by proclamations 3,000 miles away. They ignored the restriction. Within a few years the British government had to acquiesce in the breakdown of the Proclamation Line.

' Grenville's main preoccupation was to raise a colonial revenue. The Seven Years' War had doubled the British national debt and driven taxation to unprecedented levels. The cost of colonial administration and defense had risen from £70,000 in 1748 to £350,000 in 1763. Still more money would be needed, for it had been decided to station an army of 10,000 permanently in the colonies to guard against possible French attempts at reconquest and to give protection against Indian attacks. It seemed only fair that the lightly taxed and obviously prosperous colonists should bear part of the burden—between a third and a half—of their own defense. And when they failed to reply constructively to Grenville's invitation to suggest alternative ways of raising the money, he felt doubly justified in taxing them.

Grenville's Sugar Act, passed in April 1764, increased duties on various colonial imports, while reducing the duty on foreign molasses from sixpence a gallon (imposed by the Molasses Act of 1733) to threepence. But whereas the 1733 measure had been a dead letter the Sugar Act was to be strictly enforced. So were the trade laws generally. Grenville was determined to revitalize the inefficient and venal colonial customs service, which brought in less than a quarter of the amount it cost to run. He ended the practice whereby customs officials remained in England, while delegating their duties to a colonial deputy; he sought to check smuggling by stricter clearance and bonding procedures and by employing naval patrols; to counter the notorious leniency of colonial juries towards smugglers he transferred jurisdiction in revenue cases to vice-admiralty courts. Finally came the Currency Act of 1764, extending to all colonies the ban on legal-tender paper money imposed on New England in 1751.

In America Grenville's program was comprehensively disliked. The prospect of a standing army in their midst kindled the colonists' suspicions; so did the denial of jury trial in revenue cases. To a people-already suffering from a postwar depression, new taxes and the deflationary effects of the Currency Act seemed to spell economic ruin. New England merchants were especially aggrieved since the Sugar Act, by outlawing their trade with the French and Spanish West Indies, would cut off their best source of specie. The new controls were all the more unacceptable because past British neglect and preoccupation had allowed the American communities·a large measure of political and economic freedom. They were unfortunately timed in other senses too. Now that the French menace had been removed, the colonists felt less dependent upon British protection. And, however much London might complain of the British taxpayer's burden and contend that the colonists had been the greatest beneficiaries of the war, they were conscious of having helped substantially to win it. The war had indeed given the colonists new confidence in their military prowess and their ability to manage their own affairs. Psychologically, they were ready for less imperial control, not more.

Even more important, perhaps, in shaping the colonial reaction to British policy was the influence of a conspiracy-minded, revolutionary tradition imported from England itself. From the 1730s onward, the colonists had become progressively more imbued with the extreme libertarian ideology first propounded by seventeenth-century radicals like Harrington and Sidney and subsequently modernized by the early eighteenth-century Whig opposition. The writings of Whig pamphleteers, especially John Trenchard's *Cato's Letters* (1720), enjoyed a wide currency in the colonies and taught the colonists—as Burke put it in assessing the effect on them of the widespread study of law—to "snuff the approach of Tyranny in every tainted breeze". They learned that government was by its nature oppressive, that only constant vigilance could check its tendency to encroach on individual rights, and that in particular certain corrupt ministers were plotting to subvert the liberty won by the Glorious Revolution. Hence when Grenville and his successors took steps which seemed to bear out this analysis, awareness of the Whig dissenting tradition led the colonists to respond vigorously.

The Stamp Act Controversy

Colonial opposition nevertheless remained localized until Parliament passed the Stamp Act in 1765. This measure required revenue stamps to be affixed to newspapers, almanacs, broadsides, legal documents, commercial bills, ships' papers, insurance policies, tavern and marriage licenses, even playing cards and dice. It produced a widespread and violent reaction. Whereas the Sugar Act had affected only New England merchants the Stamp Act applied universally and antagonized other influential groups, lawyers, printers, and tavern-keepers among them. The first direct tax ever levied by Parliament upon the colonies, it was accordingly condemned as a dangerous and unjustified innovation. In the Virginia House of Burgesses Patrick Henry introduced a series of resolutions asserting that Americans possessed all the rights of Englishmen and claiming for the assembly the sole right to tax Virginians. The House did not endorse Henry's more extreme resolutions, but since they were printed and circulated in their entirety the impression was given that it had.

Throughout the colonies secret organizations known as the Sons of Liberty came into existence to concert opposition. Before long the Stamp Act had been nullified by mob action. Stamp agents were terrorized into resigning, supplies of stamps were destroyed, the houses of royal officials pillaged. In October 1765 representatives of nine colonies met at New York in a Stamp Act Congress, the first spontaneous intercolonial gathering and a significant milestone on the road to independence. The delegates drew up a Declaration of Rights and Grievances denouncing the Stamp Act as having "a manifest tendency to subvert the rights and liberties of the colonies" and claiming that only their own legislatures could constitutionally impose taxes upon them.

Colonial protest and riot left the British government unmoved, but economic sanctions proved more persuasive. The Stamp Act gave new impetus to the policy of nonimportation—a boycott of British goods in effect—adopted by colonial merchants after the passage of the Sugar Act. The paralysis of the American trade prompted British merchants to demand the repeal of the Stamp Act. In the spring of 1766 the Rockingham ministry complied. In America the news was rapturously received. Nonimportation was immediately abandoned. But in their rejoicing Americans tended to overlook the fact that repeal had been accompanied by the passage of a Declaratory Act, which asserted that Parliament had full authority to make laws "to bind the colonies and people of America . . . in all cases whatsoever".

The Townshend Duties

In 1767, in a fresh attempt to solve the revenue problem Charles Townshend, the gifted but self-willed Chancellor of the Exchequer in Chatham's ministry, introduced new duties on colonial imports of glass, lead, paint, paper, and tea. During the Stamp Act crisis Americans had drawn a distinction between internal and external taxes, denying Parliament's authority to impose the former upon them but conceding its right to regulate trade, even if such regulation happened to produce a revenue. Since Townshend's new duties were unquestionably 'external', he reasoned that the colonists could not logically object to them. To tighten the machinery of trade enforcement still further Townshend established an American Board of Customs Commissioners, to be stationed at Boston. He also took steps to enforce the Mutiny Act of 1765. Designed to remedy the shortage of military accommodation it required colonial assemblies to make provision for quartering and supplying British troops. Most of the colonies had grudgingly complied but New York, the headquarters of the British army in America, had refused. Consequently the New York assembly was suspended until the act was obeyed.

Townshend's measures revived the uproar in America. In his *Letters of a Pennsylvania Farmer* (1768) the Philadelphia lawyer, John Dickinson, broke new constitutional ground in arguing that even external duties were unconstitutional if imposed with the intention of raising a revenue. He also condemned the Mutiny Act for being an attempt among other things at direct parliamentary taxation, and attacked the suspension of the New York assembly as a blow at colonial liberty generally. In February 1768 the Massachusetts assembly sent out a 'circular letter', drafted by Samuel Adams, the acknowledged leader of Boston radicalism ever since the Stamp Act controversy. In calling for concerted opposition the letter denounced the Townshend duties for violating the principle of 'no taxation without representation'. Despite government efforts to prevent assemblies from endorsing the document, several promptly did so. Resistance took a more practical form when in March 1768 the colonists organized another economic boycott similar to the one apparently so effective against the Stamp Act.

In Boston serious disorders developed out of the efforts of the new Board of Customs to enforce the revenue laws. Before long the obstructionism of the townsfolk had made its task well-nigh impossible. Then in June 1768 a riot occurred when customs officials attempted to seize the sloop *Liberty*, belonging to the prominent radical, John Hancock. The dispatch of troops to the town to restore order merely increased friction. The climax came on March 5, 1770 when a detachment of British soldiers, goaded by a mob, opened fire and killed five Bostonians. Eight of the soldiers were brought to trial; six were acquitted, the other two were found guilty of manslaughter but were released after being branded in the hand. Although the soldiers had fired under extreme provocation, Samuel Adams and other propagandists sought to give the impression that there had been a 'Boston massacre'. Their version of the incident was accepted by many Americans at the time, as well as by later generations.

Despite the best efforts of men like Adams, colonial unity soon began to dissolve. Conservatives were alarmed at the increasing resort to mob action. There was also resentment at the fact that the nonimportation agreement was not being uniformly observed. Hence there was a general welcome for the olive branch held out by Townshend's successor, Lord North. On the same day as the 'Boston massacre', North secured the repeal of all the Townshend duties save that on tea which was retained "as a mark of the supremacy of Parliament". This was the signal for New York to abandon nonimportation and, despite radical protest, the remaining ports quickly followed suit.

There followed three years of comparative calm, broken only by the burning of the revenue cutter *Gaspee* off Rhode Island in 1772 and a ripple of alarm at renewed reports that the Church of England was planning to establish an American bishopric. Sam Adams continued to fulminate and set up a network of committees of correspondence in an effort to keep agitation alive. But he got little support. Prosperity had returned after the long postwar depression and most people seemed weary of contention. Smuggling, though not eradicated, was practiced more discreetly, while parliamentary taxation was an established fact.

The colonists seemed more intent, indeed, on quarreling among themselves than with Great Britain. Disputes between colony and colony over boundaries and land claims sometimes culminated in bloodshed. Even more menacing were the tensions within particular colonies. With the exception of the antirent riots in the Hudson valley in 1766 these were manifestations not of class conflict, as some historians have claimed, but of divisions between the older coastal regions and the more recently settled frontier. Thus Pennsylvania frontiersmen, mainly Scotch-Irish, complained that the Quaker oligarchy of Philadelphia denied them adequate representation in the assembly, overtaxed them, and neglected to protect them against Indian attack. Alarmed by Pontiac's uprising, six hundred frontiersmen, known as the Paxton Boys, marched on Philadelphia in 1763 to demand redress. In North Carolina in the late 1760s back-country farmers formed an association known as the Regulators which used force to counter the oppressions of tidewater officials. After a period of virtual civil war the Regulators were crushed in 1771 at the battle of Alamance by militia under the command of the royal governor. This struggle, like similar ones elsewhere, was to influence attitudes toward independence. When their tidewater oppressors backed the Revolution in 1776, many Regulators became loyalists.

The Boston Tea Party

The passage of the Tea Act of 1773, however, pushed domestic squabbles once more into the background. The act was an attempt to relieve the financial stresses of the East India Company by permitting it to export tea to the colonies direct and retail it there. It would have made tea cheaper to the consumer but by threatening colonial merchants with monopoly and the smuggling rings with extinction united those two powerful interests in opposition. Radicals found the retention of the import tax on tea objectionable on constitutional grounds also. Resistance took different forms. The tea sent to Charleston was landed, but popular pressure prevented it from being offered for sale; that consigned to New York and Philadelphia was rejected and sent back to England; at Boston on December 16, 1773 a body of men disguised as Indians, and directed by Sam Adams, boarded the tea-ships and threw their cargoes into the harbor.

The Boston Tea Party brought the dispute with the mother country to a head. Twice before, in 1766 and in 1770, colonial protest had brought about a reversal of British policy. But now, confronted with colonial defiance for a third time, the British government abandoned appeasement for coercion. It had become convinced, as had British opinion generally, that it faced a fundamental challenge to the imperial commercial and constitutional system, a challenge which could not be ignored without imperiling national prosperity and security. If control over America were to be lost, the Earl of Carlisle was to declare in March 1776, Great Britain would sink into obscurity and insignificance. Early in 1774, therefore, Parliament passed a series of Coercive Acts, dubbed Intolerable Acts in the colonies. They closed the port of Boston until the destroyed tea had been paid for, revised the Massachusetts charter so as to increase the powers of the executive, provided for the transfer to England of murder trials in law-enforcement cases, and imposed a new quartering act on all the colonies.

Far from isolating Massachusetts as intended, the Coercive Acts united the colonies in her defense. Radical propaganda, disseminated by the committees of correspondence, persuaded the colonists of the need for common action. In May 1774 the Virginia assembly sent out a call for an intercolonial meeting. On September 5 twelve colonies sent delegates to Philadelphia to the first Continental Congress. By this time colonial sensibilities had been further inflamed by the passage of the Quebec Act. This statesmanlike but ill-timed attempt to solve the problem of governing the French inhabitants of Canada was seen by the older colonies as confirmation of nefarious British designs. Recognition of the privileged position of the Roman Catholic Church in Canada seemed, especially to New Englanders, to "smell strong of popery". The continuance of the French legal system, which did not provide for trial by jury, appeared to presage autocracy. Moreover, the extension of the Quebec boundary south and west to the Ohio and the Mississippi invalidated all land claims in that region and looked like a deliberate attempt to check westward expansion.

The Continental Congress

While delegates to the Continental Congress were agreed on the need for concerted action, they were at first divided on its form. Conservatives favored the scheme of imperial federation put forward by Joseph Galloway of Pennsylvania. Galloway's Plan of Union would have tied the colonies together by a written constitution and created a continental legislature (the 'grand council') to share power with Parliament over colonial matters. But Congress rejected Galloway's proposal by one vote. It went on to endorse the 'Suffolk Resolves', adopted by a Massachusetts county convention, which had urged resistance to the Coercive Acts, demanded the formation of a rival colonial government which should retain taxes and establish a militia, and recommended stringent economic sanctions against Great Britain. Before adjourning Congress drew up a Declaration of Rights, petitioned the King and Parliament for redress, and subscribed to a Continental Association, consisting of nonimportation, nonexportation, and nonconsumption agreements, to go into effect on November 1, 1774.

During the winter of 1774–5 colonial protest developed into open, though still unavowed, rebellion. Committees of inspection were elected to ensure strict observance of the Association and to punish violators. Provincial congresses assumed the functions of government and made defensive preparations. It should have been plain that only substantial British concessions could settle the dispute peaceably. But North's Conciliation Plan of February 20, 1775 yielded nothing of substance. It promised merely that Parliament would 'forbear' to tax any colony paying the cost of its own civil administration and making a satisfactory contribution to imperial defense. In any case North's offer came too late; by the time it reached America hostilities had begun. In April 1775 General Thomas Gage, the newly appointed governor of Massachusetts, sent a party of 700 men from Boston to seize the powder and arms the colonists had been collecting at Concord, sixteen miles away. But the countryside had been aroused by Paul Revere and other emissaries from the Boston Committee of Safety. At Lexington on April 19 the British found their path barred by a body of Massachusetts militia. Shots were fired and a skirmish developed. Pushing on to Concord the British encountered a larger militia force and there was a heavy exchange of fire. After destroying the military stores the British set off on the return march to Boston, being assailed on all sides by steadily swelling American forces. Before regaining the town 273 British soldiers had been killed and wounded. The provincial forces then closed in and besieged Boston.

Radical propagandists skillfully exploited the events at Lexington and Concord to stir up patriot feeling. Hence, when the Second Continental Congress met at Philadelphia on May 10, 1775 there was no hesitation in resolving that the colonies "be immediately put into a state of defense". A Continental Army of 20,000 men was authorized and on June 15 George Washington was appointed "general and commander-in-chief of the army of the United Colonies". Washington's appointment owed more to politics than to his military experience, which was limited to service, albeit distinguished, as a Virginia militia colonel during the French and Indian Wars. It was felt that to place a Virginian in command of what was still a predominantly New England army would cement colonial unity; further, the choice of a wealthy, conservative planter would allay fears of radicalism. While all delegates were determined to preserve American rights, a majority still hoped to do so within the Empire. There was still a great residue of affection for Great Britain and a belief that the American cause enjoyed widespread British support. Some colonial leaders feared also that with the removal of British authority they might lose political control. Thus in adopting a Declaration of the Causes and Necessities of Taking Up Arms (July 6), Congress specifically disclaimed any intention of "separating from Great Britain and establishing independent States". It also adopted the Olive Branch Petition (July 5), which professed attachment to George III and begged him to prevent further hostile measures so that a plan of reconciliation might be worked out.

When Washington assumed command of the Continental Army at Cambridge, Massachusetts in early July, he found it recovering from what proved the bloodiest battle of the Revolutionary War. Known as the Battle of Bunker Hill (June 17), the engagement actually took place on neighboring Breed's Hill, which dominated Boston from the Charlestown peninsula. The British, under General William Howe, achieved their aim of dislodging the American defenders, but only after three frontal assaults and at fearful cost. Of Howe's 2,500 men more than a thousand became casualties; the Americans lost less than half that number. The chastened British made no further offensive moves. Nor were the besiegers immediately in a condition to attack. Washington had enough to do to remedy the Continental Army's deficiencies. Undisciplined and disorganized, it was short of arms and powder. By the spring of 1776 these difficulties had been partly overcome but Howe had decided to withdraw from Boston to a more favorable base. On March 17 his army, accompanied by more than a thousand loyalists, sailed off to Halifax. Thus the British relinquished for the time being their last foothold in the thirteen colonies.

Meanwhile an American invasion of Canada had been repelled. Though there was only a small British garrison there American hopes that Canadians would welcome the invaders and join the rebellion proved ill-founded. The Quebec Act had largely assuaged Canadian discontent, while the outburst of anti-Catholicism it had provoked in New England had offended Canadian opinion. Having advanced up the Champlain waterway Richard Montgomery's army captured Montreal (November 13, 1775) and then joined Benedict Arnold's forces in an attempt to take the great fortress of Quebec. The American assault, made in a heavy snow-storm on December 30, was a costly failure; Montgomery was killed and Arnold wounded. Arnold continued to besiege Quebec throughout the winter but the arrival of large British reinforcements in the spring forced him to retire. Montreal had also to be abandoned and the Americans retreated from Canada in disorder.

For more than a year after the fighting at Lexington and Concord, Congress remained reluctant to break with Great Britain. Continuing to protest their loyalty to the Crown, delegates affected to believe that coercion was the policy of a 'venal ministry', and lived in hope of a conciliatory royal gesture. But it gradually became clear that George III, no less than his ministers, was bent on subjugation. He returned no answer to the Olive Branch Petition. The king's speech to Parliament in October reaffirmed the intention of using force. The Prohibitory Act of December 22 declared the rebellious colonies to be outside the protection of the Crown and laid an embargo upon colonial trade. To John Adams, Sam's relatively conservative cousin, the measure was tantamount to the expulsion of the colonies from the empire. Meanwhile several months of fighting had weakened attachment to the mother country; the news that 30,000 German mercenaries—the so-called Hessians—were to be recruited to suppress the rebellion deepened colonial resentment. Thomas Paine's pamphlet, *Common Sense*, expressed the developing mood, while helping to convince waverers of the necessity of separation. Published in January 1776, it quickly sold 120,000 copies. A recent immigrant from England, Paine savagely and directly attacked "the royal brute" and the whole concept of monarchy, in the process disabusing Americans of the notion that they could look to George III for redress. The only alternatives, Paine insisted, were submission or independence. Meanwhile the conviction had grown that foreign aid was vital to the American cause, but that this would not be forthcoming so long as Americans shrank from independence.

The Declaration of Independence

Accordingly in the spring of 1776 colony after colony instructed its delegates to the Continental Congress to vote for separation. On April 6 Congress opened American ports to the vessels of all nations except Great Britain. On May 10 it recommended the formation of independent state-governments. Then on July 2 it unanimously approved Richard Henry Lee's resolution that "these United Colonies are, and of right ought to be, free and independent states". It was this vote, rather than the adoption of the Declaration of Independence on July 4, that formally proclaimed the birth of the United States. Thus for the past two hundred years Americans have evidently been celebrating their country's birthday on the wrong day.

The Declaration of Independence was written by Thomas Jefferson, with some assistance from Benjamin Franklin and John Adams. Its purpose was to furnish a moral and legal justification for the rebellion. Much of it consists of a lengthy enumeration of the wrongs committed against the colonists since 1763, all of them laid squarely, but somewhat unfairly, at the door of George III who was accused of seeking deliberately to establish an "absolute Tyranny over these States". But the subsequent fame of the Declaration rests upon its brief preamble, a lucid and eloquent statement of the political philosophy underlying the colonists' assertion of independence. Jefferson never claimed any originality for his handiwork; it was intended, he said, to be simply "an expression of the American mind". In proclaiming certain truths to be "self-evident" he drew upon the natural-rights philosophy that dated back to Aristotle and Cicero and had been given classic formulation in 1690 in John Locke's second *Treatise on Civil Government*. According to this, men possessed certain natural rights which Jefferson defined as "life, liberty and the pursuit of happiness". Governments were established to secure those rights, derived their just powers from the consent of the governed, and could legitimately be overthrown if they subverted the purposes they were created to serve.

Just what Jefferson meant by the celebrated phrase, "all men are created equal", still bemuses historians. Some contend that he was thinking merely of the equality Americans shared with Englishmen as subjects of the same monarch. Certainly he could not have been describing the actual state of American society, with its palpable inequalities. Nor is there any evidence that he was advocating an equality of wealth, possessions, or social condition. Yet Jefferson can hardly have been insensitive to the term's wider implications. What he may have had chiefly in mind was equality of rights and of opportunity. Nature, while endowing men with unequal capacities, had nonetheless given all equally the "inalienable rights" Jefferson enumerated. The ideal society, moreover, should seek to ensure that each individual had an equal opportunity to make the most of whatever talents he possessed. What the phrase meant to its author is, however, less important than what it came to mean to later generations of Americans. For them "created equal" has been an inspiration, an ideal, a "standard maxim", as Lincoln once remarked, "constantly looked to, constantly labored for, and even though never perfectly attained, constantly approximated and thereby constantly spreading and deepening its influence and augmenting the happiness and value of life".

Whatever its later significance, the Declaration's immediate effect was divisive. Enthusiastically greeted by those who shared Paine's conviction that it was time to part, it alienated those who could not bring themselves to renounce traditional loyalties. Precisely how opinion divided has been much debated. The best guess seems to be that at least half the population favored independence, while of the remainder neutrals outnumbered those who remained loyal to George III. Nevertheless the number of active loyalists was not inconsiderable. They were to be found in every colony. In New York and New Jersey they were probably in the majority. Only in New England, Virginia, and Maryland—the oldest colonies—were their numbers small. Proportionately loyalism was strongest among commercial and professional people, and among office-holders and the Anglican clergy. But far from being an upper-class phenomenon, as was once believed, loyalism drew adherents from all segments of society. The American Revolution was essentially a civil war which divided not only social classes but families as well. Loyalists—scornfully called Tories by their opponents—were mobbed, imprisoned, driven from their homes, deprived of their estates and other property. They were an important source of supply and intelligence to the British army; perhaps as many as 30,000 fought on the British side. After the war between 80,000 and 100,000 left the United States for Canada, Nova Scotia, the West Indies, and England.

British opinion, too, was divided on the American war, though not as much as was once believed. Though a few highly placed army and naval officers resigned their commissions rather than fight the Americans, the loyalty of the armed forces as a whole was never in question. In Parliament the policy of force was loudly criticized. Chatham had long been a friend of the colonies; Burke consistently preached conciliation; Fox paraded his American sympathies by appearing in the buff and blue of the Continental Army. But much of the criticism was simply factious. At bottom the opposition was no more willing than the government to abandon Parliament's right to legislate for the colonies, still less entertain the notion of an independent America. Once the issue had been fairly drawn between yielding and coercing, only a handful of radicals like Price and Cartwright continued to champion the American cause. As North later claimed, both Parliament and people solidly supported the American war—at least until Cornwallis's surrender at Yorktown in 1781 demonstrated the impossibility of reconquest.

The Revolutionary War

When the war began Great Britain seemed invincible. Outnumbering the United States in population by more than three to one, she possessed naval and military superiority and infinitely greater war-making potential. The Americans lacked not only an army and navy but even an effective government. An ingrained localism meant that the Articles of Confederation, adopted by the Continental Congress in 1777 but not ratified by the states until 1781, conferred only limited powers upon the central government. Though empowered to make war, it was denied the means to wage it effectively. The requisitions it made on the states for men and money produced tardy and inadequate responses. State particularism also limited the effectiveness of the Continental Army. Soldiers tended to resent commanders from other states and were reluctant to fight at a distance from their homes. Leveling tendencies, too, created disciplinary problems. Soldiers squabbled incessantly over rank and precedence; the states were reluctant to establish differential pay-scales for officers; an unmilitary familiarity existed between officers and men. Still another source of difficulty was short enlistments, the product of widespread suspicion of standing armies. Militiamen generally enlisted for only three months, would not remain a moment longer, and frequently went home before their terms expired. Even in the face of the enemy Washington was tormented by the thought that his army would melt away. His numbers never exceeded 20,000; most of the time he had hardly 5,000; at one point he commanded only a dwindling band of 2,000.

Yet the odds were not as heavily in favor of the British as they seemed. To transport and maintain a heavily equipped army across three thousand miles of ocean, and to wage war in unfriendly territory were formidable tasks. America's unfamiliar terrain, vast distances, and poor communications were ill-suited to the elaborate maneuvers, parade-ground formations, and set-piece battles the British were used to. Much of the fighting, especially in the South, took the form of guerrilla warfare, at which American militiamen proved more adept than British regulars. Moreover, the Royal Navy had been allowed to decay, and the British army was far below strength. To make matters worse, the British generals were a sorry lot: Howe was overcautious, Burgoyne blundering, Clinton dilatory, and Cornwallis reckless. However, in Lord George Germain, the North ministry had an energetic and highly competent war minister. Far from trying to run the war from London, as was long alleged, he gave his commanders wide latitude. But his excessive faith in loyalist support resulted in a debilitating dispersal of effort. Equally serious, North's government displayed a confusion of purpose; until late in the war it could not decide whether to conciliate or coerce. Yet the fundamental British difficulty was that occupation of territory brought no lasting advantage. Though every important American town fell to the British during the war, there were not enough troops to garrison them. The moment the British moved away from a subdued region, rebellion flared up in their rear. Thus if the Americans could but retain the will to fight and some capacity for doing so, they were bound to win in the end.

Military Operations: Long Island to Saratoga

Following his withdrawal to Halifax Howe planned an assault on New York City, the key to the Hudson–Champlain route to Canada and the leading center of loyalism. On July 2, 1776 his army supported by a fleet commanded by his elder brother, Admiral Lord Howe, landed on Staten Island. Washington had concentrated his forces to protect the city but his dispositions were faulty, and at the battle of Long Island (August 27) he was outflanked and heavily defeated. Only Howe's slowness in pursuit allowed him to escape complete disaster. After a brief interval during which the Howe brothers vainly offered pardons to rebels prepared to swear loyalty to the Crown, the British resumed the offensive and easily captured New York, which remained in their hands for the rest of the war. Next they overran New Jersey and chased the Americans across the Delaware. Philadelphia was Howe's for the taking but, still wedded to European conventions of warfare, he decided to go into winter quarters. This unexpected respite gave Washington an opportunity to strike at the over-extended British lines. On Christmas night 1776 he recrossed the Delaware and fell upon the unsuspecting Hessian garrison at Trenton, capturing over 1,000 prisoners. He followed this up with a similar *coup* at Princeton. These bold counterstrokes forced the British to relinquish most of their recent gains and breathed new life into the American cause.

With characteristic lethargy Howe waited until July 1777 before resuming operations. Embarking most of his army at New York he sailed into Chesapeake Bay, with Philadelphia his objective. At Brandywine Creek on September 11 he again outflanked and defeated Washington and on September 26 captured the rebel capital. A surprise American counterattack at Germantown (October 4) having failed to dislodge him, Howe prepared to spend the winter in comfort at Philadelphia while Washington withdrew to the desolate plateau of Valley Forge, twenty miles to the northwest. But despite the seeming success of the Philadelphia compaign, Howe had squandered a second opportunity to destroy Washington's army.

Meanwhile, in the woods of northern New York, disaster had overtaken British arms. General John Burgoyne, commanding the now formidable British army in Canada, planned a southward offensive aimed at controlling the Hudson valley and isolating New England. Though he later claimed otherwise, Burgoyne did not rely upon Howe's forces at New York City advancing up the Hudson to meet him. When he set off from Canada in mid-June 1777 he felt confident he could succeed independently. But he underestimated the difficulties of a wilderness campaign. Encumbered by an enormous baggage train—thirty vehicles were needed to carry "Gentleman Johnny's" resplendent wardrobe and his stock of champagne— his army found movement increasingly difficult along blocked roads and destroyed bridges. By early autumn lack of supplies and mounting American opposition had halted his advance. After British and Indian forces from Lake Ontario had failed in an attempt to join him, Burgoyne's situation became critical. His army, weakened by Canadian and Indian desertions, numbered only 5,000, barely half its original strength; his supply line stretched back two hundred miles to Canada. To the eastward the New England militia were gathering; before him stood General Horatio Gates, with 12,000 militia and 5,000 Continentals. Only a swift retreat could save the expedition. But Burgoyne gambled on breaking through the American lines to Albany, only twenty miles away. Two attempts having been repulsed with heavy loss, he found himself surrounded. At Saratoga on October 17 his exhausted soldiers laid down their arms.

The French Alliance

Saratoga was the turning-point of the struggle. It brought in France and thus transformed a local rebellion into a world war. Vergennes, the French Minister of Foreign Affairs, seeing in the American rebellion an opportunity to reverse the verdict of the Seven Years' War, had already been secretly supplying the Americans with large quantities of arms and gunpowder and providing port facilities for their privateers. But he had withheld formal recognition of American independence while the outcome of the war was in doubt. Saratoga ended French fears of an American collapse and, by prompting Lord North to make fresh concessions in the hope of luring the Americans back into the empire, gave Benjamin Franklin, the leader of the American diplomatic mission to Paris, the opportunity to obtain French recognition.

Franklin enjoyed extraordinary popularity in Paris. His fame as a scientist had gone before him; he was also lionized as a homespun revolutionary sage. He now used North's Conciliatory Propositions of February 1778— which yielded everything Americans had demanded three years before but which Congress eventually spurned—to play on Vergennes's fears of a possible Anglo-American reconciliation. The outcome on February 6, 1778 was two Franco-American treaties, one a commercial agreement, the other a defensive alliance to take effect when France went to war with Great Britain—as she did in June 1778. By the terms of the alliance France and the United States guaranteed each other's New World possessions, promised to wage war until American independence was "formally or tacitly assured", and undertook not to make peace separately.

In 1779, Spain entered the war against Great Britain though for reasons of her own and as the ally, not of the United States, but of France. The following year the Dutch followed suit, and the formation of the League of Armed Neutrality—Russia, Sweden, Denmark—meant that nearly the whole of Europe was arrayed in hostility to Great Britain. But while Great Britain's European enemies contributed indirectly to the final American victory, they were not necessarily well disposed towards the young republic. Spain, seeing it as a threat to her position in the Mississippi Valley took no part in the American war, but concentrated on expelling the British from the Caribbean and on recovering Gibraltar. Even France was slow to lend military or naval support. She had entered the war less to achieve American independence than to strike at her British rival. Thus although a French squadron arrived in American waters in 1778, it achieved nothing tangible and soon departed for the West Indies, bent on capturing British sugar islands. Three years were to elapse before the French returned to the American mainland in force.

Although Saratoga boosted American morale, the winter of 1777–8 was one of trial and dissension for the patriots. Gates's victorious army disintegrated with the return home of its militiamen; Washington's ragged, half-starved Continentals endured great privations in their Valley Forge encampment. Even Washington's own position seemed in jeopardy. There is no evidence of an organized conspiracy against him—though he and his aides believed otherwise—but both in and out of Congress there was an undercurrent of criticism. Some feared that military dictatorship might result from what John Adams had earlier called "the superstitious veneration that is sometimes paid to General Washington". Others, chagrined by Washington's repeated failures against Howe and especially by the loss of Philadelphia, began to question his military abilities and to contrast his sorry record with Gates's. Matters came to a head in November 1777 with the publication of a private letter written to Gates by General Thomas Conway, an Irish-born French officer in the Continental Army, expressing the hope that the victor of Saratoga would supersede "the weak general". But criticism was no sooner out in the open than it expired.

Washington's contribution to the American cause can hardly be overstated. He was no military genius; indeed, he lost more battles than he won. But he was a great war leader. Creating an army out of unpromising material, he kept it in being against great odds and through a long succession of dark days. Nor were steadfastness and resource the only qualities for which his country had reason to be thankful. Though frequently driven to protest at Congressional neglect, he was never less than deferential to the civil authorities. Moreover, the promptness with which he quitted the army in 1783 allayed fears that he might become a "man on horseback".

By the spring of 1778 American fortunes had begun to mend. The Continental Army had been augmented, and largely reequipped. Its organization, discipline, and drill had also improved, thanks in part to 'Baron' von Steuben's exertions. Steuben was one of a number of European sympathizers, some idealists, some soldiers of fortune, who had been attracted to the American cause. Among the best known were Lafayette and Kościuszko, who served throughout the war, and De Kalb and Pulaski, both killed in action.

France's entry had meanwhile compelled the British to go on the defensive, at least in the north. Sir Henry Clinton, Howe's successor as Commander-in-Chief, was ordered to evacuate Philadelphia and concentrate his forces at New York. When he set off overland for New York in mid-June 1778 he was closely pursued by Washington. At Monmouth Court House in New Jersey on June 28 an attack on the British rearguard failed through the incompetence of General Charles Lee, a former British officer with a talent for self-advertisement and an abiding jealousy of Washington. But for Washington's timely arrival, there might have been a serious American reverse. As it was, Clinton reached New York without further hindrance. After Monmouth there were no more major battles in the north, though Tory Rangers and Indian auxiliaries continued to wage a savage frontier war against settlers in Pennsylvania and New York.

During the first half of the war Great Britain's command of the sea had been unchallenged. The Americans had no navy worthy of the name. Eventually some fifty vessels were commissioned into the Continental navy, and almost as many into state navies, but these were not ships of the line but converted merchantmen or at best small frigates. The best-known American naval commander was the Scots-born ex-slaver, John Paul Jones. A daring and skillful frigate captain, Jones raided British shipping in the English Channel, spiked the guns at Whitehaven, and in September 1779, in a fiercely fought action off Flamborough Head, captured the British fifty-gun frigate *Serapis*—though Jones's own ship was sunk and the convoy which had been his main objective escaped. When stripped of the glamour of legend, Jones's exploits were of small military significance. More important was privateering, which at times enrolled more men than the Continental Army. Over two thousand privateers were commissioned during the war, mostly in New England. Privateering was highly profitable as well as patriotic; it founded the fortunes of such families as the Cabots of Beverley and the Derbys of Salem. But while privateers inflicted heavy damage, the threat they posed to British transatlantic supply lines had been effectively countered by 1778 through the adoption of an efficient convoy system.

It was a different story, however, once France became a belligerent. The

Royal Navy was hard put to it to contain the new and powerful French fleet. Spain's entry into the war added further to the strain. In 1779 Great Britain escaped invasion only because a Channel gale dispersed a Franco-Spanish armada. Gibraltar was besieged, a French squadron was active in the Indian Ocean, the West Indian islands of Dominica, St. Vincent, and Grenada were lost, even Jamaica was in grave danger.

Problems of War-making

The Americans were initially unable to profit from Great Britain's distresses. Far from being able to take the offensive, Washington experienced renewed difficulty in keeping an army together. The French alliance persuaded some soldiers that the fighting could safely be left to others. Many deserted or refused to reenlist. Even high-ranking officers like General Philip Schuyler felt that they could honorably resign their commissions; a dedicated patriot like the future president, James Monroe, gave up soldiering to study law. Infinitely more serious was the appearance, first of treason, then of mutiny. In 1780 Benedict Arnold, resentful of real and imagined slights at the hands of Congress, plotted to turn over the fortress of West Point to the British for £20,000. The plot miscarried when Clinton's emissary, Major John André, was captured with incriminating evidence. André was hanged as a spy, but Arnold escaped to fight for the British, his name becoming a byword for treachery. The mutiny of the Pennsylvania Line in January 1781 was the result of long-smoldering discontent with conditions of service. Food and clothing were inadequate; pay, meager to begin with and usually months in arrears, lost value as the currency depreciated. Though spurning Clinton's invitation to desert, the mutineers refused to return to duty until promised redress. Their success encouraged the New Jersey Line to mutiny in turn, but Washington stepped in to nip this second rising in the bud.

The trouble over soldiers' pay was only one indication that Congress was in desperate financial trouble. Lacking a tax revenue of its own, unsuccessful in inducing the states to comply with its requisitions, and with no hope of floating long-term domestic loans because of a nationwide shortage of specie, Congress could finance the war only by increasingly frequent issues of paper money. The states were even more prodigal, Virginia alone issuing more paper than the Continental Congress. By 1779 the country was snowed under with paper money, mostly unsecured. As its quantity increased, its value declined and prices rose in proportion. To check inflation some states experimented with price controls, but found enforcement impossible. In the spring of 1780 Congress was driven to devalue, fixing the ratio of Continental paper to specie at 40 to 1. A year later, after a second devaluation had fixed the ratio at 75 to 1, the notes became worthless—hence the expression, "Not worth a Continental".

However, the appointment in 1781 of Robert Morris, a wealthy Philadelphia merchant, as Superintendent of Finance, eased the crisis. He issued bills of credit backed by his own fortune, pressed the states for cash contributions, negotiated a French loan, and established the Bank of North America to act as the government's fiscal agent.

Military Operations: The Southern Phase

The last phase of the fighting took place in the south. Unable to win a decisive victory elsewhere the British resolved to transfer their efforts to a region whose large slave population, hostile Indian neighbors, and reputed loyalism seemed to offer better prospects. At first all went well. After Savannah had fallen to a British army (December 29, 1778), Georgia was rapidly overrun. A year later Clinton began a four-month siege which ended with the capture of Charleston and its garrison of 5,000 (May 12, 1780). Cornwallis, left in charge after Clinton's return to New York, followed this up by heavily defeating a hastily assembled American army at Camden, South Carolina (August 16). Thus in three months the British had eliminated two armies the size of the one they lost at Saratoga. Nonetheless the tide now began to turn against them. Despite appearances, the subjugation of South Carolina had been far from complete; resistance had simply gone underground. As soon as Cornwallis advanced northward into North Carolina to crush, as he supposed, the last vestiges of Southern opposition the countryside rose behind him. In North Carolina itself a loyalist force was wiped out by backwoods riflemen at King's Mountain (October 7). Next, a new American army under Greene routed a British detachment at Cowpens (January 16, 1781) and although Cornwallis inflicted a series of defeats on Greene he could not beat him decisively and, indeed, suffered so heavily in these back-country engagements that he withdrew to the coast. Thus when Cornwallis marched into Virginia in April Greene was able, with guerrilla aid, to reduce the scattered British outposts in the Carolinas one by one. By the end of the summer all Cornwallis's southern conquests had melted away. South of Virginia the British now held only Charleston and Savannah.

Up till now the Americans had been somewhat disappointed with the French alliance. The frustration born of d'Estaing's half-hearted naval operations in 1778 deepened when Rochambeau's army, which arrived in Newport, Rhode Island in the summer of 1780, remained largely inactive for more than a year. Rochambeau's officers, though respectful of Washington, did not improve relations by their lack of regard for their comrades in arms—or by their attentions to American women. But in May 1781 Washington learned that Admiral De Grasse's fleet was on its way to cooperate with him and Rochambeau. Intending originally to attack New York, he was persuaded by Rochambeau to transfer their joint operations to Virginia and make Cornwallis's army their quarry. In a rapidly executed and perfectly timed operation the Franco-American armies reached Virginia in early September, thus confronting Cornwallis with a force twice the size of his own and trapping him on the Yorktown peninsula. De Grasse had already arrived in the Chesapeake with an additional 4,000 French troops to prevent an escape by sea. The repulse of a British fleet on September 5 gave the French temporary but vital command of the sea; finally delay in dispatching a relief expedition from New York sealed Cornwallis's fate. On October 19, 1781 he and his army of 7,000 surrendered.

Peacemaking, 1781–1783

The Yorktown surrender virtually ended the American war. The departure of De Grasse and Rochambeau for the West Indies deprived the Continental Army of the power to act offensively. Great Britain, for her part, was content to remain on the defensive in America, though she recovered command of the sea and in other parts of the world won belated victories. But British opinion was now ready to concede American independence. The war had crippled trade and was ruinously expensive. Ireland, inspired by the American example, seethed with discontent; the British position in India was precarious; in Europe, Great Britain was dangerously isolated. Convinced of the futility of further effort the House of Commons adopted a motion in April 1782 to abandon coercion. North resigned, to be succeeded, first by Rockingham, then by Shelburne, both of whom favored peace with America. A chagrined George III spoke momentarily of abdication, but ultimately acquiesced in the decision to send an emissary to Paris to discuss terms with Franklin.

The peace negotiations exposed deep cracks in the Franco-American alliance. In appointing Franklin, John Jay, and John Adams as peace commissioners, Congress had specifically instructed them to do nothing without the "knowledge and concurrence" of France. But Jay, now the effective leader of the American delegation, suspected—with good reason, as it transpired—that Vergennes's aim was to ensure that an independent United States would not be strong enough to dispense with French help. Vergennes was even ready to support the Spanish claim to the trans-Allegheny region on which the United States had set its heart. Without consulting either Franklin or the French, Jay decided to open separate negotiations with Great Britain. Shelburne, seeing an opportunity to drive a wedge between the allies, responded encouragingly. After protracted negotiations the American commissioners signed a preliminary peace treaty with Great Britain on November 30, 1782. Vergennes reproved the Americans for going behind his back but accepted the outcome without undue protest. The terms of the treaty were confirmed with little change by the definitive agreement of September 3, 1783, to which France, Spain, and the Netherlands also subscribed. Great Britain formally recognized American independence and agreed that the boundaries of the United States should extend west to the Mississippi river, north to the Great Lakes, and south to the 31st parallel (the northern boundary of Florida, which Great Britain ceded to Spain). Thanks to John Adams's spirited defense of New England's interests the Americans were granted the 'liberty', though not the right, to fish the Newfoundland Banks and to dry and cure fish on the unsettled coasts of Nova Scotia and Labrador. Finally the treaty attempted to deal with two matters over which there had been prolonged wrangling during the negotiations. It was agreed that British merchants should meet with "no lawful impediment" in seeking to recover their prewar American debts, and that Congress should "earnestly recommend" to the states the restoration of confiscated loyalist property.

The peace terms bore little relation to the military situation. The British still had 30,000 troops in New York and also held Charleston and Savannah. Especially surprising was the British willingness to concede the Mississippi river boundary. Though a daring Virginian, George Rogers Clark, had seized a number of British posts in the Illinois country, the British still controlled most of the trans-Appalachian West. But Shelburne considered this and other sacrifices to be worthwhile. Besides wanting to lure the United States away from France, he nursed the hope that a generous peace might lay the foundation for an Anglo-American commercial alliance and, eventually, even some form of political reunion. Practically every clause of the peace treaty contained ambiguities, some of which were to bedevil Anglo-American relations for decades. But meanwhile the United States had won a highly advantageous peace settlement. This owed much to the uncompromising stand of Franklin, Jay, and Adams and to their skill in exploiting their opportunities. Yet diplomacy could not conceivably have won such a triumph had not a war for national independence developed into a general European conflict. Surrounded by adversaries the British had ultimately been compelled, as Vergennes remarked, not so much to make peace as to buy it.

4. *The Revolutionary Transformation,*
1776–1789

The American Revolution

During the struggle for independence and for some years thereafter Americans were engaged in reordering their society in ways which gave the period a revolutionary significance. At first glance, it is true, the American Revolution hardly deserves its name. It had none of the cataclysmic quality associated, say, with what happened in France in 1789 or in Russia in 1917. It was limited, decorous, even prosaic, with little social upheaval or class conflict, no radical reorganization of government or the economy, no challenge to existing religious beliefs, no bloodthirsty mobs, no carnivals of pillage, no descent into anarchy or dictatorship, no reign of terror. It was led, not by fanatical visionaries like Robespierre, Lenin, or Mao Tse-Tung, but by a group of conservative and mainly well-to-do gentlemen. Nor did it devour its children. The men who made it were not in turn overthrown but remained in control of what they created, dying in due course full of years and honor. One might be forgiven, therefore, for concluding, as Burke did at the time, that there was no real revolution in America, but simply a successful war of independence which ended British rule but otherwise left things pretty much as they had been.

Yet the American Revolution was a truly revolutionary event. As the first war for national independence in modern times to result in the rupture of an imperial connection it was to serve as an inspiration to other colonial peoples. The war also produced a new nation based on a body of ideas which differed from—indeed, consciously repudiated—those of the Old World. Those ideas not only affected contemporary beliefs and attitudes but were to act as a leaven on succeeding generations of Americans.

The social changes that accompanied the Revolution were not at first easy to see. Although the Great Seal of the United States—like today's dollar bills—bears the motto *novus ordo seclorum*, the Revolutionary leaders did not seek to create a new social order. All of them, even Jefferson, accepted that class distinctions were natural and inevitable. They made no attempt to redistribute wealth or to promote social equality. They evidently did not feel that the institution of indentured servitude was at variance with the new nation's libertarian ideals: in the 1780s Pennsylvania and New York even passed laws to encourage it. The abolition of quitrents and of other feudal survivals like primogeniture and entails were once thought to have produced a more fluid pattern of landownership. (Under primogeniture, the whole estate of a landowner who died intestate passed to his eldest son. Entail was a legal device for holding an estate together in perpetuity.) But although the diffusion of landownership was Jefferson's purpose in fighting a long and ultimately successful battle in Virginia against primogeniture and entails, the results should not be exaggerated. Entails had not been universal even in the tidewater South, and primogeniture applied only in the relatively rare cases of intestacy.

Nor did the sudden disappearance of the loyalists have leveling effects. Since loyalists came from all social classes, there was no question of American society being decapitated. Insofar as there was now more room at the top it was promptly occupied, not by the poor, but by the already well off. Thus in Boston prominent mercantile families such as the Higginsons, the Jacksons, and the Cabots stepped into the vacancies created by the departure of old established families like the Hutchinsons and the Olivers. Admittedly the loyalist exodus and the confiscation of Crown and proprietary lands brought substantial changes in land ownership. Huge estates became forfeit, like those of Sir John Johnson in the Mohawk Valley and of Lord Fairfax in the Northern Neck of Virginia. But except in New York, where some large estates were broken up and disposed of cheaply, confiscated land was generally sold as a unit and at prices which ordinary men could not afford. Thus some great landowning families, like the Livingstons and the Van Rensselaers in the Hudson Valley, who had been on the right side during the Revolution, were able to expand their estates substantially. So was that shrewd speculator, George Washington. Except for its loyalist component the old colonial aristocracy survived the Revolution intact, especially in Virginia. In 1787 over four-fifths of the hundred wealthiest Virginians, all owning more than 4,000 acres, had inherited their wealth.

Nevertheless the Revolution increased social mobility, at least within the middle ranks of society. The great acceleration of the westward movement, such a feature of the Revolutionary era, was one cause. Land in the west was cheaper and easier to obtain than on the seaboard. The tax records of Lunenberg county, Virginia, then on the frontier, show that about two-thirds of those who had been landless in 1764 had acquired land by 1782. However, social mobility tended to diminish once the frontier stage had passed and society became more stable.

Republican ideology, too, had social effects. If Americans continued to accept the principles of social stratification, they were not prepared to acknowledge those not based on individual merit. Hereditary privilege in all its forms, from monarchy down, was taboo. Two states forbade the creation of titles of nobility; so did the Federal Constitution of 1787. Many state constitutions explicitly prohibited hereditary office-holding. The attempt by former army officers in 1783 to form a hereditary society, the Society of the Cincinnati, met with strong condemnation. "The idea", wrote one critic, "of a man *born* [to be] magistrate, legislator or judge, is absurd and unnatural." In consequence the Society abandoned the hereditary principle, at least at the national level. Authority was forced on to the defensive, and some of the outward marks of social deference disappeared. Republican simplicity decreed less ceremony in the lawcourts; judges no longer wore wigs and scarlet robes in the English fashion. The practice of seating people in church according to rank became less common. Increasing travel, the product of turnpikes and stagecoaches, helped quicken the trend towards social informality.

The Revolutionary period also produced an upsurge of humanitarianism. Criminal codes became less harsh, a start was made in improving prison conditions, there was growing concern about the treatment of the insane. Above all, slavery for the first time came under widespread attack. Many Americans were struck by the inconsistency of claiming freedom for themselves while keeping others in bondage. Yet Revolutionary antislavery was not the product simply of newfound libertarianism. While nearly every state prohibited the slave-trade, most acted out of the conviction that it inhibited white immigration. In all the Northern states, where soil and climate had been unfavorable to the large-scale employment of slaves, steps were taken either to abolish slavery outright or to provide for gradual emancipation. In New York and New Jersey, the only two Northern states with sizable slave populations, opposition was sufficiently strong to delay the passage of gradual emancipation laws until 1799 and 1804 respectively and, even then, the process of emancipation took decades to work itself out. Moreover, freedom did not bring equality to Northern blacks: they were discriminated against in every conceivable way.

In the South, where slavery was part of the social and economic fabric, the institution was less affected. In Virginia and Maryland, with relatively few slaves and a depressed agriculture, the prevailing liberalism led some slave-holders, like George Washington and Robert Carter, to provide for manumission by deed or will. Between 1782 and 1810 the number of free blacks in Virginia rose from 2,000 to 30,000. But other Virginians, including Jefferson and Patrick Henry, though acknowledging slavery as a moral evil, took no overt action against it, contenting themselves with the vague hope that the institution would ultimately die a natural death. Further South, where the slave population was greatest, antislavery agitation had virtually no impact. All the same, the Revolution had a lasting effect upon attitudes to slavery. By revealing a fundamental contradiction in the American credo between human rights and property rights, it confronted Southern slave-holders with the need to justify the institution.

A further consequence of the Revolutionary upheaval was the strengthening of religious freedom. The principle of an ecclesiastical establishment, already eroded during the colonial period, was further weakened during the Revolution, partly by the ardent loyalism of the Anglican clergy, far more by the skepticism of the Enlightenment. Yet Americans displayed virtually none of the anticlericalism and militant secularism characteristic of the French Revolution. They not only remained a religious people, but insisted on retaining a religious dimension in their national life. Washington proclaimed a Day of Thanksgiving for the inauguration of the Constitution in 1789, another for the suppression of the Whiskey Rebellion in 1793; John Adams decreed fasts during the yellow-fever epidemic of 1798 and 1799. (Jefferson, characteristically, declared no religious observances.) All the same, American leaders affirmed their conviction that religious belief, worship, and association were strictly private affairs.

Although Congress was forbidden in the Bill of Rights (1791) to pass laws "respecting an establishment of religion or prohibiting the free exercise thereof", the triumph of religious liberty did not come easily or occur everywhere at once. In New England the Revolution left the existing religious order substantially unchanged. All the New England states except Rhode Island continued to require taxpayers to support "public Protestant worship", though non-Congregationalists could insist that their taxes went to their own denominations. The Congregational Church was not completely disestablished until 1817 in New Hampshire, 1818 in Connecticut, and 1833 in Massachusetts. But all the Southern states separated church and state in the 1780s. The fiercest struggle took place in Virginia, the main bastion of Anglicanism. It ended in 1786 with the passage of the Virginia Statute of Religious Liberty, drafted by Jefferson. This not only exempted citizens from attending and supporting places of worship and guaranteed them freedom of conscience, but also declared that their religious opinions were not to affect their civil capacities. This was a revolutionary doctrine: it repudiated the age-old European principle that a citizen's religious affiliation determined his status and function. Religious freedom also had social implications. In colonial days the fact that one church was officially favored had tended to divide society along religious lines; in Virginia especially, membership of the Anglican Church had provided the gentry with a social identity. But once all churches were equally unconnected with the state, existing patterns of association tended to crumble.

The State Constitutions

In politics, as in society, the Revolution produced no sudden or startling changes. When the royal governors departed at the outbreak of war, provincial congresses seized power. To establish a legal foundation for these makeshift governments seemed an urgent necessity to Revolutionary leaders deeply concerned for the rule of law and fearing the spread of civil disorder. Even before the Declaration of Independence was adopted, therefore, the Continental Congress recommended the colonies to establish new governments "under the authority of the people". Between 1776 and 1780 all the states but two adopted new constitutions. The exceptions were Rhode Island and Connecticut, which merely revised their old colonial charters so as to delete all reference to royal authority. Most of the new state constitutions were drawn up and put into effect by state legislatures without specific authorization from the electorate. A few were the work of specially elected conventions. Massachusetts, however, worked out an elaborate and detailed procedure to secure the explicit consent of the governed: first a convention was elected for the express purpose of framing a constitution and then its handiwork was submitted to the electorate for scrutiny and approval. This later became the standard method of constitution-making in the United States.

The preference for formal, written constitutions was not surprising. The vagueness of the unwritten British constitution had after all been largely responsible for the controversy with Britain after 1763. In any case Americans had long been accustomed to living under a set of written rules: colonial charters, governors' commissions, instructions from the Board of Trade. The new constitutions while varying in detail, resembled each other in many respects. They outlined a framework of government broadly patterned on the old colonial model. Though for a time Pennsylvania had a plural executive and, along with Georgia, a unicameral legislature, the usual provision was for a legislature consisting of two houses and for a single executive head—the governor. Instead of being nominated by the Crown the governor was henceforth to be chosen by the legislature or elected directly by the voters; in addition an elected upper house replaced the governor's appointed council. The deep suspicion of executive authority which was one of the legacies of the colonial past resulted in state governors being denied—initially at least—many of the powers enjoyed by their royal and proprietorial predecessors. Only in Massachusetts and New York was the governor given a veto; elsewhere his powers were narrowly restricted. Experience had also taught the constitution-makers to distrust the idea of an independent judiciary; accordingly in most states judges were to be appointed by the legislatures and for short terms only. And although several constitutions affirmed a principle of great subsequent importance—the separation of powers—authority was in practice largely concentrated in the legislatures, and especially in the lower houses. But the power of the assemblies was limited, first, by the requirement to hold annual elections and, second, by the inclusion of bills of rights. The Virginia Declaration of Rights, drawn by George Mason in 1776, provided the model. It enumerated those fundamental English liberties which Americans had come to regard as their own: freedom of expression, worship, and assembly, the right to jury trial, protection against cruel and unusual punishments and against search warrants, the subordination of military to civil power.

Far from being democratic, the new constitutions reflected the eighteenth-century belief that political rights should be confined to property-holders. A man without property, it was held, was not sufficiently independent to be entrusted with political power or even with the selection of those who were to exercise it. Thus while nearly all states reduced property qualifications for voting, only two (Pennsylvania and Georgia) did away with them altogether, and even they limited the franchise to taxpayers. Property qualifications for office-holding were generally even higher than those for voting, sometimes so high as to exclude all but the really wealthy.

Nevertheless the Revolution brought changes in the composition of state governments. Assemblies became larger; frontier towns and counties were granted additional representation. The result was that men of comparatively modest fortunes began to be more prominent in public life. Before the Revolution small farmers and artisans had accounted for only about 20 percent of the members of the colonial assemblies; afterward they constituted a majority in some Northern legislatures and a sizable minority in the South. The tradition of upper-class leadership by no means ended; even in the states which went furthest in liberalizing qualifications for voting and office-holding, the political order remained highly deferential. But there was now less of a correlation between high social position and the holding of public office. The first elected governors of Virginia and New York were both frontier lawyers: Patrick Henry and George Clinton. Still another indication that political power was no longer the exclusive preserve of the seaboard gentry was the transfer inland of several state capitals: from Williamsburg to Richmond, from New York City to Albany, from Philadelphia to Harrisburg, from Charleston to Columbia.

The Articles of Confederation

The task of framing new state constitutions was accomplished much more smoothly than that of creating a central government for the states as a whole. It had been obvious from the start that political unity was essential to the attainment of independence. On June 12, 1776 the Continental Congress appointed a Committee of Thirteen (one from each state) to draw up a constitution. After a month's debate the committee produced a draft constitution—the Articles of Confederation. Largely the work of John Dickinson of Pennsylvania, they provided for a central government with limited powers. It could declare war, conclude treaties and alliances, apportion the common expenses among the states, coin money, establish post offices, and regulate Indian affairs. But it lacked two of the essential attributes of sovereignty: the power to tax and the power to regulate trade. All powers not specifically granted to the Confederation were reserved to the states which, the Articles insisted, retained their "sovereignty, freedom and independence". There was no provision for a national executive or a national judiciary. The confederation's powers were to be exercised solely by Congress, a unicameral legislature in which each state had one vote. Important measures, such as treaties, needed the approval of at least nine states, and the Articles themselves could not be amended without the consent of all thirteen states. Thus the proposed Confederation was little more than what Dickinson called it—"a firm league of friendship".

But such was the hostility towards centralized authority, even of so limited a kind, that the Articles did not obtain Congressional approval until November, 1777. And because of a protracted controversy over Western land claims the unanimous consent of the states, necessary for the constitution to become effective, was not obtained until February 1781—that is, until the Revolutionary War was almost over. Yet throughout the conflict the Continental Congress functioned as a *de facto* government.

During the eight years the Articles of Confederation were in operation (1781–9) the United States had only the semblance of a national government, and at times not even that. Once independence was achieved, the states attached less importance to unity and became absorbed in their own affairs. They continued to exercise rights they had specifically relinquished, responded belatedly or not at all to Congressional requisitions, and were casual in appointing Congressional delegates. Congress, in session only intermittently, had no fixed abode. Withdrawing from Philadelphia in 1783 to escape angry soldiers demanding back pay, it drifted successively to Princeton, Annapolis, and Trenton before settling temporarily in New York in 1785. Attendance at sessions was meager and irregular; only with difficulty was a quorum scraped together to ratify the Treaty of Paris. Such executive powers as Congress possessed were exercised through special committees whose membership, like that of Congress itself, was constantly changing. Not even the appointment of three secretaries (of war, foreign affairs, and finance) could provide executive continuity. Not surprisingly Congress declined in prestige and proved incapable of solving the new nation's problems.

Nevertheless, the Confederation had one substantial success to its credit: the regulation of Western settlement. The Revolutionary period witnessed an unprecedented flood of pioneers into the trans-Appalachian region, especially Kentucky and Tennessee. Between 1775 and 1790 its population rose from a mere handful to 120,000. This made a clear-cut policy on Western land distribution and territorial government essential. Two problems were involved: that of mediating the claims of settlers and speculators and that of curbing premature attempts at political organization such as the 'state of Franklin', established in 1783 in what later became Tennessee. As early as 1779 Congress had resolved that the West would eventually be organized into new states, to be admitted to the Union as equals. But nothing could be done until the states had vacated their claims to the region. South of the Ohio this did not happen until 1802; but the territory north of the river came under the jurisdiction of the United States in 1784, when Virginia finally ceded her claims.

Congress's first attempt to legislate for the territory between the Ohio and the Great Lakes was the Ordinance of 1784, drafted largely by Jefferson. This provided for self-government from the earliest stages of settlement, the eventual division of the territory into ten or more districts (Jefferson suggested such fanciful names for them as Metropotamia and Assenisipia), each of which was to be granted statehood when its population equaled that of any of the original states. Next came the Land Ordinance of 1785, outlining a system of land sales. Government surveyors were first to divide land in the Northwest Territory into thirty-six sections each of one square mile (640 acres). Four sections in every township were to be set aside as bounty land for ex-soldiers and one for the maintenance of schools. The rest of the land was to be sold at auction in 640-acre lots at not less than one dollar an acre.

The Confederation's need for quick returns explained why the terms favored wealthy speculators rather than actual settlers. Speculative land companies like the Ohio and Scioto companies were able, indeed, to persuade Congress to sell millions of acres of unsurveyed land at less than nine cents an acre. It was, moreover, at the prompting of the companies' lobbyist, the Reverend Manasseh Cutler, that Congress agreed to a less liberal form of territorial government than Jefferson's 1784 Ordinance had envisaged. The Northwest Ordinance of 1787 provided that during the initial phase of settlement the territory would not be self-governing (as Jefferson had proposed) but would have a governor and judges appointed by Congress. When the territory had 5,000 adult male inhabitants, it could elect a legislature with limited powers. Finally when its population reached 60,000 the territory would qualify for statehood, being divided not into Jefferson's ten or more states, but into not less than three nor more than five. (In the event, it was divided into five: Ohio, Indiana, Illinois, Michigan, and Wisconsin.) The Ordinance also prohibited slavery, though Congress subsequently watered down the provision, insisting that its intention had been simply to prohibit the further importation of slaves. In practice, therefore, it was not federal action but state action that finally abolished slavery in the Northwest Territory. Nevertheless this was the first time that the United States government had acted against slavery.

Though born of speculative greed the Northwest Ordinance was an enlightened and successful measure. Few laws have had such an influence. The Ordinance established the principle that the West was not to be kept in colonial subjection, but was an integral part of the nation, eventually to be admitted to full equality with the original states. It also prescribed a set of orderly political procedures that served as a model for all the territory subsequently acquired by the United States. Those procedures were not uniformly or literally applied. Ohio, the first state to be carved out of the Northwest Territory, would be granted statehood prematurely in 1803—because a Congressional majority wanted extra votes. Conversely, because of Congressional distaste for polygamy, Mormon-dominated Utah would be denied statehood for decades after reaching the qualifying total. Until the Civil War, moreover, the need to preserve equilibrium between North and South dictated that states were admitted and territories created in pairs. Thereafter, the need to preserve the party balance, together with Congressional reluctance to abandon territorial patronage, tended to slow down the creation of new states. But, however modified by politics, the system laid down by the Northwest Ordinance was substantially adhered to until the last remaining territory in the continental United States was admitted as the state of Arizona in 1912.

The Confederation's hopes for the West could hardly be realized, however, so long as Great Britain and Spain denied the United States full control of the region. Despite promising in the peace treaty to evacuate American soil "with all convenient speed", Great Britain still clung to a number of frontier posts south of the Great Lakes in order to safeguard the fur trade and maintain contact with the Indian tribes of the Northwest. Confident that the American union would soon collapse the British sought to accelerate the process by organizing Indian resistance to American expansion and encouraging the separatist tendencies of Vermont, whose application for statehood Congress had turned down because New York claimed part of her territory. As a pretext for continuing to occupy the frontier posts Great Britain cited the American failure to observe those clauses of the peace treaty concerning the repayment of prewar debts and the restoration of loyalist property. Congress had in fact urged the states to place no obstacle in the way of recovering prewar debts, most of them owed by Southern planters to British merchants; but the states had ignored the advice. They had likewise turned a deaf ear when Congress "earnestly recommended" the return of confiscated loyalist property. A government so obviously impotent at home could scarcely command respect abroad.

Thus John Adams, sent to London in 1785 with instructions to demand the evacuation of the frontier posts and to seek a commercial treaty, was disdainfully rebuffed.

Meanwhile Spain was displaying an equal hostility to American expansion. Strengthening her ties with Southwest Indians, she schemed to create an Indian buffer state to protect her own possessions. She even seized Natchez on the east bank of the Mississippi and closed the river itself to American navigation, thus depriving Western settlers of a vital outlet for their goods. Yet in 1786 John Jay, whom Congress had appointed Secretary for Foreign Affairs, initiated a treaty with Spain whereby, in return for limited access to Spanish markets, the United States agreed to give up for twenty-five years the right to use the Mississippi. As it happened the agreement fell through; with five Southern states opposed, the treaty could not be ratified by the required nine. But Westerners were furious at Jay's willingness to sacrifice their interests to those of Eastern merchants. They began to talk of setting up an independent Western republic under Spanish protection. Some of them, like General James Wilkinson, entered into secret negotiations with Spain and accepted Spanish pensions.

Vexing though the problems of the frontier and of diplomacy were, the weakness of the Confederation was most evident in finance. Lacking the power to levy taxes, Congress was dependent on the states' willingness to respond to requisitions. But the states, heavily in debt, were reluctant to part with what little specie they possessed or to contribute more than their neighbors. Between 1781 and 1786 only about one-sixth of the money requested was actually forthcoming. This was not sufficient to meet the interest on the public debt, let alone the principal, or to cover the ordinary expenses of the government. Bankruptcy was averted only through the dexterity of Robert Morris, the Superintendent of Finance, in raising fresh loans from Holland. But when efforts were made to amend the Articles so as to give Congress authority to levy a 5 percent duty on imports, the necessary unanimity proved unattainable. In 1782 Rhode Island refused to agree; the following year it was New York's turn to object. Little wonder that in 1784 Morris resigned in despair.

Equally menacing was the state of the currency. By the end of the war the paper issued by Congress—the so-called Continental currency—had depreciated so much that it had ceased to circulate. State paper, too, had declined sharply in value. Having emerged from the war encumbered with debts, the states imposed heavy taxes to pay them off. This brought loud cries for relief from debtors, mostly farmers, already suffering from post-war deflation. As in colonial days debtors demanded an increase in paper money. Of the seven states which acceded, Rhode Island went to the greatest lengths, not only making paper money legal tender but even compelling creditors to accept it. The value of Rhode Island paper depreciated abruptly and creditors fled the state to avoid having to accept it.

In nearby Massachusetts the demand for paper money was rejected. Instead the creditors controlling the government undertook to pay off the state debt by means of taxation. This meant a heavy burden on poor farmers, especially since taxes had to be paid in scarce specie. Many who failed to pay lost their land through mortgage foreclosure; some even went to jail. By the summer of 1786 western Massachusetts was burning with discontent. When the state legislature adjourned without heeding the farmers' demands for paper money and for stay laws suspending the foreclosure of mortgages for unpaid debts, riotous mobs roamed from place to place preventing the courts from hearing debt cases. By the autumn the malcontents had found a leader in Daniel Shays, a bankrupt farmer who had been a captain in the Revolutionary War. Shays led an armed band of 1,200 toward the federal arsenal at Springfield but by February 1787 the insurgents had been scattered by the state militia. Shays's rebellion was never a serious threat to the state government, but as well as inducing the Massachusetts legislature to make concessions to debtors, it alarmed conservatives throughout the country by conjuring up the specter of social revolution. In conjunction with the events in Rhode Island, Shays's rebellion gave a crucial impetus to the movement already under way to strengthen the power of the central government.

Dissatisfaction with the Articles of Confederation had begun to develop even before they had been ratified. Merchants and shipowners believed there could be no effective retaliation against British restrictions on American trade until Congress was given power to regulate commerce. Holders of depreciated bonds were aware of the advantages to themselves of a government which could establish national credit. Speculators in Western lands were anxious for a government capable of meeting the Indian threat, creditors wanted one which might put a stop to inflationary paper-money issues.

Emergent nationalism gave a further impetus to the movement for a stronger national government. American nationalism was, admittedly, still a young and tender plant. Patrick Henry's grandiloquent claim in 1774— "The distinctions between Virginians, Pennsylvanians, New Yorkers and New Englanders are no more . . ."—was far removed from reality. Local prejudices were largely unabated. Americans still tended to give their first loyalty to their states. They generally referred to the United States in the plural. Yet there were distinct signs of growing national awareness. The Revolution, besides mixing men from different states in the Continental Army and the Continental Congress, produced a rich crop of national heroes (George Washington, Patrick Henry, Samuel Adams, Thomas Jefferson) and of national shrines (Independence Hall, Bunker Hill, Mount

Vernon). National symbols and mottoes appeared in profusion. The Continental Congress adopted the Stars and Stripes as the national flag in 1777. (No one knows who designed it: the legend that it was the work of Betsy Ross was invented by her grandson in 1870.) The bald eagle took its place on the Great Seal of the United States in 1782, as well as on medals, patterns, and furniture--though Franklin, thinking the eagle "a bird of bad moral character" and often "very lousy", would have preferred the wild turkey. Then there was the national motto, *E pluribus unum* —from many, one—soon to become, along with the goddess Liberty, a permanent feature of the nation's coins.

That nationalism struck a responsive chord was clear from the immense vogue enjoyed by the textbooks of Noah Webster, later famous for his American dictionary. In 1783, with the object of establishing 'a national language', he brought out a spelling-book which stressed how American spelling and pronunciation had diverged from British forms. National spirit also permeated the arts, especially the work of the rather tedious literary group misnamed the 'Connecticut Wits'. Timothy Dwight, later president of Yale, glorified the nation in *The Conquest of Canaan* (1785), which he claimed as the first American epic poem. In similar vein was another epic, Joel Barlow's *Vision of Columbus* (1787). The painter, John Trumbull, commemorated the Revolutionary War in such works as *The Battle of Bunker's Hill* and *The Surrender of Lord Cornwallis at Yorktown*. Nationalism also inspired the small group of political leaders who led the movement for constitutional reform. Men like Alexander Hamilton, Robert Morris, John Jay, George Washington, and James Madison were mortified at the powerlessness of Congress. They shared Hamilton's feeling that there was "something . . . contemptible in the prospect of a number of petty states, with the appearance only of unity, jarring, jealous and perverse, . . . weak and insignificant in the eyes of other nations". Only the creation of a strong central government, they believed, could secure American independence, prosperity, and prestige.

The constitutional reformers even argued that the weakness of the Articles threatened impending disintegration and chaos. For a long time historians echoed this view, but it is now accepted that the 1780s were not a period of unrelieved gloom. The postwar slump did not last long. American merchants, freed from British mercantilist restrictions, discovered new markets in Continental Europe and the Far East. Agriculture was buoyant, manufacturing began to expand, and the first American banks were founded. Though immigration was limited the population increased by a third in a decade, reaching four millions by 1790. Nor was it fair to blame all the troubles of the period on the weakness of the central government. The depression of 1784–5 was due mainly to the overimportation of British manufactures and to the drain of specie following the departure of the British and French armies. Likewise it was not the form of government but the new nation's military and economic weakness that explained its inability to secure the withdrawal of foreign troops or win respect abroad.

But if critics of the Articles exaggerated the problems of the day, their complaints were well founded. In September 1786 representatives of five states, meeting in Annapolis, Maryland, to discuss commercial problems, proposed that a convention of all the states should be held in Philadelphia the following year "to devise such further provisions as shall appear to them necessary to render the constitution of the federal government adequate to the exigencies of the Union". Congress was not at first keen on the idea but after the shock of Shays's rebellion it called upon the states to send delegates to the convention "for the sole and express purpose of revising the Articles of Confederation".

The Federal Convention

The Federal Convention met in the Philadelphia State House from May 25 to September 17, 1787. Every state was represented except Rhode Island, which declined to participate. A total of fifty-five delegates attended, the average at each session being about thirty. It was a remarkably talented gathering, despite the absence of Thomas Jefferson and John Adams, then serving as envoys to France and Great Britain respectively. With an average age of forty-four the Founding Fathers were a relatively youthful group. Some had been officers in the Revolutionary War and a large majority had served in Congress or their state legislatures. Only six had signed the Declaration of Independence.

Having unanimously chosen Washington to preside, the delegates took two crucial decisions. First, they resolved to keep their deliberations secret, thus insulating the convention from outside pressures and encouraging frank discussion. Second, though empowered only to revise the Articles of Confederation, they decided to draw up an entirely new constitution.

Virtually all the delegates were agreed on the need to strengthen the central government. But there was little disposition to centralise power to the extent of abolishing state sovereignty altogether. Hamilton's proposal for a single, consolidated government got no support. There was general agreement, too, on the need for 'balanced government'. No one branch of government should be allowed to monopolize power, nor should government be exclusively controlled by a single economic interest. Likewise a balance must be struck between property and numbers. Concerned on the one hand lest a wealthy elite should oppress the mass of the people, the delegates were on the other hand distrustful of democracy. Hence while the people must have a voice in the government, some means must be found of limiting majority rule lest it lead to the plunder of the rich.

Despite a large measure of agreement on principles and, indeed, on the framework of government, there was no unanimity on details. Delegates differed, for example, on how the executive was to be elected, what powers he should possess, how long his term of office should be, whether the legislature should consist of one house or two. Representation was the most contentious issue. Should all the states be equally represented in the federal legislature, irrespective of size, as was the case under the Articles? Or should representation be based on population, an arrangement which would give Virginia, with 747,000 people, twelve times as many representatives as Delaware, which had only 60,000?

The convention's first step was to consider a draft constitution. Largely the work of James Madison and introduced by his fellow-Virginian, Edmund Randolph, the 'Virginia Plan' provided for a national legislature of two houses, in each of which representation was to be proportionate to population. The legislature was to have wide powers: it was to elect both the executive and the judiciary and to have a veto over state legislation infringing the constitution. Though congenial to the larger states the Virginia Plan was bitterly opposed by the smaller ones, as well as by delegates who objected to the amount of power concentrated in Congress. In an effort to ensure that the smaller states would not be overwhelmed, William Paterson of New Jersey presented an alternative scheme providing for a single legislative chamber, in which each state was to have one vote. The 'New Jersey Plan' envisaged merely the amendment of the Articles of Confederation. Though Congress was to be given enlarged powers, including authority to tax and to regulate commerce, state sovereignty would be largely preserved. Disagreement about representation threatened for a time to wreck the convention, but after a month's debate compromise was reached. It gave the states equal representation in the upper house (the Senate), while providing for proportional representation in the lower house (the House of Representatives).

The conflict between large states and small was largely unreal. That Virginia was large and Maryland small mattered less than that they shared a common plantation economy based on slave-labor. State rivalries were less significant in fact than the clash of economic regions or sections, especially North and South. One sectional issue arose out of the decision to apportion seats in the House of Representatives according to population. The Southern states wanted slaves to be included in the population total when allotting Congressional seats but left out in determining liability for direct taxation. The Northern states wanted slaves excluded from representation, since they were neither citizens nor voters, but included for tax purposes since they were a species of property. The result was a second compromise, the 'three-fifths' clause, whereby a slave was counted as three-fifths of a person for the purposes of both representation and direct taxation.

A more divisive sectional issue was the proposed federal regulation of commerce. The South, dependent upon the export of staples, feared that this power might be used to tax exports. It was also concerned at the possibility of federal interference with the slave-trade. To allay such fears Congress was to be forbidden to levy export taxes or to abolish the slave-trade for at least twenty years. As a further sop to the South the consent of two-thirds of the Senate would be needed to ratify treaties—most being then of a commercial nature.

No agreement could be reached on some matters—the precise role of the proposed national judiciary, for example. Hence the delegates took refuge in evasion. It recognized, as Madison put it, that ambiguity was the price of unanimity. But once the major clashes had been resolved the task of drafting went rapidly ahead. In its final form the Constitution was a substantially modified version of the Virginia Plan. Like the government of the Confederation, the federal government was authorized to maintain an army and navy, coin and borrow money, and make treaties with foreign powers. But it was given some additional powers, notably to levy taxes and to regulate commerce. Moreover, in the famous 'elastic clause' Congress was authorized to "make all laws which shall be necessary and proper" for executing its powers. The states were deprived of some powers they had hitherto exercised: they were not to issue money, make treaties, or pass laws, such as stay laws, "impairing the obligation of contract". The Constitution and all laws and treaties made under it were declared to be the supreme law of the land, superior to any state law. Thus the federal government would no longer depend on the goodwill of the states: it could act directly, through its own officers, upon individual citizens. Its executive authority would be exercised by a single person, the President, though the Senate was to be associated with him in making important appointments and in concluding treaties. The President was to be Commander-in-Chief of the army and navy. He could veto acts of Congress, unless overridden by a two-thirds vote of both houses, and he could be removed from office only on impeachment for and conviction of "high crimes and misdemeanors". Finally, amendment of the Constitution, though still difficult, was made easier than it had been under the Confederation.

While ensuring that the will of the people would ultimately prevail, the Founding Fathers sought to check and delay its operation. Hence a variety of election processes were adopted. Members of the House were to be elected directly by the voters for periods of two years, voting qualifications being decided by the states. Senators were to be elected indirectly, by the state legislatures, for periods of six years. The President, who was to have a four-year term, was to be elected still more indirectly by a cumbrously chosen electoral college. Standing at the apex of the constitutional structure he would, it was believed, be least susceptible to popular influence. Along with this complicated system of elections went a careful division of authority—between executive, legislature, and judiciary—which reflected the convention's faith in the separation of powers theory. But the Constitution's most distinctive feature was its novel and ingenious division of sovereignty between two governments, state and federal. Fully sovereign within its own sphere, each was to operate directly upon the same political community. However, no attempt was made in the Constitution to chart the boundary between state and federal power or to decide how conflicts of jurisdiction were to be resolved. These questions would provide the staple of constitutional debate for decades to come and were not to be finally settled until the Civil War.

The Founding Fathers may not have been what Jefferson called them, "an assembly of demigods", but their wisdom, good sense, and political realism are evident from the fact that the Constitution has stood the test of time. With relatively little amendment a document devised two hundred years ago for a small, rural republic is still the fundamental law for an industrial world power. The Federal Constitution, the oldest functioning written constitution in the world, has not operated in practice exactly as expected. Some of its provisions, like the electoral-college procedure for electing the President, have become meaningless. Others, like those giving the House control over money-bills, have not proved entirely effective. Others again, like the provision that treaties require the approval of two-thirds of the Senate, have handicapped the formulation and execution of a coherent foreign policy. Then, too, the Constitution has sometimes been an obstacle to much-needed change. Yet it is not difficult to see why it should have been so venerated by Americans and so admired by others. Despite its brevity—it is only 6,000 words long—it is a model of draftsmanship: "a judicious mixture", as James Bryce remarked, "of definiteness in principles with elasticity in details". Its flexibility has been vital to its success. The Founding Fathers did not make the mistake of trying to cover every possible contingency. As one historian has remarked, they drew up a sketch, not a blueprint. That has enabled successive generations to reinterpret the Constitution in accordance with changing circumstances.

The Ratification Debate

Even after the convention had finished its work the states had still to accept it. Although the Articles of Confederation stipulated that amendments required approval by all thirteen states, the convention knew unanimity to be unattainable, and decided that the new document would become operative when ratified by only nine. Moreover, the delegates boldly bypassed the state legislatures, recommending instead that the Constitution be submitted to specially elected state conventions. Such a procedure would confer on the Constitution a status which the constitutions of all but one of the states (Massachusetts) lacked, namely, that of being based directly on popular consent.

In the struggle over ratification the friends of the Constitution—Federalists, they somewhat misleadingly called themselves—were most strongly supported by men of property and position: planters, well-to-do farmers, merchants, lawyers. Many of their Anti-Federalist opponents were small farmers, especially if they were debtors. But as with later American political contests, opinion did not divide neatly along lines of class or economic interest. Many wealthy men, like the great landowners of the Hudson Valley, were against the Constitution; many poor men, like the laborers, artisans, and tradesmen of the cities, were for it.

.The support of the two most famous men in America, Washington and Franklin, added luster to the Federalist cause; that of Madison, Hamilton, and Jay provided it with energetic political leadership. There were also men of ability on the other side: Patrick Henry, Richard Henry Lee, and George Mason of Virginia, Samuel Adams of Massachusetts, George Clinton of New York. But the Federalists possessed the initiative and had the advantage of a positive program. They were also superior in political management and in presenting their case. Even so, the opponents of ratification mounted a formidable attack. As well as claiming that the new Constitution was illegal and that there was no need to abandon the Articles of Confederation, they raised a host of specific objections, all reflecting a suspicion of centralized power: the federal government's new taxing power was potentially oppressive, the President would have too much authority and might in practice hold office for life, the Supreme Court would become an agent of federal aggrandizement, the House of Representatives (initially having only sixty-five members) would be too small to represent adequately the varied interests of so large a country. But what the Anti-Federalists objected to most was that the Constitution lacked a Bill of Rights guaranteeing popular liberties.

In some states ratification was easily achieved. Of the first five states to ratify, Delaware, New Jersey, and Georgia did so unanimously, Pennsylvania approved by a comfortable margin (43–26), and Connecticut by an overwhelming one (128–40). But in Massachusetts there was a long and spirited contest, ending in a narrow victory for the Federalists by 187 votes to 168. Maryland (63–11) and South Carolina (149–73) then fell into line and in June 1788 New Hampshire (57–47) became the ninth state to ratify. Technically the Constitution could now go into force, but without Virginia and New York it could hardly succeed. In both states the outcome was very uncertain. In Virginia, the largest and most populous state, the opposing forces were evenly balanced. Patrick Henry's eloquent attacks on the Constitution, ably seconded by Richard Henry Lee's *Letters from a Federal Farmer*, had a profound effect. But Madison's reasoned advocacy and his promise to work for amendments to the Constitution, including a Bill of Rights, turned the tide. On June 25, 1788 the Virginia convention ratified by 89 votes to 79. When the New York convention met the Anti-Federalists were thought to be in a majority. But Hamilton, for all his reservations about the Constitution, spoke "frequently, very long and vehemently" in its defense. He, Madison, and Jay, using the joint pseudonym, Publius, wrote a series of eighty-five articles for the New York press expounding and urging the adoption of the Constitution. These essays, subsequently published as the *Federalist Papers*, came to be regarded as a classic of American political thought. But they do not appear to have had a great influence on contemporary opinion. More important in softening the intransigence of the New York Anti-Federalists were Virginia's decision to ratify and the fear, sedulously cultivated by Hamilton, that New York City would secede if the state rejected the Constitution. On July 25, 1788 the New York convention approved ratification by the narrow margin of 30 to 27. North Carolina and Rhode Island still stood sulkily aloof. But the new government could now begin to function. As its last act the Congress of the Confederation ordered national elections for January 1789.

5. *The Federalist Age*, 1789–1801

The Constitution of 1787 stipulated that an official census was to be taken every ten years. The first was carried out in 1790. It revealed that the United States had a population of just under four millions. Roughly half lived in the six states south of the Mason–Dixon line—the boundary between Pennsylvania and Maryland—while the remaining half was divided almost equally between the three Middle states and the four states of New England. Included in the total were just over 750,000 blacks, all but 60,000 of them slaves; they were heavily concentrated in the Southern states, where they constituted three-eighths of the population. In the country as a whole one person in eight had been born abroad, but in cosmopolitan Pennsylvania the proportion was one in three. Virginia was easily the most populous state: with a total of 747,610 it had nearly twice as many people as its nearest rival, Pennsylvania. At the other extreme lay Rhode Island, with 68,825. The census showed the country to be still overwhelmingly rural; a mere 3.3 percent of the population lived in places of 8,000 inhabitants or more. In contrast to the large surplus of males which had characterized the population for most of the seventeenth century, the sexes were fairly evenly balanced. Finally, the population was extraordinarily youthful: about half were under sixteen.

Organizing the Federal Government

The election of 1789, the first under the Constitution, gave the Federalists control of the new government. There were large Federalist majorities in both the Senate and the House of Representatives: indeed, the bulk of those elected had been supporters of the Constitution in the Federal Convention or the state ratifying conventions. The election also resulted, as the Constitution-makers had anticipated, in the choice of George Washington as the first President. Though unanimously elected, Washington left Mount Vernon to take up his new responsibilities with the greatest reluctance, declaring that he felt like a condemned man going to the place of his execution. Washington's apprehensions were understandable. The nation he had been called upon to preside over was weak and far from united; it had an experimental form of government and an untried Constitution; burdened with debt, it was open to Indian raids and hemmed in by the empires of two great European powers. British and Spanish troops indeed still occupied parts of the national territory; the United States had no navy and its army consisted of 840 officers and men. But Washington was never one to ignore the call of duty. On April 30, 1789 he took the oath of office in New York City, the temporary seat of the federal government.

Believing that a strong executive was indispensable to the new government's success, Washington set out to invest the office of president with an aura of dignity like that surrounding European monarchies. The task was made easier by his own austere personality and his awareness of the symbolic significance of forms and ceremonies. He rode in a yellow chariot decorated with gilded nymphs and cherubs and emblazoned with his own coat of arms. His wife's weekly levees were stiff with formality: Washington would gravely bow to those present but not shake hands. Soon after convening, the first Congress spent a month discussing a proper title for the President. Vice-President John Adams, and probably Washington himself, favored some high-sounding designation like "His Highness the President of the United States and Protector of their Liberties". But Congress, thinking that too monarchical, settled for the republican simplicity of "President of the United States".

The newly ratified Constitution had provided only a general framework of government. The work of filling in gaps and clarifying ambiguities remained. In assuming this task the Federalists set a number of precedents which permanently influenced American constitutional development— sometimes in directions the Founding Fathers had not foreseen.

During the debate over the Constitution there had been much criticism of the lack of specific guarantees of popular rights. In some state conventions the Federalists had virtually had to promise to remedy the omission in order to secure ratification. Thus the first Congress adopted and submitted to the states ten constitutional amendments known as the Bill of Rights. They were duly ratified and went into force in December 1791. They went far towards reconciling Anti-Federalists to the Constitution. Nine of the amendments were concerned with the rights of the individual. They guaranteed freedom of religion, of speech, of assembly, and of the press, the right to petition and to bear arms, and immunity against arbitrary search and arrest. They also prohibited excessive bail, cruel and unusual punishments, and the quartering of troops in private houses. The tenth amendment reserved to the states all powers except those specifically delegated to the federal government.

Another necessity was to implement the rather vaguely worded clause of the Constitution authorizing a national judiciary. The Judiciary Act of 1789 established a hierarchical system of federal courts. At the top the Supreme Court of the United States was to consist of a Chief Justice and five associate justices; beneath it there were to be three circuit courts (presided over by two Supreme Court Justices and a district judge) and thirteen district courts. The Act also provided that the Supreme Court should rule on the constitutionality of state court decisions and nullify state laws which violated the Federal Constitution. Looking back, one can see the first meeting of the Supreme Court, on February 2, 1790, was a milestone in the history of jurisprudence. Yet Washington had difficulty in appointing men of distinction to so seemingly inconsequential a body.

Among the questions the Constitution had not tried to answer in detail was that of the relationship between the executive and the legislature. But the members of the Constitutional convention had evidently intended that the Senate (which initially had only twenty-two members) should function as the President's advisory council. Thus the Constitution had provided that the President was to appoint high officials and make treaties "by and with the advice and consent of the Senate". But when Washington appeared before the Senate to seek advice about a draft Indian treaty, senators refused to discuss the matter in his presence. Thereafter it became the practice for treaties to be submitted to the Senate after, and not before, they had been negotiated.

Since the Senate had insisted upon its independence Washington was forced to look elsewhere for advice. At first he relied heavily on James Madison, then a member of the House of Representatives. It was Madison who wrote most of Washington's inaugural address—and the Congressional reply to it—, drafted the Bill of Rights, and introduced the new government's first revenue bill. But Madison's dominance ended once Congress created executive departments. The State, Treasury, and War Departments were established in the autumn of 1789, along with the offices of Attorney General and Postmaster General. There was some suggestion of making the heads of executive departments responsible to Congress; had that happened something like the emerging British parliamentary system could have developed. But Madison, concerned for executive independence, ensured that the heads were made responsible to the President alone. As Secretary to the Treasury Washington chose his wartime secretary and aide-de-camp, Alexander Hamilton, who, in helping to organize the Bank of New York, had acquired a knowledge of public finance. Thomas Jefferson became Secretary of State: he was at that time minister to France and did not take up his new appointment until March 1790. At first it was Washington's practice to consult his official family individually on matters of policy. But by the end of his second term the department heads had evolved into the Cabinet, a body not mentioned in the Constitution. They met regularly, cast votes, and arrived at some kind of collective decision.

Hamilton's Financial Program

That Hamilton became the main driving force of the administration was due to a combination of factors: his own energy and ambition, Washington's conviction that it was not the function of the President to initiate legislation, Jefferson's belated return to the domestic scene, the crucial importance of finance, the fact that the Secretary of the Treasury occupied a special place among executive heads in that he was required to report direct to Congress. Hamilton was born in the West Indies in 1755, the illegitimate son of a Scottish father and a French Huguenot mother. Sent to New York as a boy he threw himself into the patriot cause while still a student at King's College (later Columbia) and went on to become a brilliant staff officer in the Revolutionary War. Afterward the thrusting young adventurer married into a great Hudson Valley 'patroon' family, the Schuylers, opened a law office in New York, and became one of the leaders of the movement for a stronger central government. Hamilton's was a many-sided personality. Charming, articulate, witty, extraordinarily able and honest (though he had a number of unethical friends), he could also be vain, petty, obstinate, and combative. Despite his meteoric rise, he was never wholly at home in his adopted country. Contemptuous of democracy, he revered wealth and believed that government was the preserve of "the rich and the well-born". Convinced also that men were governed by "ambition and interest", the main purpose of his financial policies—apart of course from the restoration of national credit—was to bind the moneyed classes to the new government.

Hamilton's financial program was set forth in a series of reports in 1790 and 1791 dealing, respectively, with public credit, a national bank, and manufactures. In his report on public credit (January 1790) Hamilton recommended, first, the funding at par of the entire domestic and foreign debt incurred by the government of the Confederation and amounting to about $56 million; second, federal assumption of the Revolutionary debts of the states, totaling some $21 million. There was virtually no opposition to the repayment of the foreign debt at face value rather than at the depreciated market-rate; such a step was obviously essential to the new government's financial standing. But the proposal to do the same for the domestic debt was bitterly attacked, especially by Southerners. Nearly all the debt was held by speculators, mostly Northern, who had bought at a steep discount when hard times had compelled the original creditors to sell. Protesting that the measure would enrich a tiny minority at the public expense Madison suggested an alternative plan which discriminated between the original holders and subsequent purchasers. Nevertheless Hamilton's measure was carried.

There was even heavier opposition, much of it sectional, to Hamilton's state debt assumption scheme. The Southern states, except for South Carolina, had provided for the repayment of their debts and objected to paying a share of the large debts owed by Massachusetts and other New England states. They also feared that assumption would expand federal power at the expense of the states. Madison, now an open opponent of the Administration, persuaded Congress in April 1790 to reject the proposal. But by August a series of political bargains with Madison and Jefferson had enabled Hamilton to reverse the verdict. In exchange for Southern votes for assumption he promised to make generous allowances to states that had already settled most of their debts and also agreed that the permanent national capital would be in the South. After a decade in Philadelphia, the seat of government would be moved to a site on the Potomac river to be chosen by President Washington.

Hamilton's next objective was the creation of a national bank. Modeled on the Bank of England, the proposed Bank of the United States would have a capital of $10 million, one-fifth to be subscribed by the government, and would serve a variety of purposes: it would act as a depository for government funds, facilitate the collection of taxes, stimulate commerce and industry—though, significantly, not agriculture—by means of loans, issue paper money, and curb excessive note issues by state banks. When the bill to charter the bank came before Congress Madison raised constitutional objections. The Constitution, he insisted, had not specifically conferred upon Congress the power to charter companies; therefore, no such power existed. Congress in fact passed the bill but when it went to Washington for signature, he had been sufficiently disturbed by Madison's arguments to consult both Jefferson and Hamilton on the constitutional question. Jefferson supported Madison, arguing for a strict construction of the Constitution and contending that Congress should be allowed no powers not expressly delegated to it. In reply Hamilton advanced the doctrine of "implied powers": though a central bank had not been authorized in so many words it was the "necessary and proper" means of exercising such explicitly granted Constitutional powers as the levying of taxes and the regulation of currency and of trade. Washington, though not wholly persuaded by Hamilton's broad constructionism, nonetheless signed the bill into law. The Bank of the United States, with a charter for twenty years, opened for business in Philadelphia in December 1791.

The last of Hamilton's state papers, the Report on Manufactures (December 1791), revealed him at his most brilliant and his most visionary. It laid down a comprehensive plan for industrialization through a system of protective tariffs, bounties, and subsidies. The aim was to bind the country together economically and make it self-sufficient. But Congress, lacking Hamilton's soaring imagination, was not ready for such bold economic planning. The Report was shelved and although Congress passed a new tariff act in 1792 it was for revenue rather than for protection.

To meet the heavy cost of his funding program and of debt assumption Hamilton needed to find more revenue than import duties would yield. Hence he proposed an excise law, among its provisions a tax on distilled liquor. The measure, passed by Congress in March 1791, bore heavily on frontier farmers. Lacking adequate transport facilities they found it difficult to dispose of their surplus corn and rye until its bulk was reduced by distillation into whiskey. In western Pennsylvania discontent with the excise boiled over in 1794 into armed resistance. Mobs terrorized federal agents and prevented the courts from functioning. At Hamilton's urging Washington called out the militia of three states. A force of 13,000 men was sent to the troubled area and rapidly suppressed the so-called Whiskey Insurrection. The new government thus showed that, unlike the Confederation, it had the power to compel obedience to its laws.

Hamilton's financial program restored public credit and ensured the success of the new government. But far from cementing the Union, as he had hoped, it served to sharpen divisions, and to give them political form. The men who made the Constitution had seen political parties as self-seeking, venal, and disruptive and had hoped that the United States would be spared them. That parties nevertheless soon arose was due to the violent conflicts engendered by the Hamiltonian system. Hamilton's blatant appeal to Northern commercial elements aroused sectional jealousies in the South and West and alienated debtors everywhere. His efforts to centralize power in the federal government provoked fears of tyranny. His admiration for the British form of government fed suspicions that he planned to reintroduce monarchy. His role in the Whiskey Rebellion conjured up the specters of a standing army and military dictatorship.

It was around Madison that opposition to Hamilton had at first centered. But once Jefferson had become convinced, as he had by 1791, that Hamilton's principles were "adverse to liberty", it was to the Secretary of State that the Republicans—as the anti-Hamiltonians were now calling themselves—looked mainly for leadership. Ideologically Hamilton and Jefferson were not as far apart as later party tradition—and most historians—would have us believe. But there is no disputing that they had sharply different visions of the American future: while Hamilton favored industrialization and hoped for a stratified society on the English model, Jefferson believed in a republic of sturdy, independent farmers. Nor can it be denied that their differences became increasingly bitter and increasingly personal. Though remaining Cabinet colleagues—at least until Jefferson resigned in December 1793—each sought to undermine the other and organize a following in Congress and in the country. To counter the influence of John Fenno, editor of the Hamiltonian *United States Gazette*, Jefferson brought the poet Philip Freneau to Philadelphia to edit a rival newspaper, the *National Gazette*. Then in the course of a "botanizing expedition" up the Hudson in the summer of 1791 Jefferson and Madison came to an understanding with some of Hamilton's political rivals in New York: Governor George Clinton, Robert R. Livingston, and Aaron Burr. Despite the forging of the New York–Virginia alliance the Republicans were not yet a national party in the modern sense; nor for that matter were their Federalist opponents. But in the election of 1792, in which Washington was again unopposed, the Republicans were sufficiently well organized to nominate Clinton as their vice-presidential candidate. He received 50 electoral votes to Adams's 77.

Foreign Affairs

During Washington's second Administration problems arising from the French Revolution and the outbreak of war in Europe sharpened party differences. The outbreak of the French Revolution had met with general approval in the United States but the execution of Louis XVI and the Jacobin reign of terror polarized public sentiment. Federalists interpreted events in France as confirming their belief that popular government tended to degenerate into mob rule. Republicans on the other hand continued to sympathize with the revolutionists, holding with Jefferson that "the tree of liberty must be refreshed from time to time with the blood of patriots and tyrants". France's declaration of war on Great Britain in February 1793 exacerbated the conflict of opinion. Hamilton and his followers regarded Great Britain as a bulwark of order, property, and religion, but Jefferson, viewing her rather as an enemy of freedom, was willing to see "half the earth devastated" to ensure the "liberty of the whole".

The European war also raised the question of American obligations to France. Under the 1778 treaty of alliance the United States was bound in case of war to help defend the French West Indies. But when Washington referred the matter to his Cabinet, Hamilton contended that the overthrow of the French monarchy had automatically invalidated the treaty. The Secretary of the Treasury was determined on neutrality not only because of his pro-British sympathies but also because British imports were the chief source of the tariff revenues on which his financial program depended. Jefferson did not want war either but argued that if the United States were to dishonor its treaty obligations, then the British should make compensatory concessions. He also believed that authority to proclaim neutrality rested solely with Congress. But Washington, yet again following Hamilton's advice, issued a presidential proclamation of neutrality (April 1793).

Meanwhile Anglo-American relations were being inflamed by happenings along the western frontier and on the high seas. Americans were incensed that the British had not kept their 1783 peace-treaty undertaking to relinquish their military posts south of the Great Lakes. No less galling to them was Great Britain's disregard of the maritime rights of neutrals. American commerce had derived a great impetus from the wartime needs of the belligerents and especially from France's decision to open trade with her West Indian colonies to neutrals. But Great Britain, unwilling to countenance such an obvious attempt to evade her blockade, issued an Order in Council in November 1793, invoking the "rule of 1756" which held that a trade illegal in peacetime remained illegal in time of war. The enforcement of this order resulted in the seizure of some 250 American vessels carrying goods from the French West Indies to France and the imprisonment of their crews.

The seizures provoked an angry American reaction and by the spring of 1794 the United States and Great Britain were close to war. But Washington, conscious that peace was the young republic's paramount need, decided to send Chief Justice John Jay to London to try to negotiate a settlement. But the British were in uncompromising mood, partly because Hamilton had secretly informed them that the United States would not join a projected League of Armed Neutrality. Jay's Treaty, signed in November 1794, fell far short of what he had been instructed to demand. The one significant British concession was a promise—this time kept—to evacuate the Northwest posts by 1796. The British also agreed to submit American claims for compensation for ship seizure to arbitration and granted American commerce limited access to the British West Indies. But in return Jay had to agree to refer the pre-Revolutionary debts and northeast boundary questions to mixed commissions. He failed to secure either the hoped-for commercial treaty or compensation for the slaves the British had carried off in 1783. Above all, he was forced tacitly to accept the British position on neutral rights at sea.

Jay's Treaty produced an uproar in the United States. Jay was burned in effigy and there were demands for his impeachment. Republicans denounced the agreement as a base surrender, Southerners objecting particularly to the provisions about prewar debts (most of the debtors were Virginia planters). Even Federalists were troubled by some of the Treaty's provisions. Only after long debate and by the narrowest of margins did the Senate ratify the document. Washington hesitated for two months before signing it, but finally did so because he could see no alternative but war.

By creating the impression that the British and the Americans were drawing closer together and might be contemplating joint action against Louisiana, Jay's Treaty induced the Spanish government to soften its attitude toward the United States. Thomas Pinckney, sent to Madrid as a special envoy, was able in October 1795 to conclude a treaty which granted the United States free use of the Mississippi and the right to deposit goods in New Orleans. Spain also accepted the American claim to the 31st parallel as the Florida boundary and promised to restrain the Indians from attacking frontier settlements. Pinckney's Treaty put an end to a decade of Spanish intrigue and Western secessionist plots: a separate Western confederacy under Spanish protection lost its point once the Mississippi had been opened to American trade.

Worn out by the burdens of the Presidency and hurt by the partisan abuse heaped upon him for his endorsement of Jay's Treaty, Washington declined to stand for reelection in 1796. His decision established a two-term presidential tradition that all his successors except Franklin D. Roosevelt were to follow. On leaving public life Washington issued a Farewell Address. On the one hand he advised Americans to "steer clear of permanent alliances with foreign nations"; on the other he warned them against "the baneful effects of the spirit of party", especially party divisions along geographical lines.

The Rise of Political Parties

The party strife Washington deprecated was made more intense by his retirement. In 1796 the Presidency became for the first time a party question. The Republicans chose Jefferson as their candidate. The Federalists, torn by factional rivalries, finally settled on John Adams. Hamilton, who disliked Adams's moderation as well as his independence, hoped to manipulate the electoral machinery so as to throw the Presidency to the Federalist vice-presidential candidate, Thomas Pinckney. As the Constitution did not then require separate balloting for President and Vice-President, each elector simply cast two votes, without specifying which candidate he favored for President. The candidate with the highest electoral vote (provided it was a majority of the total number of electors), would be President and the runner-up Vice-President. Hamilton hoped that a number of Southern Republicans, whose first votes would go to Jefferson, might be persuaded to make another Southerner, Pinckney, their second choice. But some of Adams's supporters got wind of the scheme and withheld their second ballots from Pinckney. Thus Adams with 71 electoral votes became President, but the Vice-Presidency went to Jefferson whose 68 electoral votes exceeded those of Pinckney. It was the only occasion in American history that candidates of different parties were elected President and Vice-President. Beside demonstrating the deficiencies of the electoral system the result also showed how well founded were Washington's fears of geographical divisions. Adams's electoral votes came almost entirely from the states north of Pennsylvania; Jefferson carried nearly all the South plus the two new Western states, Kentucky and Tennessee. It was ironic that New England, earlier the most democratic part of America, should have become the chief stronghold of Federalism, whereas Virginia, where society had been—and, indeed, still was—more stratified, became the most Republican.

The two parties were not, however, completely sectional. If Federalism drew its main support from New England and to a lesser extent from the Middle States, it was not without adherents in the South, especially Virginia and South Carolina. Conversely, while Republicanism had a distinct Southern and Western tinge, there were sizable Republican minorities in the North, especially in New York and even by 1800 in New England. Nor did the parties divide along strict socio-economic lines. By and large, merchants, bankers, shipowners, and manufacturers were Federalist, while farmers and planters were Republican. But with farmers making up about 90 percent of the population, the commercial and manufacturing classes were too few to account for all the votes Federalist candidates received. In fact both parties had a distinct farming constituency. How they were composed is not altogether clear, but it has been suggested that while small-scale farmers tended to support the Republicans, large commercial farmers whose crops were produced for the market were generally Federalist. Contemporaries, of whatever shade of opinion, were apt to believe that people of the "better sort" were Federalist, those of the "meaner sort" Jeffersonian. Voting returns lend support to this theory, though there was wealth on both sides, even if Federalist wealth was usually older. Certainly the Federalists were not wholly a gentlemen's party. The Federalist candidates for the New York legislature in 1800 included a baker, a porter, a bankrupt, and a mason. Many urban artisans customarily voted Federalist—at least until 1800. Northern free blacks, too, had strong Federalist sympathies, not surprisingly given the slave-holding leadership of the Republican party and the fact that prominent Federalists like Hamilton and Jay had taken the lead in demanding the abolition of slavery.

A variety of factors influenced partisan allegiance. State rivalries and local attachments were important: so were family conflicts. There were some who voted Federalist out of veneration for George Washington, others who simply followed the lead of a local magnate. Religion also played a great part. Congregationalists were overwhelmingly Federalist: Episcopalians and Quakers hardly less so. Baptists, Methodists, and Presbyterians, on the other hand, tended toward Republicanism. No one of these factors explains, however, why people voted as they did: each interacted with and qualified the others.

The Adams Administration

Of all the Founding Fathers John Adams was the most original political thinker. Temperamentally conservative, he was distrustful of democracy. In his political writings he had argued that the best form of government was one in which a strong executive held the balance between two legislative chambers representing the rich and the poor respectively. By the time he became President Adams had accumulated a varied experience of politics and diplomacy. He had been a leader of the Revolutionary movement in Massachusetts and was the author of the much-admired Massachusetts Constitution of 1780. He helped negotiate the peace treaty of 1783 and, by the time he returned to the United States in 1788 to become Washington's Vice-President, he had represented the young republic successively in France, Holland, and England.

Able, courageous, and honest, Adams nevertheless lacked political skill, particularly of the kind that the recent emergence of parties necessitated. Sharing Washington's dislike of party spirit, he could not perceive that the strong executive he favored would be impossible unless the President was the undisputed party leader. Adams thus made the mistake of retaining Washington's Cabinet, most of whose members acknowledged Hamilton as their leader and continued to look to him for advice. Even out of office—he left the Treasury in January 1795 to return to his New York law practice—Hamilton was the real power behind Adams's Administration. And although the President soon became aware of the intrigues against him he was slow to exert his authority or build up a following of his own.

The most urgent problem facing Adams's Administration was the deterioration of relations with France. The United States, so the French thought, by tacitly accepting the British view of neutral rights in Jay's Treaty had virtually become Great Britain's ally. The Directory, now in power in Paris, retaliated by refusing to receive the newly appointed American minister, Charles Cotesworth Pinckney, and by ordering the seizure of American vessels carrying British cargoes. By June 1797 more than three hundred American merchantmen had been captured. In an attempt to avert war Adams sent a special mission to France. But when it reached Paris it was greeted by three of Talleyrand's subordinates (later identified in the envoys' dispatches only as X, Y, and Z) with the news that before negotiations could begin the United States must pay a bribe of $250,000 to French officials and agree to lend France $12 million.

Though bribery was commonplace in eighteenth-century diplomacy Adams was outraged at the humiliating treatment of the commissioners. So was the country when Adams submitted the XYZ correspondence to Congress in March 1798. With war fever mounting even among Republicans, Congress abrogated the 1778 treaty of alliance with France, created a Navy Department, and voted funds for the expansion of the army and navy. Washington was appointed commanding general of the newly enlarged army, but accepted only on condition that Hamilton was made second in command and given effective control until war actually began. Formally, that never happened. But between 1798 and 1800 the United States and France fought a limited and undeclared naval war. The infant

United States navy more than held its own in a series of single-ship engagements and captured more than eighty French privateers.

War hysteria gave the Federalists an opportunity to strike both at foreign influence and at their domestic opponents. They were incensed by the fact that many recent political refugees—French Jacobins, Irish rebels, English and Welsh radicals—had become outspoken supporters of the Republican party. Hence in the summer of 1798 they rushed through a series of measures known collectively as the Alien and Sedition Acts. The Naturalization Act, designed to deprive the Republicans of immigrant votes, lengthened the residential requirement for citizenship from five years to fourteen. An Alien Act, passed in the belief that the country was swarming with foreign spies, gave the president power to deport any alien whom he deemed "dangerous to the peace and safety of the United States". Most repressive of all was the Sedition Act, intended to silence not only the "pack of imported scribblers" who had lent their pens to the Republicans, but native-born dissenters as well; it prescribed heavy fines and imprisonment for persons convicted of publishing "any false, scandalous or malicious writing" bringing into disrepute the government, Congress, or the president of the United States. To his credit Adams did not enforce the Alien Act, though fear of its provisions led several shiploads of foreigners to depart. But under the Sedition Act some twenty-five persons were arrested, including some prominent Republican editors, and ten were convicted.

Republicans denounced the Alien and Sedition Acts as arbitrary extensions of federal power and violations of the Bill of Rights. In 1798–9 the legislatures of Virginia and Kentucky adopted protest resolutions drafted respectively by Madison and Jefferson. Maintaining that the Alien and Sedition Acts were unconstitutional, the Virginia and Kentucky resolutions invoked the theory that the Constitution was a compact among the states which had delegated certain specified powers to the federal government, while retaining ultimate sovereignty. They went on to assert the right of a state to judge when infractions of the Constitution had occurred and to nullify those acts it deemed unconstitutional. Both Virginia and Kentucky, however, affirmed their attachment to the Union and took no steps to obstruct the execution of the offending Acts.

Meanwhile the High Federalist faction dominated by Hamilton was eager for an outright declaration of war on France. Such a step, it believed, would unite the country behind their leadership, while strengthening the central government. It might also open the way to foreign adventure. Hamilton, dreaming of emulating his hero, Julius Caesar, saw himself leading an expedition to seize Louisiana and the Floridas from Spain, France's ally, and then with British help going on to liberate South America. But Adams still hoped for a peaceful solution. He disliked the militarism that had infected his party and suspected Hamilton of aspiring to the role of "man on horseback". Early in 1799, therefore, in response to overtures from Talleyrand, he decided to reopen negotiations with France. When Adams's commissioners arrived in France they found Napoleon, now First Consul, in a conciliatory mood. The resulting treaty, commonly known as the Convention of 1800, settled the outstanding differences between the two countries and formally released the United States from the 1778 defensive alliance with France.

The Election of 1800

Adams's insistence on peace created a rift within his party. It was widened by his handling of Fries's "insurrection" of 1799. When a group of Pennsylvania farmers led by Captain John Fries rioted in protest against the direct federal property tax levied in 1798 in anticipation of war with France, Adams used troops to restore order but, in the eyes of the High Federalists, displayed weakness in pardoning Fries upon his conviction for treason. Finally in the spring of 1800 the schism in the Federalist party could no longer be concealed when the President, belatedly meeting intrigue with firmness, dismissed two leading Hamiltonians from his Cabinet: Secretary of State Timothy Pickering and Secretary of War James McHenry. When Adams ran for reelection in 1800 almost none of the Federalist leaders stood by him. Hamilton wrote a pamphlet declaring Adams unfit to be President and, adopting the same tactic as in 1796, hoped to defeat him by throwing support to the Federalist vice-presidential candidate, Charles Cotesworth Pinckney. The Republicans again nominated Jefferson and Aaron Burr. A vituperative campaign followed. The Republicans made much of the Alien and Sedition Acts and condemned the heavy taxes imposed to pay for the expansion of the army and navy. They also accused Adams of monarchical tendencies. The Federalists, for their part, depicted Jefferson as a Jacobin, an atheist, and a libertine. The result of the election was a narrow Republican victory: Jefferson and Burr each had 73 electoral votes, Adams 65, and Pinckney 64. Adams's defeat originated in his refusal to subordinate national interests to party ends. Perceiving that peace was essential to the security and stability of the young republic, he withstood the belligerent clamor of important elements in his own party. Yet by alienating them he sacrificed his chances of reelection. Next to the split in the Federalist ranks, the key factor was superior Republican organization and electioneering. While their opponents had remained a relatively loose association of like-minded amateurs who still equated party with faction and made little attempt to woo popular support, the Jeffersonians had been building a permanent, efficient, tightly disciplined national machine, holding popular meetings, collecting campaign funds, founding party newspapers. In New York especially they worked tirelessly to get every qualified voter to the polls—and New York's electoral votes proved crucial.

Though Adams had clearly been defeated, the identity of the next President remained in doubt for some time. Everyone knew that Jefferson was the Republican choice for President, but he and Burr had received the same number of electoral votes. The Constitution provided that in the event of a tie the choice devolved on the House of Representatives, with each state delegation casting a single vote. Since the Federalists were in a majority in the House, the decision would be up to them. Ballot after ballot was taken in the winter of 1800–1 without result. Some diehard Federalists were prepared to make Burr President—a course which Burr himself was careful neither to endorse nor to rule out. But Hamilton thought Burr, his long-standing rival in law and politics in New York, unprincipled and dangerous. Much as he distrusted Jefferson he feared Burr more. His views influenced enough Congressmen for Jefferson to be elected on the thirty-sixth ballot. To avoid another such crisis in future the twelfth amendment to the Constitution, adopted in 1804, required separate ballots for President and Vice-President.

During their twelve years in office the Federalists had achieved much. They had successfully launched the new Constitution, built a fiscal structure which safeguarded the nation's credit, avoided wars which could have caused the country to fall apart. But by 1800 the Federalist party had lost both vitality and appeal. Washington's death in December 1799 deprived it of its most effective symbol. Some of its leading financial backers were in debtors' prisons as a result of disastrous speculations. Other party leaders had had their fill of political turmoil and had withdrawn either to the bench (like Theodore Sedgwick) or to the diplomatic service (like Rufus King). Moreover a gulf had opened up between the Federalist leaders and the common people. While the Federalists felt political organization to be beneath them, their policies had resulted in their being widely associated with militarism, repression, and high taxation.

6. *Jeffersonian Republicanism,*
1801–1824

Jefferson in Power

No one could have been more unlike the irascible, cynical, and pompous John Adams than the urbane Virginia planter who succeeded him as President. Animated by the optimism of the Enlightenment and fired by an omnivorous intellectual curiosity, Thomas Jefferson displayed a greater range of talents than any other President. Besides being politician and diplomat, he was philosopher, naturalist, architect, scientific farmer, and inventor; he collected pictures and was devoted to music; in his old age he not only founded the University of Virginia, but also designed the buildings and drew up the curriculum. Among American statesmen only Lincoln has rivaled Jefferson's ability to express ideas felicitously—at least on paper, for he was no orator. Jefferson did, however, have limitations which an admiring posterity has chosen largely to ignore. He was thin-skinned and, like many other great men, had a large capacity for self-deception. A lifelong slave-holder, his eloquent affirmation of human equality co-existed with a belief in the inferiority of blacks and, indeed, of Indians. His egalitarian bias did not extend to the elevation of the common man to high political office. While asserting that education was the only safeguard of republican freedom, he had some highly selective ideas about schooling above the primary level. And although in 1798 he expressed outrage at Federalist attempts to silence Republican editors, his response to press criticism of himself in 1803 was to suggest that 'a few prosecutions of the most prominent offenders would have a most wholesome effect in restoring the integrity of the presses'.

The simplicity and informality which were to be the hallmarks of Jefferson's presidential style accorded well with the rawness of the new national capital on the banks of the Potomac to which the federal government had moved late in 1800. The Capitol, where Jefferson took the oath of office, was only half built—it remained so for decades. Washington itself, with a population of only 3,000, was little more than a muddy frontier village. Aiming to do away with anything that smacked of royal ceremonial Jefferson walked to and from his inauguration, refusing to ride in a carriage. Instead of addressing Congress in person he employed written messages, a practice that lasted until Woodrow Wilson's day. Jefferson also made a point of dressing plainly, even on formal occasions. He abolished formal weekly levees, made himself freely available to all-comers, and at state dinners ignored precedence and protocol and introduced the principle of *pêle-mêle* whereby guests seated themselves wherever there was room.

Jefferson began his term of office with a plea for harmony. 'We are all Republicans, we are all Federalists', he declared in his inaugural address. In keeping with his desire to heal divisions he refused to heed the demands of his supporters for an immediate and drastic purge of Federalists from public office. Yet he was not blind to the political uses of patronage. When appointments fell vacant he took the opportunity to change the complexion of what had been an overwhelmingly Federalist bureaucracy. By the time he left the Presidency practically all federal employees were Republicans.

Though in later years Jefferson liked to refer to his election as the 'revolution of 1800', it was hardly that. The Republicans systematically reversed a number of Federalist policies. They repealed the Naturalization Act of 1798, restoring the five-year residential qualification for citizenship. They allowed the Alien and Sedition Acts to expire, while Jefferson pardoned those still in jail for violating them. They abolished not only the hated whiskey excise but the whole system of internal taxation. In fiscal policy, indeed, Jefferson and his Secretary of the Treasury, Swiss-born Albert Gallatin, departed sharply from Hamiltonian theory and practice. Admittedly, they retained and even made use of the capstone of Federalist mercantilism, the Bank of the United States, while the thought of repudiating Hamilton's funded debt never entered their minds. But unlike Hamilton, Jefferson saw a national debt as a 'moral canker'. Gallatin devised a scheme to eliminate it completely and by the time Jefferson left office had succeeded in reducing it from $83 to $45 million. Moreover, in fulfillment of Jefferson's inaugural pledge of limited and economical government, Gallatin severely reduced government expenditure. The biggest cuts were in military and naval expenditure: the regular army was reduced from four thousand to twenty-five-hundred men and several warships were sold or laid up. These steps stemmed not only from Jefferson's passion for economy but also from his conviction that standing armies were a menace to liberty. Jefferson believed that the state militia and a handful of gunboats were all that was necessary for the defense of a country 'separated by nature and a wide ocean from the exterminating havoc' of the Old World. Ironically, his Administration was responsible for founding the United States Military Academy at West Point in 1802, though in its first decade it graduated a mere seventy cadets. Moreover, to defend American shipping in the Mediterranean from the attacks of Barbary pirates Jefferson was soon compelled to recommission a number of frigates.

The sharpest divergence from Federalism came with the Republican assault on the federal courts. Although the 1800 election gave the Republicans control of Congress as well as of the Presidency the Federalists had taken steps to entrench themselves in the judiciary. Their Judiciary Act of 1801 set up additional district courts in the new Western states and erected six new circuit courts, to be presided over by sixteen federal judges. These reforms were much needed but the haste with which the expiring Federalist Congress rushed them through stemmed from a desire to enable Adams to make the new appointments before leaving office. This he proceeded to do, filling the newly created posts with dedicated Federalists in a series of 'midnight appointments'—so-called because the President reputedly spent the last hours of his administration signing judicial commissions. At the same time he appointed his outgoing Secretary of State, John Marshall, to be Chief Justice of the Supreme Court. A distant relative of Jefferson, who detested both him and his politics, Marshall's career as Chief Justice would continue until 1835— a quarter of a century after Jefferson's retirement from public life. Consequently, while the Federalist party never won another national election, Federalist constitutional principles continued to be expounded by the Supreme Court for a period that spanned the Administrations of five Presidents. Moreover, Marshall was to prove a vital influence on the development of American constitutional law. Though his legal learning was not impressive and he had no previous judicial experience, he became the greatest of Chief Justices. By a mixture of boldness and adroitness he greatly extended the jurisdiction of the Supreme Court, thus transforming an infant and none too highly regarded institution into something more than a coordinate brand of government. At the same time he extended federal power at the expense of that of the states.

While the long-term implications of Marshall's appointment could scarcely have been foreseen in 1801, the Republicans had already singled out the federal judiciary as a target. They regarded federal courts as dangerous engines of centralization. Fresh in their minds also was the blatant partisanship of Federalist judges in cases under the Sedition Act. Moreover, they regarded the midnight appointments as an attempt to thwart the popular will. Hence they promptly repealed the Judiciary Act of 1801, thus sweeping away the newly created circuit courts and, at least in Federalist eyes, violating the constitutional provision guaranteeing tenure to federal judges during good behavior.

The war on the judiciary entered a further phase with the celebrated case of *Marbury v. Madison* (1803). The case arose from the refusal of Jefferson's Secretary of State, James Madison, to deliver a commission of office to William Marbury, one of Adams's last-minute appointments. Marbury promptly applied to the Supreme Court for a writ of mandamus, a judicial instruction to compel the performance of a legally required act. Marshall ruled that, while Madison had no right to withhold the commission, the clause of the Judiciary Act of 1789 under which Marbury had sued was contrary to the Constitution and therefore invalid. Marshall displayed great shrewdness in his choice of ground. By sacrificing Marbury and disclaiming authority to issue a writ of mandamus, he avoided a direct clash with the Administration. Yet by asserting the power of the Supreme Court to declare acts of Congress unconstitutional, he gave notice that there were limits to what a Congressional majority could do. While Marshall's doctrine of judicial review was destined to become the most distinctive feature of the American constitutional system, it had little immediate effect: for more than half a century *Marbury* v. *Madison* was the only case in which the Supreme Court declared an act of Congress unconstitutional.

Meanwhile Jefferson and his followers had been seeking to purge the judiciary by means of impeachment. Having employed it successfully in 1803 to remove a New Hampshire district judge who had become insane, they went after larger game: the rabidly partisan Justice Samuel Chase of the Supreme Court. While Chase's conduct had unquestionably been unjudicial, it was doubtful whether it met the constitutional test for impeachment—the commission of high crimes and misdemeanors. At all events, when Chase was brought to trial early in 1805 the administration failed to muster the necessary two-thirds majority for conviction. The Chase impeachment ended the Republican assault on the judiciary. Both sides could claim victory: the courts had preserved their independence, but judges learned to show greater restraint in their public pronouncements.

The Louisiana Purchase

Jefferson's greatest triumph as President, the Louisiana Purchase, involved some compromise of political principle. In 1800, as a first step towards reviving the French North American empire, Napoleon had concluded with Spain a treaty providing for the return to France of Louisiana, the vast territory extending westward from the Mississippi River to the Rockies and northward as far as Canada, but including also New Orleans to the east of the river near its mouth. The treaty was kept secret, Spain continuing to administer the territory. But news of its provisions soon leaked out. Though Jefferson was a lifelong Gallophile he was concerned at the prospect of having an enfeebled Spain replaced as a neighbor by a powerful and aggressive France. In April 1802 he wrote that while the United States had hitherto looked on France as its "natural friend", there was on the globe "one single spot" the possessor of which was "our natural and habitual enemy". That spot was New Orleans, the outlet for the products of nearly half the territory of the United States. "The day that France takes possession of New Orleans . . .", he concluded, "we must marry ourselves to the British, fleet and nation." In October 1802 Jefferson became still more alarmed when, notwithstanding the guarantees of Pinckney's Treaty of 1795, the Spanish Intendant at New Orleans closed the Mississippi to American commerce. Faced by clamorous Western demands for action Jefferson sent James Monroe as envoy extraordinary to Paris to assist Robert Livingston, the American minister. Monroe was instructed to offer $10 million for New Orleans and West Florida (the coastal strip extending eastward from the mouth of the Mississippi to the Perdido) or, if the French refused to sell, to press for a perpetual guarantee of the use of the Mississippi. Failing both, Monroe was to approach England for a defensive alliance.

The contingent instructions proved unnecessary. By the time Monroe reached Paris, Napoleon had abandoned his designs on the New World. As a preliminary to resuming control over Louisiana he had dispatched a large French army under his brother-in-law, General Leclerc, to restore French authority over the colony of Haiti, where a slave rebellion led by Toussaint l'Ouverture had been followed by the formation of a Negro republic. But when Leclerc and most of his troops succumbed to yellow fever, Napoleon abruptly decided to offer the Americans not only New Orleans but also the whole of Louisiana. Monroe and Livingston had no authority to make such a purchase but, fearing that Napoleon might withdraw the offer if they delayed, resolved to exceed their instructions. On April 30, 1803 they signed a treaty whereby the United States acquired the whole of Louisiana for approximately $15 million.

The American negotiators had made what Talleyrand rightly described as a "noble bargain". The Louisiana Purchase gave the United States a tract of some 828,000 square miles at a cost of less than three cents an acre; it more than doubled the national territory. But the treaty embarrassed Jefferson. To spend $15 million, a sum nearly twice as great as the normal annual expenditure of the federal government, was hardly compatible with the President's earlier concern for economy. More worrisome still were the constitutional aspects. According to his own doctrine of strict construction the federal government had no constitutional power to acquire additional territory or to promise full American citizenship to its inhabitants (as was provided in the treaty). Jefferson's first thought was that a constitutional amendment would be necessary to legitimize the transaction. But that would be a lengthy and uncertain procedure and in the meantime Napoleon might change his mind. Accordingly the President swallowed his constitutional scruples and submitted the treaty to the Senate. In the ratification debate the Federalists showed an equal readiness to reverse themselves on questions of constitutional interpretation. Opposed to the acquisition of an immense territory which would strengthen the agricultural interests represented by the Republican party, the erstwhile exponents of broad construction denounced Jefferson for his "implied powers" position. But the Senate overwhelmingly approved the treaty and in December 1803 the Louisiana territory was formally handed over to the United States.

Long interested in exploring the western half of the North American continent Jefferson had been planning a transcontinental expedition even before Napoleon offered to sell Louisiana. In 1803 he induced Congress to make a secret appropriation for one. The expedition, commanded by the President's secretary, Captain Meriwether Lewis, and another experienced frontiersman, William Clark, set out from St. Louis in May 1804. After following the Missouri to its headwaters, it crossed the Rocky mountains, then descended the Snake and Columbia rivers to reach the Pacific coast. After an epic journey of nearly 4,000 miles, the explorers were back in St. Louis late in 1806 with a large collection of maps, drawings, botanical and geological specimens, and a mass of data on Indian customs. Besides adding to scientific knowledge the expedition strengthened the American claim to the Oregon country and ultimately stimulated the fur trade and Western settlement.

From almost every point of view Jefferson's first term had been a huge success. His moderate domestic policy had appeased many of his Federalist opponents; the Louisiana Purchase had added greatly to his popularity. Thus, when he ran for reelection in 1804 he carried every state in the Union except Connecticut and Delaware. The Republicans also secured overwhelming majorities in both houses of Congress. During the next four years, however, Jefferson was to experience a multitude of troubles. Republican party harmony was shattered, the Federalists staged something of a revival, separatist movements threatened the Union, and, finally, the European war, renewed in 1803, brought serious difficulties with foreign countries.

Jefferson's conduct during his first term had not pleased all his supporters, notably the group of doctrinaire state-rights Republicans from Virginia led by the gifted but erratic John Randolph of Roanoke (one of his plantations was appropriately named Bizarre). The dissidents grumbled at Jefferson's failure to make a clean sweep of Federalist office-holders and felt that he had moved too far toward Federalism. Moreover, Randolph blamed Jefferson's lack of support for the failure of the Chase impeachment. But it was not until 1805 that Randolph broke with the Administration. Of the two issues responsible, each involving the use of federal funds, the first arose out of the notorious Yazoo land scandal. Randolph denounced as a compromise with fraud Jefferson's willingness to compensate speculators who had, in good faith, bought lands corruptly granted by the Georgia legislature and had lost them when the grant was rescinded. The other issue was Jefferson's somewhat devious scheme for acquiring West Florida. With the $2 million he requested from Congress the President hoped to persuade Napoleon to put pressure on Spain to hand over the colony to the United States. To Randolph the proposal was "a base prostration of the national character". The dozen or so Republicans who followed him into opposition were nicknamed by their leader the "Tertium Quids", but although they continued to harass Jefferson they hardly constituted a third party.

Meanwhile a little group of uncompromising New England Federalists, led by Timothy Pickering, had been plotting disunion. The Louisiana Purchase, with its enormous potential for western expansion, seemed likely to doom their party and their section to being a permanent minority. Early in 1804, they began to toy with the idea of a separate Northern Confederacy, consisting of New England and New York. Hamilton would have nothing to do with the scheme but his fellow New Yorker, Vice-President Aaron Burr, was more receptive. Repudiated by the Republicans for his conduct after the 1800 election and dropped as Jefferson's running mate in 1804, Burr tried to salvage his political career by courting Federalist support in his campaign for the governorship of New York. But as in 1801 Hamilton's opposition frustrated his ambition and, moreover, put paid to the projected Northern Confederacy. Burr challenged his old rival to a duel and in the ensuing encounter on July 11, 1804 Hamilton fell mortally wounded.

After serving out his term as Vice-President Burr went West and involved himself in some kind of wild conspiracy for which he unsuccessfully sought aid, first from Great Britain, then from Spain. He may have planned to detach the Mississippi Valley from the Union. Alternatively he may have intended a filibustering expedition against Spain in Mexico. Whatever the scheme was it collapsed late in 1806 when a fellow conspirator, General James Wilkinson, fearful for his own hide, decided to warn Jefferson of what was afoot. Burr was arrested and indicted for treason before Chief Justice Marshall. Jefferson vindictively wanted Burr hanged. But after a colorful trial which created a precedent for the American law of treason, the President was yet again frustrated by Marshall. Taking an uncharacteristically literal view of the Constitution the Chief Justice acquitted Burr because, in his judgment, the government had not fulfilled the constitutional requirement that no conviction for treason should occur except upon "the testimony of two witnesses to the same overt act".

It used to be thought that once Jefferson came to power the Federalist party was reduced to "a grumbling company of out-of-date gentlemen" and quickly disintegrated. In fact its decline was very gradual and not complete until the 1820s. While the party's Old Guard, loathing democracy in all its forms, was not prepared to court popular favor younger leaders made a spirited and not altogether unsuccessful attempt to defeat the Republicans with their own weapons. They created popularly based local organizations, sponsored partisan newspapers and secret political societies, and borrowed Jeffersonian techniques, rhetoric, and issues. Federalists never quite succeeded in removing the impression that Federalism stood for privilege and repression but, capitalizing on the embargo's unpopularity, made a far better showing in the presidential election of 1808 than in 1804. Jefferson's successor in the Virginia dynasty, his Secretary of State, James Madison, was comfortably elected to the presidency, but the Federalists recaptured nearly the whole of New England and even won some electoral votes in the South. They also made substantial gains in Congress. An important incidental consequence of keen party competition was an extraordinary rise in the proportion of voters going to the polls: in Massachusetts, for example, the proportion of the white adult-male population voting for governor rose from 31% in 1800 to 64% in 1809.

The Neutral Rights Controversy

During his second Administration Jefferson was increasingly preoccupied with the defense of American neutral rights at sea. By 1805, two years after their renewal of hostilities, Great Britain and France had reached stalemate. Unable to strike at each other directly the two belligerents attempted to cripple each other's trade. As the chief neutral carrier the United States could scarely avoid involvement.

The first blow to American shipping came when British prize courts tightened the rules governing neutral trade between the French West Indies and French-controlled Europe. Since 1800 the British had tolerated this provided it was not conducted direct. Accordingly, by first carrying West Indian goods to the United States and then reshipping them American vessels had been able to develop an immensely profitable "re-export" trade. But in the *Essex* decision of 1805, a British court virtually outlawed it by ruling that vessels making broken voyages between two enemy ports should be regarded as being engaged in one continuous voyage. Thereupon British warships established a virtual blockade of the American coastline and seized large numbers of American vessels carrying French West Indian cargoes.

American shipowners were indignant, but soon had far more to complain about. Napoleon's Berlin Decree (1806) proclaimed a blockade of the British Isles and closed the Continent to neutral vessels which had called at a British port. The British retaliated with Orders-in-Council extending the blockade of French-controlled ports and barring all neutral vessels from them unless they first stopped at a British port to secure a license and pay customs duties. Caught between blockade and counter-blockade American merchants found it impossible to carry on foreign trade without running the risk of seizure and confiscation by one belligerent or other.

In their disregard of American rights there was little to choose between France and Great Britain. Between 1803 and 1812 both confiscated hundreds of American merchantmen. But Americans were understandably more sensitive to injuries inflicted by the former mother country than by her Revolutionary ally. Besides, what Great Britain did affronted the national honor more deeply. Whereas the French could seize American vessels only in European ports, Great Britain's sea power enabled her to interfere with American commerce anywhere on the high seas, even within sight of the American coast. An even keener challenge to American sovereignty was implicit in the British practice of impressment. Chronically short of hands and aware of the high proportion of British-born sailors in the American merchant marine, Royal Navy captains would intercept American vessels at sea, muster the crews, and impress those suspected of being British. Between 1803 and 1812 alone a total of somewhere between 5,000 and 9,000 sailors was carried off. Had they all been indisputably British the United States would probably have protested less vehemently. But some, though British-born, were—or claimed to be—naturalized Americans. The British, however, did not recognize naturalization, holding to the doctrine of indefeasible allegiance. In any case British captains tended to discount claims to American citizenship since sailors notoriously carried false papers.

An indignant Jefferson first sought to defend American rights by diplomacy. In 1806 he sent a Maryland lawyer, William Pinkney, to London to reinforce the efforts of the American minister, James Monroe, to persuade the British to renounce impressment, modify the *Essex* decision, and pay compensation for confiscated American ships. To provide the American negotiators with a bargaining weapon Congress passed the Nonimportation Act (1806) which threatened to exclude specified British manufactures unless agreement was reached. But the Monroe–Pinkney Treaty of December 1806 contained only trifling concessions on the West India trade and none at all on impressment. Consequently Jefferson did not even trouble to submit it to the Senate.

In June 1807 the impressment controversy reached a climax in a dramatic incident off the coast of Virginia. The British frigate *Leopard* fired upon the American *Chesapeake* to compel her to stop, boarded her, and seized four alleged deserters. Since the *Chesapeake* was a warship, not a merchantman, this was the crowning indignity. When she limped back to port with her twenty-one killed and wounded, the country demanded war. But Jefferson refused to be swayed by popular clamor. He pinned his faith on "peaceable coercion"—the use of economic pressure as an alternative to war. He believed that, if the belligerents were denied American foodstuffs and American markets, they would be forced to respect American rights. Thus, the Nonimportation Act was invoked against Britain and in December 1807 Congress passed a sweeping Embargo Act, suspending commerce with the rest of the world, whether in American or in foreign vessels.

"Peaceable coercion" proved a disappointment. Although the embargo inflicted damage on Britain, it hurt the United States far more. The cessation of foreign trade brought stagnation to the seaports and depressed the American economy generally: farm prices collapsed, bankruptcies multiplied, land values fell. The South, dependent on foreign markets for its tobacco and other staples, was hard hit. Yet out of loyalty to Jefferson it suffered in comparative silence. But in mercantile New England opposition was unrestrained. New England merchants and shipowners had been exasperated when their vessels had been stopped, searched, and seized; they had also shared in the general indignation at impressment. Yet they had been willing to accept the risks of neutral trade because of its huge profits. Now, however, with their ships idling at the wharves, they bitterly denounced Jefferson's "dambargo". They felt that it sacrificed their interests for a utopian purpose and, moreover, believed it to be unconstitutional. The Constitution, observed young Daniel Webster of New Hampshire, had given Congress the power to regulate commerce, not destroy it. New England's discontent increased still further when Jefferson, faced with widespread evasion of the embargo, resorted to arbitrary powers of enforcement.

The unpopularity of the embargo not only contributed to the Federalist resurgence in the election of 1808; it produced rumblings of discontent within the Republican party. Consequently, in March 1809, a few days before Jefferson left office, Congress voted to replace the embargo with a Nonintercourse Act, prohibiting trade only with Britain and France while reopening it with other countries. It also authorized the President to restore trade with whichever of the two belligerents agreed to respect American rights.

The Nonintercourse Act proved difficult to enforce. Hence a substitute measure, Macon's Bill No. 2, was adopted in May 1810. This reopened trade with Britain and France, but offered them a bribe: if either abandoned its restrictions on American shipping, nonintercourse would be revived against the other. Napoleon at once saw a chance to divert American anger wholly against the British: in August 1810 he announced the repeal of his decrees insofar as they affected American commerce. Instead of waiting to see whether this was a genuine change of policy—which it was not—President Madison precipitately invoked nonintercourse against Great Britain.

Indians and Frontiersmen

Meanwhile anti-British feeling was mounting in the South and the trans-Appalachian west. Though Southerners and Westerners were not ship-owners, they did not regard the question of freedom of the seas as academic. They blamed British restrictions on neutral trade for the loss of their European markets and the severe agricultural depression that followed. Western frontiersmen also held the British responsible for their continuing Indian troubles. It was true that British officials had maintained contact with the tribes of the Northwest Territory ever since 1783. Concerned for the fur trade and attracted by the concept of an Indian buffer state, they had encouraged the Indians to unite to resist American expansion and had supplied them with weapons. Yet the real causes of Indian unrest were the insatiable greed of the frontiersmen and the inability or unwillingness of the federal government to protect Indian rights. Although the Northwest Ordinance had promised that Indian lands and property would "never be taken from them without their consent", the United States had in practice seized every opportunity of extinguishing Indian rights. Whenever the Indians retaliated against invading settlers and speculators, federal troops were sent to suppress them. In November 1791, the Ohio Indians inflicted a stunning reverse on Governor Arthur St. Clair's force, but a second American punitive expedition, under General Anthony Wayne, decisively defeated them at the battle of Fallen Timbers (August 20, 1794) and by the Treaty of Greenville (August 3, 1795) the Indians ceded to the United States most of what later became the state of Ohio.

Soon land-hungry frontiersmen spilled over into Indiana and the chiefs were being pressed to make further cessions. The process of dispossession was accelerated under Jefferson, who shared the popular belief that the Indians must be removed to make way for white settlement. After the purchase of Louisiana he began a drive to persuade the tribesmen to exchange their lands east of the Mississippi for others further west. His representative in these proceedings, William Henry Harrison, governor of Indiana Territory, employed a mixture of trickery, bribery, and intimidation to induce the Northwest Indians to sign away millions of acres of tribal lands. These methods were equally effective south of the Ohio. So long as Spain had occupied Louisiana she had armed and subsidized the southern tribes, but after 1804 Spanish support had ceased.

A few years later, however, a remarkable Indian leader emerged, the great Shawnee chief, Tecumseh. Determined to halt further American encroachments, and believing he could count on British aid, he began organizing a grand confederacy of all the Mississippi Valley tribes. Tecumseh's efforts were reinforced by those of his brother, a medicine man known as the Prophet, who inspired a new religion emphasizing Indian racial pride and won a fanatical following. Harrison decided he must nip this alarming resistance movement in the bud. Taking advantage of Tecumseh's absence in the South, he destroyed the chief's Indiana headquarters at the battle of Tippecanoe (November 7, 1811). The defeated Indians left on the battlefield rifles of recent British manufacture. Their discovery confirmed the frontiersmen's long-held conviction that the only security for the West was to expel the British from North America.

While the Northwest clamored for the conquest of Canada, Southern frontiersmen were anxious to take Florida from Spain, Great Britain's weak ally. Florida possessed great strategic value. It was also a haven for escaped Negro slaves and a base for marauding Indians. Jefferson's efforts to buy the territory had been rebuffed, but in 1810 American settlers in West Florida took advantage of the fact that Spain had her hands full with a French invasion. They staged a revolt, proclaimed a republic, and requested annexation by the United States. Within a month Madison had complied. A similar revolt in East Florida in 1811 was unsuccessful despite American moral and material support. But war with Great Britain, so the expansionists reasoned, might provide a better opportunity for annexation.

The War of 1812

When the Twelfth Congress assembled in November 1811—three days before the battle of Tippecanoe—a group of young Republicans, dubbed War Hawks by their opponents, seized the initiative. Coming mainly from the new Western states or from frontier regions of the Lower South, they were ardently nationalistic, believing that the United States could not consider itself an independent nation so long as it passively accepted interference with its trade. Their leader was Henry Clay of Kentucky. Elected Speaker of the House of Representatives, Clay packed key committees with fellow War Hawks like John C. Calhoun of South Carolina and Felix Grundy of Tennessee and used his influence in other ways to push the country toward war.

Madison was no War Hawk. But he despaired of a change in British policy. He may also have feared that unwillingness to go to war to assert American rights might result in his being denied his party's nomination in the 1812 election. Thus on June 1, 1812 he sent a war message to Congress listing various British offenses. Beginning with impressment, it went on to cite the harassment of shipping off the American coast, the use of "pretended blockades", and the sweeping restrictions of the Orders-in-Council. Finally it alleged that the British had incited Indian border warfare. Congress responded with a declaration of war on June 18. Two days earlier Castlereagh had announced the British government's intention to repeal the Orders-in-Council. He hoped that the reopening of the American market would alleviate the depression affecting British industry. It is sometimes argued that if there had been an Atlantic cable to transmit this news promptly to Washington war would have been averted. But the repeal of the Orders-in-Council would not have sufficed to preserve peace; the Madison Administration would also have insisted on the discontinuance of impressment, which the British would certainly have refused.

The Congressional vote on the war resolution, 19 to 13 in the Senate and 79 to 49 in the House, showed that American opinion was badly split. The division was both partisan and sectional. Nearly all Republicans backed the war; not a single Federalist did so. The South and West overwhelmingly supported the declaration; New York, New Jersey, and most of New England were solidly against. A similar cleavage was revealed in the presidential election of 1812. Madison was opposed by a "peace" Republican, De Witt Clinton of New York, who received Federalist backing. Though the President was reelected the "peace" ticket would have triumphed had Clinton carried Pennsylvania.

When news of the declaration of war reached Boston, flags flew at half-mast and the governor of Massachusetts proclaimed a public fast. New Englanders feared that war would ruin their commerce more completely even than the embargo. They also deplored the fact that the United States would be, nominally at least, on the side of Napoleonic autocracy. Men like Clay and Calhoun, on the other hand, genuinely believed that it was not Napoleon who threatened the republic, but Federalist "monarchism" and British hostility to popular self-government. They felt, indeed, that a second struggle with Britain was necessary to confirm the successes of the first.

Despite the brave talk of the War Hawks the United States was almost totally unprepared for the conflict. Republican parsimony had cut the armed services to the bone. The regular army, reduced to 6,700 men, was poorly equipped and commanded by elderly veterans of the Revolutionary War. The state militia, notoriously ill-trained and ill-disciplined, was a doubtful military asset. The United States navy had no ships of the line and only half a dozen frigates. The Treasury was almost empty, thanks to the decline of customs revenues resulting from the embargo and the Non-intercourse Act. Moreover, the refusal of the Republican majority in Congress to recharter the Bank of the United States in 1811 had deprived the government of an invaluable fiscal agency. And when war came, the Administration proved incapable of waging it effectively.

Even so, the invasion of Canada seemed to be well within American capabilities. Its long land frontier was defended only by 4,500 troops, and Great Britain could not easily spare reinforcements so long as her hands were tied by the struggle with Napoleon. With a population of only half a million, compared with seven and a half million in the United States, Canada had few reserves of manpower. Moreover the loyalty of her population was in doubt: in Lower Canada two-thirds of the people were of French descent and in Upper Canada there were many recent American immigrants. Canada was so obviously vulnerable that to Jefferson its conquest appeared "a mere matter of marching".

Nevertheless two successive American invasions ended in failure. The first, in 1812, was a complete fiasco; the Americans were not only expelled from Canada but also surrendered Detroit and other frontier posts to their pursuers. A second invasion in 1813 accomplished nothing tangible. After capturing York (Toronto) the then capital of Canada, the invaders stirred up Canadian animosity by setting fire to Parliament and a number of other public buildings before withdrawing across Lake Ontario. The last months of 1813 saw a brightening of American prospects. Commodore Oliver H. Perry's victory in the battle of Lake Erie gave the United States command of the Great Lakes and General William Henry Harrison, having retaken Detroit, defeated the British at the Battle of the Thames (October 5), in which Tecumseh was killed. But these victories came too late to retrieve American fortunes completely. When the war against Napoleon ended in 1814 the British sent out 20,000 reinforcements to Canada, thus ending American dreams of conquest.

Only at sea could the Americans derive any satisfaction from the first two years' fighting. Though the tiny United States navy was in no position to challenge British naval supremacy, its frigates, more maneuverable and more heavily armed than their British counterparts, won spectacular victories in single-ship engagements. As in the Revolutionary War, swarms of American privateers took a heavy toll, capturing 1,300 British vessels. But although these exploits were a source of understandable pride to Americans and of discomfiture to the British, they had no great strategic significance. By 1814 the Royal Navy had bottled up most of the American warships and imposed so tight a blockade as to cripple the American carrying trade, both foreign and coastwise.

Once the British were free to give their undivided attention to the American war the roles of the belligerents were reversed. By the late summer of 1814 the United States stood on the defensive everywhere. The British occupied much of the coast of Maine, a large British expedition sailed into Chesapeake Bay, swept aside American resistance, and entered Washington (August 24), putting Madison and his Cabinet to flight. In retaliation for the earlier incendiarism at York they set fire to the Capitol, the White House, and other public buildings. After inflicting this crowning humiliation the raiders launched an unsuccessful attack on Baltimore and then withdrew. A projected British offensive from Canada had meanwhile suffered a fatal check. The destruction of the British flotilla at the battle of Plattsburg (September 11) gave the Americans command of Lake Champlain and secured their northern borders. But another British invading army, composed of Peninsular veterans and commanded by Wellington's brother-in-law, Sir Edward Pakenham, was preparing for an assault on New Orleans. If it succeeded the United States stood to lose the Louisiana Territory.

As 1814 drew to a close the Madison Administration was in dire straits. The military situation was critical, the country on the verge of bankruptcy. To finance the war Gallatin had first resorted to taxation. Much against its will Congress had been persuaded to reimpose that hated Federalist impost, the excise duty, along with other internal taxes. But because of widespread evasion these measures raised only a fraction of the expected revenue. Gallatin then turned to borrowing, but with equal lack of success. New England, which controlled most of the country's capital, refused to lend. Moreover, since the Bank of the United States had expired in 1811 there was no centralized financial machinery for raising loans. Though the Treasury issued bonds nominally worth $80 million, their sale brought in less than half that sum.

To add to the crisis there were renewed rumblings of secessionism from New England. Resentful of the shift in political power that had occurred since 1800, New England Federalists saw the war as a deliberate attempt to ruin them. Throughout the conflict they defied the Administration, sometimes carrying their opposition to the verge of treason. They discouraged enlistments and refused to place state militia under federal control or to allow them to take part in the invasion of Canada. They not only boycotted federal loans but also lent money freely to Great Britain. And until the British blockade was extended to New England late in the war, Yankee merchants waxed fat by trading with the enemy, even supplying the British army in Canada with most of its food.

Federalist disaffection reached a climax in December 1814 when delegates from the New England States met at Hartford, Connecticut to consider a "radical reform of the national compact". Some of the more extreme Federalists had been urging secession but the Hartford Convention was dominated—indeed, had been convened—by moderates. Under their leadership the convention contented itself with asserting the right of nullification (in language reminiscent of the Virginia and Kentucky resolutions) and with proposing a series of constitutional amendments. These would, among other things, have abolished the three-fifths clause of the Constitution (thereby reducing the voting power of the slave states), required a two-thirds vote of both houses of Congress to admit new states or declare war, forbidden embargoes lasting more than sixty days, limited Presidents to a single term, and prohibited the election of a President from the same state as his immediate predecessor. If these amendments were rejected and the war continued a second convention was to meet in Boston in six months' time. The commissioners appointed by the Convention to go to Washington expected to dictate terms to a collapsing government. But when they arrived in the capital they were greeted by the news that American forces had won a resounding victory at New Orleans and that a peace treaty had been signed. There was nothing for the envoys to do but to steal silently back to New England.

The battle of New Orleans (January 8, 1815) demonstrated that the United States had no monopoly of incompetent generals. Pakenham's slowness delivered his army into the hands of a self-taught military genius, Andrew Jackson. His Tennessee militia routed the British and drove them back to their ships with heavy losses. The battle made Jackson a national hero, but had no effect on the outcome of the war. Peace had been made at Ghent two weeks earlier (December 24, 1814) but news of it had not yet crossed the Atlantic. Both sides, having lost the will to continue an apparently inconclusive war, were eager to end it. Moreover, since the war in Europe was over, the question of neutral rights had become academic. The peace treaty made no reference to impressment, blockades, or other maritime issues and left other disputed questions to the future. Apart from providing for the return of conquered territory the treaty did little more than proclaim that the war was over.

Nonetheless the War of 1812 had important consequences. It gave a great stimulus to New England manufactures. Tecumseh's death and Jackson's defeat of the Creeks at the battle of Horseshoe Bend (March 27, 1814) crippled Indian power east of the Mississippi and facilitated western settlement. The war inspired a great outburst of national feeling in a still feeble Union. It added a substantial group of heroes, Jackson above all, to the American pantheon and provided the United States with a national anthem—the Star-Spangled Banner which a prominent Washington lawyer, Francis Scott Key, had been inspired to write while observing the British bombardment of Baltimore—and a national symbol, Uncle Sam.

To an England locked in the great struggle with Napoleon the skirmishes in the wilds of America were an unimportant, if irritating, sideshow, soon to be forgotten. But to the United States the War of 1812 was a truly significant event. Far more than the Revolution it implanted a lasting Anglophobia in the American political consciousness: it was, after all, the only time since becoming independent that the United States has experienced the humiliation of foreign invasion. Yet paradoxically the United States emerged psychologically triumphant from the war. What was remembered was not the defeats and disappointments but the naval victories and, above all, Jackson's great triumph at New Orleans. Thus the War of 1812 on the whole merits the title of "the second war for independence". True, the reimposition of British rule had never been on the cards. But the young republic had demonstrated that it had the will and the capacity to defend its national interests, unaided, against the strongest power in the world. The war also marked the end of American dependence on the European state system. Up till now the United States had been unable to escape involvement in European wars. Her primary preoccupations had thus been foreign affairs and defense. But in 1815 Europe entered a long period of peace and the United States, having won a dominating position in North America, could afford to retreat into diplomatic isolation and concentrate on domestic affairs.

Political Transition and Postwar Nationalism

In the decade after 1815 political divisions became blurred and the two-party system ceased to operate. The Federalists, discredited by their near treasonable attempt to extract party and sectional advantage from the nation's difficulties, went into rapid decline. The Republicans, enthusiastically adopting what had once been distinctively Federalist policies, enjoyed virtually unchallenged political control. In the presidential election of 1816 the Republican candidate, James Monroe, won an easy victory over his Federalist opponent. By 1820 the Federalist party had disappeared and Monroe was reelected unopposed. The third Virginian in succession to become President, Monroe tried to promote national unity and assuage Northern resentment of the 'Virginia dynasty' by appointing John Quincy Adams of Massachusetts as his Secretary of State and by making a nationwide goodwill tour which included a visit to Federalist New England. A remark in a Boston newspaper during the visit that an 'era of good feelings' had arrived has provided historians with a convenient label for the eight years of Monroe's Administration. But the description is misleading for, despite the absence of party divisions, factional strife was endemic within the Republican party and, by 1820, sectional rivalries, too, had revived.

The immediate postwar years saw the completion of the process, under way since 1800, whereby the Republican party abandoned its traditional Jeffersonian hostility to standing armies, centralized power, and loose constructionism. At Madison's urging Congress agreed in 1816 to double naval strength and quadruple the size of the peacetime army. A new generation of party leaders, taught by the experiences of the war, came forward with a program of economic nationalism designed to promote national prosperity by linking the different sections of the country more closely and making it economically self-sufficient. The main features of the program, which its leading exponent, Henry Clay, later christened the 'American System', were tariff protection for America's infant industries, the re-creation of a national bank, and federal aid for improved transport. Though it closely resembled the program earlier advocated by Hamilton, the American System should not be seen as a revival of Hamiltonianism. It did not seek, as Hamilton had done, to advance the interests of merchants and manufacturers at the expense of those of farmers. Nor was the revived bank intended to cement an alliance between the federal government and monied interests. And far from being predicated on close trading and financial ties with Great Britain, as Hamilton's program had been, the American System's purpose was to free the United States from economic dependence on foreigners.

In 1816 Clay and his fellow nationalists persuaded Congress to pass measures which went some way towards implementing the American System. First came a tariff act, which broke new ground in aiming to provide protection rather than revenue. A relatively modest measure it was designed principally to nurture those industries (textiles and iron) which had grown up during the war and were now threatened by British dumping. There was considerable opposition from New England shipping interests, which feared that higher duties would impede foreign trade, as well as from Southern cotton planters. But Calhoun, ironically in view of his subsequent hostility to protection, strongly supported the measure. At this stage of his career a staunch nationalist, he hoped that protection might stimulate Southern industry.

In 1811, when the charter of the first Bank of the United States expired, the Republicans had refused to renew it. This decision contributed largely to the Administration's financial difficulties during the War of 1812: it was left without a secure depository for its funds or proper machinery for raising loans. Worse still, the disappearance of the bank plunged the currency into chaos. Freed from its restraining influence, large numbers of newly chartered state banks flooded the country with paper money of fluctuating value. Clay, who had opposed rechartering on constitutional grounds in 1811, now proclaimed a central bank a national necessity. With a view mainly to restoring a stable, uniform currency Congress granted a twenty-year charter to a second Bank of the United States in 1816. It was to have essentially the same structure and functions as Hamilton's bank, though its capital was increased from $10 million to $25 million and it was given wider powers over state banks.

The need to improve the country's internal transport system had been demonstrated when the British wartime blockade virtually halted coastal shipping. Poor communications also proved to be an obstacle to the westward movement and to interstate commerce. The case for 'internal improvements'—federal aid to road, canal, and waterway projects—was best put by Calhoun. Pointing to the danger of disunion if barriers to communication persisted, he declared in 1817: "Let us, then, bind the republic together with a perfect system of roads and canals." Congress narrowly passed his 'bonus bill' setting aside for internal improvements the $1.5 million paid by the Bank of the United States for its charter, but on his last day in office Madison vetoed it on strict constructionist grounds. Similar scruples led Monroe also to veto internal improvement bills. Thus while Congress continued to vote funds for one indisputably national project—the construction of the Cumberland or National Road running westward from the Potomac to the Ohio—it left the building of local roads and canals to state governments and private enterprise.

The rampant nationalism that inspired the American System was even more strikingly asserted by the Supreme Court. In a series of far-reaching decisions Chief Justice Marshall took issue with those who argued that federal power was strictly limited. The most celebrated case was *McCulloch* v. *Maryland* (1819), which involved the constitutionality of the second Bank of the United States. In delivering judgment on Maryland's attempt to impede the Bank's operations by means of a prohibitory tax Marshall drew upon Hamilton's 'implied powers' theory of the Constitution and insisted also that the national government was fully sovereign in its own sphere and was not just the creature of the states. He ruled that the establishment of a bank, though not specifically authorized by the Constitution, was nonetheless implicit in the grant of fiscal powers to Congress. Moreover, in exercising its constitutional powers Congress could adopt any appropriate means which were not explicitly prohibited by the Constitution. The states had no right to hamper the federal government in the exercise of its constitutional powers. Hence the Bank, as a legitimate federal agency, was not subject to state regulation.

If Marshall was a staunch nationalist he was equally concerned to uphold private property rights. He first did so in the case of *Fletcher* v. *Peck* (1810) which arose out of the Yazoo land scandal and involved the constitutional requirement that states may not impair the obligations of contract. Notwithstanding the corruption surrounding the affair Marshall held that the Yazoo land grant was legally a contract which the Georgia legislature could not constitutionally invalidate. This was the first occasion, incidentally, that the Supreme Court had declared a state law unconstitutional. Solicitude for the sanctity of contracts likewise shaped Marshall's decision in the famous case of *Dartmouth College* v. *Woodward* (1819). This arose when the New Hampshire legislature arbitrarily amended the Dartmouth College charter with a view to bringing the institution under state control. Daniel Webster, himself a Dartmouth graduate, argued before the Court that a charter of incorporation was a contract within the meaning of the Constitution and hence was inviolable. By upholding this doctrine Marshall not only extended constitutional protection to private endowments but, more significantly, also granted immunity to business corporations from state legislative interference.

Postwar nationalism received its fullest expression in foreign policy. Although Monroe upheld state rights in domestic affairs, he was ardently nationalistic toward foreign countries—though less aggressively than his

Secretary of State, John Quincy Adams. No one could have been better prepared for diplomacy than Adams. The eldest son of the second President, John Adams, he had acted as his father's secretary during the peace negotiations of 1783, represented his country successively in The Hague, Berlin, and St. Petersburg, helped negotiate the Treaty of Ghent, and had been United States minister to London. A thoroughgoing expansionist, Adams was among the first to express the belief that Providence intended the United States to possess the whole of the North American continent. He saw diplomacy chiefly as an instrument for hastening that end.

Adams's first step was to settle some Anglo-American disputes. The Rush–Bagot Agreement of 1817, the product of Adams's initiative, limited American and British warships on the Great Lakes to those required to enforce customs regulations. This averted a threatened arms race and set a precedent in international relations for reciprocal naval disarmament. A second agreement, the Convention of 1818, recognized American fishing rights off the coasts of Newfoundland and Labrador, established the forty-ninth parallel as the northern boundary of the Louisiana Purchase from the Lake of the Woods to the Rockies, and provided for the joint occupation of the disputed Oregon country for a period of ten years—an arrangement subsequently renewed until 1846.

A more important achievement was the acquisition of the Floridas. Between 1810 and 1813, the United States had swallowed up most of West Florida, the coastal strip running eastward from New Orleans to Mobile, but a rump of the colony, together with the whole of East Florida (the Florida peninsula), still remained under Spanish rule. As Spain was now too weak to maintain effective control, East Florida became a refuge for white outlaws and runaway slaves and a base from which Seminole Indians raided American frontier settlements. Late in 1817 the Monroe administration ordered General Andrew Jackson to chastise the Seminoles, pursuing them if necessary into Spanish territory. Taking advantage of the vagueness of his instructions Jackson promptly invaded East Florida, seized a number of Spanish forts, deposed the Spanish governor, and captured and executed two Englishmen for allegedly inciting the Indians against the whites. While Jackson's high-handed conduct won popular acclaim, his political enemies, led by Calhoun and Clay, demanded that he be dismissed. But the general found a champion in Adams, who persuaded Monroe against disciplining him. Indeed, Adams turned the incident to diplomatic advantage. In rejecting a Spanish protest he argued that Jackson's incursion was fully justified and insisted that Spain must either govern Florida effectively or cede it to the United States. The Spanish government, already facing revolts in its South American colonies, recognized that it had no choice. The Adams–Onís Treaty of 1819 provided for the cession of both the Floridas to the United States. At the same time the United States assumed the claims of its citizens against the Spanish government, which came to about $5 million. The treaty also defined the boundary between Spanish Mexico and the Louisiana Purchase: it was to run from the Sabine River in east Texas to the forty-second parallel—the present northern boundary of California—and thence due west to the Pacific. This meant that the United States gave up its shadowy claim to Texas, while Spain surrendered its equally vague claim to the Oregon country.

The revolt of Spain's South American colonies and the possibility of European intervention to restore the status quo provided the chief incentive for the Monroe Doctrine, destined later to become a cardinal principle of American foreign policy. Though American public opinion strongly sympathized with the rebellious colonists, the Monroe Administration was reluctant to antagonize Spain so long as the Florida question remained unsettled, and did not recognize the newly independent governments until 1822. By then Russia, Prussia, Austria, and France had formed a 'Holy Alliance' to suppress liberalism and uphold monarchy. After the alliance had crushed uprisings in Italy and Spain (1821–3) there were rumors that it was planning to help Spain recover its South American empire. This alarmed the United States, both for security reasons and because it hoped to extend republican institutions. The Monroe Administration was also disturbed by a Russian edict of 1821 extending the boundary of Alaska southward into the Oregon country and claiming the west coast of North America as a possible field for Russian colonization. Both developments persuaded Monroe and Adams of the need to make clear American opposition to European intervention in the Western Hemisphere.

At this juncture Great Britain sought American cooperation. Having built up a thriving trade with the former Spanish colonies, the British had no desire to see the restoration of Spanish rule. In August 1823, therefore, Canning proposed a joint Anglo-American protest against European intervention. Monroe was at first disposed to accept the offer of what amounted to an informal alliance. Jefferson and Madison, too, despite their earlier belief in nonentanglement, warmly favored the idea. But John Quincy Adams would not hear of it. Knowing that the British would in any case oppose intervention, he argued that it would be "more candid and more dignified" for the United States to act unilaterally than to appear "to come in as a cock-boat in the wake of the British man-of-war" Adams's arguments prevailed and, in his annual message to Congress on December 2, 1823, Monroe laid down the policy later known as the Monroe Doctrine. An essentially nationalistic declaration, it embodied the concept of two separate hemispheres. On the one hand it stated that the American continent was not to be considered as an area for future colonization by

European powers and that European intervention in the affairs of the New World would be regarded as a manifestation of unfriendliness towards the United States. On the other hand it assured the European powers that the United States would not involve itself in their internal affairs or interfere with their existing New World colonies. In the United States the Monroe Doctrine eventually symbolized hostility to despotism and became as sacrosanct as the Constitution itself; yet in Latin America it came to be associated with United States domination. But it had no immediate effects. The European powers, well aware that the United States lacked the power to support its grand pretensions, dismissed the declaration as arrogant bluster. In fact it was not the Monroe Doctrine but British diplomacy, backed by the might of the Royal Navy, that dissuaded the Holy Alliance from intervening in Latin America. Even in the United States the Doctrine attracted relatively little attention and was well-nigh forgotten for a generation.

Sectional Strains

Despite the postwar flowering of nationalism, sectional rivalries persisted. Already evident in the 1816 Congressional debates on the bank, the tariff, and internal improvements they became more intense as the nation grew and the different sections became economically more divergent. There were especially bitter sectional clashes over the tariff. The South, disappointed when the 1816 tariff did nothing to stimulate its own infant industries, came to feel that it was being exploited for the benefit of Northern manufacturers. When protectionists succeeded in raising tariff levels in 1824 it was against almost solid Southern opposition.

Westward expansion created additional sectional strains. Between 1810 and 1819 the population of the trans-Appalachian region more than doubled and five new states entered the Union. The move west was accompanied—indeed largely made possible—by a speculative boom. High farm prices encouraged speculative purchases of public land, generally with inflated paper money. In 1819 the speculative bubble burst. Commodity prices and land values tumbled, businesses collapsed, many state banks failed. The economic depression lasted until 1823 and, while the entire country was affected, Westerners were especially hard hit. Ignoring the real causes of the disaster, they put the blame on the deflationary policies of the Bank of the United States. In 1818 the Bank had begun, somewhat belatedly, to enforce sound banking practices and to contract credit by calling in loans and presenting the notes of 'wildcat' banks for payment. These steps, though fiscally sound, precipitated the economic downturn and generated intense Western hostility toward the Bank—'the monster' as it became known. And since the panic of 1819 coincided with the *McCulloch* decision which thwarted state attempts to cripple the Bank,

Western hatred of the Eastern 'money power' was extended to the Supreme Court.

Even more dangerously divisive was the controversy that developed over Missouri's application for admission to the Union. The territory of Missouri, situated within the Louisiana Purchase, had been settled chiefly by Southerners and about six thousand of its 66,000 inhabitants in 1820 were Negro slaves. Thus the proposed state constitution recognized and protected slavery. But when the bill to admit Missouri came before Congress in February 1819, a New York representative proposed an amendment requiring the gradual abolition of slavery as a condition of admission. The amendment passed the House on a markedly sectional vote but was defeated in the Senate. The issue was furiously debated throughout the country. Northerners bitterly attacked slavery as an evil which ought not to be allowed to spread; Southerners defended it with equal passion. But the moral and humanitarian aspects of the question were less important than the political. Since the North had now outstripped the South in population, it had a sizable majority in the House. But with eleven slave states and eleven free, the balance in the Senate was even. Which section would control the federal government in the future depended on whether slavery was to be permitted in Missouri and the rest of the Louisiana Purchase. For the time being the issue was settled by the Missouri Compromise of 1820, of which Clay was the main architect. Missouri was to be admitted as a slave state while Maine, hitherto part of Massachusetts, was to come in as a free state in order to preserve the sectional equilibrium. In addition slavery was forbidden in the Louisiana Purchase north of the line 36°30', except in Missouri itself. A further difficulty developed when Missouri included in its constitution a provision forbidding free blacks and mulattos to enter the state, but Clay once again devised an acceptable compromise which allowed Missouri to attain statehood in 1821.

The Missouri crisis brought home to leading Americans the alarming potentialities of sectional disputes over slavery. Jefferson declared: "this momentous question, like a fire-bell in the night, awakened and filled me with terror". John Quincy Adams confided to his diary that "the present question is a mere preamble—a title-page to a great, tragic volume". While these apprehensions were eventually borne out, the danger to the Union was less immediate than Jefferson and Adams imagined. The Missouri Compromise put to rest the question of slavery extension for a quarter of a century.

7. The Expanding Union, 1815–1860

Between 1815 and 1860 the United States changed faster and more completely than in the previous two centuries or in any comparable period since. Population continued to double every twenty-five years or so; by 1860 it exceeded thirty-one millions and was larger than the United Kingdom's. The country's boundaries were extended to the Pacific, the settled area was doubled, the number of states increased from eighteen to thirty-three. At the same time a rapidly growing capitalist and commercial economy replaced the simpler agrarian society of Jefferson's day. There were breathtaking improvements in transport and communication, foreign trade boomed, cities grew, immigration reached undreamt-of heights. This growth also caused the three main sections of the country to develop along different lines. A new agrarian West came into being; mass immigration and an Industrial Revolution transformed the Northeast; a new scale of cotton production gave the slave-holding South a more special character than ever. By 1850 these divergences had sharpened antagonisms to the point of threatening the Union itself.

The Transport Revolution

Better communications underlay economic growth. Road improvement came first. The earliest hard-surfaced road in the country, the sixty-six-mile-long turnpike connecting Philadelphia and Lancaster, Pennsylvania, was opened in 1794. So profitable was it that more than 4,000 miles of turnpikes were built in the next thirty years, mostly in New England and the Middle Atlantic states. Nearly all of them were built by private companies chartered for the purpose and supported by tolls. But state and local governments often helped by investing in them and the federal government financed the most famous of all turnpikes, the National (or Cumberland) Road; running across the Appalachians from Cumberland, Maryland to Wheeling, Virginia by 1818, by 1850 it had reached Vandalia, Illinois. It became a great highway for emigration; thousands of pioneer families trekked annually along its 834-mile length on horseback or by stagecoach or Conestoga wagon, accompanied by droves of cattle, sheep, and hogs. But constitutional objections and sectional and state jealousies ended federal road-building. In any case, turnpike fever subsided after 1835 or so. Thousands of miles of road were abandoned. Repair costs were high; the payment of tolls was widely evaded; above all, overland freight charges were too steep. Partly to blame, too, was competition from other forms of transport.

One stemmed from the application of steam-power to lake and river transport. As early as 1787 John Fitch had successfully demonstrated a paddle-wheeler on the Delaware River, but it was an artist and civil engineer, Robert Fulton, who made steam navigation commercially successful. In 1807, his steamboat, *Clermont*, sailed up the Hudson from New York to Albany, a distance of 150 miles, in thirty-two hours. Fulton and a business partner immediately obtained a monopoly of the waters of New York state—a grant which retarded steamboat navigation until the Supreme Court in 1824 in *Gibbons* v. *Ogden* declared such monopolies to be unconstitutional.

Steamboats made their greatest impact further west. In 1811 the first steamboat appeared on the Ohio and made a demonstration run to New Orleans. By 1830 nearly 200 were plying the Mississippi and its tributaries, and by 1855 more than 700. Freight and passenger costs plummeted, river traffic soared. St. Louis, a frontier village in 1804, rose swiftly to become the commercial pivot of the Mississippi Valley. New Orleans, the natural outlet for Western flour, corn, beef, tobacco, and lumber, grew more rapidly than any city in the country. The two decades before the Civil War were the heyday of river steamboats. The typical Mississippi steamboat was two or three decks high, 250 or even 300 feet long, and powerful enough to stem the swiftest current, yet with a draft so shallow that it could "run on a heavy dew". It was thoroughly practical and showily handsome. There was no more colorful sight in the entire Western panorama than one of these 'floating palaces', with its sumptuously furnished saloon, gilded superstructure, and twin stacks pouring out black smoke. Yet river travel remained hazardous. Unlit, poorly charted rivers, submerged rocks, sandbanks, tree-stumps, wrecks, fire, and boiler explosions took a heavy toll. More than 30 percent of all Western steamboats built before 1849 were lost in accidents of one kind or another. A safety code was enacted in 1852, but in 1858 alone, 47 Western steamboats were sunk, 19 were burned, and 9 exploded, with the loss of 259 lives.

Although the Mississippi and Ohio river systems were heavily used right up to the Civil War, canals and railroads gradually enabled the Atlantic seaports to outstrip New Orleans in the competition for Western trade. In 1816 there were only a hundred miles of canals in the entire country. But the Erie Canal (built between 1817 and 1825) opened a new era. Largely the creation of Governor De Witt Clinton of New York, it linked Albany on the Hudson with Buffalo on Lake Erie; thus New York City was connected by water with the Old Northwest. The canal was 363 miles long, had 83 locks and 18 aqueducts, and was an immediate success. Nineteen thousand boats and rafts used Clinton's 'big ditch' in 1826; within nine years it had paid for itself. Freight charges from Buffalo to New York fell from $100 to $15 a ton, travel time from twenty days to eight. This galvanized the economy of the Old Northwest and helped to give New York City the lead it established over the rival ports of Boston, Philadelphia, and Baltimore. By 1850 half of America's foreign trade was passing through New York.

The spectacular success of the Erie led to a general enthusiasm for canal-building. By 1840 a total of 3,326 miles of canals had been built at a cost of about $125 million. Private capital could not raise such sums and constitutional objections limited the amount of federal aid; the states therefore supplied most of the money—much of it borrowed from British investors. But after a panic in 1837, itself the result in part of excessive expenditure on canals which brought the states close to bankruptcy, the canal boom was over. Many projects had been undertaken in ignorance of the difficulties and expense, and even without the growing competition of railroads, heavy maintenance costs, loss of revenue through droughts, floods, and frost, and inefficient management were bound to produce a crop of failures. During the 1840s and 1850s substantial sums continued to be spent on enlargement and improvement, but there were few new canals, and even the busiest soon became obsolescent. Nevertheless canals had been crucial in expanding inland commerce and in opening up the West.

But the future belonged elsewhere. The railroad era had begun even before canal-building reached its height. The first American railroad—as distinct from a private tramway—was the Baltimore and Ohio, chartered by the city of Baltimore in 1827. The first spadeful of earth for its track was turned on July 4, 1828 by the last surviving signatory of the Declaration of Independence. A thirteen-mile stretch went into operation in May 1830 and within months steam locomotives had replaced the horses which originally drew the wagons. The struggle for Western markets, which had prompted Baltimore's action, led other cities to authorize railroad construction and by 1840 the United States had 3,328 miles of track, though little as yet west of the Appalachians.

Such was the popular enthusiasm for railroads that private capital was readily forthcoming: more than $1,250 million was invested in railroads between 1830 and 1860. State and local governments also helped with monopoly privileges, exemptions from taxation, and substantial loans. A few states, Georgia and Virginia among them, even built and operated railroads themselves. Constitutional scruples delayed federal aid for a time but in 1850, in response to pressure from the South and West, Congress made a grant of 3,736,000 acres of public land to help finance the construction of the Illinois Central Railroad from Chicago to New Orleans. During the next ten years federal land grants totaling a further eighteen million acres were made to encourage railroad building.

The mileage of 1840 almost trebled in the next ten years. Then in the 1850s came a further astonishing acceleration: by 1860 the national track mileage stood at 30,626 miles—three times more than Great Britain's. The most striking growth was in the West, notably in Ohio, Indiana, and Illinois. By 1860 all the major Northern cities were connected by rail; four great trunk lines—the New York Central, the Erie, the Pennsylvania, and the Baltimore and Ohio—linked the Atlantic seaboard with the Middle West, no fewer than eleven railroads radiated from Chicago, and it was now possible to travel by rail as far west as St. Joseph, Missouri. There was even talk of a transcontinental railroad. All the same the United States did not yet have an integrated railroad network. Rails had still not bridged such major rivers as the Ohio and the Potomac; gauge diversity still hampered through services. Nor was rail travel yet safe. In the hectic rush to lay more track little attention was paid to maintenance or to elementary safety precautions. In 1853 alone there were more than a hundred serious accidents, with 234 passengers killed and 496 seriously injured. But for all that the vast benefits of rail were obvious. Triumphing over all rivals it had solved the problem of moving goods and people cheaply over great distances, opened the way for large-scale manufacturing, and created a single interdependent market. Almost in step with it, because it made railroad operation easier, the electric telegraph, too, had forged new links across the nation. Samuel F. B. Morse had demonstrated its practicality in 1844 by sending messages by wire from Baltimore to Washington; the country had over 50,000 miles of telegraph by 1861, when it became possible to send a telegraph message from New York to San Francisco.

Foreign Trade and Shipping

As the domestic economy expanded, foreign trade boomed. Exports, still mainly cotton, tobacco, wheat, and other agricultural products, rose in value from $67 million in 1825 to $333 million in 1860; imports, largely manufactured goods, grew even faster. Much of this foreign trade was carried in American vessels. Between 1820 and 1860 the total of American registered tonnage expanded nearly fourfold from about 636,000 tons to 2,300,000. The shipyards of New York and New England turned out vessels which in speed, strength, and durability were superior to anything afloat as well as being cheap. They were also more skillfully manned. Consequently American packets and regular traders dominated the Atlantic shuttle to Liverpool and Le Havre; the American flag became a familiar sight in the roadsteads of Calcutta, Canton, Smyrna, and Rio de Janeiro;

about three-quarters of the world's whaling fleet was American. The supreme achievement of American shipbuilding was, however, the development of the clipper ship. Its sharp, uncluttered lines and huge spread of canvas gave it the speed for record-breaking passages: the *Flying Cloud*, built in Boston in 1851 by the most famous of clipper-builders, Donald McKay, sailed on her maiden voyage from New York to California via Cape Horn in eighty-nine days, making 374 miles in one day. Speed gave the clippers profitable employment in the California and Australia gold trades, and, after the repeal of the British Navigation Acts in 1849, in the China tea trade to England.

But the golden age of American shipping was not to last. Wood and sails were giving way to iron and steam. As early as 1840 a Cunard steamer inaugurated the first regular transatlantic steamship service between Liverpool and Boston. Soon British, French and German steamships monopolized the carriage of mails, cabin passengers and fine freight. In 1850 a New York shipowner attempted to restore American fortunes with a fleet of wooden paddle-steamers, but the powerful engines of the 1850s required iron hulls, which the American yards of the day could not build and the attempt collapsed in a few years. The final blow to American shipping—from which it never really recovered—was the toll taken by Confederate commerce-raiders during the Civil War. But the Civil War merely accelerated decline.

The Westward Movement

Besides expanding markets and generally tying the nation together, the transport revolution facilitated travel and settlement. Americans had of course been edging westward for more than two centuries, but at the close of the War of 1812 the frontier had nowhere advanced more than halfway across the continent. The settled area of the United States lay almost wholly within a westward-pointing triangle whose base was the Atlantic and whose apex lay at the confluence of the Ohio and the Mississippi rivers. Flanking this triangle lay two huge empty provinces, one stretching north to the Great Lakes, the other south to the Gulf of Mexico. In the succeeding quarter of a century land-hungry settlers poured into both these regions, transforming primeval forests and rolling prairies into farms and plantations. By 1850 the frontier vanguard was well beyond the Mississippi and a number of outposts existed on the Pacific coast. The nation's center of gravity had moved west several hundred miles. Only one American in seven lived west of the Appalachians in 1810, but by 1850 one in two did so. Political geography was equally transformed. In 1815 only four of the eighteen states in the Union lay beyond the Appalachians. By 1850 fifteen out of thirty were west of the mountains. The West had a distinctive ethos: it was more innovative, more self-reliant and more aggressively democratic than the East. There were also distinctively Western demands—for Indian removal, for federal aid to internal improvements and for a liberal land policy. But the West was never a wholly unified section: its southern half was slave-holding and its northern half free-soil.

White settlement meant the removal of the Indians. The War of 1812 had weakened the Indians' ability to resist. After it by a mixture of bribery and threats most of the tribes were prevailed upon to sign treaties ceding their ancestral lands. But some tribes proved recalcitrant and had to be ejected by force. The Black Hawk War of 1832, in which Abraham Lincoln served as a private in the Illinois militia, required no more than a series of skirmishes against the confederated Sacs and Foxes. But the Seminole War of 1835–42 involved large-scale operations in the Florida swamps and cost the United States 1,500 men and $50 million. The worst example of ruthlessness was the state of Georgia's expulsion of the Cherokees (see Chapter 8). The cruelty and injustice of the removal policy was strongly condemned by religious bodies supporting Indian missions and by New England intellectuals like Ralph Waldo Emerson. But most Americans accepted that the Indian was an obstacle to progress and a menace to the safety of whites.

Changes in public land policy also helped Western settlement. The Land Act of 1796 favored land companies at the expense of settlers, providing that public land be sold at auction in 640-acre lots at a minimum of $2 per acre. During the Jeffersonian period the minimum unit of sale was reduced, first to 320 acres, then to 160, while purchasers were allowed several years to pay. The credit system, however, encouraged speculation and in 1820 Congress ended it, though at the same time it further reduced the minimum purchase to 80 acres and brought down the minimum price to $1.25 per acre. A further concession to Western pressure came in the Preemption Act of 1841, which gave squatters a prior right to purchase lands on which they had settled. But although the land laws were progressively liberalized they did not—at least until the Homestead Act of 1862—provide that easy access to the public domain that Jefferson had seen as the foundation of political and economic democracy. There was no limit on purchases and no need for buyers to settle on their lands. This encouraged speculation and in places the accumulation of large estates. Moreover since the average settler found government land too dear for outright purchase and was forced to borrow at high rates, hard times tended to force him into tenancy. By and large, it is true, the West was settled by men who tilled their own soil. But the pattern of ownership was not wholly democratic.

Every new Western farm, every mile of highway, canal, and railroad linking the seaboard with the interior made it more difficult to wrest a living from New England's rocky, sterile soil. Migration was the result, though the growth of industry and towns provided some farmers with a local market for specialized crops. Those living close to the expanding cities turned to vegetable-growing and dairying, many in the Connecticut Valley to tobacco culture, those in hilly country to sheep-raising. The 'sheep craze' which swept over Massachusetts, Connecticut, and Vermont in the late 1820s was a major cause of depopulation—as it was in the Scottish Highlands. Western competition produced less dramatic results in the Middle Atlantic states but here too there was agricultural distress and disturbance of the rural population. In the South soil exhaustion intensified the problems caused by the rise of the West. Wasteful methods of cultivation had left a legacy of declining crops and exhausted fields, first in the tobacco states of Virginia, Maryland, and North Carolina, then throughout the cotton-producing regions of the Carolinas and Georgia. Agricultural reformers pleaded for the adoption of scientific methods but they made few converts when the rich virgin lands of Alabama and Mississippi beckoned. As Jefferson had noted, Americans found it cheaper to buy a new acre than to manure an old one.

Broadly speaking, pioneers tended to migrate along lines of latitude. Yet within this broad tidal pattern there were many cross-currents. The family of the future Confederate President, Jefferson Davis, headed southwest from Kentucky to Louisiana just before the War of 1812, but subsequently doubled back to settle in Mississippi. During periods of depression, moreover, many disappointed settlers went back East. Few Mississippi Valley settlers traveled long distances to their new homes: they generally came from immediately adjacent territories. Nor did they generally stay put for long. Typical of migrating frontier families was Abraham Lincoln's. The future President's father, Thomas Lincoln, was born in upcountry Virginia in 1778. Four years later he was taken to Kentucky, where in 1809 Abraham was born. By 1816 the Lincolns had drifted to Indiana where they squatted for a year in a three-sided shack before moving into a typical log cabin with a dirt floor, no windows or doors, and a loft where young Abe made his bed on a pile of leaves. This unpretentious dwelling was their only home for fifteen years before they moved once again, this time to Illinois. As the experience of the Lincolns suggests, loneliness, poverty, and a near primitive existence were the lot of many frontiersmen, at least during the early stages of settlement. But steady advance was the rule even though—contrary to what Frederick Jackson Turner's much-quoted schematic model assumed—frontier society did not pass sequentially through well-defined phases. Instead of there being successive waves of specialized settlers (as Turner believed), each more committed to permanence than the last, 'men of enterprise and capital' intending to put down roots were just as likely to be pioneers as were transient individualists.

With the advance of settlement the Northwest displaced the Atlantic seaboard as the main source of corn, wheat, cattle, sheep, and pigs. It was a land of small family farms. As the Northeast became more industrial and urban, Western farming became more commercial and more specialized. The huge increase that occurred in Western agricultural production, especially between 1840 and 1860, was due not only to the richness of the soil but also to the advance of agricultural technology. Western farmers paid little heed to Eastern advocates of scientific farming who preached the virtues of crop rotation and the use of commercial fertilizers: the abundance of land encouraged wasteful methods. But they were quick to abandon traditional ways in favor of the improved tools and labor-saving devices which now became available. In 1837 an Illinois blacksmith, John Deere, turned out a steel plow capable of cutting and turning the tightly packed prairie sod. Ten years later Deere established a plow factory at Moline, Illinois and by 1858 was manufacturing 13,000 a year. Even more important for large-scale grain production was the mechanical reaper invented in 1831 by Cyrus H. McCormick of Virginia. His farsightedness in moving his factory in 1847 to Chicago, in the heart of the grain belt, together with his superior business methods, enabled him to triumph over a rival who had independently perfected a similar device. By 1860 McCormick was turning out 20,000 reapers a year. Comparable improvements in threshing came about at the same time, the leading invention being the combined threshing and fanning machine invented by John and Hiram A. Pitts in 1834. These advances, along with the introduction of mechanical seed-drills and various types of cultivator, made it possible for Northern farmers to sustain and even to increase grain production during the Civil War, despite the heavy manpower demands of the Union army.

Many of those who went West were lured by the opportunities that accompanied the growth of towns. Indeed, the town-dweller often preceded the farmer on the frontier. Towns like Pittsburgh, Cincinnati, Lexington, Louisville, and St. Louis, planted in the late-eighteenth century as forts or trading posts, lay well ahead of the line of settlement and served as magnets for the advancing population. Not all frontier towns prospered as their founders had hoped. Many never got beyond the planning stage; others flourished briefly, then stopped growing or faded away altogether. But the more successful grew spectacularly, especially after 1830; Rochester, Buffalo, Cleveland, Detroit, and Milwaukee each doubled their population in two successive decades, while Chicago's rose from a mere 40 in 1830 to 60,000 in 1855 and to 109,000 in 1860.

In the absence of regulation either by Congress, by the state legislatures, or by the Post Office, Western pioneers were free in the early decades of the nineteenth century to devise their own names for the raw settlements they inhabited. Duplication and frequent second thoughts were a constant source of confusion. Yet the hotchpotch of Western place-names was both a tribute to the inventiveness of the settlers and an expression of their culture. Town names could be purely descriptive (Grand Rapids, South Bend), synthetic (Zanesville, Parkersburg), or exotic (Pekin, Calcutta). Settlers commemorated their European origins, mineral discoveries, and Indian attacks. Frequently they honored national leaders, especially Washington, Franklin, Jefferson, Madison, and Jackson. Names like Sioux Falls, Omaha, and Kansas City were borrowed from the Indians and others like Des Moines, Terre Haute, and Baton Rouge looked back to the French presence. The proliferation of such names as Athens, Rome, Troy, Ithaca, and Syracuse, coinciding with the early nineteenth-century Greek revival in architecture, testified alike to classical influences and to aspirations to future grandeur. Romantic invention produced some odd toponymy. There were bogus Greek names like Minneapolis, bogus Spanish names like Pasadena, meaningless Indian names like Conestoga. And some French place-names were marvelously transmogrified: thus Purgatoire became Picketwire.

Urban Growth

Though Western towns grew fastest, most towns grew rapidly. 7.2 percent of Americans lived in communities of 2,500 in 1820 and 19.8 percent in 1860. In the 1840s the total urban population grew from 1,843,500 to 3,548,000, an increase of 92 percent, greater than in any other decade before or since. The most urbanized region was the Northeast, where more than a third of the people lived in towns and cities by 1860; in Massachusetts and Rhode Island the proportion was well over half. In the South, fewer than 10 percent of the population were urban dwellers; towns were few and, except for New Orleans and Baltimore, comparatively small. In 1815 only two American cities (New York and Philadelphia) had more than 100,000 people, but by 1860 there were eight with more than 150,000. (England at the time had only seven.) New York now forged ahead of its rivals to become easily the largest and most important American city. This was not due simply to the Empire City's natural advantages—her excellent ice-free port and the deep-water navigation into the interior afforded by the Hudson—or even to the building of the Erie Canal. Equally important was the enterprise of her merchants. In 1817 they established an import auction system that ensured a rapid turnover; the following year they inaugurated the first regular, scheduled transatlantic packet service; by the end of the 1820s they had developed a 'cotton triangle' with Southern ports and Europe that gave them almost complete control of Southern commerce.

Slavery and the Cotton Kingdom

The South was transformed by the expansion of cotton production and the consequent revival of slavery. The rise of the textile industry in England and later in New England created a huge demand for cotton. At first, however, the only cotton grown in the United States was the 'sea-island'variety which needed the special climatic conditions of coastal Georgia and South Carolina. Then in 1793 came Eli Whitney's cotton gin which solved the problem of separating the seeds from the fibers of upland or short-staple cotton, and made cotton-growing practicable on almost any soil in regions with adequate rainfall and 200 continuous frost-free days. Cotton production spread, first into the Piedmont areas of South Carolina and Georgia, then into the rich lands of the Alabama–Mississippi Black Belt and the Mississippi Delta, and finally into Texas. By 1840 or so the Cotton Kingdom extended more than a thousand miles from east to west and spread six or seven hundred miles up the Mississippi Valley. Production rose phenomenally: from 3,000 bales (of 500 lbs. each) in 1790 it shot up to 100,000 in 1801, 400,000 in 1820, and nearly 4 million in 1860. As cotton cultivation expanded the center of production moved steadily west; by 1860 Mississippi was the leading cotton state and almost a third of American cotton came from west of the Mississippi River.

The South was not simply one vast cotton field. It grew other important staples, especially tobacco, sugar, and rice and raised more than half the corn produced in the United States. But it was around cotton that the economic life of the section mainly revolved. In growing it there were advantages in large-scale production. Thus large plantations tended to grow in number faster than small farms. Moreover, the fact that all staples required constant, though not necessarily skilled, attention meant that slave-labor was ideally suited to their cultivation.

At the time of the Revolution slavery had seemed moribund. But the cotton gin and the spread of cotton cultivation revitalized it. This had important consequences for sectional alignments. The Gulf states of Alabama, Mississippi, and Louisiana came to identify themselves, not with other Western states like Ohio, Indiana, and Illinois, which were settled contemporaneously, but with the slave states of the Atlantic seaboard.

Among New World slave societies, that of the Old South was the only one that did not need to sustain itself by fresh importations from Africa. Though the African slave-trade legally ended in 1808, the number of slaves in the South continued to double every thirty years, growing from 857,000 in 1800 to nearly four million in 1860. Some clandestine importations continued even after 1808—one authority has put the total between then and 1860 at 250,000—but most of the slaves in the newly opened cotton states of the Southwest came not from abroad but from soil-exhausted areas of the upper South, especially Virginia and Maryland. Sometimes slaves accompanied their migrating masters but more often they were shipped overland or by sea by professional slave-traders to auction centers like New Orleans, Natchez, and Galveston. This domestic slave-trade was a highly organized and lucrative business; on the eve of the Civil War it annually involved perhaps 80,000 slaves valued at $60 million. After the closing of the foreign slave-trade prices rose steadily. The price of a 'prime field hand' increased from $500 in 1832 to $1800 in the late 1850s.

The distribution of slaves in the Old South was distinctively different from that in the rest of the Americas. Whereas in Brazil, Cuba, and Jamaica slaves outnumbered whites they were no more than a third of the total Southern population in 1860. Only three states—South Carolina, Mississippi, and Louisiana—had a slave majority and in none of them did the slave proportion exceed 60 percent. The Old South also differed from other slave societies in that slave-holders in Brazil and the Caribbean usually owned more than 100 slaves apiece, whereas fewer than 1 percent of United States slave-holders possessed that many. (Fewer than a dozen had 500 or more.) In 1860 nearly three-quarters of Southern slave-holders owned fewer than ten. Many small farmers supervised their slaves personally, often working side by side with them. Nevertheless most slaves were owned in groups of twenty or more and were to be found on large farms or plantations.

Not all slaves were employed in growing cotton or even in agriculture. Plantations needed many slave craftsmen—carpenters, masons, bricklayers, coopers, and so on—not to mention house servants. Perhaps as many as 500,000 slaves lived in cities and towns on the eve of the Civil War. They worked in coal-mines and textile factories as well as in virtually every trade and craft, in lumber camps and on steamboats, sometimes alongside whites. In Richmond, Virginia, the Tredegar Iron Works—the largest in the South—relied heavily upon slave-labor.

The Southern states regulated the conditions of slavery by law. The various slave laws or codes reflected the anomaly that was characteristic of the institution. On the one hand slaves were defined as chattel property which could be bought, sold, inherited, bequeathed, mortgaged, or hired out. On the other, their humanity was recognized: they were acknowledged to be capable of rebelling, running away, and committing serious crimes and were made liable to punishment for such actions. In theory slaves lived under an unvaryingly harsh and repressive system. They were forbidden to hold property, to carry firearms, to congregate with others except at church, to leave their masters' premises without permission, or to give evidence against a white man in court. They could not legally marry or be taught to read and write. In practice, however, the provisions of the slave codes were widely ignored. Moreover the courts moderated some of their more draconian features.

While the severity of the codes reflected Southern fears of servile insurrection, organized slave resistance was rare. A plot in Richmond in 1801 was discovered and crushed before it came to a head. So was the conspiracy organized in 1822 by a Charleston free Negro. But it was a different story in August, 1831 when a Negro preacher, Nat Turner, who had developed mystical tendencies, led an insurrection in Southampton County, Virginia. Fifty-seven whites were killed before Turner and his followers were hunted down and executed. Although the South was untroubled by actual slave rebellions after that, rumors of imminent uprisings continued to alarm. Slave codes were tightened and night-patrols stepped up, and it was made more difficult for slaves to acquire freedom. Moreover, greater restraints were placed upon free Negroes,—there were 250,000 in the slave-holding states in 1860.

It is difficult to generalize about slave life. It depended upon the region in which slaves lived, the crop, the time of year, and the character of the individual master. Household servants had a much easier time than field hands, while the hiring system tended everywhere to enlarge slave privileges. Growing rice in the unhealthy swamps of coastal South Carolina and Georgia was more arduous than raising cotton; so was work in the Louisiana sugar plantations during the grinding season. The tradition that slaves were more humanely treated on small plantations than on large ones had elements of truth in it but was overdrawn; so was the stereotype that represented conditions in the Deep South as being much worse than those further north. Likewise the correlation between cruelty and absentee ownership suggested by the abolitionists was not universally true, though overseers were disproportionately responsible for maltreatment.

As far as purely material conditions are concerned, the life of American slaves compared favorably with that of slaves elsewhere and of the laboring classes in Europe. In general slaves were adequately if simply fed, clothed, and housed. The slave's diet of corn, pork, molasses, and greens was coarse and lacked variety, but it was better than that of many English farm laborers and infinitely superior to that of Irish or Russian peasants. Similarly, a slave's long workday was no longer than that of many Northern industrial and agricultural laborers. Where the 'task system' was employed, slaves were free for the rest of the day once the assigned work was done. Moreover, slave-holders commonly allowed slaves half a day off on Saturday, as well as the whole of Sunday. Some slaves had small plots of land and were encouraged to grow vegetables for their own use or for sale. There is no evidence to support the abolitionist charge that the rapid increase in slave numbers was due to systematic breeding. The standard practice was to allow—or at most to encourage—slaves to pair off and let nature take its course. Masters were well aware of the advantages that accrued to them from slave 'marriages': besides producing offspring they reduced the likelihood of runaways.

Yet slavery was at bottom a system of fear. Though brutality and cruelty were not the rule, neither self-interest nor public opinion could always check the violence to which even the best masters might succumb. Still less could they restrain the excesses of a drunkard or a sadist. If flogging was the commonest punishment, it was by no means the severest. Abolitionists had no need to invent stories of branding, mutilation, hanging, deliberate starvation, and torture; they simply copied them from Southern newspapers. Even so, the real degradation of slavery was not physical but psychological: it engendered feelings of dependency and helplessness and undermined the slaves' sense of their own worth. Yet slaves were not totally compliant, still less 'infantilized'. Though recognizing that resistance to slavery could rarely be violent or open, they devised a variety of mechanisms to modify and subvert it: they malingered, pilfered, broke tools, went slow, feigned sickness, pretended not to understand instructions, and sometimes ran away. Subtle and complex forms of accommodation enabled them to influence their conditions of work, to convert privileges into rights, to cushion the masters' authority, and to bind the masters to themselves in a system of mutual dependence. Despite repression, moreover, the slave community sustained an autonomous culture. Thus it escaped complete domination by the white master class. Folktales, oral traditions, dances, spirituals, religion, family ties—all showing signs of African influence—conferred a measure of dignity and psychological independence. Slave religion, far from being an echo of white evangelical Protestantism, evolved distinctive styles of worship, preaching, and participation. Despite the vulnerability of the slave family, slaves retained a strong sense of kinship. Most slaves lived in family groups, slave marriages were surprisingly stable and long-lasting, kinship patterns often survived the breakup of families by sale. For the slave, indeed, the family was one of the most important mechanisms for survival and for transmitting traditional African values.

It used to be held that slavery was an inefficient and uneconomic labor system that might well have collapsed under its own weight. But most economic historians now accept that slaves were a highly profitable form of investment and that slavery was very far from being moribund in 1860. Yet whatever profits were made by individual planters the heavy investment of Southern capital in slaves and land meant that little was available for industry or transport. Slavery was also the main cause of the South's economic dependence. Concentration on staple-crop agriculture drove Southerners to rely on Northern manufactures, Northern loans in anticipation of the harvest, Northern marketing and shipping services for their cotton and other exports. Much of a planter's profits went into Northern pockets. Not without reason did the South come to regard itself as a Northern colony. Yet although some Southern leaders urged the section to diversify its economy and develop direct trade with Europe, the dominant planter class was hostile to industrial and commercial enterprise. It regarded agriculture as the only fitting occupation for gentlemen and feared that industrialization would undermine both slavery and their own position. Although iron foundries and textile factories could be found there, the South produced less than 10 percent of America's manufactures in 1860.

The Growth of Industry

The origins of American industrialization can be traced back to 1790 when Samuel Slater, an English immigrant with a knowledge of Arkwright's machinery, built a tiny cotton-spinning mill at Pawtucket, Rhode Island. But manufacturing grew only slowly until foreign imports were cut off by the Jeffersonian embargo and the War of 1812. By the end of the war there were hundreds of small mills, mostly in New England. The founding in 1813 of the Boston Manufacturing Company by a group of wealthy Massachusetts merchants headed by Francis Cabot Lowell set the fashion of transferring capital from foreign trade to manufacturing. The factory the company built at Waltham, Massachusetts was the first in the world to combine under unified management all the operations of converting raw cotton into finished cloth. Lowell's company constantly introduced new technological improvements and established its own selling agencies instead of employing middlemen. In other ways too the group broke new ground: by hiring professional managers to direct operations and by building company towns to house their female employees. In 1823 they transferred their activities to the new industrial town of Lowell on the Merrimack and subsequently opened other mills in Massachusetts and New Hampshire, thus confirming New England's position as the country's leading cotton textile center.

From cotton manufacturing the Waltham system spread successively to other industries. Woolen manufacture, still organized on a household or domestic basis up to about 1820, was transformed thereafter by the introduction of power machinery. Ironworks multiplied. After coal and coke had replaced charcoal for smelting, iron-ore production became concentrated in western Pennsylvania and Ohio where coal and iron were both available. By mid-century the open forge and the blacksmith's shop had given way to the closed furnace and the rolling-mill. In places like Philadelphia, New York, and Lynn, Massachusetts the boot and shoe industry became progressively more mechanized and more specialized. Flour-milling and meat-packing were similarly transformed, the former concentrated mainly at Rochester and St. Louis, the latter at Cincinnati and Chicago.

Although each of the formative industries leaned heavily at first on European technology, native ingenuity and inventiveness soon made their contribution. As early as 1787 a Delaware farmer's son, Oliver Evans, built the first completely automatic flour-mill; in 1802 he constructed a high-pressure steam-engine that proved adaptable to a great variety of industrial purposes. Even more crucial to industrial development and mass production was the principle of interchangeable parts applied in 1798 to the manufacture of guns by the New Englander, Eli Whitney, the inventor of the cotton gin. This method, which involved making each part to the same precise pattern, was shortly applied to other manufactures. In 1839 Charles Goodyear discovered a means of vulcanizing India rubber—that is, of preventing it from melting, sticking, and decomposing in heat—and after further experiments developed a uniform product which made possible the growth of the rubber industry. In 1846, two years after Morse's electric telegraph had demonstrated its capabilities, communications were further revolutionized by Richard M. Hoe's steam cylinder-press which made it possible to print newspapers more quickly and more cheaply. In 1846 also Elias M. Howe of Massachusetts devised and constructed a successful sewing-machine; after being improved by Isaac M. Singer, it was applied to the manufacture of ready-made clothing and shoes. By mid-century, indeed, the reputation of the United States as the home of invention had spread abroad. At the Crystal Palace Exhibition of 1851, American inventions like Cyrus Hall McCormick's reaping machine and Samuel Colt's revolver created an immense stir. A few perceptive Englishmen glimpsed portents of America's ultimate industrial supremacy.

Industrial expansion revolutionized business. As factories grew larger and production became more mechanized the capital required rose far beyond the resources of even the wealthiest individuals. The answer to the problem was the corporation, which could accumulate capital by selling shares to large numbers of investors. The corporate form having already been used by turnpike and bridge companies, the principle of limited liability was already well established in law and in practice by the 1820s. This meant that owners of corporation stock were liable for the debts of the company only to the extent of their own investments. General incorporation laws passed in the 1830s helped further. Hitherto a corporation charter needed a special legislative grant, a practice which had been widely criticized as leading to the creation of monopolies. But, in accordance with Jacksonian equal-rights principles, corporation charters became available to all who fulfilled certain legal requirements. Though most industrial firms remained unincorporated until well after the Civil War corporations nonetheless proliferated under the new arrangements and, with the number of stockholders growing steadily, there was a tendency for ownership to become divorced from management. The way was thus open for a few aggressive businessmen and financiers, owning only a fraction of the stock, to assume control of a company, or indeed a combination of companies.

The emergence of this new business elite was accompanied by that of a class of weekly wage-earners. At first the labor force was drawn from the nearby farm population and, especially in the textile industry, included large numbers of women and children. From the 1830s, however, it consisted increasingly of immigrants. Working and living conditions, though better than in Great Britain, were unquestionably bad and deteriorated further as the factory system expanded. The working day was long—even children worked twelve hours and more—wages were low, production was progressively speeded up, and both the factories and the workers' dwellings were crowded and unhealthy. The factory girls of Lowell, it is true, were better off. Working in mills that were anything but dark and satanic, they impressed visitors with their cheerful demeanor and neat attire and lived in comfortable boarding-houses, enjoying a variety of educational and recreational facilities, and finding the time to produce their own monthly magazine, the *Lowell Offering*. But even in Lowell women worked thirteen hours a day in the summer and from daylight to darkness in the winter, discipline was strict to the point of tyranny, and in 1834 they were driven to strike against a wage cut. Six years later the reformer Orestes Brownson was to write of the Lowell girls: 'the great mass wear out their health, spirits and morals without becoming one whit better than when they commenced labor'.

Yet collective action to improve conditions was slow to develop. In Philadelphia carpenters, cordwainers, and printers had begun to band together in the 1790s. Despite the fact that the courts tended to regard combinations of workers as illegal conspiracies, other crafts followed suit in the early nineteenth century. In the late 1820s a number of craft societies established citywide federations, and in 1834 six of them united to form a National Trades' Union. The next few years brought a large gain in membership and a rash of strikes. But the depression and unemployment which followed the panic of 1837 brought about the collapse of the movement. Nor were the Working-men's parties founded in New York and Philadelphia in the late 1820s more effective. Their definition of 'working-men' was extremely broad; including everyone except bankers and speculators, the 'Workies' anticipated the Knights of Labor of later years in being designed as associations of all the producing classes. Most of the leaders were not laborers but middle-class reformers and visionaries like William Leggett, Theodore Sedgwick, and Robert Dale Owen. They were concerned not so much with working conditions but with such objectives as the removal of property qualifications for the franchise, universal free education, and the abolition of imprisonment for debt. Divided by factionalism the Working-men's parties had become defunct by about 1834.

In 1842 trade unionism won a notable judicial victory in the Massachusetts case of *Commonwealth* v. *Hunt*, which ruled that trade unions were not in themselves criminal conspiracies and legalized strikes in favor of a closed shop. But although other state courts soon accepted these principles, the legal obstacles had been only partly removed. Nor did the working day get much shorter. A number of states, beginning with New Hampshire in 1847, passed laws establishing a ten-hour day, but these measures were rendered inoperative by provisions allowing employers and workers to 'negotiate' longer hours. Similarly the child-labor laws adopted by Massachusetts, New Hampshire, and Pennsylvania were a nullity: they simply forbade the employment of children for more than ten hours a day without their parents' consent. The mid-century flood of immigrants cheapened labor and served still further to delay labor organization.

American industrial progress in the half-century before the Civil War is easy to measure by statistics. The number of people employed in manufacturing industry grew from 349,000 to 1,311,000; the capital invested in manufacturing increased from $50 million to nearly $1,000 million; the annual value of manufactured products rose from $200 million to $2,000 million. Yet the American industrial revolution was still in its early stages in 1860. Manufacturing was still largely concentrated in New England and the Middle Atlantic states and even there mainly processed the products of American farms and forests. Many products were crudely and carelessly finished. Operations were typically on a small scale; the 140,000 manufacturing enterprises employed on average fewer than ten people. The annual value of American manufactures was less than that of the United Kingdom, France, or Germany. Little was exported but foreign agricultural products and manufactures still flooded in. Not enough coal was available to supplant other sources of energy in transport, industry, or the home. Nor could iron production meet domestic needs; much of the iron for the huge railroad expansion of the 1850s came from Great Britain. America's greatest period of industrial development still lay ahead.

The Rise of Mass Immigration.

The changes overtaking the North owed much to mass immigration. Hitherto the number of arrivals from abroad had been small, never more than 10,000 a year. But after 1815 the great wave of European immigration, which was destined to span an entire century, began to gather momentum. By the early 1830s immigrants were arriving at the rate of 50,000 a year, by the early 1840s 100,000, and by the early 1850s well over 300,000. Altogether between 1815 and 1860 there were no fewer than five million arrivals, more than the entire population of the United States in 1790.

Nearly all the immigrants came from northern and western Europe—mainly Ireland, Germany, and Great Britain, with smaller numbers from Switzerland, The Netherlands, and Scandinavia. Mainly they came because of economic pressure at home: rising populations coincided with the transformation of the old agricultural order. Ireland was the most densely populated country in Europe, with an iniquitous land system that kept the mass of the peasantry chained to the margin of subsistence. The rise of large-scale farming after 1815 and the consequent clearing of estates gave emigration its initial impetus. Then the Great Famine of 1845–9 opened the floodgates. After successive failures of the potato crop one million people died from starvation and fever; many of the survivors fled panic-stricken from a seemingly doomed land. The German immigrants of the period were by contrast victims neither of oppression nor of want. That German immigration reached its peak just after the revolutions of 1848 was pure coincidence. The great majority of the emigrants were farmers from Württemberg, Baden, and Bavaria where, as in Ireland, the consolidation of farms was squeezing out the small man. Some left after being ruined by crop failures, more decided not to wait until they had been reduced to poverty, preferring to go while they still had enough capital to make a fresh start.

Other developments, too, contributed to the rise of mass immigration. Cheap books, newspapers, and emigrant guides spread popular knowledge of America. Governments, which had long frowned on emigration as a drain on national wealth, now came to see it again as a remedy for pauperism and as a safety-valve for discontent and removed legal restraints. Greater freedom to move coincided with increasing opportunities for doing so. The great expansion of transatlantic commerce reduced steerage fares to a level that all but the very poorest could afford; vessels which carried bulky cargoes like cotton or timber on the eastward voyage had space to spare going west and were glad to carry emigrants. True, the Atlantic crossing remained a harsh ordeal. Emigrants were huddled together for weeks on end in dark and unventilated steerage quarters, food was coarse and meager, epidemics frequent. The worst horrors occurred in 1847 when more than 17,000 emigrants, mostly Irish, died from ship fever. Governments attempted remedial action but regulations were difficult to enforce. Yet hardship and exploitation failed to deter the millions determined to seek a share of American prosperity.

The overwhelming majority of immigrants settled in the North, especially along the eastern seaboard and in the upper Mississippi Valley. The South was largely shunned: neither jobs nor farmland were so readily available there. Immigrants with industrial skills tended to congregate in the American centers of their crafts: coal-miners and ironworkers in Pennsylvania, potters in Ohio, textile operatives in New England. Although frontier farming needed special techniques immigrant farmers settled on virgin land in greater numbers than used to be thought, though most probably bought improved land from owners moving further west. An exceptionally high proportion of Norwegians and Swedes took up farming, settling so thickly in Wisconsin and Minnesota as to give those states a pronounced Scandinavian flavor. Germans, too, frequently became farmers, particularly in Ohio, Illinois, Wisconsin, and Iowa. Yet at least as many Germans settled in towns and cities. In the 1850s Belleville, Illinois had a German mayor, a German majority on the city council, and three German newspapers—even the local blacks spoke German. The heaviest German concentrations, however, were in big cities like Milwaukee, Cincinnati, and St. Louis, each of which had unmistakably Germanic neighborhoods. In Cincinnati's 'Over the Rhine' German signs and inscriptions were universal in shops, restaurants, churches, theaters, and beer gardens; pipe-smoking Germans, some in peasant costume, filled the streets; distinctive German organizations flourished, among them choirs, gymnastic societies, and sharp-shooting clubs.

Urban concentration was most marked among the Irish. Despite their overwhelmingly rural origin only about 8 percent settled on the land. Ill-equipped for American farming, lacking capital, and knowing nothing of agriculture except how to grow potatoes, they were repelled by the loneliness of American farm life and were loath to move to regions lacking a Catholic church. For these reasons and because they were often too poverty-stricken and demoralized to do anything else, the Irish flocked to the cities, often remaining where they happened to land. By 1860 New York contained 200,000 Irish, Philadelphia 95,000, Boston about 70,000; there were other sizable Irish colonies in St. Louis, Chicago, New Orleans, and San Francisco. The famine refugees had a naive faith in America, but became America's first slum-dwellers, crowding into garrets, cellars, tenements, old warehouses, and flimsy one-room shacks in squalid neighborhoods like Boston's North End and New York's Five Points. These areas became notorious for epidemics and high mortality-rates. A Boston investigating committee reported in 1849 that the city's Irish neighborhoods were 'the permanent abode of fever' and that 'the average age of Irish life in Boston does not exceed fourteen years'.

Without money, education, or skills, the Irish were forced into menial occupations; they became laborers, porters, carters, and waiters or, in the case of women, domestic servants. They were also prominent in digging canals and building railroads. Conditions in the construction camps were uniformly bad, accidents common; often Irish navvies were cheated of their wages by unscrupulous contractors. Yet because of the strength of anti-Irish feeling, even unskilled jobs were sometimes hard to find. 'No Irish Need Apply' was a familiar feature of job advertisements. Gradually the Irish began to find places in New England textile mills (where they displaced native-born farm girls) and in the Pennsylvania mines, while those who managed to get as far as the new city of San Francisco found prejudice less of an obstacle. But in general the Irish remained at the bottom of the pile.

Although the immigrant influx benefited the country economically, its volume and character alarmed many native-born Americans. By 1850 immigrants made up almost half the populations of New York, Chicago, Cincinnati, Milwaukee, Detroit, and San Francisco; in St. Louis they outnumbered natives two to one. More worrying than mere numbers was the loss of social unity. Americans had hitherto prided themselves on their immunity from Europe's social ills. Paupers and beggars had been few, crime comparatively rare. But mid-century poor-relief and crime statistics revealed the foreign-born to be heavily over-represented. Two-thirds of the paupers in Massachusetts in 1849 were foreigners, mostly Irish; out of 17,328 persons arrested in New York in a typical quarter in 1858, no fewer than 14,638 were foreigners, 10,477 of them Irish. Americans were also perturbed at the political consequences of immigration, among them electoral violence and voting frauds. And although many newcomers were ignorant of American institutions, they were numerous enough in places to hold the political balance.

But more than anything it was religion that fanned anti-immigrant feeling. Until 1830 or so the United States had been almost exclusively Protestant but thirty years later, thanks to Irish and German immigration, the number of Roman Catholics exceeded three million—a tenth of the population. The number of Catholic bishops and priests, convents and monasteries, schools and colleges had risen correspondingly. All this rekindled the anti-Catholicism of colonial days. Regarding the Catholic Church mainly as a political institution, closely allied moreover to European despotism, Protestants believed the Catholic faith to be incompatible with American ideals. Some overwrought zealots even saw immigration as part of a popish plot to subvert America's free institutions. The 1830s saw a flood of scurrilous anti-Catholic literature, though its popularity was probably due as much to the appeal of religious pornography as to anti-Catholicism proper. In the early 1840s fears of Romanism were further stimulated by Catholic opposition to the use of the King James version of the Bible in the public schools and Catholic demands for a share in state-school funds. To many Protestants such attitudes seemed blasphemous, divisive, and un-American. Hostility toward Catholics occasionally erupted in mob violence, notably in 1834, when the Ursuline convent at Charlestown, Massachusetts was burned, and in 1844, when Catholic churches in Philadelphia were set on fire and several Catholics were killed and injured.

Not all Americans were upset by immigration. Many still held to the traditional belief that their country had been marked out by Providence as a refuge for the Old World's oppressed. Yet in the mid-1850s fear of foreigners and Catholics resulted in the emergence of a new 'nativist' political party which enjoyed spectacular, though short-lived success. (See Ch. 11.)

8. The Politics of Egalitarianism, 1824–1844

A Society of Equals?

To Alexis de Tocqueville, author of the classic *Democracy in America* published in 1835, the distinguishing mark of Americans was "equality of condition". The whole of American society, he insisted, had "merged into the middle class", few men being either very rich or very poor. Those reputed to be wealthy were not really so by European standards. They were, moreover, generally self-made men who tended to lose their fortunes as readily as they had made them. That a general equality of condition prevailed was also the view of other European visitors like Harriet Martineau and Charles Dickens. They noted the absence of social barriers and distinctions of rank, the fact that titles were taboo save for loosely conferred honorifics like 'Judge' and 'Colonel'. They observed that manners were less formal than in Europe, that immigrants quickly learnt egalitarian attitudes, that politicians paraded their humble origins or apologized for the lack of them, that the word 'servant' was considered too demeaning and (except in the slave-holding South) the word 'master' too deferential, that even children rejected the principle of authority. Class-conscious Europeans—and, indeed, some Americans, like the writer, James Fenimore Cooper—found all this distasteful, complaining that Americans were excessively familiar, indeed intrusively curious, and in addition were lacking in refinement. But such complaints simply reinforced the assertion that in Jacksonian America every man was as good as any other.

Tocqueville's was in some respects an exaggerated picture. Recent investigations have revealed the existence of great economic inequalities, especially in Northeastern cities. At the time of Tocqueville's American visit (1831–2) New York alone had a hundred persons worth $100,000 or more and Boston seventy-five. At the other extreme immigration was creating a growing mass of pauperism. Moreover, very few of the rich were self-made men; nor were great fortunes readily lost. Then again, for all its supposed classlessness, American society was far from unstratified. Everywhere there were differences of education and status and in places like

New York, Boston, Philadelphia, and Baltimore there existed, if not a formal aristocracy, at least a wealthy elite which lived genteelly and— especially its women — displayed a fierce exclusiveness.

Nevertheless the egalitarian thesis was basically sound. Though the fact of wealth was undeniable, it did not of itself confer power or prestige. Nor were the American rich idle. Even members of fashionable coteries had to work for their living and, in a society which prized industriousness, work tended to be a leveler. Furthermore, to an extent unknown in Europe, Americans spoke alike and dressed alike. Distinctive American forms of speech, as one observer would note in 1855, were "equally distributed through all classes and localities". Just as remarkable was what one historian has called "the democracy of clothing". Even workingmen wore gloves. The British consul in Boston, observing in the early 1840s that servant girls were "strongly infected with the national bad taste for being overdressed", complained that they were "scarcely to be distinguished from their employers". Travel, too, was having equalizing effects. People not only traveled more than in Europe but traveled hugger-mugger and indeed were commonly expected to sleep together, hotel guests being assigned to beds in the order of their arrival, with two, three, or even four to a bed. Demographic factors also played a part. The United States was a youthful country in more than one sense: in 1830 nearly half the population (45 percent) was under fifteen and a third (32.6 percent) was under ten. This extraordinary youthfulness helped explain the freedom which American children enjoyed and which struck European observers so unfavorably. The labor force being relatively small, parents were necessarily preoccupied with work and children had perforce to become self-reliant. The consequence was that, as Tocqueville remarked, adolescence was unknown in America. As another visitor put it, the United States was a country without children, having only "diminutive men and women in process of growing into bigger ones".

Political Democracy

The passion for equality was most fully expressed in politics. The new Western states that entered the Union after 1812 either had white manhood suffrage from the start or, at worst, prescribed nominal taxpaying qualifications. In the older Eastern states constitutional conventions did away with remaining property qualifications for voting, though there was stubborn resistance in some places. Conservative jurists like Joseph Story and James Kent, along with Daniel Webster and former Presidents Madison and Monroe, argued that property was entitled to special political weight and influence since it provided government with most of its revenues. But by 1830 most of the states had adopted universal white manhood suffrage and by the Civil War all had done so. Women could not yet vote nor, with a few exceptions, could blacks; indeed some states disfranchised blacks while extending the vote to whites. But with these limitations the right to vote became virtually universal.

Political democracy also advanced in other ways. Property and religious qualifications for office-holding were removed or reduced; state offices, even judgeships, tended to become elective rather than appointive; the principle of majority rule was recognized in attempts to equalize electoral districts. Moreover, presidential electors came increasingly to be chosen by direct popular vote instead of by state legislatures. By 1824 only six states adhered to the older practice; by 1828 only one—South Carolina. During the 1820s the number of voters, especially in presidential elections, began to increase far more rapidly than did the population as a whole. In the presidential election of 1824, only 26.5 percent of the adult white males went to the polls, but in 1828 it rose to 56.3 percent and in 1840 reached 78 percent. This was not due wholly to the extension of the suffrage. The electorate became more politically conscious and the newly developing party organizations made strenuous efforts to 'get out the vote'. Still another consequence of the egalitarian upsurge was a change in the procedure for choosing presidential candidates. Ever since 1800 the choice had been made by secret Congressional caucuses. This system, which left nominations in the hands of an inner clique of Washington politicians, was increasingly attacked as undemocratic. By 1832 'King Caucus' had given way to a system of national nominating conventions, in which the party rank and file were represented and, at least in theory, had some say in the choice of candidates.

No less significant was the development of a more popular political style. Candidates for public office found it expedient not only to extol the common man but also to claim kinship with him. Political nicknames came into fashion: Andrew Jackson was 'Old Hickory', Thomas Hart Benton 'Old Bullion', Martin Van Buren 'the red fox of Kinderhook', and Henry Clay 'Harry of the West'. Language quickly adapted itself to the demands of mass politics. The patrician political culture of the early republic had expressed itself in words like junto, caucus, interest, and faction. But, as the historian Morton Keller has demonstrated, a political vocabulary now developed which drew heavily upon images familiar to the common man. An obscure candidate for office was a 'dark horse'; a defeated incumbent was a 'lame duck'; appropriations bills became 'pork barrels', often passed through 'logrolling', that is, reciprocal political help; politicians made 'stump speeches', sat on the fence, put planks together to make a platform; a sweeping electoral victory was a landslide. Other revealing coinages included 'buncombe' or 'bunkum' (meaning speech-making for the purpose of winning popular approval), 'gerrymandering' (a method of arranging electoral districts so as to benefit one party), and 'lobbying' (the practice of frequenting legislatures in order to influence members). Some of these examples suggest that political democracy had unfortunate side-effects. Certainly it led to a marked decline in standards of Congressional behavior. Congressmen seem to have become increasingly prone to intoxication, while perhaps in consequence debates were all too frequently marred by personal altercations and unseemly brawls.

John Quincy Adams and National Republicanism

The caucus system collapsed in 1824 when the different Republican factions could not agree on a presidential candidate. A caucus meeting attended by fewer than a third of Congressional Republicans nominated William H. Crawford of Georgia, whom President Monroe had designated as his successor. But other aspirants refused to accept the decision. A Boston gathering nominated John Quincy Adams, Monroe's Secretary of State; the Kentucky legislature named Henry Clay, the Speaker of the House; the Tennessee legislature chose a political outsider, General Andrew Jackson, the hero of New Orleans. In the election Jackson received 99 electoral votes, Adams 84, Crawford 41, and Clay 37. Since no candidate had a majority, it fell to the House of Representatives to choose a President from among the three leading candidates. Crawford, having suffered a stroke, was out of·the reckoning, along with Clay who had run fourth. But the latter, as Speaker of the House and with thirty-seven electoral votes in his gift, had the power to decide the outcome. Eagerly courted by the friends of both Adams and Jackson, Clay finally threw his weight behind Adams, who was duly elected.

Clay's choice was a logical one since Adams was an avowed supporter of the American System, whereas Jackson was not—and, moreover, was Clay's principal rival for the affections of the West. But Jackson's followers were indignant that their candidate had been denied the Presidency after having led in both popular and electoral votes. And when Adams appointed Clay as his Secretary of State—the traditional stepping-stone to the Presidency—they promptly alleged that the two had made a 'corrupt bargain'. There is no evidence for this but the Jacksonians, their eyes already on the 1828 election, raised the cry that a small clique had thwarted the popular will. The most important consequence of the controversy was the realignment of the various Republican factions into two opposing camps, the Adams–Clay wing becoming known as National Republicans, the Jacksonians as Democratic Republicans.

The son of the second President, John Quincy Adams had served successively as minister to the Netherlands, Russia, and Great Britain and had been an outstanding Secretary of State. But his Presidency was one long catalog of frustration. Talented and conscientious though he was, he was lacking both in political skill and in charisma. His long residence abroad had caused him to lose touch with his native land. Lacking warmth, Adams was ill at ease with the products of the rising egalitarianism. He would not court popularity and was too high-minded to use presidential patronage to build a personal following or even to win votes for the grandiose plan of national improvement he set forth on coming to office. The plan included a national network of roads and canals, federal support for agriculture, commerce, and manufactures, encouragement of science, literature, and the arts, and a national university. Adams was well aware that centralized programs such as this ran counter to the rising states' rights tide but, believing that people should be given not what they wanted but what was good for them, urged Congress not to be "palsied by the will of our constituents".

In the event the President's proposals were ignored or derided. Appropriations for internal improvements exceeded those voted during all previous Administrations, but fell far short of what Adams wanted. The President ran into further trouble with state-rights supporters—and indeed with Southerners and Westerners generally—when he repudiated a fraudulent treaty depriving the Creek Indians of their lands in Georgia. Nor did Congress heed Adams's call for further protection for industry. The Tariff of 1828 did indeed raise duties but in haphazard fashion; the product of political maneuvering by Congressional Jacksonians the measure referred, as John Randolph remarked, "to manufactures of no sort or kind, but the manufacture of a President of the United States".

The Jacksonians

Adams's economic nationalism united his opponents against him and provided Jackson's supporters with new allies. Sheer opportunism accelerated the rush to get on the Jacksonian bandwagon: calculating politicians, sensing the upsurge of popular support for Jackson, hastened to attach themselves to him. The first national leader to do so was Calhoun. Angered by the 'corrupt bargain' which appeared to block his path to the White House, Calhoun was also influenced by his state's growing hostility to federal power. Next, Martin Van Buren put at the disposal of the developing coalition his formidable talent for political organization. A leading member of the Albany Regency, the powerful machine which for some years had controlled New York politics, Van Buren aimed to counter the menace of sectionalism by creating a new national political party and saw in the Jackson movement an opportunity of doing so. Along with other Jacksonian lieutenants, Van Buren set to work to erect the machinery necessary to elect Old Hickory. He established committee networks radiating from Nashville (Jackson's home) and Washington and set up a nationwide chain of newspapers to bring the Jacksonian creed to the people. What that creed consisted of was unclear for Jackson avoided commitment on issues, not surprisingly given the differences among the heterogeneous groups that lined up behind him; Old Republicans, former Federalists, Southern state-righters, supporters of 'Workingmen's' movements in eastern cities. But one theme was constantly reiterated: that Jackson was the people's candidate.

Few issues other than the 'corrupt bargain' charge were put to the electorate in 1828. The campaign was indeed a poor advertisement for democracy, with partisans of both sides seeking to outdo their opponents in vilification and scurrility. The Jacksonians abused Adams as a monarchist, a hypocrite, and a parasite, charging him with squandering public money on gambling machines and, still more fantastically, with having acted as a pimp for the Czar of Russia. Adams's supporters, for their part, denounced Jackson as a frontier ruffian, a gambler, an adulterer, and a military tyrant.

All this mudslinging may have contributed to the high turnout of voters, but it seems not to have affected the result, which was an impressive, though not an overwhelming, victory for Jackson. Jackson's supporters hailed the outcome as a victory for the common man, an interpretation borne out by the tumultuous scenes which followed the new President's inauguration. Immense crowds gathered in Washington and a motley army of well-wishers, intent on shaking the general's hand, invaded the White House, clambering over the furniture and fighting for refreshments. Jackson was forced to escape from the melee via a rear door and only the placing of tubs of punch on the lawn induced the crowd to go outdoors and averted further damage. Conservatives were scandalized. Justice Story of the Supreme Court declared: "The reign of King Mob seemed triumphant." But a Jackson supporter asserted: "It was a proud day for the people. General Jackson is *their own president.*"

Jackson was certainly closer to the people than any of his six predecessors. They had come from well-established Eastern families and were educated and cultured. But Jackson had risen from poverty, had received little formal education, and was a product of the frontier. Born of Scotch-Irish immigrant parents on the Carolina frontier in 1767 and orphaned at fourteen, he was successively saddler's apprentice and schoolteacher before studying law and moving to Tennessee. Plunging into politics and land speculation he soon became a well-to-do lawyer, planter, slaveholder, and judge. Though not as rough-hewn as his enemies sometimes alleged he was a man of violent temper and strong prejudices, a celebrated duelist and a devotee of cock-fighting and horse-racing. He had only limited experience of national politics but won national renown as an Indian fighter and as the victor of New Orleans. It was as a military hero that his friends pressed his presidential claims in 1824. Jackson contributed nothing to the democratic movement that was to bear his name; indeed in Tennessee he had shown scant regard for the common man, siding with large speculators and vigorously pressing claims against debtors. Nor, before becoming President, did he attempt to formulate the ideas and policies that would become associated with Jacksonian Democracy. But once in the White House he displayed the qualities that led the plain people to see in him the embodiment of their democratic aspirations.

Jackson's Presidency

One of Jackson's first actions was to provide a lofty rationale for the practice, begun under Jefferson, of rewarding political supporters with public office. One of his lieutenants, William L. Marcy of New York, might shamelessly assert that he "saw nothing wrong with the rule that to the victor belongs the spoils of the enemy". But to the President rotation in office was "a leading principle of republicanism". Office-holders, he argued, should be periodically replaced so as to check corruption, ensure against the creation of an entrenched bureaucracy, and enable more citizens to participate in public life. The suspicion of experts that was to be a feature of Jacksonianism prompted the President's avowal that official duties were "so plain and simple that men of intelligence may readily qualify themselves for their performance". Jackson did not carry out a wholesale purge; during the eight years of his Presidency he removed no more than one-fifth of federal office-holders, some of them for just cause. (The Whigs were to be far more ruthless after their victory in 1840.) Nor, at the higher levels at least, did he make the civil service more democratic; his appointees were mainly men of education, wealth, and social position. Yet under Jackson the spoils system, already well-established in New York and Pennsylvania, became for the first time a feature of national politics. Federal patronage was systematically used to promote party discipline. And since, as a Democratic observer noted in 1838, "office-seeking and office-getting [became] a regular business, where impudence triumphed over worth", the principal result of rotation of office was to depress the standards and efficiency of the civil service.

However imperfectly acted upon, Jackson's belief in popular participation in politics represented a departure from Jefferson's doctrinaire and condescending egalitarianism. Jacksonian thought and practice also went beyond Jeffersonianism in equating the suffrage with citizenship rather than with property-holding and in glorifying the presidential office as the embodiment of the popular will. But otherwise Jacksonian Democracy was an outgrowth of Jeffersonian Republicanism and Jackson himself, a Jeffersonian in background and outlook, continued to champion the old Republican virtues of frugality, fiscal solvency, and limited government. Like Jefferson, too, he repeatedly emphasized that the federal government

was one of limited powers and promised to guard against "all encroachments upon the legitimate sphere of state sovereignty".

This was the principle Jackson invoked in 1830 in vetoing the Maysville
Road bill which provided federal aid for a sixty-mile turnpike linking two
Kentucky towns, Maysville and Lexington, and regarded by its advocates
as part of the projected National Road. Jackson held, however, that it
would be unconstitutional to appropriate federal money for a road that lay
wholly within one state. Far better to pay off the national debt and distribute the surplus among the states to enable them to finance their own
internal improvements. In fact the reasons for the veto were largely
political: wanting to strike a blow at the American System he selected a
target in Clay's own state. On other occasions he signed internal improvement bills for projects just as local in character. Nevertheless the veto
checked, if it did not stop, the movement for federal aid for internal
improvements.

Jackson's solicitude for state rights was still more strikingly demonstrated in a controversy over the removal of the Cherokee Indians from
their Georgia lands. By a series of treaties with the United States dating
back to 1791 the Cherokee in the state of Georgia had been regarded as
a nation with their own laws and customs. However neither these treaties
nor the fact that they were a literate and highly civilized people was proof
against the greed of white settlers. In 1828, after the discovery of gold on
Cherokee lands, the Georgia legislature pronounced the laws of the Cherokee Nation null and void and in effect made Indian land-titles worthless.
The tribesmen then took their case to the Supreme Court. In *Worcester
v. Georgia* (1832) Chief Justice John Marshall declared the Georgia law
unconstitutional since the federal government had exclusive jurisdiction
over the Cherokee. But when Georgia defied the Court's ruling Jackson
was reported to have said: "John Marshall has made his decision, now let
him enforce it!" Encouraged by the President's support, Georgia drove
the Cherokee from their homes at the point of the bayonet. About a
quarter of them died on the thousand-mile trek across the Mississippi, the
so-called 'Trail of Tears'. Jackson's lack of sympathy with the red man was
only to be expected from such an old Indian fighter. During his Presidency
he vigorously expedited Jefferson's program of removing all the Indian
tribes to lands west of the Mississippi. Oblivious to the suffering entailed,
Jackson defended the removal policy as being in the interests of the Indians
themselves. "The philanthropist", he unctuously declared on leaving the
Presidency, "will rejoice that the remnant of that ill-fated race has been
at length placed beyond the reach of injury and oppression, and that the
paternal care of the General Government will hereafter watch over them
and protect them."

The Nullification Crisis

A defender of state rights when it suited him, Jackson was nonetheless an uncompromising nationalist, opposed to any attempt to break up the Union. This became plain during the nullification crisis of 1832–3, the product—at least ostensibly—of South Carolina's dissatisfaction with federal tariff policy. Though protection had not been a sectional issue when the tariff act of 1816 was passed, it had become one a decade later. As New England committed itself increasingly to manufacturing its spokesmen, at first divided about tariffs, became fiercely protectionist; the South, on the other hand, grew increasingly hostile to protection as its hopes of becoming industrialized faded. Southern protests rose to a crescendo when the severely protectionist 'Tariff of Abominations' was passed in 1828. Extending protection to certain agricultural products like wool and hemp as well as to manufactures the measure was an electoral gimmick, designed by Jackson's supporters to win votes in New York, Pennsylvania, and the Western states. It provoked an especially loud outcry in South Carolina, where cotton prices had been depressed for several years. The real reasons for the state's economic decline were soil exhaustion and the competition of newly opened cotton lands further west, but South Carolinians blamed federal policy. They reasoned that while protection enriched Northern manufacturers the consequences for themselves were more expensive manufactures and lower cotton prices. Because of the attitude of his state Calhoun found it expedient to recant his earlier protectionism, along with much of his nationalism. His *Exposition and Protest*, written anonymously in 1828, denounced the Tariff of Abominations as "unconstitutional, unequal and oppressive", and went on to propose an ingenious constitutional safeguard for Southern rights: the doctrine of nullification. Echoing the constitutional doctrines of the Virginia and Kentucky Resolutions, Calhoun argued that a state could, through the instrumentality of a special convention, nullify any act of the federal government it deemed unconstitutional.

But apart from denouncing the Tariff of Abominations and endorsing the *Exposition*, South Carolina for the moment did nothing. It looked to the newly elected Jackson Administration for redress, expecting Calhoun to dominate it and indeed to succeed the apparently frail old soldier after one term. But a series of personal and political quarrels led swiftly to a breach between Jackson and his Vice-President. The great Senate debate of January 1830 on the nature of the Union served to bring their disagreement into the open. Originating in a discussion of public land policy, the debate came to center upon the question of state rights versus national power. As the Senate's presiding officer Calhoun did not speak but he listened with evident approval as his fellow South Carolinian, Robert Y.

Hayne, launched into an impassioned defence of the extreme state-rights point of view and of the theory of nullification. Hayne was opposed by Daniel Webster, now as ardent a nationalist as Calhoun had formerly been. Webster's Second Reply to Hayne, regarded as the most celebrated oration ever delivered in Congress, asserted that the Constitution was not, as the *Exposition* had it, a compact among states but one between the people. The proper authority to interpret the Constitution was the Supreme Court. The union was intended to be perpetual; nullification was treasonable and would lead to civil war. Webster's concluding words, "Liberty *and* Union, now and forever, one and inseparable", became the rallying-cry for Union troops in 1861. Where Jackson stood soon became clear. At a banquet to celebrate Jefferson's birthday in April 1830, at which state rights' sentiments were freely expressed, the President rose and, looking Calhoun straight in the eye, proposed a toast: "The Federal Union, it must be preserved."

An absurd society squabble helped complete the estrangement of the two men. Mrs Calhoun, the acknowledged leader of Washington official society, reacted to gossip about Peggy Eaton, the sprightly, alluring, and notorious wife of Jackson's Secretary of War, by leading a movement of Cabinet wives to ostracize her. Jackson, believing that the slandering of his own wife during the 1828 campaign had hastened her death, was deeply offended and demanded that Mrs Eaton be treated with respect. But while the members of the Cabinet stood in awe of the President, they feared their wives' wrath even more. Meanwhile Jackson had discovered that in 1818 Calhoun, then Secretary of War, had wanted to court-martial him for his unauthorized invasion of Florida during the Seminole War. Taxed with this revelation Calhoun attempted to explain away his conduct but merely convinced Jackson of his duplicity. In April 1831 the Cabinet was reorganized so as to exclude Calhoun's friends. Van Buren, whose maneuvers had contributed to this result, was able to ingratiate himself further with the President and in 1832 supplanted Calhoun as Vice-President and Jackson's heir-apparent.

Following the passage of a new tariff act in July 1832 the nullification controversy came to a head. Though the measure reduced duties considerably it did not go far enough to satisfy South Carolina. Yet the tariff question did not account fully—or even perhaps mainly—for the pathological fear of federal power which now seized South Carolina's dominant planter aristocracy. The rise of militant abolitionism in the North, the shock of the Nat Turner insurrection, the antislavery sentiments expressed during the Virginia legislative debates of 1832, the growing agitation for emancipation in the British West Indies, a region with which South Carolina had historical and cultural links—such a conjunction of events could not fail to arouse apprehension in a state which had a higher proportion of blacks than any other. And since the North was rapidly outstripping the South in population, the day might not be far distant when a hostile national majority might remove the safeguards provided by the Constitution for the 'peculiar institution'. Thus nullification came to be seen in South Carolina as something more than a method of checking Northern economic exploitation, namely, the means of limiting the federal government's potential power over slavery.

Despairing of redress from the Administration after the adoption of the tariff of 1832, Calhoun openly avowed his support of nullification and resigned as Vice-President in order to fight for Southern rights on the floor of the Senate. In South Carolina nullifiers won control of the legislature and a popularly elected convention meeting at Columbia in November 1832 adopted an ordinance pronouncing the tariff acts of 1828 and 1832 to be unconstitutional and hence null and void, prohibiting the collection of customs duties within the state after February 1, 1833, and warning that South Carolina would secede if the federal government used force against it.

Jackson's response was prompt and unequivocal. He sent reinforcements to Charleston harbor and privately let it be known that in the event of armed resistance he would personally lead an invasion of South Carolina and hang the nullifiers. In his Nullification Proclamation of December 10, 1832, moreover, he forthrightly endorsed the doctrine of national power as set forth for Marshall and Webster. Nullification, he asserted, was "incompatible with the existence of the Union, unauthorized by its spirit, inconsistent with every principle on which it was founded, and destructive of the great object for which it was formed". As President, he warned, it would be his duty to enforce the law. South Carolina responded with counterthreats and began to recruit a volunteer army. Jackson thereupon asked Congress for a 'force bill' empowering him to use the armed forces to collect customs duties in South Carolina. Yet, while determined to uphold federal authority Jackson was prepared to offer an olive branch: he urged Congress to make further tariff reductions. Meanwhile Calhoun and other South Carolina leaders had become uncomfortably aware of their isolation; while other Southern states continued to reiterate their opposition to protective duties, they were equally hostile to nullification. Thus there was substantial Congressional support when Clay, working with Calhoun, came forward with a compromise measure providing for the gradual reduction of all tariffs over a nine-year period to a uniform level of 20 percent. The Force Bill and the Compromise Tariff, simultaneously passed by Congress on March 1, 1833, promptly received presidential approval. On March 15 the South Carolina Convention accepted the compromise and withdrew its nullification ordinance, but defiantly nullified the Force Act— a facesaving gesture which Jackson chose to ignore. Thus the crisis ended with both sides claiming victory. Jackson had demonstrated that no state could defy federal authority with impunity. Yet the threat of nullification had enabled a single dissident state to change federal policy.

The Bank War

The struggle over nullification overlapped the other major controversy of Jackson's Presidency—the Administration's war on the Second Bank of the United States. Under the capable management of Nicholas Biddle, the urbane and talented Philadelphian who became its president in 1823, the Bank had become a prosperous and well-conducted institution, performing a number of vital economic functions. It organized the sale of government bonds and served as a repository for government funds; its bank notes provided the country with a sound paper currency; it acted as a salutary restraining influence upon state banks, checking reckless lending by periodically presenting their notes for redemption in gold and silver. Yet the Bank attracted fierce opposition. It was hated by a variety of groups for different, indeed contradictory, reasons. Agrarian debtors in the West and Southwest had long resented its restraining role; as 'soft-money' men, they wanted more paper money and easy credit. 'Hard-money' Eastern laborers, on the other hand, were hostile because the Bank itself issued paper; frequently paid in bank notes of fluctuating value they disliked all banks of issue. Rising capitalists tended to identify the Bank with privilege and monopoly; in their eyes it represented men of established wealth, intent on excluding outsiders from the opportunities provided by an expanding economy. State banks, for their part, chafed at the control the Bank exercised over their activities, while in addition New York bankers were jealous of a Philadelphia-based institution. Others alleged that the Bank of the United States represented a dangerous concentration of power; they were concerned at the extent of its control over the nation's currency and credit system and at the fact that it was not subject to effective government regulation. Finally, since it was known that Biddle made loans on easy terms to influential politicians, Clay and Webster among them, the Bank was seen as a corrupting influence in politics.

Jackson's animosity to the Bank had several sources. First, like many hard-money agrarians he was deeply suspicious of all banks and paper money and, moreover, was profoundly ignorant of the functions of central banking. "I do not dislike your Bank any more than all banks", he told Biddle in 1829. "But ever since I read the history of the South Sea Bubble I have been afraid of banks." Second, despite Marshall's judgement in *McCulloch* v. *Maryland* he continued to doubt the constitutionality of the Bank. Third, he was disturbed by reports that the Bank had been playing politics, notably by using some of its funds against him in 1828. Thus he came to the conclusion that the Bank was a "hydra of corruption—dangerous to our liberties by its corrupting influence everywhere". And once the issue was joined he was quick to personalize it, as indeed he did most disputes. "The Bank is trying to kill me", he told Van Buren, "but I will kill it."

It was not Jackson but Clay and Webster who fired the first shot in the Bank War. Believing that the Bank had more supporters than enemies and that the issue would be useful in the forthcoming election campaign, they persuaded Biddle to apply for a new charter in 1832, four years before the old one was due to expire. The recharter bill, drafted so as to meet some of the criticisms of the Bank, readily passed both houses of Congress in July 1832. Jackson promptly vetoed it. His veto message maintained that the Bank was unconstitutional, unnecessary, and undemocratic. Its proposed capital of $35 million was far more than was needed. In addition it was a dangerous monopoly operating to the advantage of a few privileged directors, some of them foreigners. Much of this was prejudiced nonsense; the Bank could not properly be described as a monopoly, neither was it over-capitalized or in danger of falling under foreign control. And as well as ignoring the Bank's economic contributions, the message was wholly negative; intent only on slaying the 'Monster', Jackson offered nothing in its place. But however feeble its economics the message was nonetheless a masterpiece of political propaganda. Addressed to the American people at large rather than to Congress it appealed to popular fears of foreign influence, of centralized government, of uncontrolled aristocratic power. It concluded with an eloquent statement of the evolving Jacksonian ideology. Accepting that inequalities existed in all societies and that each individual was entitled to "the fruits of superior industry, economy and virtue", it argued that government should not add to these advantages by granting special privileges "to make the rich richer, and the potent more powerful". This brand of *laissez-faire*, then, was his prescription for what could now be seen as the central objective of the Jacksonian movement, increased individual opportunity and social mobility.

The appeal of such a credo was evident from Jackson's resounding victory in the 1832 presidential election in which the Bank was the main issue. The campaign was also significant for two political novelties: the fact that the contestants received the endorsement of national nominating conventions and the appearance of the Antimasonic party, the first of many third parties to run a presidential candidate. Antimasonry, an egalitarian but anti-Jacksonian movement, originated in 1826 in the kidnaping and apparent murder of one William Morgan, a disgruntled freemason from western New York who had published a pamphlet purporting to expose the secrets of Masonry. When investigation met official obstructiveness there were allegations of a gigantic Masonic conspiracy to subvert the rule of law and in the late 1820s Antimasonry became a mass political movement, winning much support in the rural areas of New England and the Middle States. It complained of Masonic secrecy, exclusiveness, and aristocratic pretensions and of Masonic dominance of the two major political parties—both Jackson and Clay were Masons. In September 1831, in keeping with their claim to be the only party representing the people, the Antimasons held a national nominating convention at Baltimore—the first of its kind—and chose William Wirt of Maryland as their presidential candidate. National Republicans and Whigs followed a similar procedure in nominating Jackson and Clay respectively. Given the President's popularity his victory was never in doubt. Clay won only six states, Wirt one. Within a few years most of the Antimasons had joined the emerging Whig party.

Encouraged by his electoral triumph and fearing that delay would enable Biddle to mount a fresh Congressional campaign for recharter, Jackson decided not to wait until the Bank's charter had expired but to emasculate it immediately by removing government deposits. Action was delayed for some months because the incumbent Secretary of the Treasury could not be persuaded that the Bank was insolvent, as the President alleged. But in September 1833, a more cooperative successor, Roger B. Taney, previously the Attorney General, began to transfer the deposits to selected state banks, nicknamed 'pet banks' by Jackson's enemies because they were nearly all controlled by his supporters. The arrogant and combative Biddle was not prepared to take this lying down. He systematically called in loans and contracted credit with the aim of depressing the economy and generating an irresistible popular demand for recharter. But Jackson's response to the resulting economic recession—"Biddle's panic" his supporters dubbed it—was simply to claim that it proved his contention that the Bank possessed too much power. In the summer of 1834, after strong pressure from business, Biddle reversed his contraction policy and the Bank War came to an end. When the Bank's charter expired in 1836 it was reorganized as a state bank under the laws of Pennsylvania. It soon found itself in difficulties and in 1841 was forced into liquidation. Biddle lost his fortune, was charged with fraud, and, although subsequently acquitted, died a broken man in 1844.

The cost to the country of Jackson's Bank War victory was soon apparent. No sooner was the restricting hand of the Bank removed than state banks proliferated and, with little regard for cash reserves, flooded the country with paper money. Over-expansion of credit led to a speculative boom. Individuals borrowed heavily to buy land, state governments to finance internal improvements. The Administration, having stimulated speculation by throwing millions of acres of public land on to the market, intensified the inflationary spiral by giving its blessing to a distribution bill, first proposed by Henry Clay. Thanks largely to soaring receipts from land sales the United States found itself, for the first and only time in its history, able to pay off the entire national debt and with a large and growing Treasury surplus. Instead of reducing it by lowering land prices and tariff rates, Congress passed a measure in June 1836 distributing it to the states. By this time, however, the speculative mania had belatedly revived Jackson's hard-money instincts and in July 1836 he issued a Specie Circular declaring that only gold and silver would henceforth be accepted in payment for public lands. This change of policy abruptly curtailed land sales, started a run on the banks, and sent prices tumbling. Then in May 1837, two months after Jackson left office, a New York bank panic plunged the country into a long and severe depression. In part the trouble was imported; a financial crisis in London led British investors to withdraw funds from the United States. But Jackson's banking policies undoubtedly exacerbated the collapse.

During his eight years in the White House Jackson greatly enlarged executive authority. He made the Presidency a more effective, dramatic, and personal office. It became the focal point of the political system and assumed a plebiscitary character. For the first time the President was seen to be the undisputed head of the federal government. Whereas Monroe and John Quincy Adams had allowed Cabinet members wide discretion, Jackson insisted that they followed his orders and arbitrarily dismissed them when they did not. He also formed the habit of ignoring his offical Cabinet, consulting instead a group of political cronies known as the 'Kitchen Cabinet'. And while some members of this inner circle—notably the Kentucky editor, Amos Kendall, and Jackson's old Tennessee friend, William B. Lewis—were doubtless influential, Jackson ran his own Administration. He also transformed the Presidency from a law-enforcing office into a policy-making one. In contrast to Madison and Monroe, who owed their election to a Congressional caucus and tended in office to defer to Congress, Jackson took an independent line, vetoing twelve bills, more than all his predecessors combined, as well as making use of the pocket veto (a device to block legislation by refusing to sign bills presented in the last ten days of a Congressional session). And as we saw he showed equal contempt for the Supreme Court.

Jackson sought to justify his conduct by casting himself as the people's champion against special interests. Now that presidential electors were popularly elected he was able to claim that he was the only elected federal official who was the choice of the people as a whole. (Senators were chosen by the voters of only one state, Congressmen by the voters of only part of a state.) But some people saw him not as the people's tribune, but as a sinister figure bent on subverting the Constitution by concentrating authority in his own hands. "Though we live under the form of a republic", said Justice Story in 1834, "we are in fact under the absolute rule of a single man." Nicknaming Jackson 'King Andrew I' his opponents began to call themselves Whigs, a term reminiscent of the struggle against George III. The Whig view of the Presidency was that the President should confine himself to his administrative duties, leaving the framing of laws to Congress. They would have liked to amend the Constitution so as to abolish the presidential veto and limit Presidents to a single term. (The only two Whig Presidents, Harrison and Taylor, were to sympathize excessively with the latter objective, both dying in office shortly after having been elected.)

The 'Second Party System'

The fact that the "presidential question" became the axis around which politics revolved explains the formation of the "second party system" (the first being the Federalist–Republican system). In place of the political fluidity of the 1820s there gradually emerged two institutionalized, evenly balanced, national parties. The second party system involved the creation of an elaborate party apparatus and a new, more popular campaign style. It survived, however, only by suppressing or avoiding divisive sectional issues, especially slavery; when that no longer proved possible, the system collapsed.

The miscellaneous coalition that had elected Jackson in 1828 had nothing in common besides a desire for electoral success. Thus as Jacksonian principles became more clearly defined and new issues arose, underlying differences emerged, prompting successive desertions. The Maysville Road veto alienated some Westerners; Jackson's firmness during the nullification crisis angered the more extreme state-rights Southerners, and the Bank War and the Specie Circular drove out fiscal conservatives (one-third of the Democrats voted to recharter the Bank and a similar proportion favored soft money); the choice of a distrusted Northerner, Van Buren, as Jackson's prospective successor, was highly unpopular in the South. The net result was to make the Democratic party smaller but more homogeneous and more united. It was still, however, a coalition embracing rich as well as poor, Easterners as well as Westerners, Protestant native-born Americans as well as Catholic immigrants. Though the Democrats claimed to be the party of the common man, they were not wholly justified in doing so. Democratic leaders were often as wealthy as the Whigs. Nor did the Democrats monopolize the votes of the poor. Geographical, local, ethnic, and religious factors sometimes counted for more than class or income in determining voting behavior, while Whig leaders such as Clay and Tom Corwin of Ohio showed that they possessed Jackson's capacity to win a devoted popular following. Nonetheless Democratic support seems to have come disproportionately from the less well off: small farmers, especially in less prosperous areas and on the frontier, native-born urban laborers and immigrants, especially Irish Catholics.

The Democratic charge that Whiggery was simply latter-day Federalism was unwarranted. Some former Federalists, like Daniel Webster, did indeed become Whigs, but others, such as James Buchanan and Roger B. Taney, became fervent Jacksonians. Conversely, Whig leaders like Clay and William H. Seward had originally been Republicans. Indeed there was a sense in which the Whigs, with their emphasis on the equalizing effects of education and of widening economic opportunity, were as much the heirs of Jefferson as the Democrats. Equally oversimplified is the traditional characterization of the Whigs as the party of wealth and business. While there were many well-to-do planters, bankers, and businessmen in the Whig ranks, the party drew its support, not only from all parts of the country but from all classes, even the poorest, as the Whiggism of Abraham Lincoln and Horace Greeley testifies. In some instances, religious, ethnic, and cultural affiliations drew men to Whiggery. Protestant immigrants from Great Britain and from Ulster tended to be strongly Whig. Northern free blacks, when they were allowed to vote, were overwhelmingly so, influenced no doubt by the part Jacksonians had played in disfranchising their race. What united these disparate groups was a distinctive set of ideals and values. Whigs tended to be basically conservative; their outlook was national rather than local; they rejected Democratic negativism and believed that the federal government had a vital role to play in fostering economic development; and, rebelling against 'executive usurpation', they wanted Congressional direction of federal policy. Moreover, irritated at the way Democratic voting strength was being augmented by immigration, Whigs were sympathetic to nativism; but they displayed—or at least professed—greater solicitude than their opponents for the rights of Negroes and Indians.

Like the Democrats the Whigs took some years to develop coherence and organization. Even at the end of Jackson's second term they were still a loose coalition of National Republicans, Antimasons, and dissident Democrats, united in hostility to Jackson but with varying opinions on everything else. In the presidential election of 1836 the party could not even agree on a nominee. Consequently they adopted the strategy of nominating three candidates who might appeal to different sections of the country: Daniel Webster to New England, General William Henry Harrison of Ohio to the West, and Hugh White of Tennessee to the South. Whigs hoped that, as in 1824, no candidate would receive a majority of electoral votes and that the election would be thrown to the House. That hope was disappointed but the narrowness of Van Buren's victory demonstrated that the Whig party, disorganized as it was, was developing a popular base.

When Jackson left office in 1837 seven of the nine Supreme Court judges were his appointees, most of them Southerners favorable to state rights. In this category was Roger B. Taney, whom Jackson chose to be Chief

Justice when death ended Marshall's long tenure in 1835. Conservatives feared that Taney's appointment would bring a radical change in constitutional interpretation. Taney did in fact steer the Court away from Marshall's extreme nationalism and modified Marshall's judgments on the rights of corporations and the sanctity of contracts. His opinions were most strikingly expressed in *Charles River Bridge* v. *Warren Bridge* (1837), in which he upheld the right of a state to alter an agreement with a corporation and laid down the principle that the rights of private property were subordinate to those of the community. Yet Marshall's great precedents were not overturned. Taney not only accepted the doctrine of judicial review but also used it in several important cases. And despite his verdict on the Charles River Bridge case he was not invariably unsympathetic to property rights, nor averse on occasion to sweeping assertions of federal power.

Van Buren's Presidency

During Van Buren's term of office the potentially divisive slavery question repeatedly threatened to come to the fore. But both political parties were agreed on the necessity of suppressing it. Thus while Congress maintained the 'gag rule' to prevent the discussion of antislavery petitions (see Chapter 8), Van Buren took no action when the slave-holding republic of Texas offered itself for annexation. However in its attitude to the African slave-trade the new Administration pandered to the wishes of its Southern supporters. In June 1839, when fifty-three African Negroes on the Spanish ship *Amistad* mutinied while being taken from one Caribbean island to another and brought the vessel to American waters, Van Buren tried unsuccessfully to hand them back to their Spanish 'owners' before an American court could hear their appeal for freedom. Van Buren also flatly refused—as did all his successors right up to the Civil War—to concede the right of search, or even of visit, to British warships engaged in hunting down suspected slavers. Yet his attitude stemmed as much from sensitivity to the question of maritime rights as from a complaisant attitude toward slavery.

Plagued though he was by the rising slavery controversy and by vexing diplomatic problems, Van Buren's chief problems were economic. The depression touched off by the Panic of 1837 persisted throughout his Presidency. Sharing Jackson's *laissez-faire* and strict constructionist beliefs, he did not accept that it was the government's responsibility to revive the economy; indeed he expressly warned Americans not to look to Washington for relief. Van Buren saw his task simply as one of solving the government's financial difficulties, rather than those of the nation. There were, however, rancorous divisions within the Democratic party as to remedies. Conservatives blamed the depression on Jackson's financial policies and demanded the repeal of the Specie Circular; they also wanted to retain the system of depositing government funds in state banks. On the other hand the Locofoco wing of the party (so-called because they had used "locofoco" matches to light candles when conservatives plunged one of their meetings into darkness by extinguishing the gas) clung doggedly to Jacksonian hard-money policies and advocated the complete separation of government from private banking. After some hesitation Van Buren chose the Locofoco solution, standing by the Specie Circular and urging the passage of an Independent Treasury Bill. This measure proposed that federal funds should be withdrawn from pet banks and deposited in a number of government-owned vaults, known as subtreasuries, to be established in different parts of the country. At Calhoun's suggestion an amendment was added providing that all payments to the government be made in specie.

The Independent Treasury question occupied most of Van Buren's term. Conservative Democrats twice combined with the Whigs to defeat the measure, but it finally squeaked through in 1840. The margin of victory came from Calhoun and his militant state-rights followers, who now ended their flirtation with the Whigs to align themselves with a party whose belief in the negative state coincided with their own. Though the Independent Treasury system was to be abolished in 1841 it was restored in 1846 and lasted until 1863. It did not produce the calamitous shortage of specie predicted by its critics, though that was due only to a fortuitous combination of circumstances: the expansion of American grain exports, the California gold discoveries, and a great increase in European capital investment in American railroads. But with the 'divorce of bank and state' an important co-ordinating agency had gone, with ill effects on economic stability and the currency.

The 1840 Election and the Whig Eclipse

As the election of 1840 approached Whig hopes soared. Times were still hard and Democratic misrule could plausibly be blamed. The Whigs realized, however, that it would be preferable to concentrate this time on a single candidate instead of scattering their strength. They also sensed that it would be better to choose a relatively unknown figure than to nominate one of their leaders like Clay or Webster; who had made enemies through their close identification with particular issues. Hence they chose General William Henry Harrison. Known as 'Old Tippecanoe' after his victory over the Indians in 1811, Harrison was not a great soldier, but he was the best facsimile of Andrew Jackson the Whigs could muster. After leaving the army he had served briefly in Congress without distinction and—what now made him more 'available'—without expressing strong opinions on matters of principle. John Tyler of Virginia was chosen as vice-presidential candidate and, since the Whigs would have had difficulty in agreeing on a platform, decided to dispense with one. The Democrats renominated Van Buren on a platform which emphasized the limited powers of the federal government.

The 1840 campaign marked the coming of age of the second-party system. For the first time two sharply divided, disciplined parties took the field at national, state, and local levels. More important, the campaign established a new presidential election style—simultaneously rollicking, emotional, demagogic, and absurd. Determined to outplay the Democrats at their own game, the Whigs displayed a mastery of the techniques of mass politics. Though they did not entirely ignore serious issues—nor for that matter did the Democrats—they concentrated on personalities and blarney. They brought a carnival atmosphere into politics, holding massive outdoor rallies, barbecues, parades, and torchlight processions, introducing campaign songs and chanting slogans like "Tippecanoe and Tyler too" and "Two dollars a day and roast beef". Above all, they sought to present themselves as the true party of the people. When a Democratic editor scoffed that Harrison would be content with a pension, a log cabin, and a barrel of cider, the Whigs seized upon the characterization, portraying their candidate as a simple Western farmer who typified the plebeian virtues associated with log cabins and hard cider. Van Buren, on the other hand, was ridiculed by Whig orators as an effete Eastern aristocrat living in sybaritic luxury, wearing a corset, using eau-de-Cologne, and wasting the people's money on champagne, gold plate, and expensive carpets, Both characterizations were travesties. Harrison was descended from a distinguished Virginia family and lived the comfortable life of a country squire, whereas Van Buren, the son of a tavern-keeper, lived plainly and unostentatiously in what foreign visitors described as a somewhat shabby White House. But the log cabin became an established Whig symbol; Webster publicly lamented that he had not been born in one.

The electorate responded by turning out in unprecedented numbers. In 1840 no fewer than 78 percent of the voters went to the polls, far surpassing the previous record of 56 percent in 1828. The Whig tactics, along with the depression, gave Harrison a handsome victory and his party control of both houses of Congress.

Echoing the Whig view of a negative Presidency, Harrison professed himself ready to leave lawmaking to Congress. But he was denied the opportunity of doing so. Having delivered the longest inaugural address on record he contracted pneumonia and died after only a month in office. That brought John Tyler to the White House. The first Vice-President to attain the highest office by right of succession, Tyler dismissed doubts about his status by insisting that he was entitled to exercise the full powers of the Presidency. Congress acquiesced, thereby establishing a precedent which has endured ever since. Nevertheless there remained the question of who was to control the government and the Whig party. As Whig leader in the Senate Clay expected to be able to dictate the policies of the Administration. But Tyler was less pliable than Harrison had promised to be. Like Calhoun he had deserted the Democrats for the Whigs after the nullification crisis, but had remained at heart a supporter of state rights and of strict construction, with no sympathy for Clay's brand of economic nationalism. Nor, despite his earlier friendship for Clay, did he care for his overbearing manner. Thus when Clay formulated a legislative program based upon the American System, Tyler frustrated him.

Though a measure repealing the Independent Treasury Act received the President's signature he vetoed a bill creating a new Bank of the United States (August 1841). A second bill designed to meet his constitutional objections was then rushed through Congress only to be vetoed in turn. This provoked an open rupture between the President and the party of which he was the titular head. A special gathering of Whig Congressmen in effect expelled Tyler from the party. In addition the entire Cabinet resigned save Webster who stayed on to complete the delicate negotiations which eventually settled the Maine boundary dispute. To fill the Cabinet vacancies Tyler appointed former Democrats like himself, most of them fellow-Southerners.

Sectional jealousies combined with presidential obstruction to create difficulties for the rest of the Whig legislative program. Clay had long had a pet scheme (similar to the one enacted in 1836 but repealed the following year) for distributing the proceeds of land sales to the states. Ostensibly designed to relieve the states of the burden of debt, its real purpose was to reduce federal revenues and thus necessitate raising the tariff. But to win the votes needed for distribution a complex logrolling operation proved necessary. To obtain Western support Clay had to couple his distribution bill with something he had long opposed, a measure giving squatters a preemptive right to 160 acres of public land. Next he won Eastern votes with a bankruptcy bill relieving hard-pressed creditors. Finally to appease low-tariff Southern Whigs he agreed to an amendment providing that distribution would be suspended if tariff rates rose above the 20 percent level set in 1833. As a result of this involved maneuvering the Distribution-Preemption Bill was passed (September 4, 1841), along with the bankruptcy law. Clay hoped to get rid later on of the link between distribution and the tariff and in fact twice persuaded Congress to pass bills which did so. But on both occasions Tyler interposed a veto, thereby compelling the Whigs to choose between protection and distribution. They chose the former. In August 1842 a tariff bill was passed raising rates approximately to 1832 levels (that is, well above 20 percent), while explicitly repealing distribution. Tyler disliked high tariffs, but reluctantly signed the bill because additional revenue was urgently needed.

Thus the Whig triumph of 1840 was quickly followed by schism. After two years in office the Whigs could point to few positive accomplishments. Yet if Clay's legislative program had been emasculated, his position as Whig leader was undisputed. Tyler's desperate efforts to win over Southern Whigs had had meager results, except in his own state of Virginia. When this became evident the President sought an alternative method of restoring his political fortunes. Reviled by the Whigs as a traitor and hardly more popular with Democrats, he hoped that by placing himself at the head of the developing movement to annex Texas he might be triumphantly reelected in 1844, either as the Democratic candidate or as the nominee of a third party. That did not happen but Tyler's expansionism had far-reaching consequences. It again made slavery a political issue and thus started a trend whereby the two parties became increasingly sectional.

9. *Social and Cultural Ferment,*
1820–1860

"In the four quarters of the globe, who reads an American book? [O]r goes to an American play? [O]r looks at an American picture or statue?" The Reverend Sydney Smith's condescending query in the *Edinburgh Review* in 1820 infuriated Americans. Though well aware of their meager achievements in art and literature, they had no wish to be reminded of the fact by foreigners. After almost half a century of independence the United States was still a cultural colony of Europe and would remain one for several decades longer. The great majority of books read in the United States were by Europeans. In the absence of an international copyright agreement, cheaply produced pirated editions of favorite British authors— especially Scott and later on Dickens—were produced in the United States, to the discouragement of native writers. Such American literature as there was in 1820 was largely derivative. Music, painting, architecture, likewise reflected the influence of the Old World.

Struggle for Cultural Independence

Yet by mid-century Americans were beginning to produce an effective answer to Sydney Smith. The United States did not yet have a fully autonomous culture, but in most branches of the arts a new and genuinely American note was being struck. American painters were developing a recognizably native style, especially Asher Durand and other landscape artists of the Hudson River School, and George Caleb Bingham, who depicted everyday scenes from Missouri life. The sculptor Hiram Powers had won acclaim on both sides of the Atlantic with his marble statue of a nude female figure, *The Greek Slave*—though it should be remembered that Powers spent more than half his life in Italy. American music, it is true, still consisted largely of minstrelsy, sentimental songs, and hymn tunes. Yet by the Civil War there had appeared such works as Stephen Foster's "The Old Folks at Home", John Howard Payne's "Home, Sweet Home!", and Lowell Mason's hymn tune for "Nearer, My God, To Thee", all of them destined for enduring popularity in England as well as in the United States. Yet it was in literature that the American achievement was greatest. The solid performance of the 1820s and 1830s was the prelude to that astonishing outpouring of imaginative power of the mid-century that is known, somewhat oddly, as the American Renaissance.

The first American writer to gain an international reputation and the first to be able to live by his pen was Washington Irving. Spending much of his life abroad Irving derived much of his material from Europe and, although he sometimes gave it an American setting, he wrote in the elegant and witty style of eighteenth-century English essayists and largely for British readers. He made his mark with a burlesque *History of New York* (1809), purportedly the work of a Dutch-American, Diedrich Knickerbocker. But his most celebrated work was *The Sketch Book* (1819–20) which also drew upon the Dutch folklore of the Hudson valley and included such memorable tales as "Rip Van Winkle" and "The Legend of Sleepy Hollow". Irving's contemporary and fellow New Yorker, James Fenimore Cooper, likewise spent several years abroad and achieved wide foreign recognition. He was the first novelist to explore what was to be a perennial theme in American literature, the relationship between Indians and white men on the advancing frontier. Despite an undistinguished style, stilted dialogue, and implausible plots, Cooper was a superb storyteller and the frontiersman hero of his "Leather-Stocking Tales", the simple, courageous, idealistic Natty Bumppo, was a character of lasting significance. However, much of the popularity Cooper won with such Leather-Stocking novels as *The Last of the Mohicans* (1826) and *The Deerslayer* (1841) was dissipated when in some of his other writings he forthrightly criticized the leveling tendencies and rampant individualism of Jacksonian America.

Equally unsympathetic to democracy was the dissolute, unstable, and brilliant Edgar Allan Poe. Brought up in Virginia, Poe liked to think of himself as a Southerner, but he spent most of his adult life in the North and his writings rarely reflect Southern influences. His work reveals an abiding fascination with the macabre and the grotesque, with horror and compulsive guilt. A lyric poet and short-story writer of real originality, and incidentally one of the originators of the detective story, Poe was also a literary critic of great perception. Though widely admired during his lifetime in England and France, his literary merits were only just beginning to be appreciated in his native land when he died in 1849 at the age of forty. .

By the 1840s New England, more particularly Boston, had supplanted New York as the chief center of American letters. Historians signaled the change. In the 1820s Jared Sparks began collecting and publishing documents relating to the Revolution and in 1834 George Bancroft published the first volume of his monumental *History of the United States*, which depicted the unfolding of American democracy under divine guidance. Yet the greatest of the Boston historians were not narrowly concerned with their own country's past. William H. Prescott brought out his *History of the Conquest of Mexico* in 1839; John Lothrop Motley published *The Rise of the Dutch Republic* in 1856; Francis Parkman took as his life-work the struggle of England and France for the mastery of North America, the first volume in his great epic, *The History of the Conspiracy of Pontiac*, appearing in 1851. An equally cosmopolitan tone informed the poetry of the Boston Brahmins, the name given to the city's cultivated, upper-class coterie by one of its members, Oliver Wendell Holmes. Self-assuredly American, the Brahmin poets nevertheless felt constrained to accept Europe's cultural standards, more especially its romantic tradition. Holmes, a professor of anatomy at Harvard, displayed his versatility by writing light verse and collections of witty essays like *The Aristocrat of the Breakfast Table* (1858). A more significant literary figure, at least in his own day, was another Harvard professor, Henry Wadsworth Longfellow, who achieved extraordinary popularity throughout the English-speaking world with short poems like "The Village Blacksmith" and "The Wreck of the Hesperus", and with longer narrative pieces on historical subjects, among them *Evangeline* (1847), *The Song of Hiawatha* (1855), and *The Courtship of Miles Standish* (1858). A third Brahmin, James Russell Lowell, who succeeded to Longfellow's chair of modern languages in 1855, was an accomplished poet and critic whose best work was *The Biglow Papers* (1848), a pungent verse satire on the Mexican War written in the Yankee vernacular. Another New Englander to contribute poetry to the antislavery cause was the Quaker, John Greenleaf Whittier, whose simple sentimental verses about rural life gave him a popularity rivaling Longfellow's.

The period's romantic tendencies attained their most sophisticated expression in Transcendentalism, a body of ideas derived partly from the philosophy of Kant, partly from his English interpreters, Coleridge and Carlyle, and adhered to by a group of young Boston intellectuals. What it meant essentially was that man was capable of apprehending the truth intuitively, without the intervention of established authority. Such a concept appealed to a certain type of New Englander because it blended perfectly with the traditional Puritan emphasis on autonomous choice, yet afforded an escape from established values, especially from materialism, into the realm of idealistic action. The chief spokesman for this doctrine was the former Unitarian minister, Ralph Waldo Emerson, who preached a gospel of optimism and self-reliant individualism. The most famous of Emerson's disciples, Henry David Thoreau, attempted to put self-reliance into practice by living alone for two years in the woods at Walden Pond, near Concord, Massachusetts. From this experience, during which he discovered a sense of harmony with nature, came Thoreau's greatest work, *Walden* (1854). Thoreau carried his nonconformism a stage further by refusing to be taxed to support the Mexican War, justifying his stand in an essay on 'Civil Disobedience' (1849), destined to inspire Gandhi and other twentieth-century advocates of passive resistance.

Emerson's transcendentalism was closely linked with a belief that America offered new and richer possibilities of life. In his Phi Beta Kappa oration, *The American Scholar* (1837), he called for an indigenous culture, free from the domination of "the courtly muses of Europe". In fact Emerson's own work, and Thoreau's too for that matter, went some way toward realizing his ideal of a native literature—in the sense, that is, that it expressed distinctively American ideas and attitudes. It was however in the novels of Nathaniel Hawthorne and Herman Melville and in the poetry of Walt Whitman—the three greatest figures of the American Renaissance—that this trend was most clearly apparent.

Hawthorne was skeptical of Emerson's bland faith in moral progress; he could not shake off the belief of his Puritan ancestors that man was innately sinful. Born at Salem, Massachusetts, where his family had been established for five generations, he was steeped in Puritan traditions and his writings were an attempt to probe the Puritan mind and temperament. Most of Hawthorne's work centered upon man's tragic destiny. His masterpiece, *The Scarlet Letter* (1850), and the novel he took most satisfaction in, *The House of Seven Gables* (1851), both began in seventeenth-century New England and depicted the destructive consequences of sin, guilt, and moral self-righteousness. Even more hostile to transcendentalist optimism was Hawthorne's close friend and admirer, Herman Melville. Born in New York into shabby gentility, Melville as a youth shipped to Liverpool as a cabin-boy and later on sailed on a whaling-ship to the South Seas. These voyages provided the material for his greatest books. *Typee* (1846) and *Omoo* (1847), both of which sketched Polynesian life, could be read as straightforward narrative, but increasingly Melville combined factual description with symbolism, a trend which reached its climax in *Moby Dick* (1851), a work which baffled contemporaries but whose greatness is now universally acknowledged. The story of how the monomaniacal Captain Ahab destroyed himself and the crew of the *Pequod* in the pursuit of a gigantic white whale, *Moby Dick* is an allegorical enquiry into man's doomed struggle against the implacable forces of evil. The pessimism of Hawthorne and Melville found no echo, however, in Whitman. A largely self-educated New York journalist, Whitman drew inspiration from but gave a more mystical cast to Emerson's message of individual self-reliance. As an ardent Jacksonian Democrat he identified himself in his poetry with the ordinary mass of his countrymen. His *Leaves of Grass*, first published in 1854, employed unconventional verse-forms and words common in everyday speech in an exuberant celebration of democracy, individualism, and brotherhood—as well as of sex. However Whitman's genius, like Melville's, was not fully recognized until the twentieth century.

Americans at Worship

The emphasis on the individual that was beginning to pervade literature and the arts had a parallel in religion. Beginning around 1800 there was a fervid upsurge in evangelical Protestantism known as the Second Great Awakening, its architects being a group of itinerant evangelists—Presbyterians, Methodists, Baptists—who rode through the newly settled West preaching a simplified theology well suited to semiliterate pioneer communities. The main feature of Western revivalism was the camp-meeting. The most famous example took place at Cane Ridge, Kentucky in 1801 when 25,000 people assembled for several days of preaching and prayer. Wild emotionalism and strange physical behavior characterized such gatherings. Revivalism then spread to the East, culminating in the 1820s in an extraordinary outburst of Pentecostal enthusiasm in the 'burned-over district' of western New York, so called because it was so regularly ablaze with religious excitement. It was this region that produced the most influential revivalist preacher of the period, Charles Grandison Finney, who carried the theology and techniques of the camp-meeting to New York and other Eastern cities. The teachings of Finney and other members of the revivalist 'Holy Band' represented an uprising against orthodox Calvinism. They rejected or at least played down such Calvinist dogmas as predestination and original sin and substituted the concepts of free will and a benevolent God. Their message essentially was that each individual was capable of working out his own salvation.

The most obvious consequence of the Second Great Awakening was a quickening of interest in religion. Between 1800 and 1835 church membership increased fivefold, whereas the population multiplied only threefold. When Tocqueville arrived in the United States in 1831 he was struck by the pervasive religious atmosphere. There were more churches and more church-goers than in Europe; Sabbath observance was well-nigh universal; public meetings invariably began with a religious invocation; family prayers and Bible-reading were widespread. While some European observers wondered whether American piety was more than skin-deep, most echoed Tocqueville's verdict that there was "no country in the world where the Christian religion retained a greater influence over the souls of men".

Accompanying the boom in religion was a significant shift in the relative standing of the different Protestant denominations. In 1776 the three largest denominations had been the Congregationalists, the Presbyterians, and the Episcopalians. Half a century later the Baptists and the Methodists were well in the lead largely because, unlike other sects, they no longer insisted on formal educational qualifications from ministers and were thus better able to meet the growing demand for them. Another consequence of revivalism was the further proliferation of sects. Successive schisms fragmented both the Baptists and the Presbyterians. One dissident Presbyterian, Alexander Campbell, founded a new denomination which subsequently became known as the Disciples of Christ and which won wide support in frontier areas. The followers of a New York farmer, William Miller, believing his prophecy that the world would end on October 23, 1844, gathered in white robes on hilltops on the appointed day to await Christ's Second Coming. When nothing happened the Millerites became less definite about the date of the millennium and ultimately reorganized themselves as the Seventh Day Adventists. Far more numerous were the adherents of the Church of Jesus Christ of Latter-Day Saints, usually known as Mormons. This was founded in upper New York state in 1830 by Joseph Smith who claimed to have had a series of visions in which the angel Moroni revealed to him certain golden tablets on which sacred writings were inscribed. Subsequently published as the *Book of Mormon* these identified the American Indians as the lost tribes of Israel and prophesied the rebuilding of Zion and the reign of Christ on earth. Since the gathering of the elect was one of Mormonism's distinctive doctrines Smith and his followers established communities first in Ohio, then in Missouri, and finally in 1839 at Nauvoo, Illinois. The fierce hostility Smith had already met with increased further after his announcement in 1843 of a further revelation sanctioning a form of polygamy which he called "plural marriage". The following year Smith was lynched by a mob and soon afterwards his followers trekked westward to Utah under the leadership of Brigham Young.

The Reform Impulse

Easily the most important effect of religious revivalism was to galvanize the reform spirit. The mood of moral perfectionism it engendered filled men with a sense of responsibility not only for their own salvation but also for that of everyone else. It led ineluctably to benevolence, a determination to stamp out every form of evil, an urge to reform the social order and bring about the earthly millennium. Transcendentalist optimism about human nature also contributed to the climate of reform but it was not Transcendentalists but revivalists and their converts who undertook the task of organizing the various reform movements. In the process they imparted to reform the evangelical, emotional tone of revivalism itself.

The most striking fact about the reform ferment of the second quarter of the nineteenth century was the variety of its concerns. There were crusades for peace, temperance, education, prison reform, women's rights, antislavery, and many other moral purposes. Indeed, as Lowell unkindly put it, "every possible form of intellectual and physical dyspepsia brought forth its gospel". Some wanted to abjure the use of money, others took up phrenology, mesmerism, hydropathy, or spiritualism. But these were bizarre and extravagant exceptions to what was essentially a practical movement. Another feature of the various reform agitations was their overlapping membership. Reformers were drawn to several causes and the various benevolent societies were managed by what has been called an "interlocking directorate" of activists. Strongest in New England and in those regions of the North colonized by New Englanders, reform found hardly an echo in the South. Indeed, because of the close connection between abolitionism and reform movements, reform became anathema to Southerners. At the same time American reform had international connections. An especially close intimacy existed between American reformers and kindred spirits in Great Britain. They regularly exchanged correspondence, periodicals, and ideas. Delegates journeyed back and forth across the Atlantic, and international meetings were held like the World Antislavery Conference in London in 1840.

Utopian Experiments

Some visionaries attempted to regenerate society by establishing model cooperative communities. First in the field were various religious groups, mainly of European origin. German pietists under the leadership of George Rapp established the Harmony Society in Pennsylvania in 1804 and other German sectarians planted the community of Zoar in Ohio in 1817. Better known were the communities founded by the Shaker followers of Mother Ann Lee, an illiterate English mystic who went to America in 1774. At the height of their strength in 1826 the Shakers boasted 6,000 members in eighteen different communities stretching from New England to Kentucky. Holding their property in common, the Shakers lived simply under strict discipline, practicing celibacy and vegetarianism. They became almost as well known for their fine furniture and handicrafts and for their useful inventions (the clothes-pin and the apple-peeler among them) as for the ritualistic dances that gave them their name.

Also religious in inspiration was the Oneida community founded in upstate New York in 1848 by John Humphrey Noyes, a New Englander unfrocked for propounding "perfectionism", the doctrine of man's innate sinlessness. Noyes held that monogamy was no more compatible than private property with a true Christian life. Hence Oneida was based not only on the common ownership of property but also on 'complex marriage', a system in which each woman was regarded as the wife of each man and each man as the husband of each woman, in which procreation was selectively controlled, and in which children grew up without recognized parents. For more than thirty years the Oneida community was economically successful but Noyes's unorthodox sexual theories and practices excited the angry resentment of neighbors. In 1879, threatened with legal action, he abandoned 'complex marriage' and departed for Canada. Almost at once the communal basis of economic life was challenged and the colony entered a new era of prosperity as a joint-stock company.

Disillusion with the tendencies of the new industrialism resulted in communities based respectively upon the teachings of Robert Owen, Charles Fourier, and Étienne Cabet. Owen, a Welsh philanthropist famous for the enlightened policies followed in his model factory town in Scotland, arrived in America in 1825, to put into practice his belief that cooperative benevolence was a better basis for society than competitive greed. New Harmony colony in Indiana attracted wide attention, but the members resented Owen's paternalism as well as his hostility to religion and within two years the enterprise had collapsed. Fourier never visited the United States, but a modified version of his ideas reached Americans through the writings of Albert Brisbane, whose *Social Destiny of Man* (1840) explained the principles of "associationism", a cooperative order of small communities or "phalanxes". In the 1840s more than forty Fourierist communities were established. The most famous was Brook Farm, near Boston, founded in 1841 as a transcendentalist enterprise, but subsequently reorganized along Fourierist lines. Brook Farm attracted many New England intellectuals, among them Nathaniel Hawthorne, who satirized it in *The Blithedale Romance* (1852). But the experiment came to an abrupt end in 1847 after a disastrous fire. Interest then shifted to the French community of Icaria, founded in 1849 by followers of the utopian novelist Cabet, at Nauvoo, Illinois, recently vacated by the Mormons. Icaria prospered for a time but factional squabbles, the overthrow and death of Cabet, and the panic of 1857 brought about the ruin of the community. Rarely having more than a hundred members or so, these secular communitarian ventures had their modest moment of glory but made little permanent impression upon so individualistic a nation.

Prison and Asylum Reform

One of the earliest manifestations of humanitarian endeavor was the attempt to improve the treatment of criminals and of the mentally and physically handicapped. While American penal codes had lost much of their harshness after the Revolution prisons remained centers of overcrowding, degradation, and disease. Men and women, young and old, debtors and murderers, hardened criminals and first offenders were herded together and left to their own devices. The demand for prison reform came from local groups like the Society for Alleviating the Miseries of Public Prisons, founded in Philadelphia in 1787. Such organizations did much to popularize the notion that imprisonment should have a reformatory rather than a retributive or a deterrent purpose. Thus Pennsylvania's Eastern

State Penitentiary—the very name suggests its object—built near Philadelphia in 1829, kept criminals in solitary confinement to allow them opportunities for penitence and to avoid contamination by their fellows. But in the event the chief result was to induce mental breakdowns. The rival New York system, introduced into the new prison at Auburn in 1821, placed prisoners in individual cells at night but involved cooperative work, though in strict silence, by day. More commendable was the provision of separate facilities for juvenile offenders. When Tocqueville visited a juvenile house of refuge in Boston he was astounded to learn that the young inmates were allowed to run their own system of government and discipline. But even in the 1850s investigations revealed the existence of serious evils in local jails. Overcrowding was common, food was indescribably poor, and warders brutal; flogging had now been outlawed but prisoners were frequently subjected to a variety of cruel punishments. Moreover, despite powerful protests, public hangings were still allowed in some states as late as the Civil War.

Improvement in the treatment of the handicapped was largely the result of single-handed effort. Thomas G. Gallaudet opened the first American school for deaf mutes at Hartford, Connecticut in 1817 and before he died in 1851 had persuaded thirteen other states to set up similar institutions. Samuel Gridley Howe of Boston espoused the cause of the blind with equal fervor and success. But the greatest individual triumph was that of Dorothea L. Dix, a frail, middle-aged, Boston schoolmistress who awakened the American consciousness to the plight of the insane. In 1843 she drew up a memorial to the Massachusetts legislature detailing how, in the jails and almshouses she had visited in different parts of the state, insane persons were confined in "cages, closets, cellars, stalls, pens!", how they were frequently "chained, naked, beaten with rods, and lashed into obedience!" Having persuaded Massachusetts to appropriate money for an insane asylum, she carried out similar investigations in one state after another, finding the same appalling conditions everywhere. By 1854 she had traveled over 30,000 miles, visiting hundreds of institutions, and spurring the legislatures of fifteen states into at least some action. But Miss Dix's heroic efforts by no means solved the problem: even as late as 1850 not more than a third of the country's insane were being cared for in asylums and in some states neglect and cruelty were undiminished.

Americans at School

The most striking advances of the period came in education. Though the Founding Fathers had believed that the success of the republican experiment would depend upon the wide diffusion of knowledge public schooling was badly neglected for decades. As late as 1830 only New England and New York possessed a free public-school system and even there a stigma attached to "pauper schools". Elsewhere children had to rely on church schools or private academies. The demand for free public schools came first from urban workingmen who visualized education as a means of guaranteeing social and economic equality. Support came also from business and professional men, the clergy, and other established groups. Worried about the disorganizing effects of industrialization and immigration they were anxious for a stabilizing mechanism to keep disorderly elements in check. There was however a good deal of opposition. The emphasis on practicality and the contempt for book-learning characteristic of the colonial period persisted well into the nineteenth century. American individualism also played a part: parents gave a high priority to the education of their own children but sometimes objected to being taxed to educate those of other people. Moreover the growing number of Catholics were not prepared to support public schools in which, notwithstanding the constitutional principle of the separation of church and state, the King James version of the Bible was read, Protestant hymns sung, and Protestant religious texts used.

Nevertheless reformers made real progress. The leading crusader for universal education was Horace Mann who in 1837 became secretary of the newly established Massachusetts Board of Education. Mann looked upon education as a national panacea: It was, he announced in 1848, "the great equalizer of the conditions of men, the balance wheel of the social machinery". As this suggests, Mann's motives were ambiguous: while seeking to extend educational opportunity, he also saw the school as an agency of social control. As well as arousing public opinion to the need for better education, Mann rationalized and centralized the Massachusetts school system, reformed curricula and teaching methods, established a minimum school year (of six months), greatly increased teachers' salaries, and secured the establishment of the first state-supported American normal college—at Lexington, Massachusetts (1839). Similarly effective was the work of Henry Barnard in Connecticut and Rhode Island, Calvin Stowe in Ohio, and Calvin Wiley in North Carolina.

By 1850 or so most states had accepted the principle that free primary education should be available for all children. The country now had 80,000 elementary schools, attended by nearly 3,500,000 pupils. But progress was uneven. The South in particular lagged behind in educational expenditure and consequently in standards: illiteracy among the native white population in the South in 1850 was over 20 percent compared with 3 percent in the Middle Atlantic states and less than half of one percent in New England. Even in the North, however, there were still grave deficiencies. Most school buildings were inadequate, most teachers ill-trained and poorly paid. With rare exceptions like Massachusetts pupils were not graded according to age or ability but were taught together indiscriminately.

Moreover, Massachusetts was the only state before the Civil War to pass a compulsory school-attendance law (1852) and even that did no more than require twelve weeks of schooling a year for children between eight and fourteen.

Only to a limited extent was the principle of state support extended to secondary education before 1860. Again Massachusetts led the way with a law (1827) requiring every city, town, and district of 500 families or more to establish a high school. But even in 1860 there were still only 300 public high schools in the entire country. However, there were about 6,000 private or semiprivate academies, about half of them in the South. Most were for boys only, though Emma Willard's example in founding Troy Female Seminary (1821) was extensively followed, especially in New England and New York. Though tuition fees in private academies were generally low, only the children of the well-to-do could in practice afford to attend since board was extra. Standards varied widely. A great many academies possessed only a single teacher. At the other extreme were excellent institutions like Phillips Andover and Phillips Exeter, founded during the Revolutionary War and in size and quality not very different from colleges. At some academies the pupils wore military uniforms and received military training, the earliest example being the American Literary, Scientific, and Military Academy, founded at Norwich, Vermont in 1819 by Alden Partridge, a former superintendent of West Point. Better known were the two leading Southern military academies: the Virginia Military Institute at Lexington (1839) and The Citadel at Charleston, South Carolina (1843).

In higher education this was a period of mushroom growth. The nine colleges founded during the colonial period had increased to twenty-five by 1800. By the time of the Civil War no fewer than 516 had been established. Most of them were short-lived. Of the 186 which survived, seventeen were state universities, one being Jefferson's creation, the University of Virginia, which opened its doors in 1825. In the West, Indiana established a state university in 1821, Michigan in 1837, Wisconsin in 1848—the last two in the same year that they achieved statehood. But the vast majority of American colleges were denominational, rural, and small. Academic standards were generally low, teaching usually by rote, and the quality of the instruction often inferior to that of the best academies. In some of the leading institutions attempts were made to break away from the traditional classical curriculum, but in general innovation was successfully resisted. Moreover, little was done to improve libraries, virtually nothing to promote advanced study or research. Not until after the Civil War would the United States have any universities of the kind to be found in Europe.

The success of the lyceum movement proved the existence of a widespread popular demand for knowledge. The first lyceum was organized in

1826 at Millbury, Massachusetts by Josiah Holbrook. In 1831 the National American Lyceum was founded and within a few years had more than 3,000 branches. The lyceum began as a mutual self-improvement association, but eventually it came to concentrate on holding public lectures on literary and scientific topics and on current affairs. Among the celebrities who became familiar figures on the lyceum circuit were Emerson, Lowell, Horace Mann, the Harvard geologist Louis Agassiz, and the abolitionists Theodore Parker and Wendell Phillips. A more systematic kind of adult education was provided by mechanics' institutes and by such products of private philanthropy as the Lowell Institute in Boston (1837), the Peabody Institute in Baltimore (1857), and the Cooper Union in New York (1859). Equally noteworthy was the rapid spread of free public libraries. By 1860 more than a thousand communities had them.

The Temperance Movement

Another example of the urge for social betterment was the temperance crusade. Heavy drinking, widespread even in colonial times, became increasingly common in the early nineteenth century, the per capita consumption of spirits rising threefold between 1792 and 1823. Foreign visitors marveled at the amount Americans drank. Weddings, funerals, ordinations, elections, militia gatherings, indeed any social occasion, afforded an excuse for tippling. Ardent spirits, especially rum, corn whiskey, and hard cider were cheap and plentiful and were popularly regarded as conducive to hard work and as a preventive against disease. Nor was habitual drinking a bar to political advancement, Webster and Clay, for example, both being notoriously bibulous. As early as 1784 Dr Benjamin Rush of Philadelphia had attacked "the demon drink", chiefly on medical grounds, but it was not until the 1820s that revivalist preachers like Lyman Beecher began to challenge the traditional acceptance of alcohol and to demand complete abstinence. The American Society for the Promotion of Temperance (as it was inaccurately called) was founded in Boston in 1826 and claimed a million members and 5,000 branches by 1834. The clergymen who initially led the movement saw drink as an obstacle to individual salvation, but their lay successors were more concerned with the close connection between alcoholism and such social evils as crime, vice, and pauperism. The established classes tended, moreover, to believe that general sobriety would make for a more enlightened electorate, a more efficient work force, and a more stable social order.

The temperance movement entered a new and more dramatic phase in 1840 with the formation of the Washington Temperance Society. Organized by reformed drunkards and aiming at the redemption of those still addicted to drink, the Washingtonians quickly spread throughout the country, their meetings attracting huge crowds. The Society mobilized thousands of children into what was known as the cold-water army and relied heavily on itinerant evangelists like John B. Gough, an English-born bookbinder whose 'experience meetings' won an emotional response. Unconnected with the Washingtonians was the Irish 'apostle of temperance', Father Theobald Mathew who, during a two-year visit to the United States (1849–51), induced half a million people to sign the pledge—some, apparently, several times over. There was also a vast outpouring of temperance literature, much of it sensational and sentimental. The outstanding example was Timothy Shay Arthur's *Ten Nights in a Bar Room, and What I Saw There* (1854), a tale of depravity second in circulation only to *Uncle Tom's Cabin.*

In the 1830s moral suasion became increasingly reinforced by political action. Several states attempted to regulate the drink trade by licensing or local-option laws. More drastic was a Massachusetts law of 1838 which forbade the purchase of less than fifteen gallons of distilled liquor at a time. In 1846, thanks largely to the efforts of Neal Dow, Maine became the first state to adopt a prohibition law. During the next nine years twelve other Northern states took similar action. But enforcement was difficult and most of the laws were soon repealed or declared unconstitutional.

The Peace Crusade and Women's Rights

Less successful in winning mass support were the opponents of war. Quakers, Mennonites, and other nonresistant religious sects had long practiced pacifism but it was not until after the War of 1812 that an organized peace movement began to develop. In 1828 a Maine sea captain and farmer, William Ladd, founded the American Peace Society but serious divisions developed over the morality of defensive wars and in 1838, after the Society had tried to straddle the issue, a minority of extremists formed the Nonresistance Society which condemned all wars. Undeterred, Ladd broke new ground in 1840 with his *Essay on a Congress of Nations*, which proposed an international peacekeeping body. After Ladd's death in 1841 leadership passed to 'the learned blacksmith', Elihu Burritt of Connecticut. In 1846, with the help of the English Quaker, Joseph Sturge, he founded the League of Universal Brotherhood to work for international friendship and the abolition of war and in 1848 he held in Brussels the first of a series of World Peace Conferences which aroused great enthusiasm. Meanwhile in the United States the Mexican War had given a fillip to the peace crusade, especially in New England where the war was unpopular. But as the slavery controversy grew more intense, many zealots subordinated pacifism to abolitionism. By 1860 the American Peace Society had became virtually inoperative.

Toward another issue of the day, women's rights, the national mood remained hostile or at best indifferent. The position of American women was paradoxical. Men treated them simultaneously as superior beings and as helpless subordinates. Nowhere in the world were women so idealized, deferred to, protected. Yet they were uniformly denied social and political equality. A married woman had no legal right to her own belongings or her own earnings, nor without her husband's consent could she make a will or even assume guardianship over her own children. Married or not, a woman could neither hold office nor vote. Her educational opportunities, too, were extremely limited. In the 1820s Emma Willard and Catherine E. Beecher established female academies and in the process refuted the charge that girls could not master such subjects as mathematics and philosophy without loss of health or femininity. Then in 1837 a Massachusetts schoolteacher, Mary Lyon, founded the first American women's college, Mount Holyoke. But as late as the mid-century Oberlin College, founded on a coeducational basis in 1833, was the only institution of standing to admit women. Even so a handful of remarkable women succeeded in becoming highly educated and in entering the professions. There were novelists like Harriet Beecher Stowe and Lydia Maria Child, and journalists like Margaret Fuller, joint editor of the Transcendentalist *Dial*, and Sarah J. Hale, who made *Godey's Lady's Book* the best known of American women's periodicals. In 1849 Elizabeth Blackwell became the first qualified woman doctor in the United States, and in 1853 Antoinette Brown the first ordained woman minister.

Women were also active in reform; they constituted a majority of the members of abolitionist and temperance societies. Some female reformers, like Angelina and Sarah Grimké, Lucy Stone, and Lucretia Mott became nationally known. But when they sought a more prominent role in such movements they invariably encountered male opposition, especially from clergymen. This drove many into feminism. When ministers objected to the appearance of the Grimké sisters on abolitionist lecture platforms, Sarah responded with her *Letter on the Equality of the Sexes and the Condition of Women* (1838), a forceful restatement of many of Mary Wollstonecraft's feminist arguments. The denial of seats to American women attending the World Anti-Slavery Conference in London in 1840 had more striking consequences. Two of those excluded, Elizabeth Cady Stanton and Lucretia Mott, discovered a mutual interest in women's rights and in 1848 they summoned a convention of women at Seneca Falls, New York. Meeting on July 4 the gathering adopted a Declaration of Sentiments echoing the language of the Declaration of Independence, but asserting that "all men and women are created equal"and substituting Man for George III as the author of the various tyrannies complained of. While the document demanded the ballot it was at least as much concerned with equality in education, in marriage, in property-holding, and in employment.

One of those attending the Seneca Falls convention was Amelia

Bloomer. Though not the first to wear the costume which bears her name—a loose-fitting, short skirt with Turkish-style trousers tied at the ankle—she vigorously championed dress reform in her suffragist newspaper, the *Lily*. The 'Bloomer costume' attracted a good deal of ridicule and was soon abandoned by the few militants who wore it. One of them, Lucy Stone, attracted fresh notoriety in 1855 when, on her marriage to Henry Blackwell (Elizabeth's brother), she insisted on retaining her maiden name and on issuing with her husband a protest at the inequalities of the marriage laws. Feminists faced incessant abuse and mockery. Even some men who counted themselves liberal clung to the dogma that woman's place was in the home. Many, perhaps most, women shared this opinion, even so dedicated a pioneer of women's education as Catherine Beecher becoming an outspoken antisuffragist. Thus progress towards sexual equality was slow. By 1860 about half the states had passed laws—largely, it must be said, at the instigation of men—recognizing married women's property rights. But other social and political disabilities remained.

Antislavery and Proslavery

The reform movement which overshadowed and ultimately swallowed up the rest was antislavery. In the colonial period most Americans had accepted slavery as an economic necessity, sanctioned moreover by the Bible. The Revolution, with its emphasis on liberty and equality, produced widespread condemnation of the institution, even in the South, but by the early nineteenth century antislavery sentiment had ebbed. Antislavery societies, most numerous in the upper South, kept up a subdued agitation but aspired to nothing more than gradual emancipation. The American Colonization Society, founded in 1817 with the support of such prominent slave-holders as Henry Clay and John Marshall, aimed at colonizing free Negroes in West Africa. Under its auspices the independent republic of Liberia was founded (1822), the capital Monrovia being named after President James Monroe. The Society won adherents in the North as well as in the South. Even some men destined to become leading abolitionists believed at first that colonization might pave the way for emancipation. But many of its Southern supporters saw colonization merely as a means of ridding the country of its free blacks, regarded as potential leaders of slave revolts. The colonization idea died hard; even as late as the Civil War Lincoln favored it as a means of solving the race problem. But as early as 1830 it was apparent that colonization was a failure. It had not induced slave-holders to accept voluntary manumission; attempts to secure a Congressional appropriation had come to naught; free blacks were violently hostile, preferring, as one group put it in 1817, "being colonized in the most remote corner of the land of our nativity to being exiled to a foreign country". Of the handful of blacks colonized in Liberia most suffered great hardships. The American Colonization Society limped along until the 1860s on private contributions and on grants from Virginia and Maryland, but colonized in all only 12,000 people, a mere fraction of the black population.

The most active opponent of slavery in the 1820s was the New Jersey Quaker, Benjamin Lundy, editor of the *Genius of Universal Emancipation* (1821). Lundy favored colonization and also urged voluntary gradual emancipation upon the states. But this did not satisfy the militant young Boston printer, William Lloyd Garrison, who became his assistant in 1828. Intense, vain, humorless, and narrow-minded, Garrison was fanatical in his idealism, unsparing in his denunciation of opponents. Rejecting gradualism in any form and condemning colonization as "a conspiracy against humanity", he saw slavery as a sin and immediate emancipation as an urgent necessity. Garrison proclaimed his militancy in the first issue of his weekly newspaper, *The Liberator*, published in Boston on January 1, 1831: "I will be as harsh as truth and as uncompromising as justice . . . I do not wish to think or speak or write with. moderation . . . I am in earnest—I will not equivocate—I will not excuse—I will not retreat a single inch— AND I WILL BE HEARD."

Garrison founded the New England Anti-Slavery Society in 1832. It gained the support of such prominent Bostonians as the Unitarian clergymen, Theodore Parker and William Ellery Channing, the wealthy lawyer, Wendell Phillips, and the poet, John Greenleaf Whittier. By many contemporaries, especially in the South, Garrison came to be regarded as the personification of abolitionism. But his influence should not be exaggerated. *The Liberator*'s circulation was small and confined largely to free blacks. For a long time the main effect of Garrison's extremism was to alienate potential supporters. He deeply shocked Northern opinion by denouncing the churches for failing to adopt an abolitionist stance and by denouncing American Christianity as "heathenish, filled with apologies for sin". Equally distasteful to many were his assertions that disunion was a moral necessity and that the Constitution, by protecting slavery, was "an Agreement with Death and a Covenant with Hell".

While Garrison was fulminating against slavery from Boston, abolitionism was growing from fertile ground in other places and under other leaders. It was they rather than Garrison who undertook the vital task of spreading the immediatist doctrine and of organizing support for it. In New York a group of wealthy philanthropists headed by the brothers Arthur and Lewis Tappan played a central role. Inspired by the triumph of emancipation in Great Britain 1833 the Tappans issued a call for a national antislavery organization. In response sixty-two people from all parts of the North, Garrison among them, assembled at Philadelphia in December 1833 to form the American Anti-Slavery Society. The Society's Declaration of Sentiments, drawn up by Garrison, condemned slavery as contrary to the principles of Christianity and the Declaration of Independence, denounced colonization, and demanded immediate abolition without compensation to slave-holders.

Agents of the Society set to work to establish branches in every Northern city, town, and village. By 1840 there were nearly 2,000 with a membership of almost 200,000. The most effective of the Society's organizers was Theodore Dwight Weld, a young Presbyterian minister whose reforming zeal had been awakened by Finney's preaching. Lane Theological Seminary in Cincinnati, founded by New York evangelicals as an outpost of Western revivalism, was the scene of Weld's greatest triumph. After a famous eighteen-day debate in 1833 he converted the students and teaching staff to immediatism and when the trustees condemned his activities led a rebellious core to newly founded Oberlin College, which soon became the hub of Western abolitionism. Throughout the 1830's Weld and his band of disciples—the celebrated 'Seventy'—labored tirelessly in hundreds of Western communities, using revivalist techniques to promote the abolitionist cause.

Accompanying the growth of abolitionist societies was the wholesale distribution of antislavery literature, an activity largely financed by the Tappans and made possible by new developments in printing technology, especially the steam press. Within two years of its birth the American Anti-Slavery Society was annually circulating a million copies of such periodicals as the *Emancipator*, the *Anti-Slavery Reporter*, *Human Rights*, and *Slave's Friend* (for juvenile readers). The country was also flooded with antislavery tracts and pamphlets. Antislavery propaganda was at first addressed chiefly to the South and called upon slave-holders to repent the sin of slave-owning. But increasingly it came to be directed to the North, arguing instead that slavery was a crime and indicting not only the cruelty and depravity of slave-holders but also Southern society in general. Thus Garrison described the South as "one great Sodom". This change of emphasis may have been prompted by Southern efforts to suppress abolitionist literature. After a mob had seized and burned antislavery publications in the Charleston post office in 1835, Southern postmasters generally refused to deliver them. Jackson's Postmaster General, Amos Kendall, condoned their action, while the President himself suggested a federal law prohibiting the circulation of "incendiary publications intended to instigate the slaves into insurrection". Congress did not respond but nearly all the Southern states adopted measures to control the mails.

A more protracted Congressional controversy centered upon the circulation and presentation of monster abolitionist petitions. In 1836 alarmed Southern Congressmen and their Northern sympathizers secured the adoption of the 'gag rule' requiring all petitions relating to slavery to be automatically laid on the table without being printed or discussed. The American Anti-Slavery Society promptly stepped up its petition campaign. During the 1837–8 Congressional session no fewer than 412,000 petitions reached the House alone. The fight against the gag rule was eloquently led by former President John Quincy Adams, who had returned to Washington as a Congressman from Massachusetts. Adams had earlier been unsympathetic to abolitionism but interpreted the gag rule as a direct threat to freedom of speech and of petition. Finally in 1844 he secured its repeal.

Abolitionism was not exclusively a white man's movement. Blacks played an important and active role, contributing to the general antislavery crusade but also acting independently. Though black churches would not officially commit themselves about slavery, black clergymen like Samuel D. Cornish, Henry Highland Garnet, and Alexander Crummell became familiar figures on abolitionist platforms. Some of the most effective antislavery propagandists were escaped slaves like William Wells Brown, William and Ellen Craft, and Frederick Douglass, whose narratives brought home to Northern audiences the realities of slavery. Douglass, the most distinguished Negro of his day, also founded the first successful black newspaper, *North Star* (1847). Black participation in the antislavery movement revealed a lingering racism even among white abolitionists. Many treated blacks condescendingly and expressed doubts as to the expediency of mixing the races at public functions. Blacks deeply resented such treatment, complaining of an 'overseer attitude' and of the subordinate role invariably assigned them in joint activities.

The black community took the lead in the only effective direct action against slavery, namely, helping runaway slaves to reach safety in the North or in Canada. True, courageous white abolitionists like the North Carolina Quaker, Levi Coffin, and the Boston clergyman, Samuel J. May, assisted occasional runaways but, contrary to what was long believed, neither they nor anyone else set up a highly organized 'underground railroad' with regular staging posts and hundreds of 'conductors' to spirit Negroes out of slavery. Individual free blacks engineered a number of slave escapes. The intrepid Harriet Tubman, herself a fugitive, reputedly made more than a dozen sorties into the South and brought back more than 200 people. But the total number of fugitives was not large and mostly it was a matter of blacks giving spontaneous aid to slaves who had brought about their own liberation. The lot of those who escaped was eased by the 'personal liberty laws' passed by Northern states in an attempt to impede enforcement of the Fugitive Slave act of 1793, requiring the return of runaways. In *Prigg* v. *Pennsylvania* (1842) the Supreme Court held one such state law to be unconstitutional, but also decided that since execution of the fugitive-slave clause in the Constitution was exclusively a federal power state authorities were not required to assist. This resulted in the adoption of new and more stringent personal-liberty laws.

Stung by the violence of the abolitionist onslaught the South lashed out in its own defense. The weight of Southern opinion had always supported slavery; the Jeffersonian attitude that slavery was a necessary evil had not been widely shared. Long before the rise of militant abolitionism, and especially after the Missouri controversy, Southerners publicly defended their 'peculiar institution'. But it was not until the 1830s that a systematic proslavery ideology was formulated. In a widely read pamphlet published in 1832 Thomas R. Dew, a professor at the College of William and Mary drew on history, anthropology, economics, and religion to make the case for slavery. The civilization of the ancient world, he argued, had been based on it. Blacks had benefited from their removal from savage Africa, but being congenitally inferior to whites, would be cruelly exploited if they were set free. Slavery made democracy possible in the South since it brought all white men "down to one common level". The entire Southern economy—indeed, the nation's prosperity—depended upon slavery for only Africans could work in the Southern heat and would do so only if compelled. Above all slavery was sanctioned by the Bible, more particularly by the practice of the Old Testament Hebrews and by the injunctions of St. Paul. Dew's arguments, refined and developed in scores of books, pamphlets, magazine articles, and sermons, were later reinforced by others. In 1854 two Southern scientists, Dr Josiah C. Nott and George Gliddon, published a book entitled *Types of Mankind* purporting to prove the plural origin of the races and asserting that the Negro lay at the bottom of the scale of human creation. Governor James H. Hammond of South Carolina advanced a "mudsill" theory, arguing that in every social system a menial class was essential so as to free the more gifted for intellectual pursuits. Still more influential were the ingenious arguments of a Virginia lawyer, George Fitzhugh. In *Sociology for the South* (1854) and *Cannibals All!* (1857) Fitzhugh explicitly repudiated the principles of the Declaration of Independence, claiming that a free competitive order meant in practice the law of the jungle and the exploitation of the weak, whereas the slave system provided for the social well-being of all.

In ceaselessly reiterating the proslavery argument Southern leaders were seeking not to convert the North or even to quieten their feelings of guilt but to unify their own section and in particular to convince the nonslaveholding majority of the necessity of slavery. To make doubly sure they suppressed all criticism, indeed all discussion, of slavery. As well as banning antislavery publications, state legislatures offered large rewards for the apprehension of prominent abolitionists. By the middle 1830s it had become dangerous for anyone to express antislavery opinions in the South. At some universities professors were dismissed for daring to do so. In

Kentucky in 1845 a mob forcibly prevented the wealthy slave-owner, Cassius M. Clay, from starting an antislavery newspaper. Thus Southern critics of slavery had either to conceal their opinions or to leave. Among those who left were such prominent recruits to Northern abolitionism as James G. Birney of Alabama and the Grimké sisters of South Carolina.

Abolitionism was also at first strongly opposed in the North. Anti-Negro feeling was the cause. "The prejudice of race", Tocqueville remarked, "appears to be stronger in the states that have abolished slavery than in those where it still exists and nowhere is it so intolerant as in those states where servitude has never existed." In most Northern states blacks could not vote, sit on juries, or intermarry with whites, segregation was the rule in public places, politicians of all parties openly championed white supremacy. Abolitionists were accordingly denounced as fanatical and irresponsible agitators, bent only on fomenting disorder, with being under foreign, especially British, influence, and with having harmed the slave by provoking the South into passing more stringent slave codes. Some Northern groups had special reasons for disliking abolitionists. Irish immigrants feared the economic competition of freed Negroes flocking to the North, while Northern businessmen, especially those with Southern connections, were apprehensive lest Southerners react to abolitionist agitation by boycotting Northern products.

Northern opinion expressed itself in antiabolition riots, in many cases organized and led by prominent and respected members of the community. Abolitionists' meetings were broken up, their property attacked, their persons assaulted, their newspapers suppressed. Lewis Tappan was stoned in New York in 1834 and his house sacked; Garrison was mobbed on the streets of Boston the following year and nearly lynched; Pennsylvania Hall in Philadelphia was burned down in 1838 after it had staged an antislavery meeting. But the worst outrage was the one which gave abolitionism its martyr: the murder of the antislavery editor, Elijah Lovejoy, in November 1837 at Alton, Illinois while defending his printing-press against mob violence. Mob action had the opposite effect from that intended. Far from silencing the abolitionists it transformed them into defenders of freedom of speech and of the press and won them, if not the support, then at least the sympathy of many who had hitherto been neutral or hostile.

Internal dissension ultimately disrupted the antislavery cause. There had been ominous divisions from the outset, some resulting from clashing personalities, others from disagreement over strategy and tactics. There were sharp differences about the precise meaning of immediatism, the Garrisonians rejecting the vague and, to many, incomprehensible Weld–Tappan formula of "gradual emancipation, immediately begun". Many committed abolitionists were repelled by Garrison's sweeping condemnation of the churches and by his acerbic generalizations about slave-holders, others by his deepening commitment to various 'radical' reforms unconnected with antislavery, notably nonresistance and women's rights. Finally there was the question of moral suasion versus political action. Dissatisfaction with the equivocation of the major parties on the slavery issue led some abolitionists to demand a new antislavery party. But Garrison and his followers argued that involvement in politics would dilute the pure philanthropy of the abolitionist crusade.

The crisis came at the annual meeting of the American Anti-Slavery Society in May 1840. Following their success in placing a woman, Abby Kelley, on the Business Committee, conservatives seceded to form their own American and Foreign Anti-Slavery Society. A month earlier, other anti-Garrisonians, chiefly New Yorkers, had organized the first antislavery party, the Liberty Party, and had nominated James G. Birney for the Presidency. Birney polled only 7,000 votes in the 1840 election but four years later picked up enough support in delicately balanced New York to determine the result. Control of the antislavery movement had passed out of the hands of the moral reformers into those of politicians keen to mobilize the developing Northern sentiment against the spread of slavery. The two rival abolitionist organizations remained in being until emancipation was achieved but neither recovered fully from the schism of 1840.

What, if anything, had the abolitionists achieved by their agitation? Not the conversion of the North to abolitionism, still less to the principle of racial equality. But if abolitionist propaganda failed to persuade Northerners to love the Negro, it at least taught many to dislike and distrust the Southern slave-owner and to believe in the existence of a 'slave power' conspiracy to snuff out liberty throughout the land. Abolitionists thus paved the way for the Free Soil and Republican parties to mobilize forces which were little concerned about the welfare of the slave but were strongly opposed to the expansion of slavery and of Southern power in the territories. At the same time abolitionist denunciation infuriated the South. In short, if abolitionists did little to help the slave they did a great deal to polarize American opinion and to heighten sectional animosity.

10. Westward Expansion and Sectional Conflict, 1844–1850

Manifest Destiny

Territorial expansion reached a new peak of intensity in the 1840s. Concern for national security, supposedly threatened by British activity in Texas, California, and Oregon was one cause. But more important were the cluster of beliefs summed up in the catch phrase 'manifest destiny' coined by a New York editor in 1845. The term reflected the assumption that Providence had intended the United States to control the entire North American continent. This provided a convenient rationalization for the conquest of lesser breeds like Indians and Mexicans by land-hungry pioneers. It was a credo strikingly similar to that adopted to justify the imperialism of the European Great Powers later in the century. But running through Manifest Destiny there was also a thread of romanticism, even of idealism; it embodied the conviction that to augment American territory was the best means of promoting the spread of democratic ideals and institutions. Such ideas, often extravagantly expressed, were widely held and became the driving force of public policy. They resulted in the annexation of Texas, the settlement of the Oregon dispute, and the acquisition of California, New Mexico, and Utah.

By the 1840s the frontier has been carried halfway across the continent. There were still vast unsettled tracts of land under American jurisdiction between the Mississippi and the Rockies, but with most of the Great Plains thought to be too arid for agriculture American pioneers looked longingly at and then spilled over into the broad unoccupied expanses of fertile land that lay in the Mexican borderlands and in the Far West. The first substantial movement was directed towards Texas in response to a Mexican invitation. Soon after winning its independence from Spain in 1822, Mexico offered liberal land grants to Americans who would submit to her jurisdiction in Texas and agree to colonize a given number of settlers. By 1830 Texas had attracted nearly 20,000 Americans, mostly Southerners who brought along their Negro slaves, despite the fact that slavery was abolished in Mexico in 1829. The Mexican government, alarmed at the extent of the influx, then prohibited further American immigration and belatedly tried to enforce the laws against slavery. This caused friction between the settlers and the Mexican authorities; there was also trouble over land-titles and taxes. Matters came to a head in 1835 when the Mexican president, General Santa Anna, tightened central control. This step, which Texans rightly interpreted as an attempt to absorb them more fully into an alien culture, made rebellion inevitable. Early in 1836 they declared their independence and established a republic. Santa Anna led an army into Texas to put down the revolt. His troops overran the Alamo mission at San Antonio, killing every member of the garrison. At the nearby town of Goliad the Mexicans executed most of the defenders after they had surrendered. These atrocities only stiffened Texan resistance. In April 1836, under the rallying cry, 'Remember the Alamo', General Sam Houston's small army decisively defeated the Mexicans at the battle of San Jacinto. Santa Anna was taken prisoner and forced to sign treaties recognizing Texan independence. Mexico later repudiated Santa Anna's undertakings as having been given under duress, but made no further attempt to subdue the province.

Almost at once the new republic sought annexation to the United States. The United States had been interested for some time in acquiring Texas, both John Quincy Adams and Andrew Jackson having vainly attempted to purchase it. American opinion had strongly sympathized with the Texan struggle for independence and there was much support for annexation, especially in the South and the West. But in the North there was strong opposition: Texas was large enough to be carved up into as many as five slave states and its incorporation would both strengthen slavery and add enormously to Southern political power. Jackson thought annexation politically explosive in an election year so he shelved the issue and even delayed recognition of Texan independence until just before he retired from the presidency in 1837. His successor, Martin Van Buren, equally anxious to avoid controversy over slavery, ignored the issue throughout his term of office.

Finding her offer spurned, Texas withdrew her application for annexation and instead sought and obtained recognition, loans, and commercial treaties from France and Great Britain. The British welcomed an independent Texas: it would obstruct American expansion, provide a market for British manufactures, and relieve the Lancashire textile industry of its dependence on American cotton. As the Texans had perhaps calculated, Great Britain's growing interest in their affairs caused alarm in Washington. Accordingly in the autumn of 1843 Tyler authorized his Secretary of State, Abel P. Upshur, who like himself, was an ardent expansionist, to reopen annexation negotiations with Texas. These were on the point of completion when, on February 28, 1844, Upshur was killed by the explosion of a cannon on board the new warship, *Princeton*.

His successor, John C. Calhoun, was as keen as Tyler to acquire Texas and the treaty negotiations were speedily concluded. But submission of the treaty to the Senate coincided with the publication of a note to the British government concerning the Texan question in which Calhoun had vigorously defended slavery. This made it appear that the annexation of Texas was being sought simply to protect the South's 'peculiar institution'. Calhoun's maladroitness sealed the treaty's fate—it was rejected by 35 votes to 16—and ensured that Texas would become an issue in the forthcoming presidential election.

Meanwhile, American interest was growing in two other sparsely settled Mexican provinces: California and New Mexico. In the early 1840s California was a remote and almost empty expanse. Some sixty years earlier Spain had encouraged Franciscan friars, led by Fr. Junipero Serra, to build a chain of mission houses along the coast between San Diego and San Francisco. These had succeeded in converting the Indians and in teaching them agriculture, but in 1834 the Mexican government secularized the missions and deprived them of their lands. By this time the province had about 7,000 inhabitants, mainly descendants of Spanish colonists and mostly engaged in ranching. They conducted a modest trade in hides, furs, and tallow with vessels that came out annually from Boston with manufactured goods, but otherwise had little contact with the outside world.

In the 1830s a handful of American merchants arrived and a few years later, stimulated by Richard Henry Dana's glowing account of California in *Two Years Before the Mast* (1841) and the favorable publicity generated by John C. Frémont's Rocky Mountain explorations, the first American settlers began to trickle in. By 1845 they numbered about 700. Despite their small numbers, they were soon toying with thoughts of independence from Mexico and of absorption into the Union. The same idea had already begun to interest the Tyler Administration. Suspicion of British designs on California, though just as ill founded as in the case of Texas, sharpened the American appetite. A remarkable incident in 1842 showed which way the wind was blowing. Under the mistaken impression that the United States had gone to war with Mexico the commander of the American naval squadron in the Pacific impetuously seized the port of Monterey and proclamed the annexation of California. Although he promptly withdrew on learning the true position, and the State Department apologized to Mexico, it was now apparent that the United States had designs on California.

Manifest Destiny had nothing to do with another stream of emigration to the Mexican borderlands. Far from wishing to extend the area of American freedom, Mormons were themselves seeking freedom from religious persecution. The hostility they encountered from neighbors reached a climax in 1844 with Joseph Smith's murder. This set in motion an epic migration. Under the leadership of Smith's successor, Brigham

Young, almost the whole Mormon community, numbering 4,000 souls, set out from Nauvoo, Illinois in 1846 for the isolated Great Salt Lake Valley. There they established a quasicommunistic social order under stern ecclesiastical leadership. Though their new Zion was a barren wilderness the Mormons used irrigation to build a prosperous agriculture. They were chagrined to discover that, as a result of the Mexican War, they had again fallen under American jurisdiction. Hopes of establishing their own state of Deseret were disappointed and the area became part of the territory of Utah, organized in 1850. But federal control proved to be largely nominal. Brigham Young was appointed territorial governor and until after the Civil War ran the territory virtually as a private commonwealth for the benefit of the Mormon Church.

For very different reasons Americans were becoming aware of the potentialities of yet another part of the West—the Oregon country, a huge region stretching from California to Alaska and from the Rockies to the Pacific Ocean. At the beginning of the nineteenth century four countries— Russia, Spain, Britain, and the United States—had had claims to the area, but the contest soon narrowed down to an Anglo-American duel. In 1818 Great Britain and the United States negotiated an arrangement known as 'joint occupation', namely, that Oregon should remain open to both countries. For a time the region remained under the control of British fur traders, but in the late 1830s came a sudden surge of American interest. Returning traders and trappers and missionaries like Marcus Whitman told of a country of almost unbelievable fertility. Almost overnight Oregon became a new land of promise and pioneers set off by covered wagon on the hazardous, 2,000 mile route known as the Oregon Trail. By the end of 1845 the 5,000 American settlers in Oregon had already organized a provisional government and were demanding that the United States end joint occupation and establish exclusive jurisdiction.

The Election of 1844

The 1844 presidential election took place when Manifest Destiny was at flood-tide. Thus the Oregon and Texas questions were bound to obtrude themselves. Alarmed at the way in which Texas had become involved in the slavery controversy, the prospective candidates for the Presidency, Henry Clay and Martin Van Buren, attempted to keep it out of the campaign. They each issued statements asserting that annexation was inexpedient because it would be likely to bring war with Mexico. Clay's declaration did not prevent his becoming the choice of the Whigs; he was nominated on a platform which said nothing about Texas. But Van Buren's attitude lost him the Democratic nomination. He was passed over in favor of James K. Polk of Tennessee, an enthusiastic expansionist and the first 'dark-horse' presidential candidate. The Democratic platform caught the prevailing mood of expansionism but was cleverly designed to combine Western aspirations with those of the South. It called for 'the reoccupation of Oregon and the reannexation of Texas', a phrase which carried the dubious implication that both the proposed acquisitions had always belonged to the United States.

During the campaign domestic issues paled before that of expansionism. The Democrats made most of the running with their aggressive demands for Texas and the whole of Oregon up to 54° 40'—though the famous slogan 'fifty-four forty or fight' emerged only after the election. Clay, realizing that his equivocation on Texas was weakening his Southern support, came out belatedly with a halfhearted endorsement of annexation. That may have done him some good in the South but on balance it was a mistake for it lost him support in the North, especially in the key state of New York. Had Clay carried it, he would have been President, but Whig antislavery voters deserted to the Liberty party in sufficient numbers to throw the state to Polk. In the country at large the Democratic victory was extremely narrow. Thus, if the election gave a mandate for expansion, it was hardly a clear one. It did show, however, that antislavery was on the way to becoming a serious force in American politics; the Liberty party polled 62,300 votes, compared with only 7,069 four years before.

In November 1844 Tyler's term of office still had four months to run and he was anxious to go out in a blaze of glory. Immediately after the election he declared that the voters had shown themselves in favor of the annexation of Texas and proposed that Congress should promptly accomplish it by means of a joint resolution. That meant that annexation would require only a simple majority in both houses—something much easier to achieve than the two-thirds majority needed in the Senate to ratify a treaty. Though opposed by antislavery Congressmen and by constitutional purists who disliked this method of acquiring territory, the joint resolution finally passed the House by 120 votes to 98 and the Senate by 27 to 25. Signed by Tyler on March 1, 1845—two days before he left office—it provided for the admission of Texas to the Union on condition that it could not be subdivided into more than four additional states, and that it had to pay its own public debt. In July 1845, despite last-minute attempts by Britain to persuade the Lone Star republic to retain its independence, Texas voted to accept the American terms and in December 1845 she was admitted as a single state.

Polk and Expansionism

The Texas issue had thus been substantially settled before Polk became President. It remained to be seen whether he would be able to implement the other half of the expansionist plank of the Democratic platform, namely, the 'reoccupation of Oregon'. At first it seemed as though the new

President's policy would be 'fifty-four forty or fight'; in his inaugural address he asserted that the American title to the Oregon country was 'clear and unquestionable' and would be fully maintained. But in July 1845 he offered to divide Oregon with Britain on the line of the 49th parallel. Why he did so is unclear. Perhaps he felt that since all the American settlers in Oregon were south of that line, the area to the north was hardly worth a war. Alternatively, at a time when relations with Mexico were fast deteriorating, he may have been anxious to avoid a war on two fronts.

When the British rejected Polk's offer he withdrew it and adopted a more militant stance. Concluding that 'the only way to treat John Bull was to look him straight in the eye', he sent a message to Congress in December 1845 in which he recommended the end of joint occupation and, in a restatement of the half-forgotten Monroe Doctrine, warned that the United States would not permit a European colony to be established on any part of the North American continent. Though the warning cut little ice in London, the British were now ready to meet Polk half way; since the Hudson's Bay Company had transferred headquarters from the Columbia river to Vancouver Island, the area south of the 49th parallel was no longer worth contending for. In June 1846 the British in their turn proposed the 49th parallel as the basis of settlement and, with the United States now at war with Mexico, Polk accepted it. The Oregon Treaty, which established the 49th parallel as the boundary between the United States and Canada from the Rockies to the Straits of Vancouver and left Vancouver Island in British hands, was a fair and reasonable settlement which satisfied both claimants. The Senate ratified it by a vote of 41 to 14 on June 18, 1846. But there was an angry protest from Western Democrats at the fact that Polk had abandoned the demand for the whole of Oregon. Their sense of betrayal was soon to produce a rift within the Democratic party.

Meanwhile war had begun with Mexico. American resentment towards Mexico had been building ever since the slaughter of the Alamo garrison during the Texan Revolution. There was friction, too, over Mexico's failure to pay her debts. American citizens in Mexico claimed several million dollars in damages for property destroyed during recurrent periods of disorder and, although Mexico had finally agreed to pay $2 million compensation to the United States she soon defaulted. When Texas was annexed the Mexican government angrily broke off diplomatic relations with the United States and the Mexican press loudly demanded war. Controversy over the Texas boundary further inflamed the situation. As a Mexican province Texas had never extended beyond the Nueces River, but Texans now advanced a highly dubious claim to the Rio Grande. Mexico refused even to admit the existence of a boundary dispute; in her eyes the whole of Texas was still Mexican territory. But Polk was determined to uphold the Texan claim and in the summer of 1845 sent a detachment of troops under General Zachary Taylor to the disputed area.

The President's ambitions did not, however, stop there. He came to office determined to acquire California and New Mexico and possibly other Mexican provinces as well. Like other expansionists, he was excited by their commercial opportunities and, moreover, he was apprehensive about British designs on the Pacific coast. Polk hoped to persuade the Mexicans to sell the territory he coveted, but was prepared to use force if he could not acquire it peaceably. In November 1845 in a last attempt at negotiation he sent John Slidell, a Louisiana politician, as special emissary to Mexico. Slidell was authorized to cancel the unpaid damage claims against Mexico in return for the Rio Grande boundary and was to offer $5 million for New Mexico and a further $25 million for California. Slidell would probably have been rebuffed in any case but, arriving in Mexico City at a time when a new government had just ridden to power on a tide of anti-Americanism, he was not even received.

In January 1846, on learning of the failure of the Slidell mission, Polk ordered Taylor to advance to the Rio Grande. He may have been trying to provoke an incident that would serve as a *casus belli*. If so, he must have been disappointed because Mexican forces made no move to cross the river. By May 9 Polk's patience came to an end. He decided to ask Congress for a declaration of war on the ground that Mexico had refused to pay its debts and had insulted the United States by declining to negotiate with Slidell. But that same evening, before the war message had been sent, news arrived that Mexican troops had crossed the Rio Grande and that in the ensuing clash sixteen American soldiers had been killed or wounded. This was the pretext Polk had been waiting for, perhaps had maneuvered to bring about. Hastily revising his war message he bent the facts to suit his purpose. He declared that 'after reiterated menaces', Mexico had 'shed American blood on American soil'. Claiming that 'war exists by act of Mexico itself' he asked Congress formally to acknowledge the fact. Congress accepted Polk's version of events and on May 13, 1846 both houses voted overwhelmingly for war and for a bill authorizing the President to enroll 50,000 volunteers.

The Mexican War

Despite the promptness with which Congress responded, neither the politicians nor the people were united in support of the war. Some Congressional leaders—Calhoun, Thomas Hart Benton, and John Quincy Adams among them—saw the war as one of American aggression. Calhoun had a further objection. He complained that the President had violated the Constitution by in effect arrogating to himself the war-making power. Senator Tom Corwin of Ohio made a scathing attack on Polk, adding that, if he were a Mexican, he would ask Americans: 'Have you not room enough in your own country to bury your dead men? If you come into mine, we will greet, you with bloody hands, and welcome you to hospitable graves.'

While Taylor's early victories were enthusiastically greeted in the West and the Southwest, where expansionist fervor ran high, they were coolly received in the Northeast, especially in New England. Despite being the most populous part of the country, the Northeast supplied fewer than 8,000 volunteers against 20,000 from the South and 40,000 from the West. New England antislavery spokesmen like Emerson, Thoreau, and James Russell Lowell denounced the Mexican war as a plot to strengthen the slave-power and acquire more slave territory. In this they were mistaken. Many Southern planters were lukewarm about possible territorial gains from Mexico; they could see that New Mexico and California were unsuited to slavery and that their acquisition would be more likely to strengthen the free states than their own. Moreover, Southern politicians, like many in the North were concerned lest expansion provoke sectional controversy. Within the Democratic party. the followers both of Calhoun and of Van Buren viewed with foreboding the likely effects of the war on party unity. The Whigs had similar apprehensions but, being out of office, felt more at liberty to oppose the war. Though pleased at the triumphs of two Whig generals, Zachary Taylor and Winfield Scott, they were concerned lest a Democratic President made political capital out of a victorious war. Thus, as the war dragged on and its costs and casualties mounted, the Whigs became increasingly critical of 'Mr Polk's War'.

Posterity was to look upon the Mexican War as a shameful blot on the American record, which indeed it was. It was also to regard the contest as hopelessly unequal, with poor, defenseless Mexico no match for her vigorous young adversary. That was not the way it appeared at the time. The Mexicans entered the war confident of victory. Their regular army numbered 32,000, four times the size of that of the United States, and they doubted whether the Americans possessed either the will or the capacity to fight. But Mexican confidence was ill founded. The Mexican army, consisting mainly of Indian conscripts, was poorly led and badly organized, while its war material was antiquated. The United States had much greater reserves of manpower—its population of seventeen millions was more than twice as large as that of Mexico—and its economy was infinitely stronger, especially in industrial production. The Americans also had the more competent generals, though none had had a formal military education and only Winfield Scott was outstanding. The United States also possessed a marked superiority in subordinate officers. Among the several hundred graduates of West Point who fought side by side in the Mexican War there was a group of young men—they included Lee and Grant, Jackson and McClellan—destined to be pitted against one another as Civil War generals. The exceptionally high level of ability among the junior officers more than compensated for the fact that they led a largely amateur army. Finally the United States enjoyed command of the seas. It did not have much of a navy, but Mexico had none at all. Hence the Americans were able to import war supplies from Europe and to transport and supply an invading army across the Gulf of Mexico.

The Mexican War was the first in which an American President acted, as he was constitutionally entitled to do, as Commander-in-Chief. Although he usually consulted his Cabinet and, less frequently, his generals it was Polk himself who determined the general strategy of the war. Not content with that he also supervised and directed the work of the General Staff and of the Army and Navy Departments. In this sense, as in others, it was 'Mr. Polk's War'.

Polk initially planned only a limited war. He hoped that a few quick victories would induce the Mexicans to accede to his territorial demands. Thus the war began with the occupation of the two provinces for which he had gone to war. In the summer of 1846 Colonel Stephen W. Kearney marched unopposed into Santa Fé, proclaimed the annexation of New Mexico, and then set off on the long march across the deserts of Arizona to California. By the time he got there the province had been substantially taken over by Americans. In May there had occurred the Bear Flag revolt, whereby the American settlers in California followed the Texan example in proclaiming their independence. Colonel John C. Frémont, an army engineer then in the Far West on the latest of his exploring expeditions, soon appeared on the scene to help the rebels. Next to join in was an American naval detachment under Commodore Robert F. Stockton, whose squadron had been conveniently stationed off the California coast. Landing at Monterey in July Stockton's naval forces brought the brief era of Californian independence to an end by hoisting the Stars and Stripes. Kearney, on arriving in San Diego in December, quarreled bitterly with Stockton and Frémont over the command of the California expedition. But he succeeded both in establishing his own authority and, rather more promptly, in ending what little Mexican resistance remained.

Meanwhile Taylor was heavily engaged in northern Mexico. In the summer of 1846 he won a series of victories over Santa Anna and advanced 200 miles, thereby becoming a national hero. But when neither the conquest of New Mexico and California nor Taylor's campaign across the Rio Grande persuaded Mexico to accept defeat, the President decided he must strike at the enemy's capital. Since, however, an overland advance an Mexico City would have involved a five-hundred-mile march across deserts and mountains with ever-lengthening lines of communication Taylor was ordered to remain on the defensive in northern Mexico and to release troops for a seaborne expedition against Vera Cruz, to be commanded by General Winfield Scott. This decision might have had serious consequences for the Americans for, when Santa Anna learned of Taylor's depleted command, he headed north from central Mexico in the hope of crushing the invaders. The ensuing battle of Buena Vista (February 2–3 1847) added further luster to Taylor's reputation. He repulsed with heavy casualties an army more than three times the size of his own and compelled Santa Anna to retreat to Mexico City. With this engagement the war in northern Mexico came to an end.

Scott's thrust into the heart of Mexico was a superb feat of arms. Landing his army near Vera Cruz in February 1847, Scott captured the city after an eighteen-day siege and then advanced 260 miles over difficult terrain and against determined resistance. Having inflicted a heavy defeat on Santa Anna at Cerro Gordo in April, he then fought half a dozen pitched battles before storming the great mountain fortress of Chapultepec. By August the Americans had reached the high Mexican plateau and on September 14 they entered Mexico City. Although his army numbered no more than 10,000, half of them untrained volunteers, Scott's campaign against a numerically superior enemy had occupied only six months. By contrast a French army of 30,000 regulars was to take eighteen months in 1861–3 to reach the same objective, though faced by less formidable Mexican armies. Polk was to claim that the Mexican War vindicated the traditional American antimilitarist belief that citizen soldiers were the equals of professionals. Yet regulars had done much of the early fighting; the volunteers had needed several months' training to become effective; and some of the best volunteer regiments were commanded by West Pointers like Jefferson Davis.

The succession of American victories was all the more remarkable in view of the lack of harmony between the civil and military leaders. The Mexican war afforded striking evidence of the way politics and soldiering tended to become intertwined in the United States. The higher direction of the war from Washington was strongly influenced by politics. Polk's two leading generals, Taylor and Scott, were known Whigs who either had been or were expected to be contenders for the Presidency, and the President was anxious to prevent them from gaining political advantage from the war. Thus he tried to deny them the credit for their victories, intervened to protect two Democratic generals—one being the President's former law partner—whom Scott had court-martialed for insubordination, and sought vainly to persuade Congress to give a Democratic politician, Thomas Hart Benton, the highest command in the army. Understandably, Taylor and Scott believed themselves to be victims of political partisanship. Yet they themselves frequently acted out of political calculation and made no secret of their lack of confidence in the Administration.

Soon after the capture of Mexico City the last Mexican forces surrendered and a new government came to power prepared to make peace. Some months earlier Polk had appointed Nicholas P. Trist, chief clerk of the State Department, as peace commissioner and had authorized him to offer terms similar to those proposed in the Slidell mission. There was a long delay while Trist sought to persuade the Mexicans to negotiate. Then when negotiations were at last about to begin, Polk recalled him; he was irritated with Mexican equivocation and was no longer prepared to pay so much for the territory he wanted. Trist, however, ignored the recall, believing that to break off negotiations would be to invite anarchy and the resumption of guerrilla warfare. With Scott's approval he negotiated a settlement based on his original instructions. By the Treaty of Guadalupe Hidalgo, signed on February 2, 1848, Mexico agreed to cede California and New Mexico—about half her national territory—and to recognize the Rio Grande boundary of Texas. The United States undertook to pay $15 million for the ceded territories and to assume the claims of American citizens against Mexico, amounting to about $3¼ million.

Polk was highly incensed at Trist's disobedience, but nevertheless decided to accept the treaty. There was every reason for doing so. It gave the United States everything she had gone to war for. If it were rejected the Whig majority in Congress, which had become increasingly critical of the war, might refuse appropriations for continuing it. A further complication was that expansionists, intoxicated by the triumph of American arms, were now demanding the annexation of the whole of Mexico. Unless that demand could be stifled there would be further criticism, not only from Whigs but also from dissident Democrats. Polk therefore decided to recommend ratification of the treaty by the Senate. On May 10, 1848 it was ratified by a vote of 38 to 14.

The Mexican War brought the United States immense advantages. She gained half a million square miles of additional territory and virtually rounded out her continental boundaries. She also acquired the magnificent harbor of San Francisco, an outlet to the trade of the Orient and the mineral wealth of California. But the price of carrying the flag to the Pacific was high. The war cost nearly $100 million and more than 13,000 soldiers had died, mostly from disease. In the long term there was to be an even higher price to pay, for the Mexican War revived the long-slumbering controversy over the extension of slavery and ushered in a period of sectional strife that was to culminate in civil war. This was foretold by Ralph Waldo Emerson. 'The United States will conquer Mexico', he predicted, 'but it will be as the man who swallows the arsenic which brings him down. Mexico will poison us.'

Slavery in the Territories

The poison had already begun to work while the war was in progress. In August 1846 Polk asked Congress for $2 million to buy additional territory from Mexico when peace negotiations began. When the necessary appropriations bill was introduced into the House an obscure Pennsylvania Democrat, David Wilmot, proposed an amendment prohibiting slavery in any territory to be acquired from Mexico. The so-called Wilmot Proviso passed the House in 1846 and again in 1847, but was defeated in the Senate on both occasions. Not all its supporters were moved by antislavery feelings. Many Western Democrats voted for it because they felt that Polk was sacrificing their interests to those of the South. They were incensed by the nonfulfillment of the Democratic platform pledge of 1844 to secure the whole of Oregon as well as Texas. They also felt they had been cheated in respect of another tacit bargain: although Polk had signed into law the Walker Tariff bill which lowered rates and thus pleased the South, he vetoed two bills appropriating federal funds for navigational improvements on Western rivers and harbors. The shift in sectional alignments revealed by the vote on the Wilmot Proviso marked an important stage in the process whereby the agricultural West withdrew from its old alliance with the plantation South and forged new bonds with the industrial North.

The Wilmot Proviso set in motion a debate which became increasingly impassioned during the last months of Polk's Administration. To the question of whether Congress could and should exclude slavery from the newly acquired territories three distinct answers emerged. For the antislavery forces of the North the Wilmot Proviso became a rallying cry; Congress, they believed, had the power to exclude slavery from the territories and should exercise it. Supporters of the Proviso were to be found in both political parties. Among Democrats its strongest adherents were the New York followers of Van Buren who were known as 'Barnburners' because they were said to resemble the farmer who was willing to burn down his barn in order to get rid of rats. Their counterparts in the other major party were the 'Conscience Whigs', so-called in order to distinguish them from their more conservative colleagues, the 'Cotton Whigs' who, as businessmen with Southern connections, were alleged to have an economic stake in the preservation of slavery.

At the other extreme stood the Southern opponents of federal intervention. That Congress possessed the power to regulate or prohibit slavery in the territories had up to this time been almost universally accepted. But in the course of the Proviso debates the South for the first time challenged the doctrine of Congressional authority. In February 1847 Calhoun introduced into the Senate a series of resolutions, subsequently known as the Platform of the South, which asserted that the territories were the common property of all states; that Congress had no constitutional authority to prevent the citizens of any state from migrating there with their property, including their slave property; and that a territorial legislature, being subordinate to Congress, had no power to debar slavery. The logic of Calhoun's position was of course that Congress could not exclude slavery from any territory; thus the Missouri Compromise and similar Congressional prohibitions had all along been unconstitutional. Calhoun had no wish to overturn the Missouri Compromise; but he would not tolerate any suggestion that Congress should also debar slavery from the Mexican acquisitions.

Many Northern state legislatures endorsed the Wilmot Proviso. Most of those in the South followed Calhoun in denouncing it. But opinion in both sections was reluctant to accept either extreme. The third doctrine which now emerged represented an attempt to appeal to this middle ground. 'Popular sovereignty', as it became known, was first clearly formulated in the closing weeks of 1847 by a Democratic senator from Michigan, Lewis Cass. Another Democratic senator from the Northwest, Stephen A. Douglas, then took it up and became its chief advocate. According to the popular sovereignty formula, the question of slavery in the territories should not be decided one way or the other by Congress, but should be left to the settlers themselves.

Popular sovereignty was an ingenious and appealing dogma. It dodged the contentious question of Congressional authority and seemed to offer something to both sections. It met the Southern wish for federal nonintervention and, in theory at least, held out the prospect that slavery might be extended to some of the Mexican territories. But it could be plausibly presented to the North as an exclusion scheme since most of the settlers in the new territories were likely to come from the more populous free states. Moreover, popular sovereignty could be defended as being in the tradition of territorial self-government. As Douglas put it, the federal government had always left it to the people of the territories to decide their own school systems, tax systems, and franchise systems. Why, then, could they not be allowed to choose their own labor systems? Yet for all its apparent simplicity and fairness, popular sovereignty had serious weaknesses. It was vague on the vital question of when, precisely, the settlers of a particular territory were to be allowed to make their decision. Could the first-comers take an early vote that would settle the slavery issue once and for all, or must they wait until the population had reached a particular level? Nor did popular sovereignty take into account the moral objection to slavery that lay at the heart of Northern support of the Wilmot Proviso.

Controversy over slavery extension preoccupied Congress to the exclusion of every other issue in the summer of 1848. Polk was eager for the establishment of territorial governments in New Mexico and California, but Congress was too divided to act. The whole of the Mexican cession thus remained under military rule. Even the bill providing for territorial organization of Oregon—where everyone knew that slavery would be excluded by soil and climate—became a sectional bone of contention. Not until August 1848 was the measure passed.

The Election of 1848

In the presidential campaign of 1848 both the major parties, concerned for unity, strove desperately to avoid commitment on the issue of slavery extension. Since Polk had pledged himself not to seek a second term the potentially divisive question of his renomination did not arise. The Democrats nominated the safe and moderate Lewis Cass, the earliest proponent of popular sovereignty and a leading expansionist. The Democratic platform praised Polk's territorial acquisitions but was equivocal in its references to slavery. The Whigs were even more circumspect; resting their hopes on a military hero, General Zachary Taylor, they adopted no platform at all. As a Louisiana slave-holder Taylor could count on the warm support of Southern Whigs, while the fact that he had spent forty years in the army meant that he could plausibly be represented as a national figure. It was an advantage that he was not committed to any particular view on slavery extension, but his lack of political knowledge and experience led many to question his fitness for high office. Taylor had only recently discovered that he was a Whig and his nomination led Clay, resentful over his own rejection, to say that he wished that he too had killed a Mexican.

Antislavery groups, dissatisfied with the failure of the major parties to take a firm stand on slavery extension, decided on a new political organization. At a national convention at Buffalo, New York, in August 1848, Barnburner Democrats, Conscience Whigs, Liberty party supporters, and other dissatisfied elements coalesced to create the Free Soil party. It nominated Van Buren for the Presidency and chose Charles Francis Adams, a Massachusetts Conscience Whig and the son of John Quincy Adams, as his running mate. The new party's slogan was 'free soil, free speech, free labor and free men'. The platform attacked the aggressions of the 'slave power' and called for the restriction of slavery to its existing boundaries and for firm adherence to the Wilmot Proviso; in addition it demanded a higher tariff, free homesteads for Western settlers. and government aid to internal improvements. Like nearly all third parties in American history the Free Soil party was short-lived. Nevertheless its appearance was a political landmark. Unlike the Liberty party it stood for something more than mere opposition to slavery. It combined the moral idealism of the abolitionist crusade with an appeal to the economic interests of Northern industry and agriculture. It could thus draw support from those who sympathized with the Negro slave and from those who were less concerned with free blacks than with ensuring that the Western territories were kept free of them.

The outcome of the 1848 election was a narrow victory for Taylor. The election showed that both major parties could still attract support throughout the country. The Whigs carried eight free states and seven slave states, the Democrats seven free states and eight slave states. But any satisfaction they may have felt on that score must have been tempered by concern at the effects of Free Soil intervention. Although Van Buren did not carry a single state he polled an impressive total for a new party organized so late in the campaign. In Ohio and Indiana he cut substantially into the Whig vote and in New York drew so heavily on Democratic strength as to throw the state—and thus the election—to Taylor. In addition the Free Soilers elected ten Congressmen, enough to hold the balance of power in a closely divided House.

The Sectional Crisis

By the time Taylor was sworn in as President in March 1849, the slavery controversy had widened to include a number of ancillary questions. Northerners were demanding the abolition of slavery in the District of Columbia; Southerners were clamoring for a more efficient fugitive-slave law; Texas was claiming a portion of New Mexico—a claim necessarily involving the issue of slavery extension. Moreover, the problem of providing civil government for the territory annexed from Mexico was daily becoming more urgent because of the California gold rush. In January 1848 gold was discovered in the Sacramento Valley. Within a few weeks the news had leaked out and from all over California men dropped whatever they were doing and flocked to the diggings. By the end of the year word of the strike had spread to the eastern states and the gold rush was on. Clerks deserted their desks, soldiers their regiments, husbands their families. During the next year some 80,000 'Forty-niners' poured into California from all over the world. From the older states most traveled by covered wagon, following overland trails across the Plains and over the Rockies; at least 5,000 died en route from disease, starvation, exhaustion, and Indian attack. Others took sailing-ships round Cape Horn, an expensive journey occupying three months or more, but even so easier and quicker than traveling overland. Still others sought a short cut through the snake-infested jungles of Panama.

By the end of 1849 California had a population of 100,000, more than enough to justify statehood. It was a colorful and unique society, less individualistic than legend would have us believe but even more unstable than most frontier communities. Normal social restraints had ceased to operate. The huge influx of settlers had included a sizable number of criminals and adventurers; in the mining-camps and elsewhere crime and violence were endemic. With the military authorities unable to maintain law and order, law-abiding elements set up vigilance committees to protect life and property. But miscarriages of justice were common and there was a crying need for legitimately constituted civil government.

Taylor's lack of political understanding and his tendency to oversimplify complex problems were revealed in his attempt to avoid the territorial issue altogether by encouraging both California and New Mexico to frame constitutions and apply for immediate admission to the Union as states. That would mean that they could decide for themselves about slavery and Congress would be spared the necessity of considering the matter. Californians promptly took Taylor's advice. In October 1849 they held a constitutional convention and drafted a constitution prohibiting slavery; in March 1850, having ratified the constitution, they applied for admission to the Union as a state. A few months later the people of New Mexico followed suit.

Taylor's statehood proposal won little support and excited bitter denunciation in the South. What angered and alarmed Southerners was the prospect that the admission of California and New Mexico as free states would upset the sectional balance in the Senate. The number of free and slave states was then equal—there were fifteen of each—so that despite being in a minority in the House of Representatives the South still retained equality of representation in the Senate, and with it a measure of protection for its peculiar institution. But since none of the remaining territories was likely to become a slave state, a Northern majority, once achieved, would be permanent and might ultimately be large enough to permit a constitutional amendment abolishing slavery. By the end of 1849 a threatening secessionist movement had developed in the South, especially in South Carolina and Mississippi, the two states with the largest Negro population. Mississippi issued a call for a Southern rights convention to meet at Nashville, Tennessee in June 1850 to consider the possibility of secession. The Northern response was equally uncompromising. Every Northern legislature but one came out in favor of the Wilmot Proviso.

The Compromise of 1850

The thirty-first Congress convened in December 1849 in an atmosphere of crisis. With the Union clearly in danger, the venerable Henry Clay, newly returned to the Senate after a seven-year absence, assumed the task of piecing together a compromise. Clay appreciated, as Taylor had not, that only a comprehensive formula, covering all the issues in dispute between North and South, stood any chance of success. On January 29, 1850 Clay introduced into the Senate a set of resolutions which proposed: (1) that California be admitted as a free state; (2) that the other territories acquired from Mexico be organized with no mention of the status of slavery; (3)

that Texas abandon its claim to New Mexico; (4) that the federal government assume the Texan national debt contracted before annexation; (5) that the slave-trade in the District of Columbia be abolished; (6) that slavery in the District of Columbia was only to be abolished if the people of the District and of Maryland consented and if compensation were paid; (7) that a new and more effective Fugitive Slave Act be passed; and (8) that Congress declare that it had no power to interfere with the interstate slave-trade.

Clay's resolutions inaugurated a debate that convulsed the country for more than seven months. His plea for national reconciliation was powerfully seconded by Daniel Webster in the last great oration of his career—'the seventh of March speech'. Webster argued that the Wilmot Proviso was unnecessary because nature would exclude slavery from the territories; he also denounced the violence of the abolitionist agitation and endorsed the proposal for a new fugitive-slave act. The speech had a mixed response. While moderates praised Webster's devotion to the Union, abolitionists and Free Soilers bitterly denounced him for betraying the cause of freedom. During the Senate debate Clay's proposals came under attack by spokesmen for both sections. Calhoun, in what was to be his last speech, insisted that the South possessed a constitutional right to take slaves into the territories and demanded a constitutional amendment that would restore the political balance between the sections. William H. Seward of New York, the leader of the Conscience Whigs, believed that compromise was 'radically wrong and essentially vicious', and infuriated Southerners with his 'higher law' doctrine with its assertion that in legislating for the territories Congress should observe 'a higher law than the Constitution', the divine law which condemned slavery. Yet by early summer there were signs that popular sentiment in the country was veering towards compromise. In the North the moderates had rallied. In the South the Nashville Convention, attended by only nine of the fifteen slave states, disappointed the secessionists by adjourning to await action by Congress.

Even so, Clay's efforts to save the Union seemed at first unlikely to succeed, Taylor, clinging doggedly to his own statehood plan, remained adamantly opposed to the entire concept of compromise. Moreover, Clay made the mistake of combining his major proposals in an 'omnibus bill' in which form it attracted the opposition of all who objected to parts of it. At the end of June a dispirited Clay left Washington, his health broken and all chances of success apparently gone.

The sudden death of President Taylor on July 9 broke the deadlock. His successor, Vice-President Millard Fillmore, a moderate from New York and a friend of Clay's, threw the weight of the Administration behind the Compromise and used his powers of patronage to overcome Northern Whig opposition. A major share of the credit for the final outcome belongs to Stephen A. Douglas, who assumed the leadership of the Compromisers after Clay's withdrawal. Douglas took the crucial step of splitting up the omnibus bill into six separate measures and piloted them through Congress one by one. By the middle of September the Compromise of 1850 had become law. The key elements were those relating to the territories and to fugitive slaves. California was to be admitted as a state, and the rest of the Mexican acquisitions were to be organized into two territories, New Mexico and Utah, which would eventually be admitted into the Union 'with or without slavery as their Constitutions shall prescribe at the time · of their admission'—a phrase which, for all its vagueness, amounted to the enactment of the principle of popular sovereignty. Simultaneously, a new and more stringent Fugitive Slave Act replaced that of 1793. This measure permitted slave-owners to arrest suspected runaways without a warrant, denied alleged fugitives the right of trial by jury and the right to give evidence on their own behalf, and imposed heavy penalties for helping slaves to escape.

The passage of the Compromise was generally welcomed with relief. All over the country mass meetings pledged support. Yet neither section was altogether satisfied with it. Northerners found it difficult to stomach the new Fugitive Slave Act and some, like Emerson, publicly declared that they would refuse to obey it. Whether the South could bring itself to accept the Compromise was at first uncertain. 'Fire-eaters' like Robert Barnwell Rhett of South Carolina and William L. Yancey of Alabama were convinced that there was no future for the South in the Union, and that the only remedy was immediate secession. But Southern Unionism was still a powerful force and although four states held special conventions to consider secession, only South Carolina came down in favor and even she was not prepared to act alone. Nevertheless, Southern acceptance of the Compromise was conditional as well as reluctant. The resolutions adopted by the Georgia convention—the 'Georgia Platform'—summed up the Southern attitude. They declared that Georgia did not wholly approve of the Compromise but would abide by it as a permanent settlement of the sectional controversy. But they also gave notice that the state would resist, 'even (as a last resort) to a disruption of every tie that binds her to the Union', any future Act of Congress which repealed or modified the Fugitive Slave Act, abolished slavery in the District of Columbia, denied admission to a slave state, or prohibited the introduction of slaves into New Mexico or Utah.

On balance the North gained more than the South from the Compromise. The admission of California as a free state gave it a majority in the Senate. The new Fugitive Slave Act, by contrast, proved a hollow victory for the South; it turned out to be largely unenforceable. Moreover, although in theory slaves might now be taken into New Mexico and Utah, in practice virtually none were. Yet the real gainer from the Compromise was the Union. Had the South seceded in 1850 it might well have been able to make good its claim to independence. Eleven years later, when secession actually occurred, the South's task had become infinitely more difficult for in the meantime the North had forged ahead in wealth, population, and industrial power.

11. *The Road to Secession,*
1850–1861

Sectionalism and the South

Hopes that the Compromise of 1850 would put an end to sectional controversy over slavery proved vain. It turned out to be only an uneasy and a short-lived truce. New crises soon reawakened and intensified sectional animosities and placed increasing strains upon the Union. As the 1850s wore on, indeed, it seemed increasingly evident that, as Seward remarked in a famous speech, the slavery struggle was 'an irrepressible conflict between opposing and enduring forces'.

Some historians argue that the fundamental cause of the sectional conflict was the emergence of two divergent and incompatible economic and social systems, Northern and Southern. But such an interpretation involves an exaggerated antithesis. In many respects the North and the South closely resembled each other: in ethnic origin, language, religion, law, political structure, and political values. Yet it cannot be denied that by about 1850 they had become distinctively different. By comparison with the North the South's population was smaller and more scattered, its wealth less extensive and more concentrated, its economy less diversified, its society more stratified, its politics less aggressively egalitarian, its outlook more introspective, more backward-looking. The South had shared hardly at all in the urban and industrial growth that had transformed the Northern states: it had remained predominantly rural and agricultural. Nor had it been much affected by the huge waves of immigration that had imparted a distinctive spice to the Northern population. But if Southern white society was relatively homogeneous, one-third of the South's population consisted of Negro slaves. It was this, more than anything else, that unified the region and set it apart. The 'peculiar institution', together with the plantation system it fostered, helped to create a comparatively rigid and oligarchical society. While the democratic upheaval of the Jacksonian period had somewhat diffused political power it had not seriously weakened the political, economic, and social dominance of the planter class. Nor had the advance of democracy been accompanied by the ferment of reform that had swept over the North. Because of the close association between abolitionism and other reform movements the South had comprehensively condemned all forms of dissent. While the North effervesced, subjecting every human institution to critical examination, the South set up what one historian has called 'an intellectual blockade' against new and dangerous ideas.

Along with intolerance and like mindedness went an inveterate romanticism. Proud of its supposed descent from seventeenth-century Cavaliers and bemused by the self-image it discovered in the novels of Sir Walter Scott, the Southern planter class gave itself over to the cult of romantic chivalry. This involved, among other things, a reverential attitude and a knightly courtesy toward women, an emphasis upon the martial arts and the military tradition, and an acceptance of dueling as the normal method of settling differences affecting personal honor. Even more characteristically Southern was a dedication to agrarianism. Glorifying agriculture as the only activity worthy of free men, Southerners despised industry and commerce as mere money-grubbing occupations and sank practically all their available capital in land and slaves. The dominance of agrarianism meant that the dynamic, restless, stridently acquisitive atmosphere of the free states was absent south of the Mason–Dixon line. Life in the South was more leisurely; there was a greater attachment to locality and to family, less preoccupation with purely material success. And while the North became the home of innovation and of technological advance, the South clung to old ways even in agriculture. Finally the South was a violent region. The persistence of frontier conditions in many long-settled areas, the difficulty of policing a widely dispersed population, and, above all, the existence of slavery encouraged Southerners to resort more readily to weapons than other Americans and, moreover, to use them more savagely.

Gradually there had developed in the South a growing sense of unity and of difference from the rest of the country. This was further nourished by sectional disputes over economic issues. Southerners harshly condemned federal legislation designed to assist the North—in particular, protective tariffs. In fact the South had little reason for complaint. The compromise tariff of 1833, passed after the nullification crisis, went far to meet Southern wishes and every subsequent revision of schedules until the Civil War was in a downward direction. Yet the South continued to find in the modest degree of protection remaining to Northern industry the cause of her own economic difficulties. Southerners also believed they were being exploited in other ways. Dependent upon Northern credit to finance the growing of their staples, upon Northern commission agents to market them, and upon Northern vessels to transport them, they alleged that forty cents in every dollar received from the sale of Southern cotton ended up in Yankee pockets. Southern Commercial Conventions, held almost annually from 1837 onward, regularly heard complaints about the South's colonial status but failed to find a remedy or indeed achieve anything save the heightening of sectional prejudices.

The South's chagrin at its economic subjection was intensified by the realization that it was becoming a permanent minority. In 1790 the population of the Northern and of the Southern states had been almost exactly equal. But as early as 1820 the North had established a clear lead and by 1850 outnumbered the South by a ratio of more than three to two. Notwithstanding this handicap the South had long managed to exercise a disproportionate influence in national affairs. Nine of the first twelve Presidents were natives of the South and of the thirty-three men appointed to the Supreme Court up to 1850 no fewer than twenty were Southerners. All this time, however, the South was 'fighting against the census returns'—and losing. Its representation in Congress declined steadily from year to year. By 1850 the South was heavily outnumbered in the House and, with the admission of California as a free state, it lost parity of representation in the Senate.

It was not mere pique at loss of political influence that stirred Southerners. Nor, at bottom, was it fear of being outvoted on economic issues. It was rather that an adverse sectional balance seemed to jeopardize the institution which was the foundation of Southern society and which all Southerners, slave-holders and nonslave-holders alike, were determined to defend even if it meant the disruption of the Union. Yet the South was not alone in feeling that its vital interests were at stake in the slavery controversy. The North's growing antipathy to the slave system stemmed from the fear that the spread of slavery into the territories would close the West to free labor and thereby threaten American democratic ideals. In these circumstances mere legislative juggling which glossed over the moral divide, as the Compromise of 1850 attempted to do, could not reconcile the differences between the sections or remove their mutual suspicions.

But in the immediate aftermath of the 1850 Compromise all but a handful of extremists had had enough of discord. There was widespread relief that disunion had been averted and an equally widespread anxiety to push the slavery issue into the background. The two years or so that remained of Fillmore's Administration were thus a period of tranquility. They were also a period of prosperity. America was enjoying a prolonged boom and an atmosphere of contentment pervaded the entire country. Industry grew, the railroad network expanded, the American merchant marine was in its heyday, cotton and wheat prices were high, and immigration was adding hugely to the nation's strength. In the glow of mid-century prosperity it was possible to believe that all would yet be well with the Union.

Pierce and the Revival of Conflict

The presidential election of 1852 demonstrated the overwhelming popular desire that there should be no more strife. The Democrats nominated an obscure New Hampshire lawyer, Franklin Pierce, on a platform which unequivocally endorsed the Compromise and promised to resist any attempt to renew the slavery agitation. The Whigs, who chose General Winfield Scott as their candidate in preference to renominating Fillmore, likewise endorsed the finality of the Compromise, but with an obvious lack of enthusiasm and only after much wrangling. Having twice won the Presidency by nominating a military hero, they hoped that the prescription would work a third time. But their equivocation over the Compromise eroded their support. Pierce's sweeping victory showed that, while the mid-century crisis had severely shaken both major parties, the Democrats had been more successful in patching up their differences. One thing which strengthened them was the return of the New York 'Barnburners'. That in turn largely accounted for the poor showing of the Free Soil Party; its candidate, John P. Hale, polled only half as many votes as Van Buren had received four years before. Meanwhile, thousands of Southern Whigs, suspicious of Scott and alienated by the antislavery stance of many of their Northern colleagues, were in the process of transferring their loyalties to the Democrats. For the Whigs the 1852 election was an unmitigated disaster. Scott proved to be the last Whig presidential candidate. Under Clay and Webster—both of whom died, incidentally, in 1852—the Whig party had been a powerful force for national unity. Its impending demise was thus a national misfortune.

Meanwhile the slavery agitation was reviving. The harsh new Fugitive Slave Act of 1850 provoked continuing controversy. It had done more than anything to reconcile Southerners to the Compromise and they were determined to resist any attempt to modify or repeal it. Yet many Northerners found its provisions unacceptable and no fewer than eleven Northern states tried to obstruct or even nullify it by means of 'personal liberty laws' extending legal protection to runaways. On occasion the law was openly defied. In 1851 abolitionists at Syracuse, New York rescued a fugitive Negro from officers of the law and helped him reach freedom in Canada. Three years later a mob incited by the oratory of Wendell Phillips and Theodore Parker stormed a Boston court-house in an unsuccessful attempt to prevent a Virginian slave being sent back to his master.

Indignation over the Fugitive Slave Act also inspired the most celebrated of antislavery works, Harriet Beecher Stowe's novel, *Uncle Tom's Cabin*. Mrs Stowe knew little of slavery at first hand, though she had lived for many years at Cincinnati on the borders of a slave state. Her picture of the brutalities of slavery drew heavily on Theodore D. Weld's well-known abolitionist tract, *Slavery As It Is*, and on information she received from fugitive slaves. It was a phenomenal success, not only in the United States but also in Great Britain. Within a year of its publication in 1852 it had sold 300,000 copies and it enjoyed an even greater vogue when it was adapted for the stage. Angrily denounced in the South as a grotesquely overdrawn portrait of slavery, *Uncle Tom's Cabin* implanted in the minds of Northerners a highly favorable, indeed idealized, image of the Negro. Yet the claim that it won thousands of converts to the antislavery cause is exaggerated. The main appeal of the novel lay in its sentimentality rather than in its sociological content—that was why it remained popular long after slavery had been abolished.

If the Union was to survive, firm and decisive leadership was essential. But this was beyond the capacity of Franklin Pierce. An unknown quantity at the time of his election, he soon showed himself to be shallow, weak, and vacillating. Too easily influenced by the strong personalities in his cabinet and in Congress, and too ready to back the views of the Southern wing of his party, he espoused policies which could not fail to reopen the sectional quarrel. Pierce evidently thought that an expansionist foreign policy was the best way of distracting attention from the burning slavery issue. But by concentrating his efforts on the acquisition of Cuba, one of the few remaining places outside the United States where slavery still survived, he succeeded only in giving the impression that he was the tool of 'the slave power'. Cuba, almost the last remnant of Spain's American empire, was rich in sugar and occupied a unique strategic position; for these reasons Americans had been casting covetous eyes upon her for decades. In the early 1850s groups of Mexican War veterans, chiefly Southerners, launched a succession of filibustering expeditions with the object of seizing the island. But, like the Bay of Pigs expedition a century later, these were unsuccessful and for the same reason: the Cubans did not, as expected, rise up and help their deliverers. But enthusiasm for Cuba was undiminished especially in the South, which was stirred by the prospect of obtaining additional slave territory.

In 1854, Pierce's Secretary of State, William Marcy, instructed the American Minister to Madrid, Pierre Soulé, to offer Spain $130 million for Cuba. Should Spain decline to sell, Soulé was authorized to try other methods to 'detach' it from Spanish rule. Marcy told Soulé to discuss the Cuban problem first with the American Ministers to Great Britain and France and in October 1854, after the three men had conferred at Ostend, they sent Marcy a joint confidential dispatch. This document, dubbed the Ostend Manifesto, soon found its way into the American press. Though it did little more than echo Marcy's earlier instructions to Soulé its publication provoked such a chorus of denunciation in Northern antislavery circles that the Secretary of State felt obliged to repudiate it. Having become a sectional issue, the annexation of Cuba ceased to be a practical possibility.

The Kansas–Nebraska Act

It was not the Ostend Manifesto, however, but the Kansas–Nebraska Act, passed by Congress a few months earlier, that brought to an end the uneasy truce which had prevailed since 1850. The author of this fateful measure was Stephen A. Douglas, Democratic senator from Illinois. An energetic, aggressive, and ambitious man, 'the little giant' had risen rapidly to national prominence and was arguably the ablest of the younger generation of politicians to whom leadership had passed after the deaths of Calhoun, Clay, and Webster. Though born in Vermont, Douglas had identified himself with the West and had become its leading spokesman. In January 1854, in his capacity as chairman of the Senate Committee on Territories, he produced a bill to organize—that is, provide civil government for—a huge new Western territory in the Nebraska country, an area of the Great Plains lying west of Iowa and Missouri and stretching north to the Canadian border and west to the Rockies. Subsequently the bill was amended so as to divide the area into two territories, Kansas and Nebraska.

Since both the proposed territories lay within the Louisiana Purchase and were north of 36°30′, they were presumably closed to slavery under the terms of the Missouri Compromise of 1820. Yet Douglas's bill provided that the status of slavery in Kansas and Nebraska should be decided on the basis of popular sovereignty, that is to say, by the people living there. The Compromise of 1850 had applied that principle to the territories of New Mexico and Utah, but no one had then imagined that it applied anywhere else. Douglas now claimed, however, that popular sovereignty had 'superseded' the Missouri Compromise restriction. The original draft of his bill repealed that restriction only by implication but, at the insistence of Southern Democrats, Douglas agreed to an amendment specifically declaring the Missouri Compromise 'inoperative and void'.

Douglas's motives in introducing a bill which, at least in theory, opened to slavery a region from which it had hitherto been excluded have been much debated. Though at the time it was alleged that he was angling for Southern support for his presidential ambitions, that seems unconvincing. Douglas himself claimed that territorial organization was essential in order to remove the 'barbarian wall' of Indians blocking white settlement of the Great Plains. But it was not so much white settlement that concerned him as the route of the proposed transcontinental railroad. This had aroused acute sectional rivalry. Army surveys had indicated two possible routes, one from New Orleans to Los Angeles, the other from Chicago or St. Louis to San Francisco. As a senator from Illinois and a substantial Chicago property-owner Douglas was eager for Chicago to become the eastern terminus and was anxious to remove the main objection to a northern route, namely, that it ran through unorganized territory. Yet he knew that without Southern support his bill would probably be blocked, as had a similar one the year before.

To Douglas's mind the repeal of the Missouri Compromise was a way of satisfying Southern aspirations without injuring those of the North. Believing that slavery would go only where it paid, he was confident that, notwithstanding the apparent opening of Kansas and Nebraska to it, the peculiar institution would not in practice be extended to the two territories because their climate and soil were unsuited to the cultivation of plantation staples. Hence in exchange for a purely nominal concession on slavery, the North would secure the rich railroad prize. Douglas also genuinely believed that popular sovereignty was both the most democratic and the most efficacious way of dealing with the problem of slavery in the territories. Once the people of each territory were allowed to decide the matter for themselves by majority vote, the slavery question would cease once and for all to agitate the nation. Douglas's practical grasp of the problem of slavery extension was sound enough. Where he erred was in his inability to comprehend that, for a great and growing number of Northerners, slavery was not a practical problem but a moral one. His insensibility to that fact led him into a miscalculation that proved fatal alike to his presidential hopes, the unity of his party, and the Union.

That Douglas had blundered was apparent the moment he introduced the Kansas–Nebraska bill. In the North the Missouri Compromise had long been thought as inviolable as the Constitution. Its repeal produced a storm of popular anger. The 'Appeal of the Independent Democrats in Congress to the People of the United States',written mainly by Senators Salmon P. Chase and Charles Sumner, denounced Douglas's measure "as a criminal betrayal of precious rights; as part and parcel of an atrocious plot to exclude from a vast unoccupied region immigrants from the Old World and free laborers from our own States, and convert it into a dreary region of despotism . . .". Douglas was widely condemned as a traitor and, as he himself remarked, he could have traveled from Boston to Chicago by the light of his own burning effigies.

The Pierce Administration threw its weight behind the measure, and by the vigorous use of patronage forced it through Congress in May 1854. But in the process party loyalties disintegrated. Every Northern Whig opposed the bill, nearly every Southern Whig supported it. All the Southern Democrats voted for the bill, but, although it was an official Democratic measure, the Northern Democrats split almost exactly in half, with forty-four in favor and forty-three against. That meant that sectionalism had now virtually destroyed the Whigs and was beginning to undermine the Democratic party as well.

Antislavery, Antiforeignism, and Political Realignment

The furor over the Kansas–Nebraska Act was one of the reasons for the wholesale political realignment that took place in the mid-1850s. The feelings the Act aroused in the North resulted in the emergence of something new in American politics, a sectional, ideological party, capable of winning mass support. Spontaneous protest meetings in the spring of 1854 led to the formation of local 'anti-Nebraska' groups which gradually coalesced under the name 'Republican'. The movement originated in the Northwest, where it swept to impressive victories in the Congressional elections of 1854. It was not only on moral grounds that the new party was opposed to the spread of slavery. Following the Free Soil example, Republicanism combined a moral attack on slavery with a sophisticated ideology which glorified 'free labor' and appealed to the economic interests of the independent farmer and the small businessman. Believing that only a free, white, democratic, capitalistic society could offer individuals the prospect of economic and social advancement, its adherents were determined that their ideals, not those of the South, should prevail in the empty West.

The largest element in the Republican party consisted of former Whigs. While committed to the principle of free soil, they were not antislavery extremists. Next, there were substantial numbers of ex-Democrats, many of them old Barnburners who brought with them a Jacksonian fervor for democracy and for the Union. Least numerous, though not the least vocal, were the antislavery radicals who stressed the moral argument against slavery and saw the exclusion of slavery from the territories simply as the first step on the road to complete abolition.

But the Kansas–Nebraska Act was not the only—nor, indeed, the earliest—solvent of political stability. Even before the anti-Nebraska agitation the emergence of a new nativist political party had begun to shatter existing political allegiances. The unprecedented influx of immigrants, amounting between 1846 and 1854 to some three million, aroused widespread native-born alarm. (See Chapter 7.) Many traditional supporters of the two established political parties, but more particularly Whigs, for whom cultural homogeneity had been almost an article of faith, were disturbed by the growing religious and political influence of foreigners, especially Catholics, and alienated by the efforts of the party hierarchy to woo these newcomers. To such people the existence of a papal plot to subvert cherished American values and institutions seemed almost self-evident. Thus in the late 1840s a number of nativist secret societies sprang into existence to protect the republic against a supposed alien menace and, around 1853, having combined to form the Order of the Star-Spangled Banner, they developed into an organized, though still secret, political movement. Officially called the American party, it was popularly known as the Know-Nothing party because, when questioned by outsiders, members were required to pretend to 'know nothing'. Its aim was not to restrict immigration, except for paupers and criminals, but to limit immigrants' political influence and purify politics. Adopting slogans like 'Americans must rule America', it advocated the exclusion of foreigners and Catholics from public office, stricter naturalization laws, and literacy tests for voting.

The Know-Nothing movement enjoyed astonishing growth. Native-born Protestant artisans and small businessmen in particular flocked to join it. In the 1854 elections Know-Nothingism won striking local successes everywhere from New Hampshire to Texas and claimed 104 Congressional seats out of a total of 234. This should not be taken to mean, however, that antiforeignism was proving more effective than antislavery in the competition for the collapsing Whig vote. In places there was a tacit alliance between Know-Nothings and Republicans and, indeed, considerable overlap between them, since some Know-Nothings were antislavery and some Republicans nativist. All that was clear, perhaps, was that each of the two new parties, both the product of political paranoia, drew its strength from the same social and religious constituency. Historians have traditionally assumed that since the idea of a slave-holders' conspiracy was inherently more plausible than that of a papal conspiracy, Know-Nothingism was bound ultimately to be eclipsed by Republicanism. But that was by no means inevitable; in 1854, certainly, it seemed unlikely. Yet in fact the Know-Nothing party declined as rapidly as it had risen. The reasons were complex: its failure, once in office, to take effective action against Catholics and foreigners; the sudden decline in immigration; disagreement over secrecy; the increasing violence of its supporters; above all, the effect of the slavery issue. When, at the party's first national convention in Philadelphia in 1855, Southern Know-Nothings pushed through a resolution supporting the Kansas–Nebraska Act, Northern delegates walked out. Within a short time most Northern Know-Nothings had joined the Republicans.

By 1856, therefore, after two years of flux and confusion, the political landscape had cleared sufficiently for the emerging new alignment to be discerned. The Whig party had finally disappeared. The Democrats, though still with a national constituency, had become more Southern-oriented, having shed their Northern antislavery wing and having recruited an army of Southern ex-Whigs for whom they were the only remaining political home. The Know-Nothing party was clearly in decline—though nativism was not—and would shortly follow the Whigs into oblivion. The Republican party, rapidly gaining strength as turmoil in Kansas continued to feed suspicions of a slave-holders' conspiracy, was well on the way to becoming the dominant party in the North.

Bleeding Kansas

On the plains of Kansas, Douglas's popular sovereignty doctrine was tested and found wanting. From the moment it was opened to settlement in 1854, Kansas Territory seethed with excitement over the slavery issue. In the ensuing struggle fraud and violence proved more influential than the forces of nature on which Douglas had pinned his hopes. The rush of settlers into Kansas was to some extent part of the normal advance of the agricultural frontier. But there were also organized movements, stimulated by extremists in both sections, with the object of winning control of the territory. The New England Emigrant Aid Society, organized by antislavery zealots, gave encouragement and financial aid to some 1,240 settlers from the free states. Comparable proslavery organizations sponsored several hundred emigrants from the slave states. Thus the settlement of Kansas became a contest between North and South.

From the start settlers from the free states were in the majority and might have expected to win control of the territorial legislature in the elections due early in 1855. But the inhabitants of neighboring Missouri were determined not to have a free-soil territory next door where escaping slaves might find refuge. On election day thousands of Missourians crossed into Kansas to vote illegally, thus producing a solid proslavery legislature. This body, meeting at Shawnee, proceeded to enact a harsh slave code which, among other things, outlawed antislavery activity and prescribed the death sentence for anyone helping a slave to escape. The antislavery settlers, unable to persuade the governor to reject more than a handful of the fraudulent returns and finding their protests to President Pierce ignored, called a convention of their own at Topeka which drew up a constitution excluding slavery. In January 1856, they held elections—which the proslavery settlers boycotted—for a governor and a legislature. Thus popular sovereignty resulted in farce. Kansas now had two rival governors and two rival legislatures, each claiming to be legitimate. Pierce might well have decided to recognize neither, but while denouncing the Topeka movement as illegal, proposed that the proslavery Shawnee legislature take steps to prepare Kansas for statehood.

Violence and bloodshed now erupted in the troubled territory. In May 1856 a force of proslavery militia marched on the free-soil town of Lawrence, destroyed an antislavery press, burned down the hotel, and terrorized the inhabitants. Retribution came a few days later. A fanatical abolitionist, John Brown, led a band of followers to Pottawatomie Creek and murdered five proslavery settlers. That was the signal for further turmoil. Armed bands roamed the territory, shooting and burning indiscriminately. Southern sympathizers sent aid to the proslavery settlers. New England abolitionists sent boxes of rifles in cases marked 'books'; the weapons became known as 'Beecher's bibles' because the celebrated New England clergyman, Henry Ward Beecher, remarked that the rifle might be a more powerful moral agent in Kansas than the Bible.

Before federal troops managed temporarily to restore order, late in 1856, some 200 people had been killed. Much of the violence was of the kind characteristic of frontier regions. But the American people did not think of it that way. The newspapers not only portrayed every violent incident in Kansas in lurid terms but also placed it in the context of a struggle between slavery and freedom. Thus 'bleeding Kansas' helped drive the sections further apart.

The dramatic assault on Charles Sumner on the Senate floor in Washington on May 22, 1856 did likewise. Sumner, an antislavery senator from Massachusetts, had made a long, vituperative, and vulgar speech attacking the South in general and South Carolina in particular, and making a particularly insulting personal reference to one of the state's absent senators, Andrew P. Butler. Two days later, Butler's nephew, Congressman Preston Brooks, entered the Senate chamber and beat Sumner unconscious with a heavy stick, thus incapacitating him for more than three years. Southerners praised Brooks for his action and presented him with ornamental canes to replace the one he had broken on Sumner's head. But in Northern eyes, Sumner was a martyr to the cause of freedom.

James Buchanan, the Dred Scott Decision, and the Lecompton Constitution

The presidential campaign of 1856 opened with the news of the assault on Sumner and of the Kansas troubles still reverberating around the country. The Democrats, seeking to appeal to both sections, passed over both Pierce and Douglas because of their damaging involvement in the Kansas question, and nominated James Buchanan of Pennsylvania who, as American Minister to Great Britain, had been abroad during the recent upheavals. The Democratic platform likewise played safe. It endorsed the Kansas–Nebraska Act and popular sovereignty but avoided the thorny question of whether a territorial legislature had the power to exclude slavery before the formation of a state government. The Republicans predictably denounced the Kansas–Nebraska Act and demanded that Congress prohibit slavery in the territory. Their platform also demanded internal improvements, a Pacific railroad, and aid to industry. The Republican nomination went not to a politician but to the explorer, John C. Frémont. He had no qualifications for the presidency except that he cut a dashing figure and that his surname lent itself to an alliterative slogan: 'Free soil, Free speech, Free men and Frémont'. The Know-Nothing Party, now reduced to a largely Southern rump as a result of its quarrels over slavery, chose as its candidate former President Millard Fillmore on a platform vaguely endorsing popular sovereignty. By presenting themselves as the party of national harmony and the Republicans as the party of sectional discord, the Democrats again managed to win. But the Republicans, in their first presidential contest, did surprisingly well. Frémont carried all but five of the free states and had he taken Pennsylvania and Illinois would have won. Whether the Democratic party could stave off the Republican challenge in 1860 would depend on its ability to retain its Northern support. Yet nearly everything Buchanan did as President seemed designed to alienate Northern Democrats. Nearly sixty-six years old at the time of inauguration, he proved to be as weak and indecisive as Pierce and as susceptible to Southern influence. His Cabinet, like Pierce's, was dominated by its Southern members. Obsessed by the fear that the Southern states might secede, he gave them all they demanded.

Shortly after Buchanan came to power, the country was hit by a severe economic depression. Like nearly everything that occurred in the 1850s, it sharpened sectional differences. The South, less hard hit than the North because of the continuing demand for cotton, boasted of its economic superiority and concluded that it would be better off outside a Union prone to such economic fluctuations. In the North, on the other hand, hard times produced demands for measures frequently proposed in the past—a high tariff, a homestead act, and internal improvements—but blocked by Southern-dominated Democratic administrations. They were to be blocked again now. The tariff of 1857, far from raising duties, was a further step towards free trade. And though Congress passed a homestead bill in 1860, it was vetoed by Buchanan.

On March 6, 1857, two days after Buchanan was inaugurated, the Supreme Court delivered judgment in the case of *Dred Scott* v. *Sanford*. A collusive action designed to test the constitutionality of laws regulating the status of slavery in the territories, it concerned a Missouri slave, Dred Scott, who had been taken by his master, an army surgeon, first to Illinois, a free state, and then to Minnesota territory, where slavery had been forbidden by the Missouri Compromise. Encouraged by abolitionists, Scott sued for his freedom on the grounds that residence in a free territory had automatically made him a free man. The Supreme Court was divided but a majority agreed with two principles enunciated by Chief Justice Taney. First, Dred Scott was not a citizen of Missouri and hence was not entitled to sue in a federal court. In support of this assertion, Taney argued that the framers of the Constitution had not intended that Negroes should be citizens; on the contrary, they had shared the prevailing view that Negroes possessed 'no rights which any white man was bound to respect'. Second, Taney and his colleagues contended that Scott's temporary residence in Minnesota territory had not made him free. Slaves were property and the Fifth Amendment to the Constitution guaranteed that Congress could not deprive a person of his property 'without due process of law'. Consequently Congress had no power to pass a law prohibiting slavery in the territories, and the Missouri Compromise of 1820 had thus been unconstitutional.

The Dred Scott decision provoked a greater storm than any judicial decision before or since. While the South was elated, Northern anger was intense. Republicans alleged that Buchanan and the Supreme Court had conspired to extend slavery throughout the country, and pledged themselves to reverse the decision. At first glance the popular excitement is difficult to understand. Dred Scott's freedom was not at stake—he was shortly set at liberty—and the substantive issue decided by the Court was that a law which had already been repealed three years before had been unconstitutional. But Northern opinion, believing—with good reason—that the racist views Taney ascribed to the Founding Fathers were also his own, was deeply offended. More important, by establishing the constitutionality of slavery in all the territories, the Court cut the ground from under the Republicans. It even called in question the constitutionality of Douglas's position.

Under Buchanan events in Kansas followed a familiar pattern. The President appointed a new territorial governor, Robert J. Walker, and instructed him to encourage a statehood movement. But the free-state settlers, complaining that the voting register was fraudulent, boycotted the ensuing election for a state constitutional convention with the result that proslavery forces won it. The convention met at Lecompton in the autumn of 1857 and drew up a state constitution establishing slavery. This was referred to the electorate in such a way as to ensure the inviolability of slavery no matter how the vote went. Since the free-state settlers again refused to vote, the Lecompton Constitution was ostensibly ratified. But meanwhile the people of Kansas had enjoyed the novel experience of a fair election. Thanks to Governor Walker's boldness in throwing out fraudulent returns in the election for a new territorial legislature, the free staters—having at last agreed to take part—won it and, in a subsequent referendum, decisively rejected the Lecompton Constitution.

Buchanan nevertheless presented the document to Congress and urged the prompt admission of Kansas to statehood. That was more than Douglas could stomach. Denouncing the proceedings as a swindle and as a mockery of popular sovereignty, he and his followers joined hands with the Republican minority to block a bill admitting Kansas as a state and to force the Administration to bring in a compromise measure providing that the Lecompton Constitution should be submitted to the Kansas voters yet again. In another honest election in August 1858, the people of Kansas made their feelings plain beyond doubt; they rejected the Lecompton Constitution by six to one.

Thus ended four years of almost continuous agitation. It was now clear that free soilers had won the contest for Kansas: although slavery was still legal, it could never take root there. The federal census of 1860 showed that there were precisely two slaves in Kansas Territory, and when Kansas was admitted to the Union the following year it was with a constitution that forbade slavery. But although the Kansas issue now receded, it had greatly exacerbated sectional hatred and had split the one remaining national party.

The Lincoln—Douglas Debates

Democratic divisions were further widened by the Buchanan Administration's efforts to defeat Douglas in his campaign for reelection to the Senate in 1858. The Republican candidate was Abraham Lincoln. Born in poverty in the slave state of Kentucky in 1809, Lincoln had moved first to Indiana, then to Illinois where he eventually became a prosperous lawyer and a prominent local politician. A dedicated Whig and an admirer of Henry Clay, he served four terms in the Illinois legislature and one in Congress (1847–9). He then resumed his law practice but the Kansas–Nebraska Act brought him back into politics. After some hesitation he abandoned the moribund Whig party for the Republicans and ran unsuccessfully for the Senate in 1855. But he was still little known outside Illinois and, even within the state, was a less distinguished figure than Douglas.

Partly to offset this disadvantage Lincoln challenged his famous opponent to a series of seven joint debates. The Lincoln–Douglas debates, though taking place in isolated Illinois country towns, attracted national attention. They revealed that, while Douglas had rebelled against his own party on the issue of slavery extension, there were important differences of principle between him and Lincoln. In propounding popular sovereignty he professed to be indifferent as to whether slavery was 'voted up or voted down'. All that mattered was that there should be a genuine expression of opinion. That meant ignoring the moral aspects of slavery. Lincoln, on the other hand, considered slavery 'a moral, social and political wrong'. He accepted that the Constitution protected slavery in the states, but was adamantly opposed to its extension. In his acceptance speech before the Illinois Republican convention he had declared: 'A house divided against itself cannot stand. I believe this government cannot endure permanently, half slave and half free. I do not expect the Union to be dissolved . . . but I do expect it will cease to be divided. It will become all one thing, or all the other.' His policy, then, would be not to abolish slavery immediately, but to place it 'in the course of ultimate extinction' by preventing its further spread.

Douglas succeeded in winning reelection by a narrow margin. Faced with a redoubtable opponent, and with the bitter hostility of the Administration, he won a remarkable personal triumph. But Lincoln made himself a national figure. Moreover, he succeeded in drawing attention to the rift within the Democratic party. In the second of the joint debates, which was held at Freeport, he had asked Douglas a key question—could the people of a territory lawfully exclude slavery from its limits? In other words, could popular sovereignty be reconciled with the Dred Scott decision? Douglas's answer, which became known as the Freeport Doctrine, gave fresh offense to Southerners already outraged by his opposition to the Lecompton Constitution and ruined what chance there was of restoring Democratic unity. He declared that, in spite of the Dred Scott decision, the people of a territory could keep out slavery if they wished by refusing to enact the local police regulations without which it could not 'exist a day or an hour anywhere'.

John Brown's Raid

John Brown's Raid on Harper's Ferry added still further to sectional animosities. Born in 1800 into a New England family strongly tinged with insanity, Brown was unstable and paranoid. A fanatical abolitionist, he became obsessed with the idea that he was God's instrument to extirpate slavery. In 1859, three years after perpetrating the Pottawatomie massacre in Kansas, he deemed the time ripe for an act of terror against the South itself. Believing that the slaves were ready to rise and merely awaited a leader, he devised a plan to incite a slave insurrection intended to bring about the collapse of the whole slave system. The abolitionists who encouraged Brown and gave him financial backing may not have known exactly what he planned, but were aware of his general intention. On the night of October 16, 1859 he led a band of followers across the Potomac from Maryland into Virginia and captured Harper's Ferry arsenal. The slaves did not answer his call and the local militia, reinforced by a detachment of United States marines under Colonel Robert E. Lee, stormed the arsenal and compelled Brown to surrender. He was promptly tried for conspiracy, murder, and treason against the state of Virginia, found guilty, and executed along with six of his followers on December 2, 1859. Most people in the North, including Republican leaders like Seward and Lincoln, condemned him as a criminal. But his courage and dignity after capture and his eloquent plea for the slave from the steps of the scaffold won the admiration even of many who disapproved of his wild deeds. Abolitionists eulogized him. To Emerson, Brown was 'a new saint awaiting his martyrdom'; his death would 'make the gallows glorious like the cross'. On the day of Brown's execution funeral bells tolled throughout the North.

No single event did more to embitter the South or to convince it that there was no safety for slavery within the Union. Though the raid failed, it alarmed and horrified Southerners by reviving the recurrent nightmare of a servile insurrection. But Northern approval of the raid had even greater effects. It persuaded the South that every Northerner was implacably hostile to slavery and that the Republican party had been behind Brown and that it fully intended, despite its leaders' disclaimers, to abolish slavery. Hence the feeling grew in the slave states that secession ought not wait upon an overt act of hostility against the South by a Republican Administration but should immediately follow a Republican victory.

The Election of 1860

When the Democratic national convention met in Charleston, South Carolina on April 23, 1860 it was soon evident that the party rift was beyond repair. Douglas had the support of a majority of the delegates, but lacked the two-thirds vote needed for the presidential nomination. He was fiercely opposed by Buchanan's supporters, who had not forgiven his opposition to the Lecompton Constitution, and by Southern 'fire-eaters' who, infuriated by his Freeport Doctrine, regarded him as no better than a Republican. Douglas hoped to unite the party and secure the nomination by means of a vague endorsement of popular sovereignty, coupled with a declaration that on all questions involving slavery in the territories the party would abide by the decisions of the Supreme Court. But Southern Democrats demanded a platform providing for federal protection of slavery in the territories and when the demand was turned down the Lower South delegates marched out. Unable to make a nomination the convention adjourned to Baltimore in June. Most of the Southern delegates reappeared there but soon walked out again, this time for good. The remaining delegates then proceeded to nominate Douglas for the Presidency on a platform of popular sovereignty. The dissident Democrats held a convention of their own and nominated the then Vice-President, John C. Breckinridge of Kentucky, on a platform demanding federal protection of slavery in the territories. The wrecking of the party was now complete. With two rival Democratic candidates in the field all hope of a Democratic victory disappeared.

The Republicans, heartened by Democratic disarray, gathered in Chicago on May 16. Practical politicians rather than idealists were in control. Knowing they could rely on the antislavery vote the Republicans went out of their way to appeal to the economic aspirations of Northern industry and agriculture. The platform demanded a protective tariff, a homestead act, and government aid to a Pacific railroad. In addition it sought to rid the party of any lingering taint of nativism by declaring its opposition to the lengthening of the period of residence before immigrants could become naturalized. In dealing with slavery the Republicans sought to convey an impression of moderation. While they took a firm stand against slavery extension and denounced disunion, the 'infamous' Lecompton Constitution, and the recent clandestine reopening of the African slave-trade, they also condemned raids like those perpetrated by John Brown. Moreover, the Chicago platform specifically conceded the right of each state to control its own domestic institutions—an oblique way of acknowledging that the federal government had no power to interfere with slavery in the states.

Though by no means unknown, Lincoln was far from being the obvious Republican choice. He had had far less experience of national politics than such aspirants as Seward and Salmon P. Chase. But he had already demonstrated that he was a match for the likely Democratic choice, Douglas. His birth in a log cabin and his ability to split rails made it possible to present him as a man of the people. Finally his managers, led by Judge David Davis of Chicago, astutely packed the convention hall with noisy Lincoln supporters, and, more important, secured the support of key delegations by the promise—or half-promise—of Cabinet posts. Lincoln received the nomination on the third ballot. The Republicans were confident that they had nominated a President; they did not suspect he would turn out to be a great one.

To complicate the political picture further a fourth party appeared. This was the Constitutional Union party, made up of conservative remnants of the Whig and Know-Nothing parties. Meeting at Baltimore in May, it chose John Bell of Tennessee as its presidential candidate, with Edward Everett of Massachusetts as his running mate. It had the shortest platform on record and the vaguest: 'The Constitution of the Country, the Union of the States and the Enforcement of the Law'. Its supporters hoped that by avoiding the slavery issue and sounding a note of patriotism they would appeal to moderates in both sections. They can hardly have expected to win but hoped to secure enough electoral votes to throw the election into the House.

During the campaign the Republicans deliberately played down the slavery question, the two Democratic factions devoted themselves to attacking each other, and the Constitutional Unionists contented themselves with pious admonitions. Nevertheless there was a good deal of excitement, especially in the South, where the prospect of secession was avidly discussed. Lincoln followed the customary practice of candidates of not campaigning personally. Douglas, by contrast, campaigned energetically in every part of the country, devoting special attention to the South, where he warned repeatedly that secession was folly.

On polling-day, Lincoln won a decisive victory in the electoral college. But as usual the electoral-college vote misrepresented the feeling of the country. Lincoln received only 40 percent of the popular vote. Douglas was the only candidate to draw substantial support from all sections, but because his strength was scattered he fared badly in the electoral college. Breckinridge carried most of the South but received relatively few votes in the North despite his endorsement by Pierce, Buchanan, and a majority of Northern Democratic Congressmen. Bell drew nearly all his votes from the border states. The most sectional candidate was Lincoln. With not a single ballot cast for him in ten of the thirty-three states, his support was heavily concentrated in the free states. But there could be no doubt that Lincoln was legally and constitutionally elected. Nor had his victory been due to the divisions of his opponents. Even had they united on a single ticket, the geographical distribution of the vote was such that, while Lincoln would have had a smaller electoral majority, he would still have carried enough of the populous states to win. Whatever the election signified it was clearly not a vote for disunion. None of the four candidates supported secession. While many of Breckinridge's supporters were secessionists not all were. In any case Breckinridge polled only a minority of the votes in the fifteen slave states; even in the eleven states which were to form the Southern Confederacy, his popular majority was tiny. The combined vote for Bell and Douglas showed that Southern Unionism—or at least Unionism of a sort—was still strong. However, it was unorganized and became progressively weaker the further South one went.

The Lower South Secedes

During the campaign Southern leaders had repeatedly warned that they would not remain in the Union under a sectional Northern President. Immediately the result was announced the secession movement began. By the time Lincoln was inaugurated four months later, seven states, all from the Lower South, had seceded from the Union. South Carolina, long a hotbed of secession, was the first to go. On December 20, 1860 a specially convened state convention passed, without a dissenting vote, an ordinance of secession dissolving 'the Union now subsisting between South Carolina and other States'. In January and February 1861 six other cotton states followed suit: Mississippi, Florida, Alabama, Georgia, Louisiana, and Texas. In these states, and especially in Georgia, there was more opposition to secession than in South Carolina. While active unconditional Unionists were few, many moderates were reluctant to abandon a Union they still looked on with pride. They wanted to postpone action until Lincoln had committed a hostile act or at least until a convention of all the slave-holding states could be held to decide how best to safeguard Southern rights. But the secessionists were better organized than their opponents, as well as having a clearer idea of what they wanted. Insisting that the only protection for Southern rights was withdrawal from the Union before Lincoln's inauguration, they succeeded in carrying all before them.

The Secession Ordinances concentrated almost exclusively on the slavery issue. The South Carolina Ordinance, for example, was taken up wholly with a recital of the ways in which the non-slave-holding states had violated the constitutional rights of slave-holders: by failing to observe the Fugitive Slave Act, by permitting and encouraging abolitionist agitation and attempting to instigate slave insurrection, by trying to exclude slavery from the territories, and by 'assuming the right of deciding upon the propriety of our domestic institutions'. And now, the document concluded, twenty-five years of steadily increasing agitation had culminated in the ultimate outrage—the election to the Presidency by a purely sectional combination of a man whose declared opinions and purposes were hostile to slavery. Once he and his party took possession of the government, the guarantees of the Constitution would cease to exist for he had announced that the South would be excluded from the common territory and that war must be waged against slavery until it ceased throughout the United States.

It was thus to safeguard slavery rather than for economic reasons that the South left the Union. Whether its fears for the institution were justified has been much discussed. Certainly Lincoln would have been powerless in the short term to touch slavery in the states, even had he wished to. Yet the South had some reason to fear for the safety of slavery if it remained in the Union. The Republican victory of 1860 marked a decisive shift of political power. It meant that the period of Southern dominance of the federal government was over, and with the North growing rapidly in wealth and population it was over for good. Ultimately the North would become strong enough to carry a constitutional amendment abolishing slavery. While Lincoln repeatedly assured the South that he had no intention of interfering with the institution where it already existed, that was no comfort to slave-holders since his aim in restricting the spread of slavery was avowedly to ensure its ultimate extinction. Southerners could not guess how long abolition would take, or indeed how it would come about, but they felt instinctively that to acquiesce in the Republican triumph would be to take the first step on a road that could have only one end.

Southerners believed there was nothing revolutionary in seceding for secession was a constitutional right. Such a view was rooted in the doctrine of states' rights, which held that the Union was a compact between sovereign states which had joined together in 1787 of their own free will and which retained the power to resume their separate status whenever they saw fit. Yet although states' rights theory was invoked to justify secession, the purpose of the Southern states was not to be able to exist independently but to federate in a new Southern Union. The dream of a Southern Confederacy had fascinated Southerners for a generation or more; early in February 1861 it became a reality. Delegates from six of the seceded states met at Montgomery, Alabama, drew up a constitution for the Confederate States of America, and elected Jefferson Davis as President.

The Failure of Compromise and the Sumter Crisis

While secession was running its course in the Deep South Buchanan was paralyzed by indecision. He denied the right of secession but asserted that the federal government possessed no constitutional power to prevent it. He hoped that if a clash of arms could be avoided a way might be found to bring the seceded states back into the Union. In Congress a variety of compromise plans emerged. The one that attracted most attention was drawn up by Senator John J. Crittenden of Kentucky. It proposed a series of constitutional amendments designed to allay Southern fears about slavery. The permanence of slavery in the states was to be guaranteed; federal compensation was to be paid to owners who failed to recover their fugitive slaves; the Missouri Compromise line was to be reestablished, slavery being prohibited north of 36° 30' and protected south of it. The Crittenden Plan won wide support in the North and Southern leaders indicated that they would accept it if the Republicans did so. But Lincoln's opposition proved decisive. Though prepared to endorse the new fugitive-slave proposal and even the amendment protecting slavery in the states, he was adamantly against any compromise on slavery extension. He believed that to restore the Missouri Compromise line would encourage Southern attempts to acquire additional slave territory in Latin America and provoke a new sectional crisis. A Peace Convention which met at Washington in February 1861 at the suggestion of the Virginia legislature met with no better success. Attended by delegates from twenty-one states, its three weeks of deliberation produced only a variant of the Crittenden Plan. Congress showed little interest in it.

When Lincoln became President on March 4, 1861 there was a widespread feeling that he would not prove equal to the crisis. His gaunt, shambling appearance and social awkwardness did not inspire confidence. Nor did his lack of experience of national politics. It was widely assumed that Lincoln would be a mere cipher and that the real power in the new Administration would be William H. Seward, whom Lincoln had nominated as Secretary of State. But Lincoln quickly established his authority. His inaugural address was a skillful blend of firmness and conciliation. He asserted that the Union was perpetual, that no state could secede of its own volition, that the ordinances of secession were legally void, and that the two sections were so closely bound together that peaceful separation was impossible. While he promised that he would execute the laws in all the states, collect the federal duties, and maintain possession of federal posts, such a policy need not entail bloodshed or violence and there would be none unless 'forced on the national authority'. Moreover, he reiterated that he had no intention of interfering with slavery where it already existed.

Lincoln's caution and forbearance were designed to win time and allow Southern Unionism to reassert itself. But time was denied him for almost at once news arrived that the federal garrison at Fort Sumter in Charleston harbor, commanded by Major Robert Anderson, was running out of supplies and would soon have to surrender unless it was relieved. Lincoln now faced a cruel dilemma. Fort Sumter was, except for Fort Pickens off Pensacola, the only federal property in the South to remain in Union hands. To give it up would be tantamount to recognizing the Confederacy. Yet to attempt to reinforce it might precipitate war. For a month Lincoln hesitated. A majority of his Cabinet favored evacuation; so did the General in Chief, Winfield Scott. But on April 6, after an attempt to reinforce Fort Pickens had miscarried, Lincoln ordered the dispatch of a relief expedition to Fort Sumter. It would attempt to provision the fort peacefully and use force only if attacked. It was now Jefferson Davis's turn to make a painful choice: either to bow to federal authority by allowing Fort Sumter to be provisioned or to strike the first blow. He chose the latter. On April 12, 1861, upon Major Anderson's refusal to evacuate the fort, Confederate batteries opened fire. After a two-day bombardment Fort Sumter capitulated.

The firing on Fort Sumter ended the North's irresolution and produced an outburst of patriotic fervor. Lincoln could now count on enthusiastic support for action to preserve the Union. On April 15, he called on the state governors to furnish seventy-five thousand militia for ninety days to put down the insurrection; on April 19, he declared a blockade of the Confederate coast; early in May he enlarged the regular army and navy. These war measures set in motion a further wave of secession. Confronted with the necessity of making a choice between the Union and the Confederacy, four more slave states—Virginia, Arkansas, Tennessee, and North Carolina—passed ordinances of secession though with some reluctance and by relatively narrow margins. Strengthened by the adhesion of the Upper South the Confederacy now consisted of eleven states, and in June it moved its capital from Montgomery to Richmond.

How does one account for the North's vehement refusal to acquiesce in secession, its passionate attachment to the Union, its willingness to make war in order to preserve the country's territorial integrity? Economic motives no doubt played a part. An independent Confederacy would rob Northern manufacturers of a profitable Southern market, deprive Northern shipowners and merchants of their control of Southern trade, impose customs barriers to the free transit of Middle Western produce down the Mississippi. But infinitely more important was the fact that secession challenged the ideological basis of American nationalism as the mass of Northerners had come to understand it. They had learned from Jackson, Webster, Clay, and countless Fourth of July orators to identify the Union with liberty and democracy and to feel that the maintenance of territorial integrity was the touchstone of the experiment in popular government begun in 1776—an idea which Lincoln was to express eloquently in the Gettysburg Address. Thus the firing on Fort Sumter brought forth a nationwide upsurge. On both sides, in fact, nationalism was the central issue of the struggle now beginning. While the South contended for separate nationhood in order to maintain its distinctive way of life, the North fought to preserve the ideals the Union had come to symbolize.

12. *The Civil War*, 1861–1865

The First Modern War?

The American Civil War was by any standard one of the great wars of history—certainly the greatest to be fought between the Napoleonic Wars and the First World War. It lasted over four years and cost a million casualties, of whom 650,000 were dead. It has been called 'the first modern war', and with good reason. It was the first war to be fought by mass citizen armies rather than by professional soldiers. The Civil War also broke with the past in being an ideological contest, and thus a war of unlimited objectives. In contrast to eighteenth-century wars this was not a contest to be concluded by some kind of accommodation. Neither the Union nor the Confederacy would be satisfied with anything less than complete victory. It was not a total war in the sense in which the term is understood today for it did not entail a wholesale shift to war production; but in the last analysis victory depended upon industrial strength. In such a contest distinctions between combatants and civilians tended to become blurred. Union generals like Sherman and Sheridan enlarged the definition of a military objective to include anything that might contribute to an enemy's capacity to wage war. It was in this respect, perhaps, that the transition from older forms of warfare was most plainly visible.

But the modernity of the struggle should not be exaggerated. There was less technological innovation than has sometimes been claimed. Though the railroad and the telegraph were for the first time extensively used in military operations, the armies remained dependent on the field of battle on horse-drawn transport and mounted dispatch-riders. The ironclad warship made a dramatic debut in 1862, but Union blockading squadrons consisted almost wholly of wooden vessels, mostly propelled by sail. Neither side took full advantage of new inventions like the breech-loading rifle; hence the muzzle-loading musket—though with a rifled barrel that greatly increased its range and accuracy—remained the basic weapon of the infantryman. And while the Civil War witnessed the introduction of various precursors of modern weapons like the machine-gun, the submarine, and the underwater mine, these were too rudimentary to have any real influence on techniques of warfare.

Moreover, the Civil War witnessed little of the ruthlessness and cruelty that were to characterize twentieth-century wars. There were indeed some atrocities: the Fort Pillow massacre of 1864 in which black Union soldiers were killed after surrendering, the murders and reprisals that marked the savage guerrilla warfare along the Kansas–Missouri border, and—though this was a consequence more of overcrowding than of calculated ill-treatment—the appalling death-rate among Union prisoners of war at Andersonville. But these were exceptions. In general this was a gentlemanly war, conducted by both sides in a civilized, indeed a chivalrous, manner. Sieges and capitulations were conducted with strict regard to the rules of war; prisoners were exchanged and released on parole, especially in the first part of the war. For all the Union talk of 'rebels' and 'rebellion', captured Confederate prisoners were treated as prisoners of war; nor did the Confederacy for its part carry out its threat to put captured slave-soldiers to death.

The Confederacy and the Union

The contestants in the Civil War were unevenly matched. The North had a great preponderance of strength in manpower and economic resources. Its population of about 22,000,000 compared with the Confederacy's 9,000,000; but its margin was even greater than these figures suggest for the Southern population included about 3,500,000 Negro slaves. In industrial production the North enjoyed an enormous advantage. Four-fifths of the nation's factories lay in the North, together with most of its mineral wealth, its supply of meat and grain, its financial and banking resources, and its shipping. The North produced fifteen times as much iron as the South, thirty-eight times as much coal, and twenty-seven times as much in woolen goods. It also had a virtual monopoly of shipbuilding facilities— an advantage which made possible the rapid expansion of the small Union navy. Ultimately the North was able to become practically self-sufficient in war materials; the South, on the other hand, had to rely heavily on Europe, importing what supplies it could through a steadily tightening Union blockade.

The familiar generalization that Southerners were more accustomed to riding and shooting than Northerners and hence made better soldiers is unconvincing; boys from Vermont and Iowa could ride and shoot as well as those from South Carolina and Arkansas and—what may have counted for more—were better educated. Likewise the claim that the Confederacy had the cream of the nation's military talent is open to question. While Lee and Jackson repeatedly outshone their Union opponents, Southern generals considered as a whole were not noticeably superior and in the end it was the Union Army, led by such commanders as Grant, Sheridan, and Thomas, which turned out to have the greater depth of ability.

Nonetheless the odds against the Confederacy were not as great as they appeared. The South commanded interior lines and was fighting on familiar terrain; it possessed an extensive coastline difficult to blockade effectively; above all, it was able to wage a defensive war. Like the American colonists in 1776 the Confederacy had no need to take the initiative in order to secure independence; it had simply to withstand enemy attacks. That largely canceled out the North's numerical advantage in manpower.

Slavery and the Border States

The balance between the two sides would, moreover, change radically if the four border slave states—Maryland, Delaware, Kentucky, and Missouri—were also to secede. They had a population of more than three millions and were of immense strategic importance. Maryland and Delaware lay astride Washington's communications with the North; Kentucky controlled the Ohio river and, with Missouri, a vital stretch of the Mississippi. Delaware's loyalty to the Union was never seriously in doubt but the other three states remained doubtful for some time after Sumter. They did not follow the Upper South into the Confederacy but were opposed to coercion and refused Lincoln's call for troops.

In late April 1861 a critical situation developed in Maryland. The Sixth Massachusetts Regiment, on its way to Washington, clashed in Baltimore with a disunionist mob. Lincoln promptly sent in Federal troops, suspended habeas corpus, and ordered the imprisonment of several leading Confederate sympathizers. By these high-handed means Maryland was saved for the Union. But when in May 1861 Kentucky formally proclaimed its neutrality in the Civil War, Lincoln displayed the velvet glove. He believed the state to be crucial. 'I hope I have God on my side,' he remarked, 'but I must have Kentucky.' Yet he made no effort to send in troops, preferring to give Unionist sentiment time to reassert itself. The wisdom of his policy was shown in September 1861 when, in response to a Confederate invasion, the Kentucky legislature declared for the Union. In Missouri, where opinion was about equally divided, Unionists staged a military coup in May 1861. Fearing that secessionist sympathizers were planning to seize the federal arsenal at St. Louis, they organized a volunteer 'home guard' which attacked and captured a pro-Confederate militia camp and drove the secessionist government out of the state capital. While this vigorous action kept Missouri in the Union, it sharpened local animosities. For the next four years the state was in a turmoil as the rival factions were locked in bitter guerrilla war.

Wartime Politics and Policies

Although the North responded with virtual unanimity to the call to arms in 1861, partisanship soon reasserted itself and for the rest of the war Lincoln experienced virulent opposition. A small minority of Democrats sympathized with the Confederacy. Most numerous in those parts of the Middle West settled by Southerners, 'Copperheads', as they were nicknamed after a particularly venomous snake, strenuously opposed the war and advocated a negotiated peace which would have accepted disunion. The great majority of Democrats were loyal to the Union and gave general support to the Administration's war measures. Yet they objected to the Administration's high tariff policy and were disquieted at the way the war tended to increase federal power at the expense of the states. Many Northern Democrats were also outraged by Lincoln's Emancipation Proclamation; though devoted to the Union, they saw no reason for making abolition a war aim. The chief criticism of Lincoln, however, concerned his arbitrary tendencies. Lincoln took a broad view of executive power and believed that in wartime it could legitimately be extended. In any case he felt that strict adherence to the Constitution mattered less than the preservation of the Union. That was his justification for exercising war powers between April and July 1861 before Congress had recognized a state of insurrection. Lincoln also believed that the civil courts were inadequate to deal with treasonable or subversive activities. He therefore invoked martial law and suspended the writ of habeas corpus, at first only in specific areas but later throughout the Union, in the case of persons who discouraged enlistment or engaged in 'disloyal practices'. In all more than 13,000 persons were arrested under martial law and imprisoned for varying periods. Lincoln's suspension of civil liberties earned him the epithet of 'dictator' and was later held by the Supreme Court to have been unconstitutional.

There was also much opposition to Lincoln from within his own party. Factional differences between Radical and Conservative Republicans, especially over slavery, became more intense as the war proceeded. Radical leaders like Thaddeus Stevens of Pennsylvania, Ben Wade of Ohio, and Charles Sumner of Massachusetts had no patience with Lincoln's cautious approach to emancipation or his insistence that the war's primary purpose was to save the Union. As ardent abolitionists they wanted to stamp out slavery, immediately and without compensation.

Republicans were, however, in fundamental agreement over economic policy and during the war took the opportunity provided by the withdrawal of the South to enact their program. Two measures long sought by Western farmers were passed in 1862: the Homestead Act granted 160 acres of public land to any citizen or applicant for citizenship who occupied it for five years and the Morrill Land Grant Act made grants of public land to the states for the purpose of endowing agricultural colleges. Other measures benefited business. Beginning with the Morrill Tariff Act of 1861 a series of protective measures raised duties to an average of 48 percent, the highest ever. The Pacific Railroad Act of 1862 marked the fulfillment of another Republican campaign promise: it made lavish land grants to facilitate the building of a transcontinental railroad. Finally came the National Bank Act of 1863. Adopted primarily to provide a means of marketing government bonds to finance the war, and secondarily to establish a uniform paper currency, the Act carried through a major reform of the banking system. The chaotic state-bank system established by the Independent Treasury scheme of 1846 gave way to one which restored federal control. Upon investing one-third of its capital in government bonds, every national bank started under the new system was empowered to issue national bank notes up to 90 percent of the market value of the bonds.

These measures stimulated an already expanding economy. The war had initially depressed it: the repudiation by Southerners of nearly $300 million owed to Northern creditors, the closing of the Mississippi river traffic, and the general atmosphere of uncertainty combined to produce a severe panic. But government spending and currency inflation soon brought back prosperity. From 1862 on boom conditions prevailed. Manufacturing output greatly increased and huge profits were made, especially in the woolen and leather industries and by the railroads. Agriculture, too, was stimulated by the need to feed the Union armies and by poor harvests in Europe. Thanks to the large-scale adoption of labor-saving devices there was a spectacular increase in agricultural production.

Behind the Lines

In the North life was barely affected by the war. In many respects it was a period of normal activity and growth. Politics were not suspended; business continued as usual; theaters and other places of amusement were crowded; colleges flourished—fifteen new institutions of higher learning, including Cornell, Swarthmore, and M I T, were founded in wartime. Immigration from Europe, which fell off momentarily at the outbreak of war, soon rose again to its customary levels. Nor was there any check to Western settlement. The population of Colorado, for example, increased from 32,000 in 1860 to 100,000 in 1864. Covered wagons dotted the Great Plains as usual during the summer months; wartime mining rushes occurred in Colorado, Nevada, and Idaho; some young men—like Samuel Langhorne Clemens, later to be famous as Mark Twain—went West to escape the draft.

The Civil War had a much greater impact on the South. The Confederacy possessed comparatively few resources, most of the fighting took place on Southern soil, and the Union blockade became increasingly effective as the war wore on. Thus the war years were a period of shortages and suffering. Clothing and footwear were in short supply, even for the army; medical supplies became increasingly scarce; substitutes had to be devised for a wide range of domestic commodities such as coffee, kero-

sene, and boot polish. Moreover, shortages were accentuated as the Southern transport system deteriorated under the stress of war.

The Confederate States of America

The Constitution of the Confederate States of America was closely modeled
on the Federal Constitution of 1787; even the wording was for the most
part identical. It reflected the Southern view that there had been little
wrong with the handiwork of the Founding Fathers; the fault had lain
rather with Northerners who had distorted its meaning. The Confederate
Constitution nevertheless differed from its prototype in significant ways.
Its preamble acknowledged state sovereignty by asserting that the constitution was the work of the Confederate States, 'each state acting in its
sovereign and independent capacity'. However, the right of secession was
not explicitly mentioned. Several clauses were designed to safeguard slavery. Congress was forbidden to pass any law 'impairing the rights of property in Negro slaves', and the institution of slavery was to be recognized
and protected in any territories belonging to the Confederacy. Unlike the
Federal Constitution which had employed circumlocutory expressions
when referring to slavery, the Confederate Constitution-makers did not
hesitate to use the words 'slave'and 'slavery'. But in an attempt to conciliate foreign opinion the African slave-trade was prohibited. Other clauses
of the Constitution ruled out the kind of economic legislation Southerners
had opposed in the United States Congress: protective tariffs, bounties,
and government aid to internal improvements. Finally some institutional
reforms were introduced. The process of constitutional amendment was
simplified. The President was to hold office for six years and was to be
ineligible for reelection. To discourage the practice of adding 'riders' to
appropriation bills, the President was given the power to veto separate
items.

In choosing a President, the delegates to the Montgomery Convention
had been anxious to demonstrate their unity and avoid any appearance of
extremism which might deter the slave states of the Upper South from
seceding. Hence they passed over fire-eaters like Rhett of South Carolina
and Yancey of Alabama, as well as the able but bellicose Robert Toombs
of Georgia, in favor of Jefferson Davis of Mississippi. Davis's grave and
dignified bearing belied his humble birth: like Lincoln he had been born
in a log cabin in Kentucky. After graduating from West Point he had
become a wealthy Mississippi planter and, after serving with distinction in
the Mexican War, became successively Pierce's Secretary of War and the
South's spokesman in the Senate. An inflated notion of his own military
abilities having led him to hope for command of the Confederate armies
he accepted the Presidency reluctantly. As the leading Southern nationalist
since the death of Calhoun he was the natural choice. But the same could

hardly be said of the selection of Alexander H. Stephens of Georgia as Vice-President: Stephens had opposed secession until the moment his state had left the Union.

Despite his wide political and military experience Davis proved to be a much less successful war President than Lincoln. A proud, opinionated, and sensitive man who resented criticism, he lacked the qualities to inspire popular enthusiasm and unity of purpose. Moreover, he concerned himself excessively with military affairs. Nor did Davis's Cabinet compensate for his deficiencies. Consisting chiefly of mediocrities, its composition changed constantly.

Southerners were largely united in supporting the war; the only serious resistance came from the Unionist sympathizers in mountainous regions, such as East Tennessee. All the same, Davis encountered vigorous opposition and was as savagely abused by his own people as was Lincoln by his. Controversy centered chiefly around state rights—the doctrine that had brought the Confederacy into being. Appreciating that the war needed centralized direction Davis was prepared to sacrifice political principle to expediency; but there were many who were prepared to see the Confederacy defeated rather than abandon state rights. Its most fanatical upholder was the Vice-President, Alexander H. Stephens; deserting Richmond, the Confederate capital, early in the war for his home state of Georgia, he seized on every exercise of presidential power to denounce Davis for seeking to establish a consolidated despotism. Several state governors took a similar line. Two of the most diehard, Joseph E. Brown of Georgia and Zebulon B. Vance of North Carolina, did all they could to obstruct Davis's attempts at centralized control especially the Conscription Act of 1862. It may be too much to claim that the Confederacy died of state rights, but state obstructionism undoubtedly weakened its military effort.

The War: Bull Run to Antietam

Lincoln initially turned for advice on grand strategy to the General-in-Chief of the United States Army, Winfield Scott, the aged and infirm veteran of the War of 1812 and the Mexican War. Scott appreciated that the Union must prepare for a long struggle. His 'anaconda plan'—so-called after a large snake which crushes its prey—aimed at starving the South into submission by combining a stringent blockade with the gradual tightening of military pressure all along the Confederate land frontier. But Northern public opinion, impatient for quick results, demanded an immediate advance on Richmond.

Either swayed by this popular clamor or because he felt that a quick thrust at the rebel army would end the insurrection at a stroke, Lincoln ordered General Irvin McDowell to take the offensive in Virginia. The opposing armies, both consisting largely of raw recruits, met at Bull Run on July 21, 1861 in the first major battle of the war. The Union attack failed and demoralized Federal troops streamed back to Washington in complete disorder. But the victorious Confederates were too disorganized to pursue them. The debacle brought home to the North the gravity of the conflict and the effort needed to win it. The short-term militia men were disbanded and a huge new army of 500,000 volunteers was authorized, consisting of men enlisted for three years or the duration. The discredited McDowell was replaced by General George Brinton McClellan who had won a series of spectacular, though minor, victories in western Virginia. Only thirty-four years old, McClellan was to become the Civil War's most controversial general. A graduate of West Point he had served with distinction in the Mexican War, and had then left the army to go into railroad management. McClellan displayed good skill and energy in organizing and training the raw recruits pouring into Washington. By the autumn of 1861 he had forged this newly created Army of the Potomac into a disciplined fighting machine. But he seemed in no hurry to lead it into battle. Apart from staging an elaborate series of parades and reviews he remained inactive throughout the winter of 1861–2. Already he was beginning to display his less admirable military traits—a chronic perfectionism and a tendency to exaggerate both his own difficulties and the strength of the enemy.

As the weeks passed without any sign of a move Northern opinion became restive. In Congress there was growing criticism and distrust of McClellan, especially among the Radicals who dominated the Joint Committee on the Conduct of the War. Set up in October 1861 to investigate a minor Union reverse, the committee was soon exceeding its brief. It spent most of its energies in promoting the fortunes of generals with Radical political sympathies and in hounding commanders, particularly those West Pointers with Democratic connections who were deemed not to be prosecuting the war with sufficient vigor. McClellan became the Committee's favorite target. They disliked him for his aristocratic temper and his open contempt for politicians: they knew he had no sympathy with the Radical demand that the abolition of slavery should become a war aim; and they suspected that in order to facilitate a settlement that would restore the Union but leave slavery intact he was anxious to avoid inflicting a crushing defeat on the South. But it was not only Radicals who were dissatisfied with McClellan's inaction. Lincoln, though reluctant at first to put pressure on the general, had by January 1862 become so exasperated as to remark at a Cabinet meeting: 'If General McClellan does not want to use the army, I would like to borrow it, provided I could see how it could be made to do something.'

While the Union cause lay becalmed in the East it made spectacular progress in what ultimately proved the decisive theater—the Mississippi

Valley. The Union armies in the West were organized in two separate commands: one at Louisville, Kentucky, under Don Carlos Buell, the other at St. Louis, Missouri, under Henry W. Halleck. Facing them were scattered Confederate forces under Albert Sidney Johnston, who held a long line of forts between the Appalachians and the Mississippi River. In January 1862 an army led by one of Buell's subordinates, George H. Thomas, a Virginian loyal to the Union, broke the Confederate line in eastern Kentucky. The following month Ulysses S. Grant, commanding part of Halleck's army and a detachment of federal gunboats, captured two Confederate strongholds, Fort Henry on the Tennessee and Fort Donelson on the Cumberland. These triumphs smashed the center of the Confederate defensive line, forced Johnston to abandon Kentucky and most of Tennessee, and opened the way for a Federal advance southward.

Yet when Grant advanced southward in April he was caught off guard at Shiloh. A surprise Confederate attack drove the Union army back and only the arrival of reinforcements and the mortal wounding of Albert Sidney Johnston enabled Grant to recover his ground. Shiloh was a desperately hard-fought battle—the bloodiest to date—the Union forces lost 13,000 out of a total of 63,000, the Confederates 11,000 out of 40,000. Though a drawn battle in the tactical sense, the strategic advantage lay with the Union forces. They were able to seize their immediate strategic objective, the railroad center of Corinth, and by early June had won control of the Mississippi down as far as Memphis. Meanwhile in April a Federal expedition under Admiral David G. Farragut and General Benjamin F. Butler had captured New Orleans, the largest city and most important port of the Confederacy. Since the only places on the Mississippi remaining in Confederate hands were Vicksburg and Port Hudson, there were now only tenuous links between the three trans-Mississippi states, Louisiana, Arkansas, and Texas, and the rest of the Confederacy.

McClellan's long-delayed offensive finally got under way in March 1862. Instead of advancing overland toward Richmond he sought to approach the Confederate capital by transporting his army down Chesapeake Bay to Fort Monroe on the Virginia coast and then advancing up the peninsula formed by the York and James rivers. By the end of May McClellan was within five miles to Richmond but after fighting a bloody and inconclusive engagement with Joseph E. Johnston at Seven Pines he paused to await the arrival of McDowell's army, due to advance from the north. But Stonewall Jackson's classic campaign in the Shenandoah Valley (May 4–June 9) undermined Union strategy. Jackson's pressure created such fears for the safety of Washington that Lincoln diverted to the Valley the reinforcements on which McClellan had been relying. By skillful maneuvering and rapid marches Jackson defeated in detail two Union armies with a total strength three times his own and then slipped back to assist the defenders of Richmond, now commanded by Robert E. Lee. With perhaps 80,000 men at his disposal, compared with McClellan's 100,000, Lee fell on the invading army and, in the bitter engagements known as the Seven Days' battles (June 16—July 1), forced McClellan to retreat to Harrison's Landing on the James. Lee had removed the threat to Richmond but had failed to destroy McClellan's army and, moreover, had suffered the heavier losses. McClellan was prepared to renew the assault, but in July Lincoln decided to call off the Peninsula campaign. He had never wholly approved of it, preferring the Army of the Potomac to be between the Confederates and Washington.

Before the bulk of McClellan's army could be returned to northern Virginia Lee had marched northward, decisively defeated the impetuous and boastful John Pope at the second battle of Bull Run (August 29–30), and driven the beaten Federals back into the Washington defenses. It was an astonishing reversal of fortune. Lincoln dismissed Pope and with some misgiving put McClellan in command of all the troops around Washington. But Lee allowed no time for reorganization. Early in September he crossed the Potomac west of Washington and for the first time carried the war into the North. He hoped to rally Maryland to the Confederacy and strike a blow at Northern morale by invading Pennsylvania. McClellan outnumbered Lee two to one and he knew from an intercepted dispatch that Lee had divided his army, having detached Jackson to invest Harper's Ferry. But McClellan's characteristic caution lost him the chance of striking a decisive blow. At the battle of Antietam (September 17) McClellan stopped Lee in his tracks but failed to pursue the exhausted enemy and allowed him to fall back into Virginia. For Lincoln that was the final straw. On November 5 McClellan was dismissed and was never given another command.

The Emancipation Proclamation

Ever since the beginning of the war Lincoln had been under abolitionist pressure to attack slavery. His hatred of the institution was never in doubt but he had come to the Presidency pledged to a policy of noninterference with slavery wherever it already existed. He was, moreover, keenly sensitive to the need not to divide Northern opinion or alienate the four Union slaves states. Hence he at first opposed the demand for emancipation, continuing to execute the Fugitive Slave Act and countermanding the actions of antislavery generals like Frémont, Butler, and Hunter who had issued orders purporting to free the slaves within their commands. For a time Congress shared the President's attitude. On July 22, 1861 the House adopted the Crittenden Resolution asserting that the purpose of the war was simply to maintain the Union, not to interfere with slavery.

Yet Congressional opinion soon began to change and antislavery views gradually gained the ascendancy. In December 1861 Congress refused to reaffirm the Crittenden Resolution and proceeded to pass a number of antislavery measures. It forbade the return of fugitive slaves to rebel owners, and abolished slavery in the District of Columbia (April 1862) and the territories (June 1862). The Confiscation Act of July 1862 went even further: it freed the slaves of rebel owners and authorized the President to employ Negroes, including freed slaves, as soldiers.

Meanwhile Lincoln had been attempting his own solution of the slavery problem: gradual, compensated emancipation at federal expense, accompanied by the colonization of the freed slaves abroad. But his efforts to persuade the Border slave states to accept the plan were unsuccessful. That was one reason why he concluded in the summer of 1862 that he must give way to demands for emancipation. Another was the failure of the Peninsula campaign. It destroyed Lincoln's hopes for an early end to the war and convinced him that the Confederacy could only be defeated if every means were adopted to weaken her. Finally he was swayed by the hope that emancipation would win friends for the Union in Europe.

On July 22 Lincoln informed his Cabinet of his intention to issue an Emancipation Proclamation, but was persuaded that to do so while the military situation was unfavorable would look like an act of desperation. He therefore put the document aside to await a victory. To the nation at large he gave no hint that the great decision had been taken. Even as late as August 20, in answer to Horace Greeley's 'Prayer of Twenty Millions' urging action against slavery, Lincoln insisted that his paramount objective was not to destroy slavery but to preserve the Union; Antietam brought this phase to an end. It was not a decisive victory but enough of one for Lincoln's purpose. On September 22, 1862 he issued a preliminary Emancipation Proclamation. It declared that on January 1, 1863, unless the Confederacy surrendered in the meantime, all persons held as slaves in those areas still in rebellion would be 'then, thenceforward and forever free'. It was thus a conditional measure and, moreover, one which did not aim at a final solution of the slavery problem. Lincoln still hoped to persuade Congress to adopt gradual emancipation and colonization and regarded the Proclamation simply as a military expedient. Thus the definitive edict of January 1, 1863 was issued by the President in his capacity as Commander-in-Chief of the armed forces and as a 'fit and necessary war measure for suppressing . . . rebellion'. For that reason it applied only to areas under Confederate control. It did not proclaim freedom in the four Union slave states or in those parts of the Confederacy occupied by Union forces. It made no attempt to provoke a slave insurrection but, on the contrary, enjoined slaves to abstain from violence, 'except in necessary self-defense'.

For all its limitations the Emancipation Proclamation gave the conflict a lofty new purpose. Henceforth it was to be a war for human freedom as well as for the Union. But it at first received a mixed reception both at home and abroad. Abolitionists rejoiced but Northern Democrats denounced the Proclamation as unwarranted, unconstitutional and calculated to prolong the war by ruling out a compromise peace. Irish immigrants were particularly incensed. Although they had sprung with alacrity to the defense of the Union they were less willing to fight to free the slaves, whom they regarded as potential economic competitors. Their resentment boiled over when the Emancipation Proclamation was followed shortly by the introduction of conscription; in the New York draft riots of July 1863 a largely Irish mob terrorized the city for three days, lynching blacks, destroying property and burning down a Negro orphan asylum. In Great Britain and France antislavery zealots hailed Lincoln's momentous step but many observers, struck by the fact that the Proclamation applied only to areas which the United States did not control and failing to appreciate the constitutional restraints under which Lincoln labored, commented caustically upon the President's supposed lack of moral principle.

Contrary to popular legend the Emancipation Proclamation did not remove the bondsman's shackles at a stroke. Indeed it had little immediate effect. But as the Union armies extended their grip on the South the Proclamation gradually became a reality: hundreds of thousands of slaves abandoned the plantations and flocked to Union camps. Moreover the Proclamation helped break down opposition to the recruitment of Negro soldiers. Altogether some 186,000 blacks served in the Union armies, many of them former slaves. Black soldiers served in segregated regiments under white officers and were discriminated against in matters of pay. But they fought with great distinction and made a vital contribution to the emancipation of their race.

The War: Gettysburg, Vicksburg, and Chattanooga

McClellan's dismissal did not improve Union fortunes. The attempts of his two immediate successors to advance on Richmond and defeat Lee failed ignominiously. Ambrose E. Burnside accepted the command of the Army of the Potomac after having twice refused it on the grounds that he considered himself unfit for independent command. This self-judgment was soon vindicated by events. Having crossed the Rappahannock at Fredericksburg, Burnside launched a frontal assault on Lee's defenses and was bloodily repulsed (December 13, 1862). 'Fighting Joe' Hooker, who replaced Burnside in January 1863, was a dashing corps commander with a well-deserved reputation for intrigue. He succeeded in restoring the army's morale, which had been all but shattered at Fredericksburg, and by springtime was ready for another attempt to reach Richmond. Hooker hoped to force Lee to retreat by threatening his rear but in the grim battle of Chancellorsville (May 1–5, 1863) Lee employed the same tactics that had undone Pope at the second battle of Bull Run to win his most brilliant victory. Though outnumbered two to one, he divided his army and sent Jackson on a flanking march to roll up the exposed Federal right. Hooker was crushingly defeated but the battle cost Lee his 'right arm': Stonewall Jackson was mistakenly shot by his own men and died of his wounds.

Following Chancellorsville Lee invaded the North for a second time. If the Confederacy could win a victory on Northern soil the North might be prepared to abandon the war. In early June Lee advanced up the Shenandoah Valley, crossed the Potomac west of Washington, and headed for Pennsylvania. Hooker followed a parallel path, pivoting so as to interpose his army between Lee and Washington. On June 28, with a decisive battle impending, Hooker got into a squabble with Halleck, the General-in-Chief, and asked to be relieved of command. He was replaced by General George Gordon Meade. Almost immediately the two armies stumbled into one another at Gettysburg, Pennsylvania, and there the greatest battle of the Civil War was fought. For three days (July 1–3, 1863) Lee launched a series of desperate assaults on the Union army but Meade, occupying a strong defensive position, succeeded in holding his ground. Losses on both sides were tremendous: Union casualties numbered 23,000, those of the Confederacy 28,000. On July 4 Lee's shattered forces began the long retreat to Virginia. Meade, his own army close to exhaustion, made little attempt to pursue and Lee, much to Lincoln's chagrin, made good his escape. Nevertheless Gettysburg proved decisive. Never again was Lee strong enough to take the offensive. Several months later (November 19, 1863) Lincoln made a brief speech at the dedication of the national cemetery on the site of the great battle. It made little impact on contemporaries but the Gettysburg Address ultimately came to be recognized as one of the noblest expressions of the American democratic faith.

Immediately after Gettysburg came news of an equally significant Union triumph: Grant's capture of Vicksburg (July 4, 1863). The daring and risky campaign upon which he had embarked in April showed Grant at his best. Having skillfully transferred his army to a point fifty miles below the great fortress he cut loose from his communications, marched east to Jackson, Mississippi, to drive off a Confederate relieving force under Joseph E. Johnston and then, after inflicting heavy losses on Pemberton's force, laid siege to Vicksburg. In six weeks he had starved the city and its garrison of 30,000 into surrender. The capture of Port Hudson, the last Confederate stronghold on the Mississippi, followed on July 8. The Union armies, having gained control of the entire river, had split the Confederacy in two, thus implementing the first stage of Scott's 'anaconda plan'.

The latter half of 1863 saw further decisive battles in the West. Union forces under William S. Rosecrans fought their way into eastern Tennessee and in September occupied the strategic rail center of Chattanooga. But having advanced incautiously into Georgia Rosecrans gave his Confederate opponent, Braxton Bragg, an opportunity to strike back. In the battle of Chickamauga (September 19–20, 1863) Rosecrans's Army of the Cumberland was heavily defeated and only Thomas's stubborn defensive action saved it from complete disaster. As it was Rosecrans found himself shut up in Chattanooga. But a month later Grant, now in command of all the Union armies in the West, came to the rescue. In the twin battles of Lookout Mountain and Missionary Ridge (November 24–5, 1863) the reinforced Federal armies recaptured the heights dominating Chattanooga and drove Bragg back into Georgia. Union forces now controlled the whole of Tennessee and were poised to spilt the Confederacy yet again.

Europe and the Civil War

Although by the end of 1863 the Confederacy was obviously tottering, the outcome of the war would not necessarily be decided on the battlefields. If the South could secure European recognition and persuade Great Britain and France to intervene, Confederate independence would be certain. At the outset the South confidently expected that Great Britain in particular would be forced by her dependence on Southern cotton to intervene to break the blockade, or at least to press mediation on the North. Southerners even tried to precipitate British intervention by placing an embargo on the export of cotton in 1861 and burning a large part of the year's crop.

But Southern faith in King Cotton was misplaced. Thanks to heavy imports in the previous two years British manufacturers held large stocks of cotton when the war broke out; shortages of raw material did not become acute until 1863, by which time alternative supplies were beginning to arrive from India and Egypt. The so-called 'Lancashire cotton famine', which inflicted widespread hardship on mill-workers during the war, could not have been alleviated by breaking the blockade since it was caused primarily by overproduction. In any case Great Britain was reluctant, as a great sea power which had traditionally relied upon the blockade weapon, to question Lincoln's authority to use it. Then, too, British industry as a whole did well out of the Civil War. Northern wartime purchases produced a boom in steel, munitions, and shipbuilding, and in the manufacture of woolen textiles and boots and shoes.

Economic factors do not, however, explain why in the end neither Great Britain nor France was prepared to intervene. Nor does the Emancipation Proclamation. In the last analysis, it was the military situation in America that was crucial. The European powers were prepared to contemplate intervention only when the Confederacy seemed about to win. Had Lee's invasion of Maryland in the autumn of 1862 succeeded, Great Britain would have recognized the Confederacy. But when he was repulsed such thoughts were put aside and, after Gettysburg, virtually abandoned.

France would have followed Great Britain's lead in recognizing the Confederacy but was unwilling to act alone.

The long-standing belief that the British government gave up its plans for intervention because of fears of a working-class outcry is a myth. There is no evidence that the government took working-class sentiment into account. In any case British opinion on the Civil War was not wholly divided along class lines. True, most of the ruling classes were strongly sympathetic to the Confederacy. Despising Northerners as a breed of acquisitive vulgarians, and cherishing a sense of kinship with aristocratic Southerners, they further welcomed the break-up of the Union because it weakened a dangerous rival and would tend to discredit popular government. Ranged against the established classes were middle-class anti-slavery liberals like Bright and Cobden, who had long admired American democracy. But working-class support for the North was far from solid. The numerous pro-Northern mass meetings in Lancashire in the spring of 1863 to celebrate the Emancipation Proclamation were not wholly spontaneous and there was a substantial amount of pro-Southern—or at least anti-Northern—sentiment in trade-union and working-class circles. Since the North was avowedly fighting to preserve the Union rather than to abolish slavery, the South, it was felt, was simply fighting for independence.

There were nonetheless two occasions when Great Britain might have been drawn in. The first was in November 1861, when Captain Charles Wilkes, commanding the American frigate, *San Jacinto*, stopped the British mail steamer, *Trent*, on the high seas and removed two Confederate diplomats, Mason and Slidell, who were on their way to represent the Confederacy in Europe. The British government denounced Wilkes's action as a violation of international law and of neutral rights and demanded the release of the prisoners and an apology. Feelings ran high on both sides of the Atlantic and for several weeks war seemed unavoidable. But after the British had adopted a less threatening attitude Lincoln and Seward gave way and released the captives.

The second crisis resulted from the building of vessels for the Confederacy in British shipyards. The British Foreign Enlistment Act of 1819 forbade the construction of warships for belligerents, but Confederate agents found that the regulations could be evaded by not actually arming the vessels until they had left British waters. This loophole enabled the Confederacy to build or purchase in England a number of fast commerce-raiders like the famous *Alabama*, which slipped out of the Mersey in July 1862 and, together with her consorts, harried Northern commerce to such effect that, because of prohibitive insurance costs, the Stars and Stripes all but disappeared from the high seas. The efforts of Charles Francis Adams, the American Minister in London, to prevent the departure of the *Alabama* came to naught, but his angry protests at the building of the 'Laird

Rams' were more effective. These were not mere commerce-raiders but powerful ironclad steam warships, whose underwater rams could have crippled the wooden ships of the Union blockading squadron. In September 1863 Adams solemnly warned Lord John Russell, the British Foreign Secretary, that if the rams were permitted to sail 'it would be superfluous in me to point out to Your Lordship that this is war'. The ultimatum was unnecessary for the government had already ordered their seizure. It realized that to do otherwise would create a precedent which might be cited against Great Britain in future wars.

Grant versus Lee

Grant's triumphs in the West persuaded Lincoln that he was the warwinning general for whom he had long been searching. In March 1864 the President recalled him to Washington to assume command of all the Union armies. Grant's strategic plan for 1864 envisaged two simultaneous, coordinated campaigns: he himself would lead Meade's Army of the Potomac against Lee in Virginia while his former lieutenant in the West, William T. Sherman, was to strike at Johnston's army in northern Georgia guarding Atlanta. Grant's Virginia campaign, begun on May 3, saw some of the grimmest fighting of the war. His purpose was to outflank and destroy Lee's army but his adversary repeatedly thwarted him by a superb defensive campaign. In a month of savage battles—the Wilderness, Spotsylvania, Cold Harbor—the slaughter was frightful. Grant lost 60,000 men and Lee the proportionately heavier total of 20,000. Grant's lack of success compelled a change of strategy: he moved southward across the James in June to threaten Petersburg, a vital communications center twenty miles from Richmond. But the garrison held out long enough for Lee's army to arrive and after three futile assaults on the Confederate entrenchments Grant settled down to a siege that was to last nine months. Meanwhile in the West Sherman was making little progress. His efforts to trap Johnston's army or bring it to battle were frustrated by masterly delaying tactics.

The Election of 1864

The appalling casualties suffered by Grant's army and the Confederacy's seeming invincibility produced war-weariness in the North in the summer of 1864. There were unofficial efforts at peacemaking, notably one undertaken by the mercurial New York editor, Horace Greeley. These came to naught but peace agitation received a boost in August when the Democrats nominated George B. McClellan, the former commander of the Army of the Potomac, as their presidential candidate on a platform which denounced the war as a failure and demanded an armistice to be followed by a national convention to restore the Union by negotiation. The 'peace plank' was confused and unrealistic; indeed McClellan repudiated it. But the idea of a negotiated peace, chimerical though it was, had a considerable appeal to a people discouraged by defeat and sick of the fratricidal slaughter.

The Republicans had already renominated Lincoln in June. In an effort to stress their national character they adopted the name of the National Union party and chose Andrew Johnson, a War Democrat from Tennessee who had opposed the secession of his state, as Lincoln's running mate. The platform called for a united effort to end the rebellion and promised the extirpation of slavery. But some Republicans were dissatisfied with Lincoln's conduct of the war; they also thought that his proposals for postwar reconstruction showed the seceded states too much leniency. Thus a group of dissident Radicals held a separate convention in May and nominated General John C. Frémont for the Presidency; and even after Lincoln received the Republican nomination there were secret moves within the party to replace him. Lincoln made no concessions to his critics but by the end of August had come to share their opinion that he would probably not be reelected.

Then suddenly the military situation was transformed and with it the political outlook. On September 2, after a siege of several weeks, Sherman captured Atlanta. The effect on Northern morale was electrifying. Peace talk evaporated, Frémont withdrew from the race, and the Republicans, now united behind Lincoln, were able to exploit the ambiguity of the Democratic platform. In November Lincoln was comfortably reelected, carrying every state in the Union except three. But his popular majority, 400,000 in a total poll of over four million, was relatively slight.

The Final Campaigns, 1864–1865

The war now entered its final phase. From his base at Atlanta Sherman plunged deep into Georgia leaving a trail of devastation in his wake and making his name a byword in the South. Railroads, bridges, cotton gins, food stores, livestock—anything that might be useful to the enemy—were systematically destroyed. John B. Hood, whom Davis had placed at the head of the Confederate forces in the West instead of Johnston, attempted to force Sherman's recall by invading Tennessee. But in the battle of Nashville (December 15–16, 1864) Thomas virtually destroyed Hood's army. On December 13 Sherman reached the sea and just before Christmas captured Savannah. What remained of the Confederacy had thus been sliced in two and Lee's army was deprived of most of its food supplies. Sherman then swung north into the Carolinas. By the end of February 1865 he had captured Charleston and sealed off Wilmington, North Carolina, the Confederacy's last remaining seaport, Mobile having been taken by a naval expedition under Farragut the previous August. Johnston lacked the strength to oppose Sherman effectively and Lee, pinned down at Petersburg by Grant's remorseless pressure, was powerless to help.

With the writing on the wall for the Confederacy Jefferson Davis expressed willingness to enter into a conference 'to secure peace to the two countries'. But when Confederate Vice-President, Alexander H. Stephens, met Lincoln on a Union steamer in Hampton Roads on February 3, he learned that the only peace terms available were reunion, the abolition of slavery, and the complete disbandment of Confederate forces. Thus the conference proved fruitless.

By the beginning of April 1865 Grant's war of attrition had stretched Lee's depleted army to breaking-point. To avoid being surrounded the Confederates evacuated Petersburg and Richmond. Lee headed west in the hope of joining Johnston in the North Carolina mountains but, finding his escape route barred, surrendered to Grant on April 9 at Appomattox Court House in southern Virginia. Johnston's surrender followed on April 26 and by the end of May the last Confederate forces had laid down their arms. Lincoln did not live to witness the final scenes. On April 14, Good Friday, he was shot in a Washington theater by a fanatical Confederate sympathizer, the actor John Wilkes Booth, and died the next morning.

Lincoln's greatness was hidden from many of his contemporaries and even today is difficult to capture. His record is in some respects flawed. As President-elect he erred badly in dismissing the secession crisis as 'an artificial one' and in exaggerating the strength of Southern Unionism. As an inexperienced President, confronted with problems of unprecedented gravity, he was at first hesitant and uncertain, especially in military matters. During the first half of the war—that is, until his rapport with Grant— he failed to give his generals his complete confidence and interfered unhelpfully with them in the field. But his political touch was from the start assured. He knew when to forbear and when to act decisively. He enlarged the presidential office and, by a mixture of dexterity, patience and good humor established his authority over a divided party, over a Congress suspicious of executive power and over a Cabinet made up largely of men who had been his eager rivals for the Presidency. Lincoln's qualities of personality and style—his dignity, humility, and compassion—contributed greatly to his success as a democratic war leader, while his gifts of expression enabled him to define the national purpose in idealistic, even mystical, terms. More than anyone he saved the Union; his untimely death was truly a national tragedy.

The Civil War was less of a historical watershed than has sometimes been claimed. The United States did not, for example, change overnight from being predominantly agricultural to being predominantly industrial. Nor did the Civil War alter American social patterns or transform political parties, government or law. Nevertheless the Civil War decided a number of things that had previously been in doubt. It settled first that the United States would remain one nation. Between 1787 and 1861, as one discontented section after another threatened to secede,the survival of the Union had seemed doubtful. And if the Confederacy had won its independence, further secessions might well have followed. But Appomattox ruled out that possibility. Second, the Civil War ended the long drawn out debate on the nature of the Union. The question of the location of ultimate sovereignty, which the Founding Fathers had left unanswered in 1787, was finally settled—by force of arms rather than by force of argument—in favor of the Federal government. True, there was no formal reapportionment of power. The Federal government's functions remained limited; most of the matters concerning the individual citizen—education, welfare, law and order and so on—remained the responsibility of the states. But federal authority was greatly and, as it proved, permanently increased. Finally, though it did little to solve the problem of race relations, the Civil War at least abolished the institution whose existence had hitherto mocked American democratic pretensions. But for the war Negro slavery might have survived much longer.

13. *Reconstruction*, 1865–1877

The Legacy of War

As victors and vanquished made their way home after Appomattox, they faced contrasting prospects. Union soldiers went back to a buoyant and prosperous land. Despite four years of war the North's population and wealth had increased, its industry and agriculture were flourishing as never before. The huge Northern armies were quickly demobilized and absorbed into civilian life. Confederate soldiers, on the other hand, returned to a ruined and desolate South. One in every four Southerners of military age had been killed or wounded. The war had been fought largely on Southern soil and many ex-Confederates found their homes destroyed and their families impoverished. Large areas of the South had been systematically devastated, cities like Richmond, Columbia, and Atlanta severely damaged by bombardment and fire. The Southern economy had collapsed: plantations were overgrown, factories closed, the transport system a shambles. Most Southerners were bankrupt; Confederate bonds and currency were worthless while the abolition of slavery had deprived slave-owners of property worth perhaps $2 billion. Emancipation had produced a profound social upheaval. Hundreds of thousands of freedmen had deserted the plantations for the nearest army camp or were wandering aimlessly about. In the first few months of peace large numbers died from starvation and disease.

What the South needed was a relief and recovery program like that undertaken by the New Deal. But the notion that such matters were the responsibility of government lay far in the future. In March 1865 the federal government set up a temporary agency, the Freedmen's Bureau, to provide the ex-slaves with food, shelter, medical aid, and education and settle them on abandoned or confiscated lands. But otherwise it did not concern itself with the alleviation of distress or the restoration of the economy. Reconstruction, as Northerners defined the term, had to do rather with two complex and related problems which had been central to the Civil War but which had only been partly solved by the Union victory. The Union had been saved, but on what terms and by what process would the former Confederate states be permitted to resume their former status? Slavery had been abolished but what precisely would be the position of the freedmen in Southern society and who would decide it? When the war ended almost no one in the North had any very clear ideas about these issues.

Presidential Reconstruction

In his Second Inaugural (March 1865) Lincoln had called for a peace that would show "malice toward none . . . [and] . . . charity for all". But the terms eventually imposed on the Southern states reflected none of Lincoln's magnanimity. For varying periods they were made to suffer military occupation and outside rule. A large minority of Southern whites were disfranchised and debarred from office-holding. Treasury agents seized $30 million from the prostrate South. But compared with the fate of the vanquished in other civil wars, the ex-Confederates escaped fairly lightly. None of the political and military leaders of the Confederacy was executed or even brought to trial; a few were arrested but only Jefferson Davis, who spent two years in jail, was imprisoned for long. No one was banished, though a few went into voluntary exile. And while a number of individual estates were seized by the federal government—the best-known example being the Lee family home at Arlington, across the Potomac from Washington, which became a national cemetery—there was no mass confiscation of property.

Lincoln had begun the process of Reconstruction during the Civil War. He dismissed the question of whether the seceded states were in the Union or not as "a mere pernicious abstraction"; the essential thing was to restore them to their proper relationship with the Union as quickly as possible. He also believed that Reconstruction was an executive, rather than a legislative, function. Thus in 1862 and 1863 he appointed provisional governors for Tennessee, Louisiana, and Arkansas, large parts of which had come under Union control. Then in December 1863 he issued a proclamation outlining a general Reconstruction plan. All Confederates, except for high civil and military leaders, would be granted amnesty once they had taken an oath of loyalty to the Union. As soon as 10 per cent of the electorate of any state had taken the oath, and accepted the abolition of slavery, they might form a state government which the President would recognize.

In three Southern states Lincoln's procedure was followed but, although he recognized their new civil governments, Congress refused to seat the representatives they sent to Washington. Radical Republicans thought the 10 percent plan far too lenient and in any case considered Reconstruction to be a function of Congress. Hence, while frustrating Lincoln's plan, they prepared an alternative of their own, the Wade–Davis Bill, which Congress adopted in July 1864. This laid down more stringent conditions for the admission of the Southern states. Only when a majority of the electorate had sworn allegiance to the Union could a seceded state establish a valid government. No one who had voluntarily borne arms against the United States could participate in framing a new constitution. The new governments would also be required to prohibit slavery, debar former Confederate leaders from voting and office-holding, and repudiate the Confederate war debt. Lincoln prevented the Wade–Davis Bill from becoming law by means of a pocket veto, and was denounced by its authors for attempting to usurp the powers of Congress. With executive and legislature deadlocked, nothing further was done about Reconstruction before the end of the war.

Whether Lincoln, had he lived, could have reached a compromise with Congress must remain a matter of speculation. But it is conceivable that his prestige and political astuteness would have enabled him to do so. But his successor, Andrew Johnson, was handicapped both by his personality and by his background. Born into poverty in North Carolina, Johnson spent much of his early life in Tennessee, where he rose to political leadership as the spokesman of the nonslave-holding poor whites and as the enemy of the planter aristocracy. He became successively a Democratic congressman, governor of Tennessee, and United States senator and, when Tennessee seceded, declared for the Union, becoming the only Southerner to retain his Senate seat. In 1862 Lincoln appointed him military governor of Tennessee and in 1864 the Republicans, campaigning as the National Union party, chose him as Lincoln's running mate. Yet he remained an old-fashioned, state-rights Democrat, opposed to virtually everything the Republican party stood for, except its unionism. In particular Johnson did not share the party's idealistic concern for the freed Negro and was against increasing unduly the powers of the national government. Johnson came to the Presidency, therefore, as a political outsider, unsympathetic to the party he nominally led. Like Lincoln largely self-educated, Johnson lacked Lincoln's felicity of expression and political dexterity. A powerful stump orator, given to denouncing his opponents in crude and intemperate language, he was stubbornly devoted to his principles and uncompromising in their defense.

When Johnson became President in April 1865, most Radical Republicans assumed that he shared their views on the need for a harsh Southern policy. Overlooking his political past they seized on his reported statement during the 1864 election campaign that "treason must be made infamous, and traitors must be impoverished". But Johnson's actions soon disillusioned them. He retained Lincoln's Cabinet and adopted a Reconstruction policy that in its essentials closely resembled Lincoln's. Like Lincoln, Johnson believed that Reconstruction was an executive responsibility and, taking advantage of the fact that Congress was not in session when he took office and was not due to meet again until December 1865, he proceeded to implement his own plan of restoration without consulting Congressional leaders.

On May 29 Johnson extended a general pardon to former Confederates who were willing to take a prescribed oath of allegiance. Men who had held high office under the Confederacy or whose taxable property exceeded $20,000 in value were excluded but could obtain special pardons by petitioning the President individually. Johnson had already recognized the restored governments in four former Confederate states—Virginia, Louisiana, Arkansas, and Tennessee—which had accepted Lincoln's 10 percent plan. For the remaining seven states he appointed provisional governors, instructed to call constitutional conventions to be elected by the qualified voters, that is, those who had taken the oath. As a preliminary to readmittance to the Union these conventions were to withdraw the ordinances of secession, repudiate the Confederate and state war debts, and ratify the pending Thirteenth Amendment abolishing slavery. That done, the states could hold elections for state governments and for representatives to the United States Congress. Suffrage qualifications were left to the states, though Johnson did invite them to consider enfranchising a few qualified Negroes.

The South's response was a display of contumacy. The state conventions complied with the letter of Johnson's conditions, but only grudgingly and after much quibbling. Some merely repealed the ordinances of secession without disavowing them. Others sought to qualify their repudiation of war debts. Nearly all raised objections before ratifying the Thirteenth Amendment and none acted on Johnson's suggestion that there should be limited Negro suffrage. Moreover, in the ensuing elections Southerners defiantly chose prominent ex-Confederates. The newly elected governor of Mississippi had been a Confederate brigadier-general; the Georgia legislature even chose as United States senator Alexander H. Stephens, until recently Vice-President of the Confederacy. The election results raised doubts whether Southerners accepted the finality of defeat. Certainly they were unrepentant about secession and one Northern observer reported "an utter absence of national feeling" among them. But the President, eager to complete the work of Reconstruction, considered the seceded states to have worked their passage back.

Many Northerners felt, however, that the President was being too precipitate. There had been little vindictiveness in the North when the war ended, but Northern opinion was disturbed by the churlishness with which Johnson's leniency had been received in the South and by the character of the men Southerners had elected to office. When Southerners offered only a grudging and limited loyalty Northerners began to fear they were being cheated of the fruits of victory. Such suspicions were greatly intensified by the "Black Codes" passed in 1865 and 1866 by the new Southern legislatures. Although they varied in severity from state to state the codes had the common aim of keeping the freedman in a subordinate position. They conferred certain rights upon him: to own property, to make contracts, to sue in court, to go to school, and to enter into legal marriage. But blacks were in general prohibited from voting or serving on juries; they were not allowed to bear arms or testify against white persons; they were made liable to heavier penalties for law-breaking than were whites and they were forbidden to marry whites. In most states Negroes were excluded from occupations where they might compete with whites; in South Carolina, indeed, they were restricted to agriculture and domestic service. Most oppressive of all were the provisions against vagrancy: unemployed Negroes could be apprehended for vagrancy and, if convicted and unable to pay the fine imposed, could be hired out to planters or other employers. To Southern whites the Black Codes were designed simply to provide freedmen with needed discipline and protection and to avert the economic chaos that would otherwise ensue. But to most Northerners the Black Codes were unpleasantly reminiscent of the old slave codes and seemed like an attempt to perpetuate slavery under another name.

Congress versus President

When Congress reassembled in December 1865 it refused to seat the representatives of the reorganized Southern states. It also asserted its claim to decide policy by creating a Joint Committee on Reconstruction, with the task of ascertaining the true state of Southern feeling and deciding whether the South was ready for readmission to the Union. At this stage Congressional Republicans had no agreed Reconstruction program, but were unanimous that the South should not be allowed to resume its place in national affairs without further guarantees against renewed rebellion and a revival of slavery.

Radical Republicans like Thaddeus Stevens of Pennsylvania and Charles Sumner of Massachusetts believed these aims involved giving the former slave equality as well as freedom. Stevens, destined to become the chief architect of Radical Reconstruction, had throughout a long career been a consistent champion of Negro rights. A formidable parliamentary tactician, celebrated for his vitriolic invective, Stevens displayed a rancorous hatred toward the Southern planter aristocracy. He maintained that the federal government should treat the former Confederate states as conquered provinces, make them pay the cost of the war, and confiscate planter estates for distribution among freed blacks. Sumner, an elegant, cultured Bostonian, did not share Stevens's vindictiveness but was no less committed to racial equality. Sumner's theory of 'state suicide' held that by seceding from the Union the Southern states had forfeited their constitutional rights and that Congress could govern them as though they were territories. Thus it had the power, as well as the duty, to insist upon Negro suffrage as a condition of readmission.

But while Stevens and Sumner were animated by genuine devotion to principle, other Radicals like Benjamin F. Wade and Zachariah Chandler seem to have favored Negro rights from considerations of political expediency. If the South returned to the Union on Johnson's terms the Northern and Southern wings of the Democratic party would be reunited and Republican control of the federal government endangered. This seemed all the more likely because, with the disappearance of slavery, the three-fifths rule for apportioning Congressional seats had lapsed. Henceforth blacks were to be counted equally with whites for electoral purposes and the Southern states would be entitled to an additional fifteen seats in the House of Representatives.

It is sometimes argued that Radical views of Reconstruction stemmed from a desire to serve the interests of the economic groups which dominated the Republican party. Northern businessmen, so the theory runs, feared that the protectionist and hard-money legislation adopted during the Civil War would be repealed if the South regained its prewar political influence. But Northern financiers and manufacturers were in fact deeply divided on tariff and currency policies. So, for that matter, were Congressional Radicals. What evidently moved most Radicals was not business pressure but idealism combined with the conviction that continued Republican predominance was essential in the national interest. To enable former rebels and their Northern allies to control the national government seemed to them dangerous and absurd.

At the end of 1865, however, the Radicals constituted only a minority of the Republican party in Congress. The moderate majority, though disturbed by the results of Johnson's policy, hoped that a compromise could be found. But Johnson's maladroitness and intransigence destroyed that prospect and radicalized many moderates. Early in 1866 he openly attacked leading Radicals as traitors, even implying they had been responsible for Lincoln's death. If anything further was needed to make the breach irreparable Johnson supplied it by vetoing two measures designed to protect blacks—the Freedmen's Bureau Bill and the Civil Rights Bill. The former, passed in February 1866, sought to counteract the Black Codes by extending the life of the Freedmen's Bureau, and empowering it to instigate proceedings in military courts in cases of racial discrimination. Johnson's veto message declared the measure to be unconstitutional since it extended military rule in peacetime and, moreover, to be unnecessary since the civil courts were open and were perfectly capable of protecting the freedmen. With equal promptness Johnson vetoed the Civil Rights Bill of March 1866 bestowing citizenship upon blacks and forbidding states to discriminate against citizens on grounds of race or color. He objected that it invaded states' rights, ought not to be passed while eleven Southern states were unrepresented in Congress, and discriminated against the white race in favor of the colored. These sentiments so alienated Congressional moderates that the Radicals were able to muster the two-thirds majority required to repass both the Freedmen's Bureau Bill and the Civil Rights Bill over Johnson's veto.

To remove widespread doubts about the constitutionality of the Civil Rights Act and guard against its repeal, its provisions were incorporated in the proposed Fourteenth Amendment to the Constitution, formulated by the Joint Committee on Reconstruction in April 1866. The Amendment, the most detailed ever added to the Constitution and the most far-reaching in its implications for federal–state relationships, had four main provisions. The first section declared that all persons born or naturalized in the United States were citizens of the United States as well as of the state in which they lived and asserted that no state could abridge "the privileges and immunities" of United States citizens or "deprive any person of life, liberty or property, without due process of law", or "deny to any person within its jurisdiction the equal protection of the laws". Since subsequent judicial decisions held that the word 'person' meant a corporation as well as an individual citizen, this section came to be used to protect business against state regulation. But the charge that this was the framers' intention seems unfounded. Their aim was simply to protect the freedmen—though some were motivated less by philanthropy than by the hope that improving the lot of Negroes in the South might prevent them from moving North. The second section did not positively enact black suffrage but provided that any state which failed to do so should have its representation in the House of Representatives and in the electoral college reduced proportionately. This section was never enforced and in any case became inoperative in 1870 when the Fifteenth Amendment attempted more directly to enfranchise blacks. The third section disqualified from office all those who had joined the Confederacy after having earlier sworn to support the Constitution. Finally the fourth section upheld the validity of the national debt and invalidated the Confederate war debt, together with any claims for compensation for loss of slaves.

If it had been left to the Radicals the Fourteenth Amendment would have been even more sweeping, especially respecting Negro suffrage. But moderate Republicans succeeded in toning it down in the hope of making it more acceptable to Johnson and the South. The President, however, promptly expressed his disapproval and in effect advised the Southern states not to ratify. His advice was probably superfluous. Of the eleven ex-Confederate states, only Tennessee ratified the Amendment—though in somewhat irregular fashion—and was thereupon declared by Congress to be back in the Union. The other ten rejected it either unanimously or by huge majorities. These ten rejections were enough to defeat the Amendment, but for good measure Delaware and Kentucky also declined to ratify.

Radical Reconstruction

The Congressional elections of 1866 presented the strange spectacle of a President campaigning against the party he nominally led. With the Radicals in control of the Republican party machinery, Johnson sought to defeat them by combining conservatives from both parties in a new organization, the National Union movement. But conservative Republicans would have none of it and only those Democrats prepared to forgive his earlier apostasy came to the President's aid. A presidential speaking tour, the so-called 'swing around the circle', proved a disaster. Johnson's wild allegations against the Radicals and vulgar exchanges with hecklers seemed to many to demean the presidential office. Johnson's position was further weakened by outbreaks of racial violence in the South, the worst being that at New Orleans on July 30, in which some 200 Negroes and white Unionists were killed or injured. The Radicals pointed to the bloodshed as confirming their predictions of what would happen in the South if Johnson's leniency prevailed.

The election results were a resounding victory for the Republicans. In both houses they secured far more than the two-thirds majority needed to override presidential vetoes. The way was now open for the dominant Radicals to put into effect their own ideas on Reconstruction. Their program was embodied in the First Reconstruction Act passed over Johnson's veto on March 2, 1867. The ten ex-Confederate states which had rejected the Fourteenth Amendment were organized into five military districts, each under an army general. To be readmitted to the Union the Southern states were required to draft new state constitutions providing for Negro suffrage and the disfranchisement of ex-Confederates disqualified under the proposed Fourteenth Amendment and, in addition, new state legislatures elected under these arrangements had to ratify the Amendment itself. In the hope of frustrating the operation of the Act, the South omitted to call new constitutional conventions and, when that failed of its purpose, organized voting boycotts. But a series of supplementary Reconstruction Acts nullified all such expedients.

The Reconstruction Acts were, to say the least, of doubtful constitutionality. That was why Johnson felt justified in vetoing them: he believed they would substitute centralization for federalism. But the Radicals were determined to have no interference with their program from the executive or, indeed, the judiciary. In seeking to implement it they came close to destroying the system of checks and balances provided by the Constitution. Two measures, both passed on March 2, 1867, invaded the President's constitutional prerogatives. The first, the Tenure of Office Act, forbade him to remove civil office-holders without the consent of the Senate. It was designed to protect Johnson's Secretary of War, Edwin M. Stanton, the Radicals' leading ally in the Cabinet. The other, the Command of the Army Act, impinged on the President's powers as Commander-in-Chief; he was prohibited from issuing military orders except through the commanding general of the army—General Grant—or from relieving him or assigning him elsewhere except with the consent of the Senate.

The Radicals next attempted to shackle the Supreme Court. In December 1866, the Court held, in *ex parte Milligan*, that a resort to martial law was unconstitutional where the civil courts were open. This decision cast doubt on the validity of the military tribunals operating under the Freedmen's Bureau Act and was therefore violently denounced by the Radicals. Some of them threatened to curb the power of the Supreme Court and even to abolish it. Intimidated by these attacks the Court refused in 1867 to accept jurisdiction in two cases in which Southern states sought injunctions to restrain the President from enforcing the Reconstruction Acts. But in February 1868 the Court did agree to consider *ex parte McCardle*, which involved the use of military tribunals in Mississippi. Fearing that a review of the case might invalidate its Reconstruction legislation Congress passed a measure on March 27, 1868 depriving the Court of appellate jurisdiction in cases involving habeas corpus.

The Impeachment of Andrew Johnson

The struggle between Congress and the President now moved to a climax. For more than a year the Radicals had been looking for an opportunity to depose Johnson, but an elaborate investigation of his record had failed to yield any evidence of treason, bribery, or other crimes or misdemeanors on which impeachment charges could be based. But towards the end of 1867 the President furnished his critics with a plausible excuse. He suspended his Secretary of War, Stanton, and when the Senate had refused to concur, dismissed him in defiance of the Tenure of Office Act. Johnson's purpose, apart from wanting to rid his Cabinet of a Radical sympathizer, was to test in the courts a measure he believed unconstitutional. But there was to be no test case—at least not in Johnson's lifetime, though more than half a century after his death the Supreme Court upheld him. For several months Stanton clung to his office by the expedient of barricading himself in the War Department. Meanwhile on February 24, 1868 the House voted by 126 to 47 that Andrew Johnson "be impeached of high crimes and misdemeanors in office".

Why the Republican majority in Congress should have been anxious to remove a President whose vetoes it could override at will and whose term of office had only a year to run has been much debated. Some historians have seen the impeachment proceedings as the act of vengeful politicians bent on punishing and humiliating a hated political opponent; others as a revolutionary attempt to replace the balanced system established by the Constitution with a parliamentary form of government. But it seems more probable that impeachment was decided on because Congress believed it was the only way of implementing its Reconstruction policy. For the fact was that Johnson had taken advantage of the opportunities open to him as Chief Executive and Commander-in-Chief to delay and obstruct the implementation of the Congressional program. In June 1867, he had issued instructions to voter registration boards in the South which, if followed, would have condoned perjured oaths of allegiance and permitted the great bulk of disqualified Southern whites to vote. Congress reversed his orders in the Third Reconstruction Act passed in July, but in December he issued a Proclamation encouraging disfranchised Southern whites to take their cases to court, thereby jeopardizing the entire work of registration. The President also removed the three most Radical military commanders in the South, replacing them with Democrats or conservative Republicans. Thus by the time the Stanton affair erupted it had become plain to Congress that its purposes in the South were likely to be systematically frustrated so long as Andrew Johnson remained in the White House.

Though Johnson's real offense was his attempt to thwart the will of Congress as expressed in the Reconstruction Acts, not even the House could persuade itself that that was an impeachable offense. But the President's efforts to dismiss Stanton made it possible to frame more concrete charges. Of the eleven articles of impeachment nine dealt with Johnson's violation of the Tenure of Office Act; a tenth article alleged that he had contravened the Command of the Army Act; and the eleventh consisted of an absurd complaint that Johnson had delivered "intemperate, inflammatory and scandalous harangues" calculated to bring Congress into disrespect. In the trial before the Senate which lasted from mid-March to the end of May 1868, Johnson's lawyers had no difficulty in showing that the Tenure of Office Act did not apply to Stanton. The measure protected Cabinet members only for the term of the President who appointed them, and Stanton had been appointed by Lincoln. Nevertheless, Johnson escaped conviction by the narrowest possible margin. The vote for conviction was 35 to 19, one vote short of the required two-thirds majority. Despite immense pressure on Republican senators to vote for conviction, seven sided with the twelve Democrats and voted for acquittal. Two things explained their action. One was fear that Johnson's removal might permanently damage the Presidency. The other was distaste for Benjamin F. Wade who, as president *pro tem* of the Senate, would succeed him; not only was Wade a man of violent passions, but his high tariff and inflationary monetary opinions were also strongly opposed.

The Radicals were understandably downcast, but if the object of impeachment had indeed been to put a stop to Johnson's wrecking activities, it may be held to have succeeded. For the rest of his term the President was quiescent, and the reorganization of the South proceeded according to the Congressional plan. In the ten Southern states covered by the Reconstruction Acts 703,000 blacks and 627,000 whites were declared eligible for the franchise. Black voters outnumbered whites in five states: South Carolina, Mississippi, and Louisiana, where blacks formed a majority of the population, and Alabama and Florida, where they did not. The Radical majorities which resulted in all five state conventions were duplicated in the remaining five states when substantial minorities of white voters joined with the blacks in electing the Republican ticket. New state governments replaced those set up by Lincoln and Johnson and by June 1868 seven of the former Confederate states had fulfilled the conditions laid down in the Reconstruction Acts, including ratification of the Fourteenth Amendment, and were accordingly readmitted to the Union. The readmission of the three remaining states—Mississippi, Texas, and Virginia—was held up until 1870 by white recalcitrance.

The Election of 1868

Even before the impeachment proceedings were over the Republicans had nominated General Grant as their candidate in the presidential election of 1868. Grant was no Radical but the Radicals considered him an ideal candidate. His war record added luster to the Republican cause; and since he had no political experience or any strong views on politics he could be expected to follow the advice of Congressional leaders. The Democrats, declining to gratify Johnson's wish to become their candidate, chose Horatio Seymour, the wartime governor of New York. Although Seymour was a 'sound money' man the Democratic platform endorsed the inflationary 'Ohio idea', a proposal sponsored by an Ohio senator to redeem Civil War bonds in greenbacks. But in spite of this attempt to divert attention from Reconstruction, that remained the chief campaign issue. While the Republicans endorsed Radical Reconstruction and Negro suffrage for the South, the Democrats denounced the Reconstruction Acts as revolutionary and void and called for state regulation of the suffrage question. The Republican campaign consisted mainly of 'waving the bloody shirt', that is, of emphasizing their war record and reviling the Democrats for their alleged disloyalty. Grant carried twenty-six of the thirty-four states but his popular majority was only 300,000 and without the 700,000 Negro votes he polled in the seven reconstructed Southern states he would have been a minority President.

The significance of these figures was not lost on the Republicans. Shortly after election day they attempted to strengthen the rather vague provisions for Negro suffrage in the Fourteenth Amendment. Congress then adopted a resolution which became the basis of the Fifteenth Amendment; it provided that the right to vote should "not be denied . . . on account of race, color or previous condition of servitude". The amendment was submitted to the states in February 1869 and was declared ratified in March 1870. It proved to be the last important Radical achievement.

The Grant Administration

As President, Grant showed none of the qualities that had made him a successful general. He was in fact hopelessly unfitted for the office. He had never been much interested in politics, knew nothing of most national issues, and did not understand the American political system. He took a narrow view of the presidential office, regarding it as largely ceremonial and symbolic. Grant's political naiveté was evident in his choice of advisers. He took no account of party or popular feeling, but irresponsibly handed round appointments to men he found congenial. Of the twenty-five men he appointed to his Cabinet during his eight years in the White House, most were undistinguished and several were rascals who ultimately disgraced the Administration. Grant's lack of judgment was also revealed in his acceptance of gifts and loans from favor-seekers like the financier, Jay Cooke, and in his friendship with an unscrupulous stock-market manipulator like Jim Fisk. Although Grant was personally honest his fondness for shoddy company and his misplaced loyalty to questionable friends helped depress standards of political morality.

Grant's deficiencies were first exposed by the gold scandal of 1869. Gold having become a speculative commodity, the financier Jay Gould and Fisk devised an unscrupulous scheme to corner the market in it. Aware that success depended on inducing the Treasury to halt gold supplies temporarily, they employed Grant's brother-in-law to extract a vague presidential assurance to that effect. Their manipulation drove up the price of gold to such an unprecedented level that by 'Black Friday', September 24, 1869, the New York Stock Exchange was in a panic. Belatedly realizing what was afoot, Grant authorized the release of sufficient gold to foil the plot, but not before many speculators—though not Gould or Fisk—had been ruined and hundreds of businesses had suffered great losses. Grant had not been implicated directly but he was severely criticized for his gullibility.

For most of Grant's presidency controversy surrounded the status of greenbacks, the paper currency issued during the Civil War. Farmers and other advocates of cheap money wanted to retain, even increase, the $356 million of notes still in circulation, thus maintaining or inflating prices and lessening the burden of debt. Creditors, on the other hand, preferred a policy of gradual contraction but insisted that, if greenbacks were to be retained, the government should stabilize their value of making them redeemable in gold. In 1869 creditors won an important victory when Congress voted that Treasury bonds should be redeemed in coin (thus rejecting the Ohio idea), a decision which enriched those who had bought them with depreciated greenbacks. Shortly afterwards the Supreme Court created uncertainty by ruling that greenbacks were not legal tender for debts contracted before they had been issued. But in 1871, after Grant had appointed to the Supreme Court two justices known to be opposed to the decision, there was a rehearing and the validity of greenbacks was in all respects affirmed. As a relief measure after the Panic of 1873 the Treasury reluctantly reissued $26 million of greenbacks which had earlier been withdrawn. Similar considerations led Congress the following year to raise the greenback total to $400 million. But Grant, after characteristic vacillation, vetoed the measure under pressure from financiers. Finally creditors obtained the 'sound money' solution they wanted. The Resumption Act of 1875 provided that as from January 1, 1879 the Treasury would, on demand, redeem all legal-tender notes in gold.

The Republican leadership showed solicitude for business in other ways. By 1870 Congress had repealed all wartime excise duties except those on drink and tobacco, and in 1872 abolished the wartime income tax. But industrialists successfully resisted attempts to lower the high tariffs imposed during the war, ostensibly as emergency revenue measures, and even secured increases in some rates. Just before the presidential election of 1872 Congress lowered most duties by 10 percent in an attempt to appease Western farmers, but before the end of Grant's second term the cuts had been restored.

Skepticism about Grant was increased by his half-hearted support of civil-service reform. He momentarily heartened the reformers in 1871 by persuading Congress to establish a Civil Service Commission authorized to devise a merit system. But under pressure from spoilsmen he gave only minimal support to the new agency and in 1873 it expired through lack of funds. Equally offensive to reformers was Grant's dismissal of Attorney General E. Rockwell Hoar and Secretary of the Interior Jacob D. Cox. Their departure meant that by 1870 every Cabinet officer of ability and integrity had been ousted except for the Secretary of State, Hamilton Fish, and even he was more than once close to resigning in disgust.

Liberal Republicanism

As the presidential election of 1872 approached, dissatisfaction with Grant produced a Republican revolt. Calling themselves Liberal Republicans, the dissidents included some distinguished figures: Carl Schurz, the German revolutionary who had been successively American diplomat, Civil War general, and senator from Missouri; Justice David Davis of the Supreme Court; Charles Francis Adams, the American Minister to London during the Civil War; Gideon Welles, Lincoln's Secretary of the Navy. The movement also attracted a galaxy of influential newspaper editors. But for all its appeal to an intellectual elite, Liberal Republicanism lacked popular support. An even greater weakness was its heterogeneous character. Gathered under the same political umbrella were high protectionists, free traders, eastern conservatives, western radicals, idealistic reformers, and practical politicians. The only unifying factors were dislike of Grant and determination to deny him a second term.

The new party's contradictions were exposed at its Cincinnati convention in May 1872. Only after prolonged wrangling could it settle on a platform. Though accepting the Reconstruction Amendments to the Constitution the platform called for universal amnesty and the withdrawal of troops from the South; it also demanded civil-service reform and a resumption of specie payments on greenbacks; but the tariff plank was so equivocal as to be meaningless. After more squabbling the party chose as its presidential nominee the notoriously erratic Horace Greeley, the veteran editor of the *New York Tribune*. This was a bizarre selection for Greeley was an ardent protectionist and lukewarm to civil-service reform. Besides, after a a lifetime castigating the Democrats, he was hardly the ideal candidate to attract Democratic votes. Nevertheless the Democrats reluctantly endorsed him since they realized that they had no hope of defeating Grant with a candidate of their own. The Republicans renominated Grant unanimously and drafted a platform endorsing Radical Republicanism and a high tariff. To no one's surprise Grant won a sweeping victory. Greeley, exhausted by the campaign and desolated by defeat, died three weeks after the election. Liberal Republicanism did not long survive him.

Political Scandals

During Grant's second term one political scandal succeeded another. The first major revelations concerned the Crédit Mobilier, the construction company formed to build the Union Pacific railroad. Having made immense profits for a handful of large shareholders by charging well over twice the real construction costs, the directors had sought to avert a Congressional investigation by distributing stock at discount to influential Congressmen. All this had happened before Grant took office but, with many prominent Republicans implicated, the President could not entirely escape the odium.

Subsequent exposures revealed that the Administration itself—though not Grant personally—was deeply corrupt. The Secretary of the Treasury, the Attorney General, and the Secretary of the Interior were all forced to resign because of suspected or proven malfeasance. The Secretary of the Navy was shown to have been negligent—or worse—in awarding contracts. The Secretary of War, William W. Belknap, was found to have taken bribes from aspirants to traderships on Indian reservations; impeached by the House he escaped conviction only because Grant, "with great regret", accepted his hasty resignation. An even bigger scandal was the discovery of the "Whiskey Ring", a conspiracy of St. Louis distillers and Treasury officials to defraud the government of millions of dollars of excise duties. "Let no guilty man escape", was Grant's response to the Whiskey Ring revelations, but when the trail led to his own private secretary, the President saw to it that he was not punished.

The corruption of the Grant era was not confined to Washington. It spread throughout the country and into every level of government. Nor was it peculiar to the Republican party. Indeed, the most blatant and pervasive corruption of the period was perpetrated by Democrats—William Marcy Tweed's notorious ring in New York City. Through their control of Tammany Hall, the city's Democratic machine, and by means of an elaborate system of "kickbacks", payoffs, and bribes, Boss Tweed and his henchmen elevated graft into a fine art. In the late 1860s they plundered New York City of millions of dollars a year. By 1871, however, their misdeeds had become so flagrant as to provoke a reaction. The cartoonist, Thomas Nast, pilloried Tweed in *Harper's Weekly*, and the *New York Times* ran a series of articles exposing him. Finally a reform coalition led by the wealthy lawyer, Samuel J. Tilden, broke his power and sent him to jail, where he was to die in 1878. Asked on entering prison to state his occupation, Tweed replied in all seriousness, "Statesman". It was not quite as absurd as it may have sounded, for in contrast to the selfish rogues with whom Grant surrounded himself the Tweed Ring's activities had a redeeming side; its massive stealing provided the funds for an elaborate welfare system which embraced substantial aid to Catholic parochial schools and the large-scale distribution of food and fuel to the poor.

Reconstruction in the South

Meanwhile, as one shameful episode followed another in Washington, Radical Reconstruction ran its course in the South. Having no clearly formulated views about Reconstruction Grant was content, at least initially, to be guided by the Radical leaders in Congress. Throughout his first term he repeatedly used federal military power to suppress Southern white attempts to overthrow Republican state governments. But after 1872 or so, as the success of the Radical experiment grew more doubtful, he became increasingly reluctant to do so. Grant's gradual change of heart, mirroring that of the Northern public generally, helps explain why Southern whites were able largely to undo Radical Reconstruction by the time he left the White House.

The most novel feature of the state governments set up under the Radical plan of Reconstruction was black participation. Yet the term 'Black

Reconstruction', favored by later generations of white Southerners, is largely unwarranted. Blacks never even held public office in proportion to their numbers. No Southern state had a Negro governor. Only two Negroes won seats in the United States Senate—Hiram R. Revels and Blanche K. Bruce, both from Mississippi—and a mere fifteen served in the House of Representatives. Negroes were elected in sizable numbers to state legislatures but only in South Carolina did they make up the majority. There, indeed, blacks used their strength in the legislature to gain control of both the Republican party machinery and the apparatus of government and eventually learned to operate independently of white leaders. Black office-holders came from a variety of backgrounds. Some were Southern-born, others were from the North; perhaps a majority were ex-slaves, but a disproportionate number, especially in South Carolina, were free-born. While some black politicians were illiterate, they also included men of education and ability who had risen to positions of influence and responsibility. A good many, like Revels and Bishop Henry M. Turner, were ministers, either in the African Methodist Episcopal Church or the Baptist Church; Francis L. Cardozo of South Carolina, a graduate of the University of Glasgow, was a minister and a school principal; Robert Brown Elliott, also of South Carolina, was a prosperous lawyer. Other black leaders were planters, businessmen, artisans, or former house-servants. The one thing they had in common was that they were not fresh from the cotton fields. Taken as a whole they were probably about as well qualified for political office as their white counterparts—which may not be claiming much.

In all the reconstructed states except South Carolina, whites monopolized political leadership. Most prominent were Northerners who had moved South after the war. In the seven states reconstructed in 1868 four of the governors, ten of the fourteen senators, and twenty of the thirty-five Congressmen were from the North. Southern Democrats, followed by several generations of historians, indiscriminately applied to these new-comers the opprobrious term 'carpetbagger', implying that they were predatory adventurers prepared to make cynical use of the Negro vote. While some carpetbaggers fitted this description most were men of integrity and public spirit. Far from having gone South in search of political spoils, they had been attracted by its opportunities for investment, business, or agriculture. One of the best was Daniel H. Chamberlain, a Harvard graduate turned South Carolina planter who, as governor in 1874–6, gave his adopted state an honest and economical reform administration. Another was Adelbert Ames, a former Union general and a man of ability and sincerity; as governor of Mississippi he devoted himself to the protection of Negro rights.

Like the carpetbaggers the native Southern whites who held office in or supported the postwar Radical governments included both upright men and rogues. Their critics dubbed them 'scalawags'—a term of contempt said to have originated in Scalloway in the Shetlands where undersized cattle and horses were bred—and accused them of acting as tools of the conqueror in order to obtain office. There were indeed some notorious renegades: in Georgia, Joseph E. Brown, who had been wartime governor of the state, became Chief Justice under Radical rule. In South Carolina a former secessionist, Franklin J. Moses, Jr., suddenly became a Radical in 1867, and having been successively elected Speaker of the Assembly and governor, proceeded to disgrace both offices. But the majority of so-called scalawags were not inspired by unworthy motives. They included poor whites like those of the North Carolina and Alabama hill country who had long disliked slavery, opposed secession, and wanted an end to the dominance of the planter aristocracy. Many scalawag leaders were drawn from the ranks of well-to-do conservative planters and businessmen. Mostly prewar Whigs who had opposed secession, like James L. Alcorn, the first Reconstruction governor of Mississippi, they saw in Radical rule an opportunity to advance Southern interests and were prepared to accept Negro suffrage because they were confident of controlling it.

It is thus an oversimplification to think of Reconstruction as a period of conflict between black and white. Though racial prejudice tended to draw Southern whites together, they were to some extent divided by the sectional, party, and class tensions which had earlier characterized Southern politics and would do so again. The clash between up-country and low-country, the continuing influence of prewar political allegiances, the common people's resentment of the aristocracy—these were obscured but by no means eradicated. Nor were Southern Negroes an undifferentiated body. In South Carolina, for example, a rift opened up between two political factions which the historian Thomas Holt has labeled "blacks", meaning the mass of former slaves, and the more conservative and better-off "browns", often mulatto, who had been free since before the war.

Radical government in the South had substantial achievements to its credit. The new state constitutions were modernizing and reforming documents. The South testified to their worth by retaining them long after Reconstruction was over. They did away with property qualifications for voting and office-holding, provided for the more equal apportionment of legislative seats and for fairer tax systems, reformed penal codes and abolished imprisonment for debt, and made fuller provision for poor relief. Radical governments also repaired the ravages of war, rebuilding public buildings, roads, and bridges and restoring and expanding the Southern railroad system. They introduced universal public education with spectacular results: in South Carolina, for example, only 20,000 children (all white) had been enrolled in the public school system in 1860, but by 1873 some 50,000 white and 70,000 black pupils were at school.

There was, however, a darker side to Radical Reconstruction. Taxes rose to punitive levels and state debts soared astronomically. This was partly because the economic recovery measures and social welfare and educational programs were necessarily costly. Even so, public expenditure and debt were swollen by wholesale graft, corruption, and waste. Some of the worst examples came from South Carolina. The public printing-bill for a single session came to nearly $500,000; the legislature issued $1,590,000 worth of bonds to redeem bank notes worth $500,000; legislators charged as expenses an extraordinary range of items including wines and spirits, women's clothes, cradles, and coffins. True, the thieving of the Tweed Ring was on a far greater scale than anything that went on in the South. But wealthy New York City could afford to be dishonestly governed, whereas the impoverished South could not.

Black Aspirations and Achievements

Whereas under slavery the boundaries of interracial behavior had been clearly drawn and were well understood, the social upheaval that followed emancipation created widespread uncertainty. Only gradually did the two races adjust to the new reality, the whites by reluctantly acquiescing in the loss of their slave-property while endeavoring to maintain the color line, the blacks by cautiously exploring the limits of freedom. Ex-slaves found it difficult, even when it was not downright dangerous, to throw off the protective habits acquired during two centuries of bondage: the subservience, the forced good humor, the pretended ignorance. Even so, the freedmen soon abandoned work patterns associated with slavery. They refused, for example, to work in gangs under supervision. They exercised their option to work less hard than they had hitherto been forced to do and often insisted that their wives and children spent less time in the fields, more in the home or at school. Many freedmen displayed their independence by leaving their "white folks" and moving elsewhere, either in search of loved ones earlier sold away or because of dissatisfaction with the wages offered. Emancipated blacks generally acquired surnames and sometimes insisted in being addressed as 'mister' or 'miss'. Many couples, forbidden to marry during slavery, took the opportunity to formalize their unions, if only to legitimize their children or qualify for soldiers' pensions. Blacks also hastened to free their churches from white domination and thus indulge their wish for forms of worship they found more satisfying spiritually and emotionally.

With rare exceptions blacks did not act vengefully or assert their rights aggressively. What they wanted most was land, education and the vote—in that order. But although they were enfranchised, their other hopes were in varying degree frustrated. At the end of the war many freedmen expected 'forty acres and a mule'. This impression stemmed largely from the fact that, during the struggle, Sherman had ordered blacks to be settled on abandoned plantations on the Sea Islands off South Carolina and Georgia. But the federal government fought shy of general land distribution. Thaddeus Stevens advocated it strongly but most Congressmen, respectful of property rights, would not support so drastic a step. The most Congress would do was to modify the Homestead Act of 1862 so as to make available forty-six million acres of federal land in the South. Few Negroes benefited, however, for most of the land was of poor quality. A surprising number of blacks succeeded through their own efforts in becoming landowners, but the great majority became tenants and sharecroppers.

While the Freedmen's Bureau led the way in establishing schools for the freedmen, Northern charities and church organizations too were active in supplying funds and teachers—over 5,000 in fact. Northerners stopped short, however, of advocating racially mixed schools. The black passion for education was unmistakable. Freedmen young and old flocked to the classroom. As Booker T. Washington remarked: 'It was a whole race trying to go to school.' There were never enough schools, especially in rural areas, and school attendance was often brief and intermittent. Moreover, blacks did not always persevere when they realized that learning was hard work. Hence progress was limited and slow. At the end of the war perhaps 95 percent of Southern blacks could not read or write; in 1870 it was down to 81 percent, and in 1890 it was still 64 percent. Many of those classed as literate possessed only the rudiments of learning. Yet there was hope for the future in the fact that black education soon showed signs of self-sufficiency: as early as 1876 one-third of the teaching staff in South Carolina's black schools was black. This reflected the gains being made in higher education. Among the black colleges opened during Reconstruction—mainly through Northern philanthropy—were Fisk University, Howard University, and Hampton Institute. Institutions of this kind nurtured most of the black leaders of the next generation.

Instruments of Radical Rule

Although the Reconstruction governments initially attracted a substantial amount of white Southern support, they lacked a stable political base. Essentially puppet regimes, they depended on manipulation of the black vote and on military force. To mobilize black voters the Republicans relied on the Union League, a patriotic society founded in Philadelphia during the Civil War. During Reconstruction the League developed offshoots in the South, ostensibly to familiarize blacks with their newly won political responsibilities. But it turned out to be an agency, not for political education in the proper sense, but for carrying elections for the Republican party. League officials taught blacks that their interests were identical with those of the Republicans, instructed them who to vote for, and sometimes marked their ballot-papers for them. The League commonly falsified registration lists, too, and stuffed ballot-boxes.

While the presence of Union soldiers also helped bolster Radical rule there were too few of them to do the job alone: in November 1869 there were only 1,112 in Virginia and 716 in Mississippi. But they were reinforced by the largely black state militia who were used not only to maintain law and order but also to police elections and to protect Republican voters—a practice which contributed largely to Republican election victories.

The work of another Radical instrument, the Freedmen's Bureau, has been severely criticized—though from contradictory points of view. In its own day white Southerners accused it not only of corruption and incompetence but also of stirring up Negro discontent and of organizing the Negro vote for the Republican party. Some modern scholars, on the other hand, have charged the Bureau with letting the freedmen down, notably by collaborating with planters to keep them on the land, even at barely adequate wages, thus perpetuating their dependence on their former masters. But although some bureau agents no doubt did what contemporary critics alleged and others—perhaps a larger number—acted on the belief that blacks would work only when made to, the majority seem to have striven conscientiously to fulfill an extraordinarily difficult task. Though given inadequate powers and starved of resources the Bureau in fact accomplished a great deal during its brief existence. It dealt effectively with a massive refugee problem, took the lead in establishing the first black schools in the South, and attempted with some success to protect the freedmen from exploitation.

Undermining Radical Rule

To the majority of white Southerners Radical rule was an abomination. Bitterly resenting governmental corruption and, still more, the threat to white supremacy implied in Negro suffrage, they resorted to violent remedies. A number of secret terrorist societies appeared, the Ku Klux Klan being the most notorious. The Klan originated in Tennessee in 1866 and spread rapidly throughout the South. It had an elaborate ritual and was governed by officers with such fanciful titles as Grand Dragons, Grand Titans, Grand Cyclops, all presided over by an Imperial Wizard. In their efforts to counter the activities of the Union League the Klansmen at first confined themselves to intimidation; clad in white robes and hoods and burning fiery crosses, they rode out at night to frighten Negroes into compliance and especially into staying away from the polls. But when these methods proved ineffectual they turned to open violence. Negroes, carpetbaggers, and scalawags were shot, beaten, hanged, burned or driven out. From this to indiscriminate criminality was only a short step. By 1869 the Klan had lost all semblance of being a vigilante organization and had fallen into the hands of criminals bent on private gain and vengeance.

Congress responded to Klan violence with a series of measures designed to compel obedience to the Fourteenth and Fifteenth Amendments. The first, the Force Act of 1870, prescribed heavy penalties for anyone using force, bribery, or intimidation to prevent citizens from voting. It also placed Congressional elections under federal supervision. A second Force Act in 1871 provided for still tighter federal control and sterner punishment for offenders. Finally, the Ku Klux Klan Act of 1871 outlawed organizations like the Klan and authorized the President to suspend the writ of habeas corpus where lawlessness and terror prevailed. Grant enforced these measures vigorously. Federal troops were sent to the worst-affected areas, martial law was proclaimed, and hundreds of arrests made. By such means the Klan was effectively suppressed by the end of 1871.

Although the Force Acts easily passed Congress, they marked the peak of attempts to force Negro suffrage on the South. Many Northerners had never been enthusiastic about it. They swallowed it only as a means of protecting the freedmen from reenslavement and guarding against renewed rebellion. But by the early 1870s these bogeys had ceased to alarm and Northerners were becoming disenchanted with the results of Negro suffrage; perhaps expecting too much of newly enfranchised ex-slaves, they were disappointed at the readiness with which they acted as tools of unscrupulous white politicians. Still cherishing the ideal of local self-government, Northerners thought federal intervention in state affairs acceptable only as a last resort. They recognized, too, that only the Union army could preserve the troubled Radical regimes in the South.

By now wartime hatreds were diminishing. Some of the more extreme Radicals, like Stevens, had died; others, like Schurz, had become reconcilers. And despite Greeley's heavy defeat in the presidential election of 1872, he nonetheless spoke for many in the North when he urged that there be no more "talk of rebels and traitors", but that the hand of friendship should be held out to "Southern brethren" and "fellow countrymen". Such sentiments impelled the passage in May 1872 of an Amnesty Act restoring political rights to all but a few hundred ex-Confederates. In the same year, Congress allowed the Freedmen's Bureau to lapse.

Disillusion with Radical Reconstruction grew more widespread during Grant's second term. As the carpetbag regimes degenerated into fraud and exploitation, they excited increasing Northern repugnance. Moreover, political scandal in Washington diverted the attention of Congress and the public from the South. So did the long economic depression sparked off by the Panic of 1873. Hard times thrust new issues to the fore: after 1873 Congress spent less time discussing Reconstruction and more on tariff and monetary policies. In these circumstances Grant met little opposition when he quietly abandoned repression in the South. By no means a Radical, he had become increasingly reluctant to use the Force Acts. Recognizing that "the whole public are tired out with these outbreaks in the South", he turned a deaf ear to Radical appeals for federal protection.

The Senate's rejection of a new Force Bill in 1875 was a further sign of a diminishing desire to control Southern politics. True, Congress passed a new Civil Rights Act in 1875, guaranteeing equal rights in theaters, inns, and public conveyances, but the measure, adopted chiefly as a tribute to Sumner who had died the previous year, was merely the last gasp of an expiring crusade. It was never enforced.

Encouraged by the evidence that the Northern people had changed their minds about Reconstruction, Southerners launched fresh attempts to undermine Radical rule and restore white supremacy. Their task was simplified by the fact that most of the Southern whites who had earlier joined the Republicans had withdrawn their support. Disappointed in their hope of winning the confidence of black voters, they had also been alienated by the excesses of the carpetbag regimes. Strengthened by these defections the Democrats searched for methods of political control that would not provoke federal intervention but would nonetheless be effective in restoring 'home rule'. They found their answer in the so-called Mississippi Plan, devised in 1874 and put into effect in the following year's elections. It aimed at forcing the few remaining scalawags into the Democratic party and at inducing blacks not to vote. Where persuasion failed, illegal and extra-legal methods were employed. Rifle clubs and other semimilitary organizations openly marched and drilled in what were intended as displays of white power. Economic pressure was perhaps even more effective than force and terror. Politically active Negroes or those who simply voted the Republican ticket were refused jobs, denied tenancies, and charged high prices in the shops. These techniques, combined with shrewd political organization, gradually brought about the collapse of most of the carpetbag regimes. By 1876, the whites had recovered control of every Southern state except Louisiana, South Carolina, and Florida.

The Disputed Election of 1876 and the Compromise of 1877

By a remarkable irony the electoral votes of these three states turned out to be crucial to the outcome of the 1876 presidential election. When the returns came in the Democratic candidate, Samuel J. Tilden of New York, had a clear majority of popular votes over his Republican rival, Rutherford B. Hayes of Ohio. But neither candidate possessed a clear majority in the electoral college. Tilden was acknowledged to have 184 electoral votes, one short of a majority, and Hayes 166. But there was dispute over the nineteen electoral votes of the three Southern states still under carpetbag rule. These were claimed by both parties; all three states had submitted two sets of returns. Months of wrangling followed. Hayes needed all nineteen votes to win the Presidency, Tilden only one. Who was really entitled to the disputed votes is impossible to say, for there had been irregularities on both sides: the Democrats had resorted to intimidation while the Republicans had been guilty of fraud. The problem is to decide whether a free election would have benefited Hayes more than a fair count would have helped Tilden. Most scholars hold that Hayes was probably entitled to the votes of South Carolina and Louisiana but that Tilden probably carried Florida and ought therefore to have been President. But in February 1877 the electoral commission set up by Congress to settle the issue decided, by a strictly partisan vote of eight Republicans to seven Democrats, to award all the contested votes to Hayes.

The Democrats were indignant at what they regarded as a brazen attempt to cheat them of a prize they had rightfully won. They threatened to obstruct the formal count in Congress, thus leaving the country without a President when Grant's term expired. But hard bargaining behind the scenes between Southern Democrats and Hayes Republicans finally produced a set of informal understandings—the so-called Compromise of 1877—that broke the deadlock and averted an interregnum. In return for accepting Hayes's election the Democrats were assured that the new President would withdraw the remaining federal troops from the South, appoint a leading Southerner to his Cabinet, and look sympathetically on Southern demands for railroad subsidies. Immediately after his inauguration Hayes fulfilled the pledge to withdraw the troops. The Republican governments in Louisiana, Florida, and South Carolina promptly collapsed and Reconstruction was over.

To a far greater extent than the Civil War, Reconstruction left a legacy of sectional and racial bitterness. For the South—or at any rate the white South—Reconstruction was a traumatic ordeal, 'a long, dark, night' that left a lasting mark on the region's psychology. Moreover, along with the Civil War, it provided a facile explanation for all the South's ills. Thus by 1877 reunion had been achieved, but not reconciliation. All that had happened was that white Americans had reached a *modus vivendi* at the expense of the blacks. The North, which had never committed itself wholly to racial democracy, was now ready to put the idea into cold storage and to abandon the race problem to the South.

14. *The New South and White Supremacy, 1877–1914*

Although the South emerged from Reconstruction shorn of some of the features that had set it apart from the rest of the country, it still retained much of its distinctiveness. The 'peculiar institution' had gone, together with the plantation system. Yet planters survived as a class, even though they were less dominant politically and economically than before the war, and the plantation persisted as a unit of ownership if not of production. The South remained, moreover, a predominantly rural, agricultural and labor-intensive one-crop region. Its population was still overwhelmingly nativeborn: despite inducements by the Southern states the tides of immigration still flowed mainly to the North. In the South the social structure continued to be more stratified than in the North, less fluid, less democratic. The South also clung to a distinctive religious subculture, a heady blend of fundamentalism and revivalism that earned the region's heartland the name of the Bible Belt. Most important of all was the persistence of a unique racial pattern. As late as 1900, 90 percent of America's blacks lived in the South, where they comprised a third of the population.

While some of the old sectional peculiarities endured, new ones appeared. The traumas of defeat and military occupation unified the South politically, and obscured its sectional and class divisions. Following the collapse of Radical rule the South became, at least at the national level, a land of one-party politics: in every presidential election in the next seventy-five years, except in 1928, the 'Solid South' voted Democratic. Meanwhile a distinctive set of economic arrangements—share-tenancy and the crop-lien system—in which produce and labor took place of money, came to characterize Southern agriculture. Towards the end of the century the South had acquired some additional badges of identity: the poll-tax, the literacy test, the white primary and the lynch mob. In addition the South as a whole was cursed with an un-American level of poverty. Thus its character was as singular in this period as under the old plantation regime.

Southern Agriculture

Southern agriculture was slow to recover from the war. The South had lost a third of its horses and mules and half its agricultural machinery. With defeat came the collapse of the Confederate currency and the burden of confiscatory taxes. Not until 1879 was cotton production back to the level of 1860. By 1894 the crop was twice as large as before the war and by 1914 had almost doubled again. The exhausted soils of South Carolina and Georgia were restored by the use of fertilizers and new cotton lands were developed in Arkansas and Texas. Production of the South's other great staples—tobacco, sugar and rice—also expanded and with the advent of the railroad and the refrigerator car, vegetable- and fruit-farming sprang up in Florida and Louisiana.

Contemporaries believed that the Civil War had resulted in the breakup of the old plantations into small farms. They cited the census of 1880, which reported that since 1850 the number of Southern farms had doubled, while the size of the average farm had been halved. But the rise of the small farm was a statistical mirage. Farms were more numerous because large amounts of new acreage had been brought under cultivation. Moreover, what the census-takers counted as separate farms were often in reality subdivisions of plantations, worked by tenants or sharecroppers. The prewar type of planter, who had lived on his estates and had managed production, tended to disappear. In the lean postwar years many planters and farmers were unable to hold on to their heavily mortgaged and heavily taxed estates and ownership tended to pass to city-based businessmen, many of them Northerners, or to banks and corporations. Mainly for this reason the proportion of Southern white farmers who owned their own land fell from about four-fifths to two-thirds during the Reconstruction period and white farm tenancy rose correspondingly.

Emancipation gave blacks a mobility which white planters attempted to limit by a variety of legal and extra-legal means: antienticement laws, vagrancy laws, concerted action about hiring-terms, and sheer terrorism. But the intense competition for labor that developed after the war tended to nullify these efforts. Planters had to recognize the blacks' newly-acquired bargaining power and were thus unable, as they would have liked, to preserve their holdings as single, large-scale units worked by gangs. Only a tiny proportion of the freed blacks possessed the capital to become landowners in the immediate postwar years. The rest became wage-earning laborers or, more commonly, rented land in exchange for a share of the crop—an arrangement they generally preferred to the wage system because it gave them a measure of independence in operating their farms.

Share-tenantry and the crop-lien system which grew up alongside it became for the next half-century the distinguishing features of Southern agriculture. Both were products of the lack of an adequate credit system. Because of a chronic shortage of cash many planters could not pay wages to their laborers, while laborers could not obtain credit to become landowners or even in many cases to pay a money rent. Two broad kinds of contractual arrangements consequently developed—sharecropping and share-renting. Under sharecropping, the laborer tilled a plot belonging to his landlord in exchange for a house and a mule, tools, seed and a share of the crop, generally about half. Share-renters, by contrast, provided their own accommodation and farming supplies but paid a proportion of the crop, usually a quarter to a third, as rent. Originally most sharecroppers were black and most share-renters white, but by 1900 or so whites were in the majority in both variants of the system. Share-tenantry was inefficient and degrading, depriving both croppers and tenants of the incentive to care for the land and subjecting them to close landlord supervision.

The crop-lien system, an arrangement whereby local storekeepers furnished credit and supplies in return for a lien or mortgage on the farmer's share of the future crop, likewise had deplorable consequences. It met the farmer's need for credit but tended to perpetuate one-crop agriculture because the lien-holder tended to insist on a readily salable product, usually cotton. Concentration on cotton was bad for the soil, led to overproduction and falling prices, and made the South dependent on other sections for products it could have raised itself. The lien system also had damaging social consequences. To compensate for the risks they ran storekeepers charged high prices for supplies and high rates of interest for credit. Not infrequently they took advantage of borrowers' ignorance to inflate the amounts owed. Sharecroppers and tenants thus found themselves perpetually in debt, continuing year after year in a state of peonage, under lien to the same creditor and tied to the same plot of land. Given such a system, reminiscent in many ways of slavery, it was not surprising that the Southern farmer, whether black or white, should have remained shiftless, improvident and undernourished.

Southern Industry

After the Civil War many Southerners became convinced that their economic salvation lay in industrialization. The Old South, they reasoned, had depended too heavily on slavery and agriculture. In future the South must embrace *laissez-faire* capitalism, imitate the North and develop her own industries. By the 1880s a group of Southern editors was preaching the gospel of industrialization with almost evangelical fervor. One of them, Henry W. Grady of the Atlanta *Constitution*, gave the New South creed its classic formulation in a celebrated speech in New York in 1886. A series of industrial fairs, beginning with the Atlanta International Cotton Exposition of 1881, aimed at publicizing the South's industrial potentialities and at drawing the attention of Northern capitalists to the new opportunities it offered.

Paradoxically, the vision of an industrialized future was accompanied, and in a sense legitimized, by nostalgic devotion to an agrarian past. While propagandists for the New South advocated a new order they were careful not to repudiate the old, often embellishing their doctrines with sentimental tributes to the Old South. In this way they adapted their standpoint to the romantic impulses that were coming to dominate the Southern mind. The cult of the 'Lost Cause', expressed in annual reunions of United Confederate Veterans and in the appearance of war memorials in courthouse squares, generated a deep emotional response. Meanwhile a Southern literary revival, of which George Washington Cable's *Old Creole Days* (1879), Joel Chandler Harris's *Uncle Remus* (1881), and Thomas Nelson Page's *In Old Virginia* (1887) were characteristic products, contributed to the idealization of the *ante-bellum* plantation regime.

In the closing decades of the nineteenth century the dreams of the New South zealots seemed likely to be realized. Northern capital made possible the expansion of the Southern railroad system and stimulated coal and iron production in the Appalachian mountain regions. Between 1875 and 1900 Southern production of coal increased tenfold and that of pig iron seventeenfold. Birmingham, Alabama, situated in a region rich in iron-ore, coal, and limestone, enjoyed a meteoric rise as an iron and steel manufacturing center; Chattanooga and Knoxville, too, sprouted smokestacks and blast furnaces. Louisiana's vast sulfur deposits and the equally rich bauxite deposits of Arkansas began to be exploited and at the turn of the century the development of petroleum fields in the Southwest, especially the discovery of the great Spindletop gusher at Beaumont, Texas, in 1901, heralded the start of the modern era of oil production.

The most spectacular expansion occurred, however, in the textile industry. Southern cotton manufacturing had begun before the Civil War, but in the 1880s a movement 'to bring the spindles to the cotton' took on the character of a civic crusade. Between 1880 and 1900 the number of Southern cotton-mills, chiefly in the Carolinas, Georgia, and Alabama, rose from 158 to 416 (about half the national total), the amount of capital invested in Southern textile mills increased sevenfold, and the number of workers rose from 17,000 to 98,000. The proximity of raw cotton and an unending supply of cheap labor gave the South the advantage of lower costs and by 1904 the region was producing more cotton goods than New England, the traditional center of cotton manufacturing. Laborers in the cotton-mills consisted of poor whites recruited from the nearby hill country. Men were in a minority. In the four leading textile states in 1890, men made up 35 percent of the workers, women 40 percent, and children the remaining 25 percent. Wages were low, hours of labor long. Adult male spinners in North Carolina in the 1880s and 1890s received about a third less than in New England. Low wages were mainly responsible for the high incidence of pellagra and other dietary diseases. The mill villages of the

Appalachian Piedmont resembled industrial fiefs, owned, run, and policed by the mill companies in almost feudal fashion. Virtually all the workers lived in miserable, company-owned shanties. They were often paid in scrip, redeemable only in company-owned stores. Company schools and company churches testified to the completeness of the control exercised over the lives of the operatives. But little could be done to improve labor conditions in the face of *laissez-faire* state governments and the widespread conviction, fostered by employers, that nothing should be done to handicap Southern factories in their competition with New England. A series of strikes in the Carolinas and Georgia between 1898 and 1902, organized by fledgling textile unions, collapsed when management resorted to collective lockouts, dismissed union members, and evicted them from their homes.

Lumbering also became an important Southern industry: by the end of the century it exceeded textiles in product value. Southern forests, a powerful magnet to Northern lumber syndicates, were ruthlessly stripped. The manufacture of tobacco, the South's oldest staple crop, also experienced a boom. Between 1885 and 1900 the industry was revolutionized. The spread of bright-leaf tobacco-growing, brought about by the new fashion of cigarette smoking, combined with the aggressive tactics of a new breed of Southern entrepreneur, transferred leadership in production and manufacture from Virginia to North Carolina. Richmond, formerly the hub of the tobacco industry, yielded pride of place to the raw new towns of Durham and Winston-Salem. What had been a handicraft industry was thoroughly mechanized, and control became highly concentrated. The dominant figure was James Buchanan Duke, who displayed the same organizing drive and adopted the same ruthless methods as Carnegie and Rockefeller. Duke poured large sums into advertizing, systematically squeezed out competition by undercutting and by cornering supplies of glycerine and liquorice. In 1890 he brought together five of the leading companies to form the American Tobacco Company, which by 1904 controlled three-quarters of all tobacco production.

Though the growth of industry gave the South a more diversified economy, progress was less impressive than it seemed. At the end of the century the South had a smaller proportion of the country's factories—about 10 percent—than it had had in 1860. As late as 1910 only about 15 percent of the Southern people were engaged in manufacturing. Moreover Southern industry was not the most profitable kind. Much of it was extractive and even in the most highly developed branches of manufacturing, such as textiles, the South tended to produce unfinished goods which were sent North for final processing. That the region remained industrially backward could be mainly attributed to defeat in war and lack of capital. But a further disadvantage was the system of freight-rate and price differentials operated by Northern business interests with the object of discouraging competitors. Thus the South remained a tributary of the North, and largely in consequence continued to lag behind the rest of the nation in wealth and living standards. In 1900 when the national average in per capita wealth was $1,165, the figure for the South was only $509. Poverty brought other evils in its train—lower standards of literacy and debilitating diseases like hookworm and pellagra. Thus for all the talk of the New South, the region below the Mason–Dixon line was in reality a stagnant and economically handicapped rural corner of a booming industrial nation.

Bourbon Rule

The men who ran the post-Reconstruction Democratic administrations in the South became known to their opponents as Bourbons. But the analogy was inexact for, unlike the French royal house recalled after Napoleon's downfall, they did not represent the restoration of the old regime or seek to perpetuate its values. Mainly middle-class businessmen and industrialists rather than members of the old·planter aristocracy, their economic attitudes were similar to those of the Northern capitalists dominant in the Republican party. Thus William Mahone, whose political machine controlled Virginia politics from 1879 until his death in 1895 and who was perhaps the most powerful Southern politician of his generation, was a self-made railroad executive. Likewise the 'Triumvirate' which dominated postwar Georgia politics—Joseph E. Brown, John B. Gordon, and Alfred H. Colquitt—were prominently involved in railroads, mining, and other business enterprises. And while there were many prewar Democrats in the new governments, including some like Brown who had been prominent in the Confederacy, most of the leaders were former Whigs who had played a leading part in the 'redemption' of the South from Radical Reconstruction.

In general the Redeemers, as they liked to call themselves, pursued *laissez-faire* policies but, like the Republican regimes they succeeded, granted tax exemptions and other favors to railroads, utilities, and factory-owners. They reacted against the financial extravagances of Reconstruction by making retrenchment the cardinal virtue, cutting taxes and public expenditure. Public education, now looked upon with suspicion as a Radical innovation, was so starved of funds that, but for the help given by Northern philanthropists, notably through the Peabody Fund and the Slater Fund, the school systems established during Reconstruction might well have collapsed. As it was they were seriously crippled. The amounts spent per pupil were slashed and the average length of the school year, only a hundred days during Reconstruction, fell to about eighty days after Redemption. The South's educational problems were, admittedly, more serious than those of the North. It had proportionately more children to educate: families were bigger and there was less money available. Sparsity of settlement was a further source of expense; so was the self-imposed burden of maintaining two separate school systems, one for each race. But the South's special difficulties do not wholly account for the shortcomings of her educational system. The region's political leaders were in truth indifferent or hostile to public support of education. That explained why in 1900 Kentucky was the only Southern state with a compulsory school-attendance law, whereas every Northern state but two had them. The consequences were what might have been expected. In only three Southern states was the proportion of white children attending school more than 50 percent in 1900. And in addition to more than two and a half million black illiterates, there were more than one million white illiterates. That was 12 percent of the white population of the South. The illiteracy rate in the North Atlantic states was only 1.6 percent, and it should be remembered that most of the North's illiterates were recently arrived immigrants.

The passion for economy also had evil effects on the penal system. To save money on prison accommodation state governments adopted the practice of leasing convicts as cheap labor to railroads, mines, and lumber camps. Since there was little or no attempt to supervise convict camps the inmates were often neglected or brutally treated. Despite repeated public outcries the convict-leasing system stayed unreformed and in some states survived until the 1920s.

The reputation the Redeemer governments enjoyed for honesty in public office was undeserved. While in aggregate less public money was misappropriated than during Reconstruction, financial laxity and irregularity were widespread. During the 1880s no fewer than nine state treasurers either were convicted of defalcation or peculation, or absconded leaving unexplained deficits. Lesser officials, too, embezzled large sums. Such scandals tended to cancel out the savings from retrenchment. Moreover, they demonstrated the unsoundness of the Redeemers' case that lack of fidelity to public trust was a peculiarity of carpetbag and Negro rule.

.The parsimony of the Redeemer governments involved also the scaling-down or 'readjustment' of state debts. By the simple expedient of repudiation nine of the former Confederate states contrived to reduce their debts by about half. Supporters of repudiation argued that there was no moral obligation to repay debts largely incurred through Radical corruption and extravagance, but more conservative Redeemers were opposed to readjustment as being damaging to state honor and likely to discourage the investment of Northern capital. The issue generated sufficient controversy to bring about the temporary overthrow of the Redeemers in certain states. But if readjustment was the most divisive issue of the period there were repeated struggles in the late 1870s and early 1880s, generally of a country-versus-town character, over a score of local issues ranging from railroad regulation to lien-laws. Short-lived local parties, usually calling themselves Independents, won much support from small farmers and attempted, though with scant success, to challenge the hegemony of the wealthy classes. Such attempts testified to the persistence of class and sectional antagonisms and to the fact that the South did not become a region of exclusively one-party politics the moment Reconstruction was over. The Solid South dates in fact only from the middle 1880s, when the Democrats had quelled the last Independent revolt.

The Erosion of Black Freedom

One reason why poor white farmers failed to capture the Democratic organization was that the Redeemers used the black vote against them. When Reconstruction ended blacks in some areas were promptly disfranchised, mainly by fraud and intimidation, but elsewhere they continued to vote in large numbers. This was because the wealthy men who ruled the South were prepared to countenance voting by a race who constituted no threat to their own status and whose·political conduct they believed they could control. To attract black support they protected the freedmen's right to vote against the attacks of white farmers and also appointed blacks to minor offices. There were more black office-holders in some states than there had been during Reconstruction. Blacks also continued to sit in some state legislatures and at least one Negro Congressman was returned in every election down to 1900 with the exception of that of 1886.

Black civil rights were eroded more quickly. Supreme Court decisions deprived blacks of the guarantee of equal treatment which the Fourteenth Amendment and the Civil Rights Acts of 1866 and 1875 had sought to confer. In the *Slaughter House Cases* (1873) the Court held that the "privileges and immunities" clause of the Fourteenth Amendment did not protect state citizenship rights, which were so defined as to include all civil rights, but only the narrow group of rights flowing from national citizenship. In *United States* v. *Cruikshank* (1875) the Court decided that the Fourteenth Amendment protected the rights and privileges of citizens only when they were infringed by the action of a state. The same reasoning was followed in the *Civil Rights Cases* of 1883, when the Court ruled that the Civil Rights Act of 1875, forbidding racial discrimination in places of public resort, was unconstitutional. The decision meant in effect that the federal government had no authority to protect blacks against discrimination by private individuals. It also opened the way to social segregation.

But the Redeemers were in no more hurry to raise racial barriers than to eliminate blacks from politics. In practice, therefore, the color line was less strictly drawn than it would be in the twentieth century. In schools, churches, and places of residence, segregation had become the norm even during Reconstruction. But in hotels and theaters and on railroads and streetcars there was no uniform pattern. In some places *de facto* segregation prevailed, in others, especially in the cities, blacks and whites shared facilities on an equal basis. But with the rise of Populism in the 1890s Southern racial policies and practices became harsher. The Conservatives, alarmed at the attempts of Populist leaders to unite poor farmers of both races against them, acquiesced in the demands of poor white, racial extremists for an end to Negro voting and for rigid segregation. The Fifteenth Amendment prohibited the disfranchisement of Negroes as such, but the same result could be achieved indirectly. Mississippi showed the way in 1890 by adopting new and elaborate suffrage qualifications, including payment of a poll-tax, a literacy test, and a residential requirement. Over the next decade or so the other Southern states passed similar laws. There was little protest from the North. In 1890 Congressman Henry Cabot Lodge tried to protect the black vote by introducing a measure into the House providing for the federal supervision of elections. But after Southerners blocked what they stigmatized as the Force Bill, there was no more Northern interference. Then in 1898 the South won an even greater victory when the Supreme Court, in *Mississippi* v. *Williams*, placed its seal of approval on state laws designed to exclude blacks from the polls by indirection. Such laws proved extremely effective. They made the payment of an optional, complicated, and burdensome poll-tax a prerequisite for voting and established literacy tests so framed and administered as to disqualify Negroes who failed to satisfy local registrars of their ability not only to read but also to interpret the Constitution. Almost at a stroke the number of Negro voters was reduced to a handful. Louisiana, for example, which had 130,344 registered black voters in 1896 had only 5,320 in 1900. Moreover, between 1896 and 1915 every Southern state adopted statewide Democratic primaries and then excluded Negro voters from them—the only meaningful elections in a one-party system. Poll-taxes and literacy tests had the further consequence—in part intended—of disfranchising not only blacks but also many whites as well. Between 1897 and 1904 the number of registered white voters fell by 44 percent. To provide a loophole for poor whites through the property and literacy tests Louisiana introduced a 'grandfather clause' in 1898, giving the vote to all male adults whose fathers or grandfathers had voted before 1867. Other states followed suit. Even so many yeoman farmers and poor whites continued to be denied the ballot. Thus the Southern political structure was less democratic in the early twentieth century than it had been in 1860.

Accompanying disfranchisement and in some states running ahead of it was segregation by statute. The first of the Jim Crow laws, as they were known, was that passed by Florida in 1887, requiring separate accommodation for the races in trains. Mississippi followed suit in 1888, Texas in 1889, Louisiana in 1890, Alabama, Arkansas, Kentucky, and Georgia in

1891. When the Louisiana law was challenged in *Plessy* v. *Ferguson* (1896) the Supreme Court upheld it, ruling that Negro rights were not infringed by separate transport facilities providing that the facilities were equal. In *Cumming* v. *Board of Education* (1899) it extended the principle of "separate but equal" to schools. These historic decisions set the pattern of race relations in the South for half a century. The principle of segregation was systematically extended by state and local law to every human activity: streetcars, parks, theaters, hotels, hospitals, residential districts, even cemeteries. To some extent the Jim Crow codes simply gave legal sanction to prevailing practices, but they were more comprehensive and rigid, and more strictly enforced than anything that had gone before.

In dissenting from the Plessy decision, Justice John M. Harlan predicted that it "would stimulate aggression, more or less brutal, upon the admitted rights of colored citizens . . .". He was soon proved right. Race hatred, fanned by white-supremacy campaigns, led to a spate of mob attacks on black residential areas. In Wilmington, North Carolina in 1898 whites rampaged through the Negro ghetto, killing eleven blacks and chasing hundreds into the woods. There were similar outbreaks in Atlanta the same year and in New Orleans in 1900. Even more odious was the spread of lynching. Lynching was common, of course, in the frontier West as well as in the South. But in the West it was usually the result of the absence or weakness of the law; in the South it was resorted to in defiance of law, often after trial and conviction, in order to gratify mob passions. Lynching, which reached its peak in the 1890s, when there were 1,875 instances in the country as a whole, assumed an increasingly Southern and racial character. Comparing the decades 1889–99 and 1899–1909 one finds that the proportion of lynchings taking place in the South increased from 82 to 92 percent and the proportion of black victims from 67.8 to 88.6 percent.

Southern whites commonly defended lynching as a defense of white womanhood against Negro sexual assault. But investigation has revealed that in the period 1889–1918 rape or attempted rape was not even alleged in more than one-sixth of the cases, that many of those so accused were innocent, and that no fewer than fifty of the lynched Negroes were women, some of them pregnant. In fact the most frequent inciting cause of lynching was murder, while theft, insult, or damage to property also accounted for a substantial number of cases. Scenes of sadism and barbarity often accompanied Southern lynchings. Torture, mutilation, and burning at the stake were among the horrors perpetrated by lynch mobs in their determination to keep the Negro in his place. Not until 1918 was a Southern white convicted for his part in a lynching.

Denied the vote, legally impotent, rigidly segregated, in constant danger from individual or collective white violence, and branded as bestial and degraded by the Southern white racial credo that developed along with the caste system, blacks remained a cruelly—indeed, a uniquely—deprived minority. Fifty years after emancipation the great majority were still tied to the cotton fields in a condition of dependence, even in some cases of virtual peonage. Those who had moved to cities and towns (the proportion of black urban-dwellers more than doubled between 1870 and 1910) found themselves increasingly restricted to the more menial and less well-paid occupations. In 1865 Negro artisans and craftsmen had heavily outnumbered whites in the South, but both there and in the North trade-union pressure and the growing employment of white women, together with the racial segregation this invariably entailed, gradually excluded blacks from many skilled trades, including some they had traditionally monopolized, such as tobacco manufacturing. In addition they were almost wholly debarred from the newer industries, such as textiles.

Yet the familiar generalization that the freed blacks were hardly better off than they had been under slavery is unwarranted. There was a substantial improvement in black standards of living in the half-century after emancipation and a corresponding reduction in black mortality-rates. Economic studies have further revealed a dramatic rise in black per capita agricultural income, though most of the gain occurred in the immediate postwar years. At the same time black land-ownership continued to increase: by 1910 twenty percent of black farmers owned their land. Black businesses, too, grew markedly in number and size in the last two decades of the century, despite a high failure-rate. The most spectacular advances were made by enterprises catering for black customers. Black-owned insurance companies and banks, often originating in long-established fraternal orders or burial and mutual-benefit societies, were established in the 1880s, especially in Richmond, Virginia. Ironically, such enterprises owed much of their prosperity to the fact that whiteowned insurance companies and banks discriminated against black customers by charging higher premiums and interest-rates. Racial discrimination also worked to the advantage of those blacks offering personal services, such as undertakers, barbers and shopkeepers. The number of black businessmen, and for that matter of black professional people, was proportionately much smaller than in the white community and, in general, they were far less wealthy. But the rising black capitalist was one sign among many that the progress of the race had not been completely stultified.

Black Responses: Accommodation and Protest

That blacks should embrace the capitalist virtues of thrift, enterprise, and hard work, while accommodating themselves to white supremacy, became the basis of the doctrine evolved by Booker T. Washington, the leading Negro spokesman in the generation after Reconstruction. Born into slavery on a Virginia plantation in 1856, the son of a slave mother and a white father, Washington was head of Tuskegee Institute, a Negro college in Alabama, from 1881 until his death in 1915. At Tuskegee Washington put into practice his belief that, in the circumstances in which blacks found themselves, their education should be mainly vocational and practical rather then intellectual. Washington set forth his philosophy of race relations at the Cotton States Exposition in Atlanta in 1895 in a speech which brought him national recognition. Conspicuously ignoring the question of political rights, he advised blacks to avoid agitation for social equality and concentrate instead on economic advancement. "Cast down your bucket where you are," was his advice, "cast it down in agriculture, in mechanics, in commerce, in domestic service and in the professions." Only thus would blacks become worthy of the privileges they hoped ultimately to acquire. Washington even endorsed segregation, albeit obliquely: "In all things that are purely social we can be as separate as the fingers, yet one as the hand in all things essential to mutual progress."

Some Negro leaders strongly dissented. Black Northern intellectuals, in particular, were critical of the Atlanta Compromise, as Washington's philosophy became known. William Monroe Trotter bitterly attacked it in the pages of the Boston *Guardian* and William Edward Burghardt Du Bois, the leading black scholar of the day, subjected it to searching examination in a famous book, *The Souls of Black Folk* (1903). Du Bois argued that Washington's conciliatory approach was a betrayal of black rights and that his stress on industrial education ignored the needs of the 'talented tenth' who provided Negro leadership and might condemn blacks to permanently menial positions. In 1905 Du Bois and other militants founded the Niagara Movement, which demanded for the Negro race "every single right that belongs to a freeborn American, political, civil and social". Nevertheless the great majority of blacks accepted the Atlanta Compromise and were content with Washington's leadership.

Washington's hope that accommodation would open more widely the door of economic advancement to his race was not borne out. But his moderation secured the goodwill of Southern whites as well as the support of wealthy Northern industrialists like Carnegie and Rockefeller for his educational programs. He thus came to enjoy unrivaled power and influence, dispensing virtually all the funds provided by Northern white philanthropists for black causes. By a combination of guile and ruthlessness, he built up the 'Tuskegee Machine', an elaborate network of agencies which gave him control of most black organizations and institutions. He owned several black newspapers and determined the editorial policies of most of the rest; the leading black churches, too, looked to him for guidance. Moreover, despite his advice to blacks not to look to politics for salvation, he played an active political role, becoming Theodore Roosevelt's leading confidential adviser on political appointments, not only of blacks but of Southerners generally.

Recent research has also revealed that Washington was secretly more assertive on behalf of his race than his public utterances led one to suppose. For example, he covertly sponsored and partially financed court suits designed to test the validity of Negro disfranchisement laws and other props of the white-supremacy regime. In 1904 he was instrumental, along with others, in instigating a successful action against the exclusion of blacks from juries, and in 1911 in securing a Supreme Court decision outlawing peonage, or involuntary servitude for debt. Later generations of Negro leaders have echoed the criticisms of Du Bois and Trotter and rejected Washington's approach as being too passive and compliant. But his policy may have been the only effective one in an age of intense racial bigotry.

The 1910 census showed that America's black population was still overwhelmingly rural: three out of four blacks lived in rural areas and nine out of ten were in the South. But ever since the Civil War blacks had been leaving the land at about the same rate as the whites—and for the same reasons. They were attempting to escape rural poverty and grasp the expanded economic opportunities created by the industrial revolution. In abandoning the worn-out cotton fields of the old Confederacy blacks headed for the industrial cities of the New South and, more particularly after 1900, for those of the North. By 1910, there were more than a dozen cities with more than 40,000 Negroes. Washington and New York had 90,000 apiece; New Orleans, Baltimore, and Philadelphia over 80,000. That only one of these five cities was in the Deep South emphasized the growing northward drift of the Negro population. But while blacks outnumbered whites in Charleston, Savannah, and Baton Rouge and several other medium-sized Southern cities and represented almost one-third of Washington's inhabitants, they as yet constituted only a small minority of the population of the great Northern cities—a mere 2½ percent of that of New York, for example.

On moving North Negroes ran full tilt into uncompromising racial hostility. Alarmed at the prospect of black competition for housing and jobs, and fearing that an influx of Negro voters would strengthen corrupt political machines, whites established an increasingly rigid pattern of discrimination and exclusion. Hitherto, though concentrated in certain areas, most Northern urban Negroes had lived in mixed neighborhoods. Now, however, as the black population expanded, whites sought to confine it to particular sections—usually the least desirable ones—a practice sanctioned in some cases by municipal segregation ordinances. By 1914 the urban Negro ghetto had become a permanent feature of the American scene. In places like San Juan Hill and Harlem in New York, Philadelphia's Seventh Ward, Chicago's South Side, and Atlanta's West End were to be found

conditions henceforth increasingly characteristic of black life: slum housing, inadequate sanitation and policing, inferior education, exceptionally
high incidences of disease, infant mortality, crime and delinquency. Racial
prejudice made it difficult for blacks to secure any but the most menial
laborious jobs. Trade unions imposed racial barriers and many employers
refused to hire blacks either because of their alleged inefficiency or because
of the objections of white workers. The result was that male blacks formed
a permanent pool of unemployed, regularly drawn upon for strike-break-
ing. Negro women, however, were much in demand as domestic servants,
a circumstance that largely explained why women generally outnumbered
men among the urban black population.

Segregation now became the rule not only in the churches but also in
other areas in which the races had formerly commingled. By the early
twentieth century urban blacks in the North found themselves increasingly
debarred from hotels, restaurants, parks, and other places of public resort.
They consequently began to establish their own segregated facilities.
Negro churches grew, Negro business, civic, and welfare institutions
sprang into existence, the Negro press expanded.

The social tensions created by Negro migration to the city exploded
periodically into interracial violence. The worst examples took place in the
South, the Atlanta race riot of 1906 being especially bloody. But vicious
race riots were almost as common in Northern cities. In New York the
mutual animosities of blacks and Irish immigrants—perhaps the most deep-
seated and persistent example of inter-group hatred in American history—
produced regular clashes and in 1900 led to the worst example of racial
violence since the draft riots of the Civil War. More terrible—and its
consequences more far-reaching—was the Springfield, Illinois riot of 1908
in which two blacks were lynched, four whites were killed, and a hundred
people injured. These events, occurring a stone's throw from Lincoln's old
home and only a mile from his tomb, shocked the nation and induced a
group of white liberals, led by the editor, Oswald Garrison Villard, grandson of the abolitionist, William Lloyd Garrison, to issue a call for a conference on Lincoln's birthday in 1909. Out of it came the National
Association for the Advancement of Colored People, pledged to work for
the abolition of segregation, equal voting rights and educational opportunities for blacks, and the enforcement of the Fourteenth and Fifteenth
Amendments. Initially most of the officials of the NAACP were white, but
most of the rank and file were better-off Negroes. Most of the members
of Du Bois's declining Niagara Movement joined the new organization and
Du Bois himself became editor of its widely circulated magazine, *Crisis*.
The NAACP agitated against lynching and against discrimination in voting, education, civil rights, and housing, relying chiefly on litigation to
attain its ends. It won an important victory in 1915 when the Supreme

Court declared the Oklahoma and Maryland grandfather clauses unconstitutional, and another in 1917, when the Court invalidated a Louisville
ordinance sanctioning residential segregation. Another new organization,
the National Urban League, concerned itself with the economic plight of
urban blacks, especially in the North. It was founded in 1911 by an alliance
of conservative Negroes close to Booker T. Washington and white philanthropists and social workers. Besides acting as a social-welfare agency, the
League directed its efforts mainly at broadening black employment opportunities. But its attempts to persuade employers to engage black workers
and to break down the discriminatory attitudes of AFL unions met with
little success.

15. *Taming the West*, 1865–1900

The Wild West

By the end of the Civil War advancing pioneers had pushed the line of settlement some way beyond the Mississippi and had leapfrogged across the continent to establish a bridgehead on the Pacific coast. But between these two frontiers, fifteen hundred miles apart, a vast wilderness, comprising nearly half the continent, still awaited the settler's plow. It was a varied land, made up of three distinct physiographic provinces: the Great Plains, which extended from the ninety-eighth meridian to the foothills of the Rockies; the great mountain chains of the Rockies and the Sierras; and, between these two ranges, the Great Basin, a region of high grassy plateaus, saline sinks, and deserts. These great expanses were the home of numerous Indian tribes and of immense herds of buffalo. There was a Mormon settlement in Utah but otherwise the only whites in the region were traders, prospectors, trappers, and the like; as nomadic as the Indians they were almost as far removed from the ways of white civilization.

The West had long occupied a special place in the minds of Americans. It possessed symbolic and mythical qualities, seeming, in Walt Whitman's words, to be "the real genuine America", the region which had shaken off the European influences which predominated along the Atlantic seaboard and in which the national ideals of democracy and equality could best be realized. As the tide of settlement moved westward these notions were applied successively to different geographical regions, but the emotional response they evoked was never greater than when they came to focus upon what has ever since been known as the Wild West. It was now that the Western scene entered most profoundly into American mythology and implanted itself most firmly in the popular consciousness.

Popular conceptions of the Wild West were shaped primarily by the Western dime novels which Erastus Beadle began publishing in 1860 and which sold in huge numbers. Featuring such legendary, albeit real-life, characters as Deadwood Dick, Buffalo Bill, and Calamity Jane, these novels familiarized their readers with a world of stagecoaches and outlaws, mining rushes and cattle drives, buffalo herds and council fires. Pictorial representations of the West circulated almost as widely. The two most highly regarded Western artists drew on firsthand experience: Charles M.

Russell, 'the cowboy artist', and Frederic Remington, whose paintings and sculptures depicted Indians, cowboys, and frontiersmen with unsurpassed accuracy and feeling. But many tried to visualize the Western scene from the vantage-point of an eastern studio. This was the case with the immensely popular series of Western lithographic prints produced by Currier and Ives, which portrayed in emblematic form many of the images Americans had come to associate with the Wild West. The romantic impressions of the artists did not always correspond with reality but by emphasizing the qualities Americans admired most—manliness, individualism, self-reliance—they made the West an acceptable image of American society as a whole.

Yet the Wild West was a transitory phenomenon and, ironically, the period in which it enjoyed its greatest vogue was the one in which it was tamed. In little more than a generation the tide of white settlement swept over the whole of this vast area. By the end of the century much of the West had been brought within sound of the locomotive's whistle; the power of the Plains Indians was broken and their hunting-grounds became the domain of miners, cattlemen, and farmers; and with the division of the West into states or territories, the political organization of the continent was complete.

Earlier generations of Americans had believed that the whole area between the Missouri and the Rockies was a sterile waste, unsuitable for agriculture and thus uninhabitable—at least by white men. In the first half of the nineteenth century the region was referred to in American atlases and geographies as "the Great American Desert", the name given to it by its early explorers. This was an exaggerated description, but the Great Plains, with their flat, seemingly endless expanses, presented a forbidding contrast with earlier frontiers. Vegetation was sparse and other than along the banks of rivers there were no trees to provide shelter, fuel, fences, or shade. The climate was extreme, rainfall abnormally low—only fifteen inches a year, or about half as much as in the Mississippi Valley. In these surroundings the pioneering techniques and agricultural methods that had proved successful in the East no longer worked. Thus it was the miner and the cattleman, rather than the farmer, who formed the cutting edge of the Far Western frontier.

The Mining Frontier

The transformation of the region began with a succession of gold and silver strikes in the 1860s and 1870s. Unlike previous frontiers the miners' frontier was one which advanced from west to east: the first prospectors in any given area were usually experienced forty-niners from California. News of a strike was enough to set in motion a headlong scramble. Only a tiny fraction succeeded in striking it rich, but despite repeated disappointments countless prospectors spent a lifetime in an obsessive search for gold.

The first major strikes occurred in Colorado and Nevada. In 1858 gold was discovered in the Colorado Rockies near Pike's Peak and within a year fifty thousand people had made their way to the diggings. The boom soon collapsed, but new gold strikes west of Denver brought richer rewards and the discovery of silver near Leadville in the early 1870s opened up a new source of mineral wealth. Meanwhile the Washoe district of western Nevada had yielded an even greater prize—the Comstock Lode, the greatest single deposit of precious metals ever found in the United States. No sooner was the discovery made public in 1859 than a mob of prospectors poured in. Virginia City, perched on a steep mountainside some 7,000 feet above sea level, grew rapidly into a thriving metropolis. Mark Twain's vivid descriptions of the town in *Roughing It* gave it a lasting notoriety. In 1878, when its population reached a peak of 38,000, Virginia City could boast, among other things, four banks, six churches, several gambling-houses, and one hundred and fifty liquor stores. It required prodigies of labor and one of the greatest engineering feats of the nineteenth century, the Sutro Tunnel, to exploit the Comstock mines properly. But the scale of the effort was matched by the yield: in the twenty years after the Lode's discovery its total output of gold and silver amounted to $350 million.

The Civil War years witnessed minor gold strikes on the southern edge of the Arizona desert and major ones in Idaho and Montana. The last of the big gold rushes began in 1874 after two government expeditions had confirmed the existence of gold in the Black Hills of Dakota Territory. This was a Sioux reservation but, once news of the find was out, the army found it impossible to exclude white prospectors. Within months fifteen thousand had arrived. The ramshackle town of Deadwood, its single street lined with saloons, gambling-houses, dance-halls, and brothels, ministered to the appetites of the miners. Desperadoes of various kinds converged on Deadwood and gunfights and stagecoach robberies became almost every-day occurrences; it was here that 'Wild Bill' Hickok was murdered in the autumn of 1876. In its brief heyday Deadwood was one of the wildest and most lawless spots on earth. It soon had a rival for that distinction, how-ever, for the discovery of the famous Lucky Cuss silver mine in Tomb-stone, Arizona in 1877 precipitated a rush that launched that community on its violent career.

The population of the mining camps was unusually diverse and cosmo-politan, and was also predominantly youthful. Miners displayed an even greater propensity than Americans generally for moving about. "The min-ers of Idaho are like quicksilver" wrote the historian Hubert Howe Ban-croft. "A mass of them dropped in any locality broke up into individual globules, and ran off after any atom of gold in their vicinity." While every frontier had its share of lawless outcasts, the diggings attracted an exceptional number of riff-raff, harpies, gamblers, and prostitutes, hoping to batten on and exploit the miners. Not surprisingly the raw mining towns became notorious for their turbulence and debauchery.

Yet it was only in the early days of the gold rushes that crime, disorder, and vice flourished unchecked. When the federal government proved unable or unwilling to provide orderly government the law-abiding and responsible majority took matters into their own hands, developing informal codes of law and dispensing a rough-and-ready brand of justice. The simple democracy of the mining camps was manifested in mass meetings which adopted laws for regulating mineral claims, settling disputes, and punishing crime. It was equally demonstrated in the widespread resort to vigilantism. Though liable to produce miscarriages of justice, it was perhaps the only effective weapon against organized crime.

Throughout the mountain country mining methods developed according to a set pattern. The earliest prospectors were able to employ crude placer-mining techniques: they shoveled auriferous gravel from a stream or hillside into a wash-pan or sluice-box and swilled it round with water to isolate the grains of gold. But these individualistic methods soon became unprofitable. Most of the gold—and the silver, for that matter—was embedded deep in hard rock, locked in veins of quartz or combined with base metals or sulfur. Once the shallower deposits were exhausted, the transition had to be made to deep-level quartz-mining, which required extensive outlays of capital, machinery, and engineering skill. Western mining thus became big business and the individual prospector was transformed into a company employee, working for wages. By the end of the century the trend toward business consolidation, characteristic of the American economy generally, was manifesting itself in the mining industry, especially in copper-mining, now exceedingly profitable thanks to the huge demand for copper created by the development of electricity. The giant Anaconda Mining Corporation, the largest copper producer of its day, owned the copper mines at Butte, Montana, 'the richest hill on earth'. Most of the other Western copper mines belonged to the Guggenheim interests.

The Cattle Kingdom

While the mining frontier was being overrun another colorful but transitory drama was being enacted on the Great Plains, where the cowboy and the cattleman grazed vast herds on the open range, that is, the rich grasslands of the public domain, not yet divided up or fenced in. The range cattle industry had originated in the early days of the Spanish Empire. It was on Spanish ranches in north-eastern Mexico that the arts employed later by the Great Plains cowboy first evolved. Here, too, were developed the cowboy's picturesque, but wholly functional, costume and his distinctive tools: the broad sombrero, the shaggy, leather chaparejos, the high-heeled boots, the spurs, the high-horned, forty-pound saddle, and the lariat.

In the eighteenth century the Spaniards introduced wiry, Andalusian cattle into Texas and allowed them to run wild. So rapidly did these long-horns multiply that by the end of the Civil War an estimated five million roamed the Texas ranges. They were worth only $3 or $4 a head in their native pastures but if they could be driven to Northern meat markets they would fetch ten times as much. Early in 1866 some enterprising Texas ranchers headed their herds northward on the first of the 'long drives'— a 1,000-mile trek to Sedalia, Missouri, the terminus of the Missouri Pacific Railroad. There were heavy losses en route and the following year a more accessible railhead was chosen: Abilene, Kansas, on the Kansas Pacific Railroad, where facilities had been established for shipping live cattle to the Chicago stockyards. What paved the way for the move to Abilene was the liberalization of the Kansas cattle quarantine laws. In the spring of 1867, in a resort to a characteristic American political technique, a well-organized cattlemen's lobby persuaded the Kansas legislature to relax restrictions imposed when longhorns had been identified as carriers of Texas fever. In 1867, 35,000 head of cattle trudged north along the Chisholm Trail to Abilene; the following year the figure was 75,000; and by 1871 it had soared to 700,000.

As the railroad and the farming frontiers reached out into the Great Plains, the long drive was pushed west. New trails came into being, like the Western Trail, which led from central Texas to western Kansas and Nebraska, and the Goodnight-Loving Trail, which circled through New Mexico territory into Colorado and Wyoming. Newer railheads eclipsed Abilene: Dodge City, Wichita, and Ellsworth in Kansas, Ogallala in Nebraska, Cheyenne and Laramie in Wyoming, Miles City in Montana. Between 1866 and 1888, somewhere between six and ten million cattle were driven to these and other cow towns. Some herds were then driven onward in a second long drive to be fattened on the northern plains or, when crossed with Hereford bulls, to stock the ranches of Colorado, Wyoming, Montana, and the Dakotas. But most were shipped from the cow towns to the packing centers of the Middle West. The rise of the range cattle industry, together with the extension of the railroads and the devel-opment of the refrigerator car, changed the nation's eating habits: Amer-icans became a primarily beef-eating rather than a pork-eating people.

From afar the long drive seemed romantic, but to the cowboy romance was less evident than discomfort, danger, and monotony. For a wage of only $25 or $30 a month, he had to spend perhaps eighteen hours a day in the saddle trying to control and coax forward a sprawling mass of cattle. Throughout the grueling, two-month journey he traveled in a continuous cloud of dust, hearing little but a chorus of lowing and bellowing. Along the way he had to contend with a variety of natural and human hazards—floods, blizzards, stampedes, rustlers, Indians—any one of which could cause crippling financial loss. Little wonder that at journey's end, he went on the spree, squandering half a year's wages in a few days on the doubtful pleasures of the cattle towns.

Though it is often supposed that life in the cattle towns was as gaudy and as riotous as in the Western mining settlements, the reality was more prosaic. Saloons were no more numerous than pubs in contemporary England; Abilene had only eleven in 1871, its busiest cattle season, and Dodge City a mere thirteen in 1882, when the resident population numbered about two thousand. Moreover, the state of Kansas forbade the sale and consumption of liquor, except for "medicinal purposes", as early as 1880, forty years before national prohibition was enacted. Though this did not shut all the saloons it reduced their number and made it more difficult for liquor dealers to ply their trade: indeed at Caldwell one of them was lynched in 1882 by incensed prohibitionists.

This incident notwithstanding, the number of murders in the cattle towns never approached the figures suggested in fictional accounts. The twenty-five or so violent deaths that helped populate the famous "Boot Hill" cemetery during Dodge City's first year as a community antedated the era of the long drive; during its ten years as a cattle town (1875–84) Dodge witnessed a total of only fifteen murders. This total, low by frontier standards, reflected the fact that law and order accompanied the rise of the cattle trade: courts were established, laws passed, and professional gunmen, like the celebrated Wyatt Earp and the equally renowned "Bat" Masterson, imported to serve as police-officers.

The discovery that beef cattle could be fattened for market on the Great Plains led ultimately to the replacement of the range by the ranch. By 1880 ranching had spread northwards from Texas as far as the Canadian border. Ranchers rarely bothered to acquire legal title to what was still almost wholly the public domain, but simply appropriated and often fenced in huge tracts of grazing land and maintained their position by force. Range disputes and rustling were endemic and in the absence of law cattlemen, like miners before them, formed their own associations to provide mutual protection and introduce a measure of order. These livestock associations developed a code of rules defining land and water rights, the recording of brands, and the disposition of strays or 'mavericks'. They behaved arbitrarily and sometimes unjustly and some of the most powerful of them, such as the Wyoming Stock Growers' Association, eventually assumed quasi-governmental powers in the territories that were being organized out of the range.

The spread of ranching was only one reason for the end of the open range. By the 1880s the Great Plains were crisscrossed by railroads and were beginning to be invaded both by farmers and by sheep-herders. Since sheep were reputed to pollute drinking water and to ruin pasture by close-cropping, cattlemen felt justified in stopping at nothing in an attempt to keep them out. But despite prolonged warfare between cattlemen and sheep-herders, resulting in the deaths of scores of men and hundreds of thousands of sheep, more especially along the Colorado-Wyoming border, the contraction of the range went on. The decline was further hastened when, in the middle 1880s, the federal government began belatedly to enforce the land laws ordering the removal of illegal enclosures. About the same time the long drive received a fatal blow when the appearance of splenic fever among cattle in the stockyards of Kansas City, St. Louis, and Chicago, prompted the passage of more stringent state quarantine laws.

Meanwhile the cattle business had increasingly come to resemble the kind of large-scale corporate enterprise characteristic of American industry. The fabulous profits made during the cattle boom of the early 1880s attracted huge amounts of Eastern and European capital into ranching. The result was that the ranges became grossly overcrowded and in 1885 beef prices tumbled. Then, in 1885–6 and 1886–7, came two exceptionally severe winters during which millions of cattle starved or froze to death. The disaster ruined thousands of cattlemen and taught the survivors the need for privately owned pasturage, equipped with shelter against the elements. The old ways persisted here and there for a while but in general the cattlemen now retreated to the security of a fenced-in ranch-house and the cowboy became in effect a farmhand.

The Destruction of the Plains Indians

When miners, cattlemen, and ranchers moved into the trans-Mississippi West, they invaded the last stronghold of the American Indian and in the process wantonly destroyed his culture. At the end of the Civil War there were perhaps 300,000 Indians in the Far West. Despite their physical, linguistic, and cultural diversity they could be divided into three main groups: the fierce Plains Indians, the weak and primitive tribesmen who inhabited the deserts between the Rockies and the Sierra Nevada, and the peaceful and highly civilized farmers and herders of the Southwest. The last two of these groups were few in number and were not destined to play a prominent part in the coming conflict with the white man. It was the Plains Indians who were to offer the most implacable and sustained resistance to his advance.

The 240,000 Indians who lived on the Great Plains in 1860 belonged to a great many tribes. Between them there was sometimes fierce enmity, usually arising from cultural differences or disputes over hunting-grounds. The Utes and the Cheyenne were old foes; the Kiowa of the Black Hills lived for years in a state of continuous warfare with their Sioux, Arapaho, and Cheyenne neighbors. Such divisions prevented the Indians from presenting a united front to the white invader. So, too, did the way in which Indian group life was organized. Since the tribal unit was too large and unwieldy to engage in the central activity of the Indians, the buffalo-hunt, the basis of social organization was the tribal subdivision known as the band, consisting of between three and five hundred people. Since the different bands were largely autonomous and ordinarily had little to do with one another, it was quite common for some bands of a tribe to be at war while others remained at peace.

Unlike the tribesmen east of the Mississippi the Plains Indians were nomadic and warlike. Their way of life was determined by the fact that on the Plains the buffalo was the source of virtually all of life's necessities. The tribesmen relied on the buffalo's flesh for food, its hide for clothing, shoes, tepees, and blankets, its bones for implements and ornaments, its horns for cups, ladles, and spoons, and its sinews for thread and bowstrings. The buffalo's stomach became a water-bottle and even its dung, when dried into chips, was used as fuel. Originally the buffalo was hunted on foot but the horses introduced into the New World by the Spaniards in the sixteenth century enabled the Indians to range widely over the Plains in pursuit of the great herds. The Plains Indians were superb horsemen and, as competition for the buffalo brought them into conflict with other tribes, they became skilled and aggressive warriors. Armed with short powerful bows admirably adapted to shooting from horseback, they were formidable foes—indeed, more than a match for their white adversaries before the repeating rifle and the Colt revolver tilted the balance. Their nomadic habits, moreover, made them singularly elusive.

Apart from buffalo-hunts and religious ceremonies, war absorbed the greater part of the energies of Plains Indians. Warfare was at the same time a career, a test of manhood and honor, and the greatest source of glory. Indian youths were taught that war was the noblest of all activities. To live to old age was a reproach; to die young, fighting bravely in battle, the highest fulfillment since it ensured a happy afterlife. And just as this conception of warfare derived its sanction from a distinctive set of religious beliefs so, too, did the cruel practices which characterized the Indian conduct of war. Torture was regarded as a means whereby a captive might acquire a badge of honor and show himself worthy of divine protection; the mutilation of slain enemies was justified as a safeguard against their becoming threats in the spirit world. The frontiersman, however, knowing nothing of the culture of this primitive warrior society, was conscious of the Indian mainly as a ferocious enemy and ascribed his methods of warfare to a uniquely depraved and vicious nature.

In the Indian wars that raged intermittently on the Plains from the 1860s to the 1880s the contestants vied with each other in ruthlessness and savagery. When the eastern Sioux, led by Little Crow, went on the warpath in Minnesota in 1862 and massacred 500 settlers, retribution was swift, harsh, and indiscriminate. Over 300 Indians were publicly hanged, thirty-eight from a single scaffold. In November 1864 the American lust for revenge produced the Sand Creek Massacre in Colorado. The Cheyenne had been pillaging and murdering for more than three years but, ignoring the fact that Chief Black Kettle had now sued for peace and had been promised protection, a militia force under Colonel John M. Chivington fell on a band of several hundred Indians, men, women, and children, and butchered them indiscriminately, scalping dead braves, disemboweling pregnant women, and clubbing children to death. Such barbarities were self-perpetuating and the war in the Southwest became more and more savage until in 1868 the Cheyenne and the Arapaho were finally defeated. Meanwhile a new conflict—the Sioux War of 1865–7—had broken out further north when the army attempted to build the "Powder River Road", which would have cut across the best hunting-grounds of the western Sioux in Montana. This goaded the Sioux into action. They harassed the soldiers so successfully that the road could not be built and in December 1866 they ambushed and completely wiped out a party of eighty-two soldiers under Captain W. J. Fetterman.

The 'Fetterman Massacre' shocked the federal government into taking a fresh look at the Indian problem. In 1867 a Peace Commission toured the Plains and submitted a report blaming the Sioux and Cheyenne wars mainly on the whites and arguing that the subjugation of the Indians was likely to prove too slow and costly. Impressed by the report Congress endorsed a plan to concentrate all the Plains Indians in two large reservations, one in the Black Hills of South Dakota, the other in Indian Territory, later to become Oklahoma. But the tribesmen were reluctant to comply and more hard fighting was needed to beat them into submission. Meanwhile in 1869 a new civilian Board of Indian Commissioners had been set up, thus ending the long-standing division of authority between the Department of the Interior and the War Department. Moreover in an effort to stamp out laxity and corruption among Indian agents Grant had attempted to replace them, first with Quakers, then with the nominees of other denominations. But these innovations brought only limited improvements.

By 1875 most of the tribes had been settled on reservations but hardly had the program been completed than the Black Hills gold rush provoked a new Sioux War. It was during this conflict that Colonel George A. Custer, who had been sent to Montana to round up the Sioux, made his famous 'last stand'. Though his scouting party numbered only 265 men Custer rashly attacked a Sioux army ten times as large. Commanded by Crazy

Horse, the most accomplished of the Indian military leaders, and by Sitting Bull, this was the largest Indian army ever brought together in the United States. In the battle of the Little Big Horn on June 25, 1876, Custer and his entire command were killed. But the Sioux gained little by their victory. Shortage of food and ammunition forced them to accept defeat before the end of the year.

After this there were only a few sporadic outbreaks. In 1877 the Nez Percé took to the warpath west of the Rockies; when troops threatened to run them down a remarkable leader, Chief Joseph, conducted a retreat of 1,300 miles before being caught just short of the Canadian border. The Apaches of the Southwest continued to give trouble for some years longer, but with the capture of Geronimo and his handful of followers in 1886, organized Indian resistance ended. But there was one last tragic clash in 1890. On the Sioux reservation in South Dakota an outburst of religious excitement, centering around the so-called 'Ghost Dance', created apprehensions of an uprising. The troops sent to restore order fired indiscriminately into a milling mob at Wounded Knee, killing about three hundred Indians.

In the end the superior technology of the white man had prevailed. The railroad, the electric telegraph, and the Winchester rifle had overcome the courage, daring, and relentlessness of the tribesmen. Yet in the last analysis the conquest of the Plains Indians was the result of the mass slaughter of the buffalo. Their destruction began with the building of the transcontinental railroads. Individual hunters seized the opportunity to furnish buffalo meat to railroad construction camps: one of them, William F. (Buffalo Bill) Cody, earned his nickname by slaughtering 4,280 buffalo in eighteen months. Railroads in turn made the buffalo range more accessible and in the early 1870s buffalo-hunting became popular with Eastern and European sportsmen. A rage developed for buffalo-robes and, after the discovery by a Pennsylvania tannery that buffalo-hides could also be used to make leather, the pursuit of the great shaggy beasts became an organized business. Between 1872 and 1874 teams of professional hunters, armed with long-range rifles, killed buffalo at the rate of three million a year. In 1865 there had been two great herds of buffalo on the Great Plains, totaling 13,000,000 animals; by 1883 the southern herd had been exterminated and a scientific expedition could find only two hundred survivors of the northern herd.

Soon after the Civil War sharp divisions of opinion began to develop over federal Indian policy. Most Western frontiersmen, backed by the army, echoed the traditional view that the only good Indian was a dead Indian and argued that there would be no peace until the tribes had been decisively defeated in battle and the survivors placed in reservations under military control. Eastern idealists, on the other hand, argued that the solution to the Indian problem lay in converting the tribesmen to white ways. Believing that tribalism fostered backwardness, superstition, and immorality, they advocated the systematic eradication of Indian culture. The Indian must be weaned from his nomadic ways, encouraged to support himself by farming, acquire a knowledge of English, cut his hair, learn the value of property, and be made to understand the merit of honest labor, instead of leaving menial tasks to his women. Impressed by these views some of the leading humanitarians of the day became active in the Indian-policy reform movement. They included former abolitionists like Wendell Phillips and William Lloyd Garrison, churchmen like Bishop Henry Whipple, statesmen like Carl Schurz and the Massachusetts author, Helen Hunt Jackson, whose book, *A Century of Dishonor* (1884), was a scathing indictment of government policy towards the red man.

To frontiersmen the reformers seemed impractical and visionary. But the reform campaign, conducted through such organizations as the Indian Rights Association and the National Indian Defense Association, succeeded in the 1870s and 1880s in converting the federal government to a policy of breaking down the tribal structure with a view to assimilating the Indian to white civilization. Boarding-schools were established where Indian children might be isolated for years at a time from parental influences; Indian religious practices were outlawed; and in an effort to compel Indians to abandon their tribal customs, rations were withheld. The climax of this policy came in 1887 with the passage of the Dawes Act, which broke up reservation land into individual or family holdings. Reformers hailed the measure as heralding a new era of harmony, but its effects were deplorable. Far from creating a class of yeoman farmers, it facilitated land-grabbing by whites and thus pauperized the red man. Moreover, while it weakened the tribal structure, it did not supply any alternative form of social organization. The result was the moral and physical disintegration of a once proud race.

Spanning the Continent

Meanwhile Americans had been grappling with the problem of communication with the Far West. The settlement of Oregon and the discovery of gold in California pointed the need for a transport network that would link the Pacific coast with the East. Californian pressure for a regular overland stagecoach service led in 1857 to the award of a federal mail contract to a syndicate headed by John Butterfield, a founder of the American Express Company and the owner of stage-lines in New York. In return for an annual subsidy of $600,000, Butterfield's company undertook to provide a semiweekly mail service, in each direction, over a 2,800-mile route between St. Louis and San Francisco and to guarantee delivery within twenty-five days. The arrival on schedule of the first eastbound stagecoach in 1858 established the company's reputation. A $200 fare and the discomforts of a three-week journey kept down the number of through passengers, but by 1860 the Butterfield Overland Express was carrying a greater volume of mail than was going to California by sea.

Overland freighting on the Central Plains enjoyed a similar boom. With the help of government contracts to transport military supplies to Western army posts, the firm of Russell, Majors, and Waddell came to dominate the business in the 1850s. Encouraged by the success of its freight wagons the firm established the famous Pony Express in April 1860 to provide a faster mail service to the Pacific coast. Relays of pony-riders, operating between St. Joseph, Missouri, the western terminus of the railroads, and Sacramento, California, covered the intervening 1,966 miles in only ten days, thus demonstrating the superiority of the Central Plains route over the more circuitous southerly trail followed by the Butterfield Overland Express. But without a government subsidy the Pony Express was incapable of making a profit. In any case the service was rendered obsolete after only eighteen months; the completion of a transcontinental telegraph line on October 22, 1861 made it possible to transmit news in seconds rather than in days.

The collapse of the Pony Express helped seal the fate of another of Russell, Majors, and Waddell's enterprises – the Central Overland, California, and Pike's Peak Express Company. Started in 1859 to provide a daily stagecoach service between eastern Kansas and Denver the company had never made money. When it went bankrupt in 1862 its remaining assets were bought by the illiterate Ben Holladay, a former Indian trader from Missouri, who proceeded to organize a thriving stagecoach empire spanning most of the West. By 1866, when he sold out to the California express firm of Wells, Fargo, and Company, which had acquired the Butterfield interests west of the Rockies, Holladay controlled 5,000 miles of stage-routes. Overland staging would continue to be important for several decades longer, but with iron rails advancing rapidly across the continent its heyday was now over.

The proposal for a transcontinental railroad, first advanced in 1845, attracted increasing public support after the California gold rush. There was general agreement that the huge expense of the project made federal aid essential. But sectional jealousies about the route prevented Congress from taking action before the Civil War. The secession of the South enabled Northerners to agree on a central route and on July 1, 1862 Congress passed the first Pacific Railway Act. It chartered the Union Pacific Railroad to build westward across the continent from Omaha and authorized the Central Pacific Railroad of California to build eastward from Sacramento. Both companies were given unprecedentedly large land grants—a four-hundred-foot right of way and ten alternate sections of public land for each completed mile of track—and were granted government loans varying in amount with the difficulty of the terrain. Two years later, with the project languishing for want of capital, Congress was prevailed upon to double the land grant and reduce the loan to the status of a second mortgage. Money now flowed in from investors and construction began.

The unscrupulous shareholders of the two companies devised an ingenious scheme to enrich themselves. Instead of inviting competitive bids, they created dummy construction companies to do the actual building: the Crédit Mobilier for the Union Pacific, the Contract and Finance Company for the Central Pacific. This enabled them to charge exorbitant rates. Thus the Crédit Mobilier received $73m for construction work that had cost $50m, while the Contract and Finance Company got $120m when actual building costs amounted to only $58m. Such a device, characteristic of the business ethics of the day, meant that the two railroads were heavily burdened with debt.

Formidable problems attended railroad construction in this largely barren and uninhabited region. Everything required—ties, stone, rails, rolling-stock, machinery—had to be transported over long distances, together with food and supplies for thousands of laborers. Union Pacific construction gangs, chiefly Irish immigrants and discharged Union soldiers, had sometimes to exchange their picks for rifles to fight off marauding Plains Indians. The Central Pacific, which relied mainly on imported Chinese coolie labor, had to traverse the 7,000-foot-high slopes of the Sierra Nevada. The Union Pacific, having the advantage of an easier roadbed, built 1,086 miles of track; the Central Pacific, 689. The two lines met at Promontory Point, five miles east of Ogden, Utah in the spring of 1869; in a colorful ceremony on May 10 they were joined by a golden spike.

The terms under which government aid was granted had turned the project into a race between the two railroads and put a premium on speed of construction rather than quality. The result was that both roads soon had to be extensively resited and reconstructed. Nevertheless the successful completion of a transcontinental line was a remarkable feat of engineering.

The financial and engineering difficulties were such that many believed that only one transcontinental railroad could ever be built. But eventually the Union Pacific-Central Pacific was paralleled by four others. The Northern Pacific, stretching from St. Paul to Portland, Oregon, and the Southern Pacific, linking New Orleans with San Francisco, were completed in 1883; the following year the Atchison, Topeka, and Santa Fe pushed its tracks from eastern Kansas to San Diego; and in 1893 the Great Northern, extending westward from Duluth and St. Paul, reached the Pacific coast at Seattle. The completion of the great transcontinental lines accounted for only a fraction of Western rail construction. The five Pacific railroads each built numerous branch-lines; the Santa Fe, for example, having made connections with San Francisco and Chicago had grown into a 7,000-mile system by the end of the 1880s. At the same time a dense network, north-south as well as east-west, was built in the eleven states between the Mississippi and the 100th meridian. Here the dominant systems were those of the four major Granger lines—the Chicago, Burlington, and Quincy; the Chicago, Milwaukee, and St. Paul; the Chicago and North Western; and the Chicago, Rock Island, and Pacific—which, as their names indicated, shared Chicago as an eastern terminal; together they possessed 18,000 miles of track by 1890. In addition several thousand miles of narrow gauge railway were built, mostly in the mining mountain states. Thus Western rail mileage, which had amounted to only 3,000 miles in 1865, had increased by the end of the century to 87,000 miles, or nearly half the national total.

Although there were no more federal loans to railroads after the Crédit Mobilier scandal of 1873 all the transcontinental lines, with the exception of the Great Northern, received lavish federal land grants. So did the four Granger lines and many of the shorter Western lines. In all the federal government gave the railroads 131 million acres—a region larger than Germany or France—more than 100 million acres of which went to Western lines. The federal government's contribution ought not to be exaggerated: its land grants helped to build only about a fifth of the track laid in the West before 1900. Its efforts were matched by the states, which advanced over $200m and made land grants totaling 48 million acres, and by municipalities and counties whose desire for railroad connections led them to provide about $300 million. And in any case, most of the capital for railroad building came not from public but from private sources, European investors and New York banking-houses being the chief contributors.

Nevertheless the federal land grants were vitally important, not so much for the cash they realized—for much railroad land was not sold until the line itself had been completed—as for the basis of credit they provided, thus enabling construction to start. In the event the federal government received a substantial return on its land grants. For one thing the alternate sections of land it retained along the railroad tracks fetched twice the normal price of $1.25 an acre. For another, government traffic on the land-grant lines enjoyed a 50 percent discount. By the end of the century, moreover, the loan of $60m to the Union Pacific and Central Pacific had been repaid in full, together with interest at 6 percent, totaling more than $104 million. Thus the government turned out to have been shrewd as well as munificent.

The Farmers' Frontier

While those who settled the Great Plains were usually known as home-steaders, relatively few of them secured farms under the 1862 Homestead

Act. That measure in theory opened the West to settlement under liberal conditions, but in practice the promise of free land for the homeless turned out to be largely a delusion. Between 1862 and 1900 the government awarded to 600,000 claimants under the Homestead Act a total of 80 million acres—a mere fraction, incidentally, of the 521 million acres surrendered to the railroads and the states or sold to land jobbers. But a great many of the claimants were not bona-fide farmers but dummy registrants, acting for speculators, cattlemen, or the representatives of mining or lumber companies.

As well as inviting fraud the Homestead Act had other weaknesses. It assumed that a mere grant of land could turn an Eastern industrial laborer into a Western farmer. But to begin farming he needed capital to buy tools, seed, stock, and machinery and the resources to support himself and his family until he got a paying crop. Moreover the framers of the measure failed to realize that a 160-acre tract, more than adequate for the Mississippi Valley, was too small a unit on which to make a living on the Great Plains. (In 1890 the average size of a farm in South Dakota was 227 acres; in North Dakota, 277 acres.) Subsequent land laws served to obstruct settlement rather than to facilitate it. The Desert Land Act of 1877 allowed a settler to buy 640 acres at $1.25 an acre provided he irrigated the holding within two years and the Timber and Stone Act of 1878 permitted the purchase at $2.50 an acre of 160 acres of land "unfit for cultivation" and valuable chiefly for timber or stone. But although designed ostensibly to enable the pioneer farmer to enlarge his holding, the two measures were in fact adopted in response to pressure respectively from ranchers and lumber interests intent on plundering the public domain. Thanks to wholesale fraud in the administration of the Acts, both groups abundantly realized their aims.

Public land policy contributed far less, indeed, to the settlement of the West than the colonizing activities of the states and railroads. Western states and territories made strenuous attempts to promote settlement, stationing agents in the East and in Europe to advertize opportunities for settlers. But their efforts were overshadowed by those of the land-grant railroads. Having millions of acres for sale, and seeing in settlement a means of generating rail traffic, railroads like the Northern Pacific, the Burlington and Missouri, and the Southern Pacific spent lavishly in attempts to attract settlers from the eastern states and Europe. Their promotional literature depicted the West in alluring and extravagant terms as a land of milk and honey. In addition they held out a variety of inducements: credit sales, reduced steamship-fares, and free 'land-exploring' tickets. Some roads, like the Great Northern, provided temporary accommodation for new arrivals and even offered to educate settlers in Plains agriculture.

Railroad advertising proved remarkably effective. Large numbers of immigrants were lured to the Great Plains from the British Isles, Germany, Scandinavia, and elsewhere. Many clustered together to form compact, homogeneous settlements. By 1890 hundreds of tiny German, Swedish, and British colonies were dotted across Kansas, Nebraska, Minnesota, and the Dakotas. Nevertheless the majority of pioneers were not from abroad but from states further east, mainly those in the Mississippi Valley. Very few city-dwellers headed for the Great Plains; the notion that the West served as a safety-valve for urban discontent has little foundation in fact.

For all the glowing descriptions of colonization literature newcomers soon discovered that the Great Plains were no land of Canaan: this tree-less, arid region presented greater difficulties than any previous frontier. Yet these were overcome sufficiently to make farming possible. The press-ing problem of fencing was solved in 1874 when an Illinois farmer, Joseph F. Gliddon, put barbed wire on the market. For the first time it became possible to fence land cheaply, and by 1890 much of the Plains region had been enclosed. The water-supply problem yielded to a combination of invention and new methods of cultivation. Deeply drilled wells and steel windmills specially designed for Western conditions provided a steady though sometimes scant supply of water and 'dry farming'—a method of tillage involving deep plowing and frequent harrowing—served to check evaporation and hold water in the soil. Yet because of the large size of farms agriculture could not have been made to pay without improved farm machinery: notably the Oliver chilled-steel plow that could break the toughest sod and the McCormick reaper with its ingenious cord-binder which allowed two men and a team of horses to harvest twenty acres of wheat a day.

Farming on the Plains remained nonetheless a difficult and uncertain business. Costs were high, there was a constant threat of drought, and such vagaries of nature as tornadoes and grasshopper plagues could bring dis-aster overnight. Moreover, as the stories of Hamlin Garland illustrate, liv-ing conditions were harsh. With only a sod-house scooped out of the earth for shelter, and with the nearest neighbors perhaps miles away, families led a primitive and isolated existence. Nonetheless the population of the Middle Border, as the Northern Plains were known, steadily increased. Between 1860 and 1900 the number of white people in Kansas, Nebraska, the Dakotas, Iowa, and Minnesota rose from less than one million to more than seven million.

While Americans in general were a mobile people, Westerners were par-ticularly so. Of the settlers who entered Kansas between 1854, when it became a Territory, and 1860, only 35 percent remained in 1865. Equally characteristic of the Western population was the fact that it was predom-inantly male. In 1880 Colorado had twice as many men as women, Wyoming Territory nearly three times as many. The striking disparity between the sexes helps account for the wild and debauched behavior of many frontiersmen and the general crudeness of Western society. Yet tendencies to barbarism and primitivism were countered by the determination of most pioneers to transplant the cultural institutions of the East. Though preoccupied with material tasks, Westerners were quick to establish churches, schools, theaters, and newspapers. Initially Western society was both democratic and fluid but maturity—and especially the arrival of women—brought an increasing tendency to social stratification. Though the West has been widely regarded as the home of individualism, members of frontier communities soon found, as had miners and cattlemen before them, that they had to act collectively. Joint effort was essential to deal with problems of law enforcement, to secure protection against Indian attack, to deal with prairie fires, even to carry out normal pioneering tasks.

Political organization kept pace with settlement. By 1890 there was for the first time a continuous band of states stretching from the Atlantic to the Pacific. Utah, long denied statehood because the dominant Mormon Church continued to sanction polygamy, finally agreed to abandon it and became a state in 1896. By the end of the century only three areas within the continental United States, all of them sparsely populated, remained under territorial government: Oklahoma, Arizona, and New Mexico.

Conservation

In his annual report for 1890, the Superintendent of the Census announced that 'at present the unsettled area has been so broken into isolated bodies of settlement that there can hardly be said to be a frontier line'. A young historian, Frederick Jackson Turner, took the announcement to mean the end of the era of settlement and advanced his influential frontier thesis which argued that the receding frontier explained American democracy and the American national character. But at the time there was still a good deal of land to be settled in the West and the 'closing of the frontier' produced no dramatic changes. Its most important immediate consequence, perhaps, was to focus attention on the problem of conservation. The natural resources of the continent had hitherto seemed inexhaustible and in consequence westward-moving pioneers had left behind an ever lengthening trail of waste and devastation, wantonly slaughtering wild life, squandering mineral wealth, felling whole forests, and displaying a similarly improvident attitude towards the soil. Toward the end of the nineteenth century, however, some Americans began to awake to the fact that there were limits even to the West's physical resources.

The first form of waste to provoke a public outcry was the destruction of timberlands. Among the earliest to draw attention to the problem was the Vermont philologist and diplomat, George Perkins Marsh, whose famous book, *Man and Nature* (1864), called on Americans to profit from the experience of the Near East, where centuries of neglect and exploitation had reduced once-fertile regions to barren wastes. By 1877 Marsh's arguments were beginning to be reflected in official thinking. Apprehensions that the United States would soon face a timber famine led Franklin B. Hough, the recently appointed forestry agent in the Department of Agriculture, to prepare a report which recommended the adoption of a system of forest management like those existing in Canada and a number of European countries. But Congress was slow to act. In 1873 it passed the Timber Culture Act, which offered 160 acres of land to settlers who planted one-fourth of the area in trees. But neither this measure, nor an amending act of 1878 which modified the tree-planting requirement, lived up to the expectations of their authors. And although after Hough's report numerous bills providing for the establishment of forest reserves were introduced into Congress none was enacted before 1891 because Westerners saw forest conservation as a threat to private enterprise. Only by means of a legislative subterfuge were conservationists able to secure the passage of the Forest Reserve Act of March 1891, which enabled President Benjamin Harrison to set aside 13,500,000 acres of the public domain in the Far West. But no steps were taken to protect or administer the new reserves in any distinctive way, nor to clarify their purpose. And when in 1897, during the closing days of his administration, President Grover Cleveland set aside an additional 21,000,000 acres of forest reserves, some in already settled regions, there was such a storm of Congressional criticism as to threaten the entire timber-conservation program. Nevertheless, out of the crisis emerged a second fundamental law, the Forest Management Act of 1897, which provided for the utilization and administration of the forest reserves and made it clear that their purpose was not to lock up resources but "to furnish a continuous supply of timber for the use and necessities of the citizens of the United States". The following year Gifford Pinchot, who had studied forestry in Europe, was appointed head of the Bureau of Forestry. Under his leadership the Bureau became a powerful and efficient administrative agency staffed by trained personnel and practicing, rather than simply preaching, skilled forest management. By the time Pinchot left the Bureau in 1910 it had jurisdiction over 149 national forests, consisting altogether of about 193,000,000 acres.

Pride of place in the long campaign to persuade the federal government to develop irrigation in the West belongs to the geologist and explorer, Major John Wesley Powell, the first white man to traverse the Grand Canyon (1869). Powell's *Report on the Lands of the Arid Regions of the United States* (1878) pointed out the dangers of erosion and advocated large-scale dam and irrigation projects west of the 100th meridian, where the rainfall was less than twenty inches. He also proposed a radical change in the land laws to suit the realities of the Far Western environment: land should be apportioned, not in the traditional 160-acre squares, but in much larger units and in such a way as to guarantee access to water for a maximum number of homesteads. Had Powell's ideas been adopted the West might have escaped the sufferings of the dust bowl, but Western Congressmen, still wedded to a *laissez-faire* conservation policy, blocked his land-apportionment proposals. Nor did Powell's agitation for government development of Western water resources meet much response until the great drought of the late 1880s had reinforced his warnings that the Great Plains were turning into deserts. Finally in 1902, the year of his death, Congress passed the National Reclamation Act, which had been introduced by Senator Francis G. Newlands of Nevada. The Act accepted the principle of federal management of Western waterways, created the Bureau of Reclamation, and authorized the federal government to build and maintain irrigation projects in sixteen Western states, to be financed through the sale of land and water rights. The measure had dramatic results. By 1914 a million acres had been reclaimed for agriculture and a number of major irrigation projects had been completed, among them the Buffalo Bill Dam in Wyoming and the Theodore Roosevelt Dam in Arizona.

Unlike the conservation movement proper the demand for national parks arose from aesthetic rather than economic considerations. The idea of preserving a wilderness in its primeval state in the public interest had been a recurrent theme in American thought since the early nineteenth century. Its champions, who included George Catlin, the painter of Indians and Western scenery, and the transcendentalist philosopher, Henry David Thoreau, were not primarily concerned with providing sanctuaries for wild life or with preserving scenic beauty for its own sake. They were moved rather by the conviction that if Americans were denied opportunities of renewing contact with nature, they would in time become overcivilized and decadent.

The first national park in the United States—indeed in the world—was created in March 1872 when Congress passed an act designating two million acres of Wyoming Territory as Yellowstone National Park. As the explorers who discovered Yellowstone in 1870 had recommended, this remote, unsettled region of natural wonders, with its geysers, hot springs, waterfalls, and mountains was, in the words of the Act, "reserved and withdrawn from settlement . . . and dedicated and set apart as a public park or pleasuring-ground for the benefit and enjoyment of the people". Even so, powerful economic influences remained hostile to the national-parks concept and it required renewed efforts by conservationists before the Yellowstone formula could be extended. The most articulate champion of national parks from about 1878 onward was the Scottish-born naturalist and explorer, John Muir. Thanks largely to the campaign he organized, along with Robert Underwood Johnson, the editor of the *Century Magazine*, three new national parks were created in 1890—Yosemite, Sequoia, and General Grant, all in California. For some time, however, Congress remained unwilling to provide adequate funds for maintenance and supervision and it was left to the Army to patrol the newly created parks. It had its hands full in expelling timber-thieves and poachers, evicting squatters, and dispersing invading herds of sheep and cattle. Only with the creation of the National Park Service in 1916, two years after Muir's death, were the national parks safe from encroachment.

16. *The Growth of an Industrial Economy*, 1865–1914

The American Industrial Revolution

In the last third of the nineteenth century, rapid industrialization was the dominant American theme. Though industry had been growing for several decades before the Civil War, agriculture was still paramount in 1861. But in the postwar decades the United States made the crucial transition to a modern industrial society. In Great Britain the Industrial Revolution had spanned a century; in America only about one-third of that time. Between 1860 and 1900 industrial production increased in value from under $2,000 million a year to more than $13,000 million, the amount of capital invested in manufacturing soared from $1,000 million to nearly $10,000 million, and the number of people employed in manufacturing, mining, construction, and service occupations went up from just over 4 million to more than 18 million. The United States consequently took Great Britain's place as the leading industrial nation. By the end of the century it was making about 30 percent of the world's manufactured goods. Epitomizing the new industrial America was the smoky, sprawling city of Pittsburgh with its coke ovens and blast furnaces, its forest of factory chimneys, its self-made millionaires, and its polyglot immigrant population.

The economic revolution transformed not only the face of America but also every aspect of national life. It brought in an age of machines, electricity, and steel, national markets, and mammoth business corporations. Industrialization was an astonishing technical achievement. But it proceeded too fast to be economically and socially just. Among its consequences were great inequalities of wealth, heartless exploitation, class hostility, and a host of complex social problems.

It was once accepted that industrialization derived its main stimulus from the Civil War itself. War demand and inflation, together with wartime legislation favorable to business, were supposed to have triggered off rapid industrial growth. In fact the effects of the Civil War were less dramatic. Some economic historians, citing the indices of industrial activity, have suggested that far from advancing industrialization the Civil War actually retarded it. They have shown that in the 1860s the economy grew more slowly than in the preceding and succeeding decades and that in certain key industries, iron manufactures in particular, productivity increased only moderately. Even so, the war undoubtedly paved the way for industrial advance. It posed new problems of large-scale economic organization, encouraged innovation, created new opportunities for entrepreneurs, and provided them with the better banking system and the cheap money needed for expansion. It was surely no accident that the foundations of many great industrial fortunes were laid during the Civil War.

The main basis of industrialization was abundant natural resources. Possessing huge deposits of coal, iron, lead, copper, and manganese, giant petroleum fields, and great timber forests the United States was largely self-sufficient in essential raw materials. Territorial expansion, population growth, and the improvement of transportation and communications systems combined to create a continental domestic market. Government support for business, manifesting itself in tariff, railroad, and banking legislation and in judicial protection of corporations, created a climate in which industrial capitalism could flourish. The earlier expansion of trade and industry had generated large accumulations of capital; foreign investors contributed even more. Immigration provided a seemingly inexhaustible supply of cheap labor as well as managerial and technological ability. Broad social and cultural influences were also important, especially the emphasis American society placed on hard work, thrift, and acquisitiveness. As the English economist, Alfred Marshall, remarked apropos of America, business flourished best where there were strong incentives to economic enterprise and material achievement.

The dominant tendency of post-Civil War economic organization was the consolidation of competing enterprises into large-scale units. As well as limiting cutthroat competition, consolidation reduced manufacturing and administrative costs, permitted the coordination and specialization of business activity, and facilitated the accumulation of capital reserves. The trend towards bigness was not universal. Textiles and clothing, for example, continued to be manufactured by large numbers of small and medium-sized firms. But railroads, public utilities, and the processing of minerals came to be dominated by small groups of giant companies. Near monopolies also developed in a long list of other industries, including meat-packing, tobacco, sugar-refining, whiskey, salt, and matches. Business successively employed various forms of combination. The first was the "pool", an informal agreement between firms to limit output or divide markets. But such arrangements were unsatisfactory because they were not legally binding, and by the 1880s "pools" had virtually disappeared. Next came the "trust", an arrangement whereby stockholders in different companies deposited their shares under agreement with trustees, who could thus exercise unified control over nominally independent firms. In

1882 the Standard Oil Company of Ohio created the first trust when the stockholders of seventy-seven oil companies, producing 90 percent of the country's refined oil, transferred their stock to nine trustees. Though the American public referred to all forms of business combination as trusts, the trust, strictly speaking, was a transient phenomenon. By the early 1890s it had been largely abandoned because of attack in state courts. The giant enterprises then turned to the holding company, a device which has survived to the present day. What it meant was that a corporation owned sufficient stock in others to be able to control their operations. Henry O. Havemeyer's Sugar Refining Company (1891) was one of the first trusts to transform itself into a holding company. In 1899 Standard Oil fled from judicial attack in Ohio and secured a charter as a holding company in more hospitable New Jersey. It held stock in forty-one companies and controlled assets worth $300 million. Between 1895 and 1904 there were more than 300 major industrial mergers of this kind with an aggregate capital of over $6 billion. About 40 percent of it was accounted for by the seven largest holding companies: Amalgamated Copper, Consolidated Tobacco, American Smelting and Refining, American Sugar Refining, International Mercantile and Marine, Standard Oil, and, overshadowing them all, the first billion-dollar company, United States Steel.

Inventions and Improvements

A flood of inventions and technological innovations accompanied—indeed, made possible—the economic revolution. Concentration of ownership and control required a marked acceleration in the pace of business. American inventiveness proved equal to the challenge. Europeans made most of the key scientific discoveries on which American technology was based, but Americans, less tradition-bound and also more optimistic and adaptable, were readier to apply them. They also displayed a more searching curiosity in seeking out new techniques. One measure of the extraordinary upsurge of inventiveness was that the number of patents soared from an annual average of 2,000 in the 1850s to 13,000 in the 1870s and to 21,000 in the 1890s. Many were for trivial improvements; others proved to be impracticable or hare-brained. But Mark Twain was basically correct in regarding the volume of patents to be a significant yardstick of a nation's progress. That was why the first official act of his Connecticut Yankee on becoming the wizard at King Arthur's Court was to establish a patent office.

No invention affected American business life more than the typewriter. It was invented in 1867 by Christopher Latham Sholes, a Milwaukee printer, but six years were needed to perfect it before the Remington Gun Company agreed to market it. One of its first purchasers was Mark Twain, whose *Adventures of Tom Sawyer*, published in 1875, is believed to be the first American novel composed on a typewriter. Within a decade few American business offices were without the new machine. Other widely adopted inventions were the cash register, invented by James S. Ritty of Ohio in 1879, and the adding machine, perfected by William S. Burroughs of New York in 1891.

Meanwhile, dramatic improvements in communications made it possible to direct huge and widely scattered organizations and to operate on a national, even an international, scale. The electric telegraph, which spanned the continent by 1862, was rapidly extended after the Civil War. Whereas in Europe telegraphs were usually state-run, in the United States commercial companies operated them. By 1878 Western Union, which controlled 80 percent of the telegraph business, owned 195,000 miles of telegraph routes. A major development came in 1872 with J. B. Stearns's invention of the duplex method, whereby two messages could be sent simultaneously in the same direction on the same wire. In 1866, Cyrus W. Field, who had financed several abortive attempts before the Civil War to lay a transatlantic cable, at last brought the project to a successful conclusion. Thus, instead of taking two weeks or more to cross the ocean by steamer, news, commodity prices, and stock-market quotations were transmitted instantaneously.

Even more epoch-making was the invention of the telephone by Alexander Graham Bell, a young Scot who had come to America by way of Canada. In March 1876, Bell transmitted the first intelligible complete sentence over a line between Boston and Cambridgeport, Massachusetts, and a year later he was able to converse with New York. He and his associates established the Bell Telephone Company to develop the instrument commercially. By 1879 it had installed 56,000 telephones, including one in the White House, and fifty-five cities had local telephone networks. A long-distance telephone service was begun in 1884 and, after other inventors had improved Bell's instrument, the number of telephones installed rose by 1900 to nearly 800,000—twice the total for the whole of Europe. The American Telephone and Telegraph Company, incorporating over 100 local systems, had now taken over the entire system. Service remained expensive—New Yorkers paid an annual telephone rental of $240—but the telephone was on the way to becoming an everyday convenience.

Technological advances which facilitated the use of electricity had an even wider impact. That electricity was a source of light had been known since 1807, when Sir Humphrey Davy demonstrated his battery-driven arc lamp. But since arc lights were too dangerous for indoor use, electric light could not be employed domestically until a vacuum bulb with a durable filament had been devised. The man who solved the problem and whose name became almost a synonym for electric light was Thomas Alva Edison. Born in Ohio in 1847 Edison had little formal education. Becoming a railway newsboy at twelve and a telegraph operator at sixteen, he devoted all his spare time and money to technical experiments and invented several improvements in telegraph apparatus. The research laboratory he established at Menlo Park, New Jersey in 1876 was a milestone in the history of invention. Hitherto, inventors, working singly and motivated by scientific curiosity, had explored problems at random. But Edison's "invention factory" was based on the concept of organized team research; it set out avowedly to supply the market with new products. Edison had no pretensions to being a scientist. Generally scoffing at scientific theory—though some knowledge of it would have saved him a lot of time—he preferred, like the pragmatic American he was, to rely on trial and error.

Edison's laboratories produced scores of important inventions, the best known being the phonograph, the storage battery, the fluoroscope, the motion-picture projector, and the electric locomotive. But his most significant achievement was the incandescent carbon-filament lamp, patented in November 1879, the first commercially practicable product of its kind: its cost was negligible and it would glow brightly for as long as 170 hours. Then, when Edison designed a centrally powered electrical circuit with outlets that could be turned on and off independently, the way was open for the large-scale introduction of electric light. Edison's first power-station, serving Wall Street, New York's financial and business district, went into operation on September 4, 1882. Within six years two million electric light-bulbs had been installed in American homes and factories.

Yet the electrical revolution was far from complete. The Edison Electric Light Company, as its name implied, existed simply to provide illumination; moreover, the direct current it manufactured could not be transmitted for more than a mile or two. But George M. Westinghouse, founder in 1886 of the Westinghouse Electric Company, showed that by using alternating current and transformers, high-voltage electric current could be transmitted safely and cheaply over long distances. Accordingly, alternating current soon outstripped direct current for lighting. The electric motor invented in 1888 by the Croatian immigrant, Nikola Tesla, provided a way of converting alternating current into power and, together with dynamo improvements by the Ohio engineer, Charles F. Brush, and others, enabled factories to use electric power. Meanwhile, one of Edison's former assistants, Frank J. Sprague, had demonstrated other applications of electricity. In 1887, using the overhead trolley invented by a Belgian immigrant, Charles J. Van Depoele, he supervised the building of the first successful electrical streetcar service at Richmond, Virginia. Sprague's company, ultimately absorbed by the Otis Elevator Company, also did much to develop the electric elevator, which first appeared in 1889 and which influenced urban architecture by encouraging the building of sky-scrapers.

Railroads and their Critics

The distinctive characteristics of the new industrialization were most fully typified by the railroads. They were the key to post-Civil War economic growth and constituted the most important single economic interest in the country. In 1890 railroad revenue exceeded $1,000 million, well over twice that of the federal government; in 1897 the combined value of railroad stocks and bonds was $10,635 million, eight times greater than the national debt; ten years later one-seventh of the country's wealth was invested in railroads. Linking together distant parts of the continent, the railroads played a major role in the settlement of the West as well as making possible the exploitation of natural resources and the creation of a national market. Their needs largely accounted, moreover, for the phenomenal expansion of coal and steel production.

The generation after the Civil War witnessed the completion of a national railroad network. Railroad mileage increased from 30,000 in 1860 to 193,000 in 1900, at which date the United States had more track than the whole of Europe, and two-fifths of the world's total. Though the trans-continental lines were the most spectacular achievement, there were other important developments. The Southern railroad system, largely destroyed during the Civil War, was rebuilt and considerably extended. By 1880 the South had 16,605 miles of track, twice as much as in 1860, and by 1890 39,108. In the Mississippi Valley, too, there was great expansion, es-pecially between 1865 and 1873. In the Northeast the major emphasis was on filling in gaps and, more particularly, on developing integrated trunk-routes. Hundreds of small lines were consolidated by lease, purchase, or merger into a handful of large systems, so that long-distance travelers no longer needed to make frequent changes. By 1874 traffic between the east-ern seaboard and the Middle West was dominated by four major railroads: the New York Central, the Pennsylvania, the Erie, and the Baltimore and Ohio. The process of amalgamation spread to New England with the cre-ation of the New York, New Haven, and Hartford and the Boston and Maine and to the South through the growth of such systems as the South-ern, the Louisville and Nashville, and the Illinois Central. One corollary was the adoption of a national uniform gauge of 4 feet 8½ inches; this was virtually achieved in 1886 when the leading Southern railroads, which had hitherto preferred a five-foot gauge, fell into line. Another was the adop-tion of standard time. A major difficulty in operating train services was the astonishing variation in local times. Thus when it was noon in Chicago, it was 11.27 a.m. in Omaha, 11.50 in St. Louis, 12.09 p.m. in Louisville,

12.17 in Toledo, and 12.31 in Pittsburgh. To end the confusion the American Railway Association divided the country into four time zones with an hour's differences between each. Going into force on November 18, 1883, the change was generally accepted by the public, though Congress did not officially sanction standard time until 1918.

Simultaneously technological advances made rail travel safer and less of an ordeal. The substitution of steel rails for iron and the cutting of wider roadbeds reduced hazards while making for smoother journeys. Steel coaches replaced the early wooden box-like cars; besides being fireproof they were infinitely stronger and thus less liable to fragment or telescope in the event of a collision. Train accidents, almost a weekly occurrence in the 1850s, became increasingly rare through the introduction of new safety devices like George M. Westinghouse's air brake, patented in 1869, which made it possible to apply the brakes to every wheel simultaneously. Soon afterwards Westinghouse invented an automatic air brake, so constructed that it set itself if a carriage became detached. Eli Janney's automatic car coupler, which obviated the need for a brakeman to go between the cars and link them together, appeared in 1873 and became standard equipment on all American railroads by 1888. More important still was the interlocking telegraphic block system, first installed in 1865 on the Camden and Amboy Railroad by its chief engineer, Ashbel Welch. By dividing the track into blocks and allowing only one train at a time into a given block, it preserved a safe distance between trains. And along with greater safety came elements of comfort, indeed of luxury. An enterprising New Yorker, George M. Pullman, who had introduced the sleeping-car during the Civil War, founded the Pullman Palace Car Company in 1867. The following year he launched the first dining-car and, a few years later, parlor and drawing-room cars. In 1879 Pullman built a model town near Chicago which bore his name and housed the largest railway-car construction company in the world.

Closely connected with the growth of railroads was bridge-building. Some of the longest spanned the continent's great rivers. Particularly remarkable were the 1,057-foot suspension bridge across the Ohio at Cincinnati (opened in 1867), the two bridges over the Missouri at Kansas City (1869) and Omaha (1871), and James B. Eads's steel arch (1874) which towered over the Mississippi at St. Louis. But most celebrated of all was Brooklyn Bridge, considered by many Americans to be the greatest engineering feat of the nineteenth century. Begun in 1866 it was the work of a wire manufacturer and engineer from Germany, John A. Roebling, already famous as the architect of the Niagara Bridge, and of his son. Washington A. Roebling. The longest bridge in the world at the time it was built (1883), it had a main span of 1,595 feet and two side spans, each of 930 feet. But it was not only its length that made it a milestone in engineering technology; it was the first suspension bridge to use steel-wire cables and one of the first to be built on pneumatic caissons.

For all the benefits railroads brought, there was much to criticize in the way they were built, financed, and operated. Wasteful construction and overbuilding far beyond the needs of traffic left many roads with crushing burdens of debt. So did stock-watering—the issuance of stock in excess of the value of assets. The result was cutthroat competition accompanied by ruinous rate-wars and the granting of huge rebates—secret reductions below the published tariff—in order to secure the business of large shippers. Another evil was fraudulent management. Admittedly, railroad magnates were not all cast in the same mold. At one extreme there was the towering figure of James J. Hill of the Great Northern, a man of vision and the highest financial probity who displayed a genuine concern for the regions his railroad served. At the other extreme stood the shameless trio—Daniel Drew, Jay Gould, and Jim Fisk—who made the Erie Railroad a byword for chicanery and fraud and whose speculations finally ruined it. A more representative figure, in the sense that he was a mixture of virtues and vices, was Cornelius Vanderbilt, the cynical, crude, and far-sighted New Yorker who expanded the New York Central into a consolidated system. Already a wealthy shipowner when he turned late in life to railroads, 'Commodore' Vanderbilt not only made the New York Central prosperous but also double-tracked its lines, pioneered the use of steel rails, improved services and equipment, and reduced rates. As he showed in his unsuccessful attempt to wrest control of the Erie from Drew, he was also a ruthless competitor, with no more compunction than his rival about corrupting legislators. He manipulated stock for his own benefit and by the time of his death in 1877 had amassed a fortune of $90 million. Nor would the Commodore entertain any notion of public regulation of the way he ran his railroad. His most-quoted utterance—"Law! What do I care about law? Hain't I got the power?"—is apocryphal, but expressed his sentiments well enough.

Such an attitude intensified popular hostility towards railroad malpractices. Criticism centered chiefly on freight rates: rebates and other forms of discrimination that favored large customers at the expense of smaller competitors, the practice of charging high rates between places that were dependent on a single line to compensate for the low rates charged when railroads were in competition with each other, agreements which enabled roads to divide traffic and charge higher uniform rates. There was also widespread indignation at railroad attempts to influence or corrupt newspaper editors and public officials by granting free passes or even by outright bribery.

Beginning with Massachusetts in 1869, a number of eastern states established supervisory railroad commissions. But the first attempts at thoroughgoing state regulation came in the Middle West as a result of agitation by farmers' organizations, especially the Granger Movement. Illinois passed a regulatory measure in 1871, Iowa and Minnesota in 1874, and Missouri, Kansas, and Nebraska a few years later. These so-called Granger laws fixed maximum rates for passengers and freight, forbade various discriminatory practices, and established railroad commissions to enforce the regulations. The railroads claimed that such measures were unconstitutional because they infringed the power of Congress over interstate commerce and because rate-fixing amounted to deprivation of property without due process of law and was thus a violation of the Fourteenth Amendment. But in *Munn* v. *Illinois* (1876) and other Granger cases, the Supreme Court held otherwise. Affirming the right of a state to regulate public utilities, Chief Justice Waite declared that when private property was devoted to public use, it "must submit to be controlled by the public for the public good".

Yet state regulation was not very effective. Some of the commissioners were incompetent, a few corrupt. Regulations were often loosely drawn and the railroads often successfully challenged them in the courts. Separate state action also meant a confusing miscellany of different rate structures. Then in 1886 the Supreme Court, having grown more conservative, decisively modified the attitude it had expressed in the Munn case. In *Wabash, St. Louis, and Pacific Railroad Company* v. *Illinois* it invalidated an Illinois statute prohibiting rate discrimination on routes between New York and Illinois on the ground that it encroached on the exclusive commerce power of Congress. The decision dealt a body-blow to state regulation and left a gap which only the federal government could fill. Few Congressmen were enthusiastic for regulation but public sentiment forced them to act. The Interstate Commerce Act of 1887 prohibited pooling, rebates, discrimination, and higher charges for short hauls than for long ones over the same line and provided that all railroad charges should be "reasonable and just". It created an Interstate Commerce Commission of five members with powers to investigate the management of railroads. This was the first of the independent regulatory agencies that were to become standard features of modern American government.

The passing of the Interstate Commerce Act is often said to mark the point at which the federal government abandoned *laissez-faire* and accepted the necessity of regulating private enterprise. But it was less of an innovation than historians generally make out. For, as James Bryce pointed out, while Americans were devoted to *laissez-faire* in theory, they were accustomed to departing from it in practice. Both state and federal governments had long intervened in economic life in various ways, the former most conspicuously by allotting funds for internal improvements and by granting charters of incorporation, the latter by its involvement in public land sales and its protective tariff policies. Moreover, after the Civil War government, especially at the state level, had greatly extended its sphere of action. In any case, the immediate practical results of the Interstate Commerce Act were negligible. The railroads showed great ingenuity in frustrating its provisions and the Supreme Court reversed many of the Commission's decisions, while whittling down its powers. In particular in the Maximum Freight Rate case (1897) the Court denied it the power to fix rates. By this time supervision had become largely nominal and the Commission had been reduced mainly to an agency for collecting and publishing statistics.

Steel, Oil, and Finance

The essential element in the economic revolution was the expansion of the iron and steel industry. These two metals provided modern America with its tools and machinery, its locomotives, bridges, and railroad tracks, its engines and skyscrapers, its bicycles, motorcars, and aircraft. Between 1860 and 1900 American pig-iron production rose from 800,000 to nearly 14 million tons, steel output from negligible proportions to 11 million tons, more than the combined production of the two next most powerful industrial nations, Great Britain and Germany. Pittsburgh, surrounded by extensive coalfields and iron-beds and strategically situated at the confluence of two great rivers, was the leading center of iron and steel production. The discovery of vast ore deposits nearly a thousand miles away in the Northern Michigan peninsula and later in the fabulous Mesabi range in Minnesota did not lessen Pittsburgh's supremacy since the ore could be brought cheaply to Pennsylvania through the Soo Canal and the Great Lakes. Nevertheless, new iron and steel centers eventually developed in places like Cleveland, Detroit, Gary, Chicago, and Birmingham, Alabama. Large-scale steel manufacture waited on the development of a cheap and practical method of ridding molten pig iron of carbon, phosphorus, and other impurities. In the 1850s an Englishman, Henry Bessemer, and an American, William Kelly, simultaneously discovered what eventually became known as the Bessemer process and in 1864 the first American Bessemer plant went into operation. Four years later, another and superior method of oxidizing the impurities in iron—the open-hearth process, a joint discovery by German and French inventors—was introduced to America by a New Jersey ironmaster, Abram S. Hewitt. The new processes enabled manufacturers to boost production enormously and to reduce the price of steel from $300 a ton to $35. Hitherto steel had been used only for making small and expensive articles, but it now rapidly ousted iron. Whereas in 1880 less than one-third of American pig-iron production was converted into steel, by 1900 the proportion was four-fifths.

The greatest steel master of the age was Andrew Carnegie. Unlike most American industrial leaders he began life in poverty. The son of a Scottish hand-loom weaver he was taken to America by his parents in 1848 at the age of thirteen. After working as a bobbin-boy in a cotton-mill and then as a telegraph operator, he turned first to iron manufacturing, which made him a millionaire, and then to steel. Though without training in engineering or technology, Carnegie was quick to grasp the significance of the new processes of steel manufacture. A man of driving energy and an aggressive salesman, he rode roughshod over competitors and trade unions alike. He had the enviable gift of surrounding himself with able associates—hard-headed businessmen like Henry Clay Frick and skilled negotiators like Charles M. Schwab. Together with Frick, Carnegie created a huge vertical combine—the first of its kind—embracing coalfields, coke ovens, limestone deposits, iron mines, ore ships, and railroads, thus securing control of all the needed sources of supply. The Carnegie Company soon dominated the steel industry; its huge profits—amounting to $40 million in 1900 alone—made its founder one of the richest men in the world. When the company merged with others in 1901 to form the United States Steel Corporation, a body which controlled three-fifths of the country's steel production, Carnegie received the colossal sum of $447 million for his holdings. He then retired to devote himself to philanthropy, endowing libraries and educational institutions, and setting up trusts and foundations to support research in science, the humanities, and international affairs. In all his benefactions amounted to about $350 million.

Oil, too, became the basis of great private fortunes. Although it did not come fully into its own until the twentieth century, when the internal-combustion engine went into general use, the petroleum industry expanded rapidly after the first successful drilling in western Pennsylvania in 1859. By the 1870s production approached 20 million barrels a year. Petroleum products found a variety of uses: heat, energy, lubrication, medicine, and above all, light. Kerosene took the place of tallow and whale-oil and, as late as 1899, about 60 percent of the industry's output went into illuminating oils. Since little capital was needed for drilling or refining, thousands of small operators, many of them incompetent, entered the business. In the violently competitive conditions that ensued, there was much waste and disorder; markets were periodically glutted, prices and profits fluctuated wildly, and long-term planning was impossible.

The end of this phase was, however, signaled in 1865 when a young Cleveland merchant, John D. Rockefeller, turned his attention fully to the oil business. Destined to provide the first outstanding example of business consolidation and to become America's first billionaire, Rockefeller is comparable with Carnegie in his business methods and achievements and ultimately in the scale of his philanthropies. He was above all an organizer.

His objects—apart from amassing a fortune—were to eliminate ruinous competition and to impose order and stability. Leaving drilling to others he set out to win control of refining. In 1872 he and his associates founded the Standard Oil Company of Ohio, transformed ten years later into the first of the trusts. Rockefeller combined superb business talent with low business ethics. He introduced efficiency into production, insisted on sound financial practices, gave priority to plowing back profits, and systematized marketing and distribution. Like Carnegie, Rockfeller established a vertically integrated system of production, building his own pipelines, warehouses, and bulk containers. But he also made systematic use of the ruthless business practices of the day. As well as insisting on railroad rebates, he resorted to blackmail, espionage, and price-slashing to drive competitors into bankruptcy or to force them to join him. His object was not, however, self-aggrandizement but to persuade competitors to agree to mergers from which all would profit. His methods nevertheless made him one of the most execrated figures in the country. The first really virulent criticism came from rivals whose methods were generally no more ethical than his. But the growth of his wealth and influence, together with his apparent indifference to public opinion, led to his being more widely reviled as an all-powerful, avaricious, and coldhearted monster. As for Standard Oil, no corporation attracted so much ill will or contributed more to the growth of hostility to trusts.

What Carnegie was to steel and Rockefeller was to oil, John Pierpont Morgan was to the world of investment banking. The son of a rich international banker, Morgan was a co-founder of the leading New York banking-house, Drexel, Morgan, and Co., reorganized in 1895 as J. P. Morgan and Co. Extraordinarily self-assured and possessing outstanding financial ability, Morgan came to symbolize the growing influence of investment bankers over corporation management. Sharing Rockefeller's dislike of ruinous competition and his passion for order, Morgan used his position in the capital market to force warring corporations to abandon their mutually destructive practices. In the 1890s he played a conspicuous part in reorganizing railroads which had been reduced to bankruptcy by speculation and overexpansion. Charging huge sums for its services, the House of Morgan scaled down the capitalization of distressed roads, improved management and financial methods, and placed its own representatives on boards of directors. By 1900 more than a third of the country's railroads had been "Morganized". The great financier then turned his attention to promoting combinations in other industries, one of his most daring and spectacular being the formation of United States Steel in 1901. Morgan's methods won the trust of investors and brought them considerable benefits. But they also concentrated vast powers in his own hands. Thus he remained until his death in 1913 the preeminent figure in the entire national economy and in the public mind the unrivaled symbol of financial domination.

Big Business: Apologia and Attack

The system which produced Carnegie, Rockefeller, and Morgan did not lack fervent and eminent defenders. Conservative intellectuals, social scientists, and clergymen formulated a clear-cut rationale of rugged individualism and unbridled competition. It drew heavily on the ideas of the English philosopher, Herbert Spencer, who applied biological concepts, especially Darwin's concept of natural selection, to social theory in order to justify an extreme version of *laissez-faire*. Competitive struggle, Spencer affirmed, made for human progress; state interference on behalf of the weak and unfit merely impeded it. Spencer's philosophy had an inherent attractiveness to Americans for it interpreted sympathetically the changing conditions of their society. His ablest American exponent was William Graham Sumner, Professor of Political Science at Yale. Sumner denied that there were social dangers in the accumulation of large individual fortunes. To him business success was merely the application of the principle of the survival of the fittest. He regarded millionaires as "the naturally selected agents of society" for work which benefited all. Bishop William Lawrence of Massachusetts, too, disputed that material wealth was inimical to morality. "Godliness is in league with riches . . .", he affirmed, "the race is to the strong." Businessmen themselves may have found the intricacies of Spencer's system beyond them, but learned to apply its catch-phrases. Thus Rockefeller asserted: "The growth of a large business is merely the survival of the fittest . . .". Carnegie, however, while employing very similar language generally defended *laissez-faire* in terms derived from the Protestant ethic with its theory of the stewardship of wealth. In 1889 he argued that the man of wealth had a grave responsibility, after providing for his own family, to see that his private fortune was used for the public welfare. In accordance with that philosophy he, like Rockefeller and other millionaires, gave away much of his enormous fortune for philanthropic purposes.

Not all Americans assented to *laissez-faire* doctrines or the gospel of wealth. In the 1880s the popular suspicion and hostility directed earlier against the railroads broadened into a more general assault on trusts. To some extent the public was simply worried lest monopoly lead to higher prices and to consumer exploitation—though criticism on that score became progressively more difficult to sustain since most prices fell continuously. Economic self-interest likewise explained the antitrust stance of farmers, trade unionists, and small businessmen. But the antitrust movement derived most of its vigor from more deep-seated forebodings: Americans feared that the concentration of economic power represented by the big corporations threatened American democratic institutions and that the decline of competition meant an end to economic opportunity and individual mobility.

At a popular level the attack on the trusts was led by artists like Joseph Keppler and Thomas Nast, whose biting antitrust cartoons became a regular feature of pictorial weeklies like *Puck* and *Harper's*. The literature of antitrust may be said to have begun with Henry George's *Progress and Poverty* (1879). Born in Philadelphia, George spent years of poverty in California trying to establish himself as a journalist. Convinced that the basic source of the inequality that accompanied material progress was private landownership, George advocated a 'single tax' on the unearned increment on land. That would suffice, he believed, to restore the benevolent operation of natural economic laws. The single-tax doctrine won relatively few converts but George's plea for social justice and his insistence that men had the power to reconstruct society attracted a vast popular audience, both in the United States and in the British Isles. By 1900 *Progress and Poverty* had sold two million copies. Another dissenting voice, that of the New Englander, Edward Bellamy, preached a more radical economic philosophy. Bellamy's Utopian novel, *Looking Backward: 2000-1887* (1888), painted an alluring picture of a new cooperative order. Private enterprise, with its waste, inequality, and poverty, had given way to a socialist commonwealth in which material rewards were shared equally. The book was an instant success and a chain of 'nationalist' clubs sprang up throughout the country to propagate Bellamy's ideas. A third writer with strong social convictions was Henry Demarest Lloyd, who retired from Chicago journalism in 1885 to devote all his energies to reform. Believing that corporate power was destroying democracy he wrote *Wealth Against Commonwealth* (1894), a slashing, heavily documented though not entirely accurate attack on the prototype of monopoly, the Standard Oil Company. Though Lloyd's plea for the public ownership of monopolies evoked little response, he helped impress upon thoughtful minds the need for the government to play a larger role in the economy.

In academic circles, too, a revolt occurred against the individualism and fatalism of Social Darwinists like Sumner. In *Dynamic Sociology* (1883) the pioneer sociologist, Lester F. Ward, took issue with Sumner's basic contention that state intervention was futile. Among economists Richard T. Ely and John R. Commons attacked the orthodoxies of the *laissez-faire* school. Even more critical of the existing order was another economist Thorstein B. Veblen, the son of Norwegian immigrants in Wisconsin. Veblen's *The Theory of the Leisure Class* (1899) was a savage assault on businessmen and their pecuniary values. The millionaire captains of industry, he argued, had contributed nothing constructive; their way of life, with its 'conspicuous leisure' and 'conspicuous consumption', showed them to be essentially parasites. Veblen's irony and apparent solemnity tended to obscure his criticisms of capitalist society, but he nevertheless came to have a profound influence on economic thought.

Curbing the Trusts

As with railroad regulation, the states took the lead in antitrust legislation. In the 1880s twenty-seven states and territories, mainly in the South and West, passed laws prohibiting trusts and other forms of combination. But local regulation was never very effective. Where trusts were proceeded against—Standard Oil of Ohio was the leading example—they managed to escape control by transferring their legal headquarters to other states, notably New Jersey, Delaware, and West Virginia, which placed few restrictions upon the issuance of corporation charters. In any case the states lacked the power to curb monopolies engaged in interstate commerce. In 1888 both the major parties pledged support for federal action and in 1890, after the briefest of debates and with hardly a dissenting voice, both houses of Congress passed the Sherman Antitrust Act. Devised not by Senator John Sherman after whom it was named but by the Senate Judiciary Committee, the measure in effect attempted to give statutory power to common-law doctrine against monopoly. It declared that "every contract, combination in the form of trust or otherwise, or conspiracy, in restraint of trade or commerce among the several states or with foreign nations . . . is illegal". Persons forming such combinations were declared to be guilty of a misdemeanor punishable by fines of $5,000 and a year in jail.

It is often argued that the Sherman Act was not a genuine attempt to deal with a complex economic problem but a cynical political gesture, designed only to make the public believe that something was being done. In fact Congressmen shared the popular concern about monopoly and seem to have acted in good faith. Nonetheless little thought went into the framing of what was a brief, unspecific, and loosely worded measure. Its ambiguous phrasing and its failure to define such terms as "trust", "combination", and "restraint of trade" turned out to be serious weaknesses. These made it easier for the courts, now dominated by devotees of *laissez-faire*, to emasculate the measure when suits were brought under it. The critical decision came in *United States* v. *E. C. Knight Co.* (1895), the first case of its kind to be decided by the Supreme Court. Though it was shown that the defendants controlled 98 percent of the manufacture of refined sugar, the court held that this admitted monopoly was not a violation of the antitrust act because manufacturing was not "trade" within the meaning of the law. Not surprisingly in view of the Knight decision, the last years of the century witnessed a renewed drive towards consolidation.

Yet judicial conservatism was not the main reason why the Sherman Act remained largely a dead letter for more than a decade. The real fault was that successive administrations made only halfhearted attempts to enforce it. Between 1890 and 1901, federal law officers initiated only eighteen suits under the Sherman Act and won ten of them, while private individuals brought another eighteen, winning two. But none of the victories was against big monopolies. That was largely because of the inexpert tactics of the prosecuting attorneys. For example, it was Attorney General Olney's blundering presentation that largely accounted for the government's failure in the Knight case. That the judiciary was not invariably hostile to antitrust legislation was demonstrated in 1897 and 1898 when in two decisions the Supreme Court ruled that the Sherman Act applied to railroads. Moreover, the later history of trust prosecutions showed that the act could be invoked to obtain favorable verdicts against monopolies.

Trade Unionism: Progress and Problems

One might have expected that the consolidation of business would stimulate the consolidation of labor. Only thus could workingmen hope to combat the power of aggregated wealth. Yet trade unions developed far more slowly in the United States than in Europe. One reason was that the workforce consisted largely of immigrants divided by language, ethnic origin, and religion. In addition, both native-born and immigrant workers refused to associate with blacks. Employers thus found it easy to play off one group against another. They also used labor spies, blackmail, and even armed force to thwart union organization. They could also generally rely on the strong bias of the lawcourts in favor of capital. Small businessmen and farmers often shared the conviction of employers that trade unionism was un-American. Indeed many of the workers themselves had little sympathy with collective action. The opportunities for advancement that existed—or were believed to exist—in America undermined class-consciousness by seeming to guarantee that no one need remain a hired hand permanently. For these reasons American labor had a long history of uncertain leadership, confusion of method, and fluctuating membership.

The first steps toward a consolidated labor movement were taken in the 1860s when local craft unions coalesced to form national organizations. From national unionism to confederation was a natural development. The first attempt to combine different unions into a single body came in 1866 when William H. Sylvis, leader of the Iron Molders' Union, founded the National Labor Union. Though attaining a considerable membership, the organization lasted only six years. It was a motley conglomeration that included not only trade unions but also farmers' associations and various reform groups. Most of its leaders were visionaries or cranks, less concerned with the immediate problems of workingmen than with long-term economic and social reform. Consequently most of the unions withdrew, whereupon the rump of the federation was transformed into the short-lived National Labor Party.

Vague and diffuse Utopianism also characterized the Knights of Labor, a secret fraternal order with an elaborate ritual founded in 1869 by a group of Philadelphia garment-cutters headed by Uriah S. Stephens, a former Baptist minister. Though established by artisans, the Knights sought to unite all "toilers" in one grand association, irrespective of occupation, race, nationality, or sex. Membership was open to all deemed to be following the divine injunction: "In the sweat of thy brow shalt thou eat bread." Thus the unskilled were welcomed along with craftsmen; so were farmers and even capitalists. Only lawyers, bankers, liquor dealers, and professional gamblers were excluded. While the Knights demanded the eight-hour day, equal pay for women, and the abolition of child labor, they also put forward a long list of political demands unconnected directly with labor conditions—paper money, an income tax, the nationalization of the railroads. And although their primary purpose was "to secure to the toilers a proper share of the wealth they create", they rejected the notion that wage-earners constituted a permanent class. Instead they revived the Jacksonian individualistic ideal of wanting to make "every man his own master". Condemning strikes as "acts of private warfare", they sought to achieve their objectives through legislation and, more particularly, through the formation of producers' cooperatives. The Knights, in a word, were unwilling to come to terms with the new economic order and looked back nostalgically to a preindustrial age.

At first the Knights grew slowly; in 1878 membership was still under 10,000. Then in 1879 they elected as Grand Master Workman a Pennsylvania machinist called Terence V. Powderly. Devoted to industrial brotherhood, education, and the cooperative principle and opposed to industrial warfare, Powderly personified the idealism—and, indeed, the contradictions—of the Order. To meet the objections of the Catholic Church—he was himself a Catholic—Powderly persuaded the Knights to abandon secrecy and modify its quasi-religious character. A period of spectacular growth followed; by 1886 the membership had soared to over 700,000, mainly because of the Order's proved ability to win strikes. In 1885, to Powderly's disgust, militant local unions affiliated with the Knights forced the Wabash railway system owned by Jay Gould to restore wage cuts and recognize their union. This victory, the first of its kind in American industrial history, gave an astonishing boost to recruitment. But the gains proved ephemeral. A third strike against the Gould system in 1886 failed and union power was broken.

The Haymarket Affair in Chicago (1886) further damaged the prestige of the Knights. Chicago, a stronghold of extreme labor radicalism, had spawned among other things a tiny anarchist movement, led by German immigrants like Johann Most and August Spies who preached violent revolution. Spies called a meeting in Haymarket Square on May 4 to protest at police violence outside the McCormick Harvester plant, where a strike had been in progress for some time. At the Haymarket meeting someone threw a bomb which killed one policeman and six other persons and injured sixty-seven others. The police promptly opened fire, killing four more people. The affair sent a wave of fear through the American business community, which saw it as proof that the anarchists meant business. Responding to demands for action, the Chicago police rounded up 200 anarchists and charged eight of them with conspiracy to murder. Some at least had been guilty of incitement to violence—Spies's newspaper had even published instructions on how to make dynamite—but there was no evidence of complicity in the Haymarket Affair. Nevertheless, all eight were convicted and seven sentenced to death. One of the condemned men, an experienced bomb-maker, blew himself up in his cell, two others (Spies being one) had their sentences commuted to life imprisonment, and the remaining four were hanged. But the feeling persisted that there had been a miscarriage of justice and in 1893 the liberal Governor of Illinois, John Peter Altgeld, braved the fury of public opinion and pardoned the three surviving anarchists.

Though the Knights of Labor repudiated anarchism and had not been involved in the Haymarket Affair, the public nonetheless connected it with violence and radicalism. Meanwhile mismanagement and unfair competition had brought about the failure of most of the two hundred cooperative enterprises—chiefly mines, shoe factories, and cooperage works—the Knights had started. After 1886 the organization crumbled rapidly. Its power in the big cities drained away as workers turned once more to national craft unions. By 1893 membership had dwindled to 75,000 and the Knights' activities had come to resemble those of a friendly society.

As the Knights declined a rival movement, based upon an entirely different labor philosophy, arose in its place. Founded in 1881 by representatives of a number of craft unions and reorganized in 1886 under the name of the American Federation of Labor, the new organization repudiated the Knights' ideal of one big, centrally-controlled union. As its name implied the AF of L was a loose federation of national trade unions, each retaining a large degree of autonomy. Made up predominantly of skilled workers, it won the support of every established union except the four railway brotherhoods (engine-drivers, conductors, firemen, and trainmen). The founders of the AF of L did not share the aspirations of the National Labor Union and the Knights of Labor for political reform or a cooperative commonwealth. Theirs was a more hardheaded philosophy which concentrated on winning concrete benefits in wages, hours, and economic conditions. Unlike the Knights of Labor, they were prepared to use strikes and boycotts to attain their ends.

The dominating figure of the AF of L was Samuel Gompers, president of the organization almost continuously from 1886 until his death in 1924. Born in London in 1850 of Dutch-Jewish parentage, Gompers arrived in the United States in 1863, went into his father's trade of cigar-making, and became prominent in the cigar-makers' union. He developed a pragmatic approach to labor problems, confessing later that he stood for "pure and simple" unionism, and claiming that his philosophy could be summed up in the single word, "More". Unlike most European trade-union leaders, he accepted the existing economic system and repudiated the idea of a separate labor party. He also fought a bitter battle against Socialist influence within the labor movement. But although against direct involvement in politics Gompers encouraged workers, irrespective of party, to use their votes to reward labor's friends and to punish its enemies. He also drew up a "legislative platform" calling for the eight-hour day, employers' liability and mine-safety laws. Thanks largely to Gompers's moderation the AF of L avoided the taint of radicalism and won an accepted place in American society and experienced a steady, if unspectacular, growth.

The Growth of Industrial Conflict

Trade unionism's faltering progress helps explain the unparalleled industrial violence of the last quarter of the century. One of the most controversial episodes—the subject of Conan Doyle's *Valley of Fear*—concerned the Molly Maguires, a secret Irish labor organization in the Pennsylvania anthracite counties. In 1873, after a series of coal strikes during which mine superintendents were mysteriously murdered, railroad cars derailed, and coal-tips burned, the mine-owners called in the Pinkerton Detective Agency, which specialized in countering labor unrest. Adopting a well-tried method, a Pinkerton agent posed as a fugitive from justice, infiltrated the inner councils of the organization, and secured evidence which resulted in 1877 in the conviction and execution of nineteen of the ringleaders.

This was the prelude to a more widespread upheaval, the great railroad strike of 1877, the first industrial conflict to affect the nation as a whole. Like most major strikes of the period, it was triggered off by wage cuts which seemed doubly unjust because the railroads maintained dividends. Beginning on the Baltimore and Ohio system it spread to other major trunk-lines, paralyzing two-thirds of the country's railroad network. As the strike expanded, it was accompanied by destructive and bloody rioting. By far the worst occurred in Pittsburgh, where a pitched battle between strikers and state militia resulted in twenty-five deaths and millions of dollars' worth of damage. Order was restored only when President Hayes sent in federal troops.

The public hostility toward trade unionism produced by the events of 1877 and the Haymarket Affair was further intensified by the bitterly fought strike at Carnegie's Homestead steel plant near Pittsburgh in 1892. The strike began when a wage dispute escalated into one over collective bargaining. The plant manager, Henry Clay Frick, prepared to use strike-breakers and engaged 300 Pinkerton detectives to protect them. On July 6, as the Pinkertons approached the plant in barges, they were fired on by strikers and in the ensuing battle both sides sustained death and injury. The Pinkertons were finally forced to surrender and were marched through the streets by their jeering captors. Frick appealed to the governor of Pennsylvania for help, and the strikers were ejected by the National Guard. Public opinion was at first on the side of the strikers, partly because of the use of the hated Pinkertons, partly because Carnegie had introduced wage cuts so soon after pleading for a higher tariff on steel. But an attempt by an anarchist to assassinate Frick produced a revulsion. The strike was finally broken in November, with the result that steel unionism in the Carnegie system was destroyed.

Less bloody though in some ways more significant was the Pullman strike of 1894. The Pullman Palace Car Company, which manufactured sleeping- and parlor cars and leased them to railroads, prided itself on being a model employer. But during the depression winter of 1893–4 it introduced swingeing wage cuts, averaging about 25 percent. When the management refused to discuss grievances with a representative committee and sacked some of its members, the workers struck in protest. The strikers' cause was taken up by the militant American Railway Union, organized the previous year by Eugene V. Debs. The union decision to boycott railroads using Pullman cars led to a major railroad strike, which paralyzed traffic out of Chicago and was accompanied by sporadic violence. The railroad companies appealed for federal intervention and the Attorney General, Richard Olney, secured a federal-court 'blanket' injunction restraining anyone from interfering with the railroads or the mails or from seeking to dissuade railway employees from performing their normal duties. Then, on the pretext that the strikers were obstructing the mails—which was not strictly true—President Cleveland sent in federal troops, ignoring the protests of the prolabor governor of Illinois, John Peter Altgeld, who was ready to restore order with state militia. These federal moves quickly broke the strike. Debs defied the injunction, was sent to prison for six months for contempt, and emerged a convert to Socialism.

The Pullman strike left no doubt that the federal government was prepared to protect employers' interests at the expense of labor's. It was also significant as the first occasion on which an injunction had been used to break a major strike. It was to remain the employers' favorite weapon until it was outlawed by the Norris-La Guardia Act of 1932. Trade unionists were understandably embittered. They were particularly infuriated that the federal court had based its blanket injunction on the Sherman Antitrust Act, arguing that the American Railway Union was a combination in restraint of trade.

In the wave of prosperity that followed the Spanish-American War union membership grew rapidly. So did the number of strikes, some of them violent. Taking the lead in an employers' counteroffensive was the National Union of Manufacturers, an organization mainly of small employers which started an aggressive open-shop campaign. Its efforts were backed up by the militant American Antiboycott Association founded in 1902 to fight unionism in the courts. Not all employers were antiunion. In 1900 a group of business magnates, including Mark Hanna and J. P. Morgan, joined with Samuel Gompers and John Mitchell, president of the United Mine Workers, to form the American Civic Federation which attempted to avoid strikes and lockouts and to provide machinery for mediation and conciliation. But organized capital as a whole had little sympathy with such efforts. The strong support it gave to the coordinated antiunion activities of the National Union of Manufacturers and similar associations was one reason why trade unionism lost ground between 1904 and 1909.

Another was the bias of the courts in favor of property rights. Stemming as much from fear of social disorder as from belief in *laissez-faire*, this manifested itself in frequent antistrike injunctions and in two important boycott cases. In the Buck's Stove and Range Company case of 1907, a federal judge issued an injunction restraining AF of L officials from boycotting the products of an employer deemed to have been unfair to labor. More sweepingly, the Supreme Court ruled in the Danbury Hatters' case in 1908 that secondary boycotts—those attempting to coerce third parties into the practice—were conspiracies in restraint of trade within the meaning of the Sherman Act. When the case was retried, the Court not only decided again in favor of the employers but also affirmed that individual union members were responsible for the actions of their officials. The Supreme Court also blocked most legislative attempts to improve working conditions on the ground that they violated the liberty guaranteed by the Fourteenth Amendment. Thus in *Lochner* v. *New York* (1905) a majority of the Court held that a law establishing a ten-hour day for bakers was, besides being an excessive use of police power, an unreasonable interference with a worker's right to contract for as many hours as he chose. The *Lochner* case turned out to be the high-water mark of judicial hostility, but the courts long continued to be unsympathetic to trade unions.

While the powers of trade unions was being whittled away by the courts, their prestige suffered from radical terrorism. Among several dynamite outrages against capital, two attracted particular attention. The first occurred in 1905 when Frank Steunenberg, who had incurred the enmity of labor while governor of Idaho, was murdered by a booby-trap bomb. The man who confessed to the crime implicated three leaders of the radical Western Federation of Miners, one being William D. (Big Bill) Haywood, soon to become America's best-known labor radical. The three were kidnaped in Denver by Pinkerton detectives and spirited to Boise, Idaho, where they were tried for murder. The entire American trade-union movement rallied to their defense and, after the prosecution evidence had been destroyed by Clarence Darrow, the most famous trial-lawyer of the day, they were acquitted. But the verdict did not shake most people's opinion that the WFM leaders were men of violence. More damaging still to labor was the dynamiting in October 1910 of the *Los Angeles Times* building, owned by a leading advocate of the open shop. After a nationwide manhunt three members of the Iron Workers' Union, Ortie McManigal and J. J. and J. B. McNamara, were arrested for the crime. Liberal opinion was aroused, the AF of L, convinced that the McNamara brothers at least were innocent, raised a defense fund and again engaged Darrow. But the McNamaras finally confessed their guilt and were given long prison sentences. Subsequently forty other officials of the Iron Workers' Union were indicted on charges of conspiracy to transport dynamite and explosives. Thirty-eight were found guilty, including Frank Ryan, the union president.

In spite of its troubles with the courts and its loss of public esteem the AF of L continued to grow. By 1914 it had more than two million members—barely 11 percent of the non-agricultural work-force, but a reasonably impressive total in view of the challenge of the Industrial Workers of the World, a revolutionary anarchist-syndicalist trade-union movement, whose members were known popularly as 'Wobblies'. Founded in Chicago in 1905, the IWW was an outgrowth of the Western Federation of Miners, a militant organization which had been involved in strikes in the Rocky Mountain mining states ever since its formation in 1893. Under Haywood's leadership the IWW planned to unite the American working class, and eventually wage-earners all over the world, into one big union to wage class war against capitalism. Already strong among western miners, the Wobblies broke new ground in attempting to unionize migratory lumberjacks and harvest-hands in the Middle Western and Far Western states and immigrant textile workers in the East. The IWW never won a wide following—membership reached a peak of 60,000 in 1912—but it earned the hatred and fear of employers by its 'free speech' campaign and its aggressive leadership of strikes. The crest of its power came in 1912 when IWW organizers led a protracted strike at Lawrence, Massachusetts of 25,000 textile workers drawn from twenty-two different nationalities. When the textile companies conceded the employees' demands it seemed that the IWW would become a major force. But when it attempted to repeat its success in the Paterson, New Jersey, silkworkers' strike in 1913, the authorities forbade picketing, ordered IWW leaders out of the town, and arrested Haywood when he tried to speak. Although the IWW managed to prolong the strike for five months, lack of funds and loss of morale finally forced the strikers to surrender.

The Wobblies became the main victims of the antiradical hysteria of World War I and the Red Scare of 1919. As a result of vigilante action and federal prosecutions, membership dwindled rapidly. The movement's balladeer, Joe Hill, was executed in Salt Lake City for murder in 1915, thus providing the Wobblies with a martyr. Haywood jumped bail after his conviction for sedition in 1918 and fled to the Soviet Union, where he died in 1928. Though the Wobblies accomplished little they retain a unique place in American folklore and in left-wing revolutionary mythology. Their romantic attraction owes much to their colorful leaders—Haywood, Hill, and the redoubtable 'Mother' Jones, the most famous and popular woman in American trade-union history— the fact that they spoke for the inarticulate and the culturally alienated, and, not least, their stirring protest songs—angry, sardonic, humorous verses and parodies sung to popular melodies and hymn tunes like Ralph Chaplin's "Solidarity for Ever", sung to the tune of *John Brown's Body*, and Joe Hill's "The Preacher and the Slave", with its famous line, "You'll get pie in the sky when you die."

Industrialization and the Condition of Labor

It is often claimed that machines, factory discipline, and the increasing trend towards bigness, robbed working men of status, security, independence, and creative pride and destroyed the former close relationship between employers and the employed. This may perhaps have happened to former craftsmen, but not to those who came to factory, mill, or mine from farm labor or domestic service. For them, and more especially for the European immigrants who constituted the bulk of the American industrial labor force, the change could and often did mean liberation from inferiority and dependence. One of the most revealing facts about occupations in this period is that the number of domestic and personal servants failed to increase as rapidly as the number of industrial workers. Moreover the industrial transformation raised the working man's standard of living. This was not always understood at the time. So regularly did contemporary critics assert that the rich were getting richer and the poor poorer that it was widely accepted as proven fact. But Carroll D. Wright, the leading statistician of the day, dismissed it as "a wandering phrase, without paternity or date" and Gompers described it as "perfectly absurd". The truth is that while the rich were indeed getting richer, so were the poor, though at an infinitely slower rate. Between 1860 and 1890 real wages rose spectacularly and, though they shrank a little in the 1890s, went up again slightly between 1897 and 1914. Moreover the average working week was reduced from about 66 hours in 1860 to 55 in 1914. But labor's gains were unevenly distributed. Skilled workers gained more than the unskilled, union members more than the unorganized, Northerners considerably more than Squtherners. Even in the North average annual wages in the textile and garment industries in the first decade of the twentieth century were only $400, a long way below the $650 estimated to be the minimum subsistence level for an average-size family. This explained the high incidence of female and child labor. Moreover, in 1915 the federal Commission on Industrial Relations reported that between a third and a half of all American wage-earning families were living below the poverty line. In short the social cost of industrialization in the United States, as in Europe, was distressingly high.

17. *Society and Culture in the Industrial Era*, 1860–1910

Population Trends

Although population nearly trebled between 1860 and 1910, the rate of growth was declining. Up to 1860 population had increased by a third or more every decade. Thereafter, despite huge immigration, the rate of increase fell steadily. By the decade 1901–10 it was down to 21 percent, only a half of what it had been between 1800 and 1810. Americans were still a highly fecund people—first-generation immigrants especially—but from about 1870 the birth-rate (as in other industrialized countries) progressively declined. Families with eight to ten children were no longer so common, especially among the business and professional classes. The main cause was an increasing resort to contraception, especially by the urban middle classes, notwithstanding religious condemnation and federal and state laws forbidding the circulation of contraceptive information and devices. As late as 1915 Margaret Sanger, the New York nurse who led the birth-control movement, was indicted for sending a birth-control pamphlet through the post.

The effects of a falling birth-rate were, however, masked by an even greater fall in the death-rate. Advances in medical knowledge, the spread of preventive and curative medicine, a more nutritious diet, and improved standards of public health were the main reasons why mortality declined. There was a particularly sharp drop in deaths from such diseases as typhoid, diphtheria, scarlet fever, and tuberculosis, as well as from infants' diseases.

Population growth was not uniform throughout the nation. Even after the frontier was officially declared closed in 1890 several western states—notably Washington, Oregon, Texas, Oklahoma, and California—experienced gains far in excess of the national average. Even so, the bulk of the population continued to be concentrated north of the Ohio and east of the Mississippi—indeed, the region had almost as large a share of the population in 1910 as in 1860—47 percent as against 55 percent. This was because it contained most of the nation's tumultuously growing cities.

Urban Growth

As early as 1860 one in every six Americans was a city-dweller. New York was already the third largest city in the world and Philadelphia was bigger than Berlin. But it was only after the Civil War that the city came into its own. Railroads, heavy industry, and technological advances helped build cities and were in turn stimulated by them. American urban growth was unparalleled. By 1900 one-third of the American population were city-dwellers and no fewer than forty cities had more than 100,000 inhabitants. Unlike many European countries the United States possessed no one metropolis, but New York was preeminent, its population growing between 1860 and 1900 from just over one million to 3½ million. Chicago, despite being almost completely destroyed in the great fire of 1871, leapt into second place, its population soaring from 100,000 to 1,700,000. Some of the older coastal cities in the East, such as Boston and Baltimore, suffered a relative decline, though Philadelphia's population went up from 560,000 to 1,300,000. Elsewhere there were some astonishing examples of rapid growth: Minneapolis expanded from 2,500 to 200,000, Denver from virtually nothing to 134,000, Los Angeles from 5,000 to 100,000.

Not until 1920 would a majority of Americans live in urban areas. But from about 1870 onwards the city became the controlling influence in national life. Within its confines were to be found the lineaments of the new industrialism: factories, mills, and railway-yards, giant corporations, investment and banking institutions. As the workshop of the wage-earner the city served as a huge magnet, attracting rural and small-town folk both from within the United States and from Europe. It was equally the home of science and technology and the cradle of the creative arts. The city dramatized the inequalities of wealth that had come to characterize American life, created new social needs, and broadened the scope of governmental activity. It provided the forum for machine politics and for civic reform. And finally it produced a new sectionalism, aligning town against country in ways that were reflected in both national and state politics.

Rural depopulation complemented urban growth. While virtually the entire eastern half of the country experienced a flight from the land, it was most marked in the North Atlantic states. New England, unable to withstand competition from Western virgin lands, was worst hit. Travelers through once prosperous New England farming districts in the 1880s were struck by the number of abandoned and overgrown farms, tumbledown buildings, and deserted villages. The census of 1890 told the same story of rural depletion. Out of a total of 1,502 rural townships in New England, 932 had lost inhabitants during the previous decade, mostly to nearby cities. Though that was where displaced country folk could best find employment the appeal of the city was not exclusively economic. The bright lights of the city were equally alluring. For the swelling tides of European immigrants the city was even more of a lodestone.

The New Immigration

In the half-century after the Civil War immigration exceeded twenty-six million—five times greater than in the previous fifty years and three times greater than in the previous two and a half centuries. Up to 1880 or so immigrants came predominantly from northern and western Europe. Thereafter a growing majority—85 percent by 1914—originated in southern and eastern Europe, more particularly Austria–Hungary, Italy, and Russia. This so-called 'new immigration' brought to the United States a bewildering variety of unfamiliar types: Poles, Czechs, and Hungarians; Finns, Ukrainians, Croats, Slovaks, and Ruthenians; east European Jews; Portuguese, Italians, and Greeks; Turks, Armenians, Syrians, and Lebanese. (Another stream, smaller but more alien still, arrived from across the Pacific; Chinese were in the van, then Japanese and Filipinos. There were also sizable overland movements from Mexico and Canada.)

The 'new' immigration from southern and eastern Europe resulted basically from the same economic changes that had earlier affected the north and west of the continent—a massive population increase, the collapse of the old agricultural order, the industrial revolution. However, many emigrated to avoid compulsory military service. Others fled religious persecution, notably the Russian Jews forced out by Czarist pogroms like those of 1881 and 1904. The transition from sail to steam, virtually complete by 1870, helped swell the exodus by robbing the Atlantic crossing of its worst terrors. Steamship companies did not, as contemporaries frequently alleged, lure Europeans peasants from their homes with promises of well-paid American jobs; that was not only illegal but also unnecessary. But competition for steerage traffic certainly stimulated emigration, especially through the expansion of the prepaid passage system. In 1901 it was estimated that between 40 and 65 percent of immigrants traveled on tickets prepaid by friends and relatives in the United States or bought with remittances received from them.

To a far greater extent than the 'old' immigrant groups (except the Irish), the 'new' immigrants congregated in America's industrial cities. Agriculture held little appeal for them, since they lacked the capital to begin farming and were attracted by the high wages obtainable in factories, mines, and mills. Their preference for urban life gave American cities a strongly foreign flavor. By 1910 one-third of the population of the twelve largest cities was foreign-born and another third was made up of the children of immigrants. New York had more Italians than Naples, more Germans than Hamburg, twice as many Irish as Dublin, and more Jews than the whole of western Europe. Chicago was more cosmopolitan still.

Each group of immigrants tended to concentrate in different industries: Poles, Slovaks, and Hungarians in mining and heavy industry; Russian and Polish Jews in the garment trade; Italians in construction work or, along with the Portuguese and French-Canadians, in textiles. For the most part immigrants did the heavy, dirty, disagreeable jobs. They frequently endured long hours, exploitation, and dangerous and insanitary conditions of work. Some of the most notorious evils were to be found in the garment industry. Under the contracting-out system which characterized it men, women and children toiled for as much as sixteen hours a day in squalid tenement homes or steam-filled, ill-lit sweatshops. The terrible Triangle Fire of 1911, the worst industrial tragedy in the history of New York's Lower East Side, in which 146 lives were lost, belatedly drew attention to these evils and prompted legislative intervention. Conditions in mines and factories were in some respects worse. Though wages were higher than in Europe, so was the accident-rate. Employers tended to blame accidents on the recklessness and ignorance of immigrants, but the real faults were inadequate supervision and disregard of safety precautions. Another kind of exploitation, largely confined to Italians, was the *padrone* system. New arrivals, unfamiliar with the language and with American conditions, welcomed the help of a compatriot *padrone*, or work-boss, in finding work; but they found themselves trapped in a system that was almost the equivalent of peonage.

Poverty compelled most immigrants to live in slums. Every large American city had its teeming and congested immigrant districts, but New York's Lower East Side, with its huge concentrations of Irish, Germans, Jews, and Italians provided the most notorious example. But conditions could be just as frightful in smaller places. The novelist, Frank Norris, visiting the Pennsylvania anthracite regions during the strike of 1902 found groups of Polish miners living in tiny hovels 'not fit for dogs' and wondered why their occupants were content merely with striking. Yet immigrants generally found harsh physical surroundings easier to adjust to than the psychological trials they faced. Mostly simple, ignorant country folk, they were bewildered, overwhelmed even, by American city life. This explained why each group tended to occupy a distinct residential area and to move elsewhere when strangers appeared. A mosaic of ethnic neighborhoods thus developed, though the use of appellations like 'Little Italy' or Kleindeutschland to describe them was misleading since immigrants clustered in provincial rather than in national groups. A desire to preserve their identity and find emotional security in the company of their own kind explained also why each immigrant group established its own social institutions—churches, schools, newspapers, mutual-aid societies, and theaters.

Massive though the impact of immigration was, immigrants rarely accounted for more than a third of the population of any state and, even when they did, it was only for short periods in sparsely-populated and newly formed Western states like Nevada and North Dakota. In the country as a whole the proportion of foreign-born rose only from 13.2 percent in 1860 to 14.7 percent in 1910. Even when immigrants and their children are counted together, they never amounted to more than 35 percent of the total population. Yet Americans became increasingly uneasy about immigration. With the closing of the frontier it was no longer possible to feel that the country had room for all. There was also growing concern about immigration's changed character. The influx of motley bands of foreigners speaking strange languages and following strange customs led many Americans to suspect that their society was being radically changed—and for the worse. The 'new' immigrants came from the more backward parts of Europe and were generally poorer, less skilled, and less literate than the 'old'. Most of them, too, were strangers to democracy and representative government. Americans began to doubt whether people so alien could ever be successfully assimilated. Prejudice and fear intensified nativist hostility. There was widespread alarm about immigrant radicalism, especially after the conviction of foreign anarchists for the Haymarket bomb outrage in 1886. There was also disquiet that the United States was losing its original Protestant character. The increasingly Catholic coloring of immigration, the spectacular expansion of the Catholic parochial school system, and the growing prominence of Irish Catholic politicians, contributed to a revival of popular anti-Catholicism. The American Protective Association, founded in 1886 to restrict Catholic political power and to defend the public school system, whipped up anti-Catholic hysteria with wild talk of an imminent papal conquest. There was also increasing hostility to another prominent element in the 'new' immigration, the Jews. Vicious racist slurs and anti-Semitic cartoons appeared in the popular press; Jews found themselves increasingly excluded from clubs, hotels, summer resorts, and private schools.

The movement for immigration restriction, which developed out of these anxieties, aimed not at ending immigration but at selective controls to exclude undesirables, especially those deemed inferior and unassimilable. Trade unions supported the demand. They saw the 'new' immigrants, with their low living standards, as a threat to the American working man, and mistakenly believed that the great majority had been recruited as contract laborers by American employers to break strikes and hold down wages. But the spearhead of the restrictionist movement was the Immigration Restriction League, founded in 1894 by a group of race-conscious Boston patricians. Arguing that the 'Anglo-Saxon' element in the American population was in danger of being swamped by lesser breeds, the League campaigned vigorously for a literacy test as a means of excluding most of the 'new' immigrants.

Yet a vocal liberal minority was reluctant to abandon the long-standing tradition of asylum. They felt that the literacy test was a gauge of opportunity rather than of ability. These considerations led Cleveland, Taft, and Wilson successively to veto literacy-test bills. Yet from the 1880s onwards the immigration laws became increasingly complex and restrictive. The first federal immigration law in 1882 debarred convicts, lunatics, paupers, and persons likely to become a public charge. The first of a series of Chinese Exclusion Acts was passed the same year. Thereafter the list of excluded classes was successively enlarged. By 1907 it included contract laborers, persons suffering from contagious diseases, polygamists, prostitutes, anarchists, and persons advocating the violent overthrow of the United States government. Ellis Island, which replaced Castle Garden in 1892 as New York's immigrant landing depot, was given the task of detecting and excluding undesirables. In fact only about 2 percent of the arrivals were found inadmissible and sent back to Europe. But all immigrants were subjected to searching interrogation and scrutiny and many thousands were annually detained for inquiry for varying periods before being finally admitted to the Promised Land.

Transport, Safety, and Public-Health Problems

Of the many problems created by urban growth, none was more pressing than rapid transit. The introduction of bricks and asphalt for paving in the 1880s did something to relieve traffic congestion. The construction of adequate bridges over the waterways that intersected many cities did more. New York, whose needs were greatest, derived a substantial measure of relief from the opening of Brooklyn Bridge in 1883, but it was not until the completion of a second bridge over the East River—the Williamsburg Bridge (1903)—that the journey in and out of Manhattan became tolerable.

For the task of moving immense numbers of daily commuters to and from work the existing horse-drawn omnibus lines were too small and too slow. The elevated steam railway was the first step forward. Pioneered by New York in the early 1870s, the 'L' was subsequently adopted by other cities. But it was expensive to build, shut out light from the streets, and was prone to shower unwary pedestrians with oil and hot cinders. The 1880s saw many cities adopt cable cars, first introduced by San Francisco in 1873 to overcome her steep, hilly streets. But the real solution came when the development of the dynamo made the electric trolley a practical proposition. (See p. 299.) Cheaper to build and operate than both the overhead steam railway and the cable car, the electric trolley soon became the principal mode of urban transport. By 1890 fifty-one cities had adopted it and by 1898 the United States boasted 15,000 miles of electric-trolley line. In time the elevated railroads were electrified too. Finally, following the example of London and Budapest, Boston (1897) and New York (1904) introduced subways. Besides facilitating movement within cities, rapid transit contributed to the spread of suburbs. By 1900 New York's suburbs held over one million people, about a third as many as the city itself.

The new conditions of urban life necessitated better lighting than the dim gas lamps of pre-Civil War days provided. Electricity once more yielded a solution. Electric arc lamps, invented by Charles F. Brush and installed in 1879 in his home town of Cleveland were quickly adopted by other cities, though improved mantles enabled gas to offer a serious challenge. Better lighting made the streets safer at night, permitted factories to operate round the clock, allowed shops to stay open longer, and gave a great stimulus to theaters and restaurants. But when it came to tackling the problems of sewage disposal and a potable water-supply, cities displayed less urgency. Sewage facilities lagged behind the needs of rapidly expanding populations. In the 1870s most major cities still clung to rural sanitation methods. Waterfront cities indiscriminately discharged their untreated waste into rivers or the sea; Baltimore and New Orleans relied heavily on open gutters, Philadelphia and Washington on private cesspools. Much effort was expended in enlarging water-supplies: the number of public waterworks increased more than fivefold in the 1880s, partly in response to the destructive conflagrations at Chicago in 1871 and at Boston in 1873. But since more heed was paid to the quantity of the water-supply than to its quality pollution by sewage or industrial waste was common. Only when the connection was grasped between polluted water and typhoid epidemics did cities give the problem closer attention and even then they moved slowly.

Retailing and Advertising

Improved transport brought far-reaching changes in shopping habits. Shops in city centers offered greater variety and lower prices than the old-fashioned country store. The most striking innovation was the department store, a collection of specialty shops under one roof. Though a European rather than an American invention it was a natural outgrowth of the American competitive system. As with industry and railroads, the struggle to reduce costs and secure the benefits of large-scale operation produced a trend towards bigness. Giant department stores like Macy's of New York, Marshall Field's of Chicago, and Wanamaker's of Philadelphia succeeded through business skill, showmanship, and bold and imaginative advertising—as well as a readiness to arrange displays to attract the new armies of women shoppers.

Mail-order houses offered an even sharper challenge to the country store. These originated in the 1870s when railroads began to offer speedy and cheap transport, but their real growth dated from the establishment of rural free delivery by the post office in 1896 and the parcel-post service in 1913. The first large, successful mail-order house was established in Chicago in 1872 by Aaron Montgomery Ward, a traveling salesman who had seen an opening for a retail house that could sell direct to consumers by mail and save them the middleman's profit. His chief competitor was Sears, Roebuck, and Company, founded in 1886 and based in Chicago from 1895. The profusely illustrated Sears, Roebuck catalog, published annually from the 1890s, offered an enticing variety of manufactured goods from bicycles and jewelry to furniture and firearms.

Mass buying, which largely explained the mail-order houses' success, was also a feature of another novelty, the chain store. The first and largest of the chains was the Great Atlantic and Pacific Tea Company. Founded in New York in 1858 by two tea importers from Maine, the A. & P. gradually extended its range of grocery products and by 1915 boasted over 1,000 branches. A comparable achievement was that of Frank Winfield Woolworth, a self-educated farm-boy from upstate New York, who opened his first successful 'five-and ten-cent store' at Lancaster, Pennsylvania in 1879 and owned over 1,000 by 1911, when F. W. Woolworth Co. was incorporated. By this time the number of chain stores was increasing rapidly, especially in clothing, shoes, and drugs. Thanks to their improved retail methods, rapid turnovers, and low prices they won a substantial share of the retail market, especially in small towns.

To distribute their products on a national scale manufacturers and retailers relied heavily on advertising. The amount of money spent annually on advertising in the United States rose tenfold between 1865 and 1900. First newspapers and then periodicals came to consist increasingly of advertisements and to derive most of their income from them. In addition, billboards, hoardings, and blank walls, even mountainsides, carried the advertiser's message. Before the Civil War advertisers had written their own copy, but by 1875 the *Nation* could remark that 'the preparation and planning of advertisements of all sorts have assumed the proportions of a business by itself'. With the emergence of the advertising agent, advertisements changed their character. Whereas they had formerly been designed merely to inform a potential customer of the availability of certain goods and services, they now sought to persuade him of his need for a given product and to choose one particular brand. Advertising did more than change purchasing habits: by exploiting every human weakness and desire it became one of the foremost arbiters of taste and social values.

Urban Architecture and Planning

The concentration of business in inner-city areas presented problems to American architects, while affording them new opportunities to marry art and engineering. The result was a distinctively American architectural form—the skyscraper. The need to economize on ground area because of high land costs, the development of steel-frame construction which took the load off walls, the invention of the passenger elevator (operated first hydraulically and then in the late 1880s by electricity) all stimulated the construction of very tall buildings. So did the telephone, electric light, and clay fireproofing. Much of the pioneer work on skyscrapers was carried out in Chicago in the 1880s by a group of outstanding architects led by Louis H. Sullivan, later to become known as the father of modernism in architecture. With his partner Dankmar Adler, Sullivan designed skyscrapers like the Wainwright Building in St. Louis (1891) and Buffalo's Guaranty Building (1895). But it was not until the architectural revolution spread to New York that the skyscraper struck the popular imagination. The twenty-story Flatiron Building, built in 1902 from plans by another Chicago architect, Daniel H. Burnham, became a landmark because of its peculiar shape, and was for a time New York's tallest building. But others soon towered above it, notably the forty-seven-story Singer Building (1908) and the sixty-story Woolworth Building (1913).

In the last decades of the century the public park became a prominent feature of urban life. This was largely the achievement of a single individual, the pioneer landscape architect, Frederick Law Olmsted. Appointed chief architect of New York's Central Park in 1858, Olmsted subsequently executed similar commissions in Brooklyn, Chicago, Baltimore, and Detroit and designed the park systems of Boston, Hartford, and Louisville. Nevertheless, city planning in the broader sense was virtually unknown before 1900. Hence American cities grew haphazardly, and were generally a mere hotchpotch of architectural styles.

The Slum Problem

By far the worst evil of urban expansion, and one that went far to justify Jefferson's animadversions on city life, was the growth of the slum. The slum problem dated back to the late 1840s when, to accommodate the immigrant influx into eastern seaport cities, enterprising landlords began to convert old mansions and warehouses into tenements and to crowd makeshift buildings together in every inch of space. Conditions deteriorated still further with the invention in 1879 of the 'dumbbell tenement' so called because of the shape of its floor-plan. These grim, insanitary barracks, five or six storys high, were honeycombed with dark, tiny rooms, many without direct light, air, or drainage. Yet they sheltered scores of families and, not surprisingly, had the highest death-rates. In 1890 the Danish-born journalist, Jacob Riis, exposed the terrible conditions of slum life in his classic study, *How the Other Half Lives*. Together with other crusaders for better housing he secured the appointment of a Tenement

House Commission which uncovered fresh horrors and concluded that in 1900 slum conditions were worse than they had been half a century earlier. A comprehensive remedial law was passed the following year but, because of the opposition of vested interests, improvement was slow.

City slums were the principal nurseries of crime. Some of the foulest slum districts in New York bore names like 'Bandits' Roost' and 'Murderers' Alley'. The gangs which sallied forth from them to commit robbery and assault and to fight periodic battles with the police and each other consisted generally not of immigrants, as was popularly believed, but of their American-born children. Mainly because of urban lawlessness, crime increased alarmingly. In 1880s the country's prison population rose by 50 percent. More worrying still, the American murder-rate more than quadrupled between 1881 and 1889—and this during a period when the rate in Europe, already only half that of the United States, declined steadily. Lax law enforcement compounded the problem. Though urban police forces were increased, generally at a faster rate than the population, and specialized detective forces introduced, police administration was often tainted with corrupt municipal politics. In addition many policemen were in league with criminal elements. The Lexow investigation in New York in 1894 revealed among other things that police appointments and promotions were purchasable, and that the guardians of law and order collected monthly blackmail from gamblers and brothel-keepers and received percentages of the earnings of prostitutes, pickpockets, and thieves.

As urban problems multiplied, middle-class reformers, especially the new class of educated women, established settlement houses in slum areas to provide guidance and leadership and to bridge the developing gulf between different social classes. Toynbee Hall in the East End of London, founded in 1884 and visited by many American social workers, was their model. The first American settlement house—Neighborhood Guild on New York's Lower East Side—was opened in 1886. By 1900 there were perhaps one hundred of them. The most celebrated was Hull House, established in 1889 by Jane Addams on South Halsted Street in Chicago in the middle of a slum inhabited by a polyglot immigrant population. Besides providing social services and recreational facilities, Miss Addams and her co-workers sought to introduce foreign slum-dwellers to American ways and, moreover, to give them a sense of belonging. Jane Addams realized, however, that settlement houses solved none of the basic problems. Thus she devoted more and more of her energies—as, indeed, did Florence Kelley, another Hull House pioneer, and Lillian D. Wald, who founded the Henry Street Settlement in New York in 1893—to campaigning for better housing, improved sanitary conditions, sweatshop regulations, and the abolition of child labor.

Class Division and Social Mobility

In the latter decades of the nineteenth century American society was becoming increasingly polarized. At one extreme there was the immigrant industrial working class, at the other a new corporate aristocracy. The Census Bureau estimated in 1892 that 9 percent of American families owned 71 percent of the country's wealth. The following year the *New York Times* listed 4,047 millionaires. Thus to be counted rich one needed to be a millionaire several times over. Not all millionaires lived extravagantly: John D. Rockefeller, for example, was notoriously frugal. But others basked in self-indulgent splendor, building palatial mansions, employing liveried servants, and entertaining lavishly. By the 1880s the gulf between rich and poor was reflected in the physical appearance of the great cities. Only a few blocks away from densely packed immigrant slums stood the magnificent homes of merchant princes, railroad barons, and Wall Street bankers. New York's Fifth Avenue, the most splendid thoroughfare in the country, possessed the most impressive array of such dwellings: members of the Vanderbilt family alone had built seven of them, each costing several millions. Still more imposing were the huge mansions, absurdly called 'cottages', built by the newly rich at the fashionable summer resort of Newport, Rhode Island. Perhaps the grandest, certainly the most costly, was William K. Vanderbilt's Marble House, built between 1889 and 1892. Inspired by Versailles, it contained shiploads of Italian Renaissance paintings, Flemish tapestries, and Greek statuary.

The social exclusiveness symbolized by Newport and other fashionable resorts found many other expressions. The exclusive country club made its debut at Brookline, Massachusetts in 1882, the exclusive suburb at Tuxedo Park, New York in 1886. Though boys' boarding-schools on the model of Eton, Harrow, or Rugby had been established in the United States as long ago as the Revolutionary War, Phillips Exeter and Phillips Andover Academies being the most distinguished, they began to be numerous only in the 1880s. By 1914 they dotted the Atlantic seaboard, the heaviest concentration being in New England, the home of such well-known schools as Groton (1884), Choate (1896), and Kent (1906). The products of such schools set the tone at Harvard, Yale, and Princeton, which in turn became the model for American colleges generally in everything from slang to clothes. Rigidly exclusive Greek-letter college fraternities experienced a boom and dominated campus life. This was the heyday also of the patrician metropolitan club for men, the preeminent examples being those founded before the Civil War: the Philadelphia Club (1834), the Century in New York (1847), and the Somerset in Boston (1851). That social distinctions were becoming sharper was further suggested by a flood of books on etiquette, the novel practice of appending III and IV to surnames to indicate family continuity, and the first appearance (1888) of the New York *Social Register*, a useful but not always reliable index to upper-class status. The search for old-stock roots resulted in a fad for genealogy and in the founding of a crop of exclusive patriotic and hereditary societies: the Sons of the Revolution (1883), the Colonial Dames (1890), the Daughters of the American Revolution (1890), and the Society of Mayflower Descendants (1894). Above all, however, the rich prized aristocratic affiliations. Thus Tiffany's, the famous New York jewelers, offered to create costs of arms for those who could afford to pay. There was also a spate of marriages between American heiresses and European noblemen, one of the most publicized taking place in 1895 between Consuelo Vanderbilt and the ninth Duke of Marlborough.

Although it had long been an American conceit that society in the United States was uniquely fluid, the cult of the self-made man reached its peak only in the late nineteenth century. Horatio Alger's widely read novels popularized the notion that poor boys of modest talents commonly achieved dazzling business success through hard work, pluck, and luck. But studies of American business and financial leaders have revealed that a very high proportion were born to wealth and privilege and that, to quote William Miller, the author of one such study, the 'poor immigrant boys and poor farm boys [who] together actually made up no more than 3 percent of the business leaders' of the 1900s 'have always been more prominent in American history books than in American history'. Confirmation that the social structure was becoming increasingly rigid is provided by research into working-class mobility. Thus in Newburyport, Massachusetts, bluecollar workers and their sons rarely became managers or even foremen, the commonest type of occupational mobility being from an unskilled to a semiskilled job, or from semiskilled to skilled. And if in the country as a whole there was only a modest amount of social mobility, native-born white working-men did better than immigrants, with blacks far behind both.

Women, Marriage, and Divorce

A much-remarked feature of the changing national scene was the growing independence of women. Legislation enlarged married women's property rights, sweeping away much of the old common-law discrimination and giving married women control over their earnings and property and the right to make contracts without their husbands' consent. Industrialization, moreover, provided women with better opportunities of supporting themselves. The number of working women rose from two million in 1870 (15 percent of all American women) to eight million in 1910 (21 percent). While domestic service, factory work, and teaching accounted for the bulk of female employees, great numbers of women became shop assistants, typists, telephone operators, bookkeepers, librarians, and nurses. Nearly all gainfully employed women were unmarried or widowed. Increased employment opportunities and the spread of women's higher education brought an increase both in the average age of marriage and in the proportion of women remaining unmarried. Whereas before the Civil War early marriage was the rule for women, in 1890 only 47 percent of women between twenty and twenty-four were married. A related trend was an increased divorce-rate. From 7,380 in 1860 (1.2 per 1,000 marriages) the number of divorces rose to 83,045 in 1910 (4.5 per 1,000). This meant that divorces were increasing about five times as fast as the population and that, except for Japan, the United States had the highest divorce-rate in the world. (As late as 1905 the annual total of divorces in the United Kingdom was 831.) Two-thirds of all divorce suits were filed by women. One reason was that it was easier to get a divorce if the woman was the plaintiff, another that to be a defendant in a divorce case was socially more damaging for a woman than for a man. The soaring divorce-rate roused widespread fears for the stability of the family. Some held the alimony laws responsible, though a government inquiry in 1909 showed that alimony was awarded in only one case in eleven. Even more blamed the ease with which out-of-state visitors could obtain divorces in Western states. But while a number of wealthy Easterners were able to dissolve their marriages by sojourning briefly in the divorce colonies of the Dakotas and Nevada— Reno ultimately became the best known—the total was never large. Nearly all divorces were in fact obtained in states in which the parties normally resided. Possibly the increasing incidence of divorce was a reflection of the declining birth-rate: at all events, about half of all divorces were granted to childless couples.

The Impact of Technology on Everyday Life

For the mass of Americans the post-Civil War decades were an age of increasing comfort and convenience. A host of mechanical inventions, gadgets, and techniques transformed the conditions of life and created a 'push-button civilization'. Science and technology, besides simplifying and quickening communications, robbed travel of many of its dangers, raised living standards, released millions from back-breaking drudgery, and extended the horizons and enriched the leisure hours of the common man. Perhaps the greatest blessing was the more varied and nutritious diet made possible by new methods of preserving foods. Concentrated and canned foods made their way increasingly into American larders and, following the invention of the 'icebox' and the growth of ice-making plants in the 1870s, ice came rapidly into household use. Moreover, the development of the refrigerator car by the Chicago meat-packers, Gustavus F. Swift and Philip D. Armour, made fresh meat available throughout the year, while improving its quality and lowering its price. The refrigerator car also encouraged domestic fruit- and vegetable-growing and, together with the rise of the ocean-going steamship, led to the wider consumption of tropical and subtropical fruit. Meanwhile electric light was spreading rapidly to the suburbs and the telephone was becoming an everyday middle-class convenience. The sewing-machine had become a familiar object in the American home much earlier. Edison's phonograph, invented in 1878, was not at first popular because his rotating wax cylinders were inconvenient to store and expensive to reproduce. But a German immigrant, Emil Berliner, succeeded in recording sound on flat 'plates' or disks and then discovered a cheap method of duplicating the disks—or records as they were being called by 1896. By the end of the century the craftsmanship and ingenuity of Eldridge Johnson of New Jersey had transformed Berliner's wheezy gramophone into an acoustically superior machine—the 'victrola'. Johnson's company, the Victor Talking Machine Company, helped create and, for a time, dominated, the new recording industry. By 1914 more than 500,000 gramophones were being produced annually and sales of records approached ten million a year. Meanwhile two other inventions had gone into general use—the fountain pen, perfected by Lewis E. Waterman in 1884, and the modern safety razor with throwaway blades, invented by King C. Gillette in 1895. But no technological innovation was more characteristically American than the Kodak camera, invented by George Eastman in 1888. Eastman's little black box was the means whereby a hitherto arcane hobby was so simplified as to become a mass activity.

Entertainment, Sport, and Leisure

No less characteristic of the period was the growth of mass entertainment. Perhaps the most widely enjoyed spectacle was the traveling circus, but a new rival appeared in 1883—Buffalo Bill's Wild West Show, which brought a genuine folk hero to life and displayed to the urban world exciting glimpses of the vanishing West. As the old hostility to the stage faded away, resident stock companies appeared but, with the advent of cheaper and easier travel, they lost ground to touring companies and visiting 'stars'. Native-born Shakespearean actors like Edwin Booth and Lawrence Barrett had a devoted following, while such luminaries of the European stage as Sarah Bernhardt, Henry Irving, Tomasso Salvini, and Eleonora Duse made profitable American tours. The tastes of most playgoers ran mainly, however, to melodrama and farce. The realism that characterized the best of American fiction was absent from the American stage. In so far as contemporary social problems were dealt with at all, they were burlesqued, as in Harrigan and Hart's popular comedies of Irish and German immigrant life. The black-face minstrel show, dating back to the 1820s, reached the peak of its popularity in the two decades after the Civil

War, but declined with the rise of vaudeville, a variety show modeled on the English music-hall, though without the earthiness of the original.

In the 1890s vaudeville itself began to be challenged by motion pictures. The key inventions were Edison's Kinetoscope (1893), an apparatus for exhibiting photographs of moving objects, and Thomas Armat's projector (1896), which Edison acquired and improved. Soon after 1900 motion pictures were being commercially exhibited in every major city, usually in converted buildings known as nickelodeons, so-called because of the five-cent admission fee. The first American film to have a plot was Edwin S. Porter's *The Great Train Robbery* (1903), a one-reeler lasting ten minutes. At first producers found difficulty in escaping from the conventions of the theater, but soon began to develop their own forms, notably Westerns, slapstick comedies like Mack Sennett's *Keystone Cops*, and serials such as *The Perils of Pauline*, 'starring' Pearl White. By 1914, the 'star' system was established, Hollywood had supplanted New York as the center of the film industry, the first 'picture palace', complete with a Wurlitzer organ, had opened on Broadway; and three million people were going to the 'movies' every day. D. W. Griffith's spectacular twelve-reel Reconstruction epic, *The Birth of a Nation* (1915), with its sophisticated camera technique, realistic crowd scenes, and use of symbolism and orchestral music, marked the coming of age of the new art form.

Until the last quarter of the century the United States was without a permanent, professional symphony orchestra. However the German-born conductor, Theodore Thomas, who regularly toured the principal cities with a series of orchestras between 1869 and 1890, did much to develop interest in orchestral music. Another immigrant musician, the Polish-born Leopold Damrosch, founded the New York Symphony Orchestra in 1878 and his son and successor, Walter, persuaded Carnegie, Rockefeller, Vanderbilt, and Morgan to support it. After other wealthy industrialists had subsidized or endowed the Boston Symphony Orchestra (1881) and Thomas's Chicago Symphony Orchestra (1891), the habit spread to other cities. Opera, however, had as much difficulty as in England in establishing itself. New York's Metropolitan Opera opened in 1883, but no other American city supported a resident company. Even in New York the opera's appeal had less to do with music than with status. It served, in Henry James's words, as 'the great vessel of social salvation', providing the unmusical rich with an acceptable way of filling the dreary gap between dinner and bedtime. Light opera in English, on the other hand, found a ready audience from the moment *HMS Pinafore* sailed into Boston in 1878, the first of a whole succession of Gilbert and Sullivan productions. Thirty years later operetta was still immensely popular, whether foreign importation like Franz Lehar's *The Merry Widow* (1907) or indigenous products like Victor Herbert's *Naughty Marietta* (1900). But a new native musical form and style—the musical comedy—had by now been born. A racy, fast-moving kind of show that American audiences at once recognized as their own, the prototype was George M. Cohan's *Little Johnny Jones* (1904).

Meanwhile, spectator sports enjoyed a boom. Baseball, derived from the English game of rounders, was easily the most popular. It took on its modern form in 1845 when the first baseball club, the New York Knickerbockers, adopted a new code of rules. During the Civil War baseball was a favorite army recreation; returning soldiers made it more widely popular. The first professional team, the Cincinnati Red Stockings, was formed in 1869. The National League, organized in 1876, did much to stamp out the bribery and dishonesty that were threatening to bring the game into disrepute. In the next quarter of a century, baseball became as much a business as a sport. The National League's attempts at monopoly were thwarted only in 1901 when the American League was organized as a powerful and permanent rival. There were savage interclub wars like those which marked the rise of Standard Oil; some baseball-clubowners were as rapacious and unscrupulous as Gould and Fisk. But by the turn of the century baseball was securely established as the national game. It entered a new era of prosperity with the establishment of the so-called World Series, an annual series of contests between the champions of the two major leagues.

Until the 1880s prize fights were brutal exhibitions, outlawed in most states. But the introduction from England of the Queensberry rules—John L. Sullivan, 'the strong boy of Boston', who had won the world heavyweight title in 1882, was the first American pugilist to adopt them—brought the bare-knuckle era to an end and conferred a measure of respectability on the sport. In defeating Sullivan in 1892 another Irish-American, 'Gentleman Jim' Corbett, demonstrated the superiority of scientific boxing over mere fighting, thus raising the ring's status still further. Thanks to religious opposition, boxing was again banned in New York State between 1900 and 1910, but popular interest continued to grow, not least because of the racial feelings stimulated by the rise of the Negro heavyweight, Jack Johnson, who became world champion in 1908. Johnson's open flouting of the convention against interracial sexual liaisons—three of his four wives and most of his mistresses were white—prompted repeated attempts, vain until 1915, to find a 'white hope' to defeat him.

Racing, established in America since before the Revolution, enjoyed unexampled prosperity. Racecourses multiplied, stakes increased, valuable new races were instituted—the Kentucky Derby dates from 1875. But in the opening years of the new century, the gambling which attended the turf attracted the attention of reformers. New York, following the lead of Missouri and Illinois, prohibited on-course betting. Some of the largest racecourses were consequently closed but, after several seasons of decline, ways were found to evade the law.

Golf and tennis, introduced respectively in the 1870s and 1880s, remained sports of the well-to-do up to the First World War. Cycling, on the other hand, quickly became a popular form of recreation as well as of locomotion. By 1893 one million Americans were riding bicycles, by 1900 ten million. One consequence was an acceleration of the trend towards shorter skirts for women—though even by 1914 they had not risen much above the ankle.

The social revolution begun by the bicycle was carried a stage further by the automobile. Within a few years of the appearance of the first American gasoline-driven motor vehicle (1893), production had become concentrated at Detroit, Michigan, which was near to iron and lumber supplies and had a carriage-building industry capable of manufacturing car bodies. At first the automobile was merely a plaything of the rich and the mechanically minded, but a Michigan farm-boy, Henry Ford, conceived the idea of bringing car travel to millions. Ford's Model T made its appearance in 1908; the following year he manufactured 20,000 of them at a basic price of $850. In 1910 he opened a new factory at Highland Park, near Detroit, and in 1913 introduced the assembly-line technique which cut production time to a tenth. In 1914, the Ford Motor Company turned out more than 250,000 vehicles and the following year the country had two and a half million registered cars.

Challenge to Religion

Despite the growth of secular counterattractions, organized religion maintained its hold—at least as far as external appearances went. Churches were crowded; costly edifices were built; church membership made striking gains—between 1860 and 1910 it grew twice as fast as the population. Though the authority of the clergy had diminished, their influence was still substantial. This was the great age of the American pulpit. Some of the more prominent preachers—Phillips Brooks, Russell H. Conwell, Lyman Abbott, Henry Ward Beecher—had national reputations and their sermons were frequently front-page news. Religious books and periodicals had large sales. So great was popular interest in the Revised Version of the King James Bible that when the first instalment (the New Testament) appeared in 1881, two hundred thousand copies were sold in New York alone in less than a week, and two Chicago daily newspapers printed the entire text.

Yet despite these indications of vitality, Protestantism faced grave challenges. On the one hand, belief in the literal truth of the Bible and in the supernatural foundations of Christian theology were being undermined by the Darwinian theory of evolution, by 'Higher Criticism'—the application of historical evidence to the biblical narrative—and by the new interest in comparative religion. On the other hand, industrialization was posing questions which were difficult to answer within the framework of individual salvation, the traditional foundation of Protestant worship and theology.

The clash between science and religion reached an emotional and rancorous climax in the last two decades of the century. The retreat from orthodoxy was gradual and far from universal. Following the example of scientists like Asa Gray, liberal church leaders like Henry Ward Beecher and Lyman Abbott found ways of accommodating Darwinism to Christian belief, arguing that evolution was not incompatible with the divine creation and governance of the universe. Yet adherents to traditional religion—fundamentalists as they later became known—remained strongly entrenched in rural communities, especially in the South. Belligerently denouncing modernism they continued to insist on literal acceptance of the Genesis account of the Creation, biblical miracles, the Virgin Birth, the' physical resurrection of Christ, and his imminent return to earth. In the 1890s modernist clergymen were being charged with heresy and several professors were forced out of universities and theological seminaries because of unorthodoxy.

Churchmen were slow to adjust social ethics to the needs of industrialized society. Far from finding fault with the existing economic order most Protestant clergymen provided theological justification for it. Though Henry Ward Beecher preached a liberal theology, he was conservative in his attitudes to social problems, advocating the use of force against strikers, and insisting that poverty was the wages of sin or improvidence. Such an attitude, growing naturally out of the Protestant ethic, reflected also the fact that membership of the Protestant churches was becoming increasingly middle class. Even denominations like the Baptists and the Methodists, once the sects of the poor, had grown rich and respectable. Significantly, John D. Rockefeller was a devout member of and a generous benefactor to the Baptist church. A gulf thus developed between the churches and the urban masses. Bryce reported hearing many lamentations at the diminished attendance at city churches and concluded that, in cities like New York and Chicago, 'the bulk of the humbler classes (except the Roman Catholics . . .) are practically heathen to the same extent as in London or Berlin'.

In the 1880s a small group of clergymen attempted a reformulation of Christian ethics. Influenced by English Christian Socialists they developed what later became known as the Social Gospel, which preached that the Church had both the responsibility and the capacity to deal with social problems. The movement's first well-known spokesman was Washington Gladden, a Congregational minister at Columbus, Ohio. One of the first ministers to support trade unions, he argued in *Applied Christianity* (1886) that what was needed in industry was cooperation between capital and labor and, still more, the 'power of Christian love'. More responsible for popularizing the Social Gospel was the Reverend Charles M. Sheldon of Topeka, Kansas, whose highly successful novel, *In His Steps* (1896), described the transformation brought about when a New York congregation tried for a year to follow Christ's teachings. Yet the greatest name in the Social Gospel movement, and its most profound thinker, was Walter Rauschenbusch, author of *Christianity and the Social Crisis* (1907) and *A Theology for the Social Gospel* (1917). Unlike most other socially aware clergymen, who wanted simply to rid capitalism of its abuses, Rauschenbusch saw no alternative to a thoroughgoing reform of society on Socialist principles.

The Social Gospel, a minority creed even among the urban clergy, was not a matter of great concern to most churchgoers. More dramatic was a resurgence of revivalism. Its foremost exponent was Dwight L. Moody, a former shoe salesman from Boston who became active in city missionary work after moving to Chicago in the 1850s. Moody had little formal education, was never ordained, and lacked the support of any ecclesiastical organization. Yet he was perhaps the most successful American evangelist since Jonathan Edwards. Unlike Edwards, however, Moody did not preach hellfire but a simple message of hope and reassurance. His sermons largely ignored social issues. What concerned him was personal conversion, to be achieved through devout acceptance of the inerrancy of the Bible: 'The Bible was not made to understand!' was his reply to those who found inconsistencies in it. Moody's direct, intimate, and vivid preaching was accompanied and reinforced by Ira D. Sankey's gospel-singing. Despite a limited vocal range Sankey produced a powerful effect on congregations, especially on women, with well-loved hymns like 'Safe in the Arms of Jesus'. Following an 1875 British tour which established their fame, Moody and Sankey conducted campaigns in all the great American cities. They reached millions with their message but, as Moody himself acknowledged, their chief work was not to convert the unchurched masses but to strengthen and rekindle the faith of backsliders.

Other evangelistic organizations sought to keep religion alive by combining social with spiritual services. The Young Men's Christian Association, introduced from England in 1851, and the Young Women's Christian Association, similarly transplanted in 1858, promoted not only religious activities but also study-classes, lectures, concerts, and athletics. The Salvation Army, founded in London in 1865 by 'General' William Booth and organized in the United States in 1880, sought meanwhile to bring evangelism to the poor by establishing missions in city slums.

Christian Science was, by contrast, an indigenous American product. It owed its inspiration to the teachings of Mrs Mary Baker Eddy, a frail, ill-educated New Englander, prone to nervous ailments since childhood. Having been restored to comparative health by a mesmerist and mental healer named Phineas P. Quimby, she-set to work to systematize and develop his ideas and train spiritual healers. In *Science and Health* (1875) Mrs Eddy denied the reality of matter and asserted that sin, poverty, illness, pain, and death were delusions which would disappear when the mortal mind achieved harmony with God. In 1879 she founded the first Christian Science Association at Lynn, Massachusetts and in 1882 established the Mother Church at Boston. Though Mrs Eddy expressed her doctrines loosely, and indeed repeatedly changed them in later editions of her book, Christian Science had a wide appeal, especially to middle-class city-dwellers, perhaps because it provided relief from urban tensions. By the time the founder died in 1910—an event explained by Mrs Eddy's doctrine of 'malicious animal magnetism', whereby ill-disposed persons can cause disease in others—she had become immensely wealthy and Christian Science had 1,000 churches and a membership variously estimated at from 300,000 to 1,000,000.

Thanks largely to immigration, the Catholic Church grew spectacularly. Adherents increased from about 3,500,000 in 1860 (11 percent of the population) to more than 16,000,000 in 1910 (17 percent of the total). Twenty new dioceses were established in the 1880s alone and after the Third Plenary Council of Baltimore had made parochial schools almost mandatory for the faithful their number rose sharply. Like American society itself the Catholic Church had difficulty in assimilating newcomers from so many different cultures. Catholic immigrants from Germany, Austria–Hungary, Poland, Italy, and French Canada resented Irish dominance of the Church—nearly all the hierarchy were of Irish origin—and demanded parishes and priests of their own. Officially condemned as inconsistent with the Church's essential unity, the demand was nevertheless tacitly conceded in practice. Bitter feuds nonetheless erupted over the language of worship and the observance of cherished Old World festivals. Some of the disaffected cut loose from Rome to form independent national churches like the Polish National Catholic Church; others, particularly the Italians, were won over the Protestant proselytizers. Even so the Catholic Church retained most of its flock.

As the Church of the city and the working class Catholicism had special need to adapt to industrialization. Some members of the hierarchy—notably Archbishop Michael A. Corrigan of New York— were extremely conservative on social questions. But the outstanding figure in American Catholicism, James, Cardinal Gibbons of Baltimore, saw the need to change if the Church was to avoid defections. Sympathizing with the aspirations of labor he persuaded the Holy See in 1887 to withdraw its condemnation of the Knights of Labor. All the same Gibbons and likeminded prelates tended to minimize economic problems and saw no glaring faults in American society.

Educational Advance

In education the period was one of expansion at all levels. The ideal of free education for all, accepted in principle as early as 1850, now became a reality—at least at the elementary level. Before 1870 the only states with compulsory school-attendance laws were Massachusetts and Vermont, but by 1900 nearly all the states and territories outside the South had fallen into line. As a result the number of pupils receiving instruction in public elementary schools rose from under 7 million in 1870 to nearly 18 million in 1910, and the proportion of children of school age actually enrolled went up from 57 to 80 percent. The average length of the school year rose from 132 to 157 days and the illiteracy-rate declined from 20 to 7.7 percent. At the same time there was a striking increase in the number of public high schools—from 200 in 1865 to more than 12,000 in 1910.

These statistics concealed wide regional disparities. New York and Massachusetts supported their school systems far more generously than Middle Western states, and all other regions spent much more than the South, though even there facilities improved considerably after 1900. Throughout the country city schools were markedly better than those in rural districts. Though Americans tended to idealize the 'little red schoolhouse' as a bulwark of democracy, the rural school was often little more than a one-room shack, in which a lone individual taught formal subjects by rote to pupils of all ages. Moreover, while the general level of education was higher than in Europe, there were still serious deficiencies. More than 90 percent of American children still received only an elementary school education: the average number of years in schooling in 1914 was only 6.16. Though scores of 'normal schools' for teacher-training were founded after 1870, most teachers were unqualified and often knew little more than their older pupils. A major cause of indifferent teaching was that although American society revered education it had little regard for teachers and paid them abysmally. This explained the accelerating displacement of men teachers by women: by 1914 four out of five teachers were women. And since both sexes tended to regard teaching as a stepping-stone to something better, schools experienced frequent staff changes. A further difficulty was that school-boards tended to assume that the school's most important funtion was not so much education in the strict sense but the promotion of democracy and social and national unity.

Higher education received a stimulus from the Morrill Act of 1862 which offered generous federal land grants to the states for the support of colleges which taught 'agriculture and the mechanic arts'. Among the first crop of 'land-grant colleges' were the Universities of Illinois (1867), Minnesota (1868), and California (1868) which had a vocational emphasis but did not neglect academic subjects. The states themselves appropriated large sums and by the end of the century all but ten could boast universities of their own. Other new institutions were the product of private philanthropy. Cornell (1868), though a beneficiary of the Morrill Act, owed more to a substantial gift from the telegraph millionaire, Ezra Cornell; Johns Hopkins at Baltimore (1876) and the Drexel Institute at Philadelphia (1891) were founded by wealthy bankers, Vanderbilt (1873) and Stanford (1893) by railroad millionaires. And although — unlike the instances just cited—it did not bear the name of its chief benefactor, the faltering University of Chicago (1892) was revived by a princely endowment of $34 million from John D. Rockefeller.

Higher education for women made great strides. All the Western state universities were coeducational from the start, as were Cornell and Stanford. Conservative Easterners continued to harbor doubts about the capacity of women to benefit from a college education, but the performance of such women's colleges as Vassar (1865), Wellesley (1875), Smith (1875), and Bryn Mawr (1885), all offering courses comparable to those taken by men, refuted their prejudices. So did the success of the grudging compromise whereby some of the older men's colleges opened affiliated institutions for women: 'Harvard Annexe', for example, which was established in 1879 and which blossomed into Radcliffe College in 1894. By the end of the century four out of every five colleges and universities in the United States were open to women, and the number of women students had grown to about 25,000, about a quarter of the total.

Mere expansion did not of course imply unqualified advance. A large proportion of the 500 colleges and universities in the United States in 1900—twice as many as thirty years before—had no real claim to be institutions of higher learning. Particularly in the South and the Middle West there were many small rural colleges, often planted by denominational zeal, whose standards were merely those of a secondary school. Even at the leading universities academic purpose tended to be diluted by an inordinate emphasis on spectator sports, especially intercollegiate football, which became a mass spectacle in the 1890s. Moreover, the domination of college boards of trustees by wealthy businessmen led to some notorious invasions of academic freedom.

Even so, Bryce could rightly claim in 1888, that the United States had 'not less than fifteen and perhaps even twenty seats of learning fit to be ranked besides the universities of Germany, France and England', and that in certain respects, notably in the natural sciences, she had taken the lead. He could have added that in every branch of learning American academics had begun to acquire international reputations. Thus Yale had William Graham Sumner, the sociologist, and Willard Gibbs, greatest of all American theoretical scientists. The formidable talents of William James, Josiah Royce, and George Santayana were concentrated in Harvard's philosophy department. Johns Hopkins boasted Simon Newcomb, the world's foremost astronomer, and Basil L. Gildersleeve, the great classical philologist. Yet at the end of the Civil War American colleges had invited criticism. They were stifled by hidebound church leadership; admission standards were low; curricula were too heavily classical; history, modern languages, and economics were all neglected; there were no adequate libraries, laboratories, or scientific apparatus; professors filled several chairs at once; too little attention was given to the advancement of knowledge. These deficiencies were remedied by a remarkable group of college presidents, among them Andrew Dickson White at Cornell (1867), James McCosh at Princeton (1868), Charles W. Eliot at Harvard (1869), and Daniel Coit Gilman at Johns Hopkins (1876). Eliot's forty-year tenure transformed Harvard from a struggling and poverty-stricken college into a major university. His most radical reform was the introduction of the elective system, whereby undergraduates made their own choices from a wide range of courses. He also put postgraduate instruction on a scholarly basis and drastically reformed the medical and law schools. Eliot's innovations—especially the elective system—provoked strong opposition but eventually were widely copied. Meanwhile at Johns Hopkins, Gilman was stressing the primacy of specialized research and graduate study; many professors, having studied in Germany, introduced rigorous German academic methods including the seminar and the Ph.D. Spurred on by the example of Johns Hopkins other foundations hastened to establish graduate schools; from a mere handful in the late 1870s the number of graduate students in American universities had risen by 1898 to nearly 5,000.

A different educational contribution was that of the Chautauqua movement, successor to the earlier lyceum. Started in 1874 at Lake Chautauqua in western New York as a summer camp for teaching Sunday-school teachers, Chautauqua soon expanded into a nationwide organization for adult education. By means of correspondence courses and organized study-groups—in which 100,000 adults were enrolled by 1892—it reached out to hundreds of small-town and rural communities. Besides offering musical and dramatic entertainment it sent out itinerant lecturers, among them Mark Twain, William Jennings Bryan, and the philosopher William James.

Libraries and the Press

At the close of the Civil War the only libraries worthy of the name were in eastern cities. But by 1900 there were few communities, except in parts of the South, without a free, tax-supported public library. This owed much to private munificence, especially the millions Andrew Carnegie donated for library buildings on condition that municipalities undertook to maintain them. The last years of the century saw the climax of the process with the formation of the New York Public Library (1895), the opening of magnificient new public library buildings at Boston (1895) and Chicago (1897), and of the still more splendid Library of Congress (1897), the largest and costliest library building in the world.

By 1900 the United States had 2,190 daily newspapers and 15,813 weeklies, more than the rest of the world combined. Rotary presses and other mechanical improvements, especially the linotype machine invented in 1886, made larger newspapers possible and immensely speeded up and cheapened production. The multiplication of cooperative newsgathering agencies like the Associated Press meant a more comprehensive coverage —though at the cost of standardizing the contents of subscribing papers. The costliness of these new techniques resulted in a greater reliance of advertising, more intense competition for circulation, and a tendency toward consolidation and the development of newspaper chains. Newspapers now became vast business undertakings and in consequence leadership in journalism passed from great owner–editors like Horace Greeley of the New York *Tribune* and James Gordon Bennett of the New York *Herald*—both of whom died in 1872—to a new breed of journalistic entrepreneurs concerned less to mold opinion than to make money by catering for the newly created mass literacy.

The Hungarian-born immigrant, Joseph Pulitzer, proprietor successively of the St. Louis *Post-Dispatch* (1878) and the New York *World* (1883), best exemplified this trend. Within a year of acquiring the *World* Pulitzer had increased its circulation from 15,000 to 60,000 and by 1898 had pushed it above a million. He frankly directed his appeal to what Bryce called 'the uninstructed, uncritical mass of readers', emphasizing 'human interest' stories, making extensive use of illustrations, cartoons, and colored comics, flamboyantly exploiting crime, sex and scandal, encouraging jingoism, while at the same time crusading with ostentatious virtue against political corruption and a ,variety of other evils including brothels, gambling, and slums. Dignified and respectable newspapers like the venerable New York *Evening Post* and the Boston *Evening Transcript* still claimed a substantial readership among the educated classes but Pulitzer's 'yellow journalism' techniques were widely copied, and not only in the United States: Alfred Harmsworth's *Daily Mail*, launched in London in 1896, owed much to his example.

Magazine sales also soared, especially after Congress granted low postal rates in 1879. The leading monthlies were *Harper's*, the *Atlantic* (both antedating the Civil War), and *Scribner's* (founded in 1870). Essentially literary, these genteel journals appealed largely to the cultured middle class. So did quality weeklies like the *Nation*, founded in 1865 by the Irishborn E. L. Godkin. For thirty years the *Nation* was a powerful leader of opinion, especially on the eastern seaboard, covering public affairs, literature, and the arts. Around 1900 established periodicals began to be challenged by a new kind of magazine, designed for the mass market. Attractively printed, heavily illustrated with halftone engravings, crisply written, and packed with profitable advertisements, magazines like *Munsey's* (1891), *McClure's* (1893), and *Cosmopolitan* (1886) sold for 10 or 15 cents—less than half the price of older periodicals. Their popularity was further increased in the early 1900s by 'muckraking' articles—sensational but carefully documented exposés of political corruption, slum housing, adulterated foods, patent-medicine frauds, and other abuses. More widely read still were the *Saturday Evening Post* and the *Ladies' Home Journal*. The latter, founded in 1883 and under the brilliant editorship from 1889 of Edward. W. Bok, had a sale of two million by the turn of the century and had become the 'monthly Bible of the American home'. All the popular magazines gave new prominence to the short story, thereby contributing to the significant place of that genre in American letters. They also serialized most of the important fiction of the day.

Literature and the Arts

In literature the Civil War decade marked a watershed. Of the great pre-war figures only Whitman remained productive. Hawthorne and Thoreau were dead, Emerson's powers were fading, Melville had retired into obscurity. With their passing came a gradual shift in literary forms and themes. While romantic, moralistic, and sentimental writing persisted there was a growing tendency from about 1870 on toward literary realism. Then, around the turn of the century, the reaction against romanticism became even sharper with the emergence of a 'naturalistic' school of novelists.

The first group of imaginative writers to describe real situations—though without much attempt to analyze them—belonged to the so-called 'local-color' movement. Finding their subject-matter in the customs and dialect of their own localities, they generally concentrated on a vanishing rural past. Thus in *The Hoosier Schoolmaster* (1871) Edward Eggleston painted an evocative picture of backwoods life in the Middle West and Sarah Orne Jewett's *The Country of the Pointed Firs* depicted the disappearing social order of rural New England. Among Southern writers George Washington Cable exploited the Creole traditions of New Orleans in *The Grandissimes* (1880) while Joel Chandler Harris recorded Negro folktales in his Uncle Remus stories. The Far West, too, produced a vigorous regional literature, beginning with Bret Harte, whose descriptions of the lawless life of mining camps in such works as *The Luck of Roaring Camp* (1870) captivated the American reading public.

Out of the local-color tradition a major figure emerged—Mark Twain. Beginning his literary career as a writer of facetious Western sketches, Twain was never able during his lifetime to correct the popular impression that he was simply a frontier humorist. Born Samuel Langhorne Clemens in Hannibal, Missouri in 1835, he was successively journeyman printer, Mississippi river-pilot, and Confederate soldier before drifting to Nevada in 1861. After,an interlude of prospecting and mining and a period as newspaper reporter and popular lecturer, he achieved success with *Innocents Abroad* (1869), a hilarious account of a European tour, and *Roughing It* (1872), a vivid picture of Western frontier society. Twain was a prolific writer on all kinds of subject—he ranged from jumping frogs to Joan of Arc—and an uneven one. But three of his works have become American classics: *The Adventures of Tom Sawyer* (1876), *Life on the Mississippi* (1883), and *The Adventures of Huckleberry Finn* (1884), all of which drew on his youthful memories of his life along the great river. In *Huckleberry Finn*, the greatest American novel of the century, the Mississippi becomes a symbol of the human journey and Huck's flight to the wilderness an attempt to escape a civilization that, in taming the natural man, deprives him of his instinctive goodness. Twain achieved realism through a mixture of hyperbole, comic jargon, and satire and, in the process, evolved what earlier writers had sought in vain—a prose style close to the American vernacular and suited to the American ethos.

A realist of a very different kind was Henry James, whose brilliant literary career spanned half a century and whose meticulous examination of backgrounds and character constituted a major contribution to the development of the novel as an art form. Born in New York in 1843 of a well-to-do and prodigiously gifted family—his elder brother was the famous philosopher, William James—Henry James was fascinated by Europe from his youth. In 1876, feeling that the United States lacked the intellectual sophistication to inspire great literature, he settled for good in England. (Henry Adams, Edith Wharton, and Gertrude Stein were among other well-known writers who became expatriates.) Yet America always remained James's point of reference and many of his writings dealt with the impact of Europe upon visiting Americans. In such works as *The Americans* (1876), *Daisy Miller* (1879), and *The Portrait of a Lady* (1881) James portrayed the American as more naive than the European but also as more idealistic. In the 1890s his novels were concerned chiefly with English upper-class society, but in his last phase he returned to the conjunction of America and Europe, a theme he explored with growing subtlety and stylistic complexity in the three novels in which he brought his art to its peak: *The Wings of the Dove* (1902), *The Ambassadors* (1903), and *The Golden Bowl* (1904).

The third member of the triumvirate which dominated American letters in this period, William Dean Howells, was a friend and admirer of both Twain and James. Born in a small Ohio town he had little formal education. Nevertheless, after settling in Boston after the Civil War he became subeditor and then editor-in-chief of the *Atlantic Monthly*. Howells was the most influential critic of his day, encouraging younger—often unfashionable—novelists and introducing the American public to foreign writers such as Tolstoy, Ibsen, and Zola. A more self-conscious literary realist than Twain, Howells defined realism as 'the truthful treatment of commonplace material' and displayed it in a long series of novels—he wrote thirty-five in all—as well as in dramas, travel books, short stories, and memoirs. His finest novel, *The Rise of Silas Lapham* (1885), is a masterly psychological study of a self-made businessman. Profoundly stirred by the labor upheavals of the 1880s and 1890s, Howells developed Socialist sympathies and his later novels, beginning with *A Hazard of New Fortunes* (1890), were strongly critical of the social consequences of industrialization.

Howells's brand of realism was, however, too refined and prudish for the 'naturalists' who rose to prominence at the turn of the century. For novelists like Hamlin Garland, Stephen Crane, Frank Norris, and Theodore Dreiser, who drew their inspiration from Zola and other French writers, realism entailed exploring all aspects of human experience, no matter how sordid or disgusting. Garland exemplified this view in *Main Traveled Roads* (1891), an uncompromising portrayal of the squalor of farm life. Crane's *Maggie* (1893) described the seduction and eventual suicide of a New York slum girl, while his Civil War masterpiece, *The Red Badge of Courage* (1895), focused upon the brutality of war. Norris's best-known novel, *The Octopus* (1901), depicts the hopeless struggle of California wheat-farmers against a heartless railroad. Dreiser's first book, *Sister Carrie* (1901), treated sex so frankly that it had to be withdrawn soon after publication. Reflecting the influence of Darwinism these 'naturalistic' writers were agreed that man's fate was determined by elemental forces over which he had no control.

Though the romantic tradition persisted in painting somewhat longer than in literature a talented group of portrait- and landscape-painters displayed an uncompromising devotion to truth. The outstanding realist was Thomas Eakins of Philadelphia, perhaps the greatest figure-painter America has produced. His fascination with human anatomy and his emotional depth were both evident in his masterpiece, *The Gross Clinic* (1875), a graphic study of a surgical operation, and in his vigorous portrayal of athletic activities. The Boston-born Winslow Homer achieved similar distinction as a realistic painter of nature. Best known for his stirring seascapes, especially of the Maine coast, he also produced vivid canvases of Caribbean scenes. Some American painters chose to work abroad: the versatile and eccentric James A. McNeill Whistler, the famous society portraitist, John Singer Sargent, both of whom lived in London, and the impressionist, Mary Cassatt, who settled in Paris. It is true that few contemporaries recognized the talent of the more innovative painters, but public interest in art developed markedly. At the end of the Civil War not a single American city possessed a good art gallery. But in 1870 New York founded the Metropolitan Museum and by the end of the century most large cities had acquired sizable collections. In addition many of the new business magnates—Henry Clay Frick and J. Pierpont Morgan, for example—patronized artists and collected European art treasures.

It was long the fashion to insist that the decades following the Civil War were characterized by a materialism and a vulgarity that were inimical to intellectual and cultural activity. That was the view of critical contemporaries like Twain who called it 'the Gilded Age' and Godkin who complained that the United States had built a 'chromo civilization'. There is much truth in their criticisms. Industrialism did indeed cast long shadows. Business success was valued above intellectual achievement. Americans produced little of value in music or drama. They continued to look to Europe for inspiration in painting, sculpture, and architecture. The long list of expatriate writers and painters was a significant comment on the country's cultural atmosphere. Moreover, some of the period's finest spirits labored in obscurity. Thus, America's greatest woman poet, Emily Dickinson, was not only unappreciated in her lifetime but was also scarcely known when she died in 1886. Yet, as will have become evident from the preceding pages, this was an extraordinarily creative period in literature, philosophy, painting, science, and education. Indeed it is hard to think of one which witnessed so much American accomplishment in the life of the mind.

18. *Politics from Conservatism to Revolt, 1877–1896*

The Political System

The 1870s and 1880s have generally been dismissed as a drab and meaningless chapter in American political history. It is not difficult to see why. National politics were based not on principle but on patronage. Both Republicans and Democrats ignored or fudged the issues that grew out of social and economic change and concerned themselves mainly with obtaining and holding office. Electioneering, it has been well said, became a business and politics a trade. That implied highly organized parties and highly professional politicians. This was the heyday of the political machine and the spoils system. The general level of political morality was low, fraud and jobbery rampant. A succession of dignified mediocrities occupied the Presidency, the tedium of their Administrations unrelieved even by scandal. Likewise in Congress there were few men of distinction. Small wonder, then, that historians have generally echoed Henry Adams's verdict that "the period was poor in purpose and barren in achievement" or that they have adopted for it the glib, derogatory label supplied by the title of a minor novel, *The Gilded Age* (1873), by Mark Twain and Charles Dudley Warner.

Yet the 'Gilded Age' had its redeeming features. One was that there were still men of integrity in public life, especially in the Senate: among them were such outspoken foes of political corruption as Carl Schurz of Missouri, Lyman Trumbull of Illinois, and George F. Hoar of Massachusetts. Then again, the rise of third parties ensured that the issues the major parties sought to avoid were nonetheless publicly debated. Thus the Granger movement and the Greenback-Labor Party, fed alike by economic discontent, focused public attention on railroad regulation and the money question respectively. If, moreover, one turns from national to local politics—as one must when dealing with a period of ingrained localism—one finds that political issues were real enough. In several Middle Western states there were fierce contests over 'ethnocultural' issues—temperance, Sunday observance, Bible-reading in the public schools, and education through the medium of foreign languages. In California the appearance of the Workingmen's Party in 1878 and the American Party in 1886, both nativist and short-lived, likewise proved that politics at the local level were anything but bankrupt.

Then again, though politics may have been dismayingly dull to disillusioned patricians like Henry Adams, they do not appear to have been so to ordinary men and women. Despite the relative absence of ideological conflict, this was an age of fierce political partisanship. Political gatherings were enthusiastically and hugely attended; a higher proportion of voters went to the polls than at any other period, before or since. Political campaigns, with their apparatus of bands, parades, and banners, met important social needs. They provided the excitement that later generations derived from other sources and also enabled groups to display their solidarity.

Stalemate was the overriding political condition. The two major parties were very evenly divided. In all five presidential elections between 1876 and 1892 the winning margin in popular votes was extraordinarily close— less than 1 percent in three of them. In both houses of Congress, too, power was finely balanced and, moreover, swung repeatedly from one party to another. Except between 1889 and 1891 no party controlled the Presidency, the Senate, and the House of Representatives simultaneously. And just as the close party balance encouraged equivocation over vital issues, so the prevailing instability and the absence of a clear mandate made it difficult for parties to implement their programs.

An equally striking characteristic of the politics of the period was the slump in the power and prestige of the Presidency. The chief reason was that the executive branch was still suffering from the Congressional assault on Andrew Johnson and from Grant's virtual abdication of presidential authority. Grant's successors, undistinguished as they were, courageously resisted the more extreme Congressional pretensions, but could do little to shift the balance of power back to the White House. They did not particularly want to. They all shared the prevailing belief that the President should confine himself to executing the laws, leaving the making of them to Congress.

Political control lay with the party bosses and their highly organized and locally oriented machines. City bosses, generally men of little education and of recent immigrant origin (usually Irish), preferred not to seek political office themselves but to operate behind the scenes. State bosses, by contrast, tended to be well-educated and of old American stock. Many were United States Senators, which meant that they had at their disposal federal as well as state patronage. Thus the Pennsylvania state Republican machine was controlled in turn by Senators Matthew S. Quay and Boies Penrose, that of New York successively by Senators Roscoe Conkling and Thomas C. Platt. Comparable in scale and power were the Democratic state machines, like the one in New York dominated by Senator David B. Hill. The size and variety of the electorate and the frequency of elections put a premium on intensive organization. Moreover, the prevailing mode of voting—party tickets and the absence before about 1890 of the secret ballot—enabled political machines to exercise tight control. Corrupt voting was also facilitated by the mobility of the electorate and the casual methods of voter identification.

James Bryce, and indeed American critics, singled out city government as 'the one conspicuous failure of the United States'. Among the causes were dishonest and incompetent officials, antiquated and cumbersome forms of city government, and the indifference of voters to the actual operation of public administration. More fundamental was the breakneck speed with which American cities grew and the fact that municipal administrations lacked experience in governing large metropolitan areas. With the large-scale expansion of public utilities—water, gas, electricity, rapid transit—and the huge increase in other municipal expenditures, corrupt alliances developed between unscrupulous city officials and business interests eager for franchises and contracts. The most notorious example of municipal graft and corruption was the Tweed Ring (see ch. 13). Following Tweed's downfall in 1871, 'Honest John' Kelly—though he hardly merited his nickname—at least gave New York a respite from the grosser forms of wrongdoing. But graft reached new depths after 1886, when Kelly was succeeded as boss of Tammany Hall by another autocratic Irishman, Richard Croker, a former prizefighter and gang-leader.

Immigrant votes buttressed the power of the city boss and his machine. At a time when there were few public-welfare agencies, the bewildered foreigners who crowded into American cities desperately needed help. City bosses systematically provided it. They found jobs and accommodation for newcomers, 'fixed' things when they ran foul of the law, paid funeral expenses, organized picnics for the children, and at Christmas distributed free coal and turkeys. Unfamiliar with the ballot-box and with representative government immigrants saw nothing wrong in repaying their benefactors with votes and turned a deaf ear to attempts to overthrow boss rule. But although reformers often blamed municipal misgovernment on what one called 'ignorant foreign riffraff', boss rule was just as characteristic of cities without large foreign-born populations.

Along with machine control of politics went legislative bribery and lobbying, especially by big business. Many state legislatures were notoriously in the pay of railroad corporations and although at the federal level corruption was more subtle, it was widespread. The corrupt Congressman became a stock character in contemporary political fiction, notably in John W. De Forest's *Honest John Vane* (1875) and Henry Adams's *Democracy* (1880). Such works have encouraged historians to ascribe corruption simply to the materialism and the flexible ethical standards of the day. But a less moralistic approach would have recognized that corruption, as in eighteenth-century England, was a necessary form of accommodation, a way of getting government to work.

The Political Parties

Each of the major parties was a congeries of state and local organizations. They temporarily assumed a national character once every four years, during presidential elections. At other times they nominated candidates, raised funds, conducted campaigns, and distributed patronage with scarcely a glance outside their immediate constituencies. According to Bryce there was little to distinguish Republicans from Democrats. "Neither party", he wrote in 1888, "has any principles, any distinctive tenets . . ." Nonetheless each had its own set of affiliations. These were based less on economic interests than on complex historical, ethnic, religious, and cultural factors. The Republican party was the party of the Union, Civil War memories the cement that bound it together. It thus appealed to Union veterans and blacks, reinforcing that appeal by invoking Lincoln's name and "waving the bloody shirt", that is, identifying the Democrats with disunion. Strongest in New England·and the upper Middle West, Republicanism drew its support predominantly from the non-Southern native-born, particularly from the more pietistic branches of Protestantism—Congregationalists, Methodists, Quakers. Most of the business community voted Republican, but so did many workingmen, as well as the bulk of the better-off farmers. The Democratic party, on the other hand, was basically an alliance of the white South and the immigrant population of the big Northern cities. It could generally rely on the Catholic vote, whether urban or rural, as well as on the support of the more liturgical Protestant sects, such as the German Lutherans. The Democrats also found adherents among marginal farmers, and even among a minority of businessmen and bankers. Moreover, despite the fact that the two parties were not explicitly ideological and indeed sought to obscure their ideological identity—successfully, in Bryce's case—it was nevertheless possible to discern real and persistent differences of emphasis on questions of public policy. Thus it could be said that the Republicans, though accepting local control over local issues, believed nevertheless that an integrated economy and a nationwide society sometimes implied active, centralized government. They stood for a protective tariff, supported—or at least paid lip-service to—the ideal of racial equality, and sympathized with, without actually endorsing, Prohibition, Sabbatarianism, and immigration restriction. The Democrats, on the other hand, symbolized states' rights and limited government, preached economy and tariff reduction, and were strongly Negrophobic—not alone in the South. Both parties were plagued by chronic factionalism, the product of personal rivalries, the poverty of political issues, and the lure of spoils. Within the Republican ranks the Stalwarts, led by Conkling, were at odds with the Half-Breeds, led by James G. Blaine. The Democrats were equally divided, especially in New York, where there was fierce rivalry between Tammany Hall and two other city factions and between Tammany and David B. Hill's upstate machine. But as election day approached the parties tried, with varying degrees of success, to patch up their squabbles and present a facade of unity.

The negativism of the political system was exemplified by the presidency of Rutherford B. Hayes. While Hayes's term of office saw no repetition of the scandals which had disgraced the Grant Administration, his positive achievements were meager. Though honest and high-minded, the circumstances of the disputed election cast doubt about his title to the Presidency; even prominent Republicans echoed popular taunts about 'His Fraudulency'. Hayes weakened his position further by announcing in advance that he would serve only one term. Besides fulfilling the undertakings given to secure Southern acquiescence in his inauguration—to withdraw the remaining federal troops and to appoint a Southern Democrat to his Cabinet—Hayes tried to placate the South in other ways. But he failed to create a viable Republican party in the South. His vetoes of Democratic efforts to repeal the Force Acts, which had been designed to protect Negro voting rights, served rather to confirm Southern hostility toward the party which had presided over Reconstruction. At the same time his conciliatory Southern policy irritated Republicans.

Republican disunity increased when Hayes turned his attention to civil-service reform. Long a critic of the spoils-ridden federal bureaucracy, he laid it down on becoming President that federal office-holders should be appointed solely on merit. But he did not fully implement the merit principle. The number of appointments he made as rewards for political services seriously compromised him with reformers. So did his watering-down in 1878 of an earlier executive order forbidding political levies on federal employees. Yet Hayes's attempts to restrict Congressional control over the appointment and removal of office-holders led him into a celebrated confrontation with the Stalwarts. After sinecurism and corruption had been exposed in the New York Custom House, the President dismissed two of its leading officials, Chester A. Arthur and Alonzo B. Cornell, both of them Conkling's henchmen. Stung by this attempt to undermine his political machine, Conkling persuaded the Senate to withhold confirmation from Hayes's replacements. After a protracted struggle the President got his way. But the spoilsmen made it impossible for him to carry out his inaugural promise of a "thorough, radical and complete" reform of the civil service.

The Money Question

When the perennial currency controversy revived, Hayes consistently took a hard-money position. He helped defeat a Greenback-inspired attempt to postpone the resumption of specie payments in 1879 as provided in the Resumption Act of 1875. He was equally hostile when inflationists turned from greenbacks to a new panacea, the unlimited coinage of silver. Although in the 1790s the United States had adopted bimetallism it had in practice been on a gold standard since 1834, when Congress had fixed the legal ratio between silver and gold at sixteen to one. That is to say, sixteen grains of silver were deemed for monetary purposes to be equal in value to one grain of gold. Since under the ratio silver was underval-ued—a fact which became still more evident after the California dis-coveries of 1848 had reduced the market price of gold—and since silver ore could thus fetch more on the open market than the mint could pay, silver dollars gradually ceased to be coined. Hence the Coinage Act of 1873, demonetizing silver, merely acknowledged a long-existing reality. At the time the measure had aroused no protest, but almost immediately the expansion of silver production in Nevada, together with the adoption of the gold standard by a number of European countries, brought about a sharp fall in the commercial price of silver. But for the Coinage Act it would now have been profitable to sell silver to the mint at the old ratio. Hence Western mining interests denounced the 'Crime of '73', blaming the measure on a bankers' conspiracy to establish the gold standard. Their demand for repeal was quickly taken up by farm groups eager to increase the per capita circulation of money and thus raise commodity prices. In 1877, ignoring Hayes's warning that a return to bimetallism under the old ratio was tantamount to a debasement of the currency, the House passed a bill introduced by Richard P. ('Silver Dick') Bland of Missouri, providing for the unlimited coinage of silver at 16 to 1. But Senate amendments emasculated the measure and in the form in which it was finally passed— over Hayes's veto—the Bland–Allison Act of 1878 provided only for the monthly purchase of not less than $2 million and not more than $4 million worth of silver bullion to be coined into dollars at the legal ratio. The measure failed to add appreciably to the currency; nor did it halt the decline in the price of silver or check the downward trend in farm prices. That was mainly because successive Secretaries of the Treasury purchased only the minimum requirements. However, prosperity began to return in 1879 and the silver agitation was stilled for more than a decade.

Factionalism and Spoils

The factionalism which had troubled the Republicans throughout Hayes's Administration resulted in a protracted struggle at the party's national convention in Chicago in 1880. The Stalwarts wanted to nominate Grant for a third term, while the Half-Breeds were divided between their nominal leader, Blaine, and the Secretary of the Treasury, John Sherman. The dead' >ck was finally broken when the Blaine and Sherman forces combined to nominate a dark-horse candidate, James A. Garfield of Ohio. Born in a log cabin—the last President to boast that distinction—Garfield was a largely self-educated and self-made man. Successively college teacher, lawyer, Union soldier, and politician, he had been House minority leader during the Hayes Administration. To propitiate the Stalwarts the convention gave the vice-presidential nomination to Chester A. Arthur, Conkling's crony recently removed from office. The Democratic choice fell on General Winfield Scott Hancock, famous as a Union general at Gettysburg. Garfield emerged the victor in the closest election in the country's history: out of more than nine million votes cast, his winning margin was only nine thousand.

From the start Garfield antagonized the Stalwarts. He failed to give them the rewards they had expected for their campaign support, albeit belatedly given, and chose Conkling's great rival, Blaine, to be Secretary of State. Before long the factional struggle over the spoils was openly joined. Garfield provoked it by appointing a leading anti-Conkling Republican to Arthur's lucrative old position in the New York Custom House. That was a challenge not only to Conkling but also to senatorial courtesy, the tradition whereby senators were permitted a veto over presidential appointments in their own states. For two months there was a bitter wrangle in the Senate. Then, sensing defeat, Conkling and his New York colleague, Thomas C. Platt, resigned their Senate seats in the belief that, vindicated by reelection, they would soon return in triumph to overawe Garfield. But in a rare display of independence the New York legislature dismissed the pair. Conkling retired from politics and the Stalwart cause went into decline.

Garfield's stubborn fight promised to strengthen executive independence. But on July 2, 1881, after holding office for only four months, he was shot by a disappointed and mentally unbalanced office-seeker who, after firing the fatal bullet, proclaimed that he was a Stalwart and sought to put Arthur in the White House. That object was not immediately achieved for Garfield lingered throughout the summer, dying only on September 19.

Civil-Service Reform

Throughout his political career Arthur had been a devoted practitioner of the spoils system. But as President he surprised everyone by his independence and zeal for reform. He showed little favor to spoilsmen and vigorously prosecuted those involved in the 'Star Route Frauds', whereby the Post Office had been swindled out of $4 million. Arthur's break with his past was best demonstrated by his support of civil-service reform. For twenty years politicians like Charles Sumner and Carl Schurz, along with influential magazine editors like E. L. Godkin of the *Nation* and George W. Curtis of *Harper's Weekly*, had been denouncing the evils of political patronage and urging the creation of a nonpartisan civil service based on merit. Such a step, they claimed, would rid the public service of corruption, extravagance, and inefficiency. Civil-service reform also appealed for elitist reasons. Taking as their model the British civil service, as reformed after the Northcote–Trevelyan Report (1854), the founders of the National Civil Service Reform League (1881), mostly East Coast patricians and intellectuals, hoped that open competitive entry would result in replacing vulgar and ignorant placemen with men of breeding, character, and refinement. Thus, whereas in England civil-service reform had been an assault on aristocratic dominance, in the United States it was aimed at the excesses of democracy.

'Snivel-service' reform, as Conkling liked to call it, was for years thwarted by him and his kind. But Garfield's assassination generated so much public revulsion against the spoils system that Congress was stirred into action. The Pendleton Act of 1883 established a bipartisan Civil Service Commission to hold open competitive examinations for applicants for federal office. It also forbade the levying of political-campaign contributions of office-holders. Arthur demonstrated his sincerity by appointing a leading civil-service reformer, Dorman B. Eaton, to be chairman of the Commission. Initially the Act covered only about 14,000 federal offices (12 percent of the total) but it empowered the President to extend the 'classified' list, that is, the list of posts subject to the merit system. Every subsequent President did so, not so much from acceptance of the merit principle as from a desire to protect his own appointees against removal. Ironically, therefore, it was largely for partisan reasons that the number of classified posts rose by the end of the century to nearly 95,000 (40 percent of the total). The Pendleton Act had a further consequence, unforeseen by its authors: with political assessments on office-holders forbidden, the parties came to rely increasingly on business for campaign contributions.

Presidential Negativism

Arthur hoped to be renominated in 1884, but his nonpartisan course had alienated the Republican Old Guard without overcoming the reformers' distaste for his earlier record. Instead the Republicans nominated Blaine, a leading presidential aspirant for nearly a decade. But as well as being detested by the Stalwarts his questionable standards of political morality made him anathema to the independent and reformist wing of the Republicans. Known henceforth as Mugwumps, and including such figures as Schurz and Godkin, these reformers announced their intention of bolting the party and of supporting an honest Democrat. This declaration contributed to the choice of Grover Cleveland as the Democratic standard-bearer. Both as mayor of Buffalo and as governor of New York he had been a model of official rectitude. The platforms of the two parties closely resembled each other and, in the absence of real issues, the campaign degenerated into scandalmongering. The Republicans made much of their discovery that as a young man Cleveland had fathered an illegitimate child. The Democrats, for their part, exploited the 'Mulligan Letters', which revealed Blaine's improper activities on behalf of certain railroads when he had been Speaker of the House.

The election was almost as close as the preceding one. Cleveland scraped in by a margin of only 23,000 votes in a poll of nearly ten million. New York, the state on which the election turned, went for the Democrats by a mere 1,149 votes. The Mugwump defection to Cleveland and the votes drawn off—mainly from the Republicans—by Prohibitionist and Greenback candidates were clearly significant. But the result may equally have been decided by an incident in the last days of the campaign. At a meeting with Blaine in New York City the spokesman for a delegation of Republican clergymen, the Reverend Samuel D. Burchard, observed that the antecedents of the Democratic party were "Rum, Romanism and Rebellion". Blaine had been attempting with some success to woo the normally Democratic Irish vote with anti-British speeches and references to his Catholic mother. But his failure to disavow Burchard's indiscretion immediately enabled the Democrats to charge him with having condoned a slander on the Catholic Church.

Cleveland's Mugwump supporters looked to him to carry civil-service reform a stage further. But the Democrats, having won a presidential election for the first time since 1856, were hungry for spoils and, after trying for some months to satisfy both groups, Cleveland responded finally to the call of party loyalty. Though he was to double the number of classified jobs, he replaced about two-thirds of all federal office-holders with Democrats. Yet no amount of political pressure could weaken Cleveland's determination to provide honest and economical government. He refused to sanction an extravagant rivers and harbors bill. He compelled Western railroad, lumber, and cattle interests to disgorge a total of eighty-one million acres of public lands to which they had no legal title. He incurred the wrath of the most powerful lobby in the country, the Grand Army of the Republic, by scrutinizing private pension bills for the benefit of Civil War soldiers and vetoing those which seemed fraudulent. The pensions issue reached a climax in January, 1887 when, under pressure from the GAR, Congress passed the Dependent Pension Bill which provided pensions for all honorably discharged Union soldiers suffering from disability, irrespective of when or how contracted. Declaring the measure would make the pension-list a refuge for frauds rather than a 'roll of honor', Cleveland vetoed it.

Cleveland's courage and integrity have led historians to describe him as the outstanding President between Lincoln and Theodore Roosevelt. But that is not claiming much. In any case his achievements were almost wholly negative, like his philosophy of government. Opposed to the enlargement of governmental power, he was against federal regulation of business and deserves no credit for the measure which marked the entry of the federal government into the field of economic regulation, the Interstate Commerce Act of 1887, which he signed reluctantly. If Cleveland's attitude toward patronage and his passion for economy recalled Andrew Jackson, so did his dislike of legislation favoring special interests. He even vetoed a trivial appropriation of $10,000 for the relief of drought-stricken Texas farmers, observing that "though the people support the Government, the Government should not support the people". Yet his conception of the Presidency was anything but Jacksonian. Believing in the separation of the executive and the legislature, he was disinclined either to initiate legislation or to attempt to influence measures during their passage through Congress.

Cleveland's sole attempt at bold presidential leadership came in December 1887, when he launched a campaign for tariff reduction. He knew that he risked splitting his party and losing the next election, but felt he had a duty to raise the issue. Existing tariff rates were piling up a revenue surplus, thus encouraging extravagant public spending and tending to depress the economy by withdrawing money from circulation. Cleveland's message also asserted that, besides being a form of special privilege, the tariff fostered trusts and raised the cost of living. Though the Democratic House of Representatives responded with a measure providing for moderate reductions, the Republican majority in the Senate buried it. Nevertheless Cleveland had jolted the two parties into clarifying their attitudes to the tariff.

In the presidential election of 1888 the Democrats renominated Cleveland, while the Republicans chose Benjamin Harrison of Indiana, a colorless lawyer whose political career had been unremarkable, but who had the advantage of coming from a doubtful state, that is, a narrowly divided one. The Republicans made protection the cornerstone of their campaign and promised generous pensions to ex-soldiers. The Democrats endorsed Cleveland's tariff message but chose a leading protectionist as his running mate. The President then relapsed into his customary lethargy and made little attempt to press the case for tariff reform. Thus the election was hardly the referendum on the tariff that had seemed likely. On the eve of polling the Republicans played a cheap electioneering trick, the publication of a letter written by the British minister in Washington, Sir Lionel Sackville West. In reply to a bogus request for voting advice from a correspondent claiming to be English-born, West had foolishly expressed the view that British interests would be best served by Cleveland's reelection. Though at the time the 'Murchison Letter' was thought to have cost Cleveland many Irish-American votes, it seems in fact to have had small effect. More important was the use of money to buy votes. In the most corrupt campaign in American history both sides were guilty of flagrant illegalities, especially in doubtful states. But the Republicans could outbid their rivals since industrialists, fearful of tariff revision, contributed hugely to their campaign fund. When the results were in, Cleveland had a majority of the popular vote but Harrison won by narrowly carrying most of the doubtful states.

Having only slender Congressional majorities the Republicans apparently faced frustration for, under existing House rules, the Democratic minority could have used a variety of procedural devices to obstruct business. But the newly elected Speaker, the autocratic Thomas B. Reed of Maine, forced through a change in the rules, thus enabling the Republicans to enact their legislative program. Such was their prodigality that the fifty-first Congress (1889–91) was dubbed the 'Billion-Dollar Congress'. The Dependent Pension Bill of 1890, similar to the one Cleveland had vetoed three years before, doubled the number of pensioners and greatly increased the annual pension bill. A flood of other measures provided for lavish public works, subsidies to steamship lines, premiums to government bondholders, and the return of federal taxes paid by the Northern states since the Civil War. The Republicans also rewarded their industrialist backers with the McKinley Tariff Act (1890), which raised duties to prohibitive levels and gave protection to more products than ever. To win Western votes for the measure its Eastern sponsors had to agree to the Sherman Silver Purchase Act (1890) which required the Treasury to buy four and a half million ounces of silver each month and to pay for it by issuing notes. That pleased the silver miners since it committed the government to buying virtually all they produced. But although it increased the amount of money in circulation it did not fully satisfy those inflationists who wanted the unlimited coinage of silver. At the same time Congress attempted to propitiate the critics of monopoly by passing the Sherman Antitrust Act.

In the Congressional elections of 1890 the Republicans, though retaining control of the Senate, lost nearly half their seats in the House. Popular revulsion against the McKinley Tariff and the extravagance of the 'Billion-Dollar Congress' were blamed for the debacle, but local political controversies in the Middle West over Prohibition and religious education also contributed. The most significant development, however, was the evidence of rising farm unrest provided by the election of nine new Congressmen —Alliance-Populists—unaffiliated with either of the major parties. This foreshadowed a major political upheaval.

The Agrarian Revolt

Farm discontent grew out of adversity. After the Civil War the prices of staple crops fell steadily and massively. Wheat, which sold for $1.45 a bushel in 1866, was down to 49¢ by 1894; corn plummeted during the same period from 75¢ to 28¢ a bushel; cotton fell from 31¢ a bale in 1866 to 6¢ in 1893. Simultaneously there was a sharp rise in farm indebtedness and farm tenancy. By 1890 over a quarter of all farms worked by their owners were mortgaged and in such Middle Western states as Wisconsin, Michigan, and Iowa the proportion was nearer a half. The number of mortgages in the South was relatively insignificant but only because the value of the land was too low to serve as security and because tenancy, sharecropping, and the lien system had become distinctive features of Southern agriculture. But the number of farmers who tilled their own land was falling all over the country. By 1880 a quarter of all American farmers were tenants and by 1900 a third.

The plight of the American farmer resulted basically from an international crisis of overproduction. While American agricultural production was expanding, thanks to mechanization and to millions of additional acres coming under the plow, vast tracts of virgin land were also being brought under cultivation in Australia, Canada, Argentina, and Russia. Railways and steam navigation made it possible to transport food and raw materials quickly and cheaply over long distances and linked the different producing countries in one vast market. The increase in world production was greater than could be readily absorbed. Thus the downward spiral of prices brought distress to farmers in many parts of the world. Naturally the worst sufferers in the United States were the growers of staple crops in the South and Middle West who were accustomed to dispose of their surpluses in the world market. That meant in particular wheat farmers, who depended for 30 to 40 percent of their income on export sales, and cotton planters, who sold no less than 70 percent of their product abroad.

Farmers' difficulties were nonetheless aggravated by domestic factors and, since these were more comprehensible than those resulting from the workings of the international economy, farmers tended to focus their indignation upon them. Railroads, with their high and discriminatory freight rates, were the main target. In the South and West rates were two or three times higher than those, say, between New York and Chicago. The railroads tended to charge all that the traffic would bear and the complaint that it took one bushel of wheat or corn to pay the freight on another bushel was sometimes an understatement. Equally resented were usurious bank interest-rates: although rates were fixed by law and nominally averaged from 6 to 10 percent, commission and service charges often brought them up to 15 or even 25 percent. Manufacturing monopolies were yet another agrarian *bête noire*. Having eliminated competition from abroad and among themselves they could charge what they liked for nearly everything the farmer bought. Farmers also complained that as consumers they paid the bill for the protective tariff, and as debtors were the principal victims of a deflationary fiscal policy which, besides depressing commodity prices, kept credit tight and money dear. In short, farmers believed that they were being ruthlessly exploited by other groups and were being ignored or discriminated against by government. In addition they were victims of declining social status. Whereas those who tilled the soil had once been admired and even idealized—had not Jefferson called them "the chosen people of God"?—they were now scoffed at by city-dwellers as "hicks" and "hayseeds".

In self-defense, angry farmers turned to collective action. The first nationwide farmers' organization, the National Grange of the Patrons of Husbandry, founded in 1867, began as a social and educational association. During the depression of the early 1870s the Grange spread rapidly and by 1875 had 21,000 lodges and 800,000 members. As it grew the organization's activities expanded. To eliminate middlemen's profits Grangers established scores of marketing and consumer cooperatives—creameries, grain elevators, warehouses, and packing plants, harvester and plow factories, even banks and insurance companies. But most of these enterprises failed owing to managerial inexperience, the hostility of established businesses, and the lack of support from those they were intended to serve. Meanwhile, though remaining ostensibly nonpolitical, the Grange became politically active. It worked both within the major parties and through a number of short-lived antimonopoly and farmers' parties. In 1873 and 1874 Grangers won control of eleven Middle Western state legislatures and proceeded to enact laws to check railroad abuses (see Ch. 16). But with the return of prosperity in the late 1870s Grangerism swiftly lost strength and reverted to being simply a movement for social and educational betterment. The nascent farmers' parties either melted away or were absorbed by the Greenback Labor Party, an alliance of agrarian and labor organizations. Its demand for inflation won it a large following among Western and Southern farmers; in the Congressional elections of 1878 Greenback Labor polled over a million votes and elected fourteen Congressmen. In 1880, however, its presidential nominee, James B. Weaver of Iowa, polled only 300,000 votes and after contesting the presidential election of 1884 the party disappeared.

More significant politically were the farmers' organizations which succeeded the Grange in the 1880s and were largely modeled on it. By the end of the decade these had coalesced to form two independent regional groups: the Southern Alliance, which claimed a million members in the cotton states, and the smaller but still substantial Northwestern Farmers' Alliance, whose strength was mainly in the wheat-belt of the Middle Border—Kansas, Nebraska, Minnesota, and the Dakotas. Like the Grange the Alliances sponsored social and educational activities and went in for cooperative buying and selling. But almost from the start they were a vehicle for expressing the farmers' economic grievances. And with the return of hard times in the late 1880s their demands became more strident and more radical.

At a meeting in St. Louis in 1889 leaders of the two Alliances attempted to weld them into a single organization. But nothing came of the idea because Northerners objected to the secrecy Southerners practiced and their refusal to admit blacks as equals. Nevertheless there was agreement on certain common political objectives, including the free and unlimited coinage of silver, nationalization of the means of transportation and communication, the abolition of national banks, and the introduction of a graduated income tax. The Southern Alliance also advanced another proposal, the brainchild of Dr C. W. Macune, editor of the leading Alliance paper. This was the subtreasury plan which suggested Treasury loans in paper money equal to 80 percent of the value of the crops which farmers were to deposit in federal warehouses. This scheme, somewhat similar to one adopted during the New Deal, was intended both to solve the farm credit problem and to have a general inflationary effect.

By now farmers were ready to plunge into politics. Those in the Northwest, despairing of help from either Republicans or Democrats, concluded that the time was ripe for a new national party. As a first step they organized statewide parties under a variety of labels in Kansas, Nebraska, and the Dakotas. In the elections of 1890 they made striking gains, winning control of a number of legislatures and electing two Senators and nine Congressmen. Most members of the Southern Alliance were dubious about starting a third party, fearing it might split the Solid South and endanger white supremacy. Accordingly they set out to wrest control of the Democratic machinery from the Bourbons and, having done so, succeeded in electing two state governors and forty Congressmen.

The People's Party

After these local successes third-party advocates redoubled their efforts to form a national organization and, at a meeting in St. Louis in February 1892, dominated by farmers' representatives but attended also by delegates from the Knights of Labor, Greenbackers, and other reform groups, formally organized the People's Party. In a convention at Omaha in July the

Populists, as they were known, nominated the old Greenbacker, James B. Weaver, for President. The platform demanded the free and unlimited coinage of silver, government ownership of railroads, telegraphs, and telephones, a graduated income tax, and the subtreasury plan. Other planks were designed to diminish the political influence of big business: the secret ballot, the initiative, referendum, and recall, and the direct election of senators. Finally, in an attempt to woo industrial workers, the platform demanded a shorter working day and immigration restriction.

The Populist platform, with its call for extensive government control of the economy, struck Eastern conservatives as wildly revolutionary. Their alarm was increased by the eccentric character—at least in their eyes—of many of the Populist leaders and their intemperate language. Weaver was no radical, merely a dedicated inflationist. Nor for that matter were other leading Populists the cranks and visionaries many took them to be. But they included some extremely colorful figures. Ignatius Donnelly, for example, the author of the Omaha platform, had been an inveterate protestor for thirty years and had written an apocalyptic novel, *Caesar's Column*, foretelling the violent overthrow of capitalism. Kansas contributed an exceptionally picturesque trio: Jerry Simpson, known as 'Sockless Socrates', the long-bearded William A. Peffer, who conjured up an Old Testament prophet, and Mary Ellen Lease, a militant woman politician in an age when women politicians of any kind were rare. The 'Kansas Pythoness', as she was known, had stumped the state preaching that "Wall Street owns the country" and advising farmers to "raise less corn and more hell".

In 1892 the Populists did poorly. Weaver ran well in the Middle Border and the Rocky Mountain states, carrying four states, but his one million votes were less than 9 percent of the total. He got hardly any support in old Granger states like Iowa, Wisconsin, and Illinois, where farmers had found a new prosperity by switching from one-crop agriculture to dairying and raising corn and hogs. Nor did he make much impact on the South, where whites, remembering Reconstruction, would not abandon the Democrats and blacks could not be weaned from support of Republicanism. He failed also to win the support of the industrial working class. Though Populists talked about the "harmony of labor" between farmers and workers, the two groups in fact had different wrongs to redress and incompatible sets of priorities. Thus the 1892 election turned out to be largely a repetition of the Harrison–Cleveland duel of 1888. Both major parties evaded the currency question, the main issue—insofar as there was one— being the tariff. While Cleveland's winning margin was fairly narrow, it was the largest for twenty years.

Yet Populism was far from dead. On the contrary, the events of Cleveland's second administration intensified the spirit of rural resentment and revolt. Hardly had Cleveland been inaugurated than the Panic of 1893 sent the economy reeling and ushered in the longest and worst depression in the country's history up to that time. Thousands of firms went bankrupt, hundreds of banks shut their doors, and one railroad in every six—including some of the largest—went into receivership. By the winter of 1893–4 there were more than two and a half million unemployed. Meanwhile farm prices plunged even further downward.

Like hard-money men generally, Cleveland was convinced that the prime cause of depression was the Sherman Silver Purchase Act. It had undermined business confidence, he reasoned, by permitting holders of silver certificates to exchange them for gold, thus causing a drain on the Treasury's gold reserves. The President therefore demanded its repeal. In October 1893 he got his way but only by enlisting Republican support and by the ruthless use of patronage to bring recalcitrant Democrats into line. But most Southern and Western Democrats voted against the Administration, among them William Jennings Bryan, a young Nebraska Congressman, whose eloquent attack on the gold standard marked the emergence of a figure destined to play a prominent role in the Democratic party for the next twenty years.

Cleveland's uncharacteristic display of leadership halted neither the depression nor the drain on the Treasury. In an attempt to replenish the gold reserves he ordered the Treasury to buy gold, paying for it with bond issues. When that expedient in turn failed, he turned in desperation to a New York banking syndicate headed by J. P. Morgan and August Belmont which arranged a $62 million loan on terms which gave it a handsome profit. That saved the situation long enough for the government to float a public loan which brought the monetary crisis to an end early in 1896. But Cleveland's stubborn defense of the gold standard infuriated Populists and bimetallists. They denounced him as the tool of Wall Street.

Beyond maintaining national solvency Cleveland believed that there was little he could do to promote economic recovery. Nor did he accept that it was government's responsibility to relieve distress. That indeed was the general view, but in many cities the unemployed began demanding a public-works relief program. To dramatize the demand, Jacob S. Coxey, a prosperous Ohio businessman with Populist sympathies, organized a march of the unemployed on Washington. But only about 500 members of "Coxey's army" reached Washington (April 30, 1894) and when its leaders were arrested—for trespassing on the Capitol grounds—the movement collapsed. Shortly afterward Cleveland's action in sending federal troops to break the Pullman strike showed that he had no more sympathy with strikers than with the unemployed.

Meanwhile Cleveland suffered a sharp defeat in trying to keep his campaign pledge of tariff reform. A bill providing for a substantial drop in rates passed the House but Senate protectionists so amended it that in its final form the Wilson–Gorman Tariff Act of 1894 was barely distinguishable from the McKinley Tariff. To Populists the measure's only saving grace was that it included a provision for a 2 percent tax on incomes over $4,000. But their satisfaction turned to chagrin when in *Pollock v. Farmers' Loan and Trust Co.* (1895) the Supreme Court declared the income-tax provision unconstitutional on the ground that "direct taxes" could be apportioned among the states only on the basis of population. To the discontented this was final proof that the government was dominated by the well-to-do and powerful.

The Battle of the Standards

As the 1896 presidential election approached the monetary issue overshadowed all others. The Populist demand for free silver was taken up by sizable factions within both major parties. Western silver-mine owners, who cared nothing for inflation but were eager to raise the price of their product, helped finance a campaign run by the National Bimetallic League. The League's most effective piece of prosilver propaganda was William H. Harvey's *Coin's Financial School* (1894), a crude political tract which both in its sales and in its effects recalled *Common Sense* and *Uncle Tom's Cabin*. Presenting free silver as a cure-all, 'Professor' Coin reduced a complex question to terms farmers could readily grasp, and played also on their paranoid tendencies by representing the demonetization of silver as a conspiracy on the part of British bankers and Jewish moneylenders.

When the Republican convention met at St. Louis in June 1896, the 'goldbugs' were in firm control. The platform, besides endorsing the high tariff, called unequivocally for maintenance of the gold standard. At this a number of Western silver Republicans bolted the party. The nomination went to William McKinley, author of the Tariff Act of 1890, who had served in both houses of Congress and had thrice been governor of Ohio. McKinley owed his selection to the preconvention maneuvers of his friend and patron, Marcus Alonzo Hanna, a wealthy Cleveland industrialist and political boss. But he was not the puppet the Democrats made him out to be. While McKinley was certainly sympathetic to business he was unquestionably his own man.

Within the Democratic ranks prosilver Southerners and Westerners had been working systematically to wrest control from Cleveland and the Eastern conservatives. When the Democrats convened at Chicago they had gained enough strength to be able to dictate a platform which amounted to a wholesale repudiation of Cleveland's policies. It declared in favor of the free and unlimited coinage of silver at 16 to 1. In the debate on the platform Bryan made the celebrated "Cross of Gold" speech in which he reiterated Jeffersonian sentiments about the primary importance and worth of the farmer in society and voiced the pent-up resentment of rural America at the way in which a plutocratic government had consistently disregarded farmers' aspirations. His assault on the gold standard concluded with the words: 'You shall not press down upon the brow of labor this crown of thorns, you shall not crucify mankind upon a cross of gold.' Bryan's impassioned oratory thrilled the convention, made him the undisputed leader of the silverites, and ensured him the nomination.

Only thirty-six years of age, Bryan was the youngest man ever nominated for the Presidency by a major party: indeed, some voters were to consider him too young to be President. More than almost any other American politician, he was capable of arousing violently conflicting emotions. His supporters idolized him as "the peerless leader of the People" in their fight against exploitation, but to his critics he was an apostle of discord and a fanatical visionary. He was not in fact as radical as he sounded. He was, however, a man of limited intellectual grasp, provincial in outlook, and, in his approach to economics, naive and muddleheaded. But he was a magnificent popular orator with an instinctive sympathy for the struggling farmer and a burning conviction that traditional values were in danger of being engulfed by a corporate state.

Bryan's nomination and the inclusion of free silver in the Democratic platform placed the Populists in a quandary. The Democrats had stolen their chief issue, while ignoring such other quintessential Populist demands as the subtreasury plan and the nationalization of the railroads. By endorsing Bryan the Populists would lose their separate political identity besides in effect giving up most of their platform. Yet to run their own candidate would mean splitting the free-silver vote, thus guaranteeing a Republican victory. After an anguished debate the Populist convention voted to accept Bryan, but in a gesture of independence refused to endorse the Democratic vice-presidential candidate, a Maine banker, and chose instead the fiery and combative Tom Watson of Georgia. Silver Republicans also backed Bryan but a group of Gold Standard Democrats insisted on nominating their own candidate.

The 1896 campaign, the first for a generation in which a clear-cut issue divided the parties, was unprecedentedly emotional and vituperative. While McKinley observed the convention of staying at home and conducting a dignified 'front-porch' campaign, Bryan barnstormed the country, traveling 18,000 miles and making 600 speeches. Focusing on the silver issue and portraying the contest as one between Wall Street and the "toiling masses", indeed dramatizing it as a struggle between good and evil, Bryan roused his audiences to an enthusiasm reminiscent of revivalist meetings. Whether his tour won him votes seems doubtful. People flocked to hear him but, although moved by his oratory, were less often converted to his politics. Bryan's rancor and his deliberate attempts to whip up mass emotion convinced many that he was a dangerous demagogue. John Hay, soon to become Secretary of State, denounced him as "a half-baked glib little jackleg lawyer promising the millennium to anyone with a hole in his pants and destruction to anyone with a clean shirt". Tom Watson's incendiary harangues likewise sounded like a call to class conflict. Many clergymen, moreover, condemned Bryan's 'cross of gold' speech as blasphemous. Bryan further harmed himself by his crudely sectional appeal, especially his ill-judged reference to the East as 'the enemy's country'.

The chief result of Bryan's speeches was to infuriate and alarm industrialists and bankers. Their contributions enabled Hanna, now the chairman of the Republican National Committee, to build up an unprecedentedly large campaign fund—estimated at between $3.5 million and $16 million— many times greater than that collected by the Democrats. Hanna used the money to deluge the country with propaganda identifying Bryanism with anarchy and revolution and predicting universal ruin if the Nebraskan were elected. He dispatched an army of speakers, among them eminent economists, to refute Bryan's arguments for free silver. But in general Hanna relied on organization rather than oratory. He formed special interest committees to woo trade unionists, blacks, ethnic, and religious groups. He chartered scores of special trains to carry representatives of different groups, all expenses paid, to McKinley's home town, Canton, Ohio, to be addressed by the candidate. Republicans also 'waved the bloody shirt' to great effect, staging parades of Civil War veterans, stressing McKinley's war service, and generally identifying the Republican party with patriotism.

Polling day produced an exceptionally high turnout, fully two million more votes being cast than in 1892. McKinley won decisively, his winning margin being easily the largest since Grant defeated Greeley in 1872. Bryan swept the South and most of the West, but failed to carry such agrarian strongholds as North Dakota, Minnesota, and Iowa. More important, he did not carry a single state in the industrial Northeast: in New England, indeed, he lost every county. The flood of Republican propaganda may have contributed to the result, along with the failure of the Eastern Democratic machines to put their full weight behind Bryan. But the main reason for Bryan's defeat was that, along with businessmen, urban workingmen were repelled, frightened even, by free silver. It did not require pressure from their employers—though there was plenty of that—to make them realize that an inflationary policy designed to boost farm prices could hardly fail to cut their real wages, that if the price of wheat rose, so did the price of bread. They also shared the widespread feeling that it was dangerous, immoral even, to tinker with the currency. Many workingmen also believed that the protective tariff was as much in their interests as in those of manufacturers. Hence the Republican vote in the great industrial states increased spectacularly. In 1892 the Democrats had carried the country's twelve largest cities by a margin of 145,000 votes; in 1896 the Republicans swept them by a majority of 352,000.

The election was followed shortly by the end of the long depression. This was due not to McKinley's victory but to the normal operation of the business cycle, and to crop failures abroad. But the Republicans could plausibly claim to be the party of prosperity. Interpreting the election as a mandate for further protection they rushed through the Dingley Tariff of 1897, raising duties to record levels. After the Administration had made a half hearted attempt to obtain an international agreement for the free coinage of silver, as promised in the Republican platform, the Currency Act of 1900 put the country firmly on the gold standard, thus ending the long monetary controversy. There was little opposition for by that time the inflation the farmers had demanded had come about in a way they would never have chosen. The discovery of new mines in the Klondike and South Africa, together with the development of new extractive processes, produced an extraordinary increase in the world's gold supply and hence in the amount of money in circulation.

The election of 1896 established the Republicans as the normal majority party. This was the first time they had won the Presidency without benefit of the black vote in the South. They had succeeded in winning the confidence of the urban industrial workingman without losing that of big business. They were now to enjoy sixteen years of unbroken power. The Democrats were badly hurt by the free-silver campaign, especially by its undertones of class warfare. Throughout the next decade and a half they were to remain deeply divided. As for the Populist party, Bryan's defeat all but destroyed it. Fusion with the Democrats and the subordination of every issue to free silver demoralized the Populists and made it impossible to reestablish their separate identity. A handful of Populist Congressmen survived for a few years but Populism as a major force died in 1896. Narrow and backward-looking, the Populists had only a limited understanding of the money question. It should be remembered, however, that their faith in free silver was no more naive and misplaced than their opponents' devotion to the gold standard. Their real significance was that they were the first organized movement to identify and seek to remedy the evils of industrialism. Moreover they resembled the English Chartists in that, although themselves defeated, many of their suggested reforms were ultimately enacted. But for the moment conservatism was firmly in the saddle. For the first time in twenty years, the Republican party controlled the Presidency and had large majorities in both branches of the legislature. McKinley filled his Cabinet with wealthy men, thus assuring the business and financial community that the federal government would pursue friendly policies. In the last years of the nineteenth century the consolidation of business was carried to unprecedented lengths. Meanwhile the return of prosperity drew the teeth of agrarian discontent. In the 1900 election little was heard of free silver and McKinley again defeated Bryan, this time by an even larger margin.

19. *The Progressive Era,*
1900–1917

Progressivism: Sources and Characteristics

The most striking characteristic of Progressivism, the vigorous wave of reform that swept over the United States between 1900 and 1917, was the range of its concerns. These included government regulation of the economy; the purification of politics; tariff reduction; Prohibition; women's suffrage; municipal reform; the improvement of working conditions; child labor; housing and public health; the treatment of poverty, vice, and crime; the conservation of natural resources. As this catalog suggests, Progressivism shared some of the objectives of Populism, and indeed borrowed consciously from it. Yet there were significant differences between the two. Unlike Populism, Progressivism was the product not of economic depression but of a period of fairly general prosperity. Nor did it follow the Populist example of coming to concentrate on a single issue. Progressivism was, moreover, nationwide rather than sectional and its strongholds were the cities rather than the countryside. Unlike Populism again, Progressivism did not (except briefly in 1912) develop into a separate political organization: its adherents operated rather as pressure groups within the two major political parties. Besides being intellectually more sophisticated, Progressivism was free from the taint of radicalism that had so damaged Populism. Progressive leaders were preponderantly middle-class city-dwellers, generally comfortably off and well-educated. In exposing the seamier side of American society Progressives were not demanding a thoroughgoing transformation of the existing political and economic system. While concerned for the victims of the new industrial order—slum-dwellers and exploited factory workers—they abhorred class conflict and did not envisage any radical redistribution of wealth and power. The limitations of Progressivism were neatly suggested by Mr Dooley, the famous fictional character created by the Chicago humorist, Finley Peter Dunne, when he remarked: "The noise ye hear is not the first gun of a revolution. It is only the people of the United States beating a carpet."

The immediate origins of Progressivism are to be found in the anxieties of the 1890s. Though Americans were proud of their technological achievements many of the more thoughtful were disturbed by the rise of the trusts, the growing concentration of wealth, the spread of political corruption, the widening of social divisions, the bitterness of industrial strife, the scale and character of immigration, and the resulting loss of cultural homogeneity. Historians have often depicted Progressivism as a kind of morality play, a struggle between good and evil, a humanitarian and idealistic uprising against the entrenched power of the trusts and against corrupt machine politicians. But this interpretation fails to do justice to the complexities of Progressivism. To begin with, Progressivism was not exclusively liberal in the present-day sense of the term; it had a conservative, even a reactionary, side. Progressives generally were ambivalent toward trade unions, frequently hostile to immigration, indifferent to the plight of blacks. Then again, Progressive leaders were not the product of popular discontent but the self-appointed guardians of the public interest. For all their democratic rhetoric, they were not just aiming at restoring power to the people. What they sought was greater popular participation in govment by a better-informed electorate; and they hoped this would produce better political leadership, preferably by people like themselves. Finally, while big business and city bosses were often the targets of Progressive reform, they were on occasion its most active sponsors.

Often a simple sense of outrage at poverty, injustice, and corruption was sufficient to generate pressure for reform. But Progressivism had other, more complex, sources. Some historians, emphasizing the middle-class background of Progressive leaders, have argued that they were motivated by a desire to regain the status they had lost to the new corporate aristocracy. But there is little evidence for this and it seems that what really worried Progressives was the tendency of industrialization and centralization to destroy social harmony. Progressives were in fact inspired by a mixture of yearnings—for efficiency, for order, for social unity, for economic stability—as well as by economic self-interest. Efficiency was the watchword, for example, of conservationists. These were not nature-lovers but advocates of the systematic preservation and allocation of natural resources for current and future use. Appalled at the unrestrained and wasteful exploitation of the public domain by private interests, they wanted to substitute scientific planning by trained experts. A passion for efficiency and a faith in the expert also helped motivate municipal reformers. They were offended less by the dishonesty of city governments than by their incompetence and excessive cost. Anxiety to eliminate disorder and waste also explained why some corporate leaders—in railroads and meat-packing, for instance—actively sought an extension of federal economic regulation. Besides being preferable to the varying, and possibly more restrictive, provisions of state laws, they thought it capable of stabilizing the market by limiting competition and forcing smaller competitors to adopt higher standards. Urban political bosses, traditionally regarded as inveterate enemies of reform, likewise supported specific innovations out of self-interest. While they would have no truck with corrupt-practices laws, women's suffrage, and other proposals designed to reduce their power, they supported primary elections which they believed could be made to work to their advantage and social-welfare legislation which would benefit their immigrant, working-class constituents.

Progressivism was thus not a unified movement; indeed, it can hardly be called a movement at all. Rather did it consist of a number of distinct reform impulses aiming at divergent and sometimes contradictory goals. Its leaders were variously motivated and differed in their programs and priorities. Yet there existed a recognizably Progressive cast of mind. This united reformers as different as the Kansas editor, William Allen White, the Chicago social worker, Jane Addams, the publicist, Frederic C. Howe, the sociologist, Edward A. Ross, the philosopher, John Dewey, and, to some extent, politicians like Theodore Roosevelt and Robert M. La Follete. The Progressive mentality was, above all, moralistic. It possessed a strain of moral fervor that recalled, and indeed was largely derived from, evangelical Protestantism. Progressives translated political and economic questions into moral terms; they exhorted rather than argued; they talked not of individual improvement but of the 'general welfare'. They were essentially optimistic and rationalistic and while they did not believe progress was automatic or inevitable, they were confident that society was infinitely malleable and believed that governmental power could, and should, be harnessed to promote the public good. Public-spirited though they were, the Progressives were in many ways naive. They had an excessive faith that reform could be achieved by improvements in political machinery. They also tended to believe that no evil, once exposed, was too great to be overcome. They had mixed feelings toward cities, seeing them as centers of crime, poverty, and corruption and yet as 'the hope of the future'. Coming as many of them did from rural small towns Progressive intellectuals were nostalgic for the values of rural America and believed that national salvation depended on the preservation of those values.

The steadily growing appeal of Socialism heightened middle-class fears. Between 1901, when the Socialist Party of America was founded, and the outbreak of World War I, Socialism developed greater strength in America than in any other period, before or since. The new party, more moderate and less doctrinaire than the older-established Socialist Labor Party dominated by the Marxist intellectual, Daniel De Leon, was a coalition of groups led respectively by Eugene V. Debs, the leader of the Pullman strike, Victor L. Berger, an Austrian-born Milwaukee journalist, and Morris Hillquit, a Latvian immigrant who had become a prominent New

York labor lawyer. The SPA attracted support from many different economic, regional, and ethnic groups. Strong among the Milwaukee and Chicago Germans and New York Jewish garment-workers, it had a sizable following among native-born intellectuals and flourished in Oklahoma and other western rural states where Populism had erupted a decade earlier. In the Rocky Mountain and Pacific Northwest region, there was a more radical brand of Socialism led by revolutionary syndicalists like William Haywood of the IWW and strongly backed by migratory harvesters, lumberjacks, miners, and railroad workers. Though continually wracked by factional disputes, the party made substantial progress at the polls. Debs, the perennial Socialist presidential candidate, polled 402,000 votes in 1904 and 897,000 votes in 1912—about 6 percent of the total. In 1910 Milwaukee sent Berger to Washington as the first Socialist Congressman; four years later he was joined by Meyer London of New York. By 1912 more than fifty cities had elected Socialist mayors; besides Milwaukee they included Schenectady, New York, Butte, Montana, and Berkeley, California. Though this in fact represented the peak of American Socialism contemporaries believed it was on the point of becoming a major political force.

Progressivism did not spring into being overnight. It drew upon nearly a quarter of a century of criticism of the economic system, beginning with Henry George's *Progress and Poverty* (see p. 308). It was further stimulated by the rise of the Social Gospel movement (see p. 336–7), which demonstrated a willingness on the part of at least some clergymen to take the lead in economic and social reform. In the 1890s the Protestant churches organized a variety of philanthropic enterprises and community services and some established industrial commissions to study such questions as trade unionism, child labor, and immigration. In 1908 they coalesced to form the Federal Council of Churches of Christ in America, a body which immediately placed itself firmly on the side of social-welfare legislation.

What did most to create a climate conducive to reform were the revelations of a group of journalists known as muckrakers, a term first applied to them in 1906 by Theodore Roosevelt and intended by him as a rebuke. (He drew his metaphor from "The Man with the Muckrake" in Bunyan's *Pilgrim's Progress*, whose vision was so fixed on earthly things that he could not see the celestial crown held over him.) There had been earlier exposés of social and economic evils, but what distinguished these was that they reached a mass audience through cheap popular magazines. *McClure's* was the prototype of the muckraking magazine. In 1902 it published a series of articles by Lincoln Steffens, "The Shame of the Cities", which disclosed widespread graft and corruption in American cities. This was followed by Ida M. Tarbell's "History of the Standard Oil Company", a carefully documented assault on John D. Rockefeller and his business methods, and by Ray Stannard Baker's highly critical "Railroads on Trial". The boost these articles gave to *McClure's* circulation demonstrated the existence of a national urge for self-criticism which other magazines hastened to exploit. Soon an army of writers was scouring the land for scandal. Muckrakers denounced among other things the activities of the beef trust, insurance and patent-medicine frauds, child labor, stock-market practices, the business connections of United States senators, prostitution, and the white slave traffic. In time muckraking tended to degenerate into mere sensationalism. Moreover, muckrakers were more concerned to expose evils than to suggest how they might be cured. But they and the authors of muckraking novels like Upton Sinclair's *The Jungle* (see p. 380) undoubtedly helped stir the American conscience.

Municipal Reform

Reform began where it was most urgently needed: in the cities. Progressives believed that the remedy for boss rule and machine politics was to change the structure of city government. Besides aiming at home rule, that is, freedom from interference by state legislatures, they worked to abolish the traditional form of government—by a mayor, city council, and elected administrative officials—and to replace it with an elective commission, whose members were to be chosen for their expertise and abilities rather than their party affiliations. The commission plan, first instituted in Galveston, Texas, in 1901, in the aftermath of a devastating flood, had been adopted in one form or another by some 400 cities by 1921. A variant of it, the city-manager plan, was also widely copied: first introduced into Staunton, Virginia in 1908, it entailed turning over executive power to a trained expert. Yet personalities were as important as forms of government. Municipal improvement owed much to a new breed of reform mayors. The two most prominent were Tom L. Johnson of Cleveland and Samuel M. ('Golden Rule') Jones of Toledo, both of whom turned to politics after having made large fortunes in business. Johnson, who was converted to reform after reading Henry George, waged a prolonged campaign for home rule, just taxation, and municipal ownership of street-cars. Mayor of Cleveland from 1901 to 1909, he made it, according to Lincoln Steffens, "the best-governed city in America". As mayor of Toledo, Jones increased the wages of municipal employees, campaigned for municipal ownership of all public utilities, and established public parks and playgrounds, golf links and free kindergartens. Dying in office in 1904, his wise and humane administration was continued by his disciple, Brand Whitlock.

Progressivism in the States

Since municipal governments possessed only limited powers Progressives generally found it necessary to continue the battle for reform at the state level. Here the earliest examples of Progressivism were provided in the 1890s by Governors John P. Altgeld of Illinois and Hazen S. Pingree of Michigan. A decade later their example was being followed all over the country. In California Governor Hiram W. Johnson ended the political domination of the Southern Pacific Railroad; in the South Bourbon control was undermined by the election of Progressive governors like Jeff Davis of Arkansas (1901), James K. Vardaman of Mississippi (1903), and Hoke Smith of Georgia (1906); on the east coast reform was best represented by Governors Charles Evans Hughes of New York and Woodrow Wilson of New Jersey. But the outstanding Progressive state governor was Robert M. La Follette of Wisconsin. A fiery, uncompromising figure, La Follette carried through a sweeping program of reform during his six years as governor (1900–6). He secured from an often reluctant legislature laws providing for effective railroad regulation, income taxes, and death duties, restrictions on lobbying, regulation of banks and insurance companies, limitation of hours of labor for women and children, the merit system in state employment, and primary elections for the choice of party candidates. An important feature of La Follette's administration was the "Wisconsin Idea", a term denoting the collaboration between the state government and University of Wisconsin experts who provided the legislature with data and advice on economic and political problems and staffed the numerous state commissions appointed to regulate business. It was thanks largely to La Follette's leadership that Wisconsin became, in Theodore Roosevelt's words, "the laboratory of democracy".

Besides passing laws to regulate business corporations and protect wage-earners, state governments adopted various devices to diminish the influence of political bosses and pressure groups and thus make government more representative and democratic. William S. U'Ren of Oregon pioneered several: the initiative, which gave voters (usually not less than 5 percent of the total) the right to compel consideration of a particular measure; the referendum, which submitted legislative proposals to a direct popular vote; and the recall, a procedure whereby elected officials could be removed from office by popular vote before the expiry of their terms. By 1918 twenty states had adopted the initiative and the referendum, twelve the recall. Even more widely adopted was the direct primary, first instituted by Wisconsin in 1903; this allowed voters themselves, rather than boss-dominated conventions, to choose party candidates. A related reform was the direct election of United States senators. Selection by state legislatures was notoriously corrupt and the Senate itself had come to be regarded as the home of special interests. By 1912 twenty-nine states had passed laws virtually requiring legislatures to endorse the popular choice, as signified in a preferential primary, and the following year the Seventeenth Amendment, providing for the direct popular election of senators, was added to the Constitution.

Women's Suffrage, Prohibition, Child Welfare

Two other reforms originating in the states and aimed at purifying politics were women's suffrage and Prohibition. The movement to enfranchise women had begun during Reconstruction when feminists had attempted to secure woman suffrage as part of the Fourteenth Amendment. After that attempt failed the National Association for Woman Suffrage was founded in 1869, with Elizabeth Cady Stanton and Susan B. Anthony at its head. Almost simultaneously a rival organization appeared, the American Woman Suffrage Association, led by Lucy Stone and Julia Ward Howe, to demand equal suffrage through constitutional amendment. In 1890 the two groups coalesced to form a single national organization, the National American Woman Suffrage Association (NAWSA). As in England the movement was largely bourgeois in membership and slow to progress. As late as 1900 only Wyoming, Colorado, Utah, and Idaho had granted full voting rights to women, though in several other states women could vote in school-board elections. It is usually argued that frontier conditions, and especially the fact that women were heavily outnumbered by men, promoted sexual equality. But in fact special local circumstances explained the grant of woman suffrage in the Rocky Mountain states. Other Western states adamantly refused to follow suit.

The reasons for the lack of progress were not far to seek. Most men— and indeed most women—were either indifferent or actively hostile. Opponents objected that to involve women in the sordid business of politics would degrade them and undermine family life, that women had no need of the vote since they were already indirectly represented by their menfolk, and that they lacked the intellect to comprehend political issues. But the rise of Progressivism enabled suffragists to counter these arguments with the rhetoric of reform. The enfranchisement of women, they claimed, would tend to purify politics and strike a blow at political machines, if only by doubling the size of the electorate and advancing Prohibition. Such causes as housing, pure food and drug laws, and the abolition of child labor would also benefit. Prejudice supplied suffragists with a further argument: many thought it monstrous to deny the vote to native-born women while offering it freely to foreign-born men. NAWSA membership soared from 17,000 in 1905 to 2,000,000 in 1917. Between 1910 and 1914 seven additional states, all of them west of the Mississippi, adopted woman suffrage. Yet the proposal was heavily defeated in Middle Western states like Ohio and Wisconsin. Moreover, even where women possessed the vote, they were not the political equals of men; few were elected to office and none entered Congress before World War I. In 1912 a handful of ardent spirits, led by Alice Paul, who had spent several years in England, sought to infuse the movement with the drama and fervor of the English struggle. But since Dr Anna Howard Shaw and Mrs Carrie Chapman Catt, the dominant figures in the NAWSA, furiously denounced militancy American suffragists did not adopt such English tactics as destroying mail-boxes, slashing paintings, and interrupting public meetings, though they did picket the White House. That as late as 1913 a woman's suffrage march in Washington could be broken up by a mob perhaps indicated the persistence of public hostility. Alternatively, it signified that woman suffrage was now being taken seriously.

The Prohibition agitation gained fresh momentum from the startling increase in alcoholic consumption after the Civil War. A Prohibition party was founded in 1869 and achieved some local successes. But the main spearhead of Prohibition was the Women's Christian Temperance Union (1874), largely a creation of Frances Willard, for whom "temperance" was essentially a means of protecting the home against male drunkenness. The wife of President Hayes demonstrated her support by refusing to serve alcoholic beverages at White House functions, thus earning for herself the nickname "Lemonade Lucy". A more militant crusader was the Kansas-born Carry Nation, an unbalanced virago who became notorious by using a hatchet to destroy saloons. But if women were in the van of the movement, they were powerfully supported by the American Antisaloon League, an organization of employers concerned at the effect of insobriety on industrial efficiency. The Methodist Episcopal Church constituted a third powerful pressure group.

The war on drink displayed Progressivism's characteristic moral fervor and high-minded idealism. Earlier Prohibitionists had sought to convince Americans that alcohol was harmful to the individual: it damaged health, weakened moral fiber, generated poverty, and stimulated male lust. To Progressives it was the source of numerous social and political ills. The liquor industry represented a dangerous concentration of economic power while the saloon, besides being associated with political corruption and prostitution, demoralized the immigrant and prevented him from becoming Americanized. The Prohibitionist campaign won a warm response in the countryside, especially where Protestant fundamentalism was entrenched. Some supported it from a naive faith in the curative potentialities of legislation, others as a harmless gesture to morality. By 1900 five rural states, all but one in New England, had adopted statewide Prohibition. Between 1907 and 1915 their example was followed by 14 other states, 8 in the South (where anxiety to deny liquor to blacks provided an additional motive) and 6 in the Far West. Most of the remaining states had enacted local option, a system which allowed counties and municipalities to decide the issue by popular vote. In the cities, especially those with large German and Irish populations, Prohibition made little progress. Nevertheless by 1916 about two-thirds of the area of the United States, a region comprising half the population, was legally 'dry'. Enforcement was difficult, however, so long as drink could be imported into 'dry' territory. That led Prohibitionists to press for federal action. They won an important victory in 1913 when, over Taft's veto, Congress passed the Webb–Kenyon Act forbidding the importation of intoxicating liquors into areas where its sale was banned. But attempts to secure a national Prohibition amendment were unsuccessful until after America's entry into the war in 1917.

A notable feature of the Progressive era was a new concern for child welfare. Children now came to be recognized as being among the worst sufferers from urban growth and industrialization and a greater understanding developed of their special needs and problems. As in the Prohibition movement, and for that matter in reform activity generally, women played a prominent part. The celebrated Jane Addams of Hull House founded the first public playground in Chicago in 1893 and later combined with Jacob Riis and others in a national campaign for public playgrounds and small parks. By 1915 over 400 cities had established them. A new and more sympathetic approach to juvenile delinquency also developed. One of its leading advocates was Julia C. Lathrop, also of Hull House, but its most famous practitioner was the 'Kids' Judge'—Ben B. Lindsey of Denver, Colorado—whose juvenile court treated youthful offenders not as criminals but as products of a bad social environment who needed supervision and guidance. By 1910 children's courts modeled on Lindsey's were functioning in every major city. Meanwhile a third Hull House social worker, Florence Kelley, had taken the lead in a movement to abolish child labor. By 1900 no fewer than 1.7 million children under sixteen were wage-earners. In 1904 the National Child Labor Committee was formed to coordinate the efforts of various reform groups and to campaign for restrictive and enforcement legislation. In the next ten years twenty-five states adopted such laws—though they were not wholly effective—and in 1912 a Children's Bureau with Julia Lathrop at its head was established as a branch of the US Department of Labor. These and similar developments reflected the influence of new behavioral and educational theories. Especially important were the writings on child development and adolescence of the psychologist, G. Stanley Hall, who stressed the crucial importance for children of creative play and contact with nature and of shaping the school to the development of the child. Hall's ideas were carried a stage further by the philosopher, John Dewey, whose *School and Society* (1899) rejected classroom authoritarianism and rote-learning and urged the substitution of a child-centered school emphasizing 'learning by doing' and more closely integrated with the community to which it belonged. Dewey's progressive educational theories, first tried out by him at the Laboratory School of the University of Chicago, were enthusiastically adopted by private schools and, in the 1920s, by the public schools, though often in the latter case to the accompaniment of fierce controversy.

Theodore Roosevelt and Progressivism

A number of Progressives, having served an apprenticeship at state level, went on to become nationally prominent. Among them was Theodore Roosevelt, the first of the three Progressive Presidents. Roosevelt was born into a well-to-do New York family in 1858. Despite the fact that men of his background generally shunned politics, Roosevelt was ambitious for a political career. He served as a Republican state assemblyman from 1882 to 1884, ran unsuccessfully for mayor of New York in 1886, became a United States Civil Service Commissioner in 1889, and president of the New York City Police Board in 1895. In 1897 he entered McKinley's Administration as Assistant Secretary of the Navy but upon the outbreak of war with Spain resigned to go on active service in Cuba with the Rough Riders. Returning a popular war hero he was elected governor of New York. His mild reformism irritated the New York Republican boss, Tom Platt, and in 1900 he was shunted off into the Vice-Presidency. But in September 1901, McKinley was assassinated and Roosevelt—"that damned cowboy", Mark Hanna called him—entered the White House. At forty-two he was the youngest man to become President.

Roosevelt's flamboyant personality, boundless energy, and hunger for power contrasted markedly with the colorlessness and negativism of his post-Civil War predecessors. He in fact redefined the presidential office and gave it new dimensions. He believed that the growing international importance of the United States and the emergence of complex national economic issues called for more decisive national leadership—Hamiltonian means had become necessary to achieve Jeffersonian ends was how he put it—which only the President could supply. Conceiving the President to be "the steward of the people bound actively and affirmatively to do all he could for the people", Roosevelt held that it was not merely his right but his duty to do anything that the national interest required unless specifically forbidden by the Constitution or the laws. He dramatized the Presidency, pushed it into the center of the political stage, and used it as a pulpit from which to preach to the nation. Possessing a flair for publicity and an instinctive understanding of public opinion, Roosevelt won a huge and devoted personal following. Yet his reputation as a reformer was not entirely deserved. He was less radical than his rhetoric tended to suggest. His own inner convictions were largely conservative but he sensed the rising demand for reform and saw the need to accommodate it. Despite his faults—vanity, egotism, childish posturing—he was the first President to comprehend the economic changes which had transformed America and to recognize and work for a new balance between big business and government.

For all his native impetuosity Roosevelt at first moved cautiously. He was conscious of having become President by accident. Anxious to be elected in his own right in 1904, he dared not alienate the conservative oligarchy led by the multimillionaire banker, Senator Nelson W. Aldrich, which controlled the party machinery. In any case he had no ready-made plan of reform. Accordingly he retained most of McKinley's cabinet, announced that he would continue his predecessor's economic policies, and displayed a willingness to accept advice from the Republican Old Guard.

But he quickly showed that he was not prepared to be the puppet of big business. In his first message to Congress he referred to the "real and grave evils" of industrial consolidation and urged Congress to establish a federal agency with power to investigate the affairs of the great combinations. The proposal was strongly resisted in the Senate, but by appealing to public opinion Roosevelt induced Congress to include a Bureau of Corporations in the Department of Commerce and Labor established in 1903. A more dramatic indication of Roosevelt's determination to discipline industry came early in 1902 when he staggered Wall Street by invoking the moribund Sherman Antitrust Act against the Northern Securities Company, a giant railroad holding company organized by James J. Hill, J. P. Morgan, and E. H. Harriman. Morgan arrogantly believed that the matter could easily be adjusted and seemed surprised when the suit was vigorously prosecuted. In 1904 the Supreme Court by a 5–4 verdict upheld the government and ordered the dissolution of the company. The decision made no difference to the ownership of the railroads concerned, but demonstrated that the government could control even the greatest combinations of capital if it chose to. During Roosevelt's seven and a half years in office the government instituted suits under the Sherman Act against forty-four corporations, including some of the largest and most unpopular, such as the meat-packers, the American Tobacco Company, the Du Pont Corporation, and the Standard Oil Company. These prosecutions sent Roosevelt's stock soaring in the country and earned him the name of "trust-buster". Ironically he had no objection in principle to big business, regarding combination as a natural process, even a beneficial one, provided it could be made to subserve the public good. Hence he believed that the real answer to monopoly was regulation, not dissolution. But with Congress unwilling to pass an effective regulatory law, he was prepared to make selective use of the Sherman Act.

Roosevelt's handling of the anthracite coal strike of 1902 was equally a landmark. Whereas previous presidents had intervened in industrial disputes only to break strikes, he did so in order to obtain a negotiated settlement. Conditions in the Pennsylvania anthracite coalfields had long been deplorable but when the miners went on strike in May 1902 for higher wages, an eight-hour day, and union recognition the owners were determined to make no concessions. They contemptuously rejected an offer by John Mitchell, president of the United Mine Workers, to submit to arbitration. As the strike dragged on a coal shortage threatened, and in October Roosevelt summoned both sides to a White House conference. Mitchell was conciliatory but the mine-owners remained intransigent, even demanding federal military intervention and the prosecution of the strike leaders. Furious at the owners' arrogance Roosevelt finally compelled them to accept mediation by threatening to send in troops, not to break the strike, but to seize and operate the mines. The miners went back to work and in March 1903 the Anthracite Coal Commission awarded them a 10 percent wage increase and a reduction in hours, though they did not get the eight-hour day or union recognition.

While Roosevelt thus showed more sympathy for trade unions than any of his predecessors, it would be going too far to call him a friend of labor. He later sent troops to Arizona, Colorado, and Nevada to quell labor disturbances. Moreover he was opposed to the closed shop and the labor boycott, and was quick to condemn the use of force by strikers. In his attitude towards labor, as indeed towards public affairs generally, Roosevelt saw himself as the guardian of the national interest. His object during the coal strike, he later remarked, had been simply to give both capital and labor a "square deal". But his intervention also implied that in a major industrial dispute the interests of the public were at least as important as those of the contending parties.

By 1904, Roosevelt's bold and vigorous leadership had earned him widespread popular acclaim. He had also tightened his grip on his party by the judicious use of patronage. Hanna's sudden death in February 1904 removed the most obvious candidate for the Republican nomination but, leaving nothing to chance, Roosevelt made conciliatory gestures toward big business. Hence, when the Republican convention met, he was renominated by acclamation. The Democrats, aware of Roosevelt's appeal to reformers, made a bid for conservative support by nominating the safe and respectable Judge Alton B. Parker. It was an ill-conceived maneuver, for, whatever their reservations about Roosevelt, most conservatives still preferred the Republicans to a party which had twice nominated Bryan. Leading industrialists and bankers contributed heavily to the Republican campaign fund. The fact that two of the defendants in the Northern Securities case, Morgan and Harriman, gave $150,000 and $50,000 respectively, testified to Roosevelt's success in convincing Wall Street that his "trust-busting" was not to be taken literally. After a colorless campaign Roosevelt won a sweeping victory.

Of the lengthy agenda for reform Roosevelt presented to Congress after his reelection little was acted upon. But by a combination of persistence, flexibility, and intricate political maneuvering he won two major legislative victories. The first was the Hepburn Act of 1906, providing for stricter railroad regulation. There was an overwhelming case for such a measure. The Interstate Commerce Act of 1887 had been virtually nullified by Supreme Court decisions. The Elkins Act of 1903, promoted by the railroads themselves and aimed primarily at the rebate evil, had likewise proved ineffectual. When a new rate bill was introduced in 1905 in response to Roosevelt's urgings, Senate conservatives sought to emasculate it and it took all the President's skill to force even a compromise measure through. In its final form the Hepburn Act authorized the Interstate Commerce Commission (subject to court review) to fix just and reasonable maximum rates; extended the jurisdiction of that body to include express and sleeping-car companies, oil pipelines, ferries, terminal facilities, and bridges; forbade rebates and free passes; and presented a uniform system of accounting for all railroads. La Follette and other Congressional Progressives were critical of Roosevelt for accepting what they regarded as half a loaf. They were especially chagrined at the provision for judicial review and at the Act's failure to provide for the physical valuation of railroad property, which they believed to be the only proper basis for determining reasonable rates. But despite its limitations the Hepburn Act marked the beginning of effective railroad regulation. Within two years, the ICC had received 9,000 complaints and had reduced many rates.

The other product of presidential pressure was the passage of laws to protect public health. For several years Dr Harvey W. Wiley, chief chemist of the Department of Agriculture, had been campaigning for a pure food and drug law. He and his 'poison squad' investigators had discovered that harmful preservatives and adulterants were widely used in food processing and that patent medicines were commonly mislabeled. Yet every attempt at control had been stalled in the Senate. Attempts to secure federal regulation of slaughterhouses, prompted by concern over diseased meat, had been equally unsuccessful. But in 1906 the muckraker Samuel Hopkins Adams aroused public indignation against patent-medicine manufacturers with a series of magazine articles entitled "The Great American Fraud". Upton Sinclair's muckraking novel, *The Jungle* (1906), produced an even greater outcry, this time against the meat-packers. Sinclair's object had been to protest at the exploitation of immigrant laborers in Chicago stockyards. But, as he himself remarked, in aiming at the public's heart he had hit its stomach: the book's sickening descriptions of the way meat was prepared and processed made it a best seller. A special inquiry Roosevelt ordered into the Chicago meat-packing industry confirmed everything Sinclair had written. Congressional resistance to regulation melted away when

Roosevelt threatened publication of the investigators' report and when the meat-packers themselves, alarmed by falling sales, suddenly came out in favor of an inspection law. Both the Meat Inspection Act and the Pure Food and Drug Act became law in June 1906.

Among Roosevelt's more impressive achievements was the impetus he gave to conservation. Armed with the powers conferred by the Newlands Act of 1902 he authorized an extensive reclamation and dam-building program which brought irrigation to millions of acres of Western lands. With the enthusiastic support of Gifford Pinchot, Chief Forester in the Department of Agriculture, he made use of the Forest Reserve Act of 1891 to set aside 150 million acres of forest land, thus quadrupling the federal forest reserve. He also—with doubtful legality—closed to public entry a further 85 million acres in Alaska and the Northwest containing coal, phosphates, oil, and water-power sites. These steps brought protests from Western ranchers, mine-owners, lumbermen, and power companies eager to exploit the national domain for private gain. In 1907 their political representatives succeeded in attaching a rider to a vital agricultural appropriation bill prohibiting the President from creating further reserves in six Western states without Congressional approval. Roosevelt signed the bill but only after he had hurriedly withdrawn a further 17 million acres, a maneuver which led to cries of 'executive dictatorship'. Congress, hostile to conservation as a threat to private enterprise, was further angered when Pinchot reserved more than 2,500 water-sites by the dubious expedient of designating them as ranger stations. Roosevelt made great efforts to educate the public to the need for conservation. In 1908 he called a National Conservation Congress which led to the creation of state conservation commissions. He also appointed an Inland Waterways Commission, which studied the problems of rural life.

Roosevelt's propensity for expanding presidential power, displayed both in the conservation controversy and, more spectacularly, in his conduct of foreign policy (see Ch. 21), was not the only source of the estrangement from Congress that marked the closing years of his term. Friction arose especially out of the severe financial panic of 1907 which caused a wave of banking and business failures. In order to avert further failures Roosevelt did not hesitate to cooperate with the great bankers he had earlier castigated. After consultation with J. P. Morgan, the Secretary of the Treasury deposited millions of dollars of government funds in threatened New York banks. Then, after a group of industrialists and financiers had argued the necessity for the largest trust in the country, the United States Steel Corporation, to acquire control of the Tennessee Coal and Iron Company, Roosevelt informally sanctioned the merger. That implied that no antitrust prosecution would follow. But despite Roosevelt's accommodating attitude Wall Street and its Congressional spokesmen blamed his antibusiness rhetoric for the panic. Roosevelt, for his part, angrily retorted that the source of the trouble had been the "speculative folly and flagrant dishonesty" of those he described as "malefactors of great wealth".

Roosevelt further alienated Congressional conservatives by demanding another installment of reform. In two messages to Congress in December 1907 and January 1908, he called for the adoption of an income tax and of death duties, federal supervision of the stock market, a limitation on the use of injunctions in labor disputes, the extension of the eight-hour day, and workmen's compensation laws. He also criticized the federal courts for declaring unconstitutional a workmen's compensation law and denounced "predatory wealth" for having consistently opposed "every measure for honesty in business". Roosevelt's growing radicalism reflected his exasperation at the indifference of big business to the needs of workingmen and his concern at the rising appeal of Socialism. He had clearly traveled a long way since entering the White House. But while he had provided the growing Progressive minority within his party with a program, he had not carried the Republican Old Guard with him. Thus he left his successor a less than united party.

Despite the feelings he aroused in Republican party bosses Roosevelt was so popular with Republican voters that renomination could have been his for the asking in 1908. But after his 1904 election victory he had promised, out of respect for the two-term tradition, not to run again. He nonetheless used his control of the party machinery to secure the nomination for his friend and political heir, William Howard Taft. A member of a prominent Cincinnati family, Taft had been a federal judge, civilian governor of the Philippines, and administrator of the Panama Canal Zone before becoming Roosevelt's Secretary of War. The Democrats, having suffered disaster with a conservative candidate in 1904, turned for the third and last time to Bryan. Capitalizing on his identification with Roosevelt, Taft won comfortably, but the Democrats did much better than in 1904. More significant, however, was the substantial increase in the size of the midwestern Progressive bloc in Congress.

Taft and Republican Insurgency

Roosevelt would have been a hard man to follow in any case, but Taft was further handicapped by temperament and background. A large, corpulent, affable man of sedentary habits, his lethargy contrasted with Roosevelt's breadth of interests and exuberant vitality. His career in law and public administration had given him little experience of campaigning or speechmaking and none in handling legislatures. Taft was in fact more suited to the bench than to the hustings; his real ambition, achieved in 1921, was to become Chief Justice. His judicial training and temper having bred an awareness of the constitutional limitations on the Presidency he was unwilling to follow Roosevelt's example of expanding executive power. And although he was genuinely anxious to continue Roosevelt's policies— and indeed did so—he was by nature more conservative than the Rough Rider. He felt more at ease with the Old Guard than with Progressives and, by supporting the former in a succession of controversies, contributed to the growing split in the Republican ranks.

Even so, Taft's services to Progressivism were considerable. During his four-year Administration there were twice as many prosecutions under the Sherman Act as the Roosevelt Administration had brought in eight years. Those indicted included such giants as the General Electric Company, the American Sugar Refining Company, the International Harvester Company, and United States Steel. Taft carried on Roosevelt's conservation program, withdrawing additional forest lands and oil reserves. He supported the Mann-Elkins Act of 1910, which further extended the jurisdiction of the Interstate Commerce Commission and empowered it to take the initiative in revising railroad rates. Despite the opposition of devotees of *laissez-faire* he pushed for and obtained a law establishing postal savings banks. Besides creating the Department of Labor and the Federal Children's Bureau he approved an eight-hour day for federal employees, as well as mine-safety legislation. Finally he gave his blessing to the two constitutional amendments ratified in. 1913: the Sixteenth Amendment, authorizing a federal income tax, and the Seventeenth Amendment, providing for the direct election of United States senators. Thus, if Taft was a failure as President, it was not that he was a reactionary. but that he lacked his predecessor's political skill in holding together the opposing factions within his party.

Taft's identification with ultraconservatism began with his vacillation during the Congressional revolt against the tyrannical control of the Speaker, Joseph G. Cannon. Since he could nominate a majority of members of the Rules Committee, which decided the order of business in the House, the reactionary Cannon had virtually come to possess a veto over legislation. After an unsuccessful attempt to unseat him in 1909 a group of Progressive Republican Congressmen sought to curb his power by proposing that the Rules Committee should in future be elected by members of the House. In March 1910, after a long bitter struggle, they secured their object, thanks to Democratic support. But Taft's behavior earned him the deep distrust of the Progressives—'insurgents', as they would shortly become known. Having encouraged them to believe that he would support their assault on Cannonism, he abruptly changed his tune when the Old Guard warned him that he was imperiling his hopes for tariff reform.

Over the tariff itself Taft plunged into worse trouble. High protectionism had been a cardinal tenet of the Republican creed ever since the Civil War and most industrialists remained wedded to it. But the heresy of tariff reduction had taken firm root throughout the staunchly Republican farming regions of the Middle West. During his Presidency Roosevelt had talked a good deal about tariff reduction but had in fact shelved the question because of its disruptive potentialities. But the 1908 Republican platform had promised tariff revision and during the campaign Taft had interpreted it to mean revision downward. To fulfill the pledge he called Congress into special session early in 1909 and the House promptly passed a bill incorporating substantial reductions. But when it reached the Senate it was transformed out of all recognition. Under Aldrich's leadership protectionists made over 800 amendments restoring, and in some cases increasing, the existing high rates. Middle Western insurgent senators, battling against the Aldrich amendments, looked to Taft for help, but in vain. He had constitutional scruples about interfering in the legislative process. Moreover, he had developed an intense dislike for the insurgents, dismissing them as fanatics and demagogues. During the Payne–Aldrich Bill's committee stage Taft secured important modifications, but even in its final form it was a high tariff measure. Taft nonetheless signed it, much to the indignation of the Middle Westerners and compounded his offense by describing the measure as "the best tariff bill that the Republican party has ever passed". The Middle West was further incensed in 1911 when a reciprocity agreement Taft made with Canada seemed likely to flood the country with cheap Canadian dairy and lumber products. Over fierce opposition Taft finally secured ratification of the agreement but when he and others publicly expressed the hope that it would lead to the annexation of Canada, a resurgence of Canadian nationalism killed reciprocity stone-dead.

If anything more were needed to complete the alienation of Progressive Republicans, a squabble over conservation supplied it. The action of Richard A. Ballinger, Taft's Secretary of the Interior, in reopening to public entry certain water-sites Roosevelt had set aside as national reserves—illegally in Ballinger's view—aroused the enmity of the chief forester, Gifford Pinchot, the leading champion of conservation and one of Roosevelt's most ardent admirers. Pinchot passed on to Taft an allegation that Ballinger had connived at handing over government coal lands in Alaska to a Morgan–Guggenheim syndicate and even after a presidential investigation had upheld Ballinger Pinchot persisted in attacking him publicly as the tool of greedy businessmen. Taft thereupon dismissed Pinchot for insubordination. By this time the affair had generated nationwide controversy. Conservatives sprang to the defense of Taft and Ballinger, Progressives rallied around Pinchot. A Congressional investigation exonerated Ballinger from charges of fraud and corruption, but revealed that he was no friend of conservation. Taft was a sincere conservationist but by continuing to defend Ballinger he widened the breach with the insurgents and drove a wedge between himself and Roosevelt's followers.

Weakened by faction the Republican party suffered a massive defeat in the Congressional elections of 1910. For the first time since 1894 the Democrats captured control of the House, while making notable gains in the Senate. West of the Mississippi, however, insurgent Republicans won striking victories despite a campaign by Taft and the Old Guard to destroy them. It was clear that if Taft was renominated the Republicans faced disaster in the presidential election of 1912. Accordingly the insurgents formed the National Progressive Republican League with the object of seizing control of the Republican party and finding an alternative leader.

At first it seemed likely that their choice would fall on La Follette. No one had so consistently backed Progressive causes. But although idolized in the Middle West, he lacked national support. Thinking him too doctrinaire and extreme some Progressives began to nurse the hope that Roosevelt could be coaxed back into politics. Soon after Taft's inauguration the former President had left on an African safari; subsequently he made a lengthy tour of European capitals. All the time he was away the newspapers were full of his doings; shooting lions, hobnobbing with European crowned heads, reviewing the German army, admonishing the French to increase their birth-rate. When he returned to New York in the spring of 1910 it was to a tumultuous reception.

Though resentful at Pinchot's dismissal and disturbed by the growing split in the Republican party, which he blamed on Taft's maladroitness, Roosevelt initially had no thought of seeking renomination. He even announced his intention of keeping quiet about politics. But he was temperamentally incapable of doing so. He was still only fifty and brimming with energy and ambition. In the summer of 1910, during a Western speaking tour designed ostensibly to heal the breach in the party, he came out more strongly than ever in favor of Progressive reform. Particularly striking was a speech at Osawatomie, Kansas calling for a New Nationalism, that is, a program of social welfare, direct government, and further regulation of business. Conservatives were alarmed by his insistence that human rights must take precedence over property rights and still more by his attack on the federal courts as barriers to social justice. Though the speech was widely interpreted as an assault on Taft's conservatism Roosevelt still appeared to favor Taft's renomination. But in the course of 1911 he became completely estranged from his former protégé. He was particularly incensed when the Administration brought an antitrust suit against the United States Steel Corporation and cited as evidence its acquisition in 1907 of the Tennessee Coal and Iron Company, a step which Roosevelt had tacitly approved. In February 1912, after months of pressure from his followers to challenge Taft for the nomination and in response to a carefully arranged appeal from a group of Republican governors, Roosevelt announced his candidacy.

The Election of 1912

The ensuing struggle between Taft and Roosevelt for the Republican nomination was bitter and vituperative. Roosevelt was clearly the choice of the majority of Republican voters. In the thirteen states which held presidential primaries—it was the first time this had happened—Roosevelt won 278 delegates compared to 48 for Taft and 36 for La Follette. But Taft forces controlled the party machinery and the Republican National Committee. Thus when the Republican convention met at Chicago in June Taft won a crucial battle over contested seats and was renominated on the first ballot. Roosevelt's followers alleged that Taft's victory had been won by fraud and stormed out of the convention. In August they reconvened in Chicago to launch a new Progressive party. In an atmosphere more akin to a religious revival than a political gathering they chose Roosevelt as their standard-bearer.

The Progressive platform reflected and indeed went beyond the reformism of Roosevelt's last years in the White House. It endorsed the initiative, referendum, and recall, woman suffrage, the nomination of presidential candidates through preferential primaries, and popular review of state judicial decisions. It demanded a long list of social-welfare reforms: minimum wages for women, child-labor legislation, workmen's compensation laws, unemployment insurance, and old-age pensions. Finally it proposed new federal agencies to regulate business, industry, and the investment market. Yet at Roosevelt's insistence an antitrust plank was eliminated from the platform. Nor was there any promise to lower the tariff. These omissions testified to the new party's dependence on the financial backing of wealthy industrialists, notably George W. Perkins, a close associate of the house of Morgan, and Frank A. Munsey, the millionaire newspaper-owner. Moreover, though Roosevelt was anxious to retain the Northern black vote, which had contributed to his success in the primaries, he could not persuade the Progressive party to endorse Negro rights.

The Republican split greatly strengthened the Democrats' chances of capturing the Presidency for the first time since 1892. Thus when the Democratic convention met at Baltimore a fierce battle developed for the nomination. Champ Clark, Speaker of the House of Representatives, went to the convention with an impressive lead in delegates, but after his rivals had combined to block him Governor Woodrow Wilson of New Jersey was nominated on the forty-sixth ballot. The Democratic platform, which owed much to Bryan, still a great force in the party, denounced the Payne–Aldrich tariff and promised genuine downward revision, as well as demanding a strengthening of the antitrust laws, new banking legislation, and control of the "money trust". It endorsed the pending constitutional amendments for an income tax and the direct election of senators, called for rural credits to assist farmers, and favored exempting trade unions from prosecution under the Sherman Act.

Wilson's political rise had ben meteoric. Born in Virginia in 1856, the son of a slaveholding Scotch–Irish Presbyterian minister, he grew up in the war-ravaged South. Having graduated from Princeton and having acquired a Johns Hopkins Ph.D., he taught history and political science at Bryn Mawr, Wesleyan, and finally at Princeton, whose president he became in 1902, the first layman to preside over that stronghold of American Presbyterianism. He fought unsuccessfully to democratize Princeton by abolishing the exclusive "eating Club" system and after another losing battle with the trustees, this time over plans for a graduate school, he resigned in 1910 to accept the Democratic nomination for governor of New Jersey. His economic views had hitherto been conservative, but once installed in the governor's chair, refusing to play the passive role envisaged by the machine politicians who had engineered his nomination, he pushed through a comprehensive reform program that brought him to national attention.

Though in form a three-cornered contest—four-cornered if the Socialist candidate, Debs, is included—the 1912 campaign was in reality a duel between Wilson and Roosevelt. In his campaign speeches Wilson expounded what he called the New Freedom, an alternative reform program to Roosevelt's New Nationalism. The two were in many respects similar. But there were also significant differences. The Progressives favored protection, the Democrats tariff reduction. Wilson strongly disapproved of Roosevelt's proposed social-welfare legislation, fearing it would sap individual initiative. But the main disagreement centered on the issue of monopoly control. Whereas Roosevelt's approach was collectivist, Wilson's was essentially individualistic. The New Nationalism assumed that large corporations were an economic necessity and sought to regulate them through the expansion of federal control. The New Freedom, on the other hand, saw the trusts as unmitigated evils and assigned to the federal government the purely negative task of destroying monopoly in order to restore competition and reinvigorate small and medium-sized business.

Perhaps because the voters found it difficult to distinguish clearly between the two reform programs, the election campaign lacked excitement, at least until October, when Roosevelt was shot by a fanatic. Admiration for his courage in continuing his campaign did not, however, prevent Wilson from winning a decisive victory. He carried forty of the forty-eight states; six states went to Roosevelt and only two to Taft. Yet Wilson received only 42 percent of the popular vote. The Progressive party, despite having attracted more support than the official Republican ticket, proved to have no lasting vitality. That it was essentially Roosevelt's personal vehicle was shown by its failure to capture more than nine seats in the House and one in the Senate. Almost immediately after the election its supporters began to drift back to the Republican fold.

The Climax of Progressivism

If Wilson was a minority President he was also in some senses a sectional one. The only states in which he gained an absolute majority were in the South. Moreover, his cabinet had a marked Southern complexion. Wilson's Southern upbringing helped shaped his political outlook, particularly on racial questions. During his Administration Negroes were systematically segregated from whites in government departments; black officeholders in the South were discharged or downgraded. Thus for the first time the Southern caste system was openly endorsed by the federal government.

During his academic career Wilson had been frankly critical of the American political system. In his doctoral dissertation, *Congressional Government* (1885), he had asserted that the separation of powers meant in practice the absence of clearly formulated policies. His remedy, set forth in *Constitutional Government in the United States* (1908), was for the President to use the power inherent in his office. Roosevelt had already demonstrated that strong presidential leadership was possible: Wilson's thesis was that it was indispensable. When he became President Wilson promptly put these theories into practice. He revived the custom, in abeyance since Jefferson had dropped it, of addressing Congress in person. He exercised firmer control over legislation than any of his predecessors, sponsoring or blocking important measures, working closely with Congressional Democratic leaders, intervening at crucial moments, using patronage to facilitate passage of his program. He was of course fortunate in possessing a large Democratic majority in the House. But without his skill in driving and cajoling Congress the New Freedom could not have been translated into law.

Wilson's first test came when he called a special session of Congress to fulfill his campaign pledge of tariff reduction. The House promptly passed a bill which abolished duties on more than 100 articles and reduced them appreciably on nearly 1,000 others. To make up for the consequent loss of revenue, the recently ratified Sixteenth Amendment was invoked to impose an income tax. Rates were extremely low: a flat 1 percent on incomes over $4,000 and a graduated surtax beginning at 1 percent on incomes over $20,000 and reaching a maximum of 6 percent on incomes over $500,000. Encountering stiff opposition in the Senate, where the Democrats had only a slender majority, the bill seemed in danger of suffering the fate of the Payne–Aldrich Act. But Wilson put pressure on wavering Democrats and publicly denounced the lobbyists who were attempting to thwart the popular will. Thanks largely to his efforts the Underwood–Simmons Tariff Act became law in 1913. By no means a free-trade measure it nevertheless reversed the long-established trend toward high protection, while its income tax provisions initiated a more equitable tax policy.

Wilson's next target was reform of the banking and monetary system. This had two major defects. Firstly, each bank operated independently and there was no machinery for propping up those which ran into difficulty. Secondly, national banks could not issue notes in excess of their holdings of government bonds, so that the supply of credit was not sufficiently flexible. The panic of 1907 had focused attention on the second of these weaknesses and as an emergency measure Congress had passed the Aldrich–Vreeland Act (1908),which introduced some degree of elasticity into the currency. It also set up a National Monetary Commission, headed by Aldrich, to investigate the banking and currency systems generally. The Commission's report, issued in 1912, recommended the setting-up of a single central bank under the control of private bankers. The Democrats had denounced the proposal since it promised to strengthen the already excessive power of Wall Street. But they were not agreed on an alternative remedy. Conservatives wanted a decentralized reserve system, free from Wall Street domination, but still privately owned and controlled. The agrarian wing of the party was equally keen on decentralization but cited the 1913 report of the Pujo committee, with its sensational revelations about a "money trust" dominated by Morgan–Rockefeller interests, to demonstrate the necessity for public control. It was no easy task to satisfy both factions. But with Bryan's help Wilson finally arrived at an acceptable compromise, which was passed as the Federal Reserve Act in December 1913. It created twelve Federal Reserve Banks in different parts of the country, each owned by member banks. Supervision of the entire system was to be entrusted to a new government agency, the Federal Reserve Board, consisting of the Secretary of the Treasury, the Controller of the Currency, and five members to be appointed by the President. In addition the Act created a new type of currency: Federal Reserve notes, to be issued by the twelve regional banks on the basis of a 40 percent gold reserve.

The Federal Reserve Act was violently denounced by bankers and did not wholly satisfy advanced Progressives like La Follette. But in time it was universally acknowledged as a notable advance. The Act did not succeed in preventing bank failures or averting periodic panics and depressions—though the 1929 crash was partly due to the Federal Reserve Board's failure to make proper use of its powers—but it made it possible to mobilize the entire country's banking resources to help threatened institutions, created a new and more flexible currency, and loosened the stranglehold of a few financial giants over credit facilities.

Wilson's attempt to grapple with a third problem, the trusts, revealed that he was shifting away from the limited and largely negative reform program of the New Freedom and beginning to embrace Roosevelt's New Nationalism. His original suggestions for revision of the Sherman Antitrust Act had emphasized the statutory prohibition of monopoly; he had recommended the abolition of interlocking directorates, the definition and punishment of "hurtful restraints on trade", and a new fact-finding trade commission. But, influenced by the Boston lawyer, Louis D. Brandeis, he came to favor something akin to the vigorous administrative regulation he had condemned when Roosevelt advocated it in 1912. Wilson's revised antitrust policy was embodied in the Federal Trade Commission Act of September 1914. It established a Federal Trade Commission to police business practices; it was authorized to investigate the activities of all corporations engaged in interstate commerce and to act against those which employed unfair methods of competition. A related measure, the Clayton Act of October 1914, was a watered-down version of Wilson's original solution to the trust problem. Intended to strengthen the Sherman Antitrust Act, it prohibited certain business practices: price discrimination which tended to lessen competition or promote monopoly, discounts given on condition that purchasers refrained from buying from other suppliers, interlocking directorates in industrial firms with a capital of more than $1 million.

The Clayton Act was also designed to benefit trade unions. It declared that they were not as such to be construed as illegal combinations in restraint of trade, that peaceful strikes, picketing, and the payment of strike benefits were not illegal, and that injunctions were not to be used in labor disputes "unless necessary to prevent irreparable damage to property". Gompers hailed the Clayton Act as "the Magna Charta of labor", interpreting it to mean that trade unions could no longer be prosecuted under the Sherman Act. But the measure did not, and indeed was not intended to, change the legal position of unions. In the 1920s the courts continued to declare certain kinds of strikes and boycotts illegal.

Though Wilson had tacitly conceded that the Rooseveltian solution to the trust problem was the only effective one, he was not yet prepared to swallow the rest of the Progressive platform of 1912. Believing that reform had gone far enough he resisted pressure for a further installment. On the ground that it would unduly favor one special-interest group he blocked a bill establishing federally backed land banks to provide long-term farm credits. He refused to support a federal child-labor bill because he believed it to be unconstitutional. He would have nothing to do with a woman-suffrage amendment, pleading that only the states could determine suffrage requirements. It was only after much hesitation—for he believed it conflicted with a recently concluded international convention on safety at sea—that he signed the La Follette Seamen's Act in March 1915. Initiated by Andrew Furuseth of the International Seamen's Union the Act imposed stricter safety standards on American merchant vessels, improved sailors' wage-rates, and abolished the crime of desertion.

Yet political exigency compelled Wilson to reverse himself. The Republicans made extensive gains in the Congressional elections of 1914, regaining power in a number of key states. The virtual disintegration of the Progressive party raised, moreover, the prospect of a reunified Republican opposition. To retain the Presidency the Democrats would clearly need to win over a substantial part of Roosevelt's old following. The first indication that Wilson was seeking wider political backing was his nomination of Brandeis to the Supreme Court in January 1916. The choice of such a prominent reformer aroused intense conservative opposition but Wilson stood firm and finally secured Senate confirmation. Then followed a remarkable presidential volte-face. Notwithstanding his earlier objections Wilson gave full support to the Federal Farm Loan Act of July 1916, which set up twelve Federal Land Banks to provide long-term rural credits. The following month he forced through the Kern–McGillicuddy Act, providing workmen's compensation for federal employees, and the Keating–Owen Act, the first federal child-labor law. In September he averted a threatened rail strike by persuading Congress to pass the Adamson Act which gave the railroad brotherhoods what they most wanted: an eight-hour day. These measures, designed to woo farmers, social reformers, and trade unionists respectively, signified Wilson's complete abandonment of state rights and *laissez-faire*, the twin ideological hallmarks of the New Freedom, and his virtual adoption of the New Nationalism.

The economic and social reforms of 1916 were the last to bear the Progressive imprint. The reform impulse was now nearly exhausted and President and Congress were having to concentrate increasingly on problems created by the war in Europe. Since 1900 Progressives had translated many of their ideas into reality. They had extended the power of government to regulate business, improve conditions of work, and conserve natural resources. They had tackled some of the worst evils of industrialization and made improvements to the machinery of government. But for all their frenetic activity they had not solved the problem of monopoly or done anything to reduce inequality; nor had they stamped out boss rule or political corruption. In social welfare the United States still lagged far behind Europe. Such victories as Progressives won were generally partial and in some cases short-lived. Many of the new political devices proved a disappointment in practice and fell into disuse. A combination of conservative judicial interpretation and administrative sloth was to permit big business to make a comeback in the 1920s. Thus the problems which had exercised the Progressives would remain for a new generation of reformers to tackle during the New Deal.

20. *The United States And World Affairs, 1865–1914*

Isolationism and Indifference

The United States emerged from the Civil War with the resources to become a major world power. The population already exceeded Great Britain's and by 1871 would almost equal that of the new German Empire (38 millions as compared with 41 millions). American industry was expanding rapidly and had just demonstrated its ability to sustain a modern war. With 900,000 battle-hardened men under arms the United States could put at least as many trained soldiers in the field as any European nation, while the Union Navy was the most powerful afloat.

Yet for the next quarter of a century the United States did not assert itself overseas or play a part on the world stage commensurate with its strength. Foreign affairs excited little interest. American energies were still concentrated on settling the continent and on exploiting its natural resources. Foreign markets were not yet essential: industrial output could still be absorbed by internal demand. Distance, moreover, protected the United States from what Jefferson had called "the broils of Europe" and encouraged the insular habit, institutionalized in the Monroe Doctrine, of thinking only of the Western Hemisphere. Within it the United States was predominant; no neighbor threatened her security. Accordingly, once the Confederacy was defeated, the huge wartime army and navy were almost completely disbanded. The diplomatic service was likewise kept to a minimum. In the 1880s the United States was represented abroad by no more than twenty-five ministers (and not a single ambassador), while the staff of the State Department numbered only sixty.

Post-Civil War Diplomacy

The decade immediately after Appomattox was nonetheless one of active diplomacy. The Civil War had left behind a number of delicate international problems and, moreover, the Johnson and Grant Administrations attempted to swim against the tide by pursuing an expansionist foreign policy.

Two European powers had taken advantage of the Civil War to try to regain their lost influence in the Western Hemisphere. Spain had re-asserted its sovereignty over the Dominican Republic and Napoleon III had set up a puppet regime in Mexico and installed the Austrian Archduke Maximilian as emperor. Spain's withdrawal from the Dominican Republic in 1865 was due not to Secretary of State Seward's protests, vigorous though they were, but to the losses inflicted by guerrilla activity and yellow fever. American diplomatic pressure was, however, a factor, along with Napoleon III's declining enthusiasm for his grandiose Mexican venture, in the departure of the French expeditionary force from Mexico in 1867. By persuading Napoleon to yield to his remonstrances Seward won a remarkable diplomatic triumph. Though he had not invoked the Monroe Doctrine by name, the French evacuation served nonetheless to reaffirm its validity in the eyes of the American people.

Expansionist ardor led Seward to make several attempts to secure additional territory. He negotiated a treaty with Denmark providing for the cession of two islands in the Danish West Indies in exchange for seven and a half million dollars, but the Senate refused to ratify. Congressional hostility also proved fatal to his hopes of acquiring a naval base in the Dominican Republic. His schemes to annex the Hawaiian Islands likewise came to naught. Seward did, however, enjoy one great triumph: the purchase of Alaska from Russia in 1867 for $7,200,000. Few Americans sympathized with Seward's expansionism and, since Alaska's economic and strategic value was little appreciated, he was criticized for having made a bad bargain. Opponents referred derisively to Alaska as "Seward's icebox" and, even after the Senate had been induced to ratify the annexation treaty, he had the utmost difficulty in persuading the House to pass the necessary appropriation bill.

One of Seward's arguments for acquiring Alaska was that it would accelerate the annexation of Canada—a long-standing American objective. Resentment toward Great Britain because of her unfriendliness during the Civil War served to revive annexationist agitation but this proved counterproductive: it stimulated Canadian nationalism and strengthened the movement for Confederation. Ill-fated Fenian incursions into Canada in 1866 and 1870 had similar effects. The Fenians, members of a secret Irish-American brotherhood, hoped that by invading Canada they would involve the United States in war with Great Britain and thus bring about Irish independence. Many Americans sympathized with them and considered their forays to be well-deserved reprisals for Confederate raids on New England during the Civil War. Johnson and Grant belatedly condemned the Fenian outbreaks but, eager for the Irish vote, were not prepared to act vigorously to prevent them.

It was however the *Alabama* claims dispute that embittered Anglo-

American relations most. In American eyes the British government had been guilty of a gross breach of neutrality in allowing the *Alabama* and other Confederate commerce-raiders to be built and armed in British ship-yards. The United States insisted on compensation for the damage they had caused. The dispute dragged on for seven years. When the Americans were ready to settle, the British stubbornly refused. Then, when Great Britain became more conciliatory, it was the Americans' turn to be unac-commodating. The Johnson–Clarendon Convention of 1869 seemed to have found a solution by referring the claims to arbitration, but it con-tained no British apology and said nothing about the so-called "indirect losses" suffered by the American merchant marine, that is, the inflated insurance rates and the wholesale transfer of American tonnage to foreign flags because of the *Alabama*'s presence on the high seas. These omissions, together with partisan hostility to Johnson's administration, led the Senate to reject the Convention. In opposing it Charles Sumner, the Chairman of the Senate Foreign Relations Committee, insisted that Great Britain pay both direct and indirect damages, which he assessed at $15 million and $110 million respectively. He contended further that since Great Britain's unneutral conduct had prolonged the Civil War by two years she was liable for half the total cost of the conflict—a sum amounting to no less than $2,000 million—and hinted that if the British could not pay in cash the United States would be happy to accept Canada instead.

Sumner's intervention, by raising American public expectations to unrealistic heights and arousing British resentment, greatly increased the difficulty of reaching agreement. But when it became clear that the Grant Administration's foreign policy would be guided, not by Sumner, but by the Secretary of State, the moderate Hamilton Fish, Great Britain was prepared to renew the search for a settlement. On May 8, 1871 after pro-tracted negotiations British and American representatives signed the Treaty of Washington, which dealt comprehensively with all outstanding Anglo-American differences. It referred the Puget Sound boundary con-troversy to the German Emperor for arbitration and set up an arbitration commission to deal with the perennial fisheries dispute. The *Alabama* claims were to be submitted to an international arbitration tribunal which included representatives of the interested parties. Great Britain expressed regret in the treaty for the escape of the *Alabama* and, to guide the arbi-trators, agreed to a set of rules defining neutral obligations. These rules went beyond what was then accepted under international law and, since they were retroactive, Great Britain virtually surrendered her case in advance.

Yet when the international tribunal convened at Geneva in December 1871, Fish, who is generally given the major credit for the *Alabama* set-tlement, almost wrecked the chances of success by unexpectedly reviving the indirect claims which had not been mentioned in the Treaty of Washington. He did, however, acquiesce when the tribunal declared them invalid. The tribunal's final decision, announced on September 14, 1872, found that Great Britain had been negligent in her duty as a neutral in allowing the *Alabama* to escape and awarded the United States $15,500,000 compensation. The British accepted the verdict and paid up. The other arbitration awards were also accepted without serious protest. The settlement of the *Alabama* claims controversy is generally cited as a model of enlightened diplomacy and as a triumph for the principle of arbitration. Certainly this was the first time that nations submitted major disputes to an international tribunal and complied with its decision. But the encomiums bestowed on the settlement would be more justified if there had been a real threat of war.

Grant normally left diplomacy to Fish but in two matters attempted to take matters into his own hands. He succeeded only in demonstrating his gullibility and ignorance. Shortly after becoming President he was persuaded to lend his support to an unsavory scheme, hatched by New York speculators, for the annexation of Santo Domingo. The project became an obsession with him but, in spite of his efforts to force an annexation treaty through the Senate, it was decisively rejected (June 30, 1870). Furious with Sumner, whose hostility had been largely responsible, Grant retaliated by engineering his removal from the Senate Foreign Relations Committee. This failed to revive the Santo Domingo treaty but it did smooth the way for the ratification of the Treaty of Washington. The other foreign question to claim Grant's attention was the Cuban rebellion against Spain which began in 1868. Grant's sympathies, like those of most Americans, were with the insurgents. In 1869 he instructed Fish to recognize Cuban belligerency but the Secretary of State, fearing this would mean war with Spain, neglected to obey. A year later, when the House seemed about to pass a resolution calling for the recognition of Cuban belligerency, Fish had to threaten resignation to get a reluctant President to send a special message to Congress urging strict nonintervention. Fish also refused to be stampeded into war in 1873 when the *Virginius*, a Cuban-owned vessel illegally flying the American flag, was captured while carrying arms intended for the rebels and the Spanish authorities summarily executed fifty-three passengers and crew as pirates, eight of them Americans. He induced Spain to release the vessel and pay an indemnity.

From Introspection to Imperialism

Once the controversies bequeathed by the Civil War had been liquidated and the Cuban insurrection had subsided, foreign policy revolved around minor matters: Chinese immigration; friction with Great Britain over the fisheries, pelagic sealing in the Bering Sea, and the imprisonment of Irish terrorists claiming American nationality; a German ban on American pork products; a quarrel with Italy over the lynching of Italian immigrants in New Orleans in 1891; the Chilean war scare of 1891–2 arising from an American sailors' brawl in Valparaiso. True, even issues of this kind proved capable of briefly arousing strong popular passions. Largely for that reason successive Administrations were wont to display an aggressive chauvinism in handling them. Yet isolationism remained the keynote. Apart from James G. Blaine's tentative and largely unsuccessful attempt to revive Henry Clay's idea of Pan-American cooperation, American foreign policy in the late 1870s and 1880s was without purpose or plan.

But the last decade of the nineteenth century brought a change. The conviction that the United States had no interests to defend or advance beyond its own borders was replaced by a nationalistic eagerness to assert American power. A variety of influences—psychological, economic, and strategic—combined to turn American eyes outward. With the completion of Western settlement Americans sought fresh outlets for their expansionist energies. Although economic forces were not, as some historians have suggested, the prime cause of the new imperialism, the importance of foreign markets was increasingly appreciated by public men, especially when domestic demand fell off during periods of depression. Also influential was the fact that the leading European powers were busy carving up Africa and Asia and acquiring naval bases in the Pacific. This is not to say that American imperialism was consciously imitative. Indeed, its advocates had little or no interest in colonization or in acquiring territory for its own sake. But, influenced by the writings of English imperialists like Seeley, Froude, and Kipling, they feared that in a world of growing imperialistic rivalries the United States could find security and protection for its interests only in expansion.

The imperialism of the 1890s in some ways resembled the pre-Civil War doctrine of Manifest Destiny, but differed in its claim to scientific respectability and its emphasis on the fashionable cult of Anglo–Saxon superiority. Exponents of the new imperialism found justification for their views in Darwin's theory of evolution, holding that natural selection and the doctrine of the "survival of the fittest" applied to nations no less than to the biological world. Hence in the international "struggle for existence" victory would go to the strongest and ablest states. In a magazine article written in 1885 John Fiske, the leading American popularizer of Darwinian ideas, extolled the genius of the Anglo–Saxon race and predicted that its language, religion, and political institutions must inevitably spread "to every land on the earth's surface". Likewise in a widely read little book, *Our Country: Its Possible Future and Present Crisis* (1885), the Revd Josiah Strong, a Congregational clergyman and social reformer from Ohio, claimed that the American branch of the Anglo–Saxon race was being prepared by God for triumph in the final competition of races.

The leading theorist of expansionism was a naval officer, Captain Alfred T. Mahan. In his classic work, *The Influence of Sea Power upon History, 1660–1783* (1890), Mahan argued that sea power was the foundation of national greatness. In order to be successful in the worldwide struggle for commerce the United States must embark upon a program of mercantilist imperialism. That meant not only the rebuilding of the merchant marine and of a powerful navy to protect it, but the acquisition of naval bases and overseas colonies, especially in the Caribbean and the Pacific. Mahan's ideas had a considerable impact abroad, especially in Great Britain and Germany. Within the United States they were soon taken up by such influential politicians as Henry Cabot Lodge, Albert J. Beveridge, and Theodore Roosevelt, the last already a rising figure soon to become, in 1897, Assistant Secretary of the Navy.

The first steps toward expanding and modernizing the navy were taken before Mahan began to write. By 1880 the American navy had decayed to such an extent that it was inferior not only to those of leading European powers but also to those of several Latin American republics. In 1883 a concerned Congress voted funds for the construction of four steel cruisers, which became the nucleus of an impressive modern battle fleet. The next decade saw a steady rise in naval appropriations and by the end of the century the United States navy, with seventeen battleships and six armored cruisers, was inferior only to those of Great Britain and Germany.

The acquisition of Pacific naval bases likewise antedated Mahan's call for them. In 1878 the United States received the right to establish a naval base in the Samoan Islands. Great Britain and Germany promptly secured similar rights and for the next ten years the three powers vied with each other for control of the islands. In 1889, they established a joint protectorate and in 1899 came to an arrangement whereby Germany annexed the two largest Samoan Islands and the United States obtained the rest of the archipelago, the British being compensated elsewhere.

American ties with the Hawaiian Islands grew steadily from about 1820 when American whaling fleets and the first New England missionaries arrived. By the close of the Civil War American settlers, mainly the children of missionaries, had developed sugar and pineapple plantations and dominated the economy and government of the islands. An 1875 reciprocity treaty, permitting Hawaiian sugar to enter the American market freely and binding the Hawaiian government not to lease or dispose of any of its territory to any other power, made Hawaii economically dependent on the United States and an 1887 treaty diluted Hawaiian independence still further by granting the United States an exclusive naval base at Pearl Harbor. The American planters in Hawaii had not up to now pressed for annexation. But the McKinley tariff of 1890 wiped out the advantage reciprocity had conferred on Hawaiian sugar, and in 1891 a new native ruler ascended the throne determined to put an end to foreign domination. In January 1893, with the support of marines from the cruiser *Boston*, then at Honolulu, American residents staged a revolt, deposed the monarch, established a provisional government, and promptly dispatched a mission to Washington to seek annexation. A treaty incorporating Hawaii as a territory of the United States was concluded and sent to the Senate, but when Cleveland took office in March 1893 he withdrew it, condemning the American role in the Hawaiian revolution as morally wrong. When the Republicans returned to power in 1897 a new annexation treaty was negotiated, only for it to be blocked in the Senate by antiimperialist Democrats and domestic sugar producers. Only in July 1898, during the war with Spain, was Hawaii at last annexed by means of a joint Congressional resolution, a procedure requiring only a simple majority.

With the growth of national pride a swaggering and at times irresponsible jingoism came to characterize both official and popular attitudes to foreign affairs. From wanting to have nothing to do with the rest of the world, Americans now seemed determined to pick a quarrel with it. This was demonstrated by the Venezuelan crisis of 1895 when American belligerence almost provoked war with Great Britain. Cleveland was in general hostile to imperialism but, needing a popular issue to help his party in the 1896 election, gratuitously intervened in a longstanding Anglo–Venezuelan dispute over the British Guiana boundary. On July 20, 1895 Secretary of State Richard Olney sent Lord Salisbury a bombastic and provocative note demanding arbitration of the boundary dispute and accusing Great Britain of violating the Monroe Doctrine. Salisbury's reply to this near ultimatum flatly refused arbitration and somewhat patronizingly rejected Olney's interpretation of the Monroe Doctrine. Incensed, Cleveland sent a special message to Congress asking for authority to appoint a commission to determine the boundary line and declaring his readiness to use force to back its findings. Congress complied enthusiastically and, as Anglophobia swept the country, there were urgent demands for war. Great Britain, however, cared little about the Venezuelan question. Fearful, moreover, of the growing power of Germany and conscious of its isolation in Europe, it had no wish to make an enemy of America. As it happened, the Jameson Raid diverted its attention from Venezuela to South Africa and the Kaiser's congratulatory telegram to President Kruger made Germany rather than the United States the target for British anger. The British thus became more conciliatory toward Cleveland and after long negotiations signed a treaty with Venezuela providing for arbitration of the boundary dispute. In October 1899 the arbitration tribunal awarded Great Britain virtually all the territory in dispute. Paradoxically the Venezuelan crisis initiated an Anglo–American *rapprochement*. But it showed how touchy Americans had now become.

The Spanish–American War

The overweening nationalism of the 1890s culminated finally in war with Spain—the first occasion for more than half a century that the United States went to war with a foreign country. Yet the conflict was as much the product of idealism as of a desire to assert American power. The American people embarked upon it to free a colonial people from Old World oppression. Cuba had been smoldering ever since the suppression of the rebellion of 1868–78 and in 1895 came a second attempt to throw off Spanish rule. As in the Hawaiian revolution, American protectionism was the unintended catalyst. The Wilson–Gorman tariff of 1894 deprived Cuban sugar of its market and plunged the island into such misery as to trigger off a renewed uprising.

From the outset American opinion was strongly on the side of the rebels. American sensibilities were particularly outraged by Spain's repressive methods. In 1896 the Spanish government instituted a harsh concentration-camp policy designed to deprive the Cuban guerrillas of civilian support. Because of incompetent administration and inadequate sanitation large numbers of people died. The horrors of the camps were real enough, but it was the manner in which the struggle in Cuba was reported in the yellow press that raised American indignation to fever pitch. Two New York newspapers, Joseph Pulitzer's *World* and William Randolph Hearst's *Journal*, then engaged in a fight for circulation, vied with each other in sensationalizing the Cuban revolt. Ignoring the cruelties perpetrated by the rebels, they filled their pages with stories—true, exaggerated or simply fabricated—of Spanish atrocities. These lurid and one-sided reports were lapped up by a jingoistic public and stimulated demands for intervention. But Cleveland saw no reason to become involved. Nor did his Republican successor, William McKinley who, like most American businessmen, feared that war might jeopardize the prosperity to which the country was just returning after the 1893 depression.

But in February 1898 two dramatic events whipped the yellow press and the jingoes into fresh fury. The first was the publication of a private letter written by the Spanish minister in Washington, Dupuy De Lôme, in which he made disparaging references to McKinley. A much greater shock was the destruction of the American battleship *Maine*, blown up as she lay at anchor in Havana harbor with the loss of 260 of her crew. What caused the explosion has never been satisfactorily explained, but almost to a man Americans assumed that Spain was responsible. There were hysterical demands for war. An emotional popular slogan swept the country: Remember the Maine! To Hell with Spain! That McKinley, after weeks of hesitation, finally resorted to force was not, as was once believed, because he was too weak to resist the popular clamor. It was rather that he gradually lost confidence in Spain's readiness and capacity to end the conflict. The Spanish Government eventually agreed to American demands for an immediate armistice and for the abandonment of the concentration-camp policy, but its refusal to grant Cuban independence prompted McKinley (April 11, 1898) to send Congress a war message. On April 20 Congress overwhelmingly adopted a joint resolution recognizing Cuban independence and authorizing the President to use force to expel the Spaniards from the island. It also adopted without dissent the Teller amendment. Disclaiming any intention of annexing Cuba it reflected the crusading idealism that lay behind the demand for war.

To Secretary of State John Hay what followed was "a splendid little war", but it was really a rather absurd affair. Brief and nearly bloodless, especially on the American side, it was a hopelessly unequal contest. The formidable American Navy enjoyed some target practice against an antique Spanish armada, and the Army, blessed by an infinity of good luck, was triumphant in every skirmish.

The United States entered the war lightheartedly but almost wholly unprepared at least for land operations. The regular army totaled only 28,000 men, scattered in small detachments around the country and experienced only in quelling Indian uprisings. The President called into service 200,000 volunteers but the War Department, staffed by elderly bureaucrats, made a fearful mess of mobilizing, training, and equipping them. Bungling and inefficiency, comparable to that displayed by the British in the Crimean War, characterized the dispatch of the expeditionary force assembled to liberate Cuba. The troops, embarking for a summer campaign in the subtropics, were clad in heavy woolen uniforms; most were equipped with obsolete, single-shot Springfield rifles; the food was atrocious, especially the canned meat which was nicknamed 'embalmed beef'. Against a determined enemy the United States could scarcely have avoided disaster. But in Spain she faced an adversary even more ill-prepared and incompetent than herself.

The first engagements took place in the Far East. On May 1 Commodore George Dewey sailed into Manila harbor and blew a few decrepit Spanish warships out of the water. An American expeditionary force was then dispatched to the Philippines and, with the help of Filipino insurrectionists, captured Manila on August 13. Meanwhile 17,000 men had finally been put ashore in Cuba toward the end of June and had closed in on Santiago. At San Juan Hill, the sharpest engagement of the war, a volunteer cavalry regiment, the Rough Riders, played a conspicuous role, whereupon the newspapers made its commander, Colonel Theodore Roosevelt, into a war hero. But the decisive blow was struck at sea. Admiral Cervera's fleet, which had been blockaded in Santiago, put to sea on July 3 to avoid capture and was promptly annihilated. The Spanish forces in Cuba surrendered on July 16, by which time Puerto Rico had also been occupied. On August 12 an armistice was signed. The ten-week war had been an unbroken series of American victories. Fewer than 400 Americans were killed in battle, though more than 5,000 fell victim to disease.

During the fighting American war aims underwent a significant change. Military victory whetted the public appetite for empire. What had begun as a war to liberate Cuba became one to acquire colonies. The United States was precluded by the Teller Amendment from annexing Cuba but was in no mood to restore Spain's other colonies or, indeed, to abandon them to anyone else. This applied particularly to the Philippines, in which there had hitherto been scant American interest. According to Mr Dooley, most Americans were not clear "whether they were islands or canned goods". But expansionists demanded that the United States should keep them. McKinley hesitated at first but, after praying for divine guidance, finally yielded. The peace treaty, signed in Paris on December 10, 1898, recognized Cuban independence and provided for the cession to the United States of the Philippines, Puerto Rico, and the Pacific island of Guam.

Not all Americans welcomed the notion of a colonial empire. Prominent figures from different walks of life—writers like Mark Twain and Hamlin Garland, reformers like Jane Addams and Lincoln Steffens, university presidents like Charles W. Eliot of Harvard and David Starr Jordan of Stanford, industrialists like Andrew Carnegie, political leaders like former President Cleveland, and the senior Republican senator from Massachusetts, George F. Hoar—united in opposing the annexation of the Philippines. They appealed mainly to idealism and tradition, arguing that to place an alien people in a faroff land under American rule without its consent and without the prospect of future statehood was unconstitutional, a dangerous innovation, and a denial of the spirit of the Declaration of Independence. They also feared that a colonial empire would necessitate large armaments and the abandonment of the traditional policy of avoiding foreign entanglements. But antiimperialism also had less exalted origins. Some Democrats acted out of pure partisanship; sugar growers feared foreign competition; trade-union leaders like Gompers were concerned about a possible influx of cheap 'native' labor; Southerners like Senator Ben Tillman objected to the incorporation of any more colored peoples. But the antiimperialists failed to win a substantial popular following. The country at large seemed more in tune with the views of Lodge and Beveridge, the treaty's principal supporters. They appealed to national pride, pointed to the commercial and strategic importance of the Philippines, and predicted that if the United States did not take them some other power would. Above all, they stressed America's moral obligation to extend the benefits of Anglo–Saxon civilization to a backward people—"to take up the White Man's burden", as Rudyard Kipling had put it in a poem addressed primarily to Americans. The bitter wrangle in the Senate over the peace treaty came to an end on February 6, 1899 when it was ratified by 57 votes to 27—that is, with little to spare.

The day before the final vote on the treaty news arrived that Filipino nationalists had risen in revolt against their erstwhile deliverers. They did not want to be "uplifted and Christianized"—McKinley's words betrayed ignorance of the fact that they had long been Catholics—but preferred independence. The rebellion dragged on for three years. To suppress it required the efforts of 70,000 American troops and the expenditure of $170 million. In a savage guerrilla war, in which 4,300 American soldiers died, the United States resorted to the brutal methods practiced in Cuba by Spain. Civil government was established in 1901 and although American rule often showed little respect for Filipino customs, it produced striking material and social improvements, especially in education, public health, and public works. But Americans found the Philippines a disappointing prize. They did not, as expected, develop into a base for Oriental trade and were soon seen as a military liability.

America's colonial empire differed from those of the European powers in being largely secondhand. With the exception of Hawaii, her colonial possessions had previously belonged to other nations. They were also administered differently. Perhaps in an attempt to appear less avowedly imperialistic, the United States did not establish a separate overseas civil service or military establishment. The various territories were placed somewhat haphazardly under the control of the State, Interior, War, and Navy Departments. The acquisition of foreign dependencies presented constitutional and administrative problems to which previous American experience of territorial government offered scant guidance. But the decision of the Supreme Court in the Insular Cases of 1901 settled the constitutional status of the dependencies. The Court asserted that "the Constitution does not follow the flag"; that is, it did not automatically or immediately incorporate new possessions into the United States, nor confer upon their inhabitants the privilege of American citizenship. Rather was it for Congress to make such constitutional provision as it saw fit. In the event Hawaii (1900) and Alaska (1912) were granted territorial status and were thus implicitly promised future statehood. Puerto Rico, however, was declared to be an "unorganized" territory, its inhabitants being declared, somewhat anomalously, to be citizens of Puerto Rico, and as such entitled to the protection of the United States, but not American citizens. The island was also granted limited home rule. In 1902 similar provisions concerning government and citizenship were made for the Philippines.

Cuba meanwhile gained only nominal independence. It remained under American military occupation until 1902. The Americans built schools, put the public finances on a sound basis, and stamped out yellow fever. At the end of the war some expansionists had wanted to brush aside the Teller Amendment and annex the island, but the temptation was finally rejected, partly because of the chastening effect of the Filipino insurrection. But the United States feared that to relinquish control completely might endanger Cuba's political stability and threaten American security. The future of Cuban–American relations was defined in the Platt Amendment, passed by Congress in 1901 as a rider to an appropriation bill. It stipulated that Cuba should never make a treaty with another power that would impair its independence, would permit American intervention to preserve that independence or maintain stable government, and grant the United States a naval base. The Cubans were extremely loath to accept these limitations on their sovereignty but, being informed that the Platt Amendment was the price of American withdrawal, reluctantly agreed to incorporate it in their Constitution and embody its provisions in a treaty. Political control went hand in hand with commercial penetration. By 1914 American corporations like the American Tobacco Company and the Havemeyer sugar interests dominated the Cuba economy.

The Development of Far Eastern Policy

The claim that the Spanish–American war marked the emergence of the United States as a world power requires considerable qualification. After 1898, to be sure, the United States participated more extensively in international affairs and, indeed, became deeply involved in Latin America and the Far East. But toward Europe, the cockpit of international politics, the American attitude remained essentially isolationist. Theodore Roosevelt was intensely interested in European affairs and broke new ground by actively intervening in disputes that did not concern the United States except in the sense that they threatened world peace. Besides mediating in the Russo–Japanese War, he took a hand in the Moroccan crisis of 1905, sending delegates to the Algeciras conference, and also played a part in arranging the Second Hague Conference in 1907. But although European statesmen took him seriously both for his own qualities and as the representative of a great nation, they knew that his anxiety to cut a figure on the world stage was not widely shared by his countrymen. Thus although the Senate ratified the Algeciras Convention and the Hague Protocol, it insisted on both occasions on appending reservations to the effect that there was no intention of departing from America's traditional foreign policy. Roosevelt's diplomatic ventures were in any case not repeated.

When France and Germany were again on the verge of war over Morocco in 1911, Taft remained aloof. Nor was Wilson involved in the feverish diplomatic activity that preceded the outbreak of the First World War.

American interest in the Far East, especially China, was greatly intensified after 1898. American businessmen had visions of a vastly expanded trade with China but were alarmed at the way the great powers were scrambling for economic concessions and carving the country up into exclusive spheres of interest. If that continued China would ultimately be closed to American trade and capital investment. In 1899 McKinley's Secretary of State, John Hay, sought to protect American interests by urging the leading powers to allow equal commercial opportunities to all nations in their respective spheres of interest. Although the replies were vague and noncommittal, Hay announced that the powers had accepted the principle of the 'Open Door'. Almost immediately, in June 1900, a group of Chinese nationalists, resenting their country's semicolonial status, launched the Boxer Rebellion to drive out "foreign devils". When the Boxers overran Peking and besieged the foreign legations an international force was organized and the United States, though insisting that it was not departing from noninvolvement, contributed 2,500 troops. Hay feared that some of the powers would use the Boxer rising as a pretext for extending their influence in China. Accordingly he dispatched a circular letter (July 3, 1900) elaborating on and broadening the Open Door policy: it declared that it was American policy to preserve Chinese territorial integrity and to ensure equality of commercial opportunity, not merely in the foreign spheres of interest, but in the whole of the Chinese Empire. Most Americans were proud of what they regarded as Hay's diplomatic triumph, but the Open Door policy was in fact simply a pious hope. As Hay and his successors acknowledged, the American people would not have been prepared to back it by force and although it remained in theory the basis of American Far Eastern policy little was done to implement it. That China was not partitioned was due, not to the Open Door policy, but to the inability of the great powers to agree how the spoils should be shared out.

The Russo–Japanese War marked a further stage in American involvement in Far Eastern affairs. Roosevelt's sympathies, like those of most Americans, were initially with the Japanese, the supposed underdogs. But as one crushing Japanese victory followed another, he began to change his mind. He did not relish the thought of complete Japanese domination in eastern Asia, preferring a balance of power between Russia and Japan. An opportunity to intervene unexpectedly presented itself. Despite their victories the Japanese were on the verge of bankruptcy and desperately wanted peace. They therefore asked Roosevelt to mediate. He agreed and helped negotiate the peace treaty signed at Portsmouth, New Hampshire in September 1905—thus winning the Nobel Peace Prize. Japan gained control of Korea and southern Manchuria and annexed the southern half of the island of Sakhalin, but Roosevelt persuaded her to abandon her claim for a large financial indemnity.

Following the war relations between the United States and Japan deteriorated sharply. Americans became alarmed at the growth of Japanese power and ambitions, fearing in particular a Japanese attack on the Philippines. Anti-Japanese sentiment was particularly strong in California where an influx of 100,000 Japanese immigrants prompted hysterical talk of a "yellow peril" and a widespread demand for Japanese exclusion. The Japanese, for their part, were disenchanted by Roosevelt's peacemaking; they blamed him for robbing them of the fruits of victory. Animosity toward the United States was exacerbated when in October 1906, as the climax of a series of discriminatory measures, the San Francisco school-board ordered the segregation of Oriental children in separate schools. Japan protested at the implicit racial slur and there were anti-American riots in Tokyo. The action of the school-board was outside the jurisdiction of the federal government but, fearing that California might drag the country into war, Roosevelt persuaded the San Franciscans to rescind the segregation order in exchange for a promise to curtail Japanese immigration. This was accomplished through the Gentlemen's Agreement, an exchange of notes in 1907 and 1908 in which the Japanese government undertook not to issue passports to laborers wishing to emigrate to the United States. So that the Japanese would not interpret his attitude on the school question as weakness, Roosevelt resolved to impress them with a dramatic display of naval strength. He sent the sixteen battleships of the new navy on a 46,000 mile world cruise. The Japanese, far from responding belligerently, invited the Great White Fleet to Yokohama and gave it a tumultuous reception. The Root–Takahira agreement of 1908 further improved relations. The two powers undertook to respect each other's possessions, maintain the status quo in the Pacific, and uphold the Open Door and China's territorial integrity. What the ambiguous and contradictory declaration signified, other than a mutual desire to relieve tension, was not immediately clear. What looked at first glance like an endorsement of the Open Door was in fact a limited retreat from it since the maintenance of the status quo implied recognition of Japan's special position in southern Manchuria. The agreement was a characteristic example of Rooseveltian realism in foreign affairs. Recognizing that the United States could not effectively challenge Japan in the Far East, Roosevelt chose to back down rather than risk war.

Under Taft Far Eastern policy showed less awareness of reality. Whereas Roosevelt had tacitly given Japan a free hand in southern Manchuria Taft and his Secretary of State, Philander C. Knox, sought to revive the original concept of the Open Door by means of a policy later known as "dollar diplomacy"—aiding private enterprise in seeking markets and investment opportunities abroad. In 1911, at the instigation of the State Department, a group of American bankers agreed to join an international consortium to finance railway construction in China. But they had little real interest in China and when in 1913 Wilson repudiated dollar diplomacy and expressed strong criticism of the terms of a proposed consortium loan to China the bankers withdrew. Knox also proposed an international syndicate to lend money to China to buy all the Manchurian railroads. But this crude attempt to jockey Japan out of Manchuria served only to drive her into Russia's arms and so strengthened Russo–Japanese control of Manchuria.

The Acquisition of the Panama Canal Zone

In the Caribbean the principal aim of American policy was to build and control an interocean canal across Central America and protect the approaches to it. Such a canal had been talked about for half a century but, only with the war with Spain and the acquisition of colonies in the Pacific and the Caribbean was its importance to national security fully appreciated. There were several difficulties to overcome. One was the Clayton–Bulwer treaty of 1850, which provided that any isthmian canal constructed by either the United States or Great Britain would be jointly controlled by them and would never be fortified. That obstacle was removed by the second Hay–Pauncefote Treaty of 1901. The Boer War had exposed Britain's isolation in Europe and she was eager for American friendship. So she agreed to exclusive American control of the canal and, by implication, to its fortification.

The next problem was to decide whether to build across the Panama isthmus or through Nicaragua. The Panama route was shorter but more expensive mainly because a French company, successor to the defunct De Lesseps company which had begun construction in Panama decades before, wanted the exorbitant sum of $109 million for its rights. In 1901 a special commission appointed by McKinley recommended the Nicaraguan route. But the French company hastily lowered its price to $40 million and one of its leading stockholders, Philippe Bunau–Varilla, conducted a skillful propaganda campaign drawing American attention to the persistence of volcanic activity in Nicaragua. As a result Congress chose the Panama route.

It now remained only to obtain the consent of Colombia, which owned Panama. In January 1903 Hay signed a treaty with the Colombian chargé in Washington granting the United States a ninety-nine year lease on a canal zone six miles wide in return for a payment of $10 million and an annual rent of $250,000. The United States Senate promptly ratified the treaty but the Colombian Senate, dissatisfied with the financial provisions, voted unanimously to reject it.

Roosevelt was furious with the Colombians, fulminating in private that the 'cutthroats' and 'blackmailers of Bogota' should not be permitted "permanently to bar one of the future highways of civilization!" He even considered taking the canal zone by force. But that proved unnecessary for in November 1903 the Panamanians, long restless under Colombian rule, revolted. Roosevelt did not actually foment the insurrection but let it be known that, if one occurred, he would be sympathetic. In the event he ordered the cruiser *Nashville* to prevent Colombian forces from suppressing the revolt, using as an excuse an 1846 treaty whereby the United States had bound itself to maintain "free transit" across the isthmus. What followed was done with indecent haste. On November 13, only ten days after the uprising, Roosevelt received Bunau–Varilla, who had been largely instrumental in planning it, as the Panamanian minister. On November 18 Hay and Bunau–Varilla signed a new canal treaty on the same terms as those rejected by Colombia. The building of the canal was entrusted to United States army engineers, who began work in earnest in 1907. The first ocean steamer passed through the canal in August 1914.

Most of Roosevelt's countrymen approved of his buccaneering tactics in Panama but a vocal minority condemned them. At the time Roosevelt claimed self-righteously that he had a "mandate from civilization". Some years later he became less guarded, boasting characteristically that, instead of following "traditional, conservative methods" that entailed delay, he simply "took the Canal Zone". He was probably right in claiming to have hastened the construction of the Canal, but the long-term cost in ill will was great. No event since the Mexican War did so much to arouse distrust of the United States in Latin America.

Policing the Western Hemisphere

Having obtained the Panama Canal site Roosevelt became increasingly sensitive to possible European encroachments in the Caribbean. The frequency of revolution in the Caribbean republics and their failure to pay their foreign debts tended to provoke European intervention. One such intervention in 1902—an Anglo–German–Italian blockade of Venezuela—aroused American fears that Germany, the prime mover in the affair, was scheming to acquire Caribbean bases. Shortly afterward, when the Dominican Republic defaulted on its debts and European investors demanded action, Roosevelt decided on a radical step. If the Monroe Doctrine debarred the European powers from intervening in the Caribbean, he reasoned, then the United States must itself step in to act as policeman. This was the essence of the Roosevelt Corollary to the Monroe Doctrine, proclaimed in 1904. "Chronic wrongdoing or impotence" in the Western

Hemisphere, he asserted, "may force the United States, however reluctantly, . . . to the exercise of an international police power." That it also meant acting as an international debt-collector became clear in 1905, when the Roosevelt Corollary was first applied. Under pressure from the United States, the Dominican Republic agreed to American financial control.

Like Roosevelt, Taft was unwilling to tolerate unrest in the Caribbean that might invite European intervention. But there were financial as well as strategic motives for his Latin American policy. As in China, he and Knox encouraged American investment. They also put pressure on the Caribbean republics to replace European capital with American. That would both lessen the risk of European intervention and make profits for American bankers. Dollar diplomacy produced its clearest results in Nicaragua. In 1909 American bankers, with the encouragement of the State Department, took over the country's finances. Then in 1912 when a revolution broke out against the pro-American government and American investments were imperiled Taft sent in marines to put it down.

Woodrow Wilson came to the Presidency determined to substitute idealism for Roosevelt's "big stick" and Taft's dollar diplomacy. In October 1913 he affirmed that the United States would "never again seek an additional foot of territory by conquest" and condemned as unfair and degrading the practice of seeking economic concessions in Latin America. Wilson further promised that the United States would seek no special favors or exert undue pressure but would deal with Latin America "upon terms of equality and honor". But in fact Wilson's Administration intervened more extensively in Latin America than those of Roosevelt and Taft combined. An exponent of that frail hybrid, liberal imperialism, Wilson combined an attitude of moral superiority with a determination to defend American interests. For all his high-minded rhetoric, he could be as realistic as Theodore Roosevelt and once in office realized that the Panama Canal was so vital to American security that political instability in the Caribbean could not be tolerated. But he was also imbued with a missionary zeal to effect the salvation of others. Believing he had a duty to uplift the dictator-ridden and poverty-stricken peoples of Latin America, he sought to help them achieve stable democratic government on the American model. Wilson began by negotiating a treaty with Colombia expressing 'sincere regret' for the American role in the Panamanian revolution and offering an indemnity of $25 million. But the treaty was blocked in the Senate by Roosevelt's friends. In Nicaragua Wilson could find no alternative to Taft's policy of controlling Nicaraguan finances and maintaining a marine detachment in the Nicaraguan capital. In 1915 when a bloody revolution broke out in Haiti he sent the marines in and took control of the country. The following year the Dominican Republic became a virtual American protectorate in almost identical circumstances. In both countries American rule brought material benefits but not political stability or democratic government.

Wilson's belief that he knew what was best for foreigners led to disastrous American involvement in the tangled internal affairs of Mexico. For a time after the revolution of 1911, Mexico seemed politically stable and on the road to constitutionalism. But in February 1913 a reactionary general, Victoriano Huerta, seized power. American businessmen pleaded that recognition of Huerta's regime was essential to safeguard their Mexican investments, but Wilson refused on the ground that Huerta had come to power by force. In the hope of driving Huerta from office and establishing constitutional government Wilson first tried to isolate him diplomatically. Then in February 1914 he lifted the arms embargo imposed by Taft, hoping this step would ensure the triumph of the Constitutionalist followers of Venustiano Carranza, who were in revolt against Huerta. But it did not and in desperation the President resorted to armed intervention. A trivial incident at the Mexican port of Tampico on April 9, 1914 provided an excuse. The Mexican authorities arrested a boatload of American sailors, and released them with apologies. But Huerta turned down an American demand for a more formal apology, whereupon Wilson asked Congress for authority to use force. At this point he learned that the German steamer *Ypiranga* was nearing Veracruz with a cargo of arms for Huerta. Without waiting for Congressional approval Wilson ordered the navy to seize Veracruz to prevent the munitions being landed. In the ensuing bombardment 126 Mexican lives were lost. Carranza, whom Wilson had been trying to help, denounced this "foreign aggression" no less vigorously than Huerta and even threatened to attack the American forces if they moved inland. Only a timely offer of mediation from the ABC powers (Argentina, Brazil, and Chile) extricated Wilson from a ticklish situation.

In August 1914 the Carrancistas at last toppled Huerta but the Constitutionalist coalition at once fell apart. In the ensuing struggle between Carranza and his former lieutenant, Francisco ('Pancho') Villa, Wilson at first favored the latter believing that he was a genuine reformer and would welcome American guidance. But Villa was soon decisively defeated and in October 1914 Wilson reluctantly granted *de facto* recognition to Carranza. Villa angrily set out deliberately to embroil the United States in war with Mexico. In January 1916 his followers stopped a train in northern Mexico and shot sixteen Americans. When no reprisals followed Villa crossed the border into New Mexico, killing a further nineteen Americans. Wilson now had no alternative but to yield to popular pressure for intervention. With Carranza's grudging and ambiguous consent a punitive expedition under Brigadier-General John J. Pershing crossed into Mexico in March 1916 to hunt down Villa. For several weeks six thousand American cavalrymen chased Villa all over northern Mexico but failed to catch him. Carranza was now becoming increasingly alarmed at the presence of the American expeditionary force and when skirmishes occurred between his forces and Pershing's the two countries seemed to be drifting into war. But Wilson did not want war and in July thankfully accepted Carranza's offer to negotiate. No agreement proved possible but in February 1917 Wilson, now preoccupied with the German submarine crisis, withdrew Pershing's troops. Meanwhile the Mexicans had drawn up a new liberal Constitution. That was what Wilson had wanted all along and, for all his blunders and inconsistencies, he deserves some credit for the outcome. He had refused to become the tool of American oil interests, had forestalled European intervention, and in the end had given way when to fight might have been easier—and electorally more profitable. But in striving to help the Mexican people Wilson had shown scant regard for their traditions or their national pride. Thus he helped strengthen the resentment and suspicion of the United States already widespread throughout Latin America.

21. *The United States and the First World War*, 1914–1920

The Problems of Neutrality

The outbreak of the First World War took Americans by surprise. Like many Europeans they had believed that arbitration was replacing war as a means of settling international disputes and a major conflict to be unthinkable. Even when war came Americans shared the general European belief that it would be short and sharp. They had no inkling of the long-drawn-out horrors to come, still less that they themselves would be drawn in. The fighting was far away and seemed to threaten no vital American interest. As Woodrow Wilson remarked when he issued the routine proclamation of neutrality in August 1914, the European war was one "with which we have nothing to do, whose causes cannot touch us".

Virtually all Americans favored neutrality in 1914; keeping out of Europe's quarrels was a hallowed national tradition. But neutrality did not mean impartiality and when Wilson urged the American people to be "impartial in thought as well as in deed" he was asking the impossible. Americans were bound to take sides in a war between European countries with which nearly all of them had ties of blood. No fewer than a third of the American people were either immigrants or the children of immigrants and, for all the talk of the melting-pot, ethnic consciousness remained a powerful force. The war greatly stimulated ancestral loyalties. The largest immigrant group in the United States, the German-Americans, became loudly and uncritically pro-German. The longstanding anti-British bias of Irish-Americans was reinforced by the ruthless suppression of the Easter Rising of 1916. Memories of ancient wrongs led Jewish-Americans to express a vociferous hatred of Czardom and Polish- and Czech-Americans to support movements for national independence. The persistence of Old World ties, widely denounced as "hyphenism", or divided loyalty, made Americans conscious of their disunity and strengthened their determination to remain neutral.

Nonetheless most Americans sympathized with the Allies—or rather with Great Britain, France, and Belgium, for autocratic Russia was unpopular. There was a widespread sense of cultural affinity with England, especially on the East coast and among the social, economic, and political elite. Anglophobia was not dead, but the bickering that had long characterized Anglo-American relations had given way since 1900 to genuine friendliness and a sense of Anglo-Saxon solidarity. France was the object of a sentimental attachment that dated back to the Revolutionary War. "Gallant little Belgium" was almost universally admired. Imperial Germany, on the other hand, had become deeply distrusted. Prussian militarism appeared to threaten American democratic ideals, and the Kaiser's saber-rattling had aroused antagonism and alarm. The invasion of Belgium in disregard of solemn treaty undertakings confirmed American feelings that Germany was an international menace. This impression, confirmed by Germany's resort to submarine warfare, ultimately played a large part in the American decision to intervene. The United States, it might be said, declared war on Germany in 1917 not because American interests were threatened but because American sentiment was outraged.

The United States hoped to continue trading with all the belligerents and was determined to maintain the traditional rights of neutrals. But the major maritime belligerents, Great Britain and Germany, proved unwilling to respect those rights. Intent on destroying each other, they unilaterally modified or rewrote international maritime law to suit their own needs. Controversy over neutral rights developed first with Great Britain. Having swept German shipping from the seas, the British instituted maritime controls designed to strangle German trade. They gradually expanded the definition of contraband of war until it embraced virtually every commodity, including foodstuffs, that might be of use to the enemy. They took liberties with the traditional right of search: instead of simply stopping and searching neutral merchantmen on the high seas, as had hitherto been the practice, the Royal Navy brought suspicious vessels into port for examination. Great Britain also arbitrarily enlarged the concept of "continuous voyage" so as to prevent goods from reaching Germany through neighboring neutrals like Sweden and The Netherlands, and to increase the effectiveness of its so-called blockade—it was never officially proclaimed—mined the North Sea, thus forcing all vessels bound for Germany or neutral Europe to stop first at a British port for sailing directions.

These departures from international practice bore heavily on the United States, the principal neutral carrier. Although the British generally paid for confiscated cargoes, and for a time exempted cotton from the contraband list to conciliate the South, American shipping was subjected to lengthy delay and loss. By 1916, indeed, American trade with the Central Powers and their neutral neighbors had declined almost to vanishing-point. The United States repeatedly protested about the British blockade, refusing to accept either the British claim to be following American practice in the Civil War or the argument that new methods of trade and warfare necessitated changes in traditional maritime rules. But for all its protests the United States in practice acquiesced in the British maritime system. One reason was that, except for the Secretary of State, William Jennings Bryan, who favored none of the belligerents, the Wilson Administration was strongly pro-Ally. The American ambassador in London, Walter Hines Page, was so partial to the British cause that he watered down the protests he delivered and even advised Sir Edward Grey how to answer them. Also sympathetic to the Allies were the Texas businessman, Colonel Edward M. House, Wilson's closest and most trusted adviser, and Robert Lansing, who succeeded Bryan as Secretary of State in 1915. But the main impetus for a pro-Allied stance came from the President himself. This owed little to Wilson's ingrained Anglophilism: though a devoted admirer of English literature and of the British parliamentary system, he did not allow his private prejudices to influence policy. But he believed that a German victory was a potential threat to the United States. Hence he was not disposed to make difficulties for the British. "England is fighting our fight," he remarked to his private secretary in the autumn of 1914.

The growth of war trade with the Allies supplied a further reason for not pushing things to extremes. The United States became an Allied arsenal, shipping vast quantities of munitions, foodstuffs, and raw materials. Allied war demands stimulated American industry and agriculture alike. The depression which had gripped the country at the outbreak of war soon gave way to feverish prosperity. At first the Allies were able to pay cash for war supplies but their purchases soon became so enormous as to exhaust their financial reserves and make borrowing essential. At first the Administration frowned on loans by private bankers to belligerents. Bryan, consulted on the subject in the early days of the war by the New York banking-house of J. P. Morgan and Company, declared that, while such loans were legal, they were "inconsistent with the true spirit of neutrality". But only two months later, though still disapproving of outright loans, he sanctioned credits. Then in September 1915 the ban on loans was in turn lifted because the Administration feared the consequences for the American economy if the profitable war business collapsed. The House of Morgan floated a $500 million Anglo-French bond issue and by the time the United States entered the war American bankers had advanced a further $1,800 million to finance war purchases.

Thus the United States became increasingly bound to the Allied cause. Germany protested that the sale of war materials to the Allies was unneutral and demanded an embargo. But the United States replied that international law sanctioned such traffic. To have prohibited it because the Allies were the only belligerents capable of transporting their purchases would itself have been unneutral. If the situation operated to Germany's disadvantage, that was not because of American favoritism—the United

States was prepared in principle to sell arms to Germany—but because of British command of the seas.

The German Submarine Campaign

Though Germany resented the way Americans interpreted neutrality, there were no serious disputes with her during the first six months of the war. But the opening of the German submarine campaign abruptly changed the situation. Unable to destroy the British surface fleet, Germany decided to retaliate against the Allied blockade with the relatively new submarine weapon and to employ it in an unprecedented manner. In February 1915 Berlin announced that all enemy merchant ships entering a designated war zone around the British Isles would be sunk without warning. The proclamation also said that, since Allied merchantmen sometimes attempted to disguise their origin by flying neutral flags, neutral vessels should avoid the war zone so as not to be sunk by mistake.

The German announcement violated the long-established rule of international law that a belligerent warship could legitimately sink an enemy merchantman only after having stopped it, ascertained its identity, and made adequate provision for the safety of its passengers and crew. The Germans argued that they were justified in departing from the rules because the nature of warfare had changed: the submarine was a fragile and vulnerable craft which risked destruction at the hands of armed merchantmen if it surfaced to give the conventional warning. But such an argument cut no ice outside Germany; there were shocked protests from all over the world. Unrestricted submarine warfare seemed to most people a barbarous innovation, utterly contrary to civilized behavior.

Accordingly, though the United States had not protested when Britain had declared the North Sea a military area it promptly sent Germany a stern warning. The two cases were not identical, of course, for while the British merely interfered with trade, the Germans threatened life. Wilson's note declared that if American vessels or lives were lost through German action, the United States would hold the German government to "strict accountability". Furthermore, it would take steps to "safeguard American lives and property and to secure to American citizens the full enjoyment of their acknowledged rights on the high seas".

Wilson nevertheless did little when an American seaman was drowned in the sinking of the British steamer *Falaba* at the end of March 1915 or when the American tanker *Gulflight* was torpedoed (but not sunk) early in May. But the sinking of the giant Cunard liner *Lusitania* put an end to his hesitation. Torpedoed off the coast of Southern Ireland on May 7 while en route from New York to Liverpool, the *Lusitania* sank in less than twenty minutes with the loss of 1,198 lives, 128 of them American. News of the disaster produced an outburst of American anger and indignation.

The press rang with allegations of mass murder and there was even talk of war. But Wilson, though deeply shocked, ruled out such a step. "There is such a thing as a man being too proud to fight", he declared to a large gathering in Philadelphia. Yet the President was determined to uphold the right of American citizens to sail the seas. He sent a vigorously worded protest to Berlin demanding disavowal of the sinking and reparation for damages. The German reply was argumentative and evasive. The Germans claimed that the sinking was an act of "just self-defense" for the *Lusitania* had been offensively armed and, moreover, was carrying a large quantity of rifle ammunition when attacked. Believing that such considerations hardly excused the indiscriminate slaughter of men, women, and children, Wilson determined on a second, more threatening, protest. That was too much for Bryan. He would have preferred the Administration to ban American citizens from traveling into the war zone on ships carrying munitions and to have coupled its representations to Germany with an equally strong protest about the Allied blockade. When Wilson rejected his advice, Bryan resigned.

Diplomatic interchanges with Berlin about the *Lusitania* were still in progress when, on August 19, a German submarine sank another British steamer, the White Star liner *Arabic*, killing forty-four passengers, including two Americans. American opinion was again aroused and the Administration considered breaking off relations with Germany. The situation was made even more tense by dramatic revelations of German espionage and sabotage in the United States and of attempts by the Austro-Hungarian ambassador to foment strikes in American munitions factories. But a rupture was averted through the initiative of the German ambassador in Washington, Count Bernstorff. He expressed regret for the sinking of the *Arabic* and, though not authorized to do so, disclosed that submarine commanders had been ordered not to attack passenger ships in future unless they tried to escape or offered resistance. The German government subsequently endorsed his assurances. Wilsonian diplomacy had apparently won a signal triumph.

Nevertheless, many Americans were uneasy about Wilson's strong stand, fearing it would eventually plunge the country into war. Resolutions were introduced into Congress in February 1916, warning American citizens against traveling on armed belligerent ships. Congress seemed disposed to accept them but, in a letter to the chairman of the Senate Foreign Relations Committee, Wilson declared that he could not "consent to any abridgement of the rights of American citizens in any respect.... Once accept a single abatement of right, and many other humiliations would certainly follow, and the whole fine fabric of international law might crumble under our hands piece by piece." The President's arguments prevailed and the resolutions were defeated.

But almost at once a fresh crisis occurred—the most dangerous to date. On March 24, 1916 the French passenger steamer *Sussex* was torpedoed in the English Channel and several Americans were injured. The attack subsequently proved to have been an error by the U-boat commander, but at the time it looked like a deliberate violation of the *Arabic* pledge. In response to public clamor Wilson sent Germany a virtual ultimatum. Unless it immediately abandoned "its present methods of submarine warfare against passenger and freight-carrying vessels", the United States would be compelled to sever diplomatic relations. Once again Germany yielded. The German chancellor, Bethmann-Hollweg, was anxious to avoid war with the United States and succeeded—though for the last time—in overruling the champions of submarine warfare. On May 4 the German government informed the United States that its submarines would sink no more merchant vessels without observing the traditional rules about search and warning. The Germans qualified this so-called "*Sussex* pledge" by insisting that Wilson take strong action against the British blockade. The President ignored the demand. He seemed to have won a remarkable diplomatic victory. He had upheld American rights and averted hostilities. But, as he himself acknowledged, his stand had deprived the United States of full freedom of action in future. Germany could at any moment plunge the United States into war by going back on the *Sussex* pledge. For several months thereafter there were no more submarine sinkings and it became Great Britain's turn to give offense. The execution of the leaders of the Easter Rising of 1916 badly damaged British prestige in the United States, deeply alienated Irish-Americans, and shocked even Anglophiles. Americans were also irritated by British interference with mail bound for Europe and angered by the publication in July 1916 of a blacklist forbidding British subjects to do business with certain American firms suspected of trading with the Central Powers. Though the British had every right to take such a step, Wilson was affronted. When his protests to London produced no response, he got Congress to grant him retaliatory powers—though these were never used.

Propaganda and Preparedness

All the same the American people were becoming steadily more pro-Ally. Most of them got only Allied versions of the European war. Great Britain cut the transatlantic cable between Germany and the United States in the first week of hostilities and was thus able to censor all war news from Germany except wireless dispatches. Another Allied advantage was that American newspapers rarely had their own correspondents in Europe and tended to rely heavily on Allied-controlled news agencies. Moreover the British went to elaborate lengths to win over American opinion. The War

Propaganda Bureau flooded the United States with literature. Among those who wrote for it were famous authors well known to American readers: Joseph Conrad, Rudyard Kipling, and A. Conan Doyle. The Germans made equally strenuous efforts to persuade Americans that their cause was just. But they found it difficult to overcome American prejudices. In any case their propaganda was inept. The British propaganda campaign, on the other hand, was skillfully devised and executed. While care was taken to avoid any appearance of seeking to embroil the United States in the war, every effort was made to implant the idea that Great Britain and the United States were sister democracies and that the war pitted democracy against autocracy. Every incident calculated to depict the Germans as latter-day barbarians—the destruction of Louvain, for example, and the execution of Edith Cavell—was cleverly exploited. The shrewdest British stratagem, however—and perhaps the most unscrupulous—was the publication of the Bryce Report, a sickening but not wholly authenticated catalog of alleged German atrocities in Belgium. Bearing the name of the famous historian and former ambassador to Washington, James Bryce, a respected figure in the United States, the Report was rushed out in May 1915 so as to capitalize on the passions aroused by the sinking of the *Lusitania*.

Despite their partiality for the Allies Americans remained basically neutral and pacific. They were still reluctant, for example, to strengthen their defenses. Though a vocal minority led by Theodore Roosevelt repeatedly warned that the weakness of the armed forces put national security in jeopardy, their 'preparedness' campaign at first had little effect, except to rouse the organized hostility of peace groups. Wilson shared the instinctive dislike of many of his countrymen for arms and armaments and, believing Roosevelt's fears to be unjustified, deprecated talk of preparedness. At the beginning of 1915 he could even contemplate a cut in the military budget. But the submarine crisis brought home to him the country's military weakness. He also feared that continued opposition to preparedness when it was clearly gaining strength might give the Republicans a campaign issue. Accordingly, in July 1915 he ordered a revision of defense needs and in November presented a modest preparedness program to Congress. There were violent protests, not merely from pacifists, but also from Middle Western and Southern Progressives, who saw in the program the triumph of militarism and the end of domestic reform. In an extensive speaking tour in January 1916 Wilson tried to win support for a Continental Army of 400,000 men and "a navy second to none". The fleet building program went through essentially unchanged. But the plan for a Continental Army had to be abandoned and although the National Defense Act of 1916 doubled the size of the regular army, that still left it with only 200,000 officers and men. Moreover, when the financing of mili-

tary and naval expansion came to be discussed, Congressional Progressives rejected the Administration's tax proposals and submitted new
income and inheritance taxes designed to make the rich foot the entire
bill.

The Election of 1916

The presidential election of 1916 afforded further proof of antiwar and
neutralist feeling. Foreign policy was a key issue and the rival candidates
vied with each other as champions of peace. The Democrats enthusiastically
endorsed Wilson and made effective use of the cry "He kept us out of
war." The President made no use of the slogan himself—he said privately
that it raised false hopes—and avoided an explicit commitment to maintain
neutrality. Nevertheless he conveyed the impression that he would do so.
Peace was a persistent theme of his campaign speeches and he warned the
voters that a Republican victory could lead to intervention. In fact the
Republicans were not a war party. Their platform, while demanding the
protection of American rights, called for "a straight and honest neutrality"; that amounted to an outright repudiation of Theodore Roosevelt's
demand for a sterner policy toward Germany. The Republican candidate
was the Progressive Charles Evans Hughes, formerly governor of New
York and now an associate justice of the Supreme Court. Hughes tried to
avoid detailed discussion of the neutrality issue and as the campaign pro-
gressed it became increasingly difficult to know where he stood. He
attempted to woo German-American and Irish-American support by
stressing his commitment to peace, but accused Wilson of weakness in
defending American rights and, moreover, accepted Roosevelt's support
and endorsed some of his bellicose utterances.

The Republicans were expected to win. They were the majority party;
their defeat in 1912 had come about simply because of their split, and that
was now healed. Yet in an extremely close election Wilson scraped in.
Hughes, having learned that he had carried most of the industrial North-
East, went to bed on election night believing he had won. But next day,
when the returns from the trans-Mississippi West came in, the tide turned
in Wilson's favor. How much the peace issue *per se* helped Wilson is far
from clear. Certainly it was his domestic reforms that enabled him to put
together a new Democratic coalition. His endorsement of the eight-hour
day gave him the support of organized labor, the rural credits act won over
Middle Western farm groups, and his championing of the cause of social
justice brought to his side many independent Progressives who had voted
for Roosevelt four years before. But the most important feature of the
campaign was the way the President and his supporters fused the causes
of Progressivism and peace. These were presented as interdependent as
well as exclusively Democratic ideals. Thus if one can regard Wilson's

narrow victory as a mandate for anything, it was one for continued neutrality and a further installment of reform.

Wilsonian Peace Efforts

Wilson had long believed that the only way of ensuring that the United States stayed out of the war was to end it. That conviction, along with horror at the scale of the slaughter, led him to send House to Europe on secret missions in 1915 and 1916 to explore the possibility of a negotiated settlement. But these attempts came to nothing for both sides were confident of complete victory. To encourage the Allies to negotiate Wilson even dangled before them at one point the carrot of American co-belligerency. The House–Grey memorandum of February 22, 1916 provided that when the British and French notified him that they deemed the time ripe Wilson would issue invitations to a peace conference. If the Germans declined or if, having accepted they refused to make peace on reasonable terms, the United States would "probably"—a word subsequently inserted by Wilson—"leave the Conference as a belligerent on the side of the Allies". But the Allies were skeptical of the plan, the more so after Wilson's insertion had watered down the American undertaking. Thus they allowed his conference proposal to lapse.

In December 1916, just after his reelection, Wilson resolved to try again. He sent notes to the belligerents asking them to state their war aims; he hoped they might find common ground. But his initiative was unsympathetically received. War-weariness had led to peace talk in both Great Britain and Germany in the latter part of 1916, but both the main belligerents still believed they could deal a knockout blow. Wilson's proposal was unwelcome for other reasons. Neither British nor German leaders cared for his moralizing. They each suspected him of acting in collusion with their enemies and were embarrassed to be asked to state their war aims. Thus while neither side was prepared to return an outright refusal for fear of offending American opinion, their replies were evasive and discouraging.

Wilson nevertheless persisted. On January 22, 1917 he outlined to the Senate the kind of peace he envisaged. A conqueror's peace, he declared, would breed hatreds and future wars; the only basis for a lasting settlement was a "peace without victory", one founded on the principles of equality among nations, national self-determination, freedom of the seas, and limitation of armaments. If such a peace were made the United States would help maintain it through membership of a permanent international organization.

America Goes to War

Wilson's offer came too late. The German government, now under military domination, had already decided on a desperate throw—the resumption of unrestricted submarine warfare. The German military leaders knew this would bring the United States into the war, but believed that the submarine fleet, now numbering more than a hundred, could starve Britain into submission before American military power could be mobilized. On January 31, 1917 Bernstorff informed the State Department that from the following day German submarines would sink on sight all vessels, enemy or neutral, passenger or merchant, armed or unarmed, within a specific zone around the British Isles and in the Mediterranean. One American steamer a week would be permitted to sail in each direction through the war zone, provided it carried no contraband, was conspicuously painted in red and white stripes, and flew a special checkered flag as well as the Stars and Stripes.

Wilson promptly broke off diplomatic relations with Germany. But that was as far as he was prepared to go for the moment. He told Congress on February 3 that only "actual overt acts" would convince him that Germany really intended to carry out her threat. In the course of the next few weeks he tried a variety of diplomatic expedients to force the Germans to reconsider. He wanted history to record that if the United States finally became involved in war it was only after every alternative had been tried and because Germany had deliberately forced her in. Thus he refused at first to accept his Cabinet's advice to ask for Congressional authority to arm American merchant ships. When he finally made the request in the last week of February it was blocked in the Senate by antiwar filibusterers led by Robert M. La Follette of Wisconsin and George Norris of Nebraska. Frustrated in his hope of a demonstration of national unity which might have induced the Germans to hold their hand, Wilson angrily denounced the filibusterers as "a little group of willful men" who had "rendered the . . . United States helpless and contemptible". He than armed the ships without Congressional sanction, relying on the authority of an almost forgotten statute of 1797.

Events now carried the United States swiftly from armed neutrality to war. On February 26 news reached Washington of what many regarded as the "overt act" the President was awaiting—the torpedoing of the Cunard liner *Laconia* with the loss of twelve lives, including those of two American women. Three days later public opinion was further roused when the government published the Zimmermann telegram. Addressed to Bernstorff by the German Foreign Secretary, Arthur Zimmermann, for onward transmission to the German Minister to Mexico, the telegram had been intercepted and decoded by British naval intelligence and then turned over to the United States. In the event of war between the United States and Germany, it declared, the German Minister should propose a Mexican–German Alliance, which Mexico should then try to persuade Japan to join. The bait held out to Mexico would be the recovery of her "lost territory" in Texas, New Mexico, and Arizona. Americans were furious at Germany's blatant disregard of the Monroe Doctrine; in her search for allies she was clearly ready to extend European quarrels to the New World. Moreover, the telegram shocked Americans into a realization of the depth of German hostility and provoked a strong reaction, especially in the Southwest, a region not hitherto anti-German.

Opinion now crystallized in favor of war. Though the Russian Revolution of March 1917 did not directly influence the decision, it removed a moral obstacle to intervention. The establishment of constitutional monarchy and democracy in Russia, short-lived though this was to prove, gave ideological unity to the Allies and made it easier for Americans to regard the Allied cause as a democratic crusade. On March 12, the day the revolutionary provisional government came to power in Petrograd, an unarmed American merchant vessel was torpedoed without warning in the Atlantic. Six days later German submarines sank three more unarmed American merchantmen, causing the loss of fifteen lives. For Wilson this was the last straw. Though still reluctant to go to war, he felt that German attacks on American lives and property had to be resisted and also that as a belligerent the United States would have a bigger say in the peace.

On April 2 Wilson asked Congress to declare war. He listed German infringements of American neutral rights but went on to place the conflict on a loftier plane than mere self-interest. It was to be a crusade for righteousness. Its aim would be not merely to defeat Germany but to create a new world order. "The world", declared Wilson, "must be made safe for democracy." The United States would fight for "a universal dominion of right by such a concert of free peoples as shall bring peace and safety to all nations". Wilson's speech brought members of Congress to their feet, cheering and waving flags. Two days later the Senate passed a formal declaration of war by 82 votes to 6 and early on the morning of April 6, Good Friday, the House followed suit by 373 votes to 50.

The votes were somewhat misleading for a sizable and vocal minority would have preferred to cling to neutrality. The opponents of war were drawn from both the major parties and came preponderantly from the agricultural Middle West. Their most impassioned spokesmen were Norris and La Follette. Norris's antiwar stance reflected a Populist preference for conspiratorial explanations and a Populist prejudice toward Eastern financiers. Wall Street bankers, he alleged, had engineered America's intervention. "We are going into war upon the command of gold." La Follette complained that the Wilson Administration had practiced a one-sided neutrality and thus bore responsibility for the crisis with Germany. Pointing to Great Britain's record in Ireland, India, and Egypt, he questioned whether the Allies were waging a war for democracy and objected to his country's joining them when their war aims were not fully known. La Follette also claimed that if a popular referendum had been held war would have been rejected by ten to one. That was wishful thinking. There would certainly have been a large antiwar vote; indeed, in Middle Western German communities and perhaps such Jewish strongholds as New York's Lower East Side there may even have been antiwar majorities. But studies of public opinion suggest that Congress correctly interpreted the popular will. The American people had come to believe that American rights were in jeopardy and that their defense was more important than peace. Yet they had not wanted war and even when it came few understood what it would entail. Americans expected to fight a naval war but not a major land campaign on the Western front. Nor were they realistic about war aims. Wilson's idealistic rhetoric may have helped unite a hesitant and divided people but it contained the seeds of disillusion. By raising lofty hopes Wilson persuaded his reluctant countrymen to embrace the cause of mankind, but when those hopes were not fulfilled there was a profound sense of letdown.

In the 1930s millions of Americans came to believe that the United States had been tricked into war in 1917 by British propaganda or, alternatively, had been dragged into it, as Norris alleged at the time, by a conspiracy of bankers and munitions-makers. These were plausible theories but nonetheless mistaken. There is no disputing the scale of British propaganda but its effectiveness has been grossly exaggerated. Americans were not so naive as to swallow it whole. If they came to see the war very much as the British themselves did, that was largely because British propaganda fell on fertile ground.

Equally oversimplified and erroneous is the economic explanation of American intervention. It is true that the American economy became closely geared to Allied needs and that Wilson could not impose an embargo on war materials to the Allies or refuse to sanction loans to them without inviting the return of depression. Moreover, the fact that the United States became the arsenal and the granary of the Allies played a part in the German decision to employ the submarine. But it is untrue to say that, in order to safeguard their war profits and ensure the repayment of the huge sums they had lent to the Allies, American bankers and munitions-makers pushed Wilson into intervening when it seemed that the Allies were in grave danger of defeat. The Allies spent far more in the United States on foodstuffs than on munitions, and if munitions-makers had a stake in an Allied victory, so had farmers and for that matter workingmen and shopkeepers who owed their prosperity to the war boom. Nor were the huge sums lent to the Allies just Wall Street money; they were subscribed by over half a million individual investors. Moreover, the bulk of Allied indebtedness was secured by American and Canadian collateral; even if the Allies had been defeated, American lenders would not have lost their money. In any case there is no evidence that bankers or businessmen attempted to persuade Wilson to declare war. They did not believe American intervention was necessary to avert an Allied defeat. Indeed virtually no one in the United States was aware of the gravity of the Allied position in April 1917. Everyone believed that the Allies were winning.

It was undoubtedly the U-boat that brought the United States into the First World War. Without it there would have been no quarrel with Germany capable of producing armed conflict. If Germany had been prepared to restrict submarine warfare in the way Wilson wanted, the United States may have remained neutral. Wilson's reading of international law was at times faulty and at other times too inflexible. Refusing to recognize how much naval warfare had changed, he insisted upon an outmoded and unrealistic interpretation of neutral rights. But he spoke not merely for Americans but for the world in condemning unrestricted submarine warfare. That was why he felt that its resumption left him no alternative but war.

The American Contribution to Victory

When the United States entered the war the Allies were in dire straits. Russia had begun to slide into anarchy and civil war and would soon cease to be an effective ally. Italy was demoralized and war-weary. The French army, bled white at Verdun and incapable of an offensive, was so riddled with defeatism that ten regiments had mutinied. France and Great Britain were running out of manpower and money. Worst of all the German submarine campaign looked like achieving its object. Allied shipping losses in April amounted to nearly 900,000 tons and Great Britain had only six weeks' supply of food left. But the United States could do little to help immediately. Not for the first time Americans had gone to war without the means to wage one effectively. They had a powerful navy but it consisted mainly of battleships rather than of antisubmarine escort vessels. The United States army was too small to be capable of influencing the fighting on the Western front; it had not even grown to the modest size authorized in 1916. As soon as Wilson and his advisers learned of the weakness of the Allied military situation, they decided to raise a huge expeditionary force. But it took time to train and equip.

The United States Navy promptly sent destroyers to Ireland to assist in antisubmarine patrols. More crucial was the help given to Lloyd George by Admiral Sims and the Secretary of the Navy, Josephus Daniels, in overcoming Admiralty resistance to the convoy system. Introduced in July 1917, convoys dramatically reduced the number of sinkings.

Notwithstanding the national prejudice against conscription Congress promptly passed a Selective Service Act (May 18, 1917). In contrast to the

Civil War no hired substitutes were allowed. By November 1918 three and a half million men had been drafted. Volunteer enlistments raised the total under arms to nearly five million. But equipping this huge new army turned out to be more difficult than raising it. Ambitious programs for the production of war material developed too slowly to have an effect on the war. The manufacture of heavy guns was a case in point; American artillery units on the Western Front had to rely mainly on French 75 mm field guns. For similar reasons most of the planes flown by American pilots were British or French. The American output of tanks was negligible and a huge shipbuilding program was a costly fiasco. Yankee ingenuity on this occasion was found wanting.

Under the command of Major-General John J. Pershing, the first units of the American Expeditionary Force landed in France in June 1917. But almost a year elapsed before American soldiers were present in strength. By March 1918 there were 300,000 "doughboys" in France. Thereafter the buildup was rapid. By Armistice Day the AEF numbered more than two million men. The Allies wanted to ·use American troops piecemeal as replacements for their own battered divisions, but Pershing insisted that the American army should operate independently with its own sector of the front. The first time American forces played an important role was in helping to parry the last great German offensive of March 1918. Then in comparatively small engagements in May and June they pushed the enemy across the Marne at Château-Thierry and Belleau Wood. By September Pershing was at last strong enough to mount a major offensive. Having reduced the St. Mihiel salient, the American army launched an assault on the Meuse–Argonne area as part of a general Allied counteroffensive. The battle, lasting forty-seven days and involving 1,200,000 American troops, was the greatest in American military history. Along with British and French victories elsewhere on the Western Front the Meuse–Argonne offensive helped bring Germany to her knees.

American losses during the war came to 109,000—48,000 killed in action, 2,900 missing, and 59,000 dead from disease. These were heavy considering the length of time the United States was at war and the number of troops involved. But they were light in comparison with the losses of the other belligerents. Russia, for instance, sustained 1,700,000 battlefront deaths, Germany 1,800,000, France 1,385,000, and Great Britain 947,000. For this reason and because the United States entered so late, the Allies were to resent American claims to have "won the war". Nevertheless the Americans provided the Allies with the margin of victory. In March 1918 the Germans outnumbered the Allies on the Western Front by over 300,000; but by November American troops had given the Allies a decisive preponderance of 600,000. Even though the American troops were inexperienced their arrival in seemingly endless numbers had a profound psychological impact. It put fresh heart into the Allies and convinced the Germans that the war was lost.

The Home Front

At home the war brought unprecedented government controls. Federal agencies were created to regulate every branch of the economy. The main vehicle for coordinating industrial production was the War Industries Board, established in July 1917 and reorganized in March 1918. Under the guidance of the financier, Bernard M. Baruch, the Board brought industrial production to a high level of efficiency; it allocated scarce materials, determined priorities, standardized products, and fixed prices. The Food Administration, presided over by Herbert Hoover and given sweeping powers over the production, manufacture, and distribution of foodstuffs, succeeded in boosting food production, trebling food exports to the Allies, and persuading people to ration themselves voluntarily. The Fuel Administration under Harry A. Garfield increased coal and oil production, pegged prices, and as a conservation measure introduced daylight-saving time. In December 1917, with the railroads creaking under the strain of additional wartime traffic, the government took them over. William G. McAdoo, placed in charge of the Railroad Administration, ran the railroads as a single system, integrating timetables, modernizing equipment, standardizing track gauge, and subordinating passenger traffic to war needs. Finally, the National War Labor Board, set up to ensure the most efficient use of manpower, threw its weight on the side of the unions; in return for pledges not to strike it guaranteed collective bargaining and the closed shop and secured improvements in wages and hours.

Government control of the economy did not mean the eclipse of big business. In a striking reversal of its antitrust policy, the Administration encouraged business consolidation in the interests of expanding war production. Yet businessmen were not given *carte blanche* to pile up profits. Some individuals made large fortunes out of wartime demand, but Progressive tax policies cut deeply into higher incomes and shifted an increasing share of the tax burden on to the wealthy.

The war also made possible the enactment of other Progressive reforms. One was Prohibition. The Antisaloon League and its allies could now invoke patriotic necessity to reinforce the medical, moral, religious, and social arguments against drink. They claimed that Prohibition would conserve barley, rye, and other grains and that alcohol lowered the efficiency of war workers and the armed forces. The fact that brewing and distilling were virtually German-American monopolies intensified prejudice against the drink trade. Even before the United States entered the war half the forty-eight states were "dry" by state law or local regulation. In 1917 Congress restricted the use of foodstuffs in the manufacture of liquor, reduced the alcoholic content of beer, and forbade the sale of liquor near army camps. The Prohibition Act of 1918 went even further, forbidding the sale or manufacture of intoxicants during wartime. Finally came the Eighteenth Amendment prohibiting the sale, manufacture, or transport of alcoholic beverages. Passed by Congress in December 1917, it was ratified by the states in January 1919 and went into force a year later.

Woman suffrage, another longstanding Progressive objective, was also achieved during the war. By April 1917 women had gained the vote in only eleven states, all in the West. Shortly afterward the House again turned down an equal-suffrage amendment. But as in Great Britain, the war undermined opposition. It brought women out of the kitchen into the factories and offices and on to the land. Their contribution to the war effort made the demand for political equality hard to resist. Wilson, who had earlier felt that for women to vote was unladylike, now saw woman suffrage as "an essential psychological element in the conduct of the war for democracy". In 1917 New York became the first eastern seaboard state to enfranchise women and in January 1918 the House adopted the Nineteenth Amendment providing for woman suffrage. Southerners blocked it in the Senate for more than a year, but it was ratified in June 1919 and went into force in August 1920.

While the war paved the way for some Progressive reforms, it also led the government into actions that contradicted Progressive ideals. To stimulate patriotism and unite the nation behind the war effort, the Administration set up a Committee on Public Information. Headed by a former muckraking journalist, George Creel, the Committee whipped up hatred of Germany and of anyone thought to sympathize with her. The result was a narrow, coercive, intolerant nationalism, popularly known as 100 percent Americanism. Although the vast majority of German-Americans loyally supported the war, they became the chief victims of popular hatred. Hostility to Germans was carried to extreme, even grotesque, lengths. People with German names were bullied into Americanizing them; school-boards banned the teaching of the German language; Beethoven's music could not be played in Boston; sauerkraut even appeared on menus as liberty cabbage. Not that the Germans were the only sufferers. Pacifists, radicals, indeed anyone whose commitment to the war seemed inadequate, were abused, ridiculed, and forced into symbolic acts of conformity—buying liberty bonds or kissing the American flag.

Far from keeping the superpatriots in check the Wilson Administration egged them on by the use it made of the Espionage Act of June 1917 and the Sedition Act of May 1918. The former measure made it a crime to obstruct military recruitment or attempt to encourage disloyalty. Under its terms the Postmaster General, Albert S. Burleson, barred a number of radical periodicals from the mails, including an issue of *The Masses* for publishing a cartoon entitled "Making the World Safe for Capitalism". In November 1917 a film producer was indicted under the Act for making a film entitled *The Spirit of '76* which showed British atrocities during the American Revolution and which, it was alleged, questioned "the good faith of our ally, Great Britain". Found guilty in a case ironically entitled *U.S.* v. *The Spirit of '76*, he was sentenced to a $10,000 fine and ten years in jail (later commuted to three years). The Sedition Act went even further in restricting free expression. It imposed heavy penalties on anyone who attempted to discourage the sale of war bonds or who uttered or published 'any disloyal, profane, scurrilous language' about the government, the Constitution, or army and naval uniforms. Over 1,500 people were imprisoned under the Act, including the Socialist leader, Eugene V. Debs, who went to jail for ten years for making an antiwar speech. Yet such was the prevailing atmosphere that few Americans seemed concerned at the assault on civil liberties. Not even the Supreme Court questioned the way in which the Administration was conducting a war for freedom and democracy. It upheld both the Espionage Act and the Sedition Act.

Wilson and Peacemaking

This narrow wartime nationalism contrasted strangely with Wilson's grand vision of a new world order based on international cooperation. To him American belligerency seemed to offer an opportunity to assert moral leadership on the international scene. To preserve his freedom of action in peacemaking, as well as to honor the tradition of nonentanglement, he insisted that the United States was at war with Germany not as one of the Allies but simply as an "associated power". Wilson outlined his war aims in an address to Congress on January 8, 1918 embodying the famous Fourteen Points. Eight dealt with specific territorial questions such as the evacuation of Belgium, Romania, Serbia, and occupied parts of France, the restoration of Alsace and Lorraine to France, the creation of an independent Poland, and the granting of an opportunity for autonomous development to the peoples of Austria–Hungary and the non-Turkish nationalities of the Ottoman Empire. Five others laid down general principles of international behavior: freedom of the seas, open diplomacy, equality of economic opportunity, the reduction of armaments, and the adjustment of colonial claims. The fourteenth point—to Wilson the all-important one—provided for the creation of a League of Nations which would keep the peace by arbitrating international disputes and affording mutual guarantees of political independence and territorial integrity to all member states.

The Fourteen Points were enthusiastically received; they seemed to express the hopes and aspirations of people everywhere. But they had been promulgated without consultation with the Allied leaders and in fact ran counter to their purposes. The Allies intended a punitive peace; they wanted to extract huge indemnities from their enemies and annex part of their territories as had been arranged in inter-Allied secret treaties. The divergence between Wilson and the Allies came into the open during the negotiations that led to the end of hostilities in November 1918. Germany approached Wilson for an armistice on the basis of the Fourteen Points and subsequent additions to them. But the Allies would accept the Fourteen Points only with explicit reservations about reparations and the freedom of the seas, and would have insisted on further modifications had the United States not threatened a separate peace.

In October 1918, with the end of the war in sight, Wilson appealed for a Democratic victory in the forthcoming Congressional elections. He had decided to go in person to the peace conference and was anxious to demonstrate that the country was behind him. But the voters gave the Republicans majorities in both houses. Foreign policy had not been the main issue in the elections but, since Wilson had asked for a vote of confidence, his failure to get one could be interpreted as a repudiation of the Fourteen Points. His ill-considered appeal, by offending those Republicans who had supported his foreign policy, also made peacemaking a partisan question. Wilson made a further miscalculation in choosing the peace delegation to accompany him to Paris. Bearing in mind the recent election result and the fact that Republican support would be essential for treaty ratification, he would have been well advised to include a leading Republican. But his determination to retain undisputed control of the peace delegation led him to ignore political realities. The only Republican to be appointed was Henry White, a retired diplomat without influence in his party.

When Wilson arrived in Paris for the start of the peace conference in January 1919, he was confident of making the Fourteen Points a reality. He knew that none of the Allied leaders shared his idealism but the rapturous reception he had received during preconference tours of France, Italy, and Britain had reinforced his conviction that he embodied the hopes of humanity and could count on the support of world opinion. He was profoundly mistaken. Although they had seemed to hail Wilson as a Messiah, the Allied peoples were firmly behind their leaders in demanding a harsh peace.

Yet Wilson achieved remarkable success. He got the map of Europe redrawn so as to accord more nearly with the principle of national self-determination. He induced Clemenceau to abandon his claim to the left bank of the Rhine, though only by agreeing to a treaty—which the Senate never ratified—whereby the United States and Great Britain would come to France's aid in the event of unprovoked German aggression. But Wilson's greatest victory was the incorporation of the League of Nations as an integral part of the peace treaty. It was he who drafted the League

Covenant, Article X of which bound signatories "to respect and preserve against external aggression the territorial integrity and . . . political independence of all members of the League". To secure agreement on the League Wilson had to make concessions. He yielded to the British and French demand for huge—and, as it proved, unpayable—reparations from Germany. He acquiesced in territorial arrangements which offended against the principles of self-determination: thus Italy acquired the Austrian Tyrol and Japan the Chinese province of Shantung. And while he prevented the victors from annexing Germany's former colonies outright, his "mandate" principle gave them all the control they needed. Yet if Wilson did not secure a settlement entirely in accordance with the Fourteen Points, the Treaty of Versailles was a far more disinterested document than it would have been without his influence. And the League Covenant would not have been among its provisions.

The Senate and the Versailles Treaty

During Wilson's absence in Paris domestic opposition to the League grew steadily. Soon after he returned briefly to the United States in February 1919, Henry Cabot Lodge, chairman of the Senate Foreign Relations Committee, presented to the Senate a round robin signed by thirty-nine Republican senators, more than enough to block ratification, indicating that they could not accept the Covenant in its existing form. Wilson 'angrily denounced his Republican critics but on his return to Paris agreed to a number of modifications. These provided for the withdrawal of members from the League, declared that the acceptance of mandates was optional, and made it clear that the League could not interfere in such domestic matters as tariff or immigration policy or infringe upon the Monroe Doctrine. But Wilson would not make concessions on Article X, the main Republican target.

Thus when the President returned finally from Paris in July 1919 Republican hostility was undiminished. Some opponents of the treaty were moved by partisanship and personal animus; they were jealous of Wilson's reception in Europe and wanted to deny him a triumph which might ensure a Democratic victory at the polls in 1920. Others had genuine doubts about the Covenant; they saw Article X as a threat to national sovereignty and were opposed to an automatic commitment to adopt sanctions against aggressors. Only fourteen Republicans, however, were opposed to American participation in any international organization; led by William E. Borah of Idaho and Hiram Johnson of California they were known as the 'irreconcilables'. The rest did not want to reject the treaty but were determined to amend Wilson's handiwork. More than the requisite two-thirds of the Senate favored some form of League membership and so, it would seem, did public opinion. But Lodge's control of the Senate Foreign

Relations Committee enabled him to play for time. The Committee held lengthy hearings and gave full rein to the treaty's opponents, especially the representatives of ethnic minorities. German-Americans condemned the treaty as unjust; Irish-Americans complained that it ignored Ireland's claim to independence; Italian-Americans criticized its failure to award Fiume to Italy. Meanwhile isolationists warned of the dangers of departing from America's traditional policy of nonentanglement and liberals expressed resentment that Wilson had surrendered some of the Fourteen Points.

In the country at large, too, support for the treaty was beginning to drain away. People were becoming bored with the issue. Other worries, like the great steel strike of 1919 and the Red Scare, claimed their attention. The irreconcilables mounted a lavishly financed and increasingly effective propaganda campaign. To counter it Wilson decided to carry his case to the people. Great audiences came to hear him but in late September at Pueblo, Colorado he suffered a stroke that forced him to cancel the rest of the trip and left him a semiinvalid for the rest of his life.

In November the Senate Foreign Relations Committee recommended ratification of the treaty but with a long series of reservations. The most important provided that the United States would not apply economic or military sanctions against aggressors without the consent of Congress. Wilson, lying ill in the White House, recovered sufficiently to exert authority over his party. Believing that the reservations would fatally weaken the League, he urged the Democrats in the Senate to vote against them. When the vote was taken on November 19, 1919, the treaty with reservations was rejected by 55 votes to 38; 42 Democrats joined with 13 irreconcilables to vote it down.

There was still considerable sentiment in favor of the treaty, however, and its friends resolved to try again. They urged Wilson to save the treaty by agreeing to some of the reservations. But the President, his natural obstinacy increased by illness, refused to budge. When the treaty again came up in the Senate on March 19, 1920, some Democrats refused any longer to follow Wilson's lead and the vote was 49 to 35 in favor of the treaty with reservations. But that was seven votes short of the necessary two-thirds majority. Thus the treaty and American membership of the League were killed. Wilson believed that the election of 1920 would be "a great and solemn referendum" on the League. But it proved otherwise. The Democratic candidate, James M. Cox, did indeed call for adherence to the League, but the Republican position was deliberately vague and once elected, Warren G. Harding chose to interpret his landslide victory as a repudiation of the Treaty of Versailles. On July 2, 1921 the United States made a separate peace with Germany.

22. *After the War*, 1919–1929

The Age of Disillusion and Reaction

For the United States World War I was not the catastrophe it was for Europe. It did not leave the country exhausted, impoverished, and in turmoil or fill American towns and villages with war memorials. During the 1920s, there was no continued public observance of Armistice Day as there was in Europe. Far from wanting to commemorate the war Americans seemed eager to forget it. Yet the war had disproportionately traumatic effects. The mood of disillusionment it engendered influenced not only attitudes to the outside world (see Ch. 24) but also many aspects of social, cultural, and political life. It may be that the changes of the 1920s—the eclipse of Progressivism, the recrudescence of nativism, the technological revolution, the challenges to the existing social and moral order—would have happened anyway. Some were already in train before 1914. But the war accelerated and intensified them and also stimulated the forces of conformity and reaction that were to be dominant throughout the 1920s.

The disturbed emotional legacy of the war was first manifested in the 'Red Scare' of 1919. The Bolshevik Revolution in Russia and the formation of the Third International aroused fears of a new alien menace and kept alive the narrow, coercive nationalism of wartime. Xenophobia was no longer directed against alleged German sympathizers but against alien radicals and revolutionaries. Many Americans were alarmed at the pro-Soviet leanings of a militant faction in the American Socialist party and at the emergence of an American Communist movement, largely foreign-born in membership. An accompanying wave of industrial unrest was widely, though wrongly, interpreted as revolutionary. After Seattle had been paralyzed by a five-day general strike in February 1919 protracted and often violent strikes followed in one major industry after another: textiles, railroads, steel, coal. Public opinion became strongly antiunion, especially after the Boston police strike of September 1919 had led to an outbreak of rioting and looting. Fear of revolution increased when homemade bombs were posted to prominent politicians and industrialists and explosions occurred simultaneously in eight different cities (June 2).

The resulting wave of repression was directed against radicals and dissenters of every kind. Congress and the New York state legislature expelled duly elected Socialist members. Thirty-two states passed laws making membership of the IWW and other syndicalist organizations a criminal offense. In two cases decided in 1919—*Schenck* v. *United States* and *Abrams* v. *United States*—the Supreme Court upheld the restraints on free speech and freedom of the press imposed by the wartime Espionage and Sedition Acts. Wilson's Attorney-General, A. Mitchell Palmer, hoping to promote his presidential ambitions by assuming the leadership of an antiradical crusade, launched a series of raids against left-wing organizations in November 1919. 9,000 people were arrested and held without trial; over 500 alien radicals were deported to Russia, among them the well-known anarchists Emma Goldman and Alexander Berkman.

When it became evident that fears of revolution were unfounded, the Red Scare quickly subsided. But that hostility toward alien radicals was undiminished was shown by the celebrated Sacco–Vanzetti case. In the length of time it dragged on, the bitter feelings it aroused, and the way it polarized opinion this was the American equivalent of the Dreyfus Affair. In May 1920, two immigrant Italians, Nicola Sacco and Bartolomeo Vanzetti, admitted anarchists and wartime draft-dodgers, were arrested for armed robbery and murder in South Braintree, Massachusetts. After a trial conducted in a hostile atmosphere by a conservative judge infected with the prevailing fear of radicalism, they were convicted in July 1921 and sentenced to death. There was widespread doubt whether the evidence warranted a conviction. An impressive array of writers, intellectuals, and lawyers—some hardly less biased in the convicted men's favor than the judge had been prejudiced against them—demanded a retrial. But the verdict was upheld on appeal and, after a commission of eminent laymen had decided that the trial had been fair, Sacco and Vanzetti were executed on August 23, 1927, to the accompaniment of worldwide protest. The case inspired plays, novels, poems, and polemics, most of them eulogizing the dead men. In 1961 new ballistics tests seemed to prove that the murders had been committed with Sacco's gun. Nevertheless the two men are still widely regarded as martyrs of the class war.

The Red Scare summer of 1919 also saw a frightening outbreak of racial strife. During World War I a labor shortage in the North resulting from the decline of immigration and the expansion of war factories had led to a huge influx of Southern blacks. Northern industrial cities experienced remarkable increases in their black populations: by 1920 New York had 152,000 blacks (an increase of 66.3 percent during the decade), Philadelphia 134,000 (58.9 percent up), and Chicago 109,000 (148.2 percent up). Blacks found the North no more tolerant than the South. White workers resented the spread of black ghettoes and, when a postwar recession set in, felt that blacks threatened their jobs. A further source of friction was the militancy of returning black soldiers, no longer willing to put up with old patterns of discrimination. In July 1919 there were race riots in twenty towns and cities. The worst occurred in Chicago, where violence went on sporadically for thirteen days: 23 blacks and 15 whites were killed, 537 people injured, and 1,000 families, mostly black, were left homeless.

In these unpromising conditions the NAACP waged a long legal battle against disfranchisement, sought to break down residential segregation and the white primacy, and campaigned for a federal antilynching law. But for all its vigor, and its occasional successes, the NAACP failed to inspire or win a following among the black urban masses. Nor did other black middle-class organizations like the National Urban League. The only leader to do so was Marcus M. Garvey, the flamboyant, Jamaica-born founder of the Universal Negro Improvement Association. Contending that blacks could never hope to win equality in racially prejudiced America, Garvey advocated a "back-to-Africa" movement. Exalting everything black, he glorified the African past and told Negroes that they should be proud of their ancestry. The leaders of established Negro organizations detested Garvey as an ignorant and insincere careerist. They were also repelled by the distinction he drew between dark-skinned and light-skinned Negroes and by his contempt for the latter. But ghetto-dwellers hailed him as a savior. Though uninterested in returning to their African 'Fatherland', they responded enthusiastically to Garvey's appeals to racial pride. With funds they subscribed Garvey established a weekly UNIA newspaper and a variety of auxiliary organizations: the semimilitary Universal African Legion, the Universal Black Cross Nurses, the Black Eagle Flying Corps, and the Black Star Steamship Line. Irregularities in the management of the Black Star Line caused Garvey's downfall. In 1923 he was convicted of using the mails to defraud, imprisoned, and then deported. Garveyism thereupon collapsed and its founder later died in obscurity. But his ideas lived on to inspire the black nationalists of the 1960s.

The Palmer raids were not the only sign that the era of political conservatism, usually associated with the Republican-dominated 1920s, had begun before Woodrow Wilson left the White House. Preoccupied with the fight for the League of Nations and incapacitated by the stroke he suffered in October 1919, Wilson proposed no further reform measures during his last two years in office. In many respects his Administration pointed the direction the Republicans would follow. A bonfire of wartime controls, along with the return of the railroads to private ownership, marked the abandonment of government-imposed economic planning. Further evidence of the revival of *laissez-faire* was the sudden withdrawal of price guarantees to farmers (May 1920). In most of the 1919 strikes the Administration sided with the employers. Palmer secured federal injunctions against striking coal-miners and sent federal troops to help break the steel strike, while Wilson himself denounced the Boston police strike as "a crime against civilization". Sympathy for big business was evident also in the Justice Department's lack of vigor in prosecuting antitrust suits.

Normalcy in Action

The presidential election of 1920 showed that the country had wearied of being kept constantly on its toes. Wilsonian moral fervor, and crusading zeal, whether for domestic reform or a new world order, had gone out of fashion. Confident that the tide was running in their favor, the senatorial cabal which controlled the Republican party insisted upon a thoroughly conservative and tractable candidate. Their choice fell upon one of their less prominent colleagues, Warren G. Harding of Ohio. As his running mate the Republican convention chose Calvin Coolidge who, as governor of Massachusetts, had been credited with having broken the Boston police strike and thus had come to symbolize law and order. The Democrats, demoralized by the controversy over the League of Nations and divided also over Prohibition, nominated for President another relatively obscure Ohioan, the Progressive Governor James M. Cox. He and his running mate, Franklin D. Roosevelt, tried to make membership of the League of Nations the main campaign issue, but the voters were largely indifferent. They were more concerned about rising prices, industrial strife, and the sharp postwar recession, all of which they blamed on the party in power. Harding was ambivalent not only toward the League but toward issues generally. In a characteristically orotund speech before his nomination he had declared that "America's present need is not heroics but healing, not nostrums but normalcy, not surgery but serenity, . . . not experiment but equipoise, not submergence in internationality but sustainment in triumphant nationality." Whatever "normalcy" was supposed to mean, it was apparently what the electorate wanted. Harding won by a greater margin than any previous presidential candidate—though only 49 percent of the electorate voted, compared with 71 percent in 1916.

Harding's platitudinous oratory, intellectual shallowness, and inveterate parochialism contrasted painfully with Wilson's high-minded rhetoric, disciplined mind, and breadth of vision. An amiable, gregarious man who had been a local newspaper editor before entering politics, Harding had made little effort to outgrow his origins. As President he enjoyed the trappings of office but found complex issues beyond him. Nevertheless history has been too harsh on him. He was no bigoted reactionary. Harding freed Debs from jail and welcomed him to the White House. He put pressure on the steel companies to grant an eight-hour day. His administration carried a stage further the kind of Progressive farm legislation—farm credits and the regulation of markets—adopted during Wilson's first Administration. There were also limits to Harding's pliability: thus, he defied the powerful American Legion lobby in 1922 in vetoing a soldiers' bonus bill. Nor was Harding a crude isolationist: his support of arms limitation was crucial to the success of the Washington Conference. And although he had serious limitations he was at least aware of them—pathetically so in fact—and had the grace.to appoint men of distinction and experience to key Cabinet posts. The eminent jurist and former governor of New York, Charles Evans Hughes, became Secretary of State; Herbert Hoover, a mining engineer who had been director of wartime relief to Belgium and head of the Food Administration, was made Secretary of Commerce; Henry C. Wallace, the widely respected editor of an Iowa farm journal, was appointed Secretary of Agriculture; and the multimillionaire Pittsburgh banker and industrialist, Andrew Mellon, became Secretary of the Treasury. Equally well conceived was the choice of ex-President William Howard Taft to be Chief Justice. Unfortunately Harding gave other important posts to his political cronies, the Ohio Gang, who shared his fondness for poker and whiskey but not his sense of public responsibility. Their rascalities were to bring disgrace on the Administration.

The Harding Administration's main characteristic, personified by Mellon's presence at the Treasury, was sympathy for business and financial enterprise. It quickly met the demands of the business community for a program of reduced government spending and sweeping tax cuts. It repealed the wartime excess-profits tax and reduced the surtax on higher incomes, though not by as much as Mellon would have liked. Corporate interests were further gratified by a prompt return to the traditional Republican policy of protection. The Emergency Tariff Act of 1921 was followed a year later by the Fordney–McCumber Act which raised tariffs to unprecedented levels. Although these measures increased duties on farm products as well as on manufactured goods, they were essentially for industry's benefit. In keeping with his belief that government intervention in the economy should be kept to a minimum, Harding filled federal regulatory commissions with men more interested in cooperating with business and industry than in curbing them. As a result the Federal Trade Commission, the Interstate Commerce Commission, and similar agencies virtually ceased to function. And since a lukewarm attitude also prevailed toward the enforcement of the antitrust laws the trend toward business consolidation, temporarily checked during the Progressive period, again became marked, with mergers especially common in banking, public utilities, the automobile industry, and retailing.

The Administration also threw its weight behind the employers in industrial disputes. When a strike of West Virginia miners led to violence in 1921, Harding sent federal troops to restore order. After an even bloodier outbreak in the Illinois coalfields the following year he secured a return to work by promising a federal commission of inquiry. But although the commission revealed the desperate plight of the miners, the President ignored its recommendations. At about the same time his Attorney General ended a bitter railroad strike against wage cuts by obtaining a sweeping court injunction against picketing. Meanwhile, the Supreme Court dealt trade unionism a succession of staggering blows. In *Duplex Printing Press* v. *Deering* (1921) it ruled that the Clayton Act of 1914 had not, as hitherto supposed, conferred immunity upon trade unions from prosecution in respect of such practices as the secondary boycott, the 'blacklist', and mass picketing; nor had it exempted union funds from liability for damages caused by a strike. Already in *Hammer* v. *Dagenhart* (1918) the Supreme Court had declared the Keating–Owen Child Labor Act of 1916 unconstitutional on the ground that Congress could not use its power over interstate commerce to regulate local labor conditions. It employed similar reasoning in *Bailey* v. *Drexel Furniture Company* (1922) to strike down a second Child Labor Act, passed in 1919. (In 1924 a constitutional amendment, designed to give Congress power to regulate child labor, was submitted to the states, but was never ratified.) Finally, in *Adkins* v. *Children's Hospital* (1923) the Court invalidated a District of Columbia minimum-wage law for women.

Early in 1923 it began to emerge that Harding's unworthy appointments and administrative laxity had opened the way to extensive graft, corruption, and extortion. The head of the Veterans' Bureau, Charles R. Forbes, was shown to have misappropriated or wasted no less than $250 million; and Thomas W. Miller, the Alien Property Custodian, was also shown to have accepted bribes. Both were convicted and sent to prison. Among those implicated in Miller's corrupt activities was Jesse Smith, a member of the Ohio Gang and a confidant of the Attorney General, Harry M. Daugherty. Smith had also conducted a flourishing business in the Justice Department, selling pardons and immunity from prosecution to lawbreakers. When the facts began to come out he committed suicide. Daugherty himself was later tried for conspiracy but escaped prison when two successive juries failed to agree. The most sensational scandal involved the lease to private interests of government oil lands earlier set aside for naval use. A Senate investigating committee discovered that Harding's Secretary of the Interior, Albert B. Fall, having secured the transfer of these oil reserves to his own department, had secretly leased those at Elk Hills, California and Teapot Dome, Wyoming to two oil magnates, Edward L. Doheny and Harry F. Sinclair, receiving in return large unsecured 'loans'. Fall was subsequently convicted of receiving a bribe and was sentenced to a fine of $100,000 and a year in prison, thus becoming the first Cabinet member to be convicted on a criminal charge. Astonishingly, because of legal technicalities, Doheny and Sinclair were acquitted of bribery charges.

Harding had taken no part in these shameful transactions and knew nothing about them. But the realization that he had been betrayed by his friends may have contributed to his sudden death during a Western speaking tour, on August 2, 1923. As yet ignorant of the scandals, the public mourned the death of a beloved President. Yet even when the wrongdoing was revealed, there was no violent reaction. Public resentment, indeed, was directed less at the guilty than at the 'character assassins' who exposed them.

The prevailing laxity was one reason why the Republicans suffered less damage from Teapot Dome than might have been expected. Another was the fact that leading Democrats, too, including four members of Wilson's Cabinet, had sought political favors from corrupt interests. In any case the patent rectitude of Harding's successor, Calvin Coolidge, made it difficult to equate Republicans with corruption. Born in a Vermont hamlet the son of a shopkeeper, Coolidge personified the characteristic traits of his Puritan ancestors: thrift, industry, sobriety, honesty. Having worked his way through Amherst College, he prácticed law in nearby Northampton, Massachusetts before entering state politics. He evolved a clear-cut conservative philosophy which combined a Hamiltonian respect for the political virtue of the rich with a Jeffersonian distrust of government. National well-being, he believed, depended on business leadership; "the business of America is business", he declared. (However, he added, "the ideal of America is idealism".) Thus the federal government should limit its activities to serving business. Liberal intellectuals, repelled by the prim, narrow New Englander, told mocking stories about his alleged somnolence, complacency, and taciturnity. But to most Americans Coolidge's presence in the White House was reassuring; he became a kind of national totem figure, a cherished symbol of traditional values threatened by the forces of change.

Nationalism, Conformity, and Social Disunity

In spite of the general prosperity of the 1920s many old-stock Americans were haunted by the fear that their society was being undermined. Alarmed at the inroads being made upon èstablished beliefs and customs, they yearned to put the clock back. Hence the defensive, moralistic, intolerant temper which manifested itself in such apparently unrelated phenomena as immigration restriction, the Ku Klux Klan, religious fundamentalism, and the prohibition experiment.

The revulsion against Europe that followed the collapse of Wilsonian internationalism gave new strength to the immigration-restriction movement. So did the Red Scare and the postwar economic recession. New barriers seemed all the more necessary since the literacy test of 1917, designed to exclude immigrants from southern and eastern Europe, had manifestly failed to do so. With racialism in the ascendant, politicians,

newspaper editors, and popular writers conjured up the related specters
of racial degeneration and national decline. America's old 'Anglo-Saxon'
stock, they warned, was in danger of being swamped by hordes of 'new'
immigrants—"the weak, the broken and the mentally crippled", as one
restrictionist put it.

In response to the clamor Congress hastily passed an Emergency Quota
Act in 1921. The first measure to impose quantitative restrictions on
immigration, it set a limit of 357,000 a year and established quotas for each
eligible national group at 3 percent of the number of foreign-born residents
in the United States in 1910. That meant a drastic reduction in the number
of 'new' immigrants. The National Origins Act of 1924 tilted the balance
still further against them. As well as reducing immigration to 165,000 a
year it cut quotas to 2 percent of the number of each national group in the
United States in 1890—that is, before immigrants from southern and eastern Europe had begun to preponderate. The Act also laid down a permanent immigration policy. When it went into effect in 1929, immigration
was limited to 150,000 a year and a quota was allocated to each nationality
according to its contribution to the existing American population. In practice, about 86 percent of the quotas were allocated to the countries of
northern and western Europe. The Western Hemisphere was exempted
from these restrictions, largely because powerful Southwestern economic
interests were dependent on Mexican labor. On the other hand, the Act
totally prohibited immigration from most Asian countries. This step, terminating the Gentlemen's Agreement of 1907–8, was deeply resented in
Japan. The immigration-restriction laws of 1921 and 1924 represented a
sharp break with the past. Designed to stabilize the ethnic composition of
the American population by reducing immigration to a trickle, it amounted
to a repudiation of the asylum tradition.

Ethnic and racial tensions also explained the dramatic rise of the Ku
Klux Klan. Like the Reconstruction organization from which it took its
name, its hooded regalia, and its elaborate, secret ritual, the new Klan
originated as a Southern, white supremacist movement. It was founded in
Georgia in 1915 by a Methodist circuit rider and insurance salesman, William J. Simmons, who had been influenced by D. W. Griffith's film epic,
The Birth of a Nation, glorifying the earlier Klan. But the revived organ-
isation soon became national rather than sectional and developed broader
objectives than its forerunner. Professing to stand for Americanism, Christianity, and morality and proclaiming the virtues of the ballot-box, a free
press, and law enforcement, the Klan served as a focus for militant patriotism. Many were attracted also by its spectacular initiation ceremonies
and its paraphernalia of oaths, secret grips, passwords, and absurd titles.
But the Klan was essentially negative and exclusive. Membership was open
only to "native born, white American citizens, who believe in the tenets

of the Christian religion, and who owe no allegiance . . . to any foreign government or institution, religious or political". As time went on Klan hostility was directed, not so much against blacks, as against those other minorities—Catholics, Jews, and foreigners—who, along with drink, dancing, and short skirts, were supposedly undermining American values.

From 1920, when two professional fund-raisers took charge of recruitment, the Klan expanded phenomenally, especially in the Middle West, the South West, and the Pacific coast. By 1925 it had over two million members. Contrary to what was long believed it was not exclusively or even mainly a rural and small-town movement. Its strength lay in fast-growing cities like Dallas, Memphis, Detroit, Youngstown, Indianapolis, San Antonio, Denver, and Los Angeles, whose residential neighborhoods were being transformed by European immigrants and Southern blacks. The Klan's support came chiefly from victims of declining status: blue-collar workers, clerks, small professional and business men who were being worsted by newcomers in the competition for jobs and housing. Especially in the South Klansmen resorted to floggings, brandings, mutilation, church-burnings, even murder, in order to terrorize people deemed un-American or immoral. But the vast majority of Klan members had no part in lawlessness. Often they were themselves victims of violence. Known or suspected Klansmen were assaulted, Klan property was bombed and set on fire, Klan gatherings broken up by armed mobs. The Catholic Mayor of Boston banned Klan meetings, even in private houses, while the Chicago City Council ordered the dismissal of any municipal employee found to be a Klansman. Thus, the 'Invisible Empire''s intolerance was matched by that of its opponents.

Ostensibly nonpolitical, the Klan nonetheless controlled politics in a number of Western and South-Western states. But after reaching a peak in 1925 its political influence plummeted. Emotional fervor proved difficult to sustain without a positive program; popular opposition became more vocal and more violent. Then came a well-publicized sexual and political scandal in Indiana, the state it dominated most completely. In November 1925, David C. Stephenson, Grand Dragon of the Indiana Klan and a well-known crusader against vice, was convicted of kidnaping and raping a girl secretary, causing her to commit suicide. Failing to obtain a pardon, he exposed Klan corruption involving leading state officials. This prompted wholesale desertions from a movement which had become, in the words of one contemporary critic, "a travesty of patriotism and a blasphemous caricature of religion".

The intellectual and moral gulf between the old America and the new was perhaps most sharply defined in the famous 'monkey trial' at Dayton, Tennessee in 1925. Modernist attempts to reconcile science and religion, and the growing acceptance of modernism in schools and universities incensed those American Protestants—possibly a majority—who believed in the literal truth of the Bible. Not all defenders of the old-time religion were benighted yokels, as their critics frequently claimed; some were sophisticated and learned theologians. Nonetheless fundamentalism drew its greatest strength from rural areas in the South and the Middle West. In the South more than religion was at stake: evolution seemed to threaten the basis of white racial supremacy. Soon after the war troubled fundamentalists, led by William Jennings Bryan, launched a spirited campaign for antievolution laws, and in 1925 secured a Tennessee law forbidding the teaching in the public schools of any evolutionary theory that denied the Genesis version of the creation. Immediately afterward John T. Scopes, a young high-school biology teacher in the small town of Dayton, was arrested for violating the law. The trial attracted enormous publicity and produced a dramatic confrontation between Bryan, who had agreed to assist the prosecution, and the country's leading defense lawyer, Clarence Darrow of Chicago, an avowed agnostic. To Darrow and the American Civil Liberties Union, which financed the defense, the issue was academic freedom. But many spokesmen for Darwinism and modern science, not least the author of the biology textbook Scopes had used, were no less dogmatic and intolerant than their fundamentalist antagonists. Scopes was convicted and fined and on appeal the constitutionality of the Tennessee law was upheld—it was not repealed until 1967. Shortly afterward three other Southern states adopted antievolution laws. Yet fundamentalism had suffered a damaging blow. Bryan had claimed to be an expert on the Bible, but Darrow's withering crossexamination exposed his ignorance and muddleheadedness. A few days after the trial the Great Commoner died of a stroke.

The Prohibition experiment reflected a utopian faith that the alcohol problem could be eradicated by legislation. But the Eighteenth Amendment, effective on January 16, 1920, and the Volstead Act of 1919, passed to implement it, proved impossible to enforce. Thousands of illicit stills were seized, millions of gallons of wine and spirits were destroyed, and jail sentences for liquor offenses rose to 44,678 in 1932, by which time federal prisons were near bursting. But because of Congressional parsimony there were never enough enforcement agents—only 1,520 in 1920 and 2,836 in 1930. Mostly political appointees, they were poorly paid and thus susceptible to bribery. A more fundamental difficulty was the extent of popular opposition. A sizable minority, including both the very rich and the immigrant working class, regarded Prohibition as an intolerable infringement of personal liberty and simply defied it. Evasion took ingenious forms. "Bootleggers" smuggled in liquor from the West Indies and the Bahamas or across the Canadian and Mexican borders. Industrial alcohol was redistilled and converted into synthetic gin and whiskey, some of it poisonous, even lethal. Domestic distillers illicitly manufactured "moonshine" and "mountain dew", countless individuals brewed their own beer or made "bathtub gin", sacramental wine was diverted into non-sacramental channels, and obliging doctors supplied liquor prescriptions to chronic sufferers from "thirstitis". In small towns and rural areas the Volstead Act was fairly well observed and in the country as a whole drinking declined: there was a marked drop in alcoholism and fewer arrests for drunkenness. But in communities opposed to Prohibition, the law was flouted with impunity. "Speakeasies" (illicit saloons) and night clubs (a rather elastic term) flourished under the protection of the great city machines. In 1929 New York City possessed 32,000 speakeasies—twice the number of its saloons before Prohibition began.

The worst consequence of Prohibition was to stimulate organized crime. Attracted by huge profits, underworld gangs set out to control the illicit liquor business. They established their own breweries, distilleries, and distribution networks, surrounded themselves with private armies, intimidated or murdered competitors, and blackmailed speakeasy proprietors into paying for 'protection'. Having built liquor monopolies the gangs branched out into other 'rackets' like gambling, prostitution, and narcotics and also preyed on legitimate businesses. Their corrupt alliances with politicians, policemen, and judges enabled them to dominate certain city governments. Such methods explained the rise of Al Capone, Chicago's leading racketeer, whose depredations by 1927 brought in $60 million annually. Gangland wars were commonplace during Capone's heyday; more than 500 gang murders occurred in Chicago between 1927 and 1930, nearly all of them unpunished.

The evident failure of the Eighteenth Amendment produced a growing demand for repeal. But the 'dry' forces, particularly strong among rural fundamentalists, remained obsessively devoted to what Hoover described in 1928 as "a great social and economic experiment, noble in motive and far-reaching in purpose". However the struggle over repeal was not a simple matter of rural fundamentalist bigotry against urban cosmopolitan liberalism. Supporters of the Eighteenth Amendment included many social workers concerned about the damaging social effects of alcoholism. Its opponents numbered not only brewers and distillers but also a group of millionaire businessmen who financed the Association Against the Prohibition Amendment in the belief that a restored tax on alcohol would mean income-tax reductions. The Wickersham Commission, appointed in 1929, acknowledged that Prohibition had been a failure but somewhat illogically recommended its continuance. However, the onset of the Great Depression supplied the 'wets' with fresh arguments. The restarting of the brewing and distilling industries would, it was said, provide employment for a million men, besides benefiting the farmer, while a revived liquor tax would swell depleted federal and state revenues. In the 1932 election the Democrats advocated repeal and, immediately they had won, Congress passed the Twenty-First Amendment, repealing the Eighteenth. By December 1933, the repeal amendment had been ratified and control over drinking reverted to the states. Only seven of them, mostly Southern, voted to retain Prohibition.

Prohibition and antievolution were part of a wider movement to enforce moral and intellectual conformity by law. State legislation already prohibited various secular activities on the Sabbath, outlawed most forms of gambling, and restricted or forbade the dissemination of birth-control information and the sale of contraceptive devices. Now came a fresh crop of proscriptions, some of them bizarre. Some municipalities banned "indecent" bathing-costumes, many states made "petting" a crime, along with extramarital sexual intercourse. That indefatigable crusader against vice, Anthony Comstock, had died in 1915 but his spirit lived on in strict local censorship of books, plays, and films. Anything the authorities deemed obscene or immoral was liable to seizure or suppression. Customs officials refused to allow the importation of the works of Ovid and Rabelais, Voltaire's *Candide*, and James Joyce's *Ulysses*; the Los Angeles District Attorney's office shut down a touring performance of *Desire Under The Elms*. The motion-picture industry, reacting to adverse publicity about Hollywood sex scandals, established its own censorship board in 1922, with Harding's former Postmaster General, Will H. Hays, at its head. But the strict moral standards Hays set did not always save films from further cuts at the hands of state censors. Meanwhile censorship found an alternative target in "unpatriotic" history books. In New York and Chicago investigating committees solemnly examined textbooks alleged to be unduly sympathetic to the British point of view in 1776; Oregon and Wisconsin even banned such books from the public schools.

The social, sectional, and religious antagonisms reflected in the controversies over immigration, the Klan, and Prohibition deeply divided the Democratic party, producing a long and furious battle at its 1924 convention. Southern and Western Democrats, mostly rural, Protestant, and 'dry', favored William G. McAdoo, Wilson's Secretary of the Treasury, for the presidential nomination. The Northern wing of the party, predominantly urban and 'wet', backed Governor Alfred E. Smith of New York, a Catholic and a product of Tammany Hall. With the contending forces evenly matched, and a two-thirds majority needed for nomination, the Convention remained deadlocked for sixteen days. Finally McAdoo and Smith withdrew by mutual agreement and on the 103rd ballot the weary delegates compromised on John W. Davis, a New York corporation lawyer.

Coolidge, the Business Boom, and the Cult of Prosperity

Since the Republicans had earlier renominated Coolidge, there were now two conservative presidential candidates with virtually identical platforms. But a genuine alternative appeared when a coalition of discontented Western farmers, trade-union leaders, Socialists, and surviving Progressives nominated Robert M. La Follette as the candidate of a new Progressive Party. Its platform, denounced by Republicans and Democrats alike as dangerously radical, condemned monopoly, demanded the nationalization of the railroads and of hydroelectric power, and proposed tariff reduction, federal aid to farmers, the prohibition of injunctions in labor disputes, the popular election of judges, and the limitation of judicial review. La Follette waged a vigorous campaign, Davis a colorless one, while Coolidge hardly campaigned at all. The result was a crushing Republican victory. La Follette had hoped to win enough electoral votes to throw the election to the House of Representatives, but carried only his own state of Wisconsin. Organized labor cooled toward him during the campaign and he was further weakened by a sudden rise in farm prices. The five million votes he received were not necessarily proof of the surviving strength of Progressivism. Many who voted for him, especially German-Americans, were simply registering retroactive approval of his antiwar stand in 1917. Immediately after the election the Progressive Party began to disintegrate and after La Follette's death in 1925 it disappeared.

Coolidge's lopsided victory heralded an extension of Republican pro-business policies. In 1926 Mellon persuaded Congress to make further drastic reductions in taxation. Justified as a means of releasing funds for productive investment, they may have stimulated the stock-market speculation that preceded the 1929 Wall Street crash. Despite the cuts government expenditure was kept so low that, between 1923 and 1929, it was possible to pay off a quarter of the National Debt. Businessmen found another effective champion in Hoover. As Secretary of Commerce he urged commercial attachés abroad to seek orders for American industry and encouraged the formation of trade associations which adopted codes of fair practice, promoted efficiency, and maintained prices and profits by adjusting production to demand.

For most of the 1920s the benign Republican attitude to business seemed to be spectacularly vindicated. Once the brief depression of 1921–2 was over the country entered an era of unparalleled prosperity. Business made huge profits, jobs were generally easy to find, standards of living rose appreciably. The key to the boom was a tremendous increase in productivity resulting from technological innovation and the application of Frederick W. Taylor's theory of scientific management. Although the population increased by only about 16 percent during the decade, industrial production almost doubled. The gross national product soared from $72.4 billion in 1919 to $104 billion in 1929, and annual per capita income rose from $710 to $857.

Whereas the industrial expansion of the late nineteenth century had been based on railroads and steel, the prosperity of the 1920s rested on the growth of newer industries and on a building boom. The cutting-off of foreign supplies during World War I boosted the American chemicals industry and encouraged the manufacture of synthetic textiles and plastics. During the 1920s artificial silk (rayon), bakelite, and cellulose products like celanese, celluloid, and cellophane all became important industries. More striking still was the rise of the electricity industry. There were revolutionary technical advances: the development of new sources of power, such as steam turbines and hydroelectric plants, improvements in generator design and in methods of transmitting power, the adoption of the grid system. Electricity consumption more than doubled during the decade, mainly because of increased industrial demand. But domestic consumption shot up too. Whereas in 1912 only 16 percent of the population lived in electrically lit dwellings, the proportion had grown to 63 percent by 1927. With the price of electricity falling steadily, electrical household appliances came into general use. For the first time electric cookers, irons, refrigerators, fans, toasters, and other gadgets were mass produced. Thus refrigerator production increased from 5,000 a year in 1921 to about one million in 1930.

Another important new industry was radio. On November 2, 1920, the first broadcasting station in the United States, KDKA in East Pittsburgh, began regular services with the presidential-election returns. Unlike Great Britain, which granted a broadcasting monopoly to a public corporation, the United States allowed private enterprise to develop the new medium. Privately owned and operated stations were financed by advertisers who "sponsored" particular programs. The earliest stations were set up by the manufacturers of radio equipment but commercial broadcasting companies gradually dominated the field. The National Broadcasting Company (NBC) established the first national radio network in 1926; the Columbia Broadcasting System (CBS) created another the following year. In 1927, when the number of stations had grown to 732, Congress belatedly established a regulatory commission to license stations and assign wavelengths. Hardly more than a toy before the war, radio soon became almost a standard household fixture. According to the census of 1930, 40 percent of all American families possessed one.

The 1920s also saw aviation come of age. As early as December 17, 1903 Orville and Wilbur Wright, two young mechanics who kept a bicycle shop in Dayton, Ohio, became the first men to fly in a motor-driven machine heavier than air. Their first flight, at Kitty Hawk, North Carolina, understandably attracted little attention: it lasted a mere twelve seconds and covered only 120 feet. World War I demonstrated the new machine's feasibility, but the United States at first lagged behind Europe in developing commercial aviation. Army pilots inaugurated the first regular airmail service, between Washington and New York, in May 1918 and two years later extended it across the continent. Not until 1925, when Congress passed a measure subsidizing the carriage of mail by private airlines, did air transport begin to expand. Then in May 1927, Charles A. Lindbergh, a twenty-five-year-old airline pilot, made the first solo nonstop transatlantic flight. Leaving New York in his tiny monoplane, *The Spirit of St. Louis*, he landed in Paris thirty-three and a half hours later. Lindbergh's exploit made him a national hero and greatly stimulated popular interest in flying. Rapid progress followed. By 1930, 50,000 miles of air routes were in operation in the United States and the airlines were carrying nearly half a million passengers annually.

What contributed most to the business boom was the automobile revolution. Its architect was a Michigan farm-boy, Henry Ford. By adapting the assembly line and the conveyor belt to car production, and concentrating on a single, standardized model, the famous Model T, Ford brought the automobile to the masses. By 1925 he was producing a car every ten seconds and the Model T could be bought for only $290. There was formidable competition from other low-price car manufacturers, notably General Motors and Chrysler, who offered more stylish models. But Ford remained the industry's dominant figure. In 1920 about nine million cars were registered in the United States; by 1929 there were nearly 27 million, that is, one car for every five Americans. With production running at nearly five million cars a year, the automobile industry had become big business. It employed 447,000 workers, about 7 percent of all manufacturing wage-earners, and accounted for over 12 percent of the value of the country's manufacture. The car industry's contribution to the national economy was, however, far greater than these figures imply. It consumed 15 percent of all the steel produced in the United States, 80 percent of the rubber and nickel, 75 percent of the plate glass, as well as great quantities of leather, paint, lead, and other products. It also laid the foundation of another great industry—oil. Finally the spread of motoring stimulated public spending on roads. In the early days of the automobile there were few good, all-weather roads except in the East, but in the 1920s well over $1 billion a year was spent on highway construction and maintenance and the amount of paved road almost doubled.

Large-scale road-building was only one reason for the buoyancy of the construction industry. The accelerated movement from the countryside to the cities and from cities to suburbs led to a massive increase in residential development. The spread of suburbia provided further testimony to the influence of the automobile. Queens, one of the five New York boroughs situated across the East River from Manhattan, doubled its population in the 1920s; Grosse Pointe (Detroit) and Elmwood Park (Chicago) expanded sevenfold; the Cleveland suburb of Shaker Heights multiplied ten times. Industrial and commercial construction also went on apace. Skyscrapers proliferated, as often for reasons of prestige as from considerations of economy. By 1929 the United States had nearly 400 skyscrapers—buildings over twenty stories high. New York City had the largest number, especially of the tallest. The 102-story Empire State Building, completed in 1931 and affording office accommodation for 25,000 people, soared to 1,250 feet to become the tallest building in the world.

To most industrial workers prosperity brought substantial gains. Hours of work declined, real wages increased by 26 percent, unemployment fell from 11.9 percent in 1921 to 3.2 percent in 1929. Other benefits accrued when employers, attempting to head off labor unrest, resorted to "welfare capitalism". They improved working conditions, extended recreational facilities, introduced profit-sharing, group life insurance, and pension plans, and enabled employees to buy company stock at less than the market price. They also sponsored "company unions" which, though lacking bargaining power and possessing neither the authority nor the funds to call strikes, enabled workers' representatives to meet management to discuss individual grievances, plant safety, and productive efficiency. Simultaneously employers' organizations launched a concerted open-shop campaign. By labeling it the 'American Plan', they conveyed the impression that opposition was somehow unpatriotic and subversive. Employers also sought to prevent or suppress unionism by using strike-breakers, private police, spies, and *agents provocateurs*. These tactics, together with the antiunion bias of the courts—and indeed of public opinion—weakened the unions, especially those which had grown most during the war. Union membership fell from about 5 million in 1920 to 3½ million in 1929. Conservative union leadership was also to blame. Neither Samuel Gompers nor William Green, who succeeded him as president of the AF of L in 1924, attempted to extend the boundaries of unionism to the great mass-production industries.

Some groups lay outside the general prosperity. There were areas of more or less permanent slump, like the textile towns of New England and the Southern piedmont, and the coal-mining regions of Kentucky and Illinois. Agricultural distress, too, was widespread. During World War I agriculture had been buoyant but by 1920 a decline in foreign demand and the withdrawal of government price supports had brought a drastic fall in farm prices. Subsequently there was some recovery: dairy farmers and fruit- and vegetable-growers, in particular, did well as nearby city markets expanded. But the great mass of American farmers remained debt-ridden and depressed. The agricultural crisis prompted the formation of a bipartisan, mainly Middle Western, farm bloc in Congress. It pushed through the Capper–Volstead Act (1922), which exempted farm cooperatives from antitrust laws, and the Intermediate Credit Act (1923), which established banks to make loans to organized groups of farmers. It also proposed a complicated price-support scheme aimed at preventing exportable farm surpluses from depressing domestic prices. After several years of debate the McNary–Haugen bill embodying this scheme was passed by Congress in 1927 and in revised from in 1928. But on both occasions Coolidge vetoed it as unconstitutional, preferential legislation, calculated to encourage overproduction and set up a vast bureaucracy.

American Society in the Jazz Age

Though the new technologically dominated economy did not distribute its benefits equally, people in general had more money and more leisure. The motor car meant greater mobility and freedom and enabled the young to escape from parental supervision. Almost as important in transforming American folkways were the mass-audience films churned out by Hollywood. Cinema-going now became a national habit. The appearance in 1927 of the first full-length talking picture, *The Jazz Singer*, starring Al Jolson, swelled cinema audiences still further. Increased leisure led to a variety of fads and crazes like dance marathons and flagpole sitting and to a boom in spectator sports. Baseball, football, and boxing attracted huge crowds. Leading athletes like Babe Ruth of the New York Yankees, Harold 'Red' Grange, the University of Illinois football star, and Jack Dempsey, world heavyweight champion from 1919 to 1926, became national celebrities.

If relentless materialism and carefree pleasure-seeking were features of the decade so, too, were rebellion and protest. Spokesmen for the younger generation were fiercely critical of traditional codes of behavior. Puritanism and Victorianism became pejorative terms. There was much discussion of Freud's sexual theories, a new frankness in novels and plays, and a widespread obsession with sex which magazines, tabloid newspapers, and Hollywood (even after its gesture at self-censorship) were quick to exploit. Youthful restlessness also explained the growing popularity of jazz. The creation largely of New Orleans black musicians, jazz outgrew its local origins after 1917, spreading to Chicago, Kansas City, New York, and the West Coast to become a national idiom. While the New Orleans style survived in the bands of King Oliver and in the work of black soloists like Louis Armstrong and 'Jelly Roll' Morton, the new music gained wide acceptance only when white orchestras, notably Paul Whiteman's, adapted and diluted it. Many older people denounced jazz as crude, even degenerate, and were alarmed by the new dance forms it inspired. Even before the war the tango and the foxtrot had displaced more decorous forms. Now came the Charleston and the 'black bottom', whose frantic contortions and uninhibited embraces seemed proof to conservatives of collapsing standards of sexual morality. In fact there were probably fewer changes in sexual behavior than contemporaries believed. Much of the talk of 'flaming youth' was exaggerated. Though they thought of themselves as wild and daring, and indeed were so by earlier standards, the young of the 1920s seem from a present-day perspective.to have been fairly conventional in dress, career expectations, and lifestyles.

A much-publicized aspect of the revolt against Victorianism was women's repudiation of the restrictions traditionally placed on their appearance and behavior. They wore shorter skirts, discarded corsets, bobbed their hair, and used more cosmetics. The more daring challenged the old proprieties by demanding and sometimes asserting the right to drink and smoke in public. Some even claimed the same sexual freedom as men. These developments are frequently cited to show that this was a time of women's emancipation. But it was nothing of the kind. Beneath the appearance of change there was an underlying continuity in women's political, economic, and social status. Although the Nineteenth Amendment had nominally granted them political equality, women still played an insignificant part in politics. They were less likely than men to vote and even when they did tended to follow the political preferences of their menfolk. Female office-holding was largely a 'widows' game': of the handful of women who served in Congress in the 1920s two-thirds inherited the seats of their late husbands, most for only one term. Nor did women make appreciable progress toward economic equality. While the number of gainfully employed women rose during the decade from 8.2 million to 10.4 million the overall percentage remained more or less stable. The majority of working women were still to be found in menial occupations. Those in the professions were overwhelmingly in teaching, nursing, and other 'female jobs'; only a handful broke into male-dominated professions like law and medicine. Poorly paid in general, women earned substantially less than men even for comparable work and were rarely given managerial or supervisory positions. All this reflected the persistence of social norms which prescribed separate spheres of activity for the sexes and insisted that women's primary responsibility was to the home and the family. Only within the domestic sphere could women be said to have become more independent. Electrical household appliances and processed foods freed them from much drudgery. They bore fewer children and found it easier to escape from unsatisfactory marriages. Birth-control, increasingly practised despite statutory obstacles, brought the birth-rate down dramatically, from 27.7 percent in 1920 to 21.3 percent in 1930. In the same period the ratio of divorces to marriages rose from about one in eight to one in six.

As had long been the case, two-thirds of all divorces were granted to women.

Literature and Rebellion

Alienation and rebellion expressed themselves most sharply in literature. Disillusioned by the war and repelled by the prevailing materialism and conformity a new generation of writers launched a scathing indictment of modern civilization in general and of America in particular. Some rebels sought escape in the Bohemian atmosphere of Greenwich Village in Lower Manhattan; others became expatriates, leading more or less self-indulgent lives in Europe, chiefly in Paris. But wherever they lived the writers of the 1920s displayed a rare creativity. The most vitriolic and widely-read critic was the journalist Henry Louis Mencken, who ridiculed not only the established social, sexual, and aesthetic conventions but democracy itself, along with the mass of mankind. More restrained and sensitive was the novelist Sinclair Lewis, the first American to be awarded a Nobel Prize for literature. His *Main Street* (1920) was a satirical though affectionate portrait of small-town America, while *Babbitt* (1922) caricatured the complacent, conformist, materialistic businessmen. Another Midwesterner to expose the sterility and bigotry of small-town life was Sherwood Anderson, whose first widely successful book was *Winesburg, Ohio* (1919). More gifted were two expatriate novelists, Ernest Hemingway and F. Scott Fitzgerald. Hemingway, writing in a laconic, staccato style which was greatly admired, depicted the meaningless lives of cynical, disenchanted expatriates in *The Sun Also Rises* (1926) and exposed the sham idealism of war in *A Farewell to Arms* (1929). Fitzgerald wrote mainly about the spiritual and moral bankruptcy of the American upper class to which, ironically, he aspired. *This Side Of Paradise* (1920), describing life at Princeton among bored, callow, blasé undergraduates, was a best seller, but Fitzgerald's finest novel, *The Great Gatsby* (1926), a devastating portrait of the world of wealth, was coolly received. A third new talent, William Faulkner, had little in common with the rebels of the 'lost generation'. Unconcerned with the shortcomings of the business culture, he tried to probe the meaning of human existence by focusing on the dissolution of traditional values in his own region, the South. In *The Sound and the Fury* (1929), *As I Lay Dying* (1930), *Sanctuary* (1931), and *Light in August* (1932), Faulkner used confused time-sequences and a complex, highly symbolic, stream-of-consciousness style which baffled many readers. Ultimately, however, critics would acclaim him as the one indisputably great American novelist of the century. Another major figure to experiment with new literary techniques was the playwright, Eugene O'Neill, who combined the realism of Ibsen with the expressionist fantasies of Strindberg and Brecht to create new possibilities for the American stage. *The Emperor Jones* (1920), *Desire*

Under The Elms (1924), *Strange Interlude* (1928), *Mourning Becomes Electra* (1931), and other powerful plays established O'Neill as America's foremost dramatist.

Meanwhile, the poetic revival begun before World War I had lost none of its vitality. The Illinois trio, Carl Sandburg, Vachel Lindsay, and Edgar Lee Masters, consolidated their reputations; the New Englander, Edwin Arlington Robinson, belatedly received critical recognition with a series of long, psychological, narrative poems; Robert Frost, William Carlos Williams, and Wallace Stevens revealed their full stature. But the pre-eminent figure in poetry, and also in criticism, was T. S. Eliot. Born in St. Louis but now living permanently in London, Eliot shared with another expatriate, Ezra Pound, the leadership of a movement which broke decisively with the conventions and stereotypes of romantic nineteenth-century verse. His long, allegorical poem, *The Waste Land* (1922), lamenting the spiritual desolation of modern life, became a classic overnight and greatly influenced other poets. Finally, there was the 'Harlem Renaissance', wrongly named since this was the first substantial outpouring of black literary talent. The poetry of Langston Hughes and Countee Cullen and the prose of Claude McKay and Walter White are remarkable chiefly for their insight into the psychological effects of racial prejudice and the problem of American Negro identity. But the vogue black writing enjoyed in the white intellectual and literary world owed as much to its rebelliousness as to its artistic merit.

The Election of 1928

Coolidge remained so popular that he could have had the Republican nomination in 1928 had he wanted it. But his refusal to be a candidate opened the way for the selection of Herbert Hoover. An Iowa farm-boy orphaned at nine, Hoover epitomized the self-made man. After graduating from Stanford University he managed mining enterprises in many parts of the world and became a millionaire before he was forty. His war-relief work established his reputation as a humanitarian, while his efficient handling of the Department of Commerce won him the confidence of businessmen. The Republican platform called for continued tariff protection, tax cuts, and government economy, promised a measure of farm relief, and upheld Prohibition. The Democrats were still badly split but Al Smith, who had twice been reelected governor of New York since 1924, was so obviously the leading candidate that his claims could no longer be denied. Smith's background contrasted sharply with Hoover's. A Catholic of Irish descent, he grew up in the slums of New York's Lower East Side and left school at fifteen. Entering ward politics in 1904, his loyalty to the Tammany organization enabled him to rise by successive stages to the governorship of New York. Despite his connection with machine politics Smith won a well-deserved reputation for Progressivism. As well as modernizing the state government he promoted a mass of welfare legislation. But he remained an economic conservative, sympathetic to business and opposed to the expansion of federal power. The platform he ran on in 1928 differed only in detail from the Republican one. However, by repudiating the equivocal Democratic plank on Prohibition, and calling for the repeal of the Eighteenth Amendment, Smith created a campaign issue.

Given the prevailing prosperity no Democrat could have won the Presidency in 1928. But Al Smith had additional liabilities which ensured that he would be not only defeated but spurned. Especially in rural America his religion revived fears of popery. Though Hoover scrupulously avoided the religious issue some of his supporters made vitriolic anti-Catholic speeches, predicting that Smith's election would place the United States under papal control. Yet Smith was not simply the victim of religious bigotry. His Catholicism was just one of a complex of characteristics that made him unacceptable to old-stock Americans. His stand on Prohibition, together with his well-known fondness for drink, deeply offended many. His Tammany associations left an ineradicable stigma, notwithstanding his personal integrity. His ignorance of and indifference to the needs of the great agricultural hinterland and his insensitivity to the social and moral aspects of his candidacy showed that he was, as Henry James said of Thoreau, not merely provincial but parochial. Finally, his East Side accent, flashy appearance, and undignified mannerisms, all widely disseminated by radio and the new cinema newsreels, added to the feeling that he was not fitted to be President.

Hoover won an overwhelming victory. For the first time since Reconstruction five former Confederate states voted Republican. Yet the long-term outlook for the Democrats was not as gloomy as it seemed. Smith polled twice as many votes as Davis in 1924. Moreover, if his religion handicapped him in the South, it enabled him to break into areas of traditional Republican strength in the North. He won Massachusetts and Rhode Island, the two most urbanized—and most Catholic—states in the Union and, more significant still, carried the nation's twelve largest cities. This portended a momentous political shift which would eventually make the Democrats the normal majority party.

23. The Great Depression, 1929–1939

Origins of the Depression

The Great Depression that began in the autumn of 1929 was the worst in American history. Infinitely more severe than previous slumps, it affected more people and lasted longer. For three grim years the economy spiraled remorselessly downward. Misery and want stalked the entire country. Recovery was slow and halting. A full decade elapsed before prosperity returned. The Depression eventually affected every industrialized country except the Soviet Union as well as economically dependent parts of the world. But the American collapse was more precipitate, more complete than elsewhere, and was psychologically more damaging because it was in such contrast to what had gone before. During the 1920s Americans had enjoyed the highest standard of living ever attained anywhere. Then, almost overnight, the world's richest country was plunged into destitution.

What caused the Great Depression? Economists (as usual) disagree, but it is generally accepted that the prosperity of the 1920s had been built on shaky foundations. The most serious underlying weakness of the economy was that capacity to produce had outrun capacity to consume. One reason for this was that a substantial part of the population—farmers, for example, and workers in declining industries like coal and textiles—had not shared in the general prosperity. Another was that income was maldistributed. Profits and dividends had risen much faster than wages, while Republican tax policies had favored the wealthy. By 1929, 5 percent of the population received a third of the income. On the other hand, 71 percent of the population received incomes of less than $2,500 a year, the minimum generally thought necessary for decent comfort. The mass of the people, though better off than before, were unable to buy their share of consumer goods and thus sustain the prevailing level of mass production. In addition the American banking system was inherently unsound. Unlike most other industrialized countries, the United States had large numbers of independent banks—over 30,000 in 1921—a large proportion of them small country banks with limited assets. Inadequate regulation, incompetent and dishonest management, and the fact that only a third of the total were members of the Federal Reserve System meant that many were extremely vulnerable if a run developed. In the 1920s no fewer than 5,000 had failed. Equally faulty was the corporate structure. The proliferation of investment trusts and holding companies had opened the way to unscrupulous promoters bent on siphoning off company profits. American foreign trade, too, was precariously poised. The United States exported heavily but because of high American tariffs foreign countries could cover their adverse trade balances only through American loans. Thus, if American lending were curtailed—as happened in 1928—exports would suffer. A further element of instability was the rapid expansion of the hire-purchase system, which sustained buying power for a time but could not go on indefinitely. At the same time the Federal Reserve System's low-interest, cheap-money policy encouraged wild lending, not least for stock-market speculation. Implicit in each of these structural weaknesses was a major economic disturbance. Their conjunction explained the severity of the Depression and, along with the inadequacy of the remedies attempted, its long-drawn-out character.

Even before 1929 there were signs that all was not well with the economy, the earliest being the collapse of the great Florida land boom in 1926. In the next two years house-building slowed down, the demand for automobiles tapered off, private investment began to dry up, inventories lengthened, exports declined. But the illusion of health was preserved for a while by the extraordinary vigor of the stock-market. A speculative mania seized large numbers of people who had had no previous experience of 'playing the market'. In the prevailing 'get-rich-quick' atmosphere, they bought stocks recklessly, often on borrowed money, still more often 'on margin', that is, by paying only a fraction of the purchase price. This flood of speculation boosted stock prices to unheard-of heights. In the two years beginning in mid-1927, the average price of common stocks increased 300 percent. By the autumn of 1929 the market had so patently lost touch with reality that some large speculators began liquidating their holdings. In mid-September prices fell sharply and then on October 24 (Black Thursday) plunged downwards in a wave of panic-stricken selling. The slide was curbed for a few days but on October 29 became a stampede. The gains of months vanished in a few hours, ruining hundreds of investors, large and small. Yet this was not the end. During the next three years prices continued to drift down helplessly. In September 1929 industrials stood at 452; by November they were down to 229; by July 1932 they hit rock-bottom at 58.

The Wall Street crash set off a devastating economic collapse. Business confidence evaporated, bankruptcies and bank failures multiplied, families lost their savings and their homes, the wheels of industry and commerce slowed down progressively, farm prices fell and went on falling. By the summer of 1932 industrial production had dropped to half the 1929 level, imports and exports to only a third. Those who were lucky enough to keep their jobs suffered crippling wage cuts. Farmers, badly off to begin with, entered a new era of adversity. Unemployment reached 4 million in April 1930, nearly 7 million in October 1931, and between 12 and 15 million—about a quarter of the working population—in July 1932. There was no dole for the unemployed as in most European countries and charity payments were pitifully small—often as little as $2 or $3 a week for a family—and in some areas, like the rural South, nonexistent. There were long breadlines everywhere, and the poor scavenged for food in dustbins. Jobless men roamed the countryside looking for work or congregated on the outskirts of big cities in colonies of cardboard shacks known, ironically, as Hoovervilles.

Hoover and the Depression

During the 1928 campaign Hoover had looked forward to the early and final conquest of poverty. Yet events made a mockery of his hopes and destroyed his reputation both for economic management and for humanitarianism. Hoover was not the mean-spirited, callous man depicted by his opponents, but a sensitive soul who cared deeply about people's sufferings. Nor was he averse to using governmental power to end the Depression. To meet it he intervened in the economy more energetically than any of his predecessors. He secured a pledge from employers to maintain wage-rates and avoid layoffs, stepped up federal spending on roads, bridges, and public buildings, attempted through a newly created Federal Farm Board and its stabilization corporations to bolster grain, cotton, and other commodity prices, and tried to reduce foreign competition by raising tariffs. But Hoover believed that the remedy for economic depression lay not in government intervention but in voluntary cooperation by industry and local communities, and in what he had earlier termed "rugged individualism". In particular he insisted that unemployment relief was a problem for city and state governments and for private charity. A federal relief program, which some were advocating, would unbalance the budget, weaken local and state government, create a permanent class of public dependents, deprive the individual of a sense of responsibility, and destroy the nation's moral fiber.

Within a few months the inadequacy of Hoover's approach was apparent. Private charity and local authorities proved incapable of handling a relief problem of such dimensions. In the winter of 1930–1, relief payments, meager to begin with, were halved; and many needy families were dropped from relief rolls. But despite evidence that the President's policies were not working he was reluctant to admit failure. Believing that the country's problems were more psychological than economic he issued a stream of reassuring statements, minimizing the number of unemployed and predicting that prosperity would soon return. In the spring of 1931 it seemed briefly as though the President might be right. Production and employment began to inch upwards. Then came a fresh collapse, triggered off by the failure of the great Austrian bank, the Kreditanstalt. This produced a world financial crisis which had further devastating effects on the enfeebled American economy. This turn of events led Hoover to a fresh diagnosis of the Depression. Hitherto he had believed it had been due to excessive domestic speculation; now he claimed that its causes lay mainly outside the United States.

Not until the third winter of the Depression (1931–2), did Hoover begin to modify his cherished voluntaristic convictions, and even then only slightly. Though continuing to pin his faith on a balanced budget and on the gold standard he now grudgingly conceded that further action was needed. Having tried in June 1931 to boost American exports by declaring a moratorium on war debts, he laid before Congress a new plan in December, based upon the assumption that if business were helped to recover, the benefits would trickle down to everyone. Its central feature was the Reconstruction Finance Corporation (RFC), created in January 1932 to lend money to ailing banks, railroads, insurance companies, and other institutions. Among other antideflationary measures the Glass–Steagall Banking Act released gold to support the dollar and expanded credit facilities, the Federal Home Loan Bank Act established a system of loans to building societies, and the Relief and Construction Act empowered the RFC to lend state and municipal governments $1.5 billion for public works and a further $300 million for relief. But the President still adamantly opposed direct federal relief to individuals.

These steps succeeded in propping up the financial structure, but did not get the economy moving again. Nor were the President's earlier measures effective. By the summer of 1932 despair and bitterness were almost universal. Three years of suffering had undermined public confidence in business leadership. The President, excessively praised during his earlier career, was now execrated for his supposed coldheartedness. To the destitute Hoover's sermonizing was irrelevant. They found it hard to understand how it could be right to use federal funds to save banks and corporations, but wrong to do so in order to feed the hungry. Hoover thus became the butt of sardonic jokes, his name a synonym for misery and hardship.

Astonishingly in view of the amount of suffering there was little violent protest. In some places starving people looted food shops; in others demonstrations by strikers or the unemployed led to clashes with the police. In Iowa and surrounding states in the summer of 1932 a Farm Holiday Association tried to pressurize Congress into passing a price-support law by barricading roads to prevent farm produce from getting to market. And in the summer of 1933 Middle Western farmers armed with shotguns and pitchforks prevented court officials from foreclosing on mortgages. But the only large-scale organized protest movement was the march of 22,000 unemployed ex-servicemen on Washington in June 1932. The marchers threatened to stay there until Congress passed a bill authorizing immediate payment of a bonus due to World War I veterans in 1945. Hoover had no sympathy with a proposal that would favor one particular group and unbalance the budget. At the end of July he ordered General Douglas MacArthur to evict the bonus marchers from the vacant government buildings they had occupied. MacArthur did so with a greater display of force than the behavior of the veterans seemed to warrant. He assembled a small army equipped with machine-guns, tanks, and tear-gas and, having driven the marchers out of Washington, pursued them across the Anacostia River and burned down their shanties.

Franklin D. Roosevelt and the Early New Deal

Although Hoover's panicky resort to force added to his unpopularity, the Republicans felt obliged to renominate him as their candidate in the 1932 presidential election. With the Democrats confident of victory a keen contest developed for the Democratic nomination. Al Smith, Hoover's defeated opponent in 1928, hoped to be chosen again. The Speaker of the House of Representatives, John N. Garner of Texas, also had strong support. But the leading contender, and the eventual nominee, was Franklin D. Roosevelt, Smith's successor as Governor of New York. The Democrats chose him because he looked a winner. A member of a wealthy, long-established New York family and a distant relative of Theodore Roosevelt, he had been educated at Groton, an exclusive private school, and at Harvard. After a brief career as a lawyer he had entered politics and had risen swiftly. In 1913 he was appointed Assistant Secretary of the Navy by Woodrow Wilson and in 1920 ran unsuccessfully as the Democratic vice-presidential candidate. The following year he was stricken with poliomyelitis. This left him paralyzed from the waist down, and seemed to have ended his political career. But he recovered sufficiently to reenter politics and, against the Republican tide, was elected Governor of New York in 1928. During two terms as governor he won a reputation as a moderate reformer, and when the Depression came he vigorously attacked the problem of unemployment relief. But there had been little in his career to suggest his future greatness: indeed, some contemporaries thought him a lightweight. He was certainly something of a trimmer, temporizing when an investigation revealed Tammany corruption and repudiating his earlier internationalism in order to secure isolationist support for the presidential nomination.

In his acceptance speech at Chicago Roosevelt pledged himself to a "new deal for the American people". But neither then nor during the campaign did he define it, concentrating instead on Hoover's record. He seemed at times to echo Hoover's conservatism, especially in attacking the Administration for overspending and promising to balance the budget. The Democratic platform differed little from the Republican, except that it called for the repeal of Prohibition. All the same Roosevelt's zest and self-assurance contrasted strongly with Hoover's gloom. There was never any doubt that the Democrats would win easily. As usual the party in power got the blame for hard times and Roosevelt carried all but six of the states.

In the four months between the election and Roosevelt's inauguration, the economy took a further nosedive. Many blamed the length of the interregnum, a view which led to the adoption later in 1933 of the Twentieth Amendment, which reduced the interval to two and a half months. The Republicans attributed the severity of the new crisis to Roosevelt's refusal to cooperate with Hoover in formulating an agreed program. At all events a sudden epidemic of bank failures prompted panic-stricken withdrawals all over the country. By the time Roosevelt took office on March 4, 1933, thirty-eight states had proclaimed indefinite 'bank holidays' and the entire banking structure seemed in danger of collapse. Roosevelt's inaugural put forward no specific proposals, though in asserting confidently that "the only thing we have to fear is fear itself" he did something to meet the national yearning for hope and reassurance. Moving swiftly and decisively to deal with the banking crisis, he proclaimed a nationwide bank holiday and called Congress into special session. His Emergency Banking Relief Bill, passed in only ten hours, placed all banks under federal control and arranged for the reopening under license of those found to be solvent. On March 12 the President delivered the first of his radio "fireside chats". He told his listeners it was safe to bank their savings. They believed him and the crisis was over.

A period of hectic activity followed, known subsequently as the Hundred Days. Roosevelt peppered Congress with messages, exhortations, proposals, and draft bills. Congressmen, glad to be given a lead, responded by passing fifteen major bills affecting unemployment relief, industry, agriculture, labor, transport, banking, and the currency. This body of legislation, as unparalleled in scope and volume as in the speed with which it was enacted, was based neither on a coordinated plan nor on a particular economic theory. It was full of contradiction, duplication, and overlap. This was to become characteristic of the New Deal as a whole. While Roosevelt was unusually receptive to theories, he never became wedded to them, blithely discarding those which ceased to be serviceable. He was in short not a doctrinaire, but an experimenter, an improviser.

In shaping the New Deal the President took advice not only from his

Cabinet but also from a group of unofficial advisers—academics, lawyers, and journalists—whom he had been in the habit of consulting while Governor of New York. The most important members of this 'Brain Trust', as it became known, were Judge Samuel Rosenman, Professor Felix Frankfurter of the Harvard Law School, and three Columbia University professors, Rexford G. Tugwell, Raymond Moley, and Adolf A. Berle, Jr. Notwithstanding the conflicting expedients these men devised, the New Deal had a single overriding aim: to save American capitalism. Contemporary allegations that Roosevelt sought to introduce Socialism are absurd, though his program certainly involved an unprecedented amount of national economic planning. It also entailed public spending on a scale so massive that Roosevelt's campaign promises to balance the budget could not be kept.

Not everything Roosevelt did was new. In lending money to business through the RFC and in extending the policy of refinancing home and farm mortgages to prevent foreclosure, he simply continued what the Hoover Administration had begun. But in many respects the New Deal broke new ground. Unlike his predecessor, Roosevelt frankly accepted that unemployment relief was a national responsibility. Thus the Federal Emergency Relief Act authorized an appropriation of $500 million for direct relief in the form of grants to the states. Administration of the program was entrusted to a New York social worker, Harry Hopkins, who believed in work relief, namely, that the self-respect of the unemployed required that the government should provide them with paid jobs instead of putting them on the dole. There were all kinds of work-relief projects: road repairs, improvements to schools, parks, and playgrounds. During the winter of 1933 more than four million people were engaged on them. Another relief measure was the creation of the Civilian Conservation Corps, an organization to recruit unemployed young men for work on conservation projects. During the Hundred Days Congress set up also a Public Works Administration (PWA) with an appropriation of $3.3 billion. Under the direction of Secretary of the Interior Harold Ickes, it built schools, courthouses, hospitals, dams, bridges, roads, public buildings, even aircraft-carriers.

A more spectacular innovation was the Tennessee Valley Authority—the TVA—destined to become the best-known and most widely admired New Deal achievement. Ever since 1916, when the federal government had built a dam and two munitions plants at Muscle Shoals, Alabama, on the Tennessee River, a group of Senate Progressives led by George W. Norris of Nebraska had been vainly urging the government to use the facilities to develop power resources and to manufacture fertilizer. This proposal now became the basis of a much broader plan to develop the Tennessee River basin, a backward area covering seven states. The TVA built dams and hydroelectric plants to provide cheap electricity and embarked on a program of flood control, land reclamation, afforestation, rehousing, education, and recreation. Though cheap electricity did not attract industry on the scale that had been hoped, the TVA dramatically raised living standards throughout the region.

Meanwhile Roosevelt had ill-advisedly been making monetary experiments. Although confessing that he knew nothing about economics he allowed himself to be persuaded that devaluation could boost domestic commodity prices. Thus in April 1933 the United States went off the gold standard and some time later the Treasury began buying gold at high prices. This lowered the exchange-rate of the dollar and made American goods somewhat more competitive abroad. But domestic prices fell rather than rose.

The two main planks of the early New Deal recovery program were designed to revive agriculture and industry respectively. The Agricultural Adjustment Act (1933) attempted to raise farm prices by curtailing production. Farmers who agreed to reduce acreage or crops were to be compensated out of funds raised by levies on the producers of specified farm products. Under this program—"organized scarcity in action", one historian has called it—farmers plowed under a quarter of the growing cotton crop, slaughtered six million pigs, and destroyed part of the tobacco harvest. The success of the AAA is difficult to gauge. By 1935 national farm income had nearly doubled, but the rise was in part accounted for by drought and dust storms and the devaluation of the dollar. Most of the benefits of the AAA went to larger farmers. Tenant farmers, sharecroppers, and farm laborers generally became worse off, especially in the Cotton Belt, and many forsook the land.

The ambitious National Industrial Recovery Act (1933) was an attempt at joint economic planning by government and industry, aiming at stabilizing prices, restricting competition, expanding purchasing power, relieving unemployment, and improving working conditions. Manufacturers were encouraged to draw up codes of fair competition that would become legally binding on all in a given industry. The codes were also to include production controls and minimum-wage and maximum-hour provisions. Section 7a of the law guaranteed the right of collective bargaining. To supervise a newly created National Recovery Administration (NRA) Roosevelt appointed the flamboyant Hugh S. Johnson, a former army general. Thanks to Johnson's flair for publicity, the NRA generated great enthusiasm. But the experiment soon turned sour. The codes were too hastily drafted, took insufficient account of the complexities of American industry, and were difficult to enforce. They were, moreover, generally drawn up by big business, which took the opportunity to strengthen monopolistic practices. Even so employers disliked the encouragement given to trade unions by Section 7a. Finally the codes failed either to create new jobs or to stop prices rising faster than wages. Thus, when in 1935 the Supreme Court invalidated the NRA no one lamented its passing.

While the main emphasis of the early New Deal was on relief and recovery, it aimed also at reform. To strengthen the banking structure and prevent failures like those of the 1920s, the Glass–Steagall Banking Act of 1933 extended the Federal Reserve System, forbade commercial banks to engage in the investment business, restricted the speculative use of bank credits, and, most important of all, created the Federal Bank Deposit Insurance Corporation to guarantee individual deposits under $5,000. The Federal Securities Act of 1933 compelled full disclosure of information about new security issues and required them to be registered with the Federal Trade Commission. The Securities and Exchange Act (1934) transferred the last of these functions to a Securities and Exchange Commission which was given broad powers to regulate stock exchanges. The measure sought also to curb speculation of the 1929 variety by forbidding the buying of stocks on margin without a down payment of at least 55 percent of the purchase price.

Critics of the New Deal

At first Roosevelt enjoyed almost universal support, but as the economic crisis moderated criticism began to be heard. Conservatives had watched with growing distaste the New Deal's intervention in the economy, its tinkering with the dollar, its social experiments like the TVA, the huge cost of its relief programs, and the consequent budget deficits. Their hostility found open expression in the American Liberty League, founded in August 1934 with the financial backing of the Du Pont family and other wealthy businessmen and the support of two former Democratic presidential candidates, Alfred E. Smith and John W. Davis. The League spearheaded an organized assault on the New Deal as a threat to the American free-enterprise system.

More worrying to Roosevelt was "the thunder on the Left", to use the rather misleading term historians have employed to describe the clamor of assorted visionaries and demagogues for the transfer of income, wealth, and power to the less well off—misleading because some at least of the agitators belonged essentially to the radical Right. It was not surprising that a radical outcry should have developed. The New Deal had produced only partial recovery: there were still eleven million unemployed at the end of 1934. Nor had it brought much benefit to some of the most disadvantaged groups: sharecroppers, small farmers, the rural unemployed, the old. Such elements were not greatly attracted to either Socialism or Communism; nor, for that matter, were other Americans, except for a minority of writers, academics, and other intellectuals. But the underprivileged were ready to turn to leaders whose nostrums seemed to offer an end to the prevailing misery.

The most improbable of these competing Messiahs was Dr Francis E. Townsend, an obscure, mild-mannered, Californian medical practitioner, whose cure for the Depression was that everyone over sixty should be granted a federal monthly pension of $200 on condition that they spent it within thirty days. The experts unanimously pronounced the Townsend Plan economic illiteracy, but all over the country elderly people flocked into Townsend Clubs. By 1935 the movement claimed five million members. A more raucous figure was Father Charles E. Coughlin, a Canadian-born Catholic priest whose weekly radio broadcasts attracted huge audiences. Coughlin's message was a confusing blend of liberal Catholicism and Middle-Western Populism. Originally a New Deal supporter, he organized his own political movement in 1934, the National Union for Social Justice, advocating such measures as silver inflation and the nationalization of the banks. His hatred of international bankers grew more explicitly anti-Semitic, while his political program increasingly resembled the corporatism of Mussolini's Italy. These changes of emphasis did not, however, appear to disturb his admirers, mainly poor farmers and lower middle-class city-dwellers. The most formidable of the new leaders was the flamboyant Huey P. Long of Louisiana. Long was not a typical Southern demagogue of the Negro-baiting variety. Nor, despite his uncouth antics and often bizarre appearance, was he a hillbilly or a buffoon—though he cultivated the image of both. A shrewd, ambitious politician and an effective popular orator he became Governor of Louisiana by stirring up poor-white resentment toward the powerful corporate interests which had long dominated the state. He brought much-needed reform to Louisiana, building roads, improving education and other public services, introducing a fairer tax system, but in the process instituted a near-dictatorship. Entering the United States Senate in 1931 he supported Roosevelt for a time but ultimately became a fierce critic. In 1934 Long came out with a plan of social and economic reform under the slogan "Share Our Wealth". Vague and shifting in its details, the program aimed essentially at a guaranteed minimum wage to be achieved through the limitation of personal fortunes. Economically radical though the plan may have sounded, it was hardly egalitarian, proposing merely that no one should be allowed to inherit more than five million dollars or have an income of more than one million dollars a year. Nonetheless Long gained a steadily increasing national following and was planning to run against Roosevelt in 1936 as a third-party candidate. But in September 1935 he was assassinated.

The New Deal: Second Phase

These radical challenges to Roosevelt's position were only one reason for his tactical shift in 1935. The Congressional elections of 1934 had reinforced the Progressive bloc in Congress led by Senators Robert F. Wagner and Robert M. La Follette, Jr., who for some time had been demanding new initiatives. Early in 1935, moreover, the Supreme Court began striking down some of the most important New Deal measures. Above all, the economy was still becalmed. The result was a renewed flood of legislation so varied and extensive in character that some historians have seen it as constituting a "Second New Deal". According to them, it was more radical than the First New Deal, less concerned with relief and recovery, more focused on social and economic reform, less interested in cooperating with business, more responsive to the needs of the less well off. There was, indeed, some change of emphasis along these lines. But one should not exaggerate the sharpness of the break. There were important elements of continuity and in particular no weakening in the New Deal's commitment to preserving capitalism. Many of the 1935 reforms had, moreover, long been in preparation and some owed less to the President than to Congress. In any case it is futile to search for neat patterns in the New Deal: it remained shapeless, even chaotic, without any unifying philosophy.

Roosevelt's change of course began to produce concrete results in April 1935, when Congress established a new relief agency, the Works Progress Administration (subsequently renamed the Works Projects Administration), to replace the emergency relief scheme of 1933. While direct relief was in future to be left to local authorities, the WPA was to concentrate on providing work relief. During its eight-year history it employed a total of eight and a half million persons and spent about eleven billion dollars. Some of its projects were of doubtful value—critics applied the epithet "boondoggling" to them—and there was much extravagance, waste, and political favoritism. But under the energetic direction of Harry Hopkins the WPA built, repaired, or improved vast numbers of roads, bridges, schools, hospitals, and airport landing grounds, besides undertaking slum clearance and reforestation.

The most striking WPA projects were designed to help unemployed writers, artists, and actors. The Federal Writers' Project prepared an excellent series of state and regional guidebooks, cataloged historical records, indexed newspapers, published local histories and folklore collections, and gathered the reminiscences of elderly blacks who had been born into slavery. The Federal Arts Project gave several thousand out-of-work artists the chance to adorn post offices, schools, libraries, courthouses, and other public buildings with murals featuring scenes from American history or sympathetically depicting working-class life. Under the Federal Music Project WPA orchestras gave symphony concerts for more than a hundred million people, while offering free music classes which attracted over half a million pupils every month. A more venturesome and ultimately more controversial departure was the Federal Theater Project. Employing about 12,500 actors and technicians, its traveling companies brought drama (often experimental) as well as ballet, puppet-shows, and circuses to communities which had never before seen them. But in 1939, disturbed by the left-wing, even Marxist, coloring of many of the plays and by the New Deal propaganda which characterized the Theater's "Living Newspaper", a dramatic form dealing with current issues, Congressional conservatives cut off Federal Theater appropriations.

In welfare legislation the United States had hitherto lagged behind Europe. In 1935 no more than 27 of the 48 states had introduced old-age pensions and only one (Wisconsin) had an unemployment-insurance scheme. But the Social Security Act of 1935 created a compulsory national system of old-age pensions and a joint federal–state system of unemployment insurance, both to be financed by deductions from wages and from employers' payrolls. The Act was in many respects timid and defective. The system it introduced was unique in being financed exclusively out of current contributions rather than out of general tax revenues; hence no payments could be made until 1942. Benefits were low and were proportionate to previous income rather than being based, as in Great Britain, on minimum subsistence needs. Unemployment pay was to run for limited periods only—twenty weeks at most. Many millions of people were exempted, including those classes most in need of protection: farm laborers, casual workers, domestic servants. Worst of all, there were to be no sickness benefits: the health-insurance clauses in the original bill were dropped because of the fierce opposition of the medical profession. Even so, it was a major departure and provided a foundation on which all subsequent administrations have built.

If the Social Security Act spiked the guns of the Townsend Movement, as was partly its intention, Roosevelt's call for "the progressive taxation of wealth and of income" was calculated to do the same to Huey Long's 'Share-Our-Wealth' crusade. Not all the President's tax proposals were accepted, but the Wealth Tax Act of 1935 stepped up income-tax and sur-tax rates and levied an excess-profits tax. Though provoking an anguished outcry from conservatives the measure was a relatively moderate one, and did little to redistribute income. Nonetheless Roosevelt's tax policies, together with his criticism of the greed and selfishness of big businessmen—'economic royalists' he called them during the 1936 election campaign—completed the estrangement of the wealthy from the New Deal. In their eyes Roosevelt was a traitor to his class.

Meanwhile Congress had enacted perhaps the most sweeping reform of the New Deal period, the National Labor Relations Act of July 1935. The brainchild of Senator Robert Wagner, it received the President's backing only after the Supreme Court had invalidated the National Industrial

Recovery Act, whose Section 7a had ostensibly guaranteed collective bar-gaining. Since it had not in practice been entirely successful in doing so Roosevelt decided that more drastic safeguards were needed. The Wagner Act, as the new measure was familiarly known, threw the government's influence more positively and, as it proved, more effectively behind the right to join trade unions. It created a new National Labor Relations Board, empowered to bargain on behalf of workers and also to restrain management from using "unfair labor practices" such as blacklists and company unions. The Act greatly expanded the role of government in industrial relations and opened the way to an unprecedented growth of union membership and power.

When the Democratic convention met in June 1936 Roosevelt was renominated by acclamation on a platform praising the achievements of the New Deal. The Republican platform predictably condemned the New Deal but did not propose to repeal it; instead it accused Roosevelt of usurping the powers of Congress, and censured him for extravagance and for centralizing power in Washington. Lacking a candidate who could rival Roosevelt's popular appeal, the Republicans finally chose the able and progressive Alfred M. Landon of Kansas, the only Republican governor to survive the Democratic landslide in 1932. The campaign was bitterly fought. Roosevelt seemed to go out of his way to stir up class hatreds. The Republicans denounced him as an unprincipled demagogue. The press was heavily against the President. A *Literary Digest* poll even predicted that Landon would win. But Roosevelt won by a record margin and carried every state in the Union except Maine and Vermont. The minor parties were buried under the Roosevelt avalanche. The Democrats won three-quarters of the seats in the Senate and almost four-fifths of those in the House. Roosevelt had evidently been given a mandate for a further install-ment of reform. His second inaugural, delivered in January 1937, seemed to promise as much for it drew attention to "one-third of a nation ill-housed, ill-clad, ill-nourished". But the second term was an anticlimax. Its legislative accomplishments were meager, while the President's standing with Congress and within his party declined.

American Society during the Depression

Grim though American sufferings were during the Depression, they were not remotely comparable to those of, say, the Soviet Union in 1920–1 when famine claimed millions of lives, or of Bengal in 1943 when between one and a half and two million people starved to death. In the five worst years of the Depression (1929–33) the total reported number of deaths from starvation was 110. Nonetheless hunger probably contributed to the death of a much larger number and there was certainly a dramatic rise in reported cases of malnutrition. Even in 1935 the president of the American

Medical Association estimated that twenty million people were not getting enough to eat. The full consequences were not apparent until conscription was introduced in 1940: of the first batch of two million draftees, almost half were found to be medically unfit, largely for reasons traceable to malnutrition. All the same the death-rate continued to decline: it went down from 11.9 per thousand in 1929 to 10.8 in 1940. One reason was the discovery and use of anticoagulant and sulfa drugs. Another was the remarkable drop in deaths in childbirth: between 1934 and 1938 they fell by a quarter.

The rate of population growth, which had been slowing down ever since the Civil War, now fell even more conclusively. A decline both in natural increase and in immigration was responsible. During the early years of the Depression the marriage-rate dipped sharply, though it had recovered by about 1935. The birth-rate, which had fallen to 21 per thousand by 1930, remained below 20 per thousand throughout the following decade, despite a growing number of women of child-bearing age. Only because the death-rate fell even more sharply did the population increase by as much as 7.3 percent, less than half the rate of the previous decade. The fall in the birth-rate—and in maternity mortality—was due largely to the spread of contraception, or 'planned parenthood' as it now became known. Opposition to birth-control declined. Advice about contraception became more widely available, especially after 1936 when the federal law prohibiting the sending of contraceptive information through the mail was modified. By 1940 every state but two had repealed laws forbidding doctors to advise patients about family limitation; the exceptions were Massachusetts and Rhode Island, where official Catholic opposition prevented action. In 1929 there had been only 28 birth-control clinics in the country; by 1941 there were 746, a third of them supported by public funds. During the 1930s, moreover, the Sears, Roebuck mail-order catalog for the first time listed contraceptives.

Immigration, which had exceeded four millions in the 1920s, dropped to barely half a million in the 1930s, the lowest total for more than a century. This was the consequence, less of the immigration-quota system, than of the Depression. Few foreigners wanted to come to an economically crippled country. In some years more people left the United States than entered it. Perhaps half the new arrivals were refugees, especially German and Austrian Jews, fleeing from Nazi persecution. They included some eminent figures: Albert Einstein, the novelist Thomas Mann, the Bauhaus architect Walter Gropius, the theologian Paul Tillich, the composer Paul Hindemith. The refugee influx would have been larger but for the fact that, with millions out of work, Congress refused to grant asylum to more people than the quota system permitted.

The Depression hit not only those at the bottom of the social and economic scale. Large numbers of middle-class folk lost their jobs, their savings, and, worst of all, their sense of security. Tens of thousands of businesses went bankrupt. Doctors, lawyers, and architects saw their incomes shrink and often found themselves idle much of the time. Many college students had to abandon their studies through lack of funds or, if they completed their courses, found themselves unemployable.

One of the most striking consequences of the Depression was a kind of mass nomadism. At any given time there were perhaps as many as five million vagrants, seeking work or simply fleeing from boredom and despair. A sizable proportion—possibly a quarter—consisted of youngsters of both sexes who lived in makeshift campsites, relied on soup-kitchens for food, and moved around by stealing rides on freight trains. The number might well have been higher but for the efforts of two New Deal agencies—the Civilian Conservation Corps, which enrolled more than 2 million unemployed young men in work-camps where they were engaged in reforestation and flood-control projects, and the National Youth Administration, which gave part-time employment to over 600,000 college students and more than eight and a half million secondary-school children, thus enabling them to continue their education and, incidentally, keeping them off the job market.

Another kind of internal migration was the exodus of farmers from the Great Plains. Between 1934 and 1936 drought, overplanting, and over-grazing combined to create a huge dust bowl in Oklahoma, Arkansas, and neighboring states. In addition, the acreage reductions prescribed by the AAA and the increasing use of tractors its subsidies made possible forced large numbers of sharecroppers off the land. Tens of thousands of stricken farm families abandoned their homes, piled their belongings into ram-shackle cars, and headed west for California to become migrant laborers.

Upon black Americans the Depression had a catastrophic effect. It wiped out the modest economic advances they had made since World War I and plunged them into new depths of deprivation. In Northern cities, where they were the last to be hired, the first to be fired, unemployment among blacks was about twice that among whites. In the rural South, where most of them still lived, blacks were more dependent than whites on cotton, the crop hardest hit by the Depression. New Deal agricultural policies compounded Negro miseries; the AAA in particular displaced many Negro tenants and croppers. New Deal agencies generally discriminated against blacks. The NRA all but excluded them from skilled jobs and adopted discriminatory wage-rates; the CCC operated segregated camps; the TVA set up all-white model towns. Roosevelt proved unresponsive to demands for Negro civil rights; unwilling to antagonize the Southern Democrats whose support he needed, he even refused to endorse a federal antilynching bill. Nonetheless the New Deal won a huge Negro following and broke the traditional tie between black voters and the party of Lincoln. In 1932 nearly three-quarters of blacks had voted Republican; in 1936 over three-quarters voted Democratic. This was mainly because of the benefits blacks derived from New Deal relief and recovery programs. By 1935 nearly 30 percent of all black families were on relief—three times the proportion of whites; by 1939 over a million blacks held WPA jobs; about a third of all federal housing went to blacks; federal funds went into black schools, colleges, and hospitals. Practical help was accompanied by symbolic gestures of recognition. Prominent black leaders like Mary McLeod Bethune, William H. Hastie, and Robert C. Weaver were given important posts in the administration. A 'Black Cabinet' developed as Negro advisers and specialists were recruited to New Deal agencies. Finally, presidential inactivity on civil rights was somewhat compensated for by Eleanor Roosevelt's outspoken stand against racial bigotry.

American Indians were even more vulnerable to economic adversity. Their lot had been pathetic enough in the prosperous 1920s. The Dawes Act of 1887 had failed either to turn them into independent farmers or to integrate them into American culture. Tilling infertile land on isolated reservations, ravaged by tuberculosis, trachoma, and other ailments, the tribesmen had eked out a miserable existence. The Depression, combined with grasshoppers and drought, dealt the Indian economy a crippling blow. Hoover, keenly interested in Indian welfare, appointed philanthropic fellow Quakers to head the Indian service and, between 1929 and 1932, while slashing public expenditure generally, almost doubled appropriations for Indian relief, schools, and hospitals. Hoover's policies were the prelude to a new approach to the Indian problem. As Commissioner of Indian Affairs Roosevelt appointed John Collier, the secretary of the Indian Defense Association who, along with other reformers, had long been demanding that Indians should be encouraged to preserve their own religion, ceremonials, and crafts instead of being forced to adopt white ways. Collier's ideas formed the basis of the Wheeler–Howard (Indian Reorganization) Act of 1934. It repudiated severalty and substituted community ownership of land, restored tribal self-government, provided loans for Indian business ventures, and expanded Indian educational opportunities. But the 'Indian New Deal' was only partly successful. True, millions of acres of Indian land were brought into cultivation; agricultural productivity soared; the death-rate declined and for the first time in centuries the Indian population began to increase. But the process of detribalization was not checked and the American Indian, torn between two cultures and wracked by alcoholism, remained pitifully deprived.

Least affected by the Depression were the very rich. Those who survived the stock-market crash—and most did—hung on to their wealth through systematic, though perfectly legal, tax avoidance. A Senate committee discovered in 1933 that the millionaire banker, J. P. Morgan, and his seventeen partners had paid no federal income tax in the previous two years. Some millionaire businessmen even expanded their fortunes during the Depression, J. Paul Getty and Joseph P. Kennedy being conspicuous examples. The top 5 percent of the population went on living much as before. Fashionable resorts in Florida and the Caribbean suffered little loss of patronage and even built new luxury hotels; General Motors reported that the demand for Cadillacs had remained buoyant—though sales of Chevrolets had slumped. Yet philanthropy persisted along with conspicuous consumption. The Mellon, Kellogg, and Sloan Foundations were born in the depths of the Depression. The great individual donors, as well as contributing generously to emergency relief campaigns, made princely gifts to a variety of projects. The oil millionaire Edward S. Harkness gave vast sums to education, medicine, and the Metropolitan Museum of Art. John D. Rockefeller's benefactions made possible the reconstruction of Williamsburg, the eighteenth-century capital of colonial Virginia, and the preservation and development of national parks like Acadia in Maine and Grand Teton in Wyoming. Andrew W. Mellon, who had brought together one of the world's great art collections, gave it to the nation in 1937, together with funds to erect the National Gallery of Art in Washington, DC.

Especially in the early years of the Depression education was a prime target for retrenchment. School expenditures were slashed, sometimes by 70 percent. Thousands of teachers were sacked; those in Chicago went unpaid for more than a year. The falling birth-rate provided a reason—or at all events an excuse—for school closures. By 1938 there were 1.6 million fewer children under ten than there had been five years before. During the decade some 4,000 elementary schools, mostly rural, shut their doors. But because of the scarcity of jobs, children tended to stay at school longer, especially when helped to do so by the NYA. Between 1929 and 1935 the number of high-school students increased by a third—from four and a half million to six million—and 900 new public high schools were built. Colleges on the other hand were hit hard. During the 1920s they had doubled their enrollments, but as their income and that of prospective students dwindled, they were hard put to it to maintain numbers.

Hard times did not, as many expected, lead Americans back to religion. Church membership and attendance fell steadily throughout the 1930s. Collections were almost halved between 1930 and 1934, necessitating sharp cuts in ministerial salaries. Only a few minor cults escaped the general decline. The Oxford Group Movement (subsequently renamed Moral Rearmament), founded in England soon after World War I by an American Lutheran minister, Dr Frank Buchman, and promising spiritual regeneration through group confession, enjoyed a considerable vogue, especially among rich, elderly women. Extreme fundamentalist Protestant Churches also prospered, especially those Pentecostal and Holiness sects which saw in economic collapse a divine judgment and a portent of the Second Coming. Black slum-dwellers in particular found solace in millenarian sects. They also turned fervently to the messianic Negro evangelist Father Divine (born George Baker), who offered devotees a gospel of love and equality and organized religious communes which provided material benefits.

Predictably enough the Depression boosted crime: during the 1930s the country's prison population rose 40 percent. Burglary, larceny, and other crimes against property increased sharply, as did arrests for vagrancy and drunkenness. Violent crime, on the other hand, declined. Nonetheless a spate of kidnapings and bank holdups captured public attention. Following the abduction and murder in 1932 of the infant son of the aviator, Charles A. Lindbergh—the most celebrated case of its kind—a federal statute was passed against kidnaping. The federal government also intervened when local authorities failed to deal with gangs of heavily armed bank robbers, whose exploits terrorized whole regions. In 1934 government agents (G-men) under J. Edgar Hoover, director of the Federal Bureau of Investigation (FBI), ambushed and killed the most notorious of these "public enemies", John Dillinger, Pretty Boy Floyd, and Baby Face Nelson, and became popular heroes in consequence.

Despite hard times, leisure activities boomed. Between 1929 and 1933 the number of library books in circulation rose 40 percent. People still flocked to spectator sports: when the black boxer Joe Louis fought Max Baer for the world heavyweight championship in 1935 the gate receipts exceeded a million dollars. People kept their cars longer but by the middle of the decade were thronging the roads as never before, especially for vacations: the number of visitors at National Parks soared from six million in 1934 to sixteen million in 1938. The Depression saw an enormous increase in the popularity of radio. In 1929, twelve million families possessed sets; by 1940 the total was twenty-eight million, or 86 percent of the population. At the outset of the Depression cinemas lost a third of their patrons, but double features and a variety of giveaway schemes brought them back. Most films of the 1930s avoided social issues. What people seemed to want was escape from contemporary reality and Hollywood obliged with a stream of comedies, Westerns, costume dramas, gangster films, musical extravaganzas, and Walt Disney animated cartoons.

Escapism rather than protest was also the keynote of much of the writing of the period. Some writers and critics developed left-wing political sympathies, but relatively few addressed themselves to the crisis facing American capitalism. One who did so was John Dos Passos whose *U.S.A.*

trilogy—*42nd Parallel* (1930), *Nineteen Nineteen* (1932), and *The Big Money* (1936)—angrily assailed industrial America and its injustices. John Steinbeck, though not a political activist, brought a compassionate understanding of the plight of migrant laborers and dispossessed farmers to such novels as *In Dubious Battle* (1936), *Of Mice and Men* (1937), and the best-selling *The Grapes of Wrath* (1939)—later made into a film—which dealt with the sufferings of a migrant 'Okie' family. But the most talented writers of the decade largely ignored social problems. William Faulkner retreated into a mythical Southern past and then went off to Hollywood—as Scott Fitzgerald had done earlier—to write film scripts. Ernest Hemingway chose in the early 1930s to write about bullfighting and big-game hunting; but he was deeply affected by the Spanish Civil War, which he saw first-hand as a correspondent, and which provided the theme for his much-acclaimed novel *For Whom the Bell Tolls* (1940). Yet at the popular level the most spectacular successes were sprawling historical romances like Hervey Allen's *Anthony Adverse* (1933), Walter D. Edmonds's *Drums Along the Mohawk* (1936), Kenneth Roberts's *North West Passage* (1937), and, outselling them all, Margaret Mitchell's *Gone With The Wind* (1936), a panoramic chronicle of Civil War and Reconstruction Georgia.

The Supreme Court Controversy

Things began to go wrong for Roosevelt early in 1937 when he attempted to reform the federal judiciary. The Supreme Court, dominated by a group of archconservatives, had for some time been hostile to government intervention in economic and social affairs. In 1935 and 1936, in unusually vigorous assertions of judicial power, it struck down the twin pillars of the early New Deal—though both the NRA and the AAA were dying before the Court killed them off. In the case of *Schechter v. United States* (1935) it held the National Industrial Recovery Act to be unconstitutional because it improperly delegated legislative power to the executive. In *United States v. Butler* (1936) it invalidated the Agricultural Adjustment Act on the ground that it represented an unconstitutional misuse of the taxing power. In addition the Court ruled that a New York minimum-wage law was invalid. These and similar decisions aggrieved Roosevelt. He thought it intolerable that the Court majority, appointed by his Republican predecessors and reflecting a *laissez-faire* attitude which public opinion no longer shared, should render the national and state governments powerless to deal with pressing economic and social problems. During the 1936 election campaign Roosevelt said nothing about the Court problem, but immediately after his victory he submitted to Congress a detailed reorganization plan. It proposed that the President be authorized to appoint one additional judge for every member of the Supreme Court who passed the age of seventy without retiring. Since six of the existing justices were above that age, Roosevelt would have been able to increase the Court's membership to fifteen. The President's real motive was, of course, to secure a more sympathetic bench. But with characteristic lack of frankness he argued that reform was necessary because "aged or infirm judges" were behind with their work.

Roosevelt was confident that the "Court-packing" plan would be accepted, but the storm of protest it provoked showed that he had miscalculated. Usually so sensitive to public feeling, he failed on this occasion to appreciate that the Court was widely revered as the guardian of the Constitution and as a symbol of national unity. Roosevelt was accused, and not only by conservatives, of seeking to undermine judicial independence and of aggrandizing executive power. Even some of those who wished to curb the Court disliked Roosevelt's devious approach and insisted that the proper way of proceeding was by constitutional amendment. In Congress a long and bitter debate on the reorganization bill seriously divided the Democrats. Meanwhile a succession of events in 1937 made reform seem less necessary. Chief Justice Hughes demonstrated that, far from being behindhand, the Supreme Court was dealing promptly with cases. The conservative Justice Van Devanter announced his retirement in May, thus enabling Roosevelt to appoint a liberal in his place—Senator Hugo Black of Alabama. Most important of all, the Court itself dramatically changed course, apparently because Hughes and Justice Roberts believed that sticking to a conservative line might imperil its very existence. In a number of leading decisions between March and May it upheld such key New Deal measures as the Social Security Act and the National Labor Relations Act, and sustained a Washington state minimum-wage law virtually identical with the New York statute it had invalidated only nine months before. These decisions effectively ended the chances of the Court-reform bill. With the sudden death in July of Senator Joseph Robinson, the administration spokesman in Congress, Roosevelt abandoned the measure. But while he had sustained a major setback, deaths and retirements enabled him during the next four years to fill no fewer than seven vacancies on the Supreme Court, thus giving it a pronounced liberal character and transforming its attitude towards the extension of federal power and economic and social legislation.

Not the least important consequence of the controversy was that it provided dissident Democrats, mostly Southern conservatives, with a pretext for deserting the President. They had been uneasy for some time about the New Deal's retreat from Jeffersonian *laissez-faire*; they looked with distaste upon the bureaucrats, academics, economic pundits, and social workers who surrounded Roosevelt; some suspected the President of dictatorial tendencies and of wanting to revolutionize race relations; they also resented being constantly pressurized by zealous presidential aides, who seemed to expect Congress to rubber-stamp every proposal emanating from the White House. The critics were also emboldened by the sheer size of the Democratic majority in Congress. Lacking the incentive for unity that an effective Republican opposition would have provided, they began to express their resentments more openly and to join the emerging bipartisan anti-New Deal coalition.

The Ebbing of the New Deal

Two developments in 1937–8 further eroded Roosevelt's authority: an eruption of industrial strife and a sudden economic collapse. The 1930s saw organized labor advance spectacularly. The Norris–La Guardia Act of 1932 had restricted the power of the federal courts to issue injunctions in labor disputes and had made "yellow dog" contracts unenforceable, and the collective-bargaining guarantees of the National Industrial Recovery Act and the Wagner Act helped create an atmosphere conducive to unionism. Union membership rose from just over two million in 1933 to almost nine million in 1938. But there were bitter conflicts both within the ranks of labor and with the employers. Though the American Federation of Labor shared in the expansion, most of its leaders, wedded to the principle of craft unionism, were not greatly interested in organizing unskilled wage-earners in the mass-production industries. In 1935, a frustrated minority of union leaders formed the Committee on Industrial Organization (CIO) with the object of organizing all workers in a given industry into a single union. In 1937, upon its expulsion from the AF of L, it established itself on a more permanent basis as the Congress of Industrial Organizations. Headed by the pugnacious, bombastic, and egotistical John L. Lewis, president of the United Mine Workers, the CIO launched a vigorous campaign to organize workers in the steel, automobile, glass, rubber, and other mass-production industries. It achieved remarkable success. By the end of 1937 it had—or at all events claimed—3.7 million members, a rather larger total than the AF of L.

The CIO's organizing drives and demands for the closed shop met ferocious resistance from employers. They resorted to lockouts, strike-breakers, "company spies", and heavily armed private armies; they could usually count also on help from the local police. In the "Memorial Day Massacre" (May 30, 1937) the Chicago police clashed with five hundred strikers picketing the Republic Steel Company plant, killing ten and injuring seventy-five. Strikers responded by intimidating nonunionists, employing flying pickets, and adopting a new and dramatic 'sit-down' technique in order to seize the factories where they worked. The 'sit-down'—later renamed the 'sit-in'—was ultimately declared illegal by the Supreme Court (1939) but not before the CIO unions had demonstrated its efficacy. By the end of 1937 'sit-down' strikes had enabled the United Automobile Workers to secure union recognition from every car manufacturer except Ford (which did not capitulate until 1941). These successes came about because state and federal governments were no longer willing to use force against strikers. Roosevelt's sympathy for labor was further demonstrated when he used his influence to frustrate an attempt to persuade the Senate to condemn 'sit-downs'. But middle-class opinion, initially prolabor, was affronted by these demonstrations of union power and by what it saw as alarming assaults on property rights. Some attributed Roosevelt's complaisance to the heavy CIO financial contributions to his 1936 campaign. Moreover, evidence began to accumulate that some AF of L unions were run by racketeers and that Communists controlled a great many CIO locals. Thus public support ebbed away, not only from the unions, but also from their New Deal patrons.

The sudden downward plunge of the economy in the late summer of 1937 ended four years of partial recovery and destroyed the illusion that the depression was being beaten. Industrial production declined, the stock market fell, unemployment rose by four million. The cause of the "recession" (as it was called) was Roosevelt's attempt to return to fiscal orthodoxy. Worried about the mounting national debt and fearing another disastrous boom like that of 1929, he tried to balance the budget by sharply cutting federal spending. This promptly sent the economy into reverse. Within the Administration rival theorists urged contradictory remedies upon the President. After much hesitation he followed the advice of the Keynesians to renew heavy public spending though he did not fully accept—or, indeed, understand—the Keynesian formula for restoring prosperity by systematic deficit-financing. Congress responded to Roosevelt's request for large new appropriations for relief and public works and by the summer of 1938 the economy had resumed its slow upward climb. But public confidence in the Administration had been further weakened.

Roosevelt nonetheless succeeded in persuading Congress to approve a further modest installment of reform. A law passed in July 1937 set up the Farm Security Administration with authority to lend money to tenants and sharecroppers for the purchase of farms, to help small farmers in emergencies, and to provide camps and medical care for, and regulate the working conditions of, migratory laborers. The Wagner–Steagall Act (September 1937) established a US Housing Authority to provide federal aid for slum clearance. A new Agricultural Adjustment Act (February 1938), reviving in modified form its invalidated 1933 predecessor, sought to stabilize farm prices by fixing marketing quotas and acreage allotments and by introducing the principle of 'parity payments', whereby a Commodity Credit Corporation made loans to farmers on surplus crops which were to be stored by the government until they could be disposed of at parity during periods of shortage. Finally, a Fair Labor Standards Act

(June 1938) established a minimum wage of 25 cents an hour rising to 40 cents within two years, and a maximum working week of 44 hours, to be reduced in the same period to 40 hours. The act also forbade child labor in interstate commerce. Roosevelt had to fight hard for these measures, especially the wages and hours law, which Southern Democrats openly opposed. Other important presidential recommendations were either ignored or rejected. Congress did nothing about a proposal for seven regional authorities modeled on the TVA. It handed Roosevelt an even sharper rebuff in rejecting the Executive Reorganization Bill. A seemingly uncontroversial measure, whose purpose was to promote government efficiency and economy by regrouping the numerous federal agencies, it reawakened fears of presidential dictatorship. Early in 1938 a massive defection of conservative Democrats brought about the bill's defeat. (It was passed in revised form a year later.)

Smarting under these reverses, Roosevelt set out to purge his party of anti-New Dealers. Especially in the South, he intervened directly in Democratic primaries, appealing to the voters to replace incumbent conservatives with liberals. But he suffered a humiliating defeat. Almost all the candidates he campaigned against were overwhelmingly reelected. The 1938 Congressional elections dealt the Administration an even heavier blow. Although the Democrats retained control of both houses of Congress, the Republicans made striking gains, the first since 1928. It was clear that the New Deal had run out of steam. Roosevelt tacitly acknowledged the fact in his annual message to Congress in January 1939. For the first time since coming to office he proposed no new reforms, emphasizing instead the threat to world peace and the need for national defense.

The New Deal in Retrospect

Not even the staunchest admirers of the New Deal could claim that it had brought about more than partial recovery. By 1939 there had been great improvements in some sectors of the economy: manufacturing production, for example, had returned to the level of 1929—though critics alleged that these had occurred in spite of New Deal policies, not because of them. But investment still lagged and there remained nine and a half million unemployed—17 percent of the working population. Not until 1941 would full employment and prosperity return, and only then because of the war and rearmament. Some New Deal policies did more harm than good: the NIRA, for example, and the gold-buying experiment. New Deal agricultural policies did nothing to help the worst-off farmers. The New Deal's social-welfare program was seriously deficient. There were also major omissions, notably the failure to embark on a large-scale housing program like that carried out in Great Britain: the federal government built only 180,000 homes during the Depression.

Yet for all its failures and limitations the New Deal can claim achievements which have stood the test of time and have become part of the national consensus. It laid the foundations of the welfare state and created a new legal framework for industrial relations. It introduced much-needed controls on banks and stock exchanges. It established the principle that government had the primary responsibility for regulating the economy. And although it is too much to claim that Roosevelt saved America from revolution—there was never any real danger of one—he restored national morale. Nor were these the only changes. The New Deal permanently enlarged the role of the federal government. It gave American capitalism a more humane aspect. While it did nothing to redistribute wealth or income, it redistributed power between capital and labor. It also conferred a new status on minorities: Roosevelt appointed an unprecedented number of Catholics, Jews, blacks, and women to federal jobs. The New Deal brought about a major political realignment: by constructing a coalition that included the South, the big-city Northern machines, organized labor, the intelligentsia, and the underprivileged, it ensured that the Democrats replaced the Republicans as the normal majority party. Finally, Roosevelt raised the presidential office to a new peak of prestige and power. He revitalized and dramatized the Presidency. He expanded the President's lawmaking functions. He introduced and skillfully stage-managed the presidential press conference and was the first to master the technique of communicating directly with a mass audience by means of radio. Roosevelt's broadcasts were not as numerous as many people later believed—he made only twenty-seven in twelve years compared with Hoover's twenty-one in four—but his warm, vibrant voice and lucid, intimate style were as great a source of comfort and hope to the American people as Churchill's radio addresses would be to the British during World War II. Yet in making the White House the focus of national life Roosevelt sowed the seeds of future trouble. His expansion of executive prerogative, together with what has been called the personalization of the presidential office, marked the beginning of a process whereby the Presidency became so inflated that it eventually threatened the balance of the American constitutional system.

24. *Foreign Policy between the Wars*, 1921–1941

The Aftermath of Versailles

Throughout the interwar period the American people remained hostile to Wilsonian internationalism and were unwilling to enter into the binding commitments that membership of the League of Nations entailed. The decision to enter the war in 1917 seemed in retrospect a mistake. The peace conference at Versailles had apparently shown all the European Powers to be equally imperialistic and self-seeking. The United States, it was felt, ought never again to become involved in their seemingly endless quarrels. These attitudes gave a nationalistic emphasis to American foreign and economic policy. Congress raised barriers against both immigrants and the importation of foreign goods. The League issue was not revived, nor was there much interest in the principle of collective security.

Nonetheless the United States did not retreat into what Wilson called "sullen and selfish isolation". There was still a good deal of popular concern about world peace and disarmament, and the Republican administrations of the 1920s played an active, though independent, role in foreign affairs. The United States took the lead in a number of ways in promoting international cooperation and European economic stability. Though the League of Nations was at first cold-shouldered, American observers were soon attending Assembly meetings at Geneva. There was even some modest cooperation with the new organization. By 1930 the United States had sent delegates to more than forty League conferences on such nonpolitical questions as public health, drug trafficking, and counterfeiting. In 1934 it joined the best-known League agency, the International Labor Organization. There was also strong support for American membership of the League-sponsored World Court and, although the United States never joined, there was always an American jurist on the bench. Thus, while American foreign policy was uncommitted and uninvolved, it was not narrowly isolationist.

The Washington Conference

This was evident from the American initiative in calling the Washington Conference of 1921–2. The first major international conference to be held in the United States, the gathering had two distinct but related objects, to limit naval armaments and to ease tension in the Far East. Congressional and public opinion strongly favored disarmament (as it was loosely called) as an insurance against war, as a positive alternative to American membership of the League, and, perhaps most of all, for reasons of economy. Since the end of the war the United States had been engaged in a costly naval arms race with Great Britain and Japan. If it continued it would seriously jeopardize the Harding administration's plans for tax cuts. The reason for the huge postwar naval-expansion program was not so much rivalry with Great Britain—though a sham anti-British battle was fought for domestic purposes by American naval expansionists—as distrust of Japanese ambitions. Japan had taken advantage of World War I to secure a preponderant position in China, thus negating the American policy of the Open Door. She had also acquired the former German colonies in the Pacific and thus threatened the sea routes and the submarine cable between Hawaii and the American outposts at Guam and the Philippines. Moreover, the disproportionate size of the Japanese force sent to Siberia in 1918 in the joint Allied intervention and its reluctance to withdraw aroused American suspicions that Japan had designs on Russian territory. But if Japan had emerged as the one likely enemy of the United States, the Anglo-Japanese alliance created a further complication. Though the British had sought to modify their obligations under the alliance when it was renewed in 1911, it still bound them to go to war with the United States if Japan did so.

When the Washington Conference opened on November 12, 1921 the American Secretary of State, Charles Evans Hughes, announced a detailed plan for naval limitation. He proposed a ten-year naval holiday during which no capital ships were to be built and, in order to preserve the existing ratio of American, British, and Japanese strength at 5:5:3, called for the scrapping of a total of sixty-six battleships. Hughes's formula, which also provided a ratio of 1.75:1.75 for France and Italy, became the basis of the Five-Power Naval Treaty signed on February 6, 1922. Great Britain, beset by financial difficulties, accepted the American claim to parity without protest, thereby surrendering her traditional position of maritime supremacy. Japan, initially reluctant to accept an inferior position, agreed to do so when the United States and Great Britain promised not to strengthen their naval bases in the Philippines and Hong Kong respectively. Agreement had already been reached on a Four-Power Treaty, whereby the United States, Great Britain, France, and Japan mutually guaranteed each other's possessions in the Pacific and agreed to consult together in the event of aggression there. These vague undertakings represented a way of terminating the Anglo-Japanese alliance without unduly offending the Japanese. A third major agreement was the Nine-Power Treaty, which committed all the participating nations to respect Chinese integrity and independence and maintain the Open Door. The Senate ratified all three treaties, but approved the Four-Power Treaty by a margin of only four votes and with the reservation that it involved "no commitment to armed force, no alliance, no obligation to enter into any defense". In a series of subsidiary agreements Japan conceded all that Hughes had asked by restoring sovereignty over Shantung to China and agreeing to withdraw from Siberia.

At the time the Washington agreements were widely hailed as heralding a permanent era of peace. A decade or so later, when Japan embarked upon an aggressive course in the Far East, Hughes was bitterly criticized for weakening the American navy and leaving Guam and the Philippines exposed. Both verdicts seem excessive. The settlement undoubtedly had its weaknesses. It did nothing to limit armies or air forces. The naval limitations applied only to battleships and aircraft-carriers. No enforcement machinery was provided for by either the Four-Power Treaty or the Nine-Power Treaty, their only sanction being moral restraint. A major Far Eastern power, the Soviet Union, was excluded from the conference. Worst of all, the Washington treaties helped perpetuate the illusion that armaments, rather than insecurity, were the basic cause of international crises. Yet Hughes's achievements, however limited and ephemeral, were significant. The Washington Conference produced the first general international agreement on arms limitation. It permitted greatly reduced expenditures on armaments, gave concrete shape to what remained of American internationalism, relaxed international tensions, and stabilized the Far Eastern situation.

Since the Washington Conference simply transferred the naval arms race from capital ships to lesser craft, especially cruisers, American leaders continued to press for the extension of the Five-Power Treaty ratios to all categories of warship. In response to a call from Coolidge a naval disarmament conference met at Geneva in 1927. It was a complete failure. France and Italy refused to attend; the American and British delegations squabbled inconclusively about cruiser strengths. But after the British had indicated willingness to accept full naval parity with the United States, a renewed American initiative proved more fruitful. The London Naval Conference of 1930 produced a complicated treaty whereby the United States, Great Britain, and Japan adopted a 10:10:6.5 ratio in cruiser strength and a 10:10:7 ratio in destroyers, while Japan was granted parity in submarines. Neither France nor Italy would sign these provisions but joined the other three signatories in extending the holiday in capital-ship construction for a further five years.

The Kellogg Pact

The belief that peace could be secured by paper promises backed only by the force of world opinion was carried to its limit in the Kellogg–Briand Pact of 1928. Since the end of the war a variety of peace organizations, some realistic, others utopian, had kept up a vocal agitation and the founder of one, a Chicago lawyer named Salmon O. Levinson, had proposed an international agreement for "the outlawry of war". The idea won influential support, including that of the powerful chairman of the Senate Foreign Relations Committee, William E. Borah, the philosopher, John Dewey, and the leaders of the Carnegie Endowment for International Peace, Nicholas Murray Butler, president of Columbia University, and James T. Shotwell, a Columbia history professor. During a visit to Paris early in 1927 Shotwell persuaded the French Foreign Minister, Aristide Briand, to announce that France was ready to sign a treaty with the United States outlawing war between the two countries. The State Department, aware that Briand's purpose was to attach the United States indirectly to the French system of alliances, was at first cool to the suggestion. But American public opinion, stirred up by Borah, Jane Addams, and other peace crusaders, became wildly enthusiastic. After receiving petitions bearing two million signatures Hughes's successor as Secretary of State, Frank B. Kellogg, made a counterproposal that the projected bilateral treaty be extended to include other powers. On August 27, 1928 the Kellogg–Briand Pact was signed in Paris by the United States and fourteen other nations. It was eventually adhered to by sixty-two. Though it permitted defensive action it bound the signatories to renounce war "as an instrument of national policy". Since it had no means of enforcement the Pact was meaningless. Like Prohibition it was a monument to illusion. Leading senators were skeptical of the Pact but since public opinion was so favorable and the treaty involved no American commitment, the Senate ratified it by 85 votes to 1—though it adopted a series of "interpretations" declaring that the treaty did not impair the right of self-defense or impinge upon the Monroe Doctrine. Whereupon senators turned to the next item of business—an appropriation of $274 million for fifteen heavy cruisers.

War Debts and Reparations

If international cooperation without specific commitment was one strand of Republican foreign policy, a narrow concern for national interests was another. This explained the acrimonious diplomatic exchanges over war debts. The United States had lent the Allies (chiefly Great Britain, France, and Italy) a total of $10.35 billion, nearly all of it spent in the United States on munitions, foodstuffs, and other supplies. The Allies subsequently argued that the loans had really been part of the American contribution to victory and should therefore be canceled. That seemed to them only fair since they had borne the brunt of the fighting. The United States, on the other hand, regarded the matter purely as a business transaction and demanded repayment in full. Coolidge's reported remark: "Well, they hired the money, didn't they?", summed up American feelings. The American attitude, though legally correct, took no account of the debtors' capacity to pay. The European countries did not possess enough gold for the purpose; nor, because of high American tariffs, could they discharge their obligations in manufactured goods. Their only hope of repaying the loans was by exacting reparations from Germany as provided in the Treaty of Versailles.

The United States refused to acknowledge formally that war debts were linked to reparations, but circumstances forced it to do so in effect. When in 1923 Germany defaulted on reparations, pleading inability to pay, French troops seized the industrial Ruhr, whereupon Germany countered with a policy of uncontrolled inflation which threatened a general European economic collapse. At this point the United States intervened to stabilize the situation. An international commission under the chairmanship of a Chicago banker, Charles G. Dawes (who maintained the fiction that he was acting as a private citizen), worked out a new reparations settlement. The Dawes Plan fixed a lower scale of reparations payments and provided for a loan to Germany of $200 million, about half to come from American banks. This stopgap measure was replaced in 1929 by the Young Plan, named after another American financier, Owen D. Young. Once assured of annual reparations payments the debtor countries renegotiated settlements with the United States. Interest-rates were scaled down and repayments extended over a sixty-two-year period.

The net effect of these arrangements was to create what has aptly been called "a financial merry-go-round". Between 1923 and 1930 American investors lent Germany about $2½ billion; Germany paid a roughly equivalent sum to the Allies as reparations; the Allies in turn transferred $2.6 billion to the United States as war-debt repayments. While these curious transactions gave Europe some years of stability they rested on fragile foundations. Once the Great Depression began in 1929 the United States could no longer act as international banker and the chain of payments was broken. In 1933, when Germany halted reparations, war-debt payments to the United States virtually ceased.

Origins of the 'Good Neighbor' Policy

The 1920s brought an improvement in relations with Latin America. Following the acquisition of the Panama Canal Zone in 1903 the Caribbean had become practically an American lake. The United States repeatedly used troops to enforce its demands on its smaller neighbors. At the end of World War I Cuba, Haiti, the Dominican Republic, and Nicaragua were under American military occupation and economic penetration had transformed most of the Latin American republics into virtual American protectorates. During the 1920s American investment and economic control continued to increase but there was a gradual retreat from interventionism. Germany's defeat had removed the main threat to the eastern approaches to the Panama Canal. American statesmen, Hughes in particular, wanted moreover to lessen the hostility big-stick diplomacy had created throughout Latin America. In 1921, under pressure from Hughes, the Senate belatedly made amends for the American role in the 1903 Panamanian revolution by ratifying a treaty granting Colombia a twenty-five million dollar indemnity. Though continuing to maintain the legality of intervention in Latin America, Hughes nonetheless withdrew American troops from Cuba in 1922 and from Santo Domingo in 1924. But his disengagement policy ran into difficulties in Nicaragua. American troops left in 1925 but were ordered back the following year when a fresh revolution threatened American lives and property. Meanwhile difficulties had developed with Mexico. The United States and Mexico backed rival factions in the Nicaraguan civil war. In 1926 the Mexican Congress angered American oil companies by sharply limiting foreign ownership of Mexican land and natural resources. It also offended American Catholics by its drastic anticlerical laws. But Dwight Morrow, a New York banker sent as ambassador to Mexico, reached a compromise oil settlement and persuaded the Mexican government to moderate its church laws. The oil agreement proved short-lived but the cordial atmosphere Morrow created was more lasting.

Hoover carried the conciliation of Latin America a stage further. As President-elect he made a goodwill tour of eleven Latin American republics. In 1930 he published the Clark Memorandum, a State Department document drawn up two years earlier. While not renouncing intervention it in effect repudiated the Roosevelt Corollary with its claim of an international police power for the United States in the Western Hemisphere. In contrast to what Roosevelt, Taft, and Wilson had done, Hoover did not intervene when revolution broke out in Brazil, Cuba, and Panama in 1930–1 or when other Latin American countries defaulted on loan repayments. Hoover and his Secretary of State, Henry L. Stimson, also took steps to liquidate the remaining American protectorates in the Caribbean. American marines finally left Nicaragua early in 1933 and a treaty was signed with Haiti providing for evacuation at the end of 1934. True, the United States retained financial control in these and other countries. Nonetheless the policy of restraint towards Latin America—the 'Good Neighbor' policy as it came to be called by Franklin D. Roosevelt—was a significant break with the past.

The Far East

Meanwhile trouble had been brewing in the Far East. The Washington treaties had not removed the causes of Japanese–American tension. The Japanese still smarted at Wilson's refusal to include a racial-equality clause in the League Covenant and still more at the inferior status Japan was accorded by the tonnage ratios of the Five-Power Treaty. An even greater affront to Japanese self-esteem was the Asian exclusion clause of the 1924 American immigration law. Hughes, who opposed the law as a needless insult to a proud and sensitive people, predicted that it would "implant the seeds of an antagonism which are sure to bear fruit in future". His apprehensions were promptly borne out. The law prompted anti-American demonstrations and boycotts of American goods all over Japan and left a sense of grievance which weakened the Japanese liberals and strengthened the military clique which favored an expansionist policy on the Asiatic mainland.

By the end of the 1920s the Japanese militarists had grown stronger and were seeking an opportunity to strike. Concerned at the resurgence of Soviet power in the Far East, they were even more alarmed at the efforts of Chiang Kai-shek's Chinese Nationalists to regain control of southern Manchuria. Though Manchuria was legally under Chinese jurisdiction it had been under Japanese control for decades. The Japanese regarded the province as their "economic lifeline" and were determined to preserve their privileged position. In September 1931, the Japanese army in Manchuria, acting independently of Tokyo, resorted to force. Blaming the Chinese for an explosion on the vital South Manchuria Railway, they occupied Mukden and other Manchurian cities and proceeded to overrun the entire province. China appealed for help to the League of Nations under Article XI of the Covenant and to the United States as a signatory of the Nine-Power Treaty and the Kellogg Pact. The League shrank from the challenge: it did nothing except appoint an investigating commission. Stimson, after some initial hesitation, would have liked to cooperate with the League in defending China. But Hoover, though condemning Japanese aggression, quickly scotched any idea of joining in economic or military sanctions. Nor was Stimson any more successful in persuading the British to enter into the consultations required by the Nine-Power Treaty. Great Britain had a good deal of sympathy with Japan and in any case its new National Government was struggling to ward off economic disaster. Stimson thus had only moral weapons to fall back on. On January 7, 1932 he sent identical notes to Japan and China warning that the United States would recognize no changes in the Far East which had been brought about

by force and which impaired American treaty rights or Chinese administrative integrity. The nonrecognition principle, known variously as the
Stimson Doctrine or the Hoover–Stimson Doctrine, was unanimously
endorsed by the League. But while it angered the Japanese, it did nothing
to restrain them. Early in 1932 they reorganized Manchuria as the puppet
state of Manchukuo and responded to a Chinese boycott of Japanese goods
by attacking Shanghai.

The Manchurian crisis demonstrated the futility of the Kellogg Pact and
the inability of the Washington treaties to protect Chinese territorial integrity and the Open Door. But if Stimson's policy proved ineffectual it is
difficult to see what else he could have done, especially in view of Great
Britain's unwillingness to take a strong stand. The United States was
preoccupied with the Depression, then at its worst. Its armed forces were
in no condition to fight. Most important, the American people had no wish
to become involved. Despite their sympathy for China, they would not
have supported stronger action against Japan.

New Deal Diplomacy

By the time Roosevelt became President in March 1933 it was evident that
the precarious peace established after World War I was breaking down.
Only a few weeks earlier Japan had announced her withdrawal from the
League of Nations and Hitler had become Chancellor of Germany.
Thenceforth world tensions mounted steadily. Japan continued to
encroach on northern China; Hitler rearmed and overturned the Versailles
settlement; Mussolini sought to carve out an extensive African empire. By
1935 another war was clearly on the way. The American response was to
become increasingly pacific, nationalistic, and—to use the not wholly
accurate term then current—isolationist. The Great Depression helped
foster such an attitude by focusing attention on domestic affairs, sapping
confidence in American ability to influence world affairs, and breeding
popular distrust of bankers and big business, the two groups with the closest connections with foreign countries. Yet isolationism stemmed also from
a deeply felt abhorrence of war and a conviction that the coming struggle
involved no vital American interest. No matter what befell the rest of the
world, Americans were determined not to become involved in a second
international crusade.

Earlier in his career Roosevelt had preached internationalism; later on
he would do so again. But in 1932, fearing to lose the Democratic nomination, he had disavowed the League of Nations and insisted that war
debts must be paid in full. Once elected President, he was unwilling to
jeopardize his domestic legislative program by alienating the powerful isolationist wing of his own party. For a time Roosevelt was even more isolationist than his Republican predecessors. Hoover may have displayed a

narrow economic nationalism in signing—and defending—the high Hawley-Smoot Tariff Act of 1930, which had disastrous consequences for world trade. But he at least agreed to American participation in the World Economic Conference, due to be held in London in June 1933. Its purpose was to overcome the worldwide depression by lowering tariff barriers and by agreeing to stabilize fluctuating currencies and exchange-rates. Roosevelt at first made encouraging noises but in the end demonstrated that he was not prepared to place international economic cooperation above domestic recovery. The leader of the American delegation, the Secretary of State, Cordell Hull, had sailed for London in the hope of implementing his pet scheme for reciprocal tariff agreements. But on the eve of the conference Roosevelt ruled out such a course and then, on July 3, publicly denounced as "the old fetishes of so-called international bankers" a currency-stabilization program laboriously worked out by the conference. This was because stabilization would hamper his plans to increase domestic purchasing power by devaluing the dollar. It is doubtful whether the conference would have accomplished anything tangible in any case. All the participating countries were obsessively concerned with self-preservation. But Roosevelt's "bombshell message" effectively ended discussion and reinforced the European conviction that Americans were impossible to work with.

In 1934, when the value of the dollar had fallen to a level Roosevelt believed to be sufficiently competitive, he embraced Hull's reciprocity philosophy and persuaded Congress to pass the Trade Agreements Act authorizing the Administration to lower tariffs by up to 50 percent for countries prepared to reciprocate. In the next four years Hull negotiated reciprocity treaties with eighteen countries mainly in Latin America. The agreements won the United States some goodwill but did not fulfill Hull's expectation that they would increase American imports and revive world trade.

Still more disappointing were the results of another foreign-policy departure: the establishment of diplomatic relations with the Soviet Union. Alone among the major powers the United States had withheld recognition from the Soviet regime because of its encouragement of world revolution, its hostility to religion, and its repudiation of Czarist debts. But by 1933 businessmen hoped that recognition would help revive the economy by boosting exports to Russia. There was a feeling that Russia might prove a bulwark against Japan. Thus a Russian overture met a ready response and in November 1933 the United States formally extended recognition. In return the Russians guaranteed religious freedom to Americans in the Soviet Union, promised not to engage in propaganda or subversive activities in the United States, and undertook to negotiate a settlement of the pre-1917 debt. The hopes raised by the agreement were speedily dashed.

All the Soviet promises were in some degree broken. Nor did the expected increase in trade materialize.

In his inaugural address Roosevelt had promised to follow "the policy of the good neighbor—the neighbor who resolutely respects himself and because he does so, respects the rights of others". Intended originally to be of general application the 'Good Neighbor' policy came to be specifically associated with Latin America. It involved continuing the Coolidge–Hoover policy of withdrawal. At the seventh Pan-American conference at Montevideo in December 1933, Hull signed a convention providing that "no state has the right to intervene in the internal or external affairs of another". The Roosevelt Administration soon showed that it meant to honor this undertaking. In 1934 the United States and Cuba signed a treaty abrogating the 1903 Platt Amendment which sanctioned American intervention; in 1936 a similar treaty was signed with Panama. Meanwhile in August 1934 the last marines left Haiti and for the first time in a generation no part of Latin America was under American occupation. American liberals applauded the withdrawal policy but were soon complaining about its results. In nearly every case, notably in Nicaragua, the Dominican Republic, Haiti, and Cuba, the end of the American occupation was the signal for the establishment of a repressive dictatorship.

Yet in abandoning armed intervention in Latin America the United States had no intention of surrendering its predominant position there. Hull's reciprocal trade agreements and the establishment of the Export–Import Bank in 1934 can be regarded as variants of dollar diplomacy. They were certainly designed to strengthen American economic influence. Even so the 'Good Neighbor' policy marked a real change. Thus when disputes broke out with Latin American countries in which there were substantial American investments the United States showed unwonted restraint. In 1937 Bolivia confiscated the holdings of the Standard Oil Company; in 1938 Mexico expropriated nearly all the foreign-owned oil industry; in 1939 Venezuela demanded higher royalties from American oil companies. In all three cases, but especially in the Mexican controversy, in which hundreds of millions of dollars were at stake, American oil interests clamored for intervention. But although the State Department insisted on adequate compensation, and indeed retaliated by boycotting Mexican silver and trying to lower the value of the Mexican peso on world markets, there was no return to the big stick. Concerned at the spread of German and Italian influence in South America, the United States was now anxious to promote hemispheric unity. It was not wholly successful in doing so, mainly because Argentina remained uncooperative, but at the Pan-American Conference at Lima in December 1938 it secured acceptance of a Declaration that in the event of a threat to "the peace, security or territorial integrity of any American republic", the foreign ministers of all twenty-one republics would meet for consultation. This was less of a commitment than the United States would have liked, but it was the first time the countries of the Western Hemisphere had agreed on common action.

Isolationism Triumphant

Meanwhile American pacifism and isolationism had reached high tide. Novels, plays, and films stressed the horrors and futility of war: among them Hemingway's *A Farewell to Arms* (1929), Erich Maria Remarque's *All Quiet on the Western Front* (1929), and Robert E. Sherwood's *Idiot's Delight* (1936). Women's clubs campaigned against the manufacture of toy soldiers and other symbols of militarism. Students paraded for peace and pledged themselves never to serve in a war. The clergy, who had been prominent in blessing the crusade of 1917–18, vowed in large numbers never to repeat the error. The writings of 'revisionist' historians like Harry Elmer Barnes and Sidney B. Fay familiarized intellectuals with the notion that Germany had not been solely or even primarily responsible for the outbreak of war in 1914. Then in 1934 came a sensational magazine article, "Arms and the Man", and a popular book, *Merchants of Death*, both blaming wars on the machinations of international arms manufacturers. Pacifist organizations like the National Council for the Prevention of War and the Women's International League for Peace and Freedom led a demand for Congressional investigation of the armaments trade. In April 1934 the Senate appointed a special investigating committee under the chairmanship of an isolationist Republican, Gerald P. Nye of North Dakota. The Nye Committee's hearings exposed the lobbying activities and dubious practices of munitions-makers. It also revealed that American industrialists and financiers had made huge profits during World War I from the sale of arms to the Allies. Moreover, though no supporting evidence was adduced, the Committee's report gave the impression that the United States had entered the war in 1917 at the bidding of Wall Street bankers and munitions-makers. Walter Millis's best-selling book, *The Road to War, 1914–1917*, spread a similar message. The United States, he insisted, had not gone to war to defend high ideals or even its national interests, but had become enmeshed by virtue of its economic ties with the Allies. To a generation absorbed with economic concerns this sounded all too plausible.

The depth of isolationist feeling was shown by the final defeat of the proposal for American membership of the World Court. Although established under Article XIV of the League of Nations Covenant to settle international disputes, the Court functioned independently of the League and membership was open to all nations. Harding, Coolidge, and Hoover had all favored American membership. But Senate isolationists were opposed to what they regarded as back-door entry into the League and insisted on reservations which the other members of the Court found unacceptable. By 1930 a formula had been devised to meet American objections but isolationists repeatedly blocked any action. Finally in 1935 Roosevelt persuaded the Senate to reconsider the matter. He was confident he could win approval for what had become a greatly watered-down commitment. But in the atmosphere created by the Nye Committee investigation the isolationists, led by the newspaper editor, William Randolph Hearst, and the radio priest, Father Coughlin, were able to stir up a popular outcry. Deluged by telegrams of protest, about twenty Senators who had intended to vote for the Court protocol changed their minds and the final vote (January 29, 1935) fell short of the needed two-thirds majority.

The main result of the Nye Committee's investigation was, however, to convince Americans of the need to ensure that they would never again be drawn into war as had happened in 1917. This was the purpose of the Neutrality Acts of 1935–7, all passed by sweeping Congressional majorities. The first of the series, passed in 1935 as Mussolini prepared to attack Ethiopia, required the President, whenever he deemed a state of war to exist, to declare an arms embargo against all belligerents and empowered him to warn American citizens against traveling on belligerent ships. When the Italian attack on Ethiopia came, in October 1935, the Administration called for a moral embargo (that is, a voluntary one) on the shipment of oil and other commodities to Italy. But it refused to cooperate with the League in imposing sanctions. In February 1936 Congress passed a second Neutrality Act extending for another year the provisions of the first and prohibiting war loans and credits to belligerents. A third Neutrality Act, passed in May 1937, renewed the earlier prohibitions, made travel on belligerent ships unlawful, and added a "cash and carry" provision giving the President authority to require belligerents to pay cash for any materials bought in the United States and to carry them away in their own ships. Roosevelt was unenthusiastic about the Neutrality Acts, especially their progressive limitations on presidential discretion and their insistence that all belligerents, whether aggressors or victims of aggression, must be treated alike. But so strong was antiwar feeling that he felt obliged to surrender control of foreign policy to Congressional isolationists.

While the debate over neutrality legislation was going on the international outlook became increasingly threatening. Germany remilitarized the Rhineland (1935), Italy completed the conquest of Ethiopia, the fighting in the Spanish Civil War became internationalized, the Rome–Berlin Axis was formed (1936), and a clash between Japanese and Chinese soldiers near the Marco Polo Bridge, just north of Peking, escalated into all-out hostilities (1937).

An alarmed Roosevelt for the first time gave his undivided attention to foreign affairs. On the ground that there had been no formal declaration he chose not to recognize that a state of war existed in China and thus avoided having to impose the arms embargo required by the Neutrality Act, a step that would have injured China and helped Japan. Then, in a speech in Chicago on October 5, 1937, the President deplored the growing epidemic of world lawlessness, asserted that "mere isolation and neutrality" offered no escape, and, in a dramatic passage that attracted worldwide attention, called upon peace-loving nations to 'quarantine' the aggressors. Roosevelt may have been trying to educate his countrymen to the realities of the international situation. But his quarantine proposal remained obscure. There is no evidence that he was contemplating economic sanctions or other strong measures against Japan. He may have been thinking of breaking off diplomatic relations. Or he may simply have been thinking aloud. At all events, when his words provoked a hostile public reaction he quickly disavowed any intention of committing the United States to collective security.

The American people were patently no more ready to fight a war in Asia in 1937 than they had been in 1932—or even to risk one—and Roosevelt was not the man to run ahead of strongly expressed public opinion. Thus British approaches for joint Anglo-American action against Japan were rebuffed. And although the United States took part in the Brussels Conference called in November 1937 to consider Japan's conduct, it was no more willing than other participants to go beyond moral condemnation. The collapse of the Brussels Conference demonstrated Western impotence and seems to have encouraged the Japanese militarists to commit a fresh outrage. On December 12, 1937 Japanese planes wantonly bombed and sank the American gunboat *Panay* in the Yangtze River. There was a brief outburst of public anger in the United States but, in contrast to what had happened after the sinking of the *Maine* in 1898, a remarkable absence of war fever. The dominant reaction, indeed, was to demand the withdrawal of American ships and men from the Far East. The Administration contented itself with a protest and when the Japanese apologized and promised to pay an indemnity the incident was declared closed.

The sinking of the *Panay* had the further consequence of bringing to the House floor a constitutional amendment which had been stalled in committee for months. Sponsored by Congressman Louis Ludlow, an Indiana Democrat, it provided that, except in the case of invasion, Congress could declare war only after a national referendum had given approval. Public-opinion polls showed that the proposal enjoyed massive public support and it seemed certain to pass. But Roosevelt objected that such a referendum "would cripple any President in his conduct of our foreign relations and ...would encourage other nations to believe that they could violate American rights with impunity". White House pressure resulted in the defeat of the Ludlow amendment on January 10, 1938 by a vote of 209 to 188. But the narrowness of the margin revealed the persistence of isolationism and the strength of opposition to presidential control of foreign policy.

Despite Roosevelt's caution and hesitancy, he continued to cast about for ways of countering aggression. In January 1938 he secretly, if somewhat halfheartedly, sounded out London about holding an international conference to promulgate agreed standards of international behavior, reduce armaments, and promote economic stability by facilitating access to raw materials. But the British Prime Minister, Neville Chamberlain, dismissed the initiative because it would interfere with his appeasement policy. In any case he felt, probably rightly, that it was wisest to expect "nothing from the Americans but words". By now the totalitarian threat in Europe was coming to overshadow the Asian conflict. Hitler's annexation of Austria in March 1938 was the prelude to a campaign of threats against Czechoslovakia. In September the Munich Agreement averted war only because the Czechs, under pressure from Great Britain and France, yielded to Hitler's demands. Six months later Hitler swallowed what was left of Czechoslovakia and began a war of nerves against Poland.

With war now plainly imminent Americans were more determined than ever to stay out of it. But they had become uneasily aware of their military weakness and vulnerability. There was thus relatively little opposition, even from isolationists, when in January 1938 Roosevelt tardily called for naval rearmament. Congress responded with the Naval Expansion Act of May 1938, which authorized the expenditure over the next decade of over one billion dollars to create a navy equal to the combined fleets of Germany, Italy, and Japan. This was the largest peacetime naval appropriation ever voted, but it was less impressive than it seemed: it entailed only a 20 percent increase in the current naval building program. Early in 1939 the President secured an additional appropriation of $525 million, most of it to strengthen air defenses. But his efforts to persuade Congress to repeal the arms-embargo provisions of the 1937 Neutrality Act were unavailing. On August 5, 1939, less than a month before Hitler's invasion of Poland, Congress adjourned without having acted.

Thus American foreign policy in the 1930s was unheroic. Distracted by the Depression and disillusioned by its experiences in World War I, the United States did little to halt the dictators or to encourage others to do so. American policy may, indeed, unwittingly have helped the Axis powers and reinforced British and French appeasement. It should, however, be remembered that American attitudes were paralleled, and with less excuse, in Europe, especially in Great Britain. British policy was no less blinkered and timorous, British public opinion just as slow to wake up to the totalitarian threat, every bit as disposed to argue that the Versailles

Treaty had been unjust and that Germany and her Axis partners had legitimate grievances. In such circumstances the United States, so much further away and apparently safe from attack, can hardly be blamed for failing to give a lead.

Challenges to Isolationism

When war broke out in 1939 Roosevelt issued a proclamation of neutrality but, unlike Wilson in 1914, pointedly refrained from urging the American people to be neutral in thought as well as in action. Most Americans, while determined to stay out of the war, fervently hoped for an Allied victory. Anxious to find some way of sending arms and other supplies to the Allies Roosevelt called Congress into special session to revise the neutrality legislation. After six weeks of stormy debate Congress passed a new Neutrality Act (November 4, 1939) which repealed the arms embargo and allowed belligerents to buy arms on a 'cash and carry' basis. But it retained the ban on American loans to nations at war and, in a new provision, forbade American ships to enter certain 'combat zones', to be designated by the President. Thus while Roosevelt got essentially what he wanted, he had to make concessions to the isolationists. Nearly all Americans were satisfied with the compromise. They were confident that, with the limited aid now available, Great Britain and France were fully capable of defeating Hitler.

These optimistic assumptions were rudely shattered in the spring of 1940, when Nazi forces successively attacked and occupied Denmark and Norway, overran the Netherlands, Belgium, and Luxemburg, drove the British army into the sea at Dunkirk, captured Paris, and forced France to capitulate. The fall of France staggered Americans. Overnight they realized their country's peril. Few expected a German attack but the Nazi triumphs undermined the whole basis of American strategic thinking, namely, the implicit assumption that the Atlantic sea lanes would remain in friendly hands. Now, however, only Great Britain stood between Hitler and the complete domination of western Europe. If the British were defeated, and that seemed all too likely, an aggressive Germany would control the whole of the eastern Atlantic and, together with her Fascist ally, Italy, who entered the war in June 1940, the Mediterranean and the North African shore. If, moreover, the Axis powers acquired the British and French fleets they would have an overwhelming naval superiority over the United States.

Roosevelt's first reaction to the European disasters was to strengthen the nation's defenses. He asked for and obtained huge additional appropriations to expand the army and navy and to boost aircraft production to 50,000 a year. In June 1940 he established the National Defense Research Committee to coordinate work on new weapons. (This was the body which ultimately developed the proximity fuse and the atomic bomb.) In September, ignoring a barrage of isolationist criticism, he urged a Selective Service and Training Act on Congress. Its passage meant that, for the first time, the United States had peacetime conscription.

Meanwhile in a speech at Charlottesville, Virginia on June 10, 1940 the President announced a policy of all-out aid to Great Britain. Using an ingenious legal loophole to circumvent the Neutrality Act he ordered the War and Navy Departments to transfer 'surplus' planes, guns, and ammunition to the British whose army had lost most of its equipment at Dunkirk and who were now facing air attack, U-boat blockade, and invasion. Yet when Winston Churchill appealed urgently for fifty old American destroyers to protect the Atlantic supply line, the President hesitated. He knew there would be formidable isolationist opposition to so blatantly unneutral an act. But the suggestion that the destroyers be exchanged for bases in Great Britain's Western Hemisphere possessions offered a way out. On September 2, 1940, by an executive agreement that enabled him to bypass Congress, Roosevelt turned over fifty World War I destroyers to Great Britain in exchange for ninety-nine-year leases on air and naval bases in six British colonies ranging from the Bahamas to British Guiana. In addition the British granted similar leases in Bermuda and Newfoundland as outright gifts and, in response to American wishes, Churchill undertook never to scuttle or surrender the Royal Navy. These agreements enabled Roosevelt to represent the transaction as one which enhanced American security at little cost. Most people recognized that the bases were a major defensive asset, but many questioned the devious way Roosevelt had engineered the exchange.

Roosevelt's attempts to arouse public opinion to the nation's peril were powerfully reinforced by those of the Committee to Defend America by Aiding the Allies. Founded in May 1940, under the chairmanship of the veteran Kansas newspaper editor, William Allen White, the Committee ran an effective propaganda campaign stressing that Great Britain was the first line of American defense and urging all possible aid to her short of war. The Committee found most support on the Eastern and Western seaboards and in the South, especially among old-stock Americans who had ties with Great Britain and among those ethnic groups, particularly Jews, whose countrymen had suffered at Hitler's hands. Most of the Committee's supporters, including White, were opposed to America's entering the war but a militant faction, the New York-based Century Group, preached outright intervention.

Organized opposition to the President's foreign policy came from the America First Committee, which sprang into existence two days after the destroyers-for-bases exchange was announced. Promoted by a group of Chicago businessmen, America First won the backing of prominent men like former President Hoover, the celebrated aviator, Charles A. Lindbergh, and the isolationist senators, Gerald P. Nye and Burton K. Wheeler. Though not wholly sectional or partisan, the movement had its largest following among Middle Westerners, whose isolationism was rooted in remoteness from any potential enemy, and in the Republican party, distrustful of Roosevelt's policies, whether domestic or foreign. Believing that Hitler posed no threat to American security, America Firsters aimed at keeping out of the war and avoiding the risks inherent in helping Great Britain, but also at building up an impregnable American defense. There was nothing intrinsically absurd or unpatriotic about such an attitude—though America First's critics vehemently asserted the contrary. Yet the movement was embarrassed and its reputation tarnished by the support of questionable elements: Coughlinites and other anti-Semites, Communists (until the Soviet Union was invaded), and Nazi sympathizers like the German–American Bund.

As the 1940 presidential election approached foreign-policy issues predominated. The Republican nomination seemed at first to lie between Thomas E. Dewey, the youthful, "racket-busting", New York district attorney, and Senator Robert A. Taft of Ohio, a relentless foe of the New Deal and of Roosevelt's foreign policy. But as the Nazis overran Europe, Dewey's inexperience in foreign affairs damaged his chances. Nor did Taft's narrow brand of isolationism seem to accord with the national mood. Rather than accept Taft, the Eastern Republicans who had earlier favored Dewey threw their support to a political outsider, Wendell L. Willkie of Indiana, an internationalist and liberal-minded corporation lawyer and utilities executive, whose largely youthful and amateur supporters had mounted an extraordinarily successful grass-roots campaign. To everyone's surprise Willkie was nominated on the sixth ballot. Until the Democrats met in July, Roosevelt's enigmatic silence about a possible third term made it difficult to predict who Willkie's opponent would be. Some historians believe that the President had decided well in advance to run for reelection but, with characteristic deviousness, chose to kill off the chances of his potential rivals, even while seeming to encourage some of them. Others hold that Roosevelt was genuinely anxious to retire but when no clear successor emerged reluctantly concluded that his own candidacy was the only way to keep the party in liberal hands and ensure continuity of leadership at a time of international crisis. At all events, when Roosevelt finally indicated his availability the Democrats defied the two-term tradition and overwhelmingly renominated him. With rather less enthusiasm they accepted his choice for the vice-presidential nomination, Secretary of Agriculture Henry A. Wallace, an advanced liberal.

Although the two candidates were in essential agreement about foreign policy, that became the main campaign issue. Willkie charged that Roosevelt's reelection would plunge the country into war within six months; Roosevelt, alarmed lest his opponent had found a winning issue, replied with an extravagant promise that American boys would not "be sent into any foreign war". Yet the impression seems to have persisted that the Democrats were less isolationist than the Republicans. At all events Roosevelt suffered defections from many German-American, Italian-American, and Irish-American voters, while picking up support from Polish-Americans and other east Europeans whose homelands had been overrun. In the end Roosevelt won comfortably but Willkie ran much more strongly than Landon in 1936 and recovered much of the farm vote in traditional Republican states in the Middle West.

Lend-Lease and its Consequences

Immediately after his reelection Roosevelt discovered that it would be necessary to go beyond the legal makeshifts he had been using to help Great Britain. The British desperately needed American war supplies but were rapidly running out of money, or rather of gold and dollars. Yet the Johnson Act of 1934 forbade loans to governments in default of their World War I debts and it was doubtful whether Congress would repeal it, at least without a prolonged wrangle. Seeking some way to enable the United States to become "the arsenal of democracy"—a phrase he used in a fireside chat on December 29, 1940—the President hit upon the bold and novel formula of lending goods instead of money. When Congress assembled in January 1941, he submitted the draft of a Lend-Lease bill that would authorize him to sell, lease, or lend, under such terms as he thought fit, arms, munitions, food, and other war supplies to any country whose defense he deemed vital to that of the United States. Two months of acrimonious debate followed. Wheeler, Taft, and other isolationists denounced the proposal as a blank check to wage undeclared war. In order to overcome Congressional opposition and demonstrate to a skeptical American public that Great Britain really was on the verge of bankruptcy, the administration urged the sale of all privately owned British investments in the United States. Churchill demurred but under pressure reluctantly agreed to sell one major British asset, the American Viscose Corporation, at a price, as it turned out, well below its intrinsic value. In the end the Lend-Lease Act passed Congress comfortably and was signed by the President on March 11, 1941. Churchill's famous description of Lend-Lease as "the most unselfish and unsordid financial act of any country in all history" did not represent his true feelings. He resented the forced sale as an unnecessary political maneuver. But he ultimately thought it as a small price to pay for $7,000 million of Lend-Lease aid.

While Lend-Lease solved the financial problem of supplying Great Britain, it would be ineffective unless the Atlantic sea lanes could be kept open. By the spring of 1941 German U-boats were sinking 500,000 tons of shipping a month, twice as much as British and American shipyards could turn out. Though still reluctant to act decisively Roosevelt took a number of steps which gradually edged the United States into the Battle of the Atlantic. In justifying his actions to Congress and the American people Roosevelt often showed a lack of candor, though the charge made by unsympathetic historians that he "lied the country into war" is unworthy of serious consideration. In March 1941 Roosevelt gave permission for damaged British warships to be repaired in American dockyards and for RAF pilots to train in Florida. In April he extended the hemispheric neutrality zone, proclaimed at Panama in 1939, halfway across the Atlantic, ordered American naval patrols to comb the area for German submarines and report their presence to British warships, and sent American forces into Greenland. In June the President issued an executive order freezing all German and Italian assets in the United States. Early in July, by agreement with the Icelandic government, American marines landed in Iceland to forestall a German occupation. This gave the President a pretext in September for ordering the convoying of American vessels as far as Iceland.

Meanwhile an informal Anglo-American alliance was taking shape. Secret talks in Washington in the spring of 1941 between British and American staff officers produced agreement on the strategy to be followed if the United States entered the war. Then in August Roosevelt and Churchill, who had been corresponding privately since 1939, held the first of their wartime meetings off the coast of Newfoundland. Roosevelt would not enter into any military commitments, but joined Churchill in issuing a press release which became known as the Atlantic Charter. This was a declaration, not of specific war aims, but of general principles. They included national self-determination, equal access to trade and raw materials, international collaboration for economic advancement and social security, freedom from fear and want, freedom of the seas, and disarmament. Despite the publicity attending its birth, the Atlantic Charter was destined to have no influence on the postwar settlement. But it was unprecedented for a country still technically neutral to join with a belligerent in issuing such a document, however vague and innocuous.

Even now Roosevelt hesitated to take any step that would commit the United States to full belligerency. This was not merely because of isolationist sentiment—persistent though that was. His own indecision held him back also. But just as Lend-Lease had led to convoying, so convoying led to open hostilities. On September 4, 1941 a German submarine off Iceland fired two torpedoes at but failed to hit the US destroyer *Greer* which responded with depth-charges. Roosevelt, concealing the fact that the *Greer* had been shadowing the U-boat and reporting its position to the British, interpreted the incident as an act of piracy and seized the chance to announce that Axis submarines in American-patrolled waters would henceforth be sunk on sight. On October 9 the President asked Congress to revise the Neutrality Act so as to allow the arming of American merchant-men and to permit them to sail to belligerent ports. During the Con-gressional debate the US destroyer *Kearney* was attacked with the loss of eleven lives (October 17) and the US destroyer *Reuben James* sunk with the loss of 115 of her crew (October 31). A week later, though by slender majorities, Congress swept away all that was left of the neutrality laws except the ban on loans to belligerents and on travel on belligerent ships. The way was now clear for American merchant ships, carrying any kind of cargo, including munitions, to enter the combat zones.

By the autumn of 1941 the United States had thus become involved in an undeclared naval war with Germany. Hitler would have been fully jus-tified in taking drastic countermeasures. But he refrained from doing so. Having invaded the Soviet Union in June and with his armies besieging Moscow and Leningrad he was anxious, for the moment at least, to avoid American belligerency. The virtual repeal of the Neutrality Act might soon have forced him to order the systematic sinking of American shipping, especially since Roosevelt had extended Lend-Lease to Russia. But that is mere speculation. War was to come to the United States, not from the Atlantic, but from the Pacific.

The Road to Pearl Harbor

Almost from the start of World War II the United States and Japan were on a collision course. The United States became increasingly alarmed at Japan's aggressive designs and increasingly anxious to find some way of restraining her. Yet the administration was just as cautious and hesitant as it was toward Germany—and for the same reasons. Roosevelt was not prepared to allow Japan to dominate South-East Asia but, because of the strength of isolationism and of his own revulsion against war, did no more than react to Japanese moves. The first came in the spring of 1940, after Nazi triumphs in western Europe had whetted Japanese appetites. With France and The Netherlands prostrate the Japanese had a golden oppor-tunity to extend their 'New Order' in East Asia. They stepped up their war against China and began to cast covetous eyes on French Indo-China and the Dutch East Indies, with their rich resources of oil and rubber. Having pressured the British into closing the Burma Road, the chief supply route to Nationalist China, they browbeat the Vichy government in France into granting them bases in northern Indo-China. Then in September 1940 Japan concluded a military alliance with Germany and Italy. American public opinion, though loath to go to war with Japan, nonetheless favored denying the Japanese the raw materials she needed to wage war in China. Accordingly, Roosevelt met Japan's southward moves by gradually applying economic sanctions against her. In July 1940 he banned the export without license of a variety of strategic materials, including oil; in September he proclaimed an absolute embargo on all types of scrap iron and steel, except to the Western Hemisphere and to Great Britain; in December he cut off machine tools, chemicals, and certain other vital war materials. The United States also increased its aid to China, encouraged the British to reopen the Burma Road—which they did—, and warned the Japanese of the grave consequences of any move against British or Dutch Far Eastern possessions.

None of these steps had any discernible effect on Japanese expansionists. What deterred them for a time was the fear that, if Japan became involved in war with the United States, the Soviet Union would strike along the Manchurian border. But the Japanese–Soviet Neutrality Pact of April 1941· and, still more, Hitler's assault on Russia two months later effectively removed that threat. The Japanese promptly made fresh demands on Vichy and extorted bases in southern Indo-China. That seemed to portend an attack on Malaya and the Dutch East Indies. Consequently on July 26 Roosevelt froze all Japanese assets in the United States, closed the Panama Canal to Japanese shipping, and mobilized the Philippine militia. Then on August 1 he took the crucial step of banning oil exports to Japan. The British and Dutch governments did the same. This meant virtually a worldwide oil embargo against Japan. Since Japan's oil reserves would last only for eighteen months at most, the Tokyo government had either to abandon its expansionist dreams or go to war in order to seize the supplies its war machine needed.

The militarists in Tokyo wanted to plunge ahead recklessly but Japanese naval leaders were anxious to avoid a war they feared they might lose. At their urging the conciliatory Prime Minister, Konoye, renewed the attempt, which had been going on intermittently since March, to reach a negotiated settlement with the United States. The Japanese were ready to promise that they would refrain from further expansion in South-East Asia and would withdraw from Indo-China upon the settlement of the 'China incident'. In return they demanded an end to American aid to Chiang Kai-shek, the unfreezing of Japanese assets, and the restoration of oil supplies. The American reply, sent on September 3, 1941, summarily rejected these proposals and insisted that Japan withdraw her troops from China and abrogate the Tripartite Pact with Germany and Italy. Roosevelt's critics were later to allege that he was hellbent on war and that he rejected Konoye's approach in order to goad the Japanese into striking the first blow. But this theory will not stand examination. The President and his advisers wanted to preserve peace in the Pacific, but not at the expense of China. Moreover, they were convinced that the Japanese were bluffing.

Roosevelt's inflexibility was a godsend to the Japanese militarists. On

September 6, 1941 an Imperial Conference in Tokyo agreed to give diplomacy one last chance to secure American acceptance of Japanese demands, but to resort to war if there was no satisfactory outcome by early October—a deadline later extended to early December. Negotiations in fact continued right up to the outbreak of war, but neither side would budge on the basic issue of China. On November 26, after the rejection of their final terms, the Japanese Cabinet confirmed the decision for war. On December 7 Japanese planes carried out a devastating surprise attack on the American naval base at Pearl Harbor, Hawaii. In less than ninety minutes the bulk of the American Pacific fleet was destroyed or immobilized. Simultaneously, Japanese naval forces attacked Siam, the Philippines, Malaya, and the Dutch East Indies. The attack on Pearl Harbor, made without a declaration of war, aroused universal indignation in the United States. Even Roosevelt's bitterest critics were agreed on the need for retaliation. The day after Pearl Harbor Congress passed a resolution (with only a single dissenting vote in the House) declaring that a state of war existed with Japan. Although Japan's Axis partners, Germany and Italy, had known nothing of her intention to attack, they both declared war on the United States on December 11.

Subsequently controversy developed over responsibility for the Pearl Harbor disaster. Why, it was asked, was the attack not anticipated and adequate steps taken to repel it, especially as American experts, having broken the Japanese diplomatic code, had been privy to the secret messages passing between Tokyo and Japanese representatives in the United States? Some 'revisionist' historians, anxious to denigrate Roosevelt, have charged that the President knew precisely what the Japanese intended but deliberately exposed the fleet so as to lure the Japanese into an attack that would unite the nation behind him. But this is a fanciful and inherently absurd suggestion. The Roosevelt Administration did indeed know that the Japanese were about to attack, but the intercepted dispatches gave no hint of where the blow would fall. American leaders unanimously believed that the Japanese intended to assault Malaya, the Dutch East Indies, and possibly the Philippines. Very few believed they would be foolhardly enough to attack Hawaii. Virtually no one thought they had the capacity to do all these things simultaneously. The basic reason for the Pearl Harbor debacle was not Machiavellian plotting but miscalculation and misunderstanding, compounded by negligence and misfortune. The material in the decoded intercepts was not properly evaluated or effectively distributed. The field commanders at Hawaii should have taken more precautions than they did. Finally, when Army radar in Hawaii picked up the approaching Japanese planes, nothing was done because they were thought to be American B-17s. Consequently the treacherous act which plunged the United States into World War II left her for a time crippled in the Pacific.

25. *Global War*, 1941–1945

Civil Liberties in Wartime

Never had Americans been more determined or more united in taking up arms than in December 1941. Though they had wanted desperately to stay out of the conflict, the attack on Pearl Harbor ranged the entire nation behind the war effort. In contrast to 1917 Americans went to war in a sober, realistic frame of mind. They saw the struggle as one for national survival, rather than as a crusade for international righteousness. There was thus little of the intolerance, the hysterical excesses of the First World War. Of the two largest groups of enemy aliens—700,000 Italians and 300,000 Germans—only a few hundred were interned; the rest were freely accepted in war industries and the armed services.

There was, however, one major exception to the general pattern of restraint: the forced removal and imprisonment of the West Coast Japanese. Pearl Harbor greatly intensified an animosity long felt toward the Japanese in California and other Pacific-coast states. Wild though unsubstantiated rumors of Japanese–American sabotage and espionage generated demands for government action against a supposed fifth column. On March 21, 1942, on the advice of the army, Roosevelt ordered the removal of 112,000 persons of Japanese ancestry, 71,000 of them American citizens, from the Pacific coast to internment camps in the interior. Ironically, all but a handful of the 150,000 Japanese in Hawaii, about a third of the population, were unmolested. Even liberals acquiesced in the removal policy and the Supreme Court subsequently upheld it on the ground of military necessity. Thus the unfortunate evacuees sat out the war behind barbed wire and under armed guard. Some 5,000 renounced their American citizenship and a slightly larger number went back to Japan after the war. But the great majority remained staunchly loyal to the United States and more than 12,000 Nisei (American-born Japanese) served in the American armed forces, many with conspicuous gallantry.

Civil liberties were curbed in various other ways. Press censorship was introduced and Father Coughlin's *Social Justice* was banned from the mails, along with dozens of lesser-known publications. The Alien Registration Act of 1940—the Smith Act—did more than control aliens. The first peacetime sedition law since 1798, it prohibited the advocacy or teach-

ing of the forcible overthrow of government and membership of organizations deemed subversive. In 1942 several Nazi sympathizers were
convicted under the Act. Conscientious objectors also had a hard time.
Public opinion was overtly hostile and, unlike other democracies, the
United States refused to grant unconditional exemption to genuine pacifists. Of the 43,000 men classified as conscientious objectors most agreed
to join the army as noncombatants, usually in the ambulance service. Of
the rest, 12,000 worked without pay in Civilian Public Service camps, helping in medical research or conservation work. The remaining 6,000 were
imprisoned for long terms.

The American War Effort

War hit the United States less hard at home than it did other belligerents.
Americans did not experience invasion, occupation, or air raids. Nor did
austerity and sacrifice become part of their way of life. There were serious
shortages, especially of houses, cars, and tires, not to mention steak, whiskey, golf balls, and nylon stockings. In addition, such commodities as
meat, fats, sugar, and gasoline were rationed. But rationing was not nearly
as severe as in, say, Great Britain or Germany. Indeed, most people's
living standards rose substantially during the war. Americans ate and
dressed better than ever before. They were also healthier. The infant
mortality-rate was cut by more than a third; the 1942 overall death-rate of
10.3 per 1,000 was the lowest in the country's history. Life expectancy, virtually unchanged during the Depression, increased overall by three years
between 1941 and 1945. For blacks the gain was five years.

The war nonetheless necessitated an unprecedented national effort. In
order to wage a two-front war the armed forces had to be massively
expanded. After Pearl Harbor Congress extended liability to military service to men between 18 and 45 (later reduced to 38). Local selective-service
boards administered the law, conscripting in all 10 million men. A further
5 million joined the armed forces as volunteers. In addition, more than
200,000 women performed noncombatant duties as army and naval
auxiliaries (WACS and WAVES) or in the marine corps and the coast-
guard.

Economic mobilization, begun before Pearl Harbor, was greatly accelerated thereafter. During the war food production rose by nearly a third,
though there was little increase in the acreage under cultivation and the
number of farm workers fell. Manufacturing output almost doubled. While
maintaining a flow of goods sufficient to sustain a rising domestic standard
of living, American industry met the gargantuan needs of the country's
armed forces and sent huge Lend-Lease shipments to Great Britain and
the Soviet Union. Production of iron, steel, magnesium, aluminum and
copper doubled and trebled; that of machine tools increased sevenfold. To

meet the rubber shortage created by the Japanese capture of Malaya and the Dutch East Indies a huge new synthetic rubber industry was started; by 1943 it was producing a third more rubber than the country had been using before the war. The automobile industry halted car production and turned to the manufacture of tanks, trucks, and a novel military vehicle, the invaluable and ubiquitous jeep. The most spectacular achievements occurred in the production of planes and ships. Aircraft construction accelerated from 2,000 in 1939 to 96,000 in 1944; all told the United States turned out 300,000 aircraft during the war, 275,000 of them military. In shipbuilding the key development was the mass production of a steel cargo freighter of simple design, the "Liberty" ship, which could be built in far less time than a standard merchant ship. Largely in consequence of the Liberty-ship program American shipyards produced fifty-five million tons of merchant shipping—equivalent to two-thirds of the entire Allied merchant marine—besides a huge amount of naval tonnage.

These astonishing levels of production were achieved by centralized planning and direction. Yet the Administration's first attempts at economic mobilization were ill-conceived and fumbling. The succession of planning agencies Roosevelt set up before and after Pearl Harbor had overlapping functions and lacked authority. Not until May 1943, when the Office of War Mobilization was set up under James F. Byrnes, formerly a Supreme Court Justice, did effective machinery exist to establish priorities, allocate basic commodities, set production targets, and coordinate the economic war effort.

Vastly increased government spending, together with wage and salary raises and a scarcity of consumer goods, generated powerful inflationary pressures. The Administration countered with an antiinflation program whose chief features were the sale of war bonds, higher taxes, and price control. War-bond drives used film and radio celebrities as salesmen and became increasingly stunt-ridden. Yet the $100 billion they netted came less from small investors than from banks, insurance companies, and the like. Wartime tax policies sought to increase revenue as well as to curb inflation. In fact the government raised 41 percent of the cost of the war through taxation, compared with 33 percent in World War I. Taxes on personal incomes were increased on a steeply graduated schedule which reached a maximum of 94 percent. Corporate income-tax rates were raised to 40 percent and a 90 percent excess-profits tax was introduced. For the first time ordinary wage-earners became liable to tax: the number of taxpayers rose during the war from 13 million to 50 million. More progressive tax schedules brought a slight reduction in economic inequalities. The top 5 percent of income-earners saw their share of the national income drop from 26 percent to 16 percent. The principal beneficiaries were the upper middle and middle classes. The bottom 20 percent of the population increased their share only from 4 percent to 5.

Attempts at price control began with the creation of an Office of Price Administration in April 1941. Since Congress at first refused to give it sufficient authority prices, especially of food, rose alarmingly. In October 1942 the threat of presidential emergency action brought a comprehensive stabilization law empowering the OPA to impose a price, wage, and rent freeze. Thereafter controls became more effective, especially after Roosevelt peremptorily ordered the OPA in April 1943 to 'hold the line' against price increases. Taking the war years as a whole the cost of living went up by about 30 percent, but between April 1943 and August 1945 the increase was only 1.4 percent.

Efforts to hold down incomes were less successful. The Congressional farm bloc doggedly opposed Roosevelt's antiinflation policies and succeeded for a time in exempting farm prices from OPA control. Consequently agricultural prices doubled during the war and farm income increased fourfold. Rising food prices in turn posed a serious problem for the National War Labor Board established by Roosevelt in January 1942 to adjudicate wage disputes. The following July, faced with mounting pressure for wage increases, the Board adopted the 'Little Steel' formula—so-called because it was first applied to a group of smaller firms in the steel industry—permitting a 15 percent cost-of-living increase. But anxiety to avoid work stoppages which might hamper the war effort led the NWLB to modify the 'Little Steel' formula, granting bonuses, travel allowances, shift differentials, and other fringe benefits which increased wages without formally exceeding the limit. Moreover, strike action in 1943 led by John L. Lewis's United Mine Workers and by railwaymen led to wage settlements that openly breached the 'Little Steel' formula. Wage raises and substantial increases in overtime pay boosted average industrial earnings by 70 percent during the war, that is, more than twice as much as prices.

Trade unions grew rapidly in size during the war, and even more in unpopularity. The increase in union membership—from 8.9 million in 1940 to 14.8 million in 1945—resulted not only from the expansion of the labor force but also from the benevolent attitude of the NWLB. In response to union demands for the closed shop it worked out a compromise "maintenance of membership" arrangement which proved greatly to labor's advantage. Disturbed by this, conservative opinion was further disquieted when, early in 1943, the CIO broke new ground by organizing a Political Action Committee. But it was John L. Lewis's obdurate defiance of the government over wages that brought antiunion sentiment to a head and led to the passage, over Roosevelt's veto, of the Smith–Connally Act (June 1943) which authorized the President to seize any plant where a strike threatened to interfere with war production, made it illegal to instigate such strikes, required unions to give thirty days' notice of all strikes, and prohibited union contributions to political campaigns. In addition a number of states, especially in the South, passed "right-to-work" laws prohibiting the closed shop.

American Society in Wartime

Thanks to the war the longstanding unemployment problem was at last solved. The numbers out of work dropped from 9 million in June 1940 to 780,000 in September 1943. Indeed, it proved difficult to find enough workers for war industries. Labor shortages provided expanded opportunities for adolescents, the retired, the handicapped, and, more particularly, women and blacks. The number of women at work increased 50 percent during the war; by 1943 they constituted a third of the total work-force. Industry took most of them but large numbers went into offices and the professions, especially journalism. Women were widely employed to do what had traditionally been men's jobs: they became stevedores, shipyard riveters, mechanics, and railway signalmen and constituted 40 percent of the workers on aircraft assembly-lines. Yet women were almost invariably paid less than men for the same work. Although by the end of 1944 one-fifth of all union members were women, labor conspired with management to oppose the principle of equal pay. The federal government, too, betrayed a lingering prejudice in refusing to provide child-care centers for working mothers. Even so, the war worked a change in public attitudes to female employment. Perhaps the best proof of this is the fact that two-thirds of the women employed during the war remained at work after 1945.

During wartime more than a million blacks, many from the South, found jobs in the industrial centers of the North and West. They included a large number of women formerly employed as domestic servants. Despite higher wages black factory workers were still restricted to the more menial jobs and denied opportunities to acquire skills. In June 1941, in order to compel government action, A. Philip Randolph, the leader of the Pullman porters' union, threatened a march of 50,000 Negroes on Washington. An alarmed President responded with Executive Order 8802 forbidding racial discrimination in all defense projects and creating a Fair Employment Practices Committee. But the FEPC lacked effective enforcement powers and many of its recommendations were ignored, especially in the South.

Black migration led to riots in a number of Northern cities, the worst being the outbreak in Detroit in June 1943, when 25 blacks and 9 whites were killed. A further source of racial strife was the presence of over a million blacks in the armed forces. Blacks were admitted to the marines and the army air corps; for the first time in decades the Navy accepted them in capacities other than that of mess-waiter; several thousand were commissioned in the army, 600 in the army air force, and 50 in the navy.

But if some long-established barriers fell segregation remained the rule, not only in army regiments but even in Red Cross blood banks—ironically since a Negro, Dr Charles Drew, had invented the process for storing blood plasma: In the South, Negro soldiers were frequently humiliated and insulted by white civilians. Some high-ranking army officers made no secret of their low opinion of black troops and refused to employ them in combat roles. This treatment, which mocked Administration claims that the United States was fighting for freedom and democracy against Nazi racism, embittered many blacks and bred a new black militancy. Membership of the National Association for the Advancement of Colored Peoples rose during the war from 50,000 to 450,000. And although the NAACP succeeded in inducing the Supreme Court, in *Smith* v. *Allwright* (1944), to strike down exclusive white primary elections, blacks were becoming impatient with a legalistic approach. Hence the formation in 1943 of a new organization, the Congress for Racial Equality, advocating nonviolent direct action.

Among other social consequences of the war were earlier marriages and a great acceleration of the divorce-rate. A soaring birth-rate ensured that the population increase in the 1940s was more than twice that of the 1930s. The war also increased the mobility of an already footloose people. Twenty-seven million people, a fifth of the population, moved in four years. Young men left their homes for army training-camps. War work lured millions not only to the North but also to the South and the Pacific coast. Consequently cities like Mobile, Norfolk, San Diego, Los Angeles, and Seattle grew phenomenally. The war also boosted cinema attendance by 50 percent, created a mass market for books, and led to a revival of interest in religion.

The Grand Alliance

World War I had been more than half over before the Americans joined in and ended just as they were beginning to make a tangible military contribution. World War II, on the other hand, was at a relatively early stage when the United States became involved; it plunged immediately into the thick of the fighting and remained an active belligerent for the war's four remaining years. American casualties were relatively light: the number of dead and missing—319,000—was palpably smaller, both proportionately and absolutely, than that of all the other major belligerents. But there was no denying the scale or decisiveness of the American military contribution. The United States created unprecedentedly powerful armed forces, simultaneously undertook massive military, naval, and air operations in two distant and widely separated theaters, and spent on the war a sum roughly twice as large as all previous federal expenditure since 1789.

A further contrast to 1917–18 was the structure of cooperation that developed between the United States and the other countries fighting the Axis. During World War I the United States had fought not as one of the Allies but as an 'Associated Power', and ultimately had concluded a separate peace. In World War II, however, she fused her efforts with those of her allies, entering into an especially close relationship with Great Britain and taking the lead in forging the coalition Churchill later named 'the Grand Alliance'. This was consummated on New Year's Day, 1942, when Roosevelt, Churchill, the Soviet Ambassador Litvinov, and the representatives of twenty-three other nations at war with the Axis signed a Declaration of the United Nations. The signatories subscribed to the principles of the Atlantic Charter, promised to employ all their resources against those Axis powers with whom they were at war—the Soviet Union was still at peace with Japan— and undertook not to make a separate peace. Though merely an executive agreement rather than a treaty, the Declaration constituted a binding military commitment—the first the United States had entered into since the French alliance in 1778.

Though neither the Russians nor the Chinese shared their plans with their American allies, the Americans and the British fought the war in close collaboration, pooling their resources and coordinating strategy through the Combined Chiefs of Staff in Washington. For the most part the two countries worked together in remarkable harmony. Yet there was much tension and bickering. Roosevelt and Churchill, though parading a mutual affection, remained jealous of each other. Churchill disliked American efforts to use Lend-Lease as a lever to force Great Britain to give up imperial preference; he resented being excluded from Roosevelt's wartime attempts at a *rapprochement* with Stalin and he was affronted at the limited and subordinate role that Great Britain was assigned in the Pacific war. He was also disturbed by Roosevelt's plans for dismembering the British Empire. Roosevelt for his part was no uncritical Anglophile: like most of his countrymen he was suspicious of British imperialism and sympathized especially with demands that the British quit India. There were persistent Anglo-American differences over France and China, while the State Department—ironically in view of postwar American policy— disliked Churchill's readiness to uphold reactionary regimes in liberated Italy and Greece in order to avert Communist control. Finally there were serious disagreements over strategic planning.

Anglo-American differences were, however, trivial compared to the gulf separating the United States from its Soviet ally. Even when the Red Army was bearing the main burden of fighting the Nazis, American leaders found it difficult to overcome their repugnance for a regime which advocated world revolution and had behaved towards its small neighbors no less brutally than Hitler. The Soviet Union, for its part, could not easily forget American armed intervention in 1918 and the long refusal to extend recognition. Wartime developments imposed fresh strains. Despite having accepted the Atlantic Charter, repudiating territorial changes except with the consent of the peoples concerned, the Soviet Union demanded American recognition of its claims to territory annexed before being attacked by Hitler—the three Baltic states, the eastern half of Poland, and parts of Finland and Romania. America's attempts to maintain friendly relations with pro-Axis regimes like Vichy France and Franco's Spain and her refusal to break off relations with Hitler's ally Finland, provoked Soviet protests. Difficulties also developed over Stalin's apparent lack of appreciation for the huge quantities of American Lend-Lease supplies sent to the Soviet Union at a heavy cost in Allied ships and lives. The sorest point with the Russians, however, was the delay in establishing a Second Front. Left alone to fight the Nazis and suffering terrible losses, they suspected that the Western Allies were not so much unable to help as unwilling.

Despite the strains of the Grand Alliance Roosevelt believed that post-war security would depend on collaboration between the Great Powers and that the United States ought to take the initiative in creating a new system of international relations. Among his objectives were the reduction of tariff barriers, the reform of the world's monetary system, and the creation of a new and more effective international peacekeeping organization to replace the League of Nations. Mainly at American prompting blue-prints were drawn up for specialized international agencies to promote these ends: the Food and Agriculture Organization (FAO) in May 1943, the United Nations Relief and Rehabilitation Administration (UNRRA) six months later, the International Monetary Fund and the World Bank in July 1944. Later in 1944 a conference at Dumbarton Oaks, near Washington, made limited progress on a draft charter for the proposed United Nations Organization.

Determined to avoid the mistakes that had vitiated Wilson's efforts to take the United States into the League of Nations Roosevelt decided to separate the drafting of the charter of the United Nations from the business of peacemaking and to win prior legislative approval for the principle of American membership. His tactics were brilliantly successful. In September 1943 the House of Representatives recommended by 360 votes to 29 that the United States take the lead in establishing the United Nations Organization. In November the Senate adopted a similar resolution by 85 to 6.

The Defensive War, 1941–1942

The military outlook for the Allies when the United States entered the war in December 1941 was blacker even than in April 1917. German armies were besieging Moscow and Leningrad. The British position in North

Africa and the Middle East was highly precarious. At sea U-boats were taking a grim toll. In the Far East the Japanese were sweeping all before them. Although it was Japan that brought the United States into the war, Roosevelt and his advisers adhered to an earlier Anglo-American staff decision that priority be given to defeating Nazi Germany. The Germany-first principle was unpopular with the many Americans—especially former isolationists—who wanted prompt and stern retribution upon Japan. But it was soundly based: Germany possessed much greater military, industrial, and technological resources than Japan and was thus the more dangerous enemy. Yet something had to be done immediately to halt the Japanese advance. In the five months after Pearl Harbor Japanese forces won a spectacular series of victories, overrunning Hong Kong, Thailand, and Malaya, capturing the great Singapore naval base, and occupying the Dutch East Indies and Burma. In the Philippines 140,000 American and Filipino troops resisted stubbornly for months on Bataan peninsula and on the island of Corregidor but surrendered on May 6, 1942 in the greatest capitulation in American military history. Meanwhile Japanese forces had fanned out widely, occupying Guam and Wake Island and landing on the Gilbert and Solomon Islands as well as on the Aleutians. By the early summer of 1942 both India and Australia seemed threatened. But two decisive naval engagements turned the tide. In the Battle of the Coral Sea (May 7–9, 1942)—the first sea-battle in which there was no visual contact between the ships involved—American carrier-based aircraft turned back a Japanese naval expedition making for New Guinea. A month later (June 3–6) a Japanese invasion fleet heading for Midway Island was repulsed with heavy loss. In August American and Australian forces under General Douglas MacArthur launched an offensive to oust the Japanese from the island of Guadalcanal in the Solomons and remove the threat to communications between Hawaii and Australia. The Japanese evacuation of Guadalcanal in February 1943, after prolonged and bitter fighting, marked a turning-point in the Pacific war.

In Europe and the Mediterranean, too, the months following Pearl Harbor were a period of almost unrelieved misfortune for the Allies. A fresh German offensive on the Russian front swept to the western edge of the Caucasus oilfields; Rommel advanced to within sixty miles of the Suez Canal; in the Atlantic German U-boats sank ships faster than the Allies could build them. The United States was in no position to launch an immediate ground offensive against Germany but in August 1942 units of the Eighth Air Force joined in the bombing of Germany from British bases. In 1943 the bombing offensive was steadily intensified, huge daylight raids by American B-17s (Flying Fortresses) complementing the RAF's massive night attacks. Like their British counterparts, American air chiefs mistakenly believed that strategic bombing could be decisive. Though it caused appalling destruction and loss of life it did not shatter German morale; nor, until late in the war, did it have much effect on war production. This is not to deny the enormous tactical contribution of the Allied air forces in paving the way for the invasion of Normandy in 1944. But the cost of the air offensive was fearful: in all the Americans lost nearly 10,000 bombers in the skies over Europe.

The Mediterranean Campaigns, 1942–1943

While the Americans and the British were agreed that the defeat of Germany must take precedence, disputes arose over the best way of accomplishing it. Churchill, remembering the immense losses sustained in frontal attacks during the First World War, wanted to delay a direct military assault on Continental Europe until Germany had been weakened by air bombardment, naval blockade, and attacks on her relatively unprotected Mediterranean flank—'the soft underbelly of the Axis' as he liked to term it. But the Americans, with their different military tradition, distrusted the peripheral approach and favored a head-on thrust across the English Channel. In May 1942 Roosevelt responded to desperate Russian appeals for help with a rash promise of a "second front" in Europe before the end of the year. But Churchill pressed strongly for an Anglo-American invasion of French North Africa as a preliminary to a cross-Channel attack, and in the end had his way.

The North African campaign proved a great success. On November 8, 1942 British and American forces under General Dwight D. Eisenhower landed at Oran, Algiers, and Casablanca. French resistance ended abruptly when Eisenhower recognized the *de facto* political authority of Admiral Darlan, a notorious Nazi collaborationist and a leading member of the Vichy government. Though loudly denounced by liberals in the United States and Great Britain, the Darlan deal saved lives and put the Allies in control of Algeria and Morocco. Shortly before the landings General Montgomery's British Eighth Army had won a resounding victory over Rommel at El Alamein in Egypt. Capturing Benghazi in November and Tripoli the following January, the British pursued the enemy into Tunisia, which Eisenhower's troops had earlier entered from the west. After some fierce fighting, in which the inexperience of American soldiers was painfully exposed, the North Africa campaign reached a triumphant conclusion in May 1943 with the capture of Tunis and the surrender of the remaining German and Italian troops.

In January 1943 Roosevelt and Churchill met at Casablanca to plan the next offensive. The now familiar Anglo-American strategical differences were again aired. With a major German disaster in the making at Stalingrad, Churchill felt there was no longer any need to undertake a possibly premature cross-Channel invasion in order to save the Russians from collapse. Moreover the early prospect of clearing North Africa opened up the possibility of knocking Italy out of the war, thus adding to German difficulties in the Balkans. The United States Chiefs of Staff were, however, reluctant to accept further Mediterranean commitments, preferring either to assault western Europe or to switch resources to the Pacific. Eventually it was decided to invade Sicily even if this delayed the attack on France.

The most highly publicized product of the Casablanca conference was Roosevelt's announcement that the Allies would insist upon the unconditional surrender of the Axis. He made it clear, however, that this meant, not a punitive peace, but no negotiations over surrender terms. Though the President gave the impression that 'unconditional surrender' was the product of his own sudden impulse, he had discussed it in advance both with his military advisers and with Churchill. All had endorsed it. Two considerations led Roosevelt to favor 'unconditional surrender'. One was determination to avoid the misunderstanding and confusion that had surrounded the 1918 armistice negotiations. The other was the need to reassure the Soviet Union in the aftermath of the Darlan affair that the Western Allies had no intention of making a compromise peace. Critics subsequently alleged that the unconditional-surrender demand had stiffened Axis resistance, discouraged the anti-Nazi opposition in Germany, and prolonged the war. But none of this seems likely.

Landing in Sicily on July 9, 1943 American and British armies overran the island in little more than a month. Mussolini's downfall on July 25 brought in a new Italian government under Marshal Badoglio which soon indicated a willingness to surrender. This turn of events enabled Churchill to overcome American misgivings about a follow-up landing on the Italian mainland. This took place on September 3. Five days later the Italians signed an armistice agreement and joined the Allies in the war against Hitler. But the Germans rushed troops south to occupy Rome and set up a defensive line. The Italian campaign, instead of producing quick results, turned into a long, hard slog. Despite successive amphibious landings behind the German lines Anglo-American forces did not take Rome until June 1944 and were still fighting in Italy when the European war ended.

The Assault on Nazi-Occupied Europe

In planning for 1942 and 1943 American leaders had reluctantly deferred to Churchill. But as American strength became preponderant, strategic decisions were made increasingly in Washington. When Roosevelt and Churchill met again in Quebec in August 1943, the Americans were able to insist upon a decision to transfer the main Allied effort from the Mediterranean to a cross-Channel invasion of France. The projected assault— Operation Overlord—was scheduled for the late spring of 1944. This decision was reaffirmed at the Tehran Conference (November 28—

December 2, 1943)—the first time Roosevelt, Churchill, and Stalin had met. The President attempted to dispel the Soviet leader's distrust and received a promise of Russian help against Japan as soon as Germany was defeated. But if America's relations with the Soviet Union improved—at least on the surface—Anglo-American strategic differences persisted. American military leaders doubted whether Churchill was fully committed to Operation Overlord and some thought he was still trying to lure the United States into sideshows. They were wrong on both counts. Nonetheless a myth subsequently developed that Churchill pressed for an extension of the war to the Balkans in order to forestall the Russians. In fact he at no time advocated a major invasion of the Balkans, though in 1944, having become alarmed about Soviet expansion, he proposed a thrust through northern Yugoslavia in order to beat the Russians to Vienna. For similar reasons he urged Eisenhower to make every effort to seize Berlin and Prague. But Roosevelt and his generals would not listen. Preoccupied with winning the war, they were relatively indifferent to the political shape of postwar Europe.

The long-awaited cross-Channel invasion of France finally came on June 6, 1944. It was the greatest amphibious operation in history. Within two weeks a million Allied troops were landed. For nearly two months they were penned in to a relatively shallow bridgehead, but at the end of July burst through the German defenses and swept southward and eastward. A new Allied invasion of the French Mediterranean coast on August 15 further increased the pressure on the Germans. On August 25 Paris was liberated and by mid-September Allied forces had advanced into Belgium, Luxemburg, and Germany itself. The success of the invasion owed more than was recognized at the time to Eisenhower's gifts as supreme commander. He was not, perhaps, a great soldier. He was outshone by some of his own generals, lacking, for example, Montgomery's tactical flair and Patton's ebullient aggression. But there was no doubting his professionalism or his complete command of the forces under him. Above all, Eisenhower was a coordinator of genius, smoothing over differences whether of national or interservice origin and welding his flamboyant, jealous, and unruly subordinates into an effective team.

By the late autumn of 1944 the defeat of Nazi Germany seemed imminent. While Eisenhower's forces had been liberating France and Belgium, the Red Army had advanced to the Baltic and into Poland and Romania. But on both eastern and western fronts the Allied advance petered out and the Germans staged an astonishing rally which prolonged the war by six months. In September the British and Americans landed airborne forces in Holland in a bold attempt to straddle the Rhine, the last great barrier defending the German homeland. But it ended disastrously and in mid-December the Germans launched a desperate counteroffensive in the

Ardennes which hurled the Americans back and was checked only with great difficulty. In Europe, therefore, the year ended gloomily for the Allies.

The Pacific War, 1943–1944

On the other side of the globe, however, the Americans pressed forward irresistibly. In contrast to the European war, the fighting in the Pacific was largely an American affair. Though the original intention had been to undertake only holding operations in the Far East until Hitler had been defeated, American resources proved sufficient to launch a major counteroffensive against the Japanese-held perimeter even before the invasion of Nazi-occupied Europe had begun. In the middle of 1943 a two-pronged amphibious assault got under way. One prong, consisting of forces commanded by Admiral Chester W. Nimitz, waged an island-hopping campaign to beat a path through the central Pacific towards the Japanese home islands. The other, under General MacArthur, aimed at recovering the Philippines and making them the springboard for a final attack on Japan. During the next eighteen months these objectives were substantially achieved. In a succession of jumps Nimitz's marines seized Tarawa in the Gilbert Islands, Kwajalein and Eniwetok in the Marshalls, and, finally, Saipan in the Marianas, only 1,500 miles from Japan. In October 1944 MacArthur landed in the Philippines and by the end of February 1945 had recaptured them. Shortly afterward the British Fourteenth Army completed the reconquest of Burma. In an effort to defend the Marianas the Japanese navy put to sea only to be heavily defeated in the Battle of the Philippine Sea (June 19–20, 1944). Then in the course of the Philippines campaign it sustained an even more crushing reverse: the Battle of Leyte Gulf (October 23–5, 1944)—the greatest naval engagement in history—resulted in the virtual destruction of Japan's remaining sea power.

Wartime Politics

The presidential election of 1944 was thus fought out against a stirring military background. The Republicans were confident. They had made substantial gains in the Congressional elections of 1942, largely because of public irritation with inflation, shortages, and wartime controls. Since the elections had strengthened the hand of the conservative wing of the party it was unlikely that Wendell Willkie would receive a second presidential nomination. In fact Willkie abandoned his candidacy after having been heavily defeated in the Wisconsin presidential primary and the Republican nomination went to Thomas E. Dewey, the young, dynamic, 'racket-busting' attorney who had been elected governor of New York in 1942. As a counter to Dewey's mild progressivism and internationalism the party chose a conservative isolationist, Senator John W. Bricker of Ohio, as his running mate.

On the Democratic side, Roosevelt's renomination was unopposed. With a war still to win and problems of peace looming, he seemed indispensable. The President was visibly tired but, "as a good soldier", consented to run for a fourth term. A factional struggle developed over the choice of his running mate. The darling of the advanced liberals, the incumbent Vice-President, Henry A. Wallace, was strongly opposed by the party bosses. Roosevelt, sensing a national move to the right, did not insist on keeping him. Wallace was replaced by Senator Harry S. Truman of Missouri whose earlier career had been undistinguished but who had recently gained stature as chairman of a Senate committee investigating defense-spending. Political expediency governed the choice. Truman was the least controversial candidate and, coming from a border state, appealed to the South. During the campaign Dewey alleged that the Roosevelt Administration had "grown tired, old and quarrelsome in office", but the President's greater experience and international leadership were difficult to deny. Misgivings about Roosevelt's health were allayed by the vigor with which he campaigned and on election day he defeated Dewey with ease.

The Yalta Conference

After his inauguration Roosevelt traveled to Yalta in the Crimea for a further meeting with Stalin and Churchill. With the end of the European war in sight a variety of problems clamored for attention: the treatment of Germany, the war in the Far East, the future of Poland and other eastern European countries, and the launching of the United Nations Organization. The eight days of the Yalta Conference (February 4–11, 1945) were unexpectedly harmonious, or so it appeared. Stalin seemed ready to meet the Western leaders half-way and agreement was reached on the unconditional surrender and disarmament of Germany, the division of that country into three zones of occupation, and the trial of the Nazi leaders for war crimes. In return for a renewed and more precise commitment to enter the war against Japan Stalin was promised the return of the Kurile Islands and of southern Sakhalin, the lease of a naval base at Port Arthur, the internationalizing of the port of Darien, and recognition of Russia's preeminent interests in Manchuria. Roosevelt and Churchill also acceded to the Soviet desire for secure European frontiers. Russia got the eastern third of pre-1939 Poland, the Poles being compensated with a slice of eastern Germany. In return Stalin promised that the Communist-dominated Lublin Committee, which he had recognized as the provisional government of Poland, would be "reorganized on a broader democratic basis" so as to include members of the exiled Polish government in London and that "free and unfettered elections" would be held as soon as possible. Democratic governments through free elections were likewise promised to all the other liberated countries. In discussions on the United Nations Organization Stalin proved unexpectedly accommodating, perhaps because he attached little importance to it. He accepted the American formula for voting in the Security Council, agreeing that the veto should apply on substantive but not on procedural matters. He also withdrew his earlier claim that each of the sixteen Soviet republics should have a seat in the General Assembly. A further Russian concession enabled Roosevelt to carry his point that all countries which had signed the United Nations Declaration by February 8, 1945, or had entered the war by March 1, would be entitled to membership of the United Nations. This permitted a number of Latin American republics to become founder members of the new organization and thus strengthened the American position in it. Finally it was agreed to hold a conference at San Francisco on April 25 in order to draw up a Constitution for the United Nations Organization.

Much controversy later developed over the Yalta agreements. Critics alleged that Roosevelt, with Churchill's acquiescence, had cynically violated the principle of self-determination contained in the Atlantic Charter, betrayed the peoples of eastern Europe, and facilitated the triumph of Communism in China. But however unwise the American concessions to Russia later appeared, there seemed good reason for them at the time. American military leaders thought that Russian military assistance would shorten the war against Japan and save many American lives. It should also be remembered that with the Red Army already in control of eastern Europe Roosevelt gave away nothing (except the Kurile Islands) that the Russians would not have seized anyway.

The apparent success of Roosevelt's attempts to win Soviet cooperation persuaded him and most of the American people that a new era of international relations was beginning. But Yalta turned out to have been a false dawn. The promises of democracy and free elections in eastern Europe were never kept. It soon became clear that the Soviet Union intended to act unilaterally in the areas it occupied. In March 1945 it ruthlessly imposed a Communist regime on Romania. Then in April, after weeks of futile wrangling over the precise method of reorganizing the Polish government, the Soviet authorities in Poland rounded up a number of leading politicians who had connections with the London exiles and imprisoned them on trumped-up charges.

The European War: Final Phase

Although Allied unity was fast disintegrating the European war was brought to a triumphant conclusion. In the early months of 1945 the German position progressively collapsed. In January the Russians launched a new offensive which carried them swiftly to the Lower Oder, only forty miles from Berlin. Soon afterward other Russian armies overran East Prussia and entered Hungary. In the West American and British troops crossed the Rhine in March and raced eastward with little opposition. On April 24 Russian troops reached the outskirts of Berlin and began the systematic reduction of the city; on April 30 Hitler committed suicide; and on May 7 Germany surrendered unconditionally.

Roosevelt did not see the end of the war in Europe. On April 12, 1945 he died şuddenly at Warm Springs, Georgia. Although his strength had been visibly waning for some time, his death came as a shock. There was an immense outpouring of popular grief and a numbing sense of loss. As a war leader Roosevelt ranks high. True, he had his limitations. He was too ready to subordinate long-term political considerations to short-term military advantage. In particular, he was slow to grasp the connection between military policy and the postwar balance of power. He could be clumsy, as in his relations with Vichy France, or naively optimistic, as in his attempts to reach a rapport with Stalin. But more than any other man he was the architect of the Allied victory. He built an awesome military machine, took the critical decision to give priority to the European war and despite strong pressure stuck to it, inspired confidence throughout the nation, and infused into the Allied war effort a genuine sense of idealism.

Truman Takes Hold

The new President, Harry S. Truman, was unprepared for his enormous responsibilities. Totally inexperienced in foreign affairs, he had not been briefed about military plans or relations with the Russians. At first he simply followed Roosevelt's policies. One of his earliest decisions was to proceed as planned with the United Nations Conference on International Organization, due to begin at San Francisco on April 25. Roosevelt's determination to profit from Wilson's mistakes had led to his selecting a bipartisan delegation to represent the United States. Though nominally headed by Cordell Hull's successor as Secretary of State, Edward R. Stettinius, Jr., its two most influential members were Senators: Tom Connally, the Texan Democrat who was chairman of the Senate Foreign Relations Committee, and Arthur H. Vandenberg, a Michigan Republican who, after a long isolationist past, had been converted during the war to American participation in the United Nations.

At the San Francisco conference the rift in the Grand Alliance deepened. The American and Russian delegates wrangled for weeks and at one point the Conference nearly broke up because of disagreement over application of the voting procedure settled at Yalta. Only a desperate personal appeal by Truman to Stalin broke the logjam. Eventually on June 26 the delegates completed their work and the representatives of fifty nations formally signed the United Nations Charter. It was essentially an American creation, containing a minimum of concession to the Soviet point of view. In contrast to the protracted and bitter debate over the Treaty of Versailles in 1919 the completed charter was promptly ratified by the Senate. After only six days of debate it was approved on July 26 by a margin of 89 to 2. The lopsided vote marked the formal abandonment of isolationism. Americans, having rejected the responsibilities of world leadership a generation earlier, now realized that the role of an active world power could no longer be avoided. But it also demonstrated that they had excessive faith in the capacity of the United Nations to keep the peace.

The Reduction of Japan

Meanwhile the war in the Pacific was reaching a climax. Early in 1945 American forces made further leapfrogging advances. The Japanese resisted fanatically and American losses were appalling. The capture of Iwo Jima, a tiny volcanic island 750 miles from Tokyo, cost the marines 20,000 casualties. The battle for Okinawa, the main island in the Ryukyu chain only 360 miles from the southern tip of Japan, was the bloodiest of the Pacific war, with American casualties exceeding 50,000. These advances enabled huge American B-29 Superfortresses to intensify the air bombardment of Japan begun from the Marianas late in 1944. In a series of low-level night attacks with incendiary bombs vast areas of Japanese cities were laid waste. In one firebomb raid alone, on March 9, sixteen square miles of the most densely populated parts of Tokyo were burned out and 83,000 people killed.

By the time the European war ended, in May 1945, Japan's situation was wellnigh hopeless. Most of her navy had been sunk and her air strength destroyed. In June the Japanese government put out peace feelers. But the army leaders were determined to fight on. Thus American preparations to invade the Japanese home islands went ahead. Suicidal resistance on the model of Iwo Jima and Okinawa was anticipated. American military experts grimly predicted that the subjugation of Japan would take at least eighteen months and cost one million Allied casualties. President Truman and his advisers therefore turned to a new and terrible weapon, the atomic bomb. Ever since 1939 an international team of scientists—American, British, and Canadian—had been working feverishly and in great secrecy on the development of atomic energy for military purposes: the United States had spent more than $2 billion on the so-called Manhattan Project. On July 16, 1945 a test bomb was successfully detonated near Alamogordo, New Mexico. The news reached Truman at the Potsdam Conference, the last of the wartime meetings of Allied leaders. On July 26, along with the British Prime Minister Clement Attlee (who had succeeded Churchill) and

Chiang Kai-shek, the President issued the Potsdam Declaration calling upon the Japanese to surrender unconditionally or face 'prompt and utter destruction'. Since the Japanese failed to comply a lone American B-29 dropped the first atomic bomb on Hiroshima on August 6. The city was devastated; 80,000 of its inhabitants were killed; many others were to die of radiation aftereffects. On August 8 the Soviet Union declared war on Japan and invaded Manchuria. On August 9 a second atomic bomb—the last the Americans possessed—was dropped on Nagasaki, causing a further 35,000 deaths. After the war controversy developed over the strategic necessity for atomic weapons and still more over the morality of using them. But few expressed doubts at the time. The civilian and military leaders who took the fateful decision did so in the conviction that they were justified in using any means that promised to save Allied lives and end the war at a stroke. Some historians claim that there was no need to use such a weapon because the Japanese were on the point of surrendering. Yet Japanese army leaders wanted to fight on even after Hiroshima and Nagasaki. They were overborne, however, and on August 14 Japan accepted the Potsdam terms on condition that the emperor retained his throne. The formal surrender of all the Japanese forces took place on board the United States battleship *Missouri* in Tokyo Bay on September 2, 1945.

26. *Cold War Tensions*, 1945–1960

The Cold War

The United States emerged from World War II with unchallenged economic and military supremacy. Alone among the major belligerents it had been neither a battlefield nor the victim of air raids. Its industrial capacity dwarfed that of all other nations, its huge army was battle-hardened and superbly equipped, its navy and air force more powerful than those of the rest of the world put together. Above all, Americans had a monopoly of a new and terrifying weapon, the atomic bomb. They could thus be forgiven for supposing that their country was unassailable, that it would be possible to return the armed forces to a peacetime footing and keep military expenditure low. There seemed moreover good grounds for believing that the wartime Grand Alliance would continue to function, thus ensuring peace and stability through the United Nations.

But things were to turn out very differently. The wartime alliance disintegrated almost at once; the atomic monopoly vanished soon after. Within a short time the United States and the Soviet Union had each come to the conclusion that the other constituted a threat to its security. Fanned by mutual fear and suspicion, their rivalry split the world into two and brought about a dangerous, nerve-racking, and protracted Cold War. And although, as its name implied, this was mainly a struggle of ideologies rather than of bullets, it entailed for the United States a posture of constant vigilance, the maintenance of a huge military establishment, and the creation of a system of defensive alliances that eventually spanned every continent.

To what extent Roosevelt's sudden death in April 1945 was a contributory factor in the Cold War has been much debated. Some critics argue that it produced a sharp break in American foreign policy. Whereas—so the argument runs—Roosevelt had worked painstakingly to build up a friendly relationship with the Soviet Union, Truman promptly took a tougher line which precipitated confrontation. But in fact there was more continuity in American policy than this interpretation allows. Cracks had begun to appear in the Grand Alliance even before the end of the European war and, towards the end of his life, Roosevelt had begun to doubt whether Soviet cooperation was after all attainable. Nor did his death place an anti-Communist crusader in the White House. Knowing nothing about foreign affairs upon his sudden elevation to the Presidency, and having few opinions about them, Truman relied initially upon Roosevelt's advisers. And although he became increasingly exasperated as difficulties with the Soviet Union multiplied, both he and his newly appointed Secretary of State, James F. Byrnes, continued to hope that concession and compromise would overcome Soviet distrust.

Stalin's failure to observe the Yalta agreements about Poland and his uncooperativeness at the San Francisco conference nonetheless aroused American suspicions, while Truman's abrupt ending of Lend-Lease in May 1945 affronted the Russians. Thus when Truman, Attlee, and Stalin met at the Potsdam Conference in July the atmosphere was noticeably less cordial than at Yalta six months before. There was prolonged wrangling before even tentative agreement was reached on the issues discussed: reparations, the military occupation of Germany, and the conclusion of peace treaties with the Axis satellites. And when it came to implementing the Potsdam Agreement, disputes multiplied.

The main flash-point was Germany. The Potsdam Agreement had stipulated that Germany, though divided into four zones of occupation, was to be administered as an economic unit. But the Russians ignored this arrangement, withholding foodstuffs raised in their own, predominantly agricultural, zone from the industrialized parts of Germany and obliging the Western Allies to make good the deficiency. The Americans retaliated late in 1946 by halting the dismantling of German industrial plant intended as reparations to the Soviet Union, expanding German industrial production to promote selfsufficiency, and merging their zone of occupation with those of Great Britain and France. Thus by the end of the year the concept of unified Allied control had virtually been abandoned; instead the two main occupying powers were busily imposing their rival economic systems upon the areas they controlled.

Soviet–American relations were further inflamed by disagreement over peace terms with Hitler's allies. It took eighteen months of haggling before the treaties were signed in February 1947. Although the Western Allies pressed for generous treatment for Italy, the Soviet Union insisted upon a punitive peace. The other four treaties, involving Russia's neighbors who had fought on the Axis side, provided (like the Italian treaty) for reparations and, more important, for varying degrees of Soviet hegemony. By signing these treaties the United States in effect abandoned its attempts to get Stalin to abide by his Yalta pledge of free elections in eastern Europe.

Yet another source of discord was the problem of atomic disarmament. In June 1946, in an effort to allay Soviet anxieties about the threat of atomic warfare the United States submitted to the United Nations Commission on Atomic Energy a far-reaching plan for international control.

The United States proposed to surrender its atomic monopoly to an international agency and destroy its existing atomic stockpile; the manufacture of atomic weapons would be outlawed and there would be international inspection to ensure compliance. In American eyes this was a magnanimous proposal, but the Soviet Union refused to accept international inspection. Hence no agreement was reached. The failure of the plan, disappointing in itself, added to American disillusion with the United Nations Organization. Instead of the effective peacekeeping agency Roosevelt had envisaged, it turned out to be a forum for propaganda.

The Containment Policy

By the beginning of 1947 American frustration at the failure to reach a *modus vivendi* with the Soviet Union had given way to alarm at Soviet intentions. Accordingly, in a radical new departure, known as the 'containment' policy, the Truman Administration committed itself to resisting any further extension of Communist power and influence. The first sustained implementation of this policy came in the eastern Mediterranean. The Soviet Union had for some time been supporting Communist-led guerrillas in the Greek Civil War and had been pressing Turkey for territory and a share in the control of the Dardanelles. When Great Britain, long the dominant power in the area, informed Washington that for economic reasons it could not continue opposing these thrusts, Truman stepped promptly into the breach. On March 12, 1947 he asked Congress for $400 million for economic and military assistance to Greece and Turkey. He also set forth what became known as the Truman Doctrine, a sweeping declaration of support to all nations threatened by totalitarian aggression or subversion. Truman's request sparked off a long and bitter Congressional debate. Conservatives were concerned at the cost, liberals disliked the President's strident ideological tone. But thanks largely to the support of leading Republican internationalists like Vandenberg, Congress eventually gave the President what he wanted.

The situation in the eastern Mediterranean was, however, only the tip of the iceberg. The whole of Europe, devastated and impoverished by war, seemed likely to succumb to Communism. To avert this danger the Administration drew up a comprehensive program of economic assistance. Byrnes's successor as Secretary of State, General George C. Marshall, announced in June 1947 that if Europe could work out a joint recovery program the United States would support it. Western European countries promptly accepted Marshall's offer, but the Soviet Union and its satellites declined to participate, denouncing the scheme as American imperialism. The Marshall Plan, as it became known, ran into opposition in Congress from both right and left, but its passage was greatly helped by the Communist coup in Czechoslovakia in February 1948 and the apparent likelihood of a Communist electoral victory in Italy. On April 3, 1948 Congress passed the Economic Cooperation Act appropriating an initial $5.3 billion; subsequent appropriations brought the total cost to $13.2 billion.

The Marshall Plan proved astonishingly successful. It brought about a swift and massive economic revival in western Europe, thus restoring political stability and diminishing Communism's appeal. Moreover since Marshall-aid funds had to be spent mainly in the United States, it gave a powerful stimulus to the American economy, as indeed it had been intended to do. But the Plan's consequences were not wholly beneficial. By snapping trade ties between eastern and western Europe, it had the effect of dividing the Continent economically as well as ideologically.

The Cold War reached a perilous climax in June 1948, when the three Western occupying powers announced plans for the formation of a federal West German republic which would be sovereign in domestic affairs and would be included in the European Recovery Program. In an attempt to force the West to abandon the scheme the Soviet Union blockaded Western land routes into Berlin, which was under four-power control but was isolated deep inside the Soviet zone. Truman feared that withdrawal from Berlin would jeopardize the success of his entire European policy, but was unwilling to risk war by sending armed convoys to smash a way through. Instead, with the support of Great Britain and France, he ordered a gigantic airlift to supply the beleaguered city. This proved effective and in the spring of 1949 the Russians lifted the blockade.

The Berlin crisis demonstrated the need for a new military alliance to guard against a possible Soviet attack on western Europe. Already, in March 1948, Great Britain, France, Belgium, The Netherlands, and Luxemburg had concluded the Brussels Pact providing for a defensive alliance. But without American participation no alliance could be effective against Soviet strength. Hence the signing of the North Atlantic Treaty in Washington on April 4, 1949 by the United States, Canada, the Brussels Pact signatories, and five other European countries. The treaty provided that an armed attack on one signatory would be regarded as an attack on all and set up the North Atlantic Treaty Organization to integrate the military forces of members. Ratified by the Senate on July 21 by 82 votes to 13 the Treaty was the logical conclusion of the containment policy. It proved also that the United States was done with isolationism.

China Goes Communist

Although containment was a dramatic success in Europe, it proved much less effective in the Far East. At the end of World War II American Far Eastern policy turned on the idea that a unified and reinvigorated China would play a key stabilizing role. Thus China was accorded the status of a great power and was allocated one of the five permanent seats on the

United Nations Security Council. But if China was to live up to Washington's expectations it would be essential to end the long-drawn-out civil war between the Nationalist government of Chiang Kai-shek and the Communists led by Mao Tse-tung. In December 1945 President Truman sent General Marshall to China to try to bring the two sides together in a coalition government. But after a year of futile effort Marshall went home in disgust. This was the signal for all-out civil war. Chiang's armies fell back steadily before the Communist advance. At the same time the Nationalist government's inability to control inflation eroded its support. But although the Truman Administration was dismayed at the turn of events it still believed in Chiang's capacity to regain control. Thus it made only halfhearted efforts to help him. By the beginning of 1949 the Communists had captured Peking and Tientsin; by April they had crossed the Yangtze; by the end of May they had taken Shanghai. At the end of the year Chiang and what was left of his army had abandoned the Chinese mainland and had taken refuge on the island of Formosa.

The Chinese Communist victory profoundly shocked Americans. China had long occupied a special place in their affections. There were close economic, educational, and missionary ties with China and it had been widely believed that the Chinese were advancing under American tutelage towards Christianity and democracy. Thus the 'loss of China' was regarded as almost parricidal. It produced a violent reaction. Critics of the Administration charged that the disaster could have been averted if the United States had given unstinted support to Chiang instead of undermining his position by trying to push him into a coalition with his Communist enemies. The State Department replied that the basic reason for Chiang's defeat was that his corrupt, reactionary, and inefficient regime had lost popular support and that the United States could have saved him only by embarking on a full-scale war on the Chinese mainland—which American public opinion would not have supported.

The China debacle produced a reversal of American thinking about Japan. At the end of World War II the United States had sought to reduce Japan to the status of a second-class power, while at the same time introducing democratic reforms. Under the proconsular rule of General Douglas MacArthur, commander of the American occupation forces, Japan was stripped of her colonies and conquests, six million Japanese soldiers were disarmed and demobilized, radical land reform was accomplished, and the educational system was reshaped. A new democratic Constitution renounced war, eliminated the army from politics, and reduced the emperor to the position of a constitutional monarch. Steps were also taken to ensure against a revival of Japanese military strength. But after the Communist victory in China and the outbreak of the Korean War in 1950 the United States saw Japan as the main Asian bulwark against Communist expansion and began to revive her economic and military power. In 1951 a Japanese peace treaty was signed over the objections of the Soviet Union and in a separate security agreement the United States was granted military bases in Japan. Thus only six years after the end of World War II Japan, like Germany, had been transformed from a conquered enemy of the United States into an informal ally.

The Korean War

Although the United States had not been prepared to invade China on Chiang's behalf American troops were soon to find themselves fighting Chinese Communists in the former Japanese colony of Korea. In 1945 Soviet and American forces had occupied Korea, dividing control along the 38th parallel. The line was originally intended to be temporary but, as the Cold War developed, it became virtually an international frontier separating a Communist regime in the North from a Western-orientated republic in the South. Soviet occupation forces left in January 1949, having seen to it that the North Koreans were heavily armed; American troops were withdrawn six months later, also leaving behind a good deal of military equipment, but not of the kind that could be used offensively. In January 1950 Secretary of State Dean Acheson made a speech defining the American 'defense perimeter' in the Far East. It extended in a huge arc from the Aleutians through Japan to the Philippines, but not embracing Korea or for that matter Formosa. Whether Acheson's speech encouraged the Soviet Union to believe that the United States would not fight to prevent Communist control of the entire Korean peninsula is obscure. Nor is it known for certain whether the Russians instigated what followed. At all events, on June 24, 1950 the North Korean army launched a full-scale offensive across the 38th parallel. Truman promptly ordered General MacArthur to give air and naval support to the hard-pressed South Koreans; a few days later he authorized the use of American ground forces. The United Nations Security Council endorsed these moves and passed an American resolution condemning North Korean aggression and calling upon member states to furnish all necessary assistance to South Korea. General MacArthur was appointed to command the United Nations forces. But although sixteen nations eventually answered the United Nations call, it was essentially an American war. American generals held all the chief commands. The United States supplied 48 percent of the United Nations ground forces—43 percent were South Korean—and virtually all the air and sea forces.

Since few American troops were immediately available for service in Korea the invaders at first seemed likely to overrun the entire peninsula. But by September the front had been stabilized and MacArthur had launched a brilliant amphibious counteroffensive which in a few weeks drove the enemy out of South Korea. This meant that the aim of the United Nations 'police action' had been achieved. But MacArthur continued advancing north beyond the 38th parallel in order to secure an entirely new objective, the unification of Korea. This fateful decision, taken despite warnings of Chinese intervention, was endorsed both by the Truman Administration and by the United Nations General Assembly. For several weeks the northward thrust went well but at the end of November, as United Nations troops approached the Yalu River separating Korea and Manchuria, massive Chinese forces appeared and MacArthur's triumphant advance became a headlong retreat. Only narrowly did his army escape complete disaster. By January 1951 he had succeeded in reforming his lines in the vicinity of the 38th parallel and a seemingly endless war of attrition set in.

At this juncture disagreement between MacArthur and the President provoked a major political crisis. Following his defeat at the hands of the Chinese MacArthur pressed Truman to blockade China, bomb bases and installations in Manchuria, and support a Nationalist invasion of China from Formosa. Truman rejected all these proposals. Chastened by the Chinese intervention he was determined now to fight only a limited war to achieve the original United Nations objective of containing North Korean aggression. He believed that in the struggle with Communism Europe was more important than Asia and that an all-out war with China would necessitate the transfer of all available American forces to the Far East, thus inviting a Soviet attack on Western Europe. The Joint Chiefs of Staff agreed with the President. So did America's NATO allies. But MacArthur impatiently dismissed the concept of limited war. An imperious and flamboyant personality, he had become accustomed during his years as virtual ruler of Japan to act independently of Washington. From the start of the Korean War he had issued public statements at variance with official policy. For this he had been repeatedly rebuked. Yet in March 1951, on learning that the President was ready to seek a negotiated peace, he attempted to rouse Congress and the public against him by writing an open letter to a Republican Congressman arguing the case for an unlimited offensive against China. This was an undisguised challenge to the President's foreign policy and to the constitutional principle that the military should be subordinate to the civil power. Thus on April 11, 1951 Truman abruptly relieved the general of all his commands.

MacArthur's dismissal brought widespread and frenzied protest. Public opinion had applauded Truman's decision to intervene in Korea but, as the war became a costly stalemate, frustration crept in. To fight a limited war ran counter to the American tradition of quick, total solutions. MacArthur's strategy seemed to promise complete victory. Hence he returned home to a tumultuous reception which reached its climax when he made a melodramatic and emotional speech to a joint session of Congress vindicating his conduct. But the furor he created soon faded away, as did MacArthur himself. A Congressional investigation into the conduct of the war gave Administration spokesmen an opportunity to show that his proposed strategy was not only risky but perverse. A showdown with the Chinese, declared General Omar N. Bradley, the chairman of the Joint Chiefs of Staff, would involve the United States in 'the wrong war, at the wrong place, at the wrong time and with the wrong enemy'.

In July 1951 armistice negotiations began near the Korean battlefront. They were marked by bitter wrangling and repeated breakdowns and went on for nearly two years before a cease-fire agreement was reached. (Even today, more than forty years later, a definitive peace settlement has still not been achieved.) Meanwhile the war continued, albeit on a reduced scale, becoming steadily more unpopular in the United States. Though it succeeded in repelling aggression it turned out to be far more than the brief police action originally contemplated. By the time it was over the United States had lost 25,000 dead, 10,000 missing, and 103,000 wounded. A total of 415,000 South Koreans died in the fighting and while their country was freed from the threat of Communist tyranny, it has been ruled ever since by a right-wing government seen as equally odious by many Western critics.

Truman and Domestic Affairs

If Truman's foreign policy was bold, decisive, and, in Europe at least, highly effective, his handling of domestic problems was fumbling and erratic. His impulsiveness and snappishness led him into serious mistakes. So did his loyalty to dishonest political cronies. Moreover, his attempts to extend the New Deal created strains within the Democratic party.

In 1945 it was widely feared that the transition from war to peace would bring back hard times. Some experts predicted that, once industry had lost the stimulus of war contracts, there would be eight to ten million unemployed. But these apprehensions proved groundless. Despite sudden, drastic cuts in government spending and an extraordinarily rapid demobilization which flooded the labor market with ex-servicemen, the war was followed by a period of unparalleled prosperity. The main reason was that pent-up consumer demand took up the slack in the economy. But the federal government helped in various ways: taxes were reduced, loans were made to business, government factories and war material were disposed of at bargain prices, farm price supports were continued. In addition the Servicemen's Readjustment Act of 1944, popularly known as the GI Bill of Rights, provided financial aid to ex-servicemen for further education and training or to enable them to set themselves up in business or farming.

Although the anticipated depression did not materialize the 'reconversion' of the economy brought inflation and industrial unrest. Truman's uncertain leadership made matters worse. Having relaxed some wartime controls when Japan surrendered, he tried to reimpose them when prices began to rise. But Congress, under pressure from business, farm interests, and consumers, would not agree to effective price control. The measure eventually passed in June 1946, after protracted debate, so emasculated the powers of the Office of Price Administration that Truman vetoed it. After a month without controls had brought alarming price rises the President reluctantly accepted a substitute hardly better than the first. But when the OPA reimposed price ceilings, farmers withheld supplies and a serious meat shortage developed, along with a flourishing black market. This forced Truman's surrender. By November 1946 he had abandoned virtually all controls. The result was that in the latter half of 1946 the cost of living shot up 30 percent.

The price-control battle was fought out against a background of industrial strife. In the latter half of 1945 there were large-scale strikes in the automobile, electrical, and steel industries and in 1946 crippling stoppages in the mines and on the railroads. The strikers wanted higher wages to make up for the loss of overtime and to keep up with the rising cost of living. In most cases they went back to work after presidential fact-finding commissions had recommended substantial increases. But the miners, led by John L. Lewis, proved more obdurate, refusing to settle even after Truman had seized the mines and obtained a temporary injunction against them. Only after a federal court had imposed huge fines on Lewis and the United Mine Workers did they go back to work. Truman's course was highly capricious. In September 1945 he had encouraged union demands by suggesting that the economy could stand sizable wage increases. But when the coal strike paralyzed the economy he turned furiously on union leaders. Then, after he had failed to avert a national rail strike by seizing the railroads, he went before Congress (May 25, 1946) to ask for authority to draft the strikers into the army. The settlement of the strike made this unnecessary, but the President's proposal shocked even conservatives.

The Truman Administration's standing was further damaged by the departure of prominent New Dealers. Although in September 1945 the President had advanced a reform program which in some respects went beyond the New Deal, Roosevelt's old lieutenants felt ill at ease with him and still more with the 'Missouri Gang'—machine politicians, small-town lawyers, and businessmen—with which he surrounded himself. Two surviving New Dealers, Frances Perkins and Henry Morgenthau, Jr., resigned unobtrusively from the Cabinet in 1945. Two others left the following year to the accompaniment of controversy. Harold L. Ickes resigned in protest at Truman's nomination of a leading California oilman to be Assistant

Secretary of the Navy; Henry A. Wallace was dismissed for publicly criticizing the Administration's anti-Communist foreign policy. These episodes dismayed blacks, union leaders, and liberal intellectuals—all important elements in the Roosevelt coalition—and left the Democratic party divided.

The Congressional elections of 1946 centered on public dissatisfaction with strikes, shortages, price controls, and inflation, and, by implication, with the President's leadership. Truman was so obviously unpopular that, on the advice of party leaders, he dropped out of the campaign. But even the Republicans were surprised by the size of their victory. For the first time since 1930 they won control of both houses of Congress.

Interpreting the vote as a mandate for greater conservatism the Republican majority in the Eightieth Congress, backed by many Southern Democrats, slashed public expenditure, sharply reduced taxes in an effort to stimulate economic expansion, and ignored Truman's requests for social-welfare legislation. Further, in "a belated act of vengeance" against Franklin D. Roosevelt's long occupation of the White House, Congress adopted the Twenty-Second Amendment to the Constitution (ratified in 1951) limiting all Presidents after Truman to two terms. But the Republicans made little attempt to undo the New Deal. The one major exception was the passage of the National Management Relations (Taft–Hartley) Act of June 1947. Its avowed purpose was to restore the balance of economic power between workers and employers allegedly upset by the prounion Wagner Act of 1935 and to protect the public against union abuses. The measure outlawed the closed shop, prohibited such 'unfair' union practices as secondary boycotts and jurisdictional strikes, made unions responsible in law for breaches of contract and for acts of violence committed by members during strikes, forbade the automatic deduction of union dues from wages as well as union contributions to political campaigns, required non-Communist oaths from union officials, provided that unions must register and report on their activities, and permitted states to enact 'right-to-work' laws forbidding the union shop. In addition the law authorized the government to obtain a court injunction forcing unions to accept an eighty-day 'cooling-off' period before striking. Trade-union leaders denounced the bill as a "slave-labor act" and mounted a spirited campaign against it. Truman, eager to win back the labor support he had lost through his handling of the coal and railroad strikes, issued a blistering veto message only for Congress to repass the bill promptly over his veto.

The wooing of Northern urban dissidents, begun with the Taft–Hartley veto, was carried a stage further when the President's advisers persuaded him of the crucial importance of the Negro vote to his chances of re-election. Notwithstanding his border-state background he became an outspoken champion of civil rights. In February 1948 he sent a special message to Congress recommending legislation to end segregation in interstate travel, to make lynching a federal crime, and to establish a permanent Fair Employment Practices Commission. Nothing came of these proposals except violent Southern protest. But Truman used his executive powers to support the NAACP's attempts to break down the legal basis of segregation by bringing civil-rights suits. In July 1948, moreover, an executive order ended segregation in the armed forces.

The Election of 1948

In the spring of 1948 the Democratic party's divisions seemed to doom its chances in the forthcoming presidential election. While the right had been alienated by Truman's civil-rights program, the left was in rebellion against his foreign policy. The chief advocate of a softer line towards the Soviet Union, the dismissed Henry Wallace, was preparing to run for the presidency as the candidate of a new Progressive party. Other disgruntled Democrats, fearing certain defeat with Truman, attempted without success to interest General Eisenhower and Justice William O. Douglas in the nomination. At their convention at Philadelphia in July the Democrats resignedly renominated Truman. However, in a bitter floor fight over the platform liberals thwarted a presidential attempt to appease the South with a watered-down civil-rights plank and forced through a strengthening amendment. This provoked a walkout by thirty Southern delegates. The rebels, popularly known as Dixiecrats, held a convention at Birmingham, Alabama, where they formed the States' Rights Democratic Party and chose Governor J. Strom Thurmond of South Carolina as their presidential candidate on a militant anticivil-rights platform. Shortly afterward the Progressive party convention, attended by a motley assortment of idealists, liberals, Socialists, and Communists, formally nominated Wallace for President. The Progressive platform wanted to replace anti-Communist containment with a policy of friendship with the Soviet Union and advocated racial equality, economic planning, and public ownership of key sectors of the economy.

Encouraged by their opponents' disarray the Republicans were confident that their long years in the wilderness were almost over. They again nominated Governor Thomas E. Dewey for President and chose another liberal internationalist, Governor Earl Warren of California, as his running mate. The platform tacitly accepted the New Deal but promised greater honesty and efficiency in government. Dewey, expecting an easy victory, waged a dignified, colorless, nonchalant campaign. Truman, on the other hand, campaigned belligerently. He set out on a strenuous 'whistle-stop' tour, traveling 31,000 miles and making over 350 speeches. Depicting the Republicans as the party of hard times, he particularly castigated the "do-nothing" Republican Eightieth Congress. His tactics were crude and perhaps unfair. But they worked. Against heavy odds, confounding poll-sters and political pundits alike, Truman won. Wallace cut sufficiently into Truman's strength in New York, Connecticut, Michigan, and Maryland to throw those states to Dewey, while Thurmond deprived the Democrats of four states in the Deep South. But on balance the two extremist defections may have helped the President, the Dixiecrats by increasing Truman's appeal to black voters, the Progressives by providing (albeit involuntarily) an answer to the charge that the Administration had been 'soft on Com-munism'. No less crucial was Truman's success in holding the labor vote and in recapturing most of the Middle Western farm states.

Having become President in his own right Truman renewed his pressure for the ambitious social-reform program he had vainly urged on Congress before and which he now called the Fair Deal. But the Congressional coalition of Republicans and conservative Democrats was more effective than ever. Republicans were bitter at the way Truman had lambasted them during the campaign, Southern Democrats at his civil-rights proposals. Nor was there much popular support for reform: the country was prosperous and moreover distracted by foreign affairs and the issue of subversion. Congress agreed to modest extensions of existing social policies, raising the minimum wage, broadening social-security coverage, and voting funds for slum clearance and low-cost housing. But it turned down the rest of the Fair Deal. Southern filibustering sealed the fate of a civil-rights bill. A proposal for national health insurance was killed after having been effectively stigmatized by the American Medical Association as 'socialized medicine'. A plan for federal aid to education was lost because of wrangling over whether parochial schools should benefit. Truman also failed to secure either the enactment of a new farm price-support system (the Brannan plan) or the repeal of the Taft–Hartley Act.

With his legislative program in tatters Truman faced vexing domestic problems which made his second term even stormier than the first. There were revelations of corruption within the Administration. An unsavory army of lobbyists, known as 'five-percenters', had made a business of ped-dling influence; they bribed officials in order to obtain contracts and government loans or to smooth over tax difficulties. The President was not implicated but some White House officials were shown to have low ethical standards. There were also renewed labor troubles, especially during the Korean War. When John L. Lewis led the miners out on strike yet again in 1950, Truman was only able to settle the dispute by invoking the Taft–Hartley Act he had earlier vetoed. Then in 1952 the President's arbitrary conduct during a steel strike brought him a humiliating defeat. In order to prevent an inflationary wage settlement he seized the steel mills. But the Supreme Court declared the seizure unconstitutional—the first time since 1866 it had invalidated a presidential action.

Communist Subversion and McCarthyism

These events were overshadowed, however, by growing public alarm over Communist espionage and infiltration. During the 1930s a number of idealists, chiefly intellectuals, dismayed by the Depression and the rise of Fascism abroad, either joined the Communist party or, more commonly, became sympathetically interested in Communism and the Soviet Union. Such people were found especially in government departments, universities, the entertainment industry, and the CIO trade unions. This seemed relatively innocuous while the United States and the Soviet Union were allies, but with the onset of the Cold War Communist proclivities and associations came to be deemed incompatible with loyalty and national security. Concern about subversion originated in 1945, when hundreds of secret State Department documents were found in the offices of the Communist-sponsored magazine, *Amerasia*. More disturbing still was the disclosure in 1946 that Canadian government employees had handed over atomic secrets to a Soviet spy ring. The Canadian revelations prompted the Truman Administration in March 1947 to institute new loyalty and security checks. No spies were uncovered but several hundred federal civil servants were dismissed as security risks. In addition eleven leading Communists were prosecuted for violating the Smith Act of 1940 by conspiring to teach and advocate the overthrow of the government by force. They were convicted in October 1949 and imprisoned. The Supreme Court, in *Dennis v. United States* (1951), upheld the conviction.

Meanwhile the House Un-American Activities Committee (HUAC), which had originated in 1938 in a desire to protect the United States against Nazi penetration, had become a vehicle for ferreting out Communists in trade unions, Hollywood, and the government. The Committee became notorious for its brazen publicity-seeking, its partisan attempts to capitalize on the growing anti-Communist hysteria, its bigotry, its bullying of individuals with unconventional opinions, and its readiness to accept the frequently vague and contradictory tittle-tattle of informers and professional ex-Communists. But not all its 'victims' were innocent, as became evident when the persistence of one of its members, Congressman Richard M. Nixon of California, resulted in the exposure of Alger Hiss, a former high-ranking State Department official, as a Soviet spy. Like the British diplomats Guy Burgess and Donald Maclean who were subsequently exposed as Soviet agents, Hiss was a man of genteel background and privileged education. During the New Deal he had held various government posts before entering the State Department and becoming an adviser at international conferences, including Yalta. In 1948 Whittaker Chambers, a senior editor of *Time* magazine and a self-confessed former Communist, testified to HUAC that during the late 1930s Hiss had given him secret information for transmission to Russia. When Hiss denied the allegation he was prosecuted for perjury: the statute of limitations prevented his indictment for espionage. At his first trial (July 1949) the jury could not agree but a second trial (January 1950) resulted in his conviction and imprisonment.

The Hiss case profoundly shocked Americans. If a man of his background and reputation, vouched for during his trial by distinguished liberals including Secretary of State Dean Acheson, could betray his country, how far might not treason extend? Though some liberals continued to assert Hiss's innocence, most were stunned. The Republican right wing, for its part, saw his conviction as a God-sent opportunity to associate the entire New Deal with Communism and to attribute the disasters which had befallen American Far Eastern policy to a conspiracy in the State Department. The impact of the Hiss case was heightened by the sudden and unexpected end of the American atomic monopoly. In September 1949, years earlier than American scientists had predicted, the Soviet Union exploded an atomic device, thus depriving Americans of the sense of security they had possessed since 1945. It soon transpired that espionage had speeded up Soviet atomic production. In February 1950 it was revealed that a high-ranking British scientist, Dr Klaus Fuchs, had confessed to having systematically turned over atomic secrets to the Soviet Union between 1943 and 1947. Several of Fuchs's American accomplices were tried and convicted for espionage and two of them, Julius and Ethel Rosenberg, were executed in 1953.

These successive revelations created a pervasive atmosphere of suspicion, self-doubt, and fear. In September 1950, with only a few dissentient votes, Congress passed a drastic Internal Security (or McCarran) Bill. Truman vetoed it as an infringement of civil liberties—a view belatedly upheld by the Supreme Court in 1965—but it was repassed over his veto in 1951. The Act required the registration of Communist and Communist-front organizations, forbade the employment of Communists in defense plants, and barred anyone who had belonged to totalitarian organizations from entering the United States. An even more draconian provision authorized the establishment of concentration camps for Communists in time of national emergency. Truman's veto of the McCarran Bill intensified Republican criticisms that the Administration was 'soft on Communism'. That such a charge could plausibly be made might seem odd in view of the President's consistently anti-Communist foreign policy and his tightening of internal-security procedures. Yet the Democratic record was vulnerable. There had been a disgracefully slack attitude to Communist penetration before, during, and even after World War II. Truman and Acheson had been altogether too complacent about the problem, even after the revelations of 1949; thus the President had dismissed the Hiss investigation as 'a red herring'. Moreover, there was no denying that the Democrats had been in power while Communism was advancing in China and making inroads into the federal bureaucracy.

The scene was thus set for a talented demagogue to assume the leadership of the anti-Communist movement. He was Joseph R. McCarthy, a hitherto obscure Republican senator from Wisconsin, who was to give to the English language a new word—McCarthyism, a term meaning sensational, indiscriminate, and unsubstantiated allegations of Communist sympathies and associations. McCarthy burst into prominence in February 1950 when, in an attempt to revive his flagging political fortunes, he claimed that scores or even hundreds of known Communists were still working in the State Department. Although he never produced evidence to substantiate the charge, he endlessly reiterated and embroidered it, and exploited unthinking popular nationalism to win a mass following, especially among Midwesterners, recent immigrants from eastern Europe, and working-class Catholics. The 1950 Congressional elections demonstrated McCarthy's power: two of his senatorial critics were defeated for reelection. Thereafter few politicians were prepared to challenge him lest they too be accused of being pro-Communist. The Republican hierarchy, though privately disliking McCarthy's tactics, was nonetheless willing to use him against the Administration. Thus for four frenzied years McCarthy rode high. His witch-hunting encouraged individual states and cities to institute their own security programs and to demand loyalty oaths from their employees. In addition local inquisitorial bodies and private vigilante groups hounded suspected Communists. Several thousand people lost their jobs and hundreds were imprisoned, Communists were denied passports, a number of resident aliens were persecuted, and some prospective foreign visitors debarred. Worse still, McCarthyism poisoned American public life, demoralized and impaired the efficiency of the State Department, and gravely damaged the reputation of the United States abroad.

The Eisenhower Landslide

As the presidential election approached a troubled and overwrought America yearned for security, tranquility, and an end to partisan strife. It turned therefore to a man entirely without political experience, the genial and unassuming General Dwight D. Eisenhower. As commander of the NATO forces Eisenhower had become popularly identified with resistance to Soviet expansion but, like other soldiers who have become President, he personified the military virtues without being at all militaristic. Though less reluctant, perhaps, to enter politics than he made it appear Eisenhower finally did so in response to the urgings of the moderate, internationalist, east-coast wing of the Republican party which was anxious to deny the Republican nomination to Senator Robert A. Taft, the favorite of the conservative, neoisolationist Middle West. Though he had expected that the diadem would be thrust upon him, Eisenhower found that he had to fight for it. When the Republican convention met in July the Taft forces seemed in control and it was only narrowly that Eisenhower won the nomination. To appease the conservatives the convention chose Senator Richard M. Nixon as his running mate. On the Democratic side a wealth of contenders appeared after President Truman had declined to run for another term. But none of these secured the party's nomination, which went instead to a more genuinely reluctant candidate, Governor Adlai E. Stevenson of Illinois. The choice of a Southerner, Senator John J. Sparkman of Alabama, as the vice-presidential nominee indicated the healing of the 1948 party split over civil rights. All the same the Democratic platform contained a moderate civil-rights plank, along with an endorsement of Truman's foreign policy.

During the campaign Stevenson's wit and eloquence captivated intellectuals but failed to stir the mass of the voters. He was in any case handicapped by having to defend the now highly unpopular Truman Administration. Republican campaigners vigorously assailed Truman's record, especially in respect of Communism, corruption, and Korea. Initially Eisenhower struck a note of Olympian detachment reminiscent of Dewey in 1948, but as the campaign developed he became increasingly partisan. Moreover, having by October recognized the depth of popular discontent with the stalemate in Korea he promised to go there to bring the war to "an early and honorable end". On election day Eisenhower won a remarkable personal victory. Capturing all but nine states he made inroads into the South and won the support of substantial numbers of normally Democratic urban voters in the North, especially the Irish. But Eisenhower ran far ahead of his party: the Republicans only narrowly won control of Congress.

With his own party in power McCarthy might have been expected to call off his reckless crusade. But, temperamentally incapable of stopping, he continued his Savonarola-like outbursts, alleging that not only the State Department but also other government departments and agencies, the Protestant churches, and the exclusive Ivy League universities were all part of what he called 'the Communist apparatus'. Eisenhower, though deeply offended that the loyalty of his mentor, General Marshall, had been impugned by McCarthy, had nonetheless endorsed the senator during the 1952 campaign in the interests of party unity. Even as President Eisenhower was reluctant to criticize McCarthy directly, believing that he would eventually destroy himself—which he duly did. Early in 1954 McCarthy broadened his attack to include the Secretary of the Army and, by implication, Eisenhower himself. This led to an extended Congressional investigation. Televised hearings revealed McCarthy to millions for the ignorant, bullying charlatan he was. In December 1954 the Senate voted by 67 to 22 to censure him—not, however, for his wild allegations but for flouting senatorial convention. Thereafter his influence rapidly declined. He became increasingly addicted to drink and in May 1957 died of it.

McCarthy's eclipse did not immediately banish the postwar obsession with Communist subversion or the associated tendency to sacrifice civil liberties to the Moloch of national security. For the rest of the decade people suspected of even the vaguest sympathies with Communism, or indeed of unconventional sexual behavior, were liable to be removed from positions of trust. In 1953 the Eisenhower Administration adopted more rigorous security procedures which, among other things, denied accused persons access to the evidence against them. More than 3,000 federal employees were dismissed as security risks, and an even larger number resigned before their cases had been decided. Some decisions taken under the security program were questionable. The most celebrated was the Oppenheimer case in which an unholy alliance of narrow-minded politicians, jealous scientific rivals, and ambitious Air Force generals dragged down a distinguished physicist—though the victim himself supplied the opportunity. J. Robert Oppenheimer, known for his wartime work as 'the father of the atom bomb', had in 1949 opposed the development of the hydrogen bomb on moral and political grounds. Four years later, when due for confirmation as an adviser to the Atomic Energy Commission, his enemies linked his opposition to the hydrogen bomb to his previous Communist connections, about which he had been less than frank. After a lengthy hearing resembling a trial—though a most unjudicial one— Oppenheimer was denied security clearance and debarred from access to secret information in the possession of the AEC.

The Eisenhower Presidency

Eisenhower's conception of the Presidency was more limited than that of his two immediate predecessors. He had a strict, simplistic, almost theological, view of the Constitution. He believed that the functions of the executive were quite distinct from those of the legislature and that Roosevelt and Truman, in their attempts to influence legislation, had usurped the prerogatives of Congress. These predilections were reinforced by the fact that by temperament Eisenhower was a conciliator rather than an innovator and that his military career had accustomed him to delegate authority. But though reluctant to impose his will on Congress or even on his Administration or his party, he became worried when Senator John W. Bricker of Ohio sponsored a constitutional amendment to restrict the negotiation of executive agreements and to limit the legal effect of treaties. Convinced that the proposal would cripple the President's conduct of foreign affairs, Eisenhower strenuously opposed it. On February 26, 1954 the

Senate finally rejected the Bricker Amendment, but by only a single vote.

In domestic affairs Eisenhower adopted a middle-of-the-road approach which he labeled 'dynamic conservatism'. In practice this meant less government intervention in the economy coupled with continued federal concern for individual welfare. Eisenhower's Cabinet was packed with businessmen: its most influential members were Secretary of State John Foster Dulles, a wealthy corporation lawyer, Secretary of the Treasury George Humphrey, a millionaire Ohio business executive, and Secretary of Defense Charles E. Wilson, president of General Motors. Among measures designed to encourage business was the ending of Korean War economic controls and the granting of tax reductions and increased depreciation allowances. Partiality for private enterprise was also evident, along with a preference for decentralization, in the Administration's attitude to the development of natural resources. In 1953 Eisenhower persuaded Congress to pass the Tidelands Oil Act which, in transferring to state ownership the rich offshore oil deposits along the Gulf of Mexico and the Pacific coast, opened the door to exploitation by private interests. The following year the Administration awarded a contract for a huge new electricity plant near Memphis to the Dixon–Yates utility syndicate rather than to the TVA—though the contract was canceled after an outcry about certain dubious aspects of the deal. Furthermore, instead of seeking appropriations for a single large federal dam on the Snake River in Idaho the Administration authorized the building of a series of small dams by private enterprise.

None of this meant that Eisenhower was trying to put the clock back to the 1920s. Although he at first cut government spending, especially on defense and foreign aid, in the hope of ultimately balancing the budget, he showed some willingness to adopt Keynesian countercyclical policies when the economy faltered. Thus in 1956 he secured Congressional approval of a ten-year interstate-highway building program which ultimately cost $25 billion. Nor was there any attempt to repeal the social-welfare legislation of the previous twenty years. On the contrary Eisenhower's Presidency saw great extensions of social-security and unemployment benefits, a rise in the minimum wage, and the creation (in 1953) of a Department of Health, Education, and Welfare. In 1956, after the introduction of a more flexible system of farm price supports had failed to solve the problem of overproduction and had sharply reduced farm income, the Administration opted for a 'soil bank' plan modeled closely on the New Deal's original agricultural program.

Eisenhower's moderation matched the national mood. His mere presence in the White House helped restore political tranquility and dispel the rancors of the McCarthy period. Two serious bouts of illness in 1955 and 1956 cast doubt on his ability to serve a second term but, having made a full recovery, he was renominated by acclamation by the 1956 Republican convention. The Democrats again chose Adlai Stevenson who on this occasion sought to palliate his intellectualism by adopting a less lofty style of campaigning and by making deliberate grammatical mistakes. But he could not contend with Eisenhower's overwhelming popularity or the fact that, as a Republican campaign slogan put it, "Everything's booming but the guns." Moreover the sudden and simultaneous eruption of the Suez crisis and the Hungarian revolt in the last days of what had been a dull campaign enabled the Republicans to claim that Eisenhower's continued leadership in international affairs was indispensable. On election day the President won an even more striking victory than in 1952. It was again a highly personal triumph. For the first time since 1848 a reelected President failed to carry at least one house of Congress.

Eisenhower's Second Term.

Although Eisenhower never lost his hold on popular affections his second term brought a decline in his prestige. Shortly after his reelection the country experienced a short but sharp economic recession, the worst since the 1930s. The rise of a civil-rights agitation resulted in violent racial clashes in the South. The launching of the Soviet *Sputnik* satellite late in 1957 dealt Americans a tremendous psychological blow, shattering their complacent belief in the technological superiority of the United States. The Administration was further embarrassed in 1958 when revelations of corruption in high places contradicted its professions of purity. The most damaging case involved the President's chief assistant, Sherman Adams, who resigned after admitting that he had received gifts from a firm seeking government contracts. The following year brought a renewal of labor troubles, especially in the steel industry, which experienced its longest strike since the war. Finally, during Eisenhower's last months in office, things went badly wrong in foreign affairs.

The most vexatious problem proved to be civil rights. The black struggle for equality entered a new phase in May 1954 with the historic Supreme Court decision in *Brown v. Board of Education of Topeka* handed down by Chief Justice Earl Warren, whom Eisenhower had appointed the year before. The case marked the triumphant climax to the NAACP's long battle in the courts against racial segregation. Speaking for a unanimous Court Chief Justice Warren reversed the 1896 decision in *Plessy v. Ferguson* that segregation did not violate the Fourteenth Amendment so long as equal facilities were provided for each race. Though in practice facilities for blacks were markedly inferior, the 'separate but equal' doctrine had provided a legal sanction for segregation. Now, however, Warren explicitly repudiated it, ruling that segregation in the public schools was unconstitutional since "separate educational facilities are inherently inferior". In another decision the following year the Court laid it down that desegregation of the schools must proceed "with all deliberate speed".

Southerners indignantly denounced the *Brown* decision as a violation of state rights and as an attempt to revolutionize their social system. In the Upper South and the border states a start was made on desegregating the schools, at least in big cities like Washington, Baltimore, and St. Louis, but in the Deep South there was determined resistance from militant White Citizens' Councils. At the beginning of Eisenhower's second term, three years after the Court's ruling, less than 12 percent of the South's 6,300 school districts had been integrated and in seven Southern states not a single black pupil had been admitted to a white high school. Eisenhower had avoided expressing an opinion on the Court's decision and resisted suggestions that he should use federal power to implement it. But in September 1957 he was forced to act when mob violence and the obstructionism of Governor Orval Faubus frustrated the operation of a gradual desegregation scheme in Little Rock, Arkansas. Faced with open defiance to federal authority the President sent in a detachment of paratroops to escort Negro children to school. Nonetheless, during the rest of Eisenhower's term the pace of desegregation remained slow. Rather than accept it large numbers of white parents transferred their children to private schools or refused to send them to school at all. Some Southern communities even abolished their public school systems. More commonly they found ways of evading, rather than directly challenging, desegregation: elaborate 'pupil placement' laws made it possible to reject black applications to particular schools on grounds other than race.

Efforts to remove obstacles to black voting in the South were similarly unproductive. Although by 1956 the number of Southern blacks registered to vote had risen to 1,200,000—twice the figure in 1947—this was only a quarter of those eligible. In August 1957 Congress attempted to provide a remedy by passing the first Civil Rights Act since Reconstruction. A weaker measure than Eisenhower had originally proposed, it established a Civil Rights Commission to investigate denials of the franchise and empowered the Justice Department to sue on behalf of black voting rights. A second Civil Rights Act in 1960 extended these provisions. But neither measure proved effective. In the Deep South especially, state officials continued to prevent the great mass of qualified Negroes from voting.

Meanwhile Southern blacks themselves had begun to fight discrimination with unwonted self-confidence and tenacity. This was only partly because of the encouragement afforded by the *Brown* decision. World War II experiences had left many blacks, especially younger ones, disinclined to accept inequality any longer. The spread of television in the 1950s revealed to them for the first time how affluent middle-class white America was and thus how deprived they themselves were. Moreover the emergence of independent black African states proved a tremendous stimulus to racial pride. The outcome was a series of demonstrations against the Jim Crow laws. The most celebrated began in Montgomery, Alabama, in December 1955, when 50,000 black residents boycotted the city buses in protest against segregation. The movement was led by a young black Baptist minister, Dr Martin Luther King, Jr., who had embraced the Gandhian ideal of civil disobedience through passive resistance. Despite mass arrests and widespread intimidation the boycott was maintained until, in November 1956, the Supreme Court declared the segregation of bus passengers to be unconstitutional. The success of nonviolence led to its adoption elsewhere. In February 1960 black students at Greensboro, North Carolina began a sit-in, destined to last six months, at a lunch counter hitherto reserved for whites. The sit-in movement spread rapidly to the entire South and proved highly effective in desegregating restaurants, shops, hotels, theaters, and parks.

Dulles and the Cold War

The moderation which characterized Eisenhower's domestic policy was manifested also in foreign affairs. This was not always apparent since John Foster Dulles, Secretary of State from 1953 to 1959, had a penchant for extravagant rhetoric which conveyed an impression of recklessness. The Republican platform of 1952, which Dulles drafted, condemned the Truman Administration's "negative, futile and immoral" policy of containment and hinted at a dynamic alternative which would result in a "rollback" of Soviet power in eastern Europe, the "liberation" of captive peoples, and the "unleashing" of Chiang Kai-shek to attack the Chinese mainland. Similarly, in office Dulles continued to use language which sounded threatening and seemed to foreshadow new, tougher policies. In 1953 French opposition to his plans to rearm West Germany so as to bring her into the Western defense system led him to hint at an "agonizing reappraisal" of American policy, meaning presumably that the United States might abandon its European commitments. In 1954, in explaining the Administration's "new look" defense policy with its emphasis on atomic strike-power rather than on conventional local wars like Korea, he talked of "massive retaliation" as a more effective as well as a cheaper way of stopping aggression. And in 1957 he claimed to have "walked to the brink of war" in his attempts to bring the Communist powers to terms. Yet in practice the foreign policy of Eisenhower and Dulles, though more moralistic in tone and more rigid in application, was essentially the same as that of Truman and Acheson.

A man of extraordinary mental gifts and tireless industry, Dulles was perhaps better qualified by ancestry and experience to preside over the State Department than any of his predecessors except perhaps John

Quincy Adams. The grandson of one Secretary of State (John W. Foster) and the nephew of another (Robert Lansing), his diplomatic career had begun at the Hague Conference of 1907 and had included attendance at the Versailles Conference of 1919 and the San Francisco Conference of 1945. He had also been called upon to negotiate the Japanese Peace Treaty of 1951. Believing in personal diplomacy he spent much of his time as Secretary of State en route between Washington and foreign capitals. This did not endear him to the State Department officials and diplomatic representatives whose functions he thus made superfluous. Nor did personal contact always facilitate negotiation. Indeed some of America's European allies came to feel that Dulles's combination of self-righteousness and deviousness made him impossible to work with. But Dulles's twists were sometimes forced on him from above. For while he was allowed a good deal of latitude in the day-to-day conduct of foreign policy, ultimate control always rested with a President who was much less passive than contemporaries believed.

Immediately after his election in 1952 Eisenhower fulfilled his campaign pledge to go to Korea and soon after he took office the stalemated negotiations were reopened. North Korean demands for the repatriation of prisoners of war, including those who did not wish to return, still caused difficulty but after the United States had intimated that tactical atomic weapons would be used if the war went on the Communists gave way and an armistice was signed on July 27, 1953. It provided for a cease-fire and for a conference to settle the future of Korea. This was held at Geneva in the spring of 1954 but failed to settle anything.

With the end of the Korean war attention switched to Indo-China, where the French had been fighting since 1946 to suppress a nationalist uprising led by the Vietnamese Communist, Ho Chi Minh. At first the United States had acted impartially in what it regarded as a colonial war, but when in 1950 the Chinese Communists began supplying Ho with arms the Truman Administration saw the French as anti-Communist crusaders and started sending them economic and military aid. This was stepped up under Eisenhower until by 1954 the United States was financing about 80 percent of the French war effort. But American aid did not avert the steady deterioration of the French position. By the spring of 1954 Vietminh Communists controlled much of Vietnam and were besieging a French garrison in the remote stronghold of Dienbienphu. Eisenhower believed Indo-China to be the strategic key to Southeast Asia; if it fell to the Communists neighboring countries would, he asserted, collapse like a row of dominoes. He and his advisers discussed a plan for limited American military intervention to relieve the hard-pressed French but abandoned it when Congressional leaders expressed opposition and the British refused to take part.

Even before Dienbienphu fell (May 7, 1954) the French government had decided to end an obviously hopeless struggle. The following month negotiations at Geneva resulted in agreements for a cease-fire in Indo-China and for the partition of the country into three independent, neutral states: Laos, Cambodia, and Vietnam. However, pending elections to be held in two years, Vietnam was to be divided along the 17th parallel into a Communist north and a non-Communist south. The United States disliked the Geneva agreements as a surrender to force and refused to sign them. It did, however, promise not to disturb the settlement. But when it became apparent that the stipulated elections would result in Communist victories in both parts of Vietnam, Washington supported Ngo Dinh Diem, the authoritarian ruler of the South Vietnam republic, in his decision not to hold them. In Diem the United States believed it had found a leader capable of creating an effective non-Communist regime strong enough to withstand attempted subversion and aggression. From 1954 onwards it gave him massive financial aid and also sent military advisers to train the South Vietnamese army. Likewise in Laos it supported conservative elements in their efforts to put down civil strife. Yet in both countries Communist influence increased.

In a further move to counter Communist expansion Dulles set up the Southeast Asia Treaty Organization (SEATO) in September 1954. Composed of the United States, Great Britain, France, Australia, New Zealand, Pakistan, Thailand, and the Philippines, this new defensive alliance differed from NATO, on which it was ostensibly modeled, in that the signatories agreed only to consult one another in the event of attack and depended not on members' contributions to common defense forces but on American striking power. An even more striking weakness was that India, Burma, Ceylon, and Indonesia refused to join. Thus the organization was largely a sham.

Meanwhile Eisenhower had announced that the United States would no longer restrain the Nationalists in Formosa from attacking the Chinese mainland. But this 'unleashing' of Chiang Kai-shek produced no spectacular results since his forces proved to be too weak to do more than occupy the offshore islands of Quemoy and Matsu. When the Communists responded by bombarding the islands, a potentially dangerous situation arose. But although in 1954 Eisenhower concluded with Chiang a mutual security treaty guaranteeing Formosa, he declined to commit American forces to the defense of Quemoy and Matsu.

Following the death of Stalin in March 1953 there were signs of a thaw in the Cold War. Its most tangible consequences were the conclusion in May 1955 of the much-delayed Austrian peace treaty and the holding two months later of a summit meeting of heads of government at Geneva—the first such gathering since Potsdam ten years before. But events in Hungary in October 1956 shattered the illusion of international harmony. When the Hungarians staged an anti-Communist revolt the Soviet Union ruthlessly suppressed it and installed a new puppet regime. The United States forthrightly condemned the Soviet action but its failure to come to the aid of the Hungarian 'freedom fighters' demonstrated the emptiness of Dulles's liberationist rhetoric.

The Hungarian revolt coincided with—indeed was overshadowed by—the Suez crisis. This originated in the failure of Dulles's attempts to woo the Egyptian nationalist leader, Colonel Gamal Abdel Nasser, from his anti-Israel and pro-Soviet course. To win Egyptian friendship Dulles first put pressure on the British to withdraw their forces from the Suez canal zone, a step duly taken in 1954, and then promised to help finance a huge dam and hydroelectric power-station Nasser proposed to build on the Nile at Aswan. These gestures did nothing to deflect Nasser. He concluded an arms deal with the Soviet Union, recognized Communist China, and intensified his border raids on Israel. Piqued by this behavior Dulles abruptly withdrew the offer to finance the Aswan Dam (July 19, 1956). Nasser retaliated by nationalizing the Suez Canal, owned mainly by British and French shareholders. He reckoned that the canal profits would provide the funds for the dam project. Great Britain and France reacted furiously. They were not prepared to countenance Egyptian control of their lifeline to Middle East oil. While Dulles and, for that matter, Eisenhower, gave the impression of sympathizing with them the Americans were secretly determined to achieve a peaceful solution. The Machiavellian shifts and delays to which Dulles was consequently driven so exasperated Great Britain and France that they finally decided on unilateral military action. Without informing their American ally, but in collusion with Israel, which launched a preventive war on Egypt on October 29, the two countries announced two days later that they were sending troops to Egypt in order—so they said—to separate the belligerents and protect transit through the canal.

The Anglo-French intervention was almost universally condemned. The United States and the Soviet Union, for once on the same side, vied with each other in denunciation. But when the Russians threatened to come to Egypt's assistance Eisenhower became so alarmed that he increased his already intense pressure on Great Britain and France to call off the expedition. In the face of American hostility they had to comply. The Suez fiasco had far-reaching consequences. Nasser, notwithstanding the mauling his army suffered at the hands of the Israelis, emerged with enhanced prestige. The Soviet Union, too, strengthened its position in the Middle East. But the NATO alliance was badly shaken, while Anglo-American relations were for a time in tatters. Furthermore the collapse of British and French influence in the Middle East seemed to open the way for further Communist penetration. Eisenhower's response was to seek and obtain (March 1957) Congressional authority to give economic and military aid to any country in the Middle East threatened by a Communist takeover. This became known as the Eisenhower Doctrine. It turned out, however, that the main threat to Middle Eastern stability came from Nasser rather than the Soviet Union. The Egyptian leader attempted successively to subvert the pro-Western governments of Jordan and Lebanon, but the United States thwarted him, first by dispatching the Sixth Fleet to the eastern Mediterranean in 1957 and then by landing marines in Lebanon the following year.

With Dulles's death in the summer of 1959 Eisenhower assumed more openly the control of foreign policy he had all along possessed. In the next year or so, as the Administration's chickens came home to roost, events in different parts of the world badly damaged American prestige. In Africa the refusal of the United States to take a strong stand against its NATO ally, Belgium, during the Congo troubles enabled the Soviet Union to make bad blood between African nationalists and the West. In the Far East the conclusion of a new mutual security treaty with Japan in 1960 to replace that of 1951 failed to assuage Japanese feelings of resentment at being treated as a client state; violent anti-American demonstrations in Tokyo in June 1960 necessitated the cancellation of a projected Eisenhower visit. In Latin America the Administration's support of reactionary dictatorships fueled popular anti-Americanism. Already manifested in Vice-President Nixon's hostile reception in Venezuela in 1958, this feeling reached new heights after the Castro revolution in Cuba in 1959. The overthrow of the brutal Batista regime was at first applauded in the United States but Cuban–American relations deteriorated when Castro confiscated American property and established an avowedly Communist government. By the summer of 1960 Cuba was clearly in the Soviet orbit and the Soviet Union had gained a foothold in the Western Hemisphere. Still more humiliating for the United States was the U-2 incident. In May 1960, just before a scheduled summit meeting in Paris which had been expected to relax world tensions, the Russians announced the shooting-down within the Soviet Union of a high-flying, American U-2 reconnaissance plane. At first the State Department claimed that the pilot had lost his way while engaged on weather research, whereupon the Soviet premier, Khrushchev, produced irrefutable proof that the plane had been on a spying mission. Eisenhower could have satisfied diplomatic protocol by claiming, however implausibly, that the flight had been unauthorized. But he frankly accepted responsibility for it and indeed for others. This admission wrecked the summit meeting: it collapsed amid recrimination and insult.

Eisenhower's Presidency thus ended on a sour note. Yet the President had given his countrymen an interlude of peace. He had refused to be panicked by ultranationalists in his own party into using America's massive nuclear arsenal. Admittedly Eisenhower shares responsibility with Dulles for overextending American commitments and for what turned out to be disastrous interventions in foreign countries, notably in Iran—where the United States staged a coup to keep the Shah on his throne—and in Indo-China. But if under Eisenhower the United States lost the initiative in world affairs, this was due less to the Administration's failings than to changing global realities: the nuclear 'balance of terror', European recovery, the rise of Afro-Asian nationalism. As for domestic affairs Eisenhower met a national need in calming and sweetening the political atmosphere. True, presidential blandness and passivity meant the shelving of urgent social problems. For this reason Eisenhower's two terms are sometimes dismissed as wasted years. Yet when the activism of his successors had produced a crop of disasters and when one Presidency after another had ended in tragedy, failure, or disgrace the Eisenhower era came to be remembered as a golden age of tranquility.

27. *The Troubled Years*, 1960–1980

The 1960s and 1970s were among the most traumatic decades in American history. The country was shaken by a sequence of political assassinations and by a protracted, shabby, and shaming political scandal. A new and aggressive militancy among blacks and other discontented groups produced violent confrontations on the streets and on college campuses. A costly, frustrating, and ultimately unsuccessful war plunged the nation into turmoil, while shattering 'the illusion of American omnipotence'. These experiences left Americans divided and unsure of themselves. Some carried their rebelliousness to the point of questioning the very moral and constitutional foundations of American society. Meanwhile America's economic supremacy was being eroded: there was mounting worry about inflation, unemployment, and the threat of an energy shortage. National pride did indeed receive a boost in 1969 from the remarkable technological achievement of landing a man on the moon and from the bicentennial celebrations of 1976. But the late 1970s brought a further darkening of the economic skies as well as more humiliating reminders of the limits of American power.

The Election of 1960

As the presidential election of 1960 approached, however, the American scene was still generally tranquil. Eisenhower's popularity was undiminished, despite the failure of his summit diplomacy. But for the Twenty-second Amendment, limiting presidents to two terms, he might well have been renominated and reelected. As it was, the Republican nomination went to Vice-President Richard M. Nixon whose highly publicized official tours abroad had given him the appearance of being Eisenhower's chosen heir and whose willingness over the years to assume the burden of campaigning and fund-raising had won him the solid backing of party officials. The Democratic nomination was more keenly contested but went finally to Senator John F. Kennedy of Massachusetts. A member of a wealthy, Catholic, Boston Irish political family, Kennedy's senatorial career had been undistinguished. His frequent absences from the Senate had led some to dismiss him as a political dilettante. His failure to speak out against McCarthyism had raised doubts about his political courage. But by means of a lavish, well-organized, and energetic campaign in key primaries he demonstrated his popular appeal and disposed of his main rival, the liberal senator, Hubert H. Humphrey. Nominated on a platform which promised to continue and extend the New Deal and the Fair Deal, Kennedy promised to lead the American people toward a vaguely defined 'New Frontier'—a phrase subsequently used to describe the aims of his Administration. Mindful that his religion might prove a handicap in the South, he made a bid for Southern support by choosing as his running mate the Senate majority leader, Lyndon B. Johnson of Texas, who had himself aspired to the presidential nomination.

During the campaign Kennedy sought to defuse the religious issue by bringing it into the open. In a speech to Protestant ministers in Houston he reaffirmed his belief in the separation of Church and State, refused to be labeled the Catholic candidate for President, and called on Americans to demonstrate their freedom from bigotry by disproving the political truism that no Catholic could be elected President. Religion, however, received less emphasis during the campaign than foreign policy. While Nixon defended the record of the Eisenhower Administration and stressed his own experience of foreign affairs, Kennedy alleged that under the Republicans America's standing in the world had declined. He dwelt on an alleged missile gap, claiming that the Soviet Union had overtaken the United States in nuclear weapons, and also criticized Eisenhower for failing to deal with the Communist presence in Cuba. A novel feature of the campaign was that the candidates appeared jointly in a series of television 'debates'. These revealed few policy differences but seem to have worked to Kennedy's advantage, making him more widely known and enabling him to refute Nixon's charge that he was immature and inexperienced.

The election turned out to be one of the closest in American history. Kennedy emerged the winner with a margin of only 0.1 percent. Race and religion were crucial to the outcome. Though Kennedy had not stressed the civil-rights issue, his telephone message of sympathy to the wife of Dr Martin Luther King at a time when the black leader was in jail in Atlanta won him the bulk of the Negro vote. In the country as a whole Kennedy's Catholicism lost him more votes than it gained. But the losses were chiefly in the South, where he could afford them, whereas in the urban North his religion brought out the Catholic vote, which was probably crucial in giving him such states as Illinois and Michigan and thus putting him in the White House.

John F. Kennedy and the New Frontier

At forty-three Kennedy was the youngest man to be elected President. (Theodore Roosevelt had, however, been a year younger than Kennedy when he succeeded to the Presidency on the death of McKinley.) He saw his youth as an advantage and attempted to give his Administration an appearance of youthful vigor and innovation by including in it a number of young men, the most notable being his brother Robert, who became Attorney General, and Robert S. McNamara, the president of the Ford Motor Company, who was appointed Secretary of Defense. Yet Kennedy's promise that 'a new generation of leadership' would 'cast off old slogans and delusions and suspicions' was largely unfulfilled. Especially in foreign affairs, the policies of his Administration differed little from those of its immediate predecessors. Slow to apprehend the great changes taking place in the world balance of power—the growing split between Moscow and Peking, the recovery of Europe, the upsurge of African and Asian nationalism—Kennedy continued to strike outmoded Cold War postures. In an inaugural address devoted almost wholly to foreign affairs, he declared that the United States would 'pay any price, bear any burdens, meet any hardship, support any friend, oppose any foe to assure the survival and success of liberty'. This sweeping commitment was based on the glib and, as it proved, false assumption that American economic and military power was so overwhelming that the United States could police the entire world. Though Kennedy later showed some awareness of the limits of American power, he continued throughout his Presidency to see the Communist menace in global terms. Moreover he carried brinkmanship to more dangerous lengths even than John Foster Dulles.

Though he soon discovered that the 'missile gap' was nonexistent, Kennedy proceeded to expand and speed up the American missile program: this meant introducing a new breed of solid-fuel, intercontinental ballistic missiles and increasing the number of nuclear-armed Polaris submarines. At the same time he encouraged McNamara's efforts to strengthen conventional forces. Defense appropriations were increased to permit an expansion of army combat divisions, tactical fighter strength, strategic airlift capacity, and counterinsurgency forces. Furthermore, in an effort to overtake the Soviet Union in the 'space race', Kennedy secured a huge increase in the budget of the Apollo program, designed to land a man on the moon. After the expenditure of $24 billion, this objective was achieved on July 20, 1969, when two American astronauts set down their lunar module on the moon's surface.

The sense of global mission that lay behind Kennedy's determination to enhance America's military capacity was evident in other features of his foreign policy. Early in his Administration he announced the formation of the Peace Corps, to consist of volunteers who would participate in various economic, educational, and welfare projects in underdeveloped countries. The scheme was enthusiastically received and was a great success. In the next two years more than 5,000 Peace Corps volunteers, mostly young, helped carry American economic and technical aid to forty-six countries. Even greater expectations were aroused by the Alliance for Progress, an ambitious cooperative program designed to prevent the spread of Communism in Latin America by fostering economic development while promoting political and social reform. But in spite of the fanfare attending its inception, the scheme fell woefully short of its goals. By the end of the 1960s critics were complaining that there had been no alliance and very little progress. American aid, meager enough to begin with, soon tapered off so that economic development lagged. Nor, because of the opposition of the established classes in Latin America, did a new era of democracy emerge.

Kennedy's hopes that the Alliance for Progress would lessen Latin American fears of 'Yankee imperialism' were in any case doomed by his ill-advised decision to proceed with a plan, inherited from the Eisenhower Administration, for the overthrow of the Castro regime in Cuba. For some time the Central Intelligence Agency had been training a force of Cuban exiles for an invasion of the island. Under pressure from his advisers Kennedy reluctantly agreed to the operation, but refused American air support. On April 17, 1961 some 1,400 Cubans landed at the Bay of Pigs. The invasion was poorly planned, poorly equipped, poorly executed. The expected popular uprising failed to materialize. Thus the invaders were easily overwhelmed. The Castro regime, now more solidly established than ever, proceeded to develop closer economic and political ties with the Soviet Union. The United States, whose involvement in the operation was soon exposed, suffered a humiliating defeat.

The Bay of Pigs fiasco was chastening experience for Kennedy; it taught him to be more wary of accepting the advice of experts. But it appears to have convinced the Soviet leader, Khrushchev, that he was dealing with a weak and indecisive adversary. At all events the Soviet Union began to adopt a more aggressive posture. In June 1961 Khrushchev threatened to sign a peace treaty with East Germany, which would then control access routes to West Berlin. Kennedy, determined not to be forced out of a city which symbolized resistance to Communist encroachment, responded by calling up army reserves and strengthening civil defense. The situation became still more tense on August 13 when the East German government built the Berlin Wall to stop the flow of refugees to the West. Though this was a violation of the Four-Power Agreements on Berlin, the United States did no more than protest and strengthen its Berlin garrison. The Berlin crisis thereafter subsided, only to be succeeded a year later by an infinitely more dangerous clash. In the summer of 1962 Khrushchev decided to challenge the United States in the Western Hemisphere itself by secretly installing medium-range ballistic missiles in Cuba—a move calculated to tilt the missile balance against the United States. Thus when in

October 1962 American photographic reconnaissance planes revealed the construction of Soviet missile bases in Cuba Kennedy was in no doubt that they must be removed. But far from being panicked into belligerency, he remained calmly resolute. After rejecting proposals for an air attack and an invasion, he decided on a naval blockade to prevent the further importation of nuclear weapons into Cuba. This course would demonstrate that the United States had the will to resist Soviet pressure and yet left Khrushchev with a necessary escape route. For ten agonizing days the world held its breath while the two superpowers faced each other out. Finally, on October 29, just as a nuclear confrontation appeared inevitable, exchanges between the two leaders brought a solution. The Soviet government announced that it would dismantle the missile sites in exchange for an American pledge not to invade Cuba. But although both sides had made concessions, the general impression was that American firmness had forced the Soviet Union to back down. Hence Kennedy's standing rose, both at home and abroad.

Paradoxically the Cuban missile crisis was followed by signs of a thaw in the Cold War. Both superpowers seemed to recognize that the threat of a nuclear holocaust demanded some softening of rivalry. On the Soviet side the growing rift with China constituted a further reason for better relations with the United States. One indication of an improved climate was the establishment in June 1963 of a Moscow–Washington 'hot line'to speed up communications in times of crisis. More important was the signing a month later of a nuclear test-ban treaty by Soviet and American representatives. The first step toward international arms control since the onset of the Cold War, the treaty banned atmospheric and underwater (though not underground) tests of nuclear weapons. It was ratified by the Senate in September.

None of this meant, however, that Kennedy had weakened in his determination to resist Communist expansion. This was especially evident in his policy towards Southeast Asia, where he inherited a dangerously deteriorating situation. In Laos and South Vietnam, two of the states created out of Indo-China by the Geneva Agreement of 1954, pro-Western regimes seemed likely to succumb to the pressure of Communist guerrillas. Like Eisenhower, Kennedy believed Indo-China to be the linchpin of Southeast Asia and thus a vital American interest. After warning that the United States would not tolerate a Communist conquest of Laos, he collaborated with the Soviet Union to bring about the pacification and neutralization of the country—a result ostensibly achieved in the summer of 1962. In South Vietnam Kennedy tried to check the growing strength of the Vietcong (Vietnamese Communists) by new counterinsurgency measures accompanied by pressure on the government of Ngo Dinh Diem for political and economic reform. He stepped up military aid and, despite misgivings about direct involvement, steadily expanded the number of American military 'advisers' until by late 1963 it reached 16,000. Yet the Vietcong continued to gain ground, while Diem's repressive and corrupt regime became increasingly unpopular. After Diem had brutally suppressed Buddhist demonstrations, Kennedy decided to withhold economic aid. Then on November 1, 1963, with the acquiescence if not the encouragement of the United States, a right-wing military clique assassinated Diem and seized power. Whether Kennedy, had he lived, could have avoided being drawn further into the Vietnam vortex remains a matter for conjecture. But at the time of his death he appears to have had no alternative in mind save continued involvement.

If Kennedy's foreign-policy record was at best mixed, at home he accomplished even less. Though he had promised bold leadership 'to get America moving again', he at first acted very cautiously. To be sure he lacked effective support in Congress. Despite nominal Democratic majorities in both houses, conservative Southern Democrats consistently voted with the Republicans on many issues. Thus many of the key features of the New Frontier legislative program—health insurance for the aged (medicare), federal aid to education, the reform of the immigration laws, the creation of a Department of Urban Affairs—were either blocked or killed outright. In most cases however the margin of defeat was narrow and it may be that a President less preoccupied with foreign and defense matters and more skilled in handling Congress could have achieved more. Kennedy had come to power confident that modern techniques of economic management could simultaneously stimulate growth, curb inflation, and ensure full employment. But during his first two years in office he was forced to give priority to the threat of inflation. He used the power of his office to persuade industry and labor to keep prices and wages inside recommended guidelines. His most dramatic intervention came in 1962 when he forced the steel companies to withdraw a price increase. By the beginning of 1963, when the hoped-for growth had failed to materialize and unemployment remained high, Kennedy again showed his faith in the 'new economics' by proposing tax reductions. But again Congressional conservatives frustrated him.

It was the same story in regard to civil rights. After his death Kennedy was remembered as a fearless champion of racial equality. But he was slow to take a strong stand on the issue. When he became President he was unwilling to propose a civil-rights bill, or even to support one drafted by Congressional liberals, for fear of jeopardizing other New Frontier measures. Executive action, he believed, could do more for blacks than legislation. Thus he appointed outstanding blacks to high office: Carl Rowan became ambassador to Finland, Thurgood Marshall, the NAACP's leading lawyer, a US Circuit Court judge, Robert C. Warren head of the Housing and Home Finance Agency. Kennedy also sent troops to Mississippi in 1962 to enforce a court order directing the state university to admit a black student, and in the following year to Alabama to protect civil-rights workers. Meanwhile Attorney General Robert Kennedy, more deeply committed to civil rights than his brother—or perhaps subject to fewer restraints—, vigorously employed litigation to speed up desegregation in schools and bus terminals and to expand black voting rights. Yet black leaders remained unimpressed. They pointed to the number of known segregationists Kennedy had appointed to judgeships in the South and to his long delay in issuing an executive order desegregating federally financed housing. As late as March 1963 a disenchanted Martin Luther King was accusing Kennedy of having settled for 'token' progress in racial matters. But mounting black pressure forced the President's hand. In June 1963, following massive black demonstrations, he put the full weight of his Administration behind a sweeping civil-rights bill. The extent to which his Congressional support promptly melted away went some way to justify his earlier hesitation. But his commitment was irrevocable.

By the autumn of 1963 virtually all of Kennedy's domestic program was deadlocked. He hoped, however, that the 1964 elections would not only confirm him in office but also produce a more friendly Congress. As a first step towards attaining these ends he embarked on a speaking tour of Florida and Texas. On November 22, as he drove through Dallas, he was fatally shot by a young ex-marine of Marxist leanings but no discoverable motive. The assassin, Lee Harvey Oswald, was himself murdered two days later during a jail transfer.

Kennedy's sudden death stunned and desolated the country. He was more deeply and widely mourned even than Lincoln. In the wake of the assassination a Kennedy legend quickly took shape. The dead man was idealized, his accomplishments exaggerated to the point that he came to be thought of as one of the greatest of Presidents. In reality the Kennedy years had been richer in promise than in practical achievement. Critics have moreover complained, with some justice, that Kennedy's rhetoric aroused unrealistic expectations and that his habit of deliberately creating an atmosphere of crisis stimulated fears that were not easily allayed. Kennedy must also bear some of the blame for the troubles that subsequently befell the United States: he significantly escalated the Vietnam War and contributed to the aggrandizement of the Presidency. Yet Kennedy possessed great qualities—courage, self-awareness, a cool intelligence. He dazzled the nation with a rare blend of youth, grace, and wit. He and his wife made the White House, if not a modern Camelot, then at least the center of cultivated life as it had not been since Jefferson's day. He possessed in addition a kind of vision that made him the symbol of hope for multitudes all over the world. Finally he displayed a remarkable capacity for growth. Had he been allowed to serve two terms he might well have become a great President.

Lyndon B. Johnson and the Great Society

Kennedy's death brought to the Presidency a man of very different background and style. Lyndon Baines Johnson had been born in humble surroundings in rural Texas. After working his way through college he had been a schoolteacher before entering politics in 1937 as a fervent New Dealer. As Democratic floor leader in the Senate during the Eisenhower Administration he had exhibited great skill in political management. The tragic circumstances in which he became President placed him in a difficult position. He was always conscious of standing in Kennedy's shadow. Lacking his predecessor's poise and sophistication and knowing himself to be incapable of inspiring the devotion that—posthumously at least—the American people gave to Kennedy, Johnson was further chagrined by intimations that some of his New Frontier advisers regarded him as an interloper. Not even his sweeping electoral victory in 1964, which made him President in his own right, overcame his personal insecurity. A tough, proud, intelligent man with a compassionate understanding of the problems of poverty and deprivation, he nonetheless had some unattractive traits. His public displays of boorishness, his tendency to domineer, his childlike love òf power excited unfavorable comment. Likewise his secretiveness, his inability to be completely truthful, and his unscrupulousness in manipulating people earned him the distrust of the press. His worst faults, however, were an excessive sensitivity to criticism and a stubborn refusal to admit error or change course. These largely explained his obsession with Vietnam, which was to wreck his Presidency. He was to leave office more distrusted and more savagely criticized, especially by his own party, than almost any of his predecessors. Yet his achievements in social reform stamp him as an outstanding President. And even in foreign policy, posterity may record that he had less room for maneuver than contemporary critics would concede.

The mood of national guilt engendered by the assassination combined with the new President's legislative expertise to break the Congressional logjam holding up Kennedy's domestic program. Within a year of becoming President, Johnson had coaxed or bludgeoned Congress into adopting nearly all the New Frontier proposals, as well as some of his own. In rapid succession he secured approval of a Tax Reduction Act (the first for thirty years), mass transit legislation, and a Higher Education Facilities Act. He also repudiated his Texas background by throwing his weight behind the stalled civil-rights bill. Bipartisan support in the Senate finally overcame a three-month Southern filibuster and on July 2, 1964 Johnson signed the measure. The Civil Rights Act of 1964 was the most far-reaching measure

of its kind ever passed. It prohibited racial discrimination in hotels, restaurants, and theaters and authorized the withholding of federal funds
from agencies practising discrimination. The Attorney General was
empowered to institute suits to protect voting rights and expedite school
desegregation. An Equal Opportunities Commission was to put an end to
job discrimination based on sex, religion, or race. In August 1964, in
response to Johnson's call for an 'all-out war on poverty', Congress passed
an Economic Opportunity Act which appropriated nearly one billion dollars to provide work experience and retraining for the unemployed,
increased educational opportunities for poor children, and established a
domestic peace corps—Volunteers in Service to America (VISTA). Significant though these measures were, Johnson viewed them simply as first
steps toward the creation of the 'Great Society', a term he employed in
May 1964 to describe his vision of an America in which there was abundance and liberty for all.

In the presidential election of 1964 the two major parties were momentarily realigned on an ideological basis. Johnson's legislative triumphs
removed any doubt that he would be the Democratic candidate. He was
unanimously nominated by the party convention at Atlantic City on an
avowedly liberal platform. When the Republican convention met at San
Francisco ultraconservatives were in the saddle. Contemptuously rejecting
the spokesman of the East Coast liberal wing of the party, Governor Nelson A. Rockefeller of New York, they nominated a candidate after their
own heart, Senator Barry M. Goldwater of Arizona. A millionaire depart-
ment-store owner who was also an Air Force reserve general, Goldwater
stood for a drastic reduction in federal powers and 'total victory' in the
struggle with world Communism. By presenting the country with a clear
choice of political philosophies he hoped to bring out millions of conservatives who did not normally vote. But Goldwater's approach was too negative to win a mass following. During the campaign he alienated the elderly
by his hostility to social security and alarmed moderates by an impulsive
suggestion that atomic weapons be used to 'defoliate' North Vietnam.
President Johnson, campaigning as the candidate of peace and consensus,
had little difficulty in depicting his opponent as a dangerous extremist bent
on destroying essential social services and prepared to risk nuclear war.

The outcome of the election was a foregone conclusion. Johnson won
a landslide victory. Goldwater won only six states, five of them in the Deep
South, where he had commended himself to whites by voting against the
Civil Rights Act of 1964. Goldwater's candidacy badly damaged his party,
even in traditional Republican strongholds. The Democrats increased their
majority in the House to 155 and secured 68 seats out of 100 in the
Senate.

After his overwhelming victory Johnson moved on to new domestic triumphs. At his urging Congress enacted a series of sweeping reform measures comparable to those of the New Deal. The Medicare Act of 1965 provided medical-insurance benefits for the elderly through the social-security system, a Medicaid Act did the same for the poor. The Elementary and Secondary Education Act of 1965 made education a major federal responsibility: it authorized the expenditure of over one billion dollars and broke new ground in extending aid to church schools. The Higher Education Act of the same year granted federal assistance to colleges and universities and for the first time provided undergraduate scholarships. Johnson also secured the passage of a Voting Rights Act (1965) to checkmate continuing Southern efforts to keep blacks from the polls: it provided for federal registration of black voters in any county where fewer than 50 percent of the eligible voters participated in presidential elections. This measure, together with the Twenty-fourth Amendment to the Constitution (1964) outlawing poll-taxes, produced a dramatic increase in black voting and black office-holding in the South. Another long-sought liberal goal was attained by the adoption of a new Immigration Act (1965) which abolished the discriminatory National Origins System which had prevailed since the 1920s. Other Great Society measures to sail through Congress were laws for highway beautification, against air and water pollution, and an ambitious urban program which included the creation of a Department of Housing and Urban Development and the provision of federal funds for slum clearance.

The Warren Court and Judicial Activism

Executive and legislative attempts to promote social justice were powerfully reinforced by a remarkable series of judicial decisions. Under the leadership of Earl Warren, Chief Justice from 1953 to 1969, the Supreme Court displayed a driving concern for civil rights and individual liberties. The *Brown* decision on desegregation in 1954 was followed by other rulings against racial discrimination in voting, public parks, and housing. In *Yates v. United States* (1957) the Court held that mere membership of the Communist party, or even the advocacy of the theoretical possibility of violence, were not sufficient for a conviction on a charge of conspiracy to overthrow the government by force. In two rulings in 1962 and 1963 it declared that prayers and Bible-reading in the public schools were violations of the constitutional principle of the separation of Church and State. The Warren Court also in effect wrote a new code of criminal procedure. A series of cases beginning with *Gideon v. Wainwright* (1963) and culminating in *Miranda v. Arizona* (1966) established the right of suspects both to remain silent and to consult a lawyer (at public expense if necessary) before being interrogated. No less significant were the Court's decisions in *Baker v. Carr* (1962) and *Reynolds v. Sims* (1964): by insisting upon the equalization of electoral districts, these ended the long standing rural dominance of state legislatures. Finally the Court took an extremely liberal position in cases involving censorship and obscenity. While these examples of judicial activism were applauded by liberals, they were fiercely condemned by conservatives who objected not only to their specific implications but also to the Court's taking the lead in social reform.

The Black Revolt

Johnson's civil-rights legislation, together with the Supreme Court's desegregation and reapportionment decisions, enabled black Americans to make substantial progress in the direction of equality. Yet far from satisfying blacks, these gains served only to increase their frustration and bitterness. This was not surprising since neither the right to vote nor legal guarantees of equality of opportunity did anything directly to ameliorate their economic condition. The black unemployment-rate was still twice the national average, nearly a third of the black population lived below the poverty line (as against 13 percent of the whites), black schools and black housing were almost universally inferior. And while black purchasing power had increased, the economic gap between the races had narrowed hardly at all.

By the middle 1960s many black Americans had become critical of both the aims and the methods of the civil-rights movement. Especially among young Northern slum-dwellers there was a shift away from the moderation of the NAACP and of Martin Luther King towards the militancy of black nationalist groups. The most important of these were the Black Muslims, a puritanical religious society which rejected Christianity in favor of a form of Islam and taught that all whites were devils; the Student Nonviolent Coordinating Committee which, under the leadership of Stokely Carmichael, a twenty-five-year-old West Indian, soon departed from its original interracial character and dropped the word 'nonviolent' from its name; and the Black Panthers, a paramilitary organization founded at Oakland, California in 1966 and subsequently involved in a number of confrontations with the police. Apart from Carmichael, the most articulate of the black nationalist spokesmen were Malcolm X, who broke with the Black Muslims to found his own Organization for Afro-American Unity but was assassinated in 1965, and Eldridge Cleaver, 'minister of information' of the Black Panther party. 'Black power', the slogan adopted by the black nationalists, was a vague and ambiguous concept. To some it was simply an assertion of black consciousness and pride, to others a demand for black control of businesses, schools, and political offices in Negro communities, to a handful of extremists a call for guerrilla warfare. Yet black-power advocates were agreed in demanding separatism rather than integration, in stressing self-help rather than collaboration with white liberals, and in being ready to contemplate violence. The Vietnam War still further inten-

sified black militancy. There was resentment that blacks were doing a disproportionate share of the fighting; though making up only 11 percent of
the population, they constituted 18 percent of the American forces in Vietnam. Black leaders were moreover critical of a war that, as Martin Luther
King put it, sent blacks to 'guarantee liberties in South East Asia which
they had not found themselves in Southwest Georgia and East Harlem'.

The smoldering discontents of the black ghettoes burst forth in the most
destructive urban riots since the Civil War. The first major outbreak, in
the Watts district of Los Angeles in August 1965, left 34 dead, injured
more than 1,000, and destroyed property worth $35 million. Following
renewed riots in 1966, notably in Chicago, the summer of 1967 witnessed
major racial disturbances in more than a hundred cities. The worst took
place in July at Newark, New Jersey and at Detroit. During five days of
rioting at Newark 26 people were killed (all but two of them black) and
2,000 were injured. At Detroit, where the death-toll reached 43 and property damage amounted to half a billion dollars, the rioters looted and
burned shops, sniped at the police, and obstructed firemen. Order was
restored only when thousands of paratroops and National Guardsmen
were sent in. Then in April 1968 the assassination of Martin Luther King
at Memphis, Tennessee set off a new wave of violence all over the
country.

Following the 1967 riots President Johnson set up a commission of
inquiry. Its report, published in March 1968, blamed the troubles on 'pervasive discrimination and segregation in employment, education and housing' and concluded that further strife could be avoided only by massive
government efforts to create jobs, improve schools, and clear the slums.
But although King's death stirred Congress into passing an Open Housing
Law prohibiting racial discrimination in the sale or letting of housing,
almost nothing was done to implement the Commission's recommendations. Many whites, frightened by the urban riots and by the militancy of
the black nationalists, became indifferent or hostile to black demands.
Moreover inflation and the needs of the Vietnam War shrank the resources
available for social programs. Johnson showed his continuing concern for
racial equality by making Robert C. Warren the first black to hold a Cabinet post (Secretary of Housing and Urban Development) and Thurgood
Marshall the first to become a Supreme Court justice. But the President
was increasingly distracted by foreign affairs, especially by Vietnam.

Resistance to Communism: the Caribbean and Vietnam

Johnson's foreign policy was based upon the well-established though
oversimplified orthodoxies of the Cold War. He and his advisers believed
that the spread of Communism was invariably the consequence of a
Moscow- or Peking-based conspiracy and that the United States had a res-

ponsibility to contain Communist aggression wherever it threatened non-Communist governments and peoples. These convictions accounted for American intervention in the Dominican Republic in April 1965. Determined not to allow another Castro in the Caribbean, Johnson sent in 30,000 American troops to support the right-wing military junta in its struggle with rebels who included a number of Communists. This revival of 'Yankee imperialism' angered much of Latin America, but the United States managed to persuade the Organization of American States to provide a peacekeeping force which restored stability to the Dominican Republic and permitted Johnson to withdraw American forces.

Vietnam, by contrast, became a festering sore. Johnson had at first been reluctant to increase American involvement. During the 1964 election campaign he had resisted Goldwater's demand for the bombing of North Vietnam as a means of stopping guerrilla infiltration. But soon after his reelection it became apparent that limited American aid would not suffice to stabilize the deteriorating military and political situation. Diem's successors in Saigon had proved incapable of preventing the Vietcong from extending their grip on the countryside. Faced with the alternatives of withdrawal or of committing large numbers of American combat forces Johnson did not hesitate. He was in no doubt that Vietnam was vital to American security and believed further that if the United States withdrew no other country would feel able to rely on promises of American protection. A basis for greater involvement had already been provided by an alleged attack on American warships by North Vietnamese torpedo-boats in the Gulf of Tonkin in August 1964. Misled by Johnson's deliberately deceptive account of the incident, Congress gave virtually unanimous support to a resolution empowering the President to 'take all necessary measures to repel any armed attack against the forces of the United States and to prevent further aggression in Southeast Asia'. The 'Gulf of Tonkin Resolution' was not a declaration of war but it gave Johnson almost unlimited authority to wage one. Early in 1965 he ordered massive air assaults on North Vietnam, initially in retaliation for Vietcong raids, subsequently as part of an effort to deprive the Vietcong of outside help. Simultaneously he began a huge buildup of American ground forces. By the end of 1965 there were 180,000 troops in South Vietnam, a year later 350,000, by the end of 1967 nearly half a million. By the end of 1968 the cost of the war had increased to $30 billion a year and the United States had suffered over 200,000 casualties, including 30,000 dead. Yet this tremendous military effort failed to crush the Vietcong. While American strategic bombing caused terrible damage and casualties, it failed to cripple the enemy's predominantly agricultural economy. Likewise concentrated artillery fire and search-and-destroy missions proved ineffective in what was essentially a guerrilla war. Nor could American attempts to create an effective South

Vietnamese army overcome the apathy of the mass of the peasants.

Meanwhile at home popular opposition to the war had been mounting. Beginning in 1965 there were huge antiwar demonstrations in which college students were especially prominent. In Congress, too, there was a rising tide of criticism from a group of 'doves', many of them like Senators J. William Fulbright, Robert F. Kennedy, and Eugene McCarthy leading members of the President's own party. Some objectors argued that the Vietnam conflict was essentially a civil war in which the United States had no right to intervene, least of all on the side of a regime as repressive as that in Saigon. Others wondered whether the United States was not overextending itself; they questioned whether Vietnam or for that matter Southeast Asia generally was really vital to American security. There was concern also that the war was distracting attention from domestic problems, especially those of the black ghettoes, and that its huge costs were weakening the dollar and stimulating inflation. Above all the manner in which the war was being waged created a wave of moral revulsion: television pictures daily brought home to Americans the full horror of what was being done in their name in Vietnam—the saturation bombing, the destruction of villages, the napalm raids, the killing and maiming of civilians. Since the more deliberate cruelties and barbarities of the Vietcong were not televised, they tended to be glossed over.

It was not however until the Tet (New Year) offensive of 1968 that American opinion generally began to turn against the war. In a furious surprise assault Vietcong and North Vietnamese forces menaced every major city in South Vietnam and were repulsed only after desperate fighting. The offensive invalidated Johnson's claim that American forces were gaining the upper hand and fatally undermined his war policy. The extent of American war-weariness was revealed when Eugene McCarthy, campaigning on a peace ticket, came within an ace of defeating the President in the New Hampshire Democratic primary. The vote forced Johnson to change course. On March 31 he announced a partial halt to the air and naval bombardment of North Vietnam and at the same time declared that he would not be a candidate for reelection. On April 3 Hanoi agreed to his proposal for peace talks and in May preliminary negotiations began in Paris.

The Election of 1968

Vietnam became the dominant issue in the 1968 presidential campaign. It also produced serious divisions within the Democratic party. Party bosses and trade-union leaders endorsed the candidacy of Johnson's political heir, Vice-President Hubert Humphrey, who supported the war. Peace Democrats on the other hand divided their support between McCarthy and Robert Kennedy who had belatedly entered the race once McCarthy had shown the President to be vulnerable. With Humphrey staying out of the primaries, McCarthy and Robert Kennedy fought a protracted duel which reached a climax in the June 4 California primary which Kennedy narrowly won. But in his hour of triumph he was fatally shot by a Jordanian immigrant disturbed by Kennedy's support of Israel. Far from profiting from Kennedy's death, McCarthy weakened his candidacy by his aloofness and his ambiguous and quixotic statements. Neither McCarthy's supporters nor the shattered Kennedy forces could prevent Humphrey's nomination by the Democratic convention at Chicago in August. But Humphrey's victory only intensified party divisions. The embittered antiwar delegates complained that the party hierarchy had flouted the popular will by nominating Humphrey and by rejecting a peace plank. Even more damaging to the Democrats was the riotous confrontation that occurred outside the convention hall but in front of television news-cameras between youthful opponents of the war, some of them bent on violence, and the Chicago police who responded with unrestrained and indiscriminate brutality to the taunts and obscenities hurled at them.

The Republicans had meanwhile nominated Richard M. Nixon, whose political career had seemed at an end after his unsuccessful attempt in 1962 to become Governor of California. More surprising even than Nixon's re-emergence was the fact that he abandoned his earlier divisiveness and portrayed himself as the candidate of peace and national harmony. Although avoiding specific commitments about Vietnam he promised to bring the conflict to an early and honorable end. He also capitalized on public concern about crime and civil strife by stressing the issue of 'law and order'—a phrase widely interpreted to mean a less sympathetic attitude to civil rights for blacks. In the hope of winning white support in the traditionally Democratic South Nixon accepted Spiro Agnew, the conservative Governor of Maryland, as his running mate. This 'Southern strategy' was dictated largely by the decision of George Wallace, the Democratic Governor of Alabama, to run on an American Independent party ticket. Wallace's diehard segregationism had in fact struck a responsive chord not only in the South but also among Northern bluecollar workers. He lost some support by choosing as his running mate the belligerent General Curtis Le May, the former air-force Chief of Staff, who threatened to 'bomb North Vietnam back into the stone age'.Even so it seemed possible that Wallace would poll sufficiently well to deny either of the major-party candidates an electoral majority. The feature of the campaign was Humphrey's belated recovery. Seemingly doomed after the disastrous Chicago convention, his candidacy received a great boost just before election day when Johnson announced the complete cessation of American bombing of North Vietnam. But Nixon nonetheless emerged the winner in an extremely close election. Wallace polled nearly ten million votes and won five Southern states—the best showing by a third-party candidate since La Follette in 1924.

Nixon's Foreign Policy: Vietnamization and Détente

During the next four years, while the Paris peace talks dragged on inconclusively, President Nixon put into operation a policy of 'Vietnamization'—the phased withdrawal of American troops accompanied by the strengthening of the South Vietnamese army to enable it to carry on the struggle alone. By the beginning of 1971 almost half the 550,000 American troops in Vietnam had been withdrawn; by September 1972 only 40,000 were still there. Yet antiwar critics grew increasingly restive at what they considered the excessively slow pace of disengagement and at continuing heavy American casualties. Their dissatisfaction boiled over into outrage when the President punctuated the pullout with new tactical military initiatives. Thus his announcement in April 1970 that he had ordered American troops to attack Communist sanctuaries and supply dumps in nominally neutral Cambodia touched off renewed antiwar demonstrations on college campuses. The shooting by National Guardsmen of four protesting students at Kent State University on May 4 further inflamed the atmosphere. The Cambodian operation was soon over but there were fresh protests in May 1972 when, in response to a new Communist offensive against the tottering Saigon government, Nixon ordered the resumption of air attacks on North Vietnam and the mining of Haiphong harbor. Criticism of the war had been further heightened in mid-1971 by the publication in the *New York Times* of a series of articles based on the Pentagon Papers, secret government documents on the Vietnam War, illegally released by a former official. These revealed the miscalculation, secrecy, and organized deception that had characterized American involvement. But although Congressional 'doves' redoubled their efforts to curb the executive's war-making powers and compel unilateral withdrawal from Vietnam, they did not succeed. The Vietnamization program in fact satisfied most people.

The effort to disengage from Vietnam was part of a wider reassessment of American foreign policy. Nixon and Dr. Kissinger, his foreign-policy adviser and later Secretary of State, recognized that the assumptions which had guided American diplomacy since 1945 were no longer valid. The bipolar postwar world on which the containment policy had been predicated had given way to a different configuration of power. Among the new international realities were the deepening hostility between the Soviet Union and China, the revival of Western Europe, and the reemergence of Japan. Unlike their predecessors Nixon and Kissinger understood that this new kind of world required a more flexible diplomacy. Since enmities were not immutable, the United States ought not to become hypnotized by ideological differences and should contemplate a succession of *ad hoc* arrangements rather than permanent alignments. And since it was evident that the United States had dangerously overextended itself by attempting to police the whole world, overt interventionism ought in future to be confined to areas where American national interests were at stake.

This new approach to international affairs, subsequently known as the Nixon Doctrine, had dramatic and striking results. Ironically in view of Nixon's anti-Communist past, his Administration entered into a *rapprochement*, first with China, then with the Soviet Union. Ever since Chiang Kai-shek's expulsion from the Asian mainland in 1949 the United States had cold-shouldered and tried to isolate 'Red China'. Yet in the spring of 1971, after Peking had indicated a desire for better relations, Nixon sent Kissinger on a secret mission to China to meet Premier Chou En-lai. The United States thereupon abandoned its opposition to the admission of the Chinese People's Republic to the United Nations and after Nixon himself had visited China (February 1972) Peking and Washington exchanged diplomatic representatives. Nixon's visit to Peking was followed by an almost equally momentous one to Moscow. Like their American counterparts the Soviet leaders were anxious for a relaxation of Cold War tensions and a respite from the ruinously expensive nuclear-arms race. Détente with the Soviet Union produced few specific benefits but agreement was reached on scientific, technological, and cultural cooperation, on the sale of American wheat to Russia, and, above all, on nuclear-arms control. The United States and the Soviet Union had already (July 1, 1968) signed a nuclear nonproliferation treaty binding the signatories not to supply nuclear weapons to nations not possessing them. Nixon's Moscow visit resulted in two further agreements, both growing from the Strategic Arms Limitation Talks (SALT) which had been in progress for over two years. One treaty restricted the number of antiballistic missile systems, the other pegged for five years the number of long-range offensive missiles. The new Soviet–American understanding did not, however, extend to the strife-torn Middle East. The fact that the United States was Israel's main arms supplier while the Soviet Union gave similar support to Egypt meant that a renewed Arab–Israel conflict might result in a superpower confrontation. This danger was at its height during the Yom Kippur War of 1973, when Israel was attacked by its Arab neighbors. But Dr. Kissinger, in a characteristic display of 'shuttle diplomacy' between the rival capitals, achieved a cease-fire and even a fragile partial settlement.

Nixonian Conservatism, the Imperial Presidency, and Watergate

The flexibility that marked Nixon's foreign policy was evident also in his handling of certain domestic problems. Inheriting a legacy of inflation he attempted at first to deal with it simply by restricting the money supply.

But in August 1971, with inflation still rising along with unemployment, he abruptly abandoned his hostility to economic controls: he ordered a ninety-day freeze on wages, prices, and rents, called for a tax cut to stimulate the economy, and took the first steps toward the devaluation of the dollar. Again, having begun by proclaiming an end to unbalanced budgets, he went on to spend so heavily on defense, the space program, and the Vietnam War that he presided over the largest budgetary deficits in history. Nixon also proposed a sweeping reform of the federal welfare system: his Family Assistance Program, announced in 1969, endorsed the principle of a national minimum income for every family. But Congressional liberals, with whom the idea had originated, turned the plan down: they wanted higher cash payments and objected to a proposed requirement that welfare recipients must either work or register for job training. Another Nixonian policy with liberal roots was that of sharing federal tax revenues with state and local authorities. After lengthy debate the President's revenue-sharing program was enacted in September 1972.

Yet despite these departures from his earlier attitudes, there could be no doubting the conservative thrust of Nixon's domestic policy. Appealing to the spirit of individualism and invoking such slogans as 'self-help' and 'local control', he undermined and dismantled many of Johnson's social-welfare programs and vetoed much new health, education, and welfare legislation. Conservatism also inspired Nixon's Supreme Court appointments. Claiming that the Court's recent decisions extending the rights of accused persons had contributed to the growth of lawlessness, he promised to appoint 'judicial conservatives' as opportunities arose. Thus, when Chief Justice Earl Warren retired in 1969 Nixon replaced him with Warren E. Burger, a Minnesota judge with a reputation for sternness towards criminals. Subsequently the President was able to appoint three other conservatives to the Court, though only after two of his nominees, both Southern strict constructionists, had been rejected by the Senate as unworthy. But while the Burger Court was notably less liberal and activist than its predecessor, especially in criminal cases, some of its decisions dismayed the Administration. In *Furman v. Georgia* (1972), for example, it declared the death penalty unconstitutional in most cases (though it left the way open for more carefully drawn capital-punishment statutes); in *Roe v. Wade* (1973) it legalized abortion. Other decisions thwarted Nixon's policy of 'benign neglect' in racial matters. When the Administration sought to slow down school desegregation in Mississippi the Court, in *Alexander v. Holmes* (1969), overruled it. And in 1971 the Court upheld the practice which Nixon had denounced of busing schoolchildren to achieve racial integration.

Nixon's stand against busing, like his emphasis on law and order and his condemnation of drug and sexual permissiveness, was designed to woo

George Wallace's right-wing following. Wallace, now returned to the Democratic fold, represented the main threat to the President's reelection in 1972. But having done well in the early Democratic primaries of that year Wallace was shot and paralyzed while campaigning and had to withdraw from the race. Within the Democratic party the rift of 1968 was far from healed. To meet criticism that the party hierarchy exercised undue influence at nominating conventions the Democrats adopted a new system of delegate selection to ensure that blacks, women, and young people—but no one else—were represented in proportion to their numbers in the population. These reforms had the effect of excluding traditional party leaders from the 1972 convention and of paving the way for the nomination of George S. McGovern, a liberal senator from South Dakota who had long been an outspoken opponent of the Vietnam War. A sincere, somewhat self-righteous man, McGovern proved an inept campaigner. He suffered an early setback when it was revealed that his running mate, Senator Thomas F. Eagleton of Missouri, had undergone psychiatric treatment. McGovern's indecisive handling of the affair made matters worse; having first announced his complete support for Eagleton, he dropped him from the ticket after a few days in response to public pressure. McGovern also lost ground by first persisting with, and then abandoning, an ill-considered welfare and tax-reform program whose contradictions had already been exposed during the primaries. Nor did McGovern appear to appreciate that, in order to have any chance of beating Nixon, he had to broaden his support. He allowed the left-wing activists who had secured his nomination to dominate his campaign to the exclusion of such pillars of the New Deal coalition as the urban political machines and the big trade unions. This fact, along with McGovern's demand for an amnesty for draft-dodgers, his equivocation on such issues as abortion and the legalization of marijuana, and his statement that he would 'crawl to Hanoi' in the cause of peace, enabled the Republicans to identify him with the forces of political and cultural radicalism and alienated 'Middle America', the middle-class, middle-aged center of the electorate which included many traditional Democrats.

From such an opponent Nixon had little to fear. Despite a dismal economic record which included the doubling of unemployment and failure to end the Vietnam War, the President felt able to leave campaigning to Vice-President Agnew and other surrogates. The result of the election fully justified his confidence. He won an overwhelming victory and got a larger share of the popular vote (60.8 percent) than any previous candidate except Lyndon Johnson. But the Democrats retained their hold on the House and they even managed to pick up two extra seats in the Senate. The election results were not so much an endorsement of Nixon as a repudiation of McGovern.

Soon after his reelection Nixon stepped up air attacks on North Vietnam to new and terrible levels. Whether, as he was later to claim, the effect was to speed up the Paris peace negotiations is disputed. But at all events a cease-fire agreement was signed in January 1973. Though Nixon described it as 'peace with honor' it was in fact a thinly disguised American defeat. It provided for the withdrawal of all remaining American forces from Vietnam but not for a corresponding withdrawal of North Vietnamese troops from areas south of the 17th parallel. Nor did it settle the political future of South Vietnam or even attempt to define the cease-fire line. This fragile settlement soon broke down. The feeble and corrupt Saigon government steadily lost authority once the Americans had withdrawn. Finally, in April 1975, it surrendered unconditionally to the Communists. Thus the long-drawn out American effort to preserve the Indo-Chinese peninsula from Communism ended in utter failure.

The Vietnam War was the longest in American history and one of the most expensive. It cost the United States 56,000 lives and $141 billion. The United States dropped on Vietnam a bomb tonnage over three times more than that the Allies had used in the European and Pacific theaters combined during World War II. Abroad the war produced widespread criticism of the United States and virtually no support, even from America's allies. At home it created enormous inflationary pressures, compelled the curtailment or abandonment of much-needed social programs, and left American society more deeply divided than at any time since the Civil War.

Soon after Nixon's reelection evidence began to pile up to implicate him in what became the biggest political scandal of the century. Investigations into what had at first appeared to be a minor attempted burglary gradually revealed that the President had misused his authority to aggrandize his power and strike at his domestic enemies and that he had committed criminal acts. Only by resigning did he escape impeachment.

The expansion of presidential authority did not begin with Nixon, but had been going on for decades. Its main cause was the vastly increased importance of the United States in the world. Presidents now had more opportunity and indeed more need to exercise the wide powers in foreign policy conferred upon them by the Constitution. Moreover the coming of the Cold War and of nuclear weapons increased the necessity for prompt decision and response. Accordingly Presidents tended to act in foreign affairs without securing the approval of or even consulting other branches of government. At the same time there was a striking increase in the power of the Presidency in the domestic sphere. The growth of big government, especially the proliferation of federal regulations on economic, social, and technical matters, brought a proportionate increase in both executive enforcement and executive discretion. But if the tendency for executive power to grow at the expense of Congress could be traced back to the

Presidencies of Franklin D. Roosevelt, Truman, and Johnson it was only during the Nixon Administration that the 'imperial presidency', as it came to be known, reached its fullest development. Nixon might justifiably have claimed that, in stretching the executive war power to make war in Cambodia and Laos, he was doing no more than Truman had done in Korea and Johnson in Vietnam. But there was little or no precedent for his other centralizing activities. In the name of national security he enlarged the traditional concept of executive privilege so as to deny Congress access to government records. Whereas his predecessors had used the presidential power of impoundment (the refusal to spend funds voted by Congress) sparingly and for reasons of economy, he used it extensively and as an instrument of policy, deliberately thwarting the will of Congress by declining to spend money it had appropriated for social programs he disapproved of. Equally novel, and more sinister, were the tactics Nixon employed against domestic critics and those suspected of leaking official information to the press. These included illegal wiretapping, tampering with letters, the misuse of the FBI, the CIA, and the Internal Revenue Service for political purposes, and the creation of a special investigations unit to stop leaks and perform political espionage.

It was the incompetence of this leak-plugging unit—the so-called 'plumbers'—which exposed the extreme and dangerous lengths to which the centralization of power had been carried. On June 17, 1972 the police apprehended five men who had broken into the Democratic party headquarters in the Watergate apartment complex in Washington in order to install electronic eavesdropping devices. Along with two former White House officials they were indicted for burglary, conspiracy, and illegal wiretapping. All the accused were employed by the Committee to Reelect the President (CREEP) which was headed by Nixon's former Attorney General, John N. Mitchell. Nixon promptly denied all knowledge of the affair and, despite McGovern's attempts to make political capital out of it during the 1972 election campaign, the public seemed at first uninterested. But following the trial and conviction of the Watergate burglars in January, one of them tried to obtain leniency by telling all he knew. His example proved infectious and in the course of extensive hearings before a Senate investigating committee it emerged that some of Nixon's closest White House associates had planned the break-in and had subsequently conspired with others to cover up their involvement. More than twenty of them, including Mitchell and the President's principal advisers on domestic affairs, H. R. Haldeman and John D. Ehrlichman, were ultimately convicted and sent to jail.

For more than a year Nixon stoutly protested that he was not implicated in Watergate. But public confidence in him nonetheless drained away as newspaper and Senate investigators uncovered evidence of one presidential misdeed after another: the submission of fraudulent income-tax returns, the spending of public money on Nixon's private homes, the granting of political favors in exchange for campaign contributions. More directly damaging to Nixon's Watergate denials was his refusal, on grounds of executive privilege, to comply with the Senate committee's demands to hand over the tape recordings he had made of all conversations in his private office since 1970—evidence that would show conclusively whether or not he had known about Watergate and the cover-up. When in October 1973 Archibald Cox, the special prosecutor appointed by Attorney General Elliott Richardson to unravel the affair, attempted to subpoena the tapes, Nixon dismissed him, thus provoking both Richardson's resignation and a storm of public protest. In April 1974 Nixon attempted to placate his critics by issuing edited transcripts of the tapes. While these were inconclusive on the question of the President's role in Watergate they harmed him by exposing his pettiness, vindictiveness, and coarse language. From this point on Nixon's position steadily deteriorated, and in the summer of 1974 came the denouement. On July 24 the Supreme Court ordered him to hand over all relevant tapes to Cox's successor as special prosecutor, Leon Jaworski. By July 30 the House Judiciary Committee, which had been conducting secret impeachment hearings, had recommended three articles of impeachment charging the President with obstruction of justice, abuse of power, and refusal to comply with the Committee's subpoenas. On August 5, in compliance with the Supreme Court's ruling, Nixon made public a tape containing information 'at variance', as he put it, 'with…my previous statements'. It established that for political reasons he had halted investigations into the Watergate break-in. Most of Nixon's remaining supporters now deserted him and on August 9, with conviction on the impeachment charges certain, he resigned the Presidency. That a President who had been overwhelmingly reelected could be brought to book for his misconduct and driven from office in mid term seemed to many Americans to be cause for self-congratulation: their constitutional system, they told themselves, had been amply vindicated. Yet if the system worked it did so by chance rather than because of its intrinsic merits: but for the fact that Nixon failed to destroy the incriminating tapes, there would have been no evidence against him.

The Ford Interlude

Minutes after Nixon had bidden an emotional farewell to his staff and Cabinet, Vice-President Gerald R. Ford was sworn in as his successor. A long-serving Congressman from Michigan and a former Republican leader in the House, Ford had been appointed Vice-President under the procedures laid down in the Twenty-fifth Amendment when Vice-President Agnew had been forced to resign in October 1973 after revelations of income-tax evasion, extortion, and bribery when he was Governor of Maryland. Ford was thus the first Chief Executive to assume the office without having been elected either to the Presidency or the Vice-Presidency. Although he possessed no unusual qualities of mind—as he himself frankly acknowledged—his obvious integrity, informality, and openness initially made a favorable impression. But his standing declined abruptly when, only a month after taking office, he pardoned Nixon for all federal crimes he had 'committed or may have committed' as President. In the November Congressional elections the country showed its displeasure with the party associated with Watergate: the Republicans lost four seats in the Senate and their representation in the House fell to 139—their lowest total since 1936. Still more strikingly, perhaps, the election demonstrated widespread disenchantment with politics: only 38 percent of those eligible bothered to cast a vote. Confidence in government declined still further the following year when a succession of newspaper accounts and Senate investigating committee reports documented the improper activities of the CIA. It emerged that from the time of the Kennedy Administration onward the CIA had plotted to overthrow a number of foreign governments and assassinate their leaders and, within the United States, had illegally kept files on thousands of individuals and groups, tampered with their mail, monitored telephone calls, and infiltrated black, antiwar, and radical political movements.

There was thus precious little euphoria as the bicentennial of the American Revolution approached. Americans celebrated the nation's 200th birthday in a chastened, puzzled, introspective frame of mind. They were no longer sure that the country had lived up to the aspirations of the Founding Fathers or that the traditional national goals of freedom and economic abundance were attainable, still less that the United States could reshape the world according to its heart's desire. Vietnam had demonstrated that the United States was not omnipotent, Watergate that it was not uniquely virtuous, the 'energy crisis' that its natural resources were not infinite. In short, the old sense of boundlessness had gone. Even as they recalled the ringing phrases of the Declaration of Independence, Americans were painfully aware of the limits of liberty and of power.

Yet if President Ford could not restore his countrymen's faith in the future, he at least calmed their frayed nerves. His modest, reassuring presence helped rid the political atmosphere of rancor. Apart from that, he had little to offer. The narrow conservatism that had characterized his Congressional career was equally manifest in his Presidency. Ford's main domestic objectives were to minimize government intervention in the economy and to balance the budget. Faced, however, with a stagnant economy and a sharp rise in unemployment he was forced in March 1975 to compromise his principles: he tried to stimulate recovery with a massive tax cut—a step which achieved only modest results. But believing inflation to be a greater evil than recession he opposed increased government expenditures, vetoing a long list of social-welfare measures as well as bills designed to increase farm prices and create new jobs. Ford's approach to government was in fact essentially negative: during his two and a half year Presidency he employed the veto on no fewer than sixty-six occasions, more than any previous President except 'the great obstructionist', Grover Cleveland.

In foreign policy Ford relied even more heavily than Nixon upon the advice of Henry Kissinger. Proof of the Secretary of State's dominance within the Administration came in September 1975 when the President summarily dismissed his Secretary of Defense, James R. Schlesinger, who had long been critical of Kissinger's readiness to make concessions to the Soviet Union. In keeping with the policy of détente Ford met the Soviet leader, Leonid Brezhnev, at Vladivostock in November 1974 and agreed to a second round of SALT talks. The following August he again met Brezhnev, as well as the heads of thirty-three other governments, to sign the Helsinki Agreement whose signatories promised to respect one another's boundaries, allow freedom of travel and information, and respect human rights. Both these moves were generally approved at home. But when the Administration appealed to Congress early in 1975 to grant emergency military aid to the crumbling South Vietnamese regime and thus honor a secret undertaking made by Nixon, it got a flat refusal. That the country was in no mood for new adventures was further demonstrated in the winter of 1975–6 when Congress rejected Kissinger's proposal to send arms and equipment to anti-Communist forces in Angola which were fighting against Soviet-backed guerrillas supported by 15,000 Cuban troops.

Although Ford had earlier given the impression that his would be only a caretaker Administration, he announced early in 1976 that he would seek reelection. But he had to fight hard for his party's nomination. He had offended Republican conservatives by his pursuit of détente, by choosing Nelson A. Rockefeller as his Vice-President, and by appointing other liberals to his Cabinet. Thus he had to contend with a strong right-wing challenge for the nomination from Ronald Reagan, a former film star who had turned to politics and had twice been elected Governor of California. Only after a spirited contest and by a narrow margin did Ford emerge the winner at the Republican convention in Kansas City. Even then, he was forced to accept a party platform that in effect repudiated the foreign policy of his Administration. The field for the Democratic nomination was unusually large, but a strong showing in the primaries provided a winning margin of delegates for the former Governor of Georgia, James Earl Carter, or Jimmy Carter as he insisted on being called. Unusually for a native of the

Deep South he had the reputation of being liberal, especially on racial questions. Hitherto little known, Carter owed his swift rise largely to the fact that he had played no previous part in national politics and thus was free of the corruption and scandal that had enshrouded Washington. In the past an outsider such as he would have had little chance of securing the presidential nomination of a major party: support from the donors who had customarily financed primary campaigns would not have been forthcoming. But the Federal Election Campaign Amendments Act of 1974 changed the system, placing strict limits on individual and corporate campaign contributions and making each contender eligible for matching funds from the Treasury (up to $5 million) if he raised funds in each of twenty states in small contributions.

Given Ford's limitations and the fact that the Republican party was tainted by Watergate, any Democrat should have beaten him easily. But during a conspicuously dull campaign Carter's enigmatic personality and reluctance to declare himself on the issues raised doubts about his fitness for the Presidency and enabled Ford to make it a close race. For many voters it was a question of deciding which of two unexciting candidates they distrusted less. In the end Carter won narrowly, but a shift of 8,000 votes in Ohio and Hawaii would have tipped the election to the incumbent. Ford might also have won if the liberal Senator Eugene McCarthy, running as an independent, had succeeded in getting on the ballot in New York; as it was, though he won only 0.9 percent of the total vote, McCarthy diverted enough support from Carter to cost him four closely contested states. To a marked degree the electorate divided along class lines: the affluent and the well-educated generally voted for Ford, the socially and economically disadvantaged for Carter. In the last analysis the black vote decided the election. White Americans gave Ford a clear majority but blacks gave 92 percent of their vote to Carter and provided him with the margin of victory in half a dozen crucial states, among them New York, Pennsylvania, Louisiana, and Mississippi.

The Carter Presidency

Jimmy Carter's Presidency began on a note of optimism. Unsullied by any association with corrupt Washington, he seemed a refreshing symbol of candor, integrity, and of a return to government by the people. Yet he proved a sad disappointment. A decent, well-meaning, immensely dedicated man, he was overwhelmed by the complexity of the problems facing the country. The worst of these problems, it is true, antedated Carter's coming to office: inflation, unemployment, falling industrial productivity, the decline of presidential authority, the growth of Soviet military power, the loss of control over energy supplies. But far from providing the 'new leadership' he had promised, Carter turned out to a be a political tyro and, what was worse, one with only a limited capacity to grow into the job. Seemingly ill at ease with the power of the Presidency, he proved incapable of wielding it effectively. He gave the impression of reacting to crises rather than anticipating them and of being unable to foresee the implications of his own actions. Having been elected as an outsider, he seemed to go out of his way to remain one: instead of cultivating the powerful and independent Congressional leaders whose support was vital to his policies, he kept them at arm's length. Carter created confusion by delegating authority illogically and to too many people, sometimes of conflicting views. Thus in foreign policy there was a constant tug of war between the Secretary of State, Cyrus Vance, who favored a mild and conciliatory approach to the Soviet Union, and the National Security Adviser, Zbigniew Brzezinski, who urged a tougher line. Not surprisingly, it was sometimes difficult to know exactly what Administration policy was. As for Carter himself, he rarely looked or sounded like a President, appearing rather to be naive, capricious, and prone to error.

Although the Democrats had large majorities in both the Senate and the House virtually all of Carter's domestic policies were rejected or had to be drastically revised. Nothing came of his ideas for tax reform, government reorganization, or expanded health care. And like Nixon and Ford he found it difficult to get Congress to take the energy crisis seriously. After three years' effort he finally succeeded in pushing through an energy bill which took steps to cut oil consumption and speed up new oil exploration, but which fell far short of the comprehensive program he had recommended. As his term wore on, the President had to devote increasing attention to the state of the economy. After a free-spending start designed to restore prosperity, he was forced to change course when prices rose and to adopt a conservative, deflationary policy. Nothing he did, however, proved effective against the twin scourges of unemployment and inflation: both doubled during his Administration. And although Carter had come to office pledged to balance the budget, he proved unable to do so: by 1980 the budget deficit had soared to $50 billion.

In foreign affairs Carter began by adopting a stance very different from that of the American architects of détente. Whereas Nixon, Ford, and Kissinger had worked essentially within the European tradition of *realpolitik* the new President recalled Woodrow Wilson by speaking the language of liberal idealism. He would not be guided, he declared, by 'balance of power politics' or by 'excessive reliance on military spending' but by a concern for universal human rights. This moralistic approach, which in practice involved criticizing and withholding aid from countries deemed to have mistreated their citizens, had no effect except to irritate some of America's friends and harden the opposition of its adversaries. Before long Carter began to make exceptions in favor of oppressive but friendly regimes and in the end more or less abandoned his human-rights campaign. This demonstration of inconsistency proved to be typical of the Administration's foreign policy. Having come into office undertaking to reduce the number of American troops in Korea, Carter later rescinded the plan. After months of persuading America's NATO allies to accept the B-1 neutron bomb, he abruptly canceled it. Having discovered the presence of a Soviet combat brigade in Cuba, he demanded its withdrawal and then withdrew the demand. The most damaging of these reversals, however, was his public repudiation in March 1980 of a United States veto in the United Nations Security Council in favor of a resolution demanding that Israel dismantle its settlements on the west bank of the Jordan. The veto and its disavowal managed to infuriate both the Israelis and the Arabs besides baffling and dismaying America's allies.

Yet Carter's foreign policy had its successes. In April 1978, he persuaded a reluctant Senate, after several months of heated debate, to ratify a Panama Canal Treaty that met a longstanding Panamanian demand for greater control over the canal and provided for complete American withdrawal from the Canal Zone by the year 2000. He also carried to its logical conclusion Nixon's policy of *rapprochement* with Peking. On January 1, 1979 the United States established full diplomatic relations with the People's Republic of China, at the same time severing relations with the Chinese Nationalists in Formosa and abrogating the 1954 defense treaty with them. Carter's most notable diplomatic achievement was the Camp David agreement on the Middle East (September 1978) and the subsequent peace treaty between Egypt and Israel. By a remarkable display of pertinacity and diplomatic virtuosity, he ended thirty years of enmity between the two countries. However, the agreement left unresolved the main cause of Arab–Israeli conflict, the status of the Palestinians, and subsequent negotiations made no progress on the issue. In any case the Camp David agreement was soon overshadowed by a major American defeat in the Middle East. In January 1979, after a year of antigovernment demonstrations and crippling strikes, the Shah of Iran, a warm friend of the United States, was overthrown and the monarchy replaced by a virulently anti-Western Islamic republic. Carter could have done little to avert the Iranian revolution, though his attempts to hurry the Shah into exile only a year after having praised him effusively once again revealed his fickleness. The President's efforts to ingratiate himself with the new regime did nothing to palliate its hostility and in November 1979 the United States suffered the humiliation of having its embassy in Tehran invaded by a revolutionary mob which seized fifty-three American diplomats as hostages for the return of the Shah and his fortune.

Meanwhile, negotiations with the Soviet Union for a second Strategic Arms Limitation Treaty had been making slow progress. By the time Ford left office considerable progress had been made towards a SALT II agreement, but when Secretary of State Vance went to Moscow early in 1977 to resume negotiations the Russians bluntly rejected his proposals for new and sweeping reductions in nuclear arsenals. Not until Carter dropped his campaign for human rights were they prepared to renew the talks. Thus it was not until June 1979 that Carter and Brezhnev signed SALT II in Vienna. Essentially the same as that negotiated by Ford, the agreement aimed at maintaining a nuclear balance by requiring both superpowers to reduce their totals of long-range bombers and missile systems. The Treaty was strongly opposed in the Senate. Its critics alleged that it contained ambiguities and loopholes that would give the Soviet Union strategic advantages over the United States. The Treaty might well have been defeated anyway, but what wrecked its chances was the Soviet invasion of Afghanistan in December 1979. Overnight, the Soviet attack converted Carter to a policy of checking Communist expansion. Having come to office promising to cut the military budget, he now proposed to increase it. Moreover, he suspended the attempt to secure Senate ratification of SALT II, placed an embargo on grain sales to the Soviet Union, and attempted to organize a boycott of the Olympic Games being held in Moscow in 1980.

The Election of 1980

By the autumn of 1979 President Carter had sunk so low in public esteem that his chances even of renomination seemed remote. Most observers believed that in the 1980 presidential election he would be forced to make way as Democratic candidate for Senator Edward Kennedy, who formally entered the race in November. But the seizure of the embassy hostages in Tehran and the Soviet invasion of Afghanistan rallied the nation to the President's side for long enough to enable him to win some crucial primaries. In May 1980 the failure of an airborne attempt to rescue the hostages again sent Carter's stock tumbling, but by now he had enough convention delegates to defeat Kennedy's challenge for the nomination. He nonetheless received only a grudging and unenthusiastic endorsement from the Democratic convention in New York in August.

Long before the Republican convention met in Detroit in July it was clear that Ronald Reagan would be the nominee. In the primaries he won an impressive string of victories, defeating in the process George Bush, a New Englander of moderate beliefs who had made a fortune in Texas oil and had been successively ambassador to the United Nations and China and director of the CIA, and John B. Anderson, a relatively obscure Illinois Congressman who in a twenty-year-long political career had gradually discarded most of his early conservatism. Having nominated Reagan as its presidential candidate and chosen Bush as his running mate, the Republican convention adopted a platform that pleased right-wing zealots. It denounced the SALT II treaty as 'fatally flawed' and demanded military superiority over the Soviet Union, advocated a reduction in federal spending and in the role of the federal government generally, promised a 30 percent tax cut over a three-year period, called for more nuclear energy and the complete decontrol of oil prices, urged the restoration of capital punishment, endorsed a constitutional ban on abortion, and declared the Equal Rights Amendment (outlawing discrimination against women) to be a matter for the states.

A feature of the nominating process had been the continuing attempt by both parties to take the choice of presidential candidates out of the hands of party bosses and give a much larger voice to ordinary voters through primary elections. In 1980 more than 70 percent of the delegates to the two major party conventions were chosen in thirty-seven separate primaries which attracted unprecedentedly large turnouts. (In 1968 the proportion had been under 40 percent). Nonetheless there was widespread dissatisfaction with the outcome. Many voters were unconvinced that either Carter or Reagan was of presidential timber. In an attempt to capitalize on this feeling and win the votes of those alienated by conventional politicians, John Anderson decided to run as an independent. His views were an eclectic mixture of fiscal conservatism and trendy liberalism: While he demanded a balanced budget and severe restrictions on federal expenditure, he supported the Equal Rights Amendment, federal financing of abortions for poor women, and homosexual equality.

The campaign was an uninspiring as that of 1976. Carter concentrated on depicting his Republican challenger as a simplistic, shallow ideologue, unsympathetic to the poor, racialist in outlook, and likely to lead the United States into nuclear war. Reagan, by contrast, waged a careful, mild-mannered campaign which eschewed personal attacks, sought to focus on the President's record, and did much to deflate charges of extremism. Anderson won a devoted following on campuses and among the sophisticated and well educated but lacked mass appeal and manifestly lost ground as election day approached.

The election was generally expected to be close. In the event, however, Reagan won a sweeping victory. At sixty-nine he was the oldest man ever to win the presidency. Anderson, though polling 5.7 million votes, had no effect on the outcome. The election was the most devastating rejection of an incumbent President since Hoover's defeat in 1932. For the first time since 1954 the Republicans won control of the Senate, defeating several prominent liberals in the process; they also gained thirty-three seats in the House. The main reason for the Republican landslide was evidently the discontent produced by unemployment, inflation, and the faltering economy. But the voters seem also to have been demanding a stronger foreign policy and more decisive leadership generally. The high proportion of abstentions suggested, however, a widespread lack of enthusiasm for any of the candidates: only 53.9 percent of the electorate voted, the lowest turnout since 1948.

28. *American Society and Culture,* 1940–1980

Population, Immigration, and Mobility

Between 1940 and 1980 the population of the United States increased by 95 million to reach a total of 226 million, thus refuting the predictions of demographers during the Great Depression that the population would cease to grow and might even decline. Yet the rate of population growth continued to slow down: by the 1970s it was under 1 percent per annum, only a third of what it had been in the beginning of the nineteenth century. During and just after World War II a "baby boom" briefly reversed the long-term fall in the birth-rate but, with the introduction of a new and more effective contraceptive—the so-called "Pill"—and with the federal government providing increasing funds for birth-control, births again began to decline. Between 1955 and 1975 the birth-rate fell by more than a third, from 24.5 per 1,000 to 14.8. This reduction was in some measure offset by the continued decline in the death-rate—from 10.9 per 1,000 in 1945 to 8.9 in 1975. Thanks largely to a decrease in infant and child mortality, life expectancy at birth showed a substantial gain, rising from 62.3 years in 1940 to 73.2 years in 1977. The net effect was that, if the population was still increasing, it was becoming progressively older.

Immigration between 1940 and 1980 amounted to nearly eleven million. The national-origins quota system introduced in the 1920s remained nominally the basis of public policy until 1965 but was progressively diluted and ultimately undermined. The first exception to the system was the War Brides Act of 1946, permitting the entry of some 150,000 foreign-born wives and fiancées of American servicemen, together with their 25,000 children. Next, in an attempt to relieve the massive refugee problems created by World War II, Congress passed two Displaced Persons Acts (1948, 1950) which together provided for the admission of 410,000 persons, chiefly from central and eastern Europe, and the Refugee Relief Act (1952) permitting the entry of a further 214,000 people, most of them escapees from behind the Iron Curtain. Subsequently a series of special laws was passed and obscure legal provisions invoked to cope with fresh waves of refugees and deportees; by such means 35,000 'freedom fighters' were admitted after the Hungarian uprising of 1956 and 650,000 Cubans after Castro came to power in 1959. In all refugees accounted for a fifth of the total immigration between 1945 and 1965.

During the same period more than half the five million immigrants came from within the Western Hemisphere, especially Canada and Mexico. The main stimulus to Mexican immigration was the severe shortage of farm labor in the Southwestern states. Beginning in 1943 and continuing on an annual basis until the end of 1964 the federal government made arrangements with Mexico to import large numbers of agricultural laborers (*braceros*), who were then subcontracted to private employers. But legal entrants from Mexico were greatly outnumbered by "wetbacks"—Mexicans who swam across the Rio Grande into the United States or otherwise entered illegally. The United States Border Patrol made determined efforts to stop the wetback invasion, apprehending and deporting one million in 1954 alone. But great numbers went undetected.

After World War II the national-origins system came under increasing attack as discriminatory and as a betrayal of American ideals. Though every President from Truman onward recommended its abolition, it was not until 1965 that Congress complied. Effective on July 1, 1968 the Immigration and Nationality Act of 1965 introduced a system of preferences that favored not particular nationalities but certain specified categories: nonimmediate relatives of American citizens; persons possessing special skills or qualifications sought by American employers; and refugees. The Act did not increase total immigration. It set an annual limit of 170,000 for countries outside the Western Hemisphere, one of 120,000 for the Western Hemisphere, and restricted immigration from any one country to 20,000. Since immediate relatives of American citizens were not subject to the overall limitations annual immigration could exceed the notional total of 290,000. In practice annual arrivals during the decade beginning in 1968 averaged about 400,000. The Act somewhat increased the proportion of immigrants from those countries in southern and eastern Europe formerly discriminated against, reduced the inflow from Canada and Mexico (though the wetback problem persisted), and produced a striking increase in Asian immigration. Throughout the 1970s Asia contributed more immigrants than Europe, the two leading countries being the Philippines and South Korea. Since Asian immigrants consisted largely of highly trained and professional people—doctors, nurses, engineers, scientists, and so on—the Act had the unexpected and unsought-for result of accelerating the "brain drain" from developing countries. Finally, although refugees were assigned only 6 percent of the 170,000 Eastern-Hemisphere preferences, ways were found to admit more when sudden emergencies arose. Thus more than 200,000 Vietnamese, 60 percent of them children, were admitted 'on parole' after the end of the Vietnam War in 1975, and some 125,000 Cubans were allowed to enter when Castro suddenly—though temporarily—permitted emigration in 1980. Post-World War II immigration, though still substantial, was much smaller, both relatively and absolutely, than in the late nineteenth and early twentieth centuries. Accordingly the proportion of foreign-born in the population steadily declined, reaching an all-time low of 4.7 percent in 1970.

Mobility remained an American characteristic. In 1960 a quarter of native-born Americans were living in a different state from the one they had been born in; in California the proportion was one-half. The currents of migration were as complex as ever. People moved from countryside to city, from city to suburb, from one city to another; Southern blacks flocked to the North, while a steady stream of Northern whites went South; a renewed westward surge accelerated the long-developing shift in the center of gravity of population away from the eastern seaboard. The Far West was by a large margin the fastest-growing region, followed by the South West and the South. Migrants to these areas were attracted less by the climate—though that was an important factor in the movement of the elderly to Florida and Arizona—than by the prosperity that followed the growth of industry. The postwar years witnessed an astonishing development of the electronics and aerospace industries in California, petrochemicals and natural gas in Texas and Louisiana, the citrus-fruit industry in Florida. During the 1960s California overtook New York as the most populous state; by 1980 one American in ten lived there. Between 1950 and 1980 Texas almost doubled its population and became the third most populous state. Even faster rates of growth were recorded by such sparsely settled Western states as Nevada, Arizona, and Alaska. Until 1970 the South remained a net exporter of people. But in the 1970s every Southern state increased its population. The greatest gainer was Florida, which grew by 23 percent.

The farm population continued to dwindle. As mechanization became more widespread and agricultural technology improved the number of farmers fell from a peak of 6.8 million in 1935 to fewer than 2 million in 1980. The demand for farm labor declined even more precipitously. In 1920 one American in three had lived on a farm; in 1980 only one in twenty. The changes in agriculture helped maintain, even accelerate, the great national drift to the cities. By 1980 over three-quarters of all Americans lived in urban areas, a high proportion of them in what became known as "megalopolises"—huge areas of almost continuous urban sprawl like that between Washington, DC and Boston. Within the metropolitan areas themselves an even more extensive redistribution occurred as people deserted the cities for the suburbs. The move to suburbia, under way since the 1920s, became a mass exodus after World War II. Several influences were at work: the construction of vast new housing developments like the archetypal Levittown on Long Island, federal loans for home ownership, new roads and expressways, near-universal car ownership. Between 1950 and 1980 most American cities lost population to the suburbs, some of them drastically. In New York the loss amounted to 10 percent, in Chicago and Philadelphia 15 percent, in Boston 25 percent, in Detroit and Cleveland over 30 percent. Almost the only exceptions to this trend were the booming cities of the South and South West: Los Angeles, San Jose, Houston, Dallas, Phoenix, and Atlanta all experienced spectacular gains. By 1960 more people lived in suburbs than in the central cities; by 1980 almost half the entire American population were suburban-dwellers. Often consisting initially of little more than endless rows of standardized homes and much criticized on that account, the postwar suburbs in time acquired not only schools, churches, shopping centers, restaurants, and theaters but also a variety of retail and wholesale businesses and even industries. Thus they ceased to be merely dormitories and became socially and economically self-sufficient.

The suburban boom led to a dramatic change in the racial character of American cities. The new suburbanites were predominantly white, those who moved in to replace them largely black. Indeed the rapid influx of Negroes gave an added impetus to what came to be referred to as 'the flight' to the suburbs. The dominant theme in black migration was the trek North. Between 1940 and 1970 some 4½ million blacks left the fields and towns of the South for the industrial cities of the North and West. By 1970 about half the 24 million blacks in the United States were living outside the South; there were 1.8 million in New York City (as against 450,000 in 1940), 1.2 million in Chicago, 640,000 in Los Angeles. Within the South itself, too, industrialization drew blacks increasingly to the cities. By 1970 Atlanta, New Orleans, Birmingham, and Richmond were 40 percent black while Washington, DC, almost three-quarters white in 1940, had become almost three-quarters black.

The Urban Crisis

From the early 1960s urban problems thrust themselves increasingly on public attention. American cities, once the symbols of the country's growing industrial power, came instead to epitomize decay, pollution, and social disintegration. Though the picture of decline was sometimes overdrawn the physical, financial, and social problems faced by cities justified talk of an "urban crisis". There were several causes. The migration to the cities of blacks and other disadvantaged minorities meant a concentration of groups already suffering from poverty, high unemployment, low educational levels, and poor housing. It also placed an immense burden on expensive urban public facilities and services. Simultaneously, the exodus of middle-class whites, and the accompanying flight of industry, sharply reduced urban tax revenues. The relocation of industry in the suburbs also left cities with a legacy of abandoned and decaying buildings and factories. Compounding the problem was the fragmentation and complexity of local government: suburban autonomy generally ruled out much-needed metropolitan consolidation, while the existence of a network of overlapping and competing jurisdictions hindered cooperation even when the will existed. Despite substantial increases in state and federal aid, many cities, especially the larger ones, were in deep financial trouble. In 1975 New York City lurched from one financial crisis to another, and was saved from bankruptcy only by substantial federal loans.

The endemic housing problem of inner cities, the product of decades of governmental neglect, was made worse after the war by federal and local tax systems which discouraged landlords from making improvements. Beginning in 1949 a succession of federal Housing Acts provided billions of dollars for slum clearance, or 'urban renewal' as it was known. The Johnson Administration also introduced rent subsidies and provided federal funds to adapt derelict buildings to new uses. But although by the early 1970s federal incentives had enabled local authorities to build over two million new homes, mostly for people on lower incomes, this was far fewer than were needed. In some respects federal policy exacerbated the slum problem. Most public housing projects took the form of grim, barrack-like, high-rise apartments which soon became new slums, not least because of eligibility requirements that excluded all but the poorest and least stable elements in the population. Moreover, federally subsidized urban renewal often meant in practice the destruction of old tenements to make way for boutiques, restaurants, office-blocks, and luxury apartments. Thanks to urban renewal much of America's architectural heritage was saved and run-down neighborhoods were revitalized. But in the process large numbers of poor people were made homeless.

Slum conditions were a major cause of the frightening level of crime. Among other contributory factors were the ease with which guns could be bought, the growth of drug addiction which could often be financed only by crime, a chronic shortage of police, and the delay and difficulty in obtaining convictions. Though crime statistics were suspect, there was general agreement that the crime-rate was rising. Violent crime was very largely an urban phenomenon, with the rates increasing in proportion to the size of the city. In the 1970s one-third of all reported crimes in the United States took place in the six largest cities, though these accounted for only 12 percent of the population. In New York City, twenty times as many people were being murdered annually as in Sweden, which had roughly the same population. Yet New York, though possessing the worst record in the country for violent crime in general, had less claim than, say, Detroit or Los Angeles to be the 'murder capital' of the United States.

Of the thirty cities with the highest murder-rates in 1979, however, all but six were in the South or in Texas. As well as being concentrated in cities violent crime was committed disproportionately by the young—especially young blacks.

Economic Growth and Technological Change

Spectacular and seemingly endless economic growth marked the decades after World War II. The Gross National Product rose from $212.3 billion in 1945 to $505.9 billion in 1960 and to $2,741 billion in 1980. The principal forces sustaining this unprecedented (and possible unrepeatable) boom were massive government spending, dramatic technological advances, and a rapidly expanding home market. The stimulus provided by government was due mainly to a swollen military budget—between 1945 and 1970 60 percent of all federal spending went on defense—and to increased federal expenditure on highways, education, welfare, housing, social security, and farm subsidies. Total federal spending shot up from $10 billion in 1940 to an astronomical $580 billion in 1980. There was also a rapid development of automation, especially of computer technology. Widespread industrial application of the digital computer and the transistor (invented in 1944 and 1948 respectively) made possible a phenomenal increase in output per man-hour: it rose by between 35 and 40 percent per decade. That consumer demand kept pace with productivity was due to population growth, the general prosperity, and, most of all, the expansion of credit. Installment buying (hire purchase), a device hitherto used mainly to buy cars, became after the war an acceptable way of acquiring the increasing number and variety of consumer goods. At the same time the credit card became an American institution. First supplied on a highly selective basis by Diners' Club in 1950, credit cards soon came to be freely issued by banks and department stores as well as by credit-card companies.

Rapid economic growth was accompanied by a continuation of the trend toward industrial consolidation. The 1950s and 1960s saw a new wave of amalgamations and mergers, especially in capital-intensive, technologically advanced industries. The proportion of total corporate assets owned by the 200 leading manufacturing concerns increased from 47.2 percent in 1947 to 60.9 percent in 1968. A number of industries, notably automobiles, aluminum, chemicals, aerospace, electronics, cigarettes, and meat products, came to be dominated by a small number of large producers. Giant corporations like General Motors, Du Pont, Lockheed, International Business Machines (IBM), and American Telephone and Telegraph (AT&T) tended both to diversify into new products and to acquire foreign subsidiaries. The underlying reason for the new merger movement was that only very large corporations could afford the huge outlays required for research and development in sophisticated high-technology—and even they relied heavily on government financing. These economic imperatives compelled a significant modification of federal antitrust policy. Although the Justice Department and the Federal Trade Commission used the authority conferred by the Celler-Kefauver Antimerger Act of 1950 to block horizontal mergers that would have substantially lessened competition, they tended to condone the very much larger number of mergers that did not alter preexisting patterns of market power.

The technological revolution produced structural changes in the labor force and adversely affected trade unions. In the years immediately after the war, despite the obstacles imposed by the Taft–Hartley Act, organized labor continued the advance begun under the New Deal. By 1953 trade-union membership totaled nearly eighteen million (28 percent of the non-agricultural labor force), three million more than in 1946. Thereafter, as automation reduced the number of bluecollar jobs, notably in car-manufacturing, coal-mining, and on the railroads, unions experienced growing difficulty in maintaining their strength. By 1960 the number of whitecollar workers for the first time exceeded that of bluecollar workers; by 1980 the disparity had become enormous—50.5 million as against 30.5 million. The professional, technical, clerical, and sales workers who made up the whitecollar section proved difficult to organize. Those employed by firms which had generous welfare capitalism schemes (see p.447)—IBM and National Cash Register for instance—tended to side with management rather than with labor. Women, now a substantial proportion of white-collar workers, did not always consider themselves permanent employees and, even when they did, tended to think of trade unionism as something for men. Most state and local governments denied public employees the right to strike; some even forbade them to join trade unions. A further difficulty was the migration of industry to such traditional antiunion regions as the South and the Southwest, where 'right to work' (open-shop) laws were widespread. During the 1970s, as inflation eroded real incomes and recession threatened job security, some office and professional workers—teachers and municipal employees especially—became more amenable to trade unionism. But although by 1980 trade-union membership had climbed to twenty-three million, this was an appreciably smaller proportion of the labor force (24 percent) than in 1953.

Growing awareness of the need for solidarity in the face of continued public hostility and of an incipient decline in union strength led in 1955 to the healing of the twenty-year-old rift in the American labor movement. By this time few structural, ideological, or ethnic differences separated the American Federation of Labor from the Congress of Industrial Organizations. The expulsion of Communist-dominated unions from the CIO in 1949–50 removed a major obstacle to reunification. The death in 1952 of the presidents of both federations (William Green of the AFL and Philip

Murray of the CIO) paved the way for leaders more receptive to the idea of unity (George Meany and Walter P. Reuther respectively). Following successful merger negotiations in 1955 Meany was elected president and Reuther vice-president of the new AFL–CIO. The most serious problems facing the unions in the years after the merger were corruption and racketeering. In 1957 a Senate investigating committee under the chairmanship of Senator John L. McClellan of Arkansas uncovered gross financial chicanery in the Teamsters' Union, the largest and most powerful union in the country. The union was promptly expelled from the AFL–CIO and its president, Dave Beck, was sent to jail for stealing union funds. The McClellan Committee's revelations led to the passage of the Landrum–Griffin Act (1959), which provided for the regulation of internal union affairs, but this did nothing to reform the Teamsters. Beck's successor, James R. Hoffa, was in turn sentenced to a long jail term in 1967 for jury tampering and larceny, though he retained the presidency of the union until 1971. Freed on parole the following year after the intercession of President Nixon, Hoffa mysteriously disappeared in 1975 and is thought to have been murdered by his underworld connections. Meanwhile fresh strains had appeared in the AFL–CIO. Throughout the 1960s Reuther had been critical of Meany's conservative attitude to civil rights and in 1968, after a further dispute over the direction and aims of the labor movement, he led his United Automobile Workers out of the AFL–CIO.

As the economy continued to grow Americans lived in a world of greater affluence than any generation in history. By the 1960s average family income had more than doubled since the Great Depression, and despite the recession of the 1970s average real disposable income continued to rise. In 1970, for the first time, Americans spent less than half their income on food, clothing, shelter, and utilities. By 1976 more households had two cars than had none and as many had television sets as had indoor toilets. Yet in a theoretically classless society there remained an enormous gulf between rich and poor. According to the line drawn by the Census Bureau (it was $3,968 for a nonfarm family of four in 1970) the proportion of Americans living in poverty went down from 22 percent in 1959 to 11 percent in 1974. Yet that still meant that over twenty-five million people were officially classified as poor. Moreover, the share of the national income received by the poorest 20 percent of the population had remained relatively constant since 1870.

The American poor were not of course to be compared with the impoverished masses of India, Latin America, or Africa. They had virtually no experience of hunger, very little of homelessness; nearly all had television sets, many had cars, perhaps one in ten possessed air-conditioning. Theirs was rather the poverty of being a permanent underclass in the world's most prosperous nation. In absolute terms, poverty was not primarily a problem of race. There were three times as many poor whites as poor blacks. Poor whites were especially numerous among migrant farm laborers, tenant farmers in the Deep South, and the wretched inhabitants of Appalachia (the hill-country of West Virginia, Kentucky, and North Carolina). But whereas poor whites were mainly elderly and scattered, poor blacks and other minorities were young and huddled together. More important, the black poor were appreciably worse off than the white poor.

Minority Problems: Blacks, Chicanos, and American Indians

Was there a revolution in the fortunes of black Americans in the four decades that followed Pearl Harbor? There is no simple answer. Taking the period as a whole blacks made enormous gains. Between 1960 and 1969 alone the proportion of blacks below the poverty line fell from a half to a third. Black family income rose sharply as a proportion of white family income—from 40 percent in 1940 to 60 percent in 1970. The proportion of blacks in the professions and in technical jobs rose much faster than in the population as a whole. Black educational attainments, as measured by years of schooling and the proportion of high-school graduates going on to college, almost caught up with those of whites. A sizable black middle class emerged with a lifestyle hardly distinguishable from that of their white counterparts. Increasingly, blacks were to be seen in the offices of banks and big corporations, in the federal civil service, on campuses of leading colleges, as sports stars and television announcers, in officers' clubs, theaters, and tourist haunts. Politically, too, blacks made great strides. During the 1960s and 1970s black mayors were elected in many major cities, among them Los Angeles, Washington, Detroit, Atlanta, and New Orleans. The number of black elected officials in the country at large rose to 4,600 by 1980. Even in Mississippi, where a black trying to vote in the 1940s would have risked being lynched, there were over 200 black office-holders thirty years later.

Yet if the old taboos vanished and long-established barriers were swept away, progress was less impressive than it seemed. Even in boom times the mass of blacks formed a depressed urban proletariat which was becoming more and more segregated residentially. It was ironic, moreover, that blacks gained urban political power only when American city government was on the point of collapse. And when the 1970s brought a harsher economic climate the march towards racial equality began to falter. The white–black income gap once again began to widen. Unemployment among blacks once more crept up to twice the level for whites: among black youths it exceeded 30 percent. By 1980 the situation had become so bad that the unemployment-rate for black college graduates was higher than for white high-school dropouts. To make matters worse, city welfare departments lacked the funds to increase payments to keep pace with inflation. Meanwhile there was growing controversy over the "affirmative action" policy laid down by President Johnson in 1968. In an effort to reduce past discrimination Johnson had required all government contractors, including colleges and universities receiving federal funds, to give preferential treatment to blacks and other minorities (and, after 1971, to women). Whites who resented what they called "reverse discrimination" challenged the policy in the courts and in two leading cases the Supreme Court handed down sharply contrasting decisions. In the celebrated *Bakke* case of June 1978, the Court dismayed blacks by holding that universities could not set aside explicit quotas for racial minorities and thus exclude white applicants who might be better qualified. But it added that it was constitutionally permissible for race to be considered along with other factors in deciding on admissions. A year later, in the case of *United Steelworkers of America* v. *Weber*, the Court decided that employers could give preference to blacks in training programs for better jobs provided that white workers were not displaced or absolutely debarred from advancement and so long as affirmative action was abandoned once the racial balance had been corrected.

Blacks provided only the most conspicuous example of the new ethnic and racial self-consciousness of the 1960s. Encouraged by the black example and by the greater tolerance of diversity now being displayed by the dominant majority, other submerged minorities, mostly Mexican-Americans and American Indians, reasserted their cultural identities and demanded community power and the recognition of their special needs. Thanks to immigration and a relatively high birth-rate the Mexican-American population soared after World War II, reaching an estimated 7.2 million in 1978. Concentrated principally in five Southwestern states which had once been part of Mexico—Arizona, California, Colorado, New Mexico, and Texas—and where they formed one-sixth of the population, Mexican-Americans moved increasingly to the cities after World War II, attracted by jobs in industry. By 1970, the proportion of city-dwellers had risen to 85 percent. There were one million Mexican-Americans in Los Angeles alone, a third of the city's population; in San Antonio and El Paso the proportion was over a half. Suffering from many of the same disabilities as blacks—high unemployment, poor housing, educational segregation, discriminatory treatment at the hands of the police and in the courts—people of Mexican descent launched their own civil-rights movement. Rejecting the term "Mexican-American" as alien and demeaning they began referring to themselves as "Chicanos" and making collective efforts to improve their political and socioeconomic position and preserve their culture. Voter-registration drives resulted in 1974 in the election of Chicanos to governorships in New Mexico and Arizona and in local victories in Texas. Yet Chicanos remained severely underrepresented in state legislatures and city councils. The best-known Chicano leader was César Chávez, who led California farm workers, mostly Mexican immigrants, in a fight for better pay and conditions and the right to join a union. Chávez's grape and lettuce boycotts between 1965 and 1972 won national support and eventually secured recognition for his union, the United Farm Workers. Moreover a campaign for educational reform secured a speedup of school desegregation, the development of bilingual and bicultural courses, and an increase in the number of Chicano teachers and administrators.

The American Indian population, which had been increasing steadily since 1900, more than doubled between 1945 and 1980 to reach a total of nearly one million. The great majority lived west of the Mississippi, the largest concentrations being in Oklahoma, Arizona, and California. Hitherto a predominantly rural people, Indians moved to the cities in large numbers, encouraged by a government-sponsored relocation program aimed at integrating the Indians into white society and at relieving the chronic unemployment, illiteracy, alcoholism, and high mortality-rates of the reservations. By 1980 almost half the Indians were urban-dwellers, some living in small towns close to reservations, others congregating in large metropolitan areas like Los Angeles, San Francisco–Oakland, Tulsa, and Minneapolis. Often overwhelmed by the impersonality, loneliness, and unfamiliar work patterns of the city, urban Indians found it difficult to escape from poverty, exploitation, and discrimination. But the move to the city stimulated a sense of pan-Indian identity and younger Indian leaders, freed from the conservative restraints of tribal council communities, began to protest against their unequal status. A young Sioux intellectual, Vine Deloria, Jr., drew public attention to Indian conditions and voiced a demand for "red power" in *Custer Died For Your Sins* (1969). That same year Indian demonstrators occupied Alcatraz Island, which they offered to buy from the government for trinkets worth $24—the precise sum the Dutch had paid the Indian sachems for Manhattan Island in 1626. In 1972 an Indian march on Washington culminated in the occupation of the Bureau of Indian Affairs and in 1973 members of the militant American Indian Movement staged an armed confrontation with federal officials at Wounded Knee, South Dakota, scene of the massacre of the Sioux by United States cavalry in 1890. In addition a number of tribes in New York and New England instituted lawsuits to recover lands their ancestors had been induced to sign away. To meet Indian grievances the Nixon Administration in 1969 appointed a Mohawk-Sioux, Louis R. Bruce, as commissioner for Indian affairs and later returned 48,000 acres of sacred tribal lands to the Taos Pueblo Indians. Nixon's assurance in 1970 that the tribes would be given greater autonomy "without being cut off from Federal concern and Federal support" marked the formal abandonment of the "termination" policy adopted by the Eisenhower Administration in an ill-advised and ultimately disastrous attempt to free the Indians from federal supervision while at the same time transferring the cost of their support to state welfare systems. The Indian Self-determination Act (1975), which Congress passed in the same enlightened spirit as Nixon's announcement, marked not so much a new policy as a return to the principle of tribal restoration adopted by the New Deal.

The singling out of blacks, Chicanos, and Indians for various kinds of federal aid and protection produced a resentful reaction from ethnic groups which believed themselves to be in equal need. Americans of Polish, Slovak, Italian, and Greek origin protested that blacks and others officially classified as minorities were advancing at their expense. Thus in the late 1960s newly formed white ethnic community organizations began to echo 'black power' demands for neighborhood-improvement schemes, greater political representation, and cultural recognition. Spokesmen for the 'white ethnics' also launched an attack on the traditional melting-pot ideal, alleging that in practice it had meant not a blending of cultures but conformity to the values of the dominant WASP (White Anglo-Saxon Protestant) majority. The "new ethnicity", as it was called, produced few tangible results, largely because most descendants of south and east Europeans were at best lukewarm to the concept of cultural distinctiveness. But they showed a readiness to combine to elect political leaders of their own kind, while their support for a campaign against degrading ethnic stereotypes in the press and on television achieved some success.

The Women's Movement

Just as the participation of women in the nineteenth-century abolitionist movement had led to a demand for women's suffrage, so female involvement in the civil-rights agitation proved a spur to the women's liberation movement. The rebirth of feminism came at a time when the number of working women had already increased dramatically; that indeed was why it was able to win so much support. In 1940 only 25 percent of women over fourteen were at work, almost exactly the same proportion as in 1910 and a much smaller proportion than in other industrial countries. Nearly all the women who then worked were young, unmarried, and poor; many were blacks or foreign-born whites. But the war and the postwar decades transformed the situation. By 1970 there were 31.6 million women workers (42.8 percent of the total work-force) and 47 percent of all women held a job. Married women workers now outnumbered single ones, a large proportion of working women were over thirty-five, and the greatest growth in the female labor force was taking place among well-educated, middle-class wives. Yet women were still a depressed class. They were discriminated against both in employment and in wages. Relatively few women were in skilled crafts or the professions; in 1973 34.1 percent held clerical jobs and 21.8 were in service occupations. As well as being concentrated in low-paid, low-prestige jobs, they were paid substantially less than men even when doing the same work. Indeed, in respect of earned income women were worse off *vis-à-vis* men than were blacks *vis-à-vis* whites.

The emergence of an organized women's liberation movement dates from the publication of Betty Friedan's *The Feminine Mystique* (1963). Attacking the romanticization of domesticity and the widespread popular notion that women could attain fulfillment only through keeping house and rearing children, the book articulated the half-felt dissatisfactions of many educated, middle-class women and sparked off a national debate. In 1966 Friedan helped found the National Organization for Women (NOW), whose main goal was the ending of sexual discrimination in employment. Subsequently NOW took up other women's rights issues, including the provision of child-care centers for working mothers, legalized abortion, and paid maternity leave. It also sponsored the Equal Rights Amendment to the Constitution, first introduced ·into Congress as long ago ·as 1923. Whereas NOW relied mainly on litigation and legislation, members of more radical women's rights groups adopted militant tactics, invading male bars and restaurants and picketing events like the Miss America Pageant which in their view exploited and degraded women.

At a time when American society was unusually sensitive to the issue of equality the drive to expand women's opportunities achieved some success. A spate of federal and state equal-opportunity laws, executive orders, and court decisions swept away the legal basis of job discrimination. Many state legislatures even repealed the laws passed earlier to protect the health and safety of working women, but which were now deemed to have restricted women's opportunities. The result was the opening up of skilled trades and professions that had been traditionally male. In the 1960s small but significant numbers of women became carpenters, machinists, and electricians; the proportion of women accountants increased at four times the male rate. Women's organizations also persuaded seventeen states to make abortion easier; by 1970, over 200,000 legal abortions were being performed annually, a tenfold increase in two years. Many cities, Chicago, San Francisco, and San Jose among them, elected women mayors and in 1974 Ella T. Grasso of Connecticut became the first woman governor to be elected in her own right (all previous women governors had succeeded their husbands).

Yet these advances did not bring the goal of sexual equality appreciably nearer. In every activity women still held few of the top jobs: in 1970 they accounted, for example, for only 4.8 percent of the country's three million managers and executives. During the 1970s, moreover, the gap between men's and women's wages actually widened. At the same time women's rights advocates experienced frustrating setbacks. In 1972 Congress enacted a lavish program to make child-care facilities more widely available, but President Nixon vetoed it as a threat to the family. Likewise the Equal Rights Amendment passed by Congress in 1972 encountered stiff resistance, not least from women, when it went to the states for ratification. By 1979 thirty-five states had ratified it, but three more would have had to do so for it to have become part of the Constitution. Since, however, this had still not happened when the deadline for ratification was reached on June 30, 1982, the amendment lapsed.

Religion in American Life

The drift away from religion that had characterized the depression years was abruptly reversed after World War II. In the 1950s especially church membership soared, unprecedented sums were spent on church building, religious leaders grew in public esteem. Among intellectuals there was a new interest in Christian doctrine and biblical theology. Especially influential were the writings of Karl Barth, Paul Tillich, and Reinhold Niebuhr, spokesmen for a Protestant 'neo-orthodoxy' which repudiated belief in man's innate goodness and taught that only a religion of grace held out hope of redemption. More appealing to the unsophisticated was the simplified pietistic gospel preached by a new generation of itinerant evangelists. Of these the best known was William F. (Billy) Graham, a magnetic North Carolina Baptist whose highly organized and skillfully publicized 'crusades' attracted vast audiences in large cities. Another prominent feature of the changed religious scene was the flood of sermons and books stressing the psychological value of religion in promoting inner tranquility and strength.

By the 1950s religion had permeated every aspect of American life. Religious films like *The Ten Commandments* broke box-office records, quasireligious songs like 'I Believe' and 'The Man Upstairs' became popular 'hits'. The pledge of allegiance, recited daily by American schoolchildren, was amended to include the words "under God". How far there was a real religious revival remains uncertain. Along with genuine religious impulses there was much that was superficial. The typical American, one commentator remarked, had "developed a remarkable capacity for being serious about religion without taking religion seriously". The new religion was certainly oversimplified, doctrinally nondescript, and strongly humanistic in emphasis. For great numbers of Americans its function was simply to define their identity and provide a context of belonging in a highly mobile society. Its appeal lay not in its intrinsic truths but in the divine sanction it could confer on the American way of life.

After 1960, despite some falling-off in church attendance, church membership continued to grow, albeit at a slower pace. But there was a significant shift in the balance of religious forces. While Protestant church

68 million, the Roman Catholic total shot up from 28.6 million to 49.6 million. (By 1980 there were also 6.1 million Jews, over four million members of Eastern Orthodox churches, an estimated two million Muslims, and 60,000 Buddhists.)

Within Protestantism the waning of theological controversy and the difficulty of maintaining language barriers as European immigration declined produced a wave of denominational mergers. Between 1939 and 1960 various Methodist, Presbyterian, and Lutheran bodies united, while the formation of the United Church of Christ in 1957 joined Congregationalists to the Evangelical and Reformed Church. There were also striking changes in the relative strengths of the different Protestant sects. Methodists (who numbered 12.9 million in 1980) were displaced as the largest Protestant denomination by the Baptists (25 million), while the Lutherans (8.5 million) overtook the Presbyterians (3.6 million) to occupy third place. Even faster rates of growth were recorded by Adventist and Holiness groups and such Pentecostal churches as the Assemblies of God; together these sects claimed over 8 million members in 1980. These developments greatly strengthened the Fundamentalist wing of Protestantism and in the 1970s there was renewed evangelical activity from those who called themselves 'born-again' Christians—notably Southern Baptists, Missouri Synod Lutherans, and the Adventist–Holiness–Pentecostal coalition. But while the gospel of born-again Christianity was based upon the Old Testament it was disseminated by modern technology. By 1980 there were no fewer than 1,400 radio stations and 36 television stations devoted exclusively to spreading the message of the evangelical churches.

The doubling of the Catholic population between 1940 and 1980 meant that the United States came to have the largest national grouping of Roman Catholics in the world. The enhanced importance of American Catholicism in the eyes of Rome was reflected in the steady increase in American representation in the College of Cardinals. Before 1921 there had never been more than one American cardinal; by 1946 there were four and by 1980 eleven—a number exceeded only by Italy. Besides the growth in Catholic numbers and in Catholic educational and cultural institutions there were other signs of ecclesiastical maturity—for example, a surge of interest in contemplative monasteries and a liturgical revival which sought to revitalize corporate worship. While the growing power of the Catholic Church did not revive the frenzied anti-Catholicism of the nineteenth century, it nonetheless worried many non-Catholic liberals. Friction also resulted from the Church's refusal to countenance divorce, birth-control, or abortion, as well as from its insistence on the censorship of books, plays, and films. Yet the gulf separating Catholicism from the general life of the nation gradually narrowed, especially after Pope John XXIII's ecumenical initiatives.

Problems of Mass Education

The affluent decades after World War II saw extraordinary advances in mass education. Secondary schooling became wellnigh universal. The proportion of children between 14 and 17 attending public high school rose from two-thirds in 1940 to nearly nine-tenths in 1970, while the number of high-school graduates increased three times as fast as the population. School buildings improved, classes became smaller, teachers were better trained and better paid. Yet the schools were beset by a succession of crises. In the immediate postwar years there were not enough schools or teachers for the children of the baby boom. Hardly had lavish expenditure overcome that problem than Americans were jolted into a thorough reappraisal of the school curriculum by the successful launching of the first Soviet artificial satellite, *Sputnik* (1957). This seeming demonstration of the superiority of Soviet scientific and technological education provided fresh ammunition for those who had been complaining that, under the influence of progressive educationalists, American schools had lapsed into intellectual flabbiness and enervation. After Sputnik the schools revised their curricula so as to provide more rigorous intellectual training in the basic academic disciplines and a greater emphasis on science, mathematics, and modern foreign languages. Yet despite massive financial help from the federal government, notably through the National Defense Education Act of 1958, such improvement as resulted was short-lived. From about 1962 onwards the verbal and mathematical skills of high-school seniors, as measured by college entrance examinations, fell steadily. And in 1979 a presidential commission found that only 15 percent of high-school pupils were studying foreign languages (compared with 24 percent in 1965) and of those only one in twenty was doing so for more than two years.

Falling academic standards reflected the changed educational priorities of the 1960s. As the desegregation issue came to the fore, concern for academic excellence gave way to the feeling that the chief aim of the schools should be to solve the problems of poverty and race through the equalization of educational opportunity. Despite the Supreme Court's desegregation ruling in 1954, compliance was slow, grudging, and incomplete. The tactics of delay and evasion adopted by whites in the seventeen Southern and border states where schools had been segregated by law proved for a time highly effective. Ten years after the *Brown* ruling only two Southern states (Tennessee and Texas) had more than 2 percent of their black children in integrated schools. But the Civil Rights Act of 1964 provided the federal government with a means of enforcement by denying federal funds to segregated schools. In 1969, moreover, the Supreme Court turned down requests from Southern school districts to delay desegregation. Thus by 1974 92 percent of Southern black children attended integrated schools. In the North, where the existence of separate schools for the two races was the product of residential segregation rather than of statute, the problem proved more intractable. When in the early 1970s attempts began to be made to use compulsory busing to promote desegregation, Northern white city-dwellers turned to boycott and protest and many joined the exodus to the suburbs. Yet the Supreme Court, while backing busing plans that did not cross city limits, drew the line at schemes which involved merging predominantly black city-school districts with those of the surrounding white suburbs. Thus by 1980 school desegregation in the North was virtually at a standstill. A fifth of the nation's 6.6 million black schoolchildren still attended schools that were almost wholly black, and more than half attended schools that were more than half black.

For colleges and universities the postwar decades were a time of phenomenal growth. Mainly reponsible was the general prosperity. Tuition fees rose more slowly than family incomes, full employment made part-time jobs easier for students to get. The notion that higher education was the birthright of every American was encouraged by the 'G.I. Bill of Rights', which provided college tuition fees and maintenance grants to qualified World War II ex-servicemen (later extended to Korean War veterans). By the time the program was wound up in 1956 it had enabled several million ex-servicemen to go to college. Between 1940 and 1970 the number of American colleges and universities rose from 1,500 to 2,500 and their enrollment from 1.5 million (16 percent of the 18–21 age-group) to 7.5 million (40 percent). Of those at college in 1970 three-fifths of the whites and three-quarters of the blacks came from families with no previous experience of higher education. These statistics, to be sure, were measures of quantity rather than of quality. Unlike European universities, whose standards were fairly uniform, American colleges and universities were more varied, ranging from those which led the world as repositories of advanced learning and research to those offering courses to suit every taste and capacity.

The postwar boom in higher education created enormous problems. As universities grew in size—there were thirty-nine with over 20,000 students by 1969—they became more bureaucratic and impersonal. Moreover their eager acceptance of huge research grants from government and corporate business for scientific and technical projects (often war-related) posed a possible threat to the academic tradition of disinterested scholarship. Then again campus regulations governing students' lifestyles and behavior became increasingly incongruous as the average age of the student population rose (thanks to the disproportionate growth of graduate and professional schools) and a youth culture took shape whose distinguishing features were long hair, unkempt clothes, rock music, experimentation with hallucinatory drugs, and a scornful rejection of middle-class sexual morality.

This was the background to the mass campus uprisings of the mid-1960s—though indignation about the Vietnam War and the draft intensified student discontent. The first major upheaval, the so-called Free Speech Movement at the University of California at Berkeley in 1964, was set off by the university's attempt to restrict student political activity on the campus. But protest soon moved beyond purely local campus issues. By 1968, when there were noisy, disruptive, and sometimes violent campus demonstrations all over the country, the targets had become the entire American socioeconomic system and the university as a microcosm of it. University authorities, intimidated and bewildered by the agitation, responded with a variety of concessions. They relaxed entrance requirements (the City University of New York abolished them altogether), made a gesture to 'relevance' by introducing 'black studies' courses, conceded student representation on governing bodies, and abolishing ROTC officer-training programs. Yet the decline in student activism in the early 1970s owed less to these changes than to the ending of the draft in 1973 and to a chillier economic climate which concentrated students' minds on job security.

By the early 1970s colleges and universities had entered an era of adversity. Inflation drove up operating costs; federal support was reduced; enrollments leveled off and even declined, partly because of soaring tuition fees, partly because it had become clear that a degree was no longer a passport to a good job. Smaller colleges were forced to reduce staffs and share facilities; some even closed their doors. Almost the only institutions to go on expanding were community colleges, the public counterpart of the private two-year junior college. Originally intended for students going on to university, they became increasingly concerned with vocational courses leading to an 'associate degree'.

American Culture: Science, Literature, and the Arts

Those who feared that mass education would prove inimical to independent thought and experimentation could have drawn comfort from the continued flowering of American science. Even allowing for the contribution of foreign-born scientists, many of them refugees, American scientific and technological accomplishments in the postwar decades were phenomenal. American physicists, biochemists, and physiologists enlarged the boundaries in their fields, regularly carrying off the lion's share of Nobel prizes. American plant biologists developed the hybrid corn that has been one of the twentieth century's most important contributions to agriculture. Among numerous American advances in medical research the most significant, perhaps, were the isolation of the antibiotic streptomycin (1947) which, in conjunction with other drugs, proved effective against tuberculosis and Dr Jonas E. Salk's vaccine which, within a few years of its introduction in 1955, had virtually ended the scourge of poliomyelitis. But the most spectacular achievements were in interplanetary exploration. The historic Apollo moon landing in July 1969 and the five other moon landings that took place in the next three years were superb technological feats. And although the moon program was wound down in the 1970s, an American Skylab earth-orbiting space station yielded invaluable information about solar radiation, the earth's magnetic field, and the weather; the Telstar unmanned satellite revolutionized international telephone and television communications; while a series of space probes gave mankind the first close-up pictures of Mercury, Mars, Venus, Jupiter, and Saturn.

In literature and the arts the American record was less uniformly outstanding. The two novelists who had dominated American writing before the war, William Faulkner and Ernest Hemingway, remained productive throughout the 1950s, though without adding substantially to their reputations. Their successors defy easy classification though some saw significance in the fact that the most-discussed novels were by 'minority' authors, especially Jews and blacks. But the leading Jewish writers—Norman Mailer, Bernard Malamud, J. D. Salinger, and Saul Bellow—belonged to no one movement or genre. Only Malamud, in novels like *The Assistant* (1957) and *The Fixer* (1966), dealt with explicitly Jewish themes. Bellow's best-known works (*Dangling Man*, 1944; *The Victim*, 1947; *The Adventures of Augie March*, 1953; *Herzog*, 1964), though sometimes depicting Jewish characters, were essentially concerned with the struggles of the individual in a hostile world. Salinger, by idealizing the young while focusing on their problems in *The Catcher in the Rye* (1951) and *Franny and Zooey* (1961), won a wide following among teenagers. Mailer, having failed to repeat the success of *The Naked and the Dead* (1948), perhaps the best American novel about World War II, turned to a new and distinctive form of journalism which produced, among other works, *The Armies of the Night* (1968), a personal account of the 1967 peace march on Washington. The concept of black literature was, perhaps, less artificial since the two best-known black novelists of the period, Ralph Ellison (*The Invisible Man*, 1952) and James Baldwin (*Go Tell it on the Mountain*, 1953; *The Fire Next Time*, 1963), were concerned chiefly with race.

In the theater Eugene O'Neill ended a long silence with *The Iceman Cometh* (1946), considered by many critics to be his finest work. After his death in 1953 his autobiographical masterpiece, *The Long Day's Journey into Night*, received its first performance, as did parts of an unfinished cycle of plays with American history as their background. Among the contenders for O'Neill's mantle as America's foremost playwright two contrasting figures stood out: Arthur Miller and Tennessee Williams. Miller's *All My*

Sons (1947) and *Death of a Salesman* (1949) represented a revival of social drama, while *The Crucible* (1953) was at once a dramatization of the seventeenth-century Salem witchcraft hysteria and a commentary on America in the era of McCarthyism. Williams's plays—*The Glass Menagerie* (1944), *A Streetcar Named Desire* (1947), and *Cat on a Hot Tin Roof* (1955)— probed violence, sex, and degeneracy against a background of decayed Southern gentility.

It was, however, in poetry that postwar American literature received its finest expression. Robert Frost, whose homely verses set mainly in his cherished New England possessed a symbolic and even a metaphysical dimension, remained the most popular and widely read of twentieth-century American poets. Frost's near contemporaries included such distinguished and original poets as the impressionistic William Carlos Williams and the abstruse but rewarding Marianne Moore and Wallace Stevens. But the preeminent figure in postwar American verse, and possibly the greatest of modern poets writing in English, was Robert Lowell, whose work ranged from New England's Puritan past to the traumas of modern America and in whom technical excellence and intensity of feeling were marvelously combined.

In the visual arts the United States at last threw off its dependence upon Europe and for the first time set styles for the rest of the world. A new phase in American painting began in the mid-1940s with the emergence of abstract expressionism as the dominant art form. Ridiculed at first, it eventually carried all before it. Among its leading exponents were immigrant artists like Arshile Gorky, Willem de Kooning, and Mark Rothko, but its most influential figure was the native-born 'action painter', Jackson Pollock, whose elegant, swirling abstractions were created by dripping paint on huge raw canvases placed on the floor. In the 1960s there was a reaction against abstraction and a more traditional kind of realism seemed back in fashion. Yet the work of the leading realists had subjective and symbolic overtones. Thus the paintings of Andrew Wyeth, the most widely acclaimed of the postwar nonabstractionists, were so meticulously executed as to appear surrealist. Likewise, the haunting urban landscapes of Edward Hopper, perhaps the most important twentieth-century American painter, were more abstract than they were usually perceived to be.

The innovation and experimentation characteristic of painting was more evident still in architecture. Three interrelated factors operated to create a new architectural idiom: advances in building technology, general acceptance of the trend towards functionalism, and the emigration to the United States of some of the outstanding European exponents of modernist architecture—notably Walter Gropius, Ludwig Miës van der Rohe, Marcel Breuer, and László Moholy-Nagy, all of them associated with the German Bauhaus school. The new architecture—cold, geometric, severely functional, and making extensive use of such materials as glass, steel, and aluminum—received dramatic expression in such buildings as the United Nations Secretariat Building in New York (1950), Miës van der Rohe's Lake Shore Drive apartments in Chicago (1951), and Miës's and Philip Johnson's Seagram Building in New York (1958). Functionalism did not, however, imply a universal commitment to glass-walled, rectilinear structures. The distinctive genius of Frank Lloyd Wright, earlier demonstrated in a startlingly original series of private homes, hotels, and office buildings, flowered anew in the sweeping curves and flowing interior spaces of such designs as the Johnson Wax Company Buildings at Racine, Wisconsin and New York's Guggenheim Museum (1959). Another radical innovator to employ sculptural forms was Eero Saarinen whose soaring creations included the Gateway Arch in St. Louis and the Trans World Airline Terminal at Kennedy Airport in New York (1962).

Postwar American music was as diverse as American society itself, ranging all the way from jazz and rock to classical music and electronic experimentation. In the classical vein there were several composers of undoubted stature, among them Aaron Copland, Roy Harris, and Roger Sessions, who had come to prominence before the war, Charles Ives, belatedly recognized as a seminal figure in contemporary music, and such representatives of a younger generation as Samuel Barber and Elliott Carter. Yet there were no American names to compare with the great contemporary European quartet of Bartók, Schoenberg, Stravinsky, and Hindemith, all of whom, incidentally, emigrated to the United States in the 1940s, thereby increasing their already considerable influence on American music. Nor, despite the striking success of Gian-Carlo Menotti's operas, notably *The Medium* (1947), *The Consul* (1950), and *The Saint of Bleecker Street* (1959), did an indigenous tradition of opera composition develop. Indeed, the most significant American musical achievement was at a popular rather than at a rarefied level. The forties and fifties were the golden age of the American musical—a term which implied increasingly a synthesis not only of music but also of dance with a detailed plot. Of the many successful Broadway musicals which became popular all over the world the most outstanding, perhaps, were Richard Rodgers's and Oscar Hammerstein II's *Oklahoma* (1943) and *South Pacific* (1949), Cole Porter's *Kiss Me Kate* (1948), Leonard Bernstein's *West Side Story* (1957), and Frederick Loewe's and Alan Jay Lerner's *My Fair Lady* (1956).

Nothing had a more pervasive influence on American postwar culture than the mass media, television in particular. Television swept over America with remarkable speed. In 1946 only 16,000 Americans owned television, but by 1949 a quarter of a million sets were being installed each month and by 1953 two-thirds of all American homes possessed the new electronic wonder. Television soon took up more American leisure time than any other activity, becoming for most people the preferred form of entertainment as well as the main source of information about what was going on in the world. Beginning in 1952 television reshaped political campaigns as candidates came to rely increasingly on the new medium to reach the electorate. A further effect of television was a sharp decline in cinemagoing. In the sixties and seventies the cinema did, however, regain some popularity, largely because of the success of films featuring eroticism, violence, and space adventure—most of them designed expressly for the young.

Almost from its birth television came under heavy fire. Critics complained that programs were banal, timid, meretricious, and exploitative and alleged that they debased taste and brutalized the senses. These criticisms were part of the general assault on mass culture that developed in intellectual circles in the 1950s. Some observers, worried not only by television but also by the flood of mass-circulation magazines ranging from the horror comic to the avowedly pornographic, foresaw the operation of a kind of Gresham's Law whereby mass culture would steadily drive out more refined and enriching leisure activities.

Such fears, though understandable, were in fact exaggerated for along with the growth of mass culture and its accompanying vulgarities came a remarkable upsurge of popular interest in and appreciation of the arts. Among the many proofs of this were the enormous sales of literary classics in paperback editions, the growing number of and extensive patronage of museums and art galleries, and the widening audience for serious music—helped especially by the invention of the long-playing record (1948). One could point also to the prodigious increase in the number of symphony orchestras. By the 1970s there were hundreds of them in the United States and at least a dozen ranked with the best in the world. Grand opera, too, flourished as never before, not merely in New York but in relatively small towns like Bloomington, Indiana and Norfolk, Virginia. Ballet, virtually unknown in the United States in the 1930s, was invigorated by the emergence of three distinguished companies: the New York City Ballet, the American Ballet Theater, and the San Francisco Ballet. Still further evidence of cultural advance was afforded by the establishment of coordinated centers for the performing arts like the Lincoln Center in New York (1966) and the John F. Kennedy Center in Washington (1972), the growth of annual Shakespeare Festivals at Stratford, Connecticut, Ashland, Oregon, and San Diego, California, and the founding of the Aspen Music Festival in Colorado in 1949. Both the federal government, through the creation of the National Endowment for the Humanities (1966), and the states played a part in sponsoring the arts; so, more lavishly, did municipalities, charitable foundations, business corporations, and private individuals. Nor should the contribution of television be overlooked.

Following the passage in 1967 of the Public Broadcasting Act authorizing the creation of a noncommercial television network scores of educational television stations sprang up to provide good plays and concerts and to disseminate knowledge generally. The net result was that the scale and standard of cultural provision in the United States became the envy of the world.

29. *The Conservative Counter-Revolution, 1980–1992*

Conservatism Resurgent

The shift to the right in American politics which brought Ronald Reagan to power in 1980 had been long in the making. Ever since Nixon's election in 1968 Middle America had been recoiling from the wave of reform that had reached its crest with the aspirations of Lyndon Johnson's Great Society. It felt that the liberal panaceas of the 1960s had failed, that increasing welfare entitlements for the poor had not improved their lot and that legal sanctions for traditional moral standards had been weakened. Sidetracked for a time by the Watergate scandal, this conservative-populist upsurge gained new momentum from the need felt by many Americans in the aftermath of Vietnam and the Iranian hostage crisis to reaffirm patriotic values and to strengthen the United States against both the Soviet Union and international terrorism. In the 1970s, moreover, a variety of conservative groupings and organizations emerged as a significant force in American politics. Neo-conservatives provided the right with much-needed intellectual respectability. They were not a homogeneous group. Some, like the columnist, William F. Buckley, Jr., and the Chicago economist, Milton Friedman, had been lifelong spokesmen for private enterprise and the minimalist state; others, like the editor, Norman Podhoretz, and the writer, Michael Novak, were former liberals who had experienced a kind of conversion. The neo-conservatives overlapped with the so-called New Right which, entrenched in prestigious think-tanks like the American Enterprise Institute and the Heritage Foundation, had supplanted older, less doctrinaire opinion-formers and used new media and fund-raising techniques to advocate welfare cutbacks and statutory recognition of traditional morality. Hostility to the counter-culture and to the changes it had wrought since the 1960s in the laws and conventions governing sexual conduct, the status of women and the family, religious belief, and the treatment of criminals largely accounted for the rise of a religious right centered in the growing Protestant fundamentalist sects, whose leaders were often popular television evangelists (see p. 587). Reagan's nomination and election enabled these motley groups, together with an assortment of anti-Communists, free-marketeers, and libertarians to merge and enter the political mainstream. But although Reagan had long shared many of the sentiments of the militant right, moderate Republicans in Congress, not to mention the Democratic majority in the Lower House, retained sufficient strength to ensure that the political pendulum did not swing too violently away from the center.

Reaganomics

In domestic policy Reagan set out to reverse the course of government activism charted by Franklin D. Roosevelt during the New Deal and broadly followed by his successors, Democrat and Republican alike, during the next forty-five years. "Government", declared Reagan in his inaugural address, "is not the solution to our problem. Government *is* the problem." He aimed therefore to shrink the role of government by reducing federal spending, cutting taxes, and keeping business regulation to a minimum. He claimed that these policies, which became known as "Reaganomics", would enlarge the scope for individual initiative, promote investment, improve economic growth, and create new jobs. This was a highly contentious approach, but Reagan showed great political skill in winning public and Congressional support for it. Barely six months into his Presidency Congress had approved the essentials of his entire economic program.

Reagan's tax policies drew on the principles of "supply-side" economics, which held that high marginal rates of tax discouraged enterprise, saving, and investment, while cutting taxes would provide a spur that would not only stimulate the economy but even increase government tax revenues. In August 1981, thanks to the support of conservative Southern Democrats, Reagan persuaded Congress to reduce taxes drastically. The top rate of personal income tax was lowered from 70 to 50 percent, capital gains tax went down by a third and there were also reductions in business and inheritance taxes. Contrary to the supply-siders' predictions, the cuts produced a sharp fall in tax receipts which, together with massive increases in defense spending, generated staggering budget deficits. In 1983 the deficit exceeded $195 billion, the largest ever in peacetime. To cover it the Treasury had to borrow heavily, thus keeping interest rates high, at least until the Federal Reserve Board relaxed its tight monetary policy in 1984. But inflation tumbled from 12 percent in 1980 to less than 4 percent in 1984 and the country, after a plunge into recession in 1981–2, entered the longest peacetime period of uninterrupted economic expansion in its history. Between 1983 and 1990, while inflation remained under 4 percent and unemployment fell to 5.2 percent—its lowest level for fourteen years—the economy grew by a third and nineteen million new jobs were created.

Reagan's next priority was to trim the federal budget by reducing spending on selected domestic programs. The budget Congress approved in the summer of 1981 slashed government expenditure by $39 billion. Social security and Medicare, which benefited the elderly, were untouched; so were the lavish farm subsidies; but the cuts bore heavily on the arts, education, energy, transportation, law enforcement, and, above all, welfare spending. In the administration's view, the 1960s welfare programs designed to help the poor had actually worsened their plight. In addition they had acted as a disincentive to work and to marriage, thereby weakening character and morals and creating a self-perpetuating, dependent "underclass". Accordingly Reagan's 1981 budget made steep reductions in spending on food stamps, child-nutrition, school lunches, low-income housing, child-assistance benefits, and child day care. He assured critics, however, that he would still maintain a "safety net" for the "truly needy".

Having as governor of California resented interference from Washington, Reagan now sought to increase the autonomy of state and local governments. He gave more discretion to the states in spending federal grants and although his "New Federalism" proposals, which would have transferred to the states responsibility for over forty federal programs, were never implemented, state governments were nonetheless obliged to assume certain federal functions because of the president's budget cuts. A presidential commission was set up to consider the privatization of federal activities and assets, but in the event only CONRAIL, the government-owned freight railroad, the Alaska Railroad, and the airports in the District of Columbia were sold to the private sector.

Reagan had long believed that government regulation of the economy, besides being inefficient, often placed unnecessary burdens on business and restricted consumer choice. As President he promoted deregulation in a variety of ways. He appointed a task force on regulatory relief, suspended some existing regulations, relaxed the enforcement of others and halted the growth of regulatory budgets. He also staffed regulatory agencies with people unsympathetic to the idea of governmental control—a glaring example being his first Secretary of the Interior, James Watt, who tried to transfer public lands together with their timber and mineral resources to private ownership. In practice, however, the number of federal regulations continued to grow, though more slowly than before, and significant deregulation was achieved only in banking, oil-drilling, coal-mining, and transportation. The White House claimed that deregulation had revitalized these industries, besides saving the government money and reducing paperwork. But critics argued that such benefits, if they had indeed occurred, had been won at the cost of lowering standards of protection in health, road and air safety, and other areas.

Organized labor, already in decline, lost further ground during the Reagan years. When in August 1981, federal air traffic controllers began an illegal strike and defied the President's order to return within forty-eight hours, he dismissed them *en bloc* and ordered the hiring of hastily trained replacements. This had the effect of destroying the air traffic controllers' union. Moreover by packing the National Labor Relations Board with appointees favorable to employers Reagan tilted the balance of power in industrial disputes away from the unions, a trend intensified by deregulation. And although the 1980s saw the creation of millions of new jobs, most of them were not in the old unionized industries but in sectors and regions unfamiliar with or even hostile to organized labour—service industries or small businesses, for example, often in the Sun Belt. Thus by 1990, trade-union membership as a proportion of the work-force had fallen in a decade from 21.9 percent to 16.1 percent, the latter figure being the lowest since the 1920s.

Reagan and the "Evil Empire"

Reagan came to the Presidency lacking any experience of foreign affairs. But he brought with him an inveterate hostility to Communism which dated back to his Hollywood days, when he had witnessed at first hand Communist efforts to exert ideological pressure on the film industry by gaining control of its unions. Anti-Communism became the dominant theme of the foreign policy of his Presidency. Reverting to the Cold War postures of Truman, Dulles, and Kennedy, he characterized the Soviet Union as an "evil empire" and "the focus of evil in the modern world". He believed that the United States had fallen behind the Soviet Union in both conventional and nuclear weapons and that only from a position of military superiority could he hope for serious negotiation on the arms control treaty on which he had set his heart. Accordingly he embarked on a massive military build-up, the greatest in American history: during his first three years in office defense spending increased in real terms by 40 percent. In 1981 he decided to go forward with the production of neutron bombs and in March 1983 outlined a Strategic Defense Initiative (SDI). It became known as Star Wars after a popular space movie. SDI was a research program designed to provide an effective anti-ballistic missile shield by using lasers or particle beams to destroy missiles in flight. Many scientists doubted the effectiveness of SDI, while Congress was alarmed at the crippling cost of what turned out to be the most expensive weapons system ever devised. But with Reagan SDI remained almost an obsession. Meanwhile to counter the deployment in Eastern Europe of Soviet SS-20 intermediate-range nuclear missiles, Reagan implemented a decision taken before he became President to station in the United Kingdom and West Germany Cruise missiles capable of reaching targets in the Soviet Union. This move prompted the Soviet Union to break off the arms-control talks in progress in Geneva. Soviet–American relations worsened still further in September 1983 when the Russians shot down a Korean airliner in Soviet airspace, killing 269 passengers and crew.

Reagan hotly denied the Soviet claim that the plane had been engaged in intelligence surveillance for the United States and condemned the attack as a massacre. American anger at the incident facilitated the passage of a huge defense .authorization bill that included funds for the MX missile, the B-1 bomber, and, for the first time in more than a decade, the production of chemical weapons.

Yet the most ideological of twentieth-century American Presidents was also one of the most pragmatic. Originally an enthusiastic supporter of the embargo on wheat sales to the Soviet Union which President Carter had imposed in protest at the Soviet invasion of Afghanistan, Reagan was persuaded by America's huge grain surplus and its soaring balance of payments deficit to conclude an unprecedentedly large grain deal with Moscow in September 1983. Similarly, the objections of America's European allies led him in 1984 to abandon his strenuous opposition to the building by Western companies of a natural-gas pipeline for the Soviet Union. And despite his strident anti-Communist rhetoric he realized the importance of dialogue with the Soviet leaders and even during the Korean airliner furore attempted unsuccessfully to initiate one with Brezhnev's successor, Yuri Andropov.

In Reagan's eyes the most immediate Communist threat was to two Central American republics, El Salvador and Nicaragua. In El Salvador a military junta had seized power in 1979 but had failed to suppress left-wing insurgents who, armed by Cuba and Nicaragua, soon controlled a quarter of the country. Although right-wing death-squads, which the ruling junta countenanced and may even have abetted, were known to be systematically eliminating suspected rebels, Reagan believed that he must support the regime if El Salvador were not to be abandoned to Communism. He therefore extended substantial military and economic aid and sent in military advisers. Elections in 1984 seemed to offer the prospect of stability since the extreme right-wing presidential candidate and supposed leader of the death-squads, Roberto d'Aubuisson, was defeated by the more moderate José Napoleon Duarte. But the civil war dragged on until January 1992, when the government and the rebels signed a peace treaty which provided for political and military reforms.

The situation in Nicaragua, as Reagan interpreted it, was even more menacing. He believed that the Marxist Sandinistas, who had overthrown the brutal Somoza regime in 1979, had established a fully-fledged Communist dictatorship which served as a Soviet beachhead from which revolution could be spread throughout the Americas. Angered also by the help the Sandinistas were giving to the Salvadoran insurgents, the President directed the CIA in December 1981 to train and arm Nicaraguan counter-revolutionaries (Contras), who then launched attacks from Honduras on Sandinista strongholds. But Congress was reluctant to provide military aid for the Contras on the scale Reagan had requested.

Far from sharing his view that they were "freedom fighters" and "the moral equivalent" of America's Founding Fathers, critics alleged that many had been supporters of Somoza and likened them to the Salvadoran death-squads. They also feared that Reagan might ultimately commit American combat forces, thus turning Central America into another Vietnam. The disclosure in 1984 that the CIA had secretly mined Nicaraguan harbors crystallized these fears and provoked Congress into passing the Boland Amendment which imposed a ban on military support for the Contras.

Although Reagan stopped short of sending American troops to Nicaragua, he showed no such restraint when a Communist threat developed to the tiny Caribbean island of Grenada. In October 1983 the Prime Minister, Maurice Bishop, the leader of a left-wing government which had already incurred American displeasure by importing Cuban workers to build an airfield and by signing military agreements with Communist bloc governments, was overthrown and executed by an even more left-wing military junta. At the request of neighboring Caribbean countries Reagan dispatched American marines and paratroops to Grenada to depose the revolutionary regime. The mission was speedily and almost bloodlessly accomplished. Most Grenadans welcomed the invading Americans as liberators, and Reagan's action was warmly applauded by his fellow-countrymen. But the United Nations General Assembly "deeply deplored" it and many Latin Americans saw it as a revival of "big stick" diplomacy. The British, moreover, who had been grateful for crucial American help in ousting the Argentine invaders from the Falkland Islands in 1982, were deeply offended that Reagan had intervened in Grenada, a Commonwealth country, without consulting or even informing them.

In the Middle East American policy failed spectacularly. Its aim was to provide Israel with peaceful, stable frontiers in the hope that it would join the United States in a military alliance that would negate the Soviet Union's influence in the region and thwart the expansionist ambitions of the Russians' ally, Syria. In June 1982, with tacit American encouragement, Israel invaded Lebanon to destroy the bases used by PLO guerrillas to attack northern Israeli settlements. Lebanon dissolved into anarchy and fighting broke out between Christians and Muslims, as well as between Israeli and Syrian troops. In August the Israelis besieging Beirut agreed to withdraw to allow a combined American, French, and Italian force to supervise a PLO evacuation. But no sooner was that task accomplished and the multinational force had left than Israeli troops returned. When they did nothing to stop Christian Phalangist militia from massacring hundreds in Palestinian refugee camps, the multinational army was sent back to Beirut by the United Nations to keep the peace between the warring factions, only to find itself virtually besieged and powerless to shape events. The Pentagon advised withdrawal but the President refused, believing American prestige to be at stake. On October 23, 1983, a Muslim suicide bomber crashed a lorry packed with explosives into US Marine barracks at Beirut airport, killing 241 American servicemen. After this debacle Reagan had no option but to remove the entire peacekeeping force.

Reagan's Second Term

The Republicans approached the 1984 presidential election in understandably buoyant mood. Economic recovery was in full swing, the dollar was strong, inflation under control, and unemployment falling. The President's personal popularity, despite his frequent gaffes in public utterances and the squabbling and minor scandals that had plagued his administration, was undiminished. Unchallenged within his own party, he was renominated by acclamation by the Republican convention in August. The Democrats, on the other hand, remained deeply divided. They suffered fresh self-inflicted wounds during a long and acrimonious contest for the party's presidential nomination. Walter F. Mondale of Minnesota, a New Deal liberal who had been Carter's Vice-President, emerged the winner, defeating Senator Gary Hart of Colorado, who ran as the champion of "new ideas", and the Reverend Jesse Jackson, the first black to mount a serious challenge for the Presidency. Once nominated Mondale broke new ground by choosing a woman as his running mate: Geraldine Ferraro, a Congresswoman from New York of Italian Catholic background.

Reagan's campaign was based on his claim to have restored both the economy and the nation's pride in itself. Mondale campaigned for greater governmental concern for the weaker members of society, attacked the President's huge budget deficits and—unusually for a candidate—advocated higher taxes. Reagan remained throughout the campaign well ahead in the polls and on election day won a resounding victory, triumphing everywhere except Minnesota and the District of Columbia and amassing a record 525 electoral votes to Mondale's 13. Except for blacks, who voted in overwhelming numbers for Mondale, every section of the community preferred Reagan by large margins: the old and the young, Protestants and Catholics, organized labour and professional people. The choice of a woman as the Democratic vice-presidential candidate failed to expand the so-called gender gap—the tendency for women to vote Democratic in greater numbers than men; it may even have had a negative effect, especially in the South. At all events a majority of women voted for Reagan. The election showed that the mood of the country was profoundly conservative. Most Americans felt comfortable with Reagan and dismissed the Democrats as the party of big spending at home and weakness abroad. But the landslide did not extend to Congressional contests. The Republicans gained a handful of seats in the House, but in the Senate they had a slightly reduced majority.

Commentators reacted to Reagan's sweeping win by noting that reversals, large and small, had swiftly overtaken all four Presidents to be reelected by huge majorities during the previous half-century, and speculated whether history was about to repeat itself. To a large extent it did. While the second term brought Reagan some success, it also brought him a full measure of frustration, setback, and scandal. The President soon discovered that Congress, seeking as usual to recover lost ground after a period of presidential hegemony, was no longer the compliant body it had been during his first term. In the summer of 1985 it refused Reagan's request for military aid to the Nicaraguan Contras, rejected his deficit-cutting proposals and forced him to accept distasteful compromises over his budget. Then in December, after years of paying lip service to balanced budgets while distributing government largesse on a scale guaranteed to ensure huge deficits, Congress responded to public clamor for action by passing the Gramm–Rudman–Hollings Act which established a supposedly automatic process of cuts that would eliminate the deficit by 1991. Despite his fears that the measure would necessitate cuts in defense spending or increased taxes or both, Reagan signed it. But anyone who expected that Gramm–Rudman would instill fiscal responsibility into Washington was to be disappointed. Instead of making a genuine attempt to keep spending within the prescribed deficit limits, both the Administration and Congress looked for ways to evade them. Despite a variety of budget-accounting maneuvers, like moving items on and off the budget, the Gramm–Rudman targets were not met and the elimination of the deficit remained a pipe-dream.

Reagan had committed himself at every opportunity to tax reform but a revolt in his own party in December 1985 sidetracked the plan for which he had been campaigning vigorously all over the country. Smarting from the setback, the President lobbied hard to breathe life into a moribund, Democrat-sponsored tax bill which differed in many respects from his own but had broadly similar aims. Despite the opposition of special interests, months of intense presidential pressure resulted in the most sweeping tax revision since World War II. The Tax Reform Act of September 1986 reduced the number of tax-rate brackets from fourteen to just two, lowered the maximum individual tax-rate from 50 to 27 percent and removed more than six million low-income earners from the tax rolls. While the top rate of corporate tax was also reduced, the Act shifted much of the tax burden from individuals to corporations by sharply curtailing tax shelters and ending the various tax credits that business had used to reduce tax bills.

Earlier that year tragedy had befallen the manned space program. With fifteen shuttle missions planned, 1986 was to have been the most

ambitious year for NASA (National Aeronautics and Space Administration) since the days of the moon-landing. But just over one minute
after lift-off from Cape Canaveral on January 28 the space shuttle
Challenger exploded, killing its seven astronauts. The disaster, by casting
doubt on America's technological competence in a field which had come
to symbolize the national purpose, dealt a sickening blow to American
self-esteem. Subsequent investigation showed the cause of the tragedy to
have been an explosion in an external fuel tank resulting from the rupture of a rubber seal on one of the solid-rocket boosters. But it also
revealed that NASA had known about the seal's faulty design, yet had
allowed the shuttle to continue flying. The entire space program was
brought to a halt. Two and a half years of redesign passed before it was
resumed.

In the mid-term elections of 1986 the Republicans suffered a reverse.
Although Reagan tried, by campaigning in twenty-two states, to turn the
elections into a referendum about himself he found that he could not
translate his immense personal popularity into votes for his supporters.
Most of his favored candidates lost, and the Democrats, while increasing
their majority in the House, gained eight Senate seats to recapture the
control they had lost in 1980. The fact that he would now face an opposition Congress did not mean that Reagan had become a lame duck
President; but his scope for new initiatives was reduced.

The Reshaping of the Supreme Court

Reagan and his more ideologically committed supporters had long cherished the hope that the most enduring legacy of his Presidency would be
a more conservative Supreme Court. Such a body could be expected to
complete the unfinished business of the Reagan revolution, overturn a
generation of liberally charged judicial decisions on social issues and
shape the Court's future direction for years to come. The conservative
capture of the lower federal courts was fairly easily achieved: during his
Presidency Reagan was able to appoint a total amounting to half the circuit and district judges. But he found it more difficult to recast the
Supreme Court into a more congenial mold. Neither the appointment of
two new conservatives, Antonin Scalia and Sandra Day O'Connor—the
latter the first woman to become a Supreme Court justice—nor the promotion of Associate Justice William H. Rehnquist to the Chief
Justiceship when Warren E. Burger retired in 1986 altered the political
complexion of the Court fundamentally. It was still evenly divided, its
verdicts on significant issues often reached by a margin of five to four,
with Justice Lewis Powell voting on some occasions with the conservatives, on others with the liberals. But Powell's resignation in the summer
of 1987 gave the President the opportunity to replace a swing-voter with
a dedicated conservative. His choice of Robert Bork, a federal district

judge and a former Yale law professor, was the signal for a bruising confirmation battle. Bork's liberal opponents had no fault to find with him as a jurist or with his general competence, but blacks, women's groups, and trade unionists were affronted by the judicial philosophy and political views he had expressed in his writings and speeches. Claiming that a judge could apply broadly expressed constitutional rights only as the framers of the Constitution had intended, Bork had publicly questioned the legitimacy of the landmark Civil Rights Act of 1964—though he later modified his stand—as well as the reasoning behind Supreme Court decisions recognizing a constitutional right to privacy, from which abortion and homosexual rights were derived. Reagan contemptuously dismissed the anti-Bork campaigners as a "lynch mob", but his efforts to win support for his nominee foundered when confirmation hearings strengthened the feeling that Bork was more concerned to generalize about the law than to promote justice and, moreover, that he was out of touch with public opinion on moral issues. In the end the Senate rejected him by a vote of 58–42, the largest margin ever recorded against a Supreme Court nominee. After Bork's rejection the President nominated a second conservative, Judge Douglas Ginsburg, whose candidacy promptly crumbled when it emerged that he had earlier smoked marijuana. A third nominee, Judge Anthony Kennedy, who was deemed to share Bork's conservative outlook but not his constitutional theories, finally won the approval of a Senate by now weary of the struggle.

Reagan's appointments to the Court eventually resulted in its decisions becoming more conservative, at least on matters affecting criminal procedure, individual liberties, and civil rights. The Court ruled that coerced confessions did not necessarily invalidate trials; it also curtailed the rights of immigrants to claim asylum and of prisoners on death row to challenge the death penalty. And although in the Johnson case (1987) it expanded affirmative action by ruling explicitly that racial minorities and women could receive preferential treatment, it decided in *Wards Cove* v. *Atonio* (1987) that the onus lay with plaintiffs to prove job discrimination. Yet to the dismay and anger of many conservatives the Court did not—even after Reagan's successor, George Bush, had appointed two additional conservative justices—move nearly as far to the right on social issues as they had hoped and expected. Not for the first time Supreme Court justices surprised the Presidents who had chosen them, on this occasion by behaving with unexpected moderation. Arguing that for it to discard legal precedents without compelling reasons would jeopardize its legitimacy, the Court refused either to withdraw its earlier prohibition of any form of school prayer or to overthrow its 1973 decision in *Roe* v. *Wade*, which had established a constitutional right to abortion.

Corruption and Scandal

The 1980s witnessed a wave of corruption, in government and out, that recalled the excesses of the Grant era after the Civil War—though, like Grant, Reagan was innocent of personal wrongdoing. An unusually large number of top-level presidential appointees, including Cabinet members, were either indicted on criminal charges or resigned under a cloud. None was censured by the White House. On Wall Street fraud and deceit ran riot, encouraged—so critics alleged—by the ethos of greed that had developed out of the administration's emphasis on the pursuit of self-interest. By means of insider trading, stock manipulation, and other illegalities a number of investment bankers and arbitrageurs made vast profits, especially in the market for the high-risk, high-yield "junk-bonds" which fuelled the decade's corporate takeover boom. Reagan's deregulation policy hampered the efforts of the Securities and Exchange Commission to unravel the scandal, but in the end such prominent offenders as Michael Milken, the "junk-bond king", Ivan Boesky, and Dennis Levine were convicted, sentenced to long prison terms, fined enormous sums, and debarred from trading in securities.

In some ways an even worse financial scandal was the collapse of hundreds of thrifts—Savings and Loan Associations or S&Ls—the American equivalent of Britain's building societies. Between 1980 and 1988 no fewer than 517 S&Ls closed, four times as many as between 1934 and 1979. Most economists put the blame on the deregulation of the savings and loan industry under the Depositary Institutions Act of 1982. By giving the thrifts greater freedom in the kind of loans they could make and the securities they could buy, the measure encouraged them to speculate wildly in the commercial property market, with catastrophic results when the property boom collapsed in the late 1980s. But the damage caused by deregulation might have been contained had not Congress successively and over-generously raised the limit on federally insured individual deposits to $100,000. Thus while the thrifts were free to keep any profits they might make from speculation, taxpayers footed the bill for the losses. Adding further to the thrifts' troubles was deliberate looting by some owners. Since both political parties had been equally culpable in their neglect of the problem, as well as in protecting fraudulent S&L owners in exchange for campaign contributions, the crisis was ignored until the Bush administration chose to address it. The rescue measure it pushed through Congress in August 1989 provided $160 billion to close or merge insolvent thrifts, but the total cost to the American taxpayer over the coming thirty years was estimated at $400 billion.

Deteriorating ethical standards also invaded the world of evangelical religious broadcasting, producing a series of sexual and financial scandals. In 1987 Jim Bakker, a Pentecostal preacher and founder of the PTL

(Praise the Lord) organization, whose enterprises included a religious television network and a Christian theme park, was dismissed by his church after allegations of adultery. When details of his lavish lifestyle emerged he was indicted on charges of fraud and conspiracy and, having been convicted, was fined $500,000 and sentenced to forty-five years in prison. The following year Jimmy Swaggart, the wealthiest and most popular of the television preachers, whose sermons featured fiery denunciations of pornography and prostitution, was suspended by his Assemblies of God church, allegedly for sexual impropriety. Meanwhile the Reverend Oral Roberts, the operator of a television ministry, university, and medical center at Tulsa, Oklahoma, had outraged even some of his own flock by announcing that God would "call him home" unless $8 million was subscribed to his troubled empire. Once the required sum had been raised, Roberts disclosed that God had "spared him".

The Iran–Contra Affair

During his first term Reagan had been, in deed if not in word, prudent and watchful in his handling of foreign affairs. But in his second term these qualities deserted him for a time and a pattern developed of such confusion and misjudgment as to leave American foreign policy in turmoil and to raise fundamental doubts about the President's competence. His first blunder stemmed from his eagerness to strike a deal on arms control with the Soviet Union, led since 1985 by Mikhail S. Gorbachev, who needed such a deal in order to finance his domestic reforms. Reagan, for all his denunciation of "the evil empire", had for some time been seeking ways of reaching an agreement with the Soviet Union that would eventually eliminate the nuclear threat. A hastily convened meeting with Gorbachev in Iceland in October 1986, intended merely to pave the way for a full-scale summit, turned suddenly into a serious negotiation when the Soviet Union surprised the Americans with far-reaching proposals for nuclear arms cuts. Forgetting his own advice to be on guard when dealing with the Soviet Union, Reagan was drawn into a bidding duel which culminated in his proposing a ban on all nuclear weapons within ten years. Much to the relief of America's NATO allies, who had not been consulted about the proposal but whose defense strategy it would have undermined, the bargaining broke up when Gorbachev insisted that any agreement must include strict limits on the American Strategic Defense Initiative, a condition to which the President was immovably opposed.

Administration spokesmen attempted with some success to present the Iceland debacle as a creditable failure. But they could do nothing to disguise what soon became the most damaging episode of the Reagan years—the Iran–Contra affair. Early in November 1986, news began to trickle out that the United States, with Israeli help, had been secretly selling arms to Iran in order to secure the release of American hostages held in Lebanon by Iran-inspired Islamic terrorists—despite the fact that the Reagan administration had consistently condemned negotiation with terrorists and had repeatedly exhorted America's allies not to sell arms to Iran. During the next few months it emerged further that a group of administration officials, operating from within the White House, had channeled the proceeds of the Iran arms sales to the Nicaraguan Contras though Congress had, at various times and in various ways, forbidden such assistance. The key figure in these shadowy deals had been a relatively obscure security official, Lieutenant-Colonel Oliver P. North, who had acted with the express approval of his immediate superior, the National Security Adviser, Vice-Admiral John M. Poindexter, as well as that of the director of the CIA, William Casey. Questioned about his own role President Reagan at first claimed that his purpose in shipping arms to Iran had been, not to secure the release of hostages, but to forge new links with Teheran moderates. But he soon retracted this claim. He also affirmed that he had known nothing about the diversion of the deal's profits to the Contras. A three-man investigating commission appointed by the President accepted his explanations and did no more than reprove him for his detached style of leadership. But a joint Congressional investigating committee which held televised hearings in the spring and summer of 1987 took a harsher view. It found that Reagan had created or tolerated a climate in which secrecy, dishonesty, and disregard for the law seemed acceptable. A "cabal of zealots", as its report called those who had carried forward the Iran–Contra policy, had disregarded the opposition of senior Cabinet members, lied to Congress, and covered up their activities by burning, shredding, and altering documents. On the recommendation of a special prosecutor, criminal indictments were instituted against Poindexter and North. In 1990 Poindexter was convicted of obstructing or making false statements to Congress and served a six-month sentence; North was found guilty of similar charges but his conviction was later set aside on a technicality. For Reagan the Iranian fiasco was an unmitigated disaster. It undermined his anti-terrorist policy, soured relationships with America's allies and with Congress, and badly dented the President's aura of invincibility. Nor did the arms sales put a stop to Iranian hostage-taking.

Nonetheless Reagan was able to round off his troubled second term and restore his popularity with an arms reduction agreement, modest in comparison with what had seemed briefly within reach in Iceland, but significant all the same. Gorbachev had removed a major stumbling block in February 1987 when he had dropped the linkage between strategic nuclear weapons and Star Wars. But it took protracted and highly technical negotiations before he and Reagan were able to meet in Washington in December to sign the INF Treaty providing for the destruction of their respective intermediate-range (between 300 and 3,000 miles) land-based nuclear forces over a period of three years. Since the Soviet Union had more missiles in this category than the United States the cuts were asymmetrical—only 859 American Pershing-2 missiles were to be destroyed as against 1,752 Soviet SS-20s. Provision was also made for on-site inspection to verify adherence to the agreement. The INF Treaty deprived the two superpowers of only a small fraction of their nuclear arsenals, and deep disagreements persisted over ways of reducing the numbers of strategic long-range missiles. But it was the first time that agreement had been reached to eliminate a whole class of weapons systems.

Reaganism in Retrospect

Ronald Reagan ended his eight years in the White House more popular than when he entered it, and with a poll rating substantially higher than that of Eisenhower, his closest rival for enduring popularity in the period since World War II. Despite the vicissitudes and tribulations of his second term, when his Presidency had seemed in danger of unraveling, he still dominated the political scene. Yet the agenda he had announced on taking office had been completed only in part. As the political analyst Richard Scamman remarked, "the Reagan revolution never moved as far as many on the left feared it would, or many on the right hoped it would". Taxes had been drastically cut, yet in 1988 Americans paid only marginally less of their GNP in taxation than in 1980; the proportion of GNP that went on federal expenditure hardly altered during the period, and Reaganomics failed to reduce the scale of government intervention in the economy, though it may have checked its earlier expansion. And while Reagan presided over the longest economic recovery in the country's history, his successive tax cuts and massive military spending generated unprecedentedly large budget deficits. During the Reagan years the national debt more than doubled, reaching $2.2 trillion in 1989. At the same time, partly in consequence of the budget deficits, America's trade deficit, which had been only $20 billion in Carter's last year, soared to $150 billion in 1988. To be sure, most Americans prospered as the economy expanded but millions did not. During the Reagan years there was a widening of differentials in both income and wealth on a scale not seen since the Great Depression, though the proportion of Americans living below the poverty line actually fell from 13 percent in 1980 to 12.8 percent in 1989.

In foreign affairs Reagan's record was uneven. He tended for too long to view the world through the lens of the Cold War, especially in Central America. His preference for standing back from the day-to-day affairs of government so as to allow his advisers to reach a consensus was responsible, along with the in-fighting between the State Department and the Pentagon, for the purposelessness and disarray that characterized some aspects of his foreign policy, especially in the Middle East. His *rapprochement* with Moscow and his success in reaching agreement on the labyrinthine question of arms control were achievements of major significance, though it remains unclear whether these were due primarily to his own persistence in asserting American interests or to his good fortune in coinciding with a Soviet leadership with the courage to acknowledge the failure of the Communist system. The President could also claim some success for the Reagan Doctrine, with its support for anti-Communist insurgency around the world. When he left office the Russians were withdrawing from Afghanistan, the Cubans from Angola, and the Vietnamese from Cambodia. In Central America the Reagan Doctrine appeared to have failed, but barely a year after he had left office the Nicaraguan Sandinistas fell from power. Reagan's record in the Middle East, on the other hand, was one of unrelieved defeat and humiliation. The misconceived intervention in Lebanon was followed in 1986 by the botched bombing of Libya, which failed either to kill Colonel Gadaffi or end his support of terrorism, and in 1987 by the disastrous Iran–Contra affair.

Yet what Reagan did must be assessed not only in the realm of solid accomplishment but also in less tangible spheres. The histrionic skills he had developed during his Hollywood years stood him in good stead as President. His much-vaunted gifts as a communicator were in fact limited. He was never particularly impressive in press conferences and, except when making a prepared speech, his poor grasp of detail led him into misstatements, exaggerations, and, occasionally, politically unwise and insensitive remarks. Yet such slips did not dent his popularity or reduce his political effectiveness. Partly because he made little attempt to force Americans to face unpleasant truths, partly because he knew how to project himself both as a nice guy and as a convincing symbol of a strong and self-confident America, partly because he had the ability in moments of crisis to invoke patriotism and traditional values so as to set his fellow countrymen's doubts at rest and calm their frayed nerves he achieved a remarkable rapport with the American people and won their support for controversial policies. For a time at least he boosted their morale and gave them a pride in themselves and their country they had not had since the Kennedy era. Moreover, he restored the authority, dignity, and prestige of the Presidency after a long period of decline.

The Presidential Election of 1988

With the departure of a popular incumbent, both parties were left leaderless. There was initially a large field for the Democratic presidential nomination, but after the early favorite, ex-Senator Gary Hart, had dropped out after a sex scandal and the volatile Governor of New York, Mario S. Cuomo, had declined to enter the fray, the contest narrowed down to a duel between Governor Michael S. Dukakis of Massachusetts, the son of Greek immigrants, and the Reverend Jesse Jackson, the fiery black preacher and civil rights activist. Jackson's populist message got a ready response from poor whites as well as from members of his own race but, although he won a string of primaries, his campaign ran out of steam when it became clear that Americans were not ready to elect a black President, or at least not one who held extreme views while lacking both political and administrative experience. Dukakis won the later primaries with ease and was nominated on the first ballot at the Democratic convention in July. Jackson held on to his delegates in the hope of receiving the vice-presidential nomination, but Dukakis made a bid instead for Southern white support by choosing a conservative Texan running mate, Senator Lloyd Bentsen.

George Bush, having served self-effacingly as Reagan's Vice-President for eight years, now aimed once more for the Presidency that had eluded him in 1980. But although the President supported him, Bush was seen by right-wing Republicans not as Reagan's heir but as the embodiment of the moderate, patrician, Eastern wing of the party. He thus had to fend off right-wing challenges for the nomination from Pat Robertson, a Southern Baptist minister, faith healer, and television evangelist and then from the much more formidable Robert Dole of Kansas, the Senate minority leader. But after a shaky start Bush dominated the primaries and easily won the Republican nomination. Usually no orator Bush enhanced his standing with an eloquent acceptance speech to the convention, but then raised doubts about his judgment by choosing as his running mate Dan Quayle, a youthful Indiana senator of modest accomplishments, who promptly embarrassed his party with an unconvincing defense to charges of draft-dodging during the Vietnam War.

The uninspiring campaign finally degenerated into mud-slinging. Largely ignoring the issues, both parties spent lavishly on television advertisements attacking the opposing candidate's record. While the Democrats accused Bush of having known more about the Iran–Contra affair than he had admitted, the Republicans depicted Dukakis as weak on defense, soft on crime, negligent on pollution, and lacking in patriotism. Some observers believed that Republican negative campaigning, some of it scurrilous and incendiary, was responsible for turning the election Bush's way. Others thought that Dukakis lost crucial ground through his flabbiness in counter-attack and his rambling and apparently cold-hearted answers in a television "debate". At all events Dukakis' seventeen-point lead in the polls in July turned into a ten-point lead for Bush by October.

On polling day Bush won comfortably to become the first sitting Vice-President since Martin Van Buren in 1836 to be elected directly to the Presidency. He carried 38 states with 426 electoral votes, while Dukakis won only 10 states and the District of Columbia for a total of 112 electoral votes. However, with 46 percent of the popular vote Dukakis did much better than most recent Democratic presidential nominees; he won clusters of states in the Northeast, the Middle West and the Pacific Northwest and narrowly failed to win others, including the big states of Pennsylvania, Illinois, and Missouri. Bush won decisively in the South, the Southwest, and the Rocky Mountain states, held on to California with a margin much smaller than Reagan's in 1984, and carried nearly all the Middle Western farm belt as well as the whole of New England. But his coattails were not long enough to benefit his party in the Congressional elections; the Democrats increased their majority in the House to 89 and took 56 of the 100 seats in the Senate.

Bush and the End of the Cold War

During George Bush's Presidency the international scene was more dramatically transformed than for half a century. The Cold War ended abruptly and with it superpower domination of world affairs. Simultaneously, democratic change overtook authoritarian regimes in widely separated parts of the globe: in Nicaragua, Chile, South Africa, and, most spectacularly, in the Soviet satellites in Central and Eastern Europe and in the Soviet Union itself. Overshadowing all else was the collapse of Soviet power. Whether due, as some have argued, to the inherent unworkability in the long run of the Communist system or, as others have contended, to the pressures of four decades of American containment policy and the resulting arms race, the shriveling of the Soviet Empire marked the attainment of what had been since 1945 the principal goal of American foreign policy. But that did not imply that the United States could now afford to give foreign affairs a lower priority. Tension and turmoil persisted in many parts of the globe, notably in Central America and the Middle East. Moreover the end of the Cold War meant that the relative stability and simplicities of a bipolar world had been replaced by confusion and unpredictability.

Although Bush entered the White House with more experience of foreign affairs than almost any of his predecessors, his handling of the diplomatic crises that developed early in his Presidency was naive, uncertain, and inconsistent. His reaction to the Chinese Communist government's ruthless use of troops to crush the mass student demonstrations in favor of democracy in Tiananmen Square, Beijing, in June 1989 showed him at his worst. He joined in the worldwide condemnation of Deng Xiaoping and promptly suspended military sales to China. Nonetheless he allowed himself to believe that his acquaintanceship with the Chinese, dating from his years as ambassador to Beijing, afforded him an opportunity to change their attitudes by means of personal diplomacy, of which he was a dedicated proponent. Thus within weeks of the Tiananmen Square massacre he secretly sent his National Security adviser, Brent Scowcroft, to China in an attempt to improve relations. But the mission, which provoked a chorus of protest in the United States when news of it leaked out, did nothing to soften Chinese intransigence. Neither did Bush's other attempts to accommodate the Chinese, which included vetoing a bill extending the visas of Chinese students in the United States, and waiving a congressional ban on loans to companies doing business with China.

In Central America, on the other hand, Bush was not prepared to pay court to revolutionary Marxist regimes. Like his predecessor he clung to a simplistic geopolitical analysis of the region's ills. Hence in Nicaragua he persisted in seeing President Daniel Ortega's Sandinista government merely as the arm of Soviet and Cuban power. Accordingly he would not endorse the peace plan devised by President Oscar Arias of Costa Rica and his fellow Central American Presidents, but continued to send aid to the Contras while maintaining a blockade which all but crippled the Nicaraguan economy. Whether the damage done by the American embargo was the decisive factor in undermining support for Ortega has been questioned. At all events he was surprisingly and heavily defeated in the presidential election of February 1990 by the leader of a loose opposition coalition, Violeta Barrios de Chamorro. Washington, which had expected that the election would be rigged, as taken aback by the result and even more astounded when Ortega accepted it and surrendered power. However, the Sandinistas · still had a large following and Chamorro, faced with the necessity of reviving a shattered economy after many years of civil war, sought their support by appointing Ortega's brother, Humberto, as head of the armed forces.

In Panama Bush resorted to force in order to unseat a regime the United States had belatedly come to detest. For several years after he came to power in 1981 the Panamanian dictator, General Manuel Noriega, had been on close terms with Washington and especially with the CIA to which he had secretly supplied information about Central America. The Reagan administration, obsessed with overthrowing the Nicaraguan Sandinistas, had for long chosen to turn a blind eye to Noriega's notorious drug-trafficking. But after the Irangate disclosures in 1987 the working alliance with Noriega was abruptly terminated and in February 1988 federal grand juries in Florida indicted him of conspiring with a Colombian drug cartel to smuggle drugs into the United States. Despite the imposition of American economic sanctions Noriega remained in power and when presidential elections were held in May 1989 he nullified the results and declared his own candidate the winner. Bush then urged the Panamanian people to overthrow him, but when an attempted coup failed and the plotters were executed he took no action. Two months later he was given a golden opportunity to do so when the Panamanian National Assembly proclaimed Noriega head of state and announced that a state of war existed with the United States. On December 20, after a series of incidents including the killing of a United

States marine by Panamanian soldiers, Bush ordered the invasion of Panama. Resistance collapsed within days, but although only twenty-three American servicemen were killed, there were heavy Panamanian civilian casualties and enormous damage to property, caused mainly by looting. A center-right government was installed, headed by Guillermo Endara, the rightful winner of the May election, while Noriega, who had taken refuge in the Vatican diplomatic mission, surrendered to American forces and was taken to Miami to be charged with racketeering, cocaine-smuggling, and money-laundering. After well over a year in jail he was brought to trial and in March 1992 he became the first foreign ex-head of state to be convicted by an American jury. He was sentenced to forty years in prison. The Bush administration claimed that the overthrow of Noriega had struck a fatal blow at drug-traffickers, but in reality it made little difference to America's drug problems. While most Americans approved of Bush's intervention in Panama, liberals—and many foreign observers—were unhappy with his revival of "big stick" diplomacy in America's backyard, especially at a time when the United States was castigating the Soviet Union for using force in neighboring Afghanistan.

Of the many diplomatic problems to emerge during Bush's Presidency perhaps the most perplexing were those resulting from the Communist retreat from empire. This began early in 1989 with the Soviet withdrawal from Afghanistan after a decade of involvement in a costly civil war. Then in a speech in Strasburg in July Gorbachev in effect reversed long-established Soviet policy by declaring that any interference in the domestic affairs of other countries was inadmissible. This appeared to give a green light to the liberal reform movements under way in eastern Europe and, during the next six months, one Communist regime after another yielded to popular pressure for change. Poland and Hungary led the way, to be followed first by Czechoslovakia and Bulgaria and then by East Germany and Romania. The opening of the Berlin Wall in November 1989 removed the most tangible symbol of the Cold war and foreshadowed a rapid advance toward German reunification, duly achieved in October 1990. Meanwhile in the Soviet Union itself Gorbachev's reforms resulted not in the revitalization of the economy but in stagnation and chaos, made worse by the separatist tendencies which grew out of revived ethnic and national rivalries. An attempted *coup d'état* against Gorbachev by hard-line Communists in August 1991 failed within days, but his authority had been fatally compromised and ten of the Soviet Union's fifteen constituent republics seized the opportunity to declare their independence. By the end of the year the Soviet Union had been replaced by a loose Commonwealth of Independent States, the Soviet Communist Party had been dissolved and Gorbachev had given way as Russian President to Boris Yeltsin.

Some critics have complained that Bush should have responded more promptly to the tumultuous events in eastern Europe and the Soviet Union, and have accused him of lacking a coherent strategy for the end of the Cold War. They point to the fact that, even after the Warsaw Pact Alliance had broken up and Gorbachev had reduced military spending and withdrawn large parts of the Red Army from eastern Europe, Bush was slow to follow suit. He did not in fact do so until the last year of his Presidency. But in 1990–1 he was very conscious of the fact that the Soviet Union, besides possessing an awesome nuclear arsenal, still had the largest army in the world. In any case the disintegrating Soviet Union was an enigma to everyone and Bush may have come nearer to comprehending it than most outside observers, certainly nearer than most European leaders. In his handling of Soviet–American relations he avoided both triumphalism and rashness. He sought to facilitate the process of reform Gorbachev had initiated and to discourage him from resorting to large-scale force against opponents in the Baltic states or elsewhere in the Soviet Empire. He also persuaded Gorbachev to accept German reunification at a time when other Western leaders were opposed to it. To achieve these goals Bush again relied heavily on personal diplomacy, this time with far better success than it had achieved for him with the Chinese. He and Gorbachev transformed East–West relations by developing a rapport so close as to be called a "partnership"—though, ironically, they each did so at the cost of losing touch with their domestic constituencies. Their greatest achievement was an historic agreement to reduce stockpiles of nuclear weapons. Signed on July 31, 1991, the Strategic Arms Reduction Treaty (START) had been the subject of negotiation since 1982 and was the first to reduce, rather than simply limit, long-range nuclear arms: it provided for the reduction of strategic offensive weapons by 30 percent in three phases over seven years. This was followed in September by Bush's announcement that, since a Soviet invasion of western Europe was "no longer a realistic threat", the United States would eliminate all its tactical nuclear weapons on land and at sea in Europe and Asia. In January 1992 Bush proposed drastic reductions in the military budget and announced the cancellation or curtailment of a number of missile programs. Then in June he and Yeltsin agreed in principle to further major reductions in strategic nuclear weapons. The United States and Russia, which at that date possessed about 10,000 nuclear warheads apiece, agreed to reduce their totals by the year 2003 to 3,500 and 3,000 respectively.

The Gulf War

The first great crisis of the post-Cold War era developed in the Persian Gulf. On August 2, 1990 the Iraqi dictator, Saddam Hussein, invaded and subsequently annexed the tiny neighboring emirate of Kuwait. Besides invoking a long-standing boundary dispute, he claimed that

Kuwait had depressed world oil prices by exceeding the quota set by the Organization of Petroleum Exporting States (OPEC). These were, however, mere pretexts: the real reason for the invasion was Iraq's financial difficulties. Iraq's treasury had been drained by the eight-year war with Iran and its oil revenues, though great, were insufficient to maintain its massive military machine. The seizure of Kuwait gave Saddam control of over 20 percent of the world's oil reserves, and the potential to control nearly half by dominating the Southern Gulf states. The Bush administration may inadvertently have invited the attack. Even after the Iranian revolution had run out of steam it had remained obsessed with the threat posed by Iran and, still seeing Iraq as a crucial regional counterweight, had supplied Saddam with huge quantities of advanced military technology. Moreover, because of an understandable preoccupation with Europe after the dismantling of the Berlin Wall, the United States had failed to react vigorously to Saddam's growing belligerence.

The Iraqi leader had calculated that the rest of the world would not intervene in a dispute between Arab neighbors. But the UN Security Council promptly condemned the invasion, demanded an Iraqi withdrawal and imposed a trade and financial embargo. On August 7 President Bush dispatched military forces to Saudi Arabia to deter a possible Iraqi incursion and, with great diplomatic skill, assembled against Iraq an unprecedentedly broad international coalition, including both the Soviet Union and a number of moderate Arab countries. On November 8 the President ordered an increase of US forces in the Gulf to 400,000 so as to make possible offensive military action, and on November 29, at the urging of the United States, the UN authorized the use of force against Iraq if it did not withdraw from Kuwait by January 15.

To begin with nearly all Americans approved of Bush's handling of the crisis, but as the deadline for withdrawal approached, support began to evaporate. Peace activists, drawing on the legacy of Vietnam, held rallies to oppose war as morally unjustifiable. Some journalists and religious leaders became dubious about the impending war, fearing massive American casualties and the prospect of inflaming the whole of Islam. Many Democrats wanted more time for economic sanctions to work, while Congressional leaders were adamant that, even though the President had obtained UN sanction for military action, he had no constitutional right to commit American troops to battle without explicit Congressional approval. On January 10 Congress began debating a resolution authorizing the use of force. Two days later this passed the House fairly comfortably (250–183), but the margin in the Senate was slim (52–47).

By this time the American expeditionary force in the Gulf had grown to more than 500,000—the largest American military deployment since Vietnam. Other members of the coalition committed a further 250,000 troops, the largest contingents being supplied by Saudi Arabia, the United Kingdom, Egypt, Syria, and France. But as in the Korean War, Operation Desert Storm (as the Gulf conflict was to become known) was essentially an American war, with an American general, H. Norman Schwarzkopf, in overall command of the Allied forces. American intelligence assessments of Iraqi military capacity proved to be greatly exaggerated and in the event the Allied armies, far from being inferior in strength as the Pentagon had predicted, enjoyed a two-to-one advantage in manpower and an overwhelming superiority in military technology, technique, training, and fire-power. Accordingly the war was short, one-sided, and on the Allied side almost completely bloodless.

The fighting began on January 17 with a series of devastating air attacks on Baghdad and other Iraqi targets by Allied bombers based in Saudi Arabia and Turkey and by sea-launched Tomahawk cruise missiles. Iraqi air defenses proved vulnerable to such products of American high technology as laser-guided missiles and electronic jamming. Within days Iraq's airfields were unusable and its air force neutralized, whereupon the Allied air assault was broadened to include communications systems, power stations, missile-launching sites, and plants producing nuclear, chemical, and biological weapons. Although it emerged after the war that 70 percent of the bombs dropped on Iraq missed their targets, Allied bombing destroyed much of Iraq's infrastructure and military hardware. Saddam's only way of hitting back was by using mobile missile-launchers to fire Soviet-made SCUD missiles at Saudi Arabia and Israel. But these caused only slight damage and casualties, in part because the United States promptly installed Patriot anti-missile batteries as protection against incoming SCUDs. Nor, contrary to Saddam's hopes, did his SCUD attacks provoke the Israelis to retaliate or weaken Arab support for the coalition. And when in desperation the Iraqis deliberately released oil into the shallow waters of the Gulf and set fire to some 600 Kuwaiti oil wells, Allied military operations were unaffected, though grievous damage was inflicted on the environment.

On February 27, after five weeks of unremitting air bombardment, the Allies launched a full-scale, multipronged ground offensive against the Iraqis. Four days sufficed for General Schwarzkopf to win a stunning victory. Having induced Saddam to concentrate his forces in Kuwait by the threat of an amphibious landing, he outflanked them by surreptitiously moving much of his army inland, a maneuver which permitted a quick breakthrough into Kuwait and a deep thrust into southern Iraq. The demoralized Iraqi army was overwhelmed, losing tens of thousands of prisoners, besides 4,000 tanks and 3,000 artillery weapons. On February 27 President Bush announced a conditional cease-fire, which the Iraqis promptly accepted. The US Defense Department estimated that 100,000 Iraqi soldiers had been killed in the fighting and 300,000 had been wounded. Allied casualties were astonishingly light: fewer than 200 Allied soldiers died in combat, 137 of them American.

Whether Bush acted prematurely in calling a halt to the fighting when he did has been much debated. The cease-fire came with the Iraqi army beaten and in flight, but with enough of Saddam's Republican Guard intact to enable him to continue in power. Many people in the West subsequently wished that Allied war aims had been extended to cover his overthrow, and some have argued that had the war gone on for only a few more days, Baghdad would have fallen and Saddam and his Republican Guard would have been fatally weakened. But Bush, though prepared to encourage Iraqi dissidents to stage a palace coup, was constrained by the fact that he had no mandate for ousting Saddam and feared that neither the international coalition nor American public opinion would have condoned an overt attempt to change Iraq's internal politics.

In the United States the Gulf War victory initially evoked an outburst of patriotic fervor: for some it served to banish the specter of Vietnam. But by the time the victory parades were held in June, euphoria had given way to feelings of ambiguity and disappointment. While the President's avowed aim of liberating Kuwait had been speedily and skilfully accomplished, the war had done little or nothing to advance America's less explicit goals in the Middle East. Saddam Hussein, now widely hailed as an Islamic hero, was as firmly in control of Iraq as ever, able both to obstruct the work of UN inspectors charged with finding and destroying his weapons of mass destruction and to renew his persecution of minority Kurds and Shiites whom President Bush, incidentally, had encouraged to rebel only to abandon them. Far from improving the prospects for democracy and human rights in the Gulf States, the war propped up corrupt and despotic regimes, of which the restored Al Sabah family in Kuwait was one of the shabbiest examples. Further, the war did not bring peace and stability to the Gulf, nor pave the way for Arab–Israeli understanding. Nor, finally, did it inaugurate the "new world order" Bush had predicted. The international coalition organized against Iraq did not become the model for further acts of cooperation against threats to peace. Admittedly the disintegration of the Soviet Union removed America's chief intended partner in such efforts, but more than anything else it was the Bush administration's confused and supine response to the second great crisis in the post-Cold War era, the war in former Yugoslavia, that wrecked what hope remained of a new world order.

Bush at Bay: Recession, Taxation, Racial Tension

In the euphoria engendered by the successful conclusion of the Gulf War, George Bush's popularity soared to new heights: a Gallup poll in March

1991 found that 89 percent of the American people approved of the way he was doing his job. But it was not long before the fragility of his popularity was exposed. Immediately the Gulf War was over, the President's approval rating plummeted and went on falling until in September 1992 it reached a low of 32 percent. The main reason was that, after seven booming years, the economy turned sharply downward in the summer of 1990 and remained stagnant for the rest of Bush's Presidency. Unemployment rose inexorably, reaching 10 million in July 1992; corporate and personal bankruptcies multiplied; residential property values fell by almost a third, commercial property values by even more. While the recession spread to all parts of the country, its worst effects were on the east coast, especially New England, and the Pacific coast states; the Middle West, the Gulf States, and the Rocky Mountain region were relatively unscathed. Unlike previous recessions, whose chief victims had been factory workers, clerks, and farmers, this one cut a swathe through America's professional and managerial elite—accountants, lawyers, engineers, bankers, stockbrokers, advertizing executives, journalists, property agents, and computer technicians. Giant corporations like American Telephone and Telegraph (AT&T) and International Business Machines (IBM), which had long boasted that their employees had jobs for life, now suddenly cut tens of thousands from their payrolls.

Even while the recession was in its earliest stages, however, Bush's political fortunes had begun to decline because of his volte-face on taxes. During his 1988 election campaign he had made a clear but reckless pledge: "Read my lips: no new taxes." But by the summer of 1990 he had become persuaded that "tax revenue increases" were necessary to reduce the ballooning federal deficit, which had been further worsened by the cost of bailing out insolvent thrifts. In October, after tough bargaining with Congressional negotiators, he signed a deficit-reduction bill which raised the top rate of individual income tax from 27 to 31 percent, removed exemptions from high earners, increased taxes on gasoline, cigarettes, and alcohol, and imposed a luxury tax on items like furs and jewelry. Bush's abandonment of the main plank of his domestic policy incensed Republican Congressmen, some of whom charged him with betrayal. It also undermined his credibility with the voters.

In the fall of 1991 a judicial nomination Bush had considered routine suddenly took on the quality of melodrama. To succeed the recently retired Thurgood Marshall, the first black to be appointed to the United States Supreme Court, the President nominated Clarence Thomas, a black federal judge who had been raised in poverty in rural, segregated Georgia before graduating from Yale Law School. Whereas Marshall, throughout his long years on the Court had been a foe of racial and gender discrimination and a determined upholder of liberal values, Thomas had questioned the constitutionality of the right to abortion, criticized affirmative action programs, and spoken dismissively of civil-rights leaders. Although the American Bar Association was unusually grudging in endorsing Thomas's nomination, Bush claimed he was the best choice for the position. The conservative views that had commended Thomas to the administration ensured the opposition of the same coalition of civil-rights activists and women's organizations that had wrecked Robert Bork's chances in 1987. Yet since Thomas had the support of most blacks, he seemed likely to be confirmed without difficulty until Anita Hill, a black law professor, accused him of having sexually harassed her when they had worked together ten years earlier in the Education Department and the Equal Opportunities Employment Commission. Once Hill's allegations were made public, support for Thomas ebbed among both Democrats and Republicans. During three days of televised confirmation hearings before the Senate Judiciary Committee in which, amid scenes of extraordinary emotion, Hill reiterated her charges and Thomas angrily denied them, the nation was treated to what many saw as the unedifying spectacle of fifteen white senators, some with dubious moral records, sitting in moral judgment on the two principals. The hearings triggered off a national debate about the sexual intimidation of women at work, raised the political consciousness of women, and drove a wedge into the long-established alliance of feminists and black activists. Many members of his own race sympathized with Thomas when he characterized the proceedings as "a high-tech lynching for uppity blacks", but women were incensed by the unsparing cross-examination of Professor Hill by Republican senators and by Bush's mobilization of senior officials to cast doubt on her credibility when public opinion seemed to be swinging in her favor. The hearings failed to settle the question of who was telling the truth, and in the end a narrow majority of senators evidently decided that the danger of angering black conservatives was greater than that of incensing liberal blacks and women. The vote to confirm Thomas (52–48) was the narrowest for any nominee to the Supreme Court in the twentieth century.

The Thomas affair was the prelude to a stark reminder of the racial dimension of America's continuing urban crisis. In April 1992, four white Los Angeles policemen were charged with having savagely assaulted a black motorist, Rodney King, a year earlier. A video-tape of the incident, taken by a bystander, clearly showed King being repeatedly beaten and kicked by the police as he lay on the ground. Yet an all-white jury acquitted the four officers. The verdict, widely held to be incomprehensible and unjust, infuriated the poor blacks of Los Angeles and ignited the worst urban violence in American history. For three days mobs in predominantly black south-central Los Angeles vented their feelings in widespread rioting, looting, and burning. Order was restored only when 7,000 National Guardsmen were sent to the city. The riots left 58 people dead, 4,000 injured, 12,000 arrested, and $1 billion worth of damage.

The riots left Bush floundering. For three years he had held aloof from domestic problems, finding foreign policy more congenial. The problems of the inner cities and their impoverished black inhabitants had only intermittently captured his attention. In November 1991, appalled by the strong showing of a former leader of the Ku Klux Klan in the Louisiana gubernatorial election, he had signed a civil-rights bill not very different from one he had twice vetoed. Now, in an effort to demonstrate his involvement, he paid a brief visit to south-central Los Angeles, the first of his Presidency to any inner-city area. But he seemed more intent on responding to the symptoms of the malaise than on tackling its causes. He condemned the violence and offered federal aid to repair the damage, but went on to blame the riots and the plight of the urban poor on Lyndon Johnson's poverty programs. He also ordered the re-opening of the investigation into the King case, with the result that the four police-men were again indicted, this time for the federal offense of violating King's civil rights. Both conservatives and civil libertarians were uneasy at a second trial without any apparent new evidence, but the conviction of two of the officers of the federal offense in April 1993 served to calm the racial tensions provoked by the case.

The Election of 1992

Bush's broken promise not to raise taxes, together with his fumbling response to the stricken economy, precipitated a right-wing challenge to his renomination from Patrick Buchanan, a newspaper and television commentator and a former presidential assistant. Buchanan's avowed iso-lationism, protectionism, and xenophobia repelled many, but he suc-ceeded in articulating Republican feelings that the President was spending too much time abroad and that he had sold out on key issues. Although Buchanan harried Bush throughout the primaries and piled up a consid-erable protest vote, the loyalty of the Republican party machine ensured that the President was renominated without difficulty. Yet the nominating convention, at Houston in August, turned into a disaster for Bush. Strident speeches by Buchanan and other arch-conservatives, a platform written largely by evangelicals which promised to criminalize abortions and restore school prayers, and the stirring invocations of "family values" by Vice-President Quayle and the First Lady, Barbara Bush, gave the impression that the religious right had taken over the party.

Meanwhile the Democratic party had been redefining itself and moving nearer the political center, processes which climaxed at its nominating convention in New York in July. In the aftermath of the Gulf War many of the biggest names in the party, believing Bush to be unbeatable, had declined to run against him. This had left the way open for Bill Clinton, the young, relatively unknown governor of Arkansas, to emerge as the front-runner. A Yale law graduate and an Oxford Rhodes Scholar,

Clinton had succeeded as governor in attracting investment to his small, impoverished state, and in expanding its educational system while demonstrating a capacity, rare among Democratic politicians, to attract both black and white votes. Scandal threatened to destroy his candidacy when allegations surfaced of adultery, draft-dodging during the Vietnam War, and drug-taking. But, although many found his denials less than wholly convincing, he survived to win primaries in each of the ten largest states—the first Democratic contender to do so—and then to receive his party's nomination for the Presidency. Breaking with the tradition that a vice-presidential candidate should bring regional balance to a party ticket, Clinton made a calculated bid for the Southern vote by choosing as his running mate a fellow Southerner, Senator Al Gore of Tennessee. The choice of the moderate Gore rather than a Northern liberal of the kind the electorate had rejected in the two preceding presidential elections signaled the fact that the Democrats had abandoned their penchant for high taxes, high spending, and wholesale government intervention. Instead they offered a "new covenant", embodying such concepts as partnership between government and business, personal responsibility, and educational training, themes which Clinton expanded in an acceptance speech which focused on what he called "the forgotten middle class".

Meanwhile the political scene had been enlivened by the emergence of an independent presidential candidate, the Texan billionaire, H. Ross Perot. The founder of a highly successful computer-services company, Perot had never held public office, but he drew strength from public disaffection with the Washington political establishment. Apart from promising to eliminate the federal budget deficit and advocating televised town meetings to solve the nation's problems, Perot did not offer specific policies. His popularity grew nonetheless and he was able to by-pass the presidential primaries and the nominating process generally when an army of volunteers responded to his appeal to organize petitions to put his name on the ballot in all fifty states. Yet in July, although ahead of both Bush and Clinton in some polls, he abruptly withdrew from the race on the ground that he could not win and wished to avoid disrupting the country. The following October, barely a month before the election, he changed his mind and reactivated his campaign.

Perot campaigned in only fifteen states, but spent $60 million of his personal fortune in promoting his candidacy on television. The Democrats ran a far more spirited and professional campaign than they had in 1988. Clinton went on a series of highly effective "meet the people" bus tours in which he wooed both suburbanites and inner-city dwellers; and while distancing himself from radical black leaders like Jesse Jackson, presented himself as the champion of minorities, including women and gays. Bush's campaign was, by contrast, one of chronic ineptitude. He waited too long to begin active campaigning, failed to produce a coherent domestic agenda, resorted to undignified personal attacks, and ended by giving the impression that he was out of touch with ordinary people and everyday problems.

On election day the 55 percent turnout was the highest for twenty-four years. Clinton won decisively, capturing thirty-two states and the District of Columbia for a total of 370 electoral votes, against the president's eighteen states and 168 electoral votes. But the popular vote was much closer than the polls had predicted: Clinton got 43 percent against Bush's 38 percent and thus became the first minority President since 1968. The Democrats swept New England and took all the big industrial states in the Middle Atlantic region and, except for Indiana, in the Middle West also. They were victorious too in the Pacific coast states and eroded Republican strength in the Rocky Mountain region. But despite having two Southerners on the ticket, they made only limited gains in Republican bastions in the South: Bush won seven of the eleven former Confederate states, including the two biggest, Texas and Florida. Clinton received the overwhelming support of blacks and Jews but also ran strongly among groups which had been crucial to Republican dominance in the 1980s—Catholics, suburbanites, independents, moderates, and the young. Women voted against Bush in larger numbers than men, perhaps because of his opposition to abortion and his party's hostility to one-parent families. Perot failed to carry a single state but nonetheless did astonishingly well, winning 19 percent of the popular vote, the best showing by any independent or third-party candidate since Theodore Roosevelt's unsuccessful comeback attempt in 1912. This was the first presidential election since 1936 in which foreign policy did not figure prominently among the issues: exit polls showed that voters were concerned primarily about the economy, health care, and education.

In the Congressional elections the Democrats picked up one seat in the Senate and, although they lost nine in the House, continued to control both chambers by large margins. The number of women (47), blacks (38), and Hispanic Americans (17) elected to the House rose sharply, and in voting for the Senate four women newcomers were elected, including Carol Moseley Braun of Illinois, the first black woman to become a United States Senator. A much greater turnover than usual in House membership—no fewer than 109 newcomers were elected—was attributable partly to redistricting to take account of population shifts, but even more to popular anger that incumbent Congressmen had voted to increase their salaries and that many had helped themselves to large overdrafts at the House bank. In a further expression of an anti-incumbent mood, the voters in five states approved measures to limit the terms of members of the House and Senate.

Population and Immigration Trends

The 1990 census showed that the nation's population had grown to more than 248 million, an increase of 22 million or 9.8 percent on the 1980 count. This was the second lowest growth-rate ever recorded: only the 7.3 percent growth during the Depression decade of the 1930s was lower. The census reported increases in the proportion of people over sixty-five and of working mothers, in single-parent households, in unmarried couples sharing a household, and in persons living alone. It also revealed that the racial and ethnic composition of America's population had changed more dramatically in the 1980s than at any other time in the twentieth century. Even though it was widely accepted that the census-takers had seriously undercounted blacks, Hispanics, Asians, and Native Americans, the published statistics nonetheless showed that these groups accounted for more than half the decade's overall population increase and now made up one-quarter of the American population, compared with one-fifth in 1980. The fastest rates of growth occurred in the Sun Belt states of the West and South, the greatest proportionate gainers being Nevada (which grew by 50 percent), Florida, Arizona, and Alaska (up over 30 percent), and California (up 25 percent). The five most populous states were California—where more than one American in ten now lived—New York, Texas, Florida, and Pennsylvania. The census demonstrated further that Americans were clustering in larger and larger communities: more than 90 percent of the growth took place in metropolitan areas of more than one million people, though it was the suburbs rather than the core cities that gained population. But metropolitan growth was not universal. While cities in the Sun Belt registered spectacular gains, with Orlando, Phoenix, Sacramento, and San Diego leading the way, many in declining industrial centres in the North East lost population, the main examples being Detroit, Cleveland, Pittsburgh, and Buffalo. Meanwhile life continued to ebb from the little farm towns long cherished as the cornerstone of American life: in the 1980s, 72 percent of towns whose population was under 2,500 experienced a loss of residents.

The marked change in America's ethnic composition was attributable to immigration, which also accounted for about one-third of the population gain. During the 1980s immigration officials recorded the arrival of 7.3 million newcomers, 65 percent more than in the previous decade. Yet the official figures took no account of an illegal influx whose precise dimensions could only be guessed but which certainly ran into millions. This illegal movement must have boosted total arrivals in the 1980s to more than 10 million, a figure never reached in any previous decade. Even more striking than the scale of immigration was the change in its sources. The shift away from Europe and toward Third World countries unintentionally set in motion by the framers of the 1965 Immigration Act accelerated with time. During the 1980s Europe contributed barely 10 percent of the immigration total, while the Western Hemisphere sent 45 percent and Asia a further 41 per cent. Among countries supplying legal immigrants Mexico easily took first place with 1,655,000, the Philippines came second with 548,000, followed by China (including Taiwan and Hong Kong), Korea, Vietnam, India, El Salvador, the Dominican Republic, and Jamaica, each of which sent well over 200,000.

Despite the huge scale of Third World immigration, fears that the country was being swamped were unfounded. Although the proportion of foreign-born rose from 6.5 percent in 1980 to 7.8 percent in 1990, it remained low by comparison with the peak of 14.7 percent in 1910. Yet in some places immigration had a massive impact. Almost 70 percent of the newcomers settled in six states—California, New York, Florida, Texas, Illinois, and New Jersey—with 40 percent in California and New York alone. In the nation's two largest cities, Los Angeles and New York, more than half the residents consisted of immigrants and their children; in a dozen other cities, including Chicago, San Diego, and San Antonio, the proportion was over one-quarter. In the cities favored by immigrants distinctively different ethnic mosaics developed. Miami's was one of the least varied, its immigrants being overwhelmingly Hispanic, especially Cuban; Los Angeles was more cosmopolitan, for although two-thirds of its newcomers were Hispanic, chiefly Mexican, there were large contingents of Asians, notably Chinese, Koreans, Vietnamese, and Filipinos; in New York City the ethnic mix was bewilderingly miscellaneous, with no one group predominating but with large communities of Dominicans, Haitians, Greeks, Jamaicans, Russian Jews, and Chinese and tens of thousands of people born in Ireland, Korea, India, Columbia, and Ecuador.

Though generally lumped together in American popular consciousness, Asian immigrants had diverse ethnic, religious, and linguistic backgrounds. Yet they had much in common, being preponderantly urban in origin, English-speaking, well-educated, and highly qualified. One-half the Asians had professional or technical qualifications, with the proportion exceeding two-thirds among Filipinos and four-fifths among Indians— Asian Indians as they were known in the United States to avoid confusion with Native Americans. Almost without exception Asians settled in large cities, generally clustering in self-contained residential ghettoes and often concentrating in particular businesses and occupations—Koreans in greengrocery, for example, Indians in newsstands, gas stations, and motel management. By mobilizing the labor of the entire family Asians rose with remarkable speed up the economic ladder. The 1990 census showed that their median family income was higher than that of whites and much higher than that of blacks and Hispanics. Even more impressive were their educational achievements: one-third of Asian immigrants had completed four years of college or more, that is, twice the proportion among whites and four times that among blacks and Hispanics.

While less diverse than Asians, immigrants from Latin America and the Caribbean were far from homogeneous. Though the great majority were Hispanic, a term which implied a shared Spanish-language background, significant numbers spoke English, French, Creole, or other tongues. They were also racially and socially dissimilar. The great majority were *mestizos* (people of mixed Spanish and Indian ancestry), but mulattoes, blacks, and whites were all strongly represented. In the early 1980s a sizable proportion of newcomers from the Dominican Republic, Haiti, Jamaica, and other newly-independent Caribbean countries were professional or white-collar people, who by every measure of achievement were highly successful in the United States. But as the decade wore on they included growing numbers of the unskilled, especially women who became domestic servants. The bulk of Mexican immigrants were by contrast poor, illiterate peasants whose lack of means and skills resulted in their lagging behind other newly-arrived groups economically and socially. Educational levels were depressed, unemployment rates high, and most of those at work had low-paid, dead-end jobs. Investigators, seeking reasons why Chicanos, the nation's second largest minority group should have achieved relatively so little, pointed out that they tended to see themselves as sojourners rather than permanent residents. Maintaining strong linguistic, psychological, and family ties with Mexico through frequent visits to their homeland, many were reluctant to put down roots in the United States or even to learn English.

Renewed mass immigration brought increased ethnic and racial tensions. Miami blacks, fearful of being crowded out of jobs by newly-arrived Cubans, vented their resentment in 1980 in riots which killed eighteen people and caused $100 million worth of damage; in Texas at about the same time angry whites set fire to Vietnamese crab-fishermen's boats and houses after a dispute over fishing rights; in Detroit there were isolated attacks on Arab-Americans during the Gulf War; and during the Los Angeles riots of 1992 Korean businesses were the main targets for black and Hispanic looters and arsonists.

During the decade immigration again became the subject of lively public debate, with attention focused mainly on two questions, refugee policy and illegal immigration. Ever since 1956, when Eisenhower invoked it to admit Hungarian "freedom fighters", presidential parole had been the favored mechanism for bringing in refugees. But some critics disliked the principle it embodied of executive control; others objected to the ideological bias of successive Acts of Congress which defined refugees mainly as people fleeing from Communism. The Refugee Act of 1980 sought to address these concerns. It abolished the parole power, established an enlarged refugee quota, and brought the American definition of refugees into line with international practice by characterizing them as people who fled persecution in any country, not just those with Communist governments. But the expanded refugee quota soon proved too low and had to be successively increased. Moreover, by leaving the allocation of refugee visas to executive discretion, the Act allowed President Reagan to continue the practice of freely admitting refugee applicants from Communist countries like Cuba and the Soviet Union, while excluding asylum-seekers from elsewhere, notably El Salvador and Haiti. Then, after a military coup which deposed the popular President Aristide in September 1991 had set in motion a new and massive exodus from Haiti in flotillas of frail craft, President Bush reactivated his predecessor's policy of intercepting and summarily repatriating those aboard. Even more of the Haitian boat people were excluded when it was reported that 10 percent of those admitted were carrying the AIDS virus.

The issue of illegal immigration, dormant since the mid-1950s, came to the fore again in the late 1970s when the stream of "undocumented aliens", mainly Mexicans, rose to flood proportions. Reagan may have exaggerated when he declared in 1984 that "we have lost control of our borders", but his alarm was widely shared. Some Americans felt that illegal immigrants displaced native-born workers, others complained that they relied unduly on welfare and placed a heavy burden on schools and hospitals. But the search for a remedy was opposed by special interests and it took until November 1986 for the Immigration and Control (Simpson–Rodino) Act to pass. This granted legal status to illegal immigrants who could prove continuous residence in the United States since January 1, 1982 or before, imposed penalties on employers who knowingly employed illegal aliens and provided additional funds for immigration law enforcement. But response to the amnesty program was sluggish, mainly because many illegal aliens feared that application for legal status would result in deportation. Hence only about 1.5 million people, out of an estimated three or four million who would have been eligible, had claimed amnesty by the time the Act expired on May 4, 1988. As had been widely predicted the Act failed to stem the illegal influx. An attempted crackdown, involving expanded border controls, chain-link fences, closed-circuit television monitors and even a 14-foot ditch across the Mexican border, detected only a small fraction of illegal entrants. And despite heavy fines, employers continued to hire aliens whose documents were patently false. The conclusion in August 1992 of a draft North American Free Trade Agreement (NAFTA) between Canada, the United States, and Mexico led to predictions that the growth of the Mexican economy resulting from free trade would mean fewer Mexicans migrating to the United States. But by now, thanks to easygoing law enforcement, widespread fraud, and bureaucratic paralysis, it was not only from Mexico that illegal immigrants were flooding in. Thousands from Ireland and tens of thousands from the former Soviet Union entered on temporary visas and then went underground; Chinese smuggling rings packed increasing numbers into the holds of freighters; and illegal travel through Puerto Rico or the US Virgin Islands enabled many Caribbean islanders to reach the American mainland.

Meanwhile a variety of groups—liberals, businessmen, and Irish-Americans—had been pressing for comprehensive changes to the immigration laws. Their main concern was that more weight should be given to what immigrants could contribute to America and less to whether they had American relatives. But it proved difficult to reconcile competing claims and only after protracted debate was a compromise measure agreed to. The Immigration Act of 1990 provided that the annual ceiling on immigration (not counting refugees) would rise from 490,000 to 700,000 in 1992–4, falling to 675,000 in 1995. More than half the visas for the first three years were to be reserved for close relatives of American citizens or of permanent residents, but the numbers to be admitted because they possessed occupational skills needed in the United States was nearly tripled to 140,000 a year. The claims of politically influential ethnic groups were recognized by setting aside 40,000 visas annually for people from "traditional source countries" like Ireland, Italy, and Poland which had had little recent history of emigration and whose citizens had thus been all but excluded by the family preference system adopted in 1965. Liberals were gratified by two provisions, one granting "safe haven" to Salvadoran refugees, the other ridding the statute book of barriers, some dating back decades, against the entry of Communists, homosexuals, and sufferers from AIDS.

Social Issues: Abortion, AIDS, Drugs, Gun Control

During the Reagan-Bush era no social issue provoked such deep divisions or generated such explosive passions as abortion. Until 1973 the matter had been one for the states but in *Roe* v. *Wade* the Supreme Court had invalidated most state anti-abortion laws, decreeing that women had a constitutional right to abortion during early pregnancy. After that ruling anti-abortionists (or pro-life advocates, as they termed themselves) campaigned to overturn it, while pro-abortionists (or pro-choice supporters, as they preferred to be called) sought to extend abortion rights to the later stages of pregnancy. In the 1980s the attitudes of both sides hardened and the debate became more bitter and emotional. Pro-life organizations spent hugely on publicity, bombarded politicians with literature, attracted support from television evangelists, and introduced scores of anti-abortion bills into state legislatures. Some of the more radical pro-life protestors picketed, besieged, and at times bombed abortion clinics, while harassing and frightening off women who attended them. Pro-choice groups were slower to organize but eventually matched their opponents in everything but violence, besides enlisting women's groups, civil liberty activists, and Hollywood celebrities to lead mass demonstrations against any change in the law. The battle culminated in the summer of 1989 with the Supreme Court's decision in *Webster* v. *Reproductive Health Services*. The Court balked at overturning *Roe* v. *Wade*, as President Bush had hoped, but was deemed to have eroded it by, in effect, encouraging each state to draw up its own abortion laws. Although a few states responded by adopting new restrictions on abortion, a much larger number turned them down. Opinion polls suggested that the American people were confused about the issue: almost half of those polled believed that abortion was tantamount to murder, but 87 percent believed it should be allowed if the woman's health was in danger. The Supreme Court seemed to be equally uncertain. While in a series of cases it upheld statutes which limited the legality of abortion, it reaffirmed in *Planned Parenthood of Pennsylvania* v. *Casey* (1992) that a woman's basic right to choose an abortion was "a rule of law and a component of liberty we cannot renounce".

By far the most alarming social problem of the period was the spread of AIDS (Acquired Immune Deficiency Syndrome), a new and deadly disease for which there was no known cure or treatment. Although the first cases of AIDS to be recognized as such occurred only in 1981, more than 100,000 Americans died of it in the next ten years and between ten and fifteen times as many became infected with the Human Immunodeficiency Virus (HIV). The main groups affected were homosexual men (who accounted for 60 percent of the deaths during the decade) and intravenous drug-users, especially those sharing needles. But it was not long before the disease appeared among heterosexuals of both sexes, as well as among children. It was disproportionately common among racial minorities: in 1989 more than 85 percent of the women with AIDS in New York City were either Hispanic or black—and 90 percent of the children. The two cities worst affected were New York and San Francisco. In New York AIDS became the third largest cause of death, after cancer and heart disease, and the leading killer of women in their twenties. San Francisco had fewer cases than New York but, since it was smaller and had an unusually large homosexual population, it was more devastated: by 1985 one resident of the city died of AIDS every day and two more fell ill with it.

The fact that the first reported cases appeared among homosexuals reinforced prejudice against them and pushed a minority which had been growing in assertiveness back on to the defensive. Homosexuals reported growing numbers of unwarranted sackings, lack of promotion, and termination of leases. Gay-baiting and anti-gay violence increased; the passage of gay-rights laws was stalled and even reversed; some employers, including a number of government agencies, discriminated more often against homosexuals than against any other minority; the armed forces barred them altogether. Ignorance of and misconception about the disease affected the way its victims were treated. There were distressing stories of children suffering from AIDS being excluded from public schools or treated like pariahs when admitted, of sick people being turned out by frightened relatives, of ambulance crews refusing to take them to hospital and of undertakers being reluctant to handle their bodies. However, well-publicized disclosures that several film, theater, and sports celebrities had been AIDS victims prompted sympathy among millions of Americans and possibly a greater measure of tolerance.

The Reagan administration was slow to respond to the health emergency, and was confused and indecisive when it finally did. This was hardly surprising since not only officialdom, but a specially appointed and representative presidential commission, and even scientists and doctors were divided into opposing camps on such matters as compulsory blood testing, the confidentiality of test results, condoms, and sex education. The AIDS-testing policy Reagan announced in May 1987 stopped short of endorsing the widespread mandatory testing demanded by the extreme right, but extended compulsory testing (already required of military recruits) to inmates of federal prisons and would-be immigrants. The President also recommended that the states should test couples applying for marriage licences, but those states which considered the proposal rejected it. Congress was, if anything, even more irresolute than the administration. In 1987 it shelved legislation to ban discrimination against homosexuals and to ensure the confidentiality of blood test results, while the Senate withdrew funds from AIDS-education programs that "promote or encourage" homosexual intercourse.

Meanwhile America's drug epidemic worsened. In 1986, according to a presidential commission, drug-trafficking was "the most serious problem presented by organized crime". In the same year more than half the people arrested for serious crimes in New York City and Washington, DC were drug-users. While heroin addiction did not increase, and may even have declined, cocaine and crack, the cheap, potent, readily obtainable, and highly addictive derivative of cocaine, ensnared millions—and not just in the inner cities. Coroners' reports and statistics and hospital emergency-room admissions told of a rapidly spreading cocaine plague. Even more horrifying was the fact that in 1989 a total of 375,000 American babies were born addicted to crack or heroin.

Reagan vowed to make drug control a central theme of his Presidency and, indeed, the sum spent on fighting drug suppliers more than tripled between 1981 and 1986. Seizures of cocaine rose during the same period from two tons to twenty-seven tons, with state agencies netting almost as much. Meanwhile arrests on drug charges increased and sentences became harsher. The Administration also tried to stem the flow of drugs from supplier countries: in 1986 it sent a US Army team to Bolivia to help the authorities in their war on cocaine production. But the main focus of Reagan's drug policy throughout was interception and arrest rather than the drug prevention his wife, Nancy Reagan, was promoting in her "just say no" campaign. Amid great publicity President Bush established a new Office of National Drug Control Policy, but prevention remained, in the words of the London *Economist*, the "neglected stepchild of drug policy".

Along with concern about drugs, and largely as a result of it, fear of violent crime was widespread. A report by the Senate Judiciary Committee in 1992, after noting that violent crime had increased by 516 percent since 1960 although the population had risen by only 41 percent, called the United States "the most violent and self-destructive nation on earth". It was certainly much more violent than other developed countries. The 23,000 killings occurring in the United States in 1990 gave it a national murder rate of 95 per million per year, compared with Great Britain's rate of just 4.5 per million. Young black men committed a disproportionate share of the murders—perhaps 50 percent of the total—but they were also the commonest victims: they were ten times more likely to be murdered than their white counterparts. Nearly half of all murder victims were aged between fifteen and twenty-nine, and a rising proportion were children. There was nothing new about the American propensity to murder. What was new was that violent crime was now rampant not only in the large city ghettos but in the suburbs, small towns, and even in the hitherto peaceful countryside. At the same time it was becoming more brutal, more irrational, and more random.

In two-thirds of the murders guns were used. According to official statistics there were more than 66 million guns in circulation in the United States in 1992, though other estimates suggested that there were three or four times as many. Most of them, according to their owners, were kept at home as a sensible precaution against random crime. But guns, often semi-automatics, were commonplace in many city streets and in urban schools. Yet, although polls showed that most Americans favored stricter gun laws, the National Rifle Association found wide support for its campaign against them. Relying heavily on a dubious and misleading interpretation of the Second Amendment to the Constitution, which guarantees a citizen's right to bear arms, it saw controls on the purchase and possession of guns as an unwarranted restraint on personal liberty. It took a seven-year battle and sustained pressure from three Presidents—Reagan, Bush, and Clinton—before Congress was at last prepared in 1993 to defy the NRA and pass the Brady bill—named after the presidential press secretary shot by Reagan's would-be assassin in 1981. It was a feeble measure, requiring only a five-day waiting period for handgun purchase, and unlikely to be effective since many states already had similar laws and since most murderers did not in any case buy their weapons from gun dealers.

The intractability of these and other social problems—poverty, unemployment, homelessness, falling educational standards, and the soaring cost of health care—were only part of the reason why the optimism of the Reagan years gave way to doubt and defensiveness as Americans prepared to celebrate the 500th anniversary of Columbus's 1492 landfall. Fear of economic decline was equally responsible. While the immediate problem was the recession, long-term trends seemed even more worrying. The American economy had virtually ceased to grow for a quarter of a century; real wages, having risen sharply in the decades immediately after World War II, had then fallen steadily until by 1987 they were back to the level of 1962. The American share of gross world product had dropped from 50 percent in the late 1940s to 23 percent in 1990, its share of world trade from 22 percent to less than 10 percent. While the United States had lost some of its competitive edge in world markets, much of its industry had fallen into the hands of foreigners and, thanks to massive borrowing from abroad to finance its mounting budget deficit, the world's richest country had become its biggest debtor. Little wonder that Americans were now less sanguine about the future. They had come to realize that the American Dream would be harder to achieve than before, that their children might well be worse off than they and would bear a heavier burden in caring for the elderly. Yet the wide-ranging public debate prompted by these concerns suggested that pessimism had been overdone. Although the American economy had its weaknesses, reports of its decline had been exaggerated. It was still more than twice the size of that of its nearest competitor—Japan. Average income in the United States was still higher than in any other country, which was largely why America remained an incomparable Mecca for the world's poor. And while American dominance was no longer what it had been, the United States alone possessed the combination of economic and military resources to qualify as a superpower.

BIBLIOGRAPHY

The works listed below are not meant to form a complete bibliography. Besides serving as an acknowledgment of my debt to other scholars, they are intended to help readers who may wish to pursue further some of the topics discussed.

General

The most comprehensive bibliography of American history is Frank Freidel, ed., *The Harvard Guide to American History* (rev. edn., 1974). Convenient one-volume reference works include Thomas H. Johnson, comp., *The Oxford Companion to American History* (1966) and Eric Foner and John A. Garraty, *The Reader's Companion to American History* (1991). More detailed is Louise B. Ketz *et al.*, eds., *Dictionary of American History* (8 vols., rev., edn., 1976). A valuable statistical compilation is *Historical Statistics of the United States, Colonial Times to 1970* (3rd edn., 1989). Indispensable for biographical information is Allen Johnson *et al.*, eds., *Dictionary of American Biography* (20 vols., plus 9 supplements, 1928–94), of which American Council of Learned Societies staff, eds., *Concise Dictionary of American Biography* (4th edn., 1990) is a useful one-volume abridgment. For biographies of women see Edward T. James *et al.*, eds., *Notable American Women* (4 vols., 1971–8). The best collection of sources is H. S. Commager, ed., *Documents of American History* (10th edn., 1988). An outstanding historical atlas is *The American Heritage Pictorial Atlas of American History* (1966). Less detailed but more up-to-date is Martin Gilbert, *The Dent Atlas of American History* (3rd edn., 1993). Other useful reference works are Stephan Thernstrom, ed., *Harvard Encyclopedia of American Ethnic Groups* (1980) and Glenn Porter, *Encyclopedia of American Economic History* (3 vols., 1980). A helpful introduction to some of the main themes of American history is Dennis Welland, ed., *The United States: A Companion to American Studies* (2nd edn., 1987). For historiography see Marcus Cunliffe and Robin Winks, eds., *Pastmasters: Essays on American Historians* (1969) and Carl Degler, ed., *Pivotal Interpretations of American History* (2 vols., 1966). Important interpretative studies include David M. Potter, *People of Plenty: Economic Abundance and the American Character* (1954), Michael Kammen, *People of Paradox: An Inquiry Concerning the Origins of American Civilization* (1972) and J. R. Pole, *The Pursuit of Equality in American History* (rev. edn., 1993). On constitutional history, A. H. Kelly and W. A. Harbison, *The American Constitution: Its Origins and Development* (6th edn., 1982) is standard, but a stimulating supplement is Michael Kammen, *A Machine That Would Go Of Itself: The Constitution in American Culture* (1986). The Presidency is perceptively analyzed in Marcus Cunliffe, *American Presidents and the Presidency* (1969). The fullest treatment of presidential elections is Arthur M. Schlesinger, Jr., and Fred L. Israel, eds. *History of*

American Presidential Elections, 1789–1968, (4 vols., 1971). For the Supreme
Court see Charles Warren, *The Supreme Court in United States History* (2 vols.,
1937) and Fred L. Israel and Leon Friedman, eds., *The Justices of the United
States Supreme Court, 1789–1966: Their Lives and Major Opinions* (1969). For the
law generally see Lawrence H. Friedman, *A History of American Law* (2nd rev.
edn., 1986). Political parties are authoritatively analyzed in Arthur M.
Schlesinger, Jr., ed., *History of U.S. Political Parties* (4 vols., 1973). Richard
Hofstadter, *The American Political Tradition* (rev. edn., 1973) is a suggestive inter-
pretation of political ideas. The most convenient surveys of diplomatic history are
Alexander De Conde, *A History of American Foreign Policy* (2nd edn., 1973) and
Thomas A. Bailey, *A Diplomatic History of the American People* (10th edn.,
1980). The main themes of economic history are ably treated in Jonathan R.
Hughes, *American Economic History*, (3rd edn., 1989) and R. M. Robertson and
G. M. Walton, *History of the American Economy* (4th edn., 1979). The standard
work on economic thought is Joseph Dorfman, *The Economic Mind in American
Civilization* (5 vols, 1946–59). For the advancing frontier see Ray A. Billington
and Martin Ridge, *Westward Expansion* (5th edn., 1982). Useful one-volume sur-
veys of trade unionism are Joseph G. Rayback, *History of American Labor* (rev.
edn., 1966) and David Brody, *In Labor's Cause: Main Themes on the History of
the American Worker* (1993). On immigration see Maldwyn A. Jones, *American
Immigration* (2nd edn., 1992), and for ethnic groups in general consult Leonard
Dinnerstein *et al.*, *Natives and Strangers: Blacks, Indians and Immigrants in
America* (2nd edn., 1990). On black history the preeminent work is John Hope
Franklin and Alfred A. Moss, Jr., *From Slavery to Freedom* (7th edn., 1993). The
role of Indians is comprehensively reviewed in Wilcomb E. Washburn, *The Indian
in America* (1975) and William T. Hagan, *American Indians* (rev. edn., 1979). The
history of women is surveyed in Linda K. Kerber and Jane S. De Hart, *Women's
America* (3rd edn., 1991), Nancy Woloch, *Women and the American Experience*
(2nd edn., 1994) and Carl Degler, *At Odds: Women and the Family in America
from the Revolution to the Present* (1980). The best surveys of religion are Sydney
Ahlstrom, *A Religious History of the American People* (1972) and James W. Smith
et al., *Religion in American Life* (4 vols., 1961). Lawrence A. Cremin, *American
Education* (3 vols., 1970–88) eclipses previous treatments of the subject. On intellectual history, the best one-volume summary is Merle Curti, *The Growth of
American Thought* (3rd edn., 1964), but Vernon L. Parrington, *Main Currents in
American Thought* (3 vols., 1927–30), though outdated in some respects, is still a
rewarding classic. The best brief introduction to American literature is Marcus
Cunliffe, *The Literature of the United States* (4th edn., 1986). For a fuller treatment see Robert E. Spiller *et al.*, *Literary History of the United States* (3 vols.,
4th edn., 1974). Art, architecture, and music may be approached, respectively,
through Edgar P. Richardson, *Painting in America: 1502 to the Present* (1965),
John Burchard and Albert Bush Brown, *The Architecture of America: A Social
and Cultural History* (1966) and Irving Sablosky, *American Music* (1969).

Chapter 1

For an absorbing picture of pre-Columbian civilizations see Brian M. Fagan,
Kingdoms of Gold, Kingdoms of Jade: The Americas before Columbus (1991). The
culture of the Native American inhabitants of North America may be approached

in such works as James H. Merrell, *The Indians' New World: Catawbas and their Neighbors from European Contact to the Era of Removal* (1989) and Richard White, *The Middle Ground: Indians, Empires and Republics in the Great Lakes Region, 1650–1815* (1991). The best single-volume introduction to European exploration is David B. Quinn, *North America from Earliest Discovery to First Settlements: The Norse Voyages to 1612* (1977), but for a more comprehensive treatment see Samuel Eliot Morison, *The European Discovery of America: The Northern Voyages, A.D. 500–1600* (1971) and *The Southern Voyages, A.D. 1492–1616* (1974). Of the many recent books by environmental historians and ethnohistorians which have provided new insights into the contacts of native Americas and Europeans, two of the most suggestive are James Axtell, *The Invasion Within* (1986) and Karen O. Kupperman, *Settling with the Indians: The Meeting of English and Indian Cultures, 1580–1640* (1980), both of which focus on cultural conflict. Francis Jennings, *The Invasion of America* (1975) is an indignant account of European colonization from the Indian standpoint. Geographical influences on European settlement and development are suggested in R. H. Brown, *Historical Geography of the United States* (1948). Useful one-volume surveys of the first century and a half of white settlement include Clarence L. Ver Steeg, *The Formative Years, 1607–1763* (1964), David Hawke, *The Colonial Experience* (1966), R. C. Simmons, *The American Colonies: From Settlement to Independence* (1976), and Richard Middleton, *Colonial America: A History, 1607–1760* (1992). For the background of English expansion see Wallace E. Notestein, *The English People on the Eve of Colonization, 1603–1630* (1951) and Carl Bridenbaugh, *Vexed and Troubled Englishmen, 1500–1642* (1968). The most comprehensive account of English colonization is C. M. Andrews, *The Colonial Period of American History* (4 vols., 1934–8). Another detailed study, emphasizing social history, is Thomas J. Wertenbaker's trilogy, *The Founding of American Civilization: The Middle Colonies* (1938), *The Old South* (1942) and *The Puritan Oligarchy* (1947). The founding of the southern colonies and their subsequent development are admirably treated in W. F. Craven, *The Southern Colonies in the Seventeenth Century* (1949) and his *White, Black and Red* (1972). J. T. Adams, *The Founding of New England* (1921) is strongly anti-Puritan, but S. E. Morison's *Builders of the Bay Colony* (1930) refutes Adams's claims that the Puritans were sanctimonious killjoys. Edwin B. Bronner, William Penn's *"Holy Experiment": The Founding of Pennsylvania, 1681–1701* (1962) is a good modern study, as is Phinizy Spalding's account of Georgia, *Oglethorpe in America* (1977). For the development of British imperial regulation see, in addition to the fourth volume of Andrews, already cited, G. L. Beer, *The Colonial System* (2 vols., 1912) and Volumes 6 and 7 of L. H. Gipson's monumental work, *The British Empire before the American Revolution* (14 vols., 1936–69). The view that British mercantilism stifled colonial economic development, advanced in L. A. Harper, *The English Navigation Acts* (1939) is sharply challenged in O. M. Dickerson, *The Navigation Acts and the American Revolution* (1951). For a balanced contribution to the controversy see T. C. Barrow, *Trade and Empire: The British Customs Service in America* (1967). See also the excellent studies by James A. Henretta, *Salutary Neglect* (1972) and Michael Kammen, *Empire and Interest: The American Colonies and the Politics of Mercantilism* (1970). The tenousness of British control is demonstrated in Michael G. Hall, *Edward Randolph and the American Colonies*

(1969). The best introduction to colonial economic development is John J. McCusker and R. R. Menard, *The Economy of British America, 1607–1789* (1985). Gipson's volumes, mentioned above, are full of information on colonial agriculture, industry, and commerce. The best general study of the franchise in the colonies is Chilton Williamson, *American Suffrage from Property to Democracy, 1760–1860* (1960). Robert E. Brown has examined the relationship between the franchise and social structure in *Middle-Class Democracy and the Revolution in Massachusetts, 1691–1780* (1955) and, with B. Katharine Brown, in *Virginia, 1705–1786: Democracy or Aristocracy?* (1964). The definitive account of the rise of the assemblies is Jack P. Greene, *The Quest for Power* (1963). Good modern studies of colonial politics include Patricia U. Bonomi, *A Factious People: Politics and Society in Colonial New York* (1971), Charles S. Sydnor, *American Revolutionaries in the Making* (1965), and Gary B. Nash, *Quakers and Politics* (1968). The best study of Bacon's Rebellion is W. E. Washburn, *The Governor and the Rebel* (1957), which connects the uprising specifically with Indian relations. Other useful accounts of late seventeenth-century rebellions are David S. Lovejoy, *The Glorious Revolution in America* (1972), Jerome A. Reich, *Leisler's Rebellion* (1953), and David W. Jordan, *Maryland's Revolution of Government, 1689–1692* (1974).

Chapter 2

The great outpouring of recent scholarly work on colonial society and culture is skillfully utilized in Jack P. Greene, *Pursuits of Happiness: The Social Development of the Early Modern British Colonies and the Formation of American Culture* (1988). The range and content of that work is indicated in essays in Jack P. Greene and J. R. Pole, eds., *Colonial British America* (1984). Still valuable, however, are Daniel J. Boorstin's fascinating and provocative study, *The Americans: The Colonial Experience* (1958), James A. Henretta, *The Evolution of American Society, 1700–1815* (1973), and Richard Hofstadter, *America at 1750: A Social Portrait* (1971). Colonial population data are judiciously handled in Robert V. Wells, *The Population of the British Colonies before 1776* (1975) and Jim Potter, "The Growth of Population in America", in D. V. Glass and D. E. C. Eversley, eds., *Population in History* (1965). For immigration to the colonies see Marcus Lee Hansen, *The Atlantic Migration, 1607–1860* (1940), Bernard Bailyn, *The Peopling of British North America: An Introduction* (1986) and his *Voyagers to the West: Emigration from Britain to America on the Eve of the Revolution* (1986), and David Hackett Fischer, *Albion's Seed: Four British Folkways in America* (1989). For non-English emigration see Ned C. Landsman, *Scotland and its First American Colony, 1683–1765* (1985), which deals with New Jersey, James G. Leyburn, *The Scotch–Irish* (1962), and Jon Butler, *The Huguenots in America* (1983). David W. Galenson, *White Servitude in Colonial America: An Economic Analysis* (1981) quantifies the demographic, social, and economic characteristics of imported servants and their role in the colonial labor market. A. Roger Ekirch, *Bound for America: The Transportation of British Convicts to the Colonies, 1718–1776* (1987) is the best study of the subject. Colonial racial attitudes and the origins of black slavery are perceptively discussed in David B. Davis, *The Problem of Slavery in Western Culture* (1966), Winthrop D. Jordan, *White Over Black: American Attitudes toward the Negro* (1968), and Edmund S. Morgan, *American*

Slavery, American Freedom (1975). For the New England family see Edmund S. Morgan, *The Puritan Family* (2nd edn., 1966) and two influential, demographically based local studies: John Demos, *A Little Commonwealth: Family Life in Plymouth Colony* (1970) and Philip Greven, Jr., *Four Generations: Population, Land and Family in Colonial Andover, Massachusetts* (1970). For the position of women and children see Greven, *The Protestant Temperament: Problems of Child-Rearing, Religious Experience and Self in Early America* (1980) and Laurel Thatcher Ulrich, *Good Wives: Image and Reality in the Lives of Women in Northern New England* (1982). The shift of historical attention in recent decades from Puritan New England to the tobacco-growing Chesapeake colonies has produced a large body of distinguished work, examples of which are Thad W. Tate and D. L. Ammerman, eds., *The Chesapeake in the Seventeenth Century* (1984), Alan Kulikoff, *Tobacco and Slaves: The Development of Southern Cultures in the Tobacco Colonies, 1680–1800* (1986), Darrett B. Rutman and Anita H. Rutman, *A Place in Time: Middlesex County, Virginia, 1650–1750* (2 vols., 1984), Gloria L. Main, *Tobacco Colony: Life in Early Maryland, 1650–1720* (1983), and T. H. Breen, *Tobacco Culture* (1985), the last of which traces the ways in which agricultural practices were affected by ideology. Colonial urban life—that is, life in the five main seaports—is thoroughly treated in Carl Bridenbaugh's two books, *Cities in the Wilderness* (1938) and *Cities in Revolt* (1955). Two good studies of New England towns are O. E. Winslow, *Meetinghouse Hill* (1952) and Michael Zuckerman, *Peaceable Kingdoms* (1970). The emergence of colonial elites is described in Louis B. Wright, *The First Families of Virginia* (1964) and F. B. Tolles, *Meeting House and Counting House: The Quaker Merchants of Colonial Philadelphia* (1948). E. Digby Baltzell, *Puritan Boston and Quaker Philadelphia* (1979) focuses on the differences between the social elites of the two towns. The social structure of different colonies is analyzed in Bernard Bailyn, *The New England Merchants in the Seventeenth Century* (1955) and "Politics and Social Structure in Virginia", in J. M. Smith, ed., *Seventeenth Century America* (1959), Thomas J. Archdeacon, *New York City, 1664–1710* (1976) and Richard L. Bushman, *From Puritan to Yankee* (1967). For estimates of wealth see Alice H. Jones, *The Distribution of Wealth in America* (1979). On social mobility there are several important local studies: Kenneth A. Lockridge, *A New England Town: Dedham, Massachusetts, 1636–1736* (1970), T. H. Breen and S. Foster, "Moving to the New World", *William and Mary Quarterly*, 30 (1973), W. A. Reavis, "The Maryland Gentry and Social Mobility, 1637–1676", *William and Mary Quarterly* 14 (1957), Russell R. Menard, "From Servant to Freeholder", *William and Mary Quarterly*, 30 (1973) and Linda Bissell, "From One Generation to Another", *William and Mary Quarterly*, 31 (1974). On colonial religion the most useful guide is Sydney Ahlstrom, *Religious History of the American People* (1972). New England Puritanism has inspired a vast literature. A brief and helpful introduction is E. S. Morgan, *The Puritan Dilemma: The Story of John Winthrop* (1958). For a more detailed analysis of Puritanism Perry Miller's seminal studies, *The New England Mind* (2 vols., 1939–53) and *Errand into the Wilderness* (1956) are indispensable. For the decline in the authority of the Puritan clergy, see D. B. Rutman, *Winthrop's Boston* (1965), R. G. Pope, *The Halfway Covenant* (1969), Robert Middlekauff, *The Mathers* (1971), and J. W. Jones, *The Shattered Synthesis* (1973). The Salem witchcraft hysteria is examined in John Demos,

Entertaining Satan: Witchcraft and the Culture of Early New England (1982) and Carol Karlsen, *The Devil in the Shape of a Woman: Witchcraft in Early New England* (1987). For the Great Awakening see E. S. Gaustad, *The Great Awakening in New England* (1951), Wesley M. Gewehr, *The Great Awakening in Virginia* (1930), O. E. Winslow, *Jonathan Edwards* (1940), and Patricia U. Bonomi, *Under The Cope of Heaven* (1986). In *The Transformation of Virginia, 1740–1790* (1982) Rhys Isaac employs some of the tools of symbolic anthropology to advance the provocative thesis that the Great Awakening challenged and changed the politics of an ordered society. There are two excellent studies of the Enlightenment: Henry F. May, *The Enlightenment in America* (1976) and Henry S. Commager, *The Empire of Reason* (1977). Franklin is admirably portrayed in Verner W. Crane, *Benjamin Franklin* (1938) and, with greater awareness of Franklin's place in his time, in Esmond Wright, *Franklin of Philadelphia* (1986). Brook Hindle, *The Pursuit of Science in Revolutionary America* (1956) is standard. The classic account of the struggle for empire is Francis Parkman, *France and England in North America* (9 vols., 1869–92). The best modern surveys, both brief, are Howard H. Peckham, *The Colonial Wars, 1689–1762* (1964) and Edward P. Hamilton, *The French and Indian Wars* (1962).

Chapter 3

Good brief introductions to the Revolutionary period as a whole are provided by Edmund S. Morgan, *The Birth of the Republic, 1773–1789* (rev. edn., 1977) and by two incisive and elegantly written studies by British scholars, Esmond Wright, *Fabric of Freedom, 1763–1800* (rev. edn., 1980) and J. R. Pole, *Foundations of American Independence, 1763–1815* (1972). More detailed coverage is provided in Robert Middelkauff, *The Glorious Cause: The American Revolution, 1763–1789* (1982), which is based on the latest scholarship. For accounts of the events in both England and America which led to the Revolution see John C. Miller, *Origins of the American Revolution* (rev. edn., 1967) and Merrill Jensen, *The Founding of the Nation, 1773–1776* (1968). Edmund S. and Helen Morgan, *The Stamp Act Crisis* (rev. edn., 1963) and Pauline S. Maier, *From Resistance to Revolution* (1972) deal with the actions and motivations of the American revolutionaries. Their ideology, and especially their conviction that the British government was conspiring against American liberties, is brilliantly analyzed in Bernard Bailyn, *The Ideological Origins of the American Revolution* (1967). The role of ideas is further illustrated in Eric Foner, *Tom Paine and Revolutionary America* (1976), Pauline S. Maier, *The Old Revolutionaries: Political Lives in the Age of Samuel Adams* (1980), and Gordon S. Wood, *The Radicalism of the American Revolution* (1992). Carl Becker's classic, *The Declaration of Independence* (1922) is still valuable but Gary Wills, *Inventing America: Jefferson's Declaration of Independence* (1978) sheds important new light on the document. Recent years have seen a revival of interest in loyalism. Among its products are Wallace Brown, *The Good Americans* (1969), Robert M. Calhoon, *The Loyalists in Revolutionary America* (1973), and Mary Beth Norton, *The British-Americans: The Loyalist Exiles in England, 1774–1789* (1974). The ideology of the loyalists is examined in William H. Nelson, *The American Tory* (1961), William A. Benton, *Whig-Loyalism* (1969) and Esmond Wright, ed., *A Tug of Loyalties* (1975). Bernard Bailyn, *The Ordeal of Thomas Hutchinson* (1974) is a finely written biography which includes some penetrating observations on the nature of loyalism. Works which stress the prevalence of class conflict during the Revolution include Edward Countryman, *A People in Revolution* (1981) and Staughton Lynd, *Class Conflict, Slavery and the United States Constitution* (1968), but Richard P. McCormick, *Experiment in Independence* (1950) found little evidence of it. For general accounts of the Revolutionary War see John C. Miller, *Triumph of Freedom, 1775–1783* (1948) and John R. Alden, *The American Revolution, 1775–1783* (1954). The military campaigns are examined in detail in Piers Mackesy, *The War for America* (1964) and Don Higginbotham, *The War for American Independence* (1971). Important studies of American society in wartime include John Shy, *A People Numerous and Armed: Reflections on the Military Struggle for American Independence* (1976), Charles Royster, *A Revolutionary People at War* (1979), and Lawrence D. Cress, *Citizens at Arms* (1982). The problems of financing the war are dealt with in Clarence Ver Steeg, *Robert Morris* (1954) and E. J. Ferguson, *The Power of the Purse* (1968). On diplomatic aspects see Samuel F. Bemis, *The Diplomacy of the American Revolution* (1935) and Richard B. Morris, *The Peacemakers: The Great Powers and American Independence* (1976).

Chapter 4

The dimensions of revolutionary change are brilliantly charted in Gordon S. Wood, *The Creation of the American Republic 1775–1789* (1969) and in his *The Radicalism of the American Revolution* (1992), both of which reflect a revival of interest in ideology. Elisha P. Douglass, *Rebels and Democrats: The Struggle for Equal Political Rights and Majority Rule during the Revolution* (1955) and J. R. Pole, *Political Representation in England and the Origins of the American Republic* (1966) are among other important works stressing ideological factors. The older fashion for economic analysis survives in Forrest McDonald, *E Pluribus Unum: The Formation of the American Republic 1776–1790* (1955). The social impact of the Revolution is described and perhaps exaggerated in J. Franklin Jameson, *The American Revolution Considered as a Social Movement* (1926) and Evarts B. Greene, *The Revolutionary Generation, 1763–1790* (1943). For correctives see Jackson T. Main, *The Social Structure of Revolutionary America* (1965) and Gary Nash, *The Urban Crucible* (1974). The extent of cultural change may be gauged from Joseph J. Ellis, *After the Revolution: Profiles of American Culture* (1979) and Oscar and Lillian Handlin, *A Restless People: America in Rebellion, 1770–1787* (1982). C. P. Nettels, *The Emergence of a National Economy* (1962), which covers the period 1775 to 1815, is the best guide to economic developments. Much distinguished work has been done on the slavery issue during the Revolution. See especially David Brion Davis, *The Problem of Slavery in the Age of Revolution, 1770–1823* (1975), Duncan J. MacLeod, *Slavery, Race and the American Revolution* (1974), and Donald L. Robinson, *Slavery in the Structure of American Politics, 1765–1820* (1971). On the abolition of slavery in the North see Arthur Zilversmit, *The First Emancipation* (1967). Ira Berlin and Ronald Hoffman, eds., *Slavery and Freedom in the Age of the American Revolution* (1983) argues that the Revolution was a seminal event in the Afro-American experience. Linda K. Kerber, *Women of the Republic* (1980) and Mary Beth Norton, *Liberty's Daughters* (1980) show how the Revolution enlarged the role of women in

American society. The most complete account of state constitution-making during the Revolution is still Allan Nevins, *The American States during and after the Revolution, 1775–1789* (1967), but state politics are further illuminated in Jackson T. Main, *The Upper House in Revolutionary America, 1763–1788* (1967). Two works by Merrill Jensen, *The Articles of Confederation* (2nd edn., 1959) and *The New Nation: A History of the United States during the Confederation, 1781–1789* (1950) challenge the older view that the 1780s were a period of national decline. A good recent survey of the Confederation period is Richard B. Morris, *The Forging of the Union, 1781–1789* (1987). For the development of American nationalism see Paul C. Nagel, *One Nation Indivisible: The Union in American Thought, 1776–1861* (1964). The making of the Federal Constitution is best treated in Christopher Collier and James L. Collier, *Decision in Philadelphia* (1987) and Richard B. Morris, *Witnesses at the Creation: Hamilton, Madison, Jay and the Constitution* (1986). D. P. Szatmary, *Shays' Rebellion* (1980) is a model study. Charles A. Beard's celebrated work, *An Economic Interpretation of the Constitution of the United States* (1913), which implied that the Founding Fathers were motivated chiefly by economic self-interest, influenced historians for half a century. But Beard's methods and conclusions have been effectively challenged, notably by Robert E. Brown, *Charles Beard and the Constitution* (1956) and Forrest McDonald, *We the People: The Economic Origins of the Constitution* (1958). Other interpretations of the making of the Constitution include Edmund S. Morgan, *Inventing the People* (1988) and Michael Kammen, *Sovereignty and Liberty* (1988). For the opposition to the Constitution see Jackson T. Main, *The Antifederalists* (1961), which employs a more sophisticated economic analysis than Beard's, and Robert A. Rutland, *The Ordeal of the Constitution: The Anti-Federalists and the Ratification Struggle of 1787–1788* (1966).

Chapter 5

An impressive introduction to the period is Stanley Elkins and Eric L. McKitrick, *The Age of Federalism: The Early American Republic, 1788–1800* (1993). Still useful, however, is Nathan Schachner, *The Founding Fathers* (1954). Robert A. Rutland, *The Birth of the Bill of Rights, 1776–1791* (1955) is a judicious study. Differing views about whether the ideology of the Revolution continued to inform political debate in the decades after the new government went into operation are expressed in Joyce Appleby, *Capitalism and the New Social Order* (1984), Drew McCoy, *The Elusive Republic: Political Economy in Jeffersonian America* (1982), and Richard Buel, Jr., *Securing the Revolution: Ideology in American Politics, 1789–1815* (1974). Washington's Presidency is covered in the later volumes of Douglas Southall Freeman's monumental biography, *George Washington* (7 vols., 1948–57) and in two works by James T. Flexner, *George Washington and the New Nation, 1783–1793* (1969) and *George Washington: Anguish and Farewell, 1793–1799* (1972). Washington's role as a national father-figure is skillfully sketched in Marcus Cunliffe, *George Washington: Man and Monument* (1958). The most rewarding biographies of Hamilton are John C. Miller, *Alexander Hamilton: Portrait in Paradox* (1959), Broadus Mitchell, *Alexander Hamilton* (2 vols., 1957—62) and Forrest McDonald, *Alexander Hamilton: A Biography* (1980). For a close examination of Hamilton's political philosophy see Gerald Stourzh, *Alexander Hamilton and the Idea of Representative Government* (1970). The emergence of political parties is thoughtfully analyzed in Joseph E. Charles, *Origins of the American Party System* (1956), William N. Chambers, *Political Parties in a New Nation* (1963), and Richard Hofstadter, The *Idea of a Party System* (1969). For the way in which an opposition party emerged see Noble E. Cunningham, Jr., *The Jeffersonian Republicans: The Formation of Party Organization, 1789–1801* (1957) and Donald Stewart, *The Opposition Press of the Federalist Period* (1969). Two volumes by Samuel F. Bemis, *Jay's Treaty* (rev. edn., 1962) and *Pinckney's Treaty* (1960) remain standard, but among several other excellent works on the foreign policy of the Washington administration the following stand out: Alexander De Conde, *Entangling Alliance: Politics and Diplomacy under George Washington* (1958), Felix Gilbert, *To the Farewell Address* (1961), Paul A. Varg, *Foreign Policies of the Founding Fathers* (1970), and Gilbert Lycan, *Alexander Hamilton and Foreign Policy* (1971). The most convenient treatment of the second President is John Ferling, *John Adams: A Life* (1992). Also useful on the Adams administration are Stephen G. Kurtz, *The Presidency of John Adams: The Collapse of Federalism, 1795–1800* (1958) and Manning J. Dauer, *The Adams Federalists* (1953). Adams's foreign policy is covered in Bradford Perkins, *The First Rapprochement: England and the United States, 1795–1805* (1955), Alexander De Conde, *The Quasi-War: Undeclared War with France, 1797–1801* (1966), and William C. Stinchcombe, *The XYZ Affair* (1980). Two excellent studies of the Alien and Sedition Acts are James M. Smith, *Freedom's Fetters: The Alien and Sedition Acts and American Civil Liberties* (1956) and John C. Miller, *Crisis in Freedom: The Alien and Sedition Acts* (1951).

Chapter 6

The quarter of a century in which the Virginia dynasty dominated the Presidency is competently summarized in Marshall Smelser, *The Democratic Republic, 1801–1815* (1968) and George Dangerfield, *The Awakening of American Nationalism, 1815–1828* (1965). The fullest treatment of Jefferson's Presidency may be found in Dumas Malone, *Jefferson and His Time* (6 vols, 1948–81), but Merrill D. Peterson, *Thomas Jefferson and the New Nation* (1970) offers an excellent introduction. Jeffersonian political leadership is perceptively analyzed in Robert M. Johnstone, *Jefferson and the Presidency: Leadership in the Young Republic* (1978) and James S. Young, *The Washington Community, 1800–1829* (1966). For Jefferson's party see Noble E. Cunningham, Jr., *The Jeffersonian Republicans in Power: Party Operations, 1801–1809* (1963). For an understanding of Jeffersonian's administrative practices, Leonard D. White's path-breaking work, *The Jeffersonians: A Study in Administrative History* (1948) is indispensable. Jefferson's war on the judiciary is treated in Richard E. Ellis, *The Jeffersonian Crisis: Courts and Politics in the Young Nation* (1971) and D. O. Dewey, *Marshall versus Jefferson* (1970). On Marshall himself Albert J. Beveridge, *The Life of John Marshall* (4 vols., 1916–19) is still the essential starting-point, but excellent modern studies include R. K. Faulkner, *The Jurisprudence of John Marshall* (1968), F. N. Stites, *John Marshall: Defender of the Constitution* (1981), and G. Edward White's superb book, *The Marshall Court and Cultural Change, 1801–1835* (1991). On the exploration of the West see P. R. Cutright, *Lewis and Clark, Pioneering Naturalists* (1976). Jefferson's attitude to Indians is considered in Reginald Horsman, *Expansion and American Indian Policy, 1783–1812* (1967) and B. W.

Sheehan, *Seeds of Extinction: Jeffersonian Philanthropy and the American Indian* (1973). Various themes in Jefferson's foreign policy are treated in Lawrence S. Kaplan, *Jefferson and France* (1967), Clifford L. Egan, *Neither Peace Nor War* (1983)—which also covers Franco-American relations—and Burton Spivak, *Jefferson's English Crises: Commerce, the Embargo and the Republican Revolution* (1979). There are several useful studies of the Federalist opposition: Shaw Livermore, *Twilight of Federalism* (1962), David H. Fischer, *The Revolution of American Conservatism: The Federalist Party in the Era of Jeffersonian Democracy* (1965), and Linda K. Ferber, *Federalists in Dissent: Imagery and Ideology in Jeffersonian America* (1970). Jefferson's difficulties with his own party are capably dealt with in Norman Risjord, *The Old Republicans: Southern Conservatism in the Age of Jefferson* (1965) and Russell Kirk, *John Randolph of Roanoke* (rev. edn., 1964). The controversy over neutral rights is best treated in Bradford Perkins, *Prologue to War: England and the United States, 1805–1812* (1961) and Robert A. Rutland, *Mr. Madison's Alternatives: The Jeffersonian Republicans and the Coming of the War, 1805–1812* (1975). See also Reginald Horsman, *The Causes of the War of 1812* (1962), R. H. Brown, *The Republic in Peril: 1812* (1963) and J. C. A. Stagg's wide-ranging historical overview, *Mr. Madison's War: Politics, Diplomacy and Warfare in the Early American Republic, 1783–1830* (1984). For other treatments of Madison's role as Secretary of State and President see Irving Brant, *The Fourth President: A Life of James Madison* (1970) and Ralph L. Ketcham, *James Madison* (1990). The fighting in the War of 1812 is covered in Reginald Horsman, *The War of 1812* (1969) and Patrick C. T. White, *Nation on Trial: America and the War of 1812* (1965). Domestic opposition to the war is treated in Samuel E. Morison *et al.*, *Dissent in Three American Wars* (1970) and in James M. Banner's outstanding study, *To The Hartford Convention: The Federalists and the Origins of Party Politics in Massachusetts, 1789–1815* (1970). For postwar nationalism see Charles M. Wiltse, *John C. Calhoun, Nationalist, 1782–1828* (1944), Glyndon G. Van Deusen, *The Life of Henry Clay* (1937), and the works on John Marshall cited earlier. The best and fullest analysis of John Quincy Adams's diplomacy is Samuel F. Bemis, *John Quincy Adams and the Foundations of American Foreign Policy* (1949), but for Anglo-American relations and the formulation of the Monroe Doctrine see also Bradford Perkins, *Castlereagh and Adams: England and the United States, 1812–1823* (1964). Two books which throw light on the revival of sectionalism are Murray N. Rockband, *The Panic of 1819* (1962) and Glover Moore, *The Missouri Controversy, 1819–1821* (1953).

Chapter 7

The social and economic forces which transformed American life in the pre-Civil War decades are comprehensively analyzed in Charles Sellers, *The Market Revolution: Jacksonian America, 1815–1846* (1992), which argues that the growth of industry split a hitherto unified society. On more purely economic matters there are valuable insights in Douglas C. North, *The Economic Growth of the United States, 1790–1860* (1961) and Stuart Bruchey, *The Roots of American Economic Growth, 1607–1861* (1965). Demographic trends are usefully analyzed in Walter Nugent, *Structures in American Social History* (1981) and Maris A. Vinovskis, *Fertility in Massachusetts from the Revolution to the Civil War* (1981).

George R. Taylor, *The Transportation Revolution, 1815–1860* (1961) covers not only transport but all aspects of economic life except agriculture, which is capably treated in Paul W. Gates, *The Farmer's Age, 1815–1860* (1960). An outstanding work on the economic development of New England is Edward C. Kirkland, *Men, Cities and Transportation, 1820–1900* (2 vols., 1948). Two admirable studies which place transport developments in a broad economic context are Carter Goodrich *et al.*, *Canals and American Economic Development* (1961) and Albert Fishlow, *American Railroads and the Transformation of the Ante-Bellum Economy* (1965). State aid to economic development is treated in Oscar and Mary F. Handlin, *Commonwealth* (1949), which deals with Massachusetts, and Louis Hartz, *Economic Policy and Democratic Thought* (1954) which focuses on Pennsylvania. The most comprehensive book on commerce and shipping is John G. B. Hutchins, *The American Maritime Industries and Public Policy, 1789–1914* (1941), but see also two distinguished local studies: Samuel Eliot Morison, *The Maritime History of Massachusetts, 1783–1860* (1939). The relevant chapters of Billington and Ridge, *Westward Expansion*, cited earlier, present an excellent general account of the westward movement but it may be supplemented by Richard C. Wade, *The Urban Frontier* (1959), which emphasizes the role of cities in the growth of the West. The fullest treatment of Southern agriculture is L. C. Gray, *History of Agriculture in the Southern United States to 1860* (2 vols., 1933). The enormous range of writing on slavery can only be sampled. A useful introduction is Kenneth M. Stampp, *The Peculiar Institution* (1956), but fresh insights are provided in Eugene D. Genovese, *Roll, Jordan, Roll: The World the Slaves Made* (1975), Stanley M. Elkins, *Slavery: A Problem in American Institutional and Intellectual Life* (1959), Herbert G. Gutman, *The Black Family in Slavery and Freedom* (1976), Carl N. Degler, *Neither Black Nor White: Slavery and Race Relations in Brazil and the United States* (1971), John W. Blassingame, *The Slave Community: Plantation Life in the Antebellum South* (1973), and Richard C. Wade, *Slavery in the Cities* (1964). For slave insurrections see Eugene D. Genovese, *From Rebellion to Revolution: Afro-American Slave Revolts* (1979) and for free blacks Ira Berlin, *Slaves Without Masters* (1975). The best introduction to the economics of slavery is Harold D. Woodman, ed., *Slavery and the Southern Economy* (1966). Both the methodology and the findings of Robert W. Fogel and Stanley L. Engerman, *Time on the Cross: The Economics of American Negro Slavery* (1974), which used computer techniques to make a case for the efficiency and profitability of slavery have been largely discredited in Herbert G. Gutman, *Slavery and the Numbers Game* (1975) and Paul A. David *et al.*, *Reckoning with Slavery* (1976). Robert W. Fogel, *Without Consent or Contract* (1989) is an impressive work, not least because it addresses the moral questions ignored in *Time on the Cross*. The fullest account of the beginnings of industrialization is still Victor S. Clark, *History of Manufactures in the United States, 1607–1860* (3 vols., 1929), but see also Alfred D. Chandler, Jr., *The Visible Hand: The Managerial Revolution in American Business* (1977). For specific industries see A. H. Cole, *The American Wool Manufacture* (2 vols., 1926) and Caroline F. Ware, *The New England Cotton Manufacture* (1931). Also useful are John W. Oliver, *History of American Technology* (1956) and Roger Burlingame, *The March of the Iron Men* (1938), which emphasizes the role of invention. For the debt owed by infant American industry to European, especially British, technology see

David Jeremy, *Transatlantic Industrial Revolution: The Diffusion of Textile Technologies between Britain and America, 1790–1830s* (1981) and B. M. Tucker, *Samuel Slater and the Origin of the American Textile Revolution* (1984). Despite its age Norman F. Ware, *The Industrial Worker, 1840–1860* (1924) provides a serviceable introduction to the condition of labor, but more penetrating accounts of working-class life appear in Peter R. Knight, *The Plain People of Boston* (1971), Howard M. Gitelman, *Workingmen of Waltham* (1974), and Alan Dawley, *Class and Community: The Industrial Revolution in Lynn, Massachusetts* (1976). The Lowell girls are treated in Thomas Dublin, *Women At Work* (1977). For the European background to mass immigration see Marcus Lee Hansen, *The Atlantic Migration, 1607–1860* (1940), Kerby A. Miller, *Emigrants and Exiles: Ireland and the Irish Exodus to America* (1976), Mack Walker, *Germany and the Emigration, 1816–1885* (1964) and the extended essays in Donald Fleming and Bernard Bailyn, eds., "Dislocation and Emigration: The Social Background of American Immigration", *Perspectives in American History*, 7 (1974). Immigrant adjustment to urban America is the theme of Oscar Handlin's classic *Boston's Immigrants* (rev. edn., 1959), but less adverse pictures are painted in Robert A. Burchell, *The San Francisco Irish, 1840–1880* (1979), Dennis Clark, *The Irish in Philadelphia* (1973), Kathleen Neils Conzen, *Immigrant Milwaukee 1836–1860: Accommodation and Community in a Frontier City* (1976), and Stanley Nadel, *Little Germany: Ethnicity, Religion and Class in New York City* (1990) as well as in Theodore W. Blegen, *Norwegian Migration to America, 1825–1860* (1931), which deals with a group which settled overwhelmingly in rural regions.

Chapter 8

The best starting-point for the study of Jacksonian society and politics remains Alexis de Tocqueville, *Democracy in America* (2 vols., 1835). For a critical analysis of Tocqueville's egalitarian thesis see Edward M. Pessen, *Riches, Class and Power before the Civil War* (1973). Daniel J. Boorstin, *The Americans: The National Experience* (1965) is full of insights about pre-Civil War American society. Samuel F. Bemis, *John Quincy Adams and the Union* (1956) is the most complete account of the Adams administration. Harry L. Watson, *Liberty and Power: The Politics of Jacksonian America* (1990) is a suggestive recent overview of the events covered in this chapter. For a thoughtful analysis of the period see Edward M. Pessen, *Jacksonian America: Society, Personality and Politics* (rev. edn., 1985). The definitive biography of the dominating figure of the age is Robert V. Remini, *Andrew Jackson* (3 vols., 1977–84), while two other admirable books by Remini, *Martin Van Buren and the Making of the Democratic Party* (1959) and *The Election of Andrew Jackson* (1963) illuminate Jacksonian political organization. J. W. Ward, *Andrew Jackson: Symbol for an Age* (1959) and Martin Meyers, *The Jacksonian Persuasion* (1957) attempt from differing standpoints to define Jacksonian democracy. Donald Cole, *The Presidency of Andrew Jackson* (1993), argues that Jackson did not shape events but simply responded to the political and economic changes of the period. Arthur M. Schlesinger, Jr., *The Age of Jackson* (1945), which advances the provocative thesis that Jackson drew his main support from urban workingmen, remains a stimulating study. Its view that Whigs and Democrats were differentiated by class and wealth is challenged by Lee Benson, *The Concept of Jacksonian Democracy: New York as a Test Case*

(1961), Walter Hugins, *Jacksonian Democracy and the Working Class* (1960), D. T. Miller, *Jacksonian Aristocracy: Class and Democracy in New York, 1830–1860* (1967), and Ronald P. Formisano, *The Birth of Mass Politics, 1827–1861* (1971). Recent studies, such as those by Ashworth and Wilentz cited below, suggest nonetheless that Schlesinger was more nearly right than his critics. Richard P. McCormick, *The Second Party System* (1966) is indispensable to an understanding of the formation of parties but in recent years both the party system itself and the ideas and values of the two major parties have been completely reassessed. Among the most influential revisionist studies are Ronald P. Formisano, *The Transformation of Political Culture* (1983), Joel H. Sibley, *The Party Imperative* (1985), Daniel Walker Howe, *The Political Culture of the American Whigs* (1979), John Ashworth, *"Agrarians" and "Aristocrats": Party Political Ideology in the United States* (1983) and Jean Baker, *Affairs of Party: The Political Culture of Northern Democrats in the Mid-Nineteenth Century* (1983). Another highly impressive work is Sean Wilentz, *Chants Democratic, New York City and the Rise of the American Working Class, 1788–1850* (1984) which reinterprets Jacksonian America by tracing the emergence of conflicting class identities in the industrializing city. The most substantial biographies of Whig leaders are Maurice G. Baxter, *One and Inseparable: Daniel Webster and the Union* (1984) and Robert V. Remini, *Henry Clay: Statesman for the Union* (1991). A useful collective biography is Merrill Peterson, *The Great Triumvirate: Webster, Clay and Calhoun* (1988). Calhoun's career during the Jacksonian period may be traced in Charles M. Wiltse, *John C. Calhoun: Nullifier, 1829–1839* (1949). On the nullification controversy the outstanding work is William H. Freehling, *Prelude to Civil War* (1966) which demonstrates the connection between nullification and the slavery issue. The most exhaustive study of the Bank War is Bray Hammond, *Banks and Politics in America from the Revolution to the Civil War* (1957). Interpretations which differ from Hammond's include Robert V. Remini, *Andrew Jackson and the Bank War* (1967), J. M. McFaul, *The Politics of Jacksonian Finance* (1972), and Peter Temin, *The Jacksonian Economy* (1969), the last of which deals with economic affairs generally. On the Bank itself and its controversial president see Thomas P. Govan, *Nicholas Biddle, Nationalist and Public Banker, 1786–1844* (1959) and Jean A. Wilbur, *Biddle's Bank: The Crucial Years* (1967). On Indian removal the most provocative account is Michael F. Rogin, *Fathers and Children: Andrew Jackson and the Subjugation of the American Indian* (1975). Also useful is Ronald W. Satz, *American Indian Policy in the Jacksonian Era* (1975). John Niven, *Martin Van Buren: The Romantic Age of American Politics* (1983) does belated justice to a long-underrated president. Tyler's stormy administration is described in O. P. Chitwood, *John Tyler: Champion of the Old South* (1939) and Robert Seager II, *And Tyler Too* (1963).

Chapter 9

The most useful introduction to social and cultural trends in the ante-bellum period is Russel B. Nye, *Society and Culture in America, 1830–1860* (1974). The most authoritative treatments of the literature of the period are Vernon L. Parrington, *Main Currents of American Thought*, Vol. 2 (1927) and F. O. Matthiesen, *American Renaissance* (1941), but students should on no account miss Van Wyck Brooks's elegant and evocative surveys, *The Flowering of New*

England, 1815–1865 (1936) and *The Times of Melville and Whitman* (1947). Biographies of the period's leading imaginative writers include J. R. Mellow, *Nathaniel Hawthorne and his Times* (1980), Justin Kaplan, *Walt Whitman* (1980), and Leon Howard, *Herman Melville* (1951). For transcendentalist thought see Paul Boller, *American Transcendentalism, 1830–1860* (1974), Robert D. Richardson, Jr., *Henry Thoreau: A Life of the Mind* (1986), and Mary K. Cayton, *Emerson's Emergence: Self and Society in the Transformation of New England* (1991). Religious revivalism is perceptively analyzed in Whitney R. Cross, *The Burned-Over District* (1950), William G. McLaughlin, *Modern Revivalism: Charles Grandison Finney to Billy Graham* (1958), and Richard Carwardine, *Transatlantic Revivalism: Popular Evangelism in Britain and America, 1790–1865* (1978). Fawn M. Brodie's biography of Joseph Smith, *No Man Knows My History* (1945), though unsympathetic to its subject, provides a good account of the early history of Mormonism. See also Richard L. Bushman, *Joseph Smith and the Beginnings of Mormonism* (1988) Robert B. Flanders, *Nauvoo: Kingdom on the Mississippi* (1965), and Leonard J. Arrington, *Brigham Young: American Moses* (1985). The connection between religion and social reform is explored in John R. Bodo, *The Protestant Clergy and Public Issues, 1812–1848* (1954), Charles C. Cole, Jr., *The Social Ideas of Northern Evangelists, 1826–1860* (1954), and Timothy L. Smith, *Revivalism and Social Reform in Mid-Nineteenth Century America* (1957). Ronald G. Walters, *American Reformers, 1815–1860* (1978) is a concise and informative introduction to the subject. Mark Holloway, *Heavens on Earth* (1951) and Michael Fellman, *The Unbounded Frame: Freedom and Community in Nineteenth Century Utopianism* (1973) are useful general accounts of Utopian communities, while Arthur E. Bestor, *Backwoods Utopias* (1950) is the standard work on the sectarian and Owenite phases of communitarianism. On school reform Lawrence F. Cremin, *American Education: The National Experience, 1783–1876* (1980) is a superb overview. The movement for common schools is sympathetically portrayed in S. L. Jackson, *American's Struggle for Free Schools* (1941) and Jonathan Messerli, *Horace Mann* (1972) but Michael B. Katz, *The Irony of Early School Reform* (1968), Stanley K. Schultz, *The Culture Factory* (1973), and Carl F. Kaestle, *The Evolution of an Urban School System, 1750–1850* (1973) question whether the motives of the reformers were wholly benevolent. Abolitionism remains the subject of a great and growing literature. Good introductions, incorporating the findings of modern scholarship, include James Brewer Stewart, *Holy Warriors: The Abolitionists and American Slavery* (1976). Louis Filler, *The Crusade Against Slavery, 1830–1860* (1960), D. L. Dumond, *Antislavery* (1961), Ronald Walters, *The Anti-Slavery Appeal* (1976), and Merton L. Dillon, *The Abolitionists* (1974). Two useful collections of essays are Martin Duberman, ed., *The Antislavery Vanguard* (1965) and Lewis Perry and Richard Feldman, eds., *Antislavery Reconsidered* (1979). Other important studies include William C. Wiecik, *The Sources of Antislavery Constitutionalism in the United States, 1760–1848* (1977), Aileen S. Kraditor, *Means and Ends in American Abolitionism: Garrison and his Critics, 1834–1850* (1969), Lewis Perry, *Radical Abolitionism: Anarchy and the Government of God in Antislavery Thought* (1973), Lawrence J. Friedman, *Gregarious Saints: Self and Community in American Abolition, 1830–1870* (1983), and Bertram Wyatt-Brown, *Yankee Saints and Southern Sinners* (1985). The role of blacks in the abolitionist movement may be gathered from

Benjamin Quarles, *Black Abolitionists* and William McFeeley, *Frederick Douglass* (1990). Dorothy Sterling, *Ahead of her Time: Abby Kelley and the Politics of Antislavery* (1991) deals perceptively with the connection between abolitionism and feminism. P. J. Staudenraus, *The African Colonization Movement, 1815–1865* (1961) is standard on that subject. The unpopularity of abolitionists in the North is explored in Lorman Ratner, *Powder Keg: Northern Opposition to the Antislavery Movement, 1831–1840* (1968) and Leonard L. Richards, *"Gentlemen of Propety and Standing": Anti-Abolition Mobs in Jacksonian America* (1970) and is made more comprehensible in Leon F. Litwack's fine study of Northern racial prejudice, *North of Slavery: The Negro in the Free States, 1790–1860* (1961). Southern defenses of slavery are examined in W. S. Jenkins, *Southern Pro-Slavery Thought in the Old South* (1935), Larry E. Tise, *Proslavery: A History of the Defense of Slavery in America, 1701–1840* (1987), William J. Cooper, *The South and the Politics of Slavery, 1828–1856* (1978), and Eugene D. Genovese, *The Slaveholders' Dilemma: Freedom and Progress in Southern Conservative Thought* (1992). The notion that most slaveholding women were opposed to the slave sytem, advanced by Catherine Clinton, *The Plantation Mistress: Women's World in the Old South* (1982) and Suzanne Lebsock, *The Free Women of Petersburg* (1984), is challenged in Elizabeth Fox-Genovese, *Within The Plantation Household: Black and White Women of the Old South* (1988). For feminism and the status of women see Nancy F. Cott, *The Bonds of Womanhood* (1977), Ann Douglas, *The Feminization of American Culture* (1977), and Anne F. Scott, *The Southern Lady* (1970). Other reform movements are dealt with in Peter Brock, *Radical Pacifists in Antebellum America* (1968), F. L. Byrne, *Prophet of Prohibition: Neal Dow and his Crusade* (1961), W. J. Rorabaugh, *The Alcoholic Republic* (1979), Blake McKelvey, *American Prisons* (1936), and David J. Rothman, *The Discovery of the Asylum* (1971).

Chapter 10

Ray A. Billington, *The Far Western Frontier, 1830–1860* (1956) provides a convenient introduction to most of the themes of this chapter. The ideology of expansionism in the 1840s is analyzed in Albert K. Weinberg, *Manifest Destiny* (19353) and with rare perception in Frederick Merk's two books, *Manifest Destiny and Mission in American History* (1963) and *The Monroe Doctrine and American Expansionism, 1843–1849* (1966). Norman Graebner's *Empire on the Pacific* (1955) and his *Manifest Destiny* (1968) emphasize the economic motives for expansion, as does Thomas R. Hietala, *Manifest Design: Anxious Aggrandizement in Late Jacksonian America* (1990). A comprehensive view of the diplomacy of expansion is provided in David M. Pletcher, *The Diplomacy of Expansion: Texas, Oregon and the Mexican War* (1973). E. C. Barker, *Mexico and Texas, 1821–1835* (1928) examines American penetration of Texas, while W. C. Binkley, *The Texas Revolution* (1952) deals with the era of Texan independence. On pioneer migration across the Great Plains see Ray A. Billington, *Westward to the Pacific* (1979), John Mack Faragher, *Women and Men on the Overland Trail* (1979) and John D. Unruh, *The Plains Across* (1979). On Oregon, Francis Parkman's classic work, *The Oregon Trail* (1849) may be supplemented by David Lavender, *Westward Vision: The Story of the Oregon Trail* (1963). For the Mormon movement to Utah, see Nels Anderson, *Desert Saints* (1942) and L. H. Creer, *The Founding of an Empire* (1947). The economic development of the Mormon settlements is well described in Leonard J. Arrington, *Great Basin Kingdom* (1958) and Klaus J. Hansen, *Quest for Empire* (1967). American migration to California is covered in R. G. Cleland, *From Wilderness to Empire* (1944) and Rodman W. Paul, *California Gold: The Beginning of Mining in the Far West* (1947). A thoughtful survey of the political background to expansion is W. R. Brock, *Parties and Political Conscience: American Dilemmas, 1840–1850* (1979). Polk's role in the disputes over Oregon and the Texan boundary is authoritatively treated in Charles G. Sellers, *James K. Polk, Continentalist, 1843–1846* (1966). A. H. Bill, *Rehearsal for Conflict* (1947) is a good, brief study of the Mexican War. A more recent study, K. Jack Brauer, *The Mexican War, 1846–1848* (1974), describes the military campaigns convincingly but is uncritically nationalistic. Alternative perspectives on the war are presented in three notable books: Gene M. Brack, *Mexico Views Manifest Destiny* (1976), John H. Schroeder, *Mr. Polk's War: American Opposition and Dissent, 1846–1848* (1973), and Robert W. Johannsen, *To the Halls of the Montezumas: The Mexican War in the American Imagination* (1988). The most detailed and penetrating account of the sectional crisis arising out of the Mexican War is Allan Nevins's magisterial work, *The Ordeal of the Union* (2 vols., 1947), which spans the years 1846 to 1854. The immediate political consequences of the war are traced in John Mayfield, *Rehearsal for Republicanism: Free Soil and the Politics of Antislavery* (1980). Holman Hamilton, *Prologue to Conflict* (1964) is the standard work on the Compromise of 1850. For further perspectives on the mid-century crisis see Charles M. Wiltse, *John C. Calhoun: Sectionalist, 1840–1850* (1951) and the biographies of Webster and Clay cited in earlier chapters.

Chapter 11

Allan Nevins, *The Ordeal of the Union*, cited previously, and his *The Emergence of Lincoln* (2 vols., 1950) are indispensable for the coming of the Civil War. Newer viewpoints are brought together in another outstanding survey of the pre-Civil War decade, David M. Potter and Don E. Fehrenbacher, *The Impending Crisis, 1848–1861* (1976). For a brief but authoritative treatment see the opening chapters of James M. McPherson, *Battle Cry of Freedom: The Civil War Era* (1989). Also valuable are the interpretative essays in Eric Foner, *Politics and Ideology in the Age of the Civil War* (1980). Scholarly analyses of the sources of Southern alienation include Clement Eaton, *The Growth of Southern Civilization, 1790–1860* (1961), Avery O. Craven, *The Growth of Southern Nationalism, 1848–1861* (1953), Bertram Wyatt-Brown, *Southern Honor: Ethics and Behavior in the Old South* (1982) and John McCardell, *The Idea of a Southern Nation* (1979). Biographies of key political figures include Robert W. Johannsen, *Stephen A. Douglas* (1973) and David Donald, *Charles Sumner and the Coming of the Civil War* (1960). Lincoln's lengthening shadow is skillfully traced in Don E. Fehrenbacher, *Prelude to Greatness: Lincoln in the 1850s* (1962). Eric Foner, *Free Soil, Free Labor, Free Men: The Ideology of the Republican Party before the Civil War* (1970) is an acute analysis of Republican ideas and values, as well as of the relationship between antislavery and nativism. William Gienapp, *The Origins of the Republican Party, 1852–1856* (1987) provides the fullest account of the birth of the new party. The thesis that the political upheaval of the 1850s owed as much to anti-foreignism as to anti-Nebraska sentiment is advanced in Michael F. Holt, *Forging a Majority: The Formation of the Republican Party in Pittsburgh, 1848–1860* (1969) and *The Political Crisis of the 1850s*. By contrast, Tyler G. Anbinder, *Nativism and Slavery: The Northern Know-Nothings and the Politics of the 1850s* (1992) makes a strong case for the primacy of the slavery issue. For the issue of popular sovereignty see James A. Rawley, *Race and Politics: "Bleeding Kansas" and the Coming of the Civil War* (1969). Don E. Fehrenbacher, *The Dred Scott Case: Its Significance in American Law and Politics* (1979) is a definitive study. For the Lincoln–Douglas debates see Harry V. Jaffa, *Crisis of the House Divided* (1959). The election of 1860 and the secession of the Lower South are well covered in Kenneth M. Stampp, *And the War Came: The North and the Secession Crisis, 1860–1861* (1950) and David M. Potter, *Lincoln and his Party in the Secession Crisis* (1942). The secession movement in the South is best studied in William L. Barney, *The Road to Secession* (1972), Ralph A. Wooster, *The Secession Conventions of the South* (1962), and William Freehling, *The Road to Disunion* (1990). For Lincoln's handling of the Fort Sumter crisis see Richard N. Current, *Lincoln and the First Shot* (1963).

Chapter 12

The best and most up-to-date one-volume survey of the war is James M. McPherson, *Battle Cry of Freedom*, already cited. Also valuable are J. G. Randall and David Donald, *The Divided Union* (1961) and Peter J. Parish, *The American Civil War* (1975). Allan Nevins, *The War for the Union* (4 vols., 1959–71) is the most comprehensive, modern full-scale study. On the Union side the most exhaustive modern accounts of the fighting are Kenneth P. Williams, *Lincoln Finds a General* (5 vols., 1949–56) and Bruce Catton, *Centennial History of the Civil War* (3 vols., 1961–8). A briefer study is T. Harry Williams, *Lincoln and his Generals* (1952), which is useful on civil–military relations. Detailed accounts of military operations from the Confederate point of view are contained in Douglas S. Freeman's classic works, *R. E. Lee: A Biography* (4 vols., 1934–5) and *Lee's Lieutenants* (3 vols., 1924–44). See also Shelby Foote, *The Civil War* (3 vols., 1958–74). A briefer treatment is Frank E. Vandiver, *Rebel Brass* (1956). The common soldiers of the two armies are brought to life respectively in Bell I. Wiley, *The Life of Billy Yank* (1952) and *The Life of Johnny Reb* (1943). Battlefield experiences are recreated in Gerald E. Linderman, *Embattled Courage: The Experience of Combat in the American Civil War* (1989) and Reid Mitchell, *Civil War Soldiers: Their Expectations and Experiences* (1989). Benjamin Thomas's admirable one-volume life, *Abraham Lincoln* (1952) offers the best introduction to its subject, but it may be supplemented by David Donald's illuminating *Lincoln Reconsidered* (1956) and Philip S. Paludan, *The Presidency of Abraham Lincoln* (1994). J. G. Randall, *Lincoln the President* (4 vols., 1945–55) is the most distinguished full-length biography. Lincoln's difficulties with his party are highlighted in T. Harry Williams, *Lincoln and the Radicals* (1941) but played down in Hans L. Trefousse, *The Radical Republicans* (1969). The problem of slavery is examined in John Hope Franklin, *The Emancipation Proclamation* (1963), James M. McPherson, *The Struggle for Equality: Abolitionists and the Negro in the Civil War and Reconstruction* (1964), Louis S. Gerteis, *From Contraband to Freedom: Federal Policy towards Southern Blacks, 1861–5* (1973) and W. Cox, *Lincoln and*

Black Freedom (1981). The role of the freedmen is explored in Benjamin Quarles, *The Negro in the Civil War* (1953) and Ira Berlin *et al.*, *Freedom: A Documentary History of Emancipation 1861–1867* (2 vols., 1986–91). Aspects of wartime politics are treated in Joel H. Silbey, *A Respectable Minority: The Democratic Party in the Civil War Era* (1977) and James A. Rawley, *Lincoln and Civil War Politics* (1969). Philip S. Paludan, *A People's Contest: The Union and Civil War, 1861–1865* (1988) is a thoughtful survey of the impact of the conflict on Northern society. How Northern intellectuals reacted to the war is brilliantly described in George M. Frederickson, *The Inner Civil War* (1968). The problems of financing the Union war effort are dealt with in Bert W. Rein, *Analysis and Critique of Union Financing during the Civil War* (1962) and Bray Hammond, *Sovereignty and an Empty Purse: Banks and Politics in the Civil War* (1970). Northern opposition to the war is the theme of Frank L. Klement, *Copperheads in the Middle West* (1960) and of Edward C. Kirkland, *Peacemakers of 1864* (1927). The best accounts of the New York draft riots are Adrian Cook, *The Armies of the Streets* (1975) and Iver Bernstein, *The New York City Draft Riots* (1990). The best general histories of the Confederacy are Emory M. Thomas, *The Confederate Nation, 1861–1865* (1979) and Clement Eaton, *A History of the Southern Confederacy* (1954). Also of value are Burton J. Hendrick, *Statesmen of the Lost Cause* (1939), Charles W. Ramsdell, *Behind the Lines in the Southern Confederacy* (1944) and Escott Paul, *After Secession: Jefferson Davis and the Failure of Confederate Nationalism* (1978). Various aspects of wartime diplomacy are treated in Brian A. Jenkins, *Britain and the War for the Union* (2 vols., 1974–7), Frank L. Owsley, *King Cotton Diplomacy* (rev. edn., 1979), David P. Crook, *The North, the South and the Powers, 1861–1865* (1974), Lynn M. Case and Warren F. Spencer, *The United States and France: Civil War Diplomacy* (1970), Martin B. Duberman, *Charles Francis Adams* (1961) and Glyndon G. Van Deusen, *William H. Seward* (1967). Mary Ellison, *Support for Secession: Lancashire and the American Civil War* (1972) contends that British working-class sentiment was less favorable to the North than was long supposed, but her view is challenged in Philip Foner, *British Labor and the American Civil War* (1981).

Chapter 13

A masterly introduction to this complex and long-misunderstood period is Eric Foner, *Reconstruction: America's Unfinished Revolution, 1863–1877* (1988). Other useful surveys include Kenneth M. Stampp, *Reconstruction, 1865–1877* (1965) and John Hope Franklin, *Reconstruction after the Civil War* (1961). Among collections of revisionist essays the best are Harold M. Hyman, ed., *New Frontiers of the American Reconstruction* (1969), Kenneth M. Stampp and Leon F. Litwack, eds., *Reconstruction: An Anthology of Revisionist Writings* (1969) and Otto H. Olsen, ed., *Reconstruction and Redemption in the South* (1980). Lincoln's wartime approaches to Reconstruction are analyzed in Herman Belz, *Reconstructing the Union* (1969). The differences between Johnson and Congress over Reconstruction policy are intensively examined in Eric L. McKitrick, *Andrew Johnson and Reconstruction* (1960), La Wanda and John H. Cox, *Politics, Principle and Prejudice* (1963), William R. Brock, *An American Crisis: Congress and Reconstruction* (1963), Michael L. Benedict, *A Compromise of Principle: Congressional Republicans and Reconstruction, 1863–1869* (1974), and Martin E.

Mantell, *Johnson, Grant and the Politics of Reconstruction* (1973). Southern attitudes to Reconstruction in the immediate postwar era are carefully analyzed in Michael Perman, *Reunion without Compromise: The South and Reconstruction, 1865–1868* (1973) and Dan T. Carter, *When the War Was Over* (1985). On Johnson's impeachment see Michael L. Benedict, *The Impeachment and Trial of Andrew Johnson* (1973) and Hans L. Trefousse, *Impeachment of a President* (1975). There are several good biographies of leading Radicals, all moderately favorable to their subjects: Fawn M. Brodie, *Thaddeus Stevens* (1959), David Donald, *Charles Sumner and the Rights of Man* (1970), and Hans L. Trefousse, *Benjamin F. Wade* (1973). The protracted debates over constitutional amendments are summarized and commented on in Joseph B. James, *The Framing of the Fourteenth Amendment* (1956) and William Gillette, *The Right to Vote: Politics and the Passing of the Fifteenth Amendment* (1968). For the role of the courts see Stanley I. Kutler, *Judicial Power and Reconstruction Politics* (1968) and for that of the army James E. Sefton, *The United States Army and Reconstruction, 1865–1877* (1967). Historians have had difficulty in making Grant an interesting figure, but William S. McFeely, *Grant* (1980) is the most up-to-date and authoritative study. James M. McPherson's excellent account of Abolitionist attitudes to Reconstruction, *The Struggle for Equality* (1964) examines one strand of Northern opinion; Forrest G. Wood, *Black Scare: The Racist Response to Emancipation and Reconstruction* (1968) casts a lurid light on another. See also Stanley Coben, "Northern Businessmen and Radical Reconstruction", *Mississippi Valley Historical Review*, 46 (1959), George R. Woolfolk, *The Cotton Regency: The Northern Merchants and Reconstruction, 1865–1880* (1959), and Robert P. Sharkey, *Money, Class and Party: An Economic Study of the Civil War and Reconstruction* (1959). Monetary policy is the subject of two important books: Walter T. K. Nugent, *The Money Question during Reconstruction* (1967) and Irwin Unger, *The Greenback Era: A Social and Political History of American Finance, 1865–1879* (1974). The implementation of Reconstruction policies in the South is dealt with in Willie Lee Rose, *Rehearsal for Reconstruction: The Port Royal Experiment* (1968), George R. Bentley, *A History of the Freedmen's Bureau* (1955), William S. McFeely, *Yankee Stepfather: General O. O. Howard and the Freedmen* (1968), and Claude F. Oubre, *Forty Acres and a Mule: The Freedmen's Bureau and Black landownership* (1978). Scholarly accounts of white reaction to emancipation are James L. Roark, *Masters Without Slaves: The Planters in the Civil War and Reconstruction* (1977) and Joel Williamson, *The Crucible of Race: Black–White Relations in the American South since Emancipation* (1984). See also L. N. Powell, *New Masters: Northern Planters during the Civil War and Reconstruction* (1980). On the black codes see Theodore B. Wilson, *The Black Codes of the South* (1965). How blacks themselves responded to freedom is imaginatively described in Leon F. Litwack, *Been in the Storm So Long: The Aftermath of Slavery* (1979). For black political participation see Howard N. Rabinowitz, ed., *Southern Black Leaders of the Reconstruction Era* (1982) and Thomas C. Holt, *Black Over White: Negro Political Leadership in South Carolina during Reconstruction* (1979). Black educational progress is charted in William P. Vaughn, *Schools for All: The Blacks and Public Education in the South, 1865–1877* (1975) and Robert C. Morris, *Reading, 'Riting and Reconstruction: The Education of Freedmen in the South, 1861–1870* (1981). For Southern white participation in state politics see Richard N. Current, *Those Terrible Carpetbaggers* (1989). For attempts to preserve white supremacy by force see Allen W. Trelease, *White Terror: The Ku Klux Klan and Southern Reconstruction* (1971) and George C. Rable, *But There Was No Peace: The Role of Violence in the Politics of Reconstruction* (1984). The undoing of Reconstruction is lucidly discussed in William Gillette, *Retreat from Reconstruction, 1869–1879* (1979) and Michael Perman, *The Road to Redemption: Southern Politics, 1869–1879* (1984). The most useful study of the disputed election of 1876 is Keith I. Poliakoff, *The Politics of Inertia: The Election of 1876 and the End of Reconstruction* (1973). For the complicated behind-the-scenes manoeuvres that brought Reconstruction to an end, see C. Vann Woodward, *Reunion and Reaction: The Compromise of 1877 and the End of Reconstruction* (1951).

Chapter 14

C. Vann Woodward's classic work, *Origins of the New South, 1877–1913* (1951) is the indispensable starting-point for the history of the post-Reconstruction South. Edward L. Ayers, *The Promise of the New South: Life after Reconstruction* (1992) is a provocative new synthesis which, while not neglecting the standard topics of New South historiography, addresses some traditionally ignored, such as religion, consumer culture, music, and sport. For studies which rely heavily on quantitative methods or on economic theory and in some respects dissent from Woodward see Harold D. Woodman, "Sequel to Slavery: The New History Views the Postbellum South", *Journal of Southern History*, 43 (1977), Stephen J. DeCanio, *Agriculture in the Postbellum South* (1975), Roger L. Ransome and Richard Sutch, *One Kind of Freedom: The Economic Consequences of Emancipation* (1977), Jonathan Wiener, *Social Origins of the New South: Alabama, 1860–1885* (1978), and Gavin Wright, *Political Economy of the Cotton South* (1978). On debt peonage see Pete Daniel, *The Shadow of Slavery* (1972) and Daniel A. Novak, *The Wheel of Servitude* (1978). The idea of the New South is discussed in R. B. Nixon, *Henry W. Grady* (1943) and is examined more critically in Paul Gaston, *The New South Creed* (1970). Valuable studies of the growth of industry include James C. Cobb, *Industry and Southern Society, 1877–1984* (1984) and Patrick J. Hearden, *Independence and Empire: The New South's Cotton Mill Campaigns, 1865–1901* (1982). Reconciliation with the North is the theme of Paul H. Buck, *The Road to Reunion, 1865–1900* (1937). The politics of the New South are ably dissected in J. Morgan Kousser, *The Shaping of Southern Politics: Suffrage Restriction and the Establishment of the One-Party South, 1880–1910* (1974), William J. Cooper, Jr., *The Conservative Regime: South Carolina, 1877–1890* (1968), and William I. Hair, *Bourbonism and Agrarian Protest: Louisiana Politics, 1877–1900* (1969). The limitations placed on black freedom after Reconstruction are sympathetically chronicled in Rayford W. Logan, *The Betrayal of the Negro* (1965). For a different perspective see Eric Foner's enlightening study, *Nothing but Freedom: Emancipation and its Legacy* (1983), which shows that emancipation brought greater gains to blacks in America than to those in other former slave societies. Black economic advance is also stressed in Robert Higgs, *Competition and Coercion: Blacks in the American Economy, 1865–1914* (1977). The origins of racial segregation are traced in C. Vann Woodward, *The Strange Career of Jim Crow* (3rd edn., 1974). The ideology of white supremacy is analyzed in Idus A.

Newby, *Jim Crow's Defense: Anti-Negro Thought, 1900–1930* (1965). For accounts of how blacks fared in particular states see Vernon L. Wharton, *The Negro in Mississippi, 1877–1890* (1947), George B. Tindall, *South Carolina Negroes, 1877–1900* (1952), and Charles E. Wynes, *Race Relations in Virginia, 1870–1902* (1961). The North's abandonment of blacks is recorded in Vincent P. De Santis, *Republicans Face the Southern Question, 1877–1897* (1959) and Stanley P. Hirshson, *Farewell to the Bloody Shirt: Northern Republicans and the Southern Negro, 1877–1893* (1953). Black migration to Northern cities is covered in Florette Henri, *Black Migration: Movement North, 1900–1920* (1975), Gilbert Osofsky, *Harlem: The Making of a Ghetto, 1890–1930* (1966), and Allan H. Spear, *Black Chicago: The Making of a Negro Ghetto, 1890–1920* (1967). Black responses to discrimination and disfranchisement are dealt with in two excellent biographies, Louis R. Harlan, *Booker T. Washington* (2 vols., 1972–83) and Elliott M. Rudwick, *W. E. B. Du Bois: Propagandist of Negro Protest* (2nd edn., 1969). Liberal white responses to the race problem are recorded in Charles F. Kellogg, *History of the National Association for the Advancement of Colored People, 1909–1920* (1967) and James M. McPherson, *The Abolitionist Legacy: From Reconstruction to the NAACP* (1975).

Chapter 15

The most useful general survey of the trans-Mississippi West is Leroy R. Hafen *et al.*, *Western America* (1970). For the influence of the frontier on American development see R. A. Billington, *America's Frontier Heritage* (1966). Billington's *Frederick Jackson Turner* (1973) has a balanced assessment of Turner's celebrated frontier thesis. The mythology of the West is sensitively probed in Henry Nash Smith, *Virgin Land: The American West as Symbol and Myth* (1950). The best studies of Western mining are Rodman W. Paul, *Mining Frontiers of the Far West, 1840–1880* (1963) and William S. Greever, *The Bonanza West: The Story of the Western Mining Rushes, 1848–1900* (1963). The early history of the most notorious mining town in the Southwest is objectively traced in Odie B. Faulk, *Tombstone* (1973). For the Western cattle industry see E. E. Dale, *The Range Cattle Industry* (1930), Lewis Atherton, *The Cattle Kings* (1961), and E. S. Osgood, *The Day of the Cattleman* (1929). Readers wishing to cling to romantic illusions about cowboys will not appreciate Joe B. Frantz and Julian E. Choate, *The American Cowboy: Myth and Reality* (1955), David Dary, *Cowboy Culture: A Saga of Five Centuries* (1989) or scholarly social histories of Kansas cattle trading centers like Robert R. Dykstra, *The Cattle Towns* (1968) and Odie B. Faulk, *Dodge City* (1977). For a good survey of all forms of Western transportation from stagecoaching to railroads see Oscar O. Winther, *The Transportation Frontier: Trans-Mississippi West, 1865–1890* (1964). Detailed studies of railroads include Robert E. Riegel, *The Story of Western Railroads* (1926) and George R. Taylor and Irene D. Neu, *The American Railroad Network, 1865–1890* (1956). On the Indian Wars see Ralph K. Andrist, *The Long Death: The Last Days of the Plains Indians* (1964), Paul I. Wellman, *The Indian Wars of the West* (1954), and two works by Robert M. Utley, *The Last Days of the Sioux Nation* (1963) and *The Indian Frontier of the American West, 1846–1890* (1984). A strongly pro-Indian but unreliable popular account is Dee Brown, *Bury My Heart in Wounded Knee* (1970). Federal Indian policy is assessed in Henry E. Fritz, *The Movement for Indian Assimilation, 1860–1890* (1963) and Loring B. Priest, *Uncle Sam's Stepchildren: The Reformation of United States Indian Policy, 1865–1887* (1975). The efforts of Eastern friends of the Indian to change federal policy are traced in Robert W. Mardock, *The Reformers and the American Indian* (1970). The problems of settling different regions of the West are treated in Walter P. Webb's classic *The Great Plains* (1931), Robert G. Athearn, *High Country Empire: The High Plains and the Rockies* (1965), and C. C. Rister, *The Southwestern Frontier, 1865–1890* (1947). Federal land policy is the subject of R. M. Robbins, *Our Landed Heritage: The Public Domain, 1776–1936* (1942) and B. H. Hibbard, *A History of Public Land Policies* (1924). For Western agriculture see Fred A. Shannon, *The Farmer's Last Frontier: Agriculture, 1860–1897* (1945), Allan G. Bogue, *From Prairie to Corn Belt* (1963) and Gilbert C. Fite, *The Farmers' Frontier, 1865–1900* (1966). See also Everett Dick, *The Sod-House Frontier, 1854–1890* (1937), which emphasizes social and cultural life. The political evolution of the West is ably described in Earl S. Pomeroy, *The Territories and the United States, 1869–1890* (1947). For conservation see Frank Graham, jr., *Man's Dominion: The Story of Conservation in America* (1971), Harold T. Pinkett, *Gifford Pinchot: Private and Public Forester* (1970), and John Ise, *Our National Park Policy: A Critical History* (1970). Wallace Stegner, *Beyond the Hundredth Meridian: John Wesley Powell and the Second Opening of the West* (1953) is a fine biography of the father of Western irrigation and reclamation.

Chapter 16

The best brief introduction to the American industrial revolution is Glenn Porter, *The Rise of Big Business* (rev. edn., 1992), but Edward C. Kirkland, *Industry Comes of Age: Business, Labor and Public Policy, 1860–1897* (1956) and Thomas C. Cochran and William Miller, *The Age of Enterprise* (1942) are still valuable. Business leaders are castigated in Matthew Josephson, *The Robber Barons* (1934) and mildly hero-worshipped in Allan Nevins, *A Study in Power: John D. Rockefeller, Industrialist and Philanthropist* (2 vols.), (1953), Joseph Wall, *Andrew Carnegie* (1970), and Harold Livesay, *Andrew Carnegie and the Rise of Big Business* (1975). The inventions that made possible the economic revolution are described in Nathan Rosenberg, *Technology and American Economic Growth* (1972), while the role of individual inventors is suggested in Matthew Josephson, *Edison* (1959). Technological advances in manufacturing are covered in D. G. Houndsell, *From the American System to Mass Production* (1984). For the part played by investment bankers and financiers see Andrew Sinclair, *Corsair: J. Pierpont Morgan* (1981) and Maury Klein, *The Life and Legend of Jay Gould* (1986). The ideas of business leaders are analyzed in Edward C. Kirkland, *Dream and Thought in the Business Community, 1860–1900* (1956) and Thomas C. Cochran, *Railroad Leaders, 1845–1890* (1965). The social origins of the business elite are revealed in William Miller, ed., *Men in Business* (1956). Railroads and their contribution to economic growth are studied in Taylor and Neu, already cited, Robert W. Fogel, *Railroads and American Economic Growth* (1964), and Albro Martin, *Railroads Triumphant* (1991). Government attempts to check business monopolies are traced in William Letwin, *Law and Economic Policy in America: The Evolution of the Sherman Anti-Trust Act* (1965), Hans B. Thorelli, *Federal Antitrust Policy* (1955) and Clair Wilcox, *Public Policies towards Business*

(1960). Gabriel Kolko's *Railroads and Regulation, 1877–1916* (1965) tries to show that the movement in favor of regulation was basically a response to the railroads' own needs. For the attitude of the courts to corporate capitalism one should consult Arnold M. Paul, *Conservative Crisis and the Rule of Law: Attitudes of Bar and Bench, 1887–1895* (1960), Robert G. McCloskey, *American Conservatism in the Age of Enterprise* (1951), Sidney Fine, *Laissez-Faire and the General Welfare State* (1964), and the relevant portions of Loren P. Beth, *The Development of the American Constitution, 1877–1917* (1972). For the growth of unions see Norman J. Ware, *The Labor Movement in the United States, 1860–1895* (1929) and Gerald Grob, *Workers and Utopia* (1961), both of which focus on the Knights of Labor. For the A.F. of L. see Philip Taft, *The A.F. of L. in the time of Gompers* (1963), Bernard Mandel, *Samuel Gompers* (1963) and S. B. Kaufman's revisionist study, *Samuel Gompers and the Origins of the American Federation of Labor* (1973). Radical unionism is comprehensively covered in Melvyn Dubofsky, *We Shall Be All: A History of the Industrial Workers of the World* (1969) and, more briefly, in Patrick Renshaw, *The Wobblies* (1967). There are several excellent accounts of strikes and industrial violence: Wayne G. Broehl, Jr., *The Molly Maguires* (1964), R. V. Bruce, *1877: The Year of Violence* (1959), Henry David, *The History of the Haymarket Affair* (1936), Leon Wolff, *Lockout: The Homestead Strike of 1892* (1965), Paul Krause, *The Battle for Homestead, 1880–1892* (1992), and Almont Lindsay, *The Pullman Strike* (1942). For insights into the lives and beliefs of ordinary industrial workers, the great majority of whom were not union members, see David Brody, *Steelworkers in America* (1960) and Herbert Gutman, *Work, Culture and Society in Industrializing America* (1977). An outstanding work is David Montgomery, *The Fall of the House of Labor: The Workplace, the State and American Labor Activism, 1865–1925* (1988), which challenges a long-dominant orthodoxy by arguing that the diversity of workers' experience did not obscure or undermine the significance of class. On working women see Alice Kessler-Harris's perceptive book, *Out to Work* (1983).

Chapter 17

The growth of cities in the half-century after the Civil War is comprehensively treated in Arthur M. Schlesinger, *The Rise of the City, 1878–1898* (1933), Blake McKelvey, *The Urbanization of America, 1860–1915* (1963), Charles A. Glaab and A. Theodore Brown, *A History of Urban America* (3rd edn., 1983), Sam Bass Warner, *The Urban Wilderness: A History of the American City* (1973) and Gunther P. Barth, *City People: The Rise of Modern City Culture in Nineteenth Century America* (1980). For the "new" immigration see Oscar Handlin's evocative study, *The Uprooted* (2nd edn., 1973). For a more recent general treatment see John Bodnar, *The Transplanted: A History of Immigrants in Urban America* (1985). Important studies of immigrant community life include Rowland T. Berthoff, *British Immigrants in Industrial America, 1790–1950* (1953), Humbert S. Nelli, *The Italians in Chicago, 1880–1930* (1967), Moses Rischin, *The Promised City: New York's Jews, 1870–1914* (1962), Irving Howe, *The Immigrant Jews of New York* (1976), Audrey L. Olson, *St Louis Germans, 1850–1920* (1980), and Dino Cinel, *From Italy to San Francisco: The Immigrant Experience* (1982). Outstanding examples of comparative urban ethnic history are Thomas Kessner, *The Golden Door: Italian and Jewish Immigrant Mobility in New York City,*

1880–1915 (1977) and Josef J. Barton, *Peasants and Strangers: Italians, Rumanians and Slovaks in an American City, 1890–1950* (1975). Immigrant women and the immigrant family are now beginning to receive the attention they deserve. See, for example, Joan Younger Dickinson, *The Role of the Immigrant Women in the U.S. Labor Force, 1890–1910* (1980), Janet A. Nolan, *Ourselves Alone: Women's Emigration from Ireland, 1885–1920* (1990), Elizabeth Ewen, *Immigrant Women in the Land of Dollars* (1985), and S. J. Kleinberg, *The Shadow of the Mills: Working Class Families in Pittsburgh, 1870–1907* (1989). Roger Daniels, *Asian America: Chinese and Japanese in the United States since 1850* (1989) makes perceptive comparisons between Chinese and Japanese immigrants and between them and European immigrants. The standard work on late nineteenth-century nativism is John Higham, *Strangers in the Land: Patterns of American Nativism, 1860–1925* (rev. edn. 1963). See also Barbara M. Solomon, *Ancestors and Immigrants: A Changing New England Tradition* (1956). Urban problems are surveyed in Gordon Atkins, *Health, Housing and Poverty in New York City* (1947) and Robert H. Bremner, *From the Depths: The Discovery of Poverty in the United States* (1956). Two excellent books by Allen F. Davis describe the settlement house movement: *Spearheads for Reform* (1967) and *American Heroine: The Life of Jane Addams* (1973). The lifestyle of the new corporate aristocracy is entertainingly described in F. L. Allen, *The Big Change: America Transforms Itself, 1900–1950* (1952), and is investigated in scholarly fashion in E. Digby Baltzell, *The Protestant Establishment: Aristocracy and Caste in America* (1964) and Frederick C. Jaher, *The Urban Establishment: Upper Strata in Boston, New York, Charleston, Chicago and Los Angeles* (1982). The popular myth to rags-to-riches is examined in Irwin G. Wyllie, *The Self-Made Man in America* (1954) and John Tebbel, *From Rags to Riches: Horatio Alger and the American Dream* (1963). Systematic studies of social mobility employing a quantitative methodology have proliferated in recent decades. Among the earliest and best is Stephan Thernstrom, *Poverty and Progress: Social Mobility in a Nineteenth Century City* (1964), which tested the rags-to-riches thesis empirically and found it wanting. Similar studies include Thernstrom's *The Other Bostonians* (1973), Howard Chudacoff, *Mobile Americans: Residential and Social Mobility in Omaha, 1880–1920* (1972), and the books by Kessner and Barton cited above. For the changing position of women see the relevant chapters of William L. O'Neill, *Everyone Was Brave: The Rise and Fall of Feminism in America* (1969). Divorce can be studied in Nelson M. Blake, *The Road to Reno* (1962) and William L. O'Neill, *Divorce in the Progressive Era* (1967). The problems facing the churches in the urban age are surveyed in Paul A. Carter, *The Spiritual Crisis of the Gilded Age* (1971). How the churches responded is covered in Aaron I. Abell, *The Urban Impact on American Protestantism, 1865–1900* (1943), Henry F. May, *The Protestant Churches and Industrial America* (1949), C. H. Hopkins, *The Rise of the Social Gospel in American Protestantism* (1940), and Susan Curtis, *A Consuming Faith: The Social Gospel and Modern American Culture* (1992). For revivalism see James F. Findlay, Jr., *Dwight L. Moody, American Evangelist, 1837–1899* (1969). Educational trends are illuminated in Lawrence A. Cremin, *The Transformation of the School: Progressivism in American Education* (1961) and Merle Curti, *The Social Ideas of American Educators* (1935) but for what actually happened in the schools see David B. Tyack, *The One Best System* (1974). Higher education is admirably surveyed in Lawrence R. Veysey, *The Emergence of the American University* (1965) and Richard Hofstadter and Walter Metzger, *The Development of Academic Freedom in the United States* (1955), a book of broader scope than its title implies. The first women's colleges are surveyed in Helen Horowitz, *Alma Mater* (1984). For the period's leading educator and philosopher see Robert B. Westbrook, *John Dewey and American Democracy* (1992). Changes in the press are most conveniently studied in biographies of the new breed of newspaper owner: W. A. Swanberg, *Citizen Hearst* (1961) and George Juergens, *Joseph Pulitzer and the New York 'World'* (1965). The main currents of American thought are expertly analyzed in Henry S. Commager, *The American Mind* (1950) and Richard Hofstadter, *Social Darwinism in American Thought, 1860–1915* (2nd edn., 1959). For the period's leading social critics see John L. Thomas, *Alternative America: Henry George, Edward Bellamy, Henry Demarest Lloyd and the Adversary Tradition* (1983). On literature and the arts the most useful guides are Jay C. Martin, *Harvests of Change: American Literature, 1865–1914* (1967), Van Wyck Brooks, *New England: Indian Summer, 1865–1915* (1944) and *The Confident Years, 1885–1915* (1952), Larzer Ziff, *The American 1890s: Life and Times of a Lost Generation* (1967), and Oliver W. Larkin, *Art and Life in America* (1949).

Chapter 18

Among the most useful introductions to the politics of the late nineteenth century are H. Wayne Morgan, *From Hayes to McKinley: National Party Politics, 1877–1896* (1969) and John A. Garraty, *The New Commonwealth, 1877–1890* (1969). Despite its age James Bryce's *The American Commonwealth* (2 vols., 1895) is still indispensable for an understanding of the political system, though Jon C. Teaford, *City Government in America, 1879–1900* (1984) effectively challenges Bryce's oft-quoted dictum that the city was "the one conspicuous failure of the United States". Invaluable also are Morton Keller, *Affairs of State: Public Life in the Late Nineteenth Century* (1977), David J. Rothman, *Politics and Power: The United States Senate, 1869–1901* (1966), Leonard White's study of the workings of the federal government, *The Republican Era, 1869–1901* (1958), and Daniel J. Elazar's study of federal–state relations, *The American Partnership* (1962). The activities and methods of local bosses and machines are described in Seymour Mandelbaum, *Boss Tweed's New York* (1965), Alexander B. Callow, Jr., *The Tweed Ring* (1966), and Stephen B. Erie's revisionist analysis, *Rainbow's End: Irish-Americans and the dilemmas of Urban Machine Politics, 1840–1985* (1988). The structure and workings of the Republican and Democratic parties, respectively, are analyzed in Robert D. Marcus, *Grand Old Party: Political Structure in the Gilded Age* (1971) and J. Rogers Hollingsworth, *The Whirligig of Politics: The Democracy of Cleveland and Bryan* (1963). Mugwumps and other reform elements are assessed in John G. Sproat, *'The Best Men': Liberal Reformers in the Gilded Age* (1971), Geoffrey Blodgett, *The Gentle Reformers: Massachusetts Democrats in the Gilded Age* (1966), and Arthur Mann, *Yankee Reformers in the Urban Age* (1954). For the civil service reform movement see Ari Hoogenboom, *Outlawing the Spoils* (1968) and Gerald W. McFarland, *Mugwumps, Morals and Politics, 1884–1920* (1975). Ethno-cultural interpretations of voting behavior, characteristically based on quantitative analysis, have become influential in recent decades. Good examples are Richard J. Jensen, *The Winning of the Midwest: Social and*

Political Conflict, 1886–1896 (1971) and Paul Kleppner, *The Cross of Culture: A Social Analysis of Midwestern Politics, 1850–1900* (1970). John D. Hicks, *The Populist Revolt* (1931), though no longer the standard work on the subject, is still worth reading., The thesis advanced in Richard Hofstadter's *The Age of Reform* (1955), that the Populists were paranoid, backward-looking, and intolerant, is challenged in Norman Pollack, *The Populist Response to Industrial America* (1966) and Walter T. K. Nugent, *The Tolerant Populists* (1963). Among important biographies of Populist leaders are C. Vann Woodward, *Tom Watson, Agrarian Radical* (2nd edn., 1973), Francis B. Simkins, *Pitchfork Ben Tillman* (1944) and Martin Ridge, *Ignatius Donnelly* (1962). Lawrence Goodwyn's sweeping reinterpretation, *Democratic Promise: The Populist Movement in America* (1976) sees the Alliance cooperative movement as being central to the agrarian revolt and opens up new ways of thinking, not only about Populism but about the political system generally. Narrower in focus but just as challenging is Stephen Hahn, *The Roots of Southern Populism: Yeoman Farmers and the Transformation of the Georgia Uplands* (1983). On the election of 1896 there are several good studies: Stanley L. Jones, *The Presidential Election of 1896* (1964), Paul W. Glad, *McKinley, Bryan and the People* (1964) and Paolo E. Coletta, *William Jennings Bryan, Political Evangelist, 1860–1908* (1964).

Chapter 19

The varied nature of the Progressive movement is best shown in Arthur S. Link and Richard L. McCormick, *Progressivism* (1983). Historians have offered widely different interpretations of Progressivism, among the most stimulating being Richard Hofstadter, *The Age of Reform* (1955), which sees it as the product of a "status revolution", Samuel P. Hays, *The Response to Industrialism* (1957), which finds its origins in a desire for efficiency and order and Gabriel Kolko, *The Triumph of Conservatism* (1963), which argues that it was business-inspired. David P. Thelen, *The New Citizenship* (1972) revives an older fashion of taking progressive rhetoric at its face value. The thinking of leading Progressive intellectuals is carefully analyzed in David Noble, *The Paradox of Progressive Thought* (1958), Charles Forcey, *The Crossroads of Liberalism: Croly, Weyl, Lippmann and the Progressive Era, 1900–1925* (1961), and David W. Levy, *Herbert Croly of "The New Republic": The Life and Thought of an American Progressive* (1986). Several studies assess the contribution of particular groups to progressivism and in aggregate illuminate its multifarious character. The best accounts of the muckrakers are Louis Filler, *Crusaders for American Liberalism* (1939) and David M. Chalmers, *The Social and Political Ideas of the Muckrakers* (1964). The role of business is considered in Robert H. Wiebe, *Businessmen and Reform* (1962) and that of city bosses and their immigrant constituents in John D. Buenker, *Urban Liberalism and Progressive Reform* (1973). The contribution of the clergy may be studied in the works by May and Hopkins cited in the bibliography for chapter 17, and that of women in Paula Baker, *Gender and the Transformation of Politics: Public and Private Life in New York, 1870–1930* (1989). The women's suffrage movement is described in Eleanor Flexner, *Century of Struggle: The Women's Rights Movement in the United States* (1969), Andrew Sinclair, *The Better Half* (1965), and Aileen S. Kraditor, *The Ideas of the Women's Suffrage Movement, 1890–1920* (1965). For other specific reforms see J. H. Timberlake, *Prohibition and the Progressive*

Movement, 1900–1920 (1963), Ruth Rosen, *The Lost Sisterhood: Prostitution in America, 1900–1918* (1982), Roy Lubove, *The Urban Community: Housing and Planning in the Progressive Era* (1967), O. E. Anderson, *The Health of a Nation: Harvey W. Wiley and the Fight for Pure Food* (1958), David M. Kennedy, *Birth Control in America: The Career of Margaret Sanger* (1970), Jeremy S. Felt, *Hostages of Fortune: Child Labor Reform in New York State* (1965), and Jack Holl, *Juvenile Reform in the Progressive Era* (1971). On conservation there are two excellent studies: Samuel P. Hays, *Conservation and the Gospel of Efficiency: The Progressive Conservation Movement* (1959) and E. R. Richardson, *The Politics of Conservation: Crusades and Controversies, 1897–1913* (1962). Progressivism at the municipal and state level is explored in Zane L. Miller, *Boss Cox's Cincinnati* (1968), Melvin G. Holli, *Reform in Detroit: Hazen S. Pingree and Urban Politics* (1969), James B. Crooks, *Politics and Progressivism: The Rise of Urban Progressivism in Baltimore, 1895–1911* (1957), William D. Miller, *Memphis during the Progressive Era, 1900–1917* (1957), George E. Mowry, *The California Progressives* (1951), Robert S. Maxwell, *La Follette and the Rise of the Progressives in Wisconsin* (1956), H. L. Warner, *Progressivism in Ohio, 1897–1914* (1964), Robert B. Wesser, *Charles Evans Hughes and Reform in New York State* (1967), Richard L. McCormick, *From Realignment to Reform: Political Change in New York State, 1893–1910* (1981), and Dewey W. Grantham, *Hoke Smith and the Politics of the New South* (1958). For good regional treatments see: Russel B. Nye, *Midwestern Progressive Politics* (1951) and Dewey W. Grantham, *Southern Progressivism* (1983). Progressivism at the national level is ably surveyed in George E. Mowry, *The Era of Theodore Roosevelt, 1900–1912* (1958) and Arthur S. Link, *Woodrow Wilson and the Progressive Era, 1910–1917* (1954). Solid biographies of Roosevelt include William H. Harbaugh, *The Life and Times of Theodore Roosevelt* (1975) and Edmund Morris, *The Rise of Theodore Roosevelt* (1979), but see also John M. Blum's brilliant vignette of Roosevelt's Presidency, *The Republican Roosevelt* (2nd edn., 1977). For Taft see D. F. Anderson, *William Howard Taft: A Conservative's Conception of the Presidency* (1973) and Paolo E. Coletta, *The Presidency of William Howard Taft* (1973). The emergence of the Progressive Party and the election of 1912 are covered in George E. Mowry, *Theodore Roosevelt and the Progressive Movement* (1946). Wilson's Presidency is comprehensively covered in Arthur S. Link's definitive biography, *Wilson* (5 vols. to date, 1947–65), but there are good brief treatments in John M. Blum, *Woodrow Wilson and the Politics of Morality* (1956) and John A. Garraty, *Woodrow Wilson* (1956). Roosevelt and Wilson are intriguingly compared in John Milton Cooper, Jr., *The Warrior and the Priest* (1983). Standard interpretations of American Socialism are Howard H. Quint, *The Forging of American Socialism* (1953), David A. Shannon, *The Socialist Party of America* (1955), and Stow Parsons and Donald D. Egbert, *Socialism and American Life* (2 vols., 1952), but many of their assumptions are challenged in James Weinstein, *The Decline of Socialism in America, 1912–1925* (1967). For the best-known Socialist of the period see Nick Salvatore, *Eugene V. Debs: Citizen and Socialist* (1982).

Chapter 20

The best general survey of foreign affairs in the half-century after the Civil War is Walter LaFeber, *The American Search for Opportunity, 1865–1913* (1992). For different perspectives on the immediate postwar decades see Charles S. Campbell, *The Transformation of American Foreign Relations, 1865–1900* (1976) and Robert L. Beisner, *From the Old Diplomacy to the New, 1865–1900* (2nd edn., 1986) and on the early twentieth century, Foster R. Dulles, *America's Rise to World Power, 1898–1954* (1955) and Julius W. Pratt, *Challenge and Rejection: The United States and World Leadership, 1900–1921* (1967). Post-Civil War expansionism and the diplomatic legacies of the Civil War are treated in Ernest Paolino, *The Foundations of the American Empire: William H. Seward and United States Foreign Policy* (1973), Norman B. Ferris, *Desperate Diplomacy: William H. Seward's Foreign Policy* (1976), and Adrian Cook, *The Alabama Claims: American Politics and Anglo-American Relations* (1975). David Pletcher, *The Awkward Years: American Foreign Relations under Garfield and Arthur* (1962) tells everything one needs to know on the subject. Milton Plesur, *America's Outward Thrust: Approaches to Foreign Affairs, 1865–1890* (1971) sees the period as one foreshadowing the more active foreign policy of the 1890s. The importance of economic factors in American expansionism is stressed in William Appleman Williams, *The Tragedy of American Diplomacy* (1959) and Walter LaFeber, *The New Empire: An Interpretation of American Expansion, 1860–1898* (1963). The imperialism of the 1890s is analyzed from differing standpoints in Ernest R. May, *Imperial Democracy* (1961), David Healy, *United States Expansionism* (1970), and Peter Karsten, *The Naval Aristocracy* (1972). For the Spanish–American War the most comprehensive study is David F. Trask, *The War with Spain in 1898* (1981). H. Wayne Morgan, *America's Road to Empire: War with Spain* (1965) and his *William McKinley and his America* (1963) show that McKinley was not, as is often claimed, a spineless President bullied into war by the press and public opinion. Opposition to expansionism is covered in Robert L. Beisner, *Twelve Against Empire: The Anti-Imperialists, 1898–1900* (1968), E. Berkeley Thompson, *Anti-Imperialism in the United States: The Great Debate, 1890–1920* (1970), and Richard E. Welch, *Response to Imperialism: The United States and the Philippine–American War, 1899–1902* (1979). The suppression of the Filipino revolt is dealt with in Stuart C. Miller, *"Benevolent Assimilation": American Conquest of the Philippines, 1899–1902* (1984). The most up-to-date biography of the architect of the Open Door policy is Kenton J. Clymer, *John Hay: The Gentleman as Diplomat* (1975). Detailed studies of the results of that policy include Charles S. Campbell, Jr., *Special Business Interests and the Open Door Policy* (1951), Paul A. Varg, *The Making of a Myth: The United States and China, 1899–1912* (1968), Jerry Israel, *Progressivism and the Open Door* (1971). Marilyn B. Young, *The Rhetoric of Empire: America's China Policy, 1893–1901* (1968), and Thomas McCormick, *China Market: America's Quest for Informal Empire, 1893–1901* (1971). The best general account of Roosevelt's foreign policy is still Howard K. Beale, *Theodore Roosevelt and the Rise of America to World Power* (1956), but see also Raymond A. Esthus, *Theodore Roosevelt and International Rivalries* (1970). The deterioration of Japanese–American relations is covered in Raymond A. Esthus, *Theodore Roosevelt and Japan* (1961) and in two monographs by Charles E. Neu, *An Uncertain Friendship: Theodore Roosevelt and Japan, 1906–1909* (1967) and *The Troubled Encounter* (1975). For the acquisition of the Panama isthmus see David McCullough, *The Path Between the Seas: The Construction of the Panama Canal, 1870–1914* (1978). The workings of dollar diplomacy are analyzed in Walter V. and Marie V. Scholes, *Intervention and Dollar Diplomacy in the Caribbean, 1900–1921* (1969) and Ralph E. Minger, *William Howard Taft and United States Foreign Policy* (1975). Wilson's missionary diplomacy and the Mexican imbroglio are dealt with in P. Edward Healy, *Revolution and Intervention: The Diplomacy of Taft and Wilson with Mexico, 1910–1917* (1970), Kenneth J. Grieb, *The United States and Huerta* (1969), Robert E. Quirk, *An Affair of Honor: Woodrow Wilson and the Occupation of Vera Cruz* (1960), and Robert F. Smith, *The United States and Revolutionary Nationalism in Mexico, 1916–1932* (1972). For the rise of Anglo-American friendship see Bradford Perkins, *The Great Rapprochement: England and the United States, 1895–1914* (1968).

Chapter 21

An excellent general survey, covering neutrality, intervention and peacemaking is Daniel M. Smith, *The Great Departure: The United States and World War I, 1914–1920* (1965). A more recent overview, covering a slightly shorter period, is Robert H. Ferrell, *Woodrow Wilson and World War I* (1985). The neutrality period is most comprehensively covered in the following volumes of Arthur S. Link's *Wilson: The Struggle for Neutrality, 1914–1915* (1960), *Confusion and Crises, 1915–1916* (1964), and *Campaigns for Progressivism and Peace, 1916–1917* (1965). Also valuable are Ernest R. May, *The World War and American Isolation, 1914–1917* (1964), John M. Cooper, Jr., *The Vanity of Power: American Isolationism and World War I, 1914–1917* (1969), Patrick Devlin, *Too Proud to Fight: Woodrow Wilson's Neutrality* (1974), and Ross Gregory, *The Origins of American Intervention in the First World War* (1971). The American military contribution is analyzed in Edward M. Coffman, *The War to End All Wars: The American Military Experience in World War I* (1968), Frank Freidel, *Over There: The Story of America's First Overseas Crusade* (1964), and H. A. De Weerd, *President Wilson Fights his War* (1968). Good modern studies of the war effort include Daniel R. Beaver, *Newton D. Baker and the American War Effort, 1917–1919* (1966), Charles Gilbert, *American Financing of World War I* (1970), Robert D. Cuff, *The War Industries Board: Business–Government Relations during World War I* (1973), and George T. Blakely, *Historians on the Home Front: American Propagandists for the Great War* (1970). There are several accounts of the wartime curtailment of civil liberties, all of them critical: Horace C. Peterson and G. C. Fite, *Opponents of War, 1917–1918* (1957), Donald M. Johnson, *The Challenge to American Freedoms: World War I and the Rise of the American Civil Liberties Union* (1963), Harry N. Scheiber, *The Wilson Administration and Civil Liberties, 1918–1921* (1960), and William Preston, Jr., *Aliens and Dissenters* (1963). For wartime politics see Seward W. Livermore, *Politics is Adjourned: Woodrow Wilson and the War Congress, 1916–1918* (1966). Wartime social and cultural trends are best covered in David M. Kennedy, *Over Here: The First World War and American Society* (1980). For the role of women see Maurine Weiner Greenwald, *Women, War and Work* (1980) and Barbara Steinson, *American Women's Activism in World War I* (1982). Wilsonian diplomacy generally is shrewdly analyzed in Arthur S. Link, *Wilson the Diplomatist* (1957) and in more detail in N. Gordon Levin, Jr., *Woodrow Wilson and World Politics* (1968). Arno J. Mayer, *The Politics and Diplomacy of Peacemaking* (1967) is a comprehensive and provocative study of the Versailles negotiations. Wilson's part in them is sympathetically treated in Arthur Walworth, *America's Moment, 1918: American Diplomacy at the End of World War I* (1977). Two books by Thomas A. Bailey, *Woodrow Wilson and the Lost Peace* (1944) and *Woodrow Wilson and the Great Betrayal* (1945) put the blame on Wilson's own intransigence for the Senate's rejection of the Versailles Treaty. Ralph A. Stone, *The Irreconcilables: The Fight against the League of Nations* (1970) shows that the League's opponents were far from united and that only a few were isolationist.

Chapter 22

Of the many useful introductions to the 1920s, John D. Hicks, *Republican Ascendancy, 1921–1933* (1960) remains useful but William E. Leuchtenburg, *The Perils of Prosperity, 1914–1932* (1958) is more lively, Donald R. McCoy, *Coming of Age: The United States in the 1920s and 1930s* (1973) is more wide-ranging and Ellis W. Hawley, *The Great War and the Search for Modern Order: A History of the American People and Their Institutions, 1917–1933* (rev. edn., 1991) is more up-to-date. Highly illuminating, despite its anti-Republican bias, is Arthur M. Schlesinger, Jr., *The Crisis of the Old Order* (1957). The standard survey of economic developments is still George M. Soule, *Prosperity Decade* (1947), but it should be supplemented by Jim Potter's succinct and lucid study, *The American Economy Between the Wars* (1974). Social and cultural aspects are entertainingly treated in F. L. Allen, *Only Yesterday* (1931) and in greater depth in George H. Knoles, *The Jazz Age Revisited* (1955), John Braeman *et al.*, *Change and Continuity in America: The 1920s* (1968) and Don Kirschner, *City and Country: Rural Response to Urbanization in the 1920s* (1970). A revealing account of the growth of suburbs is Kenneth T. Jackson, *Crabgrass Frontier* (1985). Many of the stereotypes of the decade are challenged, though from differing standpoints, in Robert K. Murray, *The Politics of Normalcy* (1973), Paul A. Carter, *Another Part of the Twenties* (1977) and Paula S. Fass, *The Damned and the Beautiful: American Youth in the 1920s* (1977). Robert K. Murray, *Red Scare: A Study in National Hysteria, 1919–1920* (1955) is thoughtful and balanced. Other works which capture the postwar mood are William Tuttle, Jr., *Race Riot: Chicago and the Red Summer of 1919* (1970), R. L. Friedheim, *The Seattle General Strike* (1964), and David Brody, *Labor in Crisis: The Steel Strike of 1919* (1965). For the 1920 election see Wesley M. Bagby, *The Road to Normalcy* (1962). There are several good monographs on the Ku Klux Klan: David M. Chalmers, *Hooded Americanism* (1965), A. S. Rice, *The Ku Klux Klan in American Politics* (1962), and Kenneth T. Jackson, *The Ku Klux Klan in the Cities* (1967). The immigration restriction movement is brilliantly analyzed in John Higham, *Strangers in the Land: Patterns of American Nativism, 1860–1925* (rev. edn., 1963). Religious fundamentalism is treated in Norman F. Furniss, *The Fundamentalist Controversy, 1918–1931* (1954) and in Ray Ginger's lively account of the Scopes trial, *Six Days or Forever?* (1958). Andrew Sinclair, *Prohibition: Era of Excess* (1962) is both scholarly and entertaining, but for the wider significance of prohibition see Joseph R. Gusfield, *Symbolic Crusade* (1963). The *cause célèbre* of the decade is surveyed in Felix Frankfurter, *The Case of Sacco and Vanzetti* (1927) and G. L. Joughin and E. M. Morgan, *The Legacy of Sacco-Vanzetti* (1948), both of which assert the innocence of the accused; the contrary conclusion is reached in Francis

Russell, *Tragedy in Dedham* (1962) and David Felix, *Protest: Sacco-Vanzetti and the Intellectuals* (1964). The declining fortunes of trade unionism can be traced in Irving Bernstein, *The Lean Years: A History of the American Worker, 1920–1933* (1960). See also Robert H. Zieger, *Republicans and Labor, 1919–1929* (1969). The literature of the period is surveyed in Malcolm Cowley, *Exile's Return* (1951), Frederick J. Hoffman, *The Twenties* (1955), and Alfred Kazin, *On Native Grounds* (1942). The decade's leading iconoclast is profiled in William Manchester, *Disturber of the Peace: The Life of H. L. Mencken* (1951). For the Harding administration see Andrew Sinclair, *The Available Man* (1965), Francis Russell, *The Shadow of Blooming Grove: Warren G. Harding in his Times* (1968) and Robert K. Murray, *The Harding Era* (1969). The major political scandal of the decade is treated in Burl Noggle, *Teapot Dome: Oil and Politics in the 1920s* (1962) and J. Leonard Bates, *The Origins of Teapot Dome* (1963). The best life of Harding's successor is Donald R. McCoy, *Calvin Coolidge: The Silent President* (1988). Other important political biographies are B.C. and Fola La Follette, *Robert M. La Follette, 1855–1925* (1953), William H. Harbaugh, *Lawyer's Lawyer: The Life of John W. Davis* (1973), Richard Lowitt, *George W. Norris* (1971), Arthur Mann, *La Guardia, A Fighter against his Times, 1882–1933* (1959), and LeRoy Ashby, *The Spearless Leader: Senator Borah and the Progressive Movement in the 1920s* (1972). The 1928 election is studied in Oscar Handlin, *Al Smith and his America* (1958) and Edmund A. Moore, *A Catholic Runs for President* (1956), both of whom attribute Smith's defeat to religious prejudice. Ruth C. Silva, *Rum, Religion and Votes: 1928 Re-Examined* (1962) demonstrates the inadequacy of this interpretation.

Chapter 23

A useful introduction to the period is L. D. Chandler, *America's Greatest Depression, 1929–1941* (1970). For differing assessments of the causes of the Great Depression see Milton Friedman and Anna Schwartz, *The Great Contraction, 1929–33* (1965), which advances a monetarist thesis, and Peter Temin, *Did Monetary Forces Cause the Great Depression?* (1976), which blames the absence of a Keynesian economic policy. The stock-market collapse is analyzed in J. K. Galbraith, *The Great Crash* (3rd edn., 1972) and in Robert Sobel, *The Great Bull Market: Wall Street in the 1920s* (1968). The economic history of the period is surveyed in Broadus Mitchell, *Depression Decade* (1947). For American society during the Depression the best general account is Dixon Wecter, *The Age of the Great Depression, 1929–1941* (1948). Herbert Hoover has been the subject of three substantial studies: Joan Hoff Wilson, *Herbert Hoover: Forgotten Progressive* (1975), David Burner, *Herbert Hoover: A Public Life* (1979), and Martin L. Fausold, *The Presidency of Herbert Hoover* (1985). Several books have analyzed Hoover's efforts to solve Depression problems. Harris G. Warren, *Herbert Hoover and the Great Depression* (1959) defends the President, but Albert U. Romasco, *The Poverty of Abundance: Hoover, the Nation, the Depression* (1965) and Jordan A. Schwartz, *The Interregnum of Despair* (1970) are critical. Roger A. Daniels, *The Bonus March* (1971) is standard on that episode. The best brief general synthesis of the New Deal is Anthony J. Badger, *The New Deal: The Depression Years, 1933–1940* (1989), but William E. Leuchtenburg, *Franklin D. Roosevelt and the New Deal* (1963) remains valuable. The most distinguished biography of

Roosevelt is Frank Freidel, *Franklin D. Roosevelt* (5 vols. to date,. 1952–1977) but the best one-volume treatment up to 1940 is James MacGregor Burns, *Roosevelt: The Lion and the Fox* (1956), which is appreciative but detached. Two pro-Roosevelt works by Arthur M. Schlesinger, Jr., *The Coming of the New Deal* (1959) and *The Politics of Upheaval* (1960) are wonderfully evocative of the years up to 1936. Basil Rauch, *The History of the New Deal* (1944) advances the concept of the two New Deals and is highly favorable to Roosevelt: Edgar E. Robinson, *The Roosevelt Leadership, 1933–1945* (1955) is severely critical. The many scholarly accounts of specific New Deal policies and agencies include Ellis Hawley, *The New Deal and the Problem of Monopoly* (1966), Van L. Perkins, *Crisis in Agriculture: The Agricultural Adjustment Administration and the New Deal, 1933* (1969), Thomas K. McGraw, *TVA and the Power Fight, 1933–1939* (1971), Michael Parish, *Securities Regulation and the New Deal* (1970), John A. Salmond, *The Civilian Conservation Corps, 1933–1942* (1967), Searle F. Charles, *Minister of Relief: Harry Hopkins and the Depression* (1963), and Roy Lubove, *The Struggle for Social Security, 1900–1935* (1968). The inadequacy of New Deal responses to Southern rural poverty may be traced in David E. Conrad, *The Forgotten Farmers: The Story of Sharecroppers in the New Deal* (1965), Donald H. Grubbs, *Cry from the Cotton: The Southern Tenant Farmers Union and the New Deal* (1971), and Paul E. Mertz, *New Deal and Southern Rural Poverty* (1978). For the New Deal's relations with the unions see Irving Bernstein, *The New Deal Collective Bargaining Policy* (1950) and Charles K. McFarland, *Roosevelt, Lewis and the New Deal, 1933–1940* (1970). Jane D. Matthews, *The Federal Theater, 1935–1939* (1967) and Richard D. McKinsey, *The New Deal for Artists* (1973) survey government aid to the arts. Demagogic opponents of the New Deal have been extensively studied, notably by William Ivy Hair, *The Kingfish and his Realm: The Life and Times of Huey Long* (1991), T. Harry Williams, *Huey Long* (1969), Alan Brinkley, *Voices of Protest: Huey Long, Father Coughlin and the Great Depression* (1982), and Abraham Holtzman, *The Townsend Movement* (1963). For Roosevelt's conservative critics see George Wolfskill, *The Revolt of the Conservatives: The American Liberty League, 1933–1940* (1962) and James T. Patterson, *Congressional Conservatives and the New Deal* (1967). Essential for the court-packing controversy are Leonard Baker, *Back to Back: The Duel between FDR and the Supeme Court* (1977), the relevant sections of Paul L. Murphy, *The Constitution in Crisis Times, 1918–1969* (1972), and, above all, William E. Leuchtenburg's penetrating articles, "The Origins of Franklin D. Roosevelt's Court-Packing plan", *The Supreme Court Review* (1966), 352–99, and "Franklin D. Roosevelt's Supreme Court 'Packing' Plan", in Harold M. Hollingsworth, ed., *Essays on the New Deal* (1969), 69–115. The most useful studies of the black experience are Harvard Sitkoff, *A New Deal for Blacks* (1978), Raymond Wolters, *Negroes and the Great Depression* (1973), and John B. Kirby, *Black Americans in the Roosevelt Era* (1980). Scholarly work on women includes Lois Scharf, *To Work and to Wed* (1985), Susan Ware, *Beyond Suffrage: Women in the New Deal* (1981), and Winifred D. Wandersee, *Women's Work and Family Values, 1920–1940* (1981). Labor unions are sympathetically treated in Irving Bernstein, *The Turbulent Years: A History of the American Worker, 1933–1941* (1970) and Sidney Fine, *Sit-Down: The General Motors Strike of 1936–1937* (1969). The rise of industrial unionism is traced in Saul D. Alinsky, *John L. Lewis*

(1949) and Walter Galenson, *The CIO Challenge to the AFL* (1960). For the impact of the New Deal on cities and states see John Braeman *et al.*, *The New Deal* (2 vols., 1975), James T. Patterson, *The New Deal and the States* (1969), and L. W. Dorsett, *Franklin D. Roosevelt and the City Bosses* (1977).

Chapter 24

L. Ethan Ellis, *Republican Foreign Policy, 1921–1933* (1968) is an outstanding study. The argument advanced by William Appleman Williams, *The Tragedy of American Diplomacy* (rev. edn., 1962) that economic expansionism dominated American foreign policy in the 1920s is questioned in Joan Hoff Wilson, *American Business and Foreign Policy, 1920–1933* (1971). Also on this topic see Herbert Feis, *The Diplomacy of the Dollar: First Era, 1919–1932* (1950) and Joseph Brandes, *Herbert Hoover and Economic Diplomacy* (1962). The most thoroughgoing discussion of the Washington Conference appears in Thomas H. Buckley, *The United States and the Washington Conference, 1921–1922* (1970). Far Eastern policy is fully explored in Warren I. Cohen, *America's Response to China* (1971) and Akira Iriye, *After Imperialism: The Search for a New Order in the Far East, 1921–1933* (1965). Republican diplomacy in the 1920s may be further studied in the following biographies of Secretaries of State: Betty W. Glad, *Charles Evans Hughes and the Illusions of Innocence* (1966), *Frank B. Kellogg and American Foreign Relations, 1925–1929* (1961), and Elting E. Morison, *Turmoil and Tradition: The Life and Times of Henry L. Stimson* (1960). Valuable also are Peter G. Filene, *Americans and the Soviet Experience, 1917–1933* (1967), Alexander De Conde, *Herbert Hoover's Latin American Policy* (1951), and Robert H. Ferrell's two books, *Peace in Their Time: The Origins of the Kellogg–Briand Pact* (1968) and *American Diplomacy in the Great Depression: Hoover–Stimson Foreign Policy, 1929–1933* (1957). The most complete account of New Deal diplomacy is Robert Dallek, *Franklin Roosevelt and American Foreign Policy, 1932–1945* (1979), which is generally favorable toward the President. The Latin American policy of the United States during the New Deal is also sympathetically assessed in Edward O. Guerrant, *Roosevelt's Good Neighbor Policy* (1950) and in two detailed studies by Bryce Wood, *The Making of the Good Neighbor Policy* (1961) and *The United States and Latin American Wars, 1932–1942* (1966). For isolationism see Wayne S. Cole, *Senator Gerald P. Nye and American Foreign Relations* (1962), John E. Wiltz, *In Search of Peace: The Senate Munitions Inquiry, 1934–36* (1963), J. K. Nelson, *The Peace Prophets: American Pacifist Thought, 1919–1941* (1967) (1966). Roosevelt's attitude to the isolationists is well covered in Robert A. Divine, *The Illusion of Neutrality* (1962) and Wayne S. Cole, *Roosevelt and the Isolationists, 1932–1945* (1983). Dorothy Borg, *The United States and the Far Eastern Crisis of 1933–1938* (1964) and Arnold Offner, *American Appeasement: United States Foreign Policy and Germany, 1933–1938* (1969) agree that the main aim of American policy in face of the totalitarian threat was to avoid war. Studies of the events leading to American involvement in World War II, all more or less sympathetic to Roosevelt, include Robert A. Divine, *The Reluctant Belligerent* (1965), Basil Rauch, *Roosevelt: From Munich to Pearl Harbor* (1950), and Herbert Feis, *The Road to Pearl Harbor* (1950). Charles A. Beard, *President Roosevelt and the Coming of the War, 1941* (1948) is an unconvincing attempt by a famous historian who was also a Roosevelt-hater to show that the President manoeuvred the country into war. More deserving of the student's attention is Paul W. Schroeder, *The Axis Alliance and Japanese–American Relations, 1941* (1958), which shows how American policy, whether designedly, or not, left the Japanese with war as the only alternative to a humiliating climb-down. Another important work, utilizing Japanese sources, is R. J. T. Butow, *Tojo and the Coming of the War* (1961). The views of the protagonists in the impassioned foreign policy debate between interventionists and isolationists are covered in Wayne S. Cole, *America First: The Battle Against Intervention, 1940–1941* (1953), Walter Johnson, *The Battle Against Isolation* (1944), and Martin L. Chadwin, *The Hawks of World War II* (1968). The evolution of Lend-Lease policy is described in Warren F. Kimball, *The Most Unsordid Act: Lend-Lease, 1939–1941* (1969). The controversy that developed over American unpreparedness to meet a Japanese attack is the subject of Roberta Wohlstetter, *Pearl Harbor: Warning and Decision* (1962). For the attack itself see Gordon W. Prange, *At Dawn We Slept: The Untold Story of Pearl Harbor* (1981) and John Toland, *Infamy* (1982).

Chapter 25

The best available study of wartime mobilization is Bureau of the Budget, *The United States at War* (1946). Also useful is Eliot Janeway, *The Struggle for Survival* (rev. edn., 1968). For an overview of the watime economy see Harold G. Vatter, *The U.S. Economy in World War II* (1988). The problems of labor and agriculture respectively are dealt with in Joel Seidman, *American Labor from Defense to Reconversion* (1953) and W. W. Wilcox, *The Farmer in the Second World War* (1947). A comprehensive survey of American society in wartime has yet to be written, but some of the war's social and cultural effects are explored in Richard R. Lingeman, *Don't You Know There's a War On* (1970), John M. Blum, *V was For Victory: Politics and American Culture during World War II* (1976), and Richard Polenberg, *War and Society: The United States, 1941–1945* (1972). On the role of blacks during the war consult Neil A. Wynn, *The Afro-American and the Second World War* (1976) and A. Russell Buchanan, *Blacks in World War II* (1977). The war's impact on women is the subject of Karen Anderson, *Wartime Women* (1981) and Susan M. Hartmann, *The Home Front and Beyond* (1983). For the treatment of conscientious objectors and pacifists respectively see M. Q. Sibley and P. E. Jacob, *Conscription of Conscience: The Conscientious Objector, 1940–1947* (1952) and Lawrence S. Wittner, *Rebels Against War* (1969). The forced removal of Japanese-Americans from the Pacific Coast has produced a considerable literature, all of it critical of the authorities. The best studies are Jacobus ten Broek *et al.*, *Prejudice, War and the Constitution* (1954), Roger Daniels, *Concentration Camps, U.S.A.: Japanese-Americans and World War II* (1971), and Peter Irons, *Justice at War* (1983). The military campaigns of the war are analyzed in A. Russell Buchanan, *The United States and World War II* (2 vols., 1964). The European conflict is surveyed in Charles B. MacDonald, *The Mighty Endeavor: American Armed Forces in the European Theater in World War II* (1969). For the war in the Far East see John Toland, *The Rising Sun: The Decline and Fall of the Japanese Empire, 1936–1945* (1970), and John Dower, *War Without Mercy: Race and Power in the Pacific War* (1986). American generalship may be studied in Forrest G. Pogue, *George C. Marshall* (3 vols., 1963–1973),

David Eisenhower, *Eisenhower: At War* (1986), and William Manchester, *American Caesar: General Douglas MacArthur* (1975). A good short account of naval operations is provided by S. E. Morison, *The Two-Ocean War* (1963), while the war at sea in the Far East is vividly portrayed in Dan van der Dat, *The Pacific Campaign: The U.S.–Japanese Naval War, 1941–1945* (1991). Two excellent brief studies of the diplomacy of the Grand Alliance are Gaddis Smith, *American Diplomacy during the Second World War, 1941–1945* (2nd edn., 1985) and J. L. Snell, *Illusion and Necessity: The Diplomacy of Global War, 1939–1945* (1967). Specialized aspects of diplomacy and strategy are covered in Raymond G. O'Connor, *Diplomacy for Victory: Franklin D. Roosevelt and Unconditional Surrender* (1971), Mark A. Stoler, *The Politics of the Second Front: American Military Planning and Diplomacy in Coalition Warfare, 1941–1943* (1977), and George C. Herring, Jr., *Aid to Russia, 1941–1946* (1973). The development and deployment of atomic weapons are discussed in Stephane Groueff, *Manhattan Project: Atomic Bomb* (1967), Herbert Feis, *The Atomic Bomb and the End of World War II* (1966), and Gar Alperowitz, *Atomic Diplomacy: Hiroshima and Potsdam* (new edn., 1985). Roosevelt's record as war leader is assessed—on the whole very favorably—in Robert A. Divine, *Roosevelt and World War II* (1969), James McGregor Burns, *Roosevelt: Soldier of Freedom, 1940–1945* (1970), and Eric Larrabee, *Commander in Chief* (1988). For wartime politics see Roland Young, *Congressional Politics in the Second World War* (1956).

Chapter 26

An excellent brief introduction to postwar American foreign policy is Stephen Ambrose, *Rise to Globalism: American Foreign Policy since 1938* (6th rev. edn., 1991). The origins and history of the Cold War remain controversial. The most balanced accounts—at least in the sense that they share the blame between the two superpowers—are John L. Gaddis, *The United States and the Origins of the Cold War, 1941–1947* (1971), Adam Ulam, *The Rivals: America and Russia since World War II* (1971) and, perhaps the best survey to date, Martin Leffler's monumental *A Preponderance of Power: The Truman Administration and the Cold War* (1991). A "revisionist" interpretation, moderately critical of American policy, is presented in Walter La Feber, *America, Russia and the Cold War, 1945–1980* (1980). More avowedly revisionist are William Appleman Williams, *The Tragedy of American Diplomacy* (1959), D. F. Fleming, *The Cold War and its Origins* (2 vols., 1961), Lloyd C. Gardner, *Architects of Illusion* (1970), and Joyce and Gabriel Kolko, *The Limits of Power: The World and United States Foreign Policy, 1945–1954* (1972). Critiques of revisionism are to be found in Robert W. Tucker, *The Radical Left and American Foreign Policy* (1972) and Robert J. Maddox, *The New Left and the Origins of the Cold War* (1973). American Far Eastern policy is analyzed in Tang Tsou, *America's Failure in China, 1941–1950* (1963) and L. A. Rose, *Roots of Tragedy: The United States and the Struggle for Asia, 1945–1953* (1976). Among one-volume histories of the Korean War the best are David Rees, *Korea: The Limited War* (1964), Max Hastings, *The Korean War* (1987), and Callum A. MacDonald, *Korea: The War Before Vietnam* (1987). For the uproar over MacArthur's dismissal, see John W. Spanier, *The Truman–MacArthur Controversy and the Korean War* (1959). The fullest, as well as the best, biography of Truman is David McCullogh, *Truman* (1992), but Alonzo J. Hamby, *Beyond the New Deal: Harry S. Truman and American Liberalism* (1973) offers a good, brief treatment of Truman's domestic policies. Harold F. Gosnell, *Truman's Crises: A Political Biography of Harry S. Truman* (1980) is a sympathetic portrait, while the essays in Barton J. Bernstein, ed., *Politics and Policies of the Truman Administraion* (1966) are uniformly hostile. Good specialized studies include Susan Hartmann, *Truman and the Eightieth Congress* (1971), Irwin Ross, *The Loneliest Campaign: The Truman Victory of 1948* (1968), R. A. Lee, *Truman and Taft-Hartley* (1967), and W. C. Berman, *The Politics of Civil Rights in the Truman Administration* (1970). Truman's internal security measures are described in Alonzo L. Hamby, *The Politics of Loyalty: The White House and the Communist Issue, 1946–1952* (1969). According to Athan Theoharis, *Seeds of Repression: Harry S. Truman and the Origins of McCarthyism* (1971) and Richard Freeland, *The Truman Doctrine and the Origins of McCarthyism* (1972) those measures, along with the President's anti-Communist rhetoric, paved the way for McCarthyism. Richard Rovere, *Senator Joe McCarthy* (1959) skillfully demolishes its subject, as does Thomas C. Reeves, *The Life and Times of Joe McCarthy* (1982). Robert Griffith, *The Politics of Fear* (1970) explains McCarthy's power in the Senate, while David Caute, *The Great Fear: The Anti-Communist Purge under Truman and Eisenhower* (1978) shows that liberals, no less than McCarthy, contributed to the anti-Communist hysteria. The most detailed and objective account of the Hiss case is Allen Weinstein, *Perjury: The Hiss–Chambers Case* (1978). Early appraisals of Eisenhower's Presidency, like those of Emmet J. Hughes, *Ordeal of Power* (1963) and Peter Lyon, *Eisenhower: Portrait of a Hero* (1974) were unflattering, but Charles C. Alexander, *Holding the Line: The Eisenhower Era, 1952–1961* (1975), Elmo R. Richardson, *The Presidency of Dwight D. Eisenhower* (1979), and Robert A. Divine, *Eisenhower and the Cold War* (1981) show a renewed respect for the man. Fred Greenstein, *The Hidden-Hand Presidency: Eisenhower as Leader* (1982) carries Eisenhower's rehabilitation still further. A more measured assessment is to be found in Stephen Ambrose, *Eisenhower* (2 vols., 1985). Important biographies of other key politicians include James T. Patterson, *Mr. Republican: A Biography of Robert A. Taft* (1972), John B. Martin's two volumes, *Stevenson of Illinois* (1976) and *Adlai Stevenson and the World* (1989), and Porter McKeever, *Adlai Stevenson: His Life and Legend* (1989). The Brown desegregation decision of 1954 and its consequences are examined in Albert P. Blaustein and C. C. Ferguson, Jr., *Desegregation and the Law* (rev. edn., 1962) and, in longer perspective, by Raymond Wolters, *The Burden of Brown: Thirty Years of School Desegregation* (1984). Southern resistance to desegregation is traced in Numan V. Bartley, *The Rise of Massive Resistance: Race and Politics in the South during the 1950s* (1969) and Anthony Lewis and *The New York Times, Portrait of a Decade* (1964). Eisenhower's foreign policy is appraised in Herbert S. Parmet, *Eisenhower and the American Crusades* (1972) and in the books by Alexander and Richardson mentioned above. For Eisenhower's controversial Secretary of State, see Michael Guhin, *John Foster Dulles* (1972), which is apologetic, and Herman Finer, *Dulles Over Suez* (1964), which is fiercely critical.

Chapter 27

The best general surveys of the 1960s are William L. O'Neill, *Coming Apart* (1972), Allen J. Matusow, *The Unraveling of America* (1984), and John M. Blum,

Years of Discord: American Politics and Society, 1961–1974 (1991). Two accounts of Kennedy's Presidency by White House courtiers, Arthur M. Schlesinger, Jr., *A Thousand Days* (1965) and Theodore Sorensen, *Kennedy* (1965) are hagiographical. Henry Fairlie, *The Kennedy Promise: The Politics of Expectation* (1977) aims to debunk the Kennedy legend. Also unfriendly to Kennedy are B. Miroff, *Pragmatic Illusion: The Presidential Politics of John F. Kenndy* (1976) and Thomas C. Reeves, *A Question of Character: A Life of John F. Kennedy* (1976) and Thomas C. Reeves, *A Question of Character: A Life of John F. Kennedy* (1991). A more even-handed approach informs Herbert S. Parmet's two volumes, *Jack: The Struggle of John Fitzgerald Kennedy* (1980) and *JFK: The Presidency of John F. Kennedy* (1983). The essential conservatism of Kennedy's New Frontier is demonstrated in Jim Heath, *John F. Kennedy and the Business Community* (1969) and C. M. Brauer, *John F. Kennedy and the Second Reconstruction* (1977). Kennedy's foreign policy is sympathetically assessed by Roger Hilsman, *To Move a Nation* (1964) and is critically examined in Richard J. Walton, *Cold War and Counterrevolution* (1972). The Cuban missile crisis is graphically described in Robert F. Kennedy, *Thirteen Days* (1971) and Herbert S. Dinnerstein, *The Making of a Missile Crisis* (1976). The failure of the Alliance for Progress is charted in Jerome Levinson and Juan de Onis, *The Alliance that Lost its Way* (1970). For the strategic arms race and the attempts to check it see Harland B. Moulton, *From Superiority to Parity: The United States and the Strategic Arms Race, 1961–1971* (1972) and John Newhouse, *Cold Dawn: The Story of SALT* (1973). Historians are no more agreed about Lyndon Johnson than they are about Kennedy. Robert Caro's two books, *The Years of Lyndon Johnson: The Path to Power* (1983) and *The Means of Ascent* (1990) is the most detailed portrait, but it is flawed by the author's animus toward his subject. More understanding and also more objective are Eric F. Goldman, *The Tragedy of Lyndon Johnson* (1969), H. Y. Schandler, *The Unmaking of the President: Lyndon Johnson and Vietnam* (1977), and Robert Dallek, *Lone Star Rising: Lyndon Johnson and his Times, 1908–1960* (1990). On the political turmoil of the 1960s see also Tom Wicker, *JFK and LBJ* (1970) and Lewis Chester *et al.*, *An American Melodrama: The Presidential Campaign of 1968* (1969). Judicial activism is discussed in Bernard Schwartz, *Super Chief: Earl Warren and his Supreme Court* (1983) and Milton R. Konvitz's survey of the Warren Court's leading decisions, *Expanding Liberties* (1966). For Warren's successor as Chief Justice see Vincent Blasi, *The Burger Court: The Counterrevolution that Wasn't* (1983). Other important studies are Richard Kluger, *Simple Justice* (1976), which deals with the *Brown* decision and its aftermath, R. G. Dixon, Jr., *Democratic Representation: Reapportionment in Law and Politics* (1968) and J. H. Wilkinson III, *From Brown to Bakke: The Supreme Court and School Desegregation* (1979). The black protest movements of the 1960s are surveyed in Benjamin Muse, *The American Negro Revolution: From Nonviolence to Black Power, 1963–1967* (1969). Martin Luther King's role in the civil-rights movement has produced a growing literature, the most rewarding examples being David J. Garrow, *Bearing the Cross: Martin Luther King and the Southern Christian Leadership Conference* (1986) and Taylor Branch, *Parting the Waters: America in the King Years* (1988). For a briefer treatment see David L. Lewis, *King* (2nd edn., 1978). Other aspects of black activism are treated in August Meier and Elliott M. Rudwick, *CORE: A Study in the Civil Rights*

Movement (1973) and C. Eric Lincoln, *The Black Muslims in America* (rev. edn., 1978). Johnson's war on poverty is examined in J. D. Donovan, *The Politics of Poverty* (1967) and Sar Levitan, *The Great Society's Poor Law* (1969). The literature on America's involvement in Vietnam is enormous and overwhelmingly critical of the United States. Perhaps the best brief survey is George M. Kahin and J. W. Lewis, *The United States in Vietnam* (1967), but see also Guenter Lewy, *America in Vietnam* (1978) and George C. Herring, *America's Longest War: The United States in Vietnam, 1950–1975* (2nd edn., 1986), both of which carry the story forward to the American withdrawal. David Halberstam, *The Best and the Brightest* (1972) analyzes the liberal establishment's responsibility for the war and Frances Fitzgerald, *The Fire in the Lake* (1972) is an excellent account of the war's effect on the Vietnamese. Domestic opposition to the war is analyzed in Charles De Benedetti and Charles Chatfield, *An American Ordeal: The Antiwar Movement of the Vietnam Era* (1990). For the Dominican intervention see J. B. Martin, *Overtaken By Events* (1966). For a hostile but not unfair assessment of Richard Nixon see Gary Wills, *Nixon Agonistes: The Crisis of the Self-Made Man* (1970). In *The Imperial Presidency* (1973) Arthur M. Schlesinger, Jr., shows that Nixon's expansion of presidential power was more calculated and far-reaching than that of his predecessors. The most substantial biography is Stephen Ambrose, *Nixon* (3 vols., 1986–92), which is scholarly, thorough, and impartial. Less detailed but valuable for comparing Nixon with other American politicians of his day is Herbert S. Parmet, *Richard Nixon and his America* (1990). Nixon's foreign policy is discussed in Lloyd C. Gardner, ed., *The Great Nixon Turnabout* (1973). For the failure of American intervention in Vietnam see A. E. Goodman, *The Lost Peace: America's Search for a Negotiated Settlement of the Vietnam War* (1978). Henry Kissinger's role in shaping foreign policy has been extensively studied and variously assessed. Marvin and Bernard Kalb, *Kissinger* (1974) is uncritical of its subject and Seymour M. Hersh, *The Price of Power* (1983) extremely hostile to it. For a more balanced portrait see Walter Isaacson, *Kissinger: A biography* (1992). On Watergate and Nixon's resignation the most thoroughgoing study is Stanley Kutler, *The Wars of Watergate* (1990). The Ford interlude is covered in Richard Reeve, *A Ford Not a Lincoln* (1975). Two scholarly works on the Carter administration, both severely critical, are Betty W. Glad, *Jimmy Carter: In Search of the Great White House* (1980) and Hayes Johnson, *In the Absence of Power* (1980). American diplomacy during the Carter years is examined in Gaddis Smith, *Morality, Reason and Power* (1986).

Chapter 28

Social and cultural trends in the postwar decades are skillfully synthesized in William E. Leuchtenburg, *A Troubled Feast: American Society since 1945* (1973), W. Issel, *Social Change in the United States, 1945–1983* (1985), and William H. Chafe, *The Unfinished Journey: America since World War II* (2nd edn., 1991). Also valuable for the earlier part of the period is Max Lerner's wide-ranging analysis, *America as a Civilization* (1957). J. K. Galbraith's *The Affluent Society* (1958) and his *The New Industrial State* (1967) present an influential liberal economist's reading of socioeconomic developments. The urban crisis is explored in Nathan Glazer, ed., *Cities in Trouble* (1970), David R. Hunter, *The Slums: Challenge and Response* (1968), Mark I. Gelfand, *A Nation of Cities: The Federal*

Goverment and Urban America, 1933–1965 (1975), and Martin Anderson, *The Federal Bulldozer: A Critical Analysis of Urban Renewal, 1949–1962* (1965). For the growth of suburbs see Robert C. Wood, *Suburbia: Its People and their Politics* (1949). For the problem of poverty see Michael Harrington, *The Other America* (1962) and James T. Patterson, *America's Struggle against Poverty, 1900–1980* (1981). The rebellion of the young is considered in Kenneth Keniston's two books, *The Uncomitted: Alienated Youth in American Society* (1965) and *The Young Radicals* (1968). See also Daniel Bell and Irving Kristol, eds., *Confrontation: Student Rebellion and the Universities* (1969), Bruce Cook, *The Beat Generation* (1969), Theodore Roszak, *The Making of a Counter Culture* (1971), and Charles Reich, *The Greening of America* (1970). On education see J. Spring, *The Sorting Machine: National Educational Policy since 1945* (1976) and J. B. Conant, *The American High School Today* (1959). A sympathetic but detached account of the women's liberation movement may be found in William H. Chafe, *The American Woman* (1972). How it appeared to committed participants may be sampled in Betty Friedan, *It Changed My Life* (1985) and Kate Millet, *Sexual Politics* (1981). The limited nature of black economic gains is stressed in Sar Levitan et al., eds., *Still A Dream: The Changing Status of Blacks since 1960* (1977). The black trek to the North is recaptured in Nicholas Lemann, *The Promised Land: The Great Black Migration and How it Changed America* (1991). For black political advancement see S. F. Lawson, *Black Ballots: Voting Rights in the South, 1944–1969* (1976) and Donald R. Matthews and James W. Prothro, *Negroes and New South Politics* (1966). The persistence of ethnic self-awareness is demonstrated in Nathan Glazer and Daniel Patrick Moynihan, *Beyond the Melting Pot: The Negroes, Puerto Ricans, Jews, Italians and Irish of New York City* (2nd edn., 1970). The "new ethnicity" is examined and perhaps exaggerated in Michael Novak, *The Rise of the Unmeltable Ethnics* (1971) and Richard Krickus, *Pursuing the American Dream* (1976). Well-informed studies of Mexican-Americans include Stan Steiner, *La Raza* (1970) and M. S. Meier and F. Rivera, *The Chicanos* (1972). On American Indians consult Stuart Levine and N. O. Lurie, eds., *The American Indian Today* (1968), Alvin M. Josephy, Jr., *Red Power* (1970), and Jack O. Weddell and O. Michael Watson, eds., *The American Indian in Urban Society* (1971). The most comprehensive study of the cultural history of the immediate postwar decades is John Brooks, *The Great Leap* (1966), while Ronald Berman, *America in the Sixties* (1968) and Bernard Rosenberg and D. M. White, eds., *Mass Culture* (1957) are important for popular culture. For cultural trends during the 1970s see Peter N. Carroll, *It Seemed Like Nothing Happened* (1982) and Christopher Lasch, *The Culture of Narcissism* (1979).

Chapter 29

The groups which contributed to the conservative upsurge in American politics in the late 1970s are suggestively discussed in Gillian Peele, *Revival and Reaction: The Right in Contemporary America* (1984) and S. Blumenthal, *The Rise of the Counter-Establishment* (1986). The ideas of leading conservative thinkers are analyzed in P. Steinfels, *The Neoconservatives* (1979) and J. David Hoeveler, Jr., *Watch on the Right: Conservative Intellectuals in the Reagan Era* (1991). Reagonomics is hailed with enthusiasm in Paul Craig Roberts, *The Supply-Side Revolution* (1985) but judged a good deal more critically in Robert Lekachman, *Greed is Not Enough:*

Reagonomics (1986) and David Stockman, *The Triumph of Politics: How the Reagan Revolution Failed* (1986). Reagan's Presidency as a whole is assessed in Lou Cannon, *The Role of a Lifetime* (1991) and Joseph Hogan, ed., *The Reagan Years: The Record in Presidential Leadership* (1990). On the issue of nuclear disarmament see Strobe Talbott, *Deadly Gambits: The Reagan Administration and the Stalemate in Nuclear Arms Control* (1984). Reagan's foreign policy in Central America is among the topics examined in Walter La Feber, *Inevitable Revolutions: The United States in Central America* (rev. edn., 1984), while his attitude to the Soviet Union, along with that of other postwar Presidents, is dealt with in Warren I. Cohen, *America in the Age of Soviet Power, 1945–1991* (1994). Jane Mayer and Doyle McManus, *Landslide: The Unmasking of the President, 1984–1988* (1988) deals with the setbacks Reagan experienced during his second term. The most damaging of these is the subject of Theodore Draper, *A Very Thin Line: The Iran–Contra Affair* (1991). Though excessively sympathetic to some of the leading protagonists, James B. Stewart, *Den of Thieves* (1991) is the best available introduction to the Wall Street scandals of the 1980s, but it should be supplemented by Fenton Bailey, *The Junk Bond Revolution: Michael Milken, Wall Street and the "Roaring Eighties"* (1991). The best analysis of the thrift crisis is Paul Z. Pilzer with Robert Deitz, *Other People's Money* (1989), but see also George Akerlof and Paul Rowe: *Looting: The Economic Underworld of Bankruptcy for Profit* (1994), which puts the blame on criminal owners rather than on government deregulation. Military operations in the Persian Gulf War are analyzed in Stephen R. Graubard, *Mr. Bush's War: Adventures in the Politics of Illusion* (1992), Harry Summers, *On Strategy II: A Critical Analysis of the Gulf War* (1992) and Rick Atkinson, *Crusade: The Untold Story of the Gulf War* (1994). The Gulf episode is treated in balanced and judicious fashion and put in wider diplomatic perspective in Lawrence Freedman and Efraim Karsh, *The Gulf Conflict, 1990–1991: Diplomacy and War in the New World Order* (1993). David M. Reimers, *Still the Golden Door: The Third World Comes to America* (2nd edn., 1992), which relates the shifting sources of America's immigrants to changing public attitudes and policy, is an outstanding study. American refugee legislation is critically examined in Gil Loescher and John A. Scanlan, *Calculated Kindness: Refugees and America's Half-Open Door, 1945 to the Present* (1986). On the antifeminist movement see Mary Frances Berry, *Why ERA Failed* (1984) and Susan Faludi, *Backlash: The Undeclared War on American Feminism* (1992). The abortion controversy is recounted in Suzanne Staggenborg, *The Pro-Choice Movement: Organization and Activism in the Abortion Conflict* (1991). Randy Shilts, *And The Band Played On: Politics, Power and the AIDS Epidemic* (1987) is a compassionate and sensitive journalistic account of the AIDS problem in America up to 1985, while Dennis Altman, *AIDS and the New Puritanism* (1986) is a scholarly analysis both of the disease and of homosexual society. For the continuing urban crisis see William Julius Wilson, *The Truly Disadvantaged: The Inner City, the Underclass and Public Policy* (1987). Of the many books which paint a picture of a nation in decline those which have prompted most public discussion are Paul Kennedy, *The Rise and Fall of the Great Powers* (1987), which advanced the thesis that the United States was suffering from the "imperial overstretch" which had brought down other Great Powers, and Alan Bloom, *The Closing of the American Mind* (1987), which places the blame on rock music.

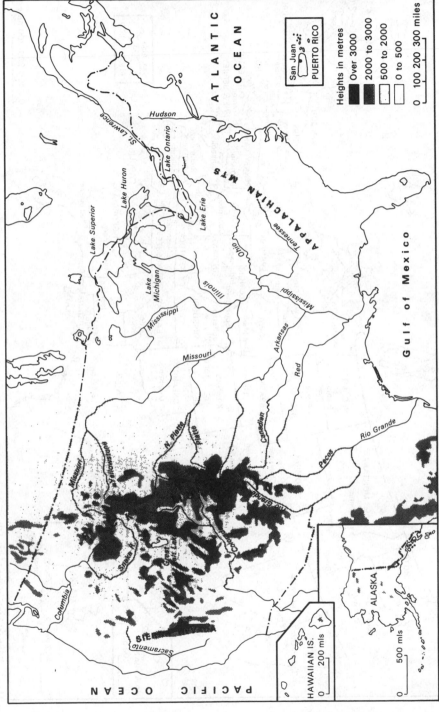

MAP 1 Physical Map of the United States (Based on Garraty, *The American Nation*. Harper and Row, 1975)

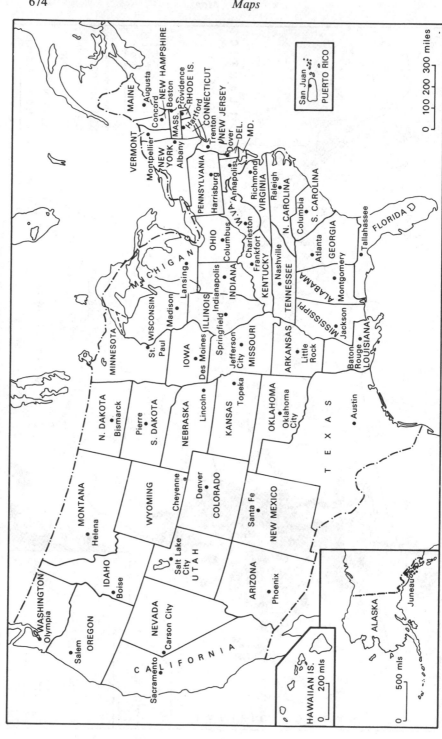

MAP 2. Political Map of the United States (Based on Garraty, *The American Nation*. Harper and Row, 1975)

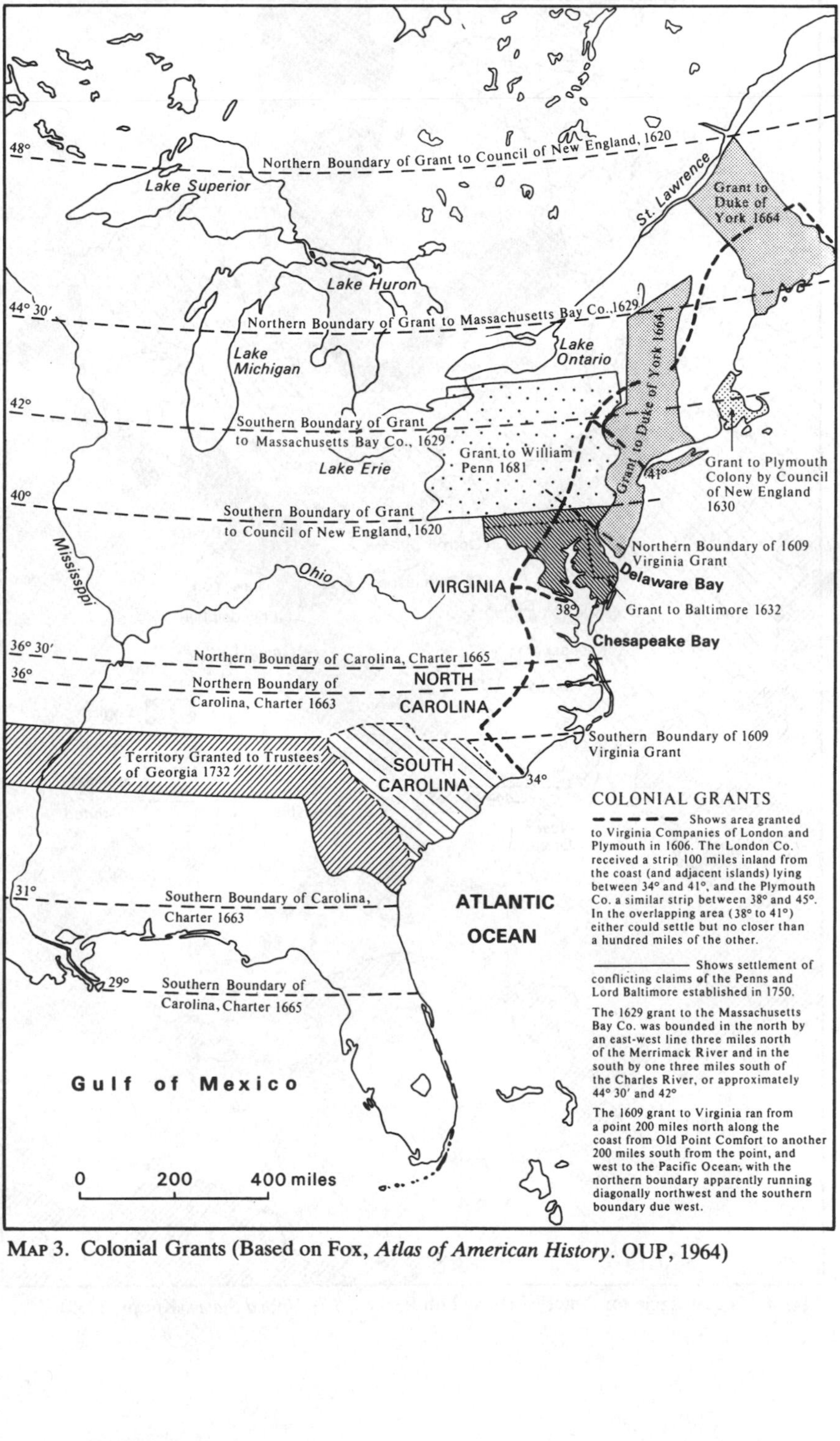

48°
Northern Boundary of Grant to Council of New England, 1620
Lake Superior
St. Lawrence
Grant to Duke of York 1664
Lake Huron
44° 30′
Northern Boundary of Grant to Massachusetts Bay Co., 1629
Lake Michigan
Lake Ontario
Grant to Duke of York 1664
42°
Southern Boundary of Grant to Massachusetts Bay Co., 1629
Grant to William Penn 1681
Lake Erie
41°
Grant to Plymouth Colony by Council of New England 1630
40°
Southern Boundary of Grant to Council of New England, 1620
Mississippi
Northern Boundary of 1609 Virginia Grant
Ohio
Delaware Bay
VIRGINIA
38°
Grant to Baltimore 1632
Chesapeake Bay
36° 30′
Northern Boundary of Carolina, Charter 1665
36°
Northern Boundary of Carolina, Charter 1663
NORTH CAROLINA
Southern Boundary of 1609 Virginia Grant
Territory Granted to Trustees of Georgia 1732
SOUTH CAROLINA
34°
COLONIAL GRANTS
Shows area granted to Virginia Companies of London and Plymouth in 1606. The London Co. received a strip 100 miles inland from the coast (and adjacent islands) lying between 34° and 41°, and the Plymouth Co. a similar strip between 38° and 45°. In the overlapping area (38° to 41°) either could settle but no closer than a hundred miles of the other.
Shows settlement of conflicting claims of the Penns and Lord Baltimore established in 1750.
The 1629 grant to the Massachusetts Bay Co. was bounded in the north by an east-west line three miles north of the Merrimack River and in the south by one three miles south of the Charles River, or approximately 44° 30′ and 42°
The 1609 grant to Virginia ran from a point 200 miles north along the coast from Old Point Comfort to another 200 miles south from the point, and west to the Pacific Ocean, with the northern boundary apparently running diagonally northwest and the southern boundary due west.
31°
Southern Boundary of Carolina, Charter 1663
ATLANTIC OCEAN
29°
Southern Boundary of Carolina, Charter 1665
Gulf of Mexico
0 200 400 miles

MAP 3. Colonial Grants (Based on Fox, *Atlas of American History*. OUP, 1964)

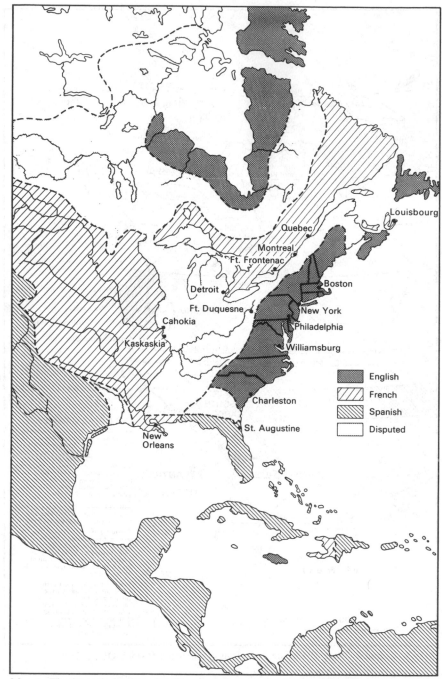

MAP 4. The Struggle for America (Based on Parkes, *The United States*. Knopf, 1959)

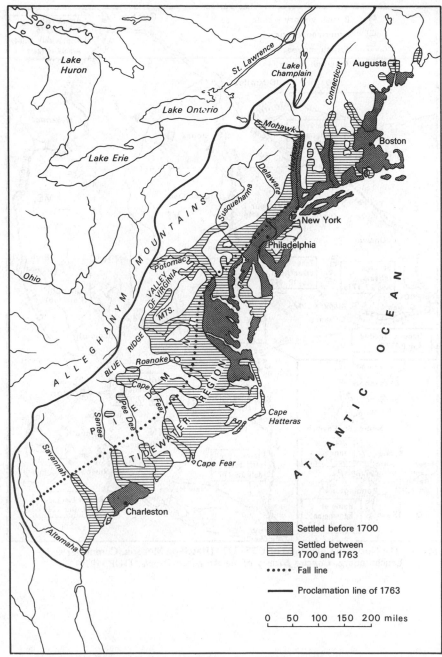

Lake Huron

Lake Ontario

Lake Erie

St. Lawrence

Lake Champlain

Augusta

Connecticut

Mohawk

Boston

Delaware

Susquehanna

New York

Philadelphia

A L L E G H A N Y M O U N T A I N S

Ohio

Potomac

VALLEY OF VIRGINIA MTS.

BLUE RIDGE

Roanoke

Cape

Pee Dee

Santee

D E L M A R

T I D E W A T E R   R E G I O N

Cape Hatteras

Cape Fear

Savannah

Altamaha

Charleston

Settled before 1700

Settled between 1700 and 1763

•••• Fall line

—— Proclamation line of 1763

0   50   100   150   200 miles

MAP 5. English Mainland Colonies, 1763 (Based on Williams *et al.*, *A History of the U.S.* Knopf, 1964)

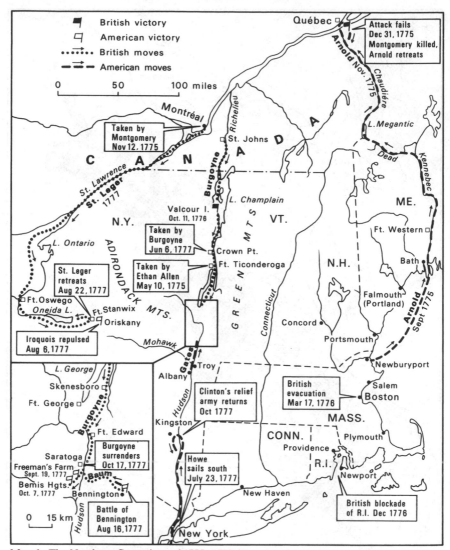

MAP 6. The Northern Campaigns of 1775–1777 (Based on Morison, Commager and
Leuchtenburg, *Concise History of the American People*. OUP, 1979)

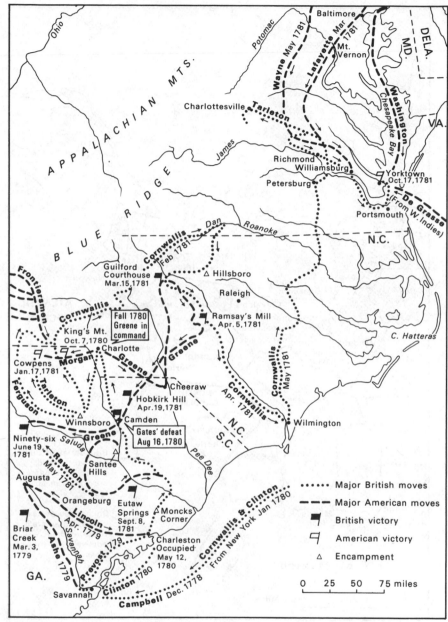

MAP 7. The Seat of the War in the South, 1779–1781 (Based on Morison, Commager and Leuchtenburg, *Concise History of the American People*. OUP, 1979)

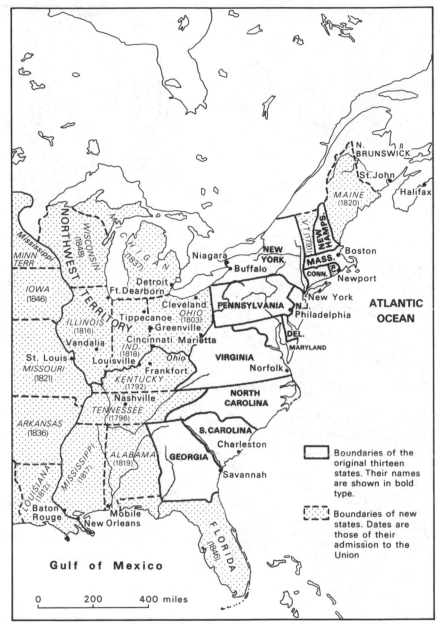

MAP 8. The New Nation (Based on Fox, *Atlas of American History*. OUP, 1964)

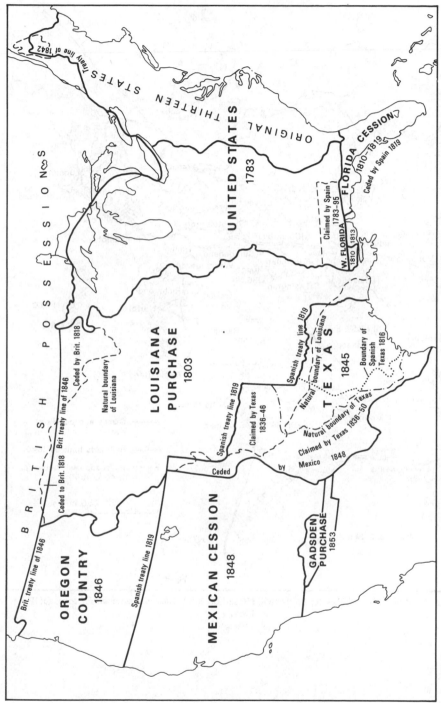

MAP 9. Growth of the United States, 1776–1853 (Based on Wesley, *Our United States: Its History in Maps*. Denoyer-Geppert Co., 1956).

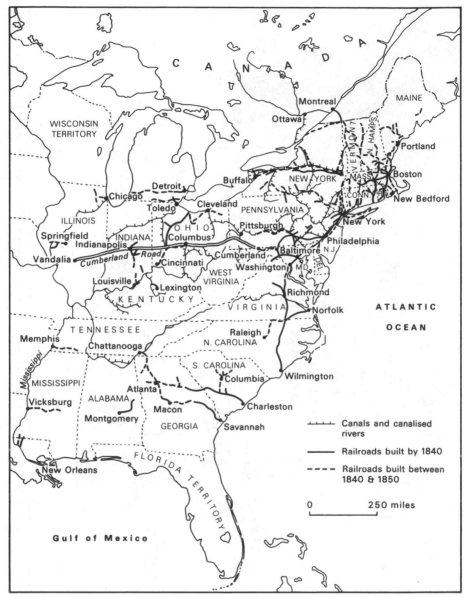

MAP 10. Railroads and Canals, 1840–1850 (Based on Fox, *Atlas of American History*. OUP 1964)

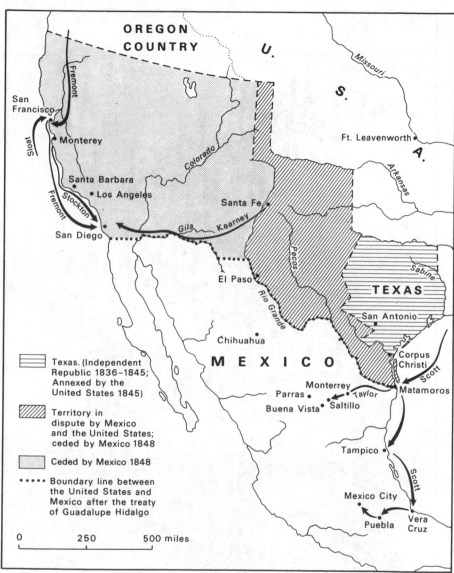

MAP 11. The Mexican War (Based on Williams *et al.*, *A History of the U.S.* Knopf, 1964)

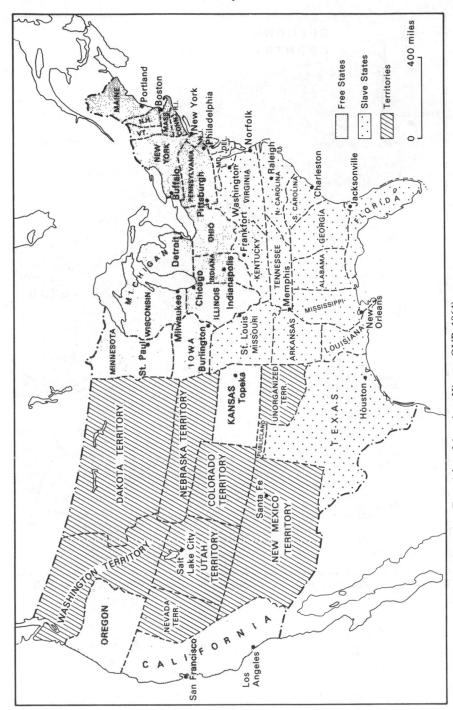

MAP 12. Eve of the Civil War (Based on Fox, *Atlas of American History*. OUP, 1964)

MAP 13. The Civil War, 1861–1865 (Based on Parkes, *The United States*. Knopf, 1959)

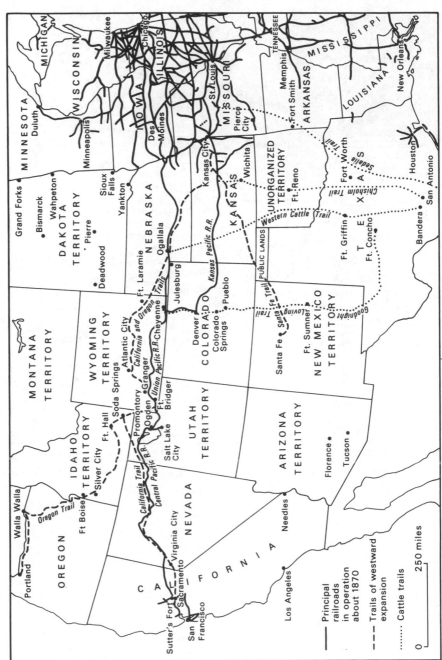

MAP 14. The New West (Based on Fox, *Atlas of American History*. OUP, 1964)

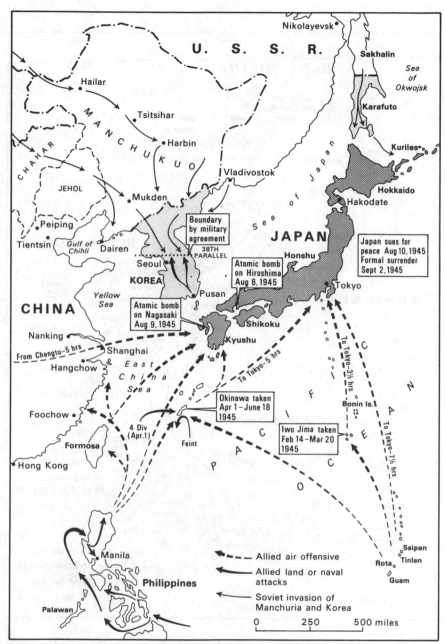

MAP 15. Final Stages of the War in the Pacific (Based on Williams *et al.*, *A History of the United States*, Knopf, 1964)

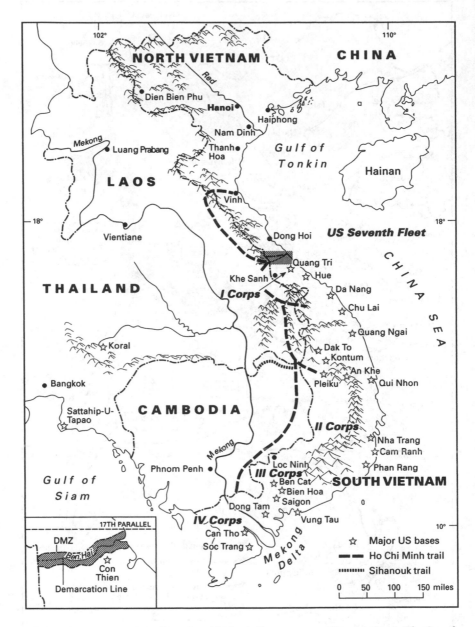

MAP 16. The Vietnam War (Based on Morison, Commager, and Leuchtenburg, *The Growth of the American Republic*, 7th ed., OUP, 1980).

TABLE 1. Population of the United States: 1790–1990

Division and State	1790	1800	1810	1820	1830	1840	1850	1860	1870	1880	1890
UNITED STATES	3,929,214	5,308,483	7,239,881	9,638,453	12,866,020	17,069,453	23,191,876	31,443,321	39,818,449	50,189,209	
New England	1,009,408	1,233,011	1,471,973	1,660,071	1,954,717	2,234,822	2,728,116	3,135,283	3,487,924	4,010,529	
Maine	96,540	151,719	228,705	298,335	399,455	501,793	583,169	628,279	626,915	648,936	
New Hampshire	141,885	183,858	214,160	244,161	269,328	284,574	317,976	326,073	318,300	346,991	
Vermont	85,425	154,465	217,895	235,981	280,652	291,948	314,120	315,098	330,551	332,286	
Massachusetts	378,787	422,845	472,040	523,287	610,408	737,699	994,514	1,231,066	1,457,351	1,783,085	
Rhode Island	68,825	69,122	76,931	83,059	97,199	108,830	147,545	174,620	217,353	276,531	
Connecticut	237,946	251,002	261,942	275,248	297,675	309,978	370,792	460,147	537,454	622,700	
Middle Atlantic	952,632	1,402,565	2,014,702	2,669,845	3,587,664	4,526,260	5,898,735	7,458,985	8,810,806	10,496,878	
New York	340,120	589,051	959,049	1,372,812	1,918,608	2,428,921	3,097,394	3,880,735	4,382,759	5,082,871	
New Jersey	184,139	211,149	245,562	277,575	320,823	373,306	489,555	672,035	906,096	1,131,116	
Pennsylvania	434,373	602,365	810,091	1,049,458	1,348,233	1,724,033	2,311,786	2,906,215	3,521,951	4,282,891	
South Atlantic	1,851,806	2,286,494	2,674,891	3,061,063	3,645,752	3,925,299	4,679,090	5,364,703	5,835,610	7,597,197	
Delaware	59,096	64,273	72,674	72,749	76,748	78,085	91,532	112,216	125,015	146,608	
Maryland	319,728	341,548	380,546	407,350	447,040	470,019	583,034	687,049	780,894	934,943	
Dist. of Columbia		8,144	15,471	23,336	30,261	33,745	51,687	75,080	131,700	177,624	
Virginia	747,610	886,149	983,152	1,075,069	1,220,978	1,249,764	1,421,661	1,596,318	1,225,163	1,512,565	
West Virginia									442,014	618,457	
North Carolina	393,751	478,103	555,500	638,829	737,987	753,419	869,039	992,622	1,071,361	1,399,750	
South Carolina	249,073	345,591	415,115	502,741	581,185	594,398	668,507	703,708	705,606	995,577	
Georgia	82,548	162,686	252,433	340,989	516,823	691,392	906,185	1,057,286	1,184,109	1,542,180	
Florida					34,730	54,477	87,445	140,424	187,748	269,493	
East South Central	109,368	335,407	708,590	1,190,489	1,815,969	2,575,445	3,363,271	4,020,991	4,404,445	5,585,151	
Kentucky	73,677	220,955	406,511	564,317	687,917	779,828	982,405	1,155,684	1,321,011	1,648,690	
Tennessee	35,691	105,602	261,727	422,823	681,904	829,210	1,002,717	1,109,801	1,258,520	1,542,359	
Alabama		1,250	9,046	127,901	309,527	590,756	771,623	964,201	996,992	1,262,505	
Mississippi		7,600	31,306	75,448	136,621	375,651	606,526	791,305	827,922	1,131,597	

Region / State									
West South Central		77,618	167,680	246,127	449,985	940,251	1,747,667	2,029,965	3,334,220
Arkansas		1,062	14,273	30,388	97,574	209,897	435,450	484,471	802,525
Louisiana		76,556	153,407	215,739	352,411	517,762	708,002	726,915	939,946
Oklahoma									
Texas						212,592	604,215	818,579	1,591,749
East North Central	51,006	272,324	792,719	1,470,018	2,924,728	4,523,260	6,926,884	9,124,517	11,206,668
Ohio	41,365	230,760	581,434	937,903	1,519,467	1,980,329	2,339,511	2,665,260	3,198,062
Indiana	5,641	24,520	147,178	343,031	685,866	988,416	1,350,428	1,680,637	1,978,301
Illinois		12,282	55,211	157,445	476,183	851,470	1,711,951	2,539,891	3,077,871
Michigan		4,762	8,896	31,639	212,267	397,654	749,113	1,184,059	1,636,937
Wisconsin					30,945	305,391	775,881	1,054,670	1,315,497
West North Central		19,783	66,586	140,455	426,814	880,335	2,169,832	3,856,594	6,157,443
Minnesota						6,077	172,023	439,706	780,773
Iowa					43,112	192,214	674,913	1,194,020	1,624,615
Missouri		19,783	66,586	140,455	383,702	682,044	1,182,012	1,721,295	2,168,380
North Dakota								2,405	36,909
South Dakota							4,837	11,776	98,268
Nebraska							28,841	122,993	452,402
Kansas							107,206	364,399	996,096
Mountain						72,927	174,923	315,385	653,119
Montana								20,595	39,159
Idaho								14,999	32,610
Wyoming								9,118	20,789
Colorado							34,277	39,864	194,327
New Mexico						61,547	93,516	91,874	119,565
Arizona								9,658	40,440
Utah						11,380	40,273	76,786	143,963
Nevada							6,857	42,491	62,266
Pacific						105,871	444,053	675,125	1,148,004
Washington						1,201	11,594	23,955	75,116
Oregon						12,093	52,465	90,923	174,768
California						92,597	379,994	560,247	864,694
Alaska									
Hawaii									33,426

Tables

Population of the United States: 1790–1990 (contd)

Division and State	1890	1900	1910	1920	1930	1940	1950	1960	1970	1980	1990
UNITED STATES	62,979,766	76,212,168	92,228,622	106,021,568	123,202,660	132,165,129	151,325,798	179,323,175	203,184,772	226,504,825	248,709,873
New England											
Maine	661,086	694,466	742,371	768,014	797,423	847,226	913,774	969,265	993,663	1,124,660	1,227,928
New Hampshire	376,530	411,588	430,572	443,083	465,293	491,524	533,242	606,921	737,681	920,610	1,109,252
Vermont	332,422	343,641	355,956	352,428	359,611	359,231	377,747	389,881	444,732	511,456	562,758
Massachusetts	2,238,947	2,805,346	3,366,416	3,852,356	4,249,614	4,316,721	4,690,514	5,148,578	5,689,170,	5,737,037	6,016,425
Rhode Island	345,506	428,556	542,610	604,397	687,497	713,346	791,896	859,488	949,723	947,154	1,003,464
Connecticut	746,258	908,420	1,114,756	1,380,631	1,606,903	1,709,242	2,007,280	2,535,234	3,032,217	3,107,576	3,287,116
Middle Atlantic	12,706,220	15,454,678	19,315,892	22,261,144	26,260,750	27,539,487	30,163,533	34,168,452	37,152,813	36,788,174	37,602,286
New York	6,003,174	7,268,894	9,113,614	10,385,227	12,588,066	13,479,142	14,830,192	16,782,304	18,190,740	17,557,288	17,990,455
New Jersey	1,444,933	1,883,669	2,537,167	3,155,900	4,041,334	4,160,165	4,835,329	6,066,782	7,168,164	7,364,158	7,730,188
Pennsylvania	5,258,113	6,302,115	7,665,111	8,720,017	9,631,350	9,900,180	10,498,012	11,319,366	11,793,909	11,866,728	11,881,643
South Atlantic	8,857,922	10,443,480	12,194,895	13,990,272	15,793,589	17,823,151	21,182,335	25,971,732	30,671,337	36,943,139	43,566,853
Delaware	168,493	184,735	202,322	223,003	238,380	266,505	318,085	446,292	548,104	595,225	666,168
Maryland	1,042,390	1,188,044	1,295,346	1,449,661	1,631,526	1,821,244	2,343,001	3,100,689	3,922,399	4,216,446	4,781,468
Dist. of Columbia	230,392	278,718	331,069	437,571	486,869	663,091	802,178	763,956	756,510	637,651	606,900
Virginia	1,655,980	1,854,184	2,061,612	2,309,187	2,421,851	2,677,773	3,318,680	3,966,949	4,648,494	5,346,279	6,187,358
West Virginia	762,794	958,800	1,221,119	1,463,701	1,729,205	1,901,974	2,005,552	1,860,421	1,744,237	1,949,644	1,793,477
North Carolina	1,617,949	1,893,810	2,206,287	2,559,123	3,170,276	3,571,623	4,061,929	4,556,155	5,082,059	5,874,429	6,628,637
South Carolina	1,151,149	1,340,316	1,515,400	1,683,724	1,738,765	1,899,804	2,117,027	2,382,594	2,590,516	3,119,208	3,486,703
Georgia	1,837,353	2,216,331	2,609,121	2,895,832	2,908,506	3,123,723	3,444,578	3,943,116	4,589,575	5,464,265	6,478,216
Florida	391,422	528,542	752,619	968,470	1,468,211	1,897,414	2,771,305	4,951,560	6,789,443	9,739,992	12,937,926
East South Central	6,429,154	7,547,757	8,409,901	8,893,307	9,887,214	10,778,225	11,477,181	12,050,126	12,804,552	14,662,882	15,176,284
Kentucky	1,858,635	2,147,174	2,289,905	2,416,630	2,614,589	2,845,627	2,944,806	3,038,156	3,219,311	3,661,433	3,685,296
Tennessee	1,767,518	2,020,616	2,184,789	2,337,885	2,616,556	2,915,841	3,291,718	3,567,089	3,924,164	4,590,750	4,877,185
Alabama	1,513,401	1,828,697	2,138,093	2,348,174	2,646,248	2,832,961	3,061,743	3,266,740	3,444,165	3,890,061	4,040,587
Mississippi	1,289,600	1,551,270	1,797,114	1,790,618	2,009,821	2,183,796	2,178,914	2,178,141	2,216,912	2,520,638	2,573,216

West South Central	4,740,983	6,532,290	8,784,534	10,242,224	12,176,830	13,064,525	14,537,572	16,951,255	19,322,458	23,743,134	26,702,793
Arkansas	1,128,211	1,311,564	1,574,449	1,752,204	1,854,482	1,949,387	1,909,511	1,786,272	1,923,295	2,285,513	2,350,725
Louisiana	1,118,588	1,381,625	1,656,388	1,798,509	2,101,593	2,363,880	2,683,516	3,257,022	3,643,180	4,203,972	4,219,973
Oklahoma	258,657	790,391	1,657,155	2,028,283	2,396,040	2,336,434	2,233,351	2,328,284	2,559,253	3,025,266	3,145,585
Texas	2,235,527	3,048,710	3,896,542	4,663,228	5,824,715	6,414,824	7,711,194	9,579,677	11,196,730	14,228,383	16,986,510
East North Central	13,478,305	15,985,581	18,250,621	21,475,543	25,297,185	26,626,342	30,309,368	36,225,024	40,252,678	41,669,738	42,008,942
Ohio	3,672,329	4,157,545	4,767,121	5,759,394	6,646,697	6,907,612	7,946,627	9,706,397	10,652,017	10,797,419	10,847,115
Indiana	2,192,404	2,516,462	2,700,876	2,930,390	3,238,503	3,427,796	3,934,224	4,662,498	5,193,669	5,490,179	5,544,159
Illinois	3,826,352	4,821,550	5,638,591	6,485,280	7,630,654	7,897,241	8,712,176	10,081,158	11,113,976	11,418,461	11,430,602
Michigan	2,093,890	2,420,982	2,810,173	3,668,412	4,842,325	5,256,106	6,371,766	7,823,194	8,875,083	9,258,344	9,295,297
Wisconsin	1,693,330	2,069,042	2,333,860	2,632,067	2,939,006	3,137,587	3,434,575	3,951,777	4,417,933	4,705,335	4,891,769
West North Central	8,932,112	10,347,423	11,637,921	12,544,249	13,296,915	13,516,990	14,061,394	15,394,115	16,324,389	17,184,066	17,659,690
Minnesota	1,310,283	1,751,394	2,075,708	2,387,125	2,563,953	2,792,300	2,982,483	3,413,864	3,805,069	4,077,148	4,375,099
Iowa	1,912,297	2,231,853	2,224,771	2,404,021	2,470,939	2,538,268	2,621,073	2,757,537	2,825,041	2,913,387	2,776,755
Missouri	2,679,185	3,106,665	3,293,335	3,404,055	3,629,367	3,784,664	3,954,653	4,319,813	4,677,399	4,917,444	5,117,073
North Dakota	190,983	319,146	577,056	646,872	680,845	641,935	619,636	632,446	617,761	652,695	638,800
South Dakota	348,600	401,570	583,888	636,547	692,849	642,961	652,740	680,514	666,257	690,178	696,004
Nebraska	1,062,656	1,066,300	1,192,214	1,296,372	1,377,963	1,315,834	1,325,510	1,411,330	1,483,791	1,570,006	1,578,385
Kansas	1,428,108	1,470,495	1,690,949	1,769,257	1,880,999	1,801,028	1,905,299	2,178,611	2,249,071	2,363,208	2,477,574
Mountain	1,213,935	1,674,657	2,633,517	3,336,101	3,701,789	4,150,003	5,074,998	6,855,060	8,283,585	11,368,330	13,658,776
Montana	142,924	243,329	376,053	548,889	537,606	559,456	591,024	674,767	694,409	786,690	799,065
Idaho	88,548	161,772	325,594	431,866	445,032	524,873	588,637	667,191	713,008	943,935	1,006,749
Wyoming	62,555	92,531	145,965	194,402	225,565	250,742	290,529	330,066	332,416	470,816	453,588
Colorado	413,249	539,700	799,024	939,629	1,035,791	1,123,296	1,325,089	1,753,947	2,207,259	2,888,834	3,294,394
New Mexico	160,282	195,310	327,301	360,350	423,317	531,818	681,187	951,023	1,016,000	1,299,968	1,515,069
Arizona	88,243	122,931	204,354	334,162	435,573	499,261	749,587	1,302,161	1,772,482	2,717,866	3,665,228
Utah	210,779	276,749	373,351	449,396	507,847	550,310	688,862	890,627	1,059,273	1,461,037	1,722,850
Nevada	47,355	42,335	81,875	77,407	91,058	110,247	160,083	285,278	488,738	799,184	1,201,833
Pacific	1,920,386	2,634,285	4,448,660	5,877,819	8,622,047	10,229,116	15,114,964	21,198,044	26,525,774	31,796,869	39,127,306
Washington	357,232	518,103	1,141,990	1,356,621	1,563,396	1,736,191	2,378,963	2,853,214	3,409,169	4,130,163	4,866,692
Oregon	317,704	413,536	672,765	783,389	953,786	1,089,684	1,521,341	1,768,687	2,091,385	2,632,663	2,842,321
California	1,213,398	1,485,053	2,377,549	3,426,861	5,677,251	6,907,387	10,586,223	15,717,204	19,953,134	23,668,562	29,760,021
Alaska	32,052	63,592	64,356	55,036	59,278	72,524	128,643	226,167	302,173	400,481	550,043
Hawaii		154,001	192,000	255,912	368,336	423,330	499,794	632,772	769,913	965,000	1,108,229

Source: *Historical Statistics of the United States and The World Almanac . . . 1982: Report of the U.S. Census Bureau, March 8, 1991*

TABLE 2. Immigration to the United States, 1820–1992

Period	
1821–1830	151,824
1831–1840	599,125
1841–1850	1,713,251
1851–1860	2,598,214
1861–1870	2,314,824
1871–1880	2,812,191
1881–1890	5,246,613
1891–1900	3,687,564
1901–1910	8,795,386
1911–1920	5,735,811
1921–1930	4,107,209
1931–1940	528,431
1941–1950	1,035,039
1951–1960	2,515,479
1961–1970	3,321,677
1971–1980	4,493,314
1981–1990	7,338,062
1991–1992	2,801,144

Source: U.S. Immigration and Naturalization Service, 1993

TABLE 3. Admission of States to the Union*

1	Delaware	Dec. 7, 1787	26	Michigan	Jan. 26, 1837
2	Pennsylvania	Dec. 12, 1787	27	Florida	Mar. 3, 1845
3	New Jersey	Dec. 18, 1787	28	Texas	Dec. 29, 1845
4	Georgia	Jan. 2, 1788	29	Iowa	Dec. 28, 1846
5	Connecticut	Jan. 9, 1788	30	Wisconsin	May 29, 1848
6	Massachusetts	Feb. 6, 1788	31	California	Sept. 9, 1850
7	Maryland	Apr. 28, 1788	32	Minnesota	May 11, 1858
8	South Carolina	May 23, 1788	33	Oregon	Feb. 14, 1859
9	New Hampshire	June 21, 1788	34	Kansas	Jan. 29, 1861
10	Virginia	June 25, 1788	35	West Virginia	June 19, 1863
11	New York	July 26, 1788	36	Nevada	Oct. 31, 1864
12	North Carolina	Nov. 21, 1789	37	Nebraska	Mar. 1, 1867
13	Rhode Island	May 29, 1790	38	Colorado	Aug. 1, 1876
14	Vermont	Mar. 4, 1791	39	North Dakota	Nov. 2, 1889
15	Kentucky	June 1, 1792	40	South Dakota	Nov. 2, 1889
16	Tennessee	June 1, 1796	41	Montana	Nov. 8, 1889
17	Ohio	Mar. 1, 1803	42	Washington	Nov. 11, 1889
18	Louisiana	Apr. 30, 1812	43	Idaho	July 3, 1890
19	Indiana	Dec. 11, 1816	44	Wyoming	July 10, 1890
20	Mississippi	Dec. 10, 1817	45	Utah	Jan. 4, 1896
21	Illinois	Dec. 3, 1818	46	Oklahoma	Nov. 16, 1907
22	Alabama	Dec. 14, 1819	47	New Mexico	Jan. 6, 1912
23	Maine	Mar. 15, 1820	48	Arizona	Feb. 14, 1912
24	Missouri	Aug. 10, 1821	49	Alaska	Jan. 3, 1959
25	Arkansas	June 15, 1836	50	Hawaii	Aug. 21, 1959

* In the case of the first thirteen states, the date given is that of ratification of the Constitution.

Source: *Historical Statistics of the United States* and *The World Almanac . . . 1982*

TABLE 4. Presidential Elections

Year	Candidates*	Parties	Popular Vote	Electoral Vote
1789	GEORGE WASHINGTON (Va.)			69
	John Adams			34
	Others			35
1792	GEORGE WASHINGTON (Va.)			132
	John Adams			77
	George Clinton			50
	Others			5
1796	JOHN ADAMS (Mass.)	Federalist		71
	Thomas Jefferson	Democratic-Republican		68
	Thomas Pinckney	Federalist		59
	Aaron Burr	Dem.-Rep.		30
	Others			48
1800	THOMAS JEFFERSON (Va.)	Dem.-Rep.		73
	Aaron Burr	Dem.-Rep.		73
	John Adams	Federalist		65
	C. C. Pinckney	Federalist		64
	John Jay	Federalist		1
1804	THOMAS JEFFERSON (Va.)	Dem.-Rep.		162
	C. C. Pinckney	Federalist		14
1808	JAMES MADISON (Va.)	Dem.-Rep.		122
	C. C. Pinckney	Federalist		47
	George Clinton	Dem.-Rep.		6
1812	JAMES MADISON (Va.)	Dem.-Rep.		128
	De Witt Clinton	Federalist		89
1816	JAMES MONROE (Va.)	Dem.-Rep.		183
	Rufus King	Federalist		34
1820	JAMES MONROE (Va.)	Dem.-Rep.		231
	John Quincy Adams	Dem.-Rep.		1
1824	JOHN Q. ADAMS (Mass.)	Dem.-Rep.	108,740	84
	Andrew Jackson	Dem.-Rep.	153,544	99
	William H. Crawford	Dem.-Rep.	46,618	41
	Henry Clay	Dem.-Rep.	47,136	37
1828	ANDREW JACKSON (Tenn.)	Democrat	647,286	178
	John Quincy Adams	National Republican	508,064	83
1832	ANDREW JACKSON (Tenn.)	Democrat	687,502	219
	Henry Clay	National Republican	530,189	49
	John Floyd	Independent		11
	William Wirt	Anti-Mason	33,108	7
1836	MARTIN VAN BUREN (N.Y.)	Democrat	765,483	170
	W. H. Harrison	Whig		73
	Hugh L. White	Whig	739,795	26
	Daniel Webster	Whig		14
	W. P. Mangum	Independent		11
1840	WILLIAM H. HARRISON (Ohio)	Whig	1,274,624	234
	Martin Van Buren	Democrat	1,127,781	60
	J. G. Birney	Liberty	7,069	–
1844	JAMES K. POLK (Tenn.)	Democrat	1,338,464	170
	Henry Clay	Whig	1,300,097	105
	J. G. Birney	Liberty	62,300	–
1848	ZACHARY TAYLOR (La.)	Whig	1,360,967	163
	Lewis Cass	Democrat	1,222,342	127
	Martin Van Buren	Free-Soil	291,263	–

* Minor candidates omitted.

Presidential Elections (cont.)

Year	Candidates	Parties	Popular Vote	Electoral Vote
1852	FRANKLIN PIERCE (N.H.)	Democrat	1,601,117	254
	Winfield Scott	Whig	1,385,453	42
	John P. Hale	Free-Soil	155,825	–
1856	JAMES BUCHANAN (Pa.)	Democrat	1,832,955	174
	John C. Frémont	Republican	1,339,932	114
	Millard Fillmore	American	871,731	8
1860	ABRAHAM LINCOLN (Ill.)	Republican	1,865,593	180
	Stephen A. Douglas	Democrat	1,382,713	12
	John C. Breckinridge	Democrat	848,356	72
	John Bell	Union	592,906	39
1864	ABRAHAM LINCOLN (Ill.)	Republican	2,213,655	212
	George B. McClellan	Democrat	1,805,237	21
1868	ULYSSES S. GRANT (Ill.)	Republican	3,012,833	214
	Horatio Seymour	Democrat	2,703,249	80
1872	ULYSSES S. GRANT (Ill.)	Republican	3,597,132	286
	Horace Greeley	Democrat; Liberal Republican	2,834,125	66
1876	RUTHERFORD B. HAYES (Ohio)	Republican	4,036,298	185
	Samuel J. Tilden	Democrat	4,300,590	184
1880	JAMES A. GARFIELD (Ohio)	Republican	4,454,416	214
	Winfield S. Hancock	Democrat	4,444,952	155
1884	GROVER CLEVELAND (N.Y.)	Democrat	4,874,986	219
	James G. Blaine	Republican	4,851,981	182
1888	BENJAMIN HARRISON (Ind.)	Republican	5,439,853	233
	Grover Cleveland	Democrat	5,540,309	168
1892	GROVER CLEVELAND (N.Y.)	Democrat	5,556,918	277
	Benjamin Harrison	Republican	5,176,108	145
	James B. Weaver	People's	1,041,028	22
1896	WILLIAM McKINLEY (Ohio)	Republican	7,104,779	271
	William J. Bryan	Democrat-People's	6,502,925	176
1900	WILLIAM McKINLEY (Ohio)	Republican	7,207,923	292
	William J. Bryan	Dem.-Populist	6,358,133	155
1904	THEODORE ROOSEVELT (N.Y.)	Republican	7,623,486	336
	Alton B. Parker	Democrat	5,077,911	140
	Eugene V. Debs	Socialist	402,283	–
1908	WILLIAM H. TAFT (Ohio)	Republican	7,678,908	321
	William J. Bryan	Democrat	6,409,104	162
	Eugene V. Debs	Socialist	420,793	–
1912	WOODROW WILSON (N.J.)	Democrat	6,293,454	435
	Theodore Roosevelt	Progressive	4,119,538	88
	William H. Taft	Republican	3,484,980	8
	Eugene V. Debs	Socialist	900,672	–
1916	WOODROW WILSON (N.J.)	Democrat	9,129,606	277
	Charles E. Hughes	Republican	8,538,221	254
	A. L. Benson	Socialist	585,113	–
1920	WARREN G. HARDING (Ohio)	Republican	16,152,200	404
	James M. Cox	Democrat	9,147,353	127
	Eugene V. Debs	Socialist	919,799	–
1924	CALVIN COOLIDGE (Mass.)	Republican	15,725,016	382
	John W. Davis	Democrat	8,386,503	136
	Robert M. LaFollette	Progressive	4,822,856	13
1928	HERBERT HOOVER (Calif.)	Republican	21,391,381	444
	Alfred E. Smith	Democrat	15,016,443	87
	Norman Thomas	Socialist	267,835	–
1932	FRANKLIN D. ROOSEVELT (N.Y.)	Democrat	22,821,857	472
	Herbert Hoover	Republican	15,761,841	59
	Norman Thomas	Socialist	881,951	–

Presidential Elections (cont.)

Year	Candidates	Parties	Popular Vote	Electoral Vote
1936	FRANKLIN D. ROOSEVELT (N.Y.)	Democrat	27,751,597	523
	Alfred M. Landon	Republican	16,679,583	8
	William Lemke	Union and others	882,479	–
1940	FRANKLIN D. ROOSEVELT (N.Y.)	Democrat	27,244,160	449
	Wendell L. Willkie	Republican	22,305,198	82
1944	FRANKLIN D. ROOSEVELT (N.Y.)	Democrat	25,602,504	432
	Thomas E. Dewey	Republican	22,006,285	99
1948	HARRY S. TRUMAN (Mo.)	Democrat	24,105,695	304
	Thomas E. Dewey	Republican	21,969,170	189
	J. Strom Thurmond	State-Rights Democrat	1,169,021	38
	Henry A. Wallace	Progressive	1,156,103	–
1952	DWIGHT D. EISENHOWER (N.Y.)	Republican	33,936,252	442
	Adlai E. Stevenson	Democrat	27,314,992	89
1956	DWIGHT D. EISENHOWER (N.Y.)	Republican	35,575,420	457
	Adlai E. Stevenson	Democrat	26,033,066	73
	Other	–	–	1
1960	JOHN F. KENNEDY (Mass.)	Democrat	34,227,096	303
	Richard M. Nixon	Republican	34,108,546	219
	Other	–	–	15
1964	LYNDON B. JOHNSON (Tex.)	Democrat	43,126,506	486
	Barry M. Goldwater	Republican	27,176,799	52
1968	RICHARD M. NIXON (N.Y.)	Republican	31,770,237	301
	Hubert H. Humphrey	Democrat	31,270,533	191
	George Wallace	American Indep.	9,906,141	46
1972	RICHARD M. NIXON (N.Y.)	Republican	47,169,911	520
	George S. McGovern	Democrat	29,170,383	17
	Other	–	–	1
1976	JIMMY CARTER (Ga.)	Democrat	40,828,587	297
	Gerald R. Ford	Republican	39,147,613	241
	Other	–	1,575,459	–
1980	RONALD W. REAGAN (Calif.)	Republican	43,899,248	489
	Jimmy Carter	Democrat	35,481,435	49
	John B. Anderson	Independent	5,719,437	–
1984	RONALD W. REAGAN (Calif.)	Republican	54,281,858	525
	Walter F. Mondale	Democrat	37,457,215	13
1988	GEORGE BUSH (Tex.)	Republican	48,881,221	426
	Michael S. Dukakis	Democrat	41,805,422	112
1992	BILL CLINTON (Ark.)	Democrat	43,682,624	370
	George Bush	Republican	38,117,331	168
	H. Ross Perot	Independent	19,217,213	–

Source: Historical Statistics of the United States and *The World Almanac . . . 1994*

TABLE 5. Justices of the United States Supreme Court

NAME *Chief Justices in Capital Letters*	Terms of Service	NAME *Chief Justices in Capital Letters*	Terms of Service
JOHN JAY, N.Y	1789–1795	Rufus W. Peckham, N.Y.	1896–1909
James Wilson, Pa.	1789–1798	Joseph McKenna, Cal.	1898–1925
John Rutledge, S.C.	1790–1791	Oliver W. Holmes, Mass.	1902–1932
William Cushing, Mass.	1790–1810	William R. Day, Ohio	1903–1922
John Blair, Va.	1790–1796	William H. Moody, Mass.	1906–1910
James Iredell, N.C.	1790–1799	Horace H. Lurton, Tenn.	1910–1914
Thomas Johnson, Md.	1792–1793	Charles E. Hughes, N.Y.	1910–1916
William Paterson, N.J.	1793–1806	Willis Van Devanter, Wy.	1914–1937
JOHN RUTLEDGE, S.C.	1795	Joseph R. Lamar. Ga.	1911–1916
Samuel Chase, Md.	1796–1811	EDWARD D. WHITE, La.	1910–1921
OLIVER ELLSWORTH, Conn.	1796–1800	Mahlon Pitney, N.J.	1912–1922
Bushrod Washington, Va.	1799–1829	James C. McReynolds, Tenn.	1914–1941
Alfred Moore, N.C.	1800–1804	Louis D. Brandeis, Mass.	1916–1939
JOHN MARSHALL, Va.	1801–1835	John H. Clarke, Ohio	1916–1922
William Johnson, S.C.	1804–1834	WILLIAM H. TAFT, Conn.	1921–1930
Brockholst Livingston, N.Y.	1807–1823	George Sutherland, Utah	1922–1938
Thomas Todd, Ky.	1807–1826	Pierce Butler, Minn.	1923–1939
Gabriel Duvall, Md.	1811–1835	Edward T. Sanford, Tenn.	1923–1930
Joseph Story, Mass.	1812–1845	Harlan F. Stone, N.Y.	1925–1941
Smith Thompson, N.Y.	1823–1843	CHARLES E. HUGHES, N.Y.	1930–1941
Robert Trimble, Ky.	1826–1828	Owen J. Roberts, Penn.	1930–1945
John McLean, Ohio	1830–1861	Benjamin N. Cardozo, N.Y.	1932–1938
Henry Baldwin, Pa.	1830–1844	Hugo L. Black, Ala.	1937–1971
James M. Wayne, Ga.	1835–1867	Stanley F. Reed, Ky.	1938–1957
ROGER B. TANEY, Md.	1836–1864	Felix Frankfurter, Mass.	1939–1962
Philip P. Barbour, Va.	1836–1841	William O. Douglas, Conn.	1939–1975
John Catron, Tenn.	1837–1865	Frank Murphy, Mich.	1940–1949
John McKinley, Ala.	1838–1852	HARLAN F. STONE. N.Y.	1941–1946
Peter V. Daniel, Va.	1842–1860	James F. Byrnes, S.C.	1941–1947
Samuel Nelson, N.Y.	1845–1872	Robert H. Jackson, N.Y.	1941–1954
Levi Woodbury, N.H.	1845–1851	Wiley B. Rutledge, Iowa	1943–1949
Robert C. Grier, Pa.	1846–1870	Harold H. Burton, Ohio	1945–1958
Benjamin R. Curtis, Mass.	1851–1857	FREDERICK M. VINSON, Ky.	1946–1953
John A. Campbell, Ala.	1853–1861	Tom C. Clark, Texas	1949–1967
Nathan Clifford, Me.	1858–1881	Sherman Minton, Ind.	1949–1956
Noah H. Swayne, Ohio	1862–1881	EARL WARREN, Cal.	1953–1969
Samuel F. Miller, Iowa	1862–1890	John Marshall Harlan, N.Y.	1955–1971
David Davis, Ill.	1862–1877	William J. Brennan, Jr., N.J.	1956–1990
Stephen J. Field, Cal.	1863–1897	Charles E. Whittaker, Mo.	1957–1962
SALMON P. CHASE, Ohio	1864–1873	Potter Stewart, Ohio	1958–1981
William Strong, Pa.	1870–1880	Byron R. White, Colo.	1962–1993
Joseph P. Bradley, N.J.	1870–1892	Arthur J. Goldberg, Ill.	1962–1965
Ward Hunt, N.Y.	1873–1882	Abe Fortas, Tenn.	1965–1969
MORRISON R. WAITE, Ohio	1874–1888	Thurgood Marshall, N.Y.	1967–1991
John M. Harlan, Ky.	1877–1911	WARREN E. BURGER, Va.	1969–1986
William B. Woods, Ga.	1881–1887	Harry E. Blackmun, Minn.	1970–
Stanley Matthews, Ohio	1881–1889	Lewis F. Powell, Jr., Va.	1972–1987
Horace Gray, Mass.	1882–1902	William H. Rehnquist, Ariz.	1972–1986
Samuel Blatchford, N.Y.	1882–1893	John Paul Stevens, Ill.	1975–
Lucius Q. C. Lamar, Miss.	1888–1893	Sandra Day O'Connor, Ariz.	1981–
MELVILLE W. FULLER, Ill.	1888–1910	WILLIAM H. REHNQUIST, Ariz.	1986–
David J. Brewer, Kan.	1890–1910	Antonin Scalia, Va.	1986–
Henry B. Brown, Mich.	1891–1906	Anthony M. Kennedy, Cal.	1988–
George Shiras, Jr., Pa.	1892–1903	David H. Souter, N.H.	1990–
Howell E. Jackson, Tenn.	1893–1895	Clarence Thomas, Va.	1991–
Edward D. White, La.	1894–1910	Ruth Bader Ginsburg, D.C.	1993–

Source: Historical Statistics of the United States and *The World Almanac . . . 1994*

INDEX

Abbott, Lyman, 335, 336
Abilene, Kan., 279, 280
Abortion, 628–9
Abrams v. *United States* (1919), 433
Acheson, Dean, 522, 530
Adams, Charles Francis, 190, 232–3, 249–50
Adams, Henry, 347, 348
Adams, John, 46, 47, 52, 61, 70, 77, 90; as
  peace commissioner, 56–7; elected
  President, 84; as President, 85–8; in
  election of 1800, 88–9
Adams, John Quincy, 178, 183; as Secretary
  of State, 108–9; and Missouri
  Compromise, 112; as President, 137–8
Adams-Onís Treaty (1819), 109
Adams, Samuel, 41, 42, 43, 74
Adams, Samuel Hopkins, 380
Adamson Act (1916), 391
Addams, Jane, 328, 370, 376, 402, 480
Adkins v. *Children's Hospital* (1923), 437
Adler, Dankmar, 327
Advertising, 326
Affirmative action, 582
AFL-CIO, 579–80
Agassiz, Louis, 167
Agnew, Spiro T., 557, 564–5
Agriculture: in colonies, 17–18; in New
  England (1815–60), 119; in the Old
  Northwest (1815–60), 120; in the South
  (1815–60), 122, post-Civil War, 260–2;
  Great Plains, 289–90; problems of post-
  Civil War, 358–60, 361; in 1920s, 447–8;
  in New Deal, 460, 467
Agricultural Adjustment Act: (1933), 460,
  471; (1938), 474
AIDS (Acquired Immune Deficiency
  Syndrome), 627, 628, 629, 630
Aix-la-Chapelle, Treaty of (1748), 34
Alabama (Confederate cruiser), 232
'*Alabama* Claims', 394–6
Alamance, battle of, 42
Alaska, purchase of, 394
Albany Plan, 34–5
Albany Regency, 138
Alcorn, James L., 253
Aldrich, Nelson W., 378
Alexander v. *Holmes* (1969), 560
Algeciras conference, 404
Alger, Horatio, 330
Alien and Sedition Acts (1798), 87, 88, 91

Alien Registration Act (Smith Act, 1940),
  499–500, 529
Allen, Hervey, 471
Alliance for Progress, 546
Altgeld, John Peter, 312, 314, 373
America First, 492–3
American and Foreign Anti-Slavery Society,
  176
American Antiboycott Association, 315
American Antisaloon League, 375
American Anti-Slavery Society, 171–2, 173,
  176
American Board of Customs
  Commissioners, 41
American Civic Federation, 315
American Civil Liberties Union, 441
American Colonization Society, 170–1
American Express Company, 285
American Federation of Labor (AF of L),
  312–3, 315, 447, 473, 474; *see also* AFL-
  CIO
American Indian Movement, 583
American Liberty League, 461
American Peace Society, 168
American Plan, 447
American Protective Association, 323
American Railway Association, 301
American Railway Union, 314–15
American Society for the Promotion of
  Temperance, 167
American System, 106–8, 137
American Telephone and Telegraph
  Company, 298, 619
American Tobacco Company, 264, 378, 404
American Viscose Corporation, 494
American Woman Suffrage Association, 374
Ames, Adelbert, 252
Amherst, Jeffrey, 35
Amish, 20
Amistad case, 151
Amnesty Act (1872), 257
Anaconda Copper Mining Corporation, 278
Anderson, John B., 570, 571
Anderson, Robert, 216
Anderson, Sherwood, 450
Andover, Massachusetts, 19
André, John, 54
Andropov, Yuri, 600
Anglophobia, 105, 399, 413
Annapolis, Md., 64, 70

Anthony, Susan B., 374
Anthracite Coal Commission, 379
Anti-Catholicism: in colonies, 43, 46; in
    1830–60, 132; in late nineteenth century,
    323; in 1928 election, 452
Antietam, battle of, 227, 228
Anti Federalists, 74–5
Anti-imperialism (1890s), 402
Antimasonic party, 146–7
Anti-semitism, 323
Antislavery movement, 170–4, 175–6
Antitrust legislation, 309–10, 436; *see also*
    Clayton Act, Sherman Antitrust Act
Apache Indians, 284
Apollo program, 545, 591
Appeal of the Independent Democrats, 202
Appomattox, Va., 235
Arabic (British steamship), 416, 417
Arapaho Indians, 283
Architecture: skycrapers, 326–7; in 1950s
    and 1960s, 592–3
Arias, Oscar, 613
Aristocracy: in colonies, 25; in post-
    Revolutionary period, 59; in 1830s,
    134–5; late ninteenth century, 329
Arizona, 66
Arlington, Va., 238
Armour, Philip D., 331
Armstrong, Louis, 448
Army: in Revolutionary War, 49, 50–1,
    52–3, 54–6; size of (1789), 77; in Jefferson
    Administration, 91; in War of 1812,
    103–5; in Mexican War, 183–7; in Civil
    War, 218, 219, 224–7, 229–31, 233, 234–5;
    in Spanish-American War, 401–2; and
    Filipino revolt, 403; and preparedness
    campaign, 418; in World War I, 425–6; in
    World War II, 504, 507–11, 513–4, 515–6;
    in Korean War, 522–4; desegregation of
    527; in Vietnam, 555–6
Arnold, Benedict, 46, 54
Art galleries, 346
Arthur, Chester A., 351, 353, 354
Articles of Confederation (1781), 49, 63–4,
    68, 69–70, 71
Assassinations: of Lincoln, 235; of Garfield,
    353; of McKinley, 377; of Huey Long,
    462; of John F. Kennedy, 549; of
    Malcolm X, 553; of Martin Luther King,
    554; of Robert F. Kennedy, 557
Association Against the Prohibition
    Amendment, 442
Atchison, Topeka and Santa Fe Railroad,
    287
Atlanta Compromise, 271
Atlantic Charter, 495, 505
Atomic bomb, 515–6, 530
Atomic Energy Commission, 533

Automobile industry: beginnings of, 335; in
    1920s, 446; trade unions in, 473–4
Aviation, 445–6

Bacon, Nathaniel, 14–15
Bacon's Rebellion, 14–15
Baer, Max, 470
Bailey v. *Drexel Furniture Company* (1922),
    437
Baker, Ray Stannard, 372
Baker v. *Carr* (1962), 552–3
Bakke case, 582
Bakker, Jim, 606
Baldwin, James, 591
Ballinger, Richard A., 384–5
Ballinger-Pinchot controversy, 384–5
Baltimore and Ohio Railroad, 115, 116
Bancroft, George, 157
Bancroft, Hubert Howe, 277
Bank of New York, 78
Bank of North America, 55
Bank of the United States (First), 80, 91,
    102, 107; (Second), 107, 108, 111–12
Barbary Company, 4
Barbary pirates, 91–2
Barbed wire, 290
Barber, Samuel, 593
Barlow, Joel, 69
Barnard, Henry, 165
Barnburners, 188, 190, 199
Barrett, Lawrence, 332
Barth, Karl, 586
Bartram, John, 29
Baruch, Bernard M., 426
Baseball, 334
Bay of Pigs invasion, 546
Beadle, Erastus, 275
Bear Flag Revolt, 185
Beck, Dave, 580
Beecher, Catherine E., 169, 170
Beecher, Henry Ward, 335, 336
Beecher, Lyman, 167
Belknap, William W., 250–1
Bell, Alexander Graham, 298
Bell, John, 212–13
Bell Telephone Company, 298
Bellamy, Edward, 308
Belleau Wood, 425
Bellow, Saul, 591
Belmont, August, 362
Bennett, James Gordon, 342
Benton, Thomas Hart, 136, 183, 186
Bentsen, Lloyd, 611
Berger, Victor L., 370, 371
Berkeley, John, Lord, 11
Berkeley, William, 14
Berkman, Alexander, 433
Berle, Adolf A., Jr., 459

Berlin airlift, 520
Berliner, Emil, 332
Bernstein, Leonard, 593
Bernstorff, Johann Heinrich, Count von, 416, 421
Bessemer, Henry, 304
Bessemer process, 304
Bethmann-Hollweg, Theobald von, 417
Bethune, Mary McLeod, 468
Beveridge, Albert J., 398, 402
Biddle, Nicholas, 145, 147
Bible Belt, 260
Bicentennial of American Independence, 565
Bill of Rights (1791), 61, 77, 78
'Billion-Dollar Conress' (1889–91), 357
Bingham, George Caleb, 156
Birmingham, Alabama, 263
Birney, James G., 175, 176
Birth-rate: 1860–1910, 319; in 1920s, 449; in 1930s, 466; in World War II, 504; after World War II, 573
Bishop, Maurice, 601
Black, Hugo, 472
Blacks: population (1790), 76; and Federalist party, 85; colonization schemes for, 170–1; in antislavery movement, 173–4; in pre-Civil War North, 175; as Civil War soldiers, 229; freedmen, 240–1, 254–5; enfranchisement of, 247–8; in Reconstruction governments, 251–2, 253; education, 255; disfranchised, 267–8; segregation of, 268–9; in post-Civil War Southern agriculture, 255; lynching, 269; violence against, 269; condition of (*c.*1910), 270; violence against (post-World War I), 433–4; and Garvey, 434; origins of jazz, 448; writers (Harlem Renaissance), 451; migration to the North, 272–3, 433, 503, 576; in the Great Depression, 467–8; and New Deal, 467–8; in World War II, 503–4; school desegregation, 535–6, 560; civil rights movement, 536–7, 548–9, 551; militant, 553–4; riots in 1960s, 554; as city-dwellers, 576; and affirmative action, 582; unemployment, 581; political gains, 581; in higher education, 581; post-World War II writers, 591
Black Codes, 240, 241
'Black Friday', 248
Black Hawk War (1832), 118
Black Hills, South Dakota, 277, 281, 283
Black Kettle (Cheyenne chief), 283
Black Muslims, 553
Black Panther party, 553
Blackwell, Elizabeth, 169
Blaine, James G., 351, 353, 355, 397
Bland, Richard P. ('Silver Dick'), 352
Bland-Allison Act (1878), 352

Bloomer, Amelia, 169–70
Board of Trade, 16
Boarding-schools, boys', 329
Boesky, Ivan, 606
Bok, Edward, 343
Boland Amendment (1984), 601
Bonus Marchers, 457
Booth, Edwin, 332
Booth, John Wilkes, 235
Booth, William, 337
Borah, William E., 430, 480
Bork, Robert, 604–5
Boston: founded, 8; colonial growth, 23; riot (1768), 41; port closed, 43; siege of, 44–5; British evacuation, 45; and War of 1812, 102; Irish in, 131; as mid-nineteenth century literary center, 157–8; and antislavery crusade, 171; population (1860–1910), 320; subway, 325; first Christian Science Church established, 338; public library, 342; police strike (1919), 432, 435; bans Ku Klux Klan, 440
Boston (cruiser), 399
Boston Manufacturing Company, 126
Boston Massacre, 41–2
Boston Tea Party, 43
Bourbons, 265
Boxer rebellion, 405
Braddock, Edward, 34
Bradley, Omar N., 524
Brady bill (1993), 631
Bragg, Braxton, 231
Brain trust, 459
Brandeis, Louis D., 390, 391
Brandywine, battle of, 50
Braun, Carol Moseley, 623
Breckinridge, John C., 211, 213
Brezhnev, Leonid, 566
Bricker, John W., 512, 533
Bridges, 301–2, 324
Bright, John, 232
Brisbane, Albert, 163
Brook Farm, 163
Brooklyn Bridge, 300–1, 324
Brown, John, 205, 210–11, 212
Brown, Joseph E., 224, 253, 265
Brown v. *Board of Education of Topeka* (1954), 535–6, 552, 588–9
Brownson, Orestes A., 128
Bruce, Blanche K., 252
Bruce, Louis R., 583
Brush, Charles F., 299, 325
Bryan, William Jennings, 341, 398; 1896 campaign, 362, 363–7; later campaigns, 379, 382, 386; Secretary of State, 414, 416; 'Monkey trial', 441
Bryce, James, 73, 303, 336, 340, 349, 350, 418

Brzezinski, Zbigniew, 568
Buchanan, James, 150, 213; elected
    President, 206; and sectional crisis, 207;
    and Kansas, 208; and secession, 213
Buck's Stove and Range Co., case of, 315
Buckley, William F., Jr., 596
Budget deficit, 597, 603, 609
Buell, Don Carlos, 226
Buena Vista, battle of, 186
Buffalo Bill, *see* Cody, William F.
Buffalo Bill Dam, 293
Buffaloes, 282, 284
Bull Run, first battle of, 224–5; second
    battle of, 227
Bunau-Varilla, Philippe, 407, 408
Bunker Hill, battle of, 45
Burchard, Samuel D., 355
Bureau of Corporations, 378
Bureau of Reclamation, 293
Burger, Warren E., 560, 604
Burgoyne, John, 50–1
Burke, Edmund, 39, 48
Burleson, Albert S., 427
Burlington and Missouri Railroad, 289
Burnside, Ambrose E., 229
Burr, Aaron, 82, 88–9, 96
Burritt, Elihu, 168
Burroughs, William S., 298
Bush, George: in election of 1980, 570;
    elected President, 611–12; foreign policy
    of, 612–15; and Gulf War, 615–18;
    domestic affairs, 618–21; in election of
    1992, 621–3; appointments to Supreme
    Court, 605
Butler, Andrew P., 206
Butler, Benjamin F., 226, 227
Butte, Mont., 278
Butterfield, John, 285
Butterfield Overland Express, 286
Byrnes, James F., 501, 518

Cabet, Étienne, 163
Cable, George Washington, 263, 343
Cabot, John, 4
Calhoun, Floride (Mrs. John C.), 143
Calhoun, John C., 109, 183; as War Hawk,
    101; nationalism of, 102, 107; supports
    Jackson, 138; nullification theories of,
    142, 144; breaks with Jackson, 143; and
    state rights, 142, 152; and annexation of
    Texas, 179; and slavery in the territories,
    188–9; and Compromise of 1850, 193
California: Spanish missions in, 179; as
    Mexican province, 179; Bear Flag revolt,
    185; gold rush, 191–2; admitted to the
    Union, 194, 198; Japanese immigrants in,
    406, 498; becomes most populous state,
    575, 624

Calvert, Cecilius (Lord Baltimore), 6
Calvert, George (Lord Baltimore), 6
Cambodia, invasion of, 558
Camden, battle of, 55
Campbell, Alexander, 161
Camp David agreement (1978), 569
Canada: French exploration and coloniza-
    tion, 13, 33; ceded to Great Britain, 35;
    Quebec Act, 43; invasion of (1775), 46;
    invasion of (1812–13), 102–3; and Rush-
    Bagot agreement, 109; Fenian raids on,
    395; reciprocity treaty (1911), 384; U.S.
    Annexation proposed, 394–5; Soviet spy
    ring in, 529
Canals, 114–15
Cannon, Joseph G., 383
Capone, Al, 442
Capper-Volstead Act (1922), 448
Cardozo, Francis L., 252
Carlisle, Frederick Howard, 5th earl of, 43
Carmichael, Stokely, 553
Carmody, Jane ('Calamity Jane'), 275
Carnegie, Andrew, 305, 306, 307, 314, 341,
    402
Carolina: founding of, 10–11; Fundamental
    Constitutions of, 10
Carpetbaggers, 252
Carranza, Venustiano, 410–11
Carroll, Charles, 26
Carter, Elliott, 593
Carter, Jimmy (James Earl): in 1976
    election, 566–7; Presidency of, 567–8;
    foreign policy of, 568–70; imposes wheat
    embargo on Soviet Union, 600; in 1980
    election, 570, 571–2
Carter, Robert, 60
Carteret, Sir George, 11
Cartwright, John, 48
Cass, Lewis, 189, 190
Cassatt, Mary, 345
Castle Garden, 324
Castlereagh, Robert Stewart, viscount, 101
Catlin, George, 293
Catt, Carrie Chapman, 375
Cattle ranching, 278–81
Caucus system, 136–7
Celler-Kefauver Antimerger Act (1950), 579
Central Intelligence Agency (CIA), 546, 565
Central Pacific Railroad, 286–7
Century of Dishonor, A (Jackson), 285
Cerro Cordo, battle of, 186
Cervera, Pascual, 401
Challenger (space shuttle) disaster, 604
Chamberlain, Daniel H., 252
Chamberlain, Neville, 490
Chambers, Whittaker, 529–30
Chamorro, Violeta Barrios de, 613
Chancellorsville, battle of, 229–30

Chandler, Zachariah, 242
Channing, William Ellery, 171
Chaplin, Ralph, 317
Charles I, King of England, 6, 7
Charles II, King of England, 10, 11, 12
Charles River Bridge v. *Warren Bridge*
    (1837), 151
Charleston, 43; British capture of (1780), 55;
    nullification crisis, 144; 1860 Democratic
    convention, 211; siege of Fort Sumter,
    216–17; Union capture of (1865), 234
Chase, Salmon P., 202
Chase, Samuel, 92
Château Thierry, 425
Chatsworth, 26
Chautauqua movement, 341
Chávez, César, 583
Cherokee Indians, expelled from Georgia,
    118, 141
Chesapeake (frigate), 98
Cheyenne Indians, 283
Chiang Kai-Shek, 483, 497, 516, 521, 537,
    539, 559
Chicago: Republican convention in (1860),
    211–12; skyscrapers, 327; fire (1871), 320,
    325; meat-packing, 127; population
    (1860–1910), 320; Haymarket affair,
    311–12, 314, 323; Hull House, 328, 376;
    immigrants in, 321; Dwight L. Moody in,
    337; gangsterism, 442; Memorial Day
    massacre, 473; race riots, 434; Democratic
    convention of 1896, 323–4, of 1968, 557
Chicanos (Mexican-Americans), 582, 625,
    626
Chickamauga, battle of, 231
Child, Lydia M., 169
Child labor: in mid-nineteenth century, 129;
    Progressives and, 376; Wilson
    Administration and, 391; Supreme Court
    and, 437
Child welfare, 376
Children's Bureau, 376, 383
Chilean war scare (1891–2), 397
China: Open Door policy in, 405, 407; and
    Manchuria, 483–4; Japan invades, 488–9;
    in World War II, 497, 595; Communist
    victory in, 521; and Korea War, 523;
    rapprochement with, 559; diplomatic
    relations restored with, 569; Bush
    administration's policy toward, 612–13
Chinese Exclusion Act (1882), 324
Chisholm Trail, 279
Chivington, J. M., 283
Choate School, 329
Chou En-lai, 559
Church of Jesus Christ of Latter-Day Saints,
    see Mormons
Christian Science, 337–8

Churchill Winston S., 476, 492, 495, 505,
    508, 509, 510
Cincinnati: meat-packing in, 127; German
    immigrants in, 131
Cities: Colonial, 23; growth of (1815–60),
    121; Western cities, 120; growth of
    (1860–1910), 320–1; immigrants in, 321–2;
    problems of, 324–5; architecture of,
    326–7; slums in, 327–8; boss rule in, 348,
    349–50; reform of, in Progressive era, 372;
    black migration to, 272–3, 433, 503, 576;
    movement to suburbs from (1920s),
    446–7, (post-World War II), 575–6;
    (1980s), 624; growth of Southern and
    Western, 576, 624; decay of, 576–8; crime
    in, 557–8
City-manager plan, 372
Civil liberties: and Alien and Sedition Acts,
    87; slavery as danger to, 175, 176; in
    World War I, 427–8; in World War II,
    499–500; and McCarthyism, 530–1
Civil-military relations: in Revolutionary
    War, 52–3; in Mexican War, 184; in Civil
    War, 225; Truman-MacArthur contro-
    versy, 523–4
Civil Rights Acts: (1866), 242–3, 267;
    (1875), 258, 267; (1957), 536; (1960), 536;
    (1964), 550–1
Civil Rights Cases (1883), 267
Civil War (*see also* Confederate States of
    America): causes of, 196–8, 213–14,
    216–17; begins at Fort Sumter, 216;
    modernity of, 218–19; Union and
    Confederacy compared, 219–20; Border
    slave states in, 220; politics in, 220–2; civil
    liberties in, 221; economic policies, 221–2;
    Emancipation Proclamation, 227–9, 232;
    military campaigns, 224–7, 229–31, 233,
    234–5; British policy toward, 231–3;
    election of 1864, 233–4; significance of,
    235–6; and industrialization, 295–6
Civilian Conservation Corps, 459, 467
Civil Service reform, 351, 354
Clark, George Rogers, 57
Clark, Champ, 386
Clark Memorandum, 482
Clark, William, 95
Class Distinctions: in colonies, 25; 1830–50,
    134–5; in late ninetenth century, 329–30
Clay, Cassius M., 175
Clay, Henry, 109, 145, 149, 150, 152, 154,
    167, 170, 190, 398; as War Hawk, 101;
    and American System, 106–7; and
    Missouri Compromise, 112; in election of
    1824, 137; and nullification compromise,
    144; in election of 1832, 147; and Bank
    War, 146; breaks with Tyler, 154–5;
    and distribution, 147, 154; and election

Clay, Henry (*cont.*):
of 1844, 180-1; and Compromise of 1850, 192-3
Clayton Antitrust Act (1914), 390, 437
Clayton-Bulwer Treaty (1850), 407
Cleaver, Eldridge, 553
Clemenceau, Georges, 429
Clemens, Samuel Langhorne, *see* Mark Twain
Clermont (steamboat), 114
Cleveland, Grover, 402; elected President (1844), 355 (1892), 361; civil-service reform, 355; pensions, 355-6; tariff, 356, 362-3; election of 1888, 356-7; and Pullman strike, 314; monetary policy, 362; and Hawaii, 399; and Venezuelan boundary, 399-400
Clinton, Bill (William Jefferson), 621-3
Clinton, De Witt, 102, 114-15
Clinton, George, 63, 74, 82
Clinton, Sir Henry, 49, 53, 54, 55
Clipper ships, 117
Clubs, men's, 329
Cobden, Richard, 232
Cody, William F. (Buffalo Bill), 275
Coercive Acts (1774), 43
Coffin, Levi, 173
Cohan, George M., 334
Coinage Act (1873), 352
Coin's Financial School (1894), 363
Cold Harbor, battle of, 233
Colleges and universities: in colonies, 31; expansion of (early 1800s), 166; in Civil War, 222; post-Civil War, 339-40; in Great Depression, 469; post-World War II boom, 589; Campus uprisings, 589-90, *see also* specific colleges and universities
Collier, John, 468
Colombia, and Panama Canal, 407-8
Colonies: agriculture in, 17-18; commerce, 18; economy, 17-18; fishing, 18; governmental structure, 13-15; manufacturing in, 17; tobacco cultivation, 18; slave trade, 18, 22; convicts transported to, 19, 21; class structure in, 25
Colonization: Spanish, 4, 33; Dutch, 4, 11; English, 3, 4-13; French, 4, 33; joint-stock companies and, 4; Portuguese, 4
Colt, Samuel, 127
Columbia Broadcasting System (CBS), 445
Columbus, Christopher, 3, 4, 632
Command of the Army Act (1867), 245, 246
Common Sense (Paine), 46
Commission on Industrial Relations (1915), 318
Committee on Public Information, 427
Committee to Defend America by Aiding the Allies, 492
Commons, John R., 308

Commonwealth v. *Hunt*, 128
Communism: sympathies with (1930s), 529; containment of, 519-21; in China, 520-1; investigations of, 529-31; collapse of, in Soviet Empire, 612
Communist party of America: established, 432; intellectuals in (1930s), 529
Communitarianism, 162-3
Compromise of 1850, 192-5, 196, 198, 199
Compromise of 1877, 259
Comstock, Anthony, 443
Comstock Lode, 277
Conan Doyle, A., 313, 418
Conciliatory Propositions, 44
Concord: battle of, 44; Thoreau in, 158
Conestoga wagon, 113
Confederate States of America: formed, 214; Constitution of, 223; Jefferson Davis as President of, 223-4; state rights and, 224
Confiscation Act (1862), 228
Congress of Industrial Organizations (CIO), 473-4, 502, 579-80
Congress for Racial Equality (CORE), 504
Conkling, Roscoe, 348, 353, 354
Connally, Tom, 514
Connecticut: founding of, 10; Fundamental Orders (1639), 10
Connecticut Wits, 69
Conrad, Joseph, 418
Conscience Whigs, 188
Conservation movement: beginnings of, 291-4; Theodore Roosevelt and, 381; Ballinger-Pinchot controversy, 384-5
Conservatism (1980s), 596-7
Constitution of the United States: framing of, 70-3; ratification, 73-5; strict and loose construction, 80, 94-5; Garrison denounces for protecting slavery, 171; *see also* Constitutional Amendments
Constitutional Amendments: Bill of Rights (first ten), 61, 77, 78; Twelfth, 89; proposed at Hartford Convention, 104; Thirteenth, 240; Fourteenth, 243-7, 257, 267; Fifteenth, 248. 257: Sixteenth. 383; Seventeenth, 373, 383; Eighteenth, 427, 441-2; Nineteenth, 427, 449; Twentieth, 458; Twenty-first, 443; Twenty-second, 526; Twenty-fourth, 552; Twenty-fifth, 564-5
Constitutional Convention (1787), 70-3
Constitutional Union party, 212
Continental Army, 45, 49, 53
Continental Association, 44
Continental Congress: First, 43; Second, 45, 63
Contraception, spread of, 319, 443, 449, 466
Contras (Nicaragua), 600-1, 608
Convention of 1800, 88

Convict-leasing system, 266
Conway, Thomas, 52
Conwell, Russell H., 335
Cooke, Jay, 248
Coolidge, Calvin, 481; and Boston police strike, 435; elected Vice-President, 435; becomes President, 438; and business, 483, 444; re-elected, 444; and war debts, 481; and Latin America, 482
Cooper, Sir Anthony Ashley (Lord Shaftesbury), 10
Cooper, James Fenimore, 134, 157
Copland, Aaron, 593
Copperheads, 221
Copper mining, 278
Coral Sea, battle of the, 507
Corbett, 'Gentleman Jim', 334
Cornell, Alonzo B., 351
Cornell, Ezra, 340
Cornwallis, Charles, 1st marquis and 2nd earl, 48, 49, 55–6
Coronado, Francisco Vasquez de, 4
Corrigan, Michael A., 338
Corwin, Thomas, 149, 184
Cotton, John, 9
Cotton States Exposition (1895), 271
Cotton Whigs, 188
Coughlin, Charles E., 462, 488, 499
Cowboys, 278–80
Cowpens, battle of, 55
Cox, Archibald, 564
Cox, Jacob D., 249
Cox, James M., 431, 435
Coxey, Jacob S., 362
Coxey's Army, 362
Crane, Stephen, 345
Crawford, William H., 137
Crazy Horse (Oglala Sioux chief), 283–4
Crédit Mobilier scandal, 250, 287, 288
Creek Indians, 138
Creel, George, 427
Crime: immigrants and, (mid-1800s), 132; and city slums (1880s), 328; gangsterism (1920s), 442; in Great Depression, 470; in cities (post-World War II), 577–8; in 1980s, 631
'Crime of '73', 352
Crisis, 273
Crittenden, John J., 215
Crittenden Compromise (1861), 215
Crittenden Resolution, 227, 228
Croker, Richard, 349
Crop-lien system, 262
Crystal Palace Exhibition (1851), 127
Cuba: U.S. attempts to acquire, 200–1; rebellion of 1868–78, 396, 400; rebellion of 1895, 400; in Spanish-American War, 401–2; Platt Amendment, 404; U.S.

occupation of, 404; Castro revolution (1959), 541; Bay of Pigs invasion, 546; immigration from, 575, 625, 626, 627
Cullen, Countee, 451
Cumberland Road (National Road), 108, 113
Cumming v. *Board of Education* (1899), 269
Cunard steamships, 117
Cuomo, Mario S., 610
Currency Act (1764), 39
Currier and Ives lithographs, 276
Curtis, George W., 354
Custer, George A., 283–4
Customs service in colonies: Grenville's reform of, 38–9
Cutler, Manasseh, 65

D'Aubuisson, Roberto, 600
Dale, Sir Thomas, 5–6
Damrosch, Leopold, 333
Damrosch, Walter, 333
Danbury Hatters case, 315
Daniels, Josephus, 424
Darrow, Clarence, 316, 441
Dartmouth College v. *Woodward* (1819), 108
Darwin, Charles, 307
Daugherty, Harry M., 437
Daughters of the American Revolution, 330
Davies, Samuel, 28
Davis, David, 212, 249
Davis, Jeff, 373
Davis, Jefferson, 119, 186, 214, 216
Davis, John W., 443, 444, 461
Dawes Act (1887), 285
Dawes Plan, 481
Dayton, Tenn., 440–1
Deadwood (Dakota Territory), 277
Deadwood Dick, 275
Death-rate: in eighteenth century colonies, 19; in colonial South, 24; late ninteenth century fall in, 319; in 1930s, 466; after World War II, 573
Debs, Eugene V., 314, 370, 371, 428, 435
Declaration of Independence, 37, 47–8
Declaration of Rights and Grievances (1765), 40
Declaration of the Causes and Necessities of Taking Up Arms, 45
Declaratory Act (1766), 40
Deere, John, 120
Deerfield, Mass., 33
De Forest, John W., 349
De Kalb, Johann, 53
Delaware: population of (1787), 71; ratifies Constitution, 74; in Civil War, 220
De Leon, Daniel, 370
De Lôme, Dupuy, 400
Deloria, Vine, jr., 583

Democratic party: principles and character
(1830s), 149; and Civil War, 220–1;
attitudes and affiliations (1880s), 350;
divisions within (1960s–1980s), 556–7,
561, 602; see *also* Elections, Political
parties
Dempsey, Jack, 448
Deng Xiaoping, 612
Dennis v. *United States* (1951), 529
Department stores, 325
Dependent Pension Bill (1887), 355–6;
(1890), 357
Depression, Great: causes of, 453–4; course
of, 454–5, 458; society in, 465–71
Desert Land Act (1877), 289
de Soto, Hernando, 4
Destroyers-for-bases deal, 492
Detroit: in War of 1812, 103; as center of
automobile industry, 335
Dew, Thomas R., 174
Dewey, George, 401
Dewey, John, 370, 376
Dewey, Thomas E., 493, 511–12, 527–8
Dickinson, Emily, 346
Dickinson, John, 41, 64
Diem, Ngo Dinh, 539, 547, 548
Dienbienphu, 538–9
Dillinger, John, 470
Dime novels, 275
Dingley Act (1897), 366; Theodore
Roosevelt and, 386; Taft and, 383–4
Direct primaries, 373
Disciples of Christ, 161
Discovery (ship), 5
Disney, Walt, 470
Displaced Persons Acts (1948, 1950), 572
Distribution Act (1836), 147–8
Divine, Father (George Baker), 470
Divorce: in 1860–1910, 331; in 1920s,
449–50; in World War II, 504
Dix, Dorothea L., 164
Dixiecrats, 527
Dodge City, Kan., 279, 280
Doheny, Edward L., 437
Dole, Robert, 611
Dollar diplomacy, 407
Dominican Republic: Spanish withdrawal
from, 394; U.S. intervention in, 409–10,
555
Donnelly, Ignatius, 361
Dos Passos, John, 470
Douglas, Stephen A.: and popular
sovereignty, 189; and Compromise of
1850, 184; and Kansas-Nebraska bill,
201–2; debates with Lincoln, 208–9; in
election of 1860, 211–13
Douglas, William O., 527
Douglass, Frederick, 173

Dow, Neal, 168
Draft (Conscription): in Civil War, 229; in
Confederacy, 224; in World War I, 424–5;
in World War II, 492, 500; abolished, 590
Dred Scott v. *Sanford*, 207
Dreiser, Theodore, 345
Drew, Charles, 504
Drew, Daniel, 302
Drug problem, 630–1
Du Bois, William E. B., 271
Duarte, José Napoleon, 600
Dukakis, Michael S., 610–12
Duke, James Buchanan, 264
Dulany, Daniel, 26
Dulles, John Foster, 534, 537–42
Dumbarton Oaks Conference (1944), 506
Dunkers, 20
Duplex Printing Press v. *Deering* (1921), 437
Du Pont Corporation, 378
Durand, Asher, 156
Dwight, Timothy, 68

Eads, James B., 301
Eagleton, Thomas F., 561
Eakins, Thomas, 345
Earp, Wyatt, 280
East India Company, 43
Eastman, George, 332
Eaton, Dorman, B., 354
Eaton, Peggy, 143
Eddy, Mary Baker, 337–8
Edison Electric Light Company, 299
Edison, Thomas Alva, 298–9, 332, 333
Edmonds, Walter D., 471
Edwards, Jonathan, 28, 29, 337
Egalitarianism, 134–5, 146–7
Eggleston, Edward, 343
Einstein, Albert, 466
Eisenhower, Dwight D., in World War II,
508, 510; in election of 1952, 531–2;
Presidency, 533–42
Eisenhower Doctrine, 541
El Salvador: civil war (1980s), 600
Election(s): of 1789, 76; of 1792, 82; of
1796, 84; of 1800, 85, 88–9; of 1804, 95;
of 1808, 97; of 1812, 102; of 1816, 106; of
1820, 106; of 1824, 137; of 1828, 139; of
1836, 150; of 1840, 152–3; of 1844, 180–1;
of 1848, 190–1; of 1852, 199; of 1856,
206–7; of 1860, 211–13; of 1864, 233–4,
239; of 1868, 247; of 1872, 249–50; of
1876, 258–9; in late nineteenth century,
348; of 1880, 353, 359; of 1884, 355, 359;
of 1888, 356–7; of 1892, 361; of 1896,
363–6; of 1900, 367; of 1904, 379; of
1908, 382; of 1912, 386–8; of 1916,
419–20; of 1920, 431, 435; of 1924, 443–4;
of 1928, 451–2; of 1932, 458; of 1936,

465; of 1940, 493–4; of 1944, 511–2; of
1948, 527–8; of 1952, 531–2; of 1956,
534–5; of 1960, 543–4; of 1964, 551; of
1968, 556–8; of 1972, 560–1; of 1976,
566–7; of 1980, 570–2; of 1984, 602–3; of
1988, 610–2; of 1992, 621–3; *see also* pp.
695–7, Table 4 Presidential Elections
Electricity, 298–300
Eliot, Charles W., 341, 402
Eliot, T. S., 451
Elkins Act (1903), 380
Elliott, Robert Brown, 252
Ellis Island, 324
Ellison, Ralph, 591
Ely, Richard T., 308
Emancipation Proclamation, 221, 227–9
Embargo Act (1807), 99
Emergency Banking Relief Act (1933), 458
Emergency Quota Act (1921), 439
Emerson, Ralph Waldo, 118, 158–9, 194,
210, 343
Endara, Guillermo, 614
England: and colonization, 3–13; colonial
policy (1600s), 15–16; Glorious Revolution
(1688), 15; after 1707, *see* Great Britain
Entails, 59
'Enumerated' Commodities, 15
Equal Rights Amendment (ERA), 571, 585,
586
Erie Canal, 114–15
Erie Railroad, 116, 302
Espionage Act (1917), 427, 428, 433
Essex decision (1805), 97
Estaing, Jean Baptiste Charles Henri Hector
comte d', 55
Ethnoculturalism, 347
Evans, Oliver, 127
Everett, Edward, 212
Executive Reorganization Bill, 475
ex parte McCardle, 245
ex parte Milligan, 245
Expatriates, 344, 345, 346
Exposition and Protest (Calhoun), 142, 143

Fair Deal, 528
Fair Employment Practices Committee, 503
Fairfax, Thomas, 6th lord, 59
Falaba (British steamship), 415
Falkland Islands, Argentine invasion of, 601
Fall, Albert B., 437
Fallen Timbers, battle of, 100
Family: in colonial America, 24–5
Farm Holiday Association, 456
Farragut, David G., 226, 234
Faubus, Orval, 536
Faulkner, William, 450, 471, 591
Federal Arts Project, 463
Federal Bank Deposit Corporation, 461

Federal Bureau of Investigation (FBI), 470
Federal Council of Churches of Christ in
America, 371
Federal Election Campaign Amendments
Act (1974), 567
Federal Emergency Relief Act (1933), 459
Federal Farm Loan Act (1916), 391
Federal Home Loan Bank Act (1932), 456
Federal Music Project, 463
Federal Reserve Act (1913), 389
Federal Reserve Board, 389–90
Federal Reserve System, 389–90, 452–3, 461
Federal Theater Project, 464
Federal Trade Commission Act (1914), 390,
436
Federal Writers' Project, 463
Federalist party: emergence of, 81–2;
principles and character of, 85; rift
within, 88; loss of support, 89; in 1796
election, 84; in 1800 election, 88–91; in
judiciary, 92–3; status of post-1800, 96–7;
and War of 1812, 102, 104; in 1816
election, 106; end of, 106
Fenians, 394
Fenno, John, 81
Ferraro, Geraldine, 602
Fetterman, W. J., 283
Field, Cyrus W., 298
'Fifty-four forty or fight', 181, 182
Fillmore, Millard: becomes President, 193;
in election of 1856, 206–7
Finney, Charles Grandison, 160, 172
Fish, Hamilton, 249, 395–6
Fisk, James, 248, 302
Fisk University, 255
Fiske, John, 397
Fitch, John, 114
Fitzgerald, F. Scott, 450, 471
Fitzhugh, George, 174
Fletcher v. *Peck* (1810), 108
Florida(s): acquired by Great Britain, 35;
ceded to Spain, 57; Jefferson's attempt to
buy, 96; revolts in (1810–11), 101; ceded
to the United States, 109; secedes, 213; in
1876 election, 259; land boom (1926),
454; population growth (1970s), 575
Floyd, Pretty Boy, 470
Flying Cloud (clipper ship), 117
Food Administration (World War I), 426
Force Act (1833), 144; (1870), 257; (1871),
257
Ford, Gerald R., 564–7
Ford, Henry, 335, 446
Ford Motor Company, 335
Fordney-McCumber Act (1922), 436
Foreign trade: in 1815–60, 116; in 1920s,
454
Forest Management Act (1897), 292

Forest Reserve Act (1891), 292, 381
Fort Donelson, 226
Fort Duquesne, 34, 35
Fort Frontenac, 35
Fort Henry, 226 ·
Fort Oswego, 35
Fort Pickens, 216
Fort Pillow massacre, 219
Fort Sumter, 216
Fort William Henry, 35
Foster, Stephen, 156
Fourier, Charles, 163
Fourteen Points, 428–9
Fox, Charles James, 48
France: settlements in New World, 33; in colonial wars, 33–4; alliance with, in Revolutionary War, 51–3, 54–7; declares war on Great Britain (1793), 82; and XYZ dispatches, 86; quasi-war with, 86–7; Convention of 1800 with, 88; and Louisiana Purchase, 93–5; and maritime rights controversy, 97–9; and Civil War, 231, 232; Mexican empire attempted, 394; in peace conference (1919), 429–30; fall of (1940), 491; Allied invasion of (1944), 510–11; in Indo-China, 496–7, 538–9; in Suez crisis, 540
Frankfurter, Felix, 459
Franklin, Benjamin, 20, 26, 29–30, 69; and the Enlightenment, 30; as inventor, 30; and Albany Plan, 35; and Declaration of Independence, 47; as diplomat, 51–2, 56; and the Federal Constitution, 74
Franklin (state), 65
Fredericksburg, battle of, 229
Freedmen's Bureau, 237, 255, 256, 257
Freedmen's Bureau Bill (1866), 242
Freeport Doctrine, 210, 211
Free Soil Party, 176, 190–1
Free Speech Movement, 590
Frelinghuysen, Theodore, J., 28
Frémont, John C., 179, 185, 206–7, 227, 234
French and Indian War, 35–6
French Revolution, 82
Freneau, Philip, 82
Freud, Sigmund, 448
Frick, Henry Clay, 305, 314, 346
Friedan, Betty, 585
Friedman, Milton, 596
Fries, John, 88
Fries's insurrection, 88
Frontier: location of (1860), 275; Turner thesis, 291; closing of, 291
Frost, Robert, 451, 592
Fugitive Slave Acts: of 1793, 173, 194; of 1850, 194, 199, 227
Fulbright, J., William 556
Fuller, Margaret, 169

Fulton, Robert, 114
Fundamentalism, 440–1
Furman v. *Georgia* (1972), 560
Furuseth, Andrew, 391

Gadaffi, Muammar al-, 610
Gage, Thomas, 44
Gag rule, 172–3
Gallatin, Albert, 91, 104
Gallaudet, Thomas G., 164
Galloway, Joseph, 44
Gangsterism, 442
Garfield, Harry A., 426
Garfield, James A., 353
Garland, Hamlin, 290, 345, 402
Garner, John N., 457
Garrison, William Lloyd, 171, 172, 175, 176, 273, 285
Garvey, Marcus M., 434
Gaspee (ship), 42
Gates, Horatio, 51
Gentlemen's Agreement (1907–8), 406, 439
George II, King of England, 35
George III, King of England, 37, 44, 45, 46, 48, 56, 149, 169
George, Henry, 308, 371, 372
Georgia, colonization of, 13
Georgia Platform, 194
Germain, Lord George, 48
German immigrants: to colonies, 20; 1815–60, 130, 131, 132; in World War I, 427
Germantown: founding of, 12; battle of, 50
Geronimo (Apache warrior), 284
Getty, J. Paul, 469
Gettysburg Address, 217, 230
Gettysburg, battle of, 230
Ghent, Treaty of (1814), 105
Gibbons, James, Cardinal, 338
Gibbons v. *Ogden* (1824), 114
GI Bill of Rights (1944), 524, 589
Gideon v. *Wainright* (1963), 552
Gilbert, Sir Humphrey, 4
Gilman, Daniel Coit, 341
Ginsburg, Douglas, 605
Gladden, Washington, 336
Glass-Steagall Banking Act: of 1932, 456; of 1933, 461
Gliddon, George, 174
Gliddon, Joseph F., 290
Glorious Revolution (1688), 15–16, 39
G-men, 470
Godey's Lady's Book, 169
Godkin, E. L., 342, 346, 354, 355
Gold: in California, 352; discoveries in late 1800s, 276–7
Goldman, Emma, 433
Goldwater, Barry M., 551, 555

Gompers, Samuel, 313, 315, 317, 402, 447
Good Neighbor policy, 481–3, 486–7
Goodnight-Loving Trail, 279
Goodspeed (ship), 5
Goodyear, Charles, 127
Gorbachev, Mikhail S., 607, 614–15
Gordon, John B., 265
Gore, Al (Albert), Jr., 622
Gough, John B., 168
Gould, Jay, 248, 302
Grady, Henry W., 262
Graham, William F. (Billy), 586
Gramm-Rudman-Hollings Act (1985), 603
Grand Army of the Republic, 355
Grandfather clause, 268
Grange, Harold ('Red'), 448
Granger laws, 303, 359
Granger Movement, 303, 347, 359
Granger railroads, 288
Grant, Ulysses S., 245; in Civil War, 226,
  230, 233, 235; elected President, 247; and
  Reconstruction, 251, 257; corruption, 248,
  250–1; re-elected, 250; and Santo
  Domingo, 396; and Indians, 283
Grasse, François Joseph Paul, comte de,
  55–6
Grasso, Ella T., 585
Great American Desert, 276
Great Atlantic and Pacific Tea Company
  (A. & P.), 326
Great Awakening, 28–9, 31; Second, 160
Great Britain (before 1707, *see* England):
  colonial policy of, 16–18; conflict with
  France and Spain, 33–4; in Seven Years'
  War, 35–6; imperial policy (1763–75),
  37–44; in Revolutionary War, 44–6,
  49–54; and Treaty of Paris (1783), 56–7,
  82–3; relations with U.S. (1780s), 66–7;
  Jay's Treaty, 83; and neutral rights, 83,
  97–9; allied with Indians (1783–1812),
  100–1; in War of 1812, 101–5; Treaty of
  Ghent, 105; Rush-Bagot agreement, 109;
  and Monroe Doctrine, 110–11; and
  Texas, 178; and Oregon question, 180,
  181–2; and U.S. Civil War, 231–3, 394;
  Alabama claims, 394–6; relations with
  U.S. in late nineteenth century, 397–8;
  Venezuelan boundary question, 399–400;
  in World War I, 413–15, 417–19, 420,
  423, 424; in peace conference (1919), 429;
  and Anglo-Japanese alliance, 478; and
  naval disarmament, 478–80; war debts,
  480–1; and appeasement, 490–1; in World
  War II, 491, 507; destroyers-for-bases
  deal, 492; lend-lease agreement with, 494;
  strategic differences with U.S., 505,
  508–9, 510; and assistance to Greece and
  Turkey, 519; in Brussels Pact, 520; in

NATO, 520; and Suez crisis, 540
Great Northern Railroad, 287, 289, 302
Great Plains, 275, 276; cattle-raising,
  278–80; railroads, 281, 285–8, Indian
  tribes, 281–5; farming on, 288–90;
  settlement of, 288–91
Greeley, Horace, 150, 342; in Civil War,
  228, 233; in 1872 election, 250, 257
Green, William, 447, 579
Greenback-Labor party, 347, 359
Greenbacks, 247
Greene, Nathanael, 55
Greenville, Treaty of, 100
Greer (US destroyer), 495
Grenada, American invasion of (1983), 601
Grenville, George, 38, 39
Grey, Sir Edward, 414
Griffith, D. W., 333
Grimké, Angelina, 169, 175
Grimké, Sarah, 169, 175
Gropius, Walter, 466
Groton School, 329
Grundy, Felix, 101
Guadalupe Hidalgo, Treaty of (1848), 187
Guam, 402, 478, 507
Gulflight (tanker), 415
Gulf of Tonkin incident, 555
Gulf War (1991), 615–18
Gun Control legislation, 631

Habeas corpus, suspension of, in Civil War,
  221
Hague Protocol, 404
Haiti, 94; U.S. intervention in, 409; U.S.
  withdrawal from, 486; refugees from, 627
Hakluyt, Richard, 4
Hale, John P., 199
Hale, Sarah J., 169
Half-Breeds, 351
Half-Way Covenant, 28
Halifax, George, 2nd earl of, 16
Halifax, Nova Scotia, 45
Hall, G. Stanley, 376
Halleck, Henry W., 226, 230
Hamilton, Alexander, 69, 75, 87; and
  Federalist Papers, 75; as Secretary of the
  Treasury, 78–81; and election of 1796, 84;
  and the Adams Administration, 86; and
  election of 1800, 88; killed in duel with
  Burr, 96
Hammer v. *Dagenhart* (1918), 437
Hammond, James H., 174
Hampton Institute, 255
Hampton Roads conference, 235
Hancock, John, 41
Hancock, Winfield Scott, 353
Hanna, Marcus Alonzo (Mark), 315, 363,
  365, 377, 379

Harding, Warren G.: in election of 1920, 431, 435; Presidency, 435–8
Harkness, Edward S., 469
Harlan, John M., 269
Harper's Ferry, 210, 227
Harper's Weekly, 251
Harriman, E. H., 378, 379
Harrington, James, 39
Harris, Joel Chandler, 343
Harris, Roy, 593
Harrison, Benjamin; campaign and election of 1888, 356–7; in election of 1892, 361; and conservation, 292
Harrison, William Henry: and Indian removal, 100; and Battle of Tippecanoe, 100; and Battle of the Thames, 103; in election of 1836, 150; elected President, 152–3
Hart, Gary, 602, 610
Harte, Bret, 343
Hartford Convention, 104–5
Harvard College (University): founding of, 31; Charles W. Eliot and, 341
Harvey, William H., 363
Hat Act (1732), 16, 17
Havemeyer, Henry O., 297
Hawaiian Islands: American economic penetration of, 398–9; annexation of, 399
Hawley-Smoot Tariff Act (1930), 485
Hawthorne, Nathaniel, 159, 163, 343
Hay, John, 365, 401, 405, 407, 408
Hay-Pauncefote Treaty (1901), 407
Hayes, Lucy Ware Webb (Mrs. Rutherford B.), 375
Hayes, Rutherford B., 313; elected President, 258–9; and civil-service reform, 351; and monetary policy, 352
Haymarket Affair (1886), 311–12, 314, 323
Hays, Will H., 443
Haywood, William D. (Big Bill), 316, 317, 371
'Headright' system, 6
Hearst, William Randolph, 400, 488
Hemingway, Ernest, 450, 471, 487, 591
Henry VII, King of England, 4
Henry, Patrick, 38, 40, 60, 63, 68
Hepburn Act (1906), 380
Hessians, 46, 50
Hewitt, Abram S., 304
Hickok, J. B. ('Wild Bill'), 277
Hill, Anita, 620
Hill, David B., 349, 351
Hill, James J., 302, 378
Hill, Joe, 317
Hillquit, Morris, 370
Hindemith, Paul, 466
Hiss, Alger, 529, 530
HIV (Human Immunodeficiency Virus), 629

Hoar, E. Rockwell, 249, 347, 402
Ho Chi Minh, 538
Hoe, Richard M., 127
Hoffa, James R., 580
Hofstadter, Richard, 25
Holbrook, Josiah, 167
Holladay, Ben, 286
Hollywood, Cal., 333
Holmes, Oliver Wendell, 158
Holt, Thomas, 253
Holy Alliance, 110
Homer, Winslow, 345
Homestead Act (1862), 118, 221, 255, 288–9
Homestead strike (1892), 314
Homosexuals, 629–30
Hood, John B., 234
Hooker, Joseph ('Fighting Joe'), 229, 230
Hooker, Thomas, 10
Hoover, Herbert, 436, 493; Food Administrator (World War I), 426; Secretary of Commerce, 444; elected President, 451–2; and the Great Depression, 455–7; in election of 1932, 458; and Latin America, 482–3; and Manchurian crisis, 483–4
Hoover, J. Edgar, 470
Hoovervilles, 455
Hopkins, Harry L., 459
Hopper, Edward, 592
Horse-racing, 334
Horseshoe Bend, battle of, 105
Hough, Franklin B., 292
House, Edward M., 414
House Un-American Activities Committee (HUAC), 529–30
Houston, Sam, 178
Howard University, 255
Howe, Elias M., 127
Howe, Frederic C., 370
Howe, Julia Ward, 374
Howe, Samuel Gridley, 164
Howe, Richard, 1st earl, 50
Howe, Sir William, 45, 49, 50, 51
Howells, William Dean, 344–5
Hudson River school of painting, 156
Huerta, Victoriano, 410
Hughes, Charles Evans, 373; in election of 1916, 419; as Secretary of State, 436, 482; and Roosevelt's Court-packing plan, 472
Hughes, Langston, 451
Huguenots, immigration of, 20
Hull, Cordell, 485
Hull House, 328, 376
Humphrey, George, 534
Humphrey, Hubert H., 544, 556–7
Hussein, Saddam, 615–18
Hutchinson, Anne, 9, 10

IBM (International Business Machines), 578, 579, 619
Ickes, Harold L., 459, 525
Immigration: to the colonies, 19–21; 1815–60, 129–33; in Civil War, 222; 1860–1910, 321; restriction of, 323–4; in 1930s, 466; 1945–80, 573–5; 1980–92, 624–8; *see also* specific ethnic groups and pp. 000–000, Table 2, Immigration to the United States, 1820–1992
Immigration laws: pre-World War I, 324; literacy test (1917), 438; National Origins (1921–4), 438–9; Displaced Persons Acts (1948–50), 573; Refugee Relief Acts (1952), of 1965, 573–5; Refugee Act (1980), 626–7; Immigration and Control (Simpson-Rodino) Act (1986), 627; of 1990, 628
Immigration Restriction League, 323
Impeachment: of Samuel Chase, 93; of Andrew Johnson, 245–7; of Belknap, 250–1; of Nixon, 562–4
Imperial Presidency, 562–3
Impressment, 98
Income tax: Civil War, 249; and Wilson-Gorman Tariff, 363; Sixteenth Amendment, 383; in World War I, 419, 426; in World War II, 501–2; reduction of (1980s), 597, 603
Indentured Servants, 21–2
Independent Treasury system, 152, 222
Indian Rights Association, 285
Indian Self-Determination Act (1975), 584
Indians, American: pre-Columbian, 2–3; first contact with Europeans, 3, 6, 32; colonial wars with, 14, 32–4; Penn's treaties with, 33; in French and Indian War, 34–5; Pontiac's rebellion, 38; in Revolutionary War, 51; removal policy toward (1783–1812), 100–1; inWar of 1812, 103, 105; removal of (post-1815), 118; Jackson's policy on, 141; culture of Great Plains, 281–2; subjugation of (1860–90), 282–4; government policy on, 284–5; and New Deal, 468; civil rights movement, 583–4; *see also* specific tribes
Indochina: Japanese occupation of, 496, 497; French defeat in, 539; partitioned, 539; *see also* Vietnam
Industrial Workers of the World (IWW; Wobblies), 316–17, 371, 433
INF (Intermediate Range Nuclear Forces) Treaty (1987), 608–9
Initiative, in state governments, 373
Insular cases (1901), 403
Intermediate Credit Act (1923), 448
Internal Security Act (McCarran Act, 1951), 530

Interstate Commerce Act (1887), 303, 304, 356, 380
Interstate Commerce Commission, 303, 304, 436
Inventions: Benjamin Franklin's, 30; 1815–60, 127; late nineteenth century, 297–300
Iran, 569, 570
Iran-Contra Affair, 607–8, 611
Irish immigrants: in 1815–60, 130, 132–3; Negrophobia of, 175; and New York draft riots, 229; in Catholic Church, 132, 338; urban concentration of, 131; as city bosses, 348; and Easter Rising, 412, 417
Iron Act (1750), 16, 17
Iron industry: in colonies, 17; early nineteenth century, 126; post-Civil War, 304; Southern, 263
Irving, Washington, 157
Isolationism, 476, 484, 487–90, 491
Ives, Charles, 593

Jackson, Andrew, 136, 150; campaign against Creek Indians, 105; and Battle of New Orleans, 105; raids into Florida, 109; in election of 1824, 137; in election of 1828, 138–9; Presidency, 140–1, 148–9; and nullification controversy, 143, 144–5; and Bank of the United States, 145–8; Indian removal, 141
Jackson, Helen Hunt, 285
Jackson, Rev. Jesse H., 602, 610–11, 622
Jackson, Thomas J. ('Stonewall'), 219, 226–7, 230
Jacksonian democracy, 139–41, 146
James I, King of England, 5
James II, King of England, 11
James, Henry, 344
James, William, 340, 341
Jameson Raid, 399
Jamestown Settlement, 5–6
Janney, Eli, 301
Japan: Russo-Japanese War, 404, 405–6; and San Francisco school segregation order, 406; Gentlemen's Agreement, 406; visit of Great White Fleet to, 406; and Open Door in China, 407; in World War I, 478; and Washington Conference of 1921–2; 478–9; and naval arms limitation, 478–9; and Immigration Act of 1924, 483; and Manchuria, 406–7, 483; invasion of China, 488–9; *Panay* bombing, 489; expansion in South-East Asia, 496–7; U.S. economic sanctions against, 497–8; Pearl Harbor attack, 498; in World War II, 507, 511, 515; atomic bombing of, 516; surrender, 516; U.S. occupation of, 521; peace treaty with (1951), 522, 538; mutual

Japan (*cont.*):
    security treaty with (1960), 541; anti-
    American riots in (1924), 483, (1960), 541
Japanese in U.S.: hostility to, 406; interned
    in World War II, 499
Jaworski, Leon, 564
Jay, John: as peace commissioner, 56–7; and
    Federal Constitution, 74–5; as Secretary
    of Foreign Affairs, 67; and Jay's Treaty,
    83
Jay's Treaty (1794), 83, 84, 86
Jazz, 448
Jefferson, Thomas, 61, 70, 73, 90, 110, 118,
    119, 359; and Declaration of
    Independence, 47–8; and slavery, 60; and
    religious liberty, 61; and Republican
    party, 81–2; elected Vice-President, 84;
    and Kentucky Resolution, 87; elected
    President, 88–9; as President, 90–1; and
    federal judiciary, 92–3; and Louisiana
    Purchase, 93–5; peaceable coercion and,
    99; and Missouri Compromise, 112
Jewett, Sarah Orne, 343
Jews: in colonies, 21; and Czarist pogroms,
    321; as immigrants, 321; hostility to, 323;
    and World War I, 412; and Ku Klux
    Klan, 440; in New Deal, 476; refugees
    from Nazi Germany, 466
Jim Crow laws, 268–9; *see also* Segregation
Johns Hopkins University, 341
Johnson, Andrew, 239; elected Vice-
    President, 234, 239; becomes President,
    239; and Reconstruction, 239–40; and
    Radicals, 242–3; impeachment of, 245–7
Johnson case (1987), 605
Johnson, Eldridge, 332
Johnson, Hiram W., 373, 430
Johnson, Hugh S., 460
Johnson, Jack, 334
Johnson, Sir John, 59
Johnson, Lyndon B., 544; elected Vice-
    President, 544; becomes President, 550;
    Great Society policies, 550–2; Dominican
    Republic intervention, 555; Vietnam War,
    555–6
Johnson, Robert Underwood, 294
Johnson, Tom L., 372
Johnson-Clarendon Convention (1869), 395
Johnston, Albert Sidney, 226
Johnston, Joseph E., 226, 230, 233, 234, 235
Joint Committee on the Conduct of the
    War, 225
Joint Committee on Reconstruction, 241,
    243
Jolson, Al, 448
Jones, John Paul, 53
Jones, Mary Harris ('Mother'), 317
Jones, Samuel L. ('Golden Rule'), 372

Jordan, David Starr, 402
Joseph (Nez Percé chief), 284
Judicial review, 93
Judiciary Act: of 1789, 93; of 1801, 92

Kansas: struggle over slavery in, 205–6;
    Lecompton Constitution, 208; statehood,
    209; immigrants in, 290; Populism in, 361
Kansas-Nebraska Act, 201–2
Kansas Pacific Railroad, 279
Kearney, Stephen W., 185
Kearney (U.S. destroyer), 496
Keating-Owen Act (1916), 391, 437
Keller, Morton, 136
Kelley, Abigail (Abby), 176
Kelley, Florence, 328, 376
Kellogg-Briand Pact (1928), 480
Kelly, 'Honest John', 349
Kelly, William, 304
Kendall, Amos, 148, 172
Kennedy, Anthony, 605
Kennedy, Edward M., 570
Kennedy, John F., 543, 550–1; elected
    President, 543–4; foreign policy of, 545–6;
    Cuban missile crisis, 546–7; Vietnam
    policy, 547–8; domestic policy, 548–9;
    assassinated, 549
Kennedy, Joseph P., 469
Kennedy, Robert F., 545, 549, 556–7
Kent, James, 135
Kent School, 329
Kentucky: settlement of, 65; resolution on
    Alien and Sedition Acts, 87; in Civil War,
    220, 226
Kentucky Derby, 334
Keppler, Joseph, 308
Kern-McGillicuddy Act (1916), 391
Key, Francis Scott, 105
Khrushchev, Nikita, 546–7
King, Martin Luther, jr., 537, 544, 549, 553,
    554
King, Rufus, 89
King Philip's War (1675–6), 10
King William's War, 33
King's Mountain, battle of, 55
King, Rodney, 620
Kipling, Rudyard, 403, 418
Kissinger, Henry A., 558, 559, 566, 568
Kitchen Cabinet, Jackson's, 148
Knights of Labor, 311–13, 338
Know-Nothing Party, 203–4, 206–7
Knox, Philander C., 406–7
Kościuszko, Tadeuz Andrzej Bonawentura,
    53
Konoye, Fumimaro, 497
Korean War, 522–4, 538
Ku Klux Klan: in Reconstruction, 256–7; in
    1920s, 439–40

Ku Klux Klan Act (1871), 257
Kuwait, 615–18

Labor: organization of, 128–9, 310–13, 315–17, 473–4, 579–80; wages and hours (1865–1914), 317–18, (1920s), 447; violence, 313–14; child, 376
Labor legislation: mid-nineteenth century, 129; in Progressive era, 390–1; in New Deal, 460, 474–5; in World War II, 502–3; post-1945, 526, 580; *see also* specific Acts
Labor unions, *see* Trade unions
Laconia (British steamship), 421
Ladd, William, 168
Lafayette, Marie Joseph Paul Yves Roch Gilbert du Motier, marquis de, 53
La Follette, Robert M., 370, 373, 380, 385, 386, 389, 421, 422, 444
La Follette, Robert M., jr., 463
La Follette Seamen's Act (1916), 391
Laird Rams, 232–3
Laissez-faire, 303–4, 307–8
Lake Erie, battle of, 103
Land Act (1796), 118
Land-grant colleges, 339
Land Ordinance of 1785, 65
Landon, Alfred M., 465
Landrum-Griffin Act (1959), 580
Lane Theological Seminary, 172
Language and speech: Americanization of, 24; absence of class patterns in, 135
Lansing, Robert, 414, 538
Lathrop, Julia C., 376
Laud, William, Archbishop of Canterbury, 7
Law: development of colonial, 31
League of Armed Neutrality, 52
League of Nations, 428, 429–30, 431, 434, 435, 476
Lease, Mary Ellen, 361
Lebanon, American intervention in (1982–3), 601–2
Leclerc, Charles, 94
Lecompton Constitution, 208
Lee, Charles, 53
Lee, 'Mother' Ann, 162
Lee, Richard Henry, 47, 74, 75
Lee, Robert E., 210, 219, 227, 229–30, 231, 233, 235
Leggett, William, 128
LeMay, Curtis, 557
Lend-Lease Act (1941), 494–5
Lenin (Vladimir Ilich Ulyanov), 58
Leopard (frigate), 98
Levant Company, 4
Levine, Dennis, 606
Levinson, Salmon O., 480

Lewis, John L., 473, 502, 525, 528
Lewis, Meriwether, 95
Lewis, Sinclair, 450
Lewis, William B., 148
Lexington, battle of, 44
Lexow investigation (1894), 328
Leyte Gulf, battle of, 511
Liberal Republicans, 249–50
Liberator, The (abolitionist newspaper), 171
Liberia, 170
Liberty party, 176, 181, 190
Liberty (sloop), 41
Libraries, 341–2
Lincoln, Abraham, 48, 118, 119, 246; and colonization of blacks, 170; debates with Douglas, 209–10; in election of 1860, 212–13; and secession crisis, 215–16; Presidency, 216, 220–2, 224–36; and civil liberties, 221; and Emancipation Proclamation, 228–9; assassination of, 235; Second Inaugural, 238; and Reconstruction, 238–9
Lincoln, Thomas, 119
Lindbergh, Charles A., 446, 470, 493
Lindsey, Ben B., 376
Literature: mid-nineteenth century, 156–60; late ninteenth century, 343–5; in 1920s, 450; in New Deal, 470–1; post-World War II, 591–2
Little Big Horn, battle of (1876), 283–4
Little Crow (Sioux chief), 283
'Little Steel' formula, 502
Litvinov, Maxim, 505
Livingston, Robert R., 82, 94
Lloyd, Henry Demarest, 308
Lloyd George, David, 424
Lochner v. *New York* (1905), 315
Locke, John; and the Fundamental Constitutions of Carolina, 10; natural-rights philosophy of, 29, 47
Locofocos, 152
Lodge, Henry Cabot, 268, 399, 402, 430
London Company, 5, 6
London, Meyer, 371
London Naval Conference (1930), 479–80
Long, Huey P., 462
Longfellow, Henry Wadsworth, 158
Long Island, battle of, 50
Lords of Trade and Plantations, 15
Loudoun, John Campbell, 4th earl of, 35
Louis XIV, King of France, 20
Louis, Joe, 470
Louisbourg (Cape Breton Island), 34, 35
Louisiana: as French colony, 33; ceded to Spain, 35–6; return to France of, 93
Louisiana Purchase, 93–5; and slavery, 112
Lovejoy, Elijah, 175
Lowell, Francis Cabot, 126

Lowell, James Russell, 158, 161, 184
Lowell, Robert, 592
Lowell, Mass., 126
Lowell Offering, 128
Loyalists, 45, 48, 57
Ludlow, Louis, 489
Lundy, Benjamin, 171
Lusitania, 415–16, 418
Lyceum movement, 166–7
Lynching, 269
Lyon, Mary, 169

McAdoo, William G., 426, 443
MacArthur, Douglas, 457, 507, 511, 521, 522, 523–4
McCarthy, Eugene, 556–7, 567
McCarthy, Joseph R., 531, 532–3
McClellan, George B.: as Civil War general, 225, 226, 227; in election of 1864, 233
McClellan, John L., 580
McClure's, 371, 372
McCormick, Cyrus H., 120, 127
McCosh, James, 341
McCulloch v. *Maryland* (1819), 108, 111, 145
McDowell, Irvin, 224
McGovern, George S., 561
Machine politics, 348
McHenry, James, 88
McKay, Donald, 117
McKinley, William: 1896 campaign and election, 363, 364, 365; and business, 366; re-elected (1900), 367; assassinated, 377; and Cuban rebellion, 400–1; in Spanish-American War, 401; and annexation of Philippines, 402, 403
McKinley Tariff Act (1890), 399
McNamara, Robert S., 545
Macon's Bill No. 2 (1810), 99
McNary-Haugen bill, 448
Macune, C. W., 360
Macy's, 325
Madison, James, 69, 78, 110; and the Federal Constitution, 75; and Republican party, 81; and Virginia Resolutions, 87; and *Marbury* v. *Madison*, 92–3; elected President, 97; and neutral rights, 99; and War of 1812, 101, 104; and suffrage requirements, 135
Mahan, Alfred T., 398
Mahone, William, 265
Mailer, Norman, 591
Mail-order houses, 325
Maine: in War of 1812, 103; becomes a state, 112
Maine (battleship), 400
Malamud, Bernard, 591
Malcolm X, 553

Manchuria: Japanese in, 406, 407, 483–4
Manifest Destiny, 177
Mann, Horace, 165
Mann, Thomas, 466
Manufactures: in colonies, 17; and War of 1812, 105, 126; Northern (post-1815), 126–9; Southern (post-1815), 126; post-Civil War, 295–7; in New South, 262–5
Mao Tse-tung, 58, 521
Marbury, William, 93
Marbury v. *Madison* (1803), 92–3
Marcy, William L., 140, 200
Marlborough, Charles Richard John, 9th Duke of, 330
Marsh, George Perkins, 291–2
Marshall, Alfred, 296
Marshall Field's, 325
Marshall, George C., 519, 521
Marshall, John, 170; as Chief Justice, 92; and Burr conspiracy trial, 96; Supreme Court decisions of, 93, 108, 141
Marshall, Thurgood, 548, 554, 619
Marshall Plan, 519
Maryland: settlement of, 6; Toleration Act (1649), 6–7; in Civil War, 220
Mason, George, 63, 74
Mason, James M., 232
Mason, Lowell, 156
Massachusetts Bay Colony: charter of, 7; General Court, 9; religious persecution in, 9; settlement of, 8; shipbuilding in, 8
Masses, The, 427–8
Masterson, William Barclay ('Bat'), 280
Mather, Cotton, 29
Mathew, Theobald, 168
May, Samuel J., 173
Mayflower (ship), 7
Mayflower Compact, 7
Mayhew, Jonathan, *A Discourse Concerning Unlimited Submission* (1750), 29
Maysville Road Bill (1830), 141
Meade, George Gordon, 230, 233
Meany, George, 580
Meat Inspection Act (1906), 381
Medicaid Act (1965), 552
Medicare Act (1965), 552
Mellon, Andrew, 436, 444
Melville, Herman, 159, 343
Mencken, H. L., 450
Menlo Park, New Jersey, 299
Mennonites, 20
Menotti, Gian-Carlo, 593
Mercantilism; theory of, 15; and English policy, 15–16; effects of, 17–18
Mesabi range, 304
Methodist Episcopal Church, 375
Meuse-Argonne battle, 425
Mexican-Americans; *see* Chicanos

Mexican War, 183–7
Mexico: Mayas and Aztecs in, 3; French intervention, 394; Wilson's policy in Revolution, 410–11; and Zimmermann Note, 421; U.S. oil interests in, 482, 486
Milken, Michael, 606
Miller, Arthur, 591–2
Miller, William (historian), 330
Miller, William (millennarian), 161
Millionaires, 329
Mining: and settlement of West, 276–8; *see also* Gold, Iron industry, Silver
Miranda v. *Arizona* (1966), 552
Mississippi v. *Williams* (1898), 268
Mississippi Plan, 258
Mississippi River: right to navigate, 67; steamboats on, 114
Missouri: application for statehood, 112; in Civil War, 220
Missouri Compromise, 112; and Kansas-Nebraska Act, 201–2; and Dred Scott decision, 207–8; and Crittenden Compromise, 215
Missouri Pacific Railroad, 279
Mitchell, John (labor leader), 315, 379
Mitchell, John N. (Attorney-General), 563
Mitchell, Margaret, 471
Model T, 446
Molasses Act (1733), 18, 38
Moley, Raymond, 459
Molly Maguires, 313
Mondale, Walter F., 602
Monmouth Court House, battle of, 53
Monroe, James, 54, 170; and Louisiana Purchase, 94; and maritime rights controversy, 98; elected President, 106; and internal improvements, 107–8; foreign policy of, 108–11
Monroe Doctrine, 110–11, 182, 393, 394, 399, 422
Monroe-Pinkney Treaty (1806), 98
Montcalm de Saint-Véran, Louis Joseph, marquis de, 35
Montgomery, Bernard L., 508, 510
Montgomery, Richard, 46
Montgomery Ward, Aaron, 326
Montreal, 46
Moody, Dwight L., 337
Moon landings, 543, 591
Moore, Marianne, 592
Moral Rearmament, 469
Moravians, 20
Morgan, house of, 386, 414
Morgan, John Pierpont (1837–1913), 362, 379, 381; and investment banking, 306–7; and railroads, 306; and American Civic Federation, 315; and art, 346
Morgan, J. Pierpont (1867–1943), 469

Morgan, William, 146
Morgenthau, Henry, Jr., 525
Mormons, 161, 179–80, 275, 291
Morrill Land Grant Act (1862), 221, 339, 340
Morris, Robert, 55, 67, 69
Morrow, Dwight, 482
Morse, Samuel F. B., 118
Morton, 'Jelly Roll', 448
Moses, Franklin J., Jr., 253
Most, Johann, 312
Motion pictures: before World War I, 333; censorship of, 443; in 1920s, 448; in 1930s, 470; in World War II, 504
Mount Holyoke College, 169
Mount Vernon, 26
Muckraking journalism, 343, 371–2
Mugwumps, 355
Muir, John, 293–4
Mulligan Letters, 355
Municipal reform, 372
Munn v. *Illinois* (1876), 303
Munsey, Frank A., 386
Murchison letter, 357
Murray, Philip, 579–80
Muscovy Company, 4
Music: before Civil War, 156; late nineteenth century, 333; symphony orchestras, 333, 463, 594; opera, 333, 593; operetta, 333; musical comedy, 333–4, 593; New Deal and, 463; post-World War II, 593, 594
Mutiny Act (1765), 41

Napoleon Bonaparte: and Louisiana Purchase, 93–5; and Berlin Decree (1806), 97; and Nonintercourse, 99
Napoleon III, 394
Nashville, battle of, 234
Nasser, Gamal Abdel, 540–1
Nast, Thomas, 251, 308
Nation, Carry, 375
Nation, The, 342
National American Woman Suffrage Association, 374–5
National Association for the Advancement of Colored People (NAACP), 273–4, 434
National Association for Woman Suffrage, 374
National Bank Act (1863), 222
National Bimetallic League, 363
National Broadcasting Company (NBC), 445
National Child Labor Committee, 376
National Civil Service Reform League, 354
National Conservation Congress (1908), 381
National Defense Act (1916), 418
National Defense Education Act (1958), 588

National Defense Research Committee, 491–2
National Gallery of Art, 469
National Indian Defense Association, 285
National Industrial Recovery Act (1933), 460–1, 467, 471
National Labor Relations Act (Wagner Act, 1935), 464–5, 472, 473
National Labor Relations Board, 465, 599
National Labor Union, 310
National Organization for Women, 585
National Origins Act (1924), 439
National Parks, 293–4, 469
National Park Service, 294
National Progressive Republican League, 385
National Reclamation (Newlands) Act (1902), 293
National Recovery Administration, 460–1
National Republicans, 137
National Rifle Association, 631
National Trades' Union, 128
National Union of Manufacturers, 315
National Union movement, 244
National Union party, 239
National Urban League, 274
National War Labor Board: (World War I), 426; (World War II), 502
National Youth Administration, 467
Nationalism, 216–17; in Revolutionary period, 68–9; after War of 1812, 106–11; Daniel Webster and, 143; and Civil War, 216–17; World War I, 427–8; in 1920s, 438; Southern, 197, 217
Nativism: (1830–60), 133; (1880–1900), 323; in Ku Klux Klan, 440
Naturalization Act (1798), 87, 91
Nauvoo, Illinois, 161, 163
Naval Expansion Act (1938), 490
Navigation Acts, 15
Navy: in Revolutionary War, 53; in quasi-war with France, 86–7; Jefferson's reduction of, 91–2; in War of 1812, 103; in Civil War, 218, 232–3; and Mahan's theories, 398; Pacific bases for, 398; expansion of (1880s), 398; in Spanish-American War, 401–2; world cruise of Great White Fleet, 406; in World War I, 418, 424; expansion (1938–41), 490–1; in World War II, 495, 507, 511
Negroes: *see* Blacks
Nelson, Baby Face, 470
Neo-conservatism, 596
Neutral rights controversy: in French Revolutionary and Napoleonic Wars, 83, 97–9; in World War I, 413–14, 415, 416–17, 420–1
Neutrality Acts: (1935–7), 488; (1939), 491

New Amsterdam, 11
New England (*see also* individual colonies and states): settlement of, 7–8; Confederation of the United Colonies of (1643), 10; Dominion of, 15; and War of 1812, 102, 104
New Deal: agricultural programs of, 460, 474; in banking and finance, 458, 460, 461; industrial and labor policies, 460–1, 464–5, 475; opposition to, 461–2, 472–3; welfare policies of, 459, 463, 464; and blacks, 467–8; and Indians, 468; ebbing of, 473–5; achievements of, 475–6
New England Emigrant Aid Society, 205
New Federalism, 598
New Freedom, 387, 390–1
New Frontier, 544, 545–9
New Hampshire: founding of, 9–10
New Haven: founding of, 10
New Jersey: colonization of, 11–12
New Jersey Line, mutiny of, 54
New Jersey Plan, 71
Newlands, Francis G., 293
New Nationalism, 385, 387, 390, 391
New Netherland, 11
New Orleans: Spanish possession of, 83–4; Jefferson's efforts to buy, 93–4; battle of, 105; and Western trade, 114; Union capture of (1862), 226; race riot in (1866), 244; Italians lynched in (1891), 397; origins of jazz in, 448
Newport, Rhode Island, 55
New York Central Railroad, 116, 302
New York City: blacks in (1690s), 22; in Revolutionary War, 50; and Erie Canal, 115; post-1815 growth of, 121; Irish in, 131; immigrants in, 322; Central Park, 327; Fifth Avenue mansions, 329; slums, 328; Public Library, 342; draft riots (1863), 229; Metropolitan Museum of Art, 346, 469; Metropolitan Opera, 333; Tweed Ring, 251, 254, 349; black population (1920), 433; speakeasies, 442; Lexow investigation, 328; settlement houses, 328; corruption in Custom House, 351; Lincoln Center, 594
New York (colony): settlement of, 11; acquired by England, 11
New York Times, 251
Newspapers: late nineteenth century, 342
Nez Percé Indians, 284
Niagara Movement, 271, 273
Nicaragua: proposed isthmian canal, 407; U.S. intervention in, 409; civil war in, 600–1
Niebuhr, Reinhold, 586
Nimitz, Chester W., 511
Nixon, Richard M.: and Hiss case, 529;

elected Vice-President, 532; in Venezuela, 541; in election of 1960, 543–4; elected President, 557; foreign policy of, 558–9; and Vietnam War, 558, 562; domestic policy, 559–61; re-election of, 561; and the Presidency, 562–3; and Watergate, 563–4; impeachment and resignation of, 564; Ford's pardon of, 565
Nonimportation, 40, 41, 44
Nonimportation Act (1806), 98, 99
Nonintercourse Act (1809), 99
Nonresistance Society, 168
Noriega, Manuel, 613–14
Norris, Frank, 322
Norris, George W., 421, 422, 423, 459
Norris, Isaac, 25
Norris-La Guardia Act (1932), 314, 473
North American Free Trade Agreement (1992), 627
North Atlantic Treaty Organization (NATO), 520
North Carolina: founded, 10–11; in Revolutionary War, 55; Regulator Movement in, 42; refuses to ratify Constitution, 75; secedes, 216; textile industry, 263; tobacco industry, 264
North, Frederick (Lord), 42, 44, 48, 49, 56
North, Oliver P., 608
Northcote-Trevelyan Report, 354
Northern Pacific Railroad, 287, 289
Northern Securities Company case, 378, 379
Northwest Ordinance, 65–6
Northwest Territory, 65–6
Northwestern Farmers' Alliance, 360
Norwegian immigrants, 131
Nott, Josiah C., 174
Novak, Michael, 596
Noyes, John Humphrey, 162
Nullification: Virginia and Kentucky Resolution and, 87; Calhoun's theory of, 142; South Carolina's Ordinance of, 144
Nullification crisis (1832–3), 142–5
Nye Committee, 487, 488
Nye, Gerald P., 487, 493

Oberlin College, 169, 172
O'Connor, Sandra Day, 604
Office of Price Administration, 502, 525
Office of War Mobilization, 501
Oglethorpe, James, 13
Ohio Company, 34, 65
Ohio Gang, 436, 437
Ohio idea, 247, 249
Oil industry, 305–6
Olive Branch Petition (1775), 45, 46
Oliver, King, 448
Olmsted, Frederick Law, 327
Olney, Richard, 310, 314, 399

Omaha platform (1892), 361
Oneida Community, 162–3
O'Neill, Eugene, 450–1, 591
OPEC (Organization of Petroleum Exporting Countries), 616
Opechancanough, 32
Open Door policy, 405
Operation Desert Storm (1991), 616–18
Oppenheimer, J. Robert, 533
Orders-in-Council: (1793), 83; (1807), 97; repeal of, 101
Order of the Star-Spangled Banner, 203
Oregon Trail, 180
Oregon Treaty (1846), 182
Ortega, Daniel, 613
Ostend Manifesto, 200, 201
Oswald, Lee Harvey, 549
Otis Elevator Company, 299
Otis, James, 38
Owen, Robert, 163
Owen, Robert Dale, 128

Pacific Railroad Act (1862), 221–2, 286
Padrone system, 322
Page, Thomas Nelson, 263
Page, Walter Hines, 414
Paine, Thomas, 46, 48
Painting: nationalism in, 69; pre-Civil War, 156; late nineteenth century, 345–6; abstract expressionism, 592; in 1960s, 592
Pakenham, Sir Edward, 104
Palmer, A. Mitchell, 433
Panama canal, 407–8, 569
Panama Canal Treaty (1978), 569
Panama: U.S. invasion of (1989), 613–14
Panay (U.S. gunboat), 489
Panic of 1819, 111
Panic of 1837, 148, 151
Panic of 1873, 257
Panic of 1893, 362
Paper money: and Currency Act (1764), 39; in Revolutionary War, 54; during the 1780s, 67–8; and Bank War, 145, 147; post-Civil War, 248–9
Paris: Treaty of (1763), 35–6; Franklin as envoy in, 51; peace negotiations in (1782–3), 56–7; Treaty of (1783), 56–7; Treaty of (1898), 402; peace conference (1919), 429–30; European summit conference (1960), 541; Vietnam peace talks in, 556, 558, 562
Parker, Alton B., 379
Parker, Theodore, 167, 171, 199
Parkman, Francis, 158
Parson's cause, 38
Partridge, Alden, 166
Patents, 297
Paterson, William, 71

Patrons of Husbandry, *see* Granger
    Movement
Patton, George, S., 510
Paul, Alice, 375
Paxton Boys, 42
Payne, John Howard, 156
Payne-Aldrich Tariff Act (1909), 383–4, 386
Peabody Fund, 265
Peaceable coercion, 99
Peace Convention (1861), 215
Peace Corps, 545–6
Peace movements: in early nineteenth
    century, 168; in Civil War, 233–4; in
    1930s, 487; Vietnam War, 556–7
Pearl Harbor, 398, 498, 499
Peffer, William A., 361
Pemberton, John C., 230
Pendleton Act (1883), 354
Penn, William: and founding of
    Pennsylvania, 12–13; Indian policy of,
    32–3
Pennsylvania: founding of, 12–13, Germans
    in, 20; Scotch-Irish in, 20–1, indentured
    servants in, 21
Pennsylvania Gazette, 30
Pennsylvania Line, mutiny of, 54
Pennsylvania Railroad, 116
Penrose, Boies, 348
Pentagon Papers, 558
People's party, *see* Populist party
Pequot War (1637), 32
Perkins, Frances, 525
Perkins, George W., 386
Perot, H. Ross, 622, 623
Perry, Oliver, H., 103
Pershing, John J., 410–11, 425
Personal liberty laws, 173–4, 199
Petroleum industry, *see* Oil industry
Philadelphia: founding of, 12; population of
    (1760), 23; Bank of the United States in,
    80; Continental Congress in, 43–4, 45, 46;
    occupied by Howe, 50; Constitutional
    Convention in, 70–3; as national capital,
    80; Catholic churches burned, 132;
    Pennsylvania Hall burned, 175; popula-
    tion (1860–1910), 320; black population
    of (1920), 433
Philippine Sea, battle of the, 511
Philippines, 478; in Spanish-American War,
    401; U.S. annexation, 402; insurrection,
    403; in World War II, 507, 511
Phillips, Wendell, 167, 199
Phillips Andover Academy, 329
Phillips Exeter Academy, 329
Phips, Sir William, 26
Phonograph, 332
Photography, 332
Pickering, Timothy, 88, 96

Pierce, Franklin: elected President, 199;
    foreign policy of, 200–1; and Kansas-
    Nebraska Act, 202; and Kansas, 205
Pike's Peak, Colorado, 277
Pilgrims, 7
Pinchot, Gifford, 292, 381
Pinckney, Charles Cotesworth, 86
Pinckney, Thomas, 83, 84
Pinckney's Treaty (1795), 83–4, 94
Pingree, Hazen S., 373
Pinkerton Detective Agency, 313, 314, 316
Pinkney, William, 98
Pitt, William (earl of Chatham), 35, 48
Pitts, John and Hiram A., 120
Pittsburgh, 34, 295; steel industry in, 304
Place-names, 120–1
Plains Indians, 281–5
Planned Parenthood of Pennsylvania v *Casey*
    (1992), 629
Platt, Thomas C., 348, 353, 377
Platt Amendment (1901), 404; abrogation
    of, 486
Plattsburg, battle of, 103
Plessy v. *Ferguson* (1896), 269, 535
Plymouth Colony, 7
Plymouth Company, 5
Pocahontas, 32
Podhoretz, Norman, 596
Poe, Edgar Allan, 157
Poindexter, John M., 608
Polish National Catholic Church, 338
Political nicknames, 136
Political parties: rise of, 84–5; in late
    nineteenth century, 350–1
Polk, James K.: elected President, 180–1;
    and expansionism, 181–2; and Mexican
    War, 183–7
Pollock, Jackson, 592
Poll-taxes, 268
Pollock v. *Farmers' Loan and Trust Co.*
    (1894), 363
Pontiac's Rebellion, 38, 42
Pony Express, 286
Pools, corporate, 296
Poor Richard's Almanac, 30
Pope, John, 227, 230
Popular sovereignty, 189, 190, 194, 201,
    202, 205
Population: colonial growth of, 19; in
    1815–60, 113; youthfulness of, 135; in
    1860–1910, 319; post-World War II, 573;
    in 1980s, 624; *see also* pp. 000–000, Table
    1, Population of the United States,
    1790–1990
Populist party, 358, 360–1
Porter, Cole, 593
Portsmouth, Treaty of, 405–6
Potsdam Conference, 515–16, 518

Potsdam Declaration, 516
Pound, Ezra, 451
Powderly, Terence V., 311
Powder River Road, 283
Powell, John Wesley, 292–3
Powell, Lewis F., Jr., 604
Powers, Hiram, 156
Powhatan, 32
Preemption Act (1841), 118
Preparedness campaign, 418–19
Prescott, William H., 158
Presidency: powers of, defined in
    Constitution, 72; Washington and, 77;
    two-term tradition, 84, 526; separate
    ballot for (Twelfth Amendment), 89;
    Hartford Convention and, 104; Andrew
    Jackson and, 148; Whig view of, 149, 153;
    post-Civil War decline in power of, 348;
    Theodore Roosevelt and expansion of
    powers of, 377, 381; Woodrow Wilson
    and, 388, succession to office, 153, 564–5;
    twentieth-century growth in authority of,
    562–3
Price, Richard, 48
Prigg v. *Pennsylvania* (1842), 173
Primogeniture, 59
Princeton, battle of, 50
Princeton University, 31, 341, 387
Princeton (USS), 178
Prison reform, 60, 163–4
Privateering, 53, 103
Proclamation Line, 38
Proclamation of 1763, 38
Progressive party: (1912), 386, 387–8;
    (1924), 444; (1948), 527–8
Progressivism, 368–70, 391–2
Prohibition: in mid-nineteenth century,
    167–8; in late nineteenth century, 374–6;
    and World War I, 426–7; in 1920s, 441–2
Prohibition Act (1918), 427
Public Broadcasting Act (1967), 595
Public Land: federal policy on, 118, 147–8,
    289; speculation in (after 1815), 111,
    (1830s), 147–8; grants of, to railroads,
    286–7; Indian claims on (1970s), 583; *see
    also* Land Ordinance (1785), Northwest
    Ordinance (1787), Land Act (1796),
    Preemption Act (1841), Homestead Act
    (1862), Desert Land Act (1877), Timber
    and Stone Act (1878)
Public health laws, 380–1
Public Works Administration, 459
Puerto Rico, 402, 403
Pujo Committee, 389
Pulaski, Casimir, 53
Pulitzer, Joseph, 342, 40
Pullman, George M., 301
Pullman Palace Car Company, 301, 314

Pullman strike (1894), 314, 362
Pure Food and Drug Act (1906), 381
Puritans: and Church of England, 7; beliefs
    of, 8; Great Migration (1630s), 8

Quakers: beliefs of, 12; in New Jersey, 12;
    in Pennsylvania, 12–13; persecution of in
    Massachusetts, 9
Quayle, Dan (J. Danforth), 611, 621
Quay, Matthew S., 348
Quebec: French settlement of, 33; capture of
    (1759), 35; during Revolutionary War, 46
Quebec Act (1774), 43, 46
Queen Anne's War, 51

Race riots: at New Orleans (1866), 244; at
    Wilmington, N.C. (1898), 269; at Atlanta
    (1898), 269; at New Orleans (1900), 269,
    (1919), 434; in World War II, 503; in
    1960s, 554; at Los Angeles (1992), 620–1
Radical Republicans: and Lincoln, 238–9;
    and Reconstruction, 238–9, 241–5
Radio, 445
Railroads: construction of (1830–60),
    115–16, (post-Civil War), 300–1;
    Transcontinental, 286–8; colonizing
    activities of, 289–90; regulation of, 302–4,
    380; hostility toward, 302; in World War I,
    426
Raleigh, Sir Walter, 4–5
Randolph, A. Philip, 503
Randolph, Edmund, 71
Randolph, John, of Roanoke, 95–6, 138
Rapp, George, 162
Rauschenbusch, Walter, 337
Readjustment of state debts, 266–7
Reagan, Ronald W.: presidential candidacy
    (1976), 566; elected President, 570–2; re-
    election of, 602–3; domestic policy, 597–9,
    603; and Supreme Court, 604–5; foreign
    policy of, 599–602, 607–9; and Iran-
    Contra affair, 607–8; presidency of,
    609–10
Reaganomics, 597–8
Recall in state governments, 373
Reconstruction, 237–59
Reconstruction Acts (1867), 244, 246, 247
Reconstruction Finance Corporation, 456,
    459
Redeemers, 265–6, 267
Redemptioners, 21
Red Scare (1919), 317, 432
Reed, Thomas B., 357
Referendum, 373
Reform movements: mid-nineteenth century,
    161 ff.
Refugee Act (1980), 626–7
Refugee Relief Act (1952), 573

Regulators, 42
Rehnquist, William H., 604
Relief and Construction Act (1932), 456
Religion: pluralistic structure of in colonial America, 26–9; in mid-nineteenth century, 160–1; and mid-nineteenth century reform, 161–2; late nineteenth-century challenges to, 335–6; and Social Gospel, 336–7; and social welfare legislation, 371; and Darwinism, 440–1; in Great Depression, 469–70; post-World War II, 586–7
Remington, Frederic, 276
Reno, Nevada, 331
Republican party (1790s–1828): beginnings of, 81–2; in 1792 election, 82; in 1796 election, 84; socioeconomic composition of, 85; and Alien and Sedition Acts, 87; in 1800 election, 88–9; and judiciary, 92–3; divisions in, 95–6; and nationalism, 106–8; factionalism in, 106; end of, 137
Republican party (1854-present): beginnings of, 203; free labor ideology of, 203; and Reconstruction, 238, 239, 241–7; principles and character (1880s), 350–1; and black vote, 247–8, 366; and urban working class vote, 366; insurgency, 383; split in (1912), 386; black desertion of (1930s), 467–8; *see also* Elections, Political parties
Resumption Act (1875), 249, 352
Reuben James (U.S. destroyer), 496
Reuther, Walter, 580
Revels, Hiram R., 252
Revere, Paul, 44
Revivalism: and Great Awakening, 28; and Second Great Awakening, 160; post-Civil War, 337; post-World War II, 586
Revolutionary War: military operations, 44–51, 50–1, 53, 55–6; loyalists in, 48; Continental Army, problems of, 49; British difficulties in, 49–50; naval operations, 53–4; financial problems, 54–5; peace negotiations, 56–7
Rhett, Robert Barnwell, 194, 223
Rhode Island: founding of, 9
Richardson, Elliott, 564
Riis, Jacob, 327, 376
Ritty, James S., 298
Roanoke Island, 5
Roberts, Kenneth, 471
Roberts, Oral, 607
Robertson, Pat, 611
Robespierre, Maximilien François Marie Isidore de, 58
Robinson, Joseph, 472
Rochambeau, Jean Baptiste Donatien de Vimeur, comte de, 55, 56
Rockefeller, John D., 305–6, 307, 329, 336,

340, 371
Rockefeller, Nelson A., 551, 556
Rockingham, Charles Watson-Wentworth, 2nd marquis, 56
Roe v. *Wade* (1973), 560, 605, 628
Roebling, John A., 301
Roebling, Washington A., 301
Roman Catholic Church: and Quebec Act, 43; and immigration, 132, 338; and public school Bible-reading controversy (1840s), 132; growth of, in late nineteenth century, 338; and labor unions, 311, 338; post-1945, 587; *see also* Anti-Catholicism
Roosevelt Corollary, 408–9; *see also* Clark Memorandum
Roosevelt, Eleanor, 468
Roosevelt, Franklin D., 457; vice-presidential candidacy (1920), 435; 1932 election, 458; banking and financial policies, 458, 460, 461; fireside chats, 458, 476; Hundred Days, 458; relief policies, 459, 463; agricultural policies, 460, 474; industrial and labor policies, 460–1, 464–5, 475; welfare policies, 464; reelection (1936), 465; and Supreme Court, 471–2; foreign policy, 484–7, 488–91, 496–8; aid to Great Britain, 491–2; 1940 election, 493–4; Lend-Lease, 494–6; in World War II, 500–3, 504–6; and Churchill, 505; Casablanca Conference, 509–10; 1944 election, 511–12; Yalta Conference, 512–13; death, 514
Roosevelt, Theodore, 370, 375; and anthracite coal strike, 378–9; in Spanish-American War, 377; and muckrakers, 371; Presidency of, 377–82; and railroad regulation, 380; and conservation, 381; and public health legislation, 380; and corporations, 378, 379, 381–2; and naval strength, 398; in Spanish–American War, 401; and Russo-Japanese War, 404, 405–6; and Moroccan crisis, 404; and Japan, 406; acquisition of Panama Canal Zone, 407–8; Corollary to Monroe Doctrine, 408–9; and preparedness, 418; and World War I, 419
Root-Takahira Agreement (1908), 406
Rosecrans, William S., 230, 231
Rosenman, Samuel, 459
Ross, Betsy, 69
Rothko, Mark, 592
Rough Riders, 401
Roughing It (Twain), 277
Royal African Company, 22
Rule of 1756, 83
'Rum, Romanism and Rebellion', 355
Rush-Bagot Agreement (1817), 109

Rush, Dr. Benjamin, 167
Russell, Charles M., 275–6
Russell, Lord John, 233
Russell, Majors and Waddell, 286
Russia: and Holy Alliance, 110; and
    Monroe Doctrine, 110; Alaska purchased
    from, 394; war with Japan (1905), 405–6;
    1917 Revolution, 422; after 1917, *see*
    Soviet Union
Russo-Japanese War, 404, 405–6
Ruth, Babe, 448
Ryan, Frank, 316

Saarinen, Eero, 593
Sac and Fox Indians, 118
Sacco-Vanzetti case, 433
Sackville West, Sir Lionel, 357
St. Clair, Arthur, 100
St. Louis, Mo., 114
Salem, Mass.: witchcraft trials at (1692), 27,
    28; Melville and, 159
Salisbury, Robert Arthur Talbot Gascoyne-
    Cecil, 3rd marquis of, 399
Salk, Jonas E., 591
'Salutary neglect', 16–17
Salzburgers, 13
Samoan Islands, protectorate over, 398
Sand Creek Massacre, 283
Sandinistas, 600, 613
San Francisco, 187; cable cars, 324;
    segregation of Oriental schoolchildren,
    406; United Nations Conference, 514
Sanger, Margaret, 319
San Jacinto, battle of, 178
San Jacinto (frigate), 232
San Juan Hill, battle of, 401
Sankey, Ira D., 337
Santa Anna, Antonio López de, 178, 185,
    186
Santo Domingo: annexation of proposed,
    396
Saratoga, battle of, 51
Sargent, John Singer, 345
Savannah: British capture of, 55
Savings and Loan Associations (S&Ls), 606
Scalawags, 253
Scalia, Antonin, 604
Scamman, Richard, 609
Schenectady, New York, 33
Schechter v. *United States* (1935), 471
Schenck v. *United States* (1919), 433
Schlesinger, James R., 566
Schools: in New England colonies, 30–1;
    private, 166; free public, 165–6; in South
    (late nineteenth century), 265–6; in late
    nineteenth century, 339; boarding, for
    boys, 329; parochial, 323; separate but
    equal facilities legalized in, 269;

Progressive educational theories in, 376–7;
    desegregation of, 535–6, 560; Bible-
    reading in declared unconstitutional, 552;
    federal aid to, 552; busing of students,
    560
Schurz, Carl, 249, 285, 347, 354, 355
Schuyler, Philip, 54
Schwab, Charles M., 305
Schwarzkopf, H. Norman, 617
Schwenckfelders, 20
Scioto Company, 65
Scopes, John T., 441
Scopes trial, 440–1
Scotch-Irish, immigration of, 20–1
Scott, Dred, 207
Scott, Sir Walter, 197
Scott, Winfield: in Mexican War, 184, 186;
    in election of 1852, 199; 'anaconda plan'
    of, 224, 230
Scowcroft, Brent, 612
Scrooby, Nottinghamshire, 7
Sears, Roebuck and Co., 326
Seattle: general strike (1919), 432
Securities and Exchange Act (1934), 461
Sedgwick, Theodore (1746–1813), 89
Sedgwick, Theodore (1780–1839), 128
Sedition Act (1918), 427–8, 433
Segregation, 267–9
Selective Service Act (1917), 424
Selective Service and Training Act (1940),
    492
Seminole War (1835–42), 118
Senators, direct election of, 373–4, 383
Seneca Falls women's rights convention
    (1848), 169
Separatists, 7
Serapis (frigate), 53
Serra, Fr. Junipero, 179
Seven Pines, battle of, 226
Seven Years' War (French and Indian War),
    35–6
Seventh Day Adventists, 161
Seward, William H., 150, 197, 210, 212; and
    Compromise of 1850, 193; as Secretary of
    State, 215; and purchase of Alaska, 394
Seymour, Horatio, 247
Shakers, 162
Sharecropping, 262
Shaw, Anna Howard, 375
Shays, Daniel, 68
Shays's rebellion, 68
Sheep-raising: in New England, 119; on
    Great Plains, 281
Shelburne, William Petty, 2nd earl of, 56
Sheldon, Charles M., 337
Sherman Antitrust Act (1890), 309–10, 315,
    378, 383, 387, 390
Sherman, John, 309

Sherman Silver Purchase Act (1890), 357, 362
Sherman, William T., 233, 234, 235, 255
Shiloh, battle of, 226
Shipbuilding: in colonies, 17; in 1820–60, 116–17
Shippen, Edward, 25
Shipping: in 1815–60, 116–17; and Civil War, 117; transatlantic steamship services, 117
Sholes, Christopher L., 297
Sidney, Algernon, 39
Silver: mining of in late 1800s, 276–7, 352; demand for unlimited coinage of, 352
Simpson, 'Sockless Jerry', 361
Sims, William S., 424
Sinclair, Harry F., 437
Sinclair, Upton, 372, 380
Singer, Isaac M., 127
Sioux Indians, 277, 283–4
Sioux War (1865–7), 283; (1875), 283–4
Skyscrapers, 327, 447
Slater Fund, 265
Slater, Samuel, 126
Slaughter House Cases (1873), 267
Slavery: development in colonies of, 22; effects of Revolution on, 60–1; as an issue in Constitutional Convention, 71–2; revival of, 122; and Missouri Compromise, 112; profitability of, 125–6; as economic institution, 123–4, 215–6; psychological effects of, 125; Southern defense of, 174–5; in the territories, 122, 188–90, 193, 198, 201–2, 203, 205–6, 207–8
Slavery As It Is (Weld), 199–200
Slaves: in the colonies, 22–3; distribution of (1815–60), 122; living conditions, 124–5; culture of, 125
Slave trade (domestic), 123
Slave trade (international): in colonial period, 18, 22; prohibited by states, 60; as constitutional issue (1787), 72; prohibited by U.S. government, 122; clandestine, 212
Slidell, John, 183
Slums, 327–8
Smith, Alfred E., 457; presidential candidacy (1924), 443; in 1928 election, 451–2; opposition to New Deal, 461
Smith, Hoke, 373
Smith, John, 5, 7
Smith, Joseph, 161, 179
Smith, Revd. Sydney, 156
Smith-Connally Act (1943), 502–3
Social Darwinism, 307, 308, 397, 398
Social Gospel, 336–7, 371
Social mobility: in colonial America, 26; in Jacksonian period, 134–5; in late

nineteenth century, 330
Social Register, 330
Social Security Act (1935), 464, 472
Socialism, 314, 370–1
Society of Colonial Dames, 330
Society of Mayflower Descendants, 330
Society of the Cincinnati, 60
Soil exhaustion, 119, 142
Solid South, 260, 267
Sons of Liberty, 40
Sons of the Revolution, 330
Soulé, Pierre, 200
South: in Revolutionary War, 55–6; in Constitutional Convention, 72–3; and tariffs, 142–4, 197; as cotton kingdom, 122–7; culture of pre-Civil War, 196–8; and sectional crisis (1848–50), 192; and Compromise of 1850, 194–5; secession of, 213–14; Black Codes, 240–1; sharecropping, 262; crop-lien system, 262; New South creed in, 262–3; industry in, 262–5; Jim Crow laws, 267–9; lynching, 269; race riots, 269; Bourbon rule in, 265–7; Populism in, 360; Progressivism in, 373; in election of 1928, 452; Dixiecrats, 527, 528; school integration in, 535—6; black voting in, 536, 581; civil rights movement, 536–7; population increase (1970s), 575; *see also* Civil War, Confederate States of America, Ku Klux Klan, Reconstruction, Slavery
South Carolina: colony founded, 10–11; blacks in (1751), 22; in Revolutionary War, 55; and Tariff of Abominations, 142–3; Nullification Ordinance of, 143–4; secessionist sentiment in, 192; secession of, 213–14; and Fort Sumter, 216; Reconstruction, 241, 252, 253, 254; 1876 election in, 259
Southeast Asia Treaty Organization (SEATO), 539
Southern Alliance, 360
Southern Commercial Conventions, 197–8
Southern Pacific Railroad, 287, 289, 373
Soviet Union: establishment of diplomatic relations with, 485–6; in World War II, 505–6, 508, 509–10, 513; Yalta Conference, 512–13; and United Nations charter, 514–15; declares war on Japan, 516; and start of Cold War, 516–19; Berlin blockade, 520; and Hungarian revolt, 539–40; and Suez crisis, 540; U-2 incident, 541; Cuban missile crisis, 546–7; nuclear test-ban treaty with, 547; détente with, 559; SALT agreement with (1972), 559, 566; SALT II agreement with (1979), 569–70; invasion of Afghanistan by, 570; Reagan and, 599–600; INF Treaty with

(1987), 608–9; Strategic Arms Reduction Treaty with (1991), 615; disintegration of, 612, 614

Spain, 177; New World exploration and colonization, 4; in colonial wars, 33; and Revolutionary War, 52; and Treaty of Paris (1783), 56–7; Louisiana ceded to, 35–6; cedes Florida to Great Britain, 35; Pinckney's Treaty (1795), 83–4; returns Louisiana to France, 93; and Florida, 101, 109–10; Adams-Onís Treaty, 109–10; and Dominican Republic, 394; *Virginius* affair, 396; and Cuban rebellion, 400–1; Spanish-American War, 400–2

Spanish-American War, 400–2

Sparks, Jared, 157

Specie Circular (1836), 148, 149, 152

Spencer, Herbert, 307

Spies, August, 312

Spoils system: Jefferson and, 91; Jackson and, 140; in late nineteenth century, 351

Spotsylvania, battle of, 233

Sprague, Frank J., 299

Sputniks, 588

Stagecoaching, 285–6

Stalin, Joseph, 505, 512–13, 514, 518, 539

Stalwarts, 351, 353

Stamp Act (1765), 40

Stamp Act Congress, 40

Standard Oil Company, 297, 306, 309, 334, 371, 379

Stanton, Edwin M., 245, 246

Stanton, Elizabeth Cady, 374

Star Route Frauds, 353–4

Star-Spangled Banner, 105

START (Strategic Arms Reduction Treaty, 1991), 615

State rights: under the Confederation, 64; at Federal Convention, 70–4; Virginia and Kentucky resolutions, 87; Jackson and, 140–1; South Carolina Nullification crisis, 142–3; and secession, 214; in the Confederacy, 224

Steamboats on rivers, 114

Stearns, J.B., 298

Steel industry: growth of (late 1800s), 304–5; Homestead strike (1892), 314; strikes in (1919), 432, 434; (1952), 528

Steerage conditions: 1815–60, 130

Steffens, Lincoln, 371, 402

Stein, Gertrude, 344

Steinbeck, John, 471

Stephens, Alexander H., 224, 235, 240

Stephens, Uriah S., 311

Stephenson, David C., 440

Steuben, Karl Wilhelm, 'Baron' von, 53

Steunenberg, Frank, 315

Stevens, Thaddeus, 221, 241, 242, 255, 257

Stevens, Wallace, 451, 592

Stevenson, Adlai E., 532, 535

Stimson, Henry L., 482, 483, 484

Stimson Doctrine, 484

Stock market crash (1929), 454–5

Stockton, Robert F., 185

Stone, Lucy, 169, 170, 374

Story, Joseph, 135, 139, 148

Stowe, Calvin, 165

Stowe, Harriet Beecher, 169

Strategic Arms Limitation Talks (SALT), 559, 566, 570, 571

Strategic Defense Initiative (Star Wars), 599

Strike(s): railroad (1877), 313; Homestead (1892), 314; Pullman (1894), 314; Southern textile (1898–1902), 264; at Lawrence, Mass. (1912), 316; at Paterson, N.J. (1913), 316; anthracite coal (1902), 378–9; of 1919, 432; Boston police (1919), 432

Strong, Josiah, 397–8

Submarine warfare, German, 413, 415–17, 421, 424

Subtreasury plan, 360–1

Suburbs, growth of, 446–7, 575–6

Suffolk Resolves, 44

Suffrage: in colonies, 13; property qualifications for, reduced (1780s), 63; widening of (post-1815), 135–6; immigrants and, 132; and Seneca Falls women's rights convention (1848), 169; ex-Confederates deprived of, 243; for blacks (Reconstruction), 243-4, (in late nineteenth century), 268, (in 1960s), 581; for women achieved, 427

Sugar Act (1764), 38

Sullivan, John L., 334

Sullivan, Louis H., 327

Sumner, Charles, 202, 206, 221, 241–2, 258, 354, 394

Sumner, William Graham, 307, 308, 340

Susan Constant (ship), 5

Sussex (French steamship), 417

Sutro Tunnel, 277

Swaggart, Jimmy, 607

Swedish immigrants, 131

Swift, Gustavus F., 331

Sylvis, William H., 310

Symphony orchestras, 333

Taft, Robert A., 493, 531–2

Taft, William Howard, 376; becomes President, 382; and Progressives, 382–5; and Republican insurgency, 384–5; in election of 1912, 386–7; and dollar diplomacy, 406–7; becomes Chief Justice, 436

Taft-Hartley Act (1947), 526, 528, 579

Talleyrand-Périgord, Charles Maurice de, 86, 94
Tammany Hall, 251, 349, 351, 443
Taney, Roger B.: as Secretary of the Treasury, 147, as Chief Justice, 150–1; and Dred Scott case, 207–8
Tappan, Arthur, 171
Tappan, Lewis, 171, 175
Tarbell, Ida M., 371
Tariff(s), 356; Hamilton's proposals on, 80; of 1792, 81; of 1816, 107, 142; of Abominations (1828), 138, 142; of 1832, 143; of 1833, 144; of 1842, 154; Walker (1846), 188; of 1857, 207; Morrill (1861), 221; McKinley Act (1890), 357; Wilson-Gorman Act (1894), 363; Dingley Act (1897), 366; Payne-Aldrich (1909), 383–4; Theodore Roosevelt and, 386; Taft and, 383–4; Underwood-Simmons (1913), 389; Emergency Tariff Act (1921), 436; Fordney-McCumber Act (1922), 436; Hawley-Smoot (1930), 485
Tariff reform: Cleveland and, 356; Theodore Roosevelt and, 384; Taft and, 383–4; Wilson and, 388–9
Tax Reform Act (1986), 603
Taylor, Frederick W., 444
Taylor, Zachary: in Mexican War, 183, 184, 185–6; elected President, 190–1; and sectional crisis, 192; death, 193
Tea Act (1773), 43
Teapot Dome scandal, 437
Tecumseh, 100–1, 103
Tehran Conference (1943), 509–10
Telegraph, 116, 298
Telephone, 298
Teller Amendment (1898), 401, 402
Temperance movements, 167–8; *see also* Prohibition
Tenement House Commission (New York), 327–8
Tennent, William, 28
Tennessee Coal and Iron Company, 381, 385
Tennessee Valley Authority, 459–60
Ten Nights in a Bar Room (Arthur), 168
Tenure of Office Act (1867), 245, 246
Tertium Quids, 96
Texas: U.S. surrenders claim to (1819), 110; American settlement in, 177–8; annexation of, 178–9, 180–1; Rio Grande boundary dispute, 182–3; 187; national debt of, 193; secession, 213; oilwells, 263; longhorn cattle herds, 279; population increase (1950–80), 575
Textile industry: in New England, 126; Southern, 263–4; in 1920s, 447
Theodore Roosevelt Dam, 293

Thomas, Clarence, 619
Thomas, George H., 226, 234
Thomas, Theodore, 333
Thoreau, Henry David, 158–9, 293, 343, 452
Thurmond, J. Strom, 527
Tiananmen Square Massacre (1989), 612
Tidelands Oil Act (1953), 534
Tilden, Samuel J., 251, 258–9
Tillich, Paul, 466, 586
Tillman, Ben, 402
Timber and Stone Act (1878), 289
Tippecanoe, battle of, 101
Tobacco: cultivation of, in colonial Virginia, 6; post-Civil War production of, 264
Tocqueville, Alexis de, 134, 135, 160, 164, 175
Tombstone, Ariz., 277
Toombs, Robert, 223
Toronto (York), burning of, 103
Tory Rangers, 53
Toussaint l'Ouverture, Pierre Dominique, 94
Townsend, Francis E., 462
Townshend, Charles, 40–1
Townshend Duties, 40–1, 42
Toynbee Hall, 328
Trade unions: beginning of, 128–9; in late nineteenth century, 319–3; in New Deal, 473–4; legislative curbs on (1947), 526; post-1945, 579–80; decline of (1980s), 598–9; *see also* National Labor Union, Knights of Labor, American Federation of Labor, Congress of Industrial Organizations
Transcendentalism, 158–9; and reform, 161
Transportation: revolution in, post-1815, 113–16; improvements, late 1800s, 324–5; *see also* Aviation, Canals, Railroads, Shipping
Treaty of Versailles (1919), 429–30
Treaty of Washington (1871), 395; (1922), 478–9
Trenchard, John, *Cato's Letters* (1720), 39
Trent affair, 232
Trenton, battle of, 50
Triangle Fire (1911), 322
Trist, Nicholas P., 187
Trotter, William Monroe, 271
Truman Doctrine, 519
Truman, Harry S.: elected Vice-President, 512; becomes President, 514; and atomic bomb, 515–16; and Cold War, 516–17; and containment policy, 519–20; and Far East, 520–2; Korean War, 522–4; domestic policies (1945–8), 524–7; reelection, 527–8; and Fair Deal, 528; and Communist subversion, 529–31
Trumbull, John, 69
Trumbull, Lyman, 347

Trusts, 296–7; hostility toward, 307–9
Tubman, Harriet, 173
Turner, Frederick Jackson, 119, 291
Turner, Nat, insurrection, 124, 143
Turnpikes, 113–114
Tuscarora War (1711–12), 32
Tuskegee Institute, 271
Twain, Mark, 222, 277, 297, 341, 343–4, 346, 347, 402
Tweed Ring, 251, 254, 349
Tweed, William Marcy, 251, 349
Two Years Before the Mast (Dana), 179
Tyler, John, 153, 154, 155
Typewriter, 297–8

U-2 incident, 541
Uncle Sam, 105
Uncle Tom's Cabin, 199–200
Unconditional surrender (World War II), 509
Underground Railroad, 173
Underwood-Simmons, Tariff Act (1913), 388–9
Unemployment: 1929–32, 455; 1937–39, 474, 475
Union League, 255–6
United Mine Workers, 315, 379, 525
Union Pacific Railroad, 250, 286–7, 288
United Nations Organization, 513, 514–15, 519
United States Steel Corporation, 297, 385
United States v. *Butler* (1936), 471
United States v. *Cruikshank* (1875), 267
United States v. *E. C. Knight Co.* (1895), 309
United States v. *The Spirit of '76* (1917), 428
United Steelworkers of America v. *Weber* (1979), 582
Upshur, Abel P., 178
U.S. Military Academy, 91
U.S. Supreme Court: established, 78; John Marshall and, 92–3, 108, 141; Jefferson and, 92–3; and Fourteenth Amendment, 267; and railroad rate-fixing, 303; and federal income tax, 363; Franklin D. Roosevelt's attempt to reform, 471–2; and civil rights, 535–6, 552–3, 605; Reagan's attempt to reshape, 604–5; *see also* specific cases and p. 000, Table 5. Justices of the United States Supreme Court
Universal Negro Improvement Association, 434
U'Ren, William, S., 373
Utah, 66, 180, 291
Utrecht, Treaty of (1713), 23

Valley Forge, 50, 52
Van Buren, Martin, 136; as political organizer, 138; elected Vice-President, 143; elected President, 150; and slavery issue, 151; and Independent Treasury, 152; in election of 1840, 153; and Texas, 178, 180; in election of 1848, 190–1
Vance, Cyrus, R. 568
Vance, Zebulon B., 224
Vandenberg, Arthur H., 514, 519
Van Depoele, Charles J., 299
Vanderbilt, Consuelo, 330
Vanderbilt, Cornelius, 302
Vanderbilt family, 329
Vanderbilt, William K., 329
Van Devanter, Willis, 472
Vardaman, James K., 373
Vaudeville, 332
Veblen, Thorstein, 308
Venezuela: boundary dispute with Great Britain, 399–400; debt controversy, 408
Vera Cruz, 186, 410
Vergennes, Charles, comte de, 51, 57
Versailles, Treaty of (1919), 429–31
Vichy, French government in, 496, 497, 506, 508, 514
Vicksburg, siege of, 230
Vietnam: Eisenhower's policy on, 538; Kennedy sends advisers to, 547–8; Johnson and U.S. involvement in, 555–6; Antiwar demonstrations, 556; Nixon and disengagement, 558; Communist victory in, 562
Villa, Francisco ('Pancho'), 410–11
Villard, Oswald Garrison, 273
Virginia: Assembly, 6; settlement of, 5–6; tobacco production in, 6; blacks in (1756), 22; population of (1787), 71; ratifies Constitution, 75
Virginia and Kentucky Resolutions, 87, 104
Virginia City, Nevada, 277
Virginia Company, 6
Virginia Plan, 71, 72
Virginius (ship), 396
Volstead Act (1919), 441–2
Voting: *see* Suffrage
Voting Rights Act (1965), 552

Wabash, St. Louis and Pacific Railroad Company v. *Illinois* (1886), 303
Wade, Benjamin F., 221, 242, 246
Wade-Davis Bill (1864), 238–9
Wagner, Robert F., 463, 464
Wagner Act: *see* National Labor Relations Act
Wagner-Steagall Act (1937), 474
Waite, Morrison, 303
Wald, Lillian D., 328
Walker, Robert J., 208
Wallace, George C., 557–8, 561

Wallace, Henry A., 493, 512, 526, 527, 528
Walpole, Robert, 16
Waltham system, 126
Wampanoag Indians, 32
Wanamaker's, 325
War debts (after World War I), 480-1
War Hawks, 101
War Industries Board, 426
War of 1812, 102-6
War of Independence, *see* Revolutionary War
Ward, Lester F., 308
Wards Cove v *Atonio* (1987), 605
Warren, Earl, 527; Chief Justice, 535, 552-3, 560
Warren, Robert C., 548-9, 554
Washington, Booker T., 255, 270-2, 274
Washington, D.C.: becomes national capital, 80, 90; burning of, 103; Library of Congress, 342; Conference (1921-2), 478-9; bonus marchers in, 457; John F. Kennedy Center, 594
Washington, George, 61, 69, 85; in French and Indian War, 34; in Revolutionary War, 45, 49, 50, 52-3, 55-6; as land speculator, 59; and slavery, 60; becomes President, 76-7; as president, 78-9, 82-4; Farewell Address of, 84; death of, 89
Washington Conference (1921-2), 478-9
Washington Temperance Society, 167-8
Watergate, 563
Waterman, Lewis E., 332
Watson, Thomas E., 364, 365
'Waving the bloody shirt', 247, 350, 365
Wayne, Anthony, 100
Wealth Tax Act (1935), 464
Weaver, James B., 359, 361
Webb-Kenyon Act (1913), 376
Webster v *Reproductive Health Services* (1989), 629
Webster, Daniel, 99, 135, 145, 150, 152, 154, 167, 199; and Dartmouth College case, 108; debate with Hayne, 142-3; and Bank War, 146; seventh of March speech, 193
Webster, Noah, 69
Welch, Ashbel, 301
Weld, Theodore Dwight, 172, 199
Welfare capitalism, 447
Welles, Gideon, 250
Wells, Fargo and Company, 286
Western Federation of Miners (WFM), 316
Western Trail, 279
Western Union, 298
Westinghouse Electric Company, 29
Westinghouse, George M., 299
Westover, Virginia, 26
West Point, 54, 91, 184
Westward movement: in Revolutionary period, 64-5; in 1815-60, 113, 117-21

Whaling, 117
Wheeler, Burton K., 493
Wheeler-Howard (Indian Reorganization) Act (1934), 468
Whig party: rise of, 148-50; philosophy of, 149-50; in election of 1836, 150; in election of 1840, 152-3; and Tyler's Administration, 153-5; and Mexican War, 184, 187, 188; and election of 1852, 199; disintegration of, 199, 202, 204
Whipple, Henry, 285
Whiskey Rebellion, 61, 81
Whiskey Ring, 251
Whistler, James A. McNeill, 345
White, Andrew D., 341
White, Henry, 429
White, William Allen, 370, 492
Whitefield, George, 28
Whiteman, Paul, 448
Whitlock, Brand, 372
Whitman, Marcus, 180
Whitman, Walt, 159, 274, 343
Whitney, Eli: cotton gin, 122; and interchangeable parts, 127
Whittier, John Greenleaf, 158, 171
Wickersham Commission, 442
Wilderness campaign, 233
Wiley, Harvey W., 380
Wilkes, Charles, 232
Wilkinson, James, 67, 96
Willard, Emma, 166, 169
Willard, Frances, 375
William and Mary College, 31
Williams, Roger, 9
Williams, Tennessee, 591-2
Williams, William Carlos, 451, 592
Williamsburg Bridge (New York), 324
Willkie, Wendell L., 493, 494, 511
Wilmot Proviso, 188, 189, 193
Winchester rifle, 284
Wilson, Charles E., 534
Wilson, Woodrow: as president of Princeton, 387; as governor of New Jersey, 373, 387; and New Freedom, 387; elected President, 386-8; domestic policy, 388-91; Latin American policy, 409-11; and World War I, 412-19, 420, 421-4; reelected, 419-20; and civil liberties, 427-8; Fourteen Points, 428-9; at Versailles Conference, 429-30; and League of Nations, 430-1; and reaction, 434-5
Wilson-Gorman Tariff Act (1894), 362-3, 400
Winthrop, John, 7, 8
Winthrop, John IV, 29
Wirt, William, 147
Wisconsin Idea, 373

Woburn Abbey, 26
Wolfe, James, 35
Women: status of, in colonies, 24–5; working conditions of (1830–60), 128; demand for equality (1830–60), 168–70; in antislavery crusade, 169, 176; suffrage movement, 169, 374–5, 427, 449; status of (1860–1910), 330–1; in Prohibition movement, 375; (1920s), 449–50; in World War II, 503; liberation movement (post-World War II), 584–6; Equal Rights Amendment, 571, 585, 586
Women's Christian Temperance Union, 375
Woolens Act (1699), 16, 17
Woolworth, Frank Winfield, 326
Worcester v. *Georgia* (1832), 141
Works Progress Administration, 463
World Anti-Slavery Conference (1840), 162, 169
World Court, 476, 487–8
Wounded Knee: Indians massacred at (1890), 284; Indian occupation of (1973), 583
Wright, Carroll D., 317

Wright, Frank Lloyd, 593
Wright, Orville, 445
Wright, Wilbur, 445
Writs of Assistance, 37
Wyeth, Andrew, 592
Wyoming Stock Growers' Association, 280

XYZ dispatches, 86

Yalta Conference, 512–13
Yamassee War (1715–18), 30
Yancey, William L., 194, 223
Yazoo land grant case, 95–6
Yeltsin, Boris, 614, 615
Yorktown, battle of, 56
Young, Brigham, 161, 179–80
Young Men's Christian Association, 337
Young Plan, 481
Young Women's Christian Association, 337
Ypiranga, s.s., 410

Zimmermann, Arthur, 421
Zimmermann telegram, 421